The Allied Occupation of Japan

TAKEMAE Eiji

Translated and adapted from the Japanese
by Robert Ricketts and Sebastian Swann

(Formerly titled *Inside GHQ: The Allied Occupation
of Japan and Its Legacy*)

Preface by John W. Dower

continuum
NEW YORK · LONDON

2003

The Continuum International Publishing Group Inc
15 East 26 Street, New York, NY 10010

The Continuum International Publishing Group Ltd
The Tower Building, 11 York Road, London SE1 7NX

First published 2002
Reprinted 2002

© Takemae Eiji 2002

This is a substantially revised and expanded version of *GHQ*,
originally published by Iwanami Shinsho (Tokyo) in 1983.

Printed in the United States of America

Library of Congress Cataloging-in-Publication Data

Takemae, Eiji, 1930–
    The Allied occupation of Japan. Formerly titled Inside GHQ : the Allied occupation of Japan and
its legacy / by Eiji Takemae ; translated and adapted from the Japanese by Robert Ricketts and Sebastian Swann.
        p.   cm.
    Includes bibliographical references and index.
    ISBN 0-8264-6247-2 (alk. paper)
    1. Japan—History—Allied occupation, 1945–1952. 2. Japan—History—1952—I. Ricketts,
Robert. II. Swann, Sebastian. III. Title.

DS389.16 .T35 2001
952.04′4—dc21

                                                                                    00-067643

The Allied Occupation of Japan ISBN 0-8264-1521-0

Contents

Contents

Illustrations, Maps and Diagrams

Maps and Diagrams

Abbreviations

AAF	Allied Air Forces (SWPA)
ABCC	Atomic Bomb Casualty Commission (US)
ABDA	American-British-Dutch-Australian Supreme Command
ACC	Allied Control Council (Germany)
ACJ	Allied Council for Japan (Tokyo)
ACJ	American Council on Japan (US)
AFL	American Federation of Labor
AFPAC	United States Army Forces in the Pacific (also USAFPAC)
AG	Adjutant General's Section (SCAP)
AIB	Allied Intelligence Bureau (SWPA)
ALF	Allied Land Forces (SWPA)
ANF	Allied Naval Forces (SWPA)
ANPŌ	Japan–US Security Treaty
ANZUS	Australia–New Zealand–United States
ARO	Alien Registration Ordinance (Japan)
ATIS	Allied Translation and Interpreters Service (SWPA/SCAP)
BCOF	British Commonwealth Occupation Force
BCW	Biological and Chemical Warfare
BRINDJAP	British and Indian Troops – Japan
CAC	Country and Area Committees (US State Department)
CAD	Civil Affairs Division (US War Department)
CAS	Civil Affairs Section (SCAP)
CASA	Civil Affairs Staging Area (CAD)
CATS	Civil Affairs Training Schools (CAD)
CCD	Civil Censorship Detachment (SCAP)
CCS	Civil Communications Section (SCAP)
CHS	Civil Historical Section (SCAP)
CIA	Central Intelligence Agency (US)
CIC	Counter-Intelligence Corps (SCAP)
CID	Civil Intelligence Division (SCAP)
CI&E	Civil Information and Education Section (SCAP)
CINC	Commander-in-Chief
CIO	Congress of Industrial Organisations (US)
CIS	Civil Intelligence Section (SCAP)
CIS	Counter-Intelligence Section (SCAP)
CLO	Central Liaison Office (Japan)

CPC	Office of the Civil Property Custodian (SCAP)
CTS	Civil Transportation Section (SCAP)
DAC	Department of the Army Civilian (US War Department)
DPRK	Democratic People's Republic of Korea
DRB	Deconcentration Review Board (US)
DS	Diplomatic Section (SCAP)
EROA	Economic Recovery in Occupied Areas (US)
ESB	Economic Stabilisation Board (Japan)
ESP	Economic Stabilisation (Dodge) Programme
ESS	Economic and Scientific Section (SCAP)
EST	Eastern Standard Time (US)
FEA	Foreign Economic Administration (US)
FEAC	Far Eastern Advisory Commission (Allied Powers)
FEC	Far Eastern Commission (Allied Powers)
FECOM	Far East Command (US)
FRUS	*Foreign Relations of the United States* (US State Department)
G-2	Intelligence Section, General Military Staff (SCAP)
GARIOA	Government Appropriation for Relief in Occupied Areas (US)
GAS	General Accounting Section (SCAP)
GDP	Gross Domestic Product
GHQ	General Headquarters (as in GHQ/SWPA, GHQ/ AFPAC, GHQ/SCAP, GHQ/FECOM)
GPA	General Procurement Agent (SCAP)
GS	Government Section (SCAP)
HCLC	Holding Company Liquidation Commission (Japan)
IDS	International Defendants Section (SCAP)
IDS	Information Dissemination Section (AFPAC)
IID	Institute of Infectious Diseases (Japan)
ICFTU	International Confederation of Free Trade Unions
IMTFE	International Military Tribunal for the Far East (Allied Powers)
IPS	International Prosecution Section (SCAP)
IRAA	Imperial Rule Assistance Association (Japan)
JCP	Japan Communist Party
JCS	Joint Chiefs of Staff (US)
JERC	Japan Education Reform Council
J Force	New Zealand Expeditionary Force – Japan (also Jayforce)
JLC	Japanese Language Council
JNR	Japan National Railways
JSP	Japan Socialist Party
JWPC	Joint War Plans Committee (JCS subcommittee)
KORYU	Korean-Ryukyus Division (SCAP)
LDP	Liberal Democratic Party (Japan)
LS	Legal Section (SCAP)

MAS	US-Japan Military Support Agreement
MG	Military Government
MGS	Military Government Section (AFPAC)
MGT	Military Government Teams (US Army)
MISLS	Military Intelligence Service Language Schools (US)
MITI	Ministry of International Trade and Industry (Japan)
MP	Military Police (US)
MS	Medical Section (FECOM, SCAP)
NATO	North Atlantic Treaty Organisation
NAVJAP	Naval Activities Japan (US)
NIH	National Institute of Health (Japan)
NHK	Nihon Hōsō Kyōkai (Japan Broadcasting Corporation)
NLP	Night-Landing Practice
NKVD	People's Commissariat of Internal Affairs (former Soviet Union)
HNMA	*History of the Nonmilitary Activities of the Occupation* (GHQ/ SCAP)
NPR	National Police Reserve (Japan)
NRS	Natural Resources Section (SCAP)
NRWU	National Railways Workers Union (Japan)
NSC	National Security Council (US)
OSS	Office of Strategic Services (US)
OWI	Office of War Information (US)
PAG	Petroleum Advisory Group (SCAP)
PH&W	Public Health and Welfare Section (SCAP)
PIO (PRO)	Public Information (Relations) Office (SCAP)
POLAD	Office of the Political Adviser (SCAP)
POW	Prisoner of War
PPS	Policy Planning Staff (US State Department)
PRC	People's Republic of China
PRJ	*Political Reorientation of Japan* (GHQ/SCAP)
PSD	Public Safety Division (SCAP)
PWB	Psychological Warfare Branch (SWPA)
PWC	Postwar Programmes Committee (US State Department)
PX	Post Exchange (US military)
RAA	Recreation and Amusement Association (Japan)
RFB	Reconstruction Finance Bank (Japan)
RG	Record Group (US National Archives)
ROC	Republic of China
ROK	Republic of Korea
RS	Reparations Section (SCAP)
RTO	Railway Transport Office (SCAP)
RYCOM	Ryukyus Command (FECOM)

SAG	Scientific Advisory Group (US)
SBI	Special Investigation Bureau (Japan)
SCAJAP	Shipping Control Authority for the Japanese Merchant Marine (US Navy)
SCAP	Supreme Commander for the Allied Powers
SCAPIN	SCAP Index
SDF	Self-Defence Forces (Japan)
SFE	Subcommittee for the Far East (SWNCC)
SOFA	Status of Forces Agreement
SRS	Statistical and Reports Section (SCAP)
SWNCC	State–War–Navy Coordinating Committee (US)
SWPA	Southwest Pacific Area (Allied Powers)
TMD	Theatre Missile Defence (US)
TS	Territorial Subcommittee (US)
UN	United Nations
USAFFE	United States Army Forces in the Far East
USAFMIDPAC	United States Army Forces in the Middle Pacific
USAFPAC	(see AFPAC)
USAFWESPAC	United States Army Forces in the Western Pacific
USAMGIK	United States Army Military Government in Korea
USAOS	United States Army Services of Supply
USCAR	US Civil Administration of the Ryukyus
WAAC	Women's Army Auxiliary Corps
WAC	Women's Army Corps
WAVES	Women Accepted for Voluntary Emergency Service
WFTU	World Federation of Trade Unions

Note on Japanese Names

Within the text the East Asian convention is followed for Japanese (Chinese and Korean) names, with the surname first, then the given name.

Acknowledgements

'The Japanese Empire and the Asia–Pacific War' (Figure 1, pages 12–13) from Charles Scribner's Sons (Mikiso Hane, *Japan: A Historical Survey*, 1972, pp. 532–33)

'The Kuril Islands' (Figure 3, page 82) from Clarendon Press, Oxford (John J. Stephan, *The Kuril Islands: Russo-Japanese Frontier in the Pacific*, 1974, p. 10).

Preface

John W. Dower

Massachusetts Institute of Technology

In much of the contemporary world outside Japan, World War II in Asia seems both long ago and yet strangely, almost perversely, recent. Great global turmoil and transformation has occurred since Japan surrendered over a half century ago, while those who remember the war personally are rapidly dwindling in number. Yet despite the gulf of time and the passing of intimate witnesses, the image of Japanese atrocities in occupied areas and against prisoners of war remains vivid. These images have, indeed, drawn renewed attention in both Asia and the West in the last several decades. What are we to make of this?

There are good reasons for the renewed fixation on Japan's war record. The conservative élites that have governed Japan with but passing interruption since the end of the war have never offered an unqualified and *sustained* apology for their country's wartime aggression and atrocities; there has been no formal counterpart to the German government's acknowledgement of Nazi depredations. Prominent Japanese, including Cabinet members, deny specific atrocities such as the Rape of Nanjing with almost metronome-like regularity, and until a few years ago government-certified textbooks sanitised treatment of the war years. It is only in the last few decades, moreover, that certain Japanese war crimes which the victors themselves chose to cover up have come to public attention. The murderous scientific experiments conducted on prisoners by 'Unit 731' in Manchuria are one such horror; the sexual enslavement of young women, mostly Koreans, to service the Emperor's soldiers and sailors is another. The brutalisation of prisoners, etched in acid in the collective memories of American and British Commonwealth veterans, never made a deep impression in a country absorbed with its own suffering and awed by the vigour and power of the Caucasian conquerors. These troubling attitudes and incidents have provoked anger and apprehension outside Japan. Beneath the country's ultra-modern façade, it is asked, have basic institutions and attitudes really changed?

That, in essence, is the underlying question addressed in this book; and the answer Takemae Eiji gives is a strong, but still qualified, yes. The horrors of the war years attract and repel us, the evasions of postwar Japanese neo-nationalists rightly alarm us – but the extraordinary and enduring changes that defeat brought to Japan are seldom well remembered or appreciated outside the defeated country itself. For six and a half years following its unconditional surrender (from August 1945 to April

1952), Japan was occupied by the victors and subjected to one of the most audacious exercises in social engineering in history. Substantive reformist policies were introduced at virtually every level of society. Even after the Cold War intervened and the reformist ardour of the victors waned, it proved impossible to set back the clock.

In the decisive, initial stages of the Occupation, these reformist policies were commonly referred to under the overarching rubric of 'demilitarisation and democratisation'. The country was to be permanently disarmed. The 'will to war' was to be eradicated by dismantling authoritarian structures and promoting liberal ideals through the legal and educational systems, the media and a broad spectrum of grassroots organisations. Although not all of the early reforms survived intact, their overall durability was ruefully acknowledged by Yoshida Shigeru, the dominant conservative politician of the early postwar period, whose own cabinets were forced to introduce much of the enabling legislation for the victors' agenda. 'There was this idea at the back of my mind', Yoshida observed when recalling his tenure as prime minister, 'that whatever needed to be revised after we regained our independence could be revised then. But once a thing has been decided on, it is not so easy to have it altered'.

There were two major reasons why Japanese conservatives found it impossible to undo all that the victors had done. The post-surrender reforms were embedded in a truly massive web of law. And, more important, unlike Yoshida and his old-guard cohorts, millions of Japanese genuinely welcomed the conquerors' so-called revolution from above. How all of this unfolded is the subject of this enlightening book.

Like the war itself, the significance of these developments is contested ground in Japan today. With varying levels of vehemence, most conservatives denounce the occupation as an exercise in cultural imperialism and 'victor's justice' that undermined the very spirit and traditions of the country. Liberals and leftists, on the other hand, argue that the victors liberated the populace from a repressive state structure and allowed *indigenous* aspirations for peace and democracy to flourish – only to turn conservative and anti-reformist once Cold War considerations came to influence Japan policy. No one, however, denies that the peculiar circumstances of the defeat and occupation profoundly changed the political, economic, social, cultural and ideological contours of the land.

Professor Takemae is uniquely qualified to guide non-Japanese through these labyrinthine developments. Fifteen years old when his country surrendered, he experienced as a teenager both the blackest years of the war and the headiest years of postwar idealism. As a young adult, he watched with dismay as the United States turned its back on reformism, aligned with the country's most conservative leaders and devoted itself to rebuilding Japan as a subordinate military and economic Cold War partner. In the 1960s, when hitherto classified materials began to become more accessible, especially in US archives, Professor Takemae emerged as one of the pioneer scholars of 'occupation studies'. By the 1970s, he was the acknowledged dean of such scholarship in Japan, helping to orchestrate an impressive range of historical research that has continued to the present day. What we have here in *Inside GHQ* is not merely a grand overview of the victors' agenda in defeated Japan, but also a compelling example of how the Occupation legacy is evaluated by someone who truly embraced the early ideals of demilitarisation and democratisation. In this book, readers encounter a Japanese counter-voice to the war apologists and conservative critics of the Occupation-era reforms.

As Professor Takemae points out, these early postwar developments were full of ironies. The relatively beneficent nature of the Allied Occupation stood in sharp contrast to the oppressive policies the Japanese themselves adopted in the areas they had occupied throughout war-torn Asia. It stood in contrast, indeed, to the emperor-system authoritarianism under which the Japanese themselves had lived until then. (It took the conquerors to empower the Emperor's erstwhile 'subjects' with the rights and privileges of being 'citizens' under a strikingly progressive new constitution that came into effect in 1947.) For many Japanese, 'defeat' became synonymous with 'liberation'.

This was but the half of it, however, for the conquerors' reformism was neither evenly nor steadfastly extended. Professor Takemae takes care to note how, in its own peculiar ways, Japan came out of the war and ensuing occupation as one of the 'divided' countries of the postwar world. Out of strategic considerations, the Ryukyu archipelago, dominated by Okinawa, was excluded from the reformist agenda and turned into a de facto American military colony – while, to the north, the Soviet Union seized four small islands off Hokkaido that had traditionally been part of Japan. These territorial issues plague Japan to the present day, as does the divisive formal as well as informal discrimination against 'minority' groups that went largely unrectified after the defeat.

Reformism also was undermined by the very modus operandi of the American-dominated Occupation, which often tended to reinforce rather than break down authoritarian and hierarchical ways of thinking and acting. Strictly speaking, the Japanese remained under military governance for over six years after World War II ended. The conquerors operated through a strict command structure that culminated in General Douglas MacArthur, the Supreme Commander for the Allied Powers. They brooked no criticism. They practised censorship and encouraged self-censorship. They were more comfortable dealing with Japanese bureaucrats than with elected legislators. *Inside GHQ* provides us with an unusually intimate and detailed analysis of the structure, personnel and all-embracing mission of this super-government. As can easily be imagined, it was not a perfect model of 'democracy' in action.

For many idealistic Japanese like Professor Takemae, the most traumatic development of the period of occupation was not the radical reform agenda, but rather the abandonment of that agenda by the United States beginning around 1947. In Japanese parlance, this Cold War change of direction is known as the 'reverse course'. It took many forms. Radical trends in the labour movement were quashed. Plans to bring additional accused top-level war criminals to trial were abandoned. Anti-trust policies aimed at promoting serious economic democratisation were jettisoned. Beginning in 1949, the purge apparatus that had been used to deny public office to individuals associated with militaristic and ultra-nationalistic organisations was turned against the political left. Within a year, this 'Red Purge' in the private as well as public sector had swept more than 20,000 union members, teachers, journalists, broadcasters, filmmakers and the like out of their jobs. By 1950, the inevitable counterpoint to the Red Purge had begun, as individuals formerly purged for their wartime associations began to be 'depurged' and return to public life. In this milieu, the civilian Old Guard personified by Yoshida Shigeru soon consolidated its position as America's new Cold War subalterns in Japan – and, indeed, in Asia.

While these developments placed obvious strains on the 'democratisation' agenda, however, they did not and indeed could not unravel the basic legal and institutional reforms that had been introduced in the first two years of defeat. Professor Takemae's comprehensive survey of these early reforms helps us understand why they proved so resilient as a whole, for it conveys how dense and pervasive this new infrastructure was. Nor did the 'reverse course' succeed in choking off popular support for the initial reformist ideals. On the contrary, such support now veered in a new (and truly ironic) direction among liberals and leftists in particular: it became associated with criticism of the America that had abandoned its original political idealism.

The single most dramatic reversal in Occupation policy was the repudiation of demilitarisation, and it is with this volte-face that we return to the issues of war and remembrance with which this preface began. Early on (and fully consistent with wartime Anglo-American pronouncements), Japan's armed forces were demobilised, virtually all military matériel was destroyed and the Imperial Army and Navy ministries were abolished. Unarmed pacifism was put forward as an ideal by which a disgraced Japan might hope to regain international trust and even admiration. In its most famous expression, pacifism was enshrined in the preamble of the new 1947 Constitution and stipulated as a binding covenant in 'Article Nine', the famous 'no war' provision. As Professor Takemae makes clear, there was from the outset some ambiguity in the phrasing of Article Nine. Nonetheless, it was generally understood that the constitutional ban on armaments excluded even the maintenance of weapons for self-defence. As late as the opening months of 1950, for example, Prime Minister Yoshida was still telling the legislature that Japan would rely on international guarantees for its security and (in a nice metaphor from feudal times) 'not employ even two swords'.

To a war-weary people who had seen most of their major cities devastated in air raids, and close to 3 million military and civilian compatriots killed, this extreme vision of 'demilitarisation' held considerable appeal. In July 1950, almost immediately after the outbreak of the Korean War, the pacifist dream was shattered. Under strong US pressure, Japan took its first step in postwar rearmament. At roughly the same time, in planning for the eventual restoration of sovereignty, the conservative government agreed to allow the United States to retain control of Okinawa and maintain an indefinite military presence throughout the nation's main islands. Before the Occupation ended in 1952, Japan had been transformed into a junior military partner of the United States – while the 'Peace Constitution' remained unrevised.

As Professor Takemae's incisive summary of post-Occupation developments reveals, time has not dissipated the tensions inherent in the circumstances under which Japan regained independence. Remilitarisation and the Constitution have become emblematic. The former symbolises a departure from early postwar ideals, a step back in the direction of the pre-surrender era. Hardly surprisingly, the conservatives who most vigorously support rearmament also tend to be the strongest deniers of Japan's 'war responsibility' and the most outspoken critics of the 'excesses' of the initial Occupation reforms, including the new Constitution. On the other hand, the fact that the 1947 Constitution survived without change to the end of the century is testimony to the continuing popular appeal of the initial vision of 'demilitarisation and democratisation'. These are contradictions within the body politic of contemporary Japan. They pull against one another. They coexist, and in their coexistence breed sophistry and cynicism.

Yet these tensions and internal struggles also remind us how greatly contemporary Japan differs from the Imperial state that ran amok prior to its defeat in 1945. Although Japan has engaged in steady remilitarisation under the eagle's wing ever since 1950, and now possesses one of the most powerful conventional forces in the world, this remains rearmament in a box. The country is still without an army or navy ministry, still without an overpowering military-industrial complex, still firmly subordinated to US grand strategy and denied autonomous decision-making. It has posed no military threat to its neighbours since the war ended, nor is it likely to do so in the future.

Indeed, the anomalous nature of this posture of 'subordinate independence' within the *Pax Americana* is, particularly to Japanese conservatives, one of the most intractable and vexing legacies of the Occupation. Every advance in military capability and redefinition of 'defensive' perimeters provokes cries of 'creeping militarism' from neighbouring Asian powers as well as from critics within the country. Every claim that Japan cannot perform certain military missions (such as sending combat troops against Iraq at the time of the Gulf War) is met with derision from erstwhile allies in the West, including the United States. Conservatives chafe at the perception that Japan remains a gelded superpower, merely 'half a state', little more than an unusually successful 'mercantile nation'. Their frustration at being unable to engage in 'normal' patriotic activity feeds the neo-nationalism that unsettles many observers today.

Professor Takemae's signal accomplishment lies in conveying the broader milieu in which these contemporary controversies have arisen. His country, he demonstrates, is far from a perfect democracy. It is a strong and viable one, however, and the early ideals of peace and democracy that inspired victor and vanquished alike in the wake of World War II still play a conspicuous role in defining the parameters of political debate. It is fair to say that the conjunction of disastrous war, defeat and occupation shaped Japan more profoundly than any other single experience in the country's twentieth-century history. And it would be difficult to find a better balance sheet of the positive and negative legacies of that experience than the one Professor Takemae gives us in the pages that follow here. His is a sober and critical analysis – and at the same time a striking exploration of how greatly his country has changed since those terrible years when Imperial Japan went on its rampage.

Introduction

Nearly two decades have elapsed since *Inside GHQ: The Allied Occupation of Japan and its Legacy* was first published in Japanese.[1] In that interval, the Cold War has dissipated, and with it the fierce US–Soviet rivalry that defined, and distorted, the postwar world order. As one menace has receded, however, another has taken its place. The devastating terrorist assaults of 11 September 2001 on the United States portend a new era of ideological and military confrontation, this time between the West and the poorest parts of the Muslim world. This crisis threatens to aggravate a host of post-Cold War tensions: nuclear proliferation, the glaring imbalance between developed and developing economies, regional and inter-ethnic conflicts and human rights abuses. As the world community calls on Japan to play a greater role in resolving these problems, the strength and resiliency of the democracy we have built on the ruins of World War II is being put to the test.

Can the nation meet this challenge? Japanese society is beset by seemingly intractable contradictions. Having at last achieved economic parity with the West, we appear to have lost our sense of national purpose and lack a coherent vision of the future. Conservative politicians have long demanded the revision of our US-inspired 'Peace' Constitution, despite strong popular support for its war-renouncing Article Nine. Today, Self-Defence Forces, illegal under that Constitution, operate in the Middle East in the name of international peace-keeping. In the wake of the recent attacks on the United States, at Washington's insistence, Tokyo has despatched armed military units to provide logistical support for US forces in Afghanistan. More than half a century after the Asia-Pacific War, however, we have yet to fully acknowledge our responsibility for that earlier conflict and make honest amends to the countries we invaded and colonised, leading our neighbors to view any foreign military role for the country with deep suspicion. Domestic problems also abound. Japanese justly pride themselves on their democratic freedoms, but even now, open criticism of the Emperor and political dissent in general are not readily condoned. Nor as a society do we easily accommodate ethnic and cultural minorities.

On 8 September 2001, Japanese celebrated the fiftieth anniversary of the signing of the San Francisco Peace Treaty that ended the Allied Occupation of Japan (1945–52), our postwar point of departure. This milestone affords a useful vantage point from which to reassess the era of defeat and occupation and its legacy of change, both to measure how far we have come as a nation and to consider the direction in which we wish to continue. That review is the ambitious task I have set for myself in this substantially revised and enlarged English edition of *Inside GHQ*.

The Allied Occupation, despite its lustre of reform and the sense of national renewal it instilled, remains a difficult period for many Japanese to come to grips with. It is the only time in our history when national sovereignty was compromised by another power. For eighty months following its surrender in 1945, Japan was at the mercy of an army of occupation, its people subject to foreign military control. Our external affairs were conducted by the American conqueror, not the Foreign Ministry. Japanese could not leave the country without special permission, which was extended only to the privileged few. Restrictions were imposed on internal migrations for the first three years, limiting freedom of movement and domicile. For four years, American soldiers ran the nation's postal system, and in the early phase of occupation, stringent information controls prohibited Japanese from communicating freely with the outside world via the mails, telephone and other media. Inside the country, too, personal letters, telecommunications, radio, press, films, photographs, song lyrics and phonograph records were monitored and censored systematically. Even news of events in the outside world was carefully filtered and managed. Criticism of Occupation policy or the Allied Powers was strictly forbidden. Moreover, Japanese were constrained, under threat of fine and imprisonment, to cooperate with their foreign overlords when ordered to do so. This affront to the national pride is difficult to forget and, for many, to forgive completely.

It is therefore an enduring and piquant irony that this temporary but degrading loss of autonomy also liberated the nation from an authoritarian régime that had suppressed the basic civil and political liberties of its own citizens and savagely invaded and oppressed its neighbours. In this brief span of time, the United States, acting for the most part alone, dramatically rewove the social, economic and political fabric of a modern industrial state, resetting its national priorities, redirecting its course of development. 'Occupation control', imposed in the name of democratisation, became a byword, and a new concept in the law of nations.

Kawai Kazuo has characterised this period as Japan's 'American interlude'.[2] Whether this interregnum was perceived as short or long, of course, depends on how and where one experienced it. For Japanese in the home islands, the six years and eight months passed quickly enough; few young people now even recognise the term *shinchūgun* (roughly, 'advancing garrison force'), a euphemism for the army of occupation. Okinawans, excluded from the postwar reforms, had to wait twenty-seven years to regain their freedom but today continue to bear the brunt of the US military presence in Japan. Koreaninhabitants of Sakhalin, still under Russian occupation, continue to await the day of liberation, as do Japan's 'invisible' minorities: disenfranchised ethnic Koreans and Chinese, indigenous Ainu and the former 'outcaste' *Buraku* people, all of whom suffer from social and institutional discrimination that Occupation reforms failed to address adequately. Migrant newcomers from the developing world inherit these problems unresolved.

The era of transformation also failed to bring closure to the thousands of Japanese children abandoned in China after the war, many of whom as adults are now seeking to reunite with parents and siblings in Japan; to the *hibakusha* victims of the atomic bombings; or to war-bereaved families. Some blame the Allied Powers for these tragedies, for the humiliation of defeat and occupation continues to rankle, and many Japanese remain ambivalent about this chapter in their history. It is easy to forget that loss of empire and the atomic bombings, like the army of occupation, were an inevitable consequence of Japan's wartime behaviour, and that the Allies' primary goal was to eliminate the possibility of Japan's ever again engaging in naked aggression. For this, all Japanese can only be grateful.

MacArthur's Headquarters
The history of GHQ, the organisation that implemented the postwar reforms, begins with the Pacific War (1941–5). Short for General Headquarters, the acronym came into wide use in the US military during that conflict and appears to have gone out of vogue not long afterwards. For historians, GHQ evokes the decade of war and Allied occupation. For Japanese, it is synonymous with more than six-and-a-half years of postwar Allied – predominantly American – rule. The term also is associated closely with the military career of General Douglas MacArthur (1880–1964), who commanded US Army forces in the Pacific and Far East during the war and later directed the Occupation as Allied Supreme Commander.[3]

GHQ was a generic designation for the various commands MacArthur held during the war. In April 1942, he established the General Headquarters, Southwest Pacific Area (GHQ/SWPA) in Melbourne, Australia, unifying under his leadership Allied forces in the region for a general counter-offensive against advancing Japanese forces. In April 1945, as Allied armies prepared to invade the Japanese home islands, American units were reorganised and placed under a single command: General Headquarters, United States Army Forces in the Pacific (USAFPAC, abbreviated hereafter as AFPAC). Located in Manila, GHQ/AFPAC became operational in June.[4] In early August 1945, MacArthur created a Military Government Section (MGS) inside AFPAC headquarters to handle non-military affairs in the areas under Allied control. In October, MGS became the core around which he built General Headquarters, Supreme Commander for the Allied Powers (GHQ/SCAP), the organisation responsible for conducting the Occupation. Many of GHQ/SCAP's top officials were trusted staff officers who had served with MacArthur in the Pacific.

A crucial but generally overlooked feature of the Occupation is its dual structure. Most Japanese mistakenly believe that there was only one General Headquarters. On 30 August 1945, upon arriving in Japan, MacArthur promptly transferred GHQ/AFPAC from Manila to Yokohama south of Tokyo. With the creation of GHQ/SCAP in Tokyo on 2 October, two headquarters organisations came into existence side by side. GHQ/AFPAC had jurisdiction over US forces in the Far East and, at the outset, about 430,000 mainly American troops in Japan. GHQ/SCAP, run initially by approximately 2,000 American bureaucrats, was responsible for the civil administration of occupied Japan. SCAP formulated basic policy in line with pre-surrender US position papers, which derived their authority from the Potsdam Proclamation of 26 July 1945. AFPAC's primary military contingent in Japan, Eighth Army, supervised the implementation of SCAP programmes at the local level. As commander in chief of both organisations, MacArthur controlled the destinies of over 74 million Japanese, including in the early months of occupation more than 2 million Koreans and Formosans, and the acronym GHQ/SCAP became synonymous both with the autocratic but charismatic general and with his headquarters staff.

MacArthur's command constituted 'an elaborate Army super-government' which, although nominally under Allied control, took its orders from Washington.[5] The Supreme Commander exercised broad discretionary powers in implementing Occupation policy, however, and often seemed a power unto himself. In principle, Occupation directives were enforced indirectly via the Japanese government, but MacArthur's staff often resorted to a combination of threat and persuasion to ensure compliance. To facilitate the task of administering Japan, GHQ/SCAP established a complement of special civil staff sections to oversee specific areas of government. Numbering about a dozen, these non-military groups were created to duplicate, in structure and function, specific Japanese ministries and agencies. As old objectives were met and new needs arose, the duties of the special staff sections were modified. Some groups were reorganised or abolished and, occasionally, new ones created.

In Japan, the conventional wisdom is that GHQ programmes were executed by inexperienced junior officers with few real qualifications for their work. The nation's first postwar education minister Maeda Tamon complained that 'Many of those who carried out the occupation administration of education were persons of extremely limited knowledge and experience in the field.' This sentiment was echoed by Kawai Kazuo in an influential book on the Occupation. Japanese educators, he asserted, had little use for the idealistic American reformers of lesser background and experience.[6] That view is patently wrong. Many military officers held advanced academic degrees and had received up to a year's intensive training in civil administration and the Japanese language at leading American universities. Moreover, SCAP recruited talented civilian experts to help run the special sections and assist in policy implementation. Thus, unlike GHQ/AFPAC, a strictly military command, GHQ/SCAP contained large numbers of non-uniformed specialists.

The competence and formal training of SCAP personnel varied, but by and large, the civilian Occupationaires were people of outstanding character and merit. They included former civil servants, financiers, labour consultants, lawyers and other professionals. PhDs abounded. Many of these experts were in uniform when the war ended and took positions in the Occupation in order to complete their service in Japan. Many remained on the job or rejoined MacArthur's headquarters after being discharged from active duty – at nearly double the salary. From 1946, SCAP relied primarily on non-military specialists to staff its huge bureaucracy; the ratio of civilian to military personnel for most of the Occupation was about four to one. Animated by a reformist zeal that was sometimes excessive, many travelled to Tokyo to put their New Deal philosophy into practice. Others came because they could not find comparably attractive work at home. Some had a genuine interest in Japan and its culture, and there were the usual adventurers and carpetbaggers, but most possessed administrative skills and expertise in some field vital to the tasks of military government.

An overwhelming majority of MacArthur's staff were Americans, although a few Australians, British and nationals of other countries could be found in specialised positions. The vast majority also were Caucasian and male, and the Occupation itself projected an unmistakable aura of white superiority reflecting the power relations governing not only victor and vanquished but also white and non-white occupier. This unstated and generally unexplored assumption has cast a long shadow over the contributions to the reform process made by Japanese Americans and women. Similarly, the role of African Americans has yet to be studied seriously. The Eighth Army, which remained segregated for most of the Occupation, included the largest all-black unit in the US Army, and black Americans were stationed across Japan. The same assumption also has obscured the role of Japanese civilians – the typists, translators, researchers, artists, expert advisers and myriad assistants – who performed SCAP's day-to-day work and accounted for more than 40 per cent of all GHQ personnel. In the prefectural Military Government Teams assigned to oversee the reform process at the grass roots, Japanese staff outnumbered the Americans, and here, many indeed were better educated than their superiors. Without the enthusiastic cooperation of these men and women, the work of occupation would have ground to a jarring halt, and yet little is known about them.

Unlike Germany and Korea, where divided Allied jurisdictions led to divided countries, in Japan proper, the United States alone exercised supreme control, and no artificial divisions were imposed on the four main islands. There, Occupation governance, conducted through existing political institutions, was indirect and relatively liberal. The first home terrain to come under foreign occupation, however, was Iwo Jima in the Ogasawaras, captured in mid-March 1945. The Ogasawaras were followed by the Kerama archipelago in the Ryukyus, which fell on 26 March, and Okinawa Island, which Allied forces had secured by 23 June. Unlike the main islands, these 'minor' territories were placed under direct US military administration, the antithesis of the democratic régime introduced in Japan proper.

Between late August and early September 1945, Soviet forces invaded and occupied southern Sakhalin and the Kuril Islands north of Hokkaido. Soviet rule there in some ways paralleled the military régime that GHQ/AFPAC established on Okinawa, which remained in US hands until 1972. In both the Kurils and the Ryukyus, civil rights were sharply curtailed or denied altogether, and life was much harsher than on the mainland, where the occupier's presence was muted. In this sense, the occupation of Japan was divided, or at least semi-divided. Today, the four southernmost Kuril islands – the so-called Northern Territories – remain under foreign control, although in the wake of the Soviet collapse, Russia has indicated a willingness to negotiate the future of certain of these territories. And in Okinawa, now a part of Japan, the US military presence continues unabated despite intense local opposition.

Historians also are prone to overlook the role of other Allied soldiers in Japan. The British Commonwealth Occupation Force (BCOF) included more than 40,000 troops from Australia, Britain, India and New Zealand. Indian soldiers were British subjects until India won its independence in 1947. During their short tenure, these colonial troops performed vital functions and gave the Occupation a cultural dimension that remains little studied. Led by an Australian, the multi-ethnic BCOF was composed of Gurkhas, Maoris, Scots, Sikhs, Welsh and half a dozen other ethnic groups and included Animists, Christians, Hindus and Muslims. Stationed in Shikoku and southwestern Japan, the Commonwealth contingent accounted at the height of its strength for nearly one quarter of all Occupation troops.

Japan's Asia–Pacific War
What social pathology propelled Japan on its course of aggression, leading to defeat and occupation by foreign armies? The Asia–Pacific War[7] did not begin with Pearl Harbor but with the Japanese invasion and occupation of Manchuria in 1931, an act that earned Tokyo international opprobrium, prompting it to withdraw in anger from the League of Nations. The creation of the puppet state of Manchukuo in March 1932 under 'Henry' Puyi, the last Qing emperor, was merely the latest in a series of colonial adventures that began in the late nineteenth century as Japan embarked on its forced march into the modern era. Manchukuo was added to a colonial empire that already included Okinawa (1879); Formosa (1895); the Kwantung Leased Territory (Port Arthur and the Liaodong Peninsula) in southern Manchuria (1905); southern Sakhalin (1905); Korea (1910); and the Pacific Mandates (1919).

In 1937, the Imperial Army launched a full-scale invasion of China. The Rape of Nanjing by the Tenth Army and the Shanghai Expeditionary Force that followed in late 1937 and early 1938 as Japanese forces drove south stunned world opinion by its savagery. For two-and-a-half months, Japanese troops under General Matsui Iwane, Commander of the China Theatre Headquarters, rampaged, engaging in an orgy of rape, pillage, arson and murder in which hundreds of thousands of Chinese reportedly were killed.[8] Japan's bellicose South Manchurian garrison, the Kwantung Army, moved westward out of Manchuria, overrunning most of Inner Mongolia by the autumn of 1938. In March 1940, as the Kwantung Army engaged in a wider campaign of annihilation against Chinese and Korean partisans in Manchuria and northern China, Imperial forces established a puppet régime in the old southern capital of Nanjing under Wang Ching-wei, a Nationalist leader who had defected from Chiang Kai-shek (Jiang Jieshi)'s Republican ranks. The Japan–China Basic Treaty of November 1940 recognised the Wang régime as the sole legitimate government of China.

Two years earlier, in November 1938, Prime Minister Prince Konoe Fumimaro had called for a 'New Order' in Asia, justifying Japanese aggression in China as necessary to combat the twin evils of Western imperialism and Communism. In December of that year, Konoe created the Asia Development Board to administer political, economic and cultural policies towards China. Japan's attempt to impose by armed might a hegemonic New Order uniting Asia in a single political and economic bloc under Imperial rule – euphemistically expressed in such slogans as 'the eight corners of the world under one roof' (that is, the world unified under the Japanese Emperor, *hakkō ichi'u*) – made a wider Asiatic and Pacific war inevitable.

Since the late 1930s, ultra-nationalist officers had insisted dogmatically that alliance with the Axis nations and military expansion into Asia were Japan's only hope of countering an attempt by the Western powers to encircle the country, sever its lifeline to oil and other natural resources and strangle the economy. To bolster its diplomatic position, Japan deepened its links with the Axis alliance through the Anti-Comintern Pact of 1936. Tokyo officially cast its lot with Germany and Italy following the signing of the Tripartite Pact in September 1940, one year after Hitler's armies had rolled across Poland igniting World War II. As in the case of Germany and Italy, Japanese leaders believed their nation had been wrongly denied its fair share of colonial spoils in the 'post-imperialist' world order that emerged from the ashes of World War I.[9] They demanded a redistribution of wealth and power in Asia commensurate with Japan's industrial and military might. This imperial ambition was clothed in the ideological garb of divine mission and spiritual destiny but rested on a shrewd practical calculation: by allying with Germany, the probable victor in the coming European conflict, Japan could assert hegemony over British, Dutch, French and Portuguese possessions in Southeast Asia after the retreat of the West European powers. Paradoxically, however, only some kind of understanding with Japan's major rivals in northern Asia and the Pacific, the Soviet Union and the United States, would free its hand in the south. The inconsistent and ultimately self-defeating policy of reaching an accommodation with Moscow and Washington while attempting to undercut their interests in Asia was, as one historian phrases it, 'more opportunistic than dogmatic and more ambiguous than systematic'.[10]

Militarily, this strategy required a major shift in emphasis. Since the Bolshevik Revolution, Imperial General Headquarters had pursued a northern policy that targeted the Soviet Union as Japan's primary enemy. During the 1930s, some 500 armed clashes erupted between Japanese and Red Army troops along the Soviet–Chinese frontier, some of them raising the prospect of war. In May 1939, Kwantung Army units engaged Mongolian forces at Nomonhan (Khalkhin Gol) on the border between Japanese-controlled Inner Mongolia and the Mongolian People's Republic ('Outer' Mongolia). At the Mongolians' request, Soviet troops intervened in June, and by August, Soviet armoured units, aircraft and flamethrowers had routed the poorly mechanised Kwantung Army at a cost to the Japanese of 20,000 dead and missing. Entire divisions suffered casualties in excess of 70 per cent, and more than 3,000 were taken prisoner. In August, Moscow and Berlin signed a non-aggression pact, forcing Tokyo to accept a diplomatic settlement to this 'four-month-long small war'. Japan's devastating defeat led military planners to focus their energies on a southward expansion.[11]

By early 1941, however, events seemed to be developing in Japan's favour. Germany had overrun most of Europe, and Britain was under attack by air and sea while the United States watched from the sidelines. On 25 April 1941, Tokyo and Moscow ratified a five-year Neutrality Pact pledging mutual non-intervention in the case of attack by a third power. Negotiated by Konoe's Foreign Minister Matsuoka Yōsuke, the architect of Japan's Tripartite agreement, the Pact could be renewed automatically, barring prior notification to the contrary, by either side. Nearly three months later, on 22 July 1941, the Nazi war machine stormed across the Soviet border in a massive display of armed might. With Great Britain and the Soviet Union expected to succumb to the Nazi onslaught, Japan now had only the United States to reckon with in the Pacific.

Washington, however, viewed Japanese aggression in China as an attempt to terminate American influence throughout Asia and responded with economic sanctions. In July 1939, the United States signalled its intention to terminate Japan's Most Favoured Nation status and subsequently outlawed the export of scrap metal. These first shots in what would become a 'cycle of mutual provocation' reinforced the determination of Imperial General Headquarters to turn to Southeast Asia as a source of raw materials.[12] In late July 1941, following the Imperial Army's march into southern French Indo-China (with the support of France's collaborationist Vichy régime), Britain, the Netherlands and the United States froze Japanese assets. For Tokyo, the final blow fell on 1 August 1941 when Washington embargoed oil exports.

To ordinary Japanese, these events confirmed the militarists' claims of 'ABCD' encirclement by the Americans, British, Chinese and Dutch. The assertion that Japan's advance into China and Southeast Asia was an act of self-defence was an egregiously self-serving argument that carried little weight outside of this country. Yet, as Assistant Secretary of State Dean Acheson later recalled, the United States badly misread Japanese intentions and the 'incredibly high risks' General Tōjō Hideki would incur to protect his country's perceived interests: 'No one in Washington realised that he and his régime regarded the conquest of Asia not as the accomplishment of an ambition but as the survival of a régime. It was a life-and-death matter to them. They were absolutely unwilling to continue in what they regarded as Japan's precarious position surrounded by great and hostile powers.'[13]

To Americans, Japan was another fascist power bent on world domination. And on the surface, the country indeed displayed similarities with the dictatorships that had evolved in Germany and Italy. The doctrine of racial supremacy, the inculcation of militarist and corporatist values and the glorification of war and territorial conquest had much in common with Nazism. Many military leaders, bureaucrats and politicians embraced the Japanese variant of national socialism, and the economy was dominated by a handful of monopoly capitalists eager to profit from military adventures. Society was tightly regimented, and the people were denied basic civil liberties and subjected to rigid police controls. The education system was geared to produce obedient subjects ready to lay down their lives for the Emperor.

Although Japan was an authoritarian society, it was not totalitarian, however, and its social and political structure differed in important ways from that of its German and Italian allies. In October 1940, Prince Konoe, prime minister for a second time from July of that year, dissolved the country's labour unions and political parties into

Photo 1. Emperor Hirohito, Supreme Commander of the Imperial Armed Forces, reviews Army troops at the Yoyogi Training Grounds in Tokyo, 8 January 1940 (Kyodo).

a mass super-organisation, the Imperial Rule Assistance Association (IRAA), which was designed to consolidate the Imperial Order at home. His primary aim, however, was to create a civilian counterpoise to the pro-war militarist cabal around General Tōjō, who replaced the Prince as premier in October 1941. In 1942, Tōjō intensified the military's efforts to recast this patriotic association in the mould of the Nazi Party and its auxiliary groupings, but the IRAA never attained the same degree of cohesiveness as its German and Italian counterparts. The Imperial Diet (Parliament) continued to convene throughout the war, although under the circumscribed conditions dictated by the national emergency. Nonetheless, about 30 per cent of Diet members refused to seek the endorsement of Tōjō's expanded IRAA in the 1942 general elections and yet managed to win seats. Many of these politicians were purged by the victors after the defeat, but some, including right-wing Socialists, would continue to play prominent roles in postwar political life.

Unlike Germany, Japan's wartime political structure was characterised by institutional continuity and stability; the same functionaries who had served the state in peacetime served it just as loyally in time of war.[14] Moreover, Japan's leadership was collective. The Emperor stood at the apex of the government and military establishment, a position enshrined in the 1890 Meiji Constitution, but did not rule directly. He leaned heavily on a group of senior statesmen and former premiers, the *Genrō*, who had played a salient role in the nation's political life through the 1930s. Although devoid of any legal or even formal status, the *Genrō* intervened in all major political decisions, advising the Emperor and mediating between Throne and government. After the 1930s, the *Jūshin*, a strategic council consisting of living former prime ministers, assumed this vital function. Real influence was wielded by political and military factions close to the Court who ruled in the Emperor's name. Power was not concentrated in one man or institution, however, and, as a wartime American writer observed, General Tōjō never enjoyed the influence wielded by a Roosevelt or Churchill, let alone a Hitler or Mussolini.[15] Tōjō led not by virtue of his personal charisma but because of his military rank and multiple Cabinet posts (in October 1941, on his accession as prime minister, he simultaneously headed the Ministries of Foreign Affairs, Home Affairs and War).

Moreover, the Japanese leadership was divided, its national socialists leaning in two opposing directions. Ultra-nationalist 'go-fast' imperialists in Tōjō's Control Faction (*Tōseiha*) found themselves at odds with the 'go-slow' social reformers in the military and bureaucracy, the so-called Imperial Way Faction (*Kōdōha*), which shared Konoe's vision of reconstructing Japan and revitalising the Imperial Order from within. Some 'reconstructionists' espoused Socialist ideals, earning them the derisive nickname 'Red fascists' or 'emperor-system Communists'. Several of the brightest young radicals found a home on the Cabinet Planning Board, which Konoe had created in 1937 to coordinate civil and military war planning at the highest level of government and rationalise the war economy (in early 1941, seventeen young bureaucrats would be arrested under an anti-subversion law for their 'left-wing progressive' ideas).[16]

Imperial General Headquarters, too, pursued a divided strategy. Until its devastating setback at Nomonhan in 1939, the Army had prepared to fight a continental war against the Soviet Union, not a war of attrition against Western armies in Southeast Asia. With sufficient reserves of petroleum and other war matériel to last at best two years, the Army General Staff shifted to a southern strategy of assuring access to the region's raw materials as a base for future expansion. Under Admiral Yamamoto Isoroku, the architect of Japan's Pacific strategy, the Imperial Navy argued instead for a series of lightning maritime offensives designed to disorientate and demoralise the Western adversary and secure an early truce on terms favourable to Japan. Tōjō and the Army were responsible for the decision to go to war, but they were not privy to the details of the planned attack on Pearl Harbor, a strictly Navy operation. Responsible directly to the Emperor, not to the Cabinet, the Imperial high command as a whole later withheld from the government – and even from its own Army and Navy ministers – negative information about the progress of the fighting.

Hirohito alone seemed to stand above these internal rivalries. Although the monarch did not have operational control, he was informed of all military decisions taken in his name, supported them, helped shape strategy, second-guessed command decisions and occasionally intervened in field operations. Presiding over the dozen or so Imperial Conferences convened between 1938 and 1945, he rarely spoke and never initiated strategy, but his presence was the enabling factor that held together the fissiparous tendencies represented there.

Many critical war choices were suggested, however, not by paramount leaders but by middle-ranking military officers, whose views percolated upward through the hierarchy via a process of consensus-building, eventually congealing at the top as policy. The crucial decision leading to war was taken at the Imperial Conference of 2 July 1941, when the government and military high command endorsed the establishment of a Greater East Asia Co-Prosperity Sphere in Asia and agreed to advance southwards, preparing for hostilities with the Anglo-American alliance should negotiations fail. When Britain, Holland and the United States suspended oil exports to Japan in August of that year, it was mid-echelon staff officers who insisted that war with the Allies was inevitable unless such restrictions were removed by a specific date. Their position, formulated in an Imperial Navy policy document, was adopted by the Imperial Conference of 6 September 1941, which set a deadline for war with Great Britain, the United States and Holland, barring a change in Allied policy by October.[17]

Hirohito expressed reservations about declaring war, and Konoe, convinced he could overturn the Conference's decision in time, intensified negotiations with Washington in hopes of finding a modus vivendi. On 5 November, another Imperial Conference set early December as the date Japan would go to war. On 26 November (Eastern Standard Time), US Secretary of State Cordell Hull issued a set of 10 conditions which Japanese leaders read as a de facto ultimatum. The so-called Hull Note called for abrogation of the Tripartite Pact, a non-aggression accord with the Allied Powers and the withdrawal of all military forces from China (including Manchuria) and French Indo-China. The Note was the point of no return. On 7 December, Japanese aircraft attacked the US Pacific Fleet headquarters at Pearl Harbor. Their objective was to prevent a flanking action against Japanese troops then deploying rapidly across Southeast Asia. The strike, a contingency action planned by Admiral Yamamoto who personally had hoped to avoid war with the West, had been in preparation since early 1941.[18]

The legacy of Imperial conquest

From late 1941, as Japanese armies pushed relentlessly into Asia, they put Western forces in the region to rout. This stunning victory over seemingly invincible European-led colonial armies enabled Japan to portray itself as a liberator of oppressed peoples, emphasising ties of blood and colour despite its own record as a colonial oppressor. Such rhetoric was potent medicine in a region where, as one historian has pointed out, roughly 500,000 British dominated 350 million Indians and 6 million Malayans; 200,000 Dutch colonists ruled 60 million Indonesians; 20,000 French soldiers and administrators controlled the lives of 23 million Indo-Chinese; and a few tens of thousands of Americans lorded it over 13 million Filipinos.[19] By mid-1942, a series of spectacular battlefield victories left Imperial forces in control of vast areas of Asia and the Pacific.

The vision of easy success was to prove ephemeral, however. Japan's leadership had no grand design for waging war, nor a backup plan for extracting itself from a quagmire should retreat become necessary. In addition the uneasy coalition of civilian and military leaders who ruled the country disagreed on the war's overall objectives. By 1943, Japanese troops were on the defensive throughout the Pacific. Factions unhappy with Tōjō's conduct of the war deposed the General in July 1944 as the Imperial Army and Navy reeled from a string of strategic defeats. Tōjō was replaced by General Koiso Kuniaki, Governor General of Korea. In April 1945 with Allied troops invading Okinawa, Koiso ceded the leadership to Admiral Suzuki Kantarō, an ageing hero of the Russo-Japanese war.

Japan also was ill-prepared to assume the burdens of a pan-Asian empire, with its leaders lacking even a rudimentary understanding of the region. It was only in September 1938 that the Cabinet Planning Board established the East Asian Institute (*Tōa Kenkyūjo*) to acquire basic knowledge about the ethnic composition, ecology and socio-economic conditions of China, Southeast Asia and the Pacific. Politico-military planning lagged even further behind. The establishment of the Asia Development Board in December 1938 enabled Tokyo to begin coordinating policy towards China, but a comparable administrative organ was not created for all of Asia until late 1942 (see below). On 25 November 1941, shortly before Japan's invasion of Southeast Asia, the Military Command and Government Liaison Council published a hastily conceived scenario for military occupation entitled 'Guidelines for the Administration of the Southern Occupied Territories'. The Guidelines laid down three principles of military government: pacification, the acquisition of natural resources and military self-sufficiency. Independence movements were to be encouraged but as a secondary objective to be pursued only after these larger goals had been achieved.[20]

Military governments subsequently were installed in the territories under Japanese control, but these worked through local-level civil administrations staffed by indigenous officials. Japanese civil affairs specialists from the Home Affairs Ministry and other government agencies in Tokyo were despatched to supervise the local bureaucracies. The Imperial Army, on the other hand, drew its military administrators largely from China, Korea and Manchuria. The Kwantung Army and Imperial forces in Korea had ample experience with the tasks of colonial rule. The hard-core military cadre sent to administer the Empire's new Southeast Asian possessions would be referred to contemptuously by local functionaries as the 'Korea clique'. Serious friction sometimes erupted between Japanese civilian and military administrators, but the military reigned supreme, promptly removing both Japanese and local bureaucrats who objected to its policies.[21]

In August 1942, the Imperial Army set up a local civil government in Burma under the radical anti-British nationalist Ba Maw, and in August 1943, that country declared its independence. In October of the same year, the Philippines established a republic under Japanese tutelage, and in December, the Provisional Government of Free India led by Subhas Chandra Bose was created in Singapore. In the East Indies, too, Mohammad Hatta, Sukarno and other nationalists collaborated with the Japanese, who pledged eventual independence to the Dutch colony. In Malaya, Japan utilised the existing British civil administration, jailing British officials and replacing them with local subordinates who underwent 're-education' and civil affairs training in Singapore. The Imperial Army helped establish and train the Indian National Army and the Burmese Independence Army. In Malaya, it created the Malay Volunteer Army and, in the Dutch East Indies, the Army for Defenders of the Homeland. More than 350,000 young Asians joined these regular armies, and some 180 officers received formal military instruction in the Japanese metropolis. Local paramilitary and vigilante groups also were formed to assist indigenous police forces, which the Japanese military retained and placed under its control.[22]

To oversee this vast empire, in November 1942, Tokyo created the Greater East Asia Ministry, which absorbed the Asia Development Board and usurped important Foreign Ministry functions, prompting Foreign Minister Tōgō Shigenori to resign in protest. In October 1943, the new Ministry brought nationalist leaders from six 'independent' nations to Tokyo to attend a Greater East Asia Council. There, Burma, China (Wang Ching-wei), Japan, Manchukuo, the Philippines and Thailand formally inaugurated the Greater East Asia Co-Prosperity Sphere (the Provisional Government of Free India attended as an observer). In British Borneo, the Dutch East Indies, British Malaya and other areas rich in petroleum, rubber, tin and bauxite, however, Imperial forces pursued a policy of 'permanent control', although here, too, they were forced to adopt the expedient of indirect rule. In Malaya, for instance, the Imperial Military Government formulated a three-pronged policy (October 1942) of using 'native princes' (sultans) as military governors, securing adequate petroleum stocks and restricting the political influence of local Chinese.[23] Chinese were repressed, and their merchant class was bled dry by forced financial 'contributions'. Japanese military administrations proved adept at manipulating popular hatred of European colonialism and exploiting inter-ethnic antagonisms.

By shattering the mystique of Western supremacy, discrediting the old colonial élite, promoting younger Asia-orientated civil and military leaders, and encouraging national languages such as Tagalog and Indonesian, the Japanese interregnum proved a major catalyst for the postwar upsurge of national independence movements. The Imperial Army's harsh repression of civilian populations everywhere, and its imposition of 'Japanisation' (forcible assimilation) programmes, however, quickly disabused many anti-colonialists of their illusions. In schools, children were taught Japanese, forced to sing the Japanese national anthem while facing towards Tokyo and perform acts of obeisance before veiled portraits of the Emperor. People were compelled to observe the Emperor's birthday and other Japanese festivals, visit shrines and bow to Japanese officials. A Japanese-style family registration (*koseki*) system was set up, and local neighbourhood associations (*tonari-gumi*) were created for mutual surveillance. Political rights were sharply curtailed and disobedience was punishable by death. Military rule often was brutal. Following the capture of Singapore in February 1942, Imperial forces arrested 70,000 Chinese and massacred tens of thousands in reprisal for alleged acts of resistance. As the mask of pan-Asianism slipped, revealing the arrogant master-race thinking behind it, the Japanese 'liberator' seemed no better, and in some ways even worse, than the Western coloniser. Among the Asian élite, sham independence generally was recognised for what it was. As one historian has expressed it, '[t]o be fêted in Tokyo did not quite make up for having one's face slapped in Rangoon or Manila'.[24]

Under Japanese rule, tens of thousands of Indonesians, overseas Chinese and Malays were drafted as 'labour recruits' (*rōmusha*) and made to perform onerous corvée duties for the occupant. Between 80,000 and 100,000 women, predominately Koreans but including other nationalities as well, were pressed into servitude in military brothels throughout Asia, only to be abandoned or killed later by retreating soldiers.[25] Enemy civilians and prisoners of war suffered inhuman treatment in internment centres in China, Borneo, Burma, the Dutch East Indies, Hong Kong, the Philippines, Malaya, Thailand and Indo-China. Korean 'auxiliaries' were mobilised to work in these camps, carrying out the orders of their Japanese superiors under threat of extreme sanction.[26] The Draconian measures Japanese garrisons introduced in the territories they occupied afford a stark contrast with the beneficent policies Japan's Allied conquerors followed after the war, and even to those Japan itself had adopted in its earlier wars on the Eurasian continent.[27] During the conflict, somewhere between 10 and 15 million Chinese are thought to have perished. About 4 million Indonesians reportedly died from war and occupation as well as an estimated 30,000 Dutch and other European inhabitants. Some 100,000 Filipinos perished in the Battle of Manila alone, and as many as 100,000 Malays are believed to have died under Japanese occupation. In French Indo-China, from 1944 to 1945, between 1 and 2 million people starved to death in famines aggravated by Japanese economic policies and forcible rice requisitions, and a similar disaster in Bengal claimed 1.5 million victims. India also reported some 180,000 war deaths. Fighting in the Pacific claimed the lives of 100,000 Americans, 30,000 Australians and 10,000 New Zealanders.[28]

The war brought disaster to Japan as well, where nearly 3 million people – almost 4 per cent of the population – died of war-related causes. At the conflict's end, Japan's major cities were charred ruins, and some 10 million people hovered near starvation. The prompt repatriation of 6.6 million soldiers and overseas Japanese compounded the nation's distress. One quarter of Japan's physical structures had been destroyed, including more than a third of its industrial machine tools, and 82 per cent of all shipping had been sunk or disabled. Industrial output stood at a mere 10 per cent of the prewar level. Agricultural production had fallen to 60 per cent, and real wages to 30 per cent. The total damage inflicted was the equivalent of 25 per cent of the national wealth.[29] The devastation wrought by Allied bombing was extensive but not total, however. Japan's rail network, hydroelectric structures and two thirds of its heavy industrial base remained intact, providing a modest foundation on which postwar recovery could begin.

The Allied reforms
Allied policy towards post-surrender Japan was strongly coloured by revulsion at its wartime transgressions and the jingoist ideology that had legitimised imperialist expansion. The victors were determined to extirpate the social values that had fed aggression and ensure that Japan would never again pose a military threat to its neighbours. To effect this sweeping transformation, GHQ/SCAP initiated in the early months of occupation an unprecedented régime of social engineering that began with a thorough-going programme of demilitarisation. The Imperial Army and Navy were disarmed and demobilised, the professional military establishment was dissolved and suspected war criminals were arrested and placed on trial. Industrial disarmament followed as factories involved in military production were razed, shut down or scheduled for reparations. Early measures were pre-emptive and designed to police and punish those responsible for the war. Virtually overnight, SCAP swept away the repressive infrastructure that had supported the prewar police state. The dreaded Special Higher Police was disbanded and the Peace Preservation Law of 1925, notorious for its suppression of civil liberties, was revoked. Occupation authorities also purged military, government and business leaders as well as teachers, media executives and medical doctors from their wartime positions, a kind of moral and ideological disarmament.

Early punitive reforms, however, also were intended to liberate, and subsequent positive policies designed to democratise built on these. Political, economic, administrative, social and cultural reforms were boldly constructive, even radical. The political project drew much of its inspiration from the US Bill of Rights, New Deal social legislation, the liberal constitutions of several European states and even the Soviet national charter. In 1946, GHQ proposed a new constitution that transferred sovereignty from the Emperor to the people in an attempt to depoliticise the Throne and reduce it to the status of a state symbol. Included in the revised charter was the famous 'no-war', 'no arms' Article Nine, which outlawed belligerency as an instrument of state policy and the maintenance of a standing army. The 1947 Constitution also enfranchised women, guaranteed fundamental human rights, strengthened the powers of Parliament and the Cabinet, and decentralised the police and local government.

During the war years, nearly 90 per cent of Japanese industrial capacity had been allocated, directly or indirectly, to military production. GHQ buttressed its liberalisation campaign with a programme of economic democratisation. This was designed to restructure Japanese capitalism by demilitarising production, decentralising and decompressing the economy, eliminating paternalism in the workplace and restoring a basic level of production. To achieve these goals, SCAP strengthened workers' rights and encouraged a free labour movement, dissolved the *zaibatsu* cartels that had dominated the pre-1945 economy, and implemented a far-reaching land reform that virtually eliminated the institution of tenancy. Finally, through a series of social and cultural reforms, the Occupation attempted to eradicate the Imperial family-state ideology that had fostered chauvinistic values and military aggression. The education system was decentralised and restructured to instill democratic ideals, and centralised control of the mass media was abolished to allow free expression. To further weaken the Imperial institution and bolster liberal government, SCAP dismantled the system of State Shintō and instrumented a strict separation of state and religion. At the same time, MacArthur's staff liberated Japan's medical and health-care systems from military control and thoroughly reorganised them in one of the unsung success stories of the Occupation.

It is a truism that democracy cannot be imposed 'from above'. Yet most Japanese, and particularly the nation's youth, disillusioned by defeat and weary of the privations and suffering of the war years, embraced the Occupation reforms with relief and genuine enthusiasm. Of course, the wartime leadership and intellectuals who had glorified militarism resisted change, and many of those who finally accepted the new régime did so grudgingly and from expedience. Conservatives manoeuvred to dilute many SCAP reforms, or to reinterpret them in ways that preserved and enhanced bureaucratic authority. The ethnic rights of Korean and Formosan minorities, for example, were not protected, and these former colonial subjects were largely excluded from the purview of reform, as were Okinawans. GHQ also failed to act decisively to eliminate social discrimination against other groups, such as the indigenous Ainu and the *Buraku* minority.

A dynamic tension quickly arose, however, between Occupation edict and persuasion on the one hand and Japanese initiative on the other, and while the relationship between occupier and occupied clearly was unequal, mutual collaboration produced salutary and lasting results. In some instances, Japanese surprised General Headquarters by pressing for reforms that did not exist in US law and went well beyond what MacArthur's staff was prepared to grant. Revisions to the Civil and Criminal Codes, women's rights guarantees, the labour reforms, land redistribution, the reorientation of education and the health and welfare reforms, in particular, were implemented, and in some instances proposed, by forward-looking Japanese men and women who used SCAP to advance their own reformationist goals, long suppressed by the old régime. Initially, they were aided in this task by government insiders, whose more conservative thinking advocated limits on change but nonetheless acknowledged its inevitability.[30] There was, in short, a powerful surge of creative energy 'from below' without which the occupier's reform projections could not have been realised. The thesis of Japan's democratisation 'from above', while accurate enough in some respects, has prevented a fuller appreciation of the diverse and imaginative ways in which Japanese from all walks of life sought to utilise the Occupation to reassert control over the destiny of their communities and the nation.

It was the active engagement of the majority that enabled the Occupation's ambitious new order to take root and flourish. Ironically, towards the end of the Allied tenure, this innovating impulse would bring large segments of the public into open conflict with the American benefactor.

The Occupation was not the simple experiment in democracy it is often portrayed to be. With the intensification of the Cold War, SCAP reined in its reform initiatives. From late 1947, US priorities shifted perceptibly from liberal social change to internal political stability and economic recovery. Demilitarisation and democratisation lost momentum and then seemed to stall. Economic deconcentration, for example, was left uncompleted as GHQ responded to new imperatives. American authorities encouraged business practices and industrial policies that have since become sources of contention between Japan and its major trade partners, notably the United States. Key administrative and education reforms were partially turned back. General Headquarters violated some of its own labour principles, which it now found constricting and inconvenient. At the same time, the government, at SCAP's instigation and with its active collaboration, began to suppress the peace movement and other popular initiatives, preventing these from playing a more prominent, and perhaps decisive, role in hastening full democratisation.

The Red Purge of 1949 and 1950 epitomised this downshifting of gears, known popularly after 1950 as the 'reverse course'. During this period, MacArthur's headquarters directed the indiscriminate dismissal of thousands of workers in the public and private sectors, many of them anti-Communists, for alleged left-wing sympathies. The Americans were assisted in this endeavour by old-school 'reform bureaucrats', men (and a few women) of some vision ensconced in key middle-echelon jobs, who accepted change as necessary but were determined to contain it within limits manageable by the state and big business. The Japanese political élite lent this movement the full force of its authority, and conservative lawmakers and businessmen applauded the return to pragmatism. This unholy alliance attempted to constrict the ideological parameters of Japanese democracy, violating the spirit, and sometimes the letter, of the postwar reforms. After 1950, with war raging in Korea and McCarthyism rampant at home, SCAP no longer defended what it had preached so fervently a few years earlier; only those philosophies it found acceptable would be permitted to compete in the marketplace of ideas. From that point forward, the responsibility for completing the early reform agenda and bringing democracy to fruition would rest on the shoulders of ordinary Japanese outside the corridors of power.

The historical significance of the Occupation
The nature and significance of the Occupation reforms remain subjects of intense debate both in Japan and abroad. Scholars using 'modernisation' as an analytical tool have emphasised the continuities between prewar and postwar society, asserting that the Occupation accelerated changes that were latent or already in train. This is the position taken by many Western researchers, but some Japanese students, too,

share this view. A prominent Japanese historian, for instance, writes that while democratisation policies improved 'the rather illogical systems' of the prewar period, ultimately, they simply transferred 'old wine into new bottles and did nothing much to change the way things were done'.[31] Other observers, the author included, have stressed the discontinuities, emphasising the dissociative impact of the postwar reforms on Japan's prewar social structure and cultural traditions.

It is true that some reform programmes displayed striking parallels with pre-defeat projects for change, and that GHQ officials borrowed – sometimes unknowingly – from the agendas that progressive-minded Japanese had advanced in the 1930s and now formulated once more in the heady, hope-charged months following the defeat. Labour and land reform proposals, for instance, had been submitted to the Imperial Diet before and even during the war. Similar attempts were made to reorganise the *zaibatsu* and the school system. Soon after the war's end, the government outlined plans for a partial reformation of the bureaucracy, welfare administration and the electoral, land-tenure and education systems. These initiatives, however, largely were designed to forestall more radical action by Allied authorities. Nothing in pre-surrender Japan could have prepared the nation for the sea change that the Occupation brought about. The wartime shortage of labour, for instance, had led large numbers of women into the workplace. This indubitably was the point of departure for later struggles to achieve gender equality, but the postwar women's movement signalled a qualitative shift away from the stance taken by war-era feminists, many of whom had collaborated with the military régime. While endogenous input was a necessary ingredient in the formula for change, it was not sufficient of itself.

A particularly strong case for the continuity thesis is the virtually uninterrupted prestige and influence enjoyed by the bureaucracy after the war. One of the trenchant ironies of the Occupation is not only that the most liberating postwar reforms were imposed by foreigners but that they were implemented by many of the junior and mid-level functionaries who had managed the affairs of empire during the war. GHQ purged its ranks but never completely broke the power of this central control apparatus, whose inbred conservatism tended to fetter the reform process as the Occupation progressed. GHQ attempted to turn this machine to its own use rather than dismantle it, seeking allies among officials who had supported labour and welfare reforms in the 1920s and 1930s in an effort to protect industrial capitalism from its own worst abuses. In their 40s at the time of surrender, a number learned English quickly and became adept at working with the American occupier. These so-called social or reform bureaucrats would support MacArthur's headquarters in its turn to the right, using GHQ's anti-Communism as a foil to achieve their own paternalistic agenda.

And yet the Allied reform programme provoked a decisive rupture with many institutional values and practices of the past. This is true not only of the retributive or 'negative' reforms, such as the elimination of the military caste and the police state, but also of GHQ's positive endeavours, especially the guarantee of basic civil liberties, women's rights, the labour and land reforms, and the revolution in health and welfare, none of which could have been completed without direct and forceful intervention on the part of MacArthur's headquarters. This disjunctive moment left an indelible imprint on postwar society that cannot be adduced solely from earlier, often feeble and piecemeal attempts at institutional streamlining.

In a sense, the attempt to plot the evolution of postwar Japan in terms of the vectors of continuity/discontinuity is simplistic, for implicit in this debate is a question of time frame. In the long sweep of history, say several centuries, the Occupation appears less significant, but in terms of the past half century or so, its reform objectives and projections determined in significant measure the character and direction of postwar social change. This transformation would have been impossible without the overarching authority of the Supreme Commander. In the absence of an Allied military presence, the constitutional order we enjoy today could not have evolved. Conservatives argue that this order was imposed at gunpoint. Perhaps, but we should remember that, as Christian Socialist Katayama Tetsu once commented in defence of the Constitution, it was imposed on reactionaries, not the people, and that most Japanese recognised that singular fact.

Of course, Occupation policies were not uniform; their force and direction varied with time and place. Nor were they equally successful. The first six to eight months had the greatest impact on democratisation. During this brief period, the authority of Japan's wartime rulers had reached its nadir and popular support for reform was at its pinnacle. In other words, in the heat of popular enthusiasm, conditions were ripe for reshaping the 'substance' of traditional Japanese institutions under the hammer of SCAP fiats. After the first two years, however, countervailing forces emerged both within General Headquarters and within Japan's ruling establishment that muted many of the achievements of the early months, restoring some degree of continuity with prewar society. In general, the Occupation began on a very high note and then, after 1947, went steadily downhill, a subject that is examined in the final section of this book. Today, more than half a century later, our understanding of these events is still incomplete, and basic research remains to be done.[32] It is my hope that the present volume will inspire younger scholars to delve deeper into the history of this short but remarkable era to shed fresh light on our 'post-modern' predicament.

The English edition

Inside GHQ is the story of how these reforms came about, of the organisation that was created in October 1945 to implement them and of the remarkable men and women who staffed it.[33] To a lesser extent, it is also the story of the Japanese who cooperated with the Occupationaires, both reform-minded individuals who embraced MacArthur's liberalising project and conservatives of various stripes. Part I traces the origins of MacArthur's headquarters to the closing days of the Asia–Pacific War. Part II details the organisation of GHQ and introduces the leading military and civilian experts who ran the Occupation. Parts III and IV examine the reforms themselves, their genesis and the complex interplay between the American and

Japanese officials who enacted them. Part V describes the fate of those projects as US objectives in Japan shifted rightward in response to Cold War pressures, culminating in the outbreak of a shooting war on the Korean peninsula, and considers their relevance for Japanese society today.

The present work differs substantially from the original monograph in several respects. Since *Inside GHQ* was published in Japanese in 1983, a number of seminal studies of the Occupation have appeared in Japanese and in English, and I have tried to incorporate their insights into these pages.[34] The basic themes developed in the original remain pertinent today, but I have broadened the analytical framework and considerably enriched the historical narrative. Explanatory information also has been added for the benefit of readers unfamiliar with contemporary Japanese history. These changes have entailed writing a new introduction, reorganising and expanding the original materials and adding a chapter on the welfare reforms and minorities and a concluding essay on the Occupation legacy. In the process, the number of chapters has grown from four to eleven.

I observe East Asian practice and transcribe Japanese, Chinese and Korean names giving the surname first, personal name last (an exception are Japanese American names, which are given in Western order). In English-language works, Japanese name order follows the preference of the author. Nationalist Chinese names are rendered in Wade-Giles romanisation, other Chinese names and place names in *pin yin*. Japanese dates fall one day later than in the United States and Europe and are used for events occurring in East Asia. Macrons are employed over long vowels in Japanese words to indicate correct pronunciation, exceptions being well-known place names and terms that have entered the English language. The original monograph did not include endnotes. In this edition, relevant Japanese and English sources are cited, but relatively inaccessible primary references have been kept to a minimum in order to avoid further encumbering an already burdened text.

Because I lost my sight in the 1970s, I have presumed on the generosity of many people in completing this project. I am especially indebted to Matsuno Masako, Naitō Kazuko (deceased) and Tanaka Kaori, my talented assistants at Tokyo Keizai University. Sasamoto Yukuo, Takano Kazumoto and Miura Yōichi helped organise the original data, took dictation and prepared the chronological tables, bibliography, glossary of acronyms and index for the Japanese version. Members of the Kokubunji and Machida Volunteer Readers groups served as my eyes. Mr Sasamoto and Ms Tanaka also read with me the many drafts of the English version.

Former GHQ officials offered valuable insights into Occupation history through personal interviews. They include Robert Amis, W. MacMahon Ball, William K. Bunce, Valery Burati, Theodore Cohen, John K. Emmerson, Beate Sirota Gordon, Benjamin Hazard, James Hoover, Charles L. Kades, William Karpinsky, Arthur R. Menzies, Jack P. Napier, Alfred C. Oppler, Mark T. Orr, Crawford F. Sams, Elliott R. Thorpe, Cecil G. Tilton and Justin Williams Sr.

I gratefully acknowledge the kind cooperation of Hoshi Ken'ichi of the National Diet Library, Tokyo; Okiyama Nobuko and Ōi Fumiko of the American Center,

Tokyo; Morimatsu Toshio of the Military History Department, National Institute of Defense Studies, Tokyo; Fujishiro Manae of the Library of Congress, Washington DC; Frank J. Shulman of the McKeldin Library, University of Maryland; and Okuizumi Eizaburō of the Japanese Section, University of Chicago Library. Eric A. Saxon provided invaluable assistance in locating materials relating to the British Commonwealth Occupation Force.

I also wish to express my gratitude to Tokyo Keizai University's Academic Publication Fund for providing a grant to offset the costs of publishing a work of this length.

Finally, I am especially indebted to Robert Ricketts and Sebastian Swann for their painstaking care in translating and adapting this work from the Japanese and to Mr Ricketts for enlarging it, under my direction, to encompass recent scholarship, including research on minorities. Mr Ricketts also undertook the formidable tasks of reorganising, revising and editing the manuscript and compiling end notes. I express my warmest thanks to John W. Dower and Sugiyama Chūhei (deceased), who read the English version and made numerous suggestions for its improvement; to Ian H. Nish who also kindly read and commented most helpfully on the text; to Joe B. Moore for skilfully editing the penultimate draft of chapter 4 and making perceptive comments on chapter 7; and to Lonny E. Carlisle, who reviewed an early version of chapters 8 and 10. Brian Southam of The Athlone Press graciously arranged for publication of the English edition, displaying quite remarkable patience and tact at the many delays in producing a final typescript. I also thank Caroline Wintersgill and Jeremy Albutt of Continuum International Group for their very enthusiastic support. My wife Atsuko deserves special mention for her constant devotion, wise counsel and energetic assistance at all stages of the work.

Takemae Eiji
Tokyo

PART I

The Allied Victory

CHAPTER 1

The Pacific War and the Origins of GHQ[1]

AMERICAN PROCONSUL

On 30 August, 1945, General Douglas MacArthur, Supreme Commander for the Allied Powers, descended from his aircraft, the *Bataan*, and stepped onto Japanese soil at Atsugi Air Base some 32 kilometres west of Yokohama. Wearing a Filipino field marshal's cap, his trademark corncob pipe in hand, he was met by Eighth Army Commander General Robert L. Eichelberger and a handful of staff officers who had preceded him. 'Melbourne to Tokyo was a long road', he told the welcoming party, 'but this looks like the payoff'. On MacArthur's orders, there was no Japanese reception party at the airfield; Japan was a defeated nation, and the General's arrival marked the start of six-and-a-half years of military occupation.[1]

MacArthur's improbable journey began in early 1942 at Bataan and Corregidor in the Philippines, then under siege by Japanese troops. On 22 February, President Franklin D. Roosevelt had ordered the General to leave his forces and proceed to Melbourne to organise the US counter-offensive against Japan in the Pacific. Accordingly, MacArthur, his family and personal staff who would form the nucleus of a new headquarters departed Corregidor on the night of 11 March, nearly two months before the fall of the island fortress. After a perilous escape by PT boat through nearly 1,000 kilometres of Japanese-held waters, the General reached Mindanao, where his party boarded a B-17 Flying Fortress and made the five-hour flight to Australia. At Adelaide Station, MacArthur told reporters with characteristic aplomb, 'I came through and I shall return.' He arrived in Melbourne on 21 March and in late April formally took charge of General Headquarters, Southwest Pacific Area, the integrated Allied command in Australia.

Nearly three-and-a-half years of savage warfare were to pass before a bomb-devastated, prostrate Japan, its war industries shattered and its major cities in ruins, finally surrendered on 15 August 1945. On that day in mid-August, as the guns fell silent, MacArthur radiated relief that the butchery was over and hailed the challenge of building a new future. In a message of that date to President Harry S. Truman, the newly appointed Supreme Commander waxed eloquent, declaring the Far East to be 'inexpressibly thrilled and stirred' by the end of the war and pledging to do everything possible to work along 'the magnificently constructive lines you have conceived for the peace of the world'.[2]

By the time he reached Tokyo, MacArthur already had established a brilliant military career. Born in 1880 in Little Rock, Arkansas, he graduated from the élite US military academy at West Point in 1903 with the highest grades ever recorded there. After a first tour of duty in the Philippines, he served as military aide to President Theodore Roosevelt and in 1914 participated in the US occupation of Vera Cruz, Mexico. During World War I, MacArthur became deputy commander of the 42nd 'Rainbow' Division and after the armistice was assigned to occupation duty in the German Rhineland, where he commanded a zone extending south of Bonn to Koblenz. From 1919 to 1922, he was Superintendent of West Point, after which he returned to the Philippines. In 1930, at age 50, MacArthur became a four-star general and the youngest Army chief of staff in US history. Two years later, in 1932, he earned notoriety by ordering his troops to forcibly evict 20,000 World War I veterans and their families, the Bonus marchers, who had squatted in makeshift camps in Washington DC demanding payment of their service bonuses. MacArthur justified this repressive measure by dismissing the Bonus march as the work of Communist agitators.

MacArthur's interest in East Asia dated from his father Arthur's tenure as Military Governor of the Philippines (1900–1). General Arthur MacArthur was a Civil War hero who had later distinguished himself in the 'Indian Wars', the bloody annihilation campaigns waged against Native Americans in the late nineteenth century. While serving in the Philippines, Arthur MacArthur suppressed with extreme cruelty a major insurrection led by the nationalist revolutionary Emilio Aguinaldo against US colonial rule (US troops introduced forms of torture that would be revived by Japanese occupiers some 40 years later). Douglas arrived in Manila in 1903 shortly after receiving his commission, and in 1905 he and his father toured Japan and the Far East on a military survey. In all, the young MacArthur was to serve four tours of duty in the Philippines. In 1935, he returned as military adviser to that country and in mid-1936, at the request of Commonwealth President Manuel L. Quezon, became Field Marshal of the Philippine Army. In 1937, he resigned his US commission to reorganise the Philippine armed forces and prepare the islands, which he considered a vital Asian asset, for a presumptive attack by Japan. In July 1941, President Franklin D. Roosevelt recalled MacArthur to active duty, incorporated the Philippine Army into a new combined American-Filipino force christened US Army Forces in the Far East (USAFFE), and placed the General in command.[3]

Four years later, on 15 August 1945, the day of Japan's capitulation, Roosevelt's successor President Truman formally appointed MacArthur Supreme Commander for the Allied Powers and ordered him to direct the postwar occupation of the defeated enemy. The General was assigned this heavy responsibility largely because he was US Theatre Commander when the war ended, but his sixteen years of experience in Asia and his role in the American occupation of the German Rhineland after World War I also recommended him for the job. MacArthur's task was awesome. He was to democratise a nation of some 74 million ruled by militarists and, in US eyes, fanatically committed to a totalitarian ideology. To discharge that duty, he was granted unusual authority. As Supreme Commander, the General 'outranked' the

Japanese prime minister and even the Emperor, widely revered as a living deity. To the Japanese, he loomed larger even than President Truman. As Theatre Commander, MacArthur's authority encompassed the Philippines, the northern Pacific and Korea, leading one historian to dub him 'the last of the great colonial overlords'.[4] His Olympian stature earned him the sobriquets of 'blue-eyed shogun' and 'Japan's saviour', and the nation's pre-eminent postwar premier, Yoshida Shigeru, called him the 'great benefactor'. MacArthur came to personify the Occupation not only to the Japanese but to the world at large.

Conservative reformer
To his staff, MacArthur, then 65, was known affectionately as the 'Old Man' or the C-in-C (Commander-in-Chief, pronounced 'sink'). To Americans he was a war hero, then a legend. An April 1946 Gallup Poll gave the General higher public approval ratings than either President Truman or Winston Churchill, and by 1948, he felt confident enough to contemplate running for president. Despite his ambitions, however, MacArthur failed to form an organisation, formulate a coherent platform or woo the Republican Party's powerful financial élite. As a former Occupation official later suggested, MacArthur's passionate commitment to a programme of revolutionary political and social reform no doubt alarmed influential conservative Republicans.[5] Ultimately, poor planning, the absence of a solid base of support and the General's inability to return home to campaign in the primaries doomed his candidature. Nonetheless, this hidden personal agenda made MacArthur hypersensitive to US public opinion for the duration of the Occupation.

MacArthur cultivated his aloof, imperious image to maximum effect. If the Japanese saw in him a saviour, he saw in himself a Caesar or Napoleon, once citing the Roman conquest of Gaul as the only example of a successful military occupation that compared favourably with his own. He interpreted his mandate broadly, sometimes working behind Washington's back, often reinterpreting policy directives to suit his own designs. Isolating himself from ordinary Japanese, the Supreme Commander met very few officials more than once, conferring mainly with the premier and the Emperor, with whom he talked many times (he met Hirohito every six months and saw Prime Minister Yoshida Shigeru on 75 occasions). MacArthur worked seven days a week, including holidays, commuting between the Dai-Ichi Building and the Embassy in a black 1941 Cadillac that he had obtained from a Manila sugar baron. He never toured Japan and left the country only twice before the Korean War, once in 1945 to Manila and again in 1948 to Seoul to attend independence ceremonies. The General abhorred staff meetings and remained inaccessible to most of his subordinates. There was no telephone in his office, and only his personal aides and Brigadier General Courtney Whitney could see him without appointment. Harbouring a deep distrust of the media, MacArthur did not hold his first official press conference as Supreme Commander until March 1947. In the course of the Occupation, he ordered several journalists expelled for their liberal reporting.

The wartime staff MacArthur brought with him to Japan was fanatically loyal, taking 'ludicrous care', as a historian has phrased it, 'that only the rosiest reports of the progress of the Occupation should reach the outside world'. The slightest criticism of GHQ was akin to sacrilege. 'He was a man', wrote one of his lieutenants, 'who suffered as much at the hands of saccharine admirers as he did from his sternest critics.' The reverse side of MacArthur's vulnerability to public opinion was a fierce distrust of higher authority that extended to his Commander-in-Chief, President Truman, who took an equally jaundiced view of MacArthur's grandstanding antics. In June 1945, an irate Truman castigated the General in his diary as 'Mr Prima Donna, Brass Hat, Five Star MacArthur', calling him 'a play actor and a bunco man'. Relations between the two would grow increasingly strained during the Occupation, culminating in MacArthur's dismissal in April 1951, at the height of the Korean War, for insubordination.[6]

MacArthur's personal life was equally reclusive. Ensconced in the US Embassy, which he referred to as the 'Big House', he lived with his second wife Jean (née Faircloth), whom he had married in 1937, and his young son Arthur. Jean's life revolved around her husband, but she reviewed parades on US and Allied holidays, did duty as titular head of the American Girls Scouts and Red Cross and generally saw more of Tokyo and Japan than Douglas. She busied herself with restoring to the Big House some of its former comforts while son Arthur 'played with family pets [four dogs], idolised John Wayne, was an eager Cub Scout, read "Joe Palooka", and drank Coke and ate B-29burgers in the PX'. Outside the manor, he was treated like royalty, photographed with Crown Prince Akihito and saluted by Japanese policemen. Also living in the Embassy compound but in separate quarters were military assistants Faubion Bowers, Lawrence E. Bunker, Sidney L. Huff and his Australian wife, and the General's wartime physician Dr Roger O. Egeberg (later replaced by Lieutenant Colonel C. C. Canada). Completing this extended Anglo-American ménage was son Arthur's governess, Englishwoman Phyllis Gibbons, who had been with the family since Manila days. On the bottom rung of the MacArthur hacienda were the usual Asian house servants and field hands. The material needs of the household were met by Japanese maids, grounds keepers and cooks proficient in both Western and Japanese cuisine. Two long-term employees attended to the General's personal wants, a Filipino houseboy and Loh Chiu, a Cantonese *amah* (whom the General insisted on calling Ah Cheu) who had joined the family in Manila in the late 1930s.[7]

Behind the General's remoteness lay an unshakable belief in his own judgment, in his personal destiny and in the innate superiority of American values and civilisation over those of the 'Orient'. Such overweening self-confidence betrayed a smug paternalism beneath which lurked a racialist impulse. Assistant secretary Bowers remarked that MacArthur often engaged in monologues out loud for the benefit of all present, assuming that 'everyone within his hearing was white, gentile and a sepulcher of silence. This was never written out *en toutes lettres*, but we all were amazingly Anglo-Saxon and Protestant'. Once, in a florid tirade, he cursed the President 'as that

Jew in the White House'. When the astounded Bowers asked to which president he was referring, the General replied brusquely, 'Truman. You can tell by his name. Look at his face . . . '[8] In 1947, MacArthur warned that a lengthy occupation might cause the occupying forces to 'assume a dominant power complex pointing to the illusion of a master race'. But the General himself was not immune from such phantasies. In 1948, during lunch with a visiting US scientific mission, he spoke about 'the veneer of civilisation over the Jap' and asserted that 'With an Oriental, we know that he is out to rob us and to agree to something as long as it suits them [sic]. We are then on guard. We should treat the Russians the same way.' In 1951, after his dismissal by Truman, he told the US Congress that the Japanese 'in spite of their antiquity measured by time, were in a very tuitionary condition. Measured by the standards of modern civilisation, they would be like a boy of twelve as compared with our [Anglo-Saxon] development of forty-five years.'[9]

MacArthur believed that America, with its 'advanced spirituality', had a civilising mission to perform, a moral obligation to free the Japanese people from 'the enslavement of feudalism'. Japan was 'the world's great laboratory for an experiment in the liberation of a people from totalitarian military rule and for the liberalisation of government from within'.[10] A devout Episcopalian, MacArthur's pronounced evangelic streak fuelled a determination to Christianise Japan – a goal that Washington policy-planners and many of his own staff viewed with faint enthusiasm.

Despite his aloofness and vanity, MacArthur possessed a radiant charisma that could charm even fierce critics who met him face-to-face. The General was a spellbinding speaker, frank and disarming, who could make his delivery with great intensity and conviction. During a visit to Japan in 1947, the head of the American Civil Liberties Union Roger N. Baldwin was forced to revise dramatically his personal assessment of the Supreme Commander. Before encountering MacArthur, Baldwin had thought him simply a puffed-up ham actor. After his interview, he exclaimed incredulously, 'Why, that man knows more about civil liberties than I do'. Such was the effect MacArthur sometimes produced on people.[11] Although a harsh taskmaster, he inspired in his staff a fierce devotion, and three high-ranking career officers in key Occupation posts would follow him into retirement in mid-1951: Crawford F. Sams, Courtney Whitney and Charles A. Willoughby.

Politically, MacArthur has been characterised as 'essentially an old-fashioned patriotic populist',[12] an outlook that enabled him to deal impartially with people of very different political persuasions. Two of his military assistants, Bonner F. Fellers and Lawrence Bunker, for example, were dyed-in-the-wool ultra-rightists. Brigadier General Charles Willoughby, SCAP's intelligence chief, was a firm believer in aristocratic privilege, not democracy. The conservative but moderate Whitney of Government Section, MacArthur's closest adviser, was in many respects the opposite. MacArthur also valued the counsel of the ardent New Dealers on his staff, such as Charles L. Kades (Government Section) and Theodore Cohen (Economic and Scientific Section) and occasionally consulted E. Herbert Norman, the left-leaning Canadian scholar and diplomat assigned to Tokyo for most of the Occupation. This

ideological flexibility gave the Supreme Commander an immense advantage in har-
nessing a vast military organisation to the tasks of civilian government. It also helps
explain how, as one Occupationaire later expressed it, 'a politically ambitious anti-
New Deal general [could] enforce an essentially New Deal programme'.[13]

MacArthur formally inaugurated his Tokyo headquarters on 2 October 1945, but
the organisational antecedents of GHQ stretch back to July 1941 and the creation
of the US Army Forces in the Far East. Headquartered in Manila and led by
MacArthur, the USAFFE consisted of American and Filipino troops. Its readiness,
and the mettle of its commander, were quickly put to the test.

WAR IN THE PACIFIC

The Japanese blitzkrieg

On 26 November 1941 (Eastern Standard Time), the day US Secretary of State
Cordell Hull delivered his list of 10 demands to the Japanese ambassador in Washington, the Imperial Navy's First Air Fleet under Admiral Nagumo Chūichi set sail
for Hawai'i from Hitokappu Bay on Etorofu Island in the southern Kurils. Nagumo's orders were to attack the US Pacific Fleet anchored near Honolulu but to
return to port should Japan–US negotiations bear fruit. The next day, 27 November, the US high command, unaware of Japan's war plans, radioed all commands in
the Pacific that negotiations with Japan had reached an impasse and warned: 'If
hostilities cannot repeat cannot be avoided the United States desires Japan commit
the first act'. In the early days of December, the Japanese Embassy began burning
codes and sensitive documents. On Friday, 5 December, Washington reportedly
picked up one of Tokyo's 'war imminent' signals, a weather broadcast ('West Wind,
Clear') indicating a break in relations with Great Britain. (It is a matter of controversy whether Japan's so-called winds' code for an impending rupture with the
United States, 'East Wind, Rain', was ever sent.) On Saturday, 6 December, the
Japanese Embassy in Washington received the Tōjō Cabinet's 14-point response to
the so-called Hull Note. The document was to be decoded, typed in diplomatic
format and presented to the State Department by 1 pm on Sunday, 7 December.
The crucial Point 14, however, was not a formal declaration of war nor even a
suspension of diplomatic relations; it simply stated that it now was 'impossible to
reach an agreement through further negotiations'. Tokyo had specifically ordered
Ambassador Nomura Kichisaburō to prepare the lengthy document in the strictest
secrecy without using an Embassy typist. As a result, Nomura's skeleton crew was
unable to meet the deadline, and the aide-mémoire was not delivered to Hull until
2 pm Eastern Standard Time (EST) the next day, even as the Japanese raid on Pearl
Harbor was unfolding. Imperial General Headquarters would not formally declare
the existence of a state of war with the United States and the British Empire until
4 pm EST.[14]

That Sunday morning at 7:55 am (Honolulu time), the first wave of 350 Japanese dive-bombers, torpedo planes and fighters launched from Imperial Navy carriers had hit Pearl Harbor without warning. Within two hours the Japanese attack force had sunk or heavily damaged 21 US Navy ships, destroyed or incapacitated 323 aircraft, killed more than 2,400 American servicemen and wounded nearly 1,200. Several hours after the devastation of Pearl Harbor, Imperial Army aircraft raided northern Luzon, the Philippines' main island, quickly destroying on the ground MacArthur's fleet of B-17s at Clark Field near Manila. Within three days, US Army Air Forces planes there had been put out of action. On 10 December, Lieutenant General Honma Masaharu's Fourteenth Army landed on Luzon. Following the arrival of the main body on 22 December, it inflicted a string of lightening defeats on the USAFFE. The Japanese Expeditionary Force seized Manila on 2 January, 1942. American and Filipino troops, 110,000-strong, retreated to the Bataan Peninsula and Corregidor, a fortified island at the mouth of Manila Bay due south of the Peninsula, where they faced the combined onslaught of 192,000 Imperial Army and Navy forces. Following MacArthur's reassignment to Australia in March, General Jonathan M. Wainwright took charge of the USAFFE.

The Philippine Army, Scouts and Constabulary accounted for 85 per cent of the 78,000 troops in Major General Edward P. King's Luzon Force on Bataan. Among the Force's 11,800 American soldiers was a large contingent of Mexican American *Caballeros* from the New Mexico National Guard who had been assigned to the Philippines in August 1941 because of their knowledge of Spanish. They were among the last troops to surrender, and many died in the battle for Bataan and its tragic sequel.[15] By early April, King's command had been cornered and was facing annihilation. Despite orders from General Wainwright to continue resisting, he capitulated on 9 April. Honma's troops lacked the logistical support needed to contain and move some 75,000 prisoners-of-war. Colonel Tsuji Masanobu directed his men to drive the starving and exhausted 'battling bastards of Bataan' on foot through dense jungle under a hot tropical sun from the Mariveles air field to Camp O'Donnell some 100 kilometres away. Japanese soldiers obeyed Tsuji's orders to show no mercy and herd their charges brutally at bayonet point (a rare few, in individual acts of courage and compassion, attempted to mitigate the harsh treatment by sharing their own rations with the captives). Accurate casualty figures do not exist, but more than 600 Americans and between 5,000 and 10,000 Filipinos are thought to have died during the Bataan Death March, many shot, bayoneted, decapitated or clubbed to death for trivial offenses. Disease and starvation took an even heavier toll. Of King's Luzon Force, 2,000 to 3,000 managed to join Wainwright's main contingent on Corregidor or escaped into the jungle. On 7 May, Wainwright himself was compelled to surrender Corregidor and the entire Philippine command, producing one of the greatest military debacles in American history. The USAFFE disintegrated, and small groups of Filipino and American combatants made their way into the mountains to organise guerrilla operations against the Japanese invader.[16]

As General Honma launched his initial attack on the Philippines in early December

1941, Imperial forces occupied Bangkok and simultaneously struck Hong Kong, Malaya, Singapore, Guam and Wake Island. The British, Canadian and Indian defenders of Hong Kong capitulated quickly, as did the tiny US Marine garrison on Guam. On 10 December (local time), Japanese fighters attacked and sunk the pride of the British Far East Fleet, the battleship HMS *Prince of Wales* and the battle cruiser HMS *Repulse*, in the Gulf of Siam. Nearly 3,000 troops died in the assault, marking the worst British naval calamity of the war. By January 1942, Imperial forces had secured all of the Malay Peninsula but Singapore. On 15 February, General Sir Arthur Percival, badly out-manoeuvred, unconditionally surrendered Singapore and its garrison of 85,000 Australian, British and Indian troops to General Yamashita Tomoyuki's army of 30,000. The fall of the 'City of the Lion' shattered the citadel of British power in the Far East, isolating British forces in India and Ceylon.

On 18 February, the carrier fleet under Admiral Nagumo that had savaged Pearl Harbor struck the main Allied supply base at Darwin on Australia's north coast, prompting Australians to consider evacuating the northern part of the continent. Canberra prepared to abandon the north and west to defend the 'Brisbane Line', the area east of a perimeter running from Brisbane to Melbourne. In early March, British and Indian troops withdrew from Rangoon, and Dutch forces surrendered Java, giving Imperial soldiers control of the Dutch East Indies and its oilfields. In April, Nagumo's flotilla chased British warships out of the Bay of Bengal, sinking several in the process. By May 1942, Japan's southward *blitzkrieg* was more or less completed, and its armies held a vast expanse of territory that stretched from the Aleutians in the North to Burma in the southwest to the Pacific islands north of Australia in the east. In addition to Korea, Manchuria and Formosa, the Greater Japanese Empire now encompassed Hong Kong, the Philippines, Thailand, Burma, Indo-China, British Malaya, the Dutch East Indies, British Borneo, the Pacific islands (Marianas, Carolines, Marshalls, Gilberts and Solomons), the Bismarck Archipelago and New Guinea (see Fig. 1). It seemed only a matter of time before the Empire added India and Australia to its acquisitions, as well.[17]

The Allied counter-offensive

Allied policy towards Japan was hammered out step-by-step in a series of summits that began with the Washington ('Arcadia') Conference of late December 1941, which produced an Anglo-American accord on grand strategy. On 1 January 1942, at the height of the Conference, the representatives of 26 associated states signed a statement of principle, the 'Declaration of the United Nations', laying the ground-work for a concerted Allied response to Axis aggression worldwide. The heart of the Declaration was the Atlantic Charter, an eight-point programme of peace aims that Churchill and Roosevelt had enunciated in mid-August 1941, and the Four Freedoms that Roosevelt had enumerated in a speech before Congress in January 1941: freedom of speech and religion and freedom from want and fear. (On the basis of the Declaration, in the autumn of 1944, Britain, Nationalist China, the Soviet Union and the United States would meet again in Washington at Dumbarton Oaks to draft the general principles of the United Nations, and in April 1945, some 50 nations would gather in San Francisco to found the new world organisation.)

The Arcadia Conference also agreed to establish the Allied Combined Chiefs of Staff, from which the US Joint Chiefs organisation would evolve. The Allied Chiefs pursued a Europe-first strategy but made provision for the formation of an American-British-Dutch-Australian (ABDA) Supreme Command in the Far East. Created on 15 January 1942, the ABDA was headquartered in Java and placed under British General Archibald Wavell, with Lieutenant General George H. Brett of US Army Air Forces as his deputy. Nationalist Chinese leader Generalissimo Chiang Kai-shek (Jiang Jieshi) was named Supreme Allied Commander in China, Thailand and Indo-China. To coordinate Allied war aims, the Pacific War Council was established in London, and shortly afterwards, an identical body was created in Washington to harmonise views on military strategy. The two Councils operated in tandem for the duration of the war, but the ABDA was short-lived. The fall of Singapore in mid-February, the Allied defeat in the Battle of the Java Sea later that month and the beginning of the British withdrawal from Burma sealed the fate of the first Combined Allied Command, which was dissolved on 25 February. With New Guinea and Australia menaced by advancing Imperial troops, Canberra, Washington and Wellington prevailed on London to relocate Allied headquarters to Australia.[18]

In the meantime, in February, the US Joint Chiefs had yielded to Army pressure and appointed MacArthur Commander-in-Chief of US Army Forces, Pacific, conferring on him a status commensurate with that of Admiral Chester Nimitz, Commander-in-Chief of the US Pacific Fleet. In March, with the concurrence of the Combined Chiefs, the American high command divided the Pacific into two great theatres, the Southwest Pacific Area (SWPA) under MacArthur in Australia and the Pacific Ocean Areas (POA) – North, Central and South Pacific – under Nimitz in Hawai'i.[19] On 18 April 1942, the Combined Chiefs established an integrated Allied Supreme Command in Melbourne, christening it General Headquarters, Southwest Pacific Area (GHQ/SWPA). MacArthur was designated to lead SWPA's Allied Land, Naval and Air Forces and plan and coordinate the counter-attack against Japan. Australia and the Netherlands played a prominent role in the new multi-national force, which also included elements from Nationalist China, the Philippines and New Zealand.[20]

As head of SWPA, MacArthur chose his general staff almost exclusively from the officers of the now defunct US Army Forces in the Far East who had fled with him from Corregidor in March 1942. These hand-picked men included Colonel Spencer B. Akin, Chief Signals Officer; Colonel Hugh Casey, Chief Engineering Officer; Colonel William F. Marquat, Chief Anti-Aircraft Officer; Lieutenant Colonel Richard J. Marshall, Deputy Chief of Staff; Colonel Richard K. Sutherland, Chief of Staff; and Colonel Charles A. Willoughby, head of SWPA intelligence (G-2). Known as the 'Bataan Crowd', this tightly knit clique would remain inseparable from the General throughout the war, often accompanying him in his four-engine C-54, nicknamed the *Bataan*. Others of MacArthur's in-group, such as Colonel Courtney

Figure 1. The Japanese Empire and the Asia–Pacific War.

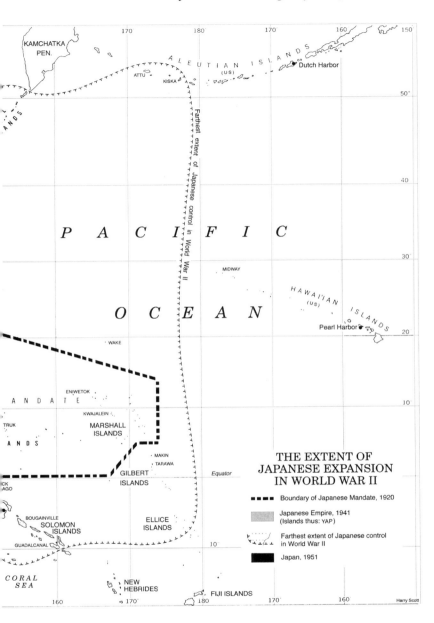

THE EXTENT OF
JAPANESE EXPANSION
IN WORLD WAR II

▪▪▪▪ Boundary of Japanese Mandate, 1920

Japanese Empire, 1941
(Islands thus: YAP)

Farthest extent of Japanese control
in World War II

Japan, 1951

Whitney and military secretary Major Bonner Fellers, who had served with the General in Manila, joined him in Australia at a later date. Most of these officers subsequently would play key roles in the occupation of Japan.[21]

On 20 July 1942, MacArthur moved GHQ/SWPA from Melbourne in the south to Brisbane on the east coast in order to quash talk of abandoning northern Australia. The continent, he announced, would be defended in New Guinea. Allied headquarters were established in Brisbane's Australia Mutual Provident Insurance Building on Queen Street. At this time, the General also regrouped the American forces under his command. He reorganised the US Army in Australia, renaming it the US Army Services of Supply (USASOS), and appointed SWPA's Deputy Chief of Staff, Lieutenant Colonel Marshall, to head it. MacArthur's primary American tactical unit was I Corps, which he entrusted to Major General Robert Eichelberger, a West Point career officer who joined SWPA in August 1942.[22] Eichelberger's I Corps initially was assigned to SWPA's Australian First Army under Sir John Lavarak.

In February 1943, MacArthur reconstituted the US Army Forces in the Far East (USAFFE), placed it under Chief of Staff Richard Sutherland and positioned it one block away from SWPA headquarters. USAFFE took over the administrative functions of the USASOS service and supply group. At the same time, MacArthur established Alamo Force as an independent command under GHQ/SWPA but assigned it administratively to USAFFE. The core of Alamo Force was the recently formed US Sixth Army led by Lieutenant General Walter Krueger. Eichelberger's I Corps had been attached to Krueger's command, and a bitter rivalry soon developed between the two leaders.[23] Thus, by early 1943, MacArthur stood astride two organisations, GHQ/SWPA and GHQ/USAFFE. Moreover, SWPA's chief of staff and deputy chief of staff did double duty as commanders of the two American organisations, USAFFE and USASOS. This dual structure of interlocking control also would characterise the General's civil and military commands in occupied Japan.

GHQ/SWPA was responsible for that part of the Pacific southwest stretching from Australia, New Guinea, the Bismarck Archipelago and the Solomon Islands to the Dutch East Indies (excluding Sumatra) and the Philippines. The theatre was too vast, however, for SWPA to mount effective counter-operations unaided. Indeed, the Allied command would be hard pressed to defend even Australia from a full-scale Japanese assault. Any SWPA offensive would hinge on the ability of US Navy units under Admiral Nimitz to divert Japanese forces into the Central Pacific and keep vital military supply routes open between the United States and Australia. In these inauspicious beginnings, MacArthur began plotting campaigns in New Guinea and the southwestern Pacific.

An early turning point
From the start, the US Navy and Army held very different views about waging war on Japan. While the Navy called for the blockade and bombardment of the Japanese

homeland based on pre-1941 contingency planning (War Plan Orange), the Army
called for a full-scale invasion on the ground. The inter-service rivalry that developed
between SWPA and POA intensified as the war progressed, with the Army and Navy
running separate campaigns, competing for human and material resources and vying
for overall control of Allied strategy. Priority initially was given to the Navy. The
architect of the Navy's Pacific strategy was Navy Chief of Staff Admiral Ernest J.
King, who insisted that the Japanese be pressed hard at every opportunity through
aggressive amphibious operations.

In early May 1942, as US forces in the Philippines went down to crushing defeat,
Nimitz's Pacific Fleet intercepted a Japanese flotilla in the Coral Sea. The Imperial
Navy was escorting troops from Rabaul, the main Japanese staging area in the
Southwest Pacific, around the eastern tip of New Guinea for an assault on Port
Moresby, jumping-off point for an invasion of Australia. The US carrier force managed to stop the Japanese but at considerable cost to itself. In June, Nimitz decimated
an Imperial carrier group heading for Midway Island, handing Japan its first major
defeat of the war and thwarting the plans of Admiral Yamamoto Isoroku, Commander of the Combined Japanese Fleets, to seize the strategic Midway base (so
serious were Yamamoto's losses that not even General Tōjō Hideki was given a full
account of the disaster). In August, US Marines landed on Guadalcanal in the
Solomons and doggedly battled desperate Japanese defenders until February 1943,
winning another major victory.

Guadalcanal had been preceded by a less celebrated but equally significant triumph in Papua, southeastern New Guinea, the target of a major Japanese ground
offensive launched in the summer of 1942. In mid-September, SWPA's Australian
7th Division finally stopped the Japanese attack directed at the Papuan capital of Port
Moresby. Entrenched at Buna on Papua's northeastern coast, Imperial troops had
scaled the precipitous, cloud-shrouded heights of the Kokoda Trail linking Buna
with Port Moresby and been turned away a mere 50 kilometres from the capital. In
November, MacArthur ordered I Corps Commander Robert Eichelberger, to capture
the Japanese beachhead, telling him simply, 'I want you to take Buna, or not come
back alive.' In early January 1943, Australian and American soldiers in Eichelberger's
Buna Force finally overwhelmed the Japanese defenders. 'Bloody Buna' handed
Japanese ground forces their most serious defeat since the 1939 rout at Nomonhan
(Khalkhin Gol) on the Manchurian-Mongolian frontier. As Nomonhan had put an
end to Imperial Japan's northern strategy, so Buna brought to naught its plans for a
general assault on Australia.[24]

These successes represented an early turning point in the war, which the Imperial
Navy had expected to win by mid-1942. Japan now was on the defensive. The
Midway and Buna–Guadalcanal victories had foiled Japanese efforts to cut Allied
supply routes and facilitated SWPA operations in the East Solomons and New
Guinea. US naval advances in the Pacific enabled MacArthur to bring forward the
timetable for SWPA's Elkton Plan, a five-stage advance up eastern New Guinea to
the huge Japanese command centre at Rabaul on the northern tip of New Britain. In

early February 1943, B-25s wiped out a Japanese convoy carrying reinforcements to New Britain in the Battle of the Bismarck Sea, allowing SWPA forces to isolate General Imamura Hitoshi, the conqueror of the Dutch East Indies. In November, the 8th New Zealand Division captured Treasury Island and US Marines stormed Bougainville, nearby strongholds in the Solomons, tightening the circle around Rabaul. By March 1944, Imamura's 100,000-strong garrison had been completely cut off by air, land and sea from other Imperial forces in the region and effectively immobilised.

At SWPA headquarters, a series of plans dubbed Reno and Musketeer were developed with the conquest of the Philippines as their ultimate objective. The Philippines lay midway between Japan and resource-laden Southeast Asia. With a large, generally pro-American population, the archipelago also offered an ideal staging ground for a sustained Allied attack on the Japanese home islands. The Reno Plan, completed in February 1943 and amended four times thereafter, called for a combined Army–Navy operation employing a strategy of 'leap-frogging' across the Pacific, beginning in New Guinea and the East Solomons and proceeding northwest towards the Philippines. Capturing a few key enemy strongholds and isolating Japanese troops on the remaining islands would accelerate the Allied drive and minimise casualties. The Musketeer Plan, a continuation of Reno V, plotted the capture of Leyte, a strategic island in the heart of the archipelago, from which Allied forces could launch an assault on Luzon, retake Manila and end the Japanese occupation.[25] Landings at Leyte Gulf were slated for 20 December 1944 and at Lingayen Bay in northwestern Luzon for 20 February 1945. Continued Allied successes in the Pacific would enable military planners to bring these dates forward by a full two months.

OBJECTIVE: THE PHILIPPINES

The Philippines under Japanese occupation
On 2 January 1942, the day Japanese expeditionary forces seized Manila, General Honma Masaharu issued a proclamation liberating the Philippines from American rule. The Imperial Army's purpose, he told the Filipino people, was 'to emancipate you from the oppressive domination of the USA, letting you establish "the Philippines for the Filipinos" as a member of the Co-Prosperity Sphere in Greater East Asia and making you enjoy your own prosperity and culture'. Japanese authorities undertook an extensive administrative reform of the government and 'reorientated' the education system to erase Western cultural influences. As part of the education reform, English, the language of instruction under the Americans, was banned, and Japanese and Tagalog were taught in public schools alongside Philippine history. In September 1943, a new Constitution was promulgated, and on 14 October, José P. Laurel declared a Japanese-sponsored Republic. Despite Laurel's militant nationalism and his efforts to ease the hardships of occupation for the common people, it was clear to most Filipinos that his was a puppet régime whose days were numbered.[26]

After the fall of Corregidor in May 1942, USAFFE survivors had taken refuge in the mountains where they organised guerrilla resistance to the Japanese occupation.[27] These soldiers were soon joined by Filipino partisans, whose ranks swelled as the people realised that Imperial troops had come not to liberate them from American domination but to impose on them a new colonial empire. On 3 January 1942, General Honma issued a proclamation decreeing death to anyone who disturbed the public tranquility or resisted Japanese forces in any manner. Military Police (*Kenpeitai*), two Filipino historians have written, 'began a career of wanton disregard of human lives. Houses with unregistered radios were raided and their occupants maimed and thrown into the dungeons of Fort Santiago, where inhuman punishments were meted out to them as daily exercise'. The people lived in constant fear of arrest and torture. Rape was common and degrading treatment a common occurrence. 'A Filipino was slapped for not bringing his residence certificate with him. He was slapped for not bowing properly to the sentry. He was slapped for not being understood by a Japanese sentry. He was slapped for having a face the Japanese did not like.'[28]

By late 1942, scattered guerrilla groups had established radio contact with GHQ/SWPA in Brisbane. Japanese forces answered peasant-based partisan operations with terror tactics, including the execution of local leaders, but Filipino *franc-tireurs* resisted tenaciously and gradually integrated their dispersed commands. Freedom fighters eventually established parallel military and civilian rule in the areas they had liberated, and Manuel Quezon, president of the US-backed government-in-exile, accorded these official recognition. Guerrilla military and administrative successes combined with the savagery of Japanese counter-insurgency operations destroyed any lingering popular support for the Greater East Asia Co-Prosperity Sphere and its innovative cultural reforms. By mid-1944, virtually the entire populace was cooperating with guerrilla forces, which American estimates placed at 270,000.[29]

Gathering intelligence on the Philippines was the job of the Allied Intelligence Bureau (AIB), which MacArthur had established in July 1942. The AIB was placed under Australian Military Intelligence Chief Colonel C. G. Roberts, with an American, Colonel Allison Ind, as his deputy. In July 1943, mounting anti-Japanese guerrilla activity prompted the AIB to create a Philippine Regional Section in its Brisbane headquarters. Colonel Courtney Whitney, a Manila lawyer and MacArthur intimate from prewar days, was picked to head the new organisation, which worked under Colonel Ind's supervision. Charged with improving communications between SWPA and the guerrilla movement, the Section inserted coastal watchers, intelligence operatives and radio teams into the Philippines via submarine and set up an underground railway enabling agents to link up Maquis units.

AIB support heralded a new phase in the Filipino struggle. Until then, coordination between partisan groups and SWPA headquarters had been haphazard, and radio contact with SWPA's G-2 Intelligence Section was sporadic. With the establishment of two-way communications, SWPA and the resistance could synchronise operations, and plans were laid for a guerrilla-led insurrection to coincide with the

Allied invasion of the islands. In the meantime, Filipinos in the United States, allowed to register for the draft in 1942, answered the call to arms with enthusiasm. Some 7,000 were mustered into the First and Second Filipino Regiments and sent to Australia for special combat training. Many of the agents the AIB infiltrated into the Philippines were Filipinos of the 1st Reconnaissance Battalion. When US troops landed in the Philippines in October 1944, Filipino Americans joined up with Maquisards behind enemy lines and fought side by side to liberate their homeland.[30]

During this period, the Filipino resistance developed various propaganda and psychological warfare techniques that the Allies subsequently would adapt for use in 'psywar' operations against Japan proper. In June 1944, as preparations for the invasion intensified, MacArthur created the Psychological Warfare Branch (PWB), SWPA and assigned his military secretary, Major Bonner Fellers, to direct its operations. Fellers was convinced that Allied propaganda could succeed only by telling the truth. At the same time, he directed the PWB to avoid direct criticism of the Emperor, who was to be portrayed as a victim of the militarists and used to achieve peace. Japanese military documents suggest that this approach was surprisingly effective in spreading doubt and disaffection among the rank-and-file as Japan's battlefront position grew desperate.[31]

The secret intelligence war
Other groups also were active in Allied intelligence as US forces island-hopped towards the Philippines. Native Americans from the southwestern Navajo (Diné) tribe were used in the field as 'Code Talkers', relaying messages encrypted in their unwritten Athapascan tongue to elude Japanese listeners. Some 3,600 Navajos were under arms during World War II, 500 of them Marines. Of the latter, a total of 420 were assigned to the Marine Signal Corps and trained as Code Talkers at a special intelligence school at Camp Elliott north of San Diego (later moved to Camp Pendleton). The Japanese never cracked the code, which was used effectively on Pacific battlegrounds. At Iwo Jima, for instance, most Marine operations were directed and monitored in Navajo, and Navajo radio networks laboured around the clock, making a major contribution to the American victory there.[32]

Second-generation Japanese Americans (Nisei) attached to the Allied Translation and Interpreters Service (ATIS) also played a crucial intelligence role. Most of the 33,000 Nisei who fought in World War II served in Europe, but several thousand were assigned to ATIS and other Pacific commands. ATIS was established in September 1942 in Brisbane under the Inter-Allied G-2 Staff, and in October, the 'pirate-featured' Colonel Sidney F. Mashbir, an American intelligence officer with a fluent command of Japanese, was named to head it.[33] The Service's duties included clandestine surveillance, code-breaking, map-reading, radio interception, order-of-battle-analysis, interrogating prisoners of war and culling information from the diaries, letters, memorabilia and other personal effects of enemy dead. A particularly vital contribution to this effort was made by Nisei who had been born in the United States, and therefore were American nationals, but who had gone to school in Japan and returned home before the outbreak of war. With their intimate knowledge of Japanese customs, geography, regional dialects and even military training, the Kibei ('returnees') proved invaluable.

In the early phase of the war, ATIS personnel studied at the Military Intelligence Language School at the Presidio in San Francisco. By virtue of their birth on American soil, second-generation Japanese Americans were US citizens. They underwent intensive language training as families and friends on the West Coast were being rounded up and incarcerated in de facto concentration camps. In February 1942, with anti-Japanese hysteria sweeping the country, President Roosevelt had issued Executive Order 9066 directing the massive 'relocation' of some 120,000 US-born citizens of Japanese descent, first-generation immigrants – barred by law from naturalising – and Aleut islanders to internment camps in remote areas of Arizona, Arkansas, California, Colorado, Idaho, Utah and Wyoming. (Pressured by Washington, Latin American governments also rounded up citizens of Japanese ancestry and shipped them to the camps.)[34]

Following the evacuation, the Military Intelligence Service Language School (MISLS) was transferred to Camp Savage, Minnesota (in 1944, it would move to nearby Fort Snelling, and in late 1945, to the Presidio of Monterey). About 1,500 Caucasians and a few Chinese and Korean Americans went through the programme, but the overwhelming majority of trainees, some 4,500, were Nisei. Since the Selective Service had classified Japanese Americans as enemy aliens, the Language School initially had to rely on volunteers. Many of the first students were Hawai'ian Nisei, who were not subject to internment. Later, large numbers were recruited directly from the camps. The MISLS eventually turned out more than 6,000 linguists of whom 3,700 were assigned on detached service to more than 130 organisations in the Pacific Theatre, including the Allied Intelligence Bureau, ATIS, Joint Intelligence (Central Pacific Ocean Area), Pacific Military Intelligence Research Section and the Psychological Warfare Branch. Nisei linguists not only suffered discrimination in the ranks but ran the risk of being mistaken for the enemy and shot by their own side, and white soldiers routinely were assigned as bodyguards to protect them.[35] Imperial forces considered the Nisei to be Japanese nationals, and capture meant certain execution as traitors.

'Paper bombs' and acts of valor

The Japanese Americans in ATIS cooperated with Feller's PWB in developing psywar posters, leaflets and newspapers, which were air-dropped on enemy positions. For instance, Lieutenant Taro ('Tom') Tsukahara, a native Californian and propaganda officer with MacArthur's staff in Brisbane and later Manila, worked closely with Japanese prisoners of war to produce convincing propaganda tracts urging Imperial troops to cease fighting. While many were designed to sow doubt and despair, others contained such messages as 'Today's foes may be tomorrow's friends', or 'We respect Japan's military valor'. These 'paper bombs' emphasised the inevitability of defeat while assuring the Japanese that the victors did not seek revenge.[36] Ironically, while

Figure 2. A 'paper bomb' prepared by Japanese-American psywar specialists. The text reads: 'If the war continues, it will bring certain destruction to the Japanese homeland. The longer the conflict lasts, the greater the task of rebuilding the country afterwards, and Japan will have lost its former power forever. Throwing one's life away for the State is easily done. Real loyalty means working hard to end the fighting and create a new nation.'

GIs demonised the enemy they were seeking to annihilate, ATIS and the PWB were engaged in an effort to understand and communicate with the Japanese as human beings. Fellers and other psywar experts later would apply the insights they gained through these operations to the task of democratising postwar Japan.

The wartime activities of Japanese American linguists were highly regarded.

Colonel Willoughby, MacArthur's G-2 chief, once boasted that a single ATIS language expert was worth one infantry battalion. He estimated that Japanese American linguists saved a million American lives and shortened the war by two years. White officers who signed the intelligence reports often took credit for these exploits, and it was not until the opening of US archives many years later that the contribution of Nisei soldiers was finally recognised. By September 1945, ATIS had translated 18,000 captured enemy documents, printed 16,000 propaganda leaflets and interrogated more than 10,000 Japanese prisoners of war.[37]

The loyalty of these servicemen was above suspicion, but a sensitivity to their cultural heritage inspired many to conspicuous acts of bravery and compassion towards the enemy. Japanese Americans entered bunkers and caves at great peril to themselves to convince frightened Japanese to surrender or to assist the wounded. In at least one case, interpreters coaxed terrified enemy soldiers out of the carcasses of dead army horses where they had burrowed to escape capture. Many former Imperial soldiers owe their lives to these intrepid individuals.

The courage displayed by Nisei soldiers in minimising enemy casualties stands in sharp contrast to the savagery displayed by American and Japanese troops in the field. To Allied soldiers, commented former Leatherneck Eugene B. Sledge, '[t]he Japanese were a fanatical enemy; that is to say, they believed in their cause with an intensity little understood by many postwar Americans – and possibly many [postwar] Japanese, as well'. To the Japanese, Allied troops were animals devoid of morality or honour. With both sides possessed by a fierce mutual hatred and primitive racialism, fighting in the Pacific was unrivalled in its sheer wanton brutality. A former US war correspondent recalled: 'We shot prisoners in cold blood, wiped out hospitals, strafed lifeboats, killed or mistreated enemy civilians, finished off the enemy wounded, tossed the dying into a hole with the dead, and . . . boiled the flesh off enemy skulls to make table ornaments for sweethearts, or carved their bones into letter openers.' Many GIs collected war trophies – ears and gold teeth – sometimes taken from the wounded. Imperial soldiers killed prisoners, booby-trapped dead comrades, feigned surrender in order to ambush Allied troops and mutilated enemy corpses. Combatants were driven by a 'cold, homicidal rage' and lust for revenge, and both sides resorted to torture and summary executions. The war, Sledge wrote, 'made savages of us all'.[38] This barbarity would reach a macabre crescendo in the final battles of the Pacific campaign.

BREACHING JAPAN'S OUTER DEFENCES

The evolution of Allied strategy

In January 1943, a year after the Arcadia Conference, British and American leaders met in Casablanca where they agreed on a formula calling for the unconditional surrender of Germany, Italy and Japan. At the Trident summit in Washington in May 1943, the Allies' Europe-first strategy was modified as Britain was forced to concede the primacy of US policy-making in the Pacific, and the Combined Chiefs laid plans for an aggressive naval campaign against Japan's island strongholds. In August 1943, at the Quadrant Conference in Quebec, Allied military leaders agreed to a timetable for the US Navy's seizure of the Gilberts, Marshalls and Carolines in the Central Pacific. From 28 to 30 November of that year, at Teheran, Churchill and Roosevelt conferred with Marshal Josef Stalin for the first time, securing from the Soviet premier a pledge to enter the war against Japan once Germany had been defeated. En route to the Teheran Conference, Churchill and Roosevelt joined Nationalist Chinese leader Chiang Kai-shek at Cairo (23 to 27 November), reiterating the demand for Japan's unconditional surrender and affirming Allied intentions to return all Japanese territories acquired by aggression after the war. The Anglo-American leadership reached consensus on a final offensive against Japan at the second Quebec (Octagon) Conference of September 1944. There, the Combined Chiefs agreed to seek Japan's unconditional capitulation via a three-pronged strategy of sea and air blockades of the home islands, intensive air bombardments and a land invasion. In late January and early February 1945, Allied leaders gathered at Malta and Yalta. At Yalta, Stalin finalised his promise to enter the war in return for certain territorial concessions (below). There, the Allies also worked out details concerning the United Nations Security Council and other UN Charter issues. The last summit of the war was convened at Potsdam in July, following Roosevelt's death, where Churchill, Chiang Kai-shek and the new US President, Harry S. Truman, served Japan with a final warning to surrender without conditions or face annihilation.[39]

Throughout 1943 and much of 1944, however, US Navy and Army strategists remained at loggerheads over the final attack on Japan. The Navy argued forcefully for a grand sweep across the Central Pacific. Having already won key victories in the Pacific, it insisted on a continuation of its deadly combination of coordinated air, sea and land assaults. In mid-May 1943, Rear Admiral Francis W. Rockwell had directed a major amphibious attack on the Japanese-held island of Attu in the Aleutians, which fell on 30 May, restoring the Aleutian chain to US control. The Japanese garrison of 2,500 went down fighting almost to the man (only 28 prisoners were taken), however, and more than 1,000 Americans died, a portent of the frenzied 'atoll war' that lay ahead. In November 1943, as agreed at Quebec in August, Admiral William F. Halsey's South Pacific Fleet captured Bougainville in the Solomons, and a huge armada under Nimitz took Makin and Tarawa in the Gilberts after a bitter struggle reminiscent in its no-holds-barred ferocity of Attu. Then, from late January 1944, Pacific Fleet amphibious forces invaded Kwajalein, Wotje and other atolls in the Marshall chain. In February, Task Force Fifty-Eight bombarded by sea and air the Imperial Navy's southern stronghold on Truk in the Carolines, the rear headquarters of the Japanese Combined Fleet and a key staging area for Japanese operations in the South Pacific. The Task Force destroyed the naval base there and isolated the Japanese garrison, neutralising a strategic segment of the Empire's outer defence perimeter.[40]

Saipan and the fall of Tōjō

In mid-June 1944, Nimitz attacked heavily defended Saipan in the Marianas, a key link in Japan's 'absolute national defence sphere'. On the evening of 6 July, Admiral Nagumo Chūichi, commander of Japan's Central Pacific Fleet, and General Saitō Yoshitsugu, responsible for the defence of Saipan, radioed their apologies to the Emperor for the impending defeat and put pistols to their heads. The next day saw some of the largest suicidal counter-attacks of the war. Retreating north, Imperial soldiers died en masse in banzai charges, or leaped from high cliffs. These acts of self-immolation, known in Japanese as 'shattering the precious jewel' (*gyokusai*), represented the highest tribute a soldier could pay to his sovereign. By the time Japan's 'Bulwark of the Pacific' fell on 9 July, almost the entire defending garrison of 30,000 had been killed (a mere 3 per cent were taken prisoner). More than 14,000 Americans, 20 per cent of all US combat troops on the island, also died in the fighting.[41]

Particularly tragic was the plight of Saipan's civilian population, which included 10,000 Japanese, 2,300 indigenous Chamorros, 1,300 Korean labourers and military prostitutes and some 900 Caroline islanders. Thousands perished, many shot or bayoneted to death by Imperial troops as they attempted to surrender to invading Marines. Large numbers retreated to the towering bluffs at Marpi Point on the island's northern tip. Ordered to kill themselves, they faithfully obeyed, two days after the official end of the fighting, preferring an 'honourable' end to the rape, torture and certain death at the hands of the Americans that Japanese propagandists had promised. As Japanese-American interpreters positioned offshore pleaded with the terrified groups of civilians to give themselves up, families clutched each other and walked into the sea or blew themselves up with hand grenades; others hurled their children from the heights onto the rocks below and then jumped after them.[42]

As US Marines battled their way across Saipan, the US Fifth Fleet under Admiral Raymond Spruance encountered Admiral Ozawa Jisaburō's Japanese Combined Fleet west of the Marianas. In the ensuing Battle of the Philippine Sea (18–20 June), the Japanese fleet lost one third of its surviving carriers and a majority of its aircraft to a deadly combination of US carrier Hellcats, battleships and submarines. Zero pilots were inexperienced, and the air battle became so one-sided that American aviators grimly dubbed it the 'Great Marianas Turkey Shoot'. In desperation, some Japanese sacrificed themselves in suicide dives against US ships, a harbinger of the organised *kamikaze* attacks that would become commonplace by the end of 1944. The engagement, 'a crushing and fatal defeat', presaged the end of the naval war in the Pacific.[43]

Meanwhile, at SWPA headquarters in Australia, MacArthur was working out the details of a ground assault on Japan which he intended to launch from the Philippines. In the spring of 1944, SWPA forces began their long westward drive towards Manila by attacking Japanese troop concentrations in the Hollandia region of Dutch New Guinea and nearby islands, which fell in April and May. In June,

Nimitz launched a massive strike against the Marianas in an effort to divert Japanese attention from MacArthur's leapfrogging advance. Military planners also hoped that the capture of strategic Pacific islands inside Japan's defence perimeter would enable the US Army Air Forces to mount long-range bombing missions against the Japanese archipelago itself. In mid-July 1944, Roosevelt flew to Honolulu to consult his top military commanders. Nimitz proposed bypassing the Philippines and taking Formosa as a forward base instead – a long-standing Navy strategy. When Roosevelt asked MacArthur bluntly, 'Douglas, where do we go from here?', the General replied, 'Leyte, Mr. President, and then Luzon.' Nimitz concurred, and Roosevelt authorised MacArthur to proceed with the liberation of the Philippines. The Navy was ordered to follow up that offensive by seizing Iwo Jima in the Ogasawara (Bonin) Islands and Okinawa, which would serve as the jumping-off point for a full-scale attack on Japan proper.[44]

The collapse of Saipan was accompanied by major setbacks for Japan in the protracted Battle of Kohima–Imphal, an ambitious but doomed attempt to cut off British and Indian forces in northeastern India and seize Bengal and Assam. These reverses precipitated the resignation of General Tōjō Hideki's Cabinet in late July. Lord Privy Seal Marquis Kido Kōichi, although personally aligned with the pro-war faction around Tōjō, helped engineer the General's departure. Also pressing for Tōjō's removal were Prince Konoe Fumimaro and Baron Hiranuma Ki'ichirō, former prime ministers and domestic reformers associated with the Imperial Way Faction (*Kōdōha*), which had opposed the military adventurism of Tōjō's Control Faction (*Tōseiha*). As senior statesmen, both Konoe and Hiranuma belonged to the august council of former heads of government, the *Jūshin*. With Tōjō's resignation, the 'peace party' around Konoe began to reassert its influence. A key backstage peace disciple was former diplomat and Anglophile Yoshida Shigeru, who held together a loose collection of political 'moderates' determined to end the war but preserve Imperial sovereignty.

On 22 July 1944, Tōjō was replaced by Koiso Kuniaki, a rather obscure Control Faction member, former chief of staff of the Kwantung Army and current Governor General of Korea. Koiso was the Emperor's choice, but he was ill-informed both about domestic politics and the situation at the front. Doubting the war could be won, he was anxious to achieve a decisive victory in the forthcoming battle for the Philippines, paving the way for peace negotiations. To coordinate policy-making between the military high command and the government, in early August 1944, Koiso established the Supreme Council for the Direction of the War, which came to function as a de facto inner war cabinet. The Council consisted of six members: the Prime Minister, the Foreign Minister, the Army and Navy Ministers and the Army and Navy Chiefs of Staff. It immediately decided to make peace overtures to the Chinese Nationalist government in Chungking (Chongqing) in an unsuccessful bid to free Imperial forces on the continent for the defence of the Philippines and the homeland. Koiso also struggled to retain Soviet neutrality through a series of secret diplomatic manoeuvres (below).

The Saipan debacle also forced the Imperial Army and Navy to coordinate their efforts and pursue a common strategy for the first time since 1941. Imperial General Headquarters elaborated plans for a series of 'victory operations' (*Shō-Go*) that would begin with the repulse of Allied invaders in the Philippines. Should the Philippine operation fail, plans called for a succession of 'final showdowns' that were in fact a succession of strategic retreats, first to Formosa and the Ryukyus, next to the home islands (except Hokkaido) and finally to Hokkaido, where the last battle would be fought. Imperial strategists decided to make their first stand on Leyte Island, which was declared a *tennōzan* (literally, 'Imperial Mountain', or decisive battle). Japan's civilian and military leaders possessed no comprehensive war plan, either for victory or for defeat, however. With the steady contraction of Japan's 'absolute defence perimeter', they desperately sought a major battlefield success with which to lever a negotiated end to the war. On this point both Prime Minister Koiso and the Emperor concurred. This unrealistic strategy would have appalling consequences.[45]

Strategic bombing

Meanwhile, in the Pacific, Japan's position was becoming untenable. The loss of Saipan was followed by the capture of Tinian and Guam in late July 1944. In September, the Octagon Conference in Quebec called for the aerial bombardment of the Japanese islands. On 10 October, Allied aircraft struck Naha, the capital of Okinawa, razing 90 per cent of the city. One month later, the Japanese mainland would come under attack from powerful B-29 long-range bombers belonging to the US Twentieth Air Force's XXI Bomber Command in the Marianas. Allied military planners expected strategic bombing to destroy Japan's 'basic economic and social fabric', and the new Super-Fortresses soon attacked its cities with devastating effect.[46]

Massive air attacks on major population centres designed to destroy civilian morale represented a new and terrible era in modern warfare. In the 1920s, Brigadier General William ('Billy') Mitchell had attempted to convince the US high command that the airplane had made the battleship obsolete. MacArthur, too, was a fervent believer in the potential of air power, and it was at his insistence that the US Army Air Forces were designated a separate command in 1935. During World War II, as he and Billy Mitchell had prophesied, control of the air became the decisive factor on the battlefield. With the escalation of aerial warfare, Axis and Allied air forces alike targeted civilian populations. In July and August 1943, British and American bombers levelled Hamburg, creating a fire storm that consumed nearly 45,000 non-combatants. In early 1945, even more terrible conflagrations engulfed Berlin, Leipzig and Dresden.

The first American air raid against Japan had occurred early in the war, in April 1942, when 16 two-engine B-25 Mitchell bombers commanded by Lieutenant Colonel James H. Doolittle lifted off precariously from the carrier USS *Hornet* in the western Pacific to launch an audacious surprise attack on Tokyo, Yokohama,

Nagoya, Osaka and Kobe. Most of the Doolittle raiders escaped to China, where several were subsequently captured. Although the attack, which targeted military installations, did little physical damage, the psychological trauma was enormous. By the autumn of 1944, having cracked Japan's outer defence shell, the United States was in a position to deploy continuously a rapidly growing fleet of land-based, four-engine Super-Fortresses with a range of 5,600 kilometres against military, industrial and civilian targets anywhere in the enemy heartland. On 17 November, more than 100 B-29s lifted off from Saipan in the first concerted air assault on Tokyo, bringing the war to the very nerve centre of the Empire. In January 1945, Major General Curtis E. LeMay, newly appointed leader of the XXI Bomber Command, proposed to replace conventional high-altitude, daylight precision targeting of major industrial and military facilities with the low-level, night-time carpet-bombing of large urban areas. In early March 1945, he substituted incendiaries for high explosives to maximise damage. His reconfigured payloads consisted of M-69 cluster bombs, each filled with a volatile mixture of jellied gasoline, phosphorus and magnesium specially designed to incinerate Japan's flimsy 'wood-and-paper' cities.

On the night of 9 March 1945, more than 300 B-29s took off from Guam on the first saturation bombing run of the war, transforming Tokyo into a raging inferno that razed 25 per cent of all buildings in an area of 25 square kilometres. LeMay later commented grimly that the 84,000 men, women and children killed in the huge fire storms, or 'red winds' (*aka-kaze*), were literally 'scorched and boiled and baked to death'. After the attack, the Japanese leader of a rescue detachment noted that the surface of Tokyo's Sumida River 'was black as far as the eye could see, black with burned corpses, logs, and who knew what else'. He continued: 'The bodies were all nude . . . and there was a dreadful sameness about them, no telling men from women or even children. All that remained were pieces of charred meat.' Three months later, MacArthur's psychological warfare chief Bonner Fellers wrote in a staff memorandum that the fire bombings were 'one of the most ruthless and barbaric killings of non-combatants in all history'.[47] LeMay, however, believed that the debilitating blitzes on Japan's population centres would shorten the war, and Nagoya, Kobe, Osaka and Kure were torched soon afterwards. By the time of Japan's surrender, 66 cities had been scourged by the massive air strikes. Nearly 40 per cent of these urban areas were reduced to ashes and 30 per cent of their inhabitants made homeless.

CLOSING IN ON THE HOME ISLANDS

The reconquest of the Philippines

As the first air attacks on Japan were being scheduled, Washington was outlining a grand strategy for the final confrontation. On 15 September 1944, the Joint Chiefs approved MacArthur's plan to invade Leyte on 20 October. On 29 September, a high-

Photo 2. Women take their noon meal in the bombed-out ruins of downtown Tokyo. Devastating US incendiary raids beginning in March 1945 reduced much of the capital to rubble. 27 May 1945 (Kyodo).

level military conference in San Francisco drew up detailed plans for the Iwo Jima and Okinawa campaigns. On 3 October, MacArthur was ordered to bring forward the invasion of Luzon from 20 February 1945 to 20 December. Nimitz was to start the Iwo Jima and Okinawa offensives on 1 February and 1 March 1945, respectively.[48]

In the fall of 1944, just before his big push on the Philippines, MacArthur regrouped the American units under his command. On 9 September, the General commissioned the Eighth Army and transferred to its control the 11th Airborne Division and other units. To the chagrin of Sixth Army Commander Krueger, Eichelberger was named head the 200,000-man force. With Eighth Army relieving Sixth Army of rearguard duties, Krueger and SWPA troops fought their way island by island from western New Guinea to Morotai in the north Molucca Sea. In mid-September, at MacArthur's insistence, US Navy amphibious forces attacked Peleliu in the Palaus east of Mindanao, a bloody offensive designed to protect SWPA's flank but which probably was unnecessary. In mid-October, victorious US Army and Navy forces converged in a vast armada off Leyte, and on 20 October, MacArthur landed at Leyte Gulf on schedule, fulfilling the pledge he had made more than two-and-a-half years earlier. His arrival was carefully stage-managed for maximum effect. Wearing aviator glasses and holding his corncob pipe, the General waded ashore and stepped up to a mobile broadcasting platform. Flanked by the new Philippine

President Sergio Osmena who had accompanied him, he announced emotionally, 'People of the Philippines, I have returned.'[49] In fact, the island's subjugation would require nearly two months of savage combat.

Imperial General Headquarters had declared Leyte a 'decisive battle' linked to the defence of the homeland, and Navy as well as Army forces were committed to the fray. As MacArthur staged his landing, Admiral Kurita Takeo left Borneo with a relief force of five battleships, including the world's largest warships, the super dread-noughts *Musashi* and *Yamato*, each displacing 63,000 tons, to challenge the US fleet and disrupt the invasion. The *Musashi* was sunk en route, forcing Kurita to with-draw temporarily, but his and other Imperial battle groups rallied to inflict substan-tial damage on Admiral Halsey's fleet before unsuccessfully engaging the American Navy on 23 October in the three-day Battle of Leyte Gulf. Rear Admiral Ōnishi Takijirō, Commander of the First Air Fleet, found himself without sufficient air support to neutralise Allied carriers. On 25 October, in desperation, he activated the first Special Attack Group (*Tokkōtai*) composed of young volunteers under orders to fly their Zeros directly into enemy vessels. The pilots sent on these flights of no return were called *kamikaze*, after the legendary 'Divine Wind' that had arisen to sink an invading Mongol fleet in the late thirteenth century. *Kamikaze* attacks would harry Allied warships until the end of the war, claiming the lives of nearly 4,000 Japanese Army and Navy airmen and hundreds of Allied personnel.[50] The Battle of Leyte Gulf ended in disaster for Kurita, eviscerating the Imperial Navy and decisively ending its ability to challenge American control of Pacific waters.

Leyte was the 'anvil' from which MacArthur intended to pound the Japanese into submission in the central Philippines.[51] Following the island's pacification in late December, the General aimed his next hammer blow at Luzon, where Imperial forces under General Yamashita Tomoyuki, the 'Tiger of Malaya', had dug in for another 'decisive battle'. On 9 January 1945, Sixth Army rendezvoused with Navy units at sea for a joint landing at Lingayen Bay in northwestern Luzon. MacArthur personally directed the fighting against Yamashita's troops. Krueger's Sixth Army led the main drive south from Lingayen to Manila, but Eichelberger also landed Eighth Army support units at Subic Bay and Nasugbu in the south and pushed northward towards the capital. By late January, US forces had outflanked the Japanese defenders and surrounded Manila. Yamashita's troops were pushed deep into the fastness of Luzon's Sierra Madre mountains, where some 100,000 soldiers, contained and weakened, would wage a bitter fight for survival until the end of the war.

Eighth Army's 11th Airborne Division under Major General Joseph M. Swing reached the southern outskirts of Manila and bogged down, just as Sixth Army units entered the capital from the north. On 7 February, MacArthur announced pre-maturely that Manila was rapidly being cleared, but hellish fighting in and around the city dragged on until early March. Holing up inside Intramuros, the old walled quarter, 20,000 Japanese soldiers and sailors ran amok. There, they tortured and massacred 1,000 defenceless civilians held hostage in Christian churches before engaging advancing Allied soldiers in a fight to the death. Filipino editor Carlos

Romulo later described the spectacle that assailed him upon returning to the old quarter: 'I saw the bodies of priests, women, children and babies that had been bayoneted for sport, survivors told us, by a soldiery gone mad with blood lust in defeat.' In all, an estimated 100,000 Filipinos perished in the battle for Manila.[52]

While Sixth Army secured Luzon, Eichelberger returned to Leyte for mopping up operations. From late February until mid-August, Eighth Army would be engaged in bloody campaigns in the central and the southern Philippines. MacArthur ordered these additional offensives without authorisation from the Joint Chiefs of Staff, who found themselves forced to accept a fait accompli, approving the operations retroactively. MacArthur's intent was to liberate all of the Philippines and protect Filipinos in outlying areas from Japanese reprisals, but Mindanao and the other islands invaded were of no strategic importance to US military planners. (One historian has observed that the Pentagon's failure to rebuke the General would postpone a showdown, encouraging a larger insubordination six years later in Korea.) Fighting in the Philippines lasted some 10 months and produced 47,000 American casualties, including nearly 10,400 battle deaths; Japanese losses were enormous, numbering some 255,800 killed and wounded. Reflecting in part Allied propaganda successes, an unprecedented 11,745 Imperial soldiers chose the ignominy of surrender to death by their own hand.[53]

Iwo Jima

Following the victory of MacArthur's armies in the Philippines, Nimitz's Navy converged on Iwo Jima in the Volcanic Islands, a part of the Ogasawara chain. Situated 1,220 kilometres due south of Tokyo, Iwo Jima occupied a position midway between the Marianas and Honshu, Japan's largest home island. The only territory in the Ogasawaras large enough to accommodate airfields, its strategic importance was immense, and the Japanese high command reinforced its fighter base there as Super-Fortresses commenced their bombing runs over Japan. Zeros regularly intercepted the US bombers flying overhead in an effort to disrupt their formations and give Tokyo early warning of impending raids. Imperial General Headquarters was determined to defend the island fortress to the last man and in October 1944 stationed 23,000 troops there under Lieutenant General Kuribayashi Tadamichi. Equipped with tanks, anti-tank weapons, heavy mortars, artillery and anti-aircraft guns, the combined Imperial Army and Navy garrison built mutually supporting complexes of pillboxes, gun emplacements and bunkers and honeycombed the island with 18 kilometres of deep tunnels, turning the rocky outpost into an impregnable fortress. Since Peleliu, Japanese island commands had abandoned frontal attacks and shoreside defences for an inland strategy of defence in depth that conserved men and forced the enemy into their well-prepared positions for a one-to-one battle of attrition.[54]

Poised for invasion were nearly 250,000 American soldiers, sailors and airmen aboard more than 800 Navy warships. The Fifth Marine Amphibious Corps, composed of the 3rd, 4th and 5th Marine Divisions and numbering 80,000 men, was the assault force. On 19 February 1945, slightly behind schedule, following five weeks of intense sea and air bombardment that completely refigured Mount Suribachi in the south, the Navy put ashore an initial 30,000 Marines. On 24 February a Marine combat patrol ran up the Stars and Stripes on Suribachi's deformed peak. Associated Press correspondent Joe Rosenthal's Pulitzer prizewinning photograph of the event came to symbolise for the Allies the high price of victory. The vastly outnumbered Japanese mounted a fierce and tenacious resistance but were slowly flushed from their positions, and on 17 March, the island was declared secured, although Kuribayashi's command bunker continued to fight on for a week. By 26 March, resistance had ceased entirely, the 23,000-strong force having been virtually wiped out. The garrison, Imperial General Headquarters reported, had gone down to 'an honourable defeat'. The nearly six-week battle for Iwo Jima saw some of the grimmest fighting of the war up to that point. The island had to be wrested from the defenders bloody yard by bloody yard, and the ratio of US casualties (6,000 dead, 25,000 wounded) to troops committed was among the highest ever sustained by the Marine Corps.[55]

The Ogasawaras, administratively a part of Metropolitan Tokyo, were the first piece of Japan's home territory to fall into Allied hands, and the islands were quickly placed under military rule. In a narrow sense, the occupation of Japan began here. The acquisition of Iwo Jima's airfields enabled the Marines to bring in Corsairs to protect the Air Force's B-29s in the air above. Forward air bases and fighter escorts greatly enhanced the effectiveness of the Super-Fortresses, which now could strike Japanese targets at lower altitudes and make emergency landings on Iwo Jima for repairs and refuelling. Indeed, the first damaged B-29 had touched down there on 4 March while the fighting still raged, and more than 2,000 would do so before the end of the war. LeMay's XXI Bomber Command subsequently renewed its incendiary attacks on Japanese cities. With the waters around the Ogasawaras free of Imperial warships, the US Navy, too, began attacking the main islands from carrier-based aircraft.

As Japanese attempted to cope with the fiery destruction that rained from the skies, they tightened their belts and adjusted to near famine conditions. Following the loss of the Philippines, American submarines intensified their silent campaign, sending one after another of Japan's commercial transports to the bottom of the sea, and the Empire's southern supply routes contracted sharply. By January 1945, almost 70 per cent of Japan's Merchant Marine had been sunk or put out of service, including nearly 60 per cent of its oil tankers, and sea links south of Formosa had been severed.[56] The Greater East Asia Co-Prosperity Sphere was being rapidly dismembered, and its markets and vital trade networks lay in disarray.

The collapse of empire threatened Japan's economic lifeline, choking off not only raw materials such as rubber, oil and mineral ores but food staples, cloth and other basic commodities. Rigid rice rationing and retrenchment measures were introduced, and the equivalent of soup kitchens were set up in the big cities, but even these efforts proved ineffectual and eventually were abandoned. In the final months of the war, the government was exhorting the population to enhance the starch content of its diet by consuming processed sawdust and grain husks, and people foraged for tea leaves, wild grasses, seeds, pumpkin stems, rats, snails, crayfish and snakes. To escape US bombing raids, young children were evacuated to the countryside where food was relatively more plentiful, but many middle and high school children were put to work in factories. Not even a large influx of colonial conscripts from Korea and Formosa could overcome the critical shortage of labour, now concentrated in war-related industries. Basic consumer goods disappeared from store shelves. As malnutrition and illness became widespread, labour productivity slumped and absenteeism soared. Despair slowly gripped the nation.

The battle of Okinawa

The island of Okinawa, some 96 kilometres long, is the largest in the Ryukyus, occupying more than half of the archipelago's land mass. Allied plans for the attack on Okinawa, code-named 'Operation Iceberg', earmarked it as a trial run for the invasion of mainland Japan. 'Iceberg' was conceived primarily as an American initiative, but at the Quebec Octagon Conference of September 1944, Churchill had insisted on a supporting role for Britain. The Prime Minister was determined to assuage the humiliating loss of Singapore in early 1942 and give London greater leverage in postwar Allied policy-making towards Japan. As a result, a British carrier squadron, Task Force Fifty-Seven under Vice Admiral Sir Bernard Rawlings, was attached to the Okinawa invasion group, and in late March, the Royal Air Force was assigned to fly air strikes against the Miyako and Yaeyama islands in the Sakishima chain south of the main island of Okinawa.

Nimitz held overall command of the invasion. Responsibility for the amphibious landings was given to US Fifth Fleet Commander Admiral Raymond Spruance. The actual assault would be carried out by the III Marine Amphibious Corps, led by Major General Roy S. Geiger, and the recently designated US Tenth Army under General Simon Bolivar Buckner, Jr, which included General John R. Hodge's XXIV Corps.[57] Buckner was responsible for all ground forces. With an armada of 1,300 ships and nearly 542,000 battle-hardened airmen, seamen and soldiers (four Army corps comprising seven divisions plus three Marine divisions), the invasion rivalled in scale the Allied landing in Normandy a year earlier. It was the largest flotilla ever assembled in the Pacific. Defending Okinawa were some 110,000 troops of the Imperial Thirty-Second Army commanded by Lieutenant General Ushijima Mitsuru. These were augmented initially by the arrival from China and Manchuria of the 15th Independent Mixed Brigade and the 9th, 28th, 24th and 62nd Divisions. Prior to the invasion, and against the advice of the Okinawa garrison, however, Imperial General Headquarters sent the crack 9th Division to defend Formosa and the Philippines, weakening Japanese defences and causing morale to plummet. Of Ushijima's force, about 24,000 belonged to an untested Okinawan home guard consisting of newly conscripted militia forces and volunteer units.[58]

Ushijima prepared for a defence in depth, concentrating his troops in the south whose complex system of escarpments and ridges was ideally suited for battling a numerically superior enemy. The Japanese strategy was to lure the invader into these heavily fortified highland positions, with their bunkers, caves, protected tunnels, trenches and other defences, and engage him in a fight to the finish at close quarters. Allied strategists, expecting a defence in force at the water's edge, intended to invade Okinawa from both sides, cut the island in two at the middle and then divide their forces, sending III Amphibious Corps northwards, Tenth Army into the south.

On 26 March, US troops landed in the Kerama islands just off Okinawa to secure the anchorage there as an emergency repair base and artillery emplacement. As American forces advanced into the Keramas, the Japanese garrison commander ordered local inhabitants to hand over all food supplies and prepare to die by their own hand. Fearing Allied reprisals, old people, women and children dutifully obeyed, killing each other in a horrible slaughter that portended the larger tragedy to come. On 28 March, a total of 329 died on Tokashiki, the largest island in the Keramas. Kinjō Shigeaki, 16 at the time, recalled the incident many years later. 'Cornered like a mouse in a trap, death was the only option left for us', he said. People tried to blow themselves up with hand grenades, but there were not enough to go around, and many failed to explode. Kinjō then watched as a middle-aged village leader snapped a limb off a nearby tree and 'turned into a madman', bludgeoning his wife and children to death. That act triggered a murderous frenzy in which families and relatives set upon each other with knives, sickles, cudgels and rocks. Kinjō recalls painfully: 'My memory tells me the first one we laid hands on was Mother. . . . When we raised our hands against the mother who bore us, we wailed in our grief. I remember that. In the end we must have used stones. To the head. We took care of Mother that way. Then my brother and I turned against our younger brother and younger sister. Hell engulfed us there.' Ultimately, only the villagers obeyed orders to kill themselves. Military units on the island avoided combat and survived. On islands where there were no soldiers, there were no group suicides of civilians.[59]

The Keramas were the second parcel of Japanese home terrain to fall to Allied forces. On 31 March, the day before the invasion of Okinawa began, Admiral Nimitz issued US Navy Military Government Proclamation no. 1. The so-called Nimitz Proclamation formally nullified Tokyo's authority over the island group and became the legal basis for the subsequent establishment of military government in the Ryukyus.

As the battle for Okinawa Island commenced, a destroyer force led by the world's mightiest battleship, the *Yamato*, broke out of Japanese waters and headed for Okinawa. The fleet was on a suicide mission, its orders being to plough through the Allied armada around Okinawa, ground the ships and join Imperial forces in defending the island. On 3 April, US carrier planes discovered and overwhelmed the *Yamato* off the coast of Kyushu, sinking the mammoth vessel and its 2,000-man crew in scenes eerily reminiscent of the Imperial Navy's destruction of the *Prince of Wales* three years earlier.[60]

On 1 April, US assault divisions landed at the Hagushi beaches on Okinawa's west coast to discover that they were unopposed. On 8 April, however, as Tenth Army pushed south, it encountered impregnable Japanese defences. The ensuing battle raged with horrifying intensity for nearly 80 days. As US soldiers advanced on the fortified positions where Japanese and Okinawan units had dug in to make a final stand, the fighting became increasingly convulsed and nightmarish. The main Japanese position was dug into the heights dominated by Shuri Castle, proud symbol of the once independent Ryukyu Kingdom. Intensive naval bombardments finally destroyed the castle, and US forces breached the Shuri Line in late May. The American breakthrough came after weeks of trench warfare and suicidal assaults and counter-assaults waged across a no-man's-land that had become a vast cesspool of mud, decomposing corpses, human excrement and maggots. US Marine Eugene Sledge later described the butchery in soul-wrenching detail, characterising it as 'too horrible and obscene even for hardened veterans'.[61]

The Imperial Army had drafted over 2,000 junior-high and high-school students between the ages of 11 and 14, formed them into a special youth unit, the Imperial Iron and Blood Corps, and sent them to the battlefront. With little or no training, boys were ordered into combat, some armed only with bamboo staves, and over 800 were slaughtered in the fighting. Of some 580 female students between the ages of 15 and 19 formed into nurses' units, more than 300 met the same fate, including nearly the entire 220-strong *Himeyuri* (Maiden Lily) Nurse Corps. Flushed out of caves where they had established field hospitals and onto high bluffs by Marine flame throwers, many killed themselves with hand grenades or leaped to their death. Miyagi Kikuko, one of the few survivors, remembered her disbelief at the sight of American soldiers pleading with the young women in Japanese to surrender. 'We thought we were hearing the voices of demons. From the time we'd been children, we'd only been educated to hate them', she said. '[W]hat we had been taught robbed us of life. . . . We never dreamt that the enemy would rescue us.'[62]

Japanese combatants behaved with utter ruthlessness. Imperial troops cut down civilians who got in their way. Islanders caught speaking their native Ryukyuan tongue were branded as spies and executed. Since most people over 60 could speak only the local dialect, hundreds were killed for that 'offence' alone. Civilians were rounded up and used as human shields. Mothers hiding in caves were ordered to strangle their babies and young children lest their cries betray their position to the Americans. Soldiers attempting to surrender were shot in the back by comrades. In the heat of battle, GIs, too, showed no quarter, incinerating with flame-throwers combatants and non-combatants alike who had taken refuge in caves and vault-like ancestral 'turtleback' tombs. Today, those walls are still scarred with the scratch marks of Okinawans who tried to claw their way through the rock. People referred to the maelstrom that ravaged their island as the 'Typhoon of Steel'. Even now, that carnage sears the memories of older Okinawans, and tales of the atrocities committed by both armies haunt the imaginations of younger generations.[63]

It took the Americans nearly three months of vicious combat, most of it at close quarters, to pacify the island. Organised resistance ceased with the ritual suicide of General Ushijima and his commanders, who disembowelled themselves within yards

Photo 3. During the height of the battle for Okinawa, a US intelligence officer questions two
young survivors of the Imperial Iron and Blood Corps. April 1945 (Kyodo).

of US lines, on 23 June. Ushijima's Chief of Staff Chō Isamu, who had ordered
many of the massacres at Nanjing in 1937, followed his leader in death. Five days
earlier, General Buckner, Tenth Army chief and US ground force commander,
had died in an artillery barrage. Some 7,400 Imperial soldiers surrendered, most of
them during mopping up operations. Casualties on both sides were staggering.

Approximately 100,000 Imperial soldiers, including Okinawan volunteers, and some 150,000 Okinawan civilians – nearly one third of the island's population – were killed or unaccounted for. Some 12,500 Americans were dead or missing and another 36,600 wounded. An additional 33,000 were listed as non-battle casualties, victims of combat fatigue, illness and other injuries.[64]

Japanese peace initiatives

The invasion of Okinawa compounded the trauma inflicted by the capture of Iwo Jima and the Philippines. These disastrous defeats toppled the government of Prime Minister Koiso, whose faltering diplomatic overtures to Nationalist China and the Soviet Union had come to naught. On 7 April 1945, Koiso resigned and was replaced by Admiral Suzuki Kantarō, 76, a retired naval hero famous for his audacity in Japan's earlier wars against China and Russia. A one-time Imperial grand chamberlain and currently President of the Privy Council (the Emperor's 'think-tank' and constitutional watchdog), Suzuki enjoyed Hirohito's full confidence. As Japan's major cities came under renewed bombardment, Lord Privy Seal Kido and Prince Konoe, both trusted Court advisers, began weighing Japan's options for ending the slaughter without compromising the Imperial institution. Both men feared that the real threat to the Throne was a domestic insurrection sparked by a Soviet declaration of war (chapter 5).

Japan's leadership as a whole deeply mistrusted Soviet intentions. Between late 1943 and late 1944, Foreign Minister Shigemitsu Mamoru had approached Moscow repeatedly in an effort to improve bilateral relations, but these overtures had been rejected. The first attempt at rapprochement was made in September 1943, following the capitulation of Italy, the second in early April 1944 and a third in September of that year. The final initiative had been authorised by Prime Minister Koiso's newly created Supreme Council for the Conduct of the War in July. In September, Foreign Minister Shigemitsu drafted a list of appeasements designed to secure a pledge of continued non-intervention. His position paper, 'Diplomatic Measures to be Taken *vis-à-vis* the Soviet Union', promised abrogation of the Tripartite Pact; a Soviet sphere of influence in Manchuria and Outer Mongolia; the transfer to Moscow of the Chinese Eastern Railway, the central and northern Kurils and southern Sakhalin; the renunciation of fishing rights in Siberian coastal waters; and permission to use the Tsugaru Strait between northern Honshu and Hokkaido. Shigemitsu's 'Diplomatic Measures' displayed a shrewd appreciation of Soviet national interests and historical grievances, but Stalin rebuffed his request to send an envoy to negotiate terms, and the Japanese proposal was never properly conveyed to the Kremlin.[65]

In early February 1945, Japanese military officials learned that Stalin was planning to discontinue the Neutrality Pact of 1941. On 5 April, Soviet Foreign Minister Viacheslav Molotov informed Ambassador Satō Naotake in Moscow that the Kremlin would not extend the agreement when it came up for renewal in April 1946. The Japanese government and military high command realised that if Germany collapsed, Soviet belligerency would make continuation of the war impossible, a fact of which Washington was aware through its intercepts of secret Japanese diplomatic traffic, compiled in daily intelligence summaries code-named 'Magic'.[66]

The Nazi capitulation of early May prompted the first discussions among members of the Supreme War Council on the need for eventual negotiations. In early June, in the strictest secrecy (not even the Emperor was informed), Foreign Minister Tōgō Shigenori brought former premier Hirota Kōki out of retirement and asked him to open talks with Soviet Ambassador Yakov Malik in Hakone outside of Tokyo. The Foreign Minister's primary concern was to negotiate a new neutrality accord, failing which he intended to request Kremlin mediation with London and Washington. Hirota came to the meeting armed with the list of concessions Shigemitsu had compiled some eight months earlier. Japan's 'peace aims' appeared vague and inconsequential, however, and Malik refused to relay them to Moscow. On Molotov's orders, the Soviet envoy broke off discussions in late June.

Until the fall of Okinawa, the Emperor himself had remained fully committed to the war effort. It was not until 22 June, the day before the Okinawa garrison went down to defeat, that an Imperial Conference officially sanctioned Tōgō's peace initiatives (chapter 5). On 10 July, the Supreme War Council, aware that Allied leaders would meet soon in Potsdam, attempted to despatch Prince Konoe to the Kremlin as 'peace ambassador'. Konoe prepared a peace offering based on the Shigemitsu concessions but offered to cede the Ogasawaras and Okinawa, as well (both already under Allied occupation). Busy preparing for Potsdam, Stalin received this approach with apparent indifference, telling Tokyo to await the outcome of the Allied summit. Japanese diplomats made similar representations to the Swedish and Swiss governments but to no effect. On balance, these diverse démarches cannot be considered serious attempts to terminate the war quickly. Rather, they were delaying tactics intended to forestall surrender and improve Japan's bargaining position.[67]

REORGANISING FOR VICTORY

The creation of USAFPAC

The Pacific War entered its final stage in early 1945, with Allied forces in control of the Pacific Rim from Southeast Asia to the waters around the Japanese archipelago. MacArthur's SWPA command and Nimitz's Pacific Fleet had effectively severed all links between Imperial armies in the Dutch East Indies and those in China. Japanese units remained scattered on islands throughout the Pacific, their situation hopeless. Soldiers from the Japanese Second, Seventeenth and Eighteenth Armies were trapped in the Solomons and New Guinea. Fragments of the Sixteenth, Nineteenth and Thirty-Second Armies were holed up in Borneo where, decimated by malaria and deprived of food and medical supplies, they engaged in a frantic struggle for survival. In the Philippines, the Fourteenth Army and the Thirty-Fifth Army had been overwhelmed by the superior forces of Krueger and Eichelberger. In the Burma/

Indo-China Theatre, Imperial soldiers were in full retreat from Admiral Lord Louis Mountbatten's forces. About eight Japanese divisions were completely cut off in the south. As starvation set in, troops resorted to cannibalism.

To speed the invasion of Japan, MacArthur insisted on the creation of a unified American command in the Pacific. Consequently, on 4 April 1945, the Joint Chiefs established the US Army Forces in the Pacific (USAFPAC, or AFPAC for short), transferred most American troops in the region to the new organisation, head-quartered in Manila, and appointed MacArthur Theatre Commander. The General was given operational control over all US military forces in the Pacific, with the exception of the Twentieth Air Force, the Alaskan Command and troops in the Southeast Pacific. By July 1945, AFPAC's nucleus consisted of the First Army, the Sixth Army, the Eighth Army, the Tenth Army, US Army Forces in the West Pacific, US Army Forces in the Mid-Pacific, the Far Eastern Air Force and some additional service commands. The Twentieth Air Force and the Pacific Fleet stood by for joint operations and logistic support. MacArthur now held two commands, GHQ/AFPAC and GHQ/SWPA, the latter still in Brisbane but consisting exclusively of Australian and Dutch troops, who were engaging the Japanese in Borneo and the East Indies.[68]

The Allied Combined Chiefs of Staff discussed a master plan for the invasion of the Japanese home islands in early February 1945 at Malta, two days before Churchill and Roosevelt met Stalin at Yalta. The Combined Chiefs estimated that the Allied offensive against Germany and Okinawa would last until the summer and that the Japanese would fight on until mid-November 1946. Based on this time-table, they approved a three-stage invasion plan. Phase One called for the blockade and bombardment of Honshu and Kyushu by air and sea from bases in the Marianas, the Philippines and Okinawa in preparation for an invasion of Kyushu. Phase Two would put troops ashore at Kagoshima and Ariake Bays in Kyushu and step up pressure on Honshu. Phase Three involved an attack on the Kanto Plain (Tokyo–Yokohama area) intended to destroy the country's administrative nerve centre and industrial base, capture Imperial General Headquarters and eliminate organised resistance in the capital region. The British Chiefs pressed for a Commonwealth role in the invasion, and at Potsdam in July, it was agreed that British air, land and sea forces would participate alongside American troops.[69]

From 'Downfall' to 'Blacklist'

On 3 April 1945, the US Joint Chiefs ordered MacArthur to coordinate planning of the final assault with Nimitz. On 8 April, the staffs of the two men met in Manila and drew up a joint plan code-named 'Operation Downfall'. The invasion of Kyushu, dubbed 'Olympic', was considered 'essential to a strategy of strangulation' and would begin on 1 December, 1945 led by the Sixth Army. The unexpected fall of Rangoon to British and Indian forces on 2 May and Germany's surrender on 8 May, however, prompted the Joint Chiefs to advance the date of the Kyushu landing ('X-Day') by one month, to 1 November. 'Coronet', the attack on the Kanto

Plain ('Y-Day'), was scheduled for 1 March 1946 with landings by the Eighth Army and Tenth Army at Sagami Bay and by the First Army on the Kujukuri coast in Chiba Prefecture. Once these beachheads had been secured, US forces would seize Tokyo, Kumagaya, Yokohama and Chiba in a 'knock-out blow to the enemy's heart' that would force capitulation. The Joint Chiefs approved 'Downfall' in principle on 25 May 1945 and on 18 June submitted it for scrutiny to America's top military leaders and Harry Truman, who had assumed the presidency following Roosevelt's death on 12 April. In urging Truman to endorse the invasion plan, Army Chief of Staff General George C. Marshall noted the hazards of a frontal assault on the Japanese homeland and pointed out that victory might hinge ultimately on a Soviet declaration of war. Truman consented to the proposed assault on Kyushu 'as the best solution under the circumstances' and authorised the military to proceed with planning for an invasion of the Tokyo region, as well. The 18 June conference also is thought to have discussed openly for the first time the possible use of atomic weapons, then nearing completion under the ultra-secret Manhattan Project.[70]

With the fall of Germany, Washington began shifting troops, weapons and munitions from the European Theatre to the Japanese front, tipping the military balance of power in favour of the Allies. Had the invasion proceeded as planned, the result would have been brutal, crushing defeat for the Empire, but the cost to Allied forces too, would have been enormous, far greater in fact than American planners could anticipate in the spring of 1945. Anglo-Saxon air and sea power gave Allied navies an overwhelming advantage, but Japan's 1.6 million ground forces outnumbered the invaders on land.[71] On 20 January, Imperial General Headquarters had issued a general policy directive, 'The Decisive Defence Plan for the Homeland' (*Ketsu-Go*), dividing Japan into seven areas, including Korea, where the final battles of the war would be fought. On 8 April, the high command sent the completed version of *Ketsu-Go* to regional field commanders, and one month later, on 8 June, the civilian and military high command issued a go-for-broke general directive, the 'Fundamental Policy for the Conduct of the War', which committed the nation to eschew surrender and fight to a collective death.

In anticipation of invasion, the Imperial Army had reorganised its home defence forces into the First Army Group (Tokyo and northern Honshu), the Second Army Group (Kyushu, central and western Honshu) and the Fifth Area Army (Hokkaido, Sakhalin Island and the Kuril archipelago). Across the country, fighter training units were being converted en masse into *kamikaze* suicide squads. By mid-July, Allied military radio intercepts code-named 'Ultra' had confirmed that Japan's military leaders were rapidly reinforcing troop strengths in the main islands and concentrating crack units on Kyushu, which was being massively fortified for a vicious finish fight. Imperial General headquarters was convinced that a victory in Kyushu was feasible. By inflicting unacceptable losses on Allied forces there, the high command believed it would be able to sue for peace on relatively favourable terms.[72]

The population, too, was prepared for total war. The National Mobilisation Law of 1938 had authorised the commandeering of all human and material resources necessary for the war effort. In late June, with the fall of Okinawa imminent, this was supplemented by a series of emergency measures. The People's Volunteer Corps Law enabled the government to raise local militias and draft all males between the ages of 15 and 60 and females from ages 17 to 40. Based on the Nazi *Volkswehr*, the Corps quickly set about mobilising elderly men, women and children, who were armed with awls and bamboo spears and ordered to fight to the last breath. The Imperial Diet also passed the Wartime Emergency Measure granting the government broad state-of-emergency powers. At the same time, the Cabinet enacted the General Superintenders Ordinance, a contingency plan assuming the collapse of central authority that divided Japan into autonomous regions to be governed by Superintenders wielding absolute administrative, political and military powers.

As Allied forces approached Japan, the civilian population readied itself for a last suicidal paroxysm. Socialised for death, Japanese were exhorted to trust in the *Yamato-damashi* – the warrior ethic, with its qualities of moral fortitude, loyalty, personal discipline and spiritual purity. In reality, such sloganeering intensified in direct proportion to the spread of apathy and doubt among a population now chronically hungry and approaching physical and psychological collapse. Morale was deteriorating rapidly and rumours of anti-war acts and even sedition proliferated Indeed, the nation's rulers feared that the spectre of defeat might trigger a revolutionary upheaval (chapter 5). But when the final call was sounded, most Japanese would have rallied to the defence of their native land, prolonging the orgy of violence and answering the incessant calls of the ideologues for 'the hundred million shattered jewels' (*ichioku gyokusai*). A ground assault on Japan proper would have spurred Imperial troops on the Asian mainland to engage advancing Allied forces in a series of last-ditch battles. The American leadership's fears of 'a score of bloody Iwo Jimas and Okinawas all across China' seemed well-founded.[73] In fact, few of Japan's top civil or military leaders took their own propagandists seriously, most realising that a decisive victory was now beyond their grasp. Japan faced annihilation, and yet ultra-rightists in the government and military, prisoners of the war psychosis they themselves had created, seemed in their public pronouncements to prefer national extinction to defeat, leaving realists scant room for manoeuvre.

With 'Downfall' near completion, MacArthur instructed his G-3 section to draft an alternative to the invasion plan should Japan surrender earlier than expected. The result was 'Operation Blacklist', a blueprint for non-belligerent occupation. Included in 'Blacklist' was a contingency plan, 'Operation Baker', for the takeover of Japan's Korean colony, as well. Finished on 16 July, 'Blacklist' was sent to Admiral Nimitz, on Guam, who compared it with a rival scenario, 'Operation Campus', that his staff had elaborated.[74] 'Campus' was the fruit of Nimitz's Pacific campaigns, particularly his victories on Iwo Jima and Okinawa. It called for the Navy and Marines to seize major ports and coastal installations around Tokyo Bay and other key shore defences, consolidating beachheads and establishing US authority there before allowing the Army to move in. 'Blacklist', however, assigned the Army the leading role; the Navy would merely provide logistical support for GIs deploying inland. MacArthur vehemently opposed the 'Campus' option. Japan still possessed enormous war potential, he asserted; it would be a strategic blunder not to send in ground troops first. After careful consideration, the Joint Chiefs endorsed MacArthur's view. 'Operation Blacklist' called for an occupation force of up to 22 divisions augmented by 2 regimental combat teams and supported by naval and air units. Three of these divisions were earmarked for Korea. Specifically, Tenth Army elements would move into Korea, Eighth Army would take northern Honshu and Hokkaido and Sixth Army would occupy western Honshu, Kyushu and Shikoku. The plan conferred on MacArthur de facto authority for implementing Allied post-defeat policy towards Japan and Korea and was to be activated upon Japan's acceptance of the Potsdam Proclamation.[75]

By the time 'Blacklist' had been finalised, Japan was being strangled and pounded by Allied forces. Admiral John S. McCain's Task Force Thirty Eight had already left Leyte Gulf and was steaming towards Tokyo Bay. The US Third Fleet and the British Pacific Fleet were blockading and shelling Japanese cities along the Pacific coast. On 17 July, as General LeMay's Super-Fortresses struck smaller urban centres across Japan, Hitachi was pummelled by a combined Anglo-American naval bombardment, the first of its kind in home waters. The next day, 1,500 American and British carrier-based fighters unleashed destruction on Tokyo. On 28 July, aircraft from the US Twentieth and Far Eastern Air Forces dropped leaflets on targeted cities, warning the inhabitants of imminent destruction in an attempt to limit civilian casualties. Residents were given 17 hours to evacuate. By this time, only five of Japan's major cities had escaped the air raids unscathed, among them Hiroshima and Nagasaki.

CAPITULATION

America's 'Baby' and Potsdam
From 17 July to 2 August, as Japan's major population centres were being pulverised and reduced to cinders, Truman, Churchill and Stalin gathered in the Cecilienhof Palace at Potsdam outside of Berlin for the last wartime Allied summit, aptly christened 'Terminal'. On 16 July, the day before the parlay began, US Secretary of War Henry L. Stimson – who had accompanied Secretary of State James F. Byrnes and Truman to the conference – handed the President a coded, one-line telegram from Washington saying, 'Baby satisfactorily born'. The cryptic message related that scientists had successfully exploded the world's first atomic device near Alamogordo, New Mexico. The plutonium-implosion test, code-named Trinity, produced an explosive yield more than 10 times greater than anticipated, 'a lightning effect', its chief administrator noted, 'equal to several suns at midday'.[76] Truman received a full report on the new bomb on 21 July, confirming its staggering destructive force.

Truman and his advisers attempted to convey the impression to Stalin that nothing unusual had happened, but they could scarcely contain their excitement.

When Stimson informed Churchill of the Alamogordo test on 17 July, the British Prime Minister reportedly 'was greatly cheered up' by the news. In September 1944, Churchill and Roosevelt had agreed at the Hyde Park Conference in London to keep development of the bomb a secret and, 'after mature consideration', to use it against Japan. Now that day had come.[77] Acquisition of atomic arms gave the United States the means to defeat Japan militarily without committing ground troops to a blood bath. It also gave new force to the impending Anglo-American ultimatum. The US delegation had yet another reason for congratulations: the secret weapon would bolster Washington's hand against Moscow in negotiating the shape of the postwar world and strengthen the Nationalist position in China.

On 26 July, Truman and Churchill, with the assent of the absent Chiang Kai-shek, issued the Potsdam Proclamation calling on Japan to surrender unconditionally or suffer the 'utter devastation of the Japanese homeland'. The 13-point document called for the elimination of the authority and influence of those who had misled Japan into embarking on world conquest and announced the occupation of Japan by the Allied Powers until a new order could be established and Japan's war-making capacity destroyed (Articles 6 and 7). The Proclamation ordered the disarmament of Imperial forces and the punishment of war criminals but pledged to encourage the revival of democratic tendencies and guarantee democratic freedoms and fundamental human rights (Articles 9 and 10). It permitted Japan to retain basic industries and participate in world trade but stipulated the payment of reparations (Article 11). The occupation was to be withdrawn when the Japanese people had established 'a peacefully inclined and responsible government' (Article 12). Finally, the Proclamation promised 'prompt and utter destruction' should Japan fail to comply with its demands, which were non-negotiable (Article 13).[78]

Truman's advisers had suggested that three additional elements be incorporated into the document, any one of which might be expected to induce an early surrender. These were a pledge in Article 12 to retain the Imperial institution, explicit mention of the atomic bomb as the agency of Japan's destruction in the event of non-compliance, and Stalin's signature. Secretary of War Stimson was the author of the first proposal, but his version of Article 12 was rejected as dangerously ambiguous (Chapter 5). Concerning the second, Churchill and Truman were determined to keep news of America's 'doomsday machine' from the Soviets. Finally, the US President had ruled against Soviet participation in the ultimatum on grounds that the Kremlin was not yet at war with Japan. In fact, Truman, in regular receipt of 'Magic' intercepts detailing Japanese efforts to secure Soviet peace mediation, was determined to discourage an independent Moscow–Tokyo venue. Consequently, Stalin would not join the Proclamation as a cosignatory until Moscow announced its war decision two weeks later. On 28 July, two days after the Potsdam statement was issued, the Marshal was told vaguely that the United States possessed a potent new weapon. Although purposely circumspect, the message's import was unmistakable, and Stalin stepped up preparations for a Soviet attack on Japan.[79]

Hiroshima and Nagasaki
The Potsdam terms produced outrage and consternation in Tokyo. The Army angrily
demanded that Foreign Minister Tōgō reject the conditions out of hand. A *Mainichi
Shinbun* headline pronounced them a 'laughable matter'. On 28 July, Prime Minister
Suzuki called a press conference and announced that his government would not
respond to the Allied proclamation, using the ambiguous and, to Washington,
provocative term *mokusatsu*, which generally means to ignore but is closer to 'no
comment'; when translated literally, however, it becomes to 'kill by silence'. The
mokusatsu statement was subsequently reported by the US media as a formal snub.
    On 6 August at 8:16 am, with no warning, the *Enola Gay*, a specially modified
B-29 deployed on Tinian, dropped a 4-ton uranium bomb nicknamed 'Little Boy'
on Hiroshima, turning 90 per cent of the city to rubble and killing as many as
130,000 people instantly or in the weeks that followed. On 9 August at 11:30 am,
another B-29 from Tinian, *Bock's Car*, dropped 'Fat Man', a 4.5-ton plutonium
bomb packing double the explosive force of the first, on Nagasaki. The device landed
wide of the target, causing less loss of life than at Hiroshima, but upwards of 70,000
are thought to have perished. The bombs exploded with a blinding flash (*pika*)
followed by an ear-splitting roar (*don*), whence the Japanese expression for the
atomic blast, *pika-don*. Those near the epicentre were vaporised, leaving behind only
a shadow engraved on a stone bridge here or a wall there. Within a radius of three
kilometres, people died quickly of first-degree burns. Many walked in a stupor,
disfigured beyond recognition and holding in front of them seared arms from which
the sloughed-off skin dangled eerily in ribbons. Radiation exposure, direct and
residual, and fallout condemned those farther from ground zero to lingering deaths
over the next few months. Precise casualty figures are impossible to compute, but
more than 200,000 people, mostly civilians, may have died in the nuclear holocaust
and its immediate aftermath. Among the obliterated, scorched and irradiated victims
were some 20,000 to 30,000 Koreans and smaller numbers of Chinese labour conscripts, more than 1,000 Japanese Americans, and a few hundred Allied prisoners of
war and Asian and European residents of the two cities.[80]
    Shortly after Hiroshima, Truman broadcast news of the blast, warning that 'We
are now prepared to obliterate rapidly and completely every productive enterprise the
Japanese have above ground in any city'. Failure to accept Allied terms, he warned,
would result in 'a rain of ruin from the air, the like of which has never been seen on
earth'. On 8 August, an Imperial Army fact-finding team led by Military Intelligence
Chief Arisue Seizō and Dr Nishina Yoshio, head of Japan's own nuclear programme,
visited Hiroshima. Nishina confirmed the weapon to be an atomic bomb. 'What I
have seen', he told Tokyo, 'is unspeakable. Tens of thousands dead. Bodies piled up
everywhere. Sick, wounded, naked people wandering around in a daze. . . . Almost
no buildings left standing.' Senior officials were horrified by the reports of carnage
from the devastated city but attempted to downplay the extent of the destruction.
The military feigned indifference. Nonetheless, on 10 August (Tokyo time), the government lodged a formal protest against the United States, via the Swiss Legation,

Photo 4. The American uranium bomb 'Little Boy' obliterates Hiroshima, 6 August 1945. Five minutes after the blast, the macabre mushroom cloud soars 17,000 metres above the stricken city. At ground zero, human beings were vaporised (Mainichi).

describing the bomb as 'having the most cruel effects humanity has ever known. . . . This constitutes a new crime against humanity and civilisation'.[81]

The use of history's most hideous weapon against non-combatants in crowded cities was indeed an unprecedented atrocity, and it represented America's moral nadir, for the bomb negated the very values the United States claimed to be fighting for.[82] The nuclear option gave President Truman the means to end the war quickly and avert heavy casualties, but, as indicated earlier, there were other alternatives. Tragically, the bomb possessed a logic of its own. The momentum generated by the $2 billion Manhattan Project pointed to a single outcome. Having built the weapon, the United States was determined to test it, and Japan, as Churchill and Roosevelt had agreed in the autumn of 1944, was the target of choice. With the fall of Berlin in early May 1945, weapons development shifted into high gear so that the device could be used in actual combat conditions before Tokyo capitulated.[83]

There were political considerations, as well. Truman's resolve was stiffened by Secretary of State Byrnes and other advisers who insisted that merely delivering a psychological shock to the Japanese leadership was not enough: demonstrating the weapon, too, was required to 'make Russia more manageable in Europe'. This intended demonstration effect was uppermost in the minds of those who chose the targets – as yet unbombed urban areas whose scale and topography would enable the military to gauge the explosive force of the weapon and its impact on a human population. Scientists such as Harvard President James B. Conant, the Manhattan Project's leading science administrator and a member of the government's atomic oversight Interim Committee, argued that a graphic test of the bomb's grotesque effects on cities was necessary to convince world leaders of the need for an effective postwar system of nuclear controls. His primary concern was the impression the bomb's actual use would have on Moscow.[84] The ethical implications of atomic weaponry appear never to have been debated seriously within the government. Technology, bureaucratic momentum and political expedience had defeated morality.

Nonetheless, some of Truman's top military advisers entertained misgivings about the wisdom of employing such a device. Fleet Admiral William D. Leahy, Truman's chief of staff, reportedly commented on the day Hiroshima was razed that the United States, too, would suffer, 'for war is not to be waged on women and children'. In his memoirs, he stated: 'It is my opinion that the use of this barbarous weapon . . . was of no material assistance in our war against Japan', adding that '[i]n being the first to use it, we had adopted an ethical standard common to the barbarians of the Dark Ages'. Under-Secretary of the Navy Ralph A. Bard believed that Tokyo should be given fair warning in view of 'the position of the United States as a great humanitarian nation' and dissented openly in a secret memorandum of 28 June 1945. Navy Chief of Staff Admiral Ernest J. King was convinced the bombing was unnecessary and immoral. Dwight D. Eisenhower, Supreme Commander of the Allied Expeditionary Force in Europe, later said that nothing could justify the use of so terrible an instrument of destruction.[85] The day after Hiroshima, even MacArthur, who may have been briefed about the bomb in Manila the day before it was dropped, reportedly was 'appalled and depressed by this Frankenstein monster'.[86]

In a war fuelled by primitive race hatreds, however, use of the bomb was not difficult to justify to most Americans. On 11 August, Truman, responding to the protest of a leading US clergyman, explained his reasoning thus: 'The only language [the Japanese] seem to understand is the one we have been using to bombard them. When you have to deal with a beast you have to treat him as a beast. It is most regrettable but nevertheless true.' The deeper, carefully concealed political dimensions of the decision to employ atomic weapons have been documented only recently.[87]

Soviet entry into the war
Stalin seriously began considering the possibility of war with Japan following the Soviet victory over German armies at Stalingrad in February 1943, a watershed in the war and in Soviet-Japanese relations.[88] In October of that year, at the Allied Foreign Ministers' Conference in Moscow, the Marshal had promised Secretary of State Hull an eventual Soviet declaration of war. In early November, in a speech commemorating the Bolshevik Revolution, he branded Japan an aggressor nation. Later that month at Teheran, the Soviet leader formally pledged to open hostilities against Japan in return for certain concessions. At Yalta in early February 1945, he refined that promise, specifying a declaration of war within 'two or three months after Germany has surrendered and the war in Europe has terminated' and outlined the conditions he expected.

The axe fell on 8 August, at 5 pm (11 pm in Tokyo), three months to the day of Berlin's capitulation, when Soviet Foreign Minister Molotov read a statement to Ambassador Satō in Moscow informing him that the USSR would consider itself at war with Japan from the next day. At 1 am (local time) on 9 August, hours before envoy Yakov Malik could formally convey that declaration to Tokyo, the Red Army struck deep into Japanese-occupied Manchuria. The attack was part of a broader Soviet offensive in the Far East ('August Storm'), which had been in preparation since late February (the order to mobilise for attack was issued to military commanders on 28 June). This 'short purifying storm' was intended to purge the entire Russian Far East and surrounding areas of the Japanese presence and ensure a Soviet role in the post-surrender disposition of Japan. Until this time, Tokyo had continued its efforts to negotiate with Moscow. The Soviet attack, complained Foreign Ministry official Kase Toshikazu, was 'the most unkind cut of all. . . . We had asked for an olive branch and received a dagger thrust instead'.[89]

Moscow had begun transferring forces from the German front to Siberia in May, following the Nazi defeat. By early August, nearly 1.6 million battle-tested troops organised in three army fronts and buttressed by the Soviet Pacific Fleet stood poised for a lightning strike against the 1 million soldiers Japan had deployed in Manchuria, Korea, southern Sakhalin and the Kurils. When the order to invade Manchuria was given, the Trans-Baikal Front attacked en masse from the Mongolian People's

Republic in the west, the First Far Eastern Front rolled in from the Soviet Maritime Province in the east, and the Second Far Eastern Front struck across the Amur River in the northeast. A fourth onslaught, launched later in the month, targeted southern Sakhalin, the Kuril Islands and northern Hokkaido, and by late August, the Red Army would occupy the Korean Peninsula down to the 38th parallel.[90] Following the Soviet seizure of the Kuriles in early September, Stalin also would press Truman for a post-defeat zone of occupation in northern Hokkaido itself, reportedly the real target of the Sakhalin–Kuril offensive (chapter 2).

Stalin bided his time, waiting to declare hostilities until the destruction of Hiroshima made early Japanese capitulation a near certainty. The full dimensions of the Soviet offensive were not immediately evident to Japan's leadership, but once the extent of the disaster became clear, the psychological jolt was comparable to that of the atomic bombings. And perhaps even more so, for the Red Army's blitz raised the appalling prospect that a Soviet attack on Japan proper would precede an Allied invasion. With or without the atomic bomb, such an outcome, it was feared, might precipitate a popular uprising and, in any event, would almost certainly entail the destruction of the Throne.

Surrender

The abrupt and dramatic Soviet entry into the conflict, coupled with the devastation of Nagasaki the same morning by a second atomic explosion, forced the Suzuki Cabinet to reconsider its earlier dismissal of the Potsdam demand for a non-negotiated surrender. On 10 August (Tokyo time), at Hirohito's insistence, the Suzuki Cabinet tentatively accepted the Potsdam terms on condition that the Allies vouchsafe the Imperial institution and its 'prerogatives'. On 11 August (EST), Secretary of State Byrnes issued a purposely vague communiqué stating that the authority of the Emperor and government would be subject to the Allied Supreme Commander but suggesting that the monarchy would not be overthrown unilaterally. To quell angry opposition from the Army and war faction, Foreign Ministry translators doctored the language of the Byrnes Note to convey the impression of an Allied commitment to Imperial sovereignty, and on 14 August, again at Hirohito's prompting, Tokyo formally agreed to capitulate, ending days of tense and convoluted deliberations (chapter 5). The Foreign Ministry immediately cabled news of the decision to Allied capitals via its legations in Switzerland and Sweden. In the meantime, Allied aircraft continued to pound Tokyo and other cities, killing an additional 1,250 people and wounding more than 1,300 between 11 and 14 August.

At noon on 15 August, the Emperor's unprecedented prerecorded radio broadcast observed disingenuously that 'the war has not necessarily developed in Our favour' (a phrase inserted by his Army Minister) and asked the people to 'endure the unendurable and bear the unbearable' in order not to prolong the conflict. This, it said, would result not only in the obliteration of the nation but also lead to the extinction of civilisation, the implied consequence of 'a new and cruel bomb which kills and maims the innocent and the power of which to wreak destruction is truly incalculable'.[91] Consummately crafted by Court advisers and leading Cabinet members, the Imperial Rescript informed the Emperor's subjects, without using the words surrender or defeat, that Japan would seek peace. It was the first time the people had heard their sovereign's voice. The recording was scratchy and the monarch's stilted, circumloquacious court language was difficult to grasp, but its impact was immediate and dramatic. To ensure that the Rescript was clearly understood, the radio announcer reread it in vernacular Japanese, but even without this assist, the message was unmistakable: Japan had agreed to surrender. That afternoon, the Suzuki Cabinet resigned, and two days later, on 17 August, the 'Imperial Cabinet' (also known as the 'surrender Cabinet') of Prince Higashikuni Naruhiko was formed.

The French-educated Higashikuni was a relatively liberal member of the Imperial family then in charge of Japan's home defences. The Prince was Hirohito's uncle by marriage, and ruling circles expected his Royal pedigree to help prepare the nation, and particularly its military leadership, for defeat and occupation. The appointment of a member of the Imperial family to head the government also fostered the impression that the Allies had endorsed the survival of the monarchy, and the Imperial Cabinet's signing of the Instrument of Surrender on 2 September reinforced this perception. Higashikuni named Prince Konoe, scion of the ancient Fujiwara line of regents, as his deputy premier and, initially, veteran diplomat Shigemitsu Mamoru as his foreign minister. One month later, on 17 September, the Prince would tap anti-Tōjō 'moderate' Yoshida Shigeru to head the Foreign Ministry, which by then had reclaimed its full powers from the defunct Greater East Asia Ministry. Higashikuni quickly set about repealing repressive wartime emergency decrees and attempting to restore the prewar Imperial status quo. Faced with the prospect of radical change, the Prince and his Cabinet were charged with the sacred mission of preserving the emperor system.

PRELUDE TO OCCUPATION

GHQ's prototype: the AFPAC Military Government Section
Japan's sudden capitulation pre-empted the Kyushu invasion plan, and MacArthur moved immediately to put 'Blacklist', the alternative to 'Operation Downfall', into effect. Completed on 8 August, the final 'Blacklist' scenario divided the occupation of Japan and southern Korea into three phases. During Phase I, Allied troops would occupy Tokyo and the Kanto Plain, Nagasaki–Sasebo, Kobe–Osaka–Kyoto, Aomori–Ominato and Seoul (Korea). In Phase II, they would move into Shimonoseki and Fukuoka, Nagoya, Sapporo and Pusan (Korea). Phase III would take US ground forces into Hiroshima and Kure, Kochi, Okayama, Tsuruga, Ōdomari (Sakhalin), Sendai, Ni'igata and, in Korea, Kunsan and Taegu. MacArthur's civil affairs specialists were equipped with an extensive preliminary blueprint for military government (chapter 5). Short of properly trained personnel and Japanese language experts, however, his staff considered plans to cooperate with existing government

agencies. In Japan, initially at least, that would mean utilising the non-military officials and institutions that had supported aggression and, in Korea, the colonial régime and its military and paramilitary minions.

In early August, the Joint Chiefs of Staff had recommended that MacArthur, as US Theatre Commander, be appointed Allied Supreme Commander in order to receive and enforce the surrender of Japan. Truman accepted that advice and on 11 August (EST), informed Churchill and other Allied leaders of his choice. Moscow proposed a power-sharing arrangement between two supreme commanders, one American, one Soviet, but Washington categorically dismissed the notion of a dual leadership. Stalin acquiesced, and on 13 August, Britain, the Republic of China and the Soviet Union agreed to confer on MacArthur sole authority for implementing the surrender terms. On 15 August (Tokyo time), MacArthur formally took up his appointment as Supreme Commander for the Allied Powers.

In early August, with surrender probable, MacArthur had ordered his staff in Manila to make concrete preparations for the occupation of Japan. General Robert Eichelberger, AFPAC's Eighth Army Commander, records in his diary a flurry of paperwork, orders, communications and organisational changes around 10 August, most of them involving Sixth and Eighth Armies, which would constitute the primary garrison force.[92] Eichelberger also records that MacArthur's staff began planning a formal surrender ceremony at this time. Since AFPAC's creation in early April 1945, the Manila-based American command had divided responsibilities for the Asian and Pacific theatres with SWPA headquarters in Brisbane. On 15 August, MacArthur reorganised AFPAC and dissolved SWPA, except for Dutch and Australian units.[93] When Allied troops began landing in Japan on 28 August, GHQ/AFPAC, with Sixth and Eighth Armies as its core, became the sole unified Allied command in the archipelago. Following Japan's formal surrender on 2 September, SWPA's remaining echelons were deactivated. Sixth Army moved into southern Honshu and Shikoku and established its base of operations in Kyoto. Eighth Army occupied central and northern Honshu and set up headquarters in Yokohama.

In the course of refining the 'Blacklist' plans, MacArthur had considered adding a G-5 civil affairs section to AFPAC's general staff to administer post-surrender Japan. He soon realised, however, that governing an Asian nation whose history, culture and values were so different from those of the West would require a far more powerful and highly structured organisation. On 5 August 1945, he established the Military Government Section (MGS) as a special staff appendage of GHQ/AFPAC to handle the civil administration of Japan. Divisions were set up inside the omnibus MGS to deal with the myriad tasks of non-military occupation. These included Administration, Economics, Finance, Operations, Personnel, Public Affairs, Public Health and Welfare, Publications and Supply. MGS was staffed by hundreds of US military experts trained in civil governance who had been hastily reassigned from Okinawa and the Philippines. About one-tenth were drawn from the pool of specialists awaiting overseas assignment at the Civil Affairs Staging Area in Monterey, California.[94]

MacArthur appointed Brigadier General William E. Crist, an experienced staff officer then deputy commander of US Military Government in the Ryukyus, to head AFPAC's Military Government Section. A graduate of West Point and the US Command and General Staff School, Crist was a China hand and former military envoy to Moscow with a background in Military Intelligence. As the Occupation began, he immediately sent half of his MGS staff to Tokyo. Some of the most outstanding of these officers later occupied key positions in the Occupation. Charles L. Kades, MGS Deputy Chief, for instance, became Deputy Chief of SCAP's Government Section (GS) and led its constitutional revision team. Others transferred from Manila to Tokyo were Alfred R. Hussey Jr., a GS officer involved in revising the Constitution; Pieter K. Roest, Chief of the GS Political Parties' Division; Cecil G. Tilton, head of the GS Local Government Division; and Justin Williams Sr, Chief of the GS Legislative Division. This élite group also included William K. Bunce, who ran the Civil Information and Education Section's Religious Division; William Karpinsky, the first head of the Labour Division, Economic and Scientific Section; Crawford F. Sams, who led the Public Health and Welfare Section; and Mark B. Williamson, Chief of the Natural Resources Section's Agricultural Division.

Military Government Section was the prototype from which General Headquarters, Supreme Commander for the Allied Powers (GHQ/SCAP) would emerge in the fall of 1945. In late September, two new civil staff sections would be created alongside MGS, and on 2 October 1945, the Section itself would be formally discontinued and its functions transferred to the new SCAP 'super-government' created to administer the occupation of Japan. Thereafter, GHQ/SCAP would exist side-by-side with but independently of AFPAC, sharing the same military general staff and headquarters building but working through a separate civil staff organisation. Former MGS divisions would be transformed into special staff sections. With the dissolution of MGS, General Crist was appointed to head SCAP's Government Section. Crist was not a member of the Bataan Gang, however, and, lacking inside connections and support, proved ineffectual in that position. He soon was reassigned for failing to launch GHQ's purge programme promptly. In mid-December, Colonel (soon to be Brigadier General) Courtney Whitney, one of MacArthur's most trusted lieutenants, stepped in to fill that vacancy. When Chief of Staff Richard Sutherland returned to the United States that month, Whitney replaced him as MacArthur's closest confidant. (Sutherland's job was taken over by Major General Richard J. Marshall, another Bataan Gang intimate then Deputy Chief of Staff.)[95]

The international context: the emerging US–Soviet confrontation

American policy for post-surrender Japan was formulated against the backdrop of a growing rivalry with the Soviet Union that would reshape power relations in Northeast Asia even before Japan's surrender. The Atlantic Charter of mid-August 1941, the basic Allied declaration of principle, had forsworn territorial aggrandisement and pledged to 'respect the rights of all peoples to choose the form of Government under which they will live'. In the Cairo Declaration, signed on 27 November and released on 1 December 1943, Chiang Kai-shek, Churchill and Roosevelt proclaimed grandly that the Allies 'coveted no gain' and haboured 'no thought of territorial expansion' in the Pacific or the Far East. The Cairo document specified, however, that Japan would be expelled from all territories it had acquired 'by violence and greed'. The Potsdam Proclamation of 26 July 1945, reiterated those principles, stipulating that '[t]he terms of the Cairo Declaration shall be carried out' (Article 8).

The Atlantic Charter and the Cairo pledge, however, applied only to the Axis powers, not to the Western imperia. With the collapse of Japanese power in Asia and the Pacific, the United States backed the return of its Western allies to colonial rule in India, Burma, Malaya, the East Indies, Borneo, Timor, New Guinea, Indo-China, Macao and Hong Kong. At the same time, Washington prepared to assume control of former Japanese mandates in the Pacific, notably the Marianas, the Marshalls and the Carolines, which it would retain as United Nations' trusteeship territories (Guam in the Marianas soon would be transformed into a major US military base and the Marshalls into an immense nuclear test range). The Soviet Union, too, while upholding the principle of self-determination for non-whites, sought to carve out its own sphere of influence in northern Korea and in the regions along China's northern and western borders.

Despite the lofty sentiments expressed at Cairo, in the last year of the conflict, Washington and Moscow jockeyed for advantage, haggling over the spoils of war. In early February 1945, Churchill and Roosevelt, determined to prevent the Kremlin from dominating postwar central Europe, met Stalin at the Crimean city of Yalta on the Black Sea. There, in a secret protocol signed on 11 February, the Allied chiefs formally agreed to three Soviet demands as a quid pro quo for a Soviet declaration of war against Japan. These were: 1 preservation of the status quo in Outer Mongolia, 2 restoration of Russian territories awarded to Japan in 1906 following the Tsar's defeat in the Russo-Japanese War and 3 the handing over to the Soviet Union of the Kuril Islands north of Hokkaido. Point 2 included extensive provisions that returned the southern half of Sakhalin Island to Soviet control; guaranteed former Tsarist rights in the Chinese port of Dairen, which was to be internationalised; leased Port Arthur to Moscow as a naval base; and promised to safeguard the USSR's 'pre-eminent interests' in Manchuria, especially the Chinese Eastern and South Manchurian railways, which were to be operated by a joint Sino-Soviet company. Moreover, the protocol specified that the 'claims of the Soviet Union shall be unquestionably fulfilled after Japan has been defeated'.[96] Although ostensibly subject to the concurrence of Chiang Kai-shek, these clandestine commitments blatantly encroached on Chinese sovereignty, violating the non-aggrandisement and self-determination principles of the Atlantic Charter and the Cairo agreement. (One also detects here an uncanny echo of the more modest concessions Japan was prepared to make to Moscow as early as 1944.)

At Potsdam, however, very different circumstances prevailed. Truman did not feel bound by Roosevelt's Yalta agreements, for with the atomic bomb, America no longer needed Soviet military support to end the war. (The British, on the other hand, believed Washington should honour its Yalta commitments.) On 27 August, Truman notified Stalin that settlement of Soviet claims would have to await a final peace settlement with Japan. By that time, however, the Red Army already had seized southern Sakhalin and key islands in the northern Kuril chain (chapter 2).

Even as the occupation of Japan began, realpolitik had begun to influence subtly the direction of reform, anticipating a new era of political and ideological confrontation in Northeast Asia. Washington effectively excluded Moscow and the other Allies from a substantive role in postwar Japan, which fell within its East Asian sphere of influence, although care was taken to include a token Commonwealth presence. America's Japan policy would become the centrepiece of a grander strategy for containing the Soviet Union, and later the People's Republic of China, and for enforcing a Pax Americana along the great arc of the Pacific Rim, from the Aleutians through Japan, southern Korea, Okinawa and Formosa and as far south as Indo-China.

CHAPTER 2

Occupation: The First Weeks

THE MAIN ISLANDS SECURED

Secret mission to Manila

On 16 August 1945, the day after Japan's capitulation, General Headquarters, US Army Forces in the Pacific (GHQ/AFPAC) instructed Tokyo to send a delegation to Manila to discuss surrender and occupation procedures. On the morning of 19 August, two medium-range bombers, white with identifying green crosses emblazoned on their wings and tails at MacArthur's request, secretly left Kisarazu military airport in Chiba across Tokyo Bay. To forestall attack by ultra-nationalist pilots opposed to surrender, an identical aircraft took off at the same time. As the decoy skirted Japan's eastern coastline, the two 'surrender planes' made their way south towards a rendezvous with US forces on Iejima, an islet off Okinawa Island.[1]

Aboard the aircraft were sixteen civilian and military leaders headed by Lieutenant General Kawabe Torashirō, Deputy Chief of the Imperial Army General Staff. Accompanying him were Rear-Admiral Yokoyama Ichirō of the Imperial Navy General Staff; Lieutenant General Arisue Seizō, Chief of Military Intelligence; Major General Amano Masakazu, Chief of Operations, Imperial General Headquarters; Navy strategist Captain Ōmae Toshikazu; and Okazaki Katsuo, Chief of the Ministry of Foreign Affairs' Investigation Bureau. At Iejima, the group boarded an American DC-3 military transport, which landed at Nichols Field in Manila in the early evening of the 19th. Met by G-2 Chief Charles A. Willoughby and Colonel Sidney F. Mashbir of the Allied Translation and Interpreters Service, the delegation was whisked immediately to a meeting with AFPAC Chief of Staff Lieutenant General Richard K. Sutherland, Deputy Chief of Staff Major General Richard J. Marshall, Willoughby and other high-ranking American staff officers. MacArthur pointedly had absented himself from the discussions, and Sutherland greeted the Japanese with 'chilly formality'. Negotiations began at 9 pm that evening and continued non-stop through the early hours of 20 August. The Americans ordered the Japanese to clear the Tokyo Bay area of all troops, repair Atsugi Air Base where MacArthur would land and remove the propellers from all fighter craft in the region to forestall *kamikaze* attacks. In return, the Japanese side asked the Americans not to enter Tokyo before 8 September to enable them to withdraw their forces and calm the populace.[2]

During the pre-surrender conference, the Japanese were shown advance copies of several documents: a draft Imperial rescript ordering compliance with the Potsdam Proclamation and an immediate ceasefire; the Instrument of Surrender; General

Order no. 1, Military and Naval, directing Imperial Headquarters to bring about the direct, unconditional surrender of military personnel to designated Allied commanders; and Allied operational requirements for entry into Japan. The Japanese agreed to the surrender formalities and gave assurances that they would comply fully with all Allied demands. MacArthur also ordered the government to establish a Central Liaison Office to handle communications with the occupying authorities (chapter 3). ATIS Chief Mashbir convinced Willoughby and MacArthur not to embarrass the Emperor by forcing him to read a prepared statement, and they concurred. Hirohito had already broadcast Japan's acceptance of the Potsdam terms on 15 August and would be permitted to issue his own rescript at the signing of the Instrument of Surrender.[3] The Americans informed the envoys that the occupation would begin on 25 August, but Lieutenant General Kawabe requested a three-day extension, pointing out that military units in Japan could not be disarmed in so short a time. The US side agreed to postpone the landing until 28 August but ordered an advance party sent to Atsugi Air Base near Yokohama on the 26th (a typhoon would delay their arrival until the 28th).

In the course of the Manila conference, Willoughby informally approached Lieutenant General Arisue Seizō, Japan's military intelligence director who was scheduled to meet the US landing party at Atsugi, and struck up an acquaintance. Arisue, like Willoughby, was an admirer of Italian dictator Benito Mussolini and had formerly served as liaison with Mussolini's régime. Moreover, the two men could communicate in German, Willoughby's first language, insuring the confidentiality of their conversation. Arisue controlled a vast clandestine information network and maintained close personal ties with the Court. On 5 September, Willoughby would recruit the aristocratic anti-Communist to set up his own spy organisation inside G-2, an opportunity the Japanese officer would seize with alacrity. Other Imperial military leaders present that day, including Lieutenant General Kawabe and Captain Ōmae, also would find places on the G-2 payroll (chapter 4).[4]

MacArthur's arrival

Its mission completed, the Japanese delegation returned to Tokyo on 20 August. Final military arrangements for the landing of US forces were completed one week before the formal surrender. On 26 August, General Robert L. Eichelberger redeployed Eighth Army from Leyte in the Philippines to Okinawa and assigned his 11th Airborne Division and 27th Infantry Division to serve as the occupation vanguard. On 26 August, however, a typhoon swept the Japanese archipelago, delaying the American disembarkation by two days. At 9 am on the 28th, led by Colonel Charles P. Tench, a forward group of 150 communications experts and engineers, backed by a minuscule force of 38 combat troops, touched down at Atsugi airfield. They secured the area for the 11th Airborne, which began landing soldiers two days later, on 30 August. From 6 am on the 30th, a military transport set down at Atsugi every three to four minutes. Many years later, an eyewitness described the scene: 'Here come these planes every three minutes. Boom! Out! Boom! Out! I never saw such majesty in my life! We barely had time to get [off] the plane when the pilot turned to get away, because here'd come the next one.' By evening, 4,200 troops had disembarked, and Eighth Army had made the short trip to Yokohama, where it set up headquarters in the abandoned Customs House.[5]

General MacArthur, Supreme Commander for the Allied Powers and AFPAC Commander-in-Chief, left Nichols Field in Manila for Atsugi on 30 August aboard his unarmed C-54 transport, the *Bataan*. A few hours earlier, he had received from Washington an outline of the 'US Initial Post-Surrender Policy for Japan' (chapter 5). With barely concealed excitement, he summarised its contents to Colonel Courtney Whitney who had accompanied him: 'First, destroy the military power. Punish war criminals. Build the structure of representative government. Modernise the constitution. Hold free elections. Enfranchise the women. Release the political prisoners. Liberate the farmers. Encourage a free economy. Abolish police oppression. Develop a free and responsible press. Liberalise education. Decentralise political power. Separate the church from the state.' The Occupation of Japan had begun.[6]

At 2 pm that afternoon, MacArthur descended from the *Bataan* with studied casualness as the 11th Airborne band struck up 'Ruffles and Flourishes'. Second-Lieutenant Thomas T. Sakamoto, a language officer with the 11th Airborne, watched the General appear at the door of the airplane 'in khaki and his well-worn garrison hat, wearing sunglasses and holding an extra long corncob pipe'. With a grand gesture, 'he hesitated a moment and gazed upward toward the horizon from left to right and took a momentary Napoleon-like pose, reminding viewers of a victor and a conqueror'. After alighting, the General held a hastily arranged press conference and then set off through the verdant countryside for Yokohama in a motorcade led incongruously by a red fire engine. The route was lined from start to finish by armed Imperial troops standing at attention a few paces apart, their backs turned and eyes averted from the passing procession – a mark of respect and security measure normally reserved for movements of the Imperial family. MacArthur's destination was the Yokohama Customs House, one of the few large buildings left standing, which Eighth Army had taken over as its temporary headquarters. Painted black like all large buildings to escape detection during night bombing raids, the structure had been stripped clean of its metal parts; even steel railings and radiators had been requisitioned for war scrap.[7] The Supreme Commander and his staff set up temporary residence in the four-storey New Grand Hotel by the Yokohama waterfront.

The US Navy had begun occupying Japanese ports and naval installations on 27 August, one day ahead of Eighth Army's advance arrival at Atsugi, with the entry of Admiral William Halsey's Third Fleet into Sagami Bay. Accompanying the Third Fleet was Admiral Bruce Frazer, Commander of the British Far East Fleet, aboard his Royal Navy flagship, HMS *Duke of York*. Halsey negotiated the warships' safe passage into Tokyo Bay with Japanese naval officers, and on the 29th, as Eighth Army troops secured Atsugi, Halsey's USS *South Dakota* docked at Yokosuka port some 24

Photo 5. Less than a month after the atomic bombings, General Douglas MacArthur desends from the *Bataan* at Atsugi Air Base outside of Tokyo to begin the Allied Occupation of Japan. 30 August 1945 (US National Archives).

kilometres away. On 30 August, the 4th Marine Regimental Combat Team and the 6th Marine Division took over the Yokosuka Naval Base, coming under Eighth Army jurisdiction. A small Commonwealth contingent consisting of 536 sailors and marines under Captain H. J. Buchanan of the Royal Australian Navy occupied and disarmed three small island fortresses guarding the entrance to Tokyo Bay and hoisted the Union Jack. By 31 August, the US 4th Marines had made contact with the 188th Parachute Glider Regiment and the 511th Parachute Infantry Regiment, which had joined forces and sped to Yokohama and Yokosuka from Atsugi to seize the docks. The 11th Airborne's 187th Parachute-Infantry Regiment remained at Atsugi to prepare the air base for the arrival of the 27th Infantry Division and other units from Okinawa. On 1 September, reconnaissance troops from the 11th Air-borne moved into Kisarazu on the Chiba side of Tokyo Bay, and on the 2nd, the 1st

Cavalry Division landed at Yokohama. Meanwhile, aircraft from the US Far Eastern
Air Force and the Third Fleet had begun flying mercy missions to over 32,000 Allied
captives held in some 100 prison camps across Japan. As Eighth Army deployed, the
Red Cross moved its headquarters from Okinawa to Yokohama and came under
General Eichelberger's control.

A bloodless occupation
The days immediately preceding and following Japan's acceptance of the Potsdam
terms were fraught with tension. In the early hours of 15 August, a group of Army
officers had entered the Imperial Palace and ransacked it in a bid to seize the phonograph recording of the Emperor's surrender address but failed to locate it. Persuaded
to abandon their revolt by Tokyo Army headquarters, the conspirators committed
suicide in front of the Palace later that morning. Rebels attempted to take over major
radio stations, but they, too, were dissuaded by superiors. These actions were part of
a plot hatched by field officers on 11 August to assassinate peace advocates in the
government and military, sequester the Emperor and stage a *coup d'état*. Following the revolt's failure, several high-ranking military officers, including the Army
Minister, General Anami Korechika, and Rear Admiral Ōnishi Takijirō, also committed suicide on the 15th.

   During this time of uncertainty, the official residences of Prime Minister Suzuki
Kantarō and Privy Council President Baron Hiranuma Ki'ichirō were firebombed by
mobs of soldiers and students intent on assassinating the statesmen. Privy Seal
Marquis Kido Kōichi, too, was in hiding. Following the Emperor's broadcast, scattered incidents of violence erupted around Tokyo. From Atsugi Air Base where
MacArthur was scheduled to land, the Sagami Air Corps leafleted Tokyo, calling on
the Japanese people to rise up against their leaders and repel the invader. The Emperor
despatched his brother Prince Takamatsu to reason with the mutineers. Incipient
revolt continued to brew, however. Some 400 soldiers from Ibaraki Prefecture seized
Ueno Hill in Tokyo. When higher authorities prevailed on them to desist, their
officers committed suicide. On 18 August, an ultra-rightist brotherhood entrenched
themselves with hand grenades atop Atago Hill north of Shiba Park and when police
attacked on 22 August, blew themselves up. Diehard officers announced plans to
form a 'government of resistance', and on the evening of 20 August, Suzuki's successor, Prince Higashikuni Naruhiko, aired a radio broadcast every hour exhorting
Young Turks to abandon plans to occupy the Imperial Palace at midnight. The
Emperor and Cabinet stood firm, however, and the military high command intervened to impose order. Troops were disarmed, and at Atsugi and other air bases,
propellers were removed from aircraft. By 23 August, the crisis had passed, and when
the first US troops arrived five days later, calm had returned to the capital region. As a
final precaution, Emperor Hirohito despatched Imperial princes overseas to persuade
the armed forces to comply with Allied orders to disarm.[8]

   Nevertheless, Japan proper had roughly 3.5 million Imperial troops under arms,
producing in Allied commanders a 'terrific psychological tension'. As Eighth Army

Commander Eichelberger remarked later, 'one undisciplined fanatic with a rifle could turn a peaceful occupation into a punitive expedition'. Such worries were soon dispelled, however. Spasms of defiance, such as anonymous stone-throwing, continued, and armed robbery and minor assaults against Occupation personnel were rife in the weeks and months after capitulation, but active resistance was neither widespread nor organised. The Americans, a few thousand in number, completed their initial deployment without violence – an astonishing achievement in the face of a heavily armed and vastly superior enemy operating on home terrain. Six weeks later, on 16 October, MacArthur could boast that: 'In the accomplishment of the extraordinarily difficult and dangerous surrender in Japan, unique in the annals of history, not a shot was necessary, not a drop of Allied blood was shed.'[9]

The occupiers were taken aback by the extent of the destruction they encountered on the ground. More than 60 cities had been subjected to carpet bombing, and in many urban centres, the only structures left standing in the wake of incendiary raids were the iron safes of non-existent shops and, here and there, tall concrete chimneys. Everything else had been reduced to ash. The chimneys belonged to burned-out public bathhouses; the safes had been acquired by businesses large and small in the wake of the disastrous 1923 Kanto earthquake to protect insurance records and other important papers from fire. In the eerie silence, there were no people; no living thing stirred.

A Canadian journalist left this account of his entry into Yokohama in December 1945: 'Before us, as far as we could see, lay miles of rubble. The people looked ragged and distraught. They dug into the debris, to clear spaces for new shacks. . . . There were no buildings in sight.' Streetcars, he wrote, 'stood where the flames had caught up with them, twisting the metal, snapping the wires overhead, and bending the supporting iron poles, as if they were made of wax. Gutted buses and automobiles lay abandoned by the roadside. This was all a man-made desert, ugly and desolate and hazy in the dust that rose from the crushed brick and mortar.'[10] Crawford F. Sams, MacArthur's public health officer, looked at the ruined landscape and noted, 'Thousands of burned bicycles lay in the ashes or along the streets in mute testimony of the speed with which the flames had swept the city.' To the north, he said, 'we could see the twisted skeletons of burned factories and mills. The heat had been so intense that massive steel girders and pillars looked like a writhing mass of reptiles flung to the ground by the hand of a giant.' Reconstruction would take years. Bowen C. Dees, who arrived in Tokyo in late 1947, was shocked to see the Ginza, Tokyo's premier shopping district, in shambles. 'An immense pile of rubble, more than head-high, filled at least two centre lanes of the Ginza for several blocks – rubble from the bombed-out buildings along and near this major street. Clearly, Japan was still in trouble.'[11]

The Surrender ceremony

The Asia-Pacific War ended formally on 2 September 1945 with the signing of the Instrument of Surrender aboard the USS *Missouri*. The battleship was anchored in Tokyo Bay some 10 minutes by launch from the New Grand Hotel on the Yokohama

Bund. Attending the brief 20-minute ceremony were representatives of nine Allied Powers, led by General MacArthur, and a delegation from the Japanese government and Imperial General Headquarters. US generals and admirals lined the deck. Sailors vied for space on crowded gun turrets, masts and smokestacks, and the initial mood was noisy and cheerful as a Navy band struck up 'Anchors Aweigh'. But when the Japanese delegation was piped on board, a sudden, hostile silence enveloped the battleship, recalled Second Lieutenant Sakamoto, the Nisei linguist who had witnessed MacArthur's landing at Atsugi. 'The whole scene', he wrote in his diary, 'was as if a huge lion had cornered a tiny, helpless-looking mouse in a cage. If ever there was a scene that brought home to me how sad a defeated nation can be – this scene was it.'[12]

The faded duty uniforms and relaxed deportment of the American participants contrasted with the stiff formality and sombre faces of the Japanese, who stood in a tight cluster on the dreadnought's deck. Representing the vanquished were Foreign Minister Shigemitsu Mamoru in striped trousers and morning coat and supported by a cane (he had lost a leg to a bomb thrown by a Korean nationalist while ambassador to China in the early 1930s) and Chief of the Imperial Army General Staff and former Kwantung Army commander General Umezu Yoshijirō in formal military dress. The hawkish Umezu had bitterly opposed Japan's surrender, and only a personal plea from the Emperor had persuaded him to represent Japan. Within less than a year, both he and Shigemitsu would stand trial for Class A war crimes. Accompanying them was Kase Toshikazu, a Harvard-educated junior diplomat and protégé of Yoshida Shigeru with flawless English, and eight other officials whose names were kept from the public for fear of reprisals.[13] After Shigemitsu and Umezu had signed for the Japanese side, MacArthur, wearing summer khakis and a shirt open at the collar, affixed his signature as Allied Supreme Commander. He was followed in turn by representatives of nine Allied nations: Australia, Britain, Canada, France, the Netherlands, New Zealand, the Republic of China, the Soviet Union and the United States.[14] In a symbolic gesture, MacArthur had flown General Arthur Percival, who had surrendered Singapore, and General Jonathan M. Wainwright, who had given up the Philippines, from a Japanese prison camp in Manchuria to attend the ceremony.

Under the terms of surrender, the Japanese side accepted the Potsdam Proclamation on behalf of the Emperor, the government and Imperial General Headquarters. The document ordered the unconditional capitulation of all Japanese military forces and commanded them to cease hostilities and surrender promptly to Allied armies. It also instructed civil and military authorities to obey and enforce all decrees issued by SCAP pursuant to the terms of the surrender and the Potsdam conditions. MacArthur immediately promulgated General Order no. 1 directing Imperial General Headquarters to surrender to designated Allied commanders in the various theatres of war in Asia. By Allied agreement, MacArthur, as AFPAC Commander-in-Chief, was to disarm Imperial troops in the Japanese main islands, the Ryukyus and Korea south of 38 degrees North latitude – a line the Americans had drawn arbitrarily two weeks earlier. General Albert B. Wedemeyer and Generalissimo Chiang Kai-shek (Jiang Jieshi) were to do the same in Formosa and Chiang in China proper (except Manchuria) and northern French Indo-China. The Soviet Union was to receive the surrender of Japanese forces in Manchuria, Korea north of the 38th parallel, Sakhalin and the Kuril Islands.

Conspicuous by his absence was the Emperor. Prime Minister Higashikuni, too, had stayed away because of his Royal blood, as did Vice Premier Prince Konoe Fumimaro, also of the Court nobility. Top officials were at pains to avoid any suggestion that the Emperor's sovereignty had been compromised by Japan's defeat. As the ceremony took place, Hirohito, in an Imperial Rescript issued in Tokyo, enjoined the nation 'to lay down . . . arms and faithfully to carry out all the provisions of the Instrument of Surrender'. At the same time, in Washington, President Truman commemorated 'V-J Day' with a plea to the American people to work with him for 'a world of peace founded on justice and fair dealing and tolerance'. A new day indeed had finally dawned.

As the ceremony aboard the *Missouri* drew to a close, nearly 2,000 American aircraft – B-29 bombers and Navy fighters – flew in formation over the battleship and the enormous US armada anchored in the bay to mark the occasion. A further element of drama was added by two American flags. One was the banner that had flown over the White House on the day Pearl Harbor was bombed; it now fluttered from the *Missouri's* mast (the same well-travelled emblem had been hoisted over Rome in September 1943 and Berlin in May 1945 following the fall of Italy and Germany). In a glass case mounted on a bulkhead near the table where the surrender documents were signed was another potent symbol: the original Stars and Stripes that Commodore Matthew Perry had flown from his flagship, the USS *Powhattan*, when it entered Uraga Bay in 1853, nearly a century earlier. Admiral Halsey had arranged for it to be flown to Japan from the museum of the US Naval Academy in Annapolis, Maryland. Perry had unfurled that flag in a sabre-rattling display of military prowess to convince Japan to open its ports to commerce with the outside world. MacArthur told the assembly that he now was unfurling the same banner in hopes that Japan would become a democratic nation:

[It is not] for us here to meet . . . in a spirit of distrust, malice or hatred. But rather it is for us, both victors and vanquished, to rise to that higher dignity which alone befits the sacred purposes we are about to serve. . . . It is my earnest hope, and indeed the hope of all mankind, that from this solemn occasion a better world shall emerge out of the blood and carnage of the past – a world dedicated to the dignity of man and the fulfillment of his most cherished wish – for freedom, tolerance and justice.[15]

MacArthur's words embodied the intrepid, liberating spirit that would remould not only Japan but the postwar world. The Japanese people, freed from 'feudalistic tyranny', were encouraged to embrace the democratic ideals that the Allied victory had infused with fresh legitimacy and vigour. In little over a year, these principles would be enshrined in a new constitution establishing popular sovereignty, guaranteeing civil liberties and renouncing war-making and armaments altogether.

ESTABLISHING THE OCCUPATION

On 28 August, as the US advance party deplaned at Atsugi, Prime Minister Higashikuni urged a 'collective confession of guilt by the whole nation'. His call for a national atonement – 'the repentance of the hundred millions' – was a thinly disguised effort to shift the blame for defeat from the Emperor and military élite to the people. Few Japanese, however, felt personally responsible for their role, active or passive, in conducting the war. On the home front, the end of the conflict was greeted generally by a strong sense of release followed by disappointment and bewilderment that Japan had lost. Anger, shame and guilt were the reaction of a minority. A station master noted that the passengers in his waiting room underwent a visible transformation as they listened to the Emperor's broadcast. 'The absolute tension that had gripped everyone gave way suddenly to resignation and relief, then turned into fear', he recorded.[16] The country's more than 2 million Korean and Formosan residents alone ecstatically celebrated the defeat, for it signalled their liberation from decades of colonial rule. The average citizen regarded the Occupation as akin to *force majeure*, the unfortunate but inevitable aftermath of a natural calamity. Where 'the military clique' was blamed, it was less for starting the war than for losing it; most Japanese were content to let General Tōjō Hideki and his confederates bear the consequences. Their primary concern was finding shelter and something to eat.

Two recently arrived American observers accurately captured the mood of the defeated nation. John K. Emmerson, a State Department Japan specialist, described the typical reaction to defeat as 'no deploring the surrender; no castigating the American enemy; no contrition'. He continued: 'This attitude explained the popular cooperation with the American reformers, which was to come; it explained the lack of hatred over the destruction we had wrought. . . . In the vacuum of defeat, the Japanese people were ready to reject the past and clutch the straw held out by the former enemy.'[17] One of the first civilian women to arrive in Tokyo, Beate Sirota, described her astonishment at the sudden reversal in attitudes she encountered among Japanese men. A former Imperial Navy officer, she wrote, caught her eye. 'Having grown up as a woman in Japan, I automatically looked down. But his response was to bow deeply. It seemed unthinkable: a Japanese serviceman deferring to me, a twenty-two-year-old Caucasian woman.' Sirota felt 'a stab of dismay at the totality of Japan's defeat'.[18]

In the field, soldiers received news of the surrender with disbelief, then chagrin. To soften the reality of defeat, officers ordered their men to 'return' their weapons, never to 'surrender' them. Each army rifle bore the Imperial crest, and soldiers had been taught that the safety of their weapons was more important than their own lives.

Ordered to toss his rifle and bayonet on a pile of discarded arms on the ground, one soldier recalled, 'I felt as if parts of my body were being ripped off. The harsh sound of metal hitting metal pierced my ears.'[19] The military categorically refused to use the term surrender. Even among the civilian population, the expression 'termination of war' (*shūsen*) was preferred to the starkness of 'defeat' (*haisen*), and 'garrison force' (*shinchūgun*) to 'army of occupation' (*senryōgun*). Such euphemisms flourished, fostering an element of ambiguity about Japan's capitulation that would persist throughout the Occupation era and well beyond, yet no one could deny that overnight an entire social order and its world view had collapsed utterly. Psychologically numbed, disorientated and disillusioned with their leaders, demobilised veterans and civilians alike struggled to get their bearings, shed the discredited ideology of militarism and embrace new values. Within days of their arrival, the American occupiers began to build the new social and political framework – Emmerson's 'straw' – within which the demolition of the Old Order and the construction of a new Japan could take place.

The phantom proclamations

The precise nature of that framework, however, was not immediately clear as the Occupation began. Would the new order be built from scratch and 'made in USA', or would it be constructed of native materials already at hand? Anticipating at best obstinacy on the part of Japanese officialdom, MacArthur had made early provision for direct military rule, including the printing of military scrip. Military governance had been the US Army's assumption until the Potsdam summit, where, on British advice, American planners had modified the proposed régime of control to allow the use of existing government offices to achieve Occupation objectives (chapter 5). The 'US Initial Post-Surrender Policy for Japan', which MacArthur had received in outline on 30 August before leaving Manila, urged him to exercise his authority through the state where possible, but it also conferred on him broad discretionary powers to intervene directly to enforce the surrender terms if necessary. Army units deploying in the field, operating on earlier assumptions of hostile occupation, had been instructed to establish full-fledged military governments in the areas they secured. These preliminary operational orders, given well in advance of MacArthur's receipt of the official US post-surrender policy, were not rescinded until 3 September, and General Headquarters would not officially adopt the modality of indirect rule until 26 September.

The Japanese learned of the Supreme Commander's early plans for military governance on the evening of 2 September, when Suzuki Tadakatsu, director of the Central Liaison Office's Yokohama branch, visited AFPAC headquarters in Yokohama. Suzuki had come to persuade MacArthur not to station combat troops in Tokyo. At GHQ/AFPAC, by chance, he saw drafts of MacArthur's first three proclamations. Addressed to the Japanese people in both languages, the orders called for the imposition of direct military rule and were to be posted in public places by Sixth and Eighth Armies as they fanned out across Japan.[20] The first decree particularly alarmed Suzuki. Its preface read: 'by virtue of the authority vested in me as Supreme Commander for the Allied Powers, I hereby establish military control over all of Japan and the inhabitants thereof'. Although the edict guaranteed personal freedoms, property rights and religious beliefs (Article 4), it subordinated the Japanese government's executive, legislative and judicial powers to SCAP authority (Article 1) and made English the official language of occupation 'for all purposes' (Article 5).

Suzuki found the second order equally distressing. Dealing with crimes and offences, it empowered the Provost Marshal and Occupation courts to prosecute and impose punishment, including the death penalty, on any Japanese who violated the surrender terms or any SCAP proclamation, order or directive; who acted 'to the prejudice of good order or the life, safety, or security of the persons or property of the United States or its Allies'; who wilfully disturbed public peace and order; or who engaged in 'any act hostile to the Allied Forces'. These stern measures, amounting to de facto martial law, would have superseded the Japanese judicial system and usurped important law-enforcement powers. The third proclamation, entitled 'Currency', made legal tender all military currency issued by Occupation forces. Moreover, military scrip was to be equivalent and interchangeable at face value with yen notes and specie issued by the Bank of Japan. The order further outlawed the export and import of all currency, coin and securities. SCAP planned to print ¥300 million in military payment certificates in 10-sen, 50-sen, ¥1, ¥5, ¥10, ¥20 and ¥100 denominations. The inflationary potential of this directive dismayed Suzuki, who feared further disruption to the battered economy.

The panic into which the impending proclamations threw Japan's top leadership was not due to their severity alone. The government had been at pains to portray the surrender as a judicious decision by the Emperor to spare the nation further suffering and bring the war to an honourable close. According to the Japanese reading, the Potsdam terms required Imperial forces to surrender unconditionally but recognised the government, which would continue to exist. The authorities had convinced the public that the cessation of hostilities would leave Japan's paramount social and political institutions, notably the emperor system, in place. Indeed, the Foreign Ministry had purposely mistranslated the Byrnes Note of August 11 in order to foster that view, a gloss that was, as Foreign Minister Shigemitsu Mamoru aptly phrased it, 'radically different' from Allied intentions (chapter 5). MacArthur's decrees placing the whole of Japan, including the Throne, under military administration threatened to expose that elaborate hoax and discredit the Imperial Cabinet of Prince Higashikuni.[21]

Indirect rule

As the edicts were to be issued the next day, Suzuki immediately contacted Okazaki Katsuo, Chief of the Central Liaison Office in Tokyo, and urged him to do everything possible to forestall implementation of the decrees. On Prime Minister Higashikuni's instructions, that night Okazaki rushed to MacArthur's suite in the

New Grand Hotel in Yokohama, hoping for a personal audience with the Supreme Commander. Arriving there at about 1 am, he insinuated his way into the hotel and entered the quarters of an American officer whom he mistook for Lieutenant General Richard Sutherland, MacArthur's chief of staff. After some initial confusion, Okazaki was led to Sutherland, who noted that the orders had already been telegraphed to field units. Acknowledging the dilemma they posed, however, Sutherland agreed to take the issue up with MacArthur.[22]

That information did little to allay the fears of the Higashikuni Cabinet, which remained in session throughout the night. Okazaki and Finance Minister Kubo Bunzō had hastily arranged for Foreign Minister Shigemitsu to meet with MacArthur the next morning. At 8:30 am on 3 September, Shigemitsu sat down with MacArthur and Sutherland to discuss the issue. The Foreign Minister entreated the General to think twice before instituting military government; should Japan be placed under military control, he said, the 'Army of Occupation . . . will be relieving the Japanese Government from the responsibility of seeing that the Occupation policy is faithfully carried out'. Shigemitsu emphasised the Emperor's determination to implement the Potsdam terms and assured the Supreme Commander that the government stood ready and eager to do his bidding. Intent on depicting Hirohito as a pacifistic sovereign who had opposed the war, he asked MacArthur to work through the government under the Emperor's directions. The General reportedly received this high-level pledge of cooperation 'with sympathy and interest' and promptly instructed Sutherland to rescind the proclamations, although some military scrip already had been issued.[23]

On 3 September, as MacArthur was cancelling the direct-rule fiats, a second crisis erupted following the landing of Eighth Army units under Brigadier General Julien W. Cunningham in Tateyama, Chiba Prefecture. After deploying, Cunningham issued a series of wide-ranging directives instructing his troops not only to disarm Japanese soldiers but also to impose controls over commodity prices, workers' salaries, rationing, education, property ownership, currency and the local courts. The central government protested immediately, and MacArthur ordered Cunningham to retract his decrees.

The Foreign Ministry highlighted Shigemitsu's 3 September meeting with MacArthur, citing it as an early turning point in the Occupation that modified the Allied régime of control in Japan's favour and arrogating credit for the alleged policy reversal. That assertion does not stand up to close scrutiny, however. MacArthur appears to have decided on some form of indirect rule well before his meeting with the Foreign Minister. The Potsdam Proclamation of July 26 had implied that the Supreme Commander might play a supervisory role rather than rule directly (chapter 5). On 28 August, AFPAC headquarters in Manila issued Operational Instruction no. 4 limiting military government to minor functions and stating that orders would be issued directly to Japanese authorities, giving them every opportunity to comply 'without further compulsion'. The decisive factor, however, was MacArthur's receipt two days later of the US Initial Post-Surrender summary with its recommendation of remote control. The adoption of this modality was inevitable, for the General lacked the human and material resources necessary to impose an effective military administration on Japan. By rescinding the early military government proclamations, MacArthur acknowledged a foregone conclusion, committing the Occupation to indirect governance in practice as well as principle.

On 22 September, President Truman unveiled the 'US Initial Post-Surrender Policy for Japan'. On 26 September, Chief of Staff Sutherland issued an AFPAC directive formally renouncing recourse to military rule 'so long as the system of enforcing the Potsdam Declaration or the surrender terms through the Japanese government works satisfactorily'. The same directive announced that special staff sections would be created inside MacArthur's headquarters to advise the Supreme Commander on civil affairs and ordered the discontinuance of AFPAC's Military Government Section. On 2 October, responsibility for administering the Occupation passed from AFPAC's military staff organisation to a new civil administration, GHQ/SCAP. As Shigemitsu had requested, the new headquarters would operate through the Cabinet, the Diet and, until a new constitution entered into force in May 1947, the Emperor, ensuring the continuity of Japan's political institutions.[24]

Footnote to Occupation: Korea
The Occupation of Japan offers a study in contrasts, ironical and tragic, with the American disposition of southern Korea (1945–8). The Cairo Declaration (27 November 1943) had announced the resolve of the United States, Great Britain and Nationalist China that 'in due course Korea shall become free and independent'. By solemn Allied pledge, Japan's defeat meant the liberation of its Korean colony from 36 years of despotic rule. But liberation was short-lived. Following the bombing of Nagasaki on 9 August, Washington's top policy group, the State–War–Navy Coordinating Committee, decided to occupy as much of Korea as possible. Consequently, the US Army's Operations Division pre-emptively fixed the 38th parallel as the line of demarcation, and this arbitrary boundary was accepted by the Soviet Union shortly after Tokyo's capitulation.[25]

'Operation Blacklist', MacArthur's contingency plan for a non-hostile occupation, included a blueprint for the seizure of southern Korea ('Operation Baker'), and on 11 August, MacArthur ordered General John R. Hodge's XXIV Corps in Okinawa to take and hold all Korean territory south of the 38th parallel. On 18 August, he appointed Hodge Commanding General, United States Army Forces in Korea. On 7 September, in his capacity as Theatre Commander, MacArthur assumed all powers over the southern half of the peninsula and delegated operational control to Hodge, who landed at Inchon on 8 September, the day US troops entered Tokyo.

American forces moving into Korea arrived not as liberators, but as occupiers, and they relied heavily on the Japanese-installed apparatus of colonial control – the police, bureaucracy and judiciary – to preserve order and, ultimately, to prevent genuine self-rule. Even before setting foot on the peninsula, Hodge had let slip an indication of the spirit that would guide American policy there, telling his officers on 4 September that Korea was an enemy of the United States, not a friend. True to his word, upon deploying, he announced that the Japanese Government-General would continue to operate until his command could replace it with a suitable American alternative. The Japanese-led police organisation similarly was retained, and Japanese functionaries were allowed to stay at their posts. Direct military rule was instituted, and English was declared to be the official language of occupation. On 2 October 1945, following popular outcry over the continuing presence of Japanese officials, GHQ/SCAP in Tokyo issued a directive formally detaching Korea from Japan's political and administrative control, but former Imperial administrators remained in the country as unofficial advisers.

American and Soviet zones of influence would be confirmed after the fact by the Big Four at the Moscow Foreign Minister's Conference in December 1945. The 'Moscow Agreement' established an international trusteeship for the Korean peninsula, gave it a five-year mandate and charged it with assisting in the formation of a provisional government. In fact, the accord legitimised a divided Korean homeland. Ironically, many of the civil affairs personnel the US Army had trained for duty in Japan became superfluous with the adoption there of indirect rule and were diverted to south Korea, which remained under direct military control until 1948, when US-engineered general elections there would install a pro-American régime. '[T]he astonishing fact', a historian has written, is 'that Korea got the occupation designed for Japan.'[26]

MacArthur's new headquarters

During September and October, Eighth Army despatched tactical units and Military Government Teams to each prefecture to ensure that Occupation policies were faithfully complied with. By late 1945, some 430,000 American soldiers had been garrisoned across Japan. With the troops in position and the basic character of the Occupation defined, MacArthur initiated a series of major organisational changes. On 8 September, advance elements of Eighth Army's 1st Cavalry Division entered Tokyo, set up camp at the Yoyogi Training Grounds and moved its staff officers into the Dai-Ichi and Yashima Hotels. The Supreme Commander accompanied the 1st Cavalry into the city and ensconced himself and his family in the US Embassy. On 17 September, MacArthur transferred AFPAC headquarters from Yokohama to Tokyo and set up his main offices on the sixth floor of the Dai-Ichi Mutual Life Insurance Building, an imposing edifice overlooking the moat and Imperial palace grounds in Hibiya, symbolic heart of the nation. The psychological significance of MacArthur's choice of location was not lost on the Japanese.

Although MacArthur was ready to work through the Japanese government, he lacked the organisational infrastructure needed to administer a foreign nation of 74 million. This Herculean task was obviously beyond the capacity of AFPAC's Military Government Section and would require an immense and highly specialised civil administrative apparatus. The task of devising a new super-organisation was assigned to Chief of Staff Sutherland, who delegated the job to Colonel Raymond C. Kramer, a former department-store executive from New York. Between mid-August and early September, Kramer came up with the idea of splitting the Military Government Section off from AFPAC and transforming it into an entirely separate headquarters that would specialise in civil affairs and operate in tandem with the Army high command. Thus was born the concept of GHQ/SCAP. In the words of a former Occupation official, Kramer's concern was 'to get a fundamentally undemocratic Army machine out of democratisation'. In that respect, his plan succeeded brilliantly.[27]

On 15 September, before moving to Tokyo, the Supreme Commander created the Economic and Scientific Section (ESS) alongside the MGS. On 22 September, following AFPAC's transfer to Tokyo, he set up the Civil Information and Education Section (CIE, or CI&E in 'Scapinese'). Both groups were established as non-military special staff sections and absorbed some MGS functions but were made independent both of that organisation and of the Military General Staff. On 2 October, MacArthur formally dissolved Military Government Section and inaugurated General Headquarters, Supreme Commander for the Allied Powers (GHQ/SCAP), which immediately assumed responsibility for administering the Japanese home islands. MGS personnel were transferred to SCAP's new staff groups or to the US Army Military Government in Korea. Nine civil staff sections, including ESS and CI&E, were set up inside the new headquarters, roughly paralleling in structure and

Photo 6. African-American GIs stroll down Ginza Boulevard, rifles slung over their shoulders, nearly a week after the first US troops entered the capital. Demobilised Imperial soldiers still in uniform look on with curiosity. 14 September 1945 (Kyodo).

function counterpart agencies in the Japanese bureaucracy. As Supreme Commander, MacArthur held two powerful commands: GHQ/AFPAC and GHQ/SCAP. The Occupation's basic administrative structure was now in place.

THE OCCUPIERS AND THE OCCUPIED

Crimes and misdemeanors

Relations between occupier and the occupied were not smooth initially. US troops comported themselves like conquerors, especially in the early weeks and months of occupation. Misbehaviour ranged from black-marketeering, petty theft, reckless driving and disorderly conduct to vandalism, assault, arson, murder and rape. Much of the violence was directed against women, the first attacks beginning within hours after the landing of advance units. In Yokohama, Chiba and elsewhere, soldiers and sailors broke the law with impunity, and incidents of robbery, rape and occasionally murder were widely reported in the press. When US paratroopers landed in Sapporo, an orgy of looting, sexual violence and drunken brawling ensued. Gang rapes and other sex atrocities were not infrequent. Victims of such attacks, shunned as outcasts, sometimes turned in desperation to prostitution; others took their life rather than bring shame to their families. Military courts arrested relatively few soldiers for these offences and convicted even fewer, and restitution for the victims was rare. Japanese attempts at self-defence were punished severely. In the sole instance of self-help that General Eichelberger records in his memoirs, when local residents formed a vigilante group and retaliated against off-duty GIs, Eighth Army ordered armoured vehicles in battle array into the streets and arrested the ringleaders, who received lengthy prison terms.[28]

According to newspaper accounts, GIs committed 931 serious offences in the Yokohama area during the first week of occupation, including 487 armed robberies, 411 thefts of currency or goods, 9 rapes, 5 break-ins, 3 cases of assault and battery and 16 other acts of lawlessness. In the first 10 days of occupation, there were 1,336 reported rapes by US soldiers in Kanagawa Prefecture alone. Americans were not the only perpetrators of such crimes. A former prostitute recalled that as soon as Australian troops arrived in Kure in early 1946, they 'dragged young women into their jeeps, took them to the mountain, and then raped them. I heard them screaming for help nearly every night'.[29] Such behaviour was commonplace, but news of criminal activity by Occupation forces was quickly suppressed. On 10 September 1945, SCAP issued press and pre-censorship codes outlawing the publication of all reports and statistics 'inimical to the objectives of the Occupation'.

'Comfort stations'

Japanese authorities, fearing the worst, had taken measures to counter the presumed rapacity of foreign soldiers – after all, Imperial troops in the field had behaved atrociously towards women. When the first GIs reached the outskirts of Tokyo, they found 'sexual comfort-stations' set aside 'to satisfy the lust of the Occupation forces'. On 18 August, three days after Japan's acceptance of the Potsdam terms, the Security Bureau of the Ministry of Home Affairs instructed law enforcement agencies across the nation to set up 'special comfort establishments', later renamed Recreation and Amusement Associations (RAAs), which were to be financed initially with public funds but run as private enterprises under police supervision. On 21 August, Prime Minister Higashikuni organised an inter-ministerial conference to coordinate this programme, and on 23 August, the Tokyo Metropolitan Police Board instructed restaurant, geisha and brothel organisations to set up local RAAs to 'cater to the amusement' of the foreign troops. Government funds were provided because, in the words of a senior Tokyo Metropolitan Police official, 'the American Army is coming to Japan. We fear that the Americans will molest our women – our wives and daughters and sisters. We need a shock absorber.' Ikeda Hayato, head of the Finance Ministry's Tax Bureau and later prime minister, set aside a budget of ¥100 million for the RAAs, noting that the money was well spent if it would 'protect the pure bloodline of the Yamato race'.[30]

Through the RAAs, the government hoped to protect the daughters of the well-born and middle classes by having lower-class women satisfy the sexual appetites of battle-weary GIs. Enlistment in the RAA ranks was hailed as a patriotic act, and the first volunteers received official thanks for their sacrifice in front of the Imperial Palace. In fact, the policy of sexual servitude was an emergency measure implemented in the name of national security, and many recruits had little choice but to comply. By the end of 1945, brothel operators had rounded up an estimated 20,000 young women and herded them into RAA establishments across the country. Early recruitment focused on geisha, bar hostesses and prostitutes, including those repatriated from military posts abroad, but the shortage of volunteers led police authorities to expand the roster to include war widows, the homeless and even high school students drafted for factory labour during the war. Eventually, as many as 70,000 are said to have ended up in the state-run sex industry.[31]

In the capital area, the first RAA brothel was the Babe's Garden in Ōmori, which was set up on 28 August, the day MacArthur's advance guard landed at Atsugi. When US troops moved into Tokyo, it quickly attracted long lines of GIs. Similar establishments, such as the Bordeaux (Ginza), the Paramount (Shinagawa), the Paradise (Tachikawa) and the Officers' Club (Sangenjaya), soon dotted the districts frequented by GIs. The RAA-run International Palace in Chiba just outside of Tokyo, one of the world's largest brothels, became known for its 'assembly-line style'. When the Association established a similar house, the Oasis of Ginza, in the heart of Tokyo for enlisted men, the US Army promptly set up a prophylactic station next door to treat venereal disease. Cabaret-style brothels, restaurants, dance halls and beer gardens all catered to GIs under the RAA umbrella. Reflecting the military hierarchy, the RAAs provided different facilities for enlisted personnel and officers. Mirroring the US Army's policy of racial segregation, they also established separate businesses for black and white GIs (chapter 3).

Panpan

The RAA was a domestic version of the extensive military brothel system that is thought to have ensnared between 80,000 and 100,000 Asian women (and possibly many more) to serve Japanese troops during the war (chapter 6). Some of these victims – Koreans, Japanese and others – continued to 'service' Occupation troops in Okinawa and elsewhere in Japan. Not all worked for the RAA. Bordellos were set up by repatriates who had run 'comfort stations' for the Japanese military abroad. The destitute former military prostitutes that staffed them were too poor or too disgraced to return to their homelands and families. As a former Occupationaire has pointed out, however, 'questions of morality did not enter into the original official Occupation attitude'. One US Marine who arrived in Nagasaki in late 1945 was stunned to discover next to the officers' quarters a house of dubious repute being run by his own command. Within days of disembarking, New Zealand troops were openly keeping women in their barracks.[32]

Prostitution was fused in the popular imagination of the early post-defeat period with black-marketeering, both activities serving as metaphors for the uprooted, anarchic conditions under which all Japanese struggled. Like Koreans and Formosans, prostitutes, known as *panpan*, represented a despised underclass against which better folk defined morality. The seemingly unrestrained behaviour of sex workers, their intimate contact with the American occupier and their survival outside of the officially sanctioned economy were unsettling to Japan's dominant élites, with their patriarchal values and notions of racial exclusivity. As one scholar has remarked, the working-class prostitute with GI customers was subversive in that she challenged the sexual authority of Japanese men while rejecting traditional female roles (propriety, monogamy, childbearing). But above all, 'the *panpan* was ... a survivor of the postwar chaos, and in this regard nearly every Japanese who lived through the war could identify with her'. Victimised by class and gender discrimination, many of these women in fact led harsh, tragic lives.[33]

Wherever there were bases there were post exchanges, and cigarettes, lipstick, nylon stockings and food were traded regularly for sexual favours. By the end of 1945, venereal diseases had become rampant (90 per cent of RAA sex workers reportedly were infected). Military discipline, however, gradually reasserted itself, and Japanese women's groups brought strong pressure to bear on GHQ to abolish this form of sexual exploitation. On 21 January 1946, Occupation authorities ordered the government to outlaw licensed and involuntary prostitution, precipitating a crackdown. In November 1945, the Institute of Infectious Diseases, forerunner of today's National Institute of Health, had established a field demonstration centre for the treatment of VD at the Yoshiwara Venereal Disease Hospital in the middle of Tokyo's traditional red-light district. By late 1946, Military Police were rounding up all women they found on the streets at night and carting them to the Yoshiwara hospital, where they were placed in barbed wire enclosures and subjected to compulsory VD examinations. Between August and November, 2,400 women were picked up at random, including night-school students, factory workers, telephone operators,

Photo 7. Women of the night ply their trade near the Ginza, autumn 1945. Prostitution, state-sponsored and voluntary, epitomised the ignominy of defeat and occupation by a foreign power (Mainichi)

GHQ employees and a Diet woman on her way home from an evening committee session. A Kyoto dragnet pulled in an Imperial princess. The humiliation was intolerable, and at least one suicide was reported. GHQ's anti-prostitution directive was formally promulgated as a Cabinet Order on 15 January 1947, and the RAA brothels were officially closed on 27 March of that year, although beer halls, cabarets and bars continued to operate until May 1949, when the RAA system finally was dismantled.[34]

The 1947 anti-prostitution ordinance did not apply to voluntary prostitution, however, and private bordellos mushroomed following the closure of the RAA establishments. At first, many RAAs simply masqueraded as 'Tea Shop Sanitation Associations' or 'Cafe Associations' or transformed themselves into 'special eating and drinking establishments', which police confined to specially zoned red-light districts. Fed by poverty, prostitution proliferated, however, and *panpan* were soon walking the streets in so-called respectable neighborhoods. By 1949, there were an estimated 59,000 prostitutes, many of them clustered around US military bases. At the insistence of Christian organisations and other anti-prostitution groups, the Ministry of Health and Welfare established special welfare homes to alleviate the distress of these women. By late 1949, more than 1,000 had found refuge in 18 such homes, but this was a tiny minority. Prostitution would not be abolished entirely until the 1956 Prostitution Prevention Law, which entered into force two years later in 1958.[35]

The sexual subjugation of women had many uses. Canadian Mark Gayn, the *Chicago Sun* correspondent, recorded in his diary that ultra-rightist racketeers had attempted systematically, and with considerable success, to corrupt high-ranking members of the Occupation with women and whisky. In a now-famous episode, Gayn interviewed Andō Akira, a gangster on intimate terms with the Emperor's brother, Prince Takamatsu, in June 1946. One of Tokyo's largest brothel owners, Andō boasted that many of his women worked in GHQ as receptionists and typists. He told Gayn that he had between 200 and 300 'American friends' inside GHQ in constant need of 'relaxation' from their labours, among them a general, a judge, several well-known officers and two members of Allied missions in Tokyo. Andō's indiscreet admissions led subsequently to his arrest by Military Intelligence for black marketeering. The 'vast and powerful nationalist underground' that Andō represented, however, continued to operate and thrive throughout the Occupation, its virulent anti-Communism insuring it a degree of immunity with Occupation security forces.[36]

Congenial occupiers or neo-colonial overlords?
Despite the absence of overt resistance, US forces trod warily in the initial weeks of occupation. Courtney Whitney recalled that during MacArthur's first meal at the New Grand Hotel, he had difficulty restraining himself from snatching the Supreme Commander's plate away and testing it for poison. One SCAP official described the early atmosphere at GHQ as tense and noted that many of his

Photo 8. Family members queue up to receive food. No rice is to be had, only a 10-day ration of soy beans. Until US emergency food stocks arrived from Manila in early 1946, Japan faced mass starvation. 15 September 1945 (Mainichi).

colleagues were afraid to enter nearby Hibiya Park for fear of bodily harm. There had been sporadic assaults on soldiers at night, and officers wore sidearms until orders came down in mid-September not to. The Japanese repaid American misgivings in kind, regarding the 'demonic and beastly' enemy with dread and loathing. Three days after capitulation, the mass-circulation daily *Yomiuri Shinbun* reported that Tokyoites expected GIs to do no less than loot, steal all available food, violate women, kill all the men and raze the city. The headmaster of a reform school outside of Tokyo told an Occupationaire that he had given his Leica camera to the first GI he encountered 'out of gratitude for not having been shot'. The man added that he would just as happily have parted with his home.[37]

An early US decision to feed Occupation forces from American supplies and allow the Japanese to consume their own meagre food stores allayed a basic fear, for Imperial forces had imposed forced food deliveries on the people they conquered. As military discipline took hold and fresh troops replaced the Allied veterans responsible for the early crime wave, violence subsided, and Japanese were quick to overlook the occupier's patronising behaviour and the ugly misdeeds of a lawless few. Happily, the worst fears of both sides proved groundless. An Australian diplomat, writing in 1946, found the GI to be a more congenial occupier than his Australian or British counterpart – whom even the Australian press characterised as rigid and unfriendly. 'We cannot compete with the Americans in Japan', he observed. 'Our soldiers do not give gum or candy and very few cigarettes in comparison with the Americans. Moreover, the Americans have a sentimentalism that makes them much easier and more friendly in manner to the Japanese'.[38]

The message that Japan was utterly at the mercy of the occupier, however, was reinforced in a thousand ways, subtle and manifest. While the average US soldier did not fit the rapacious image of wartime Japanese propagandists, Occupation personnel lived and frequently behaved like neo-colonial overlords. SCAP commandeered every large building that had not burned down to house thousands of civilians and requisitioned vast tracts of prime real estate to quarter several hundred thousand troops in the Tokyo–Yokohama area alone. The Stars and Stripes were hoisted over Tokyo (display of the Rising Sun – the 'meatball' – was banned), and the downtown area, 'Little America', was transformed into a US enclave. Leading staff officers took up residence in the stately Imperial Hotel, which Frank Lloyd Wright had designed during World War I. Field officers were assigned to the less prestigious Dai-Ichi Hotel in Shinbashi. Department of the Army civilians were billeted in more distant quarters, such as the Kanda Kaikan (the former YMCA) or the Yuraku Hotel. Entire buildings were refurbished as officers' clubs, replete with slot machines and gambling parlours installed at Occupation expense. Reflecting the military preference for elevated terrain, Army camps with such names as Jefferson Heights, Grand Heights, Palace Heights and Washington Heights became familiar landmarks to people in the capital region.

In accordance with a 3 September directive from MacArthur decreeing the transcription in romanised letters of all public notices, the signboards and street names along the road from Yokohama to Tokyo were rendered in English as well as Japanese, but in the centre of occupied Tokyo, English alone prevailed. At the Hibiya crossing in front of GHQ, even the billboards were written exclusively in the conqueror's tongue. The boulevard in front of SCAP headquarters was renamed First Avenue. Japan's national sports arena became Memorial Hall, and Tokyo's all-female opera, the Takarazuka, was rechristened the Ernie Pyle Theatre in honour of a well-known American combat journalist killed on Okinawa. American correspondents set up a press club in one of the few buildings still standing in Shinbashi, assigned it the street number 'No. 1' and renamed the street itself Shinbun (Newspaper) Alley. Bars, black-market restaurants, gambling dens, bath-houses, RAAs, and honky-tonk night spots with names like the Starlight Club and the Showboat sprang up from the ruins in downtown areas. A prime piece of Ginza real estate, the Hattori Building, was converted into the Eighth Army Post Exchange (PX), and its shelves were soon stocked with tax-free consumer items including food staples, canned delicacies, liquor, cigarettes, clothing, cameras, refrigerators and diamond rings. At the PX grill, Occupation personnel could feast on Coke, milk shakes, hot dogs, french fries and 'B-29burgers'.

Military policemen (MPs) were ubiquitous, their stern demeanours, sidearms and

Photo 9. Eighth Army promptly requisitioned the Hattori Tokei Building in Ginza as its main Post Exchange. The PX became a symbol of American affluence, attracting street urchins, impecunious young women and a variety of loiterers, Japanese and American. 22 September 1945 (Mainichi).

billy clubs an intimidating reminder of Occupation authority. Off-duty GIs thronged the streets in freshly pressed olive-drab uniforms, their servicemen's hats cocked jauntily to one side. Road traffic was dominated by nearly empty khaki-coloured, white-striped staff sedans and was nearly all American, for only the occupier had access to ample petrol – most Japanese cars and buses ran on charcoal. The occasional canvas-roofed Army truck lumbered through city streets, filled with troops en route to new postings, and 'recreation jeeps' with Japanese drivers were available to US personnel for off-duty excursions. Officers sped through downtown thoroughfares in commandeered jeeps accompanied by fashionably dressed Japanese girlfriends trailing bright scarves, their insouciance a striking contrast to the gloomy faces of the hungry, ill-clad Japanese, many of them homeless, who looked on these centurions with a mixture of awe and envy.

Jeeps, like English-language signs and MPs, became universal emblems of Occupation control. On one level, at a time of great hardship and distress for the vanquished, they symbolised the seemingly unbridled freedom of the victors to go where they wished, do as they pleased. Children associated the military vehicle with GI chocolate bars, chewing gum and candy drops, and toy jeeps became a coveted play item in many urban neighbourhoods. In outlying areas, however, Japanese read into the ubiquitous Army jeep 'more coercion than good intentions'. New expressions were coined to express this basic ambivalence. In early 1946, GHQ introduced compulsory rice deliveries to counter hoarding and black marketeering and cracked down on tax evaders. 'Jeep *kyōmai*' came to mean US-monitored rice requisitions, and 'jeep *chōzei*' referred to a visit by the Army tax officer.[39]

The conquerors arrogated to themselves privileges unimaginable to most Japanese. Entire trains and train compartments, fitted with dining cars, were set aside for the exclusive use of Occupation forces. These sped half-empty past crowded train platforms, arousing the ire and resentment of Japanese passengers forced to enter and exit packed cars via their punched-out windows rather than the doors, or look for space on carriage roofs, couplings and running boards, with tragically predictable loss of life. These luxury express coaches afforded an irresistible target for anonymous stone-throwers. During the war, retrenchment measures had closed restaurants, cabarets, beer halls and geisha houses to people in Tokyo and other large cities and cancelled theatre performances. Now, however, a vast leisure industry sprang up to cater to the needs of the foreign occupant. Reopened restaurants, and theatres together with train stations, buses and streetcars were placed off limits to Allied personnel (in part for security reasons and in part to avoid burdening already strained Japanese resources), but an elaborate and costly service infrastructure was built to the specifications of the occupying forces. Facilities reserved for Occupation troops carried large signs reading 'Japanese Keep Out' or 'For Allied Personnel Only', and in downtown Tokyo, important public buildings requisitioned for Occupation use had separate entrances for Americans and Japanese. The effect of such policies was to create a subtle but distinct colour bar between the predominantly white conqueror and the conquered 'Asiatic' Japanese.

The enclave mentality this cocooned existence fostered was reinforced by the arrival within the first six months of about 700 American families. At the height of the Occupation, some 14,800 families employed a total of 25,000 Japanese servants to ease the 'rigours' of overseas duty. Even enlisted men in the spartan quonset-hut cities that appeared overnight around the city lived like kings compared to ordinary Japanese. Japanese workers cleaned the barracks, did kitchen chores and handled other work details on base. The lowest private drew a 25 per cent hardship bonus until these special allotments were discontinued in 1949. Most military families quickly got used to a pampered lifestyle that included in addition to maids and 'boys' a whole panoply of specialised household help, from cooks and laundresses to babysitters, gardeners and masseuses. Among the perks and privileges accruing to the victors were spacious quarters equipped with swimming pools, central heating, hot running water and modern plumbing. Two contemporary observers have compared GHQ to the British Raj in its heyday. The patrician George F. Kennan, head of the State Department's Policy Planning Staff, complained bitterly during his 1948 mission to Japan that the Americans had monopolised 'everything that smacks of comfort or elegance or luxury', and denounced what he termed the 'American brand of philistinism' and the 'monumental imperviousness' of MacArthur's underlings to the sufferings of the Japanese. This conqueror's mentality also expressed itself in the bullying attitudes many top Occupation officials adopted towards the Japanese with whom they dealt. Major Faubion Bowers, MacArthur's military secretary, later commented that 'I and nearly all the Occupation people I knew were extremely conceited and extremely arrogant and used our power every inch of the way'.[40]

Enduring defeat

Japan lay prostrate. Industrial output had fallen to a mere 10 per cent of the prewar level, and as late as 1946, more than 13 million remained unemployed. Nearly 40 per cent of Japan's urban areas had been turned to rubble, and some 9 million people were homeless. The war-displaced, many of them orphans, slept in doorways and hallways, in bombed-out ruins, dugouts and packing crates, under bridges or on pavements, and jammed the hallways of train and subway stations. As the winter of 1945 descended, with food, fuel and clothing scarce, people froze to death. Bonfires were lit on the streets to ward off the chill. 'The only warm hands I have shaken thus far in Japan belonged to Americans', Mark Gayn noted in his diary in December 1945. 'The Japanese do not have much of a chance to thaw out, and their hands are cold and red.' Unable to afford shoes, many people made do with straw sandals, which cost the equivalent of four days' salary. Those with stilted wooden clogs (*geta*) felt themselves privileged. The sight of a man wearing a woman's high-buttoned shoes in the dead of winter surprised one Occupationaire but epitomised the daily struggle to keep dry and warm.[41]

Shantytowns built of scrap wood, rusted metal and scavenged odds and ends sprang up everywhere, resembling vast junk yards. The poorest searched smouldering refuse heaps for castoff items that might somehow be bartered for a scrap to eat or something to wear. Black markets (*yami'ichi*) run by Japanese, Koreans and Formosans mushroomed to replace collapsed distribution channels and cash in on inflated prices. Tokyo became 'a world of scarcity in which every nail, every rag, and even a tangerine peel [had a] market value'.[42] Black-market *yami* goods fetched prices more than 30 times higher than those for officially controlled commodities. Such markets also were awash with food stores, clothing and industrial equipment pilfered from military stockpiles by corrupt industrialists, bureaucrats and former military officers, whose illegal activities made black marketeering a low-risk, high-growth industry.

On 15 August, the Imperial Army had issued Secret Instruction no. 363 authorising the free delivery of war matériel other than armaments to local governments. Immediately, reported one observer, 'trucks, wagons, railroad cars, carts, bicycles and porters swarmed into the arsenals; documents were forged, altered or destroyed. Thousands of tons of finished products, food, textiles, raw materials and machinery were hauled away.' In this manner, men in positions of power raided and carted off an estimated 70 per cent of Japan's military stocks. An additional ¥100 billion in construction materials and machinery, turned over to the Home Ministry for safekeeping by GHQ, also disappeared mysteriously – presumably diverted by the five *zaibatsu* groups into whose care the goods had been entrusted. Many postwar firms were able to refinance themselves and begin anew thanks to this egregious betrayal of the public trust. The police and bureaucracy were intimately involved in the dispersal of national wealth, protecting the hoarders of illicit goods and harassing the consumers, who were subject to arrest. The appropriated stocks became the economic lifeline of the Old Order, and the complex alliance between corrupt bureaucrats, politicians, police and gangsters that this collective act of theft solidified enabled the élite to rebound quickly from defeat and restake its claim on political and economic power.[43]

While enterprising members of the discredited *ancien régime* made fortunes, the people foraged for a subsistence. An estimated 14.5 million Japanese were indigent, of whom some 10 million hovered on the brink of starvation. The 1945 harvest, the worst since 1910 due to typhoons and extensive flooding in mid-September, had produced only two-thirds the normal rice yield. No longer able to depend on forced rice deliveries from its Korean and Formosan colonies, Japan faced the spectre of famine. Farmers alone had sufficient to eat. Long despised by city-dwellers as crude and uneducated, they exploited this seller's market with great shrewdness, selling

Photo 10. During the early years of occupation, city dwellers went to the countryside to barter kimonos and other valuables for food. Here two boys fill a bag with freshly harvested potatoes while their parents negotiate the transaction. Farmers refused to accept cash, made nearly worthless by inflation. June 1947 (Mainichi).

their vegetables and rice to the indigent city dwellers who flocked to the countryside to barter for food (*kaidashi*). In the rural areas and at 'open-air' or 'free' markets in the cities, silk kimonos and family heirlooms changed hands for a few potatoes, some Chinese cabbages or a small bag of grain. This hand-to-mouth life, where city dwellers peeled off one layer of clothing at a time and sold it for food, was called *takenoko seikatsu*, a 'bamboo-shoot' existence (bamboo shoots are prepared for cooking by stripping off the tough outer husks one by one until the edible root is exposed).

In October, the government asked GHQ for emergency food assistance, and MacArthur authorised an initial shipment of Army wheat, which reached Tokyo from Manila in late January 1946. He eventually secured a substantial promise of food from Washington, but supplies were delayed. By May of that year, Japanese officials were unable to maintain fixed food rations, and the Supreme Commander asked again for emergency interim deliveries, pleading Japan's case in unusually strong language. The country in its present state, said a SCAP memo, 'can only be considered a vast concentration camp under the control of the Allies and foreclosed from all avenues of commerce and trade'.[44] In July, monthly rations were slashed from 9.7 days' worth of rice to 3.9 days, and even then, delivery was sometimes held up by a month or more. Other rationed goods, such as sweet potatoes, barley, biscuits and canned goods, sufficed only for 22 days. For nearly 10 days a month, there were not even sweet potatoes to eat, and people fell back on their own resources to survive.

What grain could be scavenged (usually millet or wild grass seed) was mixed with radish leaves, sweet potatoes or other filler and cooked into an unwholesome watery gruel that was minimally nourishing and intolerably bland. Half a sweet potato for a noon meal was counted a luxury (today, many still react to that particular food item with revulsion). A well-known scholar reminisces, 'In desperation, we dug up the university lawn and planted yams, which we divided among us and cooked – stems, roots and all. On Sundays we searched for grasshoppers.' Adults weakened by hunger squatted along the roadside or leaned against walls in exhaustion. Those who lay down too long risked freezing to death. Women and children were reduced to begging handouts of food. Alarmed by the prospect of famine, GHQ eventually released emergency grain held in reserve for US troops and the British Commonwealth Occupation Force as a stopgap measure, but regular food imports did not reach Japan until the autumn of 1946 (chapter 9).[45]

Although Allied authorities were at pains to deny that people were starving to death, it is estimated that in Tokyo alone more than 1,000 perished from malnutrition in the first three months of occupation. And when emergency relief supplies finally were distributed, they included foods alien to the Japanese palate. Cornmeal – 'feed that was meant for cows, pigs and chickens' – became a staple, supplemented by flour, butter, pinto beans, dried apricots and prunes, and apple and tomato juice. Powdered milk, a commodity that Americans now spurned, became standard fare in school meals for millions of children. Accustomed to a semi-starvation diet, many Japanese suffered from carbohydrate diarrhoea, and children developed allergic reactions to reconstituted skim milk, which their protein-deprived bodies could not assimilate. Nonetheless, mass starvation was averted, a remarkable achievement, although the nutritional value of food rations did not reach the level necessary to sustain healthy life until 1949.[46]

With so many enervated by hunger, contagious diseases, including cholera, diphtheria, dysentery, pneumonia, smallpox, tuberculosis, typhoid and typhus, spread rapidly, claiming the lives of tens of thousands. Starvation and epidemics, with the attending spectre of civil disorder, also constituted a major threat to the health and security of Occupation forces, and MacArthur on his own initiative directed the government to organise an emergency assistance programme. Washington eventually provided annual assistance of $400 million to buy foodstuffs, clothing, medical supplies, fertilizer and petroleum under the Army's Government Appropriation for Relief in Occupied Areas (GARIOA) programme. GARIOA ultimately distributed commodities worth $2.14 billion, which Washington later insisted that Japan repay (a $490 million settlement was finally reached in 1961).[47]

In early 1946, GHQ imposed restrictions on internal migrations, forbidding Japanese in rural areas to relocate to or seek work in urban areas. This measure, taken to counter inadequate food and housing and the threat of disease in the cities, enabled authorities to disperse potential refugees and avoid overburdening already strained relief facilities. It eliminated the need for relocation camps and soup kitchens, curbed the spread of infectious illnesses, encouraged repatriates to resettle in rural hometowns, where many took up farming, and helped maintain civil order. The emergency decree, later enacted in law, remained in force for three years, until 1 January 1949 (chapter 9).

Fraternisation

As people struggled to survive, the parade of well-fed GIs walking the streets with young Japanese women in tow heaped insult on injury. Many US church groups found this spectacle equally deplorable and pressed Occupation authorities to curb such behaviour. 'The sight of our soldiers . . . with their arms around Japanese girls is equally repugnant to Americans at home . . . as well as to most Japanese', General Eichelberger told the troops in March 1946. Public displays of affection, he warned, were 'prejudicial to good order and military discipline and will be treated as disorderly conduct'. Japanese women were promptly prohibited from riding in military vehicles, and large signs were posted warning 'No fraternisation with the indigenous personnel'. One Eighth Army general, acknowledging the inevitable, attempted to preserve the appearance of decorum by enforcing a 'six-inch rule': MPs were ordered to insert a six inch measure between GIs and their dancing partners in authorised cabarets and dance halls. The Supreme Commander, however, refused to follow the example set by US forces in Germany who issued a non-fraternisation order (enforced in May but lifted in September 1945). 'They keep trying to get me to stop all the Madame Butterflying around', he complained to Major Faubion Bowers, his aide. 'I won't do it . . . for all the tea in China', he exclaimed. Although MacArthur refused to socialise with the Japanese himself, he encouraged his staff to mix as much as they wished, and this liberal attitude permeated all levels of the Occupation.[48]

Japanese officials at first cautioned passive acceptance of Allied authority and avoidance of all personal contact with the occupier. Daily newspapers warned people to comport themselves with dignity since 'the eyes of the world are upon Japan'. Women were warned against coquetry and told not to use heavy lipstick, rouge or eyebrow pencils. They were not to walk unattended even during the day and to avoid eye contact with foreign soldiers, 'even if they say "hello" or "hey"'. At the same time, incongruously, the authorities encouraged people to learn English, which had been discouraged during the war years, in order to prevent misunderstandings with the occupiers.[49]

MacArthur's hands-off approach to Japanese-American amity was in line with official policy: Washington had instructed SCAP to control the Japanese only to the extent necessary to achieve Occupation objectives. Moreover, MacArthur was determined to avoid the loss of self-respect and self-confidence he had observed in occupied Germany after World War I. He was particularly sensitive to 'the lowering of spiritual and moral tone of a people controlled by foreign bayonets' and the master–slave mentality it gave rise to.[50] Nonetheless, for the first half of the Occupation, segregation was practised in principle, with Japanese excluded from areas reserved for Allied personnel. In September 1949, however, the Supreme Commander lifted virtually all restrictions on friendly association, 'establishing the same relations between occupation personnel and the Japanese population as exists between troops stationed in the United States and the American people'. Thereafter, hotels, inns, theatres and other public places became in bounds to US forces, and Japanese were allowed to participate in American social activities on base and even visit service clubs. The assumptions of white privilege, however, tacitly accepted by both sides, would remain unchallenged and unchanged during the Occupation, and such attitudes continue to influence subtly Japan-US relations today.

While 'fraternisation' per se was not outlawed, marriage initially was. Sexual promiscuity, wrote a former Occupationaire, was expected of white troops in a far-away Asian land, but intermarriage carried 'overtones of miscegenation', a threat to the myth of racial purity subscribed to by both sides. The first registered mixed-blood child was born in June 1946, and by mid-1948, estimates of 'Occupation babies' ranged from 1,000 to 4,000. It is worth recalling that during this period, 30 American states, including California, carried laws prohibiting racially mixed marriages, and the offspring of such unions were discriminated against in a variety of ways. In Japan, too, children of mixed parentage were treated as outcasts. Legally, many ended up in limbo: unless the American father claimed paternity and registered the birth – which the military discouraged – the child was 'illegitimate' and the mother, as an enemy alien, had no right of appeal. Moreover, SCAP censorship rules prohibited discussion of this problem until late in the Occupation. 'Both countries' a historian has noted, 'looked upon mixed marriages as a social evil, a threat to public health, safety, morals, and the general welfare.' Such children were treated accordingly, and most were secreted away in poorly funded, ill-equipped private orphanages. Children of black American fathers suffered disproportionately, being made to bear the burdens of two racist cultures.[51]

Nonetheless, many GIs defied pressure from superiors and married Japanese, and re-enlistments often were motivated by the desire to remain with a spouse or girl-friend. The US Immigration ('Oriental Exclusion') Act of 1924 was still in effect, preventing Japanese women from emigrating to the United States, even as the wife of an American national. MacArthur eventually lifted this proscription, and the 1948 War Brides Act enabled Japanese-American couples to live together in either country. One source reports that 12,000 such unions took place during the Occupation. Despite racial prejudice on both sides of the Pacific, many withstood the test of time.[52]

By contrast, the British Commonwealth Occupation Force (BCOF) in southwestern Japan rigidly enforced a ban on all forms of off-duty socialising with the enemy. BCOF troops were ordered not to enter private homes and to treat the Japanese they came into contact with as 'a conquered enemy'. Sir Alvery Gascoigne, head of the British Liaison Mission in Tokyo from 1946, expressed the Commonwealth view of inter-ethnic relations when he castigated American troops as 'youthful novices without either the background of battle or the personal experiences of the Japanese as inhuman fanatic enemies'. Worst of all, he complained, they spent ther spare time 'in undignified fraternisation'. The Commonwealth non-fraternisation decree applied equally to American Nisei personnel, who were barred from all BCOF facilities, a practice that GHQ never challenged.[53]

THE SOVIET SEIZURE OF THE KURILS

In a sense, World War II did not end for Japan on 15 August 1945. The Red Army continued to fight and seize territory in Manchuria, Korea, Sakhalin and the Kuril Islands even after the surrender. With the takeover of the Kurils on 5 September, another occupation began in earnest. Unlike other former Japanese territories in Soviet possession, the Kurils posed a special problem, for their investment and retention were clearly illegal under the Potsdam Proclamation. The occupation of the southernmost group of islands, the so-called Northern Territories, sparked a bitter diplomatic dispute between Tokyo and Moscow that continues to impede the normalisation of relations today. Past neglect by historians and recent revelations from Russian archives make this seemingly minor episode in Occupation history of special interest.

The Kuril archipelago is a sparsely populated arc of more than 30 islands and islets stretching roughly 1,200 kilometres from the northeastern tip of Hokkaido to the Kamchatka Peninsula in Siberia. Situated along the Great Circle route from the Aleutians to Japan, it is strategically significant to three major powers: Japan, Russia and the United States. Well before the era of colonial expansion, the Tokugawa Shogunate (1603–1867) controlled all of the Kurils south of Urup, including the

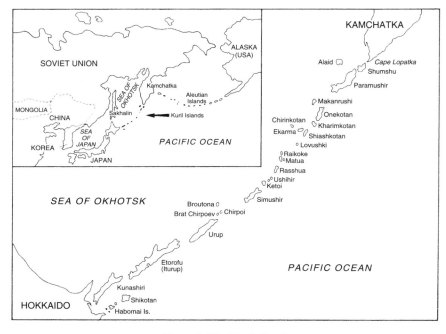

Figure 3. The Kuril Islands

four southernmost islands of Kunashiri (Kunashir), Etorofu (Iturup), Shikotan and the Habomais. In 1855, the Treaty of Shimoda signed by Edo and Moscow drew the Russo-Japanese border between Urup and Etorofu. In 1875, Tsarist Russia ceded the remaining Kurils in the Treaty of St Petersburg, in return for which Japan abandoned all claims to the island of Sakhalin, which it had occupied conjointly with Russia. In 1869, following the Meiji Restoration, the southernmost Kurils became an adminis-trative district of Nemuro City in Hokkaido. (Pre-1945 Russian reference works list the Habomai Group, located 3.7 kilometres from Hokkaido, as an extension of the Nemuro peninsula, not a part of the Kuril arc.)[54] Tsarist control of Sakhalin was brief, however. In 1906, following its victory in the Russo-Japanese War (1904–5), the Japanese Empire acquired the southern half of the island under the Treaty of Portsmouth (which also awarded it Russia's Manchurian concessions, notably Port Arthur and the Liaodong Peninsula).

The Kurils and early US–Soviet policy
Soviet designs on the Kurils surfaced in November 1940 when Foreign Minister V. M. Molotov asked Tokyo for the archipelago as the price for a non-aggression pact. Having just deployed troops in the islands that summer, the Japanese turned down the request and settled for a neutrality accord instead.[55] Following the Nazi defeat at Stalingrad in early 1943, Stalin again turned his attention to Sakhalin, the

Kurils and Manchuria. The Marshal is thought to have mentioned Soviet interest in the northern arc to Roosevelt at the Teheran Conference in late November of that year, for in mid-January 1944, Roosevelt told US members of the Allied Pacific War Council that the Kremlin wanted all of Sakhalin 'returned' and the Kurils 'turned over' to the USSR after the war. The Kurils re-emerged as a policy issue in December 1944 when Stalin included the islands, together with southern Sakhalin, in a list of concessions he outlined to US Ambassador Averell W. Harriman in Moscow as a condition for entering the war against Japan.[56]

Stalin's claims were substantive. He wanted control of the Kurils to protect Siberia's Pacific littoral, the Maritime Provinces, from external attack; ensure unrestricted access to the Pacific; and safeguard the Soviet fishing industry in the Sea of Okhotsk. Moscow also nurtured a long list of historical grievances, notably the Russo-Japanese War (1904–5), which had stripped Russia of southern Sakhalin and its Manchurian concessions and given Japan coastal fishing rights. This affront to Russian pride was compounded by Japan's Siberian intervention in support of anti-Bolshevik forces (1918–22); the Imperial Army's unsuccessful assault on Soviet armies at Lake Kashan (Changkufeng on the Siberia–Manchuria border, 1938) and Nomonhan (1939); the aggressive overfishing of Siberian waters; and Tokyo's support of Axis expansionism. Acquisition of the Kurils and southern Sakhalin would not only assuage past humiliations but protect the Soviet Far East from postwar Japanese revanchism.[57]

American planners first considered the Kuril question in a study of May 1943 conducted by the Territorial Subcommittee, a high-level US policy group, which recommended that Japan retain administrative control of the islands but under international supervision. Should that approach fail, the study said, the southern Kurils should remain in Japan's possession; handing them over to the Soviet Union outright would violate the Atlantic Charter. In late December 1944, George H. Blakeslee, head of the State Department's Inter-Divisional Area Committee on the Far East, concluded in a memorandum on the Kuril problem that Japan should retain the southern isles for economic and historical reasons, that Moscow should administer the central and northern Kurils under international trusteeship and that Japan should be assured of fishing rights in the northern arc. Curiously, this memorandum was not included in the briefing papers prepared for the Yalta Conference of early February 1945. Had Roosevelt been aware of Japan's historical claims to the southern Kurils, he might have dealt more forcefully with Stalin at that summit.[58]

The Yalta protocol

The Yalta Conference took place between 4 and 11 February at the Livadia Palace overlooking the Black Sea. On 8 February, Roosevelt, accompanied by Harriman and interpreter Charles E. Bohlen, met secretly with Stalin and Molotov for about 30 minutes. Churchill was not consulted and did not attend. There, Roosevelt agreed 'with breathtaking despatch', as one historian has phrased it, to Stalin's terms that southern Sakhalin be returned and that the Kurils be traded to the Soviet Union for a declaration of war. Churchill regarded the agreement as an American affair but later approved it.[59] On 11 February, Churchill, Roosevelt and Stalin signed the secret protocol. Point 3 of the 'Agreement Regarding Japan' stated simply, 'The Kuril islands shall be handed over to the Soviet Union'. The American leader managed to keep the Yalta text hidden even from his own State Department, and the full contents of the accord were not revealed until Moscow publicised it a year later, in February 1946, in support of its territorial claims.

The awarding of the Kurils to Moscow violated previous Allied statements of principle. The Atlantic Charter and the Cairo Declaration authorised the victors to return only those territories Imperial Japan had seized 'by violence and greed'. While this stipulation applied to southern Sakhalin, a Japanese war trophy, it clearly did not extend to the Kurils, which Tsarist Russia had ceded to Japan peacefully in 1875. Scholars have concluded that Roosevelt acceded to Stalin's demands because he mistakenly assumed that the Kurils, too, had been wrested from Russia in 1905.[60] Recent research suggests, however, that the American leader genuinely supported Moscow's irredentist claims.

Even before Stalin clarified Soviet intentions, Roosevelt had been prepared to cede the island territory to Moscow. On 4 October 1943, he told Secretary of State Cordell Hull on the eve of Hull's departure for Moscow that 'the Kuriles really should go to Russia'. The next day, at a secret staff conference of State Department policy experts, he proposed that 'the Kurils be handed over to Russia' in exchange for a Soviet declaration of hostilities. (British officials apparently had reached the same conclusion.)[61] Aware of Stalin's 1940 request for the arc, Roosevelt acknowledged the Kremlin's legitimate security concerns in the northern region. His own postwar defence strategy called for surrounding Japan with a series of 'strategic strong points' to discourage future aggression. Soviet control of the Kurils would serve as a deterrent in the north and earn Moscow's good will.

The Joint Chiefs of Staff generally seem to have concurred with Roosevelt, believing that the archipelago was not worth a serious row with the Soviets despite its strategic value. When Ambassador Harriman told the Joint Chiefs just before the Yalta summit that the Soviet premier insisted on southern Sakhalin, the Kurils and concessions in Manchuria and the Mongolian People's Republic, the military high command raised no objections. The British Chiefs of Staff also saw no reason to quibble. In late July 1945 at Potsdam, the Allied Combined Chiefs indicated to Soviet military leaders that they did not wish to become involved militarily in the Kurils or other territories north of the Japanese archipelago, a diversion that would weaken their forces.[62]

The Potsdam Proclamation did not mention the Kurils per se but stated that 'The terms of the Cairo Declaration shall be carried out and Japanese sovereignty shall be limited to the islands of Honshu, Hokkaido, Kyushu, Shikoku and such minor islands as we determine' (Article 8). Ignorant of the Yalta protocol, the State Department took 'such minor islands' to mean the Kurils. An undated State

Department memorandum discussed at a meeting on 30 July 1945 noted that the Potsdam document 'does not include an intention to eliminate Japan's sovereignty over the Liu Chiu [*Ryukyu*] and Kuril islands as they are "minor islands". There is more grounds for supposing that [it] intends to eliminate Japan's sovereignty over Southern Sakhalin which is hardly a "minor island".' The document concluded, however, that 'The Department's policy has not favoured the elimination of Japan's sovereignty in any of these three areas'.[63]

Final diplomatic moves
Roosevelt's death in April and the ascension of Harry S. Truman to the American presidency effectively voided the Yalta agreement. With surrender imminent, the US Joint Chiefs appear to have had second thoughts about the value of the island territory. On 11 August, the US Navy was ordered to occupy the central and southern Kurils. On 15 August, Truman cabled Stalin an advance copy of General Order no. 1 directing Japanese units to surrender to Allied commanders in the areas where they were deployed. Missing was any reference to the Kurils. This omission probably was intentional. General Order no. 1 had been drafted by the Army General Staff's Strategy and Policy Group, whose leading members now viewed the island chain as a strategic asset that should remain at least partially within the US control sphere. These staff officers seem purposely to have left open the possibility of an American takeover of the chain.[64]

Reading into Truman's message evidence of a reversal on the Yalta promises, on 15 August, Stalin ordered Marshal Aleksander Vasilevsky, Commander of the Soviet Far Eastern Forces, to prepare to take and hold the Kuril chain. On 16 August, he replied to Truman's cable, demanding that the entire northern arc be incorporated into the Soviet area of responsibility. He also insisted that the northern half of Hokkaido, above a line running from Kushiro on the east coast to Rumoi on the west, be included in that zone. Moscow's demand for a Hokkaido foothold has been explained as a gambit designed to manipulate Washington into acquiescing to Soviet control of the Kurils and southern Sakhalin. A zone of occupation in Japan proper was a long-standing Soviet goal, however, and the Kremlin appears to have been deadly earnest, for on 18 August, Stalin ordered the First Far Eastern Army and the Pacific Fleet to prepare an invasion of northern Hokkaido and the southern Kurils. Russian archival materials opened since the collapse of the USSR indicate that Hokkaido itself was in fact the ultimate objective of the Soviet advance. The Red Army had begun its attack on southern Sakhalin on 11 August, before Japan's decision to surrender, and by 25 August, it held the entire island. The impending assault on the Kurils apparently was the second phase of a two-pronged offensive directed against Japan's northern home island.[65]

On 18 August, Truman replied to Stalin's message of the 16th, agreeing to the Marshal's request to modify General Order no. 1 and include the Kuril arc in the Soviet control sphere. Truman's quick resolution of the Kuril surrender issue reflected a pressing concern that Soviet troops, then nearing P'yŏngyang, might push south of the 38th parallel, contesting US plans to occupy southern Korea. In the same message, the President categorically rejected the Soviet demand for northern Hokkaido (although the Joint Chiefs actually had planned for that contingency – chapter 3), but countered with a request for US air-base rights in the central Kuril group. On 22 August, Stalin told Truman that he would not insist on occupying part of Hokkaido but flatly rebuffed the American bid for air facilities in the islands, noting angrily that such demands usually were made of conquered states, not allies. The same day, the Soviet leader ordered his Far East Commander Marshal Vasilevsky to abandon plans for the invasion of Hokkaido. In flagrant violation of the Potsdam terms, however, he also instructed Internal Affairs (NKVD) Commissar Lavrenty Beria to prepare to transport captured Imperial soldiers to Soviet territory for hard labour.[66]

At this point, the State Department and the Joint Chiefs decided to drop the matter, in effect suspending America's incipient northern strategy. The United States would not oppose Soviet movement into the islands, sealing the arc's fate, but Washington was not prepared to condone outright annexation. On 27 August, Ambassador Harriman handed Stalin a message from Truman dropping the request for air bases but stating that final disposition of the territorial problem would have to await a peace treaty with Japan. Stalin was outraged by what he perceived as American duplicity but did not pursue the issue, accelerating instead the invasion of the archipelago, in progress since mid-August.

The Soviet–Japanese War

On 15 August 1945, three hours after Hirohito broadcast his Rescript ending the war, Marshal Vasilevsky, Soviet Far East Commander, ordered Major General Aleksei Gnechko, Commander of the Kamchatka Defence Zone, to take Shumshu, Paramushir, Onekotan and other islands in the northern group by 25 August. Major General Porfiry Dyakov, Commander of the 101st Rifle Division, and Captain Demitry Ponomarev, Commander of the Petropavlovsk Naval Base, led the assault force consisting of 8,800 men, including one marine battalion and two rifle regiments, supported by 80 aircraft and 64 naval vessels. It set sail from Kamchatka on 16 August.[67]

Shumshu and Paramushir were defended by Japan's 91st Division under Lieutenant General Tsutsumi Fusaki, who commanded a force of 23,000 men, some 200 light and heavy artillery pieces, 85 tanks and 8 aircraft.[68] With news of Japan's capitulation, the Imperial garrison prepared to surrender to the nearest Allied forces, which it assumed would be American. At day break on 18 August, 8,300 Soviet forces struck Shumshu without warning, taking the Japanese completely by surprise. Tsutsumi did not expect the Red Army to attack as he was preparing to lay down arms. Believing the invader to be Americans, his soldiers repelled the initial onslaught at the water's edge with devastating effectiveness, costing Soviet forces an estimated 2,000 lives. Tsutsumi's main contingent was concentrated in well-fortified positions in the interior for a defence in depth, but on 19 August, Lieutenant

General Higuchi Ki'ichirō, Commander of the Fifth Area Army in Sapporo, ordered him to 'stop fighting, hand over weapons and begin negotiations'. Intent on taking the island, Soviet troops pressed the attack, however, and bitter fighting raged for an additional two days, wasting many more lives on both sides. The battle witnessed the last *kamikaze* attacks of the war, as one of Tsutsumi's three aircraft ploughed into a Soviet escort fleet. Hostilities finally ended on 20 August. Three days later, a Japanese delegation led by Tsutsumi, his Chief of Staff Yanagioka Takeshi, and Suizu Mitsuru, the Fifth Area Army's Chief of Staff, signed a formal truce with Generals Gnechko and Dyakov and Vice Admiral Alexander Frolov of the Soviet Pacific Fleet. On 24 August, Japanese soldiers began surrendering their arms.[69]

On 25 August, the Soviets secured Paramushir and on 26 August took Matsuwa (Matua) in the central Kurils. By 27 August, a Soviet naval squadron had advanced southward, moving into position off Urup at the southern end of the central group, but no landings were made until the 31st. Between 27 and 31 August, the squadron patrolled the offing, keeping an eye out for US forces. Whether, up to that point, the Soviet military had intended to occupy the four islands south of Urup is unclear. According to Suizu Mitsuru, who subsequently served as Vice Admiral Frolov's interpreter and guide, the Soviet fleet commander stated unequivocally that all islands south of Urup were in the American sphere of control and out of bounds to Soviet forces.[70] Encountering no American presence, however, units of the Soviet Pacific Fleet under Captain Viktor Leonov began occupying the southernmost group – Kunashiri, Etorofu, Shikotan and the Habomais – as well. The last of these territories, the five Habomais and their smaller islets, were occupied by Soviet troops between 3 and 5 September, presenting Japan and the United States with a fait accompli that would prove impossible to undo.[71]

Soviet historians have insisted that the occupation of the southern Kurils was completed by 1 September 1945, a claim that defies the facts and appears to be a deliberate falsification.[72] The southernmost islands were seized after Japan and the Allied Powers, including the USSR, had signed the surrender documents on 2 September. The reason for this duplicity seems clear enough. On 2 September, as the Instrument of Surrender was being initialled aboard the *Missouri*, Stalin delivered his own victory speech to the Soviet people. In it, the Marshal stated baldly that 'southern Sakhalin and the Kuril Islands have been transferred to the Soviet Union, and will henceforth serve . . . as a means for linking the Soviet Union with the ocean and as a base for our defence against Japanese aggression'.[73] By bringing forward the official date of the archipelago's seizure, Moscow obviously hoped to legitimise the Kuril annexation.

Life under Soviet rule
The inhabitants of the southern Kuril group included Ainu, Nivhks (Gilyak) and Oroks (Uilta), native peoples who had first inhabited this territory; Japanese settlers and Imperial troops; Korean conscript labourers; and a small number of Russians and

other ethnic groups. Japan had pursued a policy of forcible assimilation toward the indigenous population, and the Soviet occupiers feared open opposition to their rule.[74] According to a Hokkaido Police report of October 1945, 600 Soviet troops landed on Etorofu on 28 August; another 8,000 were deployed on Kunashiri and 600 on Shikotan on 1 September; and 239 occupied the Habomais – 19 on Suisho, 200 on Shibotsu and 20 on Taraku – on 3 September. Estimates placed the total Soviet garrison in the southern islands at more than 9,400.[75]

Some 50,400 Imperial soldiers, including 24,000 survivors of Tsutsumi's 91st Division, surrendered in the Kurils. Soviets authorities disarmed them, confiscating weapons, ammunition and other war matériel. Enlisted personnel and low-ranking officers were sent to labour camps in Kamchatka, Sakhalin and Magadan. Staff officers were declared war criminals and sent to special high-security prisons in Khabarovsk. Nearly 18,000 Japanese civilians, including some 2,000 seasonal workers, many of them presumably Koreans, lived in the southern Kurils. Cut off from the home islands, they found themselves at the mercy of Soviet troops and propaganda. When Red Army officers in Kunashiri spread rumours that the islands would become a part of the USSR and that local inhabitants would be made Soviet citizens, many islanders fled to Hokkaido rather than await an uncertain repatriation. By 10 October 1945, an estimated 4,000 had risked their lives to escape. Nemuro City has compiled the stories of these survivors, who describe a climate of insecurity and fear, with reports of occasional rape and physical assault and widespread looting by occupying troops. Islanders suffered from a lack of food and other winter provisions. Moreover, communication with Soviet authorities was difficult in the absence of interpreters.[76] Unlike Manchuria, where Japanese were singled out for rape and pillage, however, systematic violence against the civilian population appears to have been exceptional. Petty theft was rife, but this was due more to the impoverished condition of Soviet troops and their low level of education than to a penchant for lawlessness. An exception was the murder of the mayor of Tomari Village on Kunashiri, who was shot two weeks after the surrender under circumstances that remain unclear.[77]

As Soviet troops deployed, they seized or destroyed telephone and telegraph installations and banned ship movements into and out of the islands. Land and sea communications, including cables, passed into Soviet hands, and contact with Hokkaido was prohibited. The Habomais had belonged administratively to Nemuro City in Hokkaido, but they, too, were cut off. Radio stations and newspapers were closed down and postal and freight services suspended. Four freighters that left Nemuro port for the southern Kurils between late August and early September were seized by the Red Army and requisitioned for military use. The Soviets searched and recorded the contents of all public offices and occupied the municipal branch offices on each island. All Japanese government institutions except public schools were closed and their officials dismissed. Police stations, district forestry offices, town and village government buildings and post offices were taken over for barracks and other military facilities.

Soviet authorities initially cooperated with local government officials to restore order. In Kunashiri, they sponsored elections for village mayors to serve as auxiliaries for the occupation. Some native policemen were sent to Sakhalin and the Soviet mainland for retraining, a measure that was widely resisted. Many Japanese law enforcement officers disposed of their uniforms, donned civilian clothes and tried to escape to avoid such transfers. A series of military government proclamations assured the islanders of their safety so long as they did not resist Soviet rule and carried on normally. The extent to which these orders regulated life varied from one district to the next, but a typical example is the decree issued on 13 September to the villagers of Tomari on Kunashiri:

Since Japan has surrendered to the Soviet Union, the Kuril Islands are now Soviet territory. The Red Army has no desire to use force against law-abiding citizens and will extend every assistance to those who obey their commanding officers.

1 All Japanese local administrative organs, district offices and police and military reserve units will be disbanded. All hamlet mobile assets and official documents must be brought to Soviet Garrison Headquarters by 15 September.

2 Inhabitants of each hamlet will elect a local headman to serve as mayor under the guidance of the Soviet garrison commander.

3 Tomari inhabitants may: a) engage in fishing, agriculture, manufacturing and lumbering; b) use roads between 6 am and 8 pm; and c) attend schools and visit shrines between 6 am and 6 pm.

4 The following activities are prohibited by order of Garrison Headquarters: a) unauthorised voyages of over six nautical miles from the coast; b) unauthorised journeys to Furukamappu and Shiranuka; c) unauthorised public meetings; d) the possession of wireless sets; e) harbouring Japanese soldiers.[78]

The proclamation issued the same day in Tomari's Furukamappu District, however, was far more restrictive. The local military commander outlawed flying the Japanese flag and the ownership of private property. No family could possess more than one horse. Rice was rationed at 1.8 *go* (0.324 litres) each week for those under 15 and over 60, and at 3.5 go (0.63 litres) for everyone else. Daily wages for labourers assigned to enlarge Soviet dock facilities were fixed at ¥7 for men and ¥5 for women.

In some areas, the scope of daily activities was drastically curtailed. On Taraku in the Habomais, for instance, a decree of 5 September prohibited all activities not specifically authorised by the Red Army and ordered women and children to remain at home at all times unless instructed otherwise. Those allowed out were to walk quietly with their hands open and in front of them. The order warned that anyone running would be shot.[79]

Although Soviet military rule brought hardships, it also enabled residents to return to former peacetime pursuits. Deep-sea fishing was prohibited but coastal trawling allowed. Islanders caught salmon, crabs, clams, scallops and a variety of small fish, and canneries flourished. With Soviet encouragement, they also harvested kelp, *nori* and other types of seaweed used for producing glue, iodine and agar. Forestry, farming, cattle-breeding and light manufacturing also were encouraged, and the authorities contracted out military work to local companies. Residents endured the harsh conditions under Soviet rule until late 1948, by which time Japanese repatriation out of the Kurils had been completed.

PART II

Organising the Occupation

CHAPTER 3

The Occupational Dynamic

THE ALLIED CONTROL MECHANISM

A zonal occupation?

Washington originally envisaged a post-surrender role in Japan for the Soviet Union and other Allies similar to that projected for Germany. Some degree of Soviet cooperation, in particular, it was reasoned, would give the United States greater say in Soviet-held postwar Europe. The Allies, too, assumed a zonal occupation. That was the prize Britain eyed when it secured a place in the American invasion force. The Free French, the Dutch and the Portuguese, anxious to recover their colonial domains, also coveted a part in the final assault on Japan and its post-defeat administration. When US Ambassador Averell W. Harriman met Stalin to discuss Japan's fate in late May 1945, the Soviet leader insisted firmly on a major role in its postwar disposition. Assuming a German-style four-power occupation, he asked for an agreement specifying which areas would be allotted to each Ally.[1] Washington, its troops bogged down on Okinawa and anxious for a Soviet military commitment against Japan, was in no position to dictate terms, and the Pentagon began drafting contingency plans for a divided occupation.

In June, America's supreme policy-making body, the inter-departmental State–War–Navy Coordinating Committee (SWNCC), decided for military reasons to deny other countries a controlling voice in the occupation of Japan's home islands, but official US policy continued to give lip support to the principle of Allied participation. Stalin pressed his demands for a post-surrender role with particular energy. On 11 August, Moscow tentatively accepted Truman's proposal to appoint MacArthur Allied Supreme Commander. In a meeting that day with Ambassador Harriman, however, Foreign Minister V. M. Molotov made a counter-proposal calling for two paramount leaders: Marshal Aleksandr Vasilevsky, Commander of the Soviet Far Eastern Forces, would share Allied authority with MacArthur. Harriman sniffed at the suggestion and walked out of the meeting. Preoccupied with events in Eastern Europe, Stalin agreed to a unitary American command in Japan but, as indicated earlier, on 16 August requested a Soviet sphere of control in the northern half of Hokkaido. President Truman curtly dismissed that demand on 18 August (chapter 2).[2]

On the same day (18 August), however, Truman approved a SWNCC proposal to invite Allied involvement in Japan on American terms: associated occupation armies would be integrated into a US command structure. Washington and London were particularly keen to include Chinese troops in order to soften the appearance of

Photo 11. General Headquarters, SCAP. The Dai-Ichi Mutual Life Insurance Building, Tokyo. The view is from Hibiya Park in front of the Imperial Palace (US National Archives).

white victors dictating the peace to a conquered 'Oriental' people. Consequently, Nationalist China was asked to contribute 60,000 troops, but the outbreak of civil war on the continent prevented the Chiang Kai-shek (Jiang Jieshi) régime from complying. The Soviet Union initially was requested to supply 175,000 soldiers and aviators, later downgraded to 70,000.[3] Unwilling to place its forces under US control, Moscow ignored Washington's lukewarm offer of inclusion. American planning also called for 135,000 Commonwealth troops, subsequently reduced to 65,000. Australia, Britain, India and New Zealand each agreed to provide a brigade group, and a force of more than 40,000 eventually was sent to Japan.

In the meantime, the Pentagon's Joint War Plans Committee had completed its scenario for a zonal occupation, 'Ultimate Occupation of Japan and Japanese Territory' (JWPC-385/1), which was submitted to the Joint Chiefs of Staff on 16 August. The plan called for a Soviet Zone in Hokkaido and northeastern Honshu (Tohoku); a US Zone in central Honshu, including the Kanto, Shin'etsu, Tokai, Hokuriku and Kinki regions; a Nationalist Chinese Zone in Shikoku; and a British Zone in western Honshu (the Chugoku region) and Kyushu. Tokyo would be administered jointly by the United States, the Soviet Union, Britain and the Republic of China (ROC); the Kobe-Kyoto-Osaka region was to be governed by the United States and the ROC.

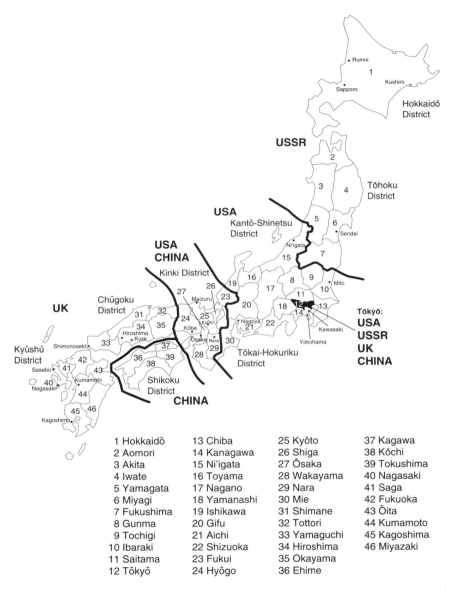

1 Hokkaidō
2 Aomori
3 Akita
4 Iwate
5 Yamagata
6 Miyagi
7 Fukushima
8 Gunma
9 Tochigi
10 Ibaraki
11 Saitama
12 Tōkyō

13 Chiba
14 Kanagawa
15 Ni'igata
16 Toyama
17 Nagano
18 Yamanashi
19 Ishikawa
20 Gifu
21 Aichi
22 Shizuoka
23 Fukui
24 Hyōgo

25 Kyōto
26 Shiga
27 Ōsaka
28 Wakayama
29 Nara
30 Mie
31 Shimane
32 Tottori
33 Yamaguchi
34 Hiroshima
35 Okayama
36 Ehime

37 Kagawa
38 Kōchi
39 Tokushima
40 Nagasaki
41 Saga
42 Fukuoka
43 Ōita
44 Kumamoto
45 Kagoshima
46 Miyazaki

Figure 4. Joint Chiefs of Staff blueprint for a Zonal Occupation (16 August 1945) and Japanese prefectures in the main islands (Hokkaidō, Honshū, Shikoku, Kyūshū).

JWPC-385/1 divided the occupation into three phases and specified desirable troop strengths for each of the participating powers. During Phase One, Allied military forces would disarm Imperial troops and quell organised resistance. In Phase Two (an estimated nine months from the completion of Phase One), occupation armies were to demilitarise Japan, rendering it permanently incapable of military aggression. During Phase Three, the Allies would administer Japan collectively. This stage was to end when it was agreed that pacification and demilitarisation had been completed.[4]

As in the case of Germany, the drafters of JWPC-385/1 hoped in part to lessen the burden of occupation by sharing it. A zonal arrangement also had the political merit of enabling Washington to demobilise rapidly, meeting public demands to bring the troops home early. Higher-level military planners, however, questioned the scheme's feasibility. Moreover, Truman, the State Department and MacArthur were flatly opposed to giving the Soviet Union or any ally so powerful a say in what they insisted must be an American show. Truman later wrote: 'I was determined that the Japanese occupation should not follow in the footsteps of the German experience. I did not want divided control or separate zones.'[5] Consequently, the plan was never presented formally to the Joint Chiefs or SWNCC, the top American policy groups. With the exception of a limited area under the jurisdiction of the British Commonwealth Occupation Force, Japan proper would be under exclusive US dominion. The occupation of the main islands was to be unitary and preponderantly American, but as indicated below, the Soviet-held Kurils and the US-controlled Ogasawara and Ryukyu chains were detached from the Japanese homeland at an early date and placed under separate military administrations. In this sense, one may speak of a divided or semi-divided occupation.

The Far Eastern Commission
Following surrender formalities, MacArthur asked Washington for a clarification of his powers, and the White House responded in a message of 6 September 1945 that the Emperor and the Japanese government were subordinate to the Supreme Commander. 'Since your authority is supreme', the directive said, 'you will not entertain any question on the part of the Japanese as to its scope.' But in fact, there were limits to MacArthur's prerogatives. The General was bound by the Potsdam terms, and his mandate was to last only until such time as Allied objectives in Japan had been achieved. He also was subject in principle to institutional restraints imposed by the machinery of occupation, although in practice, he often behaved as if these did not exist. As SCAP, MacArthur was answerable to the Far Eastern Commission (FEC), the Allied body ostensibly responsible for overseeing the administration of Japan. During MacArthur's stewardship, he received more than 100 directives from superiors, about half of which came from the FEC and half from Washington.

In the spring of 1945, SWNCC, the inter-departmental policy-making committee, proposed the creation of a multi-national high commission to formulate policy for Japan and other occupied areas in the Pacific. This control body was to be modelled on the Allied Four Power Commission established for Germany.

MacArthur and the War and Navy Departments objected strenuously, however, insisting on complete US domination of the Pacific, which they viewed as vital to America's global security interests. No 'higher commission', they argued, should be able to override the authority of the Joint Chiefs of Staff. SWNCC subsequently abandoned the idea of a superordinate Pacific-Far Eastern directorate. When Moscow suggested the creation of an Allied control body in Tokyo, complete with veto power for each of its members, Washington rejected the idea out of hand. Instead, on 21 August 1945, the State Department proposed the establishment of a Far Eastern Advisory Commission (FEAC), omitting references to the Pacific or any higher authority. An exercise in tokenism, the FEAC had no control functions and was to serve a purely advisory role concerning occupied Japan. At American insistence, the 10-member Commission finally was established on 2 October. Convening in Washington on 30 October, the body met nine more times in November and December, but its tenure was short-lived. From late December through early February 1946, at MacArthur's invitation, the FEAC toured Japan on a fact-finding mission and was reorganised soon afterwards (below).[6]

Britain and Nationalist China, unhappy with the FEAC's lack of substantive authority, participated only because of US pressure. The Soviet Union refused to take part, and as US-Soviet relations worsened, Kremlin opposition to America's monopoly of the Occupation intensified. SCAP allowed Moscow and the other Allies to establish diplomatic missions in Tokyo (the Soviets promptly despatched 400 consular officials), but these were accredited to MacArthur's headquarters, which held sole responsibility for Japan's foreign affairs, and the status of the missions remained ambiguous. Australia also demanded a major occupation role and insisted on representing all Commonwealth countries in Japan on matters pertaining to the Pacific region.

To compel Washington to share power further, London pressed for the creation in Tokyo of a five-nation central Allied Control Council, to be headed by MacArthur. The State Department considered the British idea, but in late October, MacArthur sent a strongly worded message to Secretary of State James F. Byrnes objecting to the proposal, which was quietly dropped. To placate London and secure a nominal pledge of cooperation from Moscow, American leaders recommended replacing the FEAC with a Far Eastern Commission endowed with formal authority. The Allies agreed to establish the new body on 27 December 1945 at the Four-Power Foreign Ministers' Conference in Moscow, with Great Britain, the Soviet Union and the United States signing the joint declaration and the Republic of China concurring. The so-called Moscow Agreement specified that the four Allies would cooperate 'in all matters relating to the surrender and disarmament of the enemy'. It also provided for the creation in Tokyo of a four-member consultative organ, the Allied Council for Japan, to advise MacArthur on occupation policy.

The Far Eastern Commission (FEC) held its first meeting on 26 February 1946 at the former Japanese Embassy in Washington. The Soviet Union took an active part in the organisation from its inception. The FEC's mandate was to formulate policies for implementing the Potsdam terms and to review SCAP directives and actions. It had no jurisdiction, however, over military or territorial matters, such as the occupation of the Kuril, Ogasawara and Ryukyu islands. FEC policies were transmitted to SCAP as directives by Washington. Although technically a decision-making body, the new Commission lacked operational control and in practice depended largely on American goodwill. The US tactic, an Occupation official later wrote, consisted of an 'effective three-step formula: First, grant the Allies participation in "policy" (through the FEC); second, reserve all operational matters to the Supreme Commander, an American; and third, consider everything important to be operational'.[7]

The Commission originally was composed of 11 nations: the nine Allies who had signed the Instrument of Surrender plus India and the Philippines. Founding members were Australia, Canada, France, India, the Netherlands, New Zealand, the Philippines, the Republic of China, the Soviet Union, the United Kingdom, and the United States. Burma and Pakistan joined in November 1949, bolstering the Commission's Asian representation. The FEC consisted of a secretariat, a steering committee and seven working committees and was headed by two senior US officials: Major General Frank R. McCoy, the chair and a close friend of MacArthur's, and Nelson T. Johnson, a former ambassador to China and Australia, who served as Secretary-General. The Steering Committee was headed by a New Zealander, the veteran diplomat Sir Carl Berendsen. His deputy was O. Reuchlin of the Netherlands. The subcommittees handled war reparations (First Committee); economic and financial affairs, including labour (Second Committee); constitutional and legal reform (Third Committee); strengthening of democratic tendencies (Fourth Committee); war criminals (Fifth Committee); aliens in Japan (Sixth Committee); and disarmament (Seventh Committee).[8]

The 'US Initial Post-Surrender Policy for Japan', made public on 22 September 1945, stated explicitly that while America would consult with the Allies on Occupation matters, 'in the event of any differences of opinion among them, the policies of the United States will govern'. This caveat and the FEC's lack of operational control gave the United States the upper hand. By casting its veto, Washington could prevent the body from interfering with virtually any Occupation policy. Great Britain, the Republic of China and the Soviet Union also had veto rights, but the United States could circumvent Allied opposition by issuing emergency 'interim directives' to deal with pressing problems in Japan pending an FEC review, and these it used effectively to defend American prerogatives. In February 1947, for instance, Washington issued an interim directive over the objections of other FEC members allowing limited advance transfers of Japanese war matériel as reparations. The most famous use of an emergency decree was Washington's nine-point economic stabilisation order to MacArthur in December 1948 instructing SCAP to implement the Dodge deflation programme. Interim directives, however, could not deal with 'fundamental changes in the Japanese constitutional structure, or in the regime of control, or . . . a change in the Japanese government as a whole'. Such 'reserved questions' required the formal consent of the entire Commission.

For the first two years of its existence, the FEC played a constructive albeit minor role in the Occupation, issuing nearly 50 policy directives on a diverse range of subjects, including the Constitution, land reform and demilitarisation. Its committees, especially the Fourth Committee (Strengthening of Democratic Tendencies), which was chaired successively by Soviet representatives Nikolai Novikov and Alexander S. Panyushkin, made pertinent proposals on constitutional and electoral reform, labour legislation and the purge of war collaborators. The FEC also became a forum for criticising what many delegates viewed as MacArthur's abusive use of his executive powers. Even as late as 1948, for instance, Australian, British, New Zealand and Soviet delegates took GHQ to task for ordering the Diet to revise the National Public Service Law and outlaw strikes by government workers. The Steering Committee Chair, Sir Carl Berendsen of New Zealand, frequently protested at America's domination of the Commission together with the FEC's superpower bias, which, he asserted, prevented members of smaller nations from receiving a fair hearing.[9]

The FEC was never able to challenge successfully the authority of Washington or SCAP. Headquartered in the US capital, it was financed largely by the American government. Existing control machinery in Japan and the US chain of command further weakened its independence. The Commission's late start was another factor contributing to its ineffectiveness. By the time the FEC met for the first time in February 1946, MacArthur's headquarters had either begun or already completed several key reforms, among them dissolution of the secret police, the purge and constitutional revision.

In theory, GHQ decisions and the recommendations of GHQ-sponsored special missions were forwarded via SCAP's Diplomatic Section to the State Department, which reported them to the Commission. The Commission then debated the proposals and issued a directive, making them official Allied Policy. Not only were such decisions time-consuming, however, but Washington might wait up to a year before notifying the Commission of a SCAP policy. Most FEC directives, then, were issued ex post facto. For instance, the Commission did not formally approve the 'US Initial Post-Surrender Policy for Japan' until 19 June 1947, some 19 months after the start of the Occupation, by which time the reform phase was winding down. On occasion, however, Allied proposals were adopted as policy. In December 1946, for example, Australia, Britain and New Zealand pushed through a liberal trade union charter that confirmed the right of labour organisations to participate in national politics. As Cold War tensions escalated, however, Allied advice, especially from the Soviet Union, fell increasingly on deaf ears. The influence of the FEC waned, its debates grew progressively sterile and, by 1949, the Commission no longer played a significant role.

The Allied Council for Japan

Moscow proposed that the Far Eastern Commission be located in Tokyo, believing that proximity to MacArthur would allow it to monitor the General's activities more effectively. Strong opposition from SCAP derailed that initiative, however, and the FEC was convened in Washington. As agreed upon at the Moscow Foreign

Ministers' Conference, a subsidiary agency, the Allied Council for Japan (ACJ), was established in Tokyo with four members: the British Commonwealth (Australia, India, New Zealand and Great Britain), the Republic of China, the Soviet Union and the United States. The Council first met on 5 April 1946 – with the Occupation already well under way – and gathered fortnightly thereafter to advise the Supreme Commander, who nominally served as Council chair and US delegate. SCAP permitted one Japanese representative, Asakai Kōichirō of the Central Liaison Office (and future ambassador to Washington), to attend as an observer, but required the diplomat to enter by the back door.[10]

Convening in the Meiji Insurance Building in downtown Tokyo, the ACJ held a total of 164 sessions between April 1946 and April 1952. Many of these meetings, however, were adjourned within minutes for lack of an agenda, and a full 47 of the 53 that US delegate William J. Sebald attended between 1948 and 1949 ended as soon as they began. Like the Far Eastern Commission, the Council found itself dealing with questions that had become non-issues by the time they were brought to its attention. One scholar has termed the ACJ 'a monument to futility', and the British Commonwealth delegate, noting that MacArthur's representatives treated it with 'frivolous derision', labelled the Council 'a failure, and at times a fiasco'. The body was not entirely useless, however, and in its heyday functioned as a sounding board for issues that otherwise might never have received a public airing.[11]

In principle, an objection raised in the Allied Council to SCAP implementation of a Far Eastern Commission decision required MacArthur to await FEC endorsement before issuing final orders. That was the only formal relationship between the FEC and the ACJ, however. In practice, MacArthur deplored the Council's 'meddlesome interference' and worked to deny the body any genuine consultative function. Although holding the dual posts of ACJ chair and US delegate, the General attended only the opening session. Thereafter, he assigned subordinates to represent the United States. The first American delegate was General William Marquat, head of SCAP's Economic and Scientific Section, who was followed in quick succession by George Atcheson Jr. and William J. Sebald, SCAP's State Department advisers in the Diplomatic Section. Convinced that the Soviets were using the body as a pulpit for anti-American propaganda, the Supreme Commander felt fully justified in boycotting the proceedings and instructed his representatives to respond to any perceived provocation with resolute counterforce. Anti-USSR harangues calculated to offend regularly hit the mark, drawing prompt and acerbic Soviet verbal retaliation, and the Council quickly became a platform for mutual recrimination. The Kremlin's representative persistently chided MacArthur for his rabid anti-Communism and criticised the high-handed manner in which he ran the Occupation. He also attacked GHQ policies on reparations, the bureaucracy, land reform and labour, notably SCAP's ban of the general strike planned for 1 February 1947.

Soviet-American clashes in the ACJ commanded wide public attention. Regular meetings were made public at MacArthur's request as 'a safeguard against Russian libels', and Japanese journalists, allowed in through the rear door, reported regularly

Photo 12. Australian W. MacMahon Ball, British Commonwealth representative to the Allied Council for Japan, attends the Council's second session, 17 April 1946 (US National Archives).

on the US-Soviet 'knock-down-dragout'.[12] These angry confrontations between erstwhile allies anticipated the official US policy of containing Communism by more than a year. Amplified by the media, they alerted the public to important differences in Allied opinion, and the names of the Soviet members – Lieutenant General Kuzma N. Derevyanko and Major General A. P. Kislenko – became household words. Derevyanko was the only ACJ member to question SCAP's censorship of the mass media, complaining that GHQ practised a double standard, suppressing information critical of Occupation policies and other Allies while allowing the publication of anti-Soviet material. In late May 1946, Derevyanko, in a sarcastic aside, told the Commonwealth representative, Australian W. MacMahon Ball, that 'we must, of course, believe SCAP that Japan is now fully democratic but there is not yet any democracy in the Allied Council!' In July, when the Soviet delegate challenged SCAP's labour reform project, George Atcheson, instead of refuting the Soviet allegations, labelled them 'Communist propaganda' and launched into a blistering diatribe against labour practices in the Soviet Union whose virulence stunned even the State Department's Japan specialists. Ball came to Derevyanko's

Photo 13. Other Allied representatives to the ACJ. From the left: General Kuzma Derevyanko (USSR), with trademark cigar, and George Atcheson, Jr (US). At the far right is General Chu Shih-ming (Republican China). Major General W. C. Chase (US Army), addressing Atcheson, drives home a point. 11 October 1946 (US National Archives).

defence, objecting to Atcheson's use 'of the Russian comment as a peg for a naive "individualist" attack on Communism'.[13]

Ball himself could be a vociferous critic of SCAP policy, and his pronouncements received extensive media coverage in Japan. The Commonwealth representative was quick to point out inadequacies in SCAP's economic policies, and his temerity in doing so enraged top GHQ officials. Atcheson complained archly to the State Department that Ball and Derevyanko consistently raised questions 'palpably designed to cause embarrassment'. Government Section Chief Courtney Whitney, who at MacArthur's urging employed 'sledgehammer tactics' in his appearances before the Council, belittled Ball as 'a farmer who speaks his own opinions rather than those of his native Australia or the British Commonwealth'. Under frequent censure from GHQ for his views, Ball resigned from the Council in August 1947, to be replaced by Australian diplomat Patrick Shaw and, in September 1949, by another Australian, Colonel William Hodgson. General Chu Shih-ming, the Chinese Nationalist representative, summed up the frustrations felt by non-American members of the Council when he confided to Ball, 'what is the use of saying anything? We cannot give advice without information; we cannot get information without asking questions; we can-not ask questions without the Chairman or SCAP representative telling us that we are impertinent to criticise the wonderful work of the Supreme Commander'. Gen-eral Chu, too, was lumped together in SCAP's book with Ball and Derevyanko. The Chinese delegate, Whitney fumed, should stand with his ally the United States, right or wrong.[14]

Two ACJ debates that received wide publicity were those concerning the labour and land reforms. Ball's critique of SCAP's agrarian project in May and June 1946 resulted in substantive changes to the original American proposal. General Derevy-anko enlivened that debate with demands for an even more radical land reallotment, and his attack on SCAP's labour programme in July ensured the passage of a radical Labour Standards Law. But such instances were exceptional, and the Allied Council, like its parent organisation, the Far Eastern Commission, exerted only minimal influence on the Occupation. With one exception, by 1948 the Council had virtually ceased to exercise any meaningful function.

That exception was the repatriation of Japanese prisoners of war interned in Siberia. According to US delegate William Sebald, this was the hottest political question the Council dealt with during his tenure. Sebald raised the issue in late October 1947, and it remained a point of bitter contention through 1950. On 21 December 1949, he queried Derevyanko about 376,000 missing POWs, and the next day, 22 December, some 400 people, including parents and relatives of the missing, staged a sit-in in front of the Soviet Mission in Tokyo and attempted to present a petition for the release of the prisoners. This orderly but rare display of collective anger struck a responsive chord with the public, reflecting not only outrage at the treatment of the POWs but also anger at Moscow's abrogation of the 1941 Neutrality Pact and its seizure of the southern Kurils after the war. The strong sentiments aroused by the POW issue also betrayed a deeper antipathy towards Russia dating from Tsarist days. When Sebald revived the question on 10 May 1950, the Soviet representative boycotted the ACJ and did not return for six months (the outbreak of the Korean War in June of that year no doubt explains the protracted Soviet absence).[15]

MacArthur's executive powers

MacArthur generally ignored the Far Eastern Commission, but he could not lightly dismiss the US military chain of command. The Supreme Commander was directly responsible, by order of rank, to President Truman, Commander-in-Chief of US Armed Forces; the Chair of the Joint Chiefs of Staff (Fleet Admiral William D. Leahy, followed by General Omar N. Bradley); the Army Chief of Staff (Dwight D. Eisen-hower, then Joseph L. Collins); the Secretary of War (successively, Henry L. Stimson and Robert P. Patterson); and the Secretary of the Army (Kenneth C. Royall, Gordon Gray and Frank Pace Jr). A five-star general, MacArthur outranked the Army Chief of Staff and the JCS Chair, but as Commander of US Army Forces in the Pacific he was duty-bound to obey their directives.

Despite the formal constraints on MacArthur's authority, three postwar policy

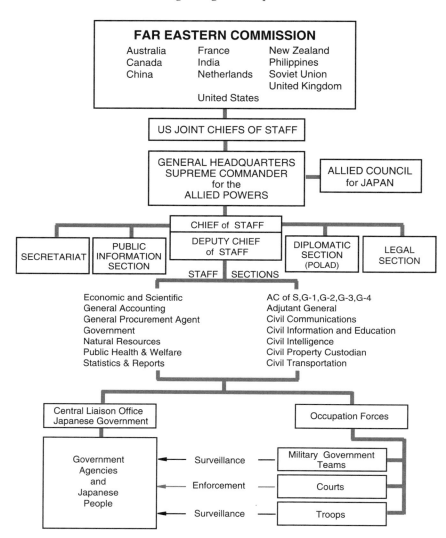

Figure 5. The machinery of the Occupation of Japan from the Far Eastern Commission through SCAP to the Japanese people, December 1948.
(Source: *Reports of General MacArthur*, 1966, p. 72)

documents, described in detail in chapter 5, gave him exceptional latitude in fulfilling his mandate as SCAP. These were the Potsdam Declaration (26 July 1945), SWNCC's 'US Initial Post-Surrender Policy for Japan' (22 September 1945) and the Pentagon's 'Basic Directive for Post-Surrender Military Government in Japan Proper' (3 November 1945). The Potsdam document was a declaration of Allied intentions towards Japan. The 'Initial Post-Surrender Policy' (SWNCC-150/4) was an enunciation of the basic goals and principles governing the Occupation. The Pentagon's 'Basic Directive' (JCS 1380/15), unlike SWNCC's more general statement, was a detailed blueprint for reform that subsumed and completed the earlier document. It was not made public until later and became the single most important external influence on MacArthur's headquarters.

While Washington formulated policy for Japan, the Supreme Commander was vested with the authority to execute that policy, and he made full use of his expanded powers, placing his personal imprimatur on nearly all aspects of the reform project. On 17 September 1945, for instance, without consulting President Truman, MacArthur announced that US garrison forces in Japan would be slashed from the 500,000 troops projected in mid-August of that year to 200,000 or less within six months. This was not a minor step. The State Department promptly upbraided the General for overstepping his bounds and attempting to dictate national policy. Dean Acheson, then facing confirmation hearings in the Senate for his appointment as Under-Secretary of State, told the press bluntly that 'the occupation forces are the instruments of policy and not the determinants of policy'. He later reflected: 'If we could have seen into the future, we might have recognised this skirmish as the beginning of a struggle leading to the relief of General MacArthur from his command on 11 April 1951.'[16]

MacArthur was under orders to carry out the Pentagon's 'Basic Directive' to the letter, but as the reform process got underway, he interpreted that document broadly, taking the initiative on matters large and small. In September 1945, fearing a breakdown in Japan's supply and distribution system, the Supreme Commander ignored a Washington policy directive not to distribute supplies to the former enemy and organised an emergency relief programme. A more striking example of executive privilege was the new Constitution, which MacArthur directed Government Section to draft and present to the Japanese in early February 1946. The completion of this centrepiece of Occupation policy was announced to Washington and the Far Eastern Commission in March as a fait accompli. In April, when the FEC demanded the right to review the constitutional draft before its promulgation, MacArthur penned an irate riposte, reminding the Commission that it was merely a policy-making body and that policy implementation in Japan was the exclusive provenance of SCAP. The FEC, he said, was not empowered 'to require prior approval of any action taken by the Supreme Commander or the Japanese Government to implement, fulfill or enforce the terms of surrender'.[17] The State Department and the Joint Chiefs, while not always pleased with MacArthur, generally deferred to him, finding it more effective to offer advice than issue orders. Relations between the self-aggrandising, imperious viceroy and the plain-spoken, pragmatic Truman, strained at the outset of the Occupation, would deteriorate steadily, however, culminating in MacArthur's forced retirement in 1951.

ESTABLISHING CONTROL

The imperative of rapid demilitarisation presented MacArthur's staff with the enormous and pressing task of decolonising the Greater Japanese Empire, disarming Imperial forces at home and abroad, establishing remote control over all government powers, destroying war equipment, assuring reparations and repatriating both overseas Japanese and foreign nationals living in Japan. These objectives, the preliminary spade work of occupation, would require a gargantuan effort lasting through 1946 and, in the case of reparations and repatriation, well beyond.

Decolonisation and disarmament
Decolonisation was accomplished physically by the Allied occupation of former Japanese colonies and mandated territories. Administratively, this was done through a series of special directives issued by SCAP that severed Japan proper from its former overseas possessions, which had accounted for nearly half of the Empire's territory, and terminated Tokyo's diplomatic relations with other states. The Cairo Declaration (27 November 1943) had limited Japanese sovereignty to Japan's four major islands and unspecified minor islands, ordained the return of Formosa, Manchuria and the Pescadores to the Republic of China, and liberated Korea. With Japan's surrender, the Supreme Commander set about disarming Imperial forces in the areas under US jurisdiction.

MacArthur's first formal directive, General Order no. 1 promulgated on 2 September 1945, authorised US Army Forces in the Pacific (AFPAC) to receive the surrender of Japanese troops in Korea south of the 38th parallel, in the Ryukyu archipelago and in Japan proper. Responsibility for detaching outlying Japanese territory from Imperial authority and overseeing its administration fell to SCAP's Government Section (GS). GS accomplished this task by issuing a directive to the Japanese government on 2 October 1945 removing Korea from Tokyo's administrative control. This was followed by another directive of 29 January 1946 terminating Japanese political and administrative dominion over former territories outside of the four major islands. GHQ also moved quickly to suspend Japan's power to deal independently with foreign governments. On 6 September 1945, MacArthur told Japanese authorities to comply with earlier instructions to close down their foreign embassies and legations and transfer all property and records to Allied representatives. On 25 October, the General ordered the recall of all Japanese diplomatic personnel from abroad, and on 4 November, he directed Tokyo to sever overseas diplomatic ties with other states and transfer all such functions to SCAP. Thereafter, GHQ handled Japan's foreign relations, a duty that would be assigned to the Diplomatic Section in April 1946.[18]

MacArthur quickly dissipated the 'terrific psychological tension' produced by the prospect of disarming and retiring some 7 million Imperial soldiers and sailors, fully half of them deployed in the home islands, by allowing the government to carry out that colossal task. Here, commented General Robert Eichelberger, 'the Emperor's

Photo 14. An end to war. Children cavort on the statues of military heroes removed from their pedestals and stored in a park pending destruction. At right is the statue of General Ōyama Iwao, a hero of the Russo-Japanese War. Tokyo, 6 September 1948 (New York Times).

prestige and proclamations were infinitely more effective than a bullying display of rifles in a land where we were feared and outnumbered'.[19] SCAP supervised and coordinated all stages of this work, but the government drew up and executed the basic plan of operations. On 13 September 1945, Imperial General Headquarters was dissolved, and the Cabinet's War and Navy Ministries were placed in charge of demobilisation activities. By December, the two Ministries, working through prefecture-level regimental headquarters, had disbanded all military forces in Japan proper. On 30 November, the War and Navy Ministries were transformed, respectively, into the First and Second Demobilisation Ministries, placed under a civilian minister and tasked with mustering out veterans returning from overseas. At the same time, prefectural regimental headquarters were reorganised into Local Assistance Bureaux and assigned to help ex-servicemen find jobs and adapt to civilian life.

In June 1946, the Ministries were downsized, renamed Demobilisation Bureaux and placed under a Demobilisation Board headed by a minister of state. A key figure in the work of the Board was Colonel Hattori Takushirō of the Army General Staff's Operations Division. He and other high-ranking colleagues, including two former chiefs of Army Operations and Military Intelligence officers, maintained lists of demobilised veterans, including some 70,000 career officers. These scrupulously kept records would enable MacArthur's intelligence chief Charles Willoughby to maintain de facto recruitment rosters for that day in the not too distant future when Japan would begin to rebuild its military.[20] In October 1947, the Demobilisation Board was disbanded and some of its functions were transferred to the Welfare Ministry's Repatriation Relief Agency.

Officers mustered out of service routinely were assigned a higher rank in order to qualify for a better pension, and these instant elevations became known as 'Potsdam promotions' (*Potsudamu shōkaku*). Over the vociferous objections of General Willoughby, however, Government Section insisted on halting the payment of military pensions and ending preferential treatment for veterans. Consequently, on 24 November 1945, GHQ's Economic and Scientific Section ordered the government to discontinue all veterans' and survivors' benefits by 1 February 1946. The Local Assistance Bureaux, by then regrouped under the Home Ministry (later, the Welfare Ministry), came to play a vital role in alleviating the distress of the Emperor's impecunious and discredited former soldiers and sailors.

The destruction of war matériel and reparations

The Japanese military had concealed arms caches in caves, tunnels, marshlands, forests and on small islands across Japan in anticipation of an Allied invasion, and in August 1945, extremist groups had hidden additional weapons for future use against the occupation army. Following the surrender, the Japanese government was instructed to collect, record and dispose of all military stores and armaments, including ammunition, small arms, heavy ordnance, tanks, aircraft and naval vessels, by burning, blowing up or dismantling them. US and British Commonwealth forces subsequently uncovered many unreported weapons caches. In November 1945, for instance, Occupation inspectors discovered a small arsenal concealed in three police stations in Aomori Prefecture consisting of a total of 1,880 rifles and bayonets, 18 light machine guns, more than 505,000 rounds of ammunition, and one case of TNT. Over 2 million tons of ammunition and munitions were exploded or dumped at sea, but scrap metal, engineering and automotive equipment and other matériel needed for economic reconstruction were returned to the Japanese government, which allocated them to leading industrial concerns. Supplies of clothing, foodstuffs, medicines and textiles also were released to the government to alleviate chronic economic shortages, although many of these goods ended up in the hands of unscrupulous black-marketeers.[21]

The Potsdam Proclamation had decreed the payment of 'just reparations in kind' to the countries Japan had ravaged, and Occupation personnel promptly began to survey all industrial machinery and plants of potential use as war reparations. The job was enormous, and tactical units were assigned to inventory the equipment and furnish armed guards to protect it. Edwin W. Pauley, a self-made US oil entrepreneur and former treasurer of the Democratic Party, was named Reparations Commissioner for Japan (he also was responsible for German reparations). On 18 December 1945, the Pauley Mission presented its recommendations to President Truman and, in April 1946, the State Department forwarded its report to the Far Eastern Commission. Pauley proposed to remove all steel capacity beyond a minimal tonnage and ship it to the countries where Imperial armies had wreaked havoc. Also slated for transfer were half of Japan's electric power capacity and virtually all of its war production facilities, such as aircraft factories, bearing and machine-tool manufacturing plants and arsenals. Pauley also recommended that the *zaibatsu* holding companies be broken up and their assets redistributed. In line with pre-surrender planning, the Mission called for production to be returned to levels obtaining between 1930 and 1934. Japanese industry was to be reorientated towards agriculture and light industry in order to allow the rest of Asia to compete more effectively against its finished goods. On 20 January 1946, GHQ issued a directive setting aside the first wartime plants for reparations, and by August 1947, more than 500 facilities had been earmarked for removal.[22]

MacArthur considered reparations 'war booty', however, and was cool to Pauley's recommendations, for the shipment abroad of Japan's modern industrial equipment threatened to retard the resumption of industrial production. Washington, too, eventually endorsed that view. With the deepening of the Cold War, it intervened to limit the scope of payments and, on 4 April 1947, issued an emergency interim directive through the Far Eastern Commission authorising advance deliveries of up to 30 per cent of scheduled reparations, which were sent over the next two years to Britain, Burma, the East Indies, Malaya, the Netherlands and the Philippines (the first load of reparations machinery did not leave Japan until January 1948, destined for China). The Allies, anxious to receive compensation promptly and in full, bitterly resented this high-handed manoeuvre but were powerless to prevent it. Changing American priorities in Japan would lead to the discontinuation of the programme in the spring of 1949, over the angry objections of the Philippines, the Republic of China and other Allies who felt they had been shortchanged. Later, the San Francisco peace settlement would require Japan to make reparations in services rather than in kind, opening the way for the resumption of large-scale Japanese investment in Southeast Asia (chapter 10).[23]

Repatriation

One of SCAP's primary responsibilities in the immediate aftermath of the war was the repatriation of overseas Japanese military personnel and civilians, and the return of foreign nationals living in Japan to their countries of origin. SCAP's G-3 Section (Repatriation Branch) had overall responsibility for arranging these massive transfers of war-displaced people. Operational control of repatriation was assumed by US Naval Forces in the Far East, but the Japanese government actually implemented – and paid for – the programme. To effect this ambitious undertaking, 14 receptions centres were set up at major ports in southwestern Japan; more than 370 seaworthy Japanese vessels, US liberty ships and Navy landing ship/tanks (LSTs) were mobilised; and Japanese seamen were hired to man them. In all, GHQ repatriated more than 8 million people, including 6.6 million overseas Japanese (more than half of them soldiers and sailors) and nearly 1 million Koreans and Chinese brought to Japan for forced labour during the war. Japanese continued to return from Southeast Asia in large numbers through 1947.[24]

The government set up special programmes to absorb Japanese returnees and find them housing and employment. Military personnel could rely on the Local Assistance Bureaux discussed above, but all repatriates were eligible for special emergency relief, including food, clothing and shelter (chapter 9). In 1946, central authorities established the Government Rehabilitation Loan, which made available short-term loans at low interest rates. Many returnees used these funds to build or repair homes or purchase farmland through the Agriculture Ministry, which had opened up vast tracts of public lands for emergency reclamation. Rural resettlement colonies absorbed tens of thousands of displaced war-sufferers, including many who had never farmed before. Postwar inflation quickly reduced the real value of interest payments, and the loans enabled millions to make a fresh start.

Chinese, Koreans and Ryukyuans were not so fortunate. The Japanese military had conscripted hundreds of thousands for supply work and corveé labour, and at the war's end, they constituted a vast colonial and semi-colonial underclass in Japan. Another 190,000 were scattered on islands across the Pacific. By the end of 1946, official repatriation from the Pacific Ocean Areas and out of Japan proper had been largely completed, and more than 1 million Chinese, Formosans, Koreans, Ryukyuans and Pacific islanders had been transported back to their respective homelands.[25] Occupation authorities strongly encouraged repatriation out of Japan. Although legally Japanese nationals, Okinawans, too, were told to 'go home'. The Occupation tailored its programmes to ethnic Japanese, and former colonials and other non-Yamato groups who insisted on remaining in Japan presented the Americans with an unwelcome problem for which little provision had been made (chapter 9).

Thousands of US nationals also found themselves in Japan in mid-August 1945, the vast majority of them Japanese Americans. Occupation sources placed the number of resident Nisei at 15,000, but not all were eligible to return to the United States. Washington automatically rescinded the citizenship of anyone who had served in the Imperial armed forces unless they could demonstrate that they had acted under duress. It also denationalised all US citizens who had voted in Japanese elections, a decision that had tragic and unintended consequences. During Japan's first postwar elections in April 1946, GHQ urged all adult men and women to turn out to vote, and many dual-national Nisei who came of age in 1946 and acted on that advice – often women – had their American citizenship revoked, making them ineligible to repatriate.[26] In May 1946, GHQ ordered the government to compile a list of Nisei residents and determined that about 10,000 were qualified to return. Of that number, roughly 5,000 eventually moved to the United States. At the same time, other Japanese Americans, recently released from internment centres, were travelling in the opposite direction, many of them Kibei who had been educated in Japan but gone back to the United States before war broke out. Outraged at the violation of their civil and political rights in the camps, they renounced their US citizenship and demanded transportation to Japan.[27]

Of the roughly 1.7 million Japanese captured by Soviet forces in Manchuria, Korea, Sakhalin and the Kurils, a majority eventually were sent home, although the last would not return from the Soviet Union until after the Occupation. In the months following the end of the conflict, Moscow had shipped as many as 700,000 POWs to labour camps in Siberia and Soviet Central Asia to alleviate chronic manpower shortages and assist in postwar reconstruction.[28] Clothed in light uniforms and subsisting on near-starvation rations, they perished in large numbers. Some 60,000 documented deaths occurred from disease, over-work, neglect or inhuman living conditions. Following a repatriation agreement signed in December 1946, Moscow allowed the return of 50,000 POWs monthly until mid-1947, but in late 1947 it suspended the programme indefinitely. The problem of the Siberian prisoners has never been resolved. Several hundred thousand had returned by late 1947, but many more did not come home until the mid-1950s, and between 300,000 and 500,000 are unaccounted for.[29]

Upon their return, former detainees were treated with suspicion. An estimated 20 to 25 per cent had participated actively in Soviet indoctrination programmes, and some became Communists, or at least professed to do so.[30] Returning POWs were herded through special screening centres set up at Maizuru and other Japan Sea ports by the Counter-Intelligence Corps to spot *aktivs* and ferret out Soviet agents. Most passively accepted these interrogations as a fact of life, but others resented them as yet another encroachment on their freedom. One returnee later described the transition from Soviet to American control in these terms: 'I wandered away from the rest, when suddenly I heard a [Japanese] female voice calling out to me. "Don't do that. Don't do that. You must not go away from the designated area. If you do that, *shinchūgun-san* [Occupation personnel] will reprimand you." Oh, my gosh, I said to myself. What is this anyway? Are they going to tell me to do this or not do that because everything has to be approved by the Honourable Occupation Personnel now, in place of the Russians I just left behind? So it was to be.'[31]

The Soviet Union's lengthy detention of Japanese POWs was an egregious violation

Photo 15. A Japanese veteran repatriated from Siberia is reunited with his family at Shinagawa Station, Tokyo. Hundreds of thousands of Japanese POWs never returned from Soviet labour camps. 1949 (Kyodo).

of Article 9 of the Potsdam Proclamation, which promised that Imperial forces would be allowed 'to return to their homes with the opportunity to lead peaceful and productive lives'. It must be noted, however, that, while Moscow carried its abusive and criminal incarceration of former Japanese soldiers to an extreme, it was not alone in seeking to profit from this vast pool of surplus labour. The British 'suspended' the repatriation of 113,500 Japanese soldiers in its Southeast Asian possessions for nearly two years, using this captive work force much as the Soviet Union had, albeit more humanely. British authorities also 'farmed out' 13,500 Japanese to Dutch colonialists in the East Indies until May 1947. London initially rejected SCAP requests to return these labour conscripts, but most had been evacuated by October 1947, although a smaller number remained in Singapore until 1948. For a year or more after the war, the Americans and the Chinese also helped themselves generously to this manpower reserve. The Communist and Nationalist régimes together retained for postwar recovery work over 100,000 former Imperial soldiers, and the Americans similarly delayed the repatriation of nearly 70,000 in the Philippines, Okinawa and the South Pacific for the 'maintenance and repair of essential installations'.[32]

INDIRECT GOVERNANCE IN JAPAN PROPER

In the Japanese home islands, MacArthur wielded his authority indirectly, via the existing civil administration. Unlike inhabitants of the Ryukyus and the Kurils, mainlanders generally did not feel themselves subject to foreign military rule. SCAP exercised indirect governance on two different levels. At the apex was GHQ's own vast civil affairs superstructure whose staff sections reflected the organisation of the Japanese bureaucracy. At the base was a network of military monitors responsible to AFPAC's Eighth Army. Linking the Allied control apparatus with Japan's governing institutions was a specially created Japanese group, the Central Liaison Office, which operated at both central and local levels.

The Central Liaison Office

During the Manila pre-surrender conference, MacArthur had ordered the Imperial government to establish a liaison organ to serve as the official channel of communications with his headquarters. On 26 August, the Foreign Ministry created the Central Liaison Office (CLO) as an external bureau. This vital institutional link played a crucial role in translating SCAP policies into action and assuring that Occupation reforms proceeded smoothly.[33] A central clearing house and message centre, the CLO transmitted SCAP orders to the government and conveyed the latter's views back to the Supreme Commander and his staff. Okazaki Katsuo, the Central Liaison Office's first director (later, vice foreign minister and foreign minister), and his deputy Shirasu Jirō, a British-educated aristocrat fluent in English, used their personal prewar connections with senior GHQ officials to plead the government's case. In their role as interested intermediaries, CLO staff – all of them Foreign Ministry officials – sometimes stubbornly resisted instructions they found objectionable and frequently manoeuvred to win concessions and soften SCAP demands.

Local CLO branch offices also were established at regional and prefectural levels to serve as the agency of contact between US Military Government (MG) Teams and local Japanese officials and to procure supplies and services for MG units. Central Liaison field offices also provided a valuable conduit between lower administrative echelons and the central government and played a pivotal role in ensuring compliance with Occupation demands locally. The most important branch office was in Yokohama, where Eighth Army Headquarters was located. Suzuki Tadakatsu, the local CLO chief, developed a close working relationship with Eighth Army Commander Eichelberger and in the early days of the Occupation, helped defuse a number of potentially explosive issues, such as crimes by US forces. Except for a brief period from 1948 to 1949 when the CLO was attached directly to the Prime Minister's Office, the liaison service remained a part of the Foreign Ministry. The CLO lost much of its influence after 1949 when GHQ's staff sections began dealing directly with their counterpart agencies in the government. The Office was formally abolished in April 1952 with the return of full sovereignty.

Fiat, persuasion, cooperation

In implementing its reform agenda, GHQ relied on a combination of fiat, persuasion and Japanese initiative. Yoshida Shigeru, prime minister during much of the Occupation, later asserted that MacArthur never gave him direct orders: 'We discussed matters fully, after which the Supreme Commander reached a decision, which I carried out.' In fact, at crucial junctures, MacArthur wrote memoranda to the government and personal letters to the prime minister virtually dictating policy. Through such private communications, the General ordered new general elections (February 1947), the execution of police reforms (September 1947), the denial to government workers of the right to strike (July 1948), the purge of the Communist Party Central Committee (June 1950) and the creation of the National Police Reserve (July 1950). Compliance invariably was prompt, Yoshida's disavowal notwithstanding.

MacArthur's headquarters also issued formal directives to the government in the form of SCAPINs (short for SCAP Index). Important SCAPINs were released to the mass media to assure the broadest possible dissemination. Understandably, Yoshida resented the Americans' overzealous recourse to these instruments of unilateralism. 'In the floodtide of their own good intentions', he wrote, Occupation officials 'were prone to ignore the feelings, history, and tradition that influenced equally well-intentioned Japanese officials.'[34] The SCAPINs were supra-constitutional occupation law. Phrased in a ponderous bureaucratic jargon, they gave rise to 'Scapinese', the idiom of occupation. To implement these fiats, on 20 September 1945 the government enacted an emergency decree, Imperial Ordinance no. 542, which allowed it to promulgate Occupation directives as Imperial edicts rather than as Diet laws. In Japanese, these enabling orders were called Potsdam Executive Decrees (*Potsudamu Chokurei*, abbreviated to the more colloquial *Potchoku*) and Potsdam Ordinances (*Potsudamu Seirei*), after the Potsdam Proclamation that gave them force of law. Subsequent to the issuance of these directives, signs emblazoned with the words 'By Order of the Occupation Forces' appeared in public places across the country, driving home the message that opposition would not be tolerated.

After the new Constitution went into effect on 3 May 1947, SCAPINs, technically issued as Imperial edicts before that date, were thenceforth implemented as Cabinet orders. GHQ produced 9,684 of these special instructions (2,204 SCAPINs and 7,480 administrative decrees), which were routed to the ministries or agencies concerned via the Central Liaison Office. On the basis of these directives, the government promulgated a total of 26 Imperial decrees and 867 Cabinet ordinances, and the National Diet enacted 804 laws. This reliance on fiat and top–down 'administrative guidance' was both ironic and counter-productive in light of the occupier's democratising mission. When GHQ set about strengthening the powers of the legislative branch in early 1946, one of its explicit objectives was 'to avoid the use of the undemocratic method of government by Imperial rescripts and ordinances'. But the very mechanism of occupation control unintentionally provided, as one scholar has expressed it, a 'working model of authoritarian governance' that was perhaps inevitable but nonetheless radically at odds with the Occupation's reformist mandate.[35]

Although GHQ staff sections relied heavily on SCAPINs, the bulk of these edicts were promulgated in the first year of occupation. In the early reform period, MacArthur's command could decide almost any issue clearly with a formal directive, but after 1947, with the duration of the occupation an unsettled question, such instruments were employed sparingly, for after independence, the government would be free to overturn anything it chose. In mid-July 1949, Washington ordered MacArthur's command to begin returning administrative powers to the government, and SCAPINs were rarely issued after that point.

Individual staff sections also generated memoranda and letters to their counterpart agencies in government. Section chiefs dispensed technical advice and made suggestions – 'non-commands with the force of commands' as one Occupationaire later described them. Government Section, for instance, urged the Foreign Ministry to dismiss certain officials for 'failing to show a proper spirit of cooperation towards Occupation policies'. (An infuriated Foreign Minister Yoshida demanded written instructions, thereby discouraging further interference.) SCAP's Public Health and Welfare Section insisted that a Welfare Ministry section chief be disciplined for questioning the wisdom of a minor proposal and the official resigned. Persuasion often proved as effective as fiat, but the line between the two could be thin. A dramatic illustration of this ambiguity occurred in December 1947 on the last day of the new Diet's first session. Parliamentary wrangling over an economic deconcentration bill had brought business to a halt. At midnight, Government Section's Justin Williams, who had been sent to observe the proceedings, stood up and proposed that the clock be stopped so that the quarrelling assembly might pass the bill before the session ended at midnight. Williams later claimed that this was not an order, simply a suggestion that the Diet follow an obscure British Parliamentary precedent. Failing to see the distinction, the Japanese legislators obediently stopped the clock (chapter 7).[36]

From mid-1946, with many basic programmes completed or well underway, MacArthur's staff increasingly sought the cooperation and advice of Japanese officials. After the early punitive phase of occupation, collaboration came to characterise the reform process, and socially minded bureaucrats, ad hoc advisory commissions and private interest groups exerted a greater influence on the formulation of policy. Mutual cooperation rather than edict or persuasion prevailed in the areas of women's rights, labour, education, religion and health and welfare.

When cooperation broke down, however, MacArthur's command could deploy more subtle means of winning compliance. One was the approval of government draft legislation by 'non-objection', such non-objection being withheld unless SCAP-proposed changes were introduced. This enabled GHQ to direct policy without being held responsible for actually doing so. Occupation authorities used this tactic, for example, to secure passage of a favourable land reform bill. Major Faubion Bowers, MacArthur's assistant military secretary, recalled many years later that on the surface everything was done through the Japanese. 'Our policy very clearly was to let the Japanese do it and keep our own noses clean in case there were repercussions. Tell "Japs" privately exactly what we want done, then watch them do it. That's the game we all had to play. It was most duplicitous and I didn't like it at all. I was appalled.'[37]

The government complied initially because the Potsdam terms obliged it to do so. Under duress, it had temporarily forfeited basic sovereign rights. Ultimately, the realisation of many early Occupation goals depended neither on fiat, persuasion or cooperation but on the proximity of Yankee bayonets. The most potent of MacArthur's many powers was that of armed intervention, and GHQ could, and did on occasion, threaten the use of military force to have its way. In January 1946, for instance, when Prime Minister Baron Shidehara Kijūrō and his Cabinet threatened to resign in protest of SCAP's Purge Directive, the Supreme Commander obliquely warned that he stood ready to appoint his own government. Shidehara backed down. On 31 January 1947, MacArthur invoked his authority as SCAP to ban a general strike by left-of-centre public- and private-sector unions planned for 1 February. In the summer of 1948, during a protracted labour dispute at the Tōhō Motion Pictures Studio in Tokyo, Eighth Army despatched troops to quell the disturbance.

In the final analysis, MacArthur's headquarters and Eighth Army garrison forces were synonymous. The Americans thought of themselves as inducing democracy, and in fact, reformist Japanese responded vigorously to SCAP's innovative projects. In key instances, however, the occupier's agenda was imposed, and Japan, as a vanquished country, had no recourse but to obey. General Order no. 1 of 2 September 1945 warned that failure to comply promptly with Allied instructions 'will incur drastic and summary punishment at the hands of Allied Military Authorities'. This was unavoidable and necessary, for in the absence of an army of occupation, GHQ and progressive Japanese could never have broken, even momentarily, the stranglehold of the immensely powerful and tenacious Old Order, with its ingrained habits of thought, entrenched political interests and steely grip on the machinery of state. Without the goad of an Allied military presence, Japan's postwar transformation could not have begun.

Military Government Teams

In Japan proper, the edifice of indirect rule reposed, at the regional, prefectural and local levels, on a substructure composed of Military Government units. Like the SCAP superstructure, these generally replicated the organisation of the prefectural and local governments with which they worked. Since occupation control was exercised through the central government, military teams were assigned the essential but secondary mission of local-level surveillance and reporting.

As Allied troops took up position across Japan, GHQ/AFPAC established Military Government (MG) Groups inside the G-1 staff sections of Sixth and Eighth armies and MG Companies at their respective division and regimental levels. When deployment was completed in October 1945, an independent Military Government Section was created in both armies at headquarters and corps levels. Under each MG Section, MG Groups and MG Companies were set up to work in tandem with prefectural and local governments. Officers qualified for civil affairs tasks were transferred out of line units and assigned to the newly created organisations. In December 1945, Eighth Army relieved Sixth Army of its occupation duties and assumed control of all MG activities, and, on 1 January 1946, it became responsible for the operational aspects of military surveillance. Military Government Headquarters, Eighth Army, was to observe and report to SCAP on local-level compliance with the flood of central government directives implementing Occupation policies. In June 1946, the MG Groups were upgraded to regional headquarters, and MG Companies became prefectural teams.[38] Military Government was now structured in a five-tier pyramid with GHQ/SCAP at the top followed by Eighth Army MG Headquarters, the MG Sections of I and IX Corps, regional MG headquarters, and prefectural MG Teams (see Fig. 6).

GHQ retained the term military government for its purported chilling effect, although it was soon apparent that such psychological ploys were unnecessary. MG units were expressly prohibited from initiating corrective action or interfering in the activities of any Japanese agency. Their task was to observe, collect information, make inspections and report regularly to higher headquarters. When MG Teams discovered that a SCAP policy was being ignored, improperly implemented or sabotaged, they were to report the details to their superiors but take no further action unless instructed. Once alerted by Eighth Army, GHQ would inform the central government of problems via the Central Liaison Office. SCAP issued a constant flow of queries and instructions, including direct orders in the form of Command Letters, to Eighth Army MG Headquarters in Yokohama, which relayed them to prefectural teams via corps-level MG Sections and MG regional headquarters. On rare occasions, however, Military Government Teams contested policy decisions by higher headquarters. In the autumn of 1948, for instance, Eighth Army Military Government Section attempted repeatedly to postpone elections for local boards of education, citing a lack of information and interest at the municipal level (GHQ overruled the Army). During the same period, Eighth Army, ordered to suppress displays of the North Korean flag, unsuccessfully demanded written orders

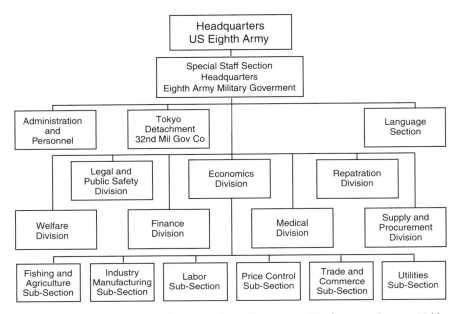

Figure 6. Organisation of Eighth Army Military Government Headquarters, January 1946.
(Source: *Reports of General MacArthur*, 1966, p. 202)

from GHQ (SCAP intelligence chiefs refused, insisting that only verbal instructions be issued).

The prefectural teams were the basic field units of occupation and, unlike Eighth Army and GHQ staff sections, were in close contact with Japanese from every walk of life. There were three types of teams – major, intermediate and minor – depending on the size and population of the prefecture to which they were assigned.[39] The staff organisations of MG units at all levels included the divisions of Economics, Civil Education, Legal and Government, Public Welfare, Civil Information, Public Health and Administration. Divisions were staffed by specialists responsible for overseeing such local government functions as natural resources; labour; commerce and trade; manufacturing and industry; finance and banking; civil information and education; religion; public health and welfare; and procurement and general administration. The typical prefectural team consisted of 7 officers, 7 Department of the Army civilians, 20 enlisted personnel and 50 specially qualified Japanese. Significantly, Japanese staff outnumbered American personnel by a ratio of roughly two to three, and it was they who did much of the team's leg-work and liaison with local inhabitants. Two areas of vital concern were the rationing of basic foodstuffs and tax collection, and here the MG Teams 'needled, cajoled and pressured' regional authorities to obey Occupation directives.[40] The Teams, together with tactical units, also cooperated with Japanese authorities in providing disaster relief, such as after the devastating earthquake that struck Ishikawa and Fukui Prefectures on 28 June 1948.

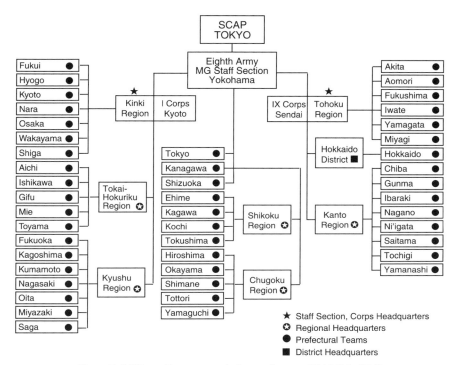

Figure 7. Military Government in Japan, January 1946–July 1948.
(Source: *Reports of General MacArthur*, 1966, p. 202)

The tremor levelled Fukui City, destroying 36,000 homes and killing some 3,800 people.

In actual practice, the Military Government system proved cumbersome. Lacking sufficient authority to operate effectively, MG personnel in the field frequently exceeded their mandate, intervening directly in local affairs. The periodic overhaul of Military Government, with its resulting organisational dislocations and personnel turbulence, also may have encouraged local teams to take matters into their own hands. MG 'suggestions', typically beginning with the words 'you should . . . ', were interpreted as direct orders by Japanese officials, as indeed they often were intended. Nozaki Hirofumi, an interpreter for the Osaka Regional Military Government Team, recalls that the MG group once ordered the dismissal of a municipal employee for ignoring a request to revise the municipal budget.[41] MG Teams also organised crackdowns on tax evasion and black-market activities, and heavy-handed attempts to settle labour disputes occasionally were reported. In November 1945, MacArthur issued a Command Letter expressly prohibiting Eighth Army interference in labour actions, yet in October 1946, an Eighth Army Military Police unit barged in on union-management talks at the Tōshiba Electric Corporation and locked out all but a handful of negotiators until a settlement could be reached. In late January 1947, a major labour federation complained to GHQ that Eighth Army had browbeaten union leaders in Fukuoka Prefecture into accepting management's terms, that miners in Hokkaido had been ordered by local MG units to call off a strike, that Occupation forces had removed machinery from a plant in Tochigi Prefecture to frustrate workers' plans to take over production, and that US troops had brandished machine guns during a labour rally in Kyushu to dissuade local miners from pursuing their grievances.[42]

A spectacular example of local military interference was a 1949 proposal by the Tokai–Hokuriku Regional MG Team to fingerprint ethnic Koreans. The request by the Team's Legal Division went directly to the regional CLO branch and, incredibly, appears to have bypassed Eighth Army MG headquarters altogether. The Central Liaison branch forwarded the plan to the Foreign Ministry which relayed it to the Attorney General's Office for a legal opinion. In late September 1949, the Attorney General rejected the scheme, noting that in Japan only criminal suspects were fingerprinted. Imposing this measure on Koreans alone, he warned, would produce 'untoward consequences'. Indeed, his Office had just banned the League of Korean Residents in Japan for political reasons and was reluctant to antagonise the Korean community further (chapter 10).[43]

From late 1948, the Occupation began to relax administrative controls, phase out monitoring operations and allow local authorities greater latitude of action. On 28 July 1949, SCAP eliminated its MG infrastructure. Military Government was redesignated Civil Affairs, the country was divided into eight Civil Affairs regions under Civil Affairs Regional Teams, and a small core of trained CA cadres began replacing more than 2,000 MG officers. The number of regional and prefectural CA Teams was reduced, and their administrative duties were substantially lightened. In November of that year, 45 prefectural Civil Affairs Teams were disbanded, and at the end of the year, I and IX Corps Civil Affairs Sections also were dissolved. In January 1950, SCAP established the Civil Affairs Section (CAS) as a special GHQ staff group and assumed direct control of the Regional Teams. Surveillance and reporting responsibilities passed from Eighth Army directly to GHQ. The CA Regional Teams were terminated on 30 June 1951 and their remaining responsibilities turned over to local governmental agencies.[44]

A DIVIDED OCCUPATION

SCAP's system of remote governance operated only in Japan proper and did not extend to Okinawa, which was administered directly, top to bottom, by the US military, or to the Kuril Islands, which were under Soviet control. The two-power zonal occupation of Korea, endorsed by the Moscow Foreign Ministers' Conference of December 1945, was similar in genesis and process to the detachment of the Ogasawaras, Ryukyus and Kurils from Japan and the imposition there of direct military rule. A product of invasion and partition, the disposition of these outlying territories affords an ironic contrast with the liberal, unitary and indirect mode of control introduced to the Japanese main islands. These 'minor' areas experienced invasion, occupation and military administration as a single, unrelenting historical moment.

The Ogasawaras

The Ogasawara (Bonin) islands technically were the first of Japan's traditional home territories to be occupied by Allied forces. The chain of some 30 volcanic islets, which includes Iwo Jima, lies roughly 1,000 kilometres due south of Tokyo Bay. The islands were discovered by Ogasawara Sadayori, a Tokugawa lord, in 1593 and surveyed by the Bakufu government in 1675, but the first inhabitants were American, British and Hawai'ian seamen and whalers who established settlements there in the early nineteenth century (the alternate name for the island group, *Bonin*, is the corruption of a Japanese word meaning 'uninhabited'). The Tokugawa government claimed possession in 1862, and the Meiji state annexed the islands in 1876. In 1880, they were incorporated administratively into Metropolitan Tokyo.

In 1944, approximately 7,700 Japanese lived there, engaged mainly in fishing and sugar-cane production. As the US Navy's Central Pacific offensive drew near, Imperial forces evacuated 6,900 islanders to Honshu. Following the capture of Iwo Jima in March 1945, the US Navy established military government over the islands and later deported the remaining 800 islanders to Japan proper to make way for expanded military facilities. The US Army, too, garrisoned troops in the islands, incorporating the Ogasawaras into the Marianas–Bonins Command. On 29 January 1946, a Government Section directive (SCAPIN-677: 'Government and Administrative Separation of Certain Outlying Areas from Japan') arbitrarily detached the island group from Japan. That year, Navy Military Government allowed 135 former inhabitants of Western ancestry to return to the islands, but other Ogasawarans were not repatriated until June 1968, some sixteen years after the end of the Occupation, following bitter and protracted protests by the displaced populace. Today, the American military continues to operate bases there.[45]

Military rule in Okinawa

Unlike the Ogasawaras, the Ryukyus are a heavily populated island chain with a long and proud history. The archipelago consists of four island groups: Amami in the north, Okinawa in the centre and Miyako and Yaeyama in the south. From the fourteenth through the sixteenth centuries, an independent kingdom centred on the Shuri Court in Okinawa unified the Ryukyus, which became a major trade hub linking the markets of China, Japan and Korea with Southeast Asia. In 1609, Kyushu's Satsuma Clan annexed the Amami islands outright and forced the Ryukyu Kingdom to accept tributary status. A period of dual subordination, during which the Ryukyus paid tribute to China and to the Satsumas, lasted until 1879, when the Meiji state seized the islands, abolished the Kingdom and made Okinawa a Japanese prefecture. With the so-called Ryukyu disposition, Okinawa became Japan's first modern colony. Ryukyuans and China's Qing Court refused to recognise Japanese suzerainty, however, and this dispute became an underlying cause of the Sino-Japanese War of 1894–5, through which Japan acquired its second colony, Formosa. Accorded semi-colonial treatment, with special restrictions and a colonial adminis-tration, Okinawa did not become a bona fide prefecture until 1920, following two decades of assimilation policies.[46]

The Ryukyus are not blessed with an abundance of arable land, and modern development was slow, forcing tens of thousands of islanders to migrate to metro-politan Japan and abroad, to the Philippines, Hawai'i and the Americas. During the Asia–Pacific War, the archipelago became a vast military base for the Imperial Army, and a sacrificial pawn in Japan's struggle for survival. The Allied invasion of April–June 1945 decimated Okinawa's indigenous population, destroyed Shuri Castle and other cultural assets, severed contact with the Japanese home islands (*hondo*) and left the local economy a shambles. In their preparation for the final assault on Japan, American authorities bulldozed abandoned villages to clear a way for the construction of B-29 air strips, military roads and storage depots. By late May 1945, 10 of 22 planned runways were under construction. The fighting had largely destroyed Okinawa's intricate system of irrigation ditches. Now Army engineers scraped off good topsoil for landfill and paved prime farmland, destroying the islanders' tradi-tional means of subsistence.[47] With no home to return to, Okinawans found them-selves squeezed into some 40 refugee camps totally dependent on the US military for food and clothing. Refugees were forced to relocate as the tactical needs of Army units changed. By 31 August 1945, roughly 250,000 Okinawans had been transferred to new camps, some of them several times, and as late as the spring of 1946, 130,000 were still without homes. Ryukyuans were not allowed to move freely inside the archipelago until March 1947, and travel to the main islands was forbidden.[48]

An ambiguous legal status
The post-surrender status of the Ryukyus had been discussed at Cairo in late November 1943, where Chiang Kai-shek proposed that China occupy the islands with the United States and administer them jointly under an international trustee-ship. A few days later, at the Teheran Conference, Josef Stalin told Roosevelt that the Ryukyus, forcibly annexed by Japan in 1879, should be 'returned' to China.[49] The Potsdam Proclamation of 26 July 1945, however, did not mention the island chain. On 31 March, with the capture of the Keramas, Admiral Chester Nimitz issued US Navy Military Government Proclamation no. 1, placing that territory under US military administration according to the law of belligerent occupation. As other areas of the archipelago fell, they, too, passed to American control.

The State Department, however, questioned the wisdom of retaining Okinawa and recommended that the islands be demilitarised and returned to Japan as one of the 'minor islands' over which Tokyo might maintain sovereignty as specified in the Potsdam terms. The danger of an international dispute over territory was greater, it reasoned, than any benefit that might accrue from the islands' future military potential. On 10 September 1945, the Joint Chiefs of Staff expressed their 'grave concern' to President Truman over the proposed return of the archipelago. The JCS memorandum produced a stalemate that would not be broken until the autumn of 1948, when Cold War concerns would convince the State Department to support a long-term American armed presence there (chapter 10). On 29 January 1946, a SCAP directive (SCAPIN-677) formally separated the Ryukyus, the Ogasawaras and other former territories south of 30 degrees North latitude from the Japanese mainland. Ironically, the Amami Islands north of Okinawa were included in the US military's Ryukyuan jurisdiction although they belonged administratively to Kagoshima Prefecture in Kyushu.[50]

Once established, however, military government in the Ryukyus lacked a clear mandate or régime of control. The military campaign officially ended on 2 July 1945, and initially, the Okinawa Group remained under Navy administration while the Amami, Miyako and Yaeyama Groups were placed under the Army's operational command. On 18 July the Navy transferred control to AFPAC, but Japan's surrender and the start of the main occupation less than a month later taxed the Army's resources, and on 21 September, the Navy again assumed responsibility, establishing the Military Government of the Ryukyu Islands. Finally, on 1 July 1946, the Army took charge one last time, reorganising the Okinawa Base Command as the Ryukyus Command.[51] One year later, on 1 January 1947, AFPAC was restructured as the Far East Command (FECOM), and a unified Ryukyus Command, complete with Military Government, was placed under the jurisdiction of GHQ/FECOM in Tokyo.

Under the new régime, Washington directives concerning the Ryukyus were issued by President Truman and transmitted via the Pentagon to MacArthur as Far East Commander. GHQ/FECOM routed Washington's orders to the Commanding General, Ryukyus Command, who passed them to the Military Government. In Tokyo, Ryukyuan affairs originally had been handled by the Korean Division in SCAP's Government Section. In February 1947, the Korean Division was abolished, and responsibility for military government in Korea and the Ryukyus was delegated to the Korean-Ryukyus Division, which was attached to the SCAP Deputy Chief of Staff. Finally, on 6 September 1948, MacArthur created the Ryukyus Military Government Section inside GHQ/FECOM.

The archipelago quickly became the forgotten stepchild of the Occupation. One historian has compared its postwar fate under US military administration to that of Asia under the wartime Greater East Asia Co-Prosperity Sphere.[52] A closer analogy is the Kuril Islands under Soviet rule.

Soviet rule in the Kurils
In annexing the Ogasawaras and the Ryukyus, the United States initially could claim military necessity. The Soviet Union occupied the Kurils, including the four island groups closest to Japan, to collect on a promise made by Roosevelt at Yalta and then defaulted on by Truman. The Potsdam Proclamation skirted the territorial issue by

limiting Japanese sovereignty to the four major islands 'and such minor islands' as the Allied powers should determine. Stalin pointed to the Yalta protocol and the Potsdam language as justification for occupying and annexing the northern archipelago. On 2 September 1945, as discussed earlier, the Marshal announced that the Kurils had been 'transferred' to the Soviet Union, and on 20 September, Moscow unilaterally declared them Soviet territory and nationalised all property there. On 2 February 1946, the islands were attached administratively to the Khabarovsk Region, and in January 1947, they were transferred to the independent Sakhalin District. Finally, on 25 February 1947, the Soviet Constitution was amended to incorporate the Kurils into the USSR, making their inhabitants Soviet citizens.[53]

During the war, Japan had been prepared to barter away the central and northern Kurils in return for a Soviet mediated peace (chapter 1), but the southernmost islands had been an integral part of Hokkaido since 1869 and were non-negotiable. Tokyo immediately contested the Soviet seizure as a breach of the Potsdam terms and international law. Despite repeated protests from Tokyo, however, Washington failed to oppose the takeover.[54] MacArthur's headquarters also accepted the fait accompli. SCAPIN-677 (29 January 1946), which detached the Ogasawaras and the Ryukyus from Japanese territory, also divested Japan of all administrative rights over the Kurils, the Habomais and Shikotan. This policy was confirmed by SCAPINs 1033 and 1033/1 of 22 June 1946 and 23 December 1948, respectively, which instructed Japanese fishing boats to restrict their activities to waters south of the Habomai Group. These directives effectively recognised Soviet possession of the northern arc. Washington and GHQ had acquiesced in a divided occupation.

Local officials in Hokkaido could do little but implore central authorities to take action, and at their urging, Tokyo lodged formal protests with GHQ via the Central Liaison Office, but to no avail. Official Japanese interest was motivated in part by an immediately practical consideration, for the government reportedly hoped to include the Kurils in the electoral register for the 1946 Lower House elections. That concern evaporated, however, in late January 1946, when, less than three months before April's general elections, SCAPIN-677 removed the Kurils from the polling lists.[55]

As a last resort, the Mayor of Nemuro, Andō Sekiten, visited Tokyo on 1 December 1945 to make a personal appeal to MacArthur. Andō carried with him a petition addressed to 'His Excellency, General MacArthur' and signed by 30,000 Hokkaido residents. It noted that the Soviet-occupied Habomais administratively were a part of Nemuro City and that Shikotan, Kunashiri and Etorofu, Japanese territory since feudal times, had been settled and inhabited by Japanese for five successive generations. The petition denounced the injustice of Soviet military rule, lamented the islanders' plight and urged the Supreme Commander to place the Habomais and the southern Kurils under US military control. As had earlier representations, the Mayor's entreaty fell on deaf ears.

The Sakhalin and Kuril repatriations

MacArthur sidestepped the Kuril territorial issue, but his staff responded immediately to pleas to return Japanese nationals stranded on Sakhalin. Occupation authorities first broached the question to the Soviet Union in October 1945, but Moscow did not welcome this 'intrusion'. During the conflict, Russians had been pulled from the island to perform various war-related duties, and the Japanese civilians there represented a vital labour resource. The Kremlin dragged its feet on the issue until several thousand Soviet settlers could be relocated to Sakhalin, and an agreement on civilian repatriation was not reached until late 1946. From December of that year through July 1949, more than 290,000 Japanese non-combatants were allowed to leave the island. This programme was finally extended to the Kurils, including the four southern islands, and in July 1947, the first group of Japanese arrived from Etorofu. Repatriation from the last of the southern Kurils, Kunashiri, was completed in October 1948, by which time a total of 170,000 had been transported to Japan. By July 1949, all Japanese had been evacuated from the Kuril chain.[56]

Not included in that massive transfer were an estimated 40,000 to 60,000 Koreans, who formed the bulk of Sakhalin's unskilled labour force. With the surrender of Japanese forces, Koreans in the northern arc were declared liberated nationals and freed from colonial rule, but while they now enjoyed certain ethnic and cultural rights, they remained virtual prisoners of the new régime. Without their labour, the economy would have collapsed in the wake of the Japanese exodus. Moreover, most Koreans were from southern Korea, then under US military occupation. Stalin saw no merit in delivering a prime labour resource to his Cold War rival. Japan, on the other hand, having forcibly relocated these workers to Sakhalin, had a moral obligation to secure their repatriation to Korea, but Tokyo remained silent on the issue. MacArthur's staff first learned of the problem in late 1945 after receiving petitions from Sakhalin Koreans. In 1947, a group of south Koreans asked SCAP to negotiate the return of this captive population, and in 1949, shortly after the Republic of Korea established a diplomatic mission in Tokyo, Seoul raised the issue again. On each occasion, the Americans discussed the problem with their Japanese and Soviet counterparts, but Japanese officials affected complete indifference, going only so far as to provide SCAP with population estimates that were greatly understated, and the Soviets ignored the US representations altogether. Steps would not be taken to resolve this issue until the 1990s (chapter 11).[57]

THE GARRISON FORCES

The Army of Occupation

The military occupation of the home islands proceeded in two phases. The first commenced on 28 August 1945 with the arrival at Atsugi of the US advance landing party and continued through the end of December. During this time, combat troops fanned out across Japan, military facilities were constructed, Allied prisoners of war were released and Imperial forces were disarmed and demobilised. The second phase began in January 1946, its objective to establish the surveillance and control mechanisms necessary to sustain a long-term occupation. This involved the reorganisation, redeployment and deactivation of American combat units.

As it became clear that Occupation goals could be met without recourse to military force, at MacArthur's behest, Washington slashed troop strength from 430,000 in late 1945 to about 200,000 in 1946. In 1947, that figure was pared further to 120,000 and by 1948 had dropped to 102,000. In 1949, the Cold War and growing social unrest in Japan prompted the Pentagon to boost US forces to 126,000, but this level fell to 115,500 in 1950 following the outbreak of fighting in Korea and massive troop transfers to the Korean peninsula. Between 1951 and 1952, however, with Japan now a rear staging area for the war, American military strength grew steadily, and when the San Francisco Peace Treaty went into effect in April 1952, 260,000 GIs were stationed on Japanese soil.

Washington complained loudly about the cost to the US taxpayer of maintaining this armed presence, and in 1948 alone, occupation forces drained the US Treasury of $600 million – about twice what it cost to occupy southern Korea (but less than half the outlay for Germany). In fact, however, the Japanese government was compelled to bear the brunt of Occupation costs, which accounted for 30 per cent of the regular budget in 1946 and remained one of the single largest budget items in the years that followed. These very substantial – and to the Japanese, unexpected and onerous – disbursments were disguised as 'war termination costs' or 'other expenses'. The State Department's top policy expert, George F. Kennan, was appalled when he arrived in Tokyo in early 1948 to discover 17,000 new housing units under construction for US personnel at government expense while millions of Japan's own war-displaced remained homeless.[58]

Sixth and Eighth armies constituted the primary military force in the early months following the surrender. Eichelberger's Eighth Army began deploying in Japan in late August and continued through September, occupying Hokkaido and the northern half of Honshu. Krueger's Sixth Army arrived in late September and took over southern Honshu and Shikoku. Eighth Army headquarters were established in Yokohama, and Eichelberger and his staff took up residence in the New Grand Hotel; Krueger set up Sixth Army command operations in the Daiken Building in Kyoto, lodging his staff in the Miyako Hotel. Sixth and Eighth Armies were reinforced by Marine contingents attached to the US Third and Fifth Fleets. In December 1945, Sixth Army was relieved of its occupation duties, and in January 1946, it was deactivated, leaving Eighth Army as the main garrison force.

In January 1947, AFPAC was reorganised as the Far East Command (FECOM). This super-command included, in addition to Eighth Army, the Far East Air Force, the Fifth Air Force, US Naval Forces in the Far East, Naval Activities Japan (NAJAP) and the air, army and naval components of the British Commonwealth Occupation Force. As FECOM commander, MacArthur's sphere of responsibility was enlarged enormously to include the Ryukyu Command, the Marianas–Bonin Command and the Philippine Command. The Ryukyus Command, as discussed earlier, was detached from the main occupation forces, with GHQ/FECOM exercising sole authority, and Okinawa was placed under the US Tenth Army, whose commander became military governor of the islands.[59]

Women in uniform

Allied forces in Japan included women's units, a fact that is not widely understood in Japan and one that most historians of the Occupation have ignored. By the spring of 1946, MacArthur's headquarters had only 453 women to 3,760 men, a ratio of eight to one, and in the field, female staff were even scarcer,[60] and with few exceptions, they found themselves confined to subordinate roles and forced to deal with traditional male attitudes. Their presence in Japan, where equality of the sexes was an alien notion, was significant, however, and their small numbers belie their importance.

The US Army had recruited female volunteers early in the war to remedy man-power shortages and perform essential non-combat work. In May 1942, following the British Commonwealth example, it set up the Women's Auxiliary Army Corps (WAAC), which was run by the Army as a support group. WAACs did not have the same legal protections as male personnel, received less pay and, if wounded, had fewer benefits. This situation was remedied with the establishment in July 1943 of the Women's Army Corps (WAC) as a regular Army command. The US Navy and Air Force also put women in uniform. Naval forces included the Women Accepted for Voluntary Emergency Service (WAVES), established in July 1942, and SPARs, female coast guard units created in November 1942, which took their name from the Coast Guard credo, *Semper Paratus* (Always Ready). The Navy inaugurated women's Marine units in February 1943.[61]

By the summer of 1945, there were 280,000 American women in uniform world-wide, 100,000 of them WACs. At war's end, many were demobilised, but 11 WAC units were assigned duty overseas, two of them in Japan. The first WAC detachments were deployed to Japan in October 1945. In September 1947, MacArthur invited WAC Director Colonel Mary A. Hallaren to inspect these outfits. They were the 8000th WAC Battalion, which included 150 women assigned to Eighth Army in Yokohama, and the 8225th WAC Battalion with more than 400 working at GHQ/AFPAC in Tokyo. With the onset of the Korean War, the number of uniformed women grew rapidly. In 1950, there were only about 600 WACs in Japan, but by mid-1951 that figure had more than quadrupled, reaching 2,600, and the number of detachments had grown from two to six.

These soldiers served as secretaries, drivers, wireless operators, intelligence opera-tives, engineers, nurses, doctors, hospital administrators and logistics specialists. Al-though most were assigned duties in the Tokyo and Yokohama areas, in 1951, a WAC group was established in Okinawa. Female units also included Japanese Americans. The first Nisei WAC contingent completed training at the Military Intelligence

Photo 16. A WAC contingent disembarks at Yokohama, 18 October 1946. The presence of Allied women in uniform was surprising to many Japanese (Kyodo).

Service Language School in November 1945, and in January 1946, 13 graduates (including one Chinese American) were assigned to Japan. Others followed as the Occupation progressed. Many of these individuals worked with local Military Government teams and played pivotal roles in explaining Japanese customs to the teams and maintaining good relations with local inhabitants. Other military women in Japan included WAVES, Marines and, following the creation of the Air Force Nurse Corps and Medical Specialist Corps in 1949, Air Force personnel.[62]

The role of service women in the Occupation is uncharted territory, but the contributions of a few exceptional individuals are well documented. An outstanding example is Army Lieutenant Ethel B. Weed who arrived in Japan with the first WAC units in October 1945. Appointed Women's Information Officer in SCAP's Civil Information and Education Section (CI&E), Weed was the chief architect of a de facto 'women's policy alliance' inside GHQ that became intimately involved in reform measures affecting women (chapter 7), and in September 1946, the War Department awarded her the Army Commendation Ribbon for her efforts on behalf of women's rights.[63] WAC Captain Eileen R. Donovan and Navy Lieutenant Commander Verna A. Carley, a WAVE with a PhD in education, are other CI&E officers who left their mark on the Occupation (chapter 4).

WACs assigned to Military Government teams also played prominent roles. Lieutenant Carmen Johnson is a typical example. Born in Wisconsin, Johnson graduated from Northern Illinois State Teachers' College, taught elementary school and worked as a Girl Scout administrator. During the war, she served in the Women's Army Auxiliary Corps with the rank of Lieutenant, working as a radar analyst in combat intelligence. After the war, she volunteered to become a clerk typist with the Fifth Air Force in Nagoya, Japan. In 1947, Johnson was appointed Women's Affairs Officer for the Shikoku Regional Military Government Team, becoming one of 27 women selected by Ethel Weed and her colleagues in GHQ to serve with the civil education branch of local MG teams across Japan. Their job was to educate Japanese women about their rights under the Constitution and encourage them to exercise their new democratic freedoms. The women chosen to do this vital work became role models for many Japanese, invigorating the postwar women's movement at the grass roots. In August 1948, women's affairs specialists were reintegrated into local MG teams as assistant civil education officers and assigned to work with their Japanese counterparts in prefectural and municipal governments.[64]

Not all of the women who served in the Occupation wore uniforms. The Army also hired female Department of the Army Civilians (DACs) to work at GHQ or serve as education and welfare officers in MG teams. Rare individuals, such as Beate Sirota (chapter 6), helped to win equal rights for women, but all of MacArthur's staff sections benefited from the talented female staff who held jobs ranging from secretaries to research assistants, public welfare specialists and intelligence analysts. GHQ and MG teams also employed large numbers of Japanese women as interpreters, translators, typists, artists and assistants in women's and youth affairs.[65]

African-American troops

America's ethnic minorities volunteered for military service in disproportionately large numbers, fighting in the Pacific alongside their white comrades-in-arms, but only African American soldiers were rigidly segregated in all-black units. The first black unit to ship overseas was the 24th Infantry Regiment, which was sent to the Pacific in April 1942. Commissioned in 1866, it was one of the Army's oldest African-American commands, tracing its history to the Civil War. The 24th Infantry served in the Solomons, including Guadalcanal and Bougainville; did garrison duty on Saipan and Tinian; and in Okinawa took part in the Keramas campaign. Apart from occasional mopping up operations, the Regiment regularly was assigned stevedore and other service tasks, white officers considering them better suited 'by temperament' to labour details than to fox holes. Bill Stevens, a black GI who fought in the Pacific, later recalled: 'Black troops were just naturally suspected of cowardice, stealing, rape, the whole racial stereotype. White commanders had no respect for black soldiers and it was obvious. Likewise, it followed that white soldiers had no respect for their black brothers in arms. In our turn, we had utter contempt for them, officers and enlisted men.'[66]

In postwar Japan, too, black GIs served ably but remained separate and unequal. The 24th Infantry Regiment was assigned garrison duty with the 25th Infantry

Division stationed in the Kansai area. The Regiment by then was the largest African-American unit in the US Army. The official Occupation attitude towards the 24th and other black commands was summed up in a secret report by MacArthur's Chief of Staff Lieutenant General Edward M. Almond. Well-known for his racial bias, Almond wrote in November 1947 that black troops required white officers to perform well but should be kept off the front lines and used for rear-area supply duties. MacArthur's attitudes towards black soldiers, too, were dismissive and paternalistic. It is not surprising then that, when President Truman issued Executive Order 9981 on 26 July 1948 establishing the principle of equality in the armed forces 'without regard to race, color, religion or national origin' and ordered all military units to integrate, the Supreme Commander refused to comply. The racial integration of US forces in Japan would have to await the arrival of General Matthew B. Ridgway, who implemented the presidential directive in 1951 (by which time the war in Korea had made integration a military necessity).[67]

Black soldiers in Japan suffered severe morale problems. By 1946, the 24th Infantry Regiment had become, in the words of one African-American officer, a 'dumping ground' for poorly trained, unmotivated newcomers, many without high school diplomas, serving under hostile or indifferent white officers. Eighth Army reserved all field positions in its black units for whites, permitting black lieutenants and captains to hold only platoon and company commands. Manipulating reductions in force, it gradually pared the percentage of black officers from 50 to 40 per cent. African Americans were not promoted at the same pace as white soldiers and were quartered as far from major urban centres as possible, where transportation was poor. 'All aspects of Jim Crow were practiced', reminisced Charles Bussey, a black officer. Enlisted men's clubs and off-duty facilities were segregated, and black soldiers were barred from white recreation areas. In Tokyo, four swimming pools were placed at the disposal of Occupation troops, but three of them were off-limits to black GIs. Racial tensions ran high in Tokyo and Kobe, and inter-racial fights were a common occurrence. General Eichelberger blamed these disturbances on African-American soldiers who, he said, 'liked to get out at night in the Mohammedan heaven furnished by some millions of Japanese girls', and suggested that black soldiers were responsible for the low ebb of morale in Eighth Army ranks.[68]

Japanese society inherited white attitudes towards African Americans, which conformed neatly to its own concepts of racial and ethnic hierarchy. To most Japanese, whites, too, were an alien presence, but whiteness was 'normative and privileged', being viewed through the distorting lens of victorious and ascendant Western culture and values. Blackness represented a more radical and regressive 'otherness', and images of black Americans were drawn from the repository of racial stereotypes generated by Western civilisation during its 400 years of global expansion. African Americans in Japan, then, were defined not by their association with Western culture but by the colour of their skin, both by the Japanese and by the white occupier.[69]

Thus, black GIs experienced discrimination both on base and off. But in the off-base establishments where they felt at home, a vital creolised counter-culture grew up. Many of Japan's leading postwar jazz artists and popular entertainers got their start in this marginalised *demi-monde* of drugs, booze and black-marketeering where the creative juices could flow freely, undisturbed by convention and the prying eyes of whites. Moreover, many African-American soldiers sympathised with the sufferings of the Japanese and related better to the culture of defeat than their white comrades.[70]

The British Commonwealth Occupation Force

Although overwhelmingly American, the army of occupation was a multi-national force. The British Commonwealth Occupation Force (BCOF) arrived in Japan in early February 1946 with 36,000 effectives, men and women, and by August, troop strength had grown to some 39,000, eventually surpassing 40,000. Stationed in southwestern Honshu and Shikoku, at full strength, the Force comprised nearly one quarter of all garrison personnel. Until recently, however, this echelon's role in the Occupation has not been widely understood in Japan. In part, this is due to the perception that the Allied Supreme Command was an exclusively American undertaking. SCAP's censorship policies, which outlawed coverage of Allied military organisations and troop movements, also are to blame. Although the Force played a relatively minor part, its presence enables us to frame the Occupation in a broader historical perspective and clarify divergences in American and Commonwealth policy towards Japan. That non-American soldiers, including Asians, were in daily contact with Japanese at the local level during this period is worthy of particular note.[71]

In late May 1945, British Foreign Minister Anthony Eden asked Prime Minister Churchill to approve planning for a British role in the Allied invasion and postwar occupation of Japan. London proposed a mixed force of Australian, British, Canadian and Indian troops, but MacArthur baulked at the idea of including Indian soldiers for reasons of 'linguistic and administrative complication'. The General suggested instead the participation of a corps composed of Australian, British and Canadian amphibious units. At Potsdam in July, the Combined Joint Chiefs agreed to furnish an assault force consisting of the British Pacific Fleet, a British Commonwealth Force of three to five divisions and British tactical air units. With Japan's surrender in mid-August, 'Operation Downfall' was cancelled and 'Blacklist', the peace plan, went into effect. In October 1945, Australia, Britain and Canada agreed to contribute a joint expeditionary force to the Occupation. Britain asked New Zealand to furnish a brigade group as well, and in late August, Wellington concurred.

Although only a supporting part was envisaged, Commonwealth leaders considered participation essential to retain some influence in the postwar disposition of Japan. Britain and Australia, in particular, hoped to see their contribution rewarded with enhanced political clout and privileged opportunities for commerce in the postwar era (indeed, to MacArthur's consternation, they would work tirelessly

Photo 17. British Commonwealth Occupation Forces march through Shimonoseki City in Yamaguchi Prefecture, southwestern Japan, September 1946. The BCOF contributed some 40,000 troops to the Occupation, making it an Allied, rather than an exclusively American, operation (Mainichi).

to include Japan in the sterling bloc). Australia originally demanded an independent role and separate command responsibility and negotiated directly with MacArthur on the matter, much to the chagrin of the British high command. A compromise solution was worked out under which Australia would lead the Commonwealth team, the Australian Commander-in-Chief reporting both to Canberra and to London.[72]

Canada had intended to take part in the Allied invasion and in fact signed the Instrument of Surrender but ultimately did not join the Occupation. During the war, Canadian troops had defended Hong Kong and later fought alongside American, not British, forces. Casualties had been relatively light, and Ottawa harboured no special desire for retribution. Moreover, the government already had accepted a role in the occupation of Germany. Having promised Canadians a quick demobilisation, it looked askance at a costly military commitment in Asia that promised few benefits (although it gladly would have seen the US monopoly on trade with Japan broken).[73] Nonetheless, Canada played an ancillary role, occupying a seat on the Far Eastern Commission in Washington, nominating a justice and prosecutor for the International Military Tribunal for the Far East (IMTFE) and signing the 1951 San Francisco Peace Treaty. During the Korean War, Canadian troops would be stationed on Japanese soil, although not as part of the Occupation.

New Zealand's participation reflected a new assertiveness in international relations that had earned the country the reputation of 'a small power rampant'. Wellington was determined to preserve its British Commonwealth defence ties, then the only guarantee of long-term external security. The need in the immediate aftermath of war to solidify Commonwealth trade relations *vis-à-vis* American economic expansion into Asia and the Pacific was another consideration. Kiwi units did not play a prominent role in the Pacific fighting, but HMNZS *Achilles* and HMNZS *Gambia* performed important early post-surrender duties in and around Japan, the latter, anchored in Tokyo Bay, representing the Royal New Zealand Navy at the surrender ceremony. Initially, New Zealand drew its occupation forces from the seasoned New Zealand Division, which had waged bitter campaigns in the Middle East and Italy. Between 1946 and 1948, Wellington contributed an Army brigade, dubbed the J Force, or Jayforce (New Zealand Expeditionary Force – Japan), together with elements of the Royal New Zealand Air Force, for a total cumulative military commitment of 12,000 men and women. Included in the Jayforce was a Maori contingent of some 270 soldiers organised in sub-units based on traditional tribal divisions. Prior to the Korean War, Occupation duty was New Zealand's primary foreign relations commitment.[74]

India, which had fought the Japanese in India, Burma, Malaya, Hong Kong and elsewhere in Southeast Asia, actively lobbied for an occupation role, both to bolster its prestige internationally and to ensure new trade opportunities. Later, New Delhi demanded, and received, a seat on the Far Eastern Commission as well as representation on the IMTFE. The days of the British Raj were numbered, and India's military leaders welcomed a chance to display their abilities, enhance political clout at home and prepare for an independent Indian Army. Moreover, India's foreign policy was based on a combination of Gandhian non-violence and the neutralist pan-Asian idealism of Jawaharlal Nehru. In contrast to Australian and New Zealand statesmen, who took a hard line on Japan, Indian leaders urged a policy of leniency and reconciliation. Participation in the Occupation eventually prompted India, which embraced a broader Asian viewpoint, to take a critical view of SCAP, especially after 1948 and the Occupation's rightward reorientation. Disagreement with Washington's Far East policy ultimately led New Delhi to refuse to sign the 1951 Peace Treaty with Japan.[75] (India signed a separate treaty in 1952.)

The first Commonwealth Force Commander was Lieutenant General (afterwards Sir) John Northcott, the former Australian Army Chief of Staff. He was replaced in mid-June 1946 by Lieutenant General (later Sir) Horace Robertson, who served until November 1951, when Lieutenant General W. Bridgeford assumed leadership. The Commonwealth Commander was under the operational control of Eighth Army and responsible to GHQ, but he also reported to the Commonwealth Joint Chiefs of Staff at Victoria Barracks, Melbourne on policy and administrative questions. Liaison with MacArthur's headquarters was provided by the British Commonwealth Sub-Area in Tokyo. The Force was assigned to the southwestern Chugoku region, relieving Eighth Army I Corps troops in Shimane, Yamaguchi, Tottori, Okayama and the island of Shikoku for duty in Kyushu and elsewhere.[76]

On 1 February 1946, the first BCOF contingent arrived in Kure from Hong Kong aboard the Australian cruiser HMAS *Hobart*. By June, a total of 39,000 BCOF troops had been deployed in southwestern Honshu, with large detachments in Kure and Fukuyama cities. At the height of the Occupation, the BCOF boasted more than

Photo 18. The BCOF high command and other dignitaries attend a ceremonial marching of the colours. At the far right is Sir Alvery Gascoigne, head of the British Liaison Mission in Tokyo. In the middle sits BCOF Commander Lieutenant General Horace Robertson. From the left are General MacArthur's son Arthur, wife Jean and General Robert L. Eichelberger, Eighth Army Commander. Tokyo, 6 August 1947 (Kyodo).

40,000 men and women in uniform and employed half as many Japanese workers. Despite its usefulness, MacArthur held the BCOF to a very subaltern position in the Occupation. Consequently, the Force exercised military control over the areas under its jurisdiction but was barred from participating directly in any phase of military government. W. MacMahon Ball later recounted the frustration and bitterness felt by many BCOF staff officers. General Robertson, known as 'Red Robbie' for his flaming red hair and moustache, 'had thought of himself as being able to play an influential part in Japan but . . . he had a very junior status and he did not have power. He discovered that he had nothing to do.' The original idea, Ball said, was that the Occupation should bring improvements in democratic rights and modern education, but 'educational reform was left entirely to the Americans! Poor old Red Robbie. It was off limits to go into a school. He couldn't go into a school in his area. He had no authority at all.'[77]

The Force's paramount mission was to guard Allied installations and Japanese military facilities awaiting destruction and to control and dispose of Japanese armaments. Among its achievements was the destruction of weapons and ordinance, particularly Japan's main chemical warfare arsenal on Ōkunojima Island, where BCOF troops laboured six months to neutralise 18,000 tons of poison gases and vesicants. The Force also arranged the return from China, Formosa, Korea and the

Ryukyus of some 750,000 Imperial 'surrendered personnel' and ran the largest repatriation centres in the country.[78] It organised land, air and sea patrols to intercept black-marketeers and illegal immigrants from Korea. It also was responsible for guarding Allied diplomatic missions assigned to SCAP headquarters. In December 1946, facing military manpower shortages within the British Empire, notably in Malaya where a Communist insurgency was in progress, London pulled about one third of the British Contingent – some 3,000 soldiers – out of Japan. By February 1947, all remaining British troops had departed, leaving Indian, New Zealand and Australian forces to carry on. In October of that year, the Indian Contingent also withdrew, followed in late 1948 by the Jayforce. The Australians alone remained until the end of the Occupation, their zone of responsibility limited to Hiroshima Prefecture.

BCOF Headquarters originally was established at Etajima in the Inland Sea, site of the former Japanese Imperial Naval Academy, but was later moved to the port city of Kure in Hiroshima Prefecture. With a supply line that stretched some 9,700 kilometres from Australia to Japan, the Force became a completely autonomous, self-sustaining Commonwealth community that in its heyday included some 700 Australian, British and Indian families for whom housing, shops, schools and hospitals were constructed.[79]

A multi-cultural legacy
Indian soldiers with BRINDJAP (British and Indian Troops – Japan) initially were led by British officers, and companies were divided into all-Hindu and all-Muslim units. The Indian Contingent was first assigned to Tottori and Shimane Prefectures but later took over many of the responsibilities of the departing British. Its main duties consisted of insuring internal security, combating black-marketeering and smuggling and preventing the illegal entry of Koreans. Gurkhas from Nepal also mounted guard at the Imperial Palace and Allied missions in Tokyo, advertising the Forces' multi-ethnic composition. Following Indian independence in August 1947, the Contingent, which now accounted for nearly one third of Commonwealth forces, nationalised its officer corps. The Indian government withdrew its troops from Japan in October of that year, following the eruption of communal violence between Muslims and Hindus at home.

Indians in Japan shared many of the problems of black GIs. Australian troops, in particular, were notorious for their bigoted behaviour. An anti-Asian 'White Australia' policy was still in effect in their country, and in 1948, the Immigration Minister saw fit to warn Parliament that 'it would be the grossest act of public indecency to permit a Japanese of either sex to pollute Australian shores'. Such supremacist attitudes coloured not only Australian relationships with the 'conquered enemy' in Japan but also Australian views of the Indian troops they served with and whom they tended to regard as just another 'aboriginal underclass'. In August 1947, tensions erupted in a full-fledged race riot that climaxed in an armed clash between Indian and Australian sappers lasting several hours.[80]

Indians were sympathetic to the Japanese, who in turn found these Asian soldiers

more congenial than their Caucasian comrades. There was occasional discrimination, but many Japanese retained a residue of wartime pan-Asianism, and an affinity
developed between the two groups. Gurkhas, in particular, proved popular with
Japanese women, leading Australian MPs to enforce the fraternisation ban in Gurkha
areas with a heavy-handed zeal. Many Indian Occupationaires returned to an
independent homeland with a keen appreciation for the order and discipline of
Japanese society and its commitment to education, science and technology.[81]

With the departure of the New Zealand Jayforce in September 1948, there
remained only a relatively small number of Australian soldiers at Hiroshima engaged
primarily in liaison work. The bulk of the Australian force left Japan in December
1951. By staying until the end, Australia secured recognition as a Pacific power, but
for the other Commonwealth participants, occupation duty conferred few long-term
rewards. London pulled its troops out too quickly to ensure any lasting benefits,
commercial or political. Withdrawal was, in the words of a historian, 'merely the first
of a long series of postwar British military retreats'. Britain's exit unintentionally
strengthened Australia's ties to the United States and frustrated New Zealand's desire
to secure a place under the British defence umbrella. By the end of the Occupation,
Wellington, too, had recognised the United States, not Britain, as holding the key to
the country's security concerns.[82]

British scholars generally have tended to regard the BCOF as a fruitless and
extravagant exercise. The conclusion of a security agreement between Australia, New
Zealand and the United States (ANZUS) in September 1951 – both a sign and
consequence of waning British influence in Asia – sounded the knell for the Force.
The BCOF's presence, however, left a multi-cultural legacy that has yet to be fully
appreciated. The racial antagonism felt by some white soldiers towards Indian troops,
and the refusal of Indians as independence approached to tolerate second-class
treatment, dramatised to Japanese who came into contact with Commonwealth
troops the evils of Western colonialism. At the same time, the unusual mixture of
ethnic and national groups, with their 'kilts, hackles, kukris, mascot goats' and
sharing a common goal, was instructive and ironical. It was, as a British Japan expert
with the Force remarked, 'English, Scots, Welsh, Australians, New Zealander
"pakehas" and Maoris, Mahrattas, Gurkhas, Sikhs, Punjabi Mussulmans, Rajputs,
Hazarawals, Jats, Madrassis and Bengalis serving together under the same flag in the
last gasp of an Empire which would never be seen again'.[83]

With the Korean War in 1950, the BCOF, by then a skeleton presence, was
infused with new life. A Commonwealth Division (Australia, Britain, Canada and
New Zealand) was created in Korea based on the BCOF model, and it used BCOF
facilities in Japan for training, reinforcement and supply. The Canadian component,
for instance, consisted of some 1,000 soldiers – mainly reinforcements and wounded
combatants. Since they were not part of the Occupation, and because Japan was not
a belligerent, armed Canadians on Japanese soil posed a delicate legal and diplomatic
problem. The British Commonwealth Occupation Force was formally disbanded
on 28 April 1952 when the San Francisco Peace Treaty came into effect but was

immediately reborn as the British Commonwealth Forces, Korea, which included the Canadian Contingent. The new Commonwealth Forces negotiated the continued use of base installations in Japan along the same lines as the United States. Later, the BCOF example would briefly serve the interests of empire once more, albeit on a more modest scale, in Borneo and Malaya.[84]

MACARTHUR'S STAFF

Following the establishment of a separate SCAP headquarters on 2 October, 1945, MacArthur found himself with dual responsibilities. As head of GHQ/SCAP, he oversaw the non-military aspects of occupation in Japan proper, but as Commander-in-Chief, GHQ/AFPAC (later, FECOM), he was responsible for occupation forces in Okinawa and southern Korea and for US Army Forces in the Philippines and the Western and Mid-Pacific. Although both general headquarters were served by a single Chief of Staff and Military General Staff (G-1 through G-4), all located in the Dai-Ichi Insurance Building, SCAP and AFPAC relied on separate civil staff sections housed in various locations in central Tokyo. Staff responsibilities often overlapped, and, in some cases, officers headed sections in both organisations.[85] This system of dual commands and interlocking staff directorates had been a characteristic of MacArthur's headquarters since SWPA days, a defining trait of the Occupation that is not widely appreciated.

MacArthur was assisted by a small personal staff originally consisting of a secretary, assistant secretary and aides-de-camp. The post of military secretary was held by Brigadier General Bonner F. Fellers. Fellers had done a tour of duty in Japan in the late 1920s and served as MacArthur's military aide in prewar Manila. He subsequently worked as military attaché in Egypt and, early in the war, took part in War Department intelligence planning before rejoining MacArthur in Brisbane in 1943. In 1944, Fellers was assigned to head SWPA's Psychological Warfare Branch. At the start of the Occupation, he became a close acquaintance of former diplomat Terasaki ('Terry') Hidenari, to whom his distant cousin, Gwendolyn, was married. Diplomat and master spy, Terasaki was a Brown University graduate who had worked as second secretary at the Japanese Embassy in Washington just before Pearl Harbor. Together with Gwendolyn and their daughter Mariko, he was repatriated to Japan in 1942. After the war, Terasaki was assigned to the Central Liaison Office and then appointed to serve as liaison between the Throne and GHQ. This connection made Fellers indispensable to MacArthur (chapter 6).

Major Faubion Bowers was MacArthur's assistant military secretary. An ardent Kabuki fan from a prewar stay in Japan, he spoke Japanese fluently, and Allied Translation and Interpreters Service Chief Sidney Mashbir considered him one of ATIS's top linguists. The gifted Bowers subsequently served as cultural mentor to many of GHQ's staff and helped rescue Kabuki from Occupation censors intent on banning the traditional drama as feudalistic. He resigned his job in late 1946 and

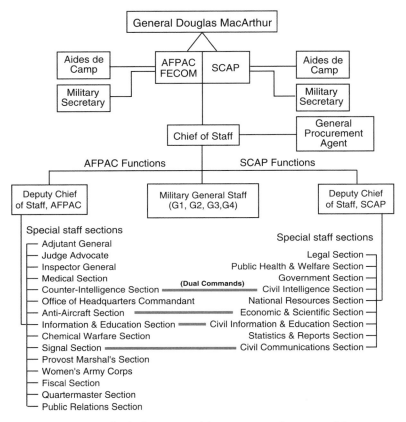

Figure 8. The dual structure of the occupation (January 1946).

joined the Civil Censorship Detachment in hopes of rescuing this ancient art form. MacArthur's Press Relations Officer for much of the war was General Legrande A. Diller, whom US correspondents dubbed 'Killer' Diller for his zeal in censoring articles to burnish the Commander-in-Chief's image. In late 1945, Diller was replaced by Brigadier General Frayne Baker[86]

The position of military secretary was abolished in November 1946 when Fellers left General Headquarters following a contretemps with MacArthur and returned to the United States to work as adviser to the Republican National Committee. Feller's departure bolstered the authority of the aides-de-camp. Among the latter were Colonel Herbert B. Wheeler and Colonel Sidney L. Huff (Huff had served with MacArthur in prewar Manila), but the General came to rely most heavily on Colonel Lawrence E. Bunker, a Harvard Law School graduate who had worked for J. P. Morgan before joining SCAP in 1946.[87]

Like Fellers, Bunker held ultra-rightist political views and later was active in the John Birch Society. A handsome, socially accomplished bachelor, he maintained friendly relations with several highly placed Japanese officials, including the aristocratic Anglophile Shirasu Jirō, CLO member and personal aide to Yoshida Shigeru. Shirasu had studied at Cambridge in the 1920s where he met and became friends with Yoshida, then a young diplomat in London. Bunker also developed a close friendship with Yoshida's daughter, Asō Kazuko, who served as her father's social secretary. Through Shirasu and Kazuko, Yoshida could approach MacArthur directly via Bunker, bypassing Government Section, whose liberal idealists disliked the conservative politician. This cosy arrangement infuriated Government Section Chief Courtney Whitney whose intense rivalry with Bunker came to a head in 1947 when the aide-de-camp issued a memorandum advising that all appointments with the Supreme Commander thenceforth would pass through his office. The memo infuriated Whitney, who in a fit of pique threatened to resign on the spot. MacArthur remonstrated with him, dramatically set fire to the memo in Whitney's presence and told him he could enter by the side door any time he pleased.[88]

Office of the 'Blue-Eyed Tycoon'

To the Japanese, MacArthur was omnipotent, and the public was stunned when President Truman relieved him of all commands for insubordination on 11 April 1951, at the height of the Korean War. His fall, however, gave Japan a valuable object lesson in the primacy of civilian control over the military in a democracy. Under MacArthur's successor, General Matthew Ridgway, the office of the Supreme Commander lost much of its lustre but became more businesslike and down-to-earth. Ridgway had commanded airborne units in Africa, Sicily and the Ardennes during World War II and held various administrative and command positions in Europe and the United States between 1945 and 1950. From December 1950 to April 1951, he led Eighth Army in Korea. An effective officer with outstanding administrative skills, the low-key Ridgway was a sharp contrast to his high-profile, grandiloquent predecessor, and he soon asserted full authority over the Occupation.

The Military General Staff

GHQ/AFPAC and GHQ/SCAP, although organisationally distinct, were physically combined in the same headquarters building. MacArthur's chiefs of staff were Lieutenant General Richard K. Sutherland (August to December 1945), Major General Richard J. Marshall (December 1945 to May 1946), Major General Paul J. Muller (May 1946 to February 1949) and Lieutenant General Edward M. Almond (February 1949 to April 1951). The Chief of Staff had jurisdiction over both headquarters but worked through two deputy chiefs, one for GHQ/AFPAC and one for GHQ/SCAP. Both commands shared the same Military General Staff: G-1 (planning, personnel and general affairs), G-2 (intelligence, security and censorship), G-3 (military operations, law enforcement and repatriation) and G-4 (budget, supply, civil aviation, oil procurement and rationing, and disarmament). The basic tasks of these sections were military, but within each a special sub-unit was established to deal with SCAP-related matters.[89]

G-1 advised the Supreme Commander on personnel policies and the administrative functions of occupation (e.g. modern management practices, manpower and organisation). Unlike most overseas military commands, however, it also regulated the entry into and exit from Japan of individuals not connected with the Occupation, including Japanese nationals. One of SCAP's earliest moves was to prohibit unauthorised travel into and out of Japan. In 1948, GHQ allowed selected Japanese to go abroad on passports issued by the Supreme Commander for purposes related to the 'reorientation or rehabilitation of Japan'. On 29 October of that year, the Soviet Union vetoed a Far Eastern Commission decision to permit expanded cultural exchanges, but with Washington's concurrence, GHQ continued to approve trips abroad by Japanese for authorised reasons. G-1 imposed especially harsh controls on movements between Japan and Korea. The travel ban worked a particular hardship on war-dispersed Korean families trying to reunite, and during the Occupation, tens of thousands of illegal entrants were rounded up and deported to southern Korea. Working through Eighth Army, G-1 functioned as a de facto immigration service until SCAP began turning this responsibility over to the Japanese in late 1949.

G-2, SCAP's intelligence arm, is examined in detail in chapter 4. G-3 advised the Supreme Commander on military operations, enforcement of the surrender terms and directives to the Japanese government. It also administered the Joint Strategic Plans and Operations Group and the Combined War Plans Committee, inter-service organisations established by the Army, Navy and Air Force to ensure cooperation in the event of a military emergency. Thus, the Section was responsible for contingency plans to forcibly suppress the general strike of 1 February 1947 and also drafted martial law and special alert plans. Another G-3 function was repatriation, which was handled by its Repatriation Branch.

G-4's responsibilities included logistics, supply, international civil aviation costs, oil imports and the disposition of surrendered Japanese war equipment and installations. These duties brought it into frequent contact with the Central Liaison Office and the Prime Minister's Office. In 1947, G-4 was assigned to oversee the return of foreign investors to Japan. In 1949, its Budget Division was taken over by the newly created Office of the Comptroller General and placed under the Deputy Chief of Staff. In October 1945, a civilian body, the Petroleum Advisory Group (PAG), was attached to the Section's Petroleum Division. PAG largely determined the orientation of Japan's postwar energy policy. Composed of oil executives from Standard Vacuum, Caltex, Shell and Tidewater Associated on loan to the Army, the Group shut down all of Japan's Pacific Coast refineries and banned private-sector oil imports, eliminating its Japanese competitors with a single blow. The British were permitted to join PAG, one of the rare exceptions to the unspoken rule that reserved

GHQ staff positions for Americans. After 1949, representatives of the major oil companies left SCAP to set up commercial branch offices in Tokyo. By the early 1960s, petroleum had replaced coal as Japan's primary fuel source, and the international producers had a firm grip on Japan's oil market.[90]

An overview of the civil staff sections

In October 1945, SCAP, in addition to its Military General Staff components, consisted basically of the Office of the General Procurement Agent, which served as the Chief of Staff's secretariat, and nine civil staff sections. These were Diplomatic Section (Office of the Political Adviser), Government Section, Civil Intelligence Section, Legal Section, Economic and Scientific Section, Civil Information and Education Section, Natural Resources Section, Public Health and Welfare Section, Civil Communications Section, and Statistics and Reports Section. In a departure from standard US military practice, most SCAP special sections were grouped below the General Military Staff and made directly responsible to the Supreme Commander through the SCAP Deputy Chief of Staff. The secretariat and civil staff groups were created, disbanded or transferred between SCAP's general and special staff sections as the need arose.[91]

GHQ was a relatively small organisation at first, but its members expanded rapidly after 1946, and by 1948, at the height of the Occupation, it had swelled to about 6,000 personnel, of whom 3,850 or 64 per cent, were civilians. In several staff sections, civilians outnumbered military people several times over. According to State Department figures, in 1948, there were a total of 4,739 employees in the 12 civil staff sections alone. Of these, 216 were commissioned officers (4.6 per cent), 312 enlisted personnel (6.6 per cent), 2,224 civilians (46.9 per cent) and 1,987 Japanese and a few ethnic Koreans and other nationalities (41.9 per cent).[92] Thus, American civilians and Japanese personnel together accounted for nearly 90 per cent of GHQ's manpower.

The large number of Japanese employees is significant, and in some staff echelons, such as Legal Section and Civil Information and Education Section (CI&E), they outnumbered Americans. Most of these individuals, although occupying subordinate positions, were not only highly qualified for the tasks they performed but firmly committed to the ideals of reform. Serving as the eyes and ears of the staff sections, Japanese brought various issues to the attention of American officials and kept them advised of Japanese views and reactions to SCAP policies. They were consulted daily on matters large and small. In 1949, for instance, CI&E Elementary School Officer Pauline Jeidy asked her Japanese subordinates about an attempt by a conservative pressure group to introduce traditional calligraphy into the elementary school curricula. The group claimed that calligraphy improved artistic ability, penmanship and moral character and was as indispensable for Oriental children as knives and forks for Westerners. Japanese staff members told her flatly that such assertions were nonsense. Jeidy consequently opposed the measure, demanding that the lobbyists substantiate their arguments.[93]

The Occupation was notorious for the bewildering variety of acronyms it generated. GHQ staff sections were generally represented by two or three letters, but
SCAP and POLAD were cumbersome, adding to the generally confused picture that
most Japanese had of the Occupation. Referred to by the Japanese as 'MacArthur's
headquarters' or simply 'headquarters', GHQ became a synonym for the most powerful organisation in the country. Diet members, bureaucrats, judges, politicians, businessmen and even trade unionists frequently justified their actions by invoking the
name of GHQ, whether they had its backing or not. Sometimes, mere allusion to
'certain quarters' was sufficient to convince an opponent of the wisdom of a course of
action. In a lighter vein, Yoshida Shigeru used to quip that GHQ stood for 'Go
Home Quickly'.

By the end of its tutelage, MacArthur's super-government had ended deep
involvement in most aspects of civil administration. There were important exceptions, however. One was the economy, where Washington took a direct hand,
micro-managing the 1949 Dodge stabilisation programme well into 1950. Another
was civil and political liberties: during the Red Purge of 1949–50, GHQ suppressed
left-of-centre publications and hounded progressives and labour activists from their
jobs. And, with the start of the Korean War, GHQ would oversee the formation of a
de facto Japanese army, the National Police Reserve.

Special missions
A host of special missions and advisory committees were organised during the Occupation to advise General Headquarters on policy matters, some of them powerful
enough to override the discretionary authority of individual staff sections. Occasionally, their members were attached to SCAP to work on specific reforms. The earliest
ad hoc group was the Pauley Mission discussed above, which arrived in Japan in
November 1945 to study the war reparations issue. In January 1946, a team headed
by Northeastern University economist Corwin D. Edwards visited to consider ways
of dismantling the giant *zaibatsu* combines. Overlapping with the Pauley group, the
Edwards Mission suggested a two-phase American-style programme of economic
deconcentration that became the basis of GHQ's *zaibatsu* dissolution programme.

Not all deputations were American. An important Allied fact-finding group was the
Australian Scientific Mission headed by Brigadier General John O'Brien, which
visited in January 1946 sponsored by the Australian government. The Australians
were intent on discovering industrial techniques and innovations of use to the
home economy and earmarking plant and equipment for future reparations. The
O'Brien group subsequently would be absorbed into the Economic and Scientific
Section's Scientific and Technical Division, another exception to the unwritten rule
of American exclusivity (chapter 4). The United Nations also despatched delegations, such as the UN Relief and Rehabilitation Agency Mission led by former US
president Herbert Hoover in the summer of 1946. Hoover recommended a school-
lunch programme to improve the health of children, a suggestion that was acted on
in December of that year.

In March 1946, two new US groups arrived in Tokyo. The first was the Advisory Committee on Labour in Japan, composed of unionists, labour economists and US Labour Department officials and sponsored by Economic and Scientific Section's Labour Division. Its final report was approved as official Occupation policy in August 1947, and some members were attached to Labour Division to help draft the enabling legislation. The second was the US Education Mission led by George D. Stoddard, which made proposals – many of them based on Japanese recommendations – to reform education. In the spring and summer of 1946, at Government Section's behest, the Metropolitan Police Mission and the Rural Policy Planning Commission came to Tokyo and urged a sweeping overhaul of the police system. Finally, in late 1946, the US Civil Service Mission under Blaine Hoover advocated bureaucratic reform and the creation of a powerful central personnel agency.

In February 1947, under the auspices of Public Health and Welfare Section, the Departments of State, War and Agriculture despatched the US Food Mission to study Japan's food and fertiliser situation. In August of that year, PH&W also hosted the US Social Security Mission under William H. Wandell, which proposed a sweeping social security reform. In July and August 1947 and again in September 1948, the National Academy of Sciences sent two US Science Advisory Groups to Japan at the invitation of the Economic and Scientific Section. Roger Adams, a chemist and Dean of Science at the University of Illinois, led the first mission whose final report made recommendations for rebuilding postwar Japanese science and technology, including reforms in higher education. In December 1947, the US Library Mission assisted the government in establishing a national book repository similar to the Library of Congress, a goal that was achieved with the passage of the National Diet Library Law on 9 February 1948. A US Cultural Science Mission visited Japan in September of that year to assess social science education.

Many of the later missions reflected a generally rightward drift in US policy towards Japan. A group led by Clifford S. Strike, a US engineer and industrial expert, spent January and February of 1947 in Japan with his firm, Overseas Consultants, Inc., re-examining the reparations program. Refuting Pauley's conclusions, the Strike Mission argued in its final report of early 1948 that reparations should be slashed drastically in order to restore domestic production and encourage economic self-sufficiency. In 1948, a group under Ralph Young of the Federal Reserve Board advocated establishing a single yen–dollar exchange rate and proposed a stabilisation plan to attack inflation and make the economy self-supporting. In January 1949, Joseph M. Dodge, a Detroit banker, arrived in Tokyo to implement the deflation. That summer, yet another mission under Columbia University tax specialist Carl S. Shoup recommended fiscal reforms to supplement the Dodge retrenchment programme. In the autumn of 1948, the Rockefeller Mission studied Japan's population problem and its implications for economic stability. The reports submitted by these embassies – drawn up in close collaboration with Japanese administrators, educators and specialists – contain a wealth of empirical data on almost every facet of Japanese society.

Missionaries were permitted to enter Japan from the start of the Occupation, but trade delegations generally were not admitted until the summer of 1947. From the beginning, however, an endless stream of educators, publishers, publicists, religious leaders, philanthropists and celebrities, some representing special constituencies, others on a lark, managed to arrange private tours of occupied Japan. Asked for a personal interview by actor Danny Kaye and New York Dodgers' manager Leo Durocher, MacArthur groused to his military aide, 'Now that the war's over, every Tom, Dick and his cat's coming over.' These 'visiting firemen' and self-styled Asia experts, as Whitney characterised them, were personally escorted by Occupation officials and accorded VIP treatment but generally shown, sometimes at considerable expense to the US taxpayer, no more than GHQ wished them to see.[94]

A few critically minded non-governmental groups also sent fact-finding missions to Tokyo to evaluate the success of specific reforms. Two of these merit passing mention. Shortly after the abortive general strike of early 1947, the left-leaning World Federation of Trade Unions sent an African American organiser to visit the recently formed National Labour Union Liaison Council (*Zenrōren*) and report on Japanese labour (chapter 6). In the spring of 1947, at MacArthur's invitation, Roger N. Baldwin, director of the American Civil Liberties Union, organised an extensive 10-week tour of Japan. He was accompanied by Thurgood Marshall of the National Association for the Advancement of Coloured People (and future Supreme Court Justice). Also representing the Japanese American Citizens' League, Baldwin and Marshall travelled at their own expense, eschewed Army chaperonage and studiously avoided pre-arranged interviews with pro-American Japanese political figures and opinion leaders. Although the civil libertarians criticised SCAP's censorship programme, their initial impression of the Occupation record generally was favourable (they would later change their views as America's Japan policy turned rightward).[95]

During the first three years of occupation, the flow of people was in one direction, for Japanese were not permitted to leave the country, but from late 1948, GHQ lifted the travel ban to initiate a series of high-level cultural exchanges. One of the most important of these was the Exchange of National Leaders Programme, financed with Government and Relief in Occupied Areas (GARIOA) funds and sponsored by the Institute of International Education, which GHQ's Civil Information and Education Section had helped establish in July 1948. In October 1948, the US National Security Council recommended bilateral visits of scholars, scientists and political leaders, and in November, the Department of the Army approved SCAP's 'Exchange of Persons Programme for Japan'. The project, which got underway in 1949, allowed influential Japanese in a variety of fields to visit the United States on specially designed study tours lasting two to six months. Closely tied to America's Cold War policy objectives in Japan, the missions were carefully prepared by the sponsoring staff sections in GHQ and concerned government agencies in Washington. Hundreds of prominent Japanese, including political leaders, were escorted personally by GHQ staff officials familiar with their areas of expertise and interests. One of the most ambitious endeavours was the Supreme Court Mission of 1951, led by Chief Justice Tanaka Kōtarō. Designed to groom pro-American leaders for the post-Occupation period, the project was part of a broader programme of ideological reorientation (chapter 8).[96]

CHAPTER 4

Inside the Special Staff Sections

SCAP's special staff sections mirrored the organisation of government ministries and, in many cases, reproduced even the administrative subdivisions of their counterpart agencies. The groups were headed initially by military men with little knowledge of civil administration and staffed by younger officers fresh out of the Army's Civil Affairs Training Schools. To meet the shortage of specialists, the War Department's Civil Affairs Division recruited qualified civilians, who began arriving in early 1946. Ranking staff officers used their personal contacts in the United States to attract experienced administrators, and at least one section chief advertised in American professional journals at his own expense.[1] United Nations and US government agencies, American universities, state school commissions, broadcasting corporations, trade unions, church groups, private firms and foundations, the American Red Cross, international aid organisations and even the Australian Army loaned staff to GHQ. By the summer of 1946, the personnel rosters of most staff groups boasted a full complement of civilian expert advisers, and by late 1947, Department of the Army civilians outnumbered their military counterparts. Moreover, throughout their stewardship, several sections invited consultants to assess the effectiveness of their programmes, providing valuable feedback.

Intense rivalries inevitably developed among GHQ's highly structured, self-contained staff groups and sub-groups, each intent on defending its authority and perceived interests. Sections contended fiercely for access to the Supreme Commander, sometimes impeding the work of reform. In October 1945, the Office of the Political Adviser, the State Department's advisory group to SCAP, convened an inter-sectional conference to clarify the respective duties of the major sections, but the staff echelons remained fiercely protective of their prerogatives. Tensions existed between the uniformed professional soldiers who ran the Military General Staff sections (G-1 through G-4) and the specialists in mufti who came to dominate SCAP's civil bureaucracy, and early in the Occupation, the former attempted unsuccessfully to arrogate the functions of the special staff sections. Brigadier General Charles A. Willoughby's G-2, in particular, was intensely jealous of Government Section's broad powers and in late 1945 manoeuvred to take over the purge and other GS duties 'lock, stock and barrel'. MacArthur sided with GS Chief Courtney Whitney, thwarting the G-2 power play,[2] and the conflict of jurisdictions was resolved in April 1946 with the creation of a separate Deputy Chief of Staff for SCAP. The new chain of command allowed the civil staff groups to report directly to the Deputy Chief and through him to the Chief of Staff and MacArthur, bypassing the Military General Staff altogether. Nonetheless, G-2

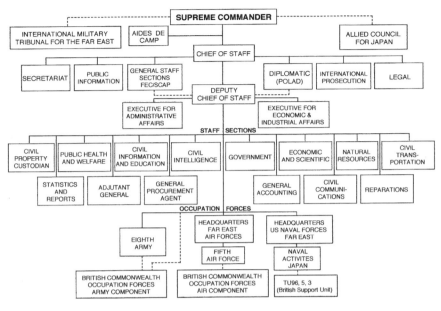

Figure 9. GHQ, SCAP, 31 December 1947.
(Source: *Reports of General MacArthur*, 1966, p. 77)

Figure 9A. General MacArthur and an aide leave GHQ as a crowd of Japanese and American GIs look on in awe, December 7, 1945 (Mainichi).

and GS would collide repeatedly over the purge, police reform, censorship and other issues.

Government Section subsequently came to wield enormous influence, in large part because its approval was required of all legislative proposals. Thus, Economic and Scientific Section (ESS), Civil Information and Education Section (CI&E) and other staff groups were compelled to negotiate each reform package with GS before approaching the central government. In mid-stream, GS usurped the labour purge being planned by ESS. GS and ESS also squared off over the issue of national subsidies to municipalities (GS won). In one instance, a CI&E branch head blatantly violated ESS labour policy by secretly collaborating with police in suppressing a major strike at the *Yomiuri Shinbun*. CI&E duplicated and then absorbed some ESS labour education functions. MacArthur generally gazed on these internecine altercations with Olympian detachment, leaving the sections to their own devices. Several staff groups even felt compelled to attach liaison officers to rival sections, but internal consensus sometimes was as difficult to achieve as agreement between American and Japanese officials.

Japanese were sensitive to these differences and proved adept at exploiting them. Yoshida Shigeru skilfully played G-2 off against GS, earning the enmity of GS Chief Whitney and his deputy Charles L. Kades. The Tokyo Metropolitan Police attempted to override an ESS policy decision outlawing police intervention in labour disputes by appealing directly to G-2. In the final stage of land-reform deliberations, the Agriculture Ministry refused to yield to Government Section on a question of principle and was backed up by the Natural Resources Section (NRS), whose chief found himself immediately embroiled in a major turf battle with Whitney.[3]

As the Occupation pressed forward, the fortunes of the various staff sections waxed and waned as the focus of GHQ's mission changed. At the outset, the Office of the Political Adviser (POLAD) seemed destined for a prominent role, but MacArthur kept the State Department team at arm's length. Once basic legal and institutional reforms got under way in early 1946, POLAD was quickly eclipsed by Government Section, which enjoyed MacArthur's full confidence throughout the Occupation. With basic reform projections more or less realised by 1947, the intelligence establishment became ascendant, playing a key, albeit often covert, role in the policy reorientation that began in late 1947 and which became known after 1950 as the 'reverse course'. Each of the other sections, too, enjoyed their day in the sun: Legal Section advised the International Military Tribunal for the Far East, Economic and Scientific Section carried out the labour and *zaibatsu* reforms, Civil Information and Education Section reorientated Japan's education system, Natural Resources Section carried out the land reform, and Public Health and Welfare Section revolutionised Japan's health care system. Other sections and consultative groups, although less conspicuous, also made significant contributions.[4]

Several staff echelons also advised US commands in Okinawa and southern Korea. Government Section initially was responsible for civil affairs in Japan, the Ryukyus and south Korea. Legal Section and Public Health and Welfare (PH&W) Section also were consulted regularly by US forces outside of Japan. These overlapping functions extended equally to personnel. Several highly qualified officers transferred out of civil affairs units in the US Army Military Government in Korea to take positions in GHQ/SCAP. Following the outbreak of war in Korea, two staff groups, PH&W and CI&E, did double duty in Japan and Korea. Finally, when Japan regained its independence in 1952, some groups arranged with the State Department to attach key personnel to the US Embassy in Tokyo. In this way, well after the dissolution of GHQ, former Occupationaires continued to monitor developments in Japan and influence US policy there.

GHQ'S STATE DEPARTMENT

In post-defeat Germany, the State Department had set up an independent adviser's office in the US Zone reporting directly to Washington on diplomatic and economic issues. The Department developed similar plans for Japan, but MacArthur baulked at the idea of an independent government agency operating outside of his command and demanded full jurisdiction. The Department relented, and on 22 September 1945, the Office of the Political Adviser was established as a personal consultant to the Supreme Commander.

Organisation and mission
One of POLAD's primary responsibilities was to study Japanese political parties and trends to ascertain whether these were compatible with occupation objectives. For this purpose, it sent the State Department a weekly report on political activities, peppered in the early days with tart references to 'the Jap people' and 'Jap political parties', and drafted confidential memoranda to President Truman concerning Japanese reactions to GHQ's 'denazification' programmes. Operating as SCAP's State Department, POLAD also represented the United States on the Allied Council for Japan. Under MacArthur's close supervision, however, the advisory group never achieved the high-profile role its counterpart enjoyed in Germany. According to State Department policy specialist George F. Kennan, the Supreme Commander had a 'violent prejudice' against the Department, and liaison between the two organisations was 'distant and full of distrust'. On his visit to Tokyo in early 1948, Kennan felt like an envoy sent to establish diplomatic relations with a 'hostile and suspicious foreign government'. This sentiment was shared by the high-ranking military men around the Supreme Commander. MacArthur's Counter-Intelligence Chief Brigadier General Elliott R. Thorpe railed against the 'soft-sell boys' in POLAD, 'most of whom had endured the hardships of the war in Washington's Foggy Bottom'.[5]

MacArthur kept the Political Adviser at arm's length physically by assigning him office space in the Mitsui Main Bank Building in Yaesu near Tokyo Station, far from GHQ. POLAD's successor, Diplomatic Section, did not get a direct telegraphic link to the State Department and permission to use its own codes until 1950. Until then, all communications were routed through MacArthur's military staff. As a result, POLAD and the State Department were kept in the dark about Government Section's constitutional drafting committee, learning of its proposed new constitution only when newspapers broke the story in early March 1946. This truncated role affords an ironic contrast to the State Department's major contribution to pre-surrender planning for Japan (chapter 5) and indicates the remarkable degree to which MacArthur succeeded in personalising his headquarters.

To resolve the anomalous status of POLAD, MacArthur created Diplomatic Section (DS) on 18 April 1946 and incorporated it into his staff. The Section's duties were limited to handling Japan's external affairs, notably relations between foreign liaison missions and the central government, but DS also recommended foreign policy for Japan and, initially, Korea. (By 1951, it oversaw the activities of 22 Allied and foreign liaison missions accredited to the Supreme Commander.) Diplomatic Section continued to be run by career Foreign Service officials on loan to General Headquarters. At State Department insistence, the Chief of Section retained the title of POLAD, and soon after DS was established, MacArthur appointed him to chair the Allied Council for Japan, which had just convened. The Political Adviser's staff also handled consular affairs, acting as a de facto US Embassy.

POLAD's early activities were varied and complex. One of its first official tasks was to draft lists of suspected war criminals. Using a copy of *Who's Who in Japan* and data provided by Washington, Robert A. Fearey, John K. Emmerson and E. Herbert Norman (then chief of Research and Analysis in SCAP's Civil Intelligence Section) compiled a list of more than 100 suspects, most of whom were arrested in late 1945. POLAD also was instrumental in freeing political prisoners, reinstating political parties, organising the first general elections and planning the purge of public officials. These reformist activities contrasted sharply with the aggressive behaviour of Mission Chiefs George Atcheson and William Sebald in the Allied Council for Japan, where they functioned as point men for MacArthur's crusade against Soviet influence in Japan. When Diplomatic Section was created in April 1946, the General ordered the Political Adviser to meet the challenge of Soviet 'sabotage and obstruction to the Occupation' and parry attacks on SCAP policy in the Council with 'equally embarrassing and revealing questions and statements'.[6]

DS remained in MacArthur's shadow for most of Occupation. Only after 1950, as negotiations over the Japanese peace settlement got underway, did it come to play a more dynamic and visible role. The State Department, on the other hand, found other ways to make its presence felt. It despatched an influential Education Mission to Tokyo, maintained a permanent labour representative inside GHQ and managed to fill some staff positions with its own people, notably in the Civil Information and Education Section's Information Division, which operated as an arm of the Department's global propaganda network (chapter 8). Towards the end of the Occupation, the State Department also actively recruited talented staff officers, many of whom embarked on careers in the Foreign Service.

Staff

Under-Secretary of State Dean Acheson, advocate of a hard peace, did not want a Japan Crowd crony providing liaison with MacArthur and appointed China hand George Atcheson to fill that position. Atcheson had joined the Foreign Service after graduating from the University of California. Attached to the US Embassy in China as an interpreter, he handled the crisis that erupted following the Japanese sinking of an American gunboat, the USS *Panay*, on the Yangtse River in 1937. In 1943, he was named adviser to General Joseph Stilwell, Chiang Kai-shek (Jiang Jieshi)'s Allied Chief of Staff, in Chongqing (Chungking). Atcheson was transferred to Tokyo to set up POLAD in September 1945, and with the creation of Diplomatic Section in April 1946, he added chief of section to his duties as Political Adviser. Despite MacArthur's jaundised view of POLAD, Atcheson became a close friend of the General and wielded considerable personal influence in SCAP until his untimely death in a plane crash off Hawai'i in August 1947.

Atcheson was succeeded by William J. Sebald, a US Naval Academy graduate. From 1925 to 1928, Sebald had served as language officer with the US Embassy in Tokyo before returning to the United States to study law at the University of Maryland. Back in Japan with a law degree in 1933, he set up practice in Kobe. In 1939, Sebald joined the Navy as a Lieutenant Commander. In late 1945, he was assigned to POLAD as Atcheson's deputy and following his superior's death in the summer of 1947 took over as Section Chief. Sebald chaired the Allied Council for Japan, and his knowledge of the country and its language made him a particularly reliable adviser. After the Occupation, he was US Ambassador to Burma and Australia and Deputy-Assistant Secretary of State.[7]

The original POLAD/DS staff included Max W. Bishop, an ambitious ultra-conservative Foreign Service officer who returned to Washington early in the Occupation to take up a senior position in the Division of Northeast Asian Affairs. There, his hawkish views would influence US policy towards Japan and Korea during the so-called reverse course. Bishop later became a member of the extreme-rightist John Birch Society. Cut from the same cloth was Dr Charles N. Spinks, a Japan expert and intelligence specialist. After earning a PhD in political science from Stanford University, Spinks taught at the Tokyo University of Commerce from 1936 to 1941. From 1942, as a Lieutenant Commander, he worked for the Office of Naval Intelligence's Far Eastern Office, publishing influential articles on Japanese education and a study on Japanese fascism.[8] In 1946, Spinks joined SCAP's Civil Intelligence Section where he directed research and analysis until moving to Diplomatic Section in 1948. A rabid anti-Communist, he kept tabs on radicals and Korean nationalists and denounced several prominent GHQ staffers as leftists. Spinks also played a role in the Red Purge of 1949–50.

Prominent in the early days was Robert A. Fearey, a Harvard-trained Japan specialist and former private secretary to Ambassador Joseph C. Grew. A member of the State Department's Japan Crowd, Fearey participated in pre-surrender planning and drafted a land-reform proposal. He left Diplomatic Section early but returned to

Photo 19. MacArthur, E. Herbert Norman of the Canadian Mission and Eighth Army Commander Eichelberger at a Canadian diplomatic function, 2 July 1947 (Mainichi).

Tokyo in 1950 as special assistant to John Foster Dulles during the peace treaty negotiations.[9] John K. Emmerson, a career Foreign Service officer, had served under Grew in prewar Tokyo but also possessed extensive wartime experience in China. In early October 1945, Emmerson and E. Herbert Norman drew attention to the plight of Japan's political prisoners and met directly with jailed Communist leaders (chapter 6). Norman was not a member of POLAD, but the Political Adviser relied heavily on his counsel in the early period of occupation. The son of Canadian missionaries, Norman had been raised in Japan, a distinction he shared with Japan experts Gordon T. Bowles (chapter 8), Eugene H. Dooman (chapter 5) and Edwin O. Reischauer. Norman's seminal scholarship on Japan's emergence from feudalism influenced Allied thinking on the country during and immediately after the war. At the outset of the Occupation, he was attached briefly to SCAP's Civil Intelligence Section and, from August 1946 to December 1950, headed the Canadian Liaison Mission in Tokyo.[10]

Meeting with Japanese Communist leaders tarred Norman and Emmerson as Communist sympathisers. After 1950, Norman became increasingly critical of the Occupation, and his alleged left-wing connections led to security investigations by Canadian and US authorities. In 1951, at the height of McCarthyism, Congressional investigators accused both men of assisting in the reconstruction of the Japan Communist Party. Emmerson's career was damaged, although he later served as deputy chief of mission in Tokyo under Ambassador Reischauer (1962–6). Norman had belonged to the Communist Party in his youth. Under recurrent pressure from Senate inquisitors, he committed suicide in Cairo in 1957.

A middle-echelon diplomat worthy of mention was Richard B. Finn, the DS legal expert. After Harvard Law School, Finn served in the Navy as a Japanese language officer. Following the war, he worked on education and constitutional reform for the Far Eastern Commission in Washington before joining the State Department and being assigned to DS. Finn coordinated GHQ's policy towards Koreans in Japan and assisted John Foster Dulles during the 1951 treaty talks. After the Occupation, he headed the State Department's Japan Division and played a central role in negotiating the reversion of Okinawa to Japan.[11]

Diplomatic Section was a small staff echelon, numbering only about three dozen Foreign Service officers. In 1948, it was composed of the Political and General Affairs Division under David C. Berger; the Executive and Administrative Division, headed by veteran Japan hand Cabot Coville and including Charles Spinks and Richard B. Finn; the Economic Liaison Division, to which the noted author and translator Edward G. Seidensticker belonged briefly; and the International Liaison Division, staffed by Richard A. Poole, who transferred from Government Section, and Eileen R. Donovan, a former education officer in Civil Information and Education Section (below). Diplomatic Section also operated two consular sections in Yokohama (U. Alexis Johnson, Ambassador to Japan, 1966–9) and Kobe (Douglas Jenkins). The Section dealt mainly with Japan's Central Liaison Office and the Foreign Ministry. It was disbanded on 28 April 1952 with the recovery of Japanese sovereignty, and its members transferred to the US Embassy in Tokyo or returned to Washington.

GOVERNMENT SECTION

Government Section was established on 2 October 1945 to advise GHQ on policies concerning the internal affairs of civil government in Japan. (Until February 1947, it had a similar responsibility for the US Army Military Government in Korea.) Its mandate was sweeping: to demilitarise and democratise the political, economic, social and cultural life of the nation. Government Section shared the Dai-Ichi Mutual Life Insurance building with MacArthur's Military General Staff, a prime location attesting to the group's central role in the Occupation. Its primary counterpart agencies in the Japanese government were the Central Liaison Office, the Home Ministry (until December 1947), the Attorney General's Office and the Prime Minister's Office.

Organisation and mission

Although Government Section was considered 'weak and ineffectual' in the first
months of duty, it soon came to epitomise the liberalising spirit of the early reform
phase of the Occupation.[12] GS revised the electoral system, enfranchised women,
drafted the 'MacArthur Constitution', purged militant nationalists from public life,
democratised the police system, restructured local government, decentralised the
bureaucracy, helped dissolve the great *zaibatsu* combines and revamped the judiciary
and Parliament. The Section's broad mission incited the envy of intelligence chief
Willoughby and led to frequent clashes with Yoshida Shigeru, the feisty foreign
minister and premier who deplored the New Deal idealists grouped around Whitney
and Kades. GS officers, in turn, regarded Yoshida as an unreconstructed reactionary.

Government Section initially consisted of two major segments, Public Administration Division, responsible for the internal administration of Japan, and Korean
Division, which exercised a similar function for the US Army Military Government
in Korea. In early 1946, Public Administration was reorganised, and in February
1947, Korean Division was disbanded. By mid-1947, the major GS divisions were
Administrative, Civil Service, Courts and Law (Legal), Governmental Powers, Legislative, Local Government, National Government, Parliamentary and Political, and
Public Administration. The Section's commitment to democratisation was tempered
by a compulsion to promote administrative efficiency that inadvertently strengthened Japanese bureaucratic control. Following Washington's decision in 1948 to rein
in the reform process, GS came under fire for its liberal sympathies, and conservatives attacked the Section's bright-eyed visionaries as 'the small group of longhaired
boys . . . who have helped General MacArthur put over his socialistic schemes'.[13]

Despite its immense authority, Government Section was a relatively small staff
group that shrunk even further as its reform objectives were achieved. In 1948, GS
had a total of 122 staff members (15 officers, 9 enlisted personnel and 98 civilians),
one tenth the size of the huge Economic and Scientific Section. In May and June
1948, with the Section's primary mission completed, Courts and Law Division and
Governmental Powers Division were transferred to Legal Section, where they were
combined, becoming Legislation and Justice Division. In late June 1948, Local
Government Division was reassigned to Eighth Army headquarters in Yokohama,
and other GS divisions were pared, merged or discontinued. In the final years of
occupation, Government Section devoted much of its energy to chasing Communists, Socialists and liberals from their jobs, intimidating the radical labour movement
and harassing ethnic Koreans. The Section was disbanded when Japan regained its
sovereignty on 28 April 1952.

Staff

Courtney Whitney, one of the strongmen of SCAP, headed Government Section for
most of the Occupation. A graduate of Columbia National Law School in Washington DC, Whitney had worked as an attorney in Manila before the war. He
was assigned to MacArthur's SWPA staff in 1943, directed the Philippine guerrilla

Photo 20. Max Bishop (DS), Courtney Whitney (GS), Charles L. Kades (GS), and William J. Sebald (DS) inspect a polling station at a primary school in Tokyo's Setagaya Ward, 10 April 1946, during Japan's first general elections (US National Archives).

movement from Brisbane and followed MacArthur to Manila and Tokyo. He was appointed Chief of Government Section in mid-December 1945, replacing Brigadier General William E. Crist. A Bataan Gang intimate, Whitney became the General's closest confidant. He spent time every day with the Supreme Commander, and it is said that even his handwriting resembled that of his mentor. The soft-spoken Whitney was described by his subordinates as a 'Knight in Shining Armour', as compared to Charles Willoughby of G-2, 'the personification of the Black Reactionary'. In fact, Whitney was a deeply conservative man prone to outbursts of anti-semitism.[14] When President Truman fired MacArthur in April 1951, Whitney resigned and followed his boss into retirement as personal adviser and biographer.[15] He was replaced by Frank Rizzo, an industrial economist with an engineering degree from Cornell

University who had done graduate work in economics, finance and international relations at New York and George Washington Universities. Rizzo was a managing partner in a New York investment bank before entering the Army in 1942. Assigned to Government Section at Kades's personal request, he became one of the few financial experts not drafted by Economic and Scientific Section. Rizzo replaced Kades as Deputy Chief of Section when the latter retired in late 1948, and when Whitney left Japan in 1951, he took over as Section Chief.

Whitney had at his service the well-known Japan specialists Dr Kenneth W. Colegrove of Northwestern University and Dr Harold S. Quigley of the University of Minnesota, then attached to G-2. The GS chief made little use of these authorities, however, and the vital work of Government Section was performed by a small cadre of outstanding subordinates handpicked by Whitney and led by Deputy Chief Colonel Charles L. Kades. Of Jewish and Spanish ancestry, Kades was born in southern New York and graduated from Cornell University and Harvard Law School. Kades was a committed New Dealer and worked as legal counsel for the Federal Public Works Administration (1933–7) and the US Treasury Department (1937–42) before going on active duty with the War Department's Civil Affairs Division (CAD). There, as Assistant Executive Officer to CAD Chief Major General J. H. Hilldring, he helped draft the Army's 'Basic Directive for Post-Surrender Military Government in Japan Proper', JCS-1380/15 (chapter 5). Later, as Deputy Chief of G-5 (Civil Affairs), Kades took part in the invasion of southern France and the Rhineland campaign. When he arrived in Tokyo on 30 August 1945, he carried with him a summary of the 'US Initial Post-Surrender Policy' and other basic Occupation documents. Described by a colleague as gregarious but not brash, Kades was thought to have 'probably the quickest intellect in GHQ'. Although not a member of MacArthur's Bataan clique, he nonetheless developed a close professional and personal relationship with Whitney, who overruled his 'brainy New Dealer' only once, and then on a matter of minor significance.[16] Kades's contribution to the liberal phase of the Occupation was seminal, and his departure in late 1948 marked the end of the reform era and the advent of realpolitik and domestic repression.

One of Kades's right-hand men in the first two years of occupation was Lieutenant Colonel Frank Hays, a Wyoming lawyer and graduate of the Chicago Civil Affairs Training School (CATS). Kades also was assisted by Lieutenant Taro ('Tom') Tsukahara, one of the small group of accomplished Japanese Americans working for GHQ. Born in Wakayama Prefecture, Tsukahara had emigrated to the United States after graduating from Japanese middle school. Interned in 1942, he later volunteered for military service and was attached to the Allied Translator and Interpreters Service in the Pacific as a psychological warfare officer. In September 1945, Tsukahara was assigned to the Civil Information and Education Section, but Kades spotted his leadership qualities and recruited him as a personal aide. The dashing, urbane Kades had a reputation as a ladies' man, and Tsukahara was sometimes called on to keep the Deputy Chief of Section out of trouble. After Kades left GHQ in late 1948,

Photo 21. Government Section's Justin Williams Sr (middle). At the far right is Yamazaki Takeshi of the House of Representatives, head of the Japanese Diet Delegation to the United States. At the left is Sakurauchi Tatsuo of the House of Councillors. The Delegation visited Washington from January to March 1950 under the Exchange of National Leaders Programme (US National Archives).

the left-leaning Tsukahara fell afoul of Willoughby's watchdogs and in 1949 was forced to return to the United States.[17]

Justin Williams Sr was another key player whose contribution left a lasting mark on Japan. Williams had taught American history and economics at the University of Wisconsin (1931–42), where he also chaired the Social Science Department. In 1942, he joined the US Army Air Forces as a First Lieutenant. After training at the University of Virginia's School of Military Government and the Yale CATS, he was assigned to AFPAC headquarters in Manila. He followed AFPAC's Military Government Section to Tokyo, where he was attached to Government Section, SCAP and asked to head the Parliamentary and Political Division. Williams was assisted by an unusually diligent and perceptive staff officer, Helen Loeb, who advised Diet leaders on basic Allied policy, provided liaison between Government Section and various Diet legislative committees and prepared reports on Diet activities and politics for internal SCAP use.[18]

Williams worked closely with Navy Commander Guy J. Swope, head of Legislative Division and later chief of National Government Division and Political Affairs Division. The epitome of the self-made man, Swope had only an elementary-school education, making him something of an oddity in GHQ, and had held a wide variety

Photo 22. An Ainu Chieftain, Miyamoto Inosuke, visits Government Section. At front left is Alfred C. Oppler, and beside him, Osborne L. Hauge. Behind Hauge is Lieutenant Colonel Frank R. Harrison. Standing in the centre behind Miyamoto is Cecil G. Tilton. Frank Rizzo is to the Chieftain's left and next to him is Tilton's assistant, Raymond Y. Aka. Guy J. Swope is at the far right in back. 22 October 1947 (US National Archives).

of jobs, including public accountant and banker. During his prewar career, he served one term in the US Congress on a New Deal ticket and was Governor of Puerto Rico. His professional experience and uncommon ability led him to Columbia University's Navy School of Military Government and landed him a job as Executive Officer in the Military Government of Saipan. He was the only GS official to head three different divisions in succession. Leaving GHQ in 1948, Swope was replaced in Political Affairs Division by Navy Lieutenant Osborne L. Hauge, a graduate of St Olaf College, Minnesota and former newspaper editor.[19]

Lieutenant Colonel Cecil G. Tilton, Chief of Local Government Division, made a singular contribution to the reform of local administration. Holding a BS and MSc from the University of California (Berkeley) and an MBA from Harvard, he had taught at the Universities of Hawai'i and Connecticut before entering the Army. After training at the University of Virginia School of Military Government, he was recruited to teach at the University of Chicago CATS. Tilton was assisted initially by John W. Maseland of Dartmouth College and Andrew J. Grajdanzev, an ardent advocate of decentralisation and home rule. Grajdanzev later played a role in drafting SCAP's land-reform programme. Tilton followed Local Government Division to Eighth Army headquarters when it was transferred there in mid-1948.

Civil service reform was the responsibility of Blaine Hoover, the personnel expert who engineered the 'defeudalising' of the Japanese bureaucracy via the National Public Service Law of 1947. Hoover left Japan but returned soon afterwards to head Government Section's new Civil Service Division. Known for his anti-labour views, he sought to curb the rights of civil servants and public employees and was responsible for incorporating an anti-strike provision in the controversial 1948 revision of the National Public Service Law.[20] Two political scientists, Lieutenant Milton J. Esman (PhD, Princeton) and Dr John M. Maki (PhD, University of Washington), a Japanese American, also worked on civil service reform and later continued university careers.[21]

Public Administration Division Chiefs included Lieutenant Colonel Carlos P. Marcum, who had been recruited from Civil Intelligence Section to help run the purge, and Lieutenant Colonel Jack P. Napier. Napier had worked in Korean Division until its discontinuance in early 1947. Doubling as GS Executive Officer, in 1949, Napier coordinated the Red Purge and GHQ's crackdown on Koreans. Although he lacked the academic credentials of others in GS, Napier proved a talented administrator who, in the words of a contemporary, brought to his duties 'all the qualities of cleverness and toughness that grim job demanded'. Hans H. Baerwald also played a major part in the purge of ultra-nationalists, later writing the definitive study of this programme.[22] One of the rare Occupationaires born in Japan, he worked initially for ATIS before joining GS as a language officer.

The 'Constitutional Convention'

The Section's best and brightest were assigned the task of drafting the so-called MacArthur Constitution in early 1946. The Steering Committee included Kades; Navy Commander Alfred R. Hussey, a graduate of Harvard and the University of Virginia Law School and practising attorney before enlisting in the Navy in 1942; Lieutenant Colonel Milo E. Rowell, a graduate of Stanford University and the Harvard Law School who had worked as an assistant US attorney in Los Angeles before the war; and Ruth Ellerman, a government analyst who served as secretary. Ellerman kept detailed notes of the proceedings, drafting an 18-page memorandum that became the Committee's official minutes. Swope and Hauge served on the Legislative Subcommittee under Frank Hays. Heading the Executive Subcommittee was Dr Cyrus H. Peake (PhD, Columbia University) who had taught two years in prewar Japan before taking up a teaching position at his Alma Mater. Frank Rizzo was the sole member of the Finance Subcommittee, and the Subcommittee on the Emperor was led by First Lieutenant George A. Nelson Jr, assisted by Navy Ensign Richard A. Poole.

Chair of the Civil Rights Subcommittee was Colonel Pieter K. Roest, Chief of Political Parties Division. After graduating from Meiden University Medical School in Holland, Roest had studied anthropology at the University of Chicago, where he received his PhD. He later pursued interests in international relations, law and economics at the University of Southern California and conducted field research in India before joining the Navy in 1942. Roest was considered a visionary, and the Steering Committee viewed his ideas as 'irrelevant, fuzzy and impractical', but his contribution to the constitutional draft's civil rights provisions was substantial.[23] Working under Roest was Dr Harry E. Wildes, who held doctorates in economics from the University of Pennsylvania and Temple University. Before the war, he had lectured at Keiō University in Tokyo (1924–5) and authored a book on Japanese society.[24]

A key member of the Civil Rights Subcommittee was 22-year-old Beate Sirota, who had grown up in Tokyo. Sirota's parents were Russian Jews who had left Vienna prior to Hitler's ascension to power. After settling in Japan, her father Leo Sirota taught piano at the Imperial Academy of Music. Austrian by birth, Sirota became a naturalised US citizen and graduated from Mills College in California before taking wartime jobs with the Federal Communications Commission's Foreign Broadcast Intelligence Service and the Office of War Information. Sirota worked briefly for *Time* magazine in New York, where she was trained as a researcher. Fluent in six languages, she was hired by GHQ as an interpreter in December 1945 and subsequently was assigned to the Civil Rights Subcommittee, where, despite her youth, she was instrumental in inscribing the rights of women and children in the 1947 Constitution.[25]

Anti-Trust economists and legal experts
Another female staffer was Eleanor M. Hadley, like Sirota a graduate of Mills College, who worked on economic policy for Japan as a State Department employee from 1944 to 1946. Recruited by GS to help with the purge of big business, Hadley also assisted Economic and Scientific Section's Anti-Trust and Cartels Division and is associated with *zaibatsu* dissolution. After leaving GHQ, she taught at Smith College, worked as a trade specialist in Washington and wrote an influential history of the dissolution programme.[26] Another officer involved in economic deconcentration was Thomas A. Bisson. After completing a BA at Rutgers University and an MA at Columbia University, Bisson had worked as a missionary in China for four years, and in the late 1930s, he accompanied Owen Lattimore to Mao Zedong's headquarters in Yenan. By the time he joined Government Section as economic adviser in 1946, he had authored three influential books on Japan and Asia.[27] Bisson worked on the economic purge and land reform, but despite the respect his ideas commanded, he had little impact on the course of the Occupation.

The Section's premier legal mind was Alfred C. Oppler, a native of Alsace–Lorraine. Oppler had studied law at the Universities of Munich, Freiburg, Berlin and Strasbourg and fought in World War I. A talented lawyer, he rose rapidly to occupy top positions in the German judiciary. His Jewish ancestry cut short a brilliant career, however, and in the 1930s, Hitler's Nuremberg laws stripped him of his citizenship.

Oppler went into hiding and emigrated to the United States in 1939. During the war, he taught at the Harvard CATS before joining the Foreign Economic Administration's German Section, where he wrote a Civil Affairs Guide on Germany. In early 1946, Government Section hired Oppler from the War Department's Civil Affairs Division to head the Courts and Law Division. He moved to Legal Section in July 1948 with the transfer there of Courts and Law (below). An expert in codified law, Oppler was eminently qualified to tackle the reform of the Japanese legal system, which had been strongly influenced by German jurisprudence.[28] Working closely with Oppler was Thomas L. Blakemore of Government Powers Division, who helped revamp the judiciary. Blakemore began his career as an Oklahoma lawyer before joining the Foreign Service. An old Japan hand who had studied law in prewar Tokyo and spoke Japanese fluently, he served as Oppler's assistant, obtaining vital feedback from Japanese jurists. After the Occupation, Blakemore passed Japan's stringent bar exam, becoming one of the few non-Japanese qualified to practise law there.

EMPIRE OF THE INTELLIGENCE TSAR

MacArthur's 'black reactionary'
GHQ's intelligence arm, G-2, eventually became the most powerful agency inside MacArthur's headquarters. G-2's prominence was due largely to the personality of its chief, Major General Charles A. Willoughby. Born in Germany in 1892 to an aristocratic family, Willoughby (né von Tscheppe und Weidenbach) emigrated to the United States at the age of 18 and joined the US Army in 1912. He fought against Pancho Villa in Mexico in 1916 and served in Europe during World War I. An anti-Communist ideologue and open admirer of fascist leaders Benito Mussolini and General Francisco Franco, he epitomised, in the words of two British writers, 'the kind of militarist the Occupation was dedicated to destroying in Japan'. In 1939, Willoughby lauded Mussolini for 're-establishing the traditional military supremacy of the white race' in Ethiopia, and upon retiring from the Army in the 1950s, he served as adviser to Franco's Falangists.[29]

Fellow Occupationaires mocked the General's stiff Prussian bearing, referring to him alternately as 'Sir Charles' and 'Baron von Willoughby'. Willoughby had been MacArthur's intelligence chief in Melbourne, Brisbane and Manila and was part of the Bataan Gang. Regarded as a martinet by his subordinates – he took a perverse pride in the epithet 'Little Hitler', and even MacArthur dubbed him 'my lovable fascist' – the volatile Willoughby nonetheless enjoyed the Supreme Commander's full confidence. This bond of trust gave him immense authority, which he used with consummate skill to inflate the powers of G-2's civil intelligence apparatus. Citing health reasons, Willoughby resigned in May 1951 following MacArthur's dismissal in April, but like Whitney, he was acting out of loyalty to the Commander-in-Chief.

Photo 23. General Charles A. Willoughby, GHQ's brooding intelligence tsar (US National Archives).

Willoughby saw no middle ground between conservatives and Communists and found abhorrent many of the reforms promoted by GHQ's civil staff groups. He objected, for instance, to the Civil Information and Education Section's draft of the Civil Liberties Directive (chapter 6). Elliott R. Thorpe, head of SCAP's Civil Intelligence Section, had to appeal to Government Section for support in clearing the measure through G-2. Thorpe sought out Kades, and the two men finally prevailed on Willoughby to approve the directive, which was promulgated on 4 October 1945.[30] Willoughby also opposed the purge and police decentralisation, attempted to censor National Diet publications and pressed for the reinstatement of Old Guard military and political leaders removed from office in the early months of occupation.

The G-2 chief decried 'the leftist infiltration' of General Headquarters, complaining that fellow travellers hired in the United States were being dumped on GHQ's civil sections. He went to great lengths to identify and discredit progressive thinkers both inside GHQ and in Japanese society at large. Utilising the FBI's blacklist, the Security Index, he placed suspected Communists and even liberals under surveillance and investigated such New Dealers as Charles Kades, Eleanor Hadley and Thomas Bisson of Government Section. Willoughby claimed, absurdly, that the parents of Beate Sirota were Russian spies when in fact they were concert pianists and refugees from Nazism with no political influence. Kades, who got along well with the General on a personal level, asked him one day, 'You see a Communist under every bed. You think I'm a Communist?' Willoughby replied, 'No, I don't think you're a Communist, but you're surrounded by Communists.' In ESS, G-2 went after anti-trust chief Edward C. Welsh and labour specialists Theodore Cohen, Anthony Costantino and Valery Burati. Willoughby ordered the Japanese police to spy on the doings of all American officials who came into their area but to keep the reports secret from local Military Government Teams. These nefarious activities prompted Government Section's Alfred R. Hussey to complain bitterly to Whitney, 'Can we, who are denied our basic civil liberties by our own officials, persuade the Japanese of the worth of the doctrines we profess?'[31] Wisely, MacArthur ignored Willoughby's accusations, which in any event rested on dubious evidence.

The intelligence apparatus in flux

During the Pacific War, MacArthur had divided his intelligence operations between two commands: Allied combat intelligence was the responsibility of GHQ/SWPA; counter-intelligence activities were assigned to US Army Services of Supply. Willoughby headed SWPA's G-2 section, and Colonel (later Brigadier General) Elliott Thorpe was placed in charge of counter-intelligence and censorship in the USAOS logistics command. When MacArthur formed AFPAC in April 1945, he maintained the division of labour between combat intelligence (G-2) and counter-intelligence (Counter-Intelligence Section). With the formation of GHQ/SCAP, he combined the AFPAC and SCAP general staff sections but kept combat intelligence and counter-intelligence apart. Thus, at the start of the Occupation, Willoughby oversaw intelligence operations in AFPAC's G-2 and Thorpe ran counter-intelligence and censorship activities in both the AFPAC Counter-Intelligence Section and SCAP's Civil Intelligence Section.

Inside AFPAC, Willoughby found himself upstaged by Thorpe's dual commands. As of January 1946, G-2 consisted solely of the Allied Translation and Interpreters Service and a War Department team responsible for evaluating operational, civil and theatre intelligence. Thorpe's multiple responsibilities as head of Counter-Intelligence Section (CIS), AFPAC and Civil Intelligence Section (CIS), SCAP, included censoring the press and media, conducting counter-espionage, freeing political prisoners, arresting war crimes suspects and planning the purge. Responsible for public safety, Thorpe's CIS commands also monitored intellectual trends, oversaw Japanese police and fire-fighting agencies and supervised reforms in prison administration. Both of his intelligence sections were located together with Willoughby's G-2 in the main SCAP headquarters building.[32]

Civil Intelligence Section originally had four components: the 441st Counter-Intelligence Corps, the Civil Censorship Detachment, a civil communications intelligence team and an interrogation unit. In January 1946, Public Safety Section was set up inside CIS, but the 441st Counter-Intelligence Corps, Civil Censorship Detachment and interrogation unit were transferred from SCAP to the AFPAC Counter-Intelligence Section. Public Safety Section was rechristened Public Safety

Division (PSD) in April 1946, and in May, it was absorbed by the Civil Intelligence Division and called Public Safety Branch. Restored to Division status again in 1948, Public Safety had jurisdiction over the courts and legal affairs, maritime safety, the penitentiary system, fire departments, courts, the Metropolitan Police Office and other law enforcement agencies. PSD later supervised the implementation of police reforms, in particular the establishment of autonomous local police units under municipal control (chapter 7).

Thorpe appeared invincible, but Willoughby eventually emerged triumphant. In early 1946, responding to cuts in the military budget and public accusations that the Army payroll was top-heavy, the Pentagon reduced in rank all officers holding wartime promotions. Willoughby accepted the loss of status, but Thorpe believed that the demotion had destroyed his effectiveness in dealing with Japanese officials and resigned in protest.[33] On 3 May 1946, Thorpe's intelligence commands in AFPAC and SCAP were abolished, and that month G-2's newly established Civil Intelligence Division (CID) absorbed their duties.

GHQ's FBI

With the emasculation of Thorpe's original commands and Willoughby's arrogation of their functions, G-2 acquired full ascendancy over the Occupation's civil and military intelligence operations. Like MacArthur, the intelligence tsar now straddled two powerful commands, AFPAC and SCAP, vastly magnifying his authority. His control of this immense, highly centralised intelligence directorate made him, in the words of one Occupationaire, 'the second most powerful American in Japan'.[34]

In June 1946, Willoughby arranged to have all official contacts between foreign liaison missions and GHQ and between Occupation forces and Japanese agencies (except diplomatic business) conducted through his office. A Japanese Liaison Unit was created inside G-2 to handle official relations with the central government. On 29 August 1946, at Willoughby's insistence, MacArthur reactivated SCAP's Civil Intelligence Section as part of an expanded intelligence apparatus designed to combat the spread of Communism in Japan and placed it under G-2. A staff echelon in name only, the resuscitated CIS was a phantom unit not even listed in GHQ's telephone directory. Its Counter-Intelligence Corps, Civil Censorship Detachment and Public Safety Division were placed under the operational control of G-2's Civil Intelligence Division, which functioned as a de facto FBI. In June 1947, following President Truman's creation of a Loyalty Review Board in the United States, Willoughby established a Loyalty Desk inside the Public Safety Division to conduct loyalty checks on Occupation personnel. A Domestic Subversion Desk also was created to ferret out 'disaffected' Americans.

On at least one occasion, Willoughby exploited his paramount position to meddle openly in Japanese politics. In the spring of 1948, G-2 leaked secret information that high-ranking officials had taken bribes from Shōwa Denkō, Japan's largest manufacturer of fertiliser, in return for channelling Reconstruction Finance Bank (RFN) funds into company coffers. The scandal, an early instance of structural corruption, implicated Prime Minister Ashida Hitoshi and key members of his coalition of Democratic, Socialist and People's Cooperative parties. Shōwa Denkō took institutionalised graft to new heights, with allegations of shady dealing reaching the higher echelons of GHQ. The web of corruption was extensive and cried out for exposure, but Willoughby's clandestine intervention in the domestic political process helped precipitate the fall of the Ashida government, the last in which Socialists would participate for over four decades.

In July 1948, as Cold War tensions escalated, G-2 instructed the Diet to submit all of its publications to GHQ censors for security. The order enraged Justin Williams, head of Government Section's Parliamentary and Political Division. Williams told the Diet to ignore the injunction, and GS Deputy Chief Kades concurred. G-2 also was accused of blatant misconduct. On 7 December, 1952, a well-known Japanese intellectual, Kaji Wataru, who had gone missing for a year, suddenly returned home to announce that he had been sequestered by an ultra-secret US intelligence unit. During the war, Kaji had belonged to a group of Japanese Communists involved in 're-educating' Imperial Army POWs in China, and after the war, he became a prominent left-wing activist and polemicist. He identified his alleged kidnappers as the Canon Unit. Also known as 'Z-Unit', the group had been set up in December 1947 under Lieutenant Colonel Jack Y. Canon and attached to Public Safety Division's Joint Special Operations Branch. Canon's work was supervised directly by Willoughby. In October 1948, the Unit comprised 26 agents, some of whom had the right to carry arms, make arrests and conduct interrogations. Unit activities are said to have included domestic counter-espionage work and secret operations against North Korea and the Soviet Union. Reliable information on Canon's activities is scarce, however, and the true story of Kaji's abduction remains an enigma.[35]

To carry out its myriad duties, G-2 employed large numbers of former Japanese officers. Among them were men who had served on the Imperial General Staff or in Military Intelligence, the Military Police and even the Special Higher ('Thought') Police. In early September 1945, Willoughby secretly enlisted the services of Lieutenant General Arisue Seizō, the Army Military Intelligence chief he had met at the pre-surrender Manila conference of 19–20 August. Unknown to anyone in GHQ but Willoughby and his closest confederates, Arisue promptly established a clandestine section inside G-2 to monitor Communist régimes in Korea, Manchuria and the Soviet Union and, at home, a domestic surveillance group to watch the Japan Communist Party and Korean nationalists. These units would continue operating until the 1970s, providing a vital conduit between American and Japanese intelligence establishments.

Arisue and his cohorts also were assigned to assist Gordon W. Prange of the University of Maryland, who had been hired by the G-2 Historical Branch to write a history of MacArthur's campaigns in the Pacific. Shelved and forgotten after its completion in 1950, part of Prange's work finally was published by the Department of the Army in 1966 as *Reports of General MacArthur*. Arisue was assigned space in Prange's offices in the Nippon Yusen Kaisha Building and given a staff of 200

Japanese, mostly former officers. His team laboured diligently, producing two of the MacArthur history tomes (vol. 2: *Japanese Operations in the Southwest Pacific Area*, Parts 1 and 2) and a voluminous official Japanese account of the war. Nisei linguist and Harvard graduate Clarke H. Kawakami headed the American staff assigned to work with the Japanese group. The resulting multi–volume Japanese history of the war comprised 184 monographs on Imperial Army and Navy operations and 18 studies of Manchuria.[36]

Working alongside Arisue were former officers of the Army and Navy General Staffs, among them Colonel Hattori Takushirō, one-time military secretary to Tōjō Hideki, former section chief in Army Operations and influential member of the postwar Demobilisation Board; Rear Admiral Nakamura Kamesaburō; Captain Ōmae Toshikazu, a highly regarded military strategist who called himself the Imperial Navy's 'number one thinker'; and Lieutenant General Kawabe Torashiro, ex-military attaché to Nazi Germany and Deputy Chief, Army General Staff. These men belonged to a core of 15 high-ranking staff officers around whom Willoughby intended to rebuild a Japanese army (chapter 9). Indeed, Americans working with this group assumed that its research activities were a cover for the covert intelligence work described above. Exempted from the purge, these men received unusually high salaries and enjoyed privileges reserved for Occupation personnel. Moreover, they maintained the strict military hierarchy, divided along service lines, of the Imperial armed forces, and Japanese subordinates were under orders to address them by their former military titles. The special treatment accorded this élite would prompt Soviet Allied Council member Kuzma Derevyanko to protest that the purge of former military officers was being conducted selectively.[37]

A vital element of the G-2 Section was the Allied Translation and Interpreters Service (ATIS) staffed largely by Japanese Americans. ATIS personnel were assigned to the International Military Tribunal for the Far East as interpreters, translators, investigators and language officers. Nisei also served with distinction in the Counter-Intelligence Corps, Military Intelligence and the Civil Censorship Detachment, where their knowledge of Japan's culture and language proved indispensable. Many felt ambivalent about their allotted role as cultural go-betweens, however. Japanese tended to look down on them as 'inferior immigrant stock' or even 'traitors to the race' (*kokuzoku*). Nisei sometimes spoke dialects from Okayama or Okinawa and, despite intensive language training, were not always adept at using honorifics and polite language, creating friction with Japanese officials. At the same time, many white Americans distrusted Nisei because of their ancestry. Without the language skills and dedication of Japanese Americans, G-2 could not have performed its intelligence duties, but discrimination kept most from rising higher than lieutenant.

The top-ranking Nisei was Lieutenant Colonel John F. Aiso, briefly one of Willoughby's top aides. Aiso was a graduate of Brown College and Harvard Law School (he was the fourth Nisei ever to attend the latter institution) and also had studied at Chūō University in Tokyo before the war. In April 1941, he was drafted by the Army and in November became head instructor at the Military Intelligence Language School in San Francisco – the first Nisei to lead a vital war-related operation. In 1944, Aiso was given the rank of Major, ending an Army policy of not commissioning Japanese Americans. In February 1946, he was assigned to G-2, where he worked on the political purge. Aiso shared Willoughby's conviction that the purge directive was being taken to extremes and administered unfairly, a position that brought him into conflict with Government Section's Kades. The feud escalated into a test of wills between Willoughby and Kades, and in February 1947, Aiso left GHQ and returned to Los Angeles. He was replaced by Major Walter Tsukamoto.[38]

The Civil Intelligence Division
G-2's central surveillance organ was the Civil Intelligence Division (CID) under Colonel Rufus S. Bratton (succeeded in 1950 by Colonel Arthur L. Lacey). Through its Civil Censorship Detachment and Counter-Intelligence Corps, the Division exercised considerable influence over the administration of the Occupation. It reportedly was able to prevent even the Central Intelligence Agency, created in 1947, from operating freely in Japan until 1950. The Civil Intelligence Division supervised the Public Safety Branch, headed by Colonel Howard E. Pulliam, the Civil Censorship Detachment under Colonel William B. Putnam and the 441st Counter-Intelligence Corps commanded by Lieutenant Colonel W. E. Homan. In late 1947, the Civil Censorship Detachment's Communications Branch and Press, Pictorial and Broadcasting Branch were both elevated to division level, and in early 1948, the CID itself was reorganised as the Civil Intelligence Section (not to be confused with the phantom CIS of August 1946), with Colonel Bratton at its head. The revitalised CIS included Pulliam's Public Safety Division, Putnam's Civil Censorship Detachment and the 441st Counter-Intelligence Corps, now under Colonel R. G. Duff. CIS was a large section, employing 1,983 people as of 1 January 1948.[39] It was formally disbanded on 9 August 1951 and its functions reconsolidated under G-2.

One of the Occupation's key intelligence tasks was monitoring and censoring the mass media, the entertainment media and other expressions of public and private opinion, a duty SCAP entrusted to the Civil Censorship Detachment (CCD). The first CCD Chief was Lieutenant Colonel Donald D. Hoover, a former journalist and public relations specialist. Hoover resigned in November 1945 after establishing the basic pattern of censorship. He was succeeded by Lieutenant Colonel C. W. Wordsworth and, from April 1946, by Colonel Putnam. The Detachment consisted of the Communications Division (H. A. Engrav), which censored the mails, telephone, telegraph and other communications media, and the Press, Pictorial and Broadcasting Division (John J. Costello), which covered the information and entertainment media. The CCD routinely opened private mail and conducted pre-publication checks of books, journals and the press. Such actions, undertaken on an emergency basis, may have been inevitable in the early stages of occupation, but their maintenance until 1949 violated the constitutional guarantees of freedom of speech and thought that GHQ was committed to uphold. After an initial preoccupation with ultra-nationalist propaganda, Occupation censors turned their attention to leftist social, political and literary commentary (chapter 8).

Counter-Intelligence was the primary responsibility of the 441st Counter-Intelligence Corps (CIC). Established to identify threats to the Occupation mission, the CIC produced detailed surveillance reports on rightist and ultra-nationalist groups, located suspected war criminals and drew up purge dockets. As the Occupation progressed, however, it increasingly monitored trade-union leaders, liberal intellectuals and Communists. After 1947, fearing links between Koreans in Japan and the Soviet-backed government in northern Korea, the CIC intensified its coverage of Korean groups.[40] CIC units originally were assigned to each prefecture, and when Military Government Teams were disbanded in 1949, Counter-Intelligence groups remained in place. Japan was redivided into 61 CIC districts, and intelligence-gathering activities were intensified. Under a top secret alert plan, 'Tollbooth', CIC units drew up lists of potential 'subversives' to be apprehended and jailed in the event of an insurrection. Blacklists included leading Socialists and Communists, progressive governors and mayors, labour leaders and Korean activists. The CIC gathered information on the proposed general strike of 1947, drew up targets for the Red Purge and, in some cases, intervened directly in government affairs. In 1951, for instance, G-2 attempted to stop Communist parliamentarians from meeting in the Diet, a practice it considered 'inimical to the occupation and to the Japanese Government'. In July, a CIC agent visited the secretary of the House of Representatives and requested that he report Communist-sponsored gatherings on a regular basis. Government Section had to intervene to stop the intimidation tactics and preserve the dignity of Parliament.[41]

LEGAL SECTION

Legal Section (LS) was created on 2 October 1945 to advise SCAP on matters of law. LS also was responsible for investigating and prosecuting war crimes and recommending rules and procedures for Occupation courts. The International Prosecution Section (IPS) was established on 8 December 1945, with LS assistance, to prosecute civilian and military leaders before the International Military Tribunal for the Far East (IMTFE) in Tokyo. The IPS and Legal Section drew up the Tribunal's guidelines, known as the Tokyo Charter. At its height, the IPS included 277 Allied attorneys, investigators and assistants and 232 Japanese. It also boasted an Investigation Branch staffed by former FBI operatives (including two agents famous for bringing gangster John Dillinger to justice).[42] Legal Section and IPS had their offices in the Meiji Building (Marunouchi district); the IMTFE took place in the refurbished War Ministry Building near Ichigaya.

The International Prosecution Section and the IMTFE

MacArthur issued the Tokyo Charter on 19 January 1946. On 29 April, the International Prosecution Section formally lodged its indictment against 28 Japanese leaders, including former premier Tōjō Hideki, for conspiring to commit crimes against peace in Asia and the Pacific between 1928 and 1945. Emperor Hirohito's name was conspicuously absent from the list of accused. Of the original 28 defendants, 2 died during the proceedings and 1 was dismissed by reason of insanity, leaving 25 to face punishment. The trial opened on 3 May, and the IPS presented its case from 4 June 1946 until 24 January 1947. The defence took charge from 24 February 1947 until 12 January 1948. Final arguments were completed on 16 April 1948. By that time, the Tribunal had held 818 court sessions during which 419 witnesses had presented testimony. The final transcript was more than 48,000 pages in length, and the exhibits ran to an additional 30,000 pages.[43]

Unlike Nuremberg, where four chief prosecutors, one from each of the occupying powers, presented the Allied case, in Tokyo there was only one chief prosecutor, Joseph B. Keenan, who had been appointed US Chief of Counsel by President Truman. He was assisted by 10 associate prosecutors from the other participating Allied nations. A graduate of Brown University and Harvard Law School, Keenan was a New Deal politician well-versed in criminal law – he had headed the Justice Department's Criminal Division in its gang-busting days – and was noted for his bureaucratic skills. He was not proficient as a prosecutor, however, and a serious drinking problem, compounded by an uncanny resemblance to comedian W. C. Fields, gave him a bad press.

Whereas the IMTFE was a rather undistinguished Bench, the Allies sent some of their brightest legal minds to Tokyo. The International Prosecution Section included Arthur Comyns-Carr assisted by the noted Buddhist scholar Christmas Humphreys (Britain), Govinda Menon and Krishna Menon (India), and the internationally recognised Soviet jurist and diplomat Dr S. A. Golunsky. The IPS also boasted an outstanding woman jurist, Grace Llewellyn Kanode, an American. The large US team included the highest-rated trial lawyer in the United States, John Fihelly of the Justice Department, and John Darsey, who had represented the Attorney General at Nuremberg. Other prosecutors, however, were of lesser calibre.[44]

Through the International Defendants Section, the Tribunal provided counsel to more than 30 attorneys (all but nine of them Japanese) in defending the accused. The American defence lawyers were dismissed by New Zealand Justice Sir Erima Harvey Northcroft as thoroughly incompetent 'almost to childishness', and many indeed seemed interested primarily in making a name for themselves. A small number of highly motivated and competent individuals, however, displayed true dedication in the difficult and unpopular task of representing Japanese suspects. One such idealist was Owen Cunningham, former head of the Des Moines College of Law, who was debarred from the proceedings at one point for an impassioned attack on the legal foundations of the Tribunal.[45]

The Nuremberg Tribunal had been conducted by four justices – one from each of

Photo 24. Judges of the International Military Tribunal for the Far East, 26 September 1947. From left to right: R. Pal (India), B. V. A. Röling (Netherlands), E. S. McDougall (Canada), Lord Patrick (UK), M. C. Cramer (US), W. F. Webb (Tribunal President, Australia), J. A. Mei (Republican China), I. Zaryanoff (USSR), H. Bernard (France), E. H. Northcroft (New Zealand) and D. Jaranilla (Philippines) (US National Archives).

the victor nations – but the IMTFE Bench consisted of 11 judges from Australia, Britain, Canada, Republican China, France, Holland, India, New Zealand, the Philippines, the Soviet Union and the United States. Nine nations had signed the Instrument of Surrender, but the criterion for participation in the Tokyo Tribunal was membership in the Far Eastern Commission, and two additional justices, one each from India and the Philippines, were added at the insistence of Britain and the United States. The Philippines and India had made significant contributions to the war effort and suffered directly from Japanese depredations; both demanded a role in bringing the aggressor to justice. The court's disparate composition made deliberation difficult, however, increasing the likelihood of a split decision.

The Tribunal was presided over by Chief Justice Sir William Flood Webb of Australia. Born in Brisbane and educated at Queens University, Webb had served as Chief Justice of the Supreme Court of Queensland and distinguished himself on the Australian Supreme Court before taking up his appointment in Tokyo. The President and at least one other justice displayed obvious bias against the defendants, however, and several members of the Bench not only were obscure but patently unqualified (chapter 6). A simple majority was sufficient to convict yet, with few exceptions, the justices believed themselves competent to rule on the guilt or innocence of the accused.[46]

The IMTFE concluded its hearings in mid-April 1948 and in November, after seven months of deliberation, the justices handed down their verdicts. The Tribunal ruled by a majority of 8 that all 25 surviving defendants were guilty of crimes against peace and sentenced 7 to hang. The judgment was not unanimous, however. Three judges, including Indian Justice Radhabinod Pal, the only jurist fully versed in international law,[47] wrote dissenting opinions. Moreover, the Tribunal was divided on the issue of the Emperor's war guilt. The IMTFE was dissolved on 12 December, and on 12 February 1949, the International Prosecution Section, too, was disbanded and its residual functions turned over to Legal Section.

Legal Section

Legal Section coordinated the activities of the IPS and was responsible for providing IMTFE defence lawyers. From 1949 to 1950, it helped determine the reduction of sentences for convicted war criminals. With the dissolution of the IMTFE, the Section shifted its focus to international law and the legal aspects of economic reconstruction, in particular exchange controls and international trade regulations. Its counterpart in the Japanese government was the Attorney General's Office.

A medium-sized section, as of February 1948, LS had 599 staff members, including 30 military officers, 17 enlisted personnel, 220 civilians and 322 support staff, mainly Japanese. It was composed of five divisions: Administrative, Law, Legislation and Justice, Philippine, and Australian. The Philippine and Australian Divisions provided liaison between GHQ/SCAP, Manila and Canberra on war crimes issues. The LS regional office in Manila closed in November 1949 after the US Military Commission in Manila handed down its last sentence. The Australian Division operated until the end of the Occupation. The Section also maintained regional branches in Fukuoka, Hiroshima, Ni'igata, Osaka, Nagoya and Sapporo. It was discontinued on 28 April 1952.

Chief of Section was Colonel Alva C. Carpenter, one of the original Bataan Gang. During the Occupation, Carpenter resigned his commission, becoming one of GHQ's rare civilian section chiefs. Among the distinguished lawyers, judges, legal scholars and experts in labour law who worked under him, four deserve special mention. Alfred C. Oppler was transferred from Government Section to Legal Section in 1948 once the basic work of the GS Courts and Law Division had been completed. As Chief of the LS Legislation and Justice Division, Oppler was responsible for examining the constitutionality of Diet legislation. He brought most of his staff with him, including Thomas Blakemore. Another top-notch legal mind Oppler tapped for his Division was Kurt Steiner, who became the LS human rights expert. A Jewish refugee from Nazism like Oppler, Steiner had graduated from the University of Vienna and fled to the United States in 1939. Joining MacArthur's headquarters in 1946, he worked as an IPS prosecutor until 1948. Steiner was well-versed in Japanese and became Oppler's deputy in 1949, heading the Civil Affairs and Civil Liberties Branch, a position he held until 1951.[48]

Leonard Appel, a University of Denver law graduate, formerly served on the National Labour Relations Board. During the war, he worked with labour movements in the Middle East and Germany as a member of the Office of Strategic

Services' Labour Division. Arriving in Tokyo in March 1946 with the US Advisory Committee on Labour in Japan, Appel helped draft the labour protection laws (chapter 7). He left Japan when the Committee's work was finished but returned in the spring of 1947, entering the LS Law Division, where he helped revise the National Public Service Law and enact the Public Corporation Labour Relations Law. The former outlined the rights and duties of government employees; the latter set out employees' rights in public enterprises, such as the Japan National Railways, Japan Telegram and Telephone, and the Japan Salt and Tobacco monopolies.

The Law Division Chief from September 1946 until the end of the Occupation was Jules Bassin. A graduate of New York City University Law School, Bassin joined LS in October 1945 after intensive training in security and intelligence, the law of military occupation and Japanese at the Harvard and University of Virginia Military Government Schools. As Law Division head, he worked on such questions as the taxation of non-Japanese nationals, the exercise of civil and criminal jurisdiction and the status and treatment of Koreans and Formosans in Japan. Bassin collaborated closely with Richard Finn of Diplomatic Section in devising GHQ's policy toward the Korean and Formosan minorities. After the Occupation, he joined the State Department, becoming legal attaché at the US Embassy in Tokyo.

Legal Section was SCAP's primary watchdog agency for civil rights. Between 1945 and 1948, Oppler's Legislation and Justice Division initiated important reforms freeing the judiciary from executive domination. The Division also tried unsuccessfully to limit the persecution of leftist groups during the Red Purge. In 1950, Oppler and Steiner collaborated on a lengthy brief criticising Prime Minister Yoshida's proposal to outlaw the Communist Party. In 1949, Bassin's Law Division suggested that Koreans be allowed to normalise their legal status and opt for full Japanese citizenship (the proposal was rejected), and in 1951, it frustrated a government attempt to classify ethnic Koreans and Formosans as aliens liable to deportation (chapter 10). In 1951, Oppler unsuccessfully opposed the enactment of the controversial Subversive Activities Prevention Law, which he considered an unconstitutional attempt to revive the 1925 Peace Preservation Law (the anti-subversion measure was passed into law in July 1952).

ECONOMIC AND SCIENTIFIC SECTION

Economic and Scientific Section (ESS) was the first special staff group to be created independently of the AFPAC Military Government Section. Established on 15 September 1945 as an autonomous staff echelon, it was assigned control over Japan's economic affairs and advised SCAP on labour, finance and industry, both in Japan and Korea. In Germany, these functions had been allocated to different staff sections in the Allied Command. In Japan, they were assumed by a single colossal bureaucracy with supervisory authority over several ministries and government agencies. ESS was responsible for *zaibatsu* dissolution, labour reform, the Dodge stabilisation programme, the reorganisation of Japan's scientific establishment and reparations (until May 1947 when a separate Reparations Section was formed).

Organisation and mission

ESS was one of the largest GHQ staff groups. In February 1948, it had 1,189 employees, including 33 military officers, 40 enlisted personnel, 599 civilians and 527 other employees, mainly Japanese. As of January 1946, it included nine major divisions: Anti-Trust and Cartels, Exports and Imports, Finance, Industry, Legal, Labour, Price Control and Rationing, Scientific and Technical, and Statistics and Research. In June 1946, ESS was augmented by the Textile Division, and between 1949 and 1950, the Divisions of Banking and Foreign Exchange, Internal Revenue, Public Finance, Tourists and Service, and Utilities and Fuels were added. Reflecting its broad mandate, ESS dealt with the Ministries of Commerce and Industry (later, International Trade and Industry), Finance and Labour and the Economic Stabilisation Board (chapter 7). The Section's offices were located in the Forestry Building behind SCAP headquarters. ESS was disbanded on 28 April 1952.

The brunt of ESS's early reform programme was borne mainly by Anti-Trust and Cartels Division and Labour Division. Anti-Trust and Cartels implemented the recommendations of the Edwards Mission (January to March 1946) for the breakup of the *zaibatsu* and sponsored a deconcentration law designed to dismantle other monopolistic practices. Labour Division, assisted by the US Advisory Committee on Labour in Japan, endeavoured to free the work force from prewar authoritarian constraints. Assisted by an ad hoc Japanese advisory group, it drafted the Labour Union Law (1945) guaranteeing workers the right to organise, engage in collective bargaining and strike and secured passage of the Labour Relations Adjustment Act (1946) and the Labour Standards Act (1947).

The Section's reform programme lost steam as US priorities switched to economic recovery. From May 1948, Anti-Trust and Cartels' deconcentration policies were ignored or reversed, and by December 1949, the dissolution programme had been abandoned (that month, Anti-Trust and Cartels was renamed the Fair Trade Division). In 1949, ESS was placed under the scrutiny of the Office of the Comptroller, a special staff group set up by order of the Department of the Army, to temper the Section's zeal for economic decentralisation. Labour Division lost its liberal élan in 1948 following the revision of the National Public Service Law denying civil servants the right to strike. By 1949, Washington's efforts to lower occupation costs and transform Japan into the capitalist powerhouse of Asia had become an all-consuming goal, economic democracy took a back seat to economic self-sufficiency and the rapid reintegration of Japan into the world economy. One of the vehicles for this transformation was the Dodge Economic Stabilisation Programme, a package of retrenchment measures introduced in 1949 to lower inflation and expand productive capacity. Responsibility for eight of the Dodge Plan's nine points devolved on ESS divisions. Consequently, ESS as a whole became increasingly involved in the details of fiscal reform, currency stabilisation and the revival of trade, while Labour Division devoted its energies to the Red Purge. A bright point in this otherwise dismal picture was the Section's leadership in liberalising scientific research, but with the 'reverse course', its democratising mission came to a halt. In the last year of occupation, ESS spearheaded an American effort to revive the Japanese armaments industry by funnelling US technological and financial support to key manufacturers for the production of military hardware (chapter 10).

Staff

ESS was first headed by Colonel Raymond C. Kramer, a former department store executive from New York.[49] While in Manila, Kramer had begun work on plans to convert the AFPAC Military Government Section into a separate headquarters, SCAP. In early September, he pushed for the creation of an independent Economic and Scientific Section and requested the services of several well-known US industrial and financial experts to staff it. During the first weeks of occupation, Kramer issued a directive freezing the assets of Hirohito's household and convinced leading *zaibatsu* to dismantle voluntarily, setting the stage for ESS's dissolution programme. Kramer resigned in December after being passed over for promotion and was replaced by Major General William F. Marquat, a career officer with no knowledge of economics whom a peer once described as 'an easygoing, affable anti-aircraft officer [who] looked and often talked like a football coach'.[50] In his youth, Marquat had been a professional boxer, then a reporter for *The Seattle Times*. During World War I, he took a commission in the Army Field Artillery. After the war, Marquat returned to journalism but re-enlisted in the late 1930s and was assigned to MacArthur's command in the Philippines, where he became the General's chief artillery officer and one of the charmed inner circle of military advisers.[51] Marquat was a hard worker and proved to be a surprisingly effective section chief. Lacking expertise in economics and scientific matters, however, he relied heavily on his division chiefs for policy advice.

The Finance and Internal Revenue Divisions were staffed by well-trained, competent specialists,[52] but the Section's top talent was concentrated in Anti-Trust and Cartels Division and Labour Division. Anti-Trust and Cartels had two outstanding chiefs, J. MacI. Henderson and Edward C. Welsh. Henderson had worked as special assistant to the US Attorney General and headed the Justice Department's West Coast Anti-Trust Division. He came to Japan with the Edwards Mission in January 1946 and, together with Raymond Vernon, Assistant Director of the US Securities and Exchange Commission, remained with ESS to help implement the anti-monopoly programme. Henderson succeeded S. W. Wheeler as head of Anti-Trust and Cartels in May 1946 and found himself responsible for dismantling the Mitsubishi conglomerate based on recommendations he had drawn up earlier. Henderson left for the Philippines in late 1946, and six months later, Edward C. Welsh stepped in to fill his shoes, remaining until the spring of 1950.

Photo 25. Raymond C. Kramer, the architect of GHQ's super-government and first chief of Economic and Scientific Section, confers with reparations expert Edwin W. Pauley (seated right) and ESS Industry Division's Joseph Z. Reday (seated left). 13 December 1945 (Kyodo).

A highly educated and motivated officer, Welsh had written a PhD dissertation at the University of Ohio on trust dissolution and the impact of monopoly on prices and, during the war, had helped administer government price controls. Imbued with a strong sense of mission, the quick and articulate economist was passionately committed to the radical dismantling of the *zaibatsu* empire. He brought with him from Washington a copy of the State Department's FEC-230 (May 1947), a confidential policy paper transmitting the Edwards Report to the Far Eastern Commission. Welsh drafted and helped clear through the Diet GHQ's anti-monopoly centrepiece, the Law on the Elimination of Excessive Concentrations of Economic Power, which was enacted in December 1947. His 'go-go' enthusiasm and radical approach to dissolution earned him the enmity of the big business lobby in Washington and seemed excessive even to the New Dealers in ESS.[53]

Labour Division chiefs were Major William Karpinsky, Theodore Cohen, James S. Killen, Chester W. Hepler and Robert T. Amis. Karpinsky was an electrical engineer from Duke University who had worked for the Labour Department and the New Jersey Mediation Service and taught at Monmouth College before joining the Army. He came to GHQ via the Harvard CATS and AFPAC's Military Government Section, Manila. Karpinsky banned police intervention in labour activities, dissolved two reactionary labour fronts, encouraged union organising, steered the Labour Union Law of December 1945 through Parliament and sponsored the visit of the US Advisory Committee on Labour in Japan. He was replaced by Theodore Cohen in January 1946.

Of Russian-Jewish stock, Cohen had studied under Hugh Borton at Columbia University, producing a 200-page Master's thesis on the Japanese labour movement. He taught briefly at City College, New York and went to work for the Foreign Economic Administration's Japanese Labour Policy Section in Washington, where he drafted Civil Affairs Guides on labour and the administration of Imperial Household property. He read and spoke Japanese fluently, a rare ability in GHQ. At 28, Cohen was GHQ's youngest division chief. In Labour Division, he supervised the drafting of the Labour Relations Adjustment Law and the Labour Standards Law and established procedures for resolving labour–management conflicts through conciliation, mediation and arbitration. Assisted by Anthony Costantino of the Division's Labour Relations Branch, he also played a central role in preventing the general strike of 1947. Following the collapse of the strike, a US reporter accused Cohen of harbouring leftist sympathies. Although MacArthur knew this to be false, he removed Cohen from Labour Division in March 1947 to avoid further controversy – and potential damage to his presidential ambitions. Cohen subsequently was appointed economic adviser to General Marquat (1947–50). This dedicated liberal had, as one journalist remarked, 'a pathological fear of being labelled red'. Cohen later remarked, 'I'd been pretty close to the Communists as a kid; some of my relatives were Communists . . . but I've been anti-Communist since I was 18 years old.'[54]

Cohen was succeeded by James S. Killen, a union organiser whom Cohen himself had recruited from the conservative American Federation of Labour. Killen began his career as a worker in the pulp and paper industry in Washington State, but by 1937 his energy, intelligence and oratory skills had won him a position as full-time union activist. He successfully organised Japanese-Canadian labourers in British Columbia, was an AFL delegate and served as assistant director of the War Production Board's Pulp and Paper Division. A self-proclaimed New Dealer, Killen also was a staunch anti-Communist. Nonetheless, as Labour Division Chief, he strongly supported the right of civil servants and public enterprise employees to bargain collectively and, within limits, to strike. He resigned from ESS in 1948 after failing to persuade MacArthur to drop plans denying civil servants these guarantees under the revised National Public Service Law. Under Killen, Labour Division began actively wooing moderate anti-Communist unions.[55]

Later Division heads Chester W. Hepler and Robert T. Amis worked to dampen many of the early labour reforms. Hepler was a graduate of Wesleyan College in Ohio. After working as a banker and accountant, he joined the Department of

Photo 26. Golda G. Stander, ESS Labour Division official. Stander was midwife to Japan's Labour Standards Law of April 1947 (Courtesy of Golda Stander).

Labour and later the Federal Employment Administration. Amis graduated from the US Naval Academy after serving in World War I. Earning a law degree from Georgetown University, he worked for the FBI and the Department of Agriculture's Resettlement Administration before becoming special assistant to Secretary of Labour Francis Perkins. During the war, he served on the War Labour Board. Amis became Labour Division Chief in 1950 at the height of the Red Purge. With the assistance of Austria-born union organiser Valery Burati, he also encouraged the development of *Sōhyō*, the General Council of Trade Unions of Japan, as a free, democratic labour federation. Despite its non-Communist origins, however, *Sōhyō* quickly became Japan's most powerful and militant national centre, opposing American policy towards Japan.[56]

Labour Division chiefs were assisted by a distinguished staff.[57] Notable among them was Golda G. Stander, who coordinated the passage of the Labour Standards Law. Stander held a Master's degree from New York City University and had worked for several New York State and Federal labour organisations, including the National Wage Stabilisation Board. In 1946, she joined ESS as head of Labour Division's Wages and Working Conditions Branch. Bitterly opposed to the Red Purge, Stander left SCAP in 1951 to work successively in the Philippines, Panama, Mexico and Peru as a labour and welfare adviser and later took up a position with US Aid for International Development. Between 1947 and 1949, Stander was assisted by Meade M. Smith. With an MA in economics from Swarthmore College in Pennsylvania, Smith joined the Labour Department's Bureau of Labour Statistics during the war and helped draft the Civil Affairs Handbook on Japanese labour.

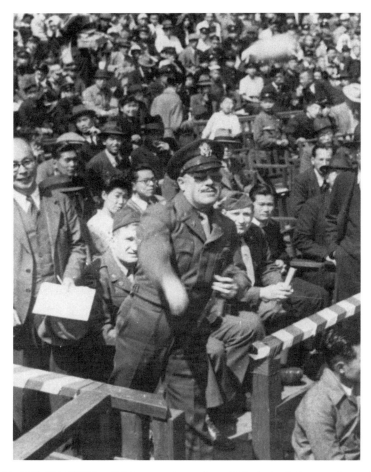

Photo 27. ESS Chief William F. Marquat. A member of MacArthur's Bataan Gang, the anti-aircraft officer was a former boxer and sports journalist who enthusiastically promoted American baseball in Japan. Here, he throws out the first ball in Japan's premier major-league opening season, 4 April 1948 (Kyodo).

Under Stander, Smith encouraged the democratisation of the women's union movement and helped write the clauses in the Labour Standards Law protecting women and minors.[58]

The Scientific and Technical Division

An important but lesser known ESS group was the Scientific and Technical Division (STD) created in mid-November 1945 to advise GHQ on science-related matters. The importance of the STD was greatly enhanced by MacArthur's destruction, on Pentagon orders, of four Japanese research cyclotrons for accelerating sub-atomic particles in late November 1945, creating outrage among US scientists and a keen awareness inside GHQ of the need for sound scientific counsel. The Division was instructed to monitor closely or eliminate scientific institutions with war potential, particularly those engaged in research in aeronautics, atomic energy and radioactivity. But it also played a constructive role in helping Japanese scientists and engineers recover from defeat and contribute effectively to economic recovery. One of STD's major accomplishments was the establishment of the Science Council of Japan, a non-governmental group of scientists elected by their peers to recommend basic science policy to the government, and the Scientific and Technical Administration Commission, a government agency charged with coordinating science policy and the forerunner of today's Science and Technology Agency.[59]

Scientific and Technical Division was unique among GHQ's staff units in that it was headed by an Australian engineer and munitions expert, Brigadier General John William Alexander O'Brien. ESS Chief Kramer had known O'Brien in Australia during the war and originally asked him to head the Industrial Division. When GHQ objected to the appointment of a non-American to that position, Kramer named the Australian to lead the Scientific and Technical Division instead. O'Brien had difficulty recruiting American officers to serve under him and so drafted several members of the Australian Scientific Mission during their visit to Tokyo in January 1946. One of these, Lieutenant Colonel Edward Allan, remained with O'Brien until the final years of the Occupation. The presence of Australians in a virtually all-American organisation posed a number of problems, personal and logistical, but O'Brien overcame them to become a valued member of ESS. He assisted the Pauley Mission in identifying plant and equipment for reparations and played a central role in reforming Japan's leading scientific organisations. O'Brien was assisted by a highly qualified American scientist, Dr Harry C. Kelly from the Massachusetts Institute of Technology's Radiation Laboratory.[60] In April 1951, another American, Dr Bowen C. Dees, replaced O'Brien as Division Chief.

In early 1946, shortly after his arrival, Kelly was placed in charge of a new STD sub-group, the Special Projects Unit (later Special Projects Branch), set up on the advice of an American nuclear physicist to investigate laboratories capable of conducting atomic research. Kelly worked closely with G-2 and reported not to O'Brien but directly to Marquat. The Special Projects Unit also worked with the Atomic Bomb Casualty Commission, a joint US–Japan scientific group created to study the medical effects of the atomic bombings. At the same time, Kelly was deeply involved in the establishment of the Science Council of Japan and the Scientific and Technical Administration Commission. He also helped Dr Nishina Yoshio, Japan's foremost nuclear scientist, rescue the Institute of Physical and Chemical Research (*Rigaku Kenkyūjo*, or *Riken*). *Riken* had been entrusted with Japan's wartime atomic development project, and its sprawling network of research laboratories was slated for destruction under the ESS *zaibatsu* dissolution programme. With Kelly's assistance, Riken was democratised and reorganised as the Scientific Research Institute (*Kagaku Kenkyūsho*). In 1950, Kelly helped SRI Director Nishina acquire radio isotopes from the United States for research purposes, and despite the constraints under which he worked, did much to enhance freedom of scientific inquiry in Japan.[61]

CIVIL INFORMATION AND EDUCATION

Civil Information and Education Section (CI&E) grew out of two different organisations. The first was Education Branch of the Public Affairs Division in AFPAC's Military Government Section (MGS). Set up in June 1945, it was staffed by teachers and academics, many of them drawn from the Civil Affairs Staging Area in Monterey. The second was AFPAC's Information Dissemination Section (IDS) headed by Bonner F. Fellers, which had been converted from Fellers' Psychological Warfare Branch on 27 August 1945 and given the task of preparing a comprehensive information policy for occupation, including a liberal school curriculum.[62] On 22 September, CI&E was cobbled together from both units and established as an independent staff group inside GHQ/AFPAC's Yokohama headquarters. On 2 October, it was incorporated into GHQ/SCAP and assigned offices in the cavernous Radio Tokyo Building in Hibiya Park.

CI&E was responsible for advising the Supreme Commander on policies relating to 'public information, education, religion and other sociological problems of Japan and Korea'. Reflecting its organisational antecedents, the Section also was assigned a propaganda mission: the dissemination of democratic ideals and principles. As of February 1948, CI&E was a medium-sized section, with 563 employees, of whom 14 were military officers, 24 enlisted personnel, 202 civilian officials and 323 general staff, predominantly Japanese. The Section worked primarily with the Education Ministry.

From October 1945 to November 1945, CI&E consisted of seven branches: Administration; Education and Religions; Press and Publications; Radio; Motion Picture; Planning and Special Projects; and Analysis and Research. Between late 1945 and January 1946, Education and Religions became two separate units, Theatre was added to Motion Pictures, becoming Motion Picture and Theatrical Branch, and Language, Library Science and Arts and Monuments were established as new branches. As the Occupation proceeded, however, CI&E became progressively centralised and complex. In June 1946, branches were upgraded to divisions, and in May 1948, the Section underwent a third reorganisation.[63] From 1948 to the end of the Occupation, it consisted of five divisions: Administration; Education; Religions and Cultural Resources; Information; and Public Opinion and Sociological Research.[64] On 3 April 1951, the Section established a CI&E staff group in the UN Unified Command in Korea. It was dissolved as a special staff group of GHQ/SCAP on 28 April 1952.

The first Chief of Section was Brigadier General Kermit ('Ken') R. Dyke, who headed CI&E from September 1945 to May 1946. Dyke was a former vice-president for promotion and research of the National Broadcasting Corporation. An advertis-

Photo 28. Kermit R. Dyke, first chief of Civil Information and Education Section, holds a press conference to announce the Shintō Directive, 16 December 1945. Immediately behind Dyke is William K. Bunce of Religions Branch. Standing at the far left is Daniel C. Imboden of Press and Publications Branch (Kyodo).

ing specialist, he had worked as a propagandist with the Office of War Information (OWI) before joining SWPA in 1943, where he directed troop information and education. His knowledge of Japan was limited, but during his short tenure, he helped free political prisoners, disband the Special Higher Police, draft the Emperor's New Year's message renouncing his divinity (1946), purge ultra-nationalists from the schools and media and write the Shintō Directive. A liberal, Dyke was labelled by conservative SCAP higher-ups as 'that damned pink', and he returned to the United States early in the Occupation.[65]

Dyke's successor, Lieutenant Colonel Donald R. Nugent, US Marine Corps, held a degree in education and a PhD in Far Eastern History from Stanford University. In 1936, he co-edited a textbook on the Pacific region[66] and, from 1937 to 1941, taught in Japan at the Wakayama Business School and Osaka Commercial College. Nugent also served as district superintendent of schools in California and taught history and economics at Menlo Junior College. Upon returning to the United States in 1941, he joined the Marines and underwent training in Japanese and psychological warfare. His academic background, Japan experience and basic knowledge of the spoken language qualified him for top positions in CI&E. Although Nugent enthusiastically implemented basic school reforms, he was a dyed-in-the-wool conservative, and beginning with the second *Yomiuri* dispute of 1946, he coordinated a steadily escalating assault on Communist influence in the labour movement, the schools and the mass media that culminated in the Red Purge of 1949–50.

Education and Religions
The CI&E mandate covered three fundamental areas of reform: education, religion and information. The Section's most pressing task was the overhaul of Japan's education system, a responsibility that initially fell to its Education and Religions Branch. On 28 November 1945, that group became two independent units, Education Branch and Religions Branch. Education Branch organised a purge to remove ultra-nationalist teachers from the schools and sponsored the visit of the first US Education (Stoddard) Mission in March 1946 to recommend basic education reforms. It was responsible for implementing the School Law and the Fundamental Education Law of 1947. The Branch also liberalised textbook certification, revised school texts, introduced social studies, initiated teacher training and vocational programmes, standardised entrance exams for public universities and promoted the establishment of new universities.

Education and Religions Branch (and later Education Branch) was led by Major (from November, Lieutenant Colonel) Harold G. Henderson. Born in New York, Henderson held a Master's degree in chemical engineering from Columbia University. While living in Japan in the 1930s, he had developed a deep interest in Japanese art and poetry and later taught Japanese literature at his Alma Mater. During the war, he served as a psychological warfare specialist with Fellers's Psychological Warfare Branch, where he composed propaganda leaflets. He worked briefly in AFPAC's Information Dissemination Section, the PWB's successor, before taking charge of Education and Religions Branch. In December 1945, he was transferred to an advisory position in CI&E after incurring MacArthur's displeasure and returned to Columbia University shortly afterwards to continue his academic career.

Henderson was assisted by two able subordinates, Navy Lieutenant (later, Lieutenant Commander) Robert K. Hall and Lieutenant Commander (afterwards, Commander) Herbert J. Wunderlich. Hall was a Harvard graduate in education with a Master's degree in Asian studies from Columbia University and a PhD from the University of Michigan. During the war, he joined the Navy and attended Princeton's Naval School of Military Government. Hall was exceptionally well-informed about Japanese education and, at the Civil Affairs Staging Area (CASA), became Education Section Chief on CASA's Occupation Planning Staff. He is best remembered for his unsuccessful crusade to substitute Latin script for Chinese characters in Japan. In early 1946, Hall was sent to Korea to advise the US Military Government on education reform, and he returned to the United States in May to take up a position at Columbia Teachers' College. Hall's Language Simplification Unit included linguist Dr Abraham M. Halpern (PhD, Chicago), who replaced Hall, and John Pelzel, who later taught cultural anthropology at Harvard. Herbert J. Wunderlich had been Dean of Student Affairs at Stanford University before entering

CI&E, where he was responsible for revising school textbooks and curricula. In 1946, he left Japan for the University of Idaho.[67]

Army Air Forces Lieutenant Colonel Mark T. Orr succeeded Nugent as Chief of Education Division in May 1946. Returning to civilian status, he stayed on as Division Chief until March 1949. Before the war, Orr had studied political science and English at the University of North Carolina, helped found and edit an academic journal (*The South and World Affairs*) and worked as a local journalist and newspaper editor. Drafted before he could complete his PhD, he trained at the University of Virginia's School of Military Government, the University of Michigan CATS and the Civil Affairs Staging Area. At CASA, he worked under Robert Hall in Education Section. Together with Nugent, Orr was one of the handful of CI&E staff officers conversant in Japanese.[68] Dr Arthur K. Loomis, who relieved Orr as Education Division Chief in March 1949, remained until March 1952. Loomis held a PhD from Colorado University and had served as superintendent of schools in Ohio during the war. He taught education at Denver University before joining CI&E in 1947.

CI&E also strove to eliminate authoritarian religious practices. The Religions Branch, upgraded to division level in June 1946, was inaugurated to sever links between religion and the state, prevent the re-emergence of ultra-nationalistic religious sects and monitor the implementation of GHQ policies among religious groups. The Religions Division Chief was Navy Lieutenant (from early 1946, Lieutenant Commander) William K. Bunce. Bunce earned a PhD in history from Ohio State University and, from 1936 to 1939, taught English at a Japanese high school in Matsuyama, Ehime Prefecture. In 1941, he became Dean of Otterbein College, Ohio before volunteering for the Navy. During the war, he served as Education Officer at the Princeton Naval School of Military Government. With the creation of AFPAC's Military Government Section in Manila, Bunce was appointed head of Education Branch in the MGS Public Affairs Division. Under his leadership, CI&E's Religions Division disestablished State Shintō and worked to ensure freedom of belief. After the Occupation, Bunce remained in Tokyo with the State Department's US Information Services (USIS), and from 1965 to 1968 headed its branch in Seoul.

Information

A third focus of reform was information. CI&E's Information Division inherited virtually intact Feller's Information Dissemination Section, taking over its functions and retaining its leading intelligence experts. CI&E's first information tsar was Bradford Smith, former head of OWI's Central Pacific Operations. A graduate of Columbia University, Smith had taught at Tokyo Imperial University and St Paul's (Rikkyō) University from 1931 to 1936 before joining the OWI during the war. He represented the State Department while serving with Feller's IDS and, following the creation of CI&E, became information adviser to CI&E Chief Dyke. It was Smith who reportedly urged Dyke to issue the Civil Liberties Directive. Smith was replaced by Don Brown, another OWI propagandist, who arrived in December 1945 and remained with CI&E as Information Division Chief until 1952. A University of Pittsburgh graduate, Brown had worked in prewar Japan for *The Japan Advertiser* (forerunner of *The Japan Times*) and spoke fluent Japanese.[69]

Information Division was responsible for ideological redirection, and in the early phase of occupation, its staff adopted liberal positions. Press and Publications Branch (PPB) censored the media of ultra-nationalistic content but also spread democratic ideals. It initially supported the workers of Japan's three largest dailies – the *Asahi, Mainichi* and *Yomiuri* – in their struggle to gain control of production, expel reactionary managers and liberalise editorial policies. PPB Chief Robert H. Berkov actively encouraged such struggles as a democratising trend. A newsman with a degree from Colorado University, Berkov worked as an OWI operative during the war. He played an important early role in freeing the mass media from totalitarian controls but was forced from his job by General Willoughby for acknowledging too freely the real origins of the 1946 Constitution.

As the Occupation grew more conservative in outlook, such positive efforts were curbed and in a few cases reversed. Major (later Lieutenant Colonel) Daniel C. Imboden, who succeeded Berkov in June 1946, took an openly antagonistic stance towards the media. An ultra-conservative ex-editor who had owned his own paper in San Luis Obispo, California, Imboden believed publishers should be free of 'outside interference' from journalists and editorial staff. He viewed media workers' efforts to liberalise management and news content as a dangerous encroachment on the owners' autonomy. As a result, from mid-1946, CI&E supported publishers in their sometimes violent efforts to reassert control over their papers. Through Imboden and others like him, media reform degenerated into a vendetta against left-wing journalists, editors and union leaders.

The Motion Picture and Drama (later, Motion Picture and Theatrical) Branch was another progressive group. From October 1945 to June 1946, it was led by David W. Conde, a Canadian-born US citizen who had served with the OWI's Psychological Warfare Branch during the war. Conde was known for his radical ideas, a zealous determination to reform Japanese cinema and a short temper. Under his leadership, the Motion Picture and Drama Branch worked to revitalise film-making and theatre by encouraging anti-militaristic and democratic themes. After leaving GHQ, Conde worked as a stringer for International News Service and Reuters until running foul of Willoughby in July 1947. He was forced to leave Japan when an article critical of SCAP's censorship programme appeared in *The St Louis Post-Dispatch*. Conde was replaced by George Gercke, one of the few Information Division staff members with actual experience in the film industry. Gercke headed the Branch from November 1946 to the end of the Occupation.[70]

Radio Branch developed 'positive' information programmes for public broadcasting and helped remould the Japan Broadcasting Corporation (NHK). It was headed initially by psychological warfare experts Irving C. Correll and Captain William V. Roth, and later by Albert C. Crews and Dwight B. Herrick, both professional NBC radiomen. The Information Division's Libraries Officer was Paul Burnette, who was succeeded by Ronald A. Mulhauser. In 1949, Mulhauser transferred to the Information Centers Branch and was replaced by Jane Fairweather, a specialist from Education Division. In the very early days of CI&E, Dr P. O. Keeny, Chief Librarian at the University of Montana and professor of library science, drafted the so-called Keeny Plan for the reform of Japan's library system. Education Division's Adult Education Officer John M. Nelson, a young educator from Kansas, helped husband the plan into the 1950 Library Law.

Women's rights and female educators

Information Division's Planning Unit (later, Planning and Programmes Branch) coordinated SCAP's propaganda effort. It expanded public access to information, promoted land reform, encouraged the labour movement and worked to improve the status of women. Initially, Captain Arthur Behrstock and Lieutenant Ethel B. Weed featured prominently in this work. Behrstock, another OWI propaganda expert, headed the Planning Unit until late 1946, when he returned to the State Department. Behrstock was succeeded by Lieutenant Colonel Wilson Gaddis, a former editor of the prewar *Japan Advertiser* and wartime Army propagandist, and John F. Sullivan who had worked for the OWI in China.[71]

Women's Information Officer Ethel Weed had been a public relations specialist in Cleveland, Ohio before undergoing six months of language training at the Northwestern University CATS. She arrived with the first WAC deployment to Japan in October 1945 and stayed on until 1952. Weed played a crucial coordinating role in drafting policy for women's rights within GHQ, and the CI&E Planning Branch became a de facto Women's Rights Desk. She worked closely with Alfred Oppler and Kurt Steiner on questions of family law in revising the Civil Code, and in early 1946, her views were reflected in a special CI&E report on the status of women in Japan. Weed solicited the opinions of prominent Japanese legal experts on the patriarchal household (*ie*) system, the symbol of male prerogative, and interceded directly with government officials to eliminate the feudalistic aspects of that system and bring the Civil Code into line with the new Constitution. Weed attracted other talented women in GHQ, and in 1946, her informal policy alliance included Beate Sirota (GS); Margaret Stone (ESS); Doris Cochrane, a State Department liaison officer and women's affairs consultant; and several staffers in CI&E, including Dr Lulu Holmes (below).[72] A group of prominent Japanese women also 'adopted' Weed. Known as 'Weeds girls', they included liberal feminists, Christian humanists and Socialists as well as Communists (chapters 6 and 7).

Women such as Captain Eileen R. Donovan of Education Division, a specialist in secondary education, also made important contributions to CI&E. Donovan graduated from Boston Teachers' College and taught history and economics at a Boston high school before joining the WACs and training at the University of Virginia School of Military Government, the University of Michigan CATS and CASA. In March 1946, she lectured to the US Education Mission on women's education and later that year proposed a liberal replacement for the Imperial Rescript on Education,

Photo 29. CI&E's Women's Information Officer Ethel B. Weed confers with Japanese women leaders. To Weed's right are Fujita Taki, President of the New Japan Women's League, Saitō Kie and Tanaka Sumiko. At the reader's far right is Suzuki Aiko. 9 October 1948. This informal 'women's policy alliance' fought for the inclusion of women's rights in the Occupation reforms (US National Archives).

triggering a wide-ranging debate within CI&E. In 1948, Donovan became the first woman officer in the US Foreign Service and was reassigned to Diplomatic Section.[73]

Other prominent women in CI&E were Dr Lulu Holmes, Dr Helen Heffernan, Dr Verna A. Carley and Dr Billie Hollingshead. Holmes, a member of Weed's informal policy group, headed Education Division's Higher Education Branch. She had taught for two years in prewar Japan at the Kobe Women's Academy, later served as Vice-President of Washington State University and was a member of the American Association of University Women. While at CI&E, she cooperated closely with her Japanese counterparts to establish the Japanese Association of University Women (chapter 8).[74] Heffernan held a Master's degree in education from the University of California and a PhD from Stanford University and had worked more than twenty years as a supervisor of primary schools in California. She joined Education Division as a textbook specialist and stayed on until December 1947. Carley had a Master's degree and PhD in teachers' training from Colorado University and was an assistant professor of education at Stanford University before taking a commission as Lieutenant Commander in the WAVES during the war. She was the Division's specialist in high school education and teachers' training from 1946 to 1948, during which time she worked on standardising university entrance exams. Hollingshead earned a

PhD in psychology from the University of Southern California and joined Education Division in 1947 from Brigham Young University. She remained with Education Division until the end of the Occupation, helping the Education Ministry and Japan Broadcasting Corporation (NHK) plan radio programmes. She also introduced the concept of on-the-job training for teacher consultants. Donovan, Hollingshead and Luana Bowles from the US Office of Education reportedly constituted 'the most well-knit team in the Division'. Finally, Elementary School Officer Pauline Jeidy, on loan from the County Schools of Ventura, California, organised conferences and workshops among primary school educators and helped develop teaching materials for students with disabilities.[75]

Other Divisions and staff
Education, Religions and Information Divisions performed the bulk of CI&E's work, but two other groups, Arts and Monuments and Analysis and Research Divisions, also performed important work. Arts and Monuments was set up in 1946 under Howard C. Hollis, curator of the Cleveland Museum of Art. In 1947, Sherman E. Lee, curator of oriental art at the Detroit Institute of Arts, replaced Hollis, and later that year, Arts and Monuments merged with Religions Division. Hollis and Lee worked closely with eminent Japanese scholars to democratise and upgrade Japanese museums and make available to the public registered works of art.[76]

Analysis and Research (from 1949, Public Opinion and Sociological Research) monitored newspapers, magazines, popular publications and radio broadcasts; produced periodic evaluations of public opinion trends; and introduced modern survey techniques to Japanese pollsters. The introduction of sociological methods to gauge Japanese acceptance of Occupation goals after 1948 led to the development of new methodologies and field-research techniques. The first Division Chief was J. R. Kennedy, who was succeeded by J. Woodall Green and Dr John W. Bennett. Bennett held a PhD in anthropology from the University of Chicago and later became a well-known scholar.[77] Serving under him was Lieutenant Herbert Passin, the son of Russian Jews who had emigrated to the United States during the Russo-Japanese War (1904–5). Passin had taught anthropology at Northwestern University and, during the war, worked as a member of the Planning and Research Division, US Department of Agriculture. He entered MacArthur's headquarters in 1946 after studying Japanese at the University of Michigan CATS. Assigned to CI&E's Analysis and Research Division, Passin brought advanced social science techniques to bear on the analysis of educational problems.[78]

The Occupation careers of other junior staff officers were equally varied.[79] Dr Joseph C. Trainor, who held a PhD in education from the University of Washington, had been a Navy Lieutenant Commander during the war. He joined CI&E as a member of the Analysis and Research Division before being appointed Deputy Chief of Education Division in June 1946. A noted Japan specialist was William P. Woodard, a graduate of the University of Chicago and the Union School of Divinity, who had worked as a missionary in Japan from 1921 to 1941. He was a CI&E liaison officer until 1949, when he was placed in charge of investigations and special projects in the Religions Division. Woodard helped Bunce draft the Shintō Directive and prepare the Religious Corporations Ordinance. His monograph remains the standard reference for CI&E's religious reforms.[80] Frank S. Baba was Programme Officer for Radio Branch from December 1945 to January 1952. Joining CI&E from the US Strategic Bombing Survey, he helped reorganise NHK, returning to the Voice of America as chief of the Japanese Service after the Occupation.

CI&E included two non-American officials: Arundel Del Re, an Italian, and Owen Gauntlett, a British subject. Del Re had studied Latin at London University and taught English at Tokyo Imperial University and Taihoku High School in Japanese-occupied Formosa from 1936 to 1943. He was employed as special adviser to Education Division because of his first-hand knowledge of the prewar school system. Gauntlett was a specialist in English language instruction and served as an adviser to Japanese educators in this important field.

A CI&E official who stirred considerable controversy was Dr Walter C. Eells of the Education Division's Higher Education Branch (1947–51). A sexagenarian when he joined GHQ, 'Hurricane' Eells was the oldest member of the Division. He held a Bachelor's degree in Greek and mathematics from Whitman College, a Master's from the University of Chicago and a PhD in education from Stanford University, where he taught before joining CI&E. Dr Eells later chaired the American Association of Junior Colleges. In Education Division, he earned notoriety for his attempts to impose centralised control on the universities, his whirlwind tours of Japanese campuses and his strident calls to purge them of 'Communist elements'.[81]

A few CI&E officials came to GHQ from the wartime internment camps for Japanese Americans. Kenneth M. Harkness (MA, Columbia Teachers' College) was Textbook Officer and special consultant to the Education Division from early 1946 until the end of the Occupation. He had served as a member of the South Dakota State Board of Education and, during the war, as an officer in the Tule Lake Relocation Camp for suspected subversives. Another education officer, Dr Rollin C. Fox, a 'roving educational ambassador' for the Kanto Military Government Region, had been principal and then superintendent of schools at the Manzanar Relocation Center (California). Like Dr Eells, Fox was a determined foe of the left-oriented Japan Teachers' Union and argued (unsuccessfully) for direct action by Military Government to curb its influence.[82]

NATURAL RESOURCES

Natural Resources Section (NRS) was created on 2 October 1945 to advise SCAP on resource policy for agriculture, fisheries, forestry, mining and geology in Japan, Korea and Japan's former Pacific territories. NRS's mandate encompassed tasks as diverse as despatching whaling fleets to the Antarctic and promoting Japanese reforestation, but one of its primary missions was to assist other staff groups in raising agricultural and marine productivity. GS, ESS and other civil sections used the data from hundreds of NRS surveys on agriculture, mining, geology, forestry and fisheries in their efforts to rebuild the economy. NRS also was responsible for emergency measures to deal with food and fuel shortages. This entailed combating the activities of black-marketeers, particularly in the early phase of occupation when frequent shortages made hoarding lucrative. To prevent such abuses, NRS devised a system of compulsory rice deliveries. Grain was purchased by the government at a pre-arranged price based on a fixed percentage of each farmer's crop. To enforce this measure, Eighth Army officers in military jeeps accompanied local officials to farms in a show of authority designed to ensure the timely requisition of rice quotas.

Headed by Lieutenant Colonel Hubert G. Schenck, NRS was a small but accomplished section. In 1948, its 265 members included 16 officers, 1 enlisted man, 132 civilians and 116 Japanese and other general personnel. NRS was composed of six divisions for most of the Occupation: Agriculture, Fisheries, Forestry, Mining and Geology, Library and Production, and Administration. In 1947, the Plans and Policies Division was created, and in mid-1951, the Agriculture and Forestry Divisions were merged. NRS dealt mainly with the Agriculture Ministry and was located in the Mitsubishi Shōji Building in Yūrakuchō. The Section ceased operations in July 1951 and was officially disbanded on 15 December of that year, at which time remaining personnel were transferred to a new unit set up inside ESS for that purpose, the Natural Resources Division.

NRS was intimately involved in GHQ's land reform project and included several agricultural experts with government and academic backgrounds. Lieutenant Colonel Hubert G. Schenck, NRS Chief for the duration of the Occupation, was a geology professor from Stanford University. Warren H. Leonard, the first head of the Agricultural Division, had been a professor of agriculture at the University of Colorado (Fort Collins). Mark B. Williamson, the third Agricultural Division Chief, had participated in a joint programme in law and soil studies at the University of Tennessee before the war. During the war, he contributed to the Civil Affairs Guide *Agriculture and Food in Japan*, and, as Acting Chief of the Civil Affairs Staging Area, developed policies to remedy post-surrender food shortages. Williamson arrived in Japan with the AFPAC Military Government Section.

Wolf I. Ladejinsky, Williamson's brilliant assistant, was an agrarian specialist and America's foremost expert on Japan's land tenure system. The son of a Jewish Ukrainian landlord, Ladejinsky emigrated to the United States, graduated from Columbia University and joined the Department of Agriculture, where he worked for the Foreign Agricultural Division's Bureau of Agricultural Economics. In the late 1930s and early 1940s, he published a series of ground-breaking articles on Japanese agriculture in *Foreign Agriculture*, the Bureau's journal. Ladejinsky drafted GHQ's main land reform proposal, but his activist role in the programme blighted his later professional life. After the Occupation, American ultra-rightist organisations blacklisted him for his involvement with this 'left-wing' measure, and during the

Eisenhower administration, he was dismissed from the Department of Agriculture as a security risk.

In his work on Japanese land reform, Ladejinsky collaborated closely with the State Department's Robert A. Fearey and, together with Dr William T. Gilmartin, Captain R. S. Hardie and Dr Lawrence J. Hewes, helped draft the land reform directives (chapter 7). Gilmartin, a passionate advocate of land reform, had a PhD in economics from the University of California. He left GHQ in June 1946 to join the World Bank, before the major land reform legislation was passed. Hardie joined NRS from Sixth Army in 1946 as land reform officer. Later that year, he became Chief of Agriculture Division's newly inaugurated Agrarian Economy Branch. Hewes, with an MBA from Harvard and a PhD in economics from George Washington University, had headed the Western Division of the Farm Stabilisation Bureau, Department of Agriculture. His detailed study of Japan's land situation was published after the Occupation.[83]

PUBLIC HEALTH AND WELFARE

US War Department pre-surrender planners had established a Health and Welfare Division to assess the public health requirements for troops involved in an eventual invasion of Japan. In early August 1945, the organisation was transplanted to AFPAC's Military Government Section as the Public Health and Welfare Division. Colonel (from April 1948, Brigadier General) Crawford F. Sams was appointed to head the new staff group. Following the transfer of MGS to Japan, AFPAC had attempted to integrate MGS's health and welfare functions into the new Civil Information and Education Section, but Sams argued that this was 'organisationally most unwise' and insisted on the creation of a separate staff echelon dedicated wholly to preventive medicine, medical care, welfare and social security.[84] Consequently, on 2 October 1945, Public Health and Welfare Section (PH&W) was created as a special staff group inside GHQ/SCAP and charged with preventing epidemic diseases, restoring basic sanitation and health-control measures and developing health and welfare policies. The immediate threat to public health came from starvation and the outbreak of contagious diseases aggravated by malnutrition and unsanitary conditions. PH&W initiated emergency relief operations and a nation-wide programme of dusting with DDT, produced vaccines and strove to improve general sanitation. These emergency measures spared Japan the agony of a major famine and forestalled the large-scale outbreak of epidemic diseases.

Overworked and understaffed, PH&W never exceeded 150 people. As of February 1948, it had only 92 employees consisting of 12 officers, 2 enlisted personnel, 56 civilian officials and 22 Japanese staff. Despite its small size, however, the Section was highly specialised and boasted a large number of divisions: Dental Affairs, Health and Welfare Statistics, Medical Service (originally Hospital Administration), Medical Supply, Nursing Affairs, Social Security, Veterinary Affairs, Welfare and

Legal Adviser's Office. Also attached to PH&W was the Atomic Bomb Casualty Commission, set up to study the medical effects of atomic radiation on human beings. PH&W staff included doctors, public health officials, dentists, quarantine experts and nutrition specialists. International relief workers, Rockefeller Foundation employees and American Red Cross personnel also were attached to the section on loan. Lawyers worked in the Section's Legal Adviser's Office drafting revisions of Japan's health and welfare regulations. PH&W was located in SCAP's main headquarters in the Dai-Ichi Insurance Building. It worked primarily with the Health and Welfare Ministry but also dealt with the Labour and Education Ministries.

PH&W's accomplishments reflected the dynamic leadership of Section Chief Crawford Sams. Born in East Saint Louis, Illinois, Sams received a BA in psychology from the University of California (Berkeley, 1925) and an MSc and an MD from the Washington University School of Medicine in St Louis (1927, 1929). He completed postgraduate work at the Walter Reed Army Medical School in Washington (1931) and graduated from the Command and General Staff School at Fort Leavenworth, Kansas (1937). In the late 1930s, he served as Assistant Surgeon in the Panama Canal Department, where he was responsible for public health and malaria control. During the war, Sams was Chief Surgeon and Acting Chief of Staff to the US Military Mission in North Africa (Cairo) and Theater Surgeon, US Army Forces in the Middle East, working in Tunisia, Libya and Sicily. From late 1944 to early 1945, he was sent to the European Front to assess the medical needs of wounded US troops, refugees and prisoners of war. In February 1945, he returned to Washington as Chief of the Programme Branch in the War Department's Logistics Division, where he formulated medical-aid policies for the anticipated Allied invasion of Japan. In July 1945, on the recommendation of Civil Affairs Division Chief Hilldring, Sams was transferred to GHQ/AFPAC in Manila and placed in charge of the MGS Public Health and Welfare Division. During the early part of the Occupation, he also served as Health and Welfare Adviser to US Army Military Government in Korea (1945 to 1948).[85]

Sams was assisted by several highly competent subordinates. Lieutenant Colonel Harry G. Johnson, Chief of the Medical Service Division, was a physician from Rochester, New York, who remained in Japan after the Occupation to run a private practice in Yokohama. Lieutenant Colonel Dale B. Ridgely, Chief of Dental Affairs Division, was an Army Dental Corps officer handpicked by Sams to serve with him in AFPAC's Military Government Section in Manila. Major Grace E. Alt, Chief of PH&W's Nursing Affairs Division, entered GHQ with an MSc in public health and welfare from Johns Hopkins Nursing Institute. Before the war, she worked for nine years in a missionary hospital in Korea. Forced by Japanese colonial authorities to leave the colony, she returned to the United States, joined the WACs and went through the Army's Civil Affairs Training programme.[86] Alt was replaced by Public Health Nursing Consultant Virginia M. Ohlson in April 1949. The Welfare Division, which planned the welfare and socal security reforms, was headed initially by Lieutenant Commander Arthur D. Bouterse and later by

Colonel Nelson B. Neff, who remained until early 1950, when he was replaced by Irving H. Markuson.

PH&W also advised US commands in Okinawa and southern Korea. In Korea, this role ended in March 1948, but in June 1950, following the outbreak of war on the peninsula, the Section became deeply involved in civil relief planning there, setting up a temporary PH&W Field Organisation. In September of that year, PH&W/SCAP despatched personnel to establish a PH&W staff section inside the UN Unified Command, the team returning to Tokyo once GHQ/Korea had recruited its own staff. In March 1951, having received reports of an alleged plague epidemic in the Democratic People's Republic, Sams personally led a secret mission into northern Korea with the intention of locating, drugging and kidnapping an enemy soldier stricken with the disease in order to determine its pathology. The small party travelled in a Navy landing craft refitted as a medical laboratory but abandoned the mission when Sams learned from Korean agents en route that the illness was hemorrhagic smallpox, not plague.[87]

Sams was fiercely loyal to MacArthur and an open admirer of Willoughby. Following the Supreme Commander's dismissal by Truman in April 1951, the PH&W Chief followed Willoughby's example and tendered his resignation (MacArthur's cashiering effectively had ended Sams's hopes of becoming Surgeon General of the Army). Sams's legacy to the Occupation was a mixed one, his brilliant achievements in public health being offset by his collaboration with Japan's wartime biological warfare experts and his uncritical support of the Atomic Bomb Casualty Commission. He returned to the United States in May 1951 and was replaced by his Deputy Chief, Colonel Cecil S. Mollohan. On 30 June, PH&W was absorbed into a new SCAP staff group, Medical Section, which was transferred from the Far East Command under FECOM Theater Surgeon General Edgar E. Hume. Public Health and Welfare Division, Medical Section, gradually phased out its activities, turning them over to concerned Japanese agencies. The Division included the branches of Preventive Medicine, Medical Service, Welfare, Supply and Narcotics Control. It was discontinued together with Medical Section on 28 April 1952. Even after the Occupation, however, former PH&W personnel continued to monitor Japanese developments in their field. Before returning to the United States in 1951, Sams had arranged with the Rockefeller Foundation to retain fourteen Foundation specialists to serve as public health and welfare advisers to the Japanese government, and with State Department cooperation, the advisory group was attached to the US Embassy in Tokyo.[88]

OTHER STAFF SECTIONS

Civil Affairs

Civil Affairs Section (CAS) was set up in July 1949 by Eighth Army to supervise the replacement of military personnel by civilian officials in prefectural Military Government Teams. CAS was transferred to MacArthur's headquarters on 1 January

1950, becoming a civil staff echelon in its own right, and was assigned office space in the Mitsubishi Building (Marunouchi district). Its primary function was to oversee the reorganisation of civil affairs activities in line with SCAP's policy of devolving administrative responsibility to the Japanese government.

In July 1950, CAS was given the task of organising Japan's National Police Reserve, a 75,000-strong force formed at MacArthur's command following the outbreak of war in Korea. Under the guidance of CAS Chief Major General Whitfield P. Shepard and his executive officer, Colonel Frank Kowalski Jr, the NPR evolved into the forerunner of the Self-Defence Forces, formed in July 1952. Before joining GHQ, Shepard had been responsible for military training at Fort Benning, Georgia, where he earned a reputation as a rigid disciplinarian. In Japan, he headed a US military advisory group before being appointed Chief of CAS, Eighth Army. Shepard was largely responsible for having CAS transferred to GHQ/ SCAP and, in 1951, was named SCAP Deputy Chief of Staff. Kowalski was a West Point graduate with a Master's degree from the Massachusetts Institute of Technology. During World War II, he was attached to General Dwight Eisenhower's general staff and placed in charge of military training. Assigned to Japan in 1947, he commanded MG teams in Kyoto and Osaka before joining CAS in 1950.

CAS consisted of Administrative, Economics, Legal and Government, and Social Affairs Divisions.[89] Following its creation in 1949, CAS continued, on a reduced scale, the oversight duties of Military Government units through its Civil Affairs Regional Teams. In June 1951, the Section was relieved of all surveillance duties and its personnel were trimmed further, its primary mission now being to supervise the National Police Reserve. CAS was disbanded on 28 April 1952.

Public Information
The Public Information Office (PIO) was designated a special staff section in February 1950, late in the Occupation. Until then, GHQ/AFPAC's Public Relations Section (created in January 1946 and redesignated Public Information Section, Far Eastern Command in May 1947) acted as SCAP's publicity organ, handling the release of information to national and international media.[90] The PIO had its offices in the Radio Tokyo Building, which it shared with Civil Information and Education Section. The Office was staffed by press and public relations officials whose job was to develop contacts with foreign correspondents and Japanese news agencies to ensure favourable coverage of the Occupation.

PIO consisted of four divisions: News, Pictures, Operations, and Radio and Communications. It was headed by MacArthur confidant Brigadier General Frayne Baker. A graduate of the Army War College, Baker had been a quartermaster officer during World War I and later commanded the 32nd Infantry Division at Camp Livingston, Louisiana. In 1941, he was appointed G-3 Assistant Chief of Staff for US Army Air Forces in the Far East (Manila), where he became a part of MacArthur's Bataan Gang. A 'genial, white-haired North Dakota National Guardsman', the conservative and manipulative Baker kept the press in line by threatening to withhold Army food and billeting privileges and, in some cases, by withdrawing or refusing to renew accreditations. In 1946, he overstepped his authority, interceding clumsily in a newspaper strike and, following a series of contretemps, was forced out of this sensitive position in March 1948. He was succeeded at PIO by Colonel Marion P. Echols and Colonel George P. Welch. The Section was dissolved on 28 April 1952.

Civil Communications
Civil Communications Section (CCS) was established on 2 October 1945 to demilitarise and modernise Japan's communications grid, including domestic and international postal, broadcasting, wireless and telecommunications networks. In executing these tasks, CCS broke the monopoly formerly exercised by the Japanese military over radio and telecommunications by dissolving or converting to non-military uses the wireless, telegram and telephone branches of the Imperial Army and Navy. The Section also revived and reorganised public radio, which had been used as a propaganda organ of the military. It dismantled the International Electrical Communications Company and the Japanese Telegraph and Telephone Construction Company, the two industrial giants in the communications field. It also modernised the postal system and introduced advanced telegraph technology. The Section was located inside the main SCAP headquarters. Its counterpart agency was the Communications Ministry.

The first CCS Chief was Major General Spencer B. Akin, who held that position until 1947. A graduate of the Army War College, Akin had served as chief signals officer at divisional, corps and general staff level before joining MacArthur in prewar Manila. Like Marquat and Willoughby, he was among the handful of officers who had come off Corregidor with the General in March 1942. Chief Signals Officer at GHQ/ SWPA in Australia, Akin followed MacArthur to Manila and Tokyo. He was replaced in 1947 by Brigadier General George I. Back. Under Akin, CCS reorganised Japan's postwar broadcasting system. Two important CCS memoranda drafted, respectively, by C. A. Feissner, Chief of Research and Development Division, and his deputy, Colonel P. F. Hannah, laid down guidelines for removing the Japan Broadcasting Company (*Nippon Hōsō Kyōkai*, or NHK) from military control, ended NHK's broadcasting monopoly and established procedures allowing private radio stations to go on the air for the first time.[91]

CCS initially consisted of the Industry, Radio, Telephone and Telegraph Divisions. In late 1946, the Analysis Division and Postal Division were created, the latter after overseas postal operations had resumed in September. The Broadcast Division also was established at this time.[92] From 1950 to 1951, CCS transferred most of its staff duties to Japanese counterpart groups and, after July 1951, became a consultant to Japanese telecommunications agencies. The Section was formally disbanded on 3 October 1951, and its remaining duties were transferred to FECOM's Communications Section and SCAP's Adjutant General's Office.

Civil Transportation

Civil Transportation Section (CTC) was established on 7 September 1946 under GHQ/AFPAC's Transportation Division and assigned offices in the Bank of Chosen Building in the Marunouchi district. Its counterpart agency was the Japanese Transport Ministry. Transferred to GHQ/SCAP as a special staff section in late 1947, CTS advised GHQ on the utilisation and rehabilitation of Japan's land transport facilities. The US Navy's Shipping Control Authority for the Japanese Merchant Marine (SCAJAP) assumed responsibility for Japanese shipping, freeing CTS to concentrate on restoring the rail system, an urgent priority in light of the extensive destruction caused by wartime bombing. As a result of the Section's efforts, one third of all war-damaged railway equipment had been repaired by July 1947. Other CTS functions were the augmentation of Japanese truck and bus fleets, the requisitioning of US Army surplus trucks for civilian needs and the organisation of special rail transport for Occupation personnel, a task CTS inherited from G-4 in late 1946.[93]

The first CTS Chief was Brigadier General Frank S. Besson, a West Point graduate with an MSc from MIT. During the war, Besson served as Chief Transportation Officer for American Forces in the Western Pacific and later as Eighth Army Transportation Officer and Director of the Third Military Railway Service. Appointed CTS Chief in 1945, Besson concurrently headed AFPAC's Transportation Division. In late 1949, he was replaced by Colonel H. T. Miller, another West Point graduate who had served as Deputy Chief of the Army Transportation Office. CTS boasted several other outstanding executive officers, as well.[94]

The Section included the divisions of Rail Transportation, Road Transportation, Municipal Transportation, Plans, Policies and Requirements, Water Transportation and, from 1948, Highways. It also was charged with streamlining the railway system under the Dodge stabilisation programme. From mid-1949, CTS phased out its operational duties and subsequently served as an advisory body to the Japanese government. CTS was discontinued on 30 June 1951, and its remaining functions were transferred to the FECOM's Transportation Section.

Reparations and Civil Property Custodian

Inaugurated on 8 May 1947, the Reparations Section (RS) advised SCAP on the removal and shipment of wartime plant and equipment to countries that had suffered the brunt of Japanese aggression. RS was located in the Kokubu Building in Marunouchi and dealt with the Reparations Agency in the Prime Minister's Office. The Section created the Reparations Technical Advisory Committee to ensure the orderly transfer of this matériel, and within two years, the RTAC had restored ¥150 million worth of assets to Allied governments, corporate persons and foreign nationals. Reparations Section coordinated its programme with Economic and Scientific Section's Industrial Division, but its importance waned as Washington's enthusiasm for industrial transfers cooled. Initially, US policy had called for a strict regimen designed to facilitate economic decentralisation by relocating the bulk of Japanese heavy industry to the war-ravaged countries of Asia (chapter 3). With the intensification of the Cold War and increased US intervention in the Japanese economy after 1948, these proposals were softened dramatically. RS was disbanded on 13 December 1948, and its duties were absorbed by the Civil Property Custodian.

The Civil Property Custodian (CPC) was formally established on 8 March 1946 but did not commence operations until later that year. CPC advised SCAP on the disposition of property and assets in Japan belonging to the Allied powers, enemy nations and former Japanese colonies. The Section was authorised to seize the property of ultra-nationalist institutions and war criminals and all precious metals, jewels and foreign currency held by the central government; appropriate and auction off Japanese real estate owned by German nationals; seize from the government illegally acquired foreign films; and operate US bank vaults in Tokyo and Osaka, a responsibility CPC took over from Eighth Army in late 1949. CPC worked closely with Reparations Section and the ESS Industrial Division on reparations, being responsible for the custody, control and maintenance of equipment slated for removal.

The first CPC Chief was Brigadier General Patrick H. Tansey, a West Point graduate who had served in the War Department's Logistics Division. In 1949, Tansey was put in charge of supplying US Army Forces in southern Korea. He was later succeeded by Brigadier General John F. Conklin. Original CPC sub-units included Comptroller, Foreign Property, Property Liquidation and Legal Divisions. Housed in the Teikoku Sōgo Building in Hibiya, the Office was enlarged in 1947 with the establishment of the Patent Division and again in 1948 following the creation of the Reparations Property Division. CPC worked largely with the Central Liaison Office and the Finance Ministry. It was dissolved on 1 March 1952, and remaining staff functions and personnel were transferred to Government Section.

Minor groups
The Statistics and Reports Section, established on 2 October 1945, collected data on the Occupation and published the *Monthly Summation of Non-Military Activities in Japan and Korea* (edited for Japan alone after 1948). Reorganised as the Civil Historical Section (CHS) on 1 January 1950, the Section compiled the 55-volume *History of the Nonmilitary Activities of the Occupation of Japan* (1952). Edited by William E. Hutchinson, this vast compendium was produced hastily and, for the most part, by amateurs, and many of its sections were never completed. Moreover, the volumes lacked objectivity, describing SCAP as the sole source of Occupation-era policies and refraining from unfavourable judgments, direct or implied, of General Headquarters. The series was never properly organised and remained classified until the late 1960s.[95] CHS was dissolved on 29 February 1952.

Lesser civil staff sections were the General Accounting Section (24 January 1946 to 28 April 1952), SCAP's accountant, and the General Procurement Agent (22 May 1946 to 1 May 1950), which was responsible for obtaining materials and manpower for US Army forces in Japan. General Accounting (GAS) was located in the

Mitsubishi Shōji Building, General Procurement (GPA) with SCAP in the Dai-Ichi Mutual Life Insurance Building. GAS worked with the Cabinet Secretariat, GPA with the Special Procurement Agency in the Prime Minister's Office.

To address specific problems, ad hoc committees occasionally were convened to consider questions ranging from currency exchange rates to measures against Communism. Some groups, like the ESS committee that stabilised the yen–dollar ratio, were intramural. Others, such as the top-secret Committee on Counter-Measures against Communism in the Far East, were high-powered, inter-service organisations involving SCAP, Eighth Army and the Far East Command. The Counter-Measures Committee was set up in May 1951 to coordinate a broad array of anti-Communist programmes and met regularly until early 1952. It exemplified the hard-line approach of General Matthew B. Ridgway, who replaced MacArthur as SCAP in the spring of 1951. The Committee served as a sounding board for various proposals designed to diminish Communist influence in Japan, but its advocacy of direct intervention in Japan's internal affairs just as the Occupation was divesting itself of administrative duties limited its effectiveness, and few of its recommendations were implemented.[96]

PART III

The Early Reforms

CHAPTER 5

The Genesis of Reform

With the machinery of occupation in place, MacArthur set about carrying out basic political, institutional, economic and cultural reforms. An overview of US wartime planning for post-surrender Japan is essential for understanding the reform process, its promise, its internal inconsistencies and limitations, and its outcome. Unlike planning for the German occupation, which was driven in large part by a desire for revenge, the dynamics of American policy-making for postwar Japan were complex, reflecting the pull of competing views of Asia and America's long-term interests there within the various branches of government.

Washington's early reform projections and the care with which they were elaborated also afford an illuminating contrast with Japan's own impromptu planning for the wartime administration of occupied Asia. Imperial Japan did not produce a basic plan for military occupation until a few weeks before its invasion and seizure of Southeast Asia. The 'Guidelines for the Administration of the Southern Occupied Territories' of November 1941, however, contained no enunciation of guiding pan-Asian principles. They were rather an ad hoc statement of concrete goals designed to secure Japan's short-term military and economic interests in the region. By contrast, American pre-surrender planning for Japan began in a very general sense with a declaration of overarching principles formulated more than a year and a half before hostilities broke out. These tenets were applicable in theory to any occupied territory. Moreover, they laid down a framework that delineated basic rights and obligations and was anchored in international law. By the time of Japan's surrender, a detailed master plan for occupation tailored to that country's precise conditions and requirements had been perfected and formulated both as a general statement of purpose and as a comprehensive and detailed military directive. The mission of MacArthur and his headquarters was to carry out those instructions in spirit and to the letter.

POLICY PLANNING FOR POSTWAR JAPAN

In September 1939, following Hitler's invasion of Poland and the outbreak of a generalised war in Europe, the US State Department brought together a small group of experts to begin planning for the eventuality of American involvement. The military, too, initiated its own contingency exercises at about the same time. In July 1940, after the fall of France, General Allen W. Gullion issued *The United States Army and Navy Manual of Military Government and Civil Affairs*. Gullion drew heavily on a 1920 military report by Colonel I. L. Hunt, a legal affairs officer and the chief civil administrator for the US occupation of the German Rhineland after World War I. Hunt believed that the greatest single shortcoming of his mission had been the lack of able and well-trained civil affairs specialists, and his report listed a number of concrete proposals designed to rectify that difficulty for future operations. General Gullion's 1940 monograph also reviewed the 1907 Hague Convention on the law of military occupation, which defined the authority of the occupying power and the rights and duties of the occupied. Specifically, Gullion's handbook urged the retention of existing governmental agencies, provided for freedom of speech and press 'to the extent that military interests are not prejudiced', called for the annulment of 'laws which discriminate on the basis of race, color, creed or political opinions', and ordained the liberation of political prisoners.[1]

The Army and Navy Manual defined military government as 'the supreme authority exercised by an armed force over the lands, property and the inhabitants of enemy territory.' Civil affairs was defined as the military control of civilians in an occupied area. This military master plan for occupation described the organisation of military rule and stipulated the creation of civil affairs staff sections. It detailed civil affairs responsibilities in areas such as administration, law enforcement, public health, censorship, public finance and banking, education, labour, agriculture, industry and commerce, and displaced persons. It also outlined the training of civil affairs personnel; general planning for the control of civil affairs; the issuance of proclamations, orders and instructions; and the creation of military commissions and courts. The Manual would become the touchstone for military planners in organising the postwar occupations of Italy, Germany and Japan.

The Territorial Subcommittee (1942–3)

US planning for post-surrender Asia began shortly after the outbreak of the Pacific War. On 28 December 1941, President Roosevelt created the Advisory Committee on Postwar Foreign Policy to devise reconstruction programmes for occupied enemy territories. Staffed by influential members of the State Department, the Council on Foreign Relations, Army and Navy officers and Congressional leaders, the Advisory Committee set up five inter-departmental subcommittees to explore foreign policy options in a postwar world that few then could envisage with any certainty. One of these was the Territorial Subcommittee (TS), which was formed on 7 March 1942. Planning for Japan began in the TS, where issues such as unconditional surrender, the Imperial institution, economic policies and Japan's post-defeat boundaries were discussed for the first time. TS position papers were prepared by the State Department's Division of Special Research, which had been set up in February 1941 to assist in formulating US foreign policy. The Division would become the centre for US post-surrender planning on Asia.

Sharp ideological differences soon emerged within the Territorial Subcommittee between a pro-China group and a pro-Japan group. The so-called China Crowd was led by Dr Stanley Hornbeck, director of the State Department's Division of Far Eastern Affairs, and John Carter Vincent of the Divisions's China Desk. Hornbeck had a reputation as 'an anti-Japanese bigot', but bigotry in the wartime government was in ample supply. (Captain H. L. Pence of the Security and Technical Sub-committee and later head of the Navy's Occupied Areas Section advocated 'the almost total elimination of the Japanese as a race.') Pro-China hardliners in the Territorial Subcommittee believed that Japanese imperialism stemmed from two sources: a totalitarian Emperor-centred political system and the domination of heavy industry by a coterie of giant financial and industrial combines, the *zaibatsu*. The Throne, Hornbeck said, was 'deistic feudalism.' To prevent Japan from ever again posing a military threat, his group urged the elimination of the emperor system and the enfeeblement of Japanese capitalism, the latter to be accomplished by destroying the *zaibatsu* and rebuilding a light rather than heavy industrial base. Like most Americans, the China Crowd assumed that Republican China, not Japan, would emerge as the postwar leader of Asia. They intended to strengthen Chinese industrial capitalism and transform that country into America's principal trade partner in Asia. The China experts, advocates of a severe peace, also were radical reformers who pressed for fundamental changes in Japan's political and economic structure.[2]

In contrast, the Japan Crowd were proponents of a soft peace. They argued for a liberalised restoration of the prewar régime that assured the continuity of the monarchy, divested of its anti-democratic features; a demilitarised body politic; and a revitalised industrial economy. Dean of the Japan experts was Joseph C. Grew, the venerable former ambassador to Japan, then Special Assistant to Secretary of State Cordell Hull. The locus of Grew's power was the Japan Desk in the Far Eastern Affairs Division. Among this select but conservative group was Grew's former chargé d'affaires in Tokyo, Eugene H. Dooman, the son of missionaries, who was fluent in both written and spoken Japanese. Other members were Grew's private secretary in Tokyo, Robert A. Fearey; Joseph W. Ballantine, a former counsellor at the Tokyo Embassy; Earle R. Dickover, a Foreign Service officer with diplomatic experience in Tokyo; and Cabot Coville, a Japanese language officer and former Embassy secretary. Coville drafted the first position papers on Japan in which he proposed three guiding principles for post-defeat policy: a rigid disarmament, a viable economy and a humanised Throne.[3] This, in essence, is very close to what Japan eventually got.

As ambassador from 1932 to 1942, Grew had associated with a group of aristocrats close to the Throne that included Prince Konoe Fumimaro, prime minister in the late 1930s and briefly in the early 1940s, and such 'moderate' conservatives as Yoshida Shigeru and Baron Shidehara Kijūrō. Grew shared the so-called peace party's belief that the emperor system alone stood in the way of the twin evils of fascism and Communism. Dooman viewed the Emperor as 'a living manifestation of the racial continuity of the Japanese people' and believed that without the Throne, Japan would, quite simply, fall apart.[4] The Japan faction condemned the cancer of militarism but held that its cause was not the Imperial system or the *zaibatsu* per se, but the 'military clique' and their fanatic followers who had manipulated these institutions for their own chauvinistic ends. The Japan experts opposed abolishing the monarchy and imposing radical economic and political reforms. Dismantling the armed forces and purging the jingoists from public life, they argued, would be sufficient to prevent Japan from again threatening the peace. The Japan Crowd received intellectual and moral support for its ideas on the Emperor from such Japan experts as John F. Embree of the University of Chicago, author of the first anthropological study on Japan in English then on loan to the State Department.[5]

The debate between the two factions in the Territorial Subcommittee defined the parameters of postwar US policy toward Japan. The TS was dissolved in December 1943, by which time its work had devolved to other groups, but the basic dynamism engendered by this rivalry continued to influence post-surrender issues. In the closing weeks of the war, the China Crowd would achieve ascendancy in the State Department, and its presence was reflected in the first wave of radical reform in occupied Japan. From mid-1947, however, the Japan Crowd would re-enter the arena and, in 1948, successfully engineer an abrupt policy shift to the right.

The Inter-Divisional Area Committee on the Far East (1943–4)

In August 1942, as the Territorial Subcommittee pursued its task, the State Department set up inside the Division of Special Research an independent intra-departmental think tank, the East Asia Policy Study Group, to develop concrete proposals for postwar Japan.[6] The Study Group was chaired by Dr George H. Blakeslee, a Wilsonian idealist and Far East expert who taught political science at Clark University and would later serve as US delegate to the Far Eastern Commission. Blakeslee's secretary was Dr Hugh Borton, a Quaker and Japan specialist who taught Japanese studies at Columbia University. Borton had worked in Tokyo with the American Friends' Service Committee in the late 1920s. There, he had been befriended by the British diplomat and eminent Japanologist Sir George Sansom, who became his mentor. Borton also pursued graduate studies at Tokyo Imperial University, spoke and read Japanese and authored two influential works on Japan.[7] Other prominent members of the Study Group included such Grew intimates as Robert Fearey and Cabot Coville, both of whom would later work for the Office of the Political Adviser in Tokyo. Joseph Grew also joined this select group. The fate of the Emperor was a subject of particular concern to these Japanophiles. Borton, for instance, drafted a memorandum proposing to retain an emasculated Throne in order to 'assure the good behaviour of the Japanese people' and secure the cooperation of the bureaucracy in carrying out Allied reforms, a position Grew warmly endorsed. Hirohito, Borton said, reigned but did not rule and was not personally responsible for the war. Moreover, the Imperial institution was potentially a moderating force and should be reformed, not eliminated.[8] This essentially is the position that MacArthur himself would adopt at the start of the Occupation.

On 20 October 1943, the State Department established an integrated intra-departmental planning group for Japan, the Inter-Divisional Area Committee on the Far East, with Blakeslee as chair and Borton as secretary. Popularly known as the Far Eastern Area Committee, this group was one of nine country and four area committees (Country and Area Committees, or CACs) inaugurated in the summer and autumn of 1943 to coordinate post-defeat planning for specific enemy nations at the administrative level. The Far Eastern Area Committee dealt exclusively with Japan and, between October 1943 and July 1945, would meet a total of 221 times. Committee documents included position papers on political problems and the institution of the Emperor (CAC-93e), unconditional surrender (CAC-267), demilitarisation (CAC-185), postwar military government and education reform (CAC-238) and a wide variety of other topics.[9]

CAC proposals were forwarded to the Postwar Programmes Committee (PWC), the State Department's highest decision-making body for post-defeat issues, which was created on 15 January 1944. Staffed by the Secretary of State, the Under-Secretary and his assistant secretaries and various division chiefs, the PWC considered the political implications of CAC recommendations, and those it approved became official Department policy. PWC/CAC memoranda on Japan were extensive, covering non-military fields from politics and economics to education and culture. Of particular significance was a PWC/CAC document entitled 'The Post War Objectives of the United States in Regard to Japan' (CAC 116b/PWC 108b). Drafted in May 1944, this was the first comprehensive attempt to delineate occupation objectives and programmes, and it would become the basis for the definitive 'US Initial Post-Surrender Policy for Japan', made public on 22 September 1945.

The PWC/CAC paper on 'Post-War Objectives' defined America's policy goals in Japan as preventing that country 'from being a menace to the United States and the other countries of the Pacific area' and establishing 'a government which will respect the rights of other states and Japan's international obligations.' To achieve these fundamental objectives, the study proposed a three-phase occupation. During the first stage, Japan's armed forces would be disarmed and disbanded and its military and naval installations destroyed, and the country would undergo 'the stern discipline of occupation' under military government. The second period was to be one of 'close surveillance' in which there would be military inspections to prevent rearmament, economic controls to thwart the development of war potential, and measures to encourage democratic and liberal thought and to establish a civil government 'actually responsible to the people.' US Army bases would be established 'to prevent aggression and facilitate military policing.' During the final phase, the United States would realise its ultimate aim: a Japan 'properly discharging its responsibilities in the family of peaceful nations.' Few military occupations have had their mandate framed so broadly.

The 'Post-War Objectives' further stipulated that, in accordance with the 1943 Cairo Declaration, Japan would 'withdraw from Manchuria, the Mandated Islands and all areas under Japanese military occupation' and be deprived of 'Korea, Formosa and islands obtained since the beginning of the First World War.' The country would be limited to Honshu, Hokaido, Shikoku and Kyushu and certain adjoining islands. The PWC/CAC series contained other 1944 policy studies that would shape later occupation programmes, including 'Freedom of Worship' (15 March 1944), 'Nullification of Obnoxious Laws' (22 March), 'Political Parties or Agencies' (23 March),

'Occupation Problems: War Criminals' (24 March), 'Military Government: Treatment of Political Prisoners' (14 June), 'Abolition of Militarism and Strengthening of Democratic Processes' (9 May) and 'Political Problems: Institution of the Emperor' (9 May).

Military Government schools

While the State Department was drafting post-surrender policy, the War and Navy Departments were creating special training programmes to turn out the military governors and civil administrators needed to implement occupation reforms. In May 1942, the War Department set up the School of Military Government at the University of Virginia, Charlottesville, which offered, among other subjects, a comprehensive course in the international law of occupation. Jules Bassin, Chief of Law Division in GHQ's Legal Section and MacArthur's final arbiter on questions of military law under belligerent occupation, received his training there. In January 1943, the Navy Department organised the Office for Occupied Areas (later, Occupied Areas Section) to deal with civil governance and established its own Naval School of Military Government and Administration at Columbia (a 36-week course) and later, in October 1944, at Princeton (an eight-week course). The Princeton school was designed specifically to produce military governors. Many Navy trainees were conscientious objectors, accounting for 10 out of the initial class of 57 at Columbia. The same presumably was true of the Army schools. The Military Government schools offered instruction in the geography, history, culture, economy and government of Germany, Japan and other areas slated for occupation. In the Pacific region, Army schools focused narrowly on Japan, while Navy schools initially studied Formosa, an early invasion target, but also Indonesia, Korea and the Philippines before turning their attention later in the war to Okinawa and Japan. Trainees generally studied for two months, taking crash courses in international law, psychology, civil administration, political science and the Japanese language. (Columbia University awarded graduates with sufficient undergraduate credits who completed its nine-month course an MA in International Administration.)[10]

In March 1943, the War Department inaugurated the Civil Affairs Division (CAD) to plan for the military administration of occupied areas. General John F. Hilldring was appointed to lead CAD, which would later draft the military blueprint for the occupation of Japan, JCS-1380/15. Hilldring's assistant executive officer was Lieutenant Colonel Charles L. Kades, later Deputy Chief of GHQ's Government Section. In the summer of 1944, the Civil Affairs Division set up Civil Affairs Training Schools (CATS) at Harvard, Yale, Chicago, Stanford, Michigan and Northwestern Universities. There, young military officers studied under such pioneers in the field of Japanese studies as Harvard's Serge Elisséeff, the first Westerner to graduate from Tokyo Imperial University; Sir George Sansom, the leading Western authority on Japan who taught at the Yale CATS; and Columbia University's Hugh Borton, who lectured on contemporary Japan. Top policy-planners, such as Ballantine and Dooman, also were frequent speakers. Graduates of the Military

Government schools went on to six months of advanced study at the CATS, which provided intensive language training combined with area studies focusing on the economies, local governments and education systems of enemy countries.[11] An estimated 1,500 civil administrators would be required for Japan, of whom the Army was to provide three quarters, the Navy the rest.

In addition to formal instruction, teaching staff organised wake-of-battle exercises and specific problem-solving sessions involving role-playing to prepare students for every possible contingency. At the University of Michigan CATS, Mark T. Orr, later a division head in GHQ's Civil Information and Education Section, found these exercises of particular benefit. Orr was designated chief planner for a simulation whose target was the city of Sendai in Miyagi Prefecture, northeastern Japan. 'The school exercises assumed that we would follow the fighting troops during an invasion of Japan. . . . We were to plan for re-establishing law and order and as much as possible normal functioning of the government and the life of the population', he recalled.'After the troops had gone through Sendai, we then would come behind with military government.' The University of Michigan had collected maps, charts and other information on the Sendai region. Had the Allies invaded, the 'big, fat report' that Orr and his team compiled from this data would have provided a detailed guide for the establishment of military rule in Sendai, one tailored to specific local conditions.[12] The CATS conducted similar exercises for each of Japan's major cities and prefectures.

Cecil G. Tilton was one of the first instructors at the University of Chicago CATS, which was attended by 60 to 70 officers. 'It was hell', Tilton reminisced later. 'I cannot tell you. Not one officer wanted to be there. Oh, they hated it. They had to learn Japanese five hours a day. The Japanese instructors, they were merciless.' Tilton eventually worked at all of the CATS except Stanford.[13] After six months of basic studies, trainees were required to submit a specialised paper on some aspect of occupation administration. As his graduation report for the Harvard CATS, Captain (later Major) William Karpinsky, for instance, wrote the extensive 'Survey of Japanese Labour' (7 March 1945), impressing his superiors sufficiently to get him appointed Labour Division Chief in GHQ's Economic and Scientific Section immediately after the war.

After initial training, incipient civil administrators spent two months at the Joint Army–Navy Civil Affairs Staging Area (CASA), Presidio of Monterey, California, where they completed their studies. CASA's Occupation Planning Staff continued to generate policy proposals for post-defeat Japan. It was there, for example, that basic education reforms were discussed and refined. More than 1,000 CASA trainees were appointed to civil affairs positions in Japan, although the majority remained in their posts only through the early phase of occupation. The War and Navy Departments also set up the Military Intelligence Service Language School to train Japanese language specialists (chapter 1). Despite these measures, civil administrators were a scarce commodity as planning for the Occupation reached completion. When MacArthur's AFPAC headquarters in Manila created the Military Government

Section in early August 1945, Brigadier General Crist, the new MGS commander, found himself desperately understaffed. During the week of 20 August, about one tenth of the recently trained CASA officers were rushed from Monterey to Manila. Crist sent half of the freshly minted Japan hands to Sixth and Eighth Armies and kept the other half for Military Government Section, which was transferred to Yokohama at the end of the month. Large numbers originally designated for Japan subsequently were diverted to southern Korea. In May 1946, with the Occupation under way, the Army established the School for Government of Occupied Areas at Carlisle Barracks, Pennsylvania as an emergency measure to meet the shortage of qualified civil affairs experts.[14]

Handbooks and Guides

Special studies, handbooks and guides were used as teaching materials in the Military Government schools. These were prepared by an inter-departmental Joint Editorial Committee on Civil Affairs Studies representing the State Department, the Navy, the Army and the Office of Strategic Services (OSS). The Joint Committee was chaired by Lieutenant Colonel James Shoemaker of the War Department's Civil Affairs Division. A professor of economics at the University of Hawai'i before the war, Shoemaker knew most of the available East Asian experts. He quickly farmed out the Committee's work to those best qualified for the task. Civil Affairs Handbooks were compiled between the spring of 1944 and 1945 based on data provided by the State Department, the Office of War Information (OWI), the OSS, the Foreign Economic Administration (FEA) and other government agencies. The work of compiling and editing the volumes was performed largely by the OSS Research and Analysis Branch. The 25-tome Handbook series covered such areas as population, government and administration, legal affairs, money and banking, natural resources, agriculture, industry, labour, foreign commerce, transportation systems, communications, public health and sanitation, public welfare, public safety, education, cultural institutions and the Japanese administration of occupied areas in Burma, Malaya, the Philippines and Thailand.

Whereas the Handbooks were compilations of essential facts, Civil Affairs Guides included policy alternatives for occupation administrators based on the surveys, analyses and statistics presented in the Handbooks. Prepared between the summer of 1944 and the autumn of 1945, the Guides focused on concrete subjects of special relevance for civil administration. These included the fishing industry, the police system, aliens, the control of wages and inflation, electric power, public information, local government, the revival of political parties, food rationing and price controls, water supply and sewage disposal, and radio broadcasting. The Guides were drafted by specialists from the OSS, the FEA and the departments of State, War, Treasury and Agriculture. CAD originally had planned some 70 civil affairs monographs, and about 50 were commissioned, but Japan's early surrender pre-empted the completion of many, and only about 40 Guides actually were published.[15]

Three Guides, in particular, all issued in July 1945, influenced subsequent occupation policies. Theodore Cohen, who replaced Karpinsky as Labour Division Chief in GHQ's Economic and Scientific Section, drafted 'Trade Unions and Collective Bargaining in Japan' while in Washington. Cohen's Guide was based in good part on the Master's thesis he had written under Hugh Borton at Columbia, 'The Japanese Labour Movement, 1918–1938.' Cohen's proposals were incorporated into the two basic US policy directives governing the Occupation (see below). Based on this Guide, Philip Sullivan of the State Department's Division of International Labour drew up a policy paper entitled 'The Treatment of Japanese Workers' Organisations', which was adopted as official US labour policy for Japan in December 1945. By that time, however, many of Cohen's recommendations already had found their way into Japan's new Labour Union Law.[16]

A second influential Guide was written by Dr Wolf I. Ladejinsky, then with the US Department of Agriculture, who had been recruited specifically to study Japanese agriculture. Disagreements within the State Department over land policy, however, resulted in only part of the Guide being published: 'Agriculture and Food in Japan.' Ladejinsky's land reform text, 'Adjustments in Systems of Land Tenure', was not approved, but Robert Fearey would bring it to MacArthur's attention in late 1945. Ladejinsky derived his inspiration, and many of his concrete ideas, from the radical reform projects of prewar Japanese agronomists.[17] CATS instructor Cecil Tilton, later head of Government Section's Local Government Division in SCAP, prepared 'Local Government in Japan', whose recommendations later would influence the reform of local government.

SWNCC and initial post-surrender policy (1945)

In July 1944, the US Navy's capture of Saipan breached Japan's defence perimeter, bringing Tokyo within range of Army Air Force B-29s. At that point, the State Department began finalising detailed plans for occupation, focusing on the political and psychological pre-conditions for victory. By late 1944, Military Government training was in full swing, and a variety of committees and groups in Washington were drafting postwar programmes for Japan. To coordinate planning among civilian and military agencies, the State–War–Navy Coordinating Committee (SWNCC, pronounced 'swink') was created in December 1944. SWNCC was a top-secret organisation whose existence was officially denied until 1946, but rumours of the Committee's work spread through Washington as it began evaluating occupation proposals in the spring of 1945. Full-time members included assistant under-secretaries of the State, War and Navy Departments supported on an ad hoc basis by a battery of experts.

State Department policy drafts drawn up earlier by the Postwar Programmes Committee and the Country and Area Committees were transferred to SWNCC, which reviewed them for final approval. SWNCC's Subcommittee for the Far East (SFE) formulated its own set of proposals for Japan. The SFE was chaired successively by Eugene H. Dooman, John Carter Vincent, James K. Penfield and

Hugh Borton. Many SFE recommendations later were adopted as Occupation policy. Harvard professor and future ambassador to Japan Edwin O. Reischauer, for instance, drafted the SWNCC-209 document group on the Imperial institution, and Borton prepared the SWNCC-228 series on reforming Japan's government system.

In early 1944, Joseph Grew became Chief of the Far Eastern Affairs Division, replacing Hornbeck, leader of the China Crowd's pro-Nationalist (*Guomindang*) faction. Japanophile Joseph Ballantine was appointed Grew's deputy director. This power shift transferred control over America's Asia policy from the China hands to the Japan hands. In late November 1944, Secretary of State Hull retired and was replaced by Under-Secretary Edward R. Stettinius. In December, Stettinius elevated Grew to Under-Secretary of State and named his protégé Eugene Dooman to head the SFE. Grew now was ideally placed to track and influence the evolution of US policy towards Japan.

SWNCC's War and Navy representatives worked out policy on military matters while its State Department members drew up plans for civil governance. At this time, the Joint Chiefs of Staff (JCS) set up two lower-level planning groups, the Joint Civil Affairs Committee and the Joint War Planning Committee, to evaluate the impact of military and non-military policies on US armed forces. Both committees worked closely with the Subcommittee for the Far East in preparing SWNCC drafts. The Joint Chiefs approved all SWNCC decisions. Once ratified by SWNCC and the JCS, SFE documents were signed by the President, becoming official policy.

As planning proceeded, however, civilian and military officials diverged in their approach to occupation. In January 1945, CAD Chief Hilldring learned of JCS plans to invade Japan. Preoccupied with the concrete details of mapping out a military administration for post-surrender areas, he resumed work on an earlier directive for military government dating from late 1943. Army planning also would be influenced strongly by the Morgenthau proposals for Germany of late 1944 (below). Seizing the initiative, on April 6 1945, the Civil Affairs Division asked SWNCC to work up a short general statement of policy goals to allow the Army to begin drafting general orders for field commanders and a definitive military government directive for Japan.[18] This task was undertaken by SWNCC's Subcommittee for the Far East. From these initiatives would emerge two basic policy documents for post-defeat Japan: a concise enunciation of general principles produced by SWNCC and a military directive to the supreme commander drafted by CAD.

Acting on Hilldring's request of early April, Dooman, Blakeslee, Borton and other SFE members prepared a document based on the earlier 'Post-War Objectives of the United States in Regard to Japan', which had been drafted by the Postwar Programmes Committee. The new guideline, completed on 19 April, was entitled 'Summary of United States Initial Post-Defeat Policy Relating to Japan' (SWNCC-150). The SFE 'Summary' called for unconditional surrender and recommended that the territorial boundaries of post-surrender Japan be defined according to the Cairo Declaration. The policy proposal advocated the establishment of a military régime with full powers of government to administer Japan directly, and specified its objectives and relationship to an occupation army. The military administration was to eradicate Japanese militarism, strengthen democratic tendencies among the people and encourage the development of liberal political groups. To implement these goals, however, occupation authorities would 'utilise the Japanese administrative machinery and, so far as practicable, Japanese public officials', making them 'responsible for the carrying out of the policies and directives of the military government'.

The 'Summary of United States Initial Post-Defeat Policy' went on to detail the 'Initial Tasks of Military Government'. Described in several clauses, these goals became the core of the wide-ranging directives that MacArthur's headquarters would issue to the Japanese government in the early months of occupation. The SFE article on the 'Nullification of Obnoxious Laws', for instance, was later expanded into the Civil Liberties Directive of 4 October 1945, which freed political prisoners and abolished restrictions on political and civil liberties. The Purge Directive of 4 January 1946 was based on a clause in the 'Summary' calling for the dissolution of 'existing political parties, including totalitarian, political and quasi-political organisations and ultra-nationalistic societies'. This formed the framework for another SCAP directive of 4 January 1946 ordering the dissolution of ultra-nationalist organisations and groups that opposed occupation policy. The 'Summary''s 'Freedom of Worship' provision became the Shintō Directive of 15 December 1945, which eliminated state sponsorship of Shintoism and separated religion and state. A 'Public Media' clause called for the democratisation of press and radio, the use of the media to promote a full understanding of occupation aims and the banning of propaganda hostile to Allied forces and personnel. Paradoxically, this proposal also laid the groundwork for SCAP's Press and Radio Codes of 19 and 22 September 1945, which authorised MacArthur's staff to ban criticism of occupation policies and purge the mass media.

The SFE 'Summary' ordained the elimination of ultra-nationalism and the development of democratic ideas. This stipulation would generate a series of major directives, issued between October and December 1945, instructing the government to arrest war criminals, democratise the courts and legal system, impose war reparations, democratise the economy and reorientate the schools. The 'Summary' also prohibited the manufacture of armaments, mandated the dissolution of 'specialised facilities for the production or repair of implements of war or aircraft of any type' and ordered the destruction of heavy industrial capacity exceeding normal peacetime requirements.

The SFE document called for the encouragement of trade unions among industrial and agricultural workers and the promotion of 'a wide distribution of income and of the ownership of the means of production and trade'. Although the framers of the 'Summary' outlined a programme of economic recovery, they did not intend that the country should become a strong economic competitor. A key provision entitled 'The Control of the Japanese Economy' specified measures to protect essential national public services, finance and banking, the production and distribution of key commodities, and exports and imports, but these measures were designed merely 'to meet the needs of the occupation forces and to prevent starvation and such disease and civil unrest as would interfere with the operations of military government'. The bottom line was clear: 'No steps shall be taken by the military government which would raise the standard of living of the Japanese people to a standard out of line with that of neighbouring peoples'.

The Morgenthau Plan, the German Directive and SWNCC-150/1
In the meantime, Civil Affairs Division continued work on its military directive, relying not only on SWNCC planning papers but also on an earlier CAD proposal. In October 1943, the Division, in cooperation with the Army's Military Government schools, had drafted a preliminary set of policy recommendations for the post-defeat control of Japan. Of much sterner stuff than the State Department scenarios, the CAD document called for the arrest as war criminals of the Emperor and his household, elder statesmen (*Jūshin*), privy councillors, Imperial Diet members, the prime minister, Cabinet ministers, high-ranking bureaucrats, senior magistrates, and prefectural governors. The plan recommended that occupation authorities requisition private property and labour and utilise lower-echelon government officials, the courts and the police to enforce military government decrees. Formulated mainly by middle-ranking staff officers, these policy ideas were rejected as Draconian by top War Department officials, but they are instructive for the light they cast on the comparatively benign Allied policies actually implemented. Reflecting the archetypal military approach to civil government, the 1943 CAD proposals resembled the punitive post-surrender plans subsequently drawn up for Germany.

In August 1944, with President Roosevelt's backing, Secretary of the Treasury Henry J. Morgenthau began work on a set of policy recommendations for Germany. The so-called Morgenthau Plan called for radical 'denazification', to include the destruction of centralised state power, direct military rule, a zonal occupation and the dismantling of heavy industry. Advocating a hard peace, the Plan intended to dismember Germany and reduce it to 'a country primarily agricultural and pastoral in its character'.[19] Morgenthau insisted that the programme should apply in principle to Japan, as well. On 1 September, the Treasury Department submitted a memorandum entitled 'Directives for the Occupation of Germany'. Urging denazification, reparations and an economic 'hands-off' policy, it was officially endorsed by Roosevelt and Churchill on 15 September at the Octagon Conference in Quebec and remained in effect for about one month before critics in the President's Cabinet, appalled by the proposal's vindictiveness, discreetly removed it from circulation.[20]

Nonetheless, the Civil Affairs Division utilised the Morgenthau document in preparing an early version of the Army's occupation directive to General Eisenhower in Europe, the 'US Basic Directive for Germany' (JCS-1067). Later, Charles Kades and other sturdy New Dealers on the CAD staff would refer to JCS-1067 when drafting the Army's instructions to General MacArthur in Japan: the 'Basic Directive for Post-Surrender Military Government in Japan Proper' (JCS-1380). Inevitably, some of the former's language, and many of its concepts, would filter into JCS-1380, leaving a clear trace in the tough economic sanctions the latter envisaged for Japan. There, as in Germany, the Allies initially would refuse responsibility for inflation and economic rehabilitation, delegating economic control to local governments.[21]

On 15 March 1945, Morgenthau convinced Roosevelt to set up the Informal Policy Committee on Germany charged with coordinating policy for the German occupation. The Committee resurrected the Morgenthau proposals and formally endorsed them. Chief among these was the abolition of a central German government, a measure that per force would necessitate direct military rule. More importantly, the Informal Policy Committee took planning for Germany out of the hands of SWNCC, which thenceforth would formulate postwar policy for Japan and Korea alone. On Morgenthau's advice, the White House urged SWNCC to pattern its basic directive for Japan on the German model, but the new division of labour ensured that SFE policy-making subsequently would follow a different trajectory, one defined by two new and crucial policy assumptions: 1 unconditional surrender would not entail the annihilation of the Japanese state; 2 as a result, the occupation would be carried out indirectly via existing governmental agencies and institutions, although the degree and modality of indirect control remained to be defined.[22]

On 12 April 1945, following the death of President Roosevelt, Morgenthau lost his patron, his constituency and his clout. Roosevelt's successor, Harry S. Truman, quickly got rid of the Treasury official and his protégés, inviting the counsel of men like Grew, Secretary of State Henry L. Stimson and Russian specialist Averell W. Harriman. With the unconditional surrender of Germany on 8 May, Allied forces implemented plans for direct military governance, and the United States turned its full attention to Asia. The SFE 'Summary', now known as SWNCC-150, had been completed on 19 April, a few days after Roosevelt's death. On 3 May and again on 11 June, important clauses were inserted into the draft. The first was the 'revolutionary' injunction to 'favour a wider distribution of ownership, management and control of the economic system'. The second was the restatement of an earlier principle that the Occupation would 'encourage the development of democratic organisations in labour, industry and agriculture'.[23]

On 12 June 1945, SWNCC formally adopted the SFE 'Summary of United States Initial Post-Defeat Policy Relating to Japan', incorporating the New Deal tenets of economic democracy but with few other revisions, and designated it SWNCC-150/1 – the first draft of the US Initial Post-Defeat Policy for Japan (after 15 August, 'Post-Defeat' would become 'Post-Surrender'). In the fluid final months of the war, however, American policy towards Japan would undergo even more dramatic changes. SWNCC-150/1 went through a final round of rewriting that was to modify its basic thrust in important ways, particularly with regard to the nature of military government and the régime of control. Many of these changes can be traced to the Potsdam Proclamation.

<h1 style="text-align:center">POTSDAM</h1>

The Emperor

Following Germany's surrender, the United States intensified preparations for the invasion of Kyushu and Honshu, a campaign that military planners estimated would be enormously costly in human life. As American troops battled the Japanese, other Allied armies would have to search out and destroy diehard Imperial soldiers in China and Southeast Asia. To Under-Secretary of State Joseph Grew, this prospect was terrifying. Only an early surrender could prevent that apocalyptic scenario, and the key to a quick capitulation in Grew's mind was the Emperor, who, he believed, had secretly desired peace all along. The monarch's cooperation would provide a vital rallying point for 'moderate' and 'liberal' elements in Japan and assure a peaceful transition to occupation. On 12 December 1944, in testimony before the Senate Foreign Relations Committee, Grew had compared the Emperor to a queen bee. 'Remove the queen from the swarm, the hive would disintegrate', he told Committee members.[24] Grew also was convinced that rapid termination of the conflict would pre-empt Soviet entry into the war, decisively limiting Moscow's postwar role in the region.

Interrogation reports by Captain Ellis M. Zacharias, head of the Psychological Warfare Section in the Office of Naval Intelligence, and the State Department's John K. Emmerson indicated that many Japanese prisoners of war shared Grew's view. Emmerson later recalled: 'It was difficult to persuade these shamed and sickened veterans even to think about losing the war, a consequence for the homeland no loyal subject of the Emperor would at first contemplate.' With some effort, however, he succeeded in coaxing the bewildered captives to visualise the unimaginable. 'Soldiers in the field', he noted, 'fought in obedience to the Emperor's command. Should the Emperor, in his divine wisdom, order them to lay down their arms, they would of course do so . . . . It was that simple.'[25]

On 28 May 1945, Grew visited President Truman with a proposal, drafted at his request by Eugene Dooman, for bringing the war to a quick conclusion. The Under-Secretary of State hoped the President would include it in a speech he was scheduled to give on 31 May. His argument, in brief, was that the Allies' unconditional surrender demand should be modified to allow Japan the possibility of retaining the Imperial institution. The proposal's logic was both subtle and compelling. America's primary goal, he told Truman, was to destroy totally Japan's military machine and blot out the cult of militarism in order to 'render it impossible for Japan again to threaten world peace'. But he warned that 'the Japanese are a fanatical people and are capable . . . of fighting to the last ditch and the last man' and noted that the cost in American lives then would be unpredictable. 'The greatest obstacle to unconditional surrender by the Japanese', he continued, 'is their belief that this would entail the destruction or permanent removal of the Emperor and the institution of the Throne.' Grew recommended that Japan be allowed to determine its own political structure to afford the country a means of saving face. He suggested that, in the wake of the fire-bombing of Tokyo in March, a public statement on the monarchy would have a profound psychological impact. The Emperor had signed the declaration of war but was not war-minded and probably had no choice but to humour the war faction. 'Japan', he asserted, 'does not need an Emperor to be militaristic nor are the Japanese militaristic because they have an Emperor.' Finally, Grew told Truman that the monarchy could 'become a cornerstone for building a peaceful future for the country'. Reworking the unconditional surrender formula to imply preservation of the Throne would induce an early capitulation. The President listened carefully and seemed to concur, noting that his own thoughts had been following the same line of reasoning.[26]

Truman instructed Grew to take his ideas to Secretary of War Henry Stimson and the military high command. On 29 May, the Under-Secretary of State conferred with Stimson, who agreed in principle with his proposal on the Japanese monarchy but noted that it would be premature for the President to make such an overture to the Japanese at that time. Stimson ascribed his hesitation to 'certain military reasons' – almost certainly an oblique reference to the development of the atomic bomb. On 16 and 18 June, Grew again put his proposal to 'clarify' the meaning of unconditional surrender before Truman, asking him to time the announcement of the modified surrender terms with the fall of Okinawa which was imminent (the fighting ended on 23 June). On 18 June, however, the President demurred, replying he would wait to reach a decision until he had met Churchill and Stalin at Potsdam in mid-July. The same day, in a meeting with the Joint Chiefs, he approved their invasion plan for Japan, 'Operation Downfall'. Landings on Kyushu on 1 November 1945 were to be followed by an assault on Honshu on 1 March 1946. Other key issues discussed that afternoon, described in the minutes as 'certain other matters', are believed to have included Soviet participation in the war, the use of atomic weapons and Grew's proposed statement on the Emperor.[27]

The Stimson Memorandum
With presidential approval of a ground invasion, Secretary of War Stimson warmed to Grew's ideas on the Throne. A quick end to the fighting and a smooth transition to peace, he believed, would not only save lives and curb Soviet influence in Japan but give the Army exclusive control of the occupation. Misgivings about the rigidity of the unconditional surrender formula were shared by many of Truman's top military officials. The Joint Chiefs of Staff believed generally at this point that a softening of the surrender terms and a Soviet attack on Japan would be sufficient to achieve peace. '[T]he impact of Russian entry on the already hopeless Japanese may well be the decisive action levering them into capitulation', a JCS memorandum had stated in the late spring of 1945.[28] Members of the British Imperial General Staff held similar views.[29]

On 2 July, after the top-secret Interim Committee, the President's atomic bomb oversight body, had recommended the use of nuclear weapons against Japan, Stimson presented Truman with the draft of a statement to the Japanese redefining the terms of surrender. The idea for a final declaration of Allied intentions had originated with Army Chief of Staff General George C. Marshall and been endorsed by the government in early June. Truman insisted that the American side present it for approval to the Potsdam Conference, scheduled to begin on 17 July, rather than issue it unilaterally. Stimson's draft, 'Proclamation by the Heads of State US-UK-[USSR]-China', had been prepared by the Army General Staff's Strategy and Policy Group under the supervision of Assistant Secretary of War John J. McCloy and was based largely on the 'Summary of United States Initial Post-Defeat Policy Relating to Japan', which SWNCC had adopted on 12 June. The proclamation called on Japan 'to surrender and permit the occupation of her country' in order to bring about 'complete demilitarisation for the sake of future peace'.[30]

In a note that accompanied his Potsdam draft, entitled 'Memorandum for the President – Proposed Programme for Japan', Stimson warned Truman of the consequences of 'a last ditch defence such as has been made on Iwo Jima and Okinawa'. Should that come to pass, he said, 'we shall . . . have to go through with an even more bitter finish fight than in Germany'. In Paragraph 5 of the so-called Stimson Memorandum, the Secretary of War wrote, 'I personally think that if in saying this we should add that we do not exclude a constitutional monarchy under her present dynasty, it would substantially add to the chances of acceptance.' Paragraph 12 of Stimson's Potsdam proclamation draft was in the same vein:

> The occupying forces of the Allies shall be withdrawn from Japan as soon as our objectives are accomplished and there has been established beyond doubt a peacefully inclined, responsible government of a character representative of the Japanese people. This may include a constitutional monarchy under the present dynasty if it be shown to the complete satisfaction of the world that such a government will never again aspire to aggression.[31]

The State Department, however, was sharply divided over the issue of the Emperor. Assistant Secretaries Archibald MacLeish, poet and former Librarian of Congress now in charge of public and cultural relations, and Dean G. Acheson were staunch abolitionists adamantly opposed to maintaining any vestige of Imperial sovereignty. In MacLeish's words, 'the institution of the Throne is an anachronistic, feudal institution, perfectly adapted to the manipulation and use of anachronistic, feudal-minded groups within the country. To leave that institution intact is to run the grave risk that it will be used in the future as it has been used in the past'. Acheson, who would replace Grew as Under-Secretary in August, argued that the Japanese sovereign 'should be removed because he was a weak leader who had yielded to the military demand for war and who could not be relied upon'. (He would later recant, acknowledging that 'I very shortly came to see that I was quite wrong'.)[32] Despite these objections, Grew's retentionist view prevailed, and on 2 July, Truman and his Cabinet reviewed and approved the Stimson Potsdam text with Paragraph 12 (Article 12 in the official draft) intact.[33]

On 3 July, Truman replaced Secretary of State Edward Stettinius with James F. Byrnes. Aligned with the China Crowd, Byrnes was a hard-nosed realist with immoderate political ambitions who favoured a tough peace. With the ascension of Byrnes to power, Grew's days as Under-Secretary were numbered. On 5 July, acting on his own initiative, Grew personally handed the new Secretary of State a copy of Stimson's unofficial Potsdam draft. The next day, 6 July, Byrnes left for Berlin without formally committing himself to the Stimson document. Former Secretary of State Cordell Hull earlier had explicitly advised against retaining the Emperor. Public sentiment against Hirohito was running high, Hull told Byrnes, and cited a June Gallup Poll indicating that two-thirds of the American public would have the sovereign arrested or executed. A guarantee of Imperial immunity, he cautioned, smacked of appeasement and was likely to whet the appetite for vengeance in the United States and Allied nations. To make his point with greater force, on 16 July, Hull cabled Byrnes – then in Potsdam – warning of 'terrible repercussions' at home if the Japanese monarchy were spared and urged the Secretary of State to postpone a final decision until after 'the climax of allied bombing and Russia's entry into the war'.[34]

Potsdam and the Throne
On 17 July, Churchill, Stalin and Truman met in the once plush Berlin suburb of Potsdam to coordinate strategy towards a defeated Germany, outline post-defeat policy for Poland and the Balkans and adopt a common approach to Japan. On 16 July, Truman had been informed of the successful Trinity Test at Alamogordo, New Mexico. With the acquisition of a nuclear capability, the United States could now bring Japan to its knees without sacrificing additional Allied lives, and Truman and Byrnes, with Hull's admonition ringing in their ears, saw no need for a formal pledge to retain the Emperor. This conclusion received unexpected support from another quarter. On 18 July, in a memorandum to the President, the Joint Chiefs noted that Stimson's Article 12 contained a dangerous ambiguity: it could be read either as a veiled threat to remove the 'present dynasty' or as 'a commitment to continue the institution of the Emperor and Emperor worship'. Top military leaders now believed that while a flexible approach to retention of the Imperial institution was essential, no change in status should be suggested or implied before the end of hostilities. Stimson reluctantly agreed, and all explicit references to the Throne were struck from Article 12.[35]

Other important changes would appear in the text before its final release. The Proclamation followed generally the points outlined in the 'Summary' (SWNCC-150), which the Japan Crowd's Subcommittee for the Far East had prepared between April and June at the request of the Civil Affairs Division. But the final document was the work of colonels on the Army General Staff, and its stern tenor reflected CAD's military preoccupations. In late July, British officials made five last-minute proposals at Potsdam that not only moderated the tone of the Proclamation but later would require Washington to readjust its plans for military government. London, like Grew, had advocated modifying the surrender terms to allow the Japanese some leeway for manoeuvre, although it was careful not to incur American displeasure by pressing the point. Now the British unobtrusively presented their case.

The US draft read 'Democratic tendencies among the Japanese people shall be supported and strengthened'; the British suggested, 'The Japanese Government shall remove all obstacles to the revision and strengthening of democratic tendencies among the Japanese people.' Instead of calling on the Japanese people to surrender, as Washington had done, London's revision called on the 'Government of Japan'. Moreover, the British draft limited unconditional surrender to the Japanese armed forces, whereas the American version had included the Emperor and the government. The US document provided for the occupation of Japanese territory; the British modified that to 'points in Japanese territory to be designated by the Allies', suggesting that Japan might retain some degree of internal sovereignty. In late July, after the Proclamation had been issued, a State Department memorandum noted in retrospect that while these changes left the status of the Imperial State uncertain, they appeared to assume 'that a Japanese government will continue and will be responsible for carrying out the [Potsdam] terms'. This was at odds with the American demand for the transfer of all governmental authority to the Allies. Furthermore, whereas Washington insisted that Japan 'obey all directives which may be given by the Allied Powers', the British seemed to offer Tokyo a chance to end the war by agreeing to the Potsdam text, giving the document an ostensibly contractual character. Despite reservations, Truman and his staff consented to these amendments, which had the merit of preserving the basic intent of the US call for complete and immediate capitulation while making Allied demands more palatable to Tokyo.[36]

The British position was understated but consistent. It had been articulated by Sir George Sansom, Minister at the British Embassy in Washington from 1942 to 1945. Sansom believed that the Allies could best promote democracy in Japan through limited reforms that left basic institutions, including the monarchy, intact. He opposed direct military occupation as 'both unnecessary and unwise', barring hostile resistance from the Japanese. London generally endorsed the views of its senior Japan specialist. Although the extent of British influence on the evolution of US policy towards the Emperor should not be exaggerated, it is safe to say that Sansom, Borton and Grew worked together to save the monarchy, with Sansom and the Foreign Office discreetly endorsing the views of the Japan Crowd to all who would listen. This influence was particularly manifest in the British alterations to the Potsdam language.[37]

All guarantees for the safety of the Throne, however, had been excised from Article 12, which now read: 'The occupying forces of the Allies shall be withdrawn from Japan as soon as these objectives have been accomplished and there has been established in accordance with the freely expressed will of the Japanese people a peacefully inclined and responsible government.' One Occupationaire has insisted that the

Photo 30. The Big Three, Churchill, Truman and Stalin, at Potsdam (Kyodo).

phrase 'freely expressed will of the Japanese people' was retained at the insistence of the Japan Crowd as a 'psychological stratagem' intended to imply that the Imperial institution might be preserved should the Japanese people so desire.[38] On 11 August, Secretary of State Byrnes would use similar language in a note to the Japanese designed to imply a loosening of the surrender terms (below). At Potsdam, however, neither Truman, his staff nor the Joint Chiefs entertained any such subtle design.

On 26 July, Churchill and Truman issued the 13-point Potsdam Proclamation ordering Japan to surrender unconditionally or face 'prompt and utter destruction' – a cryptic reference to the atomic bomb. The document was released hastily, as soon as Hiroshima had been scheduled for destruction. It gave no warning of the weapon nor did it allude to the expected entry of the Soviet Union into the war. The document appeared to allow Japan some freedom of action, but in fact, its demands were irreducible. The government of Suzuki Kantarō had two choices: accept the Potsdam demands in their entirety and order Imperial forces to cease fighting immediately or invite total ruin and a dictated peace. Despite the text's ambiguities, in the minds of the Anglo-American leadership, the sole 'condition' for Japan's survival was speedy and unreserved compliance. 'The following are our terms', the Allies proclaimed. 'We will not deviate from them. There are no alternatives. We shall brook no delay.' The Proclamation pledged to dismantle the Greater Japanese Empire, disarm and demilitarise the nation, deliver stern justice to war criminals and exact war reparations. It decreed a military occupation but also guaranteed such basic liberties as freedom of speech, religion and thought and pledged to nurture the emergence of a democratic, peacefully inclined government. The document was not a legal instrument. Its proposals amounted to neither an armistice nor a treaty. It was, quite simply, the Allies' last warning.

THE EMPEROR AND SURRENDER

Revolution and the 'Peace Party'
The Japanese government failed to deliver a clear response to the Potsdam Proclamation. On 6 August, an atomic bomb laid waste to Hiroshima. On 8 August, the Soviet Union declared war on Japan, and on 9 August, as Soviet tanks rolled into Manchuria, a second nuclear explosion obliterated large parts of Nagasaki. Defeat was an intolerable notion to the Japanese leadership, but as the end drew near, officials close to the Throne entertained another, even more compelling reason for alarm: it was conceivable that the Soviet declaration of war would spark insurrection at home, precipitating the overthrow of the Imperial Order from within.

The spectre of revolution had been raised in early 1945 by the so-called Yoshida Anti-War (*Yoshida Hansen*) Group, a loose coalition of 'moderate' political leaders and upper-class Japanese, thoroughly conservative in outlook but opposed to the war itself for a variety of reasons. The group had been formed in 1942 by Yoshida Shigeru, China hand and former ambassador to Rome (1930–2) and London (1936–38), who was regarded in some circles as an old-style liberalist. In fact, Yoshida had defended Japan's Manchurian adventure in Europe and worked to secure Mussolini's support for the Imperial cause. He was, as one observer quipped, 'no man of peace, and he carried no taint of democracy'.[39] Nonetheless, Yoshida worked tirelessly offstage to bring the war to an end and preserve the monarchy. In April 1945, he and two other 'peace plotters' would be arrested for their pains by Military Police. Yoshida was freed in May, and the incident served to establish his anti-war credentials, facilitating his rehabilitation and rise to prominence during the Occupation.

Associated with the Yoshida Anti-War Group were Court adviser and former premier Prince Konoe Fumimaro; Admiral Suzuki Kantarō, premier from April to August 1945; Count Makino Nobuaki, an Imperial confidant and Yoshida's father-in-law; Ikeda Seihin, a Mitsui *zaibatsu* financier and Yoshida intimate; parliamentarian and ex-minister of education Hatoyama Ichirō; and Ueda Shunkichi, a former bureaucrat and emperor-system ideologue. Konoe and Makino were members of the 'peace group' that Grew had frequented before the war (Makino had represented Japan at the 1919 Versailles Peace Conference where he fought unsuccessfully for the insertion in the treaty of an anti-discrimination clause). The anti-war party believed broadly that the gravest danger to the Throne came from three sources: the 'military clique' that had usurped power and which was said to harbour Communistic leanings; the Communist movement outside of Japan's borders; and a revolutionary conflagration inside the country kindled by an Allied victory. The United States, the group believed, would offer Japan a general peace, keep the Communists at bay and preserve the Imperial State, or *kokka-taisei* ('national polity', usually shortened to *kokutai*) – the euphemism for Imperial rule.

In early 1945, leading members of the Yoshida Group attempted to persuade the Emperor to end the war. In February, Hirohito discreetly consulted his senior statesmen, the *Jūshin*, about the course of the fighting.[40] Prince Konoe seized this opportunity to present a sharply dissenting view in his Memorial to the Throne, which Yoshida had helped draft. Delivered on 14 February, the Memorial argued that:

> Japan has already lost the war. . . . From the standpoint of maintaining Japan's Imperial system, that which we have most to fear is not defeat itself but, rather, the threat inherent in the possibility that a Communist revolution may accompany defeat. . . . I feel that conditions within Japan and those prevailing abroad are rapidly progressing towards such an eventuality.[41]

The Emperor and War

Konoe's plea was an oblique attack on General Tōjō Hideki's expansionist Control Faction (*Tōseiha*), the military cabal in power. The Prince's conspiracy theory followed broadly the political line of the discredited Imperial Way Faction (*Kōdōha*), which regarded the Soviet Union as the real enemy and had opposed war with the West. (Committed to direct action to achieve its goal of internal reconstruction, the faction was in no sense liberal, having lost ascendancy only after the bloody *coup d'état* attempt of 26 February 1936.) Hirohito sided with Tōjō and then-Prime Minister Koiso Kuniaki, rejected Konoe's arguments and pressed emphatically for 'one more military gain' to strengthen Japan's hand in future negotiations and improve the monarchy's chances of surviving defeat.[42] Imperial recalcitrance at this crucial juncture prolonged the agony of war, making inevitable the debacle of Okinawa and the devastation of Hiroshima and Nagasaki.

By February 1945, Imperial armies were in retreat across Southeast Asia. MacArthur had captured Leyte, invaded Luzon and was about to take Manila, and a US task force had converged on Iwo Jima. Indian and British troops were manoeuvring to take Mandalay and Rangoon. Particularly worrisome was a report in mid-February that Moscow might abrogate the Neutrality Pact and enter the war against Japan. And yet Hirohito clung tenaciously to his obsession with one last victory. When MacArthur invaded Luzon in early January, the Emperor had argued for a vigorous head-on confrontation with the enemy and pressed Army Chief of Staff Umezu Yoshijirō to challenge General Yamashita Tomoyuki's strategy of attrition (despite Royal prodding, Umezu refused to intervene). As late as May, with Imperial forces engaged in a bloody and futile rearguard action in Okinawa, Hirohito was still hoping for a military success there. When defeat loomed inevitably, he dreamed incredibly of striking a decisive blow at Allied armies in southern China and Burma, by then no longer major theatres of operations.[43]

Hirohito's views on the war reflected those of most of his senior military advisers.

Japan's isolation and deteriorating war situation paradoxically confirmed the bureaucratic and military establishments in their determination to defend the homeland to the death. On 6 June, in the presence of Hirohito, an Imperial Conference including the Supreme Council for the Conduct of the War, the Cabinet and the Privy Council President adopted a crucial position paper, 'Fundamental Policy for the Conduct of the War', which explicitly committed the nation to fight to extinction rather than accept surrender. Two days later, on 8 June, the Emperor officially endorsed that policy.[44]

The bleak prospect of a frenzied finish fight on home soil galvanised the 'peace party', including Lord Privy Seal Marquis Kido Kōichi and Foreign Minister Tōgō Shigenori. Kido, in particular, shared the fears of Konoe and Yoshida's anti-war group that civil insurrection was a greater peril to the Throne than military defeat. In May, without the Emperor's knowledge, Tōgō had obtained the reluctant consent of the Supreme War Council to put out secret peace feelers to the Soviet Union. As discussed in chapter 1, in early June, former premier Hirota Kōki met Ambassador Yakov Malik near Tokyo, but the Soviet envoy gave the overture a chilly reception. By late June, the peace faction had prevailed upon the Suzuki Cabinet and Hirohito to seek the formal mediation of Moscow, which alone had the diplomatic weight to intercede effectively on Japan's behalf. With the fall of Okinawa now a certainty, the Emperor appears to have undergone a change of heart. The war, he realised, could not continue without endangering the Throne. On 22 June, Hirohito convoked another Imperial Conference. Breaking with tradition, he addressed the gathering first, urging that concrete plans to end the war be drawn up and implemented speedily.[45] The Japanese leadership had badly misread Moscow's intentions, however, and these démarches proved unrealistic and ineffectual. Between 17 and 21 July, with the Potsdam Conference in progress, Ambassador Satō Naotake in Moscow repeatedly warned Tōgō that Japan's only hope was to meet all Allied conditions for surrender while demanding assurances for the survival of the Imperial institution. His pleas fell on deaf ears. At that point, not even so-called peace advocates were willing to consider a non-negotiated settlement. The Potsdam Proclamation of 26 July hardened the government in its resolve.

The Emperor and Peace
On 9 August, with two cities levelled by atomic bombs and Soviet troops overrunning Manchuria, Konoe's ominous scenario of February seemed palpably near at hand. Continued resistance almost certainly would bring about a Soviet invasion of Japan proper before the Anglo-American expeditionary force could position itself to land. In mid-morning of that day, which a historian has termed 'perhaps the most critical in Japanese history', the six-member Supreme Council for the Conduct of the War convened to consider options for terminating the war.[46] Present were Prime Minister Suzuki; Foreign Minister Tōgō; Navy Minister Admiral Yonai Mitsumasa, a former prime minister, Suzuki's deputy and an avowed peace disciple; Army Minister General Anami Korechika, a stubborn hardliner; the conservative Navy Chief of Staff

Admiral Toyoda Soemu; and the hawkish Army Chief of Staff Umezu Yoshijirō. Foreign Minister Tōgō now was convinced that Japan had no choice but to accept the Potsdam terms and surrender without negotiations, news of Nagasaki's destruction, received during the deliberations, having steeled his determination. Echoing Ambassador Satō's proposals of late July, the Foreign Minister posed a sole condition for capitulation: that an understanding be reached allowing the Imperial system to continue. Suzuki initially agreed with his foreign minister, as did Navy Minister Yonai.

Earlier, however, Yonai had proposed a negotiated peace plan based on four conditions: 1 that Imperial sovereignty be preserved, 2 that Imperial General Headquarters disarm and demobilise all Japanese forces, 3 that Japan not be subject to Allied occupation and 4 that the government itself be allowed to punish war criminals. Anami, Toyoda and Umezu strongly supported the Yonai Plan, even though its author no longer did, and stood resolutely opposed to Tōgō's single demand. If the four conditions could not be met, the military proposed to continue fighting until the Allies relented. In any event, interposed Umezu, it would be difficult if not impossible to secure the surrender of Imperial troops to Allied forces. Suzuki, too, seemed swayed by this rhetoric. When the question was put to the Cabinet in the afternoon, Yonai and Anami took opposing positions, and after more than seven hours of debate, the ministers found themselves at an impasse.[47]

Consultations continued at various levels throughout the day but ended inconclusively. Finally, shortly before midnight, at Suzuki's request, an Imperial Conference was convened in the Palace's underground bomb shelter adjoining the library with the Emperor himself in attendance. Suzuki now wrongly presented the Yonai Plan as representing a general consensus, an interpretation that Tōgō contested vigorously. The Foreign Minister countered that there was no time to negotiate such demands. Preservation of the Imperial line, he insisted, was the sole criterion for surrender. After Yonai had again expressed agreement with Tōgō, Privy Council President Baron Hiranuma Ki'ichirō, a former premier and old-school nationalist, took the floor. Hiranuma generally supported Tōgō but insisted that the sole condition for capitulation be an explicit Allied pledge, not an implicit understanding, that the Throne would be spared. He was demanding, as one student of history has aptly expressed it, 'the retention of real, substantive political power in the hands of the Emperor, so that [Hiranuma] and the "moderates" might go on using it to control the people'.[48]

Generals Anami and Umezu and Admiral Toyoda stood their ground, however, and again a stalemate was reached. At this point, Prime Minister Suzuki, acting on Hiranuma's suggestion, took the unusual step of approaching the Throne for guidance. In the early morning hours of 10 August, Hirohito spoke emotionally but without hesitation, saying that the time had come to 'bear the unbearable' and 'accept the Allied proclamation on the basis outlined by the Foreign Minister'. Upon receiving the Emperor's 'sacred decision' (*seidan*), the Council agreed to accept the Potsdam terms on condition that they did not compromise the position of the

Imperial institution and proposed to ask for a clarification of Allied intentions regarding the Throne. The Cabinet ratified the Conference's decision, making it official, and the Suzuki government informed Washington, London, Chungking (Chongqing) and Moscow of its tentative assent, contingent on Allied recognition of Imperial continuity, through Japanese legations in Berne and Stockholm.[49]

The Foreign Ministry's Kase Toshikazu drafted the original English note, making acceptance conditional on 'the understanding that the said declaration does not comprise any demand which prejudices the constitutional status of the Emperor'. Baron Hiranuma, however, was adamant that the archaic expression *taiken* ('powers inherent in the Throne') be substituted for 'constitutional status of the Emperor'. This term Kase deftly glossed as 'prerogatives'. Thus, the final text read, 'with the understanding that the said declaration does not comprise any demand which prejudices the prerogatives of His Majesty as a Sovereign Ruler'.[50]

As soon as Washington received the note, Japan Crowd stalwarts Eugene Dooman (SWNCC Subcommittee for the Far East) and Joseph Ballantine (Far Eastern Affairs Division, State Department) prevailed on Secretary of State Byrnes to respond to the Japanese query with an implied softening of the Allied terms. With the consent of Truman and Stimson, Byrnes decided to issue a Delphic statement suggesting a great deal but promising nothing. The proposed text could be construed broadly as a vague assurance that the monarchy would not be abolished unilaterally but stopped short of actually guaranteeing Royal prerogatives, or even that Hirohito would continue as sovereign. In a note dated 11 August, Byrnes instructed the Swiss chargé d'affaires in Washington to inform Tokyo via Berne that: 'From the moment of surrender, the authority of the Emperor and the Japanese Government to rule the state shall be subject to the Supreme Commander of the Allied Powers who will take such steps as he deems necessary to effectuate the surrender terms.' The penultimate paragraph read: 'The ultimate form of government of Japan shall, in accordance with the Potsdam Declaration, be established by the freely expressed will of the Japanese people.' The British and Nationalist Chinese governments gave their concurrence immediately, but Soviet Foreign Minister V. M. Molotov complained that the text was incompatible with the principle of unconditional surrender. Soviet agreement eventually was obtained, however, and the Secretary of State had the statement transmitted to Tokyo.[51]

On 12 August, as waves of B-29s blasted Tokyo and other cities, Army Minister Anami and the war party manoeuvred behind the scenes to obstruct acceptance of the Byrnes Note and build consensus for a continuation of the war. Privy Council President Hiranuma, too, rejected the Allied reply, which he astutely perceived was not a pledge of security for the Throne. To make the message more palatable to the adversaries of a quick peace, the Foreign Ministry's Treaty Bureau had purposely toned down its translation of the text. In the Japanese version, the Note simply enjoined the Emperor and government to continue 'to carry out their functions under certain restrictions'. Treaty Bureau translators omitted all reference to Byrnes' stipulation that the Emperor and the government would be subject to the Allied

Supreme Commander, conveying the impression that the surrender was an agreement between consenting parties. The statement 'The ultimate form of government of Japan shall, in accordance with the Potsdam Declaration, be established by the freely expressed will of the Japanese people' posed a special difficulty. The Bureau got around this by noting that the 'g' in government was lower case and therefore did not include the monarchy and rendered the Japanese text accordingly.[52]

Privy Seal Kido lobbied intensely for acceptance of the Foreign Ministry translation and Tōgō managed to win over Prime Minister Suzuki, but their opponents saw through the Ministry's subterfuge. On 13 August, the Cabinet deadlocked on the issue of Imperial sovereignty, prompting Suzuki once again to refer the question to the Emperor. To compound the peace faction's difficulties, early in the morning of 14 August, Allied aircraft dropped leaflets on Tokyo publicising the texts of the Japanese and American diplomatic exchanges, increasing the possibility of insubordination and even revolt by diehard militarists. That morning, at Hirohito's urging, a second Imperial Conference was convened in his presence in the Palace air raid shelter. There, the monarch delivered his final verdict: 'I have studied the terms of the Allied reply and have concluded that they constitute a virtually complete acknowledgment of the position We maintained in the note despatched several days ago. In short, I consider the reply to be acceptable.'[53] At the same time, he ordered an Imperial rescript prepared for broadcast to the nation the following day and recorded the message shortly before midnight. The broadcast was aired at noon on 15 August.

FINALISING POST-SURRENDER PLANS

The US initial post-surrender policy

When the Potsdam Proclamation was issued, SWNCC's Subcommittee for the Far East was refining its 'Summary of United States Initial Post-Defeat Policy Relating to Japan' (SWNCC-150/1). The SFE 'Summary' had envisaged an initial period of direct rule by military government, but as a result of the British amendments, the Potsdam document now implied that existing governmental institutions might implement Allied policy. On 1 August, John Balfour, the British chargé in Washington, wrote to the State Department suggesting that it would be preferable 'for the Allies, instead of assuming all the functions of government in Japan, to work through a Japanese administration'. In a memorandum to Grew dated 6 August, Joseph Ballantine, the Far Eastern Affairs Division Chief, discussed the contradiction between 'complete control' by the Allies, as supposed by SWNCC-150/1, and the 'supervisory role' implicit in the modified Potsdam text. He suggested a scenario where, circumstances permitting, 'The Japanese administrative structure would be used to the fullest extent but all policies would be decided by the supreme commander'.[54]

As surrender became imminent, activity at the State Department intensified. When the Department received notice of Japan's conditional acceptance of the Potsdam terms on 10 August, it finalised a draft Instrument of Surrender (SWNCC-21/3). On 12 August, the SFE issued a modified version of its 'Summary' (SWNCC-150/2) in a first attempt to clarify the principle of indirect rule, but Truman asked for further changes. On 14 August (EST), the Suzuki Cabinet notified Washington of its final acceptance of the Potsdam conditions, and US planning reached fever pitch. Assistant Secretary of War General John J. McCloy, SWNCC's War Department representative, believed that legally the post-surrender policy document would have to be harmonised with the letter and spirit of the Potsdam Proclamation. On 22 August, bypassing the Subcommittee for the Far East completely, McCloy on his own authority inserted the phrase, 'the Supreme Commander will exercise his authority through Japanese governmental machinery and agencies, including the Emperor', into a revised draft, which was adopted as SWNCC-150/3. The new version represented a compromise between pro-China and pro-Japan factions. It retained the reformist vitality of the former but acceded to the indirect occupation advocated by the latter. Moreover, the document explicitly instructed the Supreme Commander not to remove the Emperor without consulting Washington.[55]

Thereafter, only minor alterations would be made to the plan. General MacArthur received it in substance by radio on 29 August (30 August, Tokyo time). On 31 August, SWNCC-150/4 was formalised, incorporating a few last-minute suggestions from the Joint Chiefs and other agencies, and on 6 September, President Truman endorsed the text and forwarded a copy to General MacArthur. On 22 September, the White House publicly issued SWNCC-150/4/A as the directive 'US Initial Post-Surrender Policy for Japan'. The next day (24 September, Tokyo time), the full text appeared in Japanese newspapers.

With the war over, the Japan Crowd, having laboured mightily to save the monarchy, plummeted from grace. Grew resigned on 15 August, and the next day his arch-adversary Dean Acheson replaced him as Acting Under-Secretary of State (the appointment would be confirmed in late September). Dooman, Grew's proxy on the Subcommittee for the Far East, was replaced by China specialist John Carter Vincent, who also took over the Far Eastern Affairs Division from Japan-hand Joseph Ballantine. George Atcheson Jr, another China expert, was appointed special envoy to GHQ/SCAP in Tokyo, where he set up the Office of the Political Adviser (POLAD). Atcheson was named to the post because, in his own words, he was 'familiar with State Department policy but unfamiliar with Japan'.[56] Henceforth, with the US policy-making apparatus controlled by advocates of a harsh peace, the fate of the Emperor and the actual implementation of the Occupation reforms would depend on General Douglas MacArthur. In one sense, however, the Japan hands already had scored their biggest victory, for they had committed the Occupation to working through the bureaucracy whose entrenched conservatism would preserve a high degree of continuity with the wartime régime and work to blunt the radical thrust of many Allied reforms. In late 1947, the Japan Crowd would re-emerge from obscurity to consolidate that victory (chapter 10).

The SWNCC Directive

By the time the machinery of Occupation was in place, three control documents existed for the post-defeat administration of Japan. The 'US Initial Post-Surrender Policy for Japan' (SWNCC-150/4/A) released on 22 September 1945 described the structure and objectives of the Occupation. The earlier Potsdam Proclamation was a restatement of these principles in condensed form. The Army's 'Basic Directive for Post-Surrender Military Government in Japan Proper' (JCS-1380/15) of 3 November, on the other hand, was a 'how-to' guide for translating those principles into action. It was a military directive based on the two earlier policy statements, and it became the Occupation Bible.

The SWNCC text's key provisions defined Allied authority and its relation to the Japanese government and outlined sweeping political and economic reforms. Japan would be governed indirectly, but there was a crucial proviso: while the Supreme Commander would 'exercise his authority through Japanese governmental machinery and agencies, including the Emperor', he was not committed to back the Emperor or any other government authority. 'The policy is to use the existing form of Government in Japan, not to support it.'

Individual liberties and democratic processes were to be strengthened by guaranteeing freedom of speech, religion and political association, and all people unjustly imprisoned on political grounds were to be freed. A wide spectrum of economic measures would destroy 'the existing economic basis of Japanese military strength' and prevent its revival. These included the dissolution of 'large industrial and banking combinations'; the promotion of labour, industrial and agricultural organisations and other democratic forces; and the resumption of international trade. 'Changes in the form of Government initiated by the Japanese people or government' to modify Japan's 'feudal and authoritarian tendencies' were to be permitted and even encouraged. The Supreme Commander was authorised to 'intervene only where necessary to ensure the security of his forces and the attainment of all other objectives of the Occupation', even if such changes involved 'the use of force by the Japanese people or government against persons opposed thereto.'

Conservative Japanese complained of the harshness of such measures, but they were fairly magnanimous compared with Allied terms for Germany. Washington faced the imposing task in Japan of translating these general prescriptions into workable policies. SWNCC was caught unprepared by Japan's early capitulation and, apart from the Initial Post-Surrender Policy, had not developed specific guidelines for administering the country. To remedy this situation, between October 1945 and March 1946, the Subcommittee for the Far East hastily completed a series of remarkably comprehensive and detailed policy recommendations. Many of these, including the paper on military government (SWNCC-52), were based on the Army's 'Basic Directive' for post-surrender Japan.[57]

The military directive and the reform process

JCS-1380/15, the 'Basic Directive for Post-Surrender Military Government in Japan Proper', issued in its final form on 3 November 1945, was a very different document. A larger, more detailed and much tougher version of SWNCC's Initial Post-Surrender Policy, the 'Basic Directive' gave the Supreme Commander even greater power to reorient Japan politically, economically and ideologically. The Directive was top secret and remained so until the latter part of the Occupation. It was not sent to President Truman or the Far Eastern Commission but went directly to MacArthur, who received an early version (JCS-1380/5) in mid-September. The manual went through a total of 15 revisions before it was finalised. Later modifications were worked out in conjunction with SWNCC's Subcommittee for the Far East, now run by the China Crowd, which substantially expanded and refined the Directive's provisions. The text of 3 November covered almost every aspect of Japanese society. In its details, the document was the radical reform that the China hands, military hardliners and New Deal idealists had worked so assiduously to achieve. As Occupationaire Theodore Cohen later wrote, the 'Basic Directive' constituted the real 'ideology' of occupation. It was, he noted, 'in great part a New Deal document. . . . MacArthur, who disliked the New Deal in the abstract admired it in the reality of JCS-1380/15'.[58]

The 'Basic Directive' also was a direct military order defining the framework within which MacArthur was to operate. In fact, the Supreme Commander was given wide latitude to interpret it in light of actual conditions, enhancing his broad discretionary powers, but the 'Basic Directive' remained his guidebook. JCS-1380/15 was, as Cohen wrote, 'a powerful reform stream running through clearly defined channels. Its commander did not seek to break the channel walls but rode the stream along its pre-determined course.' Indeed, perhaps only a personality as strong as MacArthur could have navigated so skilfully the powerful, contending currents that churned and propelled this surge tide of reform.

The 'Basic Directive' was the master plan from which GHQ's special staff sections worked in implementing policy for Japan. They did this by breaking up the text and following the instructions contained in each paragraph. The executive officer of each staff group would compile an assignment schedule, define responsibilities and parcel out specific paragraphs for implementation in a kind of scissors-and-paste operation. Cohen recalled afterwards: Economic and Scientific Section 'split up these paragraphs . . . and then in some of the bigger divisions, even the sentences were broken down: this sentence to this branch, and that sentence to that branch.' On the basis of these paragraphs, clauses and phrases, ESS and other staff sections drew up Command Letters to Eighth Army and SCAPINs to the government.[59]

Although the general contours of policy were set in Washington, the details often were elaborated at the junior staff level, and many SCAPINs signed by the Supreme Commander actually were drafted by branch or division heads. Nor were they necessarily verbatim copies of the 'Basic Directive'. Where precise instructions were lacking or ambiguities arose, a section chief normally commissioned an internal staff study. Compiled in consultation with specialists in other GHQ sections and their Japanese advisers, staff studies often evolved into lengthy treatises with concrete recommendations for action. Staff sections communicated their policy proposals to other sections via memoranda and 'check sheets' – inter-sectional circulars seeking the concurrence of concerned groups in GHQ. Where disagreements arose, inter-staff conferences, occasionally attended by Eighth Army representatives, were convened to hammer out a coherent policy approach. The conclusions, endorsed by the section chief, then were forwarded to the Deputy Chief of Staff and the Supreme Commander for approval.

After the early reform phase of occupation, unilateralism became the exception, and policy formulation, from written instruction to implementation, involved some degree of Japanese participation. A section typically initiated a reform process via close consultation with in-house Japanese advisers and its counterpart agency in the government. Japanese officials, for their part, relied heavily on broadly constituted ad hoc consultative bodies composed of bureaucrats and non-government experts, thereby assuring a constant influx of ideas from academics, political action groups, professional associations and informed citizens (many of whom were meeting simultaneously with GHQ officers or their Japanese assistants). Thus, even where Allied policy was imposed, it was the bold outlines that prevailed; Japanese input, usually from a variety of sources, invariably modified the details. In several cases, the government, private advisory groups and even individuals prevailed on Occupation staff to approve measures that exceeded their section's original mandate. One historian has asserted that 'GHQ in Tokyo was little more than an enforcement agency for policies set in Washington',[60] but in fact, between 1946 and 1948, MacArthur's super-government, forced to make many of its own decisions, sought Japanese advice and, until Occupation policy towards Japan shifted rightward in 1948, strove to incorporate liberal Japanese views into its reform projections. The nuts-and-bolts dynamics of this complex process, the subject of chapters 6 through 9, too often escape the notice of historians concerned exclusively with the 'big picture'.

THE LEGITIMACY OF OCCUPATION CONTROL

Surrender: unconditional or negotiated?

On 2 September, the Instrument of Surrender placed Japan under Allied military jurisdiction and stated unequivocally that 'The authority of the Emperor and the Japanese Government to rule the state shall be subject to the Supreme Commander for the Allied Powers who will take such steps as he deems proper to effectuate these terms.'[61] The Japanese government hewed to a different interpretation, however. In concluding his pre-recorded radio address of 15 August, Hirohito had proclaimed that, 'Since it has been possible to preserve the structure of the Imperial State, We shall always be with ye, our good and loyal subjects.'[62] The same day, Prime Minister

Suzuki noted in his resignation speech to the nation that Japan's acceptance of the Potsdam terms had been contingent upon retaining the principle of Imperial sovereignty. On 24 August, Hirohito, repeating the subtext of his 15 August pronouncement, exhorted the people to 'make manifest the innate glory of Japan's [Imperial] national polity'. Even 'liberal' political commentator and future prime minister Ishibashi Tanzan assumed continuity of the Throne when, on 1 September, he urged a return to the 'democratic' principles of the Emperor Meiji's Charter Oath of 1868 and the Imperial Constitution of 1890.[63] In the minds of the nation's leaders, then, capitulation presupposed Allied assent to Baron Hiranuma's singular condition: retention of the Imperial Order and the substantive political power that it embodied. The Byrnes Note, its ambiguity compounded by the Foreign Ministry's deliberate mistranslation, was cited as proof of that contention.

The Byrnes Note indeed had purposely encouraged such an interpretation – but without making a clear commitment – in order to hasten Japanese acceptance of the Potsdam demands. And the Proclamation itself, although intended as an ultimatum, displayed a certain flexibility of construction. As indicated above, on British advice, US policy-makers had revised the text to allow a broader reading of its provisions, and this modification produced some initial confusion even in Washington.[64] On 29 August, Eugene Dooman of the Subcommittee for the Far East told SWNCC that the State Department considered the surrender a contractual agreement, not an unconditional renunciation of national sovereignty. By early September, however, Dooman and the Japan Crowd were on their way out the door. The China Crowd parsed the Potsdam document as an ultimatum: Tokyo's surrender was absolute and without conditions. All of Japan's institutions, including the Throne, were well within the purview of reform. President Truman and Secretary of State Byrnes had adopted this as the official US position all along, and the victorious powers subsequently ratified it as official Allied policy (below).[65]

In his memoir, Assistant Secretary of State Dean Acheson confessed that the Potsdam language disturbed him deeply. 'Regarded not as an ultimatum but as an invitation to negotiate, it would [I feared] lead us into a trap both at home and in Japan', he wrote in terms reminiscent of the Joint Chiefs' Potsdam memorandum to Truman of 18 July (p. 217). The Proclamation was merely a statement of Allied intentions. It was the deep secret of the atomic bomb, he realised later, that explained its seemingly contradictory character. For the bomb, not the Proclamation, was the real ultimatum, but only Truman and a handful of American and British high officials knew that at the time.[66] The document did not acquire the force of an ineluctable demand until the obliteration of Hiroshima on 6 August, almost two weeks after its publication. In that sense, the atomic bombings destroyed ex post facto any grounds that might have existed for a contractual gloss.

On 6 September, President Truman and the Joint Chiefs cabled MacArthur a message clarifying his powers. The communication was in response to queries from the Supreme Commander and State Department officials who were alarmed by Japan's refusal on 17 August to obey a directive to close its diplomatic missions in neutral states (the Japanese said the request did not conform to any of the Potsdam provisions). The text is worth citing at length:

> The authority of the Emperor and the Japanese Government to rule the State is subordinate to you. . . . Our relations with Japan do not rest on a contractual basis, but on an unconditional surrender. . . . Since your authority is supreme, you will not entertain any question on the part of the Japanese as to its scope. . . . The statement of intentions contained in the Potsdam Declaration will be given full effect. It will not be given effect, however, because we consider ourselves bound in a contractual relationship with Japan as a result of that document.[67]

'Control of Japan', the President and military high command told MacArthur, 'shall be exercised through the Japanese Government to the extent that such an arrangement produces satisfactory results. This does not prejudice your right to act directly if required. You may enforce the orders issued by you by the employment of such measures as you deem necessary, including the use of force.' This broad grant of authority was fully consistent with the stated intent of the Potsdam document and the 'US Initial Post-Surrender Policy'.

At the same time, Tokyo's acceptance of the Potsdam terms compelled the occupying forces to honour certain self-imposed obligations with respect to the defeated enemy. For instance, Japanese compliance was predicated on an Allied pledge, derived from the Atlantic Charter, to assure limited sovereignty on the home islands, not to enslave the Japanese people or destroy the nation and to end the régime of control and restore full independence once occupation objectives, as defined at Potsdam, had been attained (Articles 8, 10 and 12). To this extent, a principle of mutual trust and good faith was implied. It was understood by both sides, however, that a Japanese refusal to carry out Allied policies could be met by military force.[68]

The Byrnes Note, mistranslation aside, reiterated that clear limits would be imposed on the authority of Japan's existing institutions to govern. By accepting the Potsdam conditions, Japan's collective leadership formally acknowledged the paramount authority of the Allied Supreme Commander. The Proclamation also required Japan to adopt a peacefully inclined and responsible form of government 'in accordance with the freely expressed will of the Japanese people'. The Allied Powers, not the government, however, would be the final judge of whether that had been accomplished.[69] In other words the Occupation sought to ally itself with liberal and progressive forces among the people against the old régime. The 'US Initial Post-Surrender Policy' gave GHQ dominion over the nation's governing institutions but also, in principle at least, empowered the people to revolutionise those same institutions from within. 'Changes in the form of Government initiated by the Japanese people or government in the direction of modifying its feudal and authoritarian tendencies', it read, 'are to be permitted and favored. In the event that the effectuation of such changes involves the use of force by the Japanese people or government

against persons opposed thereto, the Supreme Commander should intervene only
where necessary to ensure the security of his forces and the attainment of all other
objectives of the occupation.'

  In short, MacArthur's headquarters possessed, in the words of one commentator,
'the unilateral power to approach the people of Japan without consultation, advice
from, or support of the Japanese Government'.[70] MacArthur personally saw in the
tenor of this provision an invitation to bloodshed and for that reason considered it
extreme. Nevertheless, this mandate would produce a bold new experiment in popular sovereignty, a massive shifting of power from the state to the people, which
Government Section's Charles Kades later characterised as 'the Revolution of 1945'.
Ironically, the Supreme Commander subsequently would side with the state against
the people, preventing that democratic process from running its full course.[71]

The Occupation and international law
Japan's capitulation produced an anomalous situation, for the régime of control the
Allies introduced after 15 August 1945 had no precedent in international law.
Japan's surrender, unlike that of Germany, took place before the imposition of
occupation rule and did not entail the destruction of centralised authority. As a
result, Allied forces were able to utilise the machinery of state and avert recourse to
armed intervention.

  International law, however, defines occupation as wartime control under belligerent conditions. Unlike subjugation or conquest, military occupation does not transfer sovereignty to the occupying power, only the authority to exercise some of the
rights of sovereignty, and then for a limited time. Article 43, Section III of the 1907
Hague Convention With Respect to the Laws and Usages of War on Land stipulates
that the occupant must respect the laws in force in the controlled territories and
forbids interference with existing political institutions. The 1918 occupation of
the German Rhineland by the United States and France deviated somewhat from the
norm in that it began after a negotiated armistice had ended hostilities. Legally, the
victors could hold German territory only until such time as Berlin had paid war
reparations and fulfilled other armistice obligations. Although this instance fell
somewhere in between a belligerent and a peaceful occupation, there was no transfer
of sovereignty, and the occupying powers were constrained to work through the local
administration.[72]

  In this sense, the occupation of Japan was unique. Unconditional surrender was a
forced cessation of hostilities, not a negotiated truce. Until 28 April 1952, when the
San Francisco Peace Treaty restored Japanese independence, the country legally was
in a state of war with the occupying powers. The Allied régime of 'occupation
control' constituted a novel form of post-defeat political and military authority.
Under this modus operandi, the Emperor and the Japanese government were subordinated to the Allied Supreme Commander but only to the extent necessary to
enforce the Potsdam conditions and secure a peace settlement. In October and
November 1945, GHQ issued directives placing Japan's external affairs under Allied

jurisdiction, but the nation's sovereignty was compromised only until such time as MacArthur's headquarters had achieved these goals. Occupation control, then, introduced a new concept into international law.

Japan recovered its autonomy in stages. For example, Occupation officials outlawed the *Hinomaru*, the Rising Sun Flag, in late August 1945, but on 28 December, GHQ issued a directive allowing the emblem to be flown for three special New Years' celebrations. In March 1948, that permission was extended to all national holidays, and in early 1949, the ban was lifted entirely. From 1948, GHQ allowed Japanese to travel abroad for specified purposes on passports authorised by the Supreme Commander, and in January 1950, it permitted the government itself to process applications for foreign travel, although SCAP's consent was still required. By that time, American authorities had begun turning over to the government many of the administrative duties they had assumed. In February 1950, Washington invited Tokyo to establish 'overseas agencies' in the United States and empowered these to report to the Japanese Foreign Ministry but with no exercise of consular or diplomatic functions. At the same time, Washington and GHQ inaugurated the Exchange of National Leaders Programme, financed with Government and Relief in Occupied Areas (GARIOA) funds, to promote visits by Japanese leaders to the United States (chapter 3), and Japan was encouraged to participate in international technical agreements and conferences, subject to Occupation approval. Washington also authorised the use of international communications services by private citizens for the first time and condoned direct dealings between the central government and foreign diplomatic missions in Japan. From August 1951, Tokyo was able to negotiate with other countries on its own behalf. Participation in the San Francisco Peace Conference in September of that year was a decisive step in Japan's recovery of world citizenship. Full independence was restored on 28 April 1952.[73]

Revisionist interpretations
The Foreign Ministry's deceptive translation of the Byrnes Note enabled the government to maintain the fiction that Japan had surrendered with Imperial sovereignty intact. It also allowed conservative scholars to assert that the surrender was negotiated and therefore conditional and contractual. From this premise derives the argument that the Potsdam Proclamation had no legal authority to curtail Japanese sovereignty, that SCAP's power was circumscribed by international conventions on war and that constitutional reform, in particular, violated the law of belligerent occupation and was null and void.[74] The 'Initial Post-Surrender Policy' and the 'Basic Directive' were dismissed as internal US government documents lacking international legitimacy. In recent years, these claims have provided an excuse for increasingly vehement attacks on the Constitution's peace provisions by revisionist historians, right-wing politicians and born-again nationalists of various leanings. Such arguments display an ignorance of what actually transpired in the weeks leading up to Japan's capitulation. They also misrepresent the historical context that

produced the Potsdam Proclamation and other policy instruments defining the character of the Occupation.

By accepting the Potsdam document and signing the Instrument of Surrender, Japanese leaders knowingly placed the country's ruling institutions under Allied authority. Moreover, as co-signatories to these documents, other Allied powers formally ratified the occupation-control régime. On 25 April 1945, before the Occupation commenced, the representatives of 50 countries gathered in San Francisco to establish the United Nations, producing a Charter that validated policies and actions taken by Allied governments against the Axis powers during and after World War II (Article 107). Adopted on 26 June 1945, the UN Charter entered into force on 24 October of that year. In June 1947, the Far Eastern Commission, the Allied control body for Japan, issued its own 'Basic Post-Surrender Policy for Japan'. Initialled by 11 participating nations, nine of which also had signed the Instrument of Surrender, this document was a replica of the 'US Initial Post-Surrender Policy'. Finally, the San Francisco Peace Treaty, concluded on 8 September 1951 by 49 nations, including Japan itself, and implemented in April 1952, added a final cachet of legitimacy to the Allied control mechanism. Japanese critics of the Occupation, through flawed logic and a distorted historical vision, ignore these salient facts.

CHAPTER 6

The Political Reforms

The first eight months of occupation laid the foundations for parliamentary democracy and left the boldest imprint on Japanese society. During this period, the reformist zeal of Occupation officials burned brightest, and popular enthusiasm for change was at its zenith. A flurry of SCAP directives dismantled the military establishment, tried wartime leaders and purged the political, business and intellectual élite. During these early months, civil liberties were instituted, the electoral system was reformed, the first Lower House elections were held and a new constitution was drawn up and presented to the people. All of these advances were accomplished by Occupation decree, but newly elected lawmakers would adapt parts of the Constitution to Japanese conditions and promulgate it as their own creation. As the Old Order was repressed, Imperial subjects shed their traditional reticence in the face of public authority and learned to become citizens, and through their empowerment a new democratic ethos emerged. Central to this process was the position of the monarchy, which was retained but stripped of its autocratic powers. In preserving the emperor system, however, MacArthur's headquarters also perpetuated a powerful and transcendent symbol around which a conservative hegemony would later coalesce.

CIVIL LIBERTIES

Humanising the Emperor
In MacArthur's mind, the survival of the Imperial institution was one of the conditions upon which the success of the Occupation hinged, and the General approached this issue with calculated tact. Uncertainty over the Emperor's fate also loomed large in the minds of Japan's ruling élite, whose cooperation was vital to the Americans in the early reform period. As if to reassure governing conservatives, on 21 September 1945, MacArthur told the US media that, by retaining the Japanese sovereign, the United States had saved lives, money and time. The Supreme Commander's press statement targeted another audience as well: the China Crowd and other advocates of a hard peace in Washington.

On 27 September, at the end of the first month, Hirohito paid MacArthur an official visit at the General's quarters in the US Embassy. The content of the 40-minute tête-à-tête was secret, but on 29 September, at GHQ's behest, Japan's major dailies ran a photograph of this historic moment taken by a US military photographer. The picture was accompanied by an unprecedented *New York Times* interview with the sovereign in which Hirohito criticised General Tōjō Hideki for failing to issue a formal declaration of war on the United States before attacking Pearl Harbor (in fact, as indicated below, the Emperor had personally assented to that decision). Front-page coverage, with the photo prominently displayed, caused a national sensation, for the monarch was sacrosanct, a 'manifest deity' (*akitsu-mikami*), and loyal subjects were taught to avert their eyes even from the veiled Imperial portraits kept in schools and public offices. For the authorities, the graphic image was sacrilege. The diminutive Hirohito, a youngish 44, stood stiffly in formal 'claw-hammer' morning coat, cravat and striped pants next to a relaxed, avuncular MacArthur, 65, dressed casually in khaki with no insignia of rank, hands in hip pockets, collar open. Appalled, Home Minister Yamazaki Iwao and his Police Bureau censors ordered the papers confiscated and attempted to suppress the demeaning photo by invoking Japan's *lèse-majesté* law, Crimes Against the Imperial Household. MacArthur's headquarters acted quickly and decisively, ordering the government to rescind the ban and cease all efforts to censor, suppress or control the media. The unique 'photo opportunity' was MacArthur's idea, and the skilfully stage-managed event succeeded brilliantly. The Emperor's act of homage to the Supreme Commander demonstrated to all that the General wielded supreme authority and yet was not indifferent to the feelings of the defeated. Moreover, GHQ's prompt intervention in defence of freedom of the press provided a dramatic public demonstration of the Occupation's commitment to democratic reform.

Later, MacArthur told his aides that Hirohito had offered to take full responsibility for the war, a myth that he cultivated assiduously and later repeated in his autobiography, but the Japanese record of the encounter indicates no such admission. Having just pointed the finger of guilt at Tōjō, Hirohito is unlikely to have suddenly pointed it at himself. Nonetheless, the Emperor's contrite posture reportedly moved MacArthur to the 'very marrow' of his bones. Rather than engage in mutual recriminations, each man appeared intent on flattering the other and making the best of an awkward situation. Shortly afterwards, the General confided to aide Faubion Bowers, who had received the Emperor at the Embassy, 'I could have humiliated him, publicly exposed him, but what for? I fought the war; he ended it. He deserves respect, the magnanimous gesture a noble defeated enemy deserves. Besides, with him as figurehead, our job is so much more easy.' This impromptu aside no doubt summed up MacArthur's real feelings on the subject.[1]

Working with the government and Court, GHQ oversaw further efforts to 'humanise' the Emperor without impugning the moral authority of the Throne. On New Year's Day 1946, Hirohito formally renounced his divinity in a deftly crafted Imperial Rescript. 'The ties between Us and Our people', the Royal statement said, 'are not predicated on the false conception that the Emperor is divine and that the Japanese people are superior to other races and fated to rule the world.' He also pledged 'to construct a new Japan through thoroughly being pacific'.

The idea for a 'declaration of humanity' had been considered by both Japanese and Americans separately, the Japanese side being particularly anxious to pre-empt an anticipated SCAP directive on the subject. The actual text appears to have had its roots in a discussion held in late November between Major Harold G. Henderson, a Japan specialist then Chief of Education and Religions Branch in the Civil Information and Education Section (CI&E), and Dr Reginald H. Blyth, an eminent British scholar of Zen Buddhism and Japanese literature. Interned in Japan during the war, Blyth had just been made instructor at the élite Peers School, the training ground of the Japanese aristocracy, and English tutor to Crown Prince Akihito. Acting as liaison with the Court, Blyth worked through Admiral Yamanashi Katsunoshin, President of the Peers School, to sound out Hirohito's advisers, who seized on the idea as 'a heaven-sent door'. They then agreed on a draft rescript drawn up by Blyth, possibly with Admiral Yamanashi's help, and showed it to CI&E Chief Kermit R. Dyke. Dyke presented the proposal to MacArthur, who endorsed it enthusiastically. The drafting process was complex and involved many hands, including those of Prime Minister Shidehara, who had replaced Higashikuni in October; Yoshida Shigeru, his Foreign Minister; Education Minister Maeda Tamon; and Hirohito himself. Dyke and MacArthur personally approved the final version.[2]

Couched in simple language, the Emperor's so-called renunciation of divinity appeared to be a firm and unprecedented statement of democratic principle, but the real message lay cleverly buried in the text. Hirohito's traditional New Year's greeting highlighted two concerns foremost in the monarch's mind. The heart of the Rescript was the first six paragraphs, in which he pledged to return to the Emperor Meiji's Charter Oath of 1868. The Oath had 'bestowed' democracy upon the people and enjoined the nation to seek wisdom and knowledge throughout the world in order to strengthen the foundations of Imperial rule (in English, this was rendered misleadingly as 'the welfare of the Empire'). Nowhere did Hirohito explicitly deny the ancestral myth of Imperial descent from the Sun Goddess (Amaterasu Ōmikami). Later it would be explained by Court officials that the Emperor's 'renunciation' meant simply that he was not a god in the Western sense. In a Japanese context, he remained a deity incarnate. In addition to this adroit reaffirmation of Imperial sovereignty, so obvious to Imperial conservatives, Hirohito managed a well-placed rhetorical jab at his political foes, exhorting the people to beware of gradually spreading 'radical tendencies in excess' and the accompanying 'confusion of thoughts'. None of this appeared in the Blyth version; it had been added by the Japanese side in the drafting process and somehow escaped SCAP's notice, the first of many such dazzling displays of textual slight of hand.[3]

MacArthur, deeply moved by Hirohito's self-effacing act of submission on 27 September, declared himself highly pleased with the monarch's New Year's statement. By it, the Supreme Commander asserted, '[h]e squarely takes his stand for the future along liberal lines'. Ironically, to Imperial conservatives MacArthur's paean appeared to confer SCAP's personal cachet on the Emperor's pledge to make the Meiji Charter Oath the basis of the postwar state, a truly astounding idea in view of stated Allied objectives. A devout Episcopalian, the General's positive assessment of Hirohito may have reflected an unconscious respect for the religious aura surrounding the Emperor's person. In any event, MacArthur's September press comments, his meeting with the sovereign and the latter's New Year's address may be seen as the opening moves in a campaign to shield the Emperor from war crimes prosecution and harness the Imperial charisma to Occupation goals.[4]

Japan's 'Bill of Rights' and the Five Great Reforms
Allied policy called for the removal of all restrictions on free speech and thought, and following the deployment of US troops, SCAP issued a press and radio code (19 and 22 September) and took other steps to liberate the mass media from state control. The Imperial Cabinet of Prince Higashikuni Naruhiko, however, reminded the public that while freedom of speech would be recognized, it should conform to the spirit of the 1925 Peace Preservation Law, under which criticism of the monarchy was sanctionable in extreme cases by death. The *lèse-majesté* statute remained on the books, and as late as 3 October 1945, Home Minister Yamazaki's police censors were threatening to imprison anyone who spoke out against the Emperor.

Following the establishment of GHQ/SCAP on 2 October 1945, MacArthur took more resolute steps to protect basic civil and political freedoms. On 4 October, the Civil Information and Education Section issued the Civil Liberties Directive (SCAPIN-93: 'Removal of Restrictions on Political, Civil and Religious Liberties') to encourage the 'revival and strengthening of democratic tendencies' as mandated by the Potsdam Proclamation. Heralded by SCAP as the 'Magna Carta for Japan' and known widely as the Japanese Bill of Rights, this order abolished the Peace Preservation Law and all other ordinances and regulations restricting 'freedom of thought, religion, assembly and speech' or operating 'unequally in favor of or against any person by reason of race, nationality, creed, or political opinion'. The directive also ordered the release of all political prisoners by 10 October; the abolition of secret police organs, including the Home Ministry's notorious Special Higher Police (*Tokkō Keisatsu*); the dismissal of the Minister of Home Affairs and the chief of the Ministry's Bureau of Police, the heads of the Tokyo and Osaka Metropolitan Police Boards, and prefectural police chiefs; and the removal of all barriers to 'the unrestricted discussion of the Emperor, the Imperial Institution and the Imperial Japanese Government'. As a result of this decree, nearly 5,000 officials in the Home Ministry and law-enforcement agencies were dismissed, and the Japan Communist Party (JCP), driven underground and persecuted under the Peace Preservation Law, suddenly resurfaced as a legitimate political organisation. Moreover, GHQ took special pains to emphasise that the directive's free-speech guarantees extended to discussion of the emperor system as well. CI&E's Captain Arthur Behrstock promptly summoned representatives of Japan's major dailies, including the *Asahi*, *Mainichi* and *Yomiuri*, and made this point clear.[5]

On 5 October, the day after the directive's promulgation, the Higashikuni Cabinet resigned en masse. The Peace Preservation Law was the state's primary weapon against the Emperor's enemies. With the statute gone, its guardians dismissed and Communists organising freely, Higashikuni's government could not fulfil its sacred office to vouchsafe the Imperial status quo. On 9 October, the relatively moderate Baron Shidehara Kijūrō acceded to the premiership. The Shidehara Cabinet included several ministers who had been jailed or placed under house arrest for their 'liberalist' views during the war, including Ashida Hitoshi (Welfare), Maeda Tamon (Education) and Yoshida Shigeru (Foreign Affairs). All three were outspoken Imperial conservatives, but they had opposed the war, and their presence was widely seen as heralding the start of a new order.

GHQ had turned its attention to civil liberties following US press reports in early October that political prisoners were still detained under appalling conditions. The well-known philosopher Miki Kiyoshi, incarcerated for harbouring a Communist friend, had died in the Tokyo Detention House on 26 September, and the health of others was precarious. Many of those imprisoned were Communists, anarchists and Korean nationalists. Koreans, liberated by Japan's defeat, took the lead in pressing for their release. Since September, the Korean community had leafleted and organised rallies demanding freedom for all political detainees.

Between 1 and 3 October, French correspondent Robert Guillain and two American journalists, learning that Communists were still in jail, visited Fuchū Prison outside of Tokyo and interviewed several leaders there.[6] Alerted by these reports, John K. Emmerson of the Political Adviser's Office (POLAD) brought the plight of these men to MacArthur's attention. On 5 October, the day after the Civil Liberties Directive, Emmerson and E. Herbert Norman, the Canadian scholar and diplomat

Photo 31. Koreans celebrate the release of political prisoners in front of GHQ, 15 October 1945. They are waving the Korean national banner and the Stars and Stripes. Koreans and Communists both welcomed the Occupation army as liberators (US National Archives).

then attached to Civil Intelligence Section, drove to Fuchū Prison and met prominent Communists incarcerated there, including Tokuda Kyūichi, Shiga Yoshio and
Korean activist Kim Ch'ŏn-hae. On 7 October, the two men escorted Tokuda, Shiga
and Kim to SCAP headquarters for a day-long debriefing on the Party's postwar
plans – and then returned them to jail. The three leaders were among the 439
Communists, Korean nationalists, liberal intellectuals and religious pacifists freed on
10 October. Police were forced to suspend immediately the surveillance of another
2,060 'subversives'. On 19 December, GHQ formally reinstated the civil rights of
these individuals with a directive, 'Restoration of Electoral Rights to Released Political Prisoners'.[7] To test the water, on the day of their release, Tokuda, Shiga and other
freed comrades, writing in the first postwar edition of *Akahata* (The Red Flag), hailed
the 'democratic revolution' brought about by the Occupation forces, pledged to
overthrow the emperor system and called for a united front under Communist
leadership. Democracy indeed had arrived.

In line with the broad US commitment to support progressive forces, Emmerson
recommended to the State Department a positive policy of encouraging all political
tendencies that might be united in creating a democratic Japan, including the Communist Party. This approach, he said, served America's long-term interests in Asia
better than a negative policy of repressing the left. The so-called Emmerson Plan
commanded wide respect in SCAP in the early days of occupation. Initially, GHQ
was willing to regard the JCP as a potential ally in combating militarists and the Old
Guard, and the Party returned the compliment by characterising the US garrison
force as a 'liberation army'. Emmerson ran into strong opposition, however, from
POLAD Chief George Atcheson and intelligence officers in G-2, who saw Communism as the antithesis of democracy and an impediment to the Occupation's
objectives. With his ideas in poor repute, Emmerson returned to Washington in
February 1946.[8]

On 11 October 1945, Prime Minister Shidehara Kijūrō, who had formed his
government two days earlier, paid his first visit to MacArthur. The General told
Shidehara to liberalise the Meiji Constitution and then handed the surprised premier
a paper listing five fundamental reforms to be implemented immediately. The Five
Great Reforms, as they became known, were 1 the enfranchisement of women, to
make 'government directly subservient to the well-being of the home' (pre-surrender
planning had made no such provision), 2 the encouragement of labour unions and
the abolition of child labour practices, 3 the reform of education, 4 the elimination
of 'secret inquisition and abuse' that had oppressed the people, and 5 promotion
of a 'wide distribution of income and ownership of the means of production and
trade'. With the exception of the first point, these measures, included in substance
in Washington's 'Initial Post-Surrender Policy for Japan', belonged to the urgent
changes that MacArthur had outlined passionately to Courtney Whitney on 30
August en route to Atsugi.

A liberal Japanese agenda

MacArthur's choice of priorities also reflected the long-standing demands of liberal Japanese. Indeed, the Supreme Commander had assigned these particular policies pride of place at the recommendation of a select group of Japanese advisers hand-picked from a list of potentially pro-American opinion leaders compiled in Washington between 1944 and 1945. In late September 1945, for example, CI&E's Captain Arthur Behrstock and Lieutenant Taro Tsukahara approached the husband-and-wife team of Katō Kanjū, a left-wing Socialist imprisoned for his views, and Katō Shizue, a radical feminist also jailed for her liberal opinions, for advice on trade unions and the status of women. When asked to become an adviser to GHQ, Katō Kanjū agreed and recommended three other Socialists as well. Lieutenant Tsukahara personally accompanied the Katōs to General Headquarters, where they met Occupation officials, including Lieutenant Ethel Weed, the CI&E Women's Information Officer. Both Katōs would be elected to the Lower House on a Socialist ticket in the first general elections of 1946. GHQ also solicited the views of right-wing Socialists who had refused to cooperate with the militarists, among them Matsuoka Komakichi, Nishio Suehiro and Christian social reformer Suzuki Bunji. Two liberal labour specialists, Suehiro Izutarō and Ayusawa Iwao, were tapped by Economic and Scientific section, and CI&E Chief Dyke recruited prominent educator Kaigo Tokiomi and Kishimoto Hideo, a Harvard-trained scholar of religion, to assist his section with education and religion reforms. In similar fashion, a number of other outstanding intellectuals lent their knowledge and prestige to the multifaceted task of building democracy. Without their wise counsel and enthusiastic backing, many GHQ initiatives would have fallen wide of the mark.[9]

Pressure for fundamental change also came from the people. Even before the Occupation began, women, for instance, had organised to press for basic freedoms. On 25 August 1945, three influential feminists established the Women's Postwar Counter-Measures Committee (*Sengo Taisaku Fujin I'inkai*) to renew the fight for universal suffrage. They were 85-year-old Ichikawa Fusae, founder of the prewar Women's Suffrage League; Akamatsu Tsuneko, a shopfloor union organiser who had headed the Women's Division in the prewar Japan General Federation of Labour; and liberal educator Kawasaki Natsu. On 10 September, the Committee presented a list of five demands, including the right to vote, to GHQ and the Higashikuni government. Although Higashikuni was favourably disposed towards the proposals, opposition from Vice Premier Prince Konoe Fumimaro frustrated the initiative. Nonetheless, on 10 October, the newly formed Shidehara Cabinet agreed in principle to enfranchise women and lower the voting age and indicated its intention to revise the Lower House Electoral Law accordingly. MacArthur's strong endorsement of universal suffrage the next day thus came as no surprise to Ichikawa's group, which shortly afterwards formed the New Japan Women's League (*Shin Nihon Fujin Dōmei*).[10]

The Supreme Commander was personally committed to the 'essential equality' of the sexes, but the presence of a political action group advocating the same liberal project may have convinced him to place that measure at the top of his list of five reforms. In any event, the franchise was an idea whose time had come. MacArthur's intervention ensured that it arrived sooner rather than later, and perhaps more completely. Other SCAP reforms, too, found well-organised public constituencies determined to hasten their implementation. The demands put forward by prewar labour leaders, agrarian reformers, liberal educators, professional organisations and private citizens' groups were welcomed by middle-ranking 'social-reform' bureaucrats, many of them in the Home and Welfare Ministries, who had supported forward-looking social policies in the 1930s in order to preserve public order and enhance basic governance. Consequently, in some instances, the first faltering steps towards institutional reform would be taken well before GHQ had organised its own agenda (chapter 7).

Testing the limits of reform

By May 1946, the first heady wave of reform had swept the country. The civil rights directives of late 1945 had been rigorously enforced, establishing fundamental civil and political liberties, which now were codified in a draft constitution (below). The new national charter divested the monarchy of its former powers and manifest claims to divinity but nonetheless guaranteed it a secure place in the new political order. Anxious to define the parameters of change on its own terms, the government now cracked down on critics of the Emperor by invoking the Meiji-era *lèse-majesté* law, which was still in force. GHQ's response to official censorship, some nine months after the start of the Occupation, now was surprisingly restrained and nuanced.

In the spring of 1946, urban dwellers were fighting mass hunger. Chronic food shortages had produced widespread discontent, and demonstrations for the free delivery of rice and other food stores erupted across the nation. On 19 May, more than 250,000 demonstrators staged the People's Rally for Obtaining Food. Converging on the Imperial Plaza in front of the Palace (now popularly called the People's Plaza), they demanded entrance to the Palace kitchens, which reportedly were stocked with rice and other staple provisions. During the protest, which became known as Food May Day, Matsushima Shōtarō, a factory worker and member of the Communist Party, hoisted a placard reading: 'Imperial Edict: The Emperor system has been preserved. I, the Emperor, have eaten my fill, but you, his subjects, may starve to death! Signed: (Imperial Seal).' The reverse side of the sign demanded that Hirohito give a public accounting of the food shortages.

This expression of popular frustration and rage alarmed both GHQ and the government. The next day, 20 May, MacArthur denounced what he termed 'mass violence' and 'intimidation', and on 24 May, the Emperor addressed the nation in his second and final radio broadcast of the Occupation era, exhorting Japanese to 'stand aloof from individual interests'. Scarce food supplies, he said in language reminiscent of wartime propaganda, should be distributed fairly, 'the distress shared by all'. The authorities did not stop there, however. With SCAP watching from the sidelines, in late June, the government applied the *lèse-majesté* statute and indicted the placard-wielding Matsushima for impairing the dignity of the Emperor. In November, he was sentenced to eight months' imprisonment (ironically, the government pardoned him immediately under an Imperial amnesty commemorating the new Constitution).

GHQ intervened only to the extent of having the charges against Matsushima changed to libel, for by the spring of 1946, MacArthur had decided to retain the Imperial institution and exempt the Emperor from war crimes prosecution (below). In June, roughly a month after the placard incident, Donald R. Nugent, Chief of Civil Information and Education Section, reportedly killed a CI&E proposal to encourage critical public discussion of the Throne. Nugent was said to be acting on secret instructions from Washington in mid-April to avoid direct attacks on the emperor system for fear of strengthening Communist and ultra-nationalist tendencies. In August, as Matsushima's trial wore on, G-2 Chief Charles Willoughby intervened at Yoshida Shigeru's request to suppress a new film critical of the monarch, overriding a CI&E decision to approve it (chapter 8).

SCAP had no intention of condoning blatant suppression of free speech, however. In October 1946 when the Yoshida Cabinet reluctantly dropped *lèse-majesté* charges against the Communist Party organ *Akahata*, MacArthur praised the action as conducive to 'the free criticism of officials and institutions', and he eventually ordered the statute struck from the Criminal Code, which was revised in October 1947 over the strenuous objections of Yoshida and his Liberal Party. Nonetheless, General Headquarter's vacillatory behaviour in allowing the placard demonstrator to be dragged through the courts over a period of months sent a mixed message to the Japanese public, reflecting the Occupation's new stance in support of the Emperor and its growing distrust of the Communist Party.[11]

THE TOKYO WAR CRIMES TRIBUNAL

In June 1945, representatives of Britain, France, the Soviet Union and the United States met in London to discuss the issue of trying German war crimes under existing international law. Britain favoured a quick 'executive' solution, Churchill proposing to shoot the German leaders summarily. The Soviets and the French were not convinced that there was sufficient legal precedent for such a trial. Nonetheless, the Allies bowed to US pressure and in August 1945 signed the Charter for the Nuremberg Trials. Armed with this instrument, the four nations convened the Nuremberg International Military Tribunal in November to try Nazi military and civilian leaders for offences against peace, the laws of war and humanity. Article 11 of the Potsdam Proclamation (26 July) committed the Allied Powers to conduct similar trials in Japan, and as soon as the Occupation commenced, SCAP ordered the Japanese government to locate suspected war criminals. On 11 September, US Military Police rounded up the first 39 suspects.[12]

At the top of SCAP's list was General Tōjō Hideki, one of the chief architects of Japan's military expansion and prime minister for most of the war. Tōjō saw American agents coming for him from a window in his home and shot himself with his service revolver in an effort to cheat justice, but he was nursed back to health by US Army doctors and subsequently indicted. Without him, the Tokyo War Crimes Tribunal would not only have been deprived of its star witness, it would have been unthinkable, for the General was to be made responsible for the war in a scenario scripted by American and Japanese officials to shield the Emperor from prosecution.

On 6 October 1945, Washington directed MacArthur to proceed with the trials of the major suspects, and in early November, the Supreme Commander instructed Elliott Thorpe's Counter-Intelligence Section and POLAD to compile further lists of suspects. Names also had been suggested by the US State Department, the Australian and Chinese governments and various Allied agencies. Japanese officials close to the Throne, too, collaborated with MacArthur's headquarters in naming names, hoping to steer Occupation authorities away from Hirohito. MacArthur made the final decision on whom to detain. By the time US prosecutors arrived in Japan in early December 1945, 103 warrants had been issued. A total of 1,128 suspects accused of a wide range of offences eventually would be incarcerated in Tokyo's Sugamo Prison, where more than half remained for the duration of the trial.

This irony of fortunes was not lost on the Japanese people. Built in the late 1920s, Sugamo was one of the country's most modern prisons, and when the war ended it held 60 political prisoners. The German spy Richard Sorge and his contact, the brilliant journalist Ozaki Hotsumi, had been executed at Sugamo in 1944. Now the tables were turned: Ozaki was a martyr, and Japan's wartime leaders were on trial for their lives; seven would meet Ozaki's fate on the Sugamo gallows.[13]

On 19 January 1946, MacArthur inaugurated the International Military Tribunal for the Far East (IMTFE) and on 15 February approved the appointment of 11 justices by each of the nations on the Far Eastern Commission. Sir William F. Webb, Chief Justice of the Australian Supreme Court, was Tribunal President. The chief prosecutor and US chief counsel was Truman-appointee Joseph B. Keenan, who was assisted by 10 associate prosecutors. Chosen to mount the defence was University of Tokyo professor Takayanagi Kenzō, a jurist of international repute who had studied at Harvard Law School and London's Middle Temple and was considered Japan's leading authority on Anglo-American law. The tall, erudite legal scholar conducted his defence before the Tribunal in English, lending an aura of dignity to the proceedings that otherwise might have been lacking. He was assisted by Uzawa Sōmei, a renowned legal expert and President of Meiji University, and Kiyose Ichirō, an arch-conservative but highly competent defence counsel who had been elected eight times to the prewar Diet.[14]

Following the Nuremberg precedent, the Tokyo Charter, promulgated on 26 April 1946, listed three types of criminal wartime activity: Class A crimes against peace, including the planning, initiating or waging of a declared or undeclared war of aggression; Class B conventional war crimes involving violations of the customary laws of war, including the maltreatment of civilians and prisoners of war; and Class C crimes against humanity, such as extermination, enslavement, deportation, persecution on political or religious grounds, and other acts of inhumanity. British Associate Prosecutor Arthur Comyns-Carr prepared the indictments, which contained a total of 55 counts: 36 for Class A transgressions, 16 for Class B offences and 3 for those falling in Class C. The indictment extended the period of liability backward from the signing of the Instrument of Surrender (2 September 1945) to 1 January 1928, when the 'criminal, militaristic clique' that had conspired to commit those wrongs achieved political supremacy.

In general, the Tokyo Charter stipulated that individuals would be held personally accountable for illegal acts they had committed, including those ordered by military superiors and the state. Class C violations held leaders who had planned such depredations responsible for the actions of subordinates and the rank-and-file military personnel who carried them out. In Germany, four Allied Powers had tried Nazi leaders for the Holocaust and related horrors under Class C crimes against humanity, but in Japan this category became blurred with Class B offences, and most of the so-called B/C war crimes covering conventional brutalities and murder were tried in local military tribunals throughout Asia. In Japan, B/C suspects were arraigned before the Yokohama Military Tribunal.

The Class A war crimes trial in Tokyo was a showcase production that initially riveted the attention of the nation and the world. Of those accused of Class A crimes, 28 were indicted on 29 April 1946 by the IMTFE. The Tribunal began on 3 May 1946 and did not conclude its arguments until 16 April 1948, but eight more months would elapse before the last of the verdicts was read on 12 November. By that time, public interest in the proceedings had slackened perceptibly. Among those tried were Tōjō and top military leaders, Foreign Minister Tōgō Shigenori and Marquis Kido Kōichi, the Emperor's closest adviser. Hirota Kōki, former foreign minister and premier, also was arraigned, as was Matsuoka Yōsuke, the architect of Japan's Axis alliance with Germany and Italy. The indictments included two men who had signed the Instrument of Surrender on behalf of Japan: career diplomat Shigemitsu Mamoru, former ambassador to Moscow and London and foreign minister from August to September 1945, and General Umezu Yoshijirō, former chief of the Army General Staff (1944–1945). Tōjō's successor, Koiso Kuniaki (prime minister, July 1944–April 1945), too, was placed on trial. Such members of the aristocracy and Royal family as Baron Hiranuma Ki'ichirō and Hirohito's uncle Field Marshal Prince Nashimoto Morimasa also were detained, and Hiranuma was indicted. Prince Konoe, thrice prime minister in the late 1930s and early 1940s, also came under suspicion. The Prince would have been apprehended as well but swallowed poison in the early morning hours of 16 December 1945, the day he had been ordered to turn himself in. In the suicide note he left for his son, he protested, 'The winner is too boastful, the loser too servile.'[15]

Of the original 28 accused, two died during the proceedings and one was placed

Photo 32. Japanese Class A war crimes suspects listen impassively to Tribunal proceedings. From left to right (front row): Doihara, Hata, Hirota, Minami, Tōjō, Oka, Araki, Mutō, Hoshino, Kaya, Kido, and Kimura. Back row (left to right): Hashimoto*, Koiso, Ōshima*, Matsui, Tōgō*, Satō, Shigemitsu, Shimada, Suzuki and Itagaki (Mainichi). (*Partially obscured)

under psychiatric care, leaving 25 to face sentencing. Eight of the 11 Allied justices found all of the accused guilty of some of the 55 charges against them – a blanket finding that did not occur at Nuremberg. All but two of the defendants were convicted of 'conspiracy to wage aggressive war'. The verdicts delivered from 4 November to 12 November 1948, condemned seven to death and ordered 18 to serve prison terms ranging from seven years to life. Capital punishment was decreed for Tōjō, Hirota and five generals. The condemned appealed the decision to MacArthur, who personally consulted Allied representatives in Tokyo on 22 November. Australia, Canada and France indicated that they would not oppose mitigation of the sentences. B. N. Chakravarty of India asked that all death sentences be commuted to life imprisonment, and Baron Lewe von Aduard of the Dutch Mission recommended lesser punishments for five prisoners. MacArthur turned down all requests for clemency. As a last resort, defence lawyers appealed to the US Supreme Court, which dismissed the motion for lack of jurisdiction – a decision that MacArthur hailed as a reconfirmation of his authority as SCAP.[16]

The seven condemned men were executed by hanging in Sugamo Prison on 23 December 1948. The sentences of the remaining 18 were later commuted, and in 1958, 10 remaining defendants, already paroled, were freed unconditionally. Veteran diplomat Shigemitsu Mamoru, released in late 1950, became foreign minister in 1954 and played a central role in securing Japan's entry into the United Nations. On 24 December, the day after the executions, the Tribunal released 19 Class A suspects who also had been held but not indicted.

The reasons for suspending prosecution at this point are unclear (in Germany, smaller trials had continued after the major suspects had been tried), but public ennui and the reorientation of Occupation priorities with the deepening of the Cold War are no doubt largely responsible. Among those freed were Kishi Nobusuke, a former Manchukuo bureaucrat and prominent member of the Tōjō Cabinet, and the notorious right-wing racketeers Kodama Yoshio and Sasagawa Ryōichi. Upon their release, these men were placed under purge constraints, but GHQ found their anti-Communism sufficiently useful to overlook their wartime misconduct and reactionary ideas. They subsequently joined the 'vast and powerful nationalist underground' of which journalist Mark Gayn had warned in 1946. After the Occupation, these figures were catapulted back into public life. Kishi, who had been responsible for the enslavement of tens of thousands of Chinese labourers in Manchukuo in the late 1930s, would become prime minister in 1957.[17]

Victor's justice?
In December 1946, the UN General Assembly formally endorsed the Nuremberg Charter as international law, conferring fresh legitimacy on the Tokyo Charter. Both instruments, however, purported to derive their authority from the Kellogg–Briand (Paris) Pact of 27 August 1928, formally the General Treaty for the Renunciation of War, which abjured belligerency as an instrument of national policy. Japan was a signatory. Indeed, aware of its treaty obligation, Tokyo had purposely categorised its attacks on China as 'incidents' to avoid a declaration of war (ironically, school texts and most history books still use that deceptive word today). The legal validity of this and other assertions of jurisdiction, however, were challenged by defence attorneys and at least one Allied justice. A major problem, critics contended, was the Tribunal's mandate to seek convictions based on legal precepts not yet established in international law at the time the offences occurred, notably the crime of conspiracy to commit aggression and crimes against humanity. The Tribunal's self-proclaimed mission seemed to conflict with its claim to be rooted in the 'expression of international law existing at the time'.

Specifically, Chief Defence Counsel Takayanagi argued that the Kellogg–Briand Pact, while it renounced war, neither defined aggression nor made it an actionable offence. He also noted that criminal conspiracy was an exclusively Anglo-American doctrine, one with the potential to make even innocent acts of cooperation subject to 'the innate prejudices or social ideas of an unknown judge'. President Webb concurred, declaring in a final separate opinion that creating 'a crime of naked conspiracy based on the Anglo-American concept' was tantamount to 'judicial legislation'. Justice Radhabinod Pal of India, the only member of the Bench trained in international jurisprudence, asserted that conspiracy could not be considered a crime under current world law. Pal also attacked the charge of 'crimes against peace' as retroactive legislation that made the Tribunal an instrument of political, not judicial, power. These contradictions did not necessarily invalidate the proceedings, however. A majority of the justices, including the liberal Dutch jurist Bert V. A. Röling who criticised the trial on other grounds, argued convincingly that the magnitude of the transgressions committed and the imperatives of morality and justice compelled the Allies to make new rules and render judgment after the fact.[18]

Defence chief Takayanagi also challenged the legality of prosecuting individuals for obeying the orders of superiors or implementing policies of state, a position that Justice Pal of India strongly endorsed. Not surprisingly, perhaps, many of the professional military men in MacArthur's headquarters also agreed heartily. SCAP's intelligence chiefs Willoughby and Thorpe, for example, objected both to the trial and its premises, which they derided in private as vindictive ex post facto law. Thorpe wrote afterwards that 'the business of trying these people before a completely prejudiced court of angry men from the Allied nations that had suffered at Japanese hands smacked strongly of hypocrisy'. The State Department's George F. Kennan, head of the powerful Policy Planning Staff, criticised the proceedings as 'political' and 'ill-conceived'.[19]

The Tokyo Tribunal took the argument of individual responsibility to a new extreme, introducing the notion, absent at Nuremberg, of 'negative criminality': failure to take positive steps to prevent atrocities and other breaches of the laws of war. Takayanagi reminded the Bench that American members of the Commission of Responsibilities at the Versailles Peace Conference in 1919 had heatedly opposed this concept, and French Justice Henri Bernard and Justice Röling of Holland both attempted to narrow the scope of the charge. Nonetheless, a slim majority sentenced Hirota Kōki to death on this count (he also was found guilty of conspiracy). Hirota had been foreign minister during the 1937 Nanjing massacre. Matsui Iwane, the commanding general at Nanjing, was hanged on that charge alone.[20]

There were also unsettling questions about the qualifications and objectivity of the Bench. Pal was the only expert in international law; the Nationalist Chinese justice, Mei Ju-ao, although holding a law degree from the University of Chicago, had never served as a magistrate (in China, he was a politician); the Soviet justice, Major General I. M. Zaryanov, spoke neither Japanese nor English, the official languages of the trial. Justice Delfin Jaranilla of the Philippines was a survivor of the Bataan Death March, and President Webb had personally investigated and tried Japanese atrocities in Australia. Such experiences cast serious doubt on the impartiality of both men. Janarilla was predictably hawkish on most of the issues before the court, demanding stiffer punishments, and the proud, arrogant Webb bullied defence witnesses and counsel. Webb's credibility came into question again when he returned to Australia from 12 November to 12 December 1947, missing 22 consecutive days of court proceedings. (It should be noted that all of the justices were absent part of the time, for periods ranging from two weeks to two months. Webb missed a total of 53 days, Pal 109 days.) New Zealand Justice Sir Erima Harvey Northcroft, a member of the New Zealand Supreme Court, felt that Webb was unqualified on other grounds, as well. The President, he said, had 'an indifferent knowledge of the rules of evidence' and was not only unreliable and vain but stupid into the bargain. Northcroft led a revolt by the British and Canadian justices, Lord Patrick and Edward S. McDougall, who threatened to resign unless Webb were removed. Smelling a scandal and unnecessary complications with the Americans, their respective governments promptly vetoed this move.[21]

The Cairo Declaration had condemned the 'enslavement of the people of Korea', yet no Korean justice participated in the judgment, and two of the three Asians on the Bench, Pal and Jaranilla, represented at the start not independent nations but colonies of Britain and the United States (the Philippines acquired full independence on 4 July 1946, shortly after the trial began, and India became independent in August 1947). The British, Dutch and French members of the Bench represented imperialist powers with extensive colonial possessions in Asia, and the Anglo-Saxon bloc, which alone accounted for five of the 11 justices, collectively defended in practice the prerogatives of empire. With the exception of the Philippines and Burma, which was allowed to place a prosecutor on the British team, none of the other Southeast Asian countries that had suffered under the Japanese was given a voice in the trial. The Indictment, too, failed to take adequately into account the wartime experiences of these countries. The associate prosecutor for the Philippines, Pedro Lopez, took exception with the document for not addressing the establishment of puppet régimes. 'In many ways', two British writers conclude, 'the Tribunal was the last bastion of colonialism.'[22]

Moreover, the Allies prevented representatives of the Japanese people from taking any positive part in the proceedings or conducting their own trials, despite calls from progressive intellectuals for people's courts. This shortsighted policy made it difficult then and later for many Japanese to confront their nation's war responsibility. Moreover, the physical organisation of the Tribunal, which took place in the former War Ministry Building in Ichigaya, sent an unmistakable message to the conquered, for the building was rigorously segregated. Allied jurists, prosecutors and staff entered by the front door, Japanese lawyers and defendants by the rear. Toilets were segregated, with those in the basement reserved for Japanese, from lawyers to maintenance personnel. Inside the court room, even Japanese and American defence counsels were seated separately, and the gallery, too, was divided into sections for Japanese and non-Japanese.[23]

There were procedural flaws, the most serious of which was the simple majority required to pass a sentence of death. All capital verdicts but one were approved by seven of the 11 justices. In the case of Hirota, however, the decision was six to five; the former diplomat was sent to the gallows by a one-vote majority. Justice Röling, who supported a verdict of not guilty, argued that the Tribunal had failed convincingly to prove Hirota guilty of even a single charge. The Bench was divided on other issues as well, and five justices issued separate opinions, three of them dissenting. President Webb, while voting with the majority, submitted a concurring opinion expressing grave reservations about the absence of the Emperor as a defendant, a flaw that he cited as an argument for commuting the death sentences. Jaranilla of the Philippines, however, in another individual opinion, not only endorsed the majority judgment but called for harsher punishments in some cases.

Bernard, Röling and Pal filed dissenting views. Bernard protested vigorously that gross procedural errors had invalidated the judgments; he also objected on the grounds that the Japanese sovereign had escaped indictment. Röling dissented on the definition of aggressive war and the doctrine of civilian responsibility for military crimes and contested five convictions, including that of Hirota. He also believed that the fire-bombings of Tokyo and other urban centres from early 1945, as well as the atomic destruction of Hiroshima and Nagasaki, had violated the laws of war. In the most famous of the dissenting opinions, Justice Pal not only shared the misgivings of Bernard and Röling but offered a book-length critique of the trial's premises and acquitted all of the defendants on all counts.[24]

Right-wing Japanese intellectuals seized on Pal's anti-colonial, anti-Communist views in an effort to discredit the Tribunal and its findings. It was true that Japan stood accused of aggression in an Asia whose broad political, economic and social contours had been moulded by more than a century of Western imperialism. More-over, Japan's expansionist policies in China, like Western colonial practice, had been motivated partially by anti-Communism. Ultra-nationalists, however, wielded the accusation of 'victor's justice' in order to obscure the root issue of Japan's war guilt, implicitly justifying their country's wartime record. But that was the position of a minority. Popular interest in the Tribunal waned as the proceedings dragged on, and there was no strong public reaction to the verdicts. Few people thought that the trial was fair, only that it was inevitable, and the condemned leaders were widely seen as scapegoats. Yet a perceptible shift of opinion had occurred since the defeat, and despite the Tribunal's glaring defects, there was a broad tacit understanding of the need for some kind of reckoning. Some progressive scholars and writers openly supported the judgments; others called for independent trials by the Japanese them-selves. Nearly 40 years later, a noted philosopher who remains critical of the victors' overweening self-righteousness and arrogant belief in the superiority of Western values pronounced the Tribunal revolutionary in its intent to establish in inter-national law the legal norms necessary to prevent war. Therein lies the real signifi-cance of the Tokyo Tribunal.[25]

CRIMES OF COMMISSION AND OMISSION

Class B and C war crimes

Japanese maltreatment of prisoners of war and interned enemy civilians was notori-ous. The brutality routinely meted out to Allied captives forced to work on the Burma–Thailand Railway, for instance, defied description. Some 12,000 Allied prisoners and as many as 70,000 Asian internees may have died building the 412-kilometre rail link through dense jungle. Whereas only about 4 per cent of US and British POWs held by German and Italian troops died in captivity, the average rate of death for those in Japanese hands was 27 per cent. More than 34 per cent of Australian POWs perished in internment camps. No comparable statistics exist for captive Asian civilians, but death rates there undoubtedly were even higher.[26]

The transgressions committed by Imperial troops against interned enemy soldiers and civilians were extreme and abhorrent. Yet there was nothing innately 'Japanese' about such behaviour. Troops on both sides committed atrocities in the heat of battle (chapter 1). In the case of Japanese combatants, however, several factors conspired to make such conduct inevitable and pervasive. In 1929, Japan had signed the Geneva Convention Concerning the Treatment of Prisoners of War, but the Imperial Diet never formally ratified it. The Emperor's troops were not even told of its existence, for suicide was preferable to surrender. The Field Service Code (*Senjinkun*) of 8 January 1941 ordered soldiers: 'Do not accept the humiliation of capture alive'. This injunction was literally pounded into recruits' consciousness, and the 'civilian instinct' was virtually extinguished in the ranks. Orders were to be followed exactly and absolutely, and brutal physical punishment was the price exacted for the slightest deviation. Personal responsibility for obeying unjust orders was an alien concept. With no sense of their own human rights, Japanese troops had little reason to honour those of enemy prisoners. These ingrained attitudes were compounded by feelings of inferiority and repressed animosity towards Western POWs and a strong sense of superiority towards Asian internees, leading Japanese captors to treat both groups with brutal contempt, albeit for different reasons. This 'combination of regimentation, brutalisation and racism' produced a dehumanising psychology of cruelty that was amplified by a general war psychosis and the increasing desperation of Japan's military position in the field.[27]

Massacres, murder, death marches, torture, cannibalism, forced labour, starvation, systematic ill treatment and other horrors committed by Japanese soldiers were prosecuted in less spectacular military trials conducted by Australian, British, Dutch, Filipino, French, Nationalist Chinese and US courts acting independently on the authority of the Potsdam Proclamation. From October 1945 to April 1951, about 5,700 Japanese were brought before 49 Allied military tribunals in Batavia (now Jakarta), Hong Kong, Kuala Lumpur, Manila, Manus, Rabaul, Saigon, Shanghai, Yokohama and elsewhere in Asia. A total of 4,405 were convicted, of whom 904 were executed and 475 given life sentences.[28] At the Yokohama Tribunal alone, run by the Eighth Army at its Yokohama headquarters, 2,214 suspects had been apprehended for B/C offences by mid-1947. Of the more than 1,000 brought to trial there, 124 were condemned to death, and 62 received life sentences.

The B/C trials got underway immediately and punishment was swift. The Yokohama Court began hearing cases on 18 December 1945 and hanged its first criminal in early March 1946. The last case was disposed of in October 1949, after the close of the IMTFE. In the Philippines, where the United States conducted separate trials, two high-ranking Japanese were executed just before the Tokyo Tribunal began. General Yamashita Tomoyuki, who had masterminded the capture of Singapore from Commonwealth forces in February 1942, was hanged on 23 February 1946 for the Rape of Manila after losing an appeal to the US Supreme Court. Lieutenant General Honma Masaharu, who had seized the Philippines from MacArthur in

Photo 33. 'This is the man who beat me.' An American soldier, flown in from Manila, testifies against his former captor at the Yokohama Tribunal for Class B and C War Crimes, 27 May 1946. American plaintiffs were encouraged to be confrontational and dramatise their accusations (Mainichi).

1942, was executed by firing squad on 3 April 1946 for the Bataan Death March and other alleged atrocities.

The Soviet Union is believed to have tried as many as 10,000 former Japanese soldiers in separate clandestine tribunals. Some 3,000 may have been executed secretly – more than three times the number shot or hanged by the other Allies combined. Among those prosecuted were 12 soldiers and scientists belonging to the notorious Unit 731 (see below) and other Kwantung Army biological and chemical warfare groups. In December 1949, they received prison sentences of up to 20 years. In China, however, the People's Liberation Army prosecuted only 45 of 1,108 Japanese war crimes suspects and did not execute a single one. Preferring self-criticism and 're-education' to forced confession, the People's Republic encouraged the accused to reflect on their actions and repent. The trials took place after the mid-1950s, and detainees subsequently were returned to Japan.[29]

Most of those jailed or executed for Class B and C crimes undoubtedly deserved their fate, but justice was not administered evenly. Generals Honma and Yamashita, for instance, were tried by US Army officers, not lawyers, acting on direct orders from MacArthur. Due process was ignored, and the rules of evidence were suspended. Both officers were charged with 'command responsibility' for atrocities committed by their troops, but neither ordered those actions nor even had knowledge of them at the time. No evidence was ever adduced linking Honma to the Bataan Death March. Yamashita was accused of massacres committed in the Philippines in September 1944 while he was stationed in Manchuria. In February 1945, he was in Baguio some 240 kilometres from Manila when the capital was sacked by troops he earlier had ordered to withdraw. The US Supreme Court upheld the sentences even though two dissenting justices denounced the trials as 'legalised lynching'. In the stern judgment of a contemporary observer, 'Homma and Yamashita – MacArthur's chief adversaries – were tried and convicted by kangaroo courts which flouted justice with the Supreme Commander's approval and probably at his urging'.

In other cases, the severity of sentences reflected the rank of the Allied victim, offences against officers being punished more harshly than those against enlisted men. In one well-documented instance, an Allied military court tried and hanged an apparently innocent man after a flawed and perfunctory investigation. In 1951, Lieutenant General Nishimura Takuma, commander of the Konoe Imperial Guards in Malaya, was executed by an Australian court on Manus Island, Papua New Guinea, for allegedly ordering the massacre of 110 Australian and 45 Indian soldiers at Parit Sulong in 1942. The death sentence was carried out even though Nishimura did not match the only eyewitness description of the officer in charge, and despite the fact that a Japanese of lesser rank had already confessed to the crime. In the view of one writer, Nishimura was railroaded because the Australians, bent on revenge, were determined to execute the highest-ranking Japanese they could find.[30]

Issues of guilt and innocence were sometimes complex. Among the B and C suspects were 148 Koreans and 173 Formosans, Japanese colonial subjects forced to work in internment camps as 'auxiliaries' to alleviate Japanese labour shortages. Of these, 42 were executed. Many of their crimes, however, were carried out under direct orders from Japanese superiors on pain of death. Indeed, as defeat neared, Japanese forces reportedly were told not only to destroy documents relating to the maltreatment of POWs but, where possible, to shift the blame for such behaviour onto colonial soldiers. With the return of Japanese sovereignty in 1952, Japanese war criminals became eligible for pensions and other veterans' benefits, but Korean and Formosan war criminals resident in Japan were barred from receiving any form of state assistance, war-related or other (see chapter 10).[31]

Several Japanese Americans also became tragically enmeshed in Japan's war machine, and two were later tried by US courts for treason. One of these was Iva Ikuko Toguri, a Nisei born in Los Angeles, who had worked for Radio Tokyo during the war and was pressured by US journalists after the defeat to claim she was 'Tokyo Rose'. Toguri had gone to Japan to visit a sick relative on the eve of the Pacific conflict and was one of a dozen English-speakers subsequently pressed into making propaganda broadcasts for Japan. Toguri rejected Japanese demands to renounce her American nationality, however. Apprehended in September 1945, she was confined in Sugamo's Blue Prison for women but was released after one year for lack of sufficient evidence to support Class B or C charges. Rearrested upon her return to the United States, she was convicted of treason in 1949 on the basis of evidence that was later retracted. She was sentenced to 10 years' imprisonment and a $10,000 fine and was stripped of her US citizenship. Toguri was pardoned in early 1977 by President Gerald Ford.[32]

Brutalities committed against Asian internees received less attention than those perpetrated against Caucasians, and entire categories of crimes against Asians escaped close scrutiny by the war crimes trials. Two prominent examples are forced labour and sexual slavery. Dutch tribunals in the Netherlands East Indies prosecuted Japanese for compelling white Dutch women to serve as military prostitutes, but the private entrepreneurs and military officials who organised and exploited non-white 'military comfort women' (*jūgun-ianfu*) on a massive scale were never brought to justice. From the late 1930s, Japanese military leaders had been directly implicated in procuring Asian women – listed as 'military supplies' – for the brothels they licensed throughout the war zone to 'service' Imperial forces. From 1930 to 1945, it is estimated that between 80,000 and 100,000 – and perhaps as many as 200,000 – women, most of them between the ages of 14 and 18, were mobilised for this purpose. About 80 per cent are believed to have been Koreans; 10 per cent Chinese, Burmese, Dutch, Filipinas, Indonesians, Malayans, Formosans and Vietnamese; and 10 per cent Japanese. Ostensibly set up to prevent reoccurences of the Rape of Nanjing, the military brothel system proved ineffectual in curbing the rapacity of soldiers in the field – indeed, there is evidence that the military condoned sexual violence against women to whet the aggression of its combat units. The war crimes trials failed to address this question, and the plight of the 'comfort women' did not become a public issue in Japan until the early 1990s (chapter 11).[33]

Crimes of omission

The case of the 'comfort women' was one of several crimes of omission. The war crimes trials were distinguished as much by the nature of the depredations they chose to ignore as by those they prosecuted. A defence bid to raise the issue of the atomic bombings, a command decision that Justice Pal compared to the actions of top Nazi war criminals, was summarily rejected. (Justice Röling implicitly concurred with Pal, later writing that 'from the Second World War, above all two things are remembered: the German gas chambers and the American atomic bombings.')[34] The US terror bombings of major Japanese cities also were discounted, as was the Soviet Union's unilateral declaration of war against Japan in violation of the bilateral Neutrality Pact of 1941, which was legally binding until April 1946. Dominated by Western colonial powers, the Tribunal turned a blind eye to abuses Japan committed in its Korean and Formosan colonies, of which slave labour and forced prostitution were but two examples. The Class B and C trials failed to consider Allied war crimes, including the murder of Japanese POWs and the battlefield destruction of hospitals.

Another group that escaped prosecution were leaders of the infamous biological warfare (BW) groups that operated in China and northern Manchuria under Lieutenant General Ishii Shirō. Ishii had established a research laboratory in Tokyo and a bacterial production plant at Pingfang near Harbin, Manchuria in 1932. From 1940, his Manchurian command, the Kwantung Army's Unit 731, began field-testing toxins by dropping them from aircraft on Chinese villages in Chejiang, Hunan and other provinces. Unit 731 tested anthrax, botulism, bubonic plague, cholera, dysentery, ganders, smallpox, typhoid and tuberculosis pathogens and later conducted grisly medical experiments using gas gangrene, syphilis, frostbite, pressure chambers and vivisections. The subjects, described by their tormentors as *maruta*, or 'logs' (the same term Nazi executioners used for their victims) included Chinese, Koreans, Manchurians, Mongolians and a small number of Allied prisoners of war (Americans, Australians, British, Dutch and New Zealanders). An estimated 3,000 were killed at Pingfan alone. At the war's end, the Japanese government gave Unit 731 cadre top evacuation priority, enabling these scientists to reach Japan before other Army groups, after disposing of evidence, including their human guinea pigs.[35]

US Army Intelligence had received word of Ishii's BW research in late 1944 and the spring of 1945. In September 1945, the US Army Chemical Warfare Service at Camp Detrick, Maryland sent a microbiologist to Tokyo to investigate Ishii and his cohorts. Over the next two years, three more BW specialists would be sent to debrief members of the 'Ishii infrastructure' and collect information. In July 1946, following the second BW mission to Tokyo, the Pentagon ordered MacArthur to protect all scientific intelligence impinging on US national security. The Army was determined not to allow such information to fall into the hands of the Soviets, who also had shown an interest in Ishii. On 8 May 1947, Ishii offered to share his knowledge and data with the Americans in return for immunity from prosecution for himself and his colleagues and asked the US Army to hire him as a bio-war expert.

The Japanese had attempted to conceal the facts of human experimentation from US investigators, but by this time, it was clear that living human beings had been used in laboratory and field tests. Nonetheless, MacArthur, Willoughby and Colonel Alva C. Carpenter of Legal Section, presumably acting on higher instructions, decided not to prosecute Ishii. On 22 May 1947, two weeks after Ishii's offer of cooperation, Legal Section issued SCAPIN-1699 ordering the Japanese government to exempt Ishii and six of his collaborators from arrest as war crimes suspects. On 20 June, Dr Norbert H. Fell, a US bacteriologist who had debriefed Ishii in early May, wrote in his final report that the 'data on human experiments, when we have correlated it with the data we and our allies have on animals, may prove invaluable'. Fell was personally interested in using the Ishii archives to develop effective vaccines for anthrax, plague and glanders. He concluded: 'It is hoped that individuals who voluntarily contributed this information will be spared embarrassment because of it.' That same month, a report by Willoughby's Military Intelligence Section (Far East Command) praised Ishii as 'pro-American and [someone who] respects the mental culture and physical science of the US'. On 1 August 1947, SWNCC's Subcommittee for the Far East formally recommended against trying the Ishii group. In a paper of that date, the Subcommittee concluded that 'the value to the US of Japanese BW data is of such importance to national security as to far outweigh the value accruing from "war crimes" prosecution'. Ishii was true to his word. In November 1947, the last US bio-war mission to Tokyo took home to Camp Detrick 15,000 pathology slides from more than 500 of Ishii's victims, as well as test protocols and autopsy reports on 850 cadavers. Japan's leading bio-war scientist subsequently received a large retirement pension from the government (this despite SCAP's order of November 1945 to end such payments by 1 February 1946) and lived quietly at his country estate in Chiba Prefecture until his death in 1964.[36]

Unit 731 was not the only Japanese BW operation in China. Other groups included Unit 100 (Changchun), Unit Ei-1644 (Nanjing), Unit 2646 (Hailar, Inner Mongolia) and Unit 9420 (Singapore), some of which were under Ishii's command. Not one of the cadre of top-level officers and scientists who actually directed the gruesome experiments ever faced a US or British military tribunal. Certainly, Ishii and at least two other bio-warriors, Lieutenant General Wakamatsu Yūjirō (Unit 100) and Major General Kitano Masaji (Units 731 and Ei-1644), deserved to be tried as war criminals and punished accordingly.

The 'leader in the crime'
The most glaring omission of all was the Emperor. President Webb in his separate concurring opinion complained that the 'leader in the crime, though available for trial, had been granted immunity'. Justice Bernard of France echoed that concern, writing in his dissenting brief that failure to indict Hirohito was one of three serious defects that justified nullification of the Tokyo Tribunal. Webb acquiesced in the immunity decision, citing 'the best interests of all the Allied Powers', but stressed that the monarch's role in beginning and ending the war was incontrovertible.[37] Considering the high ideals espoused by the Tribunal, it is indeed astounding that the Emperor was not even called upon to testify. Between March and April 1946, five Imperial Court officials, fearing just such a summons, formally put a number of questions to Hirohito and recorded his answers. The resulting statements were recorded over five sessions lasting a total of eight hours. The partially amended 'Imperial Soliloquy' was circulated among MacArthur's top staff but mysteriously disappeared soon afterwards, and a copy did not resurface until after the sovereign's death in 1989. In the document, Hirohito, looking back on his decision of late 1941 to approve the military's war plans, affirmed that he had made the proper choice. Had he not permitted the armed forces to take prompt action, he stated, Allied demands would have led to an even more brutal war and Japan would have been crushed utterly.[38]

There was no moral or legal justification for making an exception of Hirohito. Recent scholarship indicates that while the sovereign did his best to avoid war with the Western powers, his primary concern was not humanitarian but military: whether or not Japan could emerge victorious. Vested with the power of supreme command (*tōsuiken*), Hirohito was as firmly committed as his military commanders to achieving Japanese hegemony in Asia; the question was one of timing and means. When the dictates of empire made war in the Pacific inevitable, the Japanese sovereign threw his full support to General Tōjō in whom, as he later admitted, he had complete trust. Hirohito was informed of military contingency planning for war at least six years before Pearl Harbor. He received the Imperial Navy's battle plan for the assault on the US Pacific Fleet in early November 1941, a full month in advance (not even the Imperial Army had the details). He ordered the preparations for war and signed the declaration of war (which, delayed by human error, did not reach Washington until *after* Japan had initiated hostilities). As the Pacific conflict progressed, the monarch monitored combat operations, participated in top-level planning sessions, was privy to key military discussions and presided over Imperial Conferences. His Army and Navy ministers briefed him frequently and thoroughly on administrative matters pertaining to the war, and the Army and Navy chiefs of staff informed him in person of military developments.[39]

Although Hirohito did not dictate policy, he was able to influence the agenda for important policy debates, and on occasion he exercised his Royal prerogative to grill the military high command and support or oppose specific policies. The sovereign was as integral to the decision-making process as Tōjō or any other wartime leader. As discussed earlier, in February 1945, Hirohito dismissed a direct appeal by his top adviser to terminate the conflict at an early date, insisting that Japan first improve its military position in the field. He continued to eschew serious efforts for peace until the atomic bombings and the entry of the Soviet Union into the war left no other alternative (chapter 5). By virtue of his position, Hirohito was more than a mere co-conspirator, however, for it was in his name that state policy was made. Indeed, the Emperor's instructions to the nation's fighting men was to 'consider an order from your superior as an order from Myself'. As a military official remarked laconically to the Imperial Vice Chamberlain in early November 1945, 'it is obvious that, as the ruler, he bears responsibility for the nation's war unless he is a robot'.[40] Certainly, if senior advisers and officials such as Hiranuma, Kido, Shigemitsu and Tōgō could be tried, convicted and sentenced for crimes against the peace, so should their supreme leader have been. Several of these men had actively sought to end the war while their sovereign chased the chimera of 'one more victory'.

Allied opinion on the subject of the Emperor was vitriolic. In a Gallup Poll of 29 June 1945, one third of Americans queried wanted Hirohito executed summarily, and one fifth favoured imprisonment or exile. Only 3 per cent supported his retention and use by the Allies. On 18 September, Congress introduced a joint resolution demanding that the monarch stand trial as a war criminal, and on 29 November, the Joint Chiefs of Staff informed MacArthur that Hirohito was not immune from prosecution and ordered the Supreme Commander to gather evidence for a possible trial. The Australians, in particular, were determined to bring the Emperor to justice, and on 21 January 1946, Canberra's representative to the United Nations War Crimes Commission in London formally recommended that the Japanese sovereign be brought up on war crimes charges.

MacArthur's headquarters baulked. Four days later, on 25 January, the Supreme Commander replied to the Joint Chiefs' directive of November. In a secret telegram to Army Chief of Staff Dwight D. Eisenhower (below), MacArthur stated that 'no specific and tangible evidence has been uncovered with regard to [Hirohito's] exact activities' and recommended against arraignment. (Indeed, as argued below, MacArthur's top lieutenants had conspired with the Court to conceal such evidence.) This message was probably the determining factor in Washington's decision not to try the monarch. In late January, when members of the Far Eastern Advisory Commission (FEAC)'s fact-finding mission visited Tokyo and broached the issue to SCAP, they were told that attempting to place Hirohito on trial would provoke a violent reaction among the public, possibly endangering the Occupation mission. According to Sir Carl Berendsen, the New Zealand member, MacArthur called the Emperor 'a cipher, a puppet rather than a leader', implying that he was not worth pursuing in court.[41]

On 30 January, the State Department cabled the US Embassy in London ordering it to oppose the Australian move to indict the Emperor. Great Britain, equally determined to spare the Japanese monarchy, cooperated with Washington, working behind the scenes to postpone consideration of the measure. Undeterred, Australian Associate Prosecutor Sir Alan Mansfield redoubled his efforts to persuade Britain, India and New Zealand to follow Canberra's lead, but his quest ended abruptly in early April when it became clear that neither Washington nor the recently empanelled Far Eastern Commission, successor to the FEAC, intended to press charges.[42] The final word from Washington came on 17 June 1946 in the form of SWNCC-55/7, a basic policy document that explicitly removed the Emperor as a war crimes suspect. The next day, 18 June, Chief Prosecutor Keenan publicly confirmed that Hirohito would not stand trial.

Saving the Emperor
Keenan's anti-climactic announcement was the denouement to a concerted effort on the part of the Throne, Japanese civilian and military leaders and the highest echelons of SCAP to protect the person of the Emperor and preserve the Imperial dynasty. Efforts to exculpate the sovereign, however, pre-dated the surrender.

At the Imperial Conferences of 9–10 August and 14 August, Hirohito had made his 'sacred decision' (*seidan*) to end the fighting (although, by then, he had prolonged the war's agony for half a year). In the weeks following defeat, this 'sacred decision' would form the central motif in a scrupulously fabricated narrative of high drama designed to foster the image of 'a figurehead Emperor who dared face down his own fanatic militarists, usurp their power, and compel them by sheer strength of will to surrender a defeated country to a superior enemy'.[43] Shigemitsu Mamoru, Shidehara and other high officials sounded this theme constantly in their encounters with MacArthur and his staff. But they were preaching to the choir.

These distortions and embellishments fit the scenario scripted in wartime Washington by the Japan Crowd. Hugh Borton, Joseph Ballantine and Joseph Grew had lobbied on behalf of the monarchy, arguing that the Japanese sovereign was an unwilling pawn of the militarists (chapter 5). They blamed Tōjō and the 'military clique' for the war and portrayed the Emperor as a crypto-pacifist who could play a useful postwar role. Inside GHQ, a key proponent of this Royalist 'wedge' strategy was MacArthur's military secretary and psychological operations specialist, Brigadier General Bonner F. Fellers. Fellers believed that the Emperor had a 'mystic hold' on his people and that he had been manipulated and misused by 'gangster militarists'. Like Grew, he was convinced that the Imperial institution was the spiritual core of the nation and therefore indispensable in securing a speedy surrender and smooth transition to democratic government. On 1 October 1945, Fellers recommended to MacArthur that 'in the interest of peaceful occupation and rehabilitation of Japan, prevention of revolution and communism . . . positive action be taken to prevent the indictment and prosecution of the Emperor as a war criminal'. On 2 October, he justified that course of action in a rambling memorandum, part of which read: 'If the Emperor were tried for war crimes the governmental structure would collapse and a general uprising would be inevitable.' He warned 'there would be chaos and bloodshed . . . and the period of occupation would be prolonged and we would have alienated the Japanese'.[44]

Fellers coordinated this strategy with Terasaki Hidenari, the spouse of Fellers' cousin Gwendolyn, Court liaison to SCAP and head of the Foreign Ministry's Information Bureau. Acting as intermediary between MacArthur and the Throne, Terasaki also worked with the Tokyo Tribunal's International Prosecution Section (IPS), secretly conveying to Roy Morgan, Chief of the IPS Investigative Division, the views of the Court and gathering information about IPS intentions towards the Emperor. With Hirohito's blessings, Terasaki gave Morgan the names of diplomats and high-ranking military officers who had played a leading part in the war. Terasaki also wondered why Army Lieutenant General Arisue Seizō, Willoughby's protégé, had not been indicted. Through these efforts, conducted simultaneously on several fronts, Hirohito betrayed his loyal subordinates in order to purchase immunity for himself.[45]

With the connivance of Terasaki and Willoughby, Fellers appears to have buried potentially incriminating evidence against the monarch, including the so-called Imperial Soliloquy mentioned above. He also attempted to stifle talk of abdication, an option that some of the Court were entertaining seriously. In early October, for instance, Prince Higashikuni had personally proposed that course of action to Hirohito, his nephew by marriage, and, in late October, Prince Konoe had embarrassed both the Imperial household and SCAP by raising the question publicly. Fellers bluntly told the Palace to contain such loose talk. On 27 February 1946, however, Prince Mikasa, Hirohito's younger brother, urged the monarch to step down, and Higashikuni leaked details of Palace discussions to the press. Leading liberals, including Nanbara Shigeru, President of Tokyo Imperial University, and even such conservative constitutional scholars as Sasaki Sōichi favoured abdication. Yabe Teiji, law professor at Tokyo Imperial University, urged this path as the best means of deflecting pressure from the Allies and preserving the Throne itself. MacArthur's staff campaigned against abdication, which was officially shelved in September 1946, but the issue was revived again in 1948 as the Tokyo Tribunal prepared to render its verdict and one last time in late 1951 on the eve of Japanese independence.[46]

Ultimately, the decision to protect the Throne was MacArthur's. On 25 January, the General informed his superiors in Washington in magniloquent prose that reproduced the gist of the Fellers Memorandum but rather extravagantly embroidered on its apocalyptic vision, that if the Emperor were to be tried, the Japanese would regard this:

> as the greatest betrayal in their history and the hatreds and resentments engendered by this thought will unquestionably last for all measurable time. A vendetta for revenge will thereby be initiated whose cycle may well not be complete for centuries, if ever. The whole of Japan can be expected . . . to resist the action either by passive or semi-active means. . . . [It] is not inconceivable that all government agencies will break down . . . and a condition of underground chaos and disorder amounting to guerrilla warfare in the mountains and outlying regions result.

MacArthur continued: 'I believe all hope of introducing modern democratic methods would disappear and that when military control finally ceased some form of intense regimentation probably along Communistic lines would arise for the mutilated masses.' This turn of events, he said, would make it 'absolutely essential' to augment the occupational forces by at least 1 million and install a complete civil service of up to several hundred thousand. 'An overseas supply under such conditions would have to be set up on a war basis', he declared. The Supreme Commander's exculpatory peroration was freighted with an emotional vigour that few in Washington felt prepared to challenge.[47] MacArthur's personal intervention saved the Emperor, a decision whose long-term consequences for Japanese society remain a subject of passionate debate (chapter 11).

EMPOWERING THE PEOPLE

GHQ followed up its Civil Liberties Directive with a series of measures designed to empower the people. The human rights order of 4 October 1945 had removed all restraints on organised political activity, and political parties reformed almost overnight, each with its roots in the past, each articulating its particular vision of the future. MacArthur's headquarters gave a further nudge to democratisation by ordaining the revision of the Election Law in late 1945 and supervising Japan's first postwar elections in April 1946. Finally, SCAP's purge directives of January 1946 removed from office the most prominent enemies of democracy, creating the conditions for the emergence of a new political leadership.

Political parties
The Japan Communist Party, reorganised in early October 1945, became the first
political grouping to re-emerge. In December, it elected Tokuda Kyūichi chair,
reconfirmed the Party's policy of overturning the Imperial institution and called for
the establishment of a broad popular front uniting workers, farmers and the urban
poor. In the nation's factories, it attempted to set up inter-shop councils as a base for
the formation of a national labour organisation. Tokuda and Shiga Yoshio, editor of
the Party organ *Akahata*, were intent on using the Occupation army to help achieve
their programme. Thus, the JCP espoused gradual reform rather than revolutionary
change. This tendency emerged more clearly after Nosaka Sanzō returned to Japan
from Yenan, China in early January 1946. In late February, Nosaka summed up the
new line neatly in two slogans: 'peaceful democratic revolution' and the 'lovable
Communist Party'.[48]

The Japan Socialist Party (JSP) was created on 2 November 1945 by non-
Communist proletarian and peasant groups of various persuasions. SCAP considered
the JSP a liberalising force, but the Party was an unwieldy conglomeration of
incompatible ideological tendencies. Some members, such as Asanuma Inejirō, a
future chair of the Party who would be assassinated in 1960, had supported the
wartime régime. Left-wing Socialists, such as Katō Kanjū, Kuroda Hisao and Suzuki
Mosaburō, had been arrested in late 1937 for opposing the war effort. Another left-of-
centre Socialist politician and activist was Matsumoto Ji'ichirō, head of the *Buraku*
liberation organisation, who had served in the wartime Diet on a ticket independent
of the militarists. Takano Minoru, future secretary general of the Socialist-dominated
labour front *Sōdōmei* (Japan Federation of Labour) and later *Sōhyō* (General Council
of Trade Unions of Japan), was a radical shopfloor organiser. Labour movement elders
Takano Iwasaburō, Abe Iso'o and Kagawa Toyohiko oversaw the formation of the new
grouping, but right-wing Socialists, such as Hirano Rikizō, Nishio Suehiro, Matsuoka
Komakichi and Mizutani Chōzaburō, seized the initiative. Hirano, a founding
member of the ultra-nationalist Imperial Way Society (*Kōdōkai*), had headed the
right wing of the prewar peasant movement; Nishio maintained close ties with the
zaibatsu; and all had held seats in the wartime Diet, although opposing the Tōjō war
cabal's Imperial Rule Assistance Association. The JSP chose as its chair Katayama
Tetsu, a Christian Socialist and former adviser to the labour movement, who would
head a Socialist-led coalition government from June 1947 to February 1948.

Reflecting the Party's heteroclyte composition, the Socialist platform was a
hodgepodge of contending ideas but nonetheless included bold recommendations
for human rights legislation; political, economic and labour reforms; a land redistribution scheme; and a new cultural and educational programme. On the question of
the Emperor, the Socialists were divided. In late August 1945, Hirano, Nishio and
Mizutani had secretly explored with conservative leaders Ashida Hitoshi and
Hatoyama Ichirō the possibility of joining ranks, and when the Communists
attempted to woo the JSP into forming a popular front in late 1945, the Party's
virulently anti-Communist right-wing frustrated the overture.[49]

Three conservative parties, two of them heirs to the prewar *Seiyūkai* (Friends of Democratic Government Party) and *Minseitō* (Constitutional Democratic Party), also formed in short order. In contrast to the JCP and JSP, all three drew their leaders from the wartime Diet and, while differing in their evaluation of the militarists and the war, were firmly committed to the Imperial institution. The Japan Liberal Party, the first conservative grouping to reappear, was formed on 9 November by Hatoyama Ichirō, an experienced politician associated with the Yoshida Anti-War Group who had held prewar Cabinet posts. The Liberals included Ashida Hitoshi, who had resigned from the Foreign Ministry in 1932 in protest of the Manchurian adventure and subsequently ran the English daily *The Japan Advertiser*; Ishibashi Tanzan, Keynesian economist and editor of the *Tōyō Keizai Shinpō* (Oriental Economist); prewar politician Kōno Ichirō; and Yoshida Shigeru. The Liberal leadership had been critical of the war faction, and the Party registered the largest gains in the first postwar elections of April 1946, but Kōno would be purged soon afterwards (Ishibashi would meet the same fate a year later). In early May, Liberal President Hatoyama, too, was purged, throwing control of the Party to Yoshida, who capitalised on the Liberal's electoral triumph to form his first cabinet in May 1946. The Liberal Party changed its name to Democratic Liberal Party in March 1948 and then back again to Liberal Party in March 1950 but remained essentially the same organisation. In March 1947, Ashida Hitoshi broke ranks to form the centrist Democratic Party, which joined Katayama's Socialist-led coalition in June 1947. From March to October 1948, Ashida would head his own coalition government.

The Japan Progressive Party, established in November 1945, drew the bulk of its membership from the Imperial Rule Assistance Association, a reactionary state-run organisation set up in October 1940 merging the major prewar parties into a single pro-military bloc to assist Imperial rule. The Progressives' nominal head, however, was ex-foreign minister Shidehara Kijūrō, who had replaced Prince Higashikuni as premier in early October 1945. An Anglophile known for his scholarly grasp of English, Shidehara had advocated a policy of peaceful diplomacy in the late 1920s. He would remain in office until May 1946. The Progressive Party was disbanded in March 1947, its ranks decimated by war crimes arrests and the purge, and its leadership joined Ashida's Democratic Party, created the same month.

The third conservative formation was the Japan Cooperative Party, the only new political organisation of the early postwar period. Founded on 18 December, the Cooperative Party drew its strength from Japan's small middle class, espoused a corporatist ideology and situated itself to the 'extreme left' of the conservative mainstream. The Cooperatives' ranks, too, were thinned by the purge, however, and, in March 1947, the group was reorganised as the People's Cooperative Party under the leadership of centrist Miki Takeo (prime minister, 1974–6). The People's Cooperatives participated in both the Katayama and Ashida coalition Cabinets.[50]

Electoral reform

MacArthur was faced with the difficult task of eliminating the wide-ranging powers of ultra-conservative wartime Diet members, 80 per cent of whom had been seated in the 1942 election with the endorsement of the Imperial Rule Assistance Association (IRAA) and the Tōjō Cabinet. To accomplish this, SCAP directed the government to revise voting requirements and broaden the electorate. Enacted on 17 December 1945, the Lower House Election Law lowered the voting age from 25 to 20, vastly expanding the range of representation; reduced the age requirement for candidates from 30 to 25 years; and gave the vote to women, the disenfranchised half of the population. The new statute more than doubled the size of the voting population. Under the prewar system, Japan had multi-member, medium-size precincts, but voters could cast a ballot for only one candidate. The enhanced Election Law now provided a limited plural vote for two or three of the candidates competing for 10 to 14 seats in each of Japan's 46 electoral districts and increased the size of the constituencies, thereby opening the way for newcomers.[51]

Some GHQ officials had advocated a more far-reaching American-style reform. They argued that Japan's write-in ballot system – ballots were blank instead of printed as in the United States – and the new large, multi-member precincts with limited plural balloting still inhibited political expression. They urged the creation of medium-sized electoral districts where people could vote for as many candidates as there were seats, door-to-door canvassing and the introduction of printed ballots. But they failed to convince MacArthur and Government Section's Whitney, who felt strongly that the Occupation should avoid even the appearance of tinkering with the electoral system. Whitney's orders to Eighth Army commander Eichelberger, charged with supervising the polling, echoed this sentiment: 'Remember that this is a Japanese election under a Japanese law. . . . The charge that [it] is being conducted under the threat of Yankee bayonets must not be permitted to arise.'[52]

On 6 March 1946, the government publicised a summary of its revisions to the draft constitution MacArthur had submitted in February (below), and soon afterwards, the Supreme Commander directed the Shidehara Cabinet to schedule Lower House elections for April. To MacArthur, general elections were a pre-condition for enactment of the new national charter: only a Parliament truly reflecting the popular will could legitimately promulgate the Constitution. As indicated below, a purge of the political élite had just begun in January, however, and the newly convened Far Eastern Commission, worried that Old-Guard politicians would use their influence to retain their seats in Parliament, urged GHQ to postpone the balloting until the dismissals could run their course. In fact, the FEC also was upset that MacArthur had not consulted it about constitutional reform. The Supreme Commander ignored the advice and proceeded as planned.

In many respects, the polling of 10 April 1946 was a resounding success that altered the composition of the Lower House, bringing many new faces to the fore. Three-quarters of eligible voters cast a ballot and returned only six Tōjō-era representatives. About 80 per cent of those elected were running for the first time, including

Photo 34. Female Socialist candidate Katō Shizue delivers a campaign speech to a crowd of impoverished Tokyoites, many of them women. The shantytown is one of several that sprang up around the National Diet Building (background). 8 April 1946 (Kyodo).

independents, candidates from minor parties and women. A total of 257 parties, many of them tiny regional groups, fielded prospective lawmakers, although only 32 would actually win a seat in the National Diet. The Liberal Party made the greatest gains, garnering a slim plurality of 140 out of 464 Lower House seats. It was followed by the Progressives, with 94 seats, the Socialists with 92 and the Cooperatives with 14. Before the election, the Communists had modified their call for the overthrow of the emperor system, urging its peaceful elimination instead, but despite the immense prestige it enjoyed among the intelligentsia, the Party captured only 5 seats. Smaller political groupings took a total of 38 seats, however, and 83 independents also were elected. Although conservatives outnumbered progressives by a ratio of seven to three, a redistribution of political power had nonetheless taken place.[53]

Contrary to predictions, large numbers of female voters – 66 per cent of those eligible, or some 14 million – turned out at the polls (79 per cent of eligible males also cast a ballot). The new Election Law's multi-member constituencies with plural voting encouraged many citizens to write in women as their second or third choices, and a total of 39 out of 79 female candidates were voted into office. Among them was Katō Shizue, a Christian humanist and Socialist, follower of American birth-control advocate Margaret Sanger and one of 'Weed's Girls', the group of forward-looking Japanese women working with CI&E's Ethel Weed. In March, at Weed's suggestion, Katō and other feminists had formed the Women's Democratic Club (*Fujin Minshu Kurabu*) to promote the participation of women in politics. Included in this group were Akamatsu Tsuneko; Hani Setsuko, liberal educator and social critic; Matsuoka Yōko, a graduate of Swarthmore College (1939) and literary critic who in February 1947 would help re-establish the Japan PEN Club; Miyamoto Yuriko, Communist and novelist of the proletarian school; writer Sata Ineko; feminist author and Marxist critic Yamakawa Kikue; and Yamamoto Sugi, medical doctor and women's rights activist.[54] The Women's Democratic Club, Ichikawa Fusae's New Japan Women's League and other feminist organisations mobilised to get out the vote, but the overwhelming majority of women who cast a ballot were unaffiliated. Their newfound sense of empowerment was reflected in the stunning polling results. MacArthur gave the female parliamentarians his personal endorsement, sending each a letter of congratulations and meeting a group of 35 on 20 June.

The elections changed the social composition of the Diet, adding farmers, physicians, teachers, writers and a former prostitute (who captured 250,000 votes). They also brought marginalised groups such as *Buraku* people into the political arena. In the second general elections of 1947, 10 members of this persecuted former outcaste group would win seats in the Lower and Upper Houses, among them Matsumoto Ji'ichirō, head of the National Committee for *Buraku* Liberation. Ironically, however, some 650,000 Koreans and 30,000 Formosans and Chinese, former Imperial subjects with nominal Japanese nationality, found themselves excluded from the balloting on the grounds that their household registers were maintained in Formosa and Korea, not Japan proper (chapter 9).

As the Far Eastern Commission had foreseen, many conservative lawmakers

Photo 35. Japan's first women parliamentarians take their seats in the Lower House, 16 May 1946. The introduction of universal suffrage made women eligible to vote and hold office, and a total of 39 female candidates were elected in the nation's first postwar elections (Kyodo).

managed to elude the purge and return to office. Purgees marshalled money and influence to name replacements, often relatives or friends, and have them elected, and right-of-centre parties captured more than half of the 466 Lower House seats. On 19 April, the victorious Liberal Party led the Socialists, Cooperatives and Communists in forming a four-party coalition calling for the resignation of the Shidehara Cabinet, which had been unable to wrestle inflation under control or restart the economy. The Shidehara government finally fell in late May. Liberal Party leader and Foreign Minister Yoshida Shigeru became prime minister and formed his cabinet on 22 May with support from Shidehara's Progressives. The new Election Law favoured women and smaller political parties, but in March 1947, Yoshida revised it to restore the pre-surrender electoral precincts and replace limited-plural balloting with a single vote, producing bitter controversy (chapter 7). Yoshida's conservatives used their parliamentary majority to railroad the bill through the Diet, setting an unhappy precedent that has since encouraged governments to ignore minority views in enacting unpopular legislation.[55]

The purge of public officials
The Potsdam Proclamation had ordained the removal from authority and influence 'of those who have deceived and misled the people of Japan'. Consequently, on 4 January 1946, MacArthur's staff issued two purge directives to the government:

SCAPIN-548 ('Abolition of Certain Political Parties, Associations, Societies, and Other Organisations') and SCAPIN-550 ('Removal and Exclusion of Undesirable Personnel from Public Office'). Appalled at the prospect of losing key legislators, the entire Shidehara Cabinet announced that, unless the purge orders were retracted, it would resign, allowing Shidehara to form a new government. When Foreign Minister Yoshida informed MacArthur of this, the General quipped stiffly that, should the Cabinet dissolve itself, 'Thereafter Baron Shidehara may be acceptable to the Emperor for reappointment as prime minister, but he will not be acceptable to me.' MacArthur's veiled threat to appoint his own government had the desired effect, and the ministers withdrew their resignations.[56]

The 'political purge' was carried out by Government Section, a duty that vastly enhanced its influence within GHQ. General Willoughby, ever jealous of his prerogatives, attempted to narrow the range of the programme and wrest control of it from GS. Whitney had just been appointed GS Section Chief in December, and Willoughby was anxious to assert his authority over a potential rival. More to the point, Willoughby was alarmed at the thought of removing potential anti-Communist allies from the political arena. Max Bishop in the Political Adviser's Office argued forcefully for disqualifying only war crimes suspects. MacArthur backed Whitney, however, and the purge rolled on, expanding in intensity and scope from 1946 to 1947. Charles Kades, GS Deputy Chief, drafted the exclusion orders, which applied to individuals in fixed purge categories covering the period from 1931, when Japan invaded Manchuria, to 1945. About 77 per cent of those affected were career military men, many of them lower ranking officers, and members of veterans' associations. The directives listed seven 'removal and exclusion' categories, barring from public life such 'active exponents of militant nationalism and aggression' as war criminals, professional military officers, leaders of ultra-nationalist and terrorist societies, influential IRAA members, officials of overseas financial and economic organisations involved in Japanese expansion, governors of former Japanese colonies and occupied territories, and a vague grab-bag of 'additional militarists and ultra-nationalists'. Kades later commented: 'We didn't enjoy the purge. It was not constructive work like the Constitution or the reformation of the code of civil procedure, criminal procedure and family law . . . but we were in the Army and those were our orders.'[57]

Political figures were a prime target, and the purge disqualified more than 600 conservative party cadres and lawmakers from running for office in the April 1946 balloting. Five members of the Shidehara Cabinet were removed from their posts just before the election, and a year later, five more ministers were dismissed from the Yoshida Cabinet. The purge was implemented administratively, not by judicial proceeding, and it was unilateral: there were neither hearings nor due process, and appeal on limited grounds was possible only after one had been debarred. Some notable exceptions were made, however, for Japanese in key positions whose services were deemed vital to the Occupation mission. As indicated earlier, Willoughby, in particular, used this loophole to recruit former Imperial Army and Navy staff officers for use by G-2 in its archival and intelligence work.

Photo 36. Prime Minister Yoshida Shigeru, elder statesman and pre-eminent politician of the Occupation era (Kyodo).

A purge order with far-reaching consequence was that signed for Liberal Party founder and president Hatoyama Ichirō, one of Japan's most senior parliamentarians. As minister of education from 1932 to 1934, Hatoyama had suspended Takigawa Yukitoki, a well-known law professor at Kyoto Imperial University, for his liberal views, prompting the resignation of the university president and 36 faculty members. During the war, however, Hatoyama had opposed the formation of the IRAA, winning election to the 1942 Diet as an unofficial candidate. On 4 May 1946, the day before he was to become premier, SCAP purged Hatoyama as a rightist collaborator, invoking the ambiguous 'additional militarists and ultra-nationalists' category.[58] This bolt from the blue catapulted his lieutenant Yoshida Shigeru into the premiership. Hatoyama the parliamentarian took a back seat until his depurge and rehabilitation in 1951; Yoshida the wily bureaucrat became the dominant figure in national politics for the duration of the Occupation, forming five cabinets between 1946 and 1954. (After the Occupation, Hatoyama would return to political life, heading three conservative governments between 1954 and 1957, and Yoshida's fortunes would wane accordingly.)

The political first phase of the purge was complemented and expanded by the 'education' purge of May 1946, which was overseen by Civil Information and Education Section (chapter 8). A year later, in January 1947, the second phase of the purge got underway, merging these efforts with a less ambitious 'economic' purge, which weeded out 1,535 captains of industry, finance and commerce. GHQ simultaneously extended the removal exercise to local government officials and media moguls. MacArthur initially assigned the economic purge to Economic and Scientific Section (ESS), but G-2, the G-4 Petroleum Advisory Group, SCAP's civil engineers and other Occupation agencies objected strenuously to a broadening of the exclusion lists, which they claimed endangered the success of their work. The removal orders ultimately were applied only to executives, financiers and others in 'key positions of high responsibility', not to operational managers, in order to avoid hampering the recovery of industrial production. In late August 1946, MacArthur transferred responsibility for this phase of the programme from ESS to Government Section, where the purge machinery was already in place, and in January 1947, the Yoshida government promulgated the enabling Cabinet legislation.[59]

The government, and even the British, protested that the purge would steam out of control, producing 'chaos, confusion and Communism', but to no avail. In early 1947, Yoshida, who had wearily resigned himself to the mass dismissals, told his Finance Minister Ishibashi Tanzan, recently blacklisted for 'continuous obstructionism toward occupation economic objectives', to imagine simply that he had been bitten by a mad dog. Yoshida also lamented the active part played by many 'obnoxious' Japanese in the exclusion programme. Liberals and leftists, men and women, denounced ultra-rightists to Government Section, especially during the media purge, resulting in the removal of many chauvinist elements from the press and publishing world. An unexpected result was the exclusion from public life of feminist Ichikawa Fusae for having cooperated with the wartime régime (she had led the Greater Japan Women's Association). Australia, New Zealand and the USSR, however, complained that the purge policy was not radical enough. The Soviet member of the Allied Council for Japan, Kuzma Derevyanko, advocated destroying the leadership of middle-of-the-road political parties, including the Socialists, as well, and took the Occupation to task for not pursuing its elimination objectives more aggressively. Ultimately, SCAP screened a total of 717,415 individuals, forcing 201,815 from key positions in public life, but even that figure was modest compared to the Allied purge in Germany, which dismissed twice that number.[60]

The purge-by-category approach amounted to a presumption of guilt by association and was doubtless unfair, and even some liberalists were snared in its fine meshes and forced, in Kades's words, to take 'early retirement' from public affairs. While many purgees richly deserved their fate, others were simply unlucky, such as governors and mayors debarred because their position had conferred on them another title which fell, ex officio, in a targeted category. Despite its inequities, however, the exclusion campaign effected a change of leadership in key areas of social, political and economic life. Many of the middle-echelon officials who had loyally served the Imperial state managed to retain their positions or find comparable work, but the purge decisively ended the political ascendancy of the officer corps and other reactionary elements in society, clearing the way for younger political and business leaders relatively untainted by ultra-rightist ideology. These latter would become the driving force behind postwar Japan's rapid economic recovery and its emergence as a democratic nation.

On the debit side, many who should have been purged found bolt-holes in municipal government or private enterprise. Among the latter, firms such as the advertising giant Dentsū (the name dates from 1955) hired so many former police, military officers and bureaucrats from the former puppet state of Manchukuo that its Tokyo headquarters was nicknamed the 'Second Manchurian Railway Building'. Paradoxically, the purge also strengthened the national bureaucracy, which was assigned the task of screening those slated for removal and administering the dismissals, albeit under the close scrutiny of SCAP. Conservative mid-echelon functionaries who escaped careful scrutiny attempted to impede the reform process or co-opt it to serve their own interests. Despite its achievements, the exclusion programme also suffered from the internal inconsistency of attempting to attain a democratic objective through essentially authoritarian means. This dilemma became palpably real after late 1949 when the purge machinery was cranked up again to cull from the public and private sectors Japanese now suspected of harbouring leftist sentiments (chapter 10).

A NEW CONSTITUTION

The primary impediment to reform was the Prussian-inspired Constitution of the Empire of Japan, which had been promulgated in 1889, entering into force in 1890. The Meiji Constitution invested the Emperor, 'sacred and inviolable', with supreme political power, including legislative authority. The Cabinet was responsible to the sovereign, not to the Imperial Diet, which functioned as an advisory organ. The duty of the prime minister, Cabinet members, Privy Councillors and the Lord Keeper of the Privy Seal was to assist the monarch in carrying out the Imperial will. The House of Peers consisted of non-elected members – mainly Imperial princes, hereditary nobles, Royal nominees and large taxpayers – and enjoyed equal power with the House of Representatives, which was composed primarily of wealthy industrialists and landlords and defended the interests of the affluent and powerful. Both bodies excluded women.

Under this system of monarchical quasi-absolutism, the people enjoyed few civil liberties. Police powers were extensive, and real political authority was wielded by a tiny cabal close to the Throne. This group included the *Genrō*, or elder statesmen; the *Jūshin*, former premiers and ex-presidents of the Privy Council; Imperial family and Court officials; and officers of the Imperial General Staff. These advisers either belonged to or were under the sway of the military, the industrial combines and top bureaucrats. Important decisions of state were made not in the Imperial Diet but behind the Chrysanthemum Curtain, at a far remove from the public eye. Moreover, as Commander-in-Chief of the armed forces, the Emperor enjoyed the prerogative of supreme command, a power outside the purview of Cabinet and Diet and not subject to civilian control. Consequently, Army and Navy leaders held themselves accountable solely to the Emperor.

Faced with the daunting task of revamping this system, MacArthur encouraged the government to amend the Imperial charter in line with democratic principles. When the Japanese side failed to produce an acceptable proposal, SCAP worked up its own between 4 and 10 February 1946 and presented it to an astonished government on 13 February. After a complex process of review and revision, a modified version of the American draft was announced to the public on 6 March as the work of the Shidehara Cabinet. The government submitted its own revised draft to the Diet on 21 June. Following several months of deliberation and debate, the new Constitution was promulgated on 3 November – the Emperor Meiji's birthday – and went into effect on 3 May 1947.

The Constitution of Japan, consisting of 11 Chapters and 103 Articles, renounced the Meiji charter's authoritarian Prussian legacy, replacing it with liberal Anglo-American legal concepts. Chapter I (Articles One through Eight) unilaterally and dramatically transferred political power from the Emperor – now reduced to 'the symbol of the State and the unity of the nation' with no 'powers related to government' – to the people, 'with whom resides sovereign power' (Article One). Chapter II consisted solely of Article Nine, which renounced war as a sovereign right of the state and forever outlawed the maintenance of armed forces. Chapter III (Articles 10 through 40) detailed the rights and duties of the people. The guarantees enshrined in these 31 articles ensured basic human and civil liberties, including equality under the law, freedom of thought and expression, and due process. One of the many dramatic changes was gender equality. Article 14 made men and women equal under the law and prohibited discrimination based on sex. Article 24 was equally far-reaching. It stated that marriage was to be based on mutual consent and gave women an equal voice in 'property rights, inheritance, choice of domicile, divorce and other matters pertaining to marriage and the family'. The provisions of this article were radical even by US standards: only the constitutions of then-Communist countries such as the USSR and Poland guaranteed sexual equality in family life.[61]

The new Constitution also boldly recast the machinery of government. Chapter IV (Articles 41 through 64) made the National Diet, consisting of elected representatives in both houses, the highest elected body and organ of state power. Membership qualifications were to be fixed by law, but discrimination based on creed, sex, social status, family origin, education, property or income was prohibited. Subsequent chapters separated and defined the legislative, executive and judiciary functions of government. Chapter V (Articles 65 through 75) invested the Cabinet with executive power but made it collectively responsible to the Diet, and a majority of its members had to be chosen from among incumbent parliamentarians. The authority of the prime minister, who was empowered to appoint and dismiss state ministers, also was strengthened. Chapters VI through IX (Articles 76 through 96) dealt variously with the judiciary, finance, local government and amendments. Chapter X (Articles 97 through 99) concerning supreme law, affirmed that the fundamental rights guaranteed by the Constitution 'are fruits of the age-old struggle of man to be free' and noted that they 'are conferred upon this and future generations in trust, to be held for all times inviolate'. Chapter XI (Articles 100 through 103) consisted of supplementary provisions for ratification.

Early proposals

Initially, neither Washington nor MacArthur had intended to replace the Meiji Constitution; both expected the government to democratise the existing charter itself. As discussed earlier, the 1907 Hague Convention expressly prohibited an occupying power from altering the political structure of an occupied state, and the 1941 Atlantic Charter had proclaimed the right of all peoples to self-determination. Unilaterally tampering with the Imperial Constitution would have left SCAP, and the United States, open to charges of violating international law.

On 4 October 1945, MacArthur personally suggested to Prince Konoe, minister of state in the Higashikuni Cabinet, that he attempt to liberalise the Meiji charter. Konoe took the assignment seriously, but on 14 October, Higashikuni's successor Shidehara Kijūrō independently entrusted the same task to Matsumoto Jōji, a former professor of commercial law at Tokyo Imperial University and his new minister of state. Working in total secrecy, Matsumoto set up the Committee to Study Constitutional Problems on 25 October and appointed a panel of distinguished legal experts and high-ranking bureaucrats to assist him. Members of the Legislation Bureau, the Cabinet's legislative watchdog body, also participated. Among the academics was Minobe Tatsukichi, Professor Emeritus of Tokyo Imperial University. Minobe was the author of a constitutional theory that held the Emperor to be an organ of the state, not its divine embodiment, and in 1935, he had been forced to resign from the House of Peers following an acrimonious debate over charges that the Emperor-as-organ concept denied the Imperial family-state tenet. Nonetheless, along with his erudite colleagues on the Committee, Minobe believed that Imperial rule and the Meiji Constitution that had established it in law were entirely compatible with democratic principles and did not require fundamental revision.

In late October, as it became clear that Konoe would be charged with war crimes, SCAP distanced itself from the Prince. On 1 November, MacArthur publicly disavowed the Konoe project, and although the beleaguered court noble eventually submitted an outline of his ideas to the Emperor in late November, his work ended there. Full responsibility for constitutional revision now shifted to the Matsumoto Committee, but its élitist orientation, its grounding in German legal theory and solid commitment to the status quo – notably the principle of Imperial sovereignty – gave it a decidedly conservative cast. Substantive reform, clearly, was not on Matsumoto's agenda.

Momentum for constitutional revision was not generated by SCAP alone. Powerful pressures for a fundamental overhaul of the national charter were building at the grass roots, and from late 1945 through March 1946, private associations and even individuals spontaneously published constitutional proposals, a number of them original and far-sighted. The mass media gave extensive coverage to many of these, reflecting a new popular commitment to change. Private groups included the Constitutional Research Association (*Kenpō Kenkyūkai*), the Constitutional Discussion Group (*Kenpō Kondankai*) and the Japan Bar Association. Influential liberals, such as Takano Iwasaburō, labour leader, scholar and founder of the Ōhara Institute for Social Research, put forward radical proposals that included strong human rights guarantees and advocated abolishing the Imperial institution. Favouring a US-type republican system, Takano helped draft proposals by the Constitutional Research Association and the Socialist Party, as well. Matsumoto Ji'ichirō, Socialist leader of the *Buraku* liberation movement, published a personal document advocating a Union of Japanese Republics, each with its own government structure.[62]

Four political parties also published drafts. The Communist Party argued for the abolition of the emperor system and proposed an extensive bill of human and social rights that drew heavily on the 1936 Soviet ('Stalin') Constitution. The Socialists advocated what amounted to a 'symbolic emperor' without governmental powers. Katō Kanjū, the well-known Socialist leader and polemicist, suggested that the monarchy was the 'symbol of national harmony' and that retaining a politically powerless sovereign for purely ceremonial purposes was 'neither unnatural nor irrational'.[63] The right-of-centre Liberals and Progressives sought to preserve the Imperial dynasty and its prerogatives, although they took pains to cast their proposals in a liberal idiom. Many of the above projects, personal and collective, made detailed recommendations for human, social, political and economic rights, but only one demanded political equality for women, and those of Takano and the Communist Party alone called for eliminating the Throne.

SCAP scrutinised all of these proposals. The document unveiled by the Constitutional Research Association on 27 December 1945, in particular, held its attention. The Association's key members included Takano and a young constitutional scholar, Suzuki Yasuzō. Following his purge from Kyoto Imperial University, Suzuki had studied the popular constitutions (*shigi kenpō*) of the Meiji-era Freedom and People's Rights Movement. (Soon after the surrender, E. H. Norman had urged him to develop a personal critique of the Imperial institution and elaborate his own constitutional draft.) The Association studied various national charters, including the American and German Weimar models, and its proposal, while stopping short of abolishing the emperor system, stripped the monarchy of all government powers and made the Cabinet the highest organ of state power. Significantly, under Suzuki's influence, the Association drew much of its inspiration from grass-roots *shigi kenpō* initiatives that the Meiji oligarchs had ignored or suppressed. Ōuchi Hyōe, a Marxist economist formerly of Tokyo Imperial University (he had been dismissed for his views), critiqued the document and contributed a section on public finances. On 11 January 1946, Lieutenant Colonel Milo E. Rowell of Government Section prepared an extensive analysis of the Association's proposal for GS Chief Whitney. Rowell praised its 'outstanding liberal provisions' on popular sovereignty and human rights and concluded that, despite shortcomings, its ideas were 'democratic and acceptable'. Whitney signed Rowell's memorandum, an indication of serious Government Section interest.[64]

Meanwhile, in early January 1946, Washington had put the finishing touches on a policy guide for the political reform of Japan, the 14-page 'Reform of the Japanese Governmental System' (SWNCC-228). The document outlined broad goals for Occupation policy, including constitutional amendments and even the adoption of a new constitution 'in a manner which will express the free will of the Japanese people'. It also affirmed that the Allies were 'fully empowered to insist that Japanese basic law be so altered as to provide that in practice the government is responsible to the people'. The SWNCC guideline's view of the emperor system was explicit and emphatic: 'The Japanese should be encouraged to abolish the Emperor Institution or to reform it along more democratic lines.' The policy paper emphasised, however, that the Supreme Commander should order the government to take such action 'only as a last resort'. Knowledge that these reforms had been imposed by the Allies, it warned, would undermine their future acceptance by the Japanese people. The State Department issued the final version of SWNCC-228 on 7 January, and MacArthur received it on 11 January.[65]

On 17 January, members of the soon-to-be-reorganised Far Eastern Advisory Commission (chapter 3) visited MacArthur's headquarters on a fact-finding mission. At a conference with Whitney, Kades and other Government Section officials, Senator Tomas Confessor, the Philippine FEAC representative, pointedly asked GS why constitutional change was not on SCAP's agenda. On 29 January, the delegation met MacArthur. Responding to a similar query, the Supreme Commander told the FEAC mission that suggestions for such reform had been made to the government but that the Moscow Agreement had taken matters out of his hands. Echoing SWNCC-228, he also noted that 'a constitution, no matter how good, no matter how well written, forced upon the Japanese by bayonet would last just as long as bayonets were present'. Nonetheless, Confessor's bold question of 17 January triggered a process that would culminate in the writing of a model constitution.[66]

The 'MacArthur Constitution'

MacArthur was in a quandary. The Four Power Moscow Agreement of December 1945 had entrusted constitutional revision to the Far Eastern Commission, the FEAC's successor; any changes SCAP contemplated would have to be cleared with

Photo 37. Members of the Far Eastern Advisory Commission arrive in Yokohama on 9 January 1946 to observe the Occupation in action. From the bottom left, in ascending order, are Frank R. McCoy (US), Lieutenant General Chu Shih-ming (Republican China), Francis Laoste (France), Major J. Plimsol (Australia), and Nelson T. Johnson (US). At the right, from the bottom up, are Sir Carl Berendsen (New Zealand), Sir George Sansom (UK), Thomas Confessor (Philippines), R. Saksans (India), Colonel L. M. Cosgrove (Canada), and Dr D. Kat Angelino (Netherlands). Confessor's blunt queries on constitutional reform were one factor prompting MacArthur to draft a new constitution. The FEAC was reorganised as the Far Eastern Commission in February 1946 (US National Archives).

that body. To escape Allied, and particularly Soviet, scrutiny, a new constitution had to be produced before the new Commission convened its first session in late February. Moreover, it would need to be presented as a Japanese initiative. Whitney was particularly anxious that SCAP meet that deadline. He believed the Matsumoto Committee incapable of producing an acceptable draft. Unless MacArthur acted immediately, the reorganised Far Eastern Commission was likely to impose its own, much harsher document, which might well abolish the emperor system (in point of fact, the Commission never pressed the issue of Imperial continuity).

Shortly after the FEAC meeting in Tokyo, Whitney ordered a review of SCAP's prerogatives to determine whether MacArthur had the power to revise the Meiji charter. Kades prepared the staff advisory, which informed the General that 'you have authority from the Allied Powers to proceed with constitutional reform', but only until such time as 'the Far Eastern Commission promulgates its own policy decision on this subject'. Whitney forwarded this finding to MacArthur on 1 February. On that day, however, the daily *Mainichi Shinbun* secretly acquired and published one of the Matsumoto Committee drafts. Essentially a rewording of the Meiji Constitution, this conservative document retained the principle of Imperial sovereignty and introduced no substantive changes. The Japanese media derided it as an exercise in tokenism that had misread the mood of the nation. The *Mainichi* scoop clinched Whitney's arguments and set constitutional revision in motion. On that same day, the GS chief ordered a reorganisation of the Section's Public Administration Division in preparation for a 'constitutional convention' (Whitney's term).

Sometime in the next three days, MacArthur reached a decision. On 3 February, he instructed Whitney to produce a constitutional text incorporating three non-negotiable principles. In his message, pencilled on yellow note paper and entitled 'Three Basic Points', the General outlined his ideas on the new charter. Point I, the first paragraph of the so-called MacArthur Notes, stated that the Emperor would be head of state but that his powers would derive from the constitution and be subject to the basic will of the people. Point II renounced Japan's sovereign right to wage war – 'even for preserving its own security' – and to maintain armed forces. The third paragraph, Point III, called for the abolition of 'the feudal system of Japan' and the reform of the peerage. Point I was consistent with SWNCC-228 and Point III with SCAP's Potsdam mandate. Point II, renunciation of the right of belligerency echoed many US and British wartime pronouncements about total and complete disarmament for Japan, but its inclusion in the constitutional draft was a remarkable innovation. Linking a depoliticised monarchy with radical pacifism was a masterful stroke of political engineering that would effectively assure the survival of the Imperial institution, albeit in a very different form.[67]

On 4 February, Whitney assigned the drafting of the document to his restructured Public Administration Division and ordered it completed by 12 February, Abraham Lincoln's birthday. In fact, the document was finished in exactly one week's time, slightly ahead of schedule. Between 4 and 10 February, a GS Steering Committee chaired by Deputy Chief Kades and eight working subcommittees acted as an ad hoc constitutional convention. Sequestered in a ballroom at the top of the Dai-Ichi Insurance Building, the group laboured day and night to produce a series of drafts, each of which was discussed with the Steering Committee and revised after extensive debate.

The work began by collating the liberal Japanese proposals and comparing them with other national charters, including the constitutions of France, the Scandinavian countries, the Soviet Union, the United States and Weimar Germany. The subcommittees worked with a high sense of purpose in an informal and congenial atmosphere free of interference from 'upstairs'. MacArthur remained aloof from the drafting process but closely followed the work in progress through Whitney. The group also toiled in absolute secrecy. Washington was not informed of the endeavour, nor initially were other SCAP sections. SWNCC-228 was consulted but used primarily as reference. Nor was Japanese input solicited. A plea by Lieutenant Milton J. Esman of the Executive Committee to dispense with secrecy and seek the advice of forward-looking Japanese scholars resulted in his temporary banishment from the project.

The Civil Rights Subcommittee
The Steering Committee consisted of Kades, who wrote the anti-war clauses; Commander Alfred R. Hussey Jr, who drafted the Preamble; and Milo Rowell, who also served on the Judiciary Committee with Hussey. They were assisted by Ruth Ellerman, who was appointed chief secretary (Ellerman, who would later play a role in the labour reforms, was one of four women contributing in some capacity to the work of the convention). This core group coordinated the progress of the eight subcommittees (Legislative, Executive, Civil Rights, Judiciary, Local Government, Finance, Emperor and Enabling Provisions, and The Preamble) and fashioned the respective reports into an integrated text. This they carefully fitted within the skeletal framework of the Imperial Charter, for SCAP was at pains to preserve the appearance of legal continuity with Meiji law in deference to the Hague Convention. In some areas, the GS team went beyond MacArthur's terse handwritten instructions. On 10 February, Whitney submitted the draft to the Supreme Commander, who approved it the following day, on 11 February, and ordered it presented to the unsuspecting Japanese on 13 February.

The architects of the MacArthur draft were Kades, Hussey and Rowell – all highly able and experienced lawyers – who strove to produce a model document that would set a new world standard of government. The actual reform provisions themselves, however, were elaborated by the individual subcommittees. A prime example was the Civil Rights Subcommittee, which wrote a full one third of the 92 articles appearing in the MacArthur draft. These articles, eventually encoded as Chapter III of the Constitution, 'Rights and Duties of the People', effectively demolished the social basis of 'the feudal system of Japan' as the MacArthur Notes had insisted. The Subcommittee was led by Colonel Pieter K. Roest and included Dr Harry Emerson Wildes and 22-year-old Beate Sirota, a naturalized US citizen who had grown up in Tokyo and spoke Japanese fluently. None of the three had legal training, but all had extensive experience living in other cultures and an acute awareness of the importance of universal human rights legislation.

Sirota was particularly distressed by the position of women in Japanese society. From childhood experience, she knew that they 'had always married men chosen for them by their parents, walked behind their husbands, and carried their babies on their backs'. 'Husbands', she noted, 'divorced wives just because they could not have children. Women had no property rights.' In translating the Japanese Civil Code, she discovered that 'Women are to be regarded as [legally] incompetent' (Article Four). Determined not to omit anything 'that might benefit Japanese women in the future', Sirota rushed through Tokyo in a jeep, requisitioning from university and other libraries a dozen or so European constitutions. These she parsed, but the most useful for her purposes were the Weimar Constitution, the Soviet Constitution and the charters of the Scandinavian countries. Based on these, she drafted two key provisions guaranteeing equality of the sexes in society and in the family, which eventually became Articles 14 and 24.[68]

Sirota proposed seven additional articles according women and children extensive social welfare rights, including free education and medical and dental care. Specifically, she wanted protective legislation to 'aid expectant and nursing mothers, promote infant and child welfare, and establish just rights for illegitimate and adopted children, and for the underprivileged'. Despite strong support from her colleagues on the Civil Rights Subcommittee, however, these proposals were eliminated at the insistence of Kades and Rowell, who found them too specific and 'not constitutional material'. Rowell argued that the social guarantees also were controversial and would arouse stiff opposition from the Japanese, perhaps even endangering the SCAP draft in its entirety. He added, 'You cannot impose a new mode of social thought on a country by law.' But wasn't that exactly what SCAP's constitutional convention was proposing to do, Sirota wondered. The debate pitted idealist against pragmatist, and the clash of opinion became so heated that Whitney finally intervened, siding with his deputy chief. 'To this day', Sirota wrote later, 'I believe that the Americans responsible for the final version of the draft of the new constitution inflicted a great loss on Japanese women.' Nevertheless, when bilateral negotiations over the final form of the text began, Kades gave Sirota his full support. During the all-night joint session of 4–5 March, the Japanese argued fiercely against the draft's equal rights provisions, but Kades stood firm. 'There is no way in which the article can be faulted', he insisted, and the Japanese side gave in.[69]

In the context of the times, Sirota's contribution to the text was revolutionary. The US Constitution contains no explicit protections for women. In 1972, after a debate spanning 50 years, the US Congress finally passed the Equal Rights Amendment, but the measure failed to obtain the necessary ratification of 38 states by 1982 and was never incorporated into the Constitution. Japan's national charter protects the position of women in marriage and in the family and in this respect is more progressive even than most European charters.

Esman's call for active Japanese participation in the drafting process was rejected, but, while Japanese were not present physically, many of their ideas were very much alive in the minds of the GS working committees. The popular constitutional proposals submitted by various Japanese groups have already been discussed, but there were other avenues of influence, as well. As a member of Weed's informal policy alliance, Sirota, for instance, was certainly aware of the demands of the Japanese women's movement through activists such as Katō Shizue, who frequented the Weed group. The Civil Rights Subcommittee's labour provisions (Articles 27 and 28), too, may have been enriched indirectly by Japanese input. Article 27 states that 'All people shall have the right and the obligation to work. Standards for wages, hours, rest and other working conditions shall be fixed by law. Children shall not be exploited.' Article 28 stipulates that 'The right of workers to organise and bargain collectively is guaranteed.' Nearly identical demands had been advanced in late 1945 by the Japanese Labour Legislation Commission, an ad hoc consultative group of union activists, reform bureaucrats and liberal academics created by the Shidehara Cabinet. The Commission worked closely with Economic and Scientific Section's Labour Division in enacting the Labour Union Law of 22 December. In the drafting process, Labour Division consulted frequently with Government Section, which was kept informed of the Japanese proposals, particularly the insistence on fixed working standards. Labour Division Chief William Karpinsky later asserted that many of the principles formulated conjointly by the Labour Legislative Commission and Labour Division found their way into the GS constitutional draft.[70]

The accuracy of that statement cannot be corroborated, but it is reasonable to assume that Japanese ideas percolated into the MacArthur text from many sources. Unlike the Soviet and Weimar charters, the US Constitution contains no explicit labour rights guarantees. The inclusion of such provisions in Japan's 1946 Constitution probably reflects not only the influence of European and Soviet models but also the long-standing Japanese demands incorporated, with GS concurrence, into the Labour Union Law some six weeks before Government Section's constitutional convention took up its work.

Japan's 'second surrender'

On 13 February, officials of the Shidehara government, as yet unaware of the MacArthur draft, met with GHQ officials in the Sun Room of Foreign Minister Yoshida Shigeru's official residence in Azabu, Tokyo. They were there, they thought, to discuss the final Matsumoto draft. Present for the Japanese side were Yoshida, Matsumoto, Shirasu Jirō (adviser to the Central Liaison Office), and the Foreign Ministry's interpreter Hasegawa Motokichi. All of the Japanese knew English well. Representing Government Section were Whitney, Kades, Hussey and Rowell. Shirasu, Yoshida's 'front man', acted as go-between for the two sides in intensive negotiations that would extend into early March.

Whitney immediately stunned the Japanese by telling them that the Matsumoto effort was 'wholly unacceptable as a document of freedom and democracy'. The Americans then abruptly handed the Japanese the MacArthur draft. Whitney explained:

> The Supreme Commander . . . being fully conscious of the desperate need of the people of Japan for a liberal and enlightened Constitution that will defend them

from the injustices and the arbitrary controls of the past, has approved this document and directed that I present it to you as one embodying the principles which in his opinion the situation in Japan demands.[71]

Whitney and company then adjourned to the sunlit garden. When the urbane British-educated Shirasu joined Whitney's group later, the General delivered 'one more psychological shaft', remarking that he had been enjoying the warmth of Japan's atomic sunshine. At that instant, a B-29 bomber happened to roar overhead, leaving, in Whitney's words, 'an indescribable but profound' impression.[72]

After the Japanese had read the draft, Whitney continued his psychological assault, noting that MacArthur 'has been unyielding in defence of your emperor against increasing pressure from outside to render him subject to war criminal investigations'. But, he warned, 'The Supreme Commander is not omnipotent. He feels that acceptance of the provisions of this new Constitution would render the Emperor practically unassailable'. Whitney went on to say that the Japanese were under no compulsion to accept SCAP's constitutional draft but added bluntly – and without MacArthur's authorisation – that, if they did not accept it before the next elections, the Supreme Commander was prepared to submit this statement of principles directly to the people. 'By this instrument', Whitney said, the Supreme Commander 'has offered Japan, a nation in defeat, the opportunity to assume moral leadership among the other nations of the world.'

The Japanese side reacted with shock and dismay, characterising the MacArthur text as 'thoroughly alien', 'something out of the ordinary' and 'no small embarrassment'. The minutes of the 13 February conference, however, show Whitney anxious to avoid any overt suggestion of force. Like the Supreme Commander and his closest aides, he was intent on saving the Royalists from themselves. The consequences of outright rejection were clear, he said. 'General MacArthur feels that this is the last opportunity for the conservative groups, considered by many to be reactionary, to remain in power. . . . I cannot emphasize too strongly that the acceptance of the draft Constitution is your only hope of survival.' Whitney's psychological ploy, as it turned out, was simple good advice.[73]

Matsumoto informed the Shidehara Cabinet of the content of the American version on 19 February. Several ministers objected strenuously, but Welfare Minister Ashida Hitoshi argued that mounting pressure from popular pro-democracy forces made acceptance unavoidable. Should General Headquarters take the Matsumoto and MacArthur drafts to the people, he said, the Japanese public would vote overwhelmingly for the SCAP document, humiliating the government and no doubt precipitating its fall. Furthermore, MacArthur was prepared to see the charter promulgated as the work of the government. (In fact, he could not do otherwise. SWNCC-228 had warned against imposing basic reforms unilaterally, and MacArthur had to convince the Far Eastern Commission that he was acting within his authority.) Nonetheless, the Cabinet asked Shidehara to make a final personal appeal to the Supreme Commander. First, however, the Prime Minister asked

Whitney for more time. The GS Chief gave the Japanese side until 22 February (not by coincidence George Washington's birthday) to reach agreement on the GHQ text.

On 21 February, Shidehara met MacArthur in one of the most significant personal encounters of the General's career in Japan. The two men shared some common ground, and the discussion lasted three hours. Shidehara was known as a 'liberalist'. As foreign minister from 1924 to 1927 and again from 1929 to 1931, he had advocated peaceful diplomacy and cooperation with China as opposed to the policy of coercion advocated by hard-liners in the military. Genuine anti-militarism was not an option in Shidehara's day, but he consistently opposed the bellicose policies of the war cabal. Unable to prevent the Manchurian invasion in late 1931, he resigned, retiring from the forefront of political life. Shidehara's meeting with MacArthur dealt mainly with Article Nine. The Premier noted that he approved of the anti-belligerency concept in principle but expressed reservations about the wisdom of an absolute ban on waging war or maintaining armed forces. MacArthur replied that Australia and the Soviet Union feared that Japan might one day embark on a war of vengeance. Japan therefore should avoid even the appearance of rebuilding its armed forces. If the government rejected the peace clauses, he said, it would never regain the trust of the international community; Japan had nothing to lose and everything to gain by accepting the pacifist article. Shidehara reluctantly agreed. Uppermost in his mind was Whitney's warning that anything less than full compliance could jeopardise the Emperor's personal safety as well as the future of the Throne.[74]

Popular sovereignty, non-belligerency and basic civil liberties were bitter pills to swallow, but the Old Guard reluctantly conceded defeat. On 22 February, the Cabinet agreed that acquiescence was ultimately in the ruling élite's best interests and tentatively accepted the MacArthur document as the basis for a Japanese text. No one, however, seemed to grasp fully the political import of the American model – indeed, the English version had not been circulated. By 5 March, however, at least some of its implications had become clear. On that date, Shidehara's ministers wept openly when the Prime Minister informed them they had no choice but to endorse formally a summary government draft based on the American transcript. Given the document's revolutionary implications, its acceptance, one historian has written, represented Japan's second surrender. On 6 March, the government made the text public, formally submitting to the Japanese people the draft of 'a new and enlightened constitution' that preserved the Throne but left it 'without governmental authority or state property, subject to the people's will, a symbol of the people's unity'.[75]

THE EMPEROR AND ARTICLE NINE

'Imperial democracy'
The most compelling reason for official Japanese acceptance was uncertainty about the fate of the Emperor, a concern that MacArthur's headquarters fully shared. Chapter I of the MacArthur version, entitled simply 'The Emperor', established the

principle of popular sovereignty and made the monarch the symbol of the state. The Byrnes Note of 11 August 1945 had implied vaguely that the Japanese people might be permitted to determine the fate of the monarchy themselves, but SWNCC-228 of 7 January 1946 made that point explicit. Preservation of the Throne also was consistent with the Initial Post-Surrender Policy (SWNCC-150/4A), which authorised Occupation authorities to work through, without necessarily supporting, existing governmental institutions. None of these documents made an unequivocal commitment to the emperor system, however, and from late 1945 through early 1946, there were indications that a significant segment of Japanese opinion actually was indifferent to the monarchy, despite the Supreme Commander's extravagant predictions of governmental breakdown and social chaos should the Emperor be tried for war crimes. Once again, the final decision would be MacArthur's.

As indicated above, at his first meeting with Hirohito on 27 September 1945, the Supreme Commander had professed to be deeply moved by the Emperor's alleged offer to accept sole responsibility for the war. The General later recalled that he decided then to exempt the sovereign from war crimes prosecution. These are questionable assertions, however, and independent research has never substantiated them. The evidence suggests that MacArthur, in basic sympathy with his military secretary Bonner Fellers, had made up his mind to retain the emperor system at a much earlier date. In any case, a series of rapidly converging events, all of them a potential threat to Imperial sovereignty, spurred MacArthur to action in late January 1946. These included lobbying by the China Crowd in Washington for a punitive peace, the Joint Chiefs' war crimes query of November 1945, Allied public opinion, the Australian crusade to indict Hirohito, SWNCC-228 of early January, the Tokyo visit of the Far Eastern Advisory Commission in mid-January and rumours from within the Palace itself of a possible abdication. On 25 January, as discussed, MacArthur cabled the Pentagon advising against indictment, and a week later, following the premature release of the Matsumoto Constitution and the adverse public reaction to it, decided to work up a charter of his own – one that would anchor a politically powerless but intact Imperial system firmly within the framework of a democratic and radically demilitarised body politic. In early February, when Whitney and Kades charged Government Section's drafting committee with the task of producing a new national charter, a staff officer asked if it were to be assumed that Hirohito would not be tried as a war criminal. Whitney and Kades reportedly confirmed that supposition, noting that the Emperor had rendered service and support to the Occupation.[76]

The draft of Article One on the Emperor delivered up by the GS Committee shortly afterwards, however, exceeded what even MacArthur had envisaged. The General's notes had called for a constitutional monarch to serve as head of state. Lieutenant George A. Nelson and Ensign Richard A. Poole, in consultation with the Steering Committee, made the sovereign 'the symbol of the State and of the Unity of the People', eliminating any political role but preserving the prestige of the Imperial institution and its potent ideological ('spiritual') dimension. The origins of this clause are not clear. One historian has suggested three convergent sources which by

February 1946 had been assimilated as 'givens' by the drafting committee. These were the British monarchy, derivative American wartime conceptions and post-surrender Japanese proposals.[77]

As noted in chapter 5, the Royalist views of Sir George Sansom were shared by his disciple Hugh Borton, friend Joseph Grew and other highly placed Japan specialists. Britain's softening of the Potsdam language to suggest the possibility of indirect rule, and imply some degree of post-defeat Imperial continuity, reflected that viewpoint. It seems safe to say that Grew and, indeed, most American policy-makers implicitly used the British monarchy as their point of reference when considering the Japanese system. English theorists had long posited the Crown as an abstract integrative symbol necessary to deflect class antagonisms and maintain domestic order. The 1931 Statute of Westminster, drafted by Arthur Balfour, greatly enlarged on that interpretation, proclaiming the Royal institution, in addition, 'the symbol of the British Commonwealth'. In 1942, Grew used a similar argument when he wrote that Japan's Imperial system should be preserved 'as a symbol' and enlisted in the cause of peace. Japan specialist Helen Mears sounded a similar note in a 1943 essay on the Emperor, who was, she said, a 'symbolic leader' representing 'the idea of national unity'.[78] Fellers couched his ideas in a similar idiom. Moreover, Grew, who had read Mears's essay and recommended it highly to friends, maintained a correspondence with MacArthur and discreetly advised him to tread softly on issues affecting the Throne.

Finally, on the Japanese side, liberal and progressive thinkers also grasped the utility of a reformed monarchy. As indicated above, the Socialists and the Constitutional Research Association both had advocated retaining the emperor system but divesting the sovereign of his secular powers and restricting his duties to purely ceremonial functions. Conservatives, for whom such Imperial symbolism signified something quite different, would later appropriate this discourse, investing it with their own ultra-traditionalist meanings. In 1932, Satomi Kishio, a commentator on the Imperial system, had defined the monarchy as 'the highest symbol in Japanese society and state'. In 1962, Satomi noted that the new Constitution had simply codified what already existed as 'an unwritten category'. There is evidence that the Matsumoto Committee consulted Satomi's writings in October 1945. Yoshida Shigeru, too, afterwards noted matter-of-factly that this 'is what Japanese Emperors have always been'.[79] In any event, when the concept of a 'symbolic emperor' sprung fully formed and conceptually untroubled from the American drafting board, it found immediate acceptance on all sides.

Whatever the origins of the symbolic emperor system, Hirohito, under intense pressure to abdicate by early 1946, also understood its usefulness. On 22 February, he gave his unreserved consent to the MacArthur constitutional draft. When the government announced the outline of the new Constitution on 6 March, the Emperor, in the pre-surrender tradition, issued an Imperial rescript ordering the government to 'revise drastically' the Meiji charter. On 20 June, Hirohito personally presented the finalised draft to the National Diet as an amendment to the 1890

Imperial Constitution. And, on 3 November, it was another Imperial rescript –
vetted by Occupation censors – that promulgated the new charter. This was done with
SCAP's full concordance. Indeed, at MacArthur's behest, Whitney had assigned
Chapter I of the Constitution to the monarchy 'in deference to the Emperor and his
place in the hearts of the Japanese people'. Thus, with Occupation encouragement,
the sovereign was able to place his imprimatur on the document, fusing, in the words
of one scholar, 'revolution from above' with 'imperial democracy'.[80]

The tradition of divine right died hard. The crowds that gathered in front of the
Imperial Palace to celebrate the birth of the Constitution in early November 1946
were cheering the Emperor, not their revised national charter. As well they might, for
some nine months earlier, on 19 February 1946, at the urging of CI&E's Kermit
Dyke, Hirohito had begun a five-year pilgrimage around the country designed to
bolster his personal popularity and ensure the preservation of the dynasty. The idea
of a Royal tour is thought to have originated with British Japanophile Reginald
Blyth, who, with Dyke's assent, sounded out the Imperial household through his
primary conduit to the Palace, Peers' School Principal Yamanashi Katsunoshin. The
Emperor readily agreed, and MacArthur embraced the proposal with enthusiasm.
The sovereign was accompanied on his regal peregrinations by Imperial household
staff and protected by a phalanx of US Military Police in Army jeeps, that puissant
Occupation symbol now inextricably associated in the popular imagination with the
Imperial charisma.

The Emperor embarked on his 'auspicious visitations' (*gyōkō*) with famine looming, strikes proliferating and the war crimes trials in full session, touring isolated farm
and fishing villages, factories, mines, schools and hospitals. His zeal for the task was
unmistakable, and, in the words of one historian, 'not even enlightened statesmen
could have matched this performance'. The reaction of his erstwhile subjects was
described as frenzied. At government expense, Hirohito eventually visited every prefecture except Okinawa (he would not reach Hokkaido until 1954), interrupting his
trips only briefly in 1948 when GHQ asked him to assume a low profile prior to the
war crimes judgments. From the start, the Imperial cavalcade drew hostile comment
from the Communist Party and the Far Eastern Commission in Washington, where
objections were raised by Australia, New Zealand and the Soviet Union. In late 1947,
an American correspondent warned that 'Japanese emperor-worship is like a stout
tree that bends before a Western breeze but does not break'. SCAP's efforts to
democratise the monarch, he wrote, 'bid fair to make him an even greater symbol
of Japanese nationalism than ever before'. Prophetic words, indeed.[81]

Article Nine
Chapter II of the 'MacArthur Constitution' was entitled 'Renunciation of War'.
This, too, was cause among Imperial conservatives for weeping and the gnashing of
teeth. The first clause of the 'no-war, no arms' provision read: 'Aspiring sincerely to
an international peace based on justice and order, the Japanese people forever
renounce war as a sovereign right of the nation and the threat or use of force as means

Photo 38. Flanked by American MPs and Japanese police officials, Emperor Hirohito visits Ōgaki City in Gifu Prefecture, 25 October 1946. The GHQ-sponsored Imperial tours were designed to give the monarchy a democratic face lift and counter Allied efforts to make the sovereign testify before the Tokyo Tribunal (Kyodo).

of settling international disputes'. The second clause stipulated that: 'In order to accomplish the aim of the preceding paragraph, land, sea and air forces, as well as other war potential, will never be maintained. The right of belligerency of the State will not be recognized.'

SCAP derived the title and spirit of Chapter II from the Kellogg–Briand (Paris) Pact of 1928 – the same instrument of international law to which the Tokyo War Crimes Tribunal traced its legitimacy. The so-called Pact of Paris required the 65 nations (including Japan) that eventually ratified it to 'condemn recourse to war for the solution of international controversies, and renounce it as an instrument of national policy in their relations with one another' (Article One). Contracting parties agreed that the settlement of all disputes or conflicts 'shall never be sought except by pacific means' (Article Two). Nor was radical disarmament a novel concept. The Moscow Foreign Ministers' Conference, for instance, had discussed a proposal to prohibit Japan from possessing arms for 25 years, and during the war, both Washington and London had made similar pronouncements. MacArthur's initial proposal went far beyond such considerations, however. In his three 'musts' of constitutional revision, the General had included a phrase that specifically banned wars 'even for preserving [Japan's] own security'. From this flowed naturally the notion of permanent disarmament. Kades, however, personally considered the principle that a country could not defend itself from external aggression troubling, unrealistic and legally dubious. He promptly excised this phrase from the GS draft, thereby altering the content of MacArthur's memo and opening an area of ambiguity that would generate intense constitutional debate over 'legitimate self-defence' in the years to come. Kades later explained his decision as follows. 'I thought the elimination of "even for preserving its own security" from Point II of the MacArthur notes left Japan with its inherent right of self-preservation.' Had he pondered the issue more deeply at the time, he noted, 'I probably would have written in: "except to repel invasions or suppress insurrection".'[82]

There can be no doubt, however, that Japan had foresworn the right of national self-defence. Both MacArthur and Yoshida Shigeru were convinced at the time that such was the case. On 26 June 1946, Prime Minister Yoshida told the House of Representatives' Special Committee on the Constitution that Japan had renounced 'the right of armed self-defence as well as of belligerency'. He asserted that 'self-defence' had been used by the militarists to justify Japan's recent wars of aggression. Yoshida remained consistent in his views of the non-belligerency clauses through early 1950, and even after the Korean War, he steadfastly opposed rearmament (albeit not from pacifist principle: Yoshida was not against remilitarisation at some future date but felt that publicly endorsing such a policy prematurely would exacerbate international distrust and frustrate his hopes of ending the Occupation quickly – see chapter 10). As late as 1961, Yoshida asserted that he still adhered to the view that Article Nine did not require amendment. Until 1950, MacArthur, too, defended Article Nine in its entirety, rejecting out of hand a Pentagon overture to partially rearm in 1948 (chapter 10). More importantly, however, many Japanese also were committed to a strict pacifist interpretation. When Japan, at SCAP's insistence, began rearming in mid-1950, most people believed that the government was violating the Constitution; there was a deep sense of betrayal, and the public reacted with indignation and angry protest.[83]

The precise origins of Article Nine remain obscure. According to Shidehara, the war-renouncing clause was the brainchild of MacArthur. MacArthur later attributed the idea to Shidehara, as did Justin Williams Jr, although recent scholarship casts doubt on that thesis. Political scientist Theodore McNelly believes that Article Nine was first suggested by Whitney and Kades, and Kades himself, in an article written before his death, lent support to that view.[84] There are other possibilities, as well. Japan's was not the first charter to draw its inspiration from the Kellogg–Briand Pact. The Philippine Constitution of November 1935 had claimed that distinction 11 years earlier by renouncing war as a means of conducting national policy. MacArthur had just been appointed military adviser to the Philippines when the charter was promulgated, leading some scholars to assert that the origins of Japan's war-renouncing clauses are to be sought in the 1935 Philippine Constitution.[85]

Article Nine, of course, was a far more explicit and radical renunciation of belligerency than the Pact of Paris. Whatever its exact lineage, Chapter II had stamped on it the bold, iconoclastic style of MacArthur. Certainly, the Supreme Commander's lavish praise for the anti-war article suggests a creator's pride. The General lauded Article Nine as one of the Occupation's most important contributions to Japan and to humanity. It was, he boasted at the time, 'one further step in the evolution of mankind, under which nations would develop, for mutual protection against war, a yet higher law of international social and political morality'. MacArthur even recommended that the United Nations adopt Japan's anti-war clauses. 'Thereby', he said, 'may we further universal adherence to that higher law in the preservation of peace which finds full and unqualified approval in the enlightened conscience of the peoples of the world.'[86]

Article Nine indeed reflected the aspirations of a war-weary world for a lasting peace. Its originality lies in the premise that peace and security are better secured through diplomacy and the non-violent resolution of international conflicts than the stockpiling of armaments and war matériel. In other words, world peace actively pursued by an aware citizenry and its democratically elected representatives is the surest means of national self-defence – a revolutionary proposition, surely, but one that embodied the highest ideals of the immediate postwar world. It is small wonder that so many Japanese, spiritually exhausted and disillusioned by 15 years of militarism culminating in humiliating defeat, would embrace this pacifist Constitution as their own.[87]

'Japanising' the constitution

After 13 February, when MacArthur's headquarters handed its draft to the government, the document underwent a series of revisions. The Japanese side presented their first revisions to Government Section on 4 March. Following intense bilateral negotiations, the government publicly announced its amended version on 17 April. Submitted to the 90th Imperial Diet on 20 June, the charter underwent further modification and was finally passed by both houses on 7 October.

Occupation censors worked hard to disguise SCAP's role in drafting the document and maintain the fiction that it was an exclusively Japanese endeavour. On the face of it, this thin pretence was difficult to uphold. A Canadian journalist expressed the reaction of many observers, Japanese and foreign, when he called it an alien instrument imposed by force and then 'represented as a native product, when any Japanese high school student simply by reading it could perceive its foreign origin'.[88] In a sense, however, the document was readily understandable, for the language was familiar. Unlike the Meiji Constitution, which had been written intentionally in a laboured, archaic legalese (*bungotai*) difficult for ordinary Japanese to comprehend, the new charter was phrased in the vernacular tongue (*kōgotai*), partly as a result of intense lobbying by citizens' groups such as the People's National Language Alliance (*Kokumin no Kokugo Renmei*).

In yet another sense, the final result, although close in form and substance to the MacArthur model, was more than a simple translation of the English text. A group of Japanese officials led by Satō Tatsuo, Deputy Director of the Cabinet Legislation Bureau and a member of the defunct Matsumoto Committee, carefully reworked the

GHQ version, subtly 'Japanising' it in the process. Satō was assisted in this effort by Irie Toshirō, Director of the Cabinet Legislation Bureau, and Kanamori Tokujirō, the author of the Liberal Party's early constitutional proposal and, from June 1946, Matsumoto's replacement as minister of state in the Yoshida Cabinet.[89] Despite the undeniably foreign flavour of parts of the document, Satō and his colleagues used the ambiguities of Japanese syntax to alter or nuance the connotation of the original English. Government Section acquiesced to many changes in wording in order to preserve the main features of its draft. Kades's standing orders from Whitney were to pose no objection to any Japanese proposal that did not violate basic principles. In general, the government succeeded in imparting to the text an 'illocutionary force' not present in the English, implying that the state, supported by the people, is responsible for ensuring democracy and civil liberties. The MacArthur version made the people alone ultimately responsible for their form of government.[90]

Some government changes were obvious and inevitable, such as the substitution of a bicameral legislature for the GHQ-proposed unicameral body (MacArthur's staff had assumed that abolition of the peerage would entail the elimination of the House of Peers). SCAP agreed to the modification on condition that both lower and upper houses consist of elected members and that the House of Representatives dominate the House of Councillors. The Japanese side also scrapped an article, dubbed the 'Red Provision', that would have enabled the government to nationalise the country's land and natural resources.[91]

In several instances, however, Japanese jurists attempted to weave a conservative bias into the text by deleting passages and manipulating phraseology. In some cases, the government's finest legal minds failed to achieve their aims. For example, Irie, Kanamori and Satō tried to substitute *shikō* ('highest'), an archaic weasel word devoid of substantive meaning, for the perfectly clear *shuken* ('sovereignty') to dilute the potency of the Anglo-American doctrine of popular will. The use of vague phrases to rob concrete rights guarantees of their content was a common ploy. In late June, two Lower House members, Communist Nosaka Sanzō and Socialist Kuroda Hisao, spotted the disparity in the Japanese and English drafts and demanded an explanation. Shortly afterwards, on 2 July, the Far Eastern Commission issued a policy paper ('Basic Principles for Japan's New Constitution') asking for a clear statement that sovereign power resides in the people. Whitney promptly despatched Kades to meet Satō's group and press for an unambiguous rendering of the phrase 'sovereignty rests with the people'. At Kades's insistence, the Japanese side reluctantly agreed to the change, abandoning this attempt to preserve a suggestion of Imperial authority and weaken the thrust of Article One. Satō and company employed other ruses, such as placing the war-renouncing and no-arms clauses in the Preamble instead of in Chapter II, but these, too, failed.[92]

In a few instances, representatives of the people had their say. The Socialist Party presented a motion to abolish the peerage, and surprisingly the Diet passed it, eliminating the ranks and special privileges of 913 families. Barons, marquises, dukes and princes passed into history, and another pillar of Imperial authority crumbled. The

Socialists also successfully inserted Article 25 in Chapter III ('Rights and Duties of the People') guaranteeing the public 'the right to maintain the minimum standards of wholesome and cultured living'. A second clause obligated the state to 'use its endeavours for the promotion and extension of social welfare and security, and of public health'. At the centre of this initiative was Katō Shizue, the Socialist feminist and Upper House representative, who fought an uphill battle, remarkably similar to that waged a few months earlier by Beate Sirota, to secure virtually the same guarantees: the protection of mothers and the rights of working women. 'Women's uniqueness', Katō said, 'must be recognized and provisions for the special protection of pregnancy, birth and care for children must be stated clearly.' Like Sirota, Katō lost the battle, but in Article 25, the Socialists introduced a general statement of principle extending social protection to all people.[93] Katō and other women, both inside and outside of MacArthur's headquarters, would carry this struggle into the legislative arena in 1947, winning important victories in the Civil and Criminal Code reforms, the passage of the Labour Standards Law and the establishment of a Women's and Minors' Bureau inside the new Labour Ministry (chapter 7).

Elsewhere, however, Japanese legal experts, employing a kind of legislative legerdemain, registered subtle but significant gains, one of which vitiated a provision in Chapter VIII on local self-government that would have granted municipalities a substantial degree of home rule (chapter 7). Another flick of the draftman's wrist effectively wrote Korean and Formosan residents out of the Constitution. This was accomplished between early March and June 1946 when the government submitted its final draft to the Diet. Satō and colleagues deleted or altered two key articles that the Civil Rights Subcommittee had inserted in the MacArthur version protecting the rights of foreigners in general. This very deliberate revision, part of a seemingly minor debate that SCAP lost perhaps without fully realising it, denied these minorities equal protection under the law (chapter 9).

Article Nine modified

The Japanese side scored another victory by artfully manipulating the wording of Article Nine to suggest a finely shaded interpretation different from the purport of the original English. This modification has been attributed to Ashida Hitoshi, but Kanamori Tokujirō is probably the real author. In late June, following the government's submission to the Diet of its fourth and final draft, Ashida was elected to head the Lower House's Special Committee on Revision of the Imperial Constitution. From 25 July to 20 August, he also chaired a Lower House subcommittee charged with producing an amended version of the government draft.

In a complex process that remains unclear, Ashida placed qualifying phrases at the beginning of each of Article Nine's clauses. At the head of the renunciation of war paragraph was added 'Aspiring sincerely to an international peace based on justice and order'. In front of the 'no-arms' clause was added 'For the above purpose', which was later changed to 'In order to accomplish the aims of the preceding paragraph'. But Ashida also had reversed the order of the clauses in the government draft, so that

Photo 39. From riches to working garb. The abolition of the peerage and postwar inflation forced many former aristocrats to earn a living the hard way. Here Prince Kaya Tsunenori and his wife sell ice cream from a small shop in Kamakura owned by the Prince. 31 July, 1948 (New York Times).

the 'no-arms' provision came first, the stronger 'no-war' statement second. Kanamori suggested delicately that the renunciation of war should come before that of arms, telling the House subcommittee in convoluted but carefully contrived language that the change might enable Japan to retain a military capability for its own defence. Kanamori's proposal carried the day, although only he and Satō Tatsuo appear to have understood its full implications. The article as finally adopted read:

> Aspiring sincerely to an international peace based on justice and order, the Japanese people forever renounce war as a sovereign right of the nation and the threat or use of force as a means of settling international disputes.
> *In order to accomplish the aims of the preceding paragraph*, land, sea, and air forces, as well as other war potential, will never be maintained. The right of belligerency of the state will not be recognised [author's italics].

Article Nine conceivably could now be construed as renouncing the maintenance of armed forces *only* as a means of settling international disputes. In other words, abjuring the right of belligerency in aggressive war did not necessarily nullify the right to deter aggression against Japan. Ashida later insisted that this had been his intention all along, although there is no evidence to support such an assertion. In any event, he claimed sole credit for the additions, which subsequently became known as the 'Ashida Amendment'. On 3 November 1946, the day the Constitution was promulgated, he proclaimed that Article Nine applied to wars of aggression only and did not preclude the threat or use of force to defend the nation from external attack. Kades, who assumed that Japan would be able to maintain at least a home guard, understood the change and approved it immediately, and without informing Whitney or MacArthur. In 1954, when Japan's Self-Defence Forces were created, the new Defence Agency would invoke the Ashida Amendment to defend the constitutionality of the SDF, telling the Lower House that Article Nine does not prohibit military preparedness to ensure national security.[94]

Like Washington, the Far Eastern Commission had been kept in the dark about the MacArthur Constitution, but once informed, it made a number of recommendations. Among these were demands for a clear statement on popular sovereignty, a strengthening of the universal suffrage clause, insuring the primacy of the Diet and the selection of a majority of cabinet members and the prime minister from sitting legislators. With respect to the Ashida Amendment, the FEC raised a major objection. On 21 September 1946, at the 27th meeting of the Commission, Dr S. H. Tan, Nationalist China's representative, noted in alarm that the 'Article has been so revised . . . as to permit of an interpretation which might in effect permit the maintenance by Japan of land, sea and air forces for purposes . . . such as, for instance, self defense.' Tan suggested that militarist elements planned to rearm using the loopholes in the revised peace clauses. The Canadian delegate and deputy chair of the Third Committee (Constitutional and Legal Reform), Ralph E. Collins, agreed with Tan and recommended that the Commission introduce a Soviet-proposed stipulation that all Cabinet members be civilians (*bunmin*). On 25 September, the Commission adopted that proposal as a safeguard against a government attempt to circumvent Article Nine's ban on a standing military. SCAP bowed to FEC pressure and prevailed on the Japanese to incorporate into Article 66 the phrase, 'The Prime Minister and other Ministers of State must be civilians.'[95] The insertion of this clause was paradoxical, however, for it implied the existence of the very armed forces whose authority it was designed to deny, a nuance that has not escaped the contemporary foes of Article Nine.

Constitutional review

When the Japanese government unveiled its outline draft on 6 March 1946, a stunned FEC responded by demanding the right to 'pass on' the final text and determine whether it was consistent with the Potsdam Proclamation. The great haste with which SCAP had orchestrated the drafting process, it said, raised questions about the extent to which the document represented the 'freely expressed will of the Japanese people'. MacArthur ignored the request, and on 10 April, the FEC passed a resolution demanding that GHQ send a representative to Washington to report in person. This time, the Supreme Commander replied, telling the Commission that, in Japan, he alone was vested with executive powers and that his decisions were not subject to FEC approval. Members took this as an affront to the dignity of the Allied body, but the American representative successfully forestalled further action on the issue, and all members but the Soviet Union approved the document in principle on 25 September 1946.

Australia and New Zealand were not placated, however, and at their insistence, on 17 October, the FEC called for a review of the Constitution within one to two years of its entry into effect. MacArthur notified Yoshida of this in January 1947, but the Japanese premier took no action. A constitutional review, he feared, would encourage liberal and left-of-centre opinion to demand a clearer statement of the Emperor's status, stronger labour guarantees and other measures at odds with the conservative position. At MacArthur's request, the FEC decision was not announced publicly in Japan until March 1948, and when it was, as Yoshida had foreseen, it prompted several proposals for radical reform from private groups. One of these, the Public Law Forum (*Kōhō Kenkyūkai*), recommended changing the conservative *Nihon kokumin* ('Japanese nationals') to *Nihon jinmin* ('Japanese people'); strengthening the popular sovereignty clause; making the Emperor the emblem, not the symbol, of the state; and prohibiting individuals as well as the nation from waging war. Yoshida and MacArthur discouraged these dangerous thoughts, and a popular review of the national charter never took place. The FEC began its pro forma scrutiny of the Constitution in January 1949, completing it in early May of that year. The Commission raised three points for clarification: the position of aliens under the Constitution, the power of the Supreme Court in constitutional matters and rules for the dissolution of the House of Representatives. But this was a footnote to history that passed without public notice or official comment.[96]

PART IV

The Later Reforms

CHAPTER 7

Institutional and Economic Reforms

With the purge and war crimes trials underway, a democratically elected Diet in place and a new constitution being deliberated, SCAP turned its attention to the institutional mainstays of the Old Order: police and local government, the bureaucracy, labour controls, the *zaibatsu*, and landlordism. The reform of these systems was carried out under the close supervision of GHQ by the first Yoshida Cabinet (May 1946–May 1947) and its successor, a tripartite coalition headed by Socialist Katayama Tetsu, which governed from June 1947 to February 1948. The Katayama coalition – the only Socialist-dominated government of the Occupation period – included right-wing Socialists and two conservative parties, the Democrats and the People's Cooperatives. MacArthur's New Dealers welcomed the centrist Katayama, whom they viewed as Japan's first truly democratic prime minister and, during his stewardship, established a close working relationship with the government. Katayama was replaced by Ashida Hitoshi in March 1948, by which time, the major administrative and economic reforms had been implemented.

LOCAL GOVERNMENT AND THE BUREAUCRACY

GHQ had relied on the police, local government and bureaucracy to carry out its early reform objectives, and these institutions received minimal attention during the first phase of the Occupation. The police and the bureaucracy, in particular, were too entrenched, too vital to public order and too central to the implementation of SCAP's liberalising project to be immediately and drastically overhauled. By 1947, however, they had become a threat to the continued success of the reform effort, and MacArthur's headquarters set about diffusing this concentration of bureaucratic power.

The police state

Organised under the Home Ministry's Police Bureau, the prewar police system was the backbone of the powerful and highly centralised state created during the Meiji era. Together with the Imperial Army, it emerged as one of the twin bulwarks of militarism during the 1930s. The police were a paramilitary organisation wielding judicial and semi-judicial powers and broad administrative authority in addition to their responsibility for maintaining public order. They had been trained, in the words of SCAP analysts, 'to protect the government from the people', and their duties covered every aspect of public and private life. Many police functions, such as the surveillance and censorship of individuals and organisations, government officials and even elections, clearly were incompatible with a democratic society. Law-enforcement agencies worked through a national network of local neighbourhood associations (*tonari-gumi*) that functioned collectively as a communal spy system. Imposed first in Formosa, Korea and Manchuria, the *tonari-gumi* were reorganised in Japan proper in 1940 by Imperial Ordinance no. 17 and placed under the Imperial Rule Assistance Association. In the eyes of SCAP, the 'block organisations' were a 'feudalistic . . . institution, by means of which the personal lives, activities and even the thoughts of the people of Japan were brought under the effective overall control of a mere handful of central government officials'.[1]

Police control was an integral facet of Japanese modernisation. In 1887, the Meiji government enacted the Peace Preservation Law to curb popular dissent in general and suppress the Freedom and People's Rights Movement, then advocating civil liberties and a democratic constitution, in particular. The law was overhauled and strengthened in 1925 and then reinforced again in 1928 to deal with Communists, anarchists, union organisers, liberals, and virtually anyone whose beliefs challenged the legitimacy of Japan's emperor-centred 'national polity' or the sanctity of private property. Political and ideological control was the domain of the Special Higher Police (*Tokkō Keisatsu*), created in 1911 to combat socialist and anarchist ideas and whose roots lay in the elaborate internal espionage system perfected by the old feudal régime. Between 1928 and 1942, more than 65,000 Japanese reportedly were arrested by the 'thought police' under the Peace Preservation Law. Communists, Socialists, anarchists, Korean nationalists, Christians, pacifists and liberal thinkers of various hues were ruthlessly repressed, and under the heel of the *Tokkō*, freedom of thought, expression and assembly virtually ceased to exist. Many detainees were summarily tortured and forced to recant their alleged 'thought crimes' via a process of forced conversion (*tenkō*), and a few died in the process. Some, such as Communist organiser Tokuda Kyūichi who endured 18 years of imprisonment and thought reform, managed to remain true to their beliefs, but others emerged from prison in 1945 broken men. Repression peaked in the years 1931–3, when some 10,000 people were jailed for ideological deviation, but continued unabated until the end of the war. The Military Police (*Kenpeitai*) added military authority to the panoply of police powers and competed with the Special Higher Police in enforcing the rule of law through terror and brutality.

Dismantling this police state and creating a modern decentralised system of democratic law enforcement became a top SCAP priority in 1947. MacArthur disbanded the Special Higher Police on 4 October 1945, but the Instrument of Surrender had exempted general police forces from disarmament and dissolution. On 17 October, MacArthur's staff ordered the Military Police dismantled and directed the civil police to take over their duties. GHQ purged police ranks from January 1946, but surveys taken in May and June indicated that more than 600 former police officers and Special Higher Police had found asylum in the labour sections of prefectural governments.

Amid Japan's chaotic post-surrender conditions, however, police forces were in disarray. Demoralised by defeat, ranks had thinned due to voluntary departures and illness, and disaffection was widespread. At Takasaki in Gunma Prefecture, police went on strike for two days in November to protest against unfair rationing practices, and in December, 50 out of 600 officers of the Imperial Guard demanded democratisation of the Guards Section and the dismissal of their chief. Such labour actions were unprecedented and, before the defeat, unimaginable. Nonetheless, the police retained many of their authoritarian powers of enforcement. In late 1945, the government asked SCAP to augment police manpower, which then stood at about 94,000 effectives, and fully re-equip the force. Worried that a refurbished and confident constabulary would hamper the implementation of reform policies, GHQ rejected the proposition.[2] Occupation authorities were well aware that the expansion of German police forces after World War I had hastened the remilitarisation of Germany under the Nazis. They were determined not to repeat that mistake.

The Police Law
A Civil Affairs Guide, 'The Japanese Police System Under Allied Occupation', provided a blueprint for remoulding the law-enforcement establishment. Compiled by the Research and Analysis Branch of the Office of Strategic Services, it was not published until 28 September 1945. The Guide analysed the prewar police system, detailing its many abuses and problems, but the manual's primary focus was on the task of maintaining internal order in post-defeat Japan. This concern pinpointed a dilemma at the very heart of occupation control: the principle of indirect rule necessitated close cooperation with and even reliance on the traditional forces of order. GHQ was committed to dismantling authoritarian police controls but was constrained to preserve and work through the existing system of law-enforcement in order to do so.

The Guide was sceptical about the Occupation's ability to completely eliminate police interference in the political process. The only sure means of preventing the abuses of the past, it noted, was to ensure civilian control by guaranteeing freedom of expression and encouraging public scrutiny and criticism of guardians of the peace. To create a force that served the people, not the state, the Guide proposed to limit police authority, purge ultra-nationalist elements, re-educate law-enforcement personnel, improve working conditions, abolish third-degree methods and other authoritarian procedures and decentralise police powers.[3]

To implement these recommendations, in the autumn of 1945, the Civil Intelligence Section's Public Safety Division commissioned two in-depth studies on the police by Lewis J. Valentine of the New York City Police Department and Oscar G. Olander, head of the Michigan State Police Force. The Metropolitan Police Mission arrived in Japan in March 1946. Assisted by Frank Meals of the US Coast Guard, Valentine and Olander submitted their final reports in June, recommending a radical decentralisation of police administration and operations. Public Safety Division had insisted on a two-track reform for rural and urban areas. Accordingly, the two police specialists proposed the establishment of autonomous Municipal Police forces based on the New York City model in towns and cities of more than 50,000 people, and the creation of a National Rural Police system to serve rural agglomerations of less than 50,000. In both instances, police were to be subject to the authority of elected government officials.

G-2's Charles Willoughby and Public Safety Division Chief Colonel Howard E. Pulliam reportedly forwarded the plan to the Yoshida Cabinet, suggesting rather deviously that it present the proposal to SCAP as a Japanese initiative. On 28 February 1947, Yoshida responded with a counter-plan that was based generally on the two reports but retained many of the old system's centralised features and proposed to boost overall police strength from 94,000 to 125,000. The Yoshida Plan immediately produced 'a certain pulling and hauling' between G-2 and Government Section. Willoughby favoured a strong *gendarmerie* sufficiently centralised to deal with civil disorders and national emergencies stemming from the 'Communist menace'. With some emotion and considerable hyperbole, Pulliam asserted that, as Hammurabi, Ghengis Khan and Cesare Borgia had relied on a centralised police, Japan could do no less. Whitney, on the other hand, demanded a radical deconcentration of authority and stoutly opposed the Yoshida Plan. An internal GS memorandum of 17 July 1947 compared the Japanese police to the Gestapo and warned that 'the maintenance of a centralised police force is a complete repudiation of the basic tenets of the Occupation and of the principles of the new Constitution'. The memorandum urged a 'full and final' decentralisation. Failure to act on the matter, it warned, constituted a threat to the future of the democratic project in Japan.[4]

Following the passage of the Local Autonomy Law in April 1947, police reform became a pressing issue that increasingly pitted Government Section against the Occupation's intelligence establishment. The inter-sectional quarrel was part of a long-running feud to determine ascendancy over basic policy, and it produced a flurry of check sheets that circulated among staff groups, carrying the battle into every corner of MacArthur's command. On 3 September, Prime Minister Katayama wrote to the General promising to revise the Yoshida Plan, which he did. While Katayama's provisions for a gradual decompression of police powers were a clear improvement over the earlier proposal, these, too, failed to satisfy Whitney. At this point, MacArthur stepped into the fray with a compromise that provided for limited centralised control via a national constabulary with circumscribed operational duties and a decentralised, independent police force at the municipal level. In a letter to the Prime Minister dated 16 September, the Supreme Commander asserted that deconcentrating the police system 'in accordance with the principle of local autonomy embodied in the Constitution' would avoid 'the potentiality of a police state' while satisfying 'all requirements of public safety'.[5] In fact, some degree of centralised authority had been preserved, but the initial victory went to Whitney's Government Section. MacArthur gave Katayama 90 days to carry the provisions in the Diet.

The Police Law was enacted on 17 December 1947, meeting MacArthur's deadline, and went into effect on 8 March the following year. It established a centrally directed National Rural Police force of 30,000 with administrative authority at the prefectural level and above and operational jurisdiction only in rural areas and municipalities with fewer than 5,000 inhabitants. The bulk of the nation's law-enforcement duties were assigned to an independent Local Municipal Police of 95,000 with administrative and operational responsibility for cities, towns and villages larger than 5,000. Moreover, women were now eligible to apply for these positions, and within a relatively short time, 2,000 uniformed female police officers were on duty in Tokyo alone, a startling reversal of traditional sex-linked roles.

The National Rural Police, financed by the central government, were placed under the Prime Minister's Office rather than the Home Ministry and made accountable to a National Public Safety Commission. Designed to guarantee the neutrality of police in political affairs, the Commission was composed of members appointed by the prime minister but remained independent of the Cabinet. The country was divided into six police regions, with public safety commissions organised at the national, regional, prefectural, and local levels, each tier enjoying a degree of independence. In a state of national emergency, however, the prime minister was authorised to take control of all law-enforcement bodies, subject to Diet approval. The administrative authority of the national police stopped at the prefectural level, where elected governors working through prefectural public safety commissions exercised operational control. The prefectural commissions were independent of the National Public Safety Commission, their members being nominated by the governor with the consent of the prefectural assembly. Below the prefecture, the Local Municipal Police maintained order in most of the nation's cities, towns and villages. They were financed locally and overseen by politically neutral municipal public safety commissions whose members were appointed by an elected mayor subject to the approval of the local assembly. By early 1948, there were nearly 1,400 local autonomous police forces across Japan.

The Police Law and the Police Duties Execution Law of 1948, which reformed police procedure, transformed Japan's law-enforcers from an élite group loyal to the Emperor and the state into a citizen's constabulary responsible, in principle, to the general public. Police functions were restricted to such duties as preserving public order, protecting lives and property, crime prevention and traffic control. Torture, illegal detention and other abusive practices were abolished. Law officers were expressly prohibited from suppressing political dissent or engaging in any form of 'thought-control'. As pre-surrender police controls dissolved under SCAP's watchful eye, the baton replaced the sabre, the traditional symbol of gendarme authority. In many respects, the police reform represented a clean break with the past. Although Government Section had won the battle, however, in the long run, the government and Willoughby's G-2 would win the war. Their combined opposition to a complete overhaul of the peace-keeping establishment would ensure the restoration of a high degree of centralised authority after 1951 (chapter 11).

Photo 40. Female law-enforcement officers on parade after graduating from the police academy. The unprecedented sight of policewomen directing traffic and patrolling neighbourhood streets epitomised the sweeping change in values that accompanied many Occupation reforms. Tokyo, 27 April 1947 (Kyodo).

Restructuring local government

Police reform was part of a broader attack on a system of authoritarian control that had its pinnacle in the Home Ministry and its base in 1.3 million neighbourhood *tonari-gumi* associations. The Prussian-inspired local government structures that relayed orders from the apex of this pyramidal edifice to the bottom were administered by the Home Ministry's Local Affairs Section. The Ministry appointed all prefectural governors, career bureaucrats whose chief ambition was to secure a post in Tokyo. Local officials were bound by a web of restrictive financial and legal regulations. SCAP characterised the Japanese administrative system as 'a monster that reached with thousands of tentacles into the home and private life of every individual Japanese'. Government Section was charged with the task of slaying this Medusa by decentralising local government and promoting municipal self-rule. Ironically, the machinery of SCAP's own highly centralised super-government, which depended on the Japanese bureaucracy to carry out its directives, tended to narrow the parameters of reform. Nonetheless, MacArthur was committed to the principle of autonomous local self-government, which he proclaimed 'a schoolhouse for democracy', and under Cecil G. Tilton, the GS Local Government Division laboured mightily from early 1946 through late 1947 to restructure municipal administration.

Local-government reform proceeded in three phases. The first consisted of a series of organic laws that revised prefectural, city, town and village codes, including those for Metropolitan Tokyo and Hokkaido. Submitted to the Diet in early July 1946, these bills contained a number of innovations, such as the right of local residents to recall public officials and demand the enactment of legislation and the right to manage local elections. Other features, however, reflected Japanese proposals for local reform that had been advanced since the 1920s. Among these were the strengthening of the power of local assemblies and the direct election of mayors and other local officials by expanded popular vote. The organic laws were drafted by SCAP's constitutional reformers, passed by the Imperial Diet and entered into force on 27 September 1946.[6] The second and third phases of local reform were the passage of the Local Autonomy Law in April 1947 and the dissolution of the Home Ministry in December 1947. Collectively, these statutes constituted the implementing legislation for the Constitution's local self-government provisions (Chapter VIII, Articles 92 through 95).

Local autonomy and the Constitution

Local Government Division's mandate was to create a grass-roots democracy by taking the administration of local affairs away from central authorities and placing it in the hands of the people. Division Chief Cecil Tilton was an ardent devolutionist whose basic tenet was 'a local answer for local problems'. In February 1946, he had drafted an early version of the MacArthur Constitution's Chapter VIII on the powers of local government, but GS Deputy Chief Charles Kades and the Steering Committee found his proposals too radical. Tilton planned to make the prefectures virtually independent of central authority by granting them the right to tax and maintain their own police forces. Municipalities also would wield broad powers of government not specified in the Constitution or parliamentary legislation. He envisaged 'something like a Greek city state', complained Kades, who dismissed Tilton's 'Chapter on Local Government' as excessive. The state, Kades asserted later, 'had a very important part to play in government. It couldn't abdicate to the localities.' Tilton enjoyed the strong backing of the Steering Committee's Lieutenant Colonel Milo Rowell, however, and the final version of Chapter VIII was a compromise between Rowell, 'a strong home-rule man', and Kades, 'a warm central government man'. The GS draft of 13 February 1946, stipulated that local public entities be responsible to local assemblies; that city, town and village officials and assembly members be elected by direct public vote; and that communities manage their own property, internal affairs and administration. At the same time, it gave local inhabitants the right to draft their own home-rule 'charters', a kind of de facto local constitution.[7]

Predictably, the Home Ministry stubbornly opposed this unprecedented award of autonomous powers. The traditional bureaucratic ethos was summed up by the expression *kanson-minpi*, 'revere officialdom, despise the people'. The Ministry found the idea of making public officials the servants, not the masters, of the people incomprehensible, and the public election of prefectural and local officials was anathema. To preserve its autocratic authority, the Ministry argued forcefully that municipal self-rule should be based on the principle of local collective responsibility to the state and that this 'communal spirit' be made explicit in the Constitution. When Government Section rejected the proposal, the Ministry ostensibly endorsed the idea of autonomy but clung tenaciously to its own interpretations of statist principle, which it managed to insinuate into the government's constitutional draft.

The Home Ministry was particularly alarmed by GHQ's home-rule clause: 'The inhabitants of metropolitan areas . . . shall be secure in their right . . . to frame their own charters within such laws as the Diet may enact.' In the government's first official revision of 4 March 1946, Satō Tatsuo and his team of legal experts replaced the word 'charter' with 'by-laws and regulations' and added the stipulation that 'Regulations concerning organisation and operations of local public entities shall be fixed by law in accordance with the principle of local autonomy.' Curiously, Government Section failed to challenge these modifications, led astray perhaps by the inclusion of the phrase 'principle of local autonomy'. By the time the Constitution was adopted by the Imperial Diet on 7 October, the word 'inhabitants' had been replaced by 'locally constituted public bodies', which were authorised simply to 'enact their own regulations within law' (Article 94). These changes effectively nullified the radical character of the original GS draft.[8]

Thus, the principle of local self-rule came to inhere not in the locality but in the state, which was empowered to 'grant' limited authority to the municipalities. This interpretation, so at odds with Occupation intent, nonetheless was consistent with the prewar theory of delegated powers elaborated by constitutional scholar Minobe Tatsukichi and other experts in administrative law. Municipal government,

Minobe said, derives its authority from the state and can have no existence prior to that of the state, a gloss that has been broadly endorsed by postwar Japanese scholarship. (The Communist Party, it should be noted, also opposed the notion of local autonomy, but for a different reason: no independent governing body, it argued, should mediate between the people and their representatives in Parliament.)[9]

The Local Autonomy Law
Despite this subtle shift in emphasis, Local Government Division's Tilton was determined to put teeth into the Constitution's local self-government guarantees, and he succeeded in engineering a thorough overhaul of the existing legislation affecting municipal government. Tilton's objective was to make the management of regional affairs by self-regulating local public entities relatively independent of central control, allow local residents to participate freely in municipal politics and give their representative bodies a voice in shaping national policy.[10] Constitutional interpretations notwithstanding, this far-reaching redistribution of power was codified in the Local Autonomy Law of 17 April 1947 and became effective simultaneously with the entry into force of the new Constitution on 3 May. Under the new law, the old city and local councils were dissolved; incumbent prefectural governors, town and city mayors, village heads and other local officials were dismissed; and new governors and municipal heads were elected by popular ballot. Representative assemblies were empowered to approve key appointments by local chief executives, override their veto by a two-thirds majority, and call for their resignation. Local inhabitants acquired the right of direct petition to enact or revoke legislation and the right to recall officials derelict in their duties. To further diffuse bureaucratic authority, a clear division of rights and duties was established between local and national administrations.

Tilton's success was short-lived, however. With the return of Yoshida Shigeru to power in October 1948, the central government sponsored a series of 'rectifying' laws and ordinances which over the next few years would gradually restore a substantial degree of centralised administrative control over the municipalities. National authorities imposed various duties on governors and municipal heads – a process known as 'agency delegation' (*kikan i'nin jimu*) – and arrogated the right to dismiss local executive officers who ignored or violated such directives. The Local Autonomy Law's greatest weakness, however, was its failure to provide an adequate financial base for local self-government. Required to pay for municipal police forces and build new schools in line with educational reforms, many governments were placed under insupportable fiscal strain and found themselves increasingly dependent on government subsidies, with the usual strings attached.

Central authorities played the situation both ways. During the Imperial tours organised after 1946 by the Imperial household (with SCAP approval) to popularise the Emperor, hosting municipalities spent millions of yen in local revenues to welcome and entertain the monarch and his entourage. When Government Section's Kades and Commander Guy Swope, then Chief of the Political Affairs Division, demanded an accounting of these expenses in late 1947, national officials replied that the Local Autonomy Law prohibited the central government from interfering with local finances. Swope accused the Imperial Household Agency of attempting to remove the Imperial budget from public scrutiny and abruptly put an end to the municipal disbursements.[11]

In the face of entrenched conservative opposition, then, SCAP's efforts to devolve power to the localities could only be partially successful. (It is also true that, by early 1947, MacArthur's headquarters was struggling to contain the powerful pressures for change from below that its early reforms had generated.) On 30 April 1947, the first nationwide elections for prefectural governors, mayors, village heads and local assembly representatives were held on the basis of universal suffrage. Despite SCAP's legislative recasting of local administration, at the grass roots, the neighborhood *tonari-gumi* and other mechanisms of local political control remained in the hands of the Old Guard, and most of the officials voted into office were conservative candidates.[12] Balloting alone could not break the stranglehold of the old régime, but, as an exercise in democratic process, the elections were an unprecedented event that signalled a break with the past, infusing communities everywhere with new vigour. A sign of the times was the election of 23 women to prefectural assemblies, 74 to city councils and 707 to town assemblies.

Dissolving the Home Ministry

The 1947 Local Autonomy Law prohibited the delegation of municipal duties to quasi-governmental bodies such as the *tonari-gumi*, the compulsory groups of five to ten families engaged in mutual surveillance. These tiny units at the base of Japan's Imperial system epitomised the authoritarian reach of the all-powerful Home Ministry. In the early months of occupation, local citizens' committees sprang up to challenge the authority of these formal associations, and at SCAP's insistence, on 22 January 1947, the Home Ministry rescinded Imperial Ordinance no. 17 of 1940, relinquishing its control over them, and their remaining functions, such as the issuance of residence certificates and food rationing, were gradually turned over to the municipalities. The Home Ministry encouraged the *tonari-gumi* to continue as voluntary groups, however, and the old block organisations retained many of their former local-control functions, although these no longer had the sanction of law. Government Section ordered the groups formally disbanded by 31 May 1947.[13]

Abolition of the *tonari-gumi* was aimed at loosening the Home Ministry's grip on the citizenry. Following the entry into force of the Constitution and the Local Autonomy Law on 3 May 1947, SCAP targeted the Ministry itself. Established in 1873 as the watchdog of Japan's Imperial polity, this immense control apparatus wielded broad legal and extra-legal powers over all aspects of national life and was staffed by élite career bureaucrats each considering himself 'the inviolable agent of an infallible Emperor'. Collectively, this group constituted the vital core of the national bureaucracy and a pillar of Imperial rule. The purge of January 1946 delivered a first blow to this citadel, removing 340 out of 564 officials, or 60 per cent of the Ministry's top-echelon staff.[14] On 30 April 1947, General Whitney issued a directive to the Central Liaison Office ordering the Ministry to decentralise. The agency countered that its existence was indispensable for carrying out Occupation directives and argued for a token reorganisation. In June, Kades and Guy Swope fired back a riposte comparing the dark history of the Ministry's notorious police network to the Nazi and Soviet secret police. World opinion, they asserted, would settle for nothing less than the full emancipation of the Japanese people from the Home Ministry's awesome powers.[15]

Despite ministerial evasions, delays and, in some instances, blatant obstructionism, SCAP prevailed, and in late November and early December, the Upper and Lower Houses passed a law dismantling the Ministry, which was formally dissolved on 31 December. Its functions were parcelled out to other ministries and agencies, including the Home Affairs Bureau, which was established in January 1948 and placed under the Prime Minister's Office, and the Construction Agency, which took charge of rivers, ports, water supply and drainage, roads and urban planning. The Ministry's top-ranking officials were moved to other positions in the national and prefectural governments. Many middle-echelon officials, too, successfully transferred their talents to other positions in the bureaucracy. A large number, including key security personnel, were relocated to the Attorney General's Office, created in February 1948. The Special Investigation Bureau established there soon afterwards would assume many of the internal security functions of the old Home Ministry (chapter 10).

Civil service reform

Pre-surrender planning had made bureaucratic deconcentration a key Occupation goal. Police and local government reforms were merely the first step. Only a complete reconstruction of the bureaucratic edifice itself, SCAP believed, could transform the arrogant minions of Imperial authority into humble servants of the people. On 30 January 1946, Lieutenant Milton J. Esman, a political scientist attached to the GS Public Administration Division, fired the first salvo. In a memorandum to Whitney, he urged a prompt and thorough-going reform of the bureaucracy. 'Modern democratic government requires a democratic and efficient public service', he declared. 'The present Japanese bureaucracy is incompetent to manage a modern democratic society. Only relentless pressure from Headquarters will induce the Japanese to make these essential and fundamental changes.'[16]

In early February, Esman, also a member of the GS constitutional team, introduced into the draft constitution a system of legislative controls over the bureaucracy and later recommended the visit of a high-profile US civil service mission to Japan. The views presented in the Esman Memo were shared by many in Government Section. Thomas A. Bisson, a GS economic adviser, regarded the bureaucracy as a bastion of the Old Order comparable in importance to the Tōjō war cabal, the great financial combines, reactionary political parties and large landlords. John M. Maki,

another GS official involved in government reform, warned that the bureaucrats had
so firmly ensconced themselves that only a radical reformation forcibly imposed by
SCAP could dislodge them and dissolve their power base. In July 1946, Maki drafted
a separate memorandum recommending measures to 'eliminate the militaristic and
authoritarian characteristics of Japanese government'.[17]

SCAP postponed action on the Esman Memo and Maki's recommendations until
November 1946, when, ostensibly at the request of the Japanese – who in fact were
responding to prodding from MacArthur's headquarters – it brought to Japan the
US Personnel Advisory Mission headed by Blaine Hoover to assess the problem and
propose solutions. Hoover was a personnel and management specialist who had
headed the Civil Service Assembly of the United States and Canada and worked as a
consultant to the US Civil Service Commission, but he possessed little knowledge of
Japan. In April 1947, he submitted an interim report to SCAP castigating Japan's
top-heavy administrative apparatus as feudalistic and riddled with favouritism and
factionalism. In Hoover's inimitable rhetoric, the task was to break up the 'tightly
knit, exclusive and self-perpetuating bureaucracy which exercised the powers of government over the people in the feudal concept of dynastic rule by divine right'. In its
place, he envisaged 'a body of democratically selected officials who will administer
the laws in the concept of a service to the people'.[18] The Mission issued its conclusions in June. The Hoover Report called for the creation of a National Personnel
Agency and the enactment of a national public service law to ensure fair and uniform
standards of personnel administration. It also recommended the creation of a merit
system for promotions based on performance and efficiency.

On 21 October 1947, under strong pressure from MacArthur's headquarters, the
Diet enacted the National Pubic Service Law on the basis of Hoover's proposals. The
law streamlined and modernised the Japanese bureaucracy by instituting a single
nationwide civil service examination and establishing a classified system of advancement by job category. It also assured fixed salaries and avenues of advancement and,
in principle at least, sought to eliminate favouritism and self-perpetuating distinctions based on social status. This latter was an effort to undermine the preponderant
influence of the University of Tokyo Law School as a source of upper-echelon functionaries. Hoover's attempt to transplant a US-inspired model to Japan, where very
different realities obtained, succeeded in some areas, but his attempt to eradicate
educational élitism failed dismally. And, when in 1948 he attempted to impose
American concepts of labour discipline on government employees as a group, he
caused a political furor that had domestic and even international repercussions
(see below).

In retrospect, bureaucratic reconstruction was more radical in its intentions than
in substance. As with the Home Ministry, many central administrators survived the
purge, and fierce turf battles later erupted to contain and divert the impetus for
reform. Despite its modernising influence on the civil service, which is undeniable,
SCAP ultimately was more concerned with improving bureaucratic efficiency than
with reshaping the bureaucracy itself. As a result, the apparatus of state remained

prey to the vested interests of its diverse constituencies, with each ministry and agency determined to defend against all comers its prerogatives and particularistic agenda.

ECONOMIC RECONSTRUCTION

The antecedents for Japan's dramatic postwar recovery may be traced in part to reforms begun in the 1920s and 1930s and implemented sporadically and partially until the end of the war. Pre-surrender currents for change resurfaced with fresh vitality in the postwar world, but in a radically altered national and international context. Today's prosperity rests solidly on the pedestal of economic reform that SCAP built between 1946 and 1947.

The Occupation's economic programme began as a process of 'defeudalisation' whose objective was not to promote full industrial recovery but to destroy the institutional roots of militarism and the social and economic forces that had impelled Japan on a course of imperialist adventure. The 'Initial Post-Surrender Policy' (22 September 1945) and the Joint Chiefs' 'Basic Initial Post-Surrender Directive' (3 November 1945) authorised General Headquarters to destroy Japan's economic war potential, exact reparations and, in the words of the 'Basic Directive', 'encourage the development within Japan of economic ways and institutions of a type that will contribute to the growth of peaceful and democratic forces'. Only later, after 1948, and against the backdrop of new Cold War exigencies and the reconstruction of a world market, did rapid industrial recovery become a pressing Occupation concern (chapter 10).[19]

The economic roots of aggression
US pre-surrender planning traced the economic causes of Japan's imperialist ambition to the country's narrow, undeveloped domestic market, skewed income distribution, and the ensuing export drives that had given Japanese products an unfair competitive edge in the 1930s. Japanese finished goods had undercut American and European commodities to devastating effect as a result of what was termed 'social dumping'. In this view, the mainsprings of economic expansionism were: 1 a labour force that was underpaid, overworked and docile by Western standards; 2 a few large industrial and financial combines, the *zaibatsu*, which monopolised the capital-intensive export sector of the economy via semi-feudalistic labour and management practices; and 3 a land-holding system dominated by a relatively small number of landlords, many of them absentee owners, who kept the producing tenant majority in a state of unrelieved misery.

The decisiveness of such socio-economic factors in fuelling Japanese aggression had been a subject of intense debate in US policy and academic circles. Occupation planners sided with those experts who located the underlying cause of this process in Japan's incomplete transformation into a capitalist society. Of particular concern were high ground rents that often exceeded half of a tenant's crop. These exploitative practices channelled manpower out of rural areas and into the city, supplying urban industry with a steady flow of cheap labour and enabling the *zaibatsu* to create a servile work force deprived of basic rights. This mutually reinforcing system had depressed labour costs, kept export prices artificially low and given Japanese big business a one-sided advantage in international markets.

MacArthur's staff promptly launched a three-pronged assault on the economic underpinnings of Japanese militarism. Specifically, SCAP sought to improve wages and working conditions in the cities by creating a dynamic labour movement and dissolving the *zaibatsu* oligopolies and the paternalistic labour practices on which they thrived. In the countryside, American agrarian reformers set about uprooting 'feudalistic landlordism' by restructuring the land-tenure system, transferring land to the tillers and raising farm productivity. The three democratisations – of labour, the combines and the tenancy system – would liberate productive forces and meet consumer demand while eliminating the unfair competitive position previously enjoyed by Japanese industry .

The long-term objective of these reforms was a reconstructed, non-predatory capitalist Japan fully reintegrated into the world market as a fair but subordinate trade partner. To this end, the Occupation worked to strengthen the economic and political status of workers and farmers – two groups that had the most to lose from a military resurgence – by giving them a vital personal stake in the new economy. These overarching goals converged roughly with the ideas of moderate Japanese intellectual, business and political leaders and reform-minded bureaucrats, some of them Marxists, who not only recognised the inevitability of change but actively championed it. These progressive academics and policy specialists were the natural allies of SCAP's New Deal reformers, and both Occupation idealists and the first Yoshida Cabinet turned to them for advice and assistance.

Bureaucratic reformers

It is useful to distinguish two groups whose ideas, in the context of the times, were forward-looking: intellectuals, among them former functionaries, who gathered around Yoshida Shigeru, and reform bureaucrats in the Welfare Ministry espousing a social agenda that dated from the 1920s.

Reformist intellectuals included the German-educated left-wing statistician Arisawa Hiromi; Inaba Hidezō, formerly of the wartime Cabinet Planning Board; political scientist and educator Nanbara Shigeru, a Christian liberal and the first postwar president of the University of Tokyo (1945–51); Ōkita Saburō, a liberal economist; neo-Marxian theorist Ōuchi Hyōe; Tsuru Shigeto, a Harvard-trained economist with Marxist leanings, close friend of E. H. Norman and nephew-in-law of Marquis Kido Kōichi; and Wada Hiro'o, an agrarian economist with radical leanings and, like Inaba, formerly of the Cabinet Planning Board. Some of these men had been recruited by Yoshida in the closing days of the conflict to begin planning for a different future. Arisawa and others had been members of Ōuchi's economics seminar at Tokyo Imperial University before the war. Conversant with Marxist theory, they were critical of the abuses of capitalism, which they believed could be transcended. Several, including Arisawa, Inaba and Wada, had been purged or arrested for their Socialist ideas.

A second group consisted of bureaucrats in the Welfare Ministry's Labour Policy and Social Bureaux. During the 1920s and 1930s, these officials, then with the Home Ministry, had proposed social welfare legislation designed to keep the labour and tenants' movements within bounds controllable by the state. They joined the Welfare Ministry when it separated from the Home Ministry in 1938 and were responsible for expanding workers' medical insurance and pension coverage and enacting other laws designed to reduce labour mobility and dissatisfaction and assure cooperation with the war effort. The welfare bureaucrats subsequently assumed broad powers over management and labour in an effort to allocate manpower effectively and boost productivity. They also supervised the wartime patriotic labour fronts that had absorbed the labour movement. Several months before the defeat, these pragmatists had begun considering a new labour union law as a more efficient way of regulating labour-management relations. Sound unionism, they believed was the only solution to labour radicalism and Communist influence.

Thus, as the Occupation got underway, antimilitarists in academia, business and government were contemplating some degree of institutional and economic reform. And if, in the words of one of them, such ideas 'did not have the force of imperative necessity', they nonetheless offered a degree of consensus upon which the Occupation could build.[20] Shortly after the surrender, presumably at Yoshida's behest, the Ministry of Foreign Affairs convened the first meeting of the Special Survey Committee, whose members included Arisawa, Ōkita, Ōuchi, Tsuru and Inaba. As Foreign Minister under Prime Ministers Higashikuni and Shidehara, Yoshida oversaw and coordinated the Committee's work – indeed, early economic planning appears to have taken place exclusively inside the Foreign Ministry. In March 1946, the group submitted a final report recommending the development of a viable domestic consumer market, support for labour unions, reform of the bureaucracy and financial institutions, the elimination of landlordism and the modernisation of food production. The report proposed that Japan focus on developing export industries through technological progress and advocated economic planning, with democratic reform and a strong centralised state as prerequisites.

The Special Survey Committee was ambivalent about whether 'selfish capitalism' was the best system for Japan. Its innovative blueprint for reform envisaged a civilian-orientated economy, but one based on cutting-edge technologies and centralised planning. Although many of these proposals coincided generally with GHQ's own reform agenda, they were at variance with the Occupation's early vision of Japan as a producer and exporter of cheap, labour-intensive light manufactures. Nonetheless, the Committee agreed with MacArthur's economists on the need to curb inflation, restore production in mining and other basic industries and reduce unemployment. Japanese reform functionaries, used to a wartime command economy, found intellectual common ground with their New Dealer counterparts in MacArthur's highly centralised military super-government. The Supreme Commander himself urged the government to adopt an integrated approach to economic recovery.[21]

When Yoshida replaced Shidehara as premier in May 1946, he tapped Ōuchi Hyōe to serve as his finance minister, but the Marxist academic refused, and Yoshida appointed Keynesian economist Ishibashi Tanzan to fill that position instead. Ishibashi favoured government spending to stimulate production and increase employment. Borrowing selectively from the ideas advanced by the Foreign Ministry planning group, he established the Reconstruction Finance Bank (RFB) in August to pool investment funds and channel them to heavy industry. Capital was subscribed by the Bank of Japan through the sale of RFB bonds. In December 1946, Ishibashi implemented the Priority Production Plan – the brainchild of Arisawa Hiromi – under which available capital, natural resources and labour were concentrated in coal, steel and other strategic industries. At the same time, under strong pressure from SCAP, the Economic Stabilisation Board (ESB) was created as an emergency measure to coordinate the new system of economic targeting, reconstruction financing and macro-level policy-planning. Arisawa, Inaba, Tsuru and Wada were called upon to play key roles in the life of the Board, which also imposed price and wage controls.[22] In August 1946, as the government gradually moved to restore economic planning, industrialists anxious to regroup their forces established the *Keidanren* (Federation of Business Organisations) to hasten the recovery of big business.

These were defensive actions, however, implemented a full year after the defeat and in response to powerful social forces unleashed at the grass roots by Occupation policy. The US agenda provided the framework and initial impetus for reform, but it was an independent labour movement, self-confident and buoyant, that generated the real momentum for economic democracy, making that process irreversible. Indeed, from late 1945, worker activism collided head-on with the bureaucracy–*zaibatsu* complex that had dominated the pre-surrender economy. This dramatic and unprecedented clash of interests radically shifted the axis of economic activity, realigned basic production relations and reshaped Japan's industrial policy-making process.

THE LABOUR MOVEMENT

The workers organise

The democratisation of labour was near the top of the Occupation agenda. Between 1945 and 1947, under SCAP guidance, the labour movement revived and flourished as never before. GHQ boldly encouraged trade unionism – another of MacArthur's 'schoolhouses of democracy' – which it regarded as a positive influence that would deter future aggression, imbue workers with democratic ideals and serve as a general index of political liberalisation. A labour expert with Economic and Scientific Section noted later, 'We have been accused of promoting economic trade unionism, but the purposes were political. . . . We wanted to see the Japanese unions not only as economic organisations but as a political force on the side of democracy.'[23]

SCAP cleared the way for a viable labour movement in September 1945 by abolishing the Patriotic Industrial Association (*Sanpō*) and the Patriotic Labour Association (*Rōhō*), reactionary labour fronts established by the militarists in the late 1930s to allocate labour to war industries and dampen worker activism. *Sanpō* alone grouped about 6 million employees from 87,000 companies into a vast nationwide organisation espousing a corporatist 'enterprise family' ideology.[24] Among the political prisoners released on MacArthur's orders in early October 1945 were a number of influential labour leaders, and in his first meeting with Prime Minister Shidehara shortly afterwards, the Supreme Commander told the premier to encourage unionisation. Consequently, on 24 October, Shidehara appointed a 130-member ad hoc Labour Legislation Commission composed of scholars, prewar labour activists, politicians, company presidents and Communist leaders (including the volatile Tokuda Kyūichi) to consider legislative reform. A working committee of five – two prominent academics and three bureaucrats of the Welfare Ministry's Labour Policy Bureau – drafted a labour union bill, which Economic and Scientific Section (ESS)'s Labour Division Chief William Karpinsky steered quickly into law.

In shepherding the bill through the Diet, Karpinsky relied heavily on the expertise of the Commission chair, Dr Suehiro Izutarō, former dean of Tokyo Imperial University's Law School and one of Japan's foremost legal minds, and Dr Ayusawa Iwao, a pacifist and ex-official of the International Labour Organisation in Geneva with a PhD in labour economics from Columbia University. The legislative draft owed much to the 1931 trade-union bill that social bureaucrats in the Home Ministry had written and to proposals advanced by Shidehara's Labour Legislation Commission, but Karpinsky himself acknowledged the direct influence of a union group, the *Sōdōmei* Preparatory Council, and such right-leaning Socialists as Nishio Suehiro and Matsuoka Komakichi with whom he worked closely. The postwar legislation was a collaborative effort that represented the best thinking of prewar union leaders, reform bureaucrats, academics and American labour specialists.[25]

Enacted on 22 December, the Labour Union Law was hailed as a Magna Carta for Japanese workers. Modelled loosely on the US National Labour Relations (Wagner) Act of 1935, it guaranteed the right to organise, bargain collectively and strike, and established labour relations boards at the central and prefectural levels to mediate disputes – in fact, the only truly new feature. Despite its sweeping provisions, however, the legislation had a serious defect: Article 15 enabled the courts to disband unions that 'disturbed the peace'. Theodore Cohen, who replaced Karpinsky as ESS Labour Division head in January 1946, managed to vitiate that stipulation by amending the enabling Cabinet ordinance that brought the law into effect in March 1946. The new statute gave labour unprecedented freedoms and effectively liberated workers from control of the bureaucracy. In the spring of 1946, Labour Division began purging former police officials from labour-related positions in the Welfare Ministry, then in charge of labour affairs, removing a major impediment to union organising.[26]

Some workers did not wait for GHQ's go-ahead to take remedial action. In April 1945, there were some 135,000 Korean labour conscripts working as virtual slaves in Japan's coal mines. Immediately following the surrender, they struck for more food, better treatment and back wages or simply walked off the job, actions that occasionally led to bloody clashes with Japanese police. Even before the war's end, Korean and Chinese workers had risen up in protest of inhuman living and working conditions. On 30 June 1945, for instance, some 850 Chinese at the Hanaoka Mine in Akita Prefecture rebelled against particularly brutal treatment at the hands of the Kajima Gumi (now the Kajima Corporation), killed five supervisors and fled into surrounding hills. Local authorities mobilised thousands of militia, veterans' groups, police, young men and even schoolboys to track the escapees down. In suppressing the revolt, military police and local militia are believed to have stabbed, beaten, shot or tortured to death more than 400.[27]

In November 1945, SCAP prohibited strikes in mining and other areas such as railroads and communications considered vital to the Occupation mission. Korean and Formosan conscripts, ostensibly 'liberated nationals', were forced to remain on the job until production could be stabilised. Elsewhere, however, GHQ assumed a stance of non-intervention and in many instances tacitly condoned spontaneous work stoppages. In November, MacArthur issued a Command Letter to Eighth Army ordering it not to interfere in labour disputes. As basic labour legislation was drafted, ESS despatched officials to factories and dockyards to encourage workers to organise. Travelling around the country to speak at workers' rallies, these specialists patiently explained the new policies, offering advice on bargaining, bookkeeping, the conducting of meetings, and the drawing up of employment contracts.

At first, the formation of unions owed more to necessity than to SCAP exhortation. Uncertain employment conditions, raging inflation and hunger forced workers to act collectively to protect jobs and wages. Labour organising began slowly in the near-chaotic post-defeat conditions but rapidly gathered steam, involving both white-collar and blue-collar workers. Right-wing Socialist leaders such as Nishio Suehiro and Matsuoka Komakichi advanced narrow economic agendas, stressed cooperation with management and attempted to rally workers using prewar methods, an approach that soon alienated many rank-and-file. Grass-roots labour radicalism spread rapidly in basic industries and the public sector, and left-wing Socialists such as Takano Minoru, Secretary General of the Kanto Metal Workers' Union, and Communist leaders, including Dobashi Kazuyoshi of the communications workers and Sakaguchi Yasuo of the national railway workers in Tokyo, became adept shopfloor organisers. By early 1946, union membership had reached half a million, and wages had risen between three and five times. (Spiralling inflation, however, accounted for most of these gains, which were quickly eroded by food shortfalls, black-marketeering and the absence of effective price controls.) Within a year, there were some 17,000 unions with a total membership of 4.8 million, representing about half of all non-agricultural wage earners. By February 1947, there were roughly 19,000 unions boasting more than 5 million members.[28]

Labour demonstrations and parades became commonplace, and unions sprouted up like bamboo shoots after an early spring rain. 'All I did was hand a circular to the neighbours next door and across the street, and the next thing I knew, we had us a union', wrote one contemporary. Industrial disputes broke out everywhere. The strike quickly became the symbol of the working class's new-found freedom, and employees from factory workers to school teachers and journalists availed themselves of this potent new weapon. In the autumn of 1945, Sendai telephone operators went on strike, and those who remained at the switchboards answered callers with the greeting: 'Hello, we are on strike. Long live democracy. Number please.'[29]

Japan's three major dailies, the *Asahi*, *Mainichi* and *Yomiuri*, which had been mouthpieces for the militarists, attempted to purge themselves of ultra-nationalist elements and liberalise management and editorial content. The *Asahi* and *Mainichi* succeeded in doing so with little difficulty, but at the *Yomiuri*, President Shōriki Matsutarō, a former member of the Tokyo Metropolitan Police Board and ardent ultra-nationalist, refused to budge. Staff and workers demanded that management resign to take responsibility for its blind wartime support of militarism and that editorial control and internal organisation be thoroughly democratised. When Shōriki rejected their revendications, *Yomiuri* employees formed a union and elected Suzuki Tōmin, a non-Communist, to chair it. On 25 October, rather than declare a strike, the union opted to take control of production and put out the paper themselves following Italian and French examples of worker self-managed production. In December, Shōriki was forced to accept arbitration and agreed to resign. The company was reorganised as a corporation, Baba Tsunego, a right-wing Socialist, became the publisher, and a management council was created to reform the editorial process. Thus began Japan's first 'production control' (*seisan kanri*) struggle. SCAP saw the *Yomiuri* dispute as a test case for the success of unionisation. In December, it arrested Shōriki as a suspected war criminal and lauded the workers' arbitration accord as free labour's first effective collective bargaining agreement. Shopfloor organisers flocked to the *Yomiuri* to learn first-hand about production control.[30]

MacArthur's headquarters also backed employees of Keisei Electric Railway Company when they locked out management in December and began to operate the railroad on their own. At the same time, miners at the Bibai Mine in Hokkaido took a lesson from the *Yomiuri* and Keisei actions and seized command of the mine's management rather than go out on strike and cripple output. Production control was a spontaneous response to specifically Japanese post-defeat conditions and an altered power relationship now favourable to labour. Such struggles proliferated, with workers taking charge of manufacturing and running their companies until a settlement with management could be reached. SCAP initially took a hands-off attitude, and in late January 1946, when the government attempted to prevent production takeovers using the police and public prosecutors, the ESS Labour Division, with SCAP's backing, publicly aired its objections to such tactics and backed the unions.[31]

Until late 1946, the corporate élite, still reeling from the dual shocks of defeat and occupation, had developed no coherent economic vision around which management might rally its energies and resources. Through shopfloor production struggles, the unions in effect took on that responsibility. Demanding a voice in how their companies were run, they pressed for higher wages, recovery through priority growth in basic industries and long-term, comprehensive economic planning. The Electric Power Workers Union (*Densan*), for instance, created a new industry-wide system for calculating labour costs by pegging wages to the cost of living rather than productivity. In short, during the first year of occupation, unions seized the initiative in reordering the economy, and they did this by giving their members a say in the everyday decisions that affect production, imparting substance to the ideal of economic democracy. From late 1946, however, as labour launched a major offensive to test its newly acquired power, government and big business closed ranks in what became a protracted contest to wrest the initiative for change from the unions and restore the primacy of management. In this struggle, which would culminate in the Red Purge of 1949–50, the Occupation threw its support to the conservative establishment. The first battle in that long war of attrition was fought in early 1947, with the last of SCAP's labour-reform legislation still on the drafting board.[32]

The labour offensive
By mid-1946, the upsurge in labour militancy and popular participation in mass demonstrations with clear political objectives had set off alarm bells in the corridors of the Dai-Ichi Insurance Building. Willoughby's intelligence empire, in particular, girded for battle. Successful production-control struggles, such as those at Tōshiba Rolling Stock and Japan Steel Tube in early 1946, helped radicalise the push for worker self-management. In January, 13 attempts by labour engaging 29,000 workers to take over production were recorded; by May, that number had grown to 56 involving some 39,000 workers. These initiatives received broad popular support from farmers and city consumers, and there were even attempts to forge incipient farmer–worker alliances.[33]

Two intriguing examples of such cooperation are the Tōyō Gōsei workers in Ni'igata City and the Edogawa Union in Tokyo. Tōyō Gōsei was a small chemical factory belonging to the Mitsui combine. From March through August 1946, workers took over and managed the enterprise to prevent Mitsui from closing it down. Tōyō Gōsei workers reached a barter agreement with a Ni'igata farmers' association, which supplied the factory with coal acquired via a similar contract with local mine workers, in return for fertiliser. The three-way trade benefited all parties. Edogawa Manufacturing was a small Tokyo factory producing formalin and affiliated with Mitsubishi. Formed in January 1946, the union set up elective workers' councils mirroring the structure of management and took over production in March. Edogawa Union negotiated directly with agricultural associations to supply formalin to farmers in northeastern Japan and Hokkaido, sent two envoys to Hokkaido for

Photo 41. Communist firebrand Tokuda Kyūichi delivers an oration at the first May Day celebration of the postwar era, 1 May 1946. In the back, a US intelligence officer, camera around his neck, monitors the speech. GHQ's initial tolerance of the Communist Party as a progressive force was short-lived (Kyodo).

liaison purposes and arranged with railway workers to transport the cargo. These innovative challenges to corporate authority, however, did not survive the counter-attack coordinated by SCAP and the Yoshida government in the summer of 1946.[34]

In the face of dire food shortages, agricultural producers, workers and the war displaced cooperated in setting up regional councils to uncover and seize hoarded goods, establish 'food committees' and organise voluntary grain deliveries by farmers. 'Livelihood-protection' associations grew up in local neighbourhoods in an effort to displace the *tonari-gumi* and seize control of the government rationing system. On 7 April, three days before Japan's first postwar general elections, labour leaders joined Communists, Socialists, Koreans, women's groups and the urban poor in a march on Prime Minister Shidehara's residence to demand food and jobs. A scuffle broke out in which several police were injured. On May Day, 500,000 demonstrated in the streets of Tokyo, and on 14 May, residents of Setagaya Ward in Tokyo attempted to force their way into the Palace to protest at a delay in issuing rice rations. On 15 May, George Atcheson Jr, US delegate to the Allied Council for Japan, rejected a petition submitted to the ACJ by the protesters, which he said smacked of 'Communist propaganda'. In his speech, he noted that, while the Communist Party was free to develop, 'The United States does not favour Communism at home or in Japan'. Thus, Atcheson managed to imply that all popular dissent was Communist-inspired, reflecting an emerging Occupation consensus on the need to dampen public dissent and contain radicalism.

On 19 May, more than 250,000 Tokyoites staged 'Food May Day', demanding the liberation of grain stores in the Imperial Palace, the resignation of the inept

Photo 42. Food May Day, 19 May 1946. People from all stations of life mobilise in front of the Imperial Palace to denounce food shortages and the policies of the Shidehara Cabinet. The massive display of popular anger at the conservative government alarmed Occupation officials. In the background is SCAP headquaters (Kyodo).

Shidehara government and the establishment of a democratic popular front. Demonstrators also called for the purge of war criminals, popular control of hoarded goods and worker control over production. In March 1946, MacArthur had waxed eloquent on unions, proclaiming with typical hyperbole, 'I do not think the history of labour throughout the last 2,000 years has shown such an extraordinary, magnificent development in such a short space of time.' But on 20 May, the day after the massive labour-backed food rallies, the Supreme Commander abruptly cautioned the Japanese people that 'the growing tendency toward mass violence and the physical process of intimidation under organised leadership [constitutes] a menace not only to orderly government, but to the basic purposes and security of the Occupation itself'.[35]

MacArthur's admonitions were no idle threat. SCAP promptly drafted a harsh public security ordinance and ordered the government to enact it as a Potsdam decree. On 12 June, the Cabinet issued Imperial Ordinance no. 311, which created prohibitive fines and prison terms of up to 10 years at hard labour for engaging in 'acts prejudicial to Occupation objectives'. Such acts included violations of orders of US army commanders and of all Japanese laws and ordinances promulgated to implement SCAP directives. Ironically, the first group to be tried under this ordinance were not Japanese demonstrators but 10 Koreans who broke into Prime Minister Yoshida's residence in December 1946 to present a petition demanding greater civil and political rights for the Korean minority.

In the summer of 1946, SCAP's Civil Information and Education Section (CI&E), stung by the *Yomiuri*'s enthusiastic support of the May Day and food rallies and angered at reporting it considered biased and in violation of the Press Code, encouraged the paper's publisher, Baba Tsunego, to reassert editorial control and break the grip of the union, sparking the second *Yomiuri* struggle. Here, CI&E received a decisive backstage assist from Prime Minister Yoshida Shigeru. GHQ's intervention was convoluted, however, and reveals some of the inner tensions animating its staff sections.

After taking over the paper in late 1945, Baba quickly had lost all influence over editorial policy. When the *Yomiuri* ran an article in early June suggesting that the government, and by implication GHQ, was siding with landlords against their tenants, he threatened to resign rather than brave the wrath of CI&E's press censors. At that point, an alarmed Yoshida Shigeru intervened. On 11 June, Yoshida sent his lieutenant Shirasu Jirō to General Frayne Baker, MacArthur's Public Relations Officer, with the names of six alleged Communists on the *Yomiuri* editorial staff. On his own initiative, Baker summoned the despondent Baba and handed him the list. Reassured by this gesture of support, Baba promptly fired the six, who refused, however, to vacate the editorial room and carried on as usual. In late June, over the opposition of Theodore Cohen's Labour Division, GHQ condoned massive police raids on the *Yomiuri* staff – the first of their kind since the war years – and the sacking of prominent union officials. According to Cohen, MacArthur had given CI&E Chief Donald R. Nugent a secret order to 'get the Communists out of the *Yomiuri*'. Nugent's conservative Press Division Chief, Major Daniel C. Imboden, manoeuvred behind the scenes to orchestrate the crackdown.[36]

On 21 June, Cohen recalled, police trucks sped past GHQ towards the *Yomiuri* Building sirens screaming. He followed, and by the time he arrived, 'the police were pulling people up and throwing them into the truck like they were sacks of potatoes'. When he tried to go upstairs to see what was happening, he was met by 'pairs of policemen coming down the staircase with someone in between them, that is . . . two policemen would arrest somebody and then would go running down the stairs pulling him along'. Eventually, 56 people were detained. This was intimidation, not law enforcement, Cohen decided. Angry at the use of police power to break up a strike, the Labour Division Chief called in the police authorities responsible and berated them for interfering with a labour dispute in violation of ESS policy. The Metropolitan Police backed down but complained to Eighth Army Headquarters. Eighth Army approached Willoughby, who attempted to intercede with the Supreme Commander, ultimately obliging Cohen to explain his actions to MacArthur in person.[37]

In August 1946, two great, competing labour federations came into being. The Japan Federation of Labour (*Sōdōmei*), with somewhat less than 1 million workers, was anchored in the private sector. Led by Matsuoka Komakichi, it drew its leadership chiefly from the right wing of the Socialist Party and was centralised and authoritarian in structure. The left-of-centre Japan Congress of Industrial Unions (*Sanbetsu Kaigi*), headed by Kikunami Katsumi of the All Japan News and Radio Workers' Union, was a loose council of autonomous unions set up along the lines of the US Congress of Industrial Organisations. Its leaders had close ties to the Japan Communist Party. Public and private unions affiliated with *Sanbetsu* boasted a combined membership of 1.6 million workers, representing roughly half of organised labour. Occupation authorities viewed the new labour centre with growing suspicion, which intensified when *Sanbetsu* rallied in support of the *Yomiuri* workers and called for a general offensive against the anti-labour Yoshida administration.

Strike actions were already underway on several fronts when, in September 1946, MacArthur refused to cancel a planned walkout by railroad workers, although it threatened to cripple the economy. The Supreme Commander's principled defence of a labour action forced National Railway Director Satō Eisaku, a Yoshida protégé and future prime minister, to back down on planned dismissals, handing *Sanbetsu* a major victory. Disputes proliferated. At Tōshiba, workers set up a strike head-quarters and collected strike funds from nearby factories. They published a news-paper, organised cultural and educational activities for workers' families and kept GHQ informed of their plans. When the strike was over, they loaned the balance of their fund to the hard-strapped company. In October, as strike activity reached fever pitch, Yoshida denounced the work boycotts as 'a criminal act of hostility' and characterised the left-wing union leadership as 'avowed enemies of the people in scheming the downfall of our country'. The resulting clash of wills led to SCAP's outlawing of a general strike planned for 1 February 1947. MacArthur had switched sides.[38]

The general strike ban
Unions affiliated with *Sanbetsu* had begun preparing for a general strike following the autumn labour offensive. This movement initially involved both right and left Socialists, Communists and independents and was intended to assist and amplify six ongoing labour disputes involving coal miners, newspaper and radio workers, electrical workers, seamen, national railway workers and government employees. These actions had been taken in response to rampant inflation, severe and chronic food shortages and the need for wage hikes, tax relief and job security. Among the workers' demands was the resignation of the Yoshida government. This position seemed entirely legitimate to union leaders and was formally endorsed by a policy directive emanating from the Far Eastern Commission at the end of the year. On 6 December 1946, the FEC had adopted the 16-point 'Principles for Japanese Trade Unions'. Point no. 6 stated clearly that 'Trade unions should be allowed to take part in political activities and to support political parties'. This statement was the work of the FEC's Commonwealth representatives, Australia, Britain and New Zealand, all

of which had labour governments in power at home. MacArthur believed that the FEC had gone too far and later commented disparagingly, 'Very good, but it was like giving second-grade students the calculus.'[39]

A strike organising committee, the Joint Struggle Committee of Public Employees' Unions (*Kyōtō*), was established on 26 November, and in mid-January 1947, a broader ad hoc coalition, the Joint Struggle Committee of National Labour Unions (*Zentō*), came into being to unify public and private sector workers in a single labour front. On 18 January, union leaders issued an ultimatum to the government threatening a general strike for 1 February if demands for a minimum wage system, substantive wage hikes, an end to dismissals and other reforms were not met by 31 January.

In the meantime, Labour Division's Cohen had sent ESS Chief William F. Marquat a memorandum warning that the unions were moving towards a general strike and recommending that SCAP prohibit such action immediately. Marquat took the issue straight to MacArthur. The Supreme Commander opposed issuing a formal ban and ordered ESS to deliver an informal warning instead. On 22 January, Marquat and Cohen met with strike leaders and read them a statement they had prepared outlining MacArthur's views. The document stated that SCAP would not permit 'a coordinated action by organised labour to provoke a national calamity by a general work stoppage'.[40] The organisers, sure of their cause, ignored the warning and continued to mobilise. It was inconceivable to them that GHQ, having just enshrined the rights of labour, would suddenly override the law to prevent workers from exercising those rights. On the afternoon of 31 January, MacArthur issued a formal directive outlawing the strike, and Marquat promptly summoned the union high command to General Headquarters and ordered them to call off the action.

MacArthur declared that he would not permit 'the use of so deadly a social weapon in the present impoverished and emaciated condition of Japan'. SCAP feared that the resulting shutdown of transportation, communications and other vital services would devastate the economy, disrupt food deliveries and create enormous hardships for ordinary people. More to the point, the General was convinced that the overriding objective of the general strike was a political one: to bring down the Yoshida Cabinet. As Supreme Commander he could not allow a duly elected government to be toppled by 'irresponsible' mass action. Nationwide strikes also would have vastly complicated SCAP's efforts to secure Congressional appropriations for emergency food relief and other basic aid to Japan. Finally, MacArthur had a compelling personal interest in calling off the work boycott: the resulting negative publicity would be potentially damaging to his presidential ambitions.

The labour unions quickly gave in. Had they defied SCAP's banning order, Eighth Army would certainly have broken the strike by force. Indeed, Military Police and Counter-Intelligence Corps teams had drawn up lists of names and stood ready to arrest union leaders. The resort to armed force would have been disastrous for Japan's fledgling labour movement. Theodore Cohen later recalled: 'one thing about Mac-Arthur was that he was not going to be shy. . . . MacArthur never, never took half

Photo 43. A despondent I'i Yashirō after announcing cancellation of the general strike planned for 1 February 1947. His broadcast on the evening of 31 January marked a major setback for Japan's radical labour movement but averted the threat of armed intervention by Eighth Army troops, who stood ready to break the strike at bayonet point (Kyodo).

measures that way.' 'What I was trying to explain to union leaders the week or so before', he said, 'was that an army is like a steamroller. You cannot control it delicately. Once you start driving the steamroller, everything in the way is going to be crushed. And they were likely to end up without a union movement.' Cohen concluded: 'If there had been a general strike, I think the jails would have been full.'[41] Japan, indeed, seemed to stand at the precipice.

At 8 pm. on 31 January, in an emotional public broadcast, I'i Yashirō, coordinator of the Joint Struggle Committee and a leader of the radical National Railways Workers' Union, formally cancelled the planned labour shutdown. In tears, he concluded his announcement by citing the words of Lenin, 'one step backward, two steps forward', and enjoined the working class to continue the struggle. But the strike ban was a palpable defeat for organised labour. SCAP had stepped in on behalf of a weak, unpopular government to police the workers' movement, driving home the message that there were limits beyond which labour activism would not be tolerated.

In retrospect, the decision to prohibit the general strike marked a turning point in the Occupation. By denying employees the right to strike, Occupation authorities violated the spirit and letter of their own reformist legislation, but given the conditions of the day, that decision probably was unavoidable. Had MacArthur called out the troops, as he was prepared to do, the result would have been the direct control of labour by the Occupation army and, possibly, the imposition of military government, an even greater setback to working people and to the country as a whole.

Nonetheless, the consequences for labour were traumatic and long-lasting. The failure discredited the radical leadership of the strike, which was criticised by the public for its confrontational tactics, and redounded to the benefit of right-wing Socialist labour organisers. More importantly, the threatened work stoppage prompted MacArthur to back the conservatives in their efforts to defuse labour militancy. His staff subsequently used the strike ruling to discourage other coordinated union struggles and to justify SCAP's intrusion into labour relations in 1948 with the anti-strike provisions of the revised National Public Service Law (below).

Aftermath

Abortion of the strike also had political repercussions. Yoshida's policies had exacerbated rather than cured inflation, producing a further decline in living standards, and popular resentment of his government was at its peak. Trade union membership now exceeded 5 million, and more than 1 million farmers had joined peasant unions, accelerating the momentum for change. Heightened labour unrest in the wake of the failed general strike coincided with popular outrage at the Yoshida government's heavy-handed reconfiguring of the 1945 Election Law, which his conservative coalition steamrollered through Parliament on 31 March 1947, producing ugly brawling on the Diet floor. The legislative revision replaced the large-constituency, plural ballot system with the traditional medium-sized constituency and single vote, which favoured Old Guard machine bosses.

On 6 February 1947, in a personal letter to Yoshida, MacArthur directed the premier to hold new general elections prior to the entry into force of the Constitution in May in order to stabilise the political situation and 'obtain another democratic expression of the people's will on the fundamental issues with which Japanese society is now confronted'.[42] Consequently, Upper and Lower House elections were held, respectively, on 20 April and 25 April. Voter dissatisfaction with the conservatives handed the Socialists a plurality in the Lower House, increasing their representation from 20 per cent to 30 per cent. Nearly four fifths of the candidates were newcomers. The Socialists captured 143 seats, the Liberals 131, the Democrats 124, the People's Cooperatives 31, the Communists 4 and smaller parties and independents 33. The postwar era's first Upper House election also gave Socialists a broad mandate. Women, however, fared poorly, winning only 15 places in the Lower House, less than half their showing of 39 seats a year earlier. In the Upper House, 10 women, including Socialist feminists Akamatsu Tsuneko and Kawasaki Natsu, were elected for the first time. Unable to find a niche in the male-dominated electoral process that governed access to the House of Representatives, many prominent women adopted the strategy of running on national tickets for the House of Councillors. The Japan Socialist Party now was the strongest political force in the National Diet. In the face of this victory, the Yoshida Cabinet resigned on 20 May, ushering in a 16-month interregnum that momentarily broke the stride of the conservative élite.

In March, Ashida Hitoshi, seeing the writing on the wall, had seceded from Liberal ranks to form the Democratic Party, and the Progressives, with their numbers

Photo 44. Socialist Katayama Tetsu confers with top advisers, 17 April 1947. From the far left, Matsuoka Komakichi, Nishio Suehiro and Katayama. On 1 June, nearly six weeks later, Katayama would inaugurate the early postwar era's only Socialist-led coalition following the resignation of the Yoshida Cabinet in May. New Dealers in GHQ hailed the Katayama victory as the advent of responsible government in Japan (Kyodo).

pruned by the purge, merged with the new political grouping in a bid to dissociate themselves from Yoshida's unpopular policies. Although Liberals and Democrats finished second and third in the polling, both lost seats. Conservative forces retained their absolute majority in both houses, but the Socialist plurality enabled Katayama Tetsu to inaugurate a Socialist-dominated coalition on 1 June, with the participation of Ashida's Democrats and Miki Takeo's People's Cooperatives. Katayama and his adviser Nishio Suehiro, soon to be Chief Cabinet Secretary, offered the defeated Liberals a portfolio, but Yoshida, leery of the JSP's influential left wing, refused to join the coalition. Yoshida's misgivings were unfounded, however, for Katayama and Nishio were determined to exclude left-wing Socialists from the Cabinet in any event. Barred from influence, the Party's Marxists became an internal opposition group. The elections represented the first full flowering of Japan's incipient postwar democracy, and a full 68 per cent of the electorate turned out for the polling, underscoring the extent of public dissatisfaction with Yoshida's neo-conservative agenda. Kades and others in Government Section actively championed the Katayama coalition, and MacArthur himself delighted in the fact that a Christian (Katayama was Presbyterian) had been chosen to lead Japan. Katayama reciprocated enthusiastically, tightening his relations with GS.

Elsewhere in General Headquarters, however, changes were afoot signalling a shift away from the Occupation's early liberalising mission. After the strike ban, Cohen had been Red-baited in the American press, and in March he was removed from ESS's Labour Division for his 'pro-labour' views and booted upstairs to serve as Marquat's economic adviser. In April, James S. Killen, a former American Federation of Labour (AFL) official with pronounced anti-Communist sentiments, took over as Division chief. Killen immediately went after the Communist-dominated *Sanbetsu*, and particularly the militant National Railways Workers' Union (*Kokurō*).

In May 1947, Killen and Richard L.-G. Deverall, head of the Division's Labour Information and Education Branch, drafted a position paper entitled 'Counteracting Communist Activities in the Labor Movement', which Chief of Section Marquat approved in June. The document urged a policy of supporting moderate forces in the union movement in a bid to undermine Communist influence. This led to the active encouragement of so-called Democratisation Leagues (*Minshuka Dōmei*, or *Mindō*), anti-Communist cells set up inside the major unions to 'bore from within' and discredit and isolate Communist leaders. Killen and Deverall met regularly with the right wing of *Kokurō*, inciting workers to 'overthrow the Red Fascists' running the union's executive committee. When the *Mindō* launched their campaign in the autumn of 1947, Killen solicited outside moral and material support from the AFL and its foreign policy arm, the Free Trade Union Committee. For Deverall, however, the real cause of the problem lay within. 'From the very beginning,' he asserted, 'the right-wing Japan Federation of Labour (*Sōdōmei*) was discriminated against by the left-wing agitators inside General MacArthur's Headquarters.' Without this Fifth Column, he implied, *Sanbetsu* could not have flourished.[43]

In February and March 1947, the leadership of the failed general strike attempted to repair some of the damage to union ranks by organising the National Labour Union Liaison Council (*Zenrōren*) to continue the work of the Joint Struggle Committee. Composed of left, right and neutralist tendencies, the Council was a brave effort to re-establish the unity of labour. Soon after its formation, *Zenrōren* was visited by Willard Townsend, the African-American founder of the US Red-caps' Union and a member of the World Federation of Trade Unions (WFTU). MacArthur intercepted Townsend before he could meet with union leaders and brought him to General Headquarters for a personal interview. Favourably impressed by the activist, the General agreed to allow a WFTU delegation to visit the new labour council, raising hopes among left-of-centre unionists that international contacts would invigorate its work.[44] *Zenrōren* was unable to staunch the growth of the *Mindō* movement, however. Thriving on the disarray in labour's ranks, this tendency gathered steam in late 1947 and early 1948 as conservative activists established 'democratisation cells' inside *Sanbetsu*. Although actively promoted by GHQ, the Democratisation Leagues also attracted the spontaneous support of Socialists, independent labour leaders and former Communist organisers. In 1949, *Sanbetsu* expelled the *Mindō* groups as anti-labour, but by then, irreparable damage had been done. A year later, in 1950, left-wing Socialists in *Sōdōmei* would join with like-minded *Mindō* groups and other democratic elements in *Sanbetsu* to form a new labour centre, *Sōhyō* (General Council of Trade Unions of Japan), and articulate the views of the non-Communist left.

THE LABOUR LAWS

Underlying SCAP's labour reforms was a New Deal ideology that strove to free labour from its authoritarian past while binding it anew with a 'web of rules' to a revitalised capitalist system. The reform project was designed to reintegrate trade unions into a pre-existing framework of industrial relations rather than empower workers to restructure hierarchical shopfloor relations themselves and create a new framework. When the union movement threatened to chart its own course, assert direct control over production and organise to achieve political objectives, SCAP intervened decisively on behalf of big business and the conservative establishment. MacArthur's headquarters was assisted in this task by Japanese social bureaucrats who had dealt with labour before the defeat. Ironically, this group, which had dissolved trade unions during the war, would help rebuild them in the early liberal phase of occupation, only to attempt once again to curb their influence after 1948. These reformationists, with a dual agenda combining reform and control, would find a home in the postwar Labour Ministry, providing a link with the pre-surrender era.[45]

Despite SCAP's aversion to radicalism, however, the Occupation's accomplishments in the domain of labour reform were substantial and, in many cases, irreversible. The institutional framework of its labour programme rested on three 'legs': the Labour Union Law (December 1945), the Labour Relations Adjustment Law (September 1946) and the Labour Standards Law (April 1947). On the American side, the driving forces behind the reform effort were Karpinsky and Cohen of ESS's Labour Division, assisted by Captain Anthony Costantino, a labour lawyer, former union activist and head of the Division's Labour Relations Branch. As in the case of the Labour Union Law, the advice and cooperation of Japanese reform bureaucrats often proved decisive, however. The Labour Standards Law, for instance, sprang fully formed from the drafting pens of Labour Policy officials in the Welfare Ministry; ESS merely gave its assent and smoothed the way for enactment. Passage of this legislative package was facilitated by an exceptionally strong assist in the Allied Council for Japan from Soviet delegate Kuzma Derevyanko, giving the reform process an international cast.

Basic legislation
The Labour Union Law of December 1945 went into effect in March 1946 and, as noted, provided the catalyst for the rapid emergence of a dynamic and powerful union movement. Subsequent legislation was the joint product of a US advisory mission on labour and Japanese reform bureaucrats. Early in his tenure, Karpinsky had requested expert assistance from Washington, and in February 1946, the

Department of the Army's Civil Affairs Division despatched the Advisory Committee on Labour in Japan. Led by government adviser Paul L. Stanchfield, the 12-member delegation included representatives from the CIO, the AFL, labour economists, Labour Department officials and a specialist on female labour, Helen Mears.[46] In June, the Committee compiled the 'First Interim Report on the Treatment of Workers' Organisations Since the Surrender', and in July, it submitted its 148-page final report, 'Labour Policies and Programmes in Japan'. SCAP approved the recommendations in August. Specifically, the advisory mission proposed a comprehensive labour relations system, a labour union law (already in force), a labour conciliation mechanism, a labour ministry, a wage policy, a labour standards law and an unemployment compensation régime. Based on these proposals, on 25 August 1946, Economic and Scientific Section directed the government to enact a labour relations law.

Draft legislation submitted by Suehiro Izutarō and Ayusawa Iwao of the Labour Legislation Commission failed to meet ESS expectations, however, and Cohen and Costantino, assisted by Stanchfield and two other members of the US labour mission now attached to ESS, wrote their own version. This the Japanese side accepted with few modifications. The Labour Relations Adjustment Law, enacted on 27 September 1946, laid down conciliation, mediation and arbitration procedures in cases where collective bargaining failed. The law was angrily condemned by labour leaders for restricting strikes by public-sector workers in certain essential services (non-essential government-enterprise employees, however, retained full rights). Nonetheless, it represented a major advance in labour–management relations, raising Japan's notoriously poor working standards to a level commensurate with ILO conventions.

The third pillar of SCAP's labour reform, the Labour Standards Law, originated with social bureaucrats in the Welfare Ministry, notably Teramoto Kōsaku, Chief of the Labour Control Section in the Labour Policy Bureau, and Matsumoto Iwakichi, a ministerial councillor. Teramoto had served in the Special Higher Police during the war – a routine assignment for career bureaucrats – and joined the Welfare Ministry after the surrender. Working closely with Dr Suehiro, the Labour Legislation Commission and union leaders, including Communists, these men drafted a comprehensive labour-protection code for industry based partly on prewar proposals shelved by the military régime and partly on the ILO conventions. A labour standards law was not high on SCAP's agenda, but Teramoto appeared at Cohen's door one day in mid-1946 with a completed draft of the legislation in hand. He won over the surprised Labour Division chief and enlisted the enthusiastic cooperation of Golda G. Stander, head of the Division's Wages and Working Conditions Branch, and her assistant, Meade Smith.

The Labour Standards Bill's extensive provisions for women and minors fired Stander's imagination, and she worked closely with Teramoto to win SCAP approval for the legislation, so much so that in ESS the Bill became known as 'Stander's and Teramoto's baby'. After successfully wooing Labour Division, Teramoto adroitly presented the reform package to the Yoshida government as a GHQ initiative and implied that opposition would not be tolerated. At this crucial juncture, Soviet intervention in the Allied Council for Japan unexpectedly accelerated the momentum for acceptance. On 10 July 1946, Derevyanko boldly challenged SCAP's labour reform programme, submitting to the ACJ a list of 22 demands. The Soviet recommendations recapitulated the basic principles advanced by the US Advisory Committee on Labour, differing largely on questions of detail, but the initiative placed the government on the defensive and forced it to publicise Teramoto's legislative draft prematurely, thereby insuring the Bill's prompt deliberation.[47]

Assisting Teramoto and Stander was Tanino Setsu, a rare female social bureaucrat who in May 1947 would become Chief of the Women's and Minors' Section in the Welfare Ministry's Labour Standards Bureau. Tanino argued that the anti-discrimination provision (Article 3) in Teramoto's draft should specifically ban unequal treatment based on sex. Teramoto rejected this proposal, insisting that the principle of gender equality was incompatible with the Bill's protective measures for women. Teramoto's views prevailed, and Article 3 omitted any reference to sex-linked discrimination, creating a basic ambiguity in the law that would allow employers and conservative lawmakers to justify lower wage scales for working women. Curiously, Stander and others in ESS objected to one of Teramoto's more innovative proposals, monthly menstrual leaves. No such guarantee existed under US law, and Stander argued that it would not only violate the principle of sexual equality but encourage absenteeism (would women past menopause also be entitled to such leave, some ESS officials wondered). With Division Chief Cohen's backing, however, the measure was retained, and the Bill was passed in both houses without major revision. The statute represented the culmination of the social bureaucrats' prewar social policy projections of the 1920s and 1930s.[48]

Enacted on 7 April 1947, the Labour Standards Law went into effect on 1 September. The statute established a maximum eight-hour work day and a 48-hour work week, guaranteed non-exploitative working conditions for women and minors, introduced the principle of equal pay for equal work, and gave labour a voice in determining shopfloor and company work regulations. It also included a non-discrimination clause, Article 3, which read 'No person shall discriminate against or for any worker by reason of nationality, creed or social status in wages, working hours and other working conditions.' Moreover, the law abolished such abusive traditional labour practices as the dormitory system, which had confined workers to closely guarded cell-like rooms known as *tako-beya* (literally 'octopus traps'), and the labour-boss (*oyabun*) system that had allowed labour contractors and brokers to pocket a part of their workers' wages in the form of payroll deductions and kickbacks. Finally, it went far beyond the US Fair Labour Standards Act, requiring employers, for instance, to give dismissed workers 30 days' advance notice as compared to 15 days in the United States. In September, Teramoto was named to head the new Labour Ministry's Labour Standards Bureau (in 1950, he would become vice minister).

Labour Division also sought to modernise employment practices. With strong backing from the Katayama Cabinet, the Employment Security Law (30 November

1947) and the Unemployment Insurance Law (1 December 1947) were enacted, setting up municipal employment offices, providing for the free mobility of labour and streamlining and democratising the prewar system of unemployment relief (chapter 9). These measures complemented a mandatory health insurance programme introduced earlier by the Workman's Compensation Insurance Law (7 April 1947), which remunerated victims of industrial accidents and disease. Labour Division also worked to improve the quality and productivity of labour by introducing modern vocational training techniques and facilities into the workplace. These sweeping reforms laid the foundations for Japan's subsequent emergence as a major economic power.

The Labour Ministry
Finally, on 1 September 1947, the Ministry of Labour was established as a service-orientated agency specialising in labour relations. This, too, ultimately was the achievement of reform-minded Japanese, in this instance Socialists. Labour ministries existed in virtually all of the world's advanced capitalist societies, and in November 1945, Shidehara's Labour Legislation Commission had urged the creation of a comparable labour-administration body. Consequently, a recommendation to that effect was attached as a rider to the Labour Union Law of December 1945. In May 1946, the new Yoshida Cabinet announced it would proceed with plans to establish a ministry, and in July, the US Advisory Committee on Labour included an identical provision in its final report. The plan foundered, however, when Welfare Minister Kawai Yoshinari pledged his absolute opposition, the Finance Ministry protested on grounds of cost and the Home Ministry, afraid of losing control of its extensive police files on labour, attempted to obstruct the measure. As the government dragged its feet, the Socialists lobbied intensively for a Cabinet-level labour agency, a Socialist goal from the prewar era. In late September 1946, Party leaders, including Socialist Diet woman Akamatsu Tsuneko, head of the Party's Women's Affairs Division, and Katō Shizue met Cohen and Government Section's Ruth Ellerman. They proposed the establishment of a viable labour ministry and the creation inside the Cabinet of an autonomous women's and minors' bureau, a long-standing item on the feminist agenda. Cohen suggested incorporating the latter into the proposed labour ministry, pledged Labour Division's backing and assured the group that GHQ, too, would support such a project. The JSP subsequently incorporated these proposals into its party platform.[49]

In the meantime, the Yoshida Cabinet, in the midst of its anti-labour crusade, came up with a revisionist proposal for a Labour Office to be created as an external agency of the reorganised Welfare Ministry. SCAP turned the proposal down, and the government resorted to delaying tactics, engaging ESS in a contest of wills. A turning point was reached with the aborted general strike. In early February 1947, lack of progress on the issue amid deteriorating labour relations spurred Cohen to action. On 10 February, the Labour Division chief conferred with Ellerman and Alfred R. Hussey Jr of GS, Ethel B. Weed of CI&E and a Public Health and Welfare officer. That afternoon, Cohen, Ellerman and Hussey met top bureaucrats from the Welfare Ministry, the Cabinet Legislation Bureau and the Central Liaison Office to consider a preliminary Cabinet order that the government had prepared and to make a counter-proposal of their own. The GHQ draft, largely the work of Cohen, called for six bureaux, among them a Women's and Minors' Bureau. The American officials curtly rejected the government plan as a poorly disguised reformulation of the earlier labour office scheme and insisted that their own version be issued as a Cabinet order. MacArthur, they said, would accept nothing short of an effective labour ministry. Negotiations quickly bogged down, and the deadlock was not broken until the collapse of the Yoshida Cabinet in May 1947 and the advent of the Socialist-led Katayama government. The Katayama Cabinet adopted the GHQ proposals with few modifications and vigorously guided the Labour Ministry Bill through the Diet, securing its passage in the autumn. (With the new Constitution now in force, the measure was promulgated as a law, not a Cabinet order.) Yonekubo Michisuke, a right-leaning Socialist parliamentarian, was named to lead the new ministry. Wartime social reform bureaucrats would dominate the Ministry, monopolising the positions of bureau chief and vice minister well into the 1960s.[50]

The Women's and Minors' Bureau
One item in the Labour Ministry Bill to which the Yoshida government had objected with particular vehemence was the creation of the Women's and Minors' Bureau. Before the war, Katō Shizue and other women's rights activists, many of them Socialists, had lobbied to endow a government bureau with broad powers to enhance the status of women. Soon after the surrender, feminist leaders revived that demand. They found an ardent ally in Lieutenant Ethel Weed, CI&E's Women's Information Officer. This talented group, dubbed 'Weed's Girls', was barred from direct participation in Occupation policy decisions, but through Weed and her associates in GHQ, it was able to articulate to Occupation authorities the needs and aspirations of Japanese women. In March 1946, Weed's informal policy alliance called for the creation of a women's bureau. This demand was incorporated in a CI&E report, 'The Status of Women in Japan', which Weed had been instrumental in drafting. Katō Shizue, a key member of 'Weed's Girls' who met frequently with the women's policy group inside GHQ, may have transmitted the request to Weed.[51] In the spring of 1946, as Weed's group began to press for a special agency to protect and promote the rights of women, the US Advisory Committee on Labour began work on its interim report. In July, Helen Mears, the Committee's only woman, included a recommendation nearly identical to Weed's in the advisory group's conclusions. A specialist on working women, Mears also was a well-known Japanologist who had lectured on Japan at the Civil Affairs Training Schools during the war.

Armed with the Mears proposal, Weed's group had two final hurdles to clear, the first an internal one. Surprisingly, the women's policy coalition ran into stiff opposition from GS Deputy Chief Kades and his liberal colleague, Alfred Hussey. In mid-August, Hussey, after consulting Kades, penned a memorandum vetoing the concept of a separate bureau for women on the grounds that it would highlight rather than resolve differences between men and women and would arouse 'serious resentment and reaction' among the Japanese. These essentially were the same arguments Kades and Milo Rowell had advanced to discourage Beate Sirota's social welfare provisions earlier that year. Hussey specifically argued against the 'encouragement of a feminist movement in Japan' and any 'direct assault on the male position' liable to incite a proverbial 'Battle Between the Sexes'.

Weed's lobby inside GHQ did not toil in isolation, however. Universal suffrage and Articles 14 and 24 of the Constitution (promulgated in November 1946) established the principle of gender equality at home, in the workplace and in society at large, and women's rights activists rallied around Weed and her American supporters. In addition to Katō Shizue, this select English-speaking group of Japanese included Kume Ai, the first female lawyer admitted to the Japanese Bar; Fujita Taki, leader of the New Japan Women's League; Tanaka Sumiko, subsequently a Socialist Diet member and scholar; and Watanabe Michiko, a well-known attorney. Moreover, these women wanted not a ministerial bureau but an independent Cabinet agency, and they went public with their demands.[52] As indicated above, when Katō and other Socialists met Cohen and Ellerman in late September 1946, the Labour Division chief convinced them to press for the creation of a specialised women's bureau inside the proposed labour ministry rather than an autonomous Cabinet-level group. GHQ included that provision in the legislative draft it presented to the government on 10 February 1947.

As Hussey had foreseen, MacArthur's headquarters encountered stubborn resistance from the government, which objected that the Labour Ministry Bill should not include 'unimportant and minute' bureaux. A Women's and Minors' Section already existed in the Welfare Ministry's Labour Standards Bureau. Transferring that to the new Labour Ministry would be sufficient, they argued. For several months, Weed's group negotiated directly with the Yoshida Cabinet, and the Japanese women's movement brought intense public pressure to bear from the outside. In the end, GHQ and the women's alliance prevailed, and on 1 September 1947, with the full backing of the Katayama government, the Women's and Minors' Bureau (WMB) came into being with the new Labour Ministry. GHQ officials were adamant that the government should not staff the new Bureau with élite bureaucrats, opening the way for the appointment of women to head the new agency.

The Bureau was composed of three sections: Women Workers, Minor Workers and Women. It's first director, Yamakawa Kikue, a well-known feminist writer and Marxist intellectual, delivered strong leadership, and as a result, women subsequently were appointed to head other Ministry bureaux as well, a landmark development. Predictably, the WMB met internal resistance from the male hierarchy. The Labour Ministry attempted on three occasions to legislate it out of existence, but by 1948, the agency had established offices in every prefecture, and opposition from women's organisations at the national and local levels and from Weed's group inside GHQ successfully derailed these efforts. Several of the Japanese women Weed employed as her assistants went on to head the WMB and later achieved social prominence. Among these were feminist leader Fujita Taki, later President of Tsuda College for Women; Takahashi Nobuko, who would serve as Japanese delegate to the ILO and ambassador to Denmark; and veteran bureaucrat Tanino Setsu, who became a well-known author and women's rights advocate.[53]

The Women's and Minors' Bureau became a focus of activity for such women's organisations as the League for Democratising Family Law and the Women's Democratic Club. These groups joined forces with Weed and others in GHQ to ensconce women's rights in the Civil and Criminal Codes, whose revision the Constitution had made mandatory. Women such as Kawasaki Natsu, a liberal educator elected to the Upper House in the April 1947 elections, fought for these reforms as members of the Judiciary and Legislative Council created by the government to study the issue. Alfred Oppler, then of Government Section, and Legal Section's Kurt Steiner played a crucial supporting role in this process, assisted by a dynamic group of forward-looking academicians. Among these were Miyazawa Toshiyoshi, a constitutional scholar at Tokyo University in whom Oppler found 'a kind of spiritual ally'; Kawashima Takeyoshi, a young Tokyo University law professor and 'courageous critic of the feudal features of Japanese society'; civil law expert Wagatsuma Sakae; and two specialists in criminal and civil procedure, Dandō Shigemitsu and Kaneko Hajime. Together, this diverse coalition realised some of the goals that Sirota and Katō had struggled for unsuccessfully a year earlier.[54]

The Criminal Code, revised on 26 October 1947, abolished the crime of adultery, which formerly had applied only to women. Under pressure from Japanese women's groups and MacArthur's headquarters, male bureaucrats and lawmakers opted to do away with this provision rather than make men equally liable under the statute. The revised Civil Code of 22 December reformed the household (*ie*) system; abolished male primogeniture and discriminatory clauses governing marriage, divorce and property rights; and enabled women, in principle at least, to register marriages under their own names. Family courts were established to settle property and child-custody disputes equitably. The de facto evisceration of the *ie* system, in particular, went well beyond what even SCAP's civil rights experts had anticipated and aroused bitter opposition from conservative lawmakers. An impassioned defence of the proposed revisions by Diet woman Kawasaki Natsu, however, swayed the members of the Judiciary and Legislative Council, and the measures subsequently passed into law.[55]

Revision of the National Public Service Law
At the tail end of the labour reforms was the 1948 revision of the National Public Service Law, the work of civil-service expert Blaine Hoover. Hoover was scandalised by the notion that government workers should be allowed to defy the state through collective bargaining and strike action. His final report of June 1947, reflecting the anti-strike provisions in the Wagner Act of 1935, had recommended that laws be passed allowing civil servants to organise but not to negotiate collectively or strike. Similarly, public enterprise workers were to have the right to organise and

Photo 45. Ex-Prime Minister Ashida Hitoshi banters with journalists as he prepares to enter the Tokyo Prosecutor's Office to answer corruption charges in the Shōwa Denkō scandal, 12 December 1948. Ashida' policies seriously weakened the labour movement and assured a conservative takeover of power that would last until the early 1990s (Kyodo).

bargain collectively but not to strike. Prime Minister Katayama strongly objected to the Hoover recommendations, for the public-sector unions constituted the Socialist Party's primary base of support. GHQ subsequently agreed to drop these proposals from its October 1947 civil service reform, to Hoover's chagrin. The American personnel specialist, however, had succeeded in convincing SCAP to set up a Civil Service Division inside Government Section and appoint him to lead it. From this position of strength, Hoover began work on a revision of the National Public Service Law, and this time his efforts were crowned with success.

In the meantime, the Katayama Cabinet collapsed. The Socialist Party had pursued a policy of nationalising major industries, but the implementing legislation it sponsored in the Diet failed to pass muster. The split between the Socialist right and left wings widened, as Marxists refused to support a supplementary budget raising railway fares in a bid to increase government revenues. Another blow was the purge of Katayama's Agriculture Minister, the right-wing Socialist Hirano Rikizō, for his wartime ultra-nationalist ties. Finally, in early March 1948, Shidehara and 30 conservative Democrats broke away from the coalition and joined Yoshida's Liberals, forming the Democratic Liberal Party. The Katayama administration disintegrated, and on 10 March, Ashida Hitoshi, the Democrat's moderate leader, inaugurated a new government. The Ashida Cabinet was built on the same three-party coalition as its predecessor (Democrats, Socialists, People's Cooperatives), and enjoyed the

continuing support of Kades and Guy Swope. MacArthur, however, had not personally endorsed the new leader's ascension to power, leaving the premier somewhat
insecure in his relations with GHQ.

Ashida's Labour Minister, Socialist Katō Kanjū, had pledged publicly not to revise
the labour laws, but the new prime minister was ill-prepared to oppose a concerted
effort by MacArthur's headquarters to amend the National Public Service Law. On
22 July 1948, the Supreme Commander sent Ashida a strongly worded letter endorsing Hoover's views and stating that strike action by government workers, 'looking
toward the paralysis of government by those who have sworn to support it, is
unthinkable and intolerable'. (MacArthur upheld the right to bargain collectively for
certain public-enterprise employees, such as National Railway workers, however.)[56]
Ashida quickly conceded defeat, and on 31 July, his government issued Cabinet
Order 201 making the Hoover plan operational pending final legislation by the Diet.
The interim order immediately denied 2.5 million workers – 40 per cent of the
nation's public employees – the right to strike and to bargain collectively, as guaranteed by Article 28 of the Constitution, and the full protection of the Labour Union
and Labour Relations Adjustment Laws. The Diet formally enacted the revised
National Civil Service Law on 3 December.[57]

MacArthur's letter of 22 July represented SCAP's first institutional encroachment
on post-reform labour relations in the public sector. The General penned the brief
the day after a dramatic six-hour, one-to-one confrontation between Hoover and
Labour Division Chief Killen that took place in his presence. Killen had entered
GHQ as a conservative (AFL) replacement for the liberal Cohen, but even he was
appalled by SCAP's intensifying anti-labour stance. Paul Stanchfield, his lieutenant
in Labour Division, agreed with him. Killen concurred that government employees
should not be allowed to go out on strike but bitterly resented Hoover's attempt to
deny them the right to bargain collectively. When the Supreme Commander, with
GS Chief Whitney's support, sided with Hoover, Killen was livid. On 30 July, the
day before Cabinet Order 201 was promulgated, he resigned in protest, and Stanchfield followed his example. MacArthur's decision, Killen believed, was 'another step
– albeit a long one – in the rather sharp swing to the right gradually evidenced in
the policies of this Headquarters'. In a press conference, he characterised that move
as 'ill-conceived' and warned that it would 'retard a healthy labour movement'.
Killen left Japan shortly afterwards, his angry departure a vivid testimony to the
Occupation's accelerating abandonment of its early reformist mission.[58]

MacArthur's support for Hoover was motivated in large part by his fear of growing
Communist influence in public-sector unions, which, GHQ held, was injecting 'a
generally discordant, fractious and disorganising element in government and industrial relations'. In December of that year, the General justified his decision to a visiting
US advisory group, asserting that in more stable countries, when labour arbitration
failed in the public services 'there was always the Army', but Japan, he said, would not
have an army for a long time.[59] The new civil service provisions amplified labour
agitation, however, exacerbating rather than remedying social turbulence.

The union movement in general condemned the strike-busting order as a violation of constitutional freedoms and basic labour law and vowed to overturn it. National Railway workers staged walkouts across the country leading to more than 100 arrests; teachers, postal employees and telecommunications workers organised massive protests; and, for the first time, millions of ordinary Japanese found themselves openly opposed to a SCAP policy. The measure also was challenged by the Soviet representative in the Allied Council for Japan in Tokyo. In the Far Eastern Commission in Washington, all members except the Americans opposed GHQ's action. Australia and the Soviet Union presented counter-proposals that would have overturned MacArthur's decision, but although the FEC debated the issue until November 1949, it was unable to force a show of hands.[60] Even the US Army and the State Department looked askance at the anti-strike provision. In practical terms, however, there was little Japanese opponents could do other than register their dissent in the streets and on the shopfloor, and the temporary Cabinet Order stood, soon to be codified in law. Its unpopularity was an underlying factor in the fall of the Ashida government, which dissolved in early October under the weight of corruption allegations in the Shōwa Denkō affair. Ironically, the implementing legislation of 3 December was rammed through the Diet by the second Yoshida Cabinet, which replaced Ashida's discredited administration on October 15.

The denial of fundamental labour rights to public workers had far-reaching social and political repercussions. It opened GHQ to accusations that it was subverting its own reforms, that prohibitive law had now become basic policy and not a limited response to emergency situations. At the same time, it made the civil service as a whole a more pliant instrument of centralised authority (an undemocratic feature that the Occupation was committed in principle to rectify). Revision of the civil service law also generated widespread anti-American sentiment, discrediting Socialists in the Ashida government such as Katō Kanjū, the hapless Labour Minister. It was one of the factors that elevated left-wing Socialist Takano Minoru to the position of Secretary General of *Sōdōmei* and contributed to Nishio Suehiro's expulsion from that labour federation in late October 1948. The more militant national centre then publicly opposed the new Yoshida Cabinet. The revised law cost Katayama Tetsu, Katō Kanjū and spouse Shizue, Mizutani Chōzaburō, Nishio and other right-wing Socialists their Diet seats in the general elections of January 1949 and shifted popular support towards the Party's left wing and the Communists. Progressive Socialists gravitated further leftward, and in January the Party split, ending its influence as a unified political force. The new Socialist Party installed non-Communist radical Suzuki Mosaburō as chairman. Talented bureaucrats such as Wada Hiro'o, Agriculture Minister under the first Yoshida Cabinet and director of the Economic Stabilisation Board under Katayama, also joined the Socialist left at this time. Finally, the no-strike provision would give public-sector employers an excuse to dismiss some 11,000 workers for various degrees of labour activism, real and imagined, during the Dodge retrenchment of 1949, producing an unprecedented wave of labour dissent and protracted social strife (chapter 10).[61]

ZAIBATSU DISSOLUTION

With the enactment of basic labour reforms, SCAP turned to the second phase of economic democratisation, *zaibatsu* dissolution. By 1946, Japan's four largest family-controlled holding companies – Mitsubishi, Mitsui, Sumitomo and Yasuda – together accounted for nearly 25 per cent of the paid-up capital of all incorporated businesses. In addition, there were six major 'new' *zaibatsu* that had tied their fortunes to the military and risen to positions of dominance in the economy: Asano, Furukawa, Ayukawa (Nissan), Ōkura, Nomura and Nakajima. In 1945, the combines collectively controlled 49 per cent of capital investment in mining, machinery and heavy industry, 50 per cent in banking and 61 per cent in shipping.[62] Thus, a few powerful families virtually monopolised basic resources, services, commerce, industrial production, banking and finance. Free enterprise was confined to a small segment of the total economy whose activities were tightly constrained by the giant industrial-financial empires. This created a dualistic economy, where a small but modernised capital-intensive industrial sector dominated a much larger labour-intensive, under-capitalised and relatively backward sector.

SWNCC's 'Initial Post-Surrender Policy for Japan' called for 'the dissolution of Japan's large industrial and banking combinations which have exercised control of a great part of Japan's trade and industry'. Washington was intent on destroying the cartels, as it had done in Germany, for two reasons. First, US policy planners were convinced that the Big Four – Mitsubishi, Mitsui, Sumitomo and Yasuda – had been in league with the militarists since the 1930s. Together with the 'new' *zaibatsu*, they stood accused of having built Japan's engine of aggression and then reaped colossal profits from wartime collusion. The destruction of this dense concentration of economic power and the industrial-military complex that sustained it was a precondition for demilitarising and democratising the economy. Yoshida Shigeru maintained close personal ties with Ikeda Seihin, chief manager of the Mitsui complex and a member of the wartime Yoshida peace group. The Prime Minister and the conservative élite around him argued that war responsibility lay not with the 'old *zaibatsu*', which they characterised as peacefully inclined, but with upstart groups of 'new' *zaibatsu* that had cashed in on military contracts and operated freely in the territories under Japanese occupation. In fact, both groups had cooperated closely with the military, profiting handsomely from the war effort, and both were thoroughly undemocratic in structure and operation. SCAP was determined to dismantle these oligopolies and break their stranglehold on the economy.[63]

A second motivating factor was America's own tradition of decartelisation dating from the Sherman Anti-Trust Act of 1890. US hostility to the monopolistic suppression of free enterprise also had produced the Clayton Anti-Trust Act of 1914. Although anti-cartel fervour cooled during the 1920s, it rekindled in the 1930s under the New Deal, culminating in the Robinson–Putman Act of 1936. This reformist zeal carried over into planning for post-surrender Japan. Inside MacArthur's headquarters, the officials most closely involved in *zaibatsu*-dissolution were either

New Dealers themselves or had helped plan the Japanese deconcentration pro-
gramme in wartime Washington. Among them were Charles Kades, Thomas
Bisson and Eleanor Hadley of Government Section, and J. McI. Henderson and
Edward C. Welsh of the Economic and Scientific Section (Anti-Trust and Cartels
Division). Welsh had served previously on the Temporary National Economic
Committee, a joint legislative-executive body set up during the 1930s to oversee US
monopoly-busting policies.

In October 1945, SCAP proposed that the *zaibatsu* dismantle themselves voluntarily. Colonel Raymond C. Kramer, the first ESS chief, met *zaibatsu* representatives,
anxious to avoid radical dismemberment, and ordered them to draw up plans for their
own demise. Reading the writing on the wall, Yasuda complied immediately and
submitted a proposal that became known as the Yasuda Plan. Mitsui and Sumitomo,
however, stalled for time, while Mitsubishi rejected the suggestion outright and
refused to cooperate. Ultimately, under firm pressure from the government, all three
would relent and adopt the Yasuda Plan as the basis for dissolution.

The Yasuda Plan was patently self-serving and full of loopholes, a transparent
'easy-out' for the *zaibatsu*. The combines were integrated vertically in a four-tiered
pyramid. At the top was a family council and, just under it, a main holding company.
The third and fourth levels consisted of major subsidiaries, below which were smaller
affiliated firms owned or controlled by the subsidiaries. The Yasuda Plan proposed to
disband the holding companies by selling family shares and forcing family members
to resign their positions in the large subsidiaries. It conveniently left these subsidiaries
and their lower-level affiliates and subcontractors intact, however, thereby preserving
the vital infrastructure of the *zaibatsu* organisation. Under the Yasuda Plan, the
controlling families could sell their stock to loyal subordinates and reclaim their
former jobs at a later time.

The Edwards Report

MacArthur originally displayed scant enthusiasm for decartelisation. On 6 November 1945, he hastily accepted the lenient Yasuda proposals and issued SCAPIN-244
('Dissolution of Holding Companies') ordering the combines to liquidate their family holdings. The State and Justice Departments were disturbed by SCAP's seemingly
lackadaisical attitude toward the *zaibatsu* empire. In January 1946, they despatched
a joint departmental mission to Japan led by Northeastern University economist
Corwin D. Edwards to report on the dissolution programme and make broad
recommendations for decentralising the economy.

In March 1946, the Edwards Mission presented a report that was highly critical of
the anti-monopoly programme. The 'Report of the Mission on Japanese Combines'
noted that the current reform left major operating subsidiaries untouched and
ignored such practices as interlocking directorates and the cross-holding of corporate
stocks. It proposed a two-stage decartelisation policy based on the US model that
would dissolve the combines and prevent the emergence of new monopolies through
tough anti-trust legislation. The Edwards Report did not stop at the dissolution of

the large family companies but urged the breakup of all economic enterprises constituting 'an excessive concentration of economic power' and a 'potential threat to competitive enterprise'. The adjective 'excessive' was applied to any economic entity deemed large enough to restrict competition or independent business activity.[64] To ensure the thorough breakdown of the giant family concerns into smaller unrelated units and prevent the divestment of assets to relatives, the report redefined a family firm to include relations by adoption and marriage. It also recommended that the government buy up real estate and other assets belonging to the holding companies at low postwar market prices and convert those assets into 10-year non-negotiable government bonds for sale to company smallholders, including executives, employees, labour unions, cooperatives and the general public. The Edwards Report also targeted the interweaving of personnel and capital assets between *zaibatsu* banks and individual subsidiaries. It recommended that preferential treatment of holding-company financial institutions by the government be outlawed; that the amount of stock held by any financial institution in a company be limited to 25 per cent; and that officials from the Ministry of Finance and state-controlled financial institutions be prevented from owning stock in private banks or finance companies, or from seeking employment in those institutions for at least two years after retiring from government.

MacArthur deeply resented Edwards's criticisms, which he viewed as outside meddling, and ESS Chief Marquat characterised the report's recommendations as too sweeping, too liberal and too unrealistic. In May 1947, after more than a year of SCAP inaction, SWNCC, the primary US policy-making body, asked the Far Eastern Commission to approve the Edwards proposals as basic Occupation policy. The FEC complied in June, drafting FEC-230, 'US Policy with Respect to Excessive Concentrations of Economic Power in Japan'. The document was kept secret so that MacArthur could present it to the government as a direct order. FEC-230 became the most controversial of the FEC's position papers, but the Commission never formally adopted it as policy.[65]

Anti-trust action and reaction
Meanwhile, SCAP, now firmly committed to the Yasuda Plan, had begun to implement it with a vengeance. In August 1946, the government set up the Holding Company Liquidation Commission (HCLC), which set out to dispose of the shares of 83 holding companies. A total of 16 were dissolved, among them all 10 of the major *zaibatsu* family companies. Some 26 conglomerates were dismantled and then restructured. Eleven were reorganised, and the remaining 30 were left intact. This offensive was accompanied by the introduction of anti-trust legislation, enacted on 12 March 1947 as the Law for Prohibition of Private Monopoly and Methods of Preserving Fair Trade (the so-called Anti-Monopoly Law). This statute prohibited the formation of holding companies, sole-agency contracts and cartels, and created the Fair Trade Commission to enforce its provisions. At the same time, GHQ conducted a moderate purge of *zaibatsu* and other top business leaders considered to

have engaged in blatantly monopolistic practices. The economic purge began in January 1947, exactly one year after the political and labour purges. By June 1947, it had removed, directly or indirectly, more than 1,500 executives and corporate officials, although they remained free to seek employment outside their former business groups.[66]

MacArthur, in an apparent reversal of roles, now became the foremost proponent of radical dissolution, ostensibly embracing the Edwards proposals he earlier had derided. His change of attitude may have been due in part to the influence of Kades and other trust-busters in Government Section who had MacArthur's confidence. The radical Edward Welsh, Chief of the ESS Anti-Trust and Cartels Division, was waging a one-man crusade against the combines. At his insistence, on 3 July 1947, GHQ ordered the disbanding of Japan's two largest trading companies, Mitsubishi Shōji and Mitsui Bussan, which together had cornered 70 per cent of Japan's prewar foreign trade. Both were giant operating subsidiaries, the only groups in fact that GHQ actually deposed directly. SCAP had decided to allow foreign firms to begin doing business in Japan in August of that year, and Welsh was intent on completing decartelisation before foreign businessmen descended on Tokyo. The Mitsubishi and Mitsui companies were broken up into some 213 successor firms, but they maintained their internal integrity, reorganising around former division and section chiefs, and within five years, they had basically reconstituted themselves.[67]

Welsh's determination to break up operating industrial firms and transform Japan into a country of small- and medium-sized businesses collided with the Katayama Cabinet's commitment to nationalisation. It also ran counter to the desperate efforts of the Economic Stabilisation Board and SCAP's own ESS to streamline production and raise productivity. ESS's Cohen, an advocate of moderate deconcentration, found Welsh's idea of using the Holding Company Liquidation Commission to oversee this massive dissolution of productive capacity 'vague and arbitrary', even 'unreal'.[68]

By mid-1947, US policy makers, too, had undergone a change of heart, but in a different direction. Now wary of undermining Japanese capitalism, they strove to restrain the pace of *zaibatsu* dissolution. MacArthur's strong stand on behalf of economic democratisation brought him and his anti-cartel programme into a head-on confrontation with Washington and US business interests. A new emphasis on economic recovery, containing Communism and strengthening conservative rule in Japan would evolve over the next year into a major reorientation of Occupation policy. SCAP's efforts to pass a new industrial deconcentration bill with more muscle than the Anti-Monopoly Law of March 1947 provided the first crucial test of this policy shift. Based on FEC-230, whose recommendations he now fully endorsed, MacArthur geared up to enact a particularly tough piece of legislation modelled on the anti-trust laws US occupation forces had implemented in Germany. The 'Bill for the Elimination of Concentrations of Economic Power', introduced to the Diet in July at MacArthur's insistence, took aim at leading subsidiary firms powerful enough to restrict market access.

MacArthur's apparent war on oligopoly raised eyebrows in Washington. The US

Chamber of Commerce, the National Association of Manufacturers and other business lobbies were alarmed, and *Fortune Magazine* denounced what it labelled 'Scapitalism'. Deconcentration also aroused the ire of James L. Kauffman, a high-powered New York corporate lawyer who had represented major US companies in prewar Japan and taught English at Tokyo Imperial University. Kauffman had been rebuffed by Welsh in the summer of 1947 when he sought an exemption for the dissolution of a company in which his client, the glassmaker Libby–Owens–Ford, had an interest. Dismayed by Welsh's 'extremist' notions, he raised the alarm in Washington with his 'Report on Conditions in Japan as of September 6, 1947'. Circulated that autumn among top policy-makers and business leaders, the Kauffman Report warned that MacArthur's 'radical reformers' and 'crackpots' were attempting to destroy big business in Japan and impose a form of Socialism on the country. Particularly unpalatable to Kauffman was the notion of allowing labour unions to acquire corporate shares. SCAP policies, he fumed, were endangering the US goal of making Japan a self-supporting anti-Communist ally. Secretary of Defense James F. Forrestal and Under-Secretary of the Army William H. Draper – both former partners of a major Wall Street investment house – lent Kauffman a ready ear. They solicited the support of Secretary of the Army Kenneth Royall and embarked on a closely coordinated campaign to eviscerate MacArthur's deconcentration bill – and sink the Supreme Commander's prospects in the 1948 presidential election.

On 1 December 1947, *Newsweek*'s foreign editor Harry F. Kern launched a broadside against MacArthur's policies. The article sparked a debate in Congress, where a Republican Senator from California, William F. Knowland, attacked the deconcentration plan on the Senate floor, brandishing a copy of FEC-230 that Draper had leaked to him. The *Newsweek* article was blistering. It quoted extensively from FEC-230 and printed generous excerpts from the Kauffman Report, reinforcing the message that SCAP's purge, reparations and deconcentration policies were extremist and incompatible with America's national interests. Earlier, Kern himself had editorialised that, unless MacArthur were stopped, 'the chances of making Japan into "the workshop of the Far East" as part of the American policy of rebuilding the world and containing Communism will have gone glimmering'. This sentiment echoed the credo of the emerging Japan Lobby, a group of wealthy industrialists, Eastern Establishment intellectuals, generals and policy experts, including key members of the original Japan Crowd, that would play a decisive role in crafting and orchestrating a basic revision of Occupation objectives (chapter 10).[69]

MacArthur harboured a deep distrust of big finance, however, and had committed himself to a course of action. In this, he enjoyed the constant support of Kades, a fierce critic of the US business lobby, who accused Kauffman of attempting to 'preserve in Japan those very institutions, influences and practices which brought on the war'. Enraged by the simultaneous attack on Occupation policy and his political ambitions, the Supreme Commander railroaded the deconcentration bill through the Diet. To get the law that MacArthur wanted, Justin Williams of Government Section's Legislative Division was despatched to monitor Upper House deliberations on the bill. On the last day of the session near midnight, Williams stood up and dramatically insisted that the adjective 'excessive' be inserted into the Elimination of Concentrations of Economic Powers Bill. He suggested that the Diet clock be stopped to gain the time needed to clear the provision and refused to budge from the spot until the legislation was passed as SCAP intended.[70] On 8 December 1947, the bill was enacted as the Law on the Elimination of Excessive Concentrations of Economic Power and put into force on 18 December, giving the Holding Company Liquidation Commission the power to ensure competition by designating and dissolving monopolistic concentrations. MacArthur's insistence on the word 'excessive' was his way of letting Washington know who was boss. The General's victory was short-lived, however. The Department of the Army, having reversed its stand on deconcentration, would effectively negate this legislation three months later, handing MacArthur a humiliating defeat (chapter 10).

LAND REFORM

The third pillar of SCAP's economic democracy programme (alongside the liberation of labour and economic deconcentration) was land reform, one of the most ambitious and successful initiatives of the Occupation. Here, the Jeffersonian ideal of independent yeoman producers – small 'independent capitalists' providing through their industry and egalitarian ownership of the means of production a solid base for the development of democratic institutions – was realised to a remarkable extent. The result was a peaceful agrarian revolution that swept aside pre-modern social relations and transformed the Japanese countryside.

In the 1930s, rural distress brought about by the collapse of the world silk market, lower rice prices – partly a consequence of importing cheaper Korean and Formosan grain – and generally depressed economic conditions had produced a rapid increase in rates of tenancy and deepened rural distress. This was accompanied by a corresponding rise in the wealth and political influence of the landlord class, which included many absentee owners. The delivery of between one third and half or more of their harvest to landlords left many tenants in great extremity. Such oppressive conditions provided a bumper crop of new recruits for the military and right-wing ideologues and accelerated agricultural colonisation by Japanese settlers in Manchukuo. Landlordism not only assured the militarists of crucial political support for their expansionist policies but helped channel rural unrest into external aggression, diffusing internal class tensions. By war's end, nearly 50 per cent of all Japanese lived in farming areas, but almost half of all land under cultivation was being worked by non-owners, and roughly 70 per cent of the nation's cultivators were involved in some degree of tenancy. Holdings were divided into small, scattered plots averaging less than 1 hectare (2.47 acres). A majority of landlords themselves owned only a few hectares, but the social, economic and political disparities that set them apart from smallholders and tenants were glaring.

Land redistribution, like the Labour Standards Law, owed much of its success to reform-minded Japanese bureaucrats. In early 1946, the Foreign Ministry's Special Survey Committee proposed the elimination of landlordism, which, like US policy-makers, it blamed for constricting the domestic market and depressing industrial wages. Paradoxically, however, Washington was divided on the land question as the Occupation began. Three distinct pre-surrender positions had emerged on this issue. The State Department's China Crowd, calling for a punitive peace, saw land reform as necessary to increase food production and eliminate reactionary elements in the countryside. Conservatives in the Japan Crowd, notably Joseph Grew and Eugene Dooman, believed that radical land reallotment would undercut conservative farm support for the Occupation. Other Japan Crowd members, notably Hugh Borton, George Blakeslee and Robert Fearey, supported land reform in principle, believing it to be the only means of alleviating rural poverty and stabilising the economy. As a result of such policy disagreements, the 'US Initial Post-Surrender Policy for Japan' did not include land reform, and the controversy remained unresolved as MacArthur established his headquarters.[71]

Indecision in Washington enabled the Shidehara administration to seize the initiative and draft a reform of its own liking. The first government proposal, however, proved too radical for conservative lawmakers in the Cabinet. On 13 October 1945, the Ministry of Agriculture publicised the outline of a reform draft prepared by Wada Hiro'o, the radical agrarian expert jailed in 1941 for his leftist views, and Tōhata Shirō, another reform bureaucrat. The Wada Plan would allow tenants to buy land held by non-absentee landowners in excess of 3 hectares; make farm rents payable as fixed cash amounts rather than in kind; and reorganise and expand the role of land commissions, the local agencies designated to buy up and redistribute tenanted land. As Yoshida later recalled, the Shidehara government greeted Wada's scheme 'with a chorus of objections' and submitted in its place a watered-down proposal that raised the ceiling on ownership to 5 hectares and added other provisions advantageous to landowners.[72]

GHQ's agrarian emancipation directives

By mid-October 1945, SCAP, too, had begun to mull the merits of land reform. When Natural Resources Section failed to move quickly on the issue, MacArthur assigned this task to Civil Information and Education Section. On 9 November, General Headquarters issued SCAPIN-257 ('Agricultural Programme') directing the government to submit a plan on its long-range food-production goals by the end of December. The plan did not concern land reform per se but was to include counter-measures for the problems of tenancy, credit, ground rents and taxes.

In the meantime, Robert Fearey, recently attached to the Political Adviser's Office in Tokyo, was dusting off a copy of the unpublished proposal that Russian-born agrarian specialist Dr Wolf I. Ladejinsky had drawn up in Washington, 'Adjustments in Systems of Land Tenure' (chapter 5). Ladejinsky's father was a Ukrainian land-lord, but his Russian experience and studies of Japanese tenancy in the 1930s had made him a believer in egalitarian land reallotment. Ladejinsky's ideas on Japanese land holding derived largely from a group of radical Japanese agronomists, including Yagi Yoshinosuke and Kawada Shirō of Kyoto Imperial University. Another formative influence on Ladejinsky was Nasu Hiroshi, an advocate of land redistribution at Tokyo Imperial University and author of the influential *Aspects of Japanese Agriculture: A Preliminary Survey* (Institute of Pacific Relations, 1941).[73]

Fearey summarised the Ladejinsky proposal in a memorandum and passed it on to POLAD Chief George Atcheson. Atcheson presented the so-called Fearey Memorandum to MacArthur, who endorsed its ideas with enthusiasm. By abolishing tenancy and alleviating rural misery, the Memorandum said, an Occupation-directed agrarian reform would not only prevent a resurgence of militarism but nip radical Socialist and Communist ambitions in the bud. The General's prewar experience in the Philippines convinced him of the merits of giving land to the tiller. His father had advocated land reform there as part of the effort to subdue Aguinaldo's national liberation movement in the early 1900s, and MacArthur himself had proposed similar action to counter the influence of Communist-dominated Hukbalahap insurgents.[74]

Fearey's recommendations also found a strong supporter in the person of William J. Gilmartin of Natural Resources Section, who added a provision covering land owned by absentee landlords. On 9 December 1945, the Supreme Commander incorporated these proposals into SCAPIN-411 ('Rural Land Reform'), drafted by CI&E's Arthur Behrstock, which instructed Shidehara to submit a comprehensive land-reform programme by 15 March 1946. The new directive was explicit: the government would buy up land from non-operating owners, sell it to the tillers and eliminate absentee landlordism by transferring their property to landless tenants. This was necessary, the document said, in order to 'exterminate those pernicious ills which have long blighted the agrarian structure'.[75]

The Imperial Diet, unreformed and still dominated by big landlords, responded by promulgating on 28 December the conservative measures it had substituted for the Wada Plan. The Agricultural Land Adjustment Law permitted landlords to retain 5 hectares, delegated the vital task of purchasing and redistributing hectarage to landlord–tenant negotiations and failed to define absentee landlords precisely. The law was scheduled to go into effect on 1 February 1946, but strong opposition from SCAP consigned the so-called first land reform to oblivion. The government's failure to draft an acceptable law transferred the initiative for reform to MacArthur's staff, which set about formulating its own agrarian programme, the so-called second land reform.

CI&E had drawn up SCAPINs 257 and 411, but now Government Section and Economic and Scientific Section also became involved. Work got under way in February 1946 and, in March, primary responsibility for the reform shifted from CI&E back to Natural Resources Section. The drafting committee included William T. Gilmartin and Ladejinsky of NRS (the latter having transferred to Japan for that purpose in December); Lieutenant W. Hicks of CI&E; and Thomas Bisson and

Dr Andrew J. Grajdanzev of GS. On 9 May, Ladejinsky completed a staff study borrowing heavily from ideas that Yagi Yoshinosuke had advanced in 1936: national expropriation of tenanted land and its sale to the tillers, compensation for landlords and entrenched tenancy rights.[76]

On 21 May, as NRS put the finishing touches on its legislative draft, Yoshida named reformist Wada Hiro'o as his new Agriculture Minister (Wada's predecessor had been purged in January). Yoshida originally had approached Tōbata Sei'ichi, a liberal non-Marxist agrarian economist at Tokyo Imperial University, but the widely respected scholar blanched at the enormity of the task of restoring food production and declined the offer. Wada's appointment thoroughly alarmed the conservatives. A man of intellectual brilliance, Wada had been jailed for three years (1941–4) under the Peace Preservation Law for attempting to insinuate Socialist ideas into the wartime Cabinet Planning Board. Before the war, he had organised study groups seeking solutions to the problems of farm tenancy and landholding. Yoshida clearly was desperate to remedy the food situation. The collapse of farm production, recent food rallies, forcible grain seizures by local 'food-control committees' and the growth of peasant–worker alliances were potent threats to his government. Although opposed to land redistribution in principle, the Prime Minister was resigned to the American reform initiative and later accounted it a great success.[77]

The irony now was nearly complete: Wada, the social radical, would implement a land redistribution programme drafted by the son of a Jewish Ukrainian landlord based on the ideas of prewar Japanese agrarian reformers. The final result, however, would go beyond what even Ladejinsky had envisaged. It remained for the Soviet and Commonwealth delegates on the Allied Council for Japan to intervene boldly, propelling the process rapidly to the left.

In late May and June of 1946, the ACJ took up the land question. On 29 May, Kuzma Derevyanko proposed a reallocation scheme that was even more far-reaching than SCAP's. The Soviet delegate urged the state to buy up and resell all tenant-cultivated land, compensate landlords only for the transfer of holdings of up to 6 hectares but at prices that amounted to de facto expropriation, confiscate everything over 6 hectares, subsidise tenant land acquisitions and complete the reform within one year. On 12 June, British Commonwealth representative MacMahon Ball unexpectedly came to GHQ's rescue. Without consulting London, which was studiously unenthusiastic about land redistribution, the Australian tabled a counter-proposal drafted by his economic adviser Eric Ward. Ward noted that the government's proposed upper limit of 5 hectares on landlord-retained land would free only 30 per cent or less of all tenanted land, whereas the 3-hectare limit favoured by Ladejinsky would liberate about half of such land. After consulting with Ladejinsky and Gilmartin, Ward proposed to lower that ceiling to one hectare, which he estimated would emancipate 70 per cent of Japan's tenant farmers. Consequently, Ball recommended that the government fix the amount of tenant-cultivated property a landlord could retain at 1 hectare, impose an absolute limit of 3 hectares (12 in Hokkaido) on all holdings and make the acquisition programme compulsory.[78]

The Derevyanko and Ball proposals were debated at length in an Allied Council meeting on 17 June, as were subsequent compromise measures submitted by Derevyanko and the Chinese delegate, General Chu Shih-ming. MacArthur was incensed at the Soviet project, which he reviled as an effort 'to disrupt Allied plans for the democratisation of Japan'. Derevyanko, he stormed, was 'endeavoring to show himself to the Japanese public and the world at large as taking the lead in, and as forcing SCAP to effect necessary . . . land and labour reforms'.[79] Determined to deflate the Soviet initiative, the SCAP team quickly adopted Ball's plan, and Ladejinsky incorporated its salient points into a new directive, which was shown informally to Agriculture Minister Wada on 28 June. MacArthur had insisted that the sweeping reform be presented as a Japanese project, and NRS Chief Hubert G. Schenck read the draft directive aloud to Wada and told him to revise the Japanese legislation accordingly. Wada, afraid the Cabinet would shrink from such a radical reform, asked NRS to make the directive public in a bid to circumvent government obstruction. Schenck, however, had instructions to keep SCAP out of the picture and refused the request. From 28 June to 9 August, the NRS team and Wada's group met 14 times to iron out a final draft, which MacArthur approved on 14 August.

The bill was submitted to the Diet on 7 September 1946, but opposition surfaced from an unexpected quarter. Andrew Grajdanzev of Government Section's Local Government Division protested that the programme was too extreme; what was needed, he said, was 'reform, not a revolution'. Grajdanzev convinced GS Chief Whitney to back his demand to clarify exceptions to the 3-hectare upper limit on holdings in a way that would benefit large landowners. Whitney also agreed to modify the composition of the land commissions to favour landlords. Wada, however, dug in his heels and refused to budge on the issue, and Schenck threw his full support to the plucky Agriculture Minister, embroiling NRS in a battle royal with the more powerful GS, which won the day. Whitney accused Schenck, in effect, of kowtowing to the Japanese and ultimately browbeat the NRS chief into compliance. Government Section obliged Wada to make exceptions to the 3-hectare limit and impose a land-price ceiling. As Diet deliberations on the amended bill proceeded, NRS abandoned its earlier strategy of secrecy, Schenck warning a Liberal Party delegation of 'dire consequences' should Parliament fail to carry the legislation. In that case, he said, the Supreme Commander would have no alternative but to issue a formal directive.[80] The law was enacted without incident on 21 October.

The agrarian legislation incorporated the key points of the NRS directive, but the nuts and bolts of reform were worked out by a highly qualified group of agronomists in the Ministry's Agricultural Administration Bureau. One of these, Ogura Takekazu, later complained that 'NRS had few reliable and capable staff members [for] land reform and other related important agricultural polic[ies]'. Neither Chief of Section Schenck nor his agrarian expert Warren Leonard had specialised knowledge of agricultural economics or social issues, Ogura said. He concluded that: 'In short, the staff members of GHQ did not appear to be able to initiate and draft the second land reform.' The details were provided by the Japanese themselves, within the parameters established by the NRS team.[81]

The quiet 'revolution'

The October 1946 reform was codified in two statutes, the Agricultural Adjustment Law and the Special Measures Law for the Establishment of Owner–Cultivators, which together incorporated most of Ladejinsky's ideas. The Ball proposals had proved decisive, however. Individual landholdings were limited to 3 hectares across the board and tenant-farmed land to 1 hectare. The law backdated landownership to November 1945 to prevent landlords from evicting their tenants. The state was authorised to purchase land belonging to absentee landlords and uncultivated holdings for redistribution to tenants, who also had the option of buying the land they worked, either immediately or over a 30-year period at low early postwar interest rates. Land prices were pegged to 1937 values, a pittance compared to the inflated prices of 1947 and 1948. Thus, tillers of the soil acquired property rights for what amounted to the cost of one salted salmon per 0.1 hectare. Moreover, annual payments for land could not exceed one third of the value of a farmer's crop, after taxes. Landlords were reimbursed for the value of their estates in long-term government bonds. Rents, limited to cash payments, were not to exceed 25 per cent of annual crop values, and tenants gained important contractual rights. The programme was implemented by tripartite village, prefectural and national land commissions composed of tenants, landlords and owner-cultivators, with tenants accounting at village and prefectural levels for 50 per cent of commission members (landlord representation was 30 per cent, owner–cultivator participation 20 per cent).[82]

The reform was largely completed between 1947 and 1948. By 1949, it had reallocated 2 million hectares of arable land, or about 80 per cent of all tenanted holdings, and rented property had fallen from the prewar figure of 46 per cent to 10 per cent. Some 57 per cent of rural families became farm owners, and 35 per cent became part-owner, part-tenants. By the end of the reform, 90 per cent of all land under crops was being cultivated by independent growers, and the number of landless tenants had declined to a mere 7 per cent of farm producers. The long-term consequence of redistribution was a steady decline in the percentage of Japanese on the land as farm mechanisation proceeded apace and high urban wages siphoned young people into the industrial work force.

The Supreme Commander was elated. The day the two reform bills became law, he issued a statement heralding the event as 'one of the most important milestones yet reached by Japan in the creation of an economically stable and politically democratic society'. With a potent MacArthurian flourish, he concluded: 'By it there will be here established the basic policy [that] those who till the land shall keep the profit of their toil. There can be no firmer foundation for a sound and moderate democracy and no firmer bulwark against the pressure of any extreme philosophy.'[83] For Japan's impoverished tenant farmers, the reform was a windfall, and MacArthur was widely

Photo 46. Farmers read an announcement on the community bulletin board declaring the start of the land reform in Saitama Prefecture, 24 June 1947. The epochal reform transformed a majority of cultivators from tenants into independent small-scale farmers, boosting agricultural production and eroding Socialist and Communist influence in the countryside (Mainichi).

acclaimed a friend and liberator. As GHQ had foreseen, the programme defused rural radicalism and kept the countryside conservative – a factor that doubtless encouraged Washington and MacArthur's critics to allow this particular assault on excessive economic concentration to run its full course.

In early February 1948, with its *zaibatsu* dissolution programme under attack, GHQ issued a new directive (SCAPIN-1855, 'Rural Land Reform') to accelerate the pace of land reallocation. Indeed, the striking success of the reform took some of the sting out of the failure of MacArthur's industrial deconcentration plan. The Occupation did not insist on redistributing forest and pasture, however, which accounted for a large percentage of rural land, and such holdings allowed many landlords to retain a degree of their former influence. Conservative governments quickly turned the reform to their advantage by paradoxically offering producers and agricultural cooperatives generous subsidies and financial incentives while pursuing industrial policies that undermined the overall position of agriculture in the economy. Today, in an age of globalism, the survival of Japanese agriculture seems uncertain, but the countryside remains a bastion of conservative sentiment.

CHAPTER 8

The Cultural Reforms

The Occupation sought to transform not only Japan's political, administrative and economic institutions but also the attitudes, values and beliefs the militarists had distorted to inculcate, in the idiom of American policy-makers, 'an extreme nationalism and a glorification of war'.[1] Redirecting an entire nation's thought processes in the short space of six and a half years was, of course, an unachievable task. Moreover, SCAP's own shifting priorities compromised that objective: after 1948, MacArthur's headquarters would retreat from its early commitment to reform, violating principles that it had struggled to establish in the first two years of occupation. Nonetheless, in many areas, the Occupation's programme of social and cultural reorientation laid the groundwork for a decisive rupture with the authoritarian past.

Washington ascribed the popular acceptance of Japanese militarism to ideological manipulation in three areas: education, religion and information. Since the Meiji era, the explicit purpose of formal instruction had been to serve the Imperial state, and children were taught absolute loyalty to the Emperor, love of country and devotion to duty. Girls and young women learned 'national morality and womanly virtues'; boys were inculcated with martial values and received paramilitary training. Ultranationalist course content was strengthened after Japan's invasion of Manchuria in 1931, and with the beginning of the Sino-Japanese War in 1937, education became overtly militaristic. Following the onset of the Pacific War, in addition to traditional military drills, boys now were taught how to fire rifles and light machine guns and hurl grenades. Unquestioning obedience to higher authority and self-sacrifice became supreme virtues. The cult of State Shintō was strengthened, and the mass media became an organ of state propaganda.

The ambitious reforms that SCAP's Civil Information and Education Section undertook from late 1945 through 1948 were an exercise in moral and psychological disarmament balanced by a positive project of institutional reform and collective re-education. Here, however, SCAP was obliged to rely extensively on Japanese administrators, intellectuals, teachers and others with hands-on expertise to achieve its basic goals. In the field of education, Occupation authorities found themselves working closely with their Japanese counterparts to implement what would turn out to be in some important respects a Japanese programme of reform.

REORIENTATING YOUNG MINDS

The State Department recommendations
State Department Asian specialists, including Japan scholars Hugh Borton and George Blakeslee, first broached the question of education reform in early 1943, advocating changes in Japan's political philosophy through 'supervision of the education system and of other media of indoctrination'.[2] In mid-July 1944, the State Department's Postwar Programmes Committee (PWC) approved a basic proposal for restructuring Japanese schooling: 'Japan: The Education System Under Military Government' (PWC-287). PWC-287 would evolve into the Occupation's master plan for education reform.[3] The policy paper asserted that traditional education had supported an authoritarian social and political régime. Universal education based on advancement by merit, while admirable in many respects, served the interests of the state, not the people. Japan's highly centralised and selective school system transformed 'the best brains of the nation' into an élite loyal to the state and big business but discouraged individual initiative and original thinking. Courses such as ethics (*shūshin*), history and military training, which taught students to 'offer [themselves] courageously to the State', were regarded as pernicious and slated for elimination.[4]

PWC-287 contained 10 recommendations. The first, that schools remain open to ensure public safety, acknowledged the role that the education system had played in maintaining internal order and sought to utilise it in establishing occupation control. Thought regimentation was to be abolished, militaristic textbooks revised and chauvinistic school curricula abandoned. Japanese educated in foreign mission schools or abroad and Japanese Americans might be used, the paper suggested, to enforce Allied education directives, and 'progressive and forward-looking Japanese' could be mobilised to prepare new textbooks and curricula. PCW-287 also called for the prohibition of nationalistic school ceremonies and observances. Finally, schools, radio broadcasting and motion pictures would be utilised to break down Japan's insularity and promote a world outlook.[5]

Nearly one year later, Washington's top policy-making body, the State–War–Navy Coordinating Committee, took a fresh look at the school question. In April 1945, it issued a control document, SWNCC-108, as the basis for a comprehensive policy statement on postwar education reform. The task of drafting this crucial document was assigned to a Japan specialist, Gordon T. Bowles. Working from PWC-287, Bowles completed his policy draft on 30 July, incorporating many of the earlier paper's recommendations.[6] His brief urged a series of radical changes, some of which went beyond the 1944 State Department proposals. First, it noted, the Education Ministry's use of textbooks recommended by the military had been a powerful influence on young minds. SWNCC-108 proposed to abolish textbooks espousing jingoism and ultra-nationalism. As a first step, it advocated replacing Shōwa-era readers, introduced in 1934 to glorify Japan's military exploits, with less objectionable Taishō-era texts compiled during the peaceful 1920s.[7]

SWNCC-108 recommended that courses in ethics, Japanese history and para-military training be removed from school curricula. It called for a ban on all forms of emperor worship in the schools, including the display of Imperial portraits (*goshin'ei*), ritual mass bowing in the direction of the Imperial Palace, formal recitations of the Meiji Imperial Rescript on Education and special convocations on national holidays. The document also decreed the purge of nationalistic teachers and administrators and the dissolution of the Education Ministry's Education Bureau, which was responsible for implementing thought-control policies. Where possible, sympathetic educators and officials willing to cooperate with the Occupation were to be retained. To instil in teachers a democratic viewpoint, the Bowles paper gave special weight to the reform of teacher's colleges. Finally, it urged a thorough decentralisation of the school system and greater educational and vocational opportunities for women.

On 19 July 1945, as Bowles was finalising SWNCC-108, the State–War–Navy Coordinating Committee forwarded a second document of equal importance to its Subcommittee for the Far East (SFE). The memorandum had been prepared at the behest of the Navy member of SWNCC, Artemus Gates, a former banker and president of Time, Inc., and reviewed by Borton and Bowles. 'Positive Policy for Reorientation of the Japanese' (SWNCC-162/D) called for major changes in 'ideologies and attitudes of mind . . . designed to bring about a Japan which would cease to be a menace to international security'. The crux of the problem, SWNCC-162/D asserted, was Japan's feudal outlook, Imperial cult and 'an extreme racial consciousness and an anti-foreign complex' which produced a chauvinistic 'common attitude of mind'.[8]

Japan's surrender on 15 August brought the planning process to a temporary halt, but on 18 August, preparations resumed in the SFE under the direction of Borton and Bowles. By then, the Bowles' SWNCC-108 proposals had been incorporated into the 'US Initial Post-Surrender Policy for Japan'. In early September, the SFE revised the second planning paper, SWNCC-162, to urge support from US civilian experts outside of the Occupation structure. Taken together, SWNCC-108 and SWNCC-162 called for a dual strategy of reforming the school system and redirecting the nation's habits of mind. These documents would form the backbone of the four implementing directives on education issued by GHQ in October and December (below). Many of the points in Bowles' study of July 1945 would be incorporated into the recommendations of the US Education Mission to Japan in early 1946. Adopted by the State–War–Navy Coordinating Committee as SWNCC-108/1 in September 1946, they would be approved by the Far Eastern Commission as official Allied policy in March 1947.[9]

The task of recasting Japan's education system was enormous. At the start of the Occupation, there were approximately 40,000 schools, 400,000 teachers and 18 million pupils. The burden of overhauling this colossal apparatus perforce would be borne largely by the Japanese. Early State Department plans to recruit Japanese-American civil affairs officers and foreign-educated Japanese to oversee reform at the central and prefectural levels were abandoned as unfeasible. GHQ might provide the framework and impetus for change, but the real work of reform would devolve on progressive Japanese educators. In the meantime, the Americans would have to work through existing institutional channels to eliminate the school system's 'pernicious' and 'obnoxious' features and win over the hearts and reorientate the minds of the nation's students and teachers.

Japan's 'educational somersault'

By the time Civil Information and Education Section had been established in the autumn of 1945, the Japanese Education Ministry already had plotted the first tentative coordinates of reform. CI&E possessed only the general guidelines laid down by the 'US Initial Post-Surrender Policy for Japan' and the two SWNCC policy drafts (108 and 162) to go by and would not issue its first formal directive to the government until late October. When the Section first approached the Education Ministry, a new Minister, Maeda Tamon, and reform-orientated bureaucrats stood ready with their own preliminary programme for change. Like most old-style liberals, Maeda's views on the Throne were solidly traditionalist.[10] Nevertheless, on 25 August 1945, before MacArthur's arrival, he suspended all laws and ordinances pertaining to military training in the schools. On 15 September, a week before CI&E was detached from AFPAC's Military Government Section as an independent staff group, the Ministry announced a comprehensive plan to revitalise education in a bid to pre-empt a more radical SCAP reform. The Ministry's 'Education Policy for the Construction of a New Japan' called for preservation of the Imperial institution, an end to militaristic and ultra-nationalistic practices and preachments in the schools and the establishment of a peace-loving nation. To this end, textbooks would be cleansed of unsuitable content, military-related instruction eliminated and a new emphasis placed on scientific education (a response to the atomic bomb). Consequently, on 3 October, the Ministry formally abolished military training in the schools, purged its bureaux and agencies of active-duty military officers and drew up plans for re-educating the nation's teachers.

Initially, CI&E was pleased. The 'US Initial Post-Surrender Policy' had authorised Japanese officials 'to exercise the normal powers of government in matters of domestic administration', and MacArthur's headquarters, not yet sufficiently organised to make informed policy proposals, appears generally to have welcomed the New Education Policy as a positive contribution to reform. Navy Lieutenant Robert K. Hall of CI&E's Education Branch termed the Japanese initiative 'the most dramatic educational somersault in modern times' and noted that the Ministry had so completely anticipated US intentions that his staff was forced to devote many hours to the systematic scrutiny of the voluntary reforms for possible omissions.[11]

Education Minister Maeda's position on the Emperor, however, while typical of many liberalists and consistent with the government's self-serving gloss of the Potsdam Proclamation, was wholly at odds with basic Occupation policy. During his brief tenure, Maeda would seek to preserve Imperial sovereignty as a basic tenet of education by reinscribing it in an ostensibly democratic discourse. In numerous public pronouncements, he stressed the importance of moral education and the primacy of the Meiji-era Imperial Rescript on Education, which he acclaimed as an inviolate pedagogical principle and a precondition for democracy. His views would be shared by his immediate successors, Abe Yoshishige (January to May 1946) and Tanaka Kōtarō (May 1946 to January 1947).[12] If GHQ looked askance at the Ministry's Imperial conservatism, the State Department took extreme umbrage at Maeda's attempt to perpetuate Royal authority in the schools. Following acerbic State Department criticisms, CI&E intervened, and the New Education Policy, fatally compromised by its commitment to the Throne, was soon superseded by sterner measures.

On 4 October, the day after Maeda announced his reform agenda, GHQ issued its Civil Liberties Directive (SCAPIN-93), toppling the Higashikuni Cabinet and ushering in the Shidehara government. As noted earlier, on 11 October, MacArthur handed Shidehara a list of basic changes he expected the new premier to make. The third of the so-called Five Great Reforms was education. On 13 October, Civil Information and Education Section summoned Maeda to its headquarters in the Radio Tokyo Building and ordered him to rewrite school texts, reorganise the school system and decentralise the Education Ministry. CI&E followed up those instructions with four 'negative' directives, largely reformulations of the earlier SWNCC planning papers, designed to tear down the impediments to liberal education and radically revise classroom content.

The first directive was 'Administration of the Educational System of Japan' (SCAPIN-178 of 22 October), a broad charter for change that outlined the Occupation's primary objectives. This basic directive ordained the rewriting of course content; the removal from the schools of militarist elements; the reinstatement of teachers and officials previously dismissed for anti-militaristic or liberal views; the prohibition of discrimination against students, teachers or officials based on 'race, nationality, creed, political opinion or social position'; and the participation of educators in all aspects of schooling, including curriculum development. The remaining directives were: 'Investigation, Screening and Certification of Teachers and Educational Officials' (SCAPIN-212 of 30 October), which specified the methods for investigating teachers and purging undesirable elements; 'Abolition of Governmental Sponsorship, Support, Perpetuation, Control and Dissemination of State Shinto' (SCAPIN-448 of 15 December) outlawing the propagation of Shintō doctrine in the classroom – a psychological assault on the foundations of Imperial authority; and 'The Suspension of Courses in Morals (<u>Shushin</u>), Japanese History, and Geography' (SCAPIN-519 of 31 December), which immediately terminated what GHQ characterised as the 'three dangerous subjects'. SCAPIN-519 also ordered the Education Ministry to collect and dispose of all objectionable textbooks and provide appropriate ones in their place.[13]

This punitive phase culminated in the education purge, which began on 7 May

1946 and rolled on for some time. By April 1949, rigorous vetting had deposed more than 3,000 unsuitable instructors, or about 1 per cent of all teachers. Even before screening began, however, the Education Ministry, under pressure from student activists, had obtained the resignation of another 116,000 wartime educators by announcing that it would suspend the pension rights of any teacher purged after a certain date. Thus, a total of 119,700 teachers, or 24 per cent of Japan's first-line educators, either were purged or resigned of their own volition, clearing the boards of objectionable elements but creating a dearth of trained professionals that would take several years to overcome.[14] As indicated above, Japanese bureaucrats and pedagogues had committed themselves at an early date to many of the measures GHQ subsequently introduced. The Education Ministry's plans fell short of the sweeping changes MacArthur's headquarters demanded, but Japanese anticipation of American intentions enabled CI&E to accomplish its mission without further recourse to formal SCAP instructions, ending the initial period of reform by decree.[15]

THE STODDARD MISSION

Origins of the Mission

GHQ balanced its retributive measures of late 1945 with a positive policy of reformation that began with the despatch to Tokyo of a high-profile group of American educators in early 1946. The US Education Mission led by George D. Stoddard remained in Japan for less than a month but in that short time produced a blueprint for the institutional reform of Japanese education. Significantly, while the Stoddard Mission's guiding principles generally recapitulated pre-surrender American planning, the details were elaborated by Japanese and US specialists working in close conjunction, and many of its conclusions reflected Japanese rather than American priorities. Indeed, the Mission affords an intimate glimpse into the dynamics of bilateral cooperation for change, for through this external agency a group of forward-looking Japanese educators were able to win grudging acceptance from their own government for liberal reform projections formulated before the war.

US planners had foreseen the need for expertise outside the Occupation structure, but the concept of an Education Mission was first floated during discussions on German school reform and ideological reorientation in May 1945, following the Nazi surrender. CI&E embraced the idea immediately. The early shortage of education specialists of high academic calibre argued strongly for a special delegation,[16] and planning for the embassy began almost as soon as the Section was established. On 24 September 1945, Brigadier General Bonner Fellers asked Major Harold G. Henderson, Chief of CI&E's Education and Religions Branch, to broach the subject to the Education Minister. A Japan scholar with prewar experience in the country and a personal friend of Maeda, Henderson informed the Minister that an American advisory group on education would visit Tokyo in the near future and suggested that the government organise a committee of experts to work with the US team. CI&E

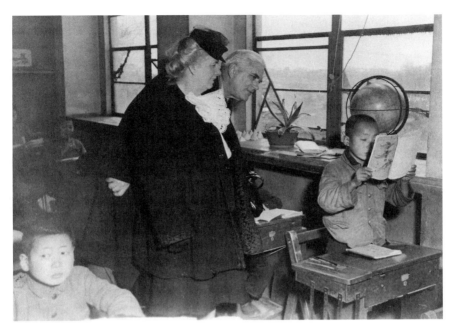

Photo 47. George D. Stoddard and Pearl A. Wanamaker of the US Education Mission visit the Nagata Elementary School in Tokyo, 15 March 1946 (US National Archives).

subsequently solicited the assistance of a small number of eminent Japanese scholars including Andō Shōji, a Japanese language specialist; Kishimoto Hideo, a leading student of religion; and Kaigo Tokiomi, a well-known educator.[17]

Henderson also asked Maeda to cooperate in selecting the Allied members of the mission, and in early October, the Education Ministry drew up a list of prospective foreign advisers that included not only Americans but distinguished British and European educators, as well. On 18 October, Henderson's deputy, Major Edward H. Farr, ordered Robert Hall to draft a staff study on Japanese education and include a roster of potential delegates. Hall was assisted by Army Air Forces Major Mark T. Orr, with whom he had worked at the Civil Affairs Staging Area in Monterey. Their task was simplified by SWNCC's Subcommittee for the Far East, which less than a week later (23 October) released a position paper, 'Education in Japan: Conclusion', formally endorsing the despatch of an education advisory team. With this authorisation and MacArthur's personal blessing, Hall and Orr proceeded with the staff study, consulting CI&E's Japanese advisers as the work progressed, but ran into difficulty when they tentatively selected Harvard President James B. Conant to lead the mission. MacArthur and Secretary of State George C. Marshall both rejected Conant's choice as 'politically inappropriate'. MacArthur reportedly feared Conant as a rival contender in the 1948 presidential elections. Conant's advocacy of the atomic bombings while a member of President Truman's Interim Committee, the atomic oversight body, was an additional disqualifying factor (chapter 1).[18] Conant's selection earned Hall and his superior, Major Henderson, the Supreme Commander's enmity, and was one of the factors leading to their subsequent reassignment.

MacArthur and Marshall approved the rest of the CI&E draft on 31 December. On 4 January 1946, GHQ cabled the War Department formally requesting an education mission to assist in drafting reforms for which, it claimed, Japanese educators were 'technically unqualified'. The need for action was urgent, for the new school year began on 1 April. The advisory group was to study four areas: 1 education for democracy, 2 'psychology in the re-education of Japan', 3 administrative reorganisation and, 4 higher education. Four independent committees would be created to recommend policy in each of these areas. In Washington, the War Department turned responsibility for the endeavour over to the State Department, which assigned Gordon Bowles, author of SWNCC-108, to help organise the Mission and accompany it to Japan. George Stoddard, a staunch advocate of 'reorientation' for Japan, Germany and Italy, currently New York State Commissioner of Education, and president-elect of the University of Illinois, was appointed to head the delegation.[19]

The Japanese and even Bowles believed that experts from other Allied countries also should be included, but MacArthur insisted that participation be limited to Americans, and the State Department concurred. (In fact, two Canadians inadvertently were included, but both represented US institutions at the time.) Bowles and a War Department observer were among the 27 members. Consisting of mainstream pedagogues, the group represented a geographical and cultural cross-section of American society, with four women, one African American, a labour education specialist from the Congress of Industrial Organisations, and Catholic and Protestant leaders (no Jewish organisation was represented). Six secretaries, all women, also were attached to the Mission.

The Committee of Japanese Educators
The Stoddard Mission marked the beginning of the second phase of education reform, that of guidance and assistance. The Americans were enjoined to encourage the Japanese to undertake basic reforms themselves, not to impose it unilaterally, and on 9 January, MacArthur instructed the Education Ministry to impanel a counterpart group of prominent Japanese academics to work with the US mission. On 2 February, the Ministry established the Committee of Japanese Educators, with four sub-committees mirroring those set up by the US Mission, and named 29 liberal academics, teachers and other professionals to staff it.

Sir George Sansom was profoundly sceptical of the venture when he learned of it. In late January, after meeting CI&E Chief Kermit R. Dyke and Henderson in Tokyo, he noted in his diary that the Japanese intellectual tradition was too firmly rooted to be easily amenable to the kind of reform the Americans were contemplating. 'They

Photo 48. Eileen R. Donovan consults members of the Committee of Japanese Educators. Seated next to Donovan is Committee Chair Nanbara Shigeru, President of Tokyo University and Japan's leading liberal educator. Several of the key education reforms endorsed by the Stoddard Mission were of Japanese origin (Mainichi).

seem to think that Japan can be supplied with a new system of education as a tailor might furnish a new suit', he wrote. Education in the United States, he observed caustically, 'is not of such a quality as to encourage one in feeling that it provides a good model for any other country.'[20] Many of the Mission's members were well-known in Japanese education circles, however, and the Committee of Japanese Educators generally welcomed this offer of assistance. The fact that the endeavour had been organised at the highest levels in Washington and stood above the Occupation and its control mechanisms gave the Mission a cachet of legitimacy.

The Committee of Japanese Educators was composed of respected scholars and dealt with its American counterparts on a basis of equality. The chair was Nanbara Shigeru, Christian President of Tokyo Imperial University and one of the country's foremost liberals. All but five of the Committee's 29 members had lived or travelled in the West, where several had earned advanced degrees. Participants included elementary and secondary school principals, university administrators and professors (including prominent feminist academics Hoshino Ai and Kawai Michi), a former Privy Councillor, an art critic, a Congregational pastor and the leader of Japan's folk art movement (Yanagi Muneyoshi). Of special significance was the involvement of far-sighted educators who had proposed democratic changes in the school system before the war. Some of the Committee's leading lights also had studied under or worked with Nitobe Inazō (1862–1933), the liberalist educator and Quaker who had introduced Western educational philosophy to Japan.[21] Nor were the Japanese dependant on the Americans. After the US team had returned home, the Japanese submitted their own official report, 'Recommendations of the Committee of Japanese Educators', to the Education Ministry. A bold restatement of their views, this document was withheld from GHQ altogether. Nineteen members of the Committee would join the Japan Education Reform Council when it was created in August 1946 to carry on the reform work.

A Japanese reform?

After a series of briefings in Washington, Hawai'i and Guam, the Stoddard Mission reached Tokyo on 5 and 6 March. Members spent the first week in briefings, the second attending lectures prepared by CI&E staff and its Japanese advisers, a few days observing conditions in the field and the last week drafting a final report. Upon its arrival, the team had received the CI&E staff study, a 132-page document entitled 'Education in Japan'. Drafted largely by Orr and Major Robert C. McAllen, it outlined the history, current status and needs of Japan's school system. Now CI&E, with Japanese assistance, prepared a series of staff lectures for the Mission, providing informed and well-reasoned arguments for reform. For instance, Captain Eileen R. Donovan, a secondary education specialist, delivered the lecture on women's colleges, noting that most Imperial universities systematically barred women from advanced study. Donovan also pointed out that the Education Ministry itself had no women in advisory or supervisory positions. She stressed the need for a school system that guaranteed women equal access to all levels of instruction, respected their right to acquire knowledge and enhanced their status in society.

In preparing her talk, Donovan had consulted female educators Hoshino Ai, then President of Tsuda College for Women, and Kawai Michi, President and founder of Keisen Women's College and former secretary general of the YWCA. Hoshino and Kawai had been instrumental in drafting the Education Ministry's 'New Comprehensive Plan for Women's Education Reform', a master plan for gender-free change published in early December 1945. Several Japanese academics, including noted philologist Andō Masatsugu and pedagogue Kaigo Tokiomi, delivered keynote speeches to the Mission, and Japanese specialists and Education Ministry bureaucrats participated in the numerous panel discussions it hosted.[22]

On 30 March 1946, after more than three weeks of activity, the US advisory group formulated its conclusions in the 'Report of the United States Education Mission to Japan', which it submitted to MacArthur as a confidential memorandum. Released to the public on 7 April, the 62-page document declared in the preface 'We do not come in the spirit of conquerors, but as experienced educators who believe that there is an unmeasured potential for freedom and for individual social growth in every human being'. The Stoddard Report recommended discontinuance of the Imperial Rescript on Education; script reform; revision of educational content (textbooks and curricula) based on the democratic principles already outlined by GHQ; a '6-3-3' school ladder with the first nine years free, coeducational and compulsory; teacher training; the reform of higher education; and administrative decentralisation.[23] A year later, on 27 March 1947, the State Department forwarded these conclusions to the Far Eastern Commission, which approved them and issued the Allied directive 'Policy for the Revision of the Japanese Educational System'. The bulk of the Stoddard recommendations were implemented in time for the new school year beginning in April 1947.

The Stoddard findings reflected the liberal American educational philosophy of the day, but in some areas they were ahead of their time. Charles S. Johnson, Chair of the Department of Social Science at Fisk University (later President of Fisk, 1946–56) and the only African-American member on the US team, stressed equality of opportunity regardless of 'gender, race, creed or color'. SCAPIN-178 ('Administration of the Educational System of Japan') of 22 October had prohibited any form of discrimination in education, but Johnson took this tenet farther. At his insistence, the stipulation 'Minority groups should be respected and valued' was written into the report's statement of purpose. Johnson also was responsible for articulating the Mission's credo: 'We believe in the power of every race and every nation to create from its own cultural resources something good for itself and for the whole world.' At a time when de facto apartheid was the norm in many areas of the United States, these were lofty ideals indeed.[24]

Stoddard acknowledged that 'negative measures will be effective only as they embody the will of the liberal Japanese', and the Mission's sweeping proposals were lauded as the epitome of the reform GHQ had been mandated to induce. On closer examination, however, some key innovations turn out to be of Japanese, not American, origin. In later years, Bowles, whose deep knowledge of Japan's culture and language enabled him to play a crucial mediating role in the Mission's work, acknowledged that roughly 60 per cent of the report's content came from the Japanese side. Through a process of intense bilateral consultations, Japanese educators managed to have their own reform objectives ratified by the Mission and presented as American conclusions.[25] In two areas, those concerning the Imperial Rescript on Education and language reform, Japanese objections to US proposals compelled the American team to tone down its final recommendations. Both sides agreed on the need for curricula and textbook revision, the revamping of higher education and teacher training, and administrative decentralisation, but in the area of systemic school reform, Japanese opinion prevailed.

The Imperial Rescript on Education
The touchstone of Japan's educational philosophy was the Imperial Rescript on Education, promulgated by the Emperor Meiji in 1890, which exalted loyalty to the sovereign, patriotism and filial piety as the supreme virtues of the people. Ceremonial recitations of the Rescript and ritual acts of obeisance before the Royal portrait and its repository (*hōanden*) were used to instil blind submission to the Throne and the Imperial state. Two manifestos of militant nationalism, the 'Cardinal Principles of the National Polity' (*Kokutai no hongi*) of March 1937 and 'The Way of the Subject' (*Shinmin no michi*) of July 1941, had been issued by the Education Ministry's Bureau of Thought Control as official interpretations of the Rescript. The Imperial

education creed was, in the words of a high-ranking CI&E official, 'one of the most significant and influential documents ever issued in Japan'.[26]

Imperial conservatives, including Maeda Tamon and Yoshida Shigeru, intended to meet the formal requirements of the Potsdam Proclamation but without, in Yoshida's words, 'altering the fundamental principles of national government laid down in the Meiji Constitution', which, it was argued, the militarists had perverted following their seizure of power. To the conservative mind, the Imperial ethos incongruously epitomised the democratic spirit. On 15 January 1946, two days after replacing Maeda as Education Minister, Abe Yoshishige told the *Mainichi Shinbun* that the government must lead the nation to true democracy by preserving the principle of the emperor-based state.[27] The ruling élite envisaged the creation of a civil society that would strengthen, not weaken, the foundations of Imperial rule; the key to this strategy was the Emperor Meiji's Rescript on Education.

Liberals, such as Nanbara Shigeru, who despite their modern views held the institution of the Throne in high esteem, nonetheless believed the old creed not only narrowly nationalistic and regressive but incompatible with democratic values. They argued for a new pronouncement on education but insisted that it bear the Royal imprimatur. Shortly after the surrender, Ariga Tetsutarō, a professor at Dōshisha University in Kyoto, had secretly drawn up a model rescript to replace the 1890 proclamation. In early December 1945, the Sixth Army Military Government commander in Kyoto obtained a copy of the Ariga draft and forwarded it to CI&E Chief Dyke with the suggestion that the Emperor promulgate it. Ariga hoped that by repudiating the ultra-nationalistic interpretation of the original, his 'Kyoto Rescript' would enable GHQ to utilise the spiritual authority of the Imperial institution in order to democratise it. Written in the same archaic Court language as the Meiji Rescript, the document's style contrasted sharply with the liberal ideals it expounded. CI&E debated the merits of issuing a revised education charter but failed to reach a consensus.

The Stoddard Mission's preliminary report called for the Rescript's 'permanent discontinuance'. On 20 March 1946, during the final round of bilateral discussions, however, the Committee of Japanese Educators submitted a written statement urging that a new rescript be promulgated alongside the new Constitution. This would prove a more effective means of motivating teachers than revoking the Meiji-era charter, it said. Japanese objections led to divided opinions among Mission members. Unable to reach a unified position, the Americans sidestepped the question of a new rescript and, at Bowles's insistence, modified their conclusion to recommend simple discontinuance. Going well beyond the 'opinions' it had expressed to Stoddard, the Japanese side later presented an even stronger defence of its case for a new charter in its official written report to the Education Ministry.[28]

Consequently, the Meiji Rescript was not rescinded but simply held in abeyance, and in late June 1946, a new Education Minister publicly advocated its resuscitation. Tanaka Kōtarō, a convert to Catholicism who had studied in Europe and was generally hailed as a liberal, broached the issue before the Lower House's Special

Committee on the Constitution. The Rescript, he told the Committee, was 'the foundation of human morality infallible for all ages and true in all places'. His attempt to reinstate the principle of Imperial sovereignty just as GHQ was attempting to replace it with that of popular sovereignty sent shock waves rippling through Civil Information and Education Section. Education Division Chief Mark Orr ordered a fresh review of the question. With no conclusion forthcoming, in August Eileen Donovan penned a scathing critique of what she termed 'the Magna Carta of Japanese national ideology'. Acknowledging GHQ's confusion on the issue and lamenting its failure to ban the Imperial credo earlier, she revived the idea of promulgating the Kyoto Rescript. The Division pressed instead for the repeal of the original charter, and on 8 October 1946, the Education Ministry reluctantly conceded the point and announced that the Rescript could no longer be considered the sole source of Japan's educational philosophy.[29]

The enactment of the 1947 Fundamental Law of Education, with its firm statement of principle, precluded the need to issue a new rescript. Yet conservatives, liberals and even the Katayama Cabinet's left-of-centre Education Minister, Morito Tatsuo (May 1947 to October 1948), who openly criticised the Rescript as 'based on feudalistic principles', hesitated to formally revoke it (like many liberals, Morito favoured a new charter). The deadlock was broken by radical politician and social historian Hani Gorō, who urged the Upper House to abolish what he said was 'an order forced on the citizenry by a despotic régime'. The Diet ultimately supported that view, and the Meiji proclamation was finally declared null and void on 19 June 1948. Six days later the Education Ministry ordered all copies removed from the nation's schools.[30]

Language Reform

Japanese and US educators appeared to lock horns on another issue: an American proposal to phase out Chinese characters (*kanji*) and replace the traditional writing system with Latin script (Roman characters, or *rōmaji*). An Education Division officer later described this episode as 'the most bizarre and disturbing' experience of his tenure.[31] The Stoddard Mission's initial script reform proposal has been portrayed as an attempt to impose foreign ways on Japan, but it coincided with a home-grown debate on language policy that dated from the Meiji era.[32] Japanese thinkers had grappled with the question of modernising their cumbersome writing system, with its two phonetic scripts (the block-style *katakana* and the cursive *hiragana*, collectively referred to as *kana*) and several thousand Chinese characters (*kanji*) in current use. Three positions emerged, two of them urging the abolition of *kanji*: full romanisation, the exclusive use of the *kana* syllabary and the simplification of *kanji*.[33]

During the final years of the war, American planners, apparently unaware of the Japanese debates, considered similar arguments. Education specialists at the Civil Affairs Staging Area in Monterey, California had concluded that Japanese school children were devoting too much classroom time to the rote memorisation of Chinese characters. To remedy that situation, Robert Hall, CASA's Education Section Chief, formulated a proposal to replace *kanji* with the native *katakana* script (the *hiragana* syllabary, too, was marked for elimination). In June 1945, he sent a memorandum to his superiors in the War Department's Civil Affairs Division urging the abolition of Chinese characters, but when CAD Chief John F. Hilldring forwarded the proposal to the State Department, it was vetoed by Japanophile Eugene Dooman, head of SWNCC's Subcommittee for the Far East. Dooman believed Hall's plan was unenforceable and dismissed its supporters as 'crack-pots, visionaries and fanatics'.[34]

Upon arriving in Tokyo, Hall promptly revived his proposal but modified it, calling now for the gradual replacement of both *kanji* and *kana* with Latin script, a position that traditionally also had found support among Japanese intellectuals. Here, however, Hall outdid himself. In late November, he ordered the Education Ministry's Textbook Bureau to reduce the number of *kanji* in use and romanise the nation's school books by stages and indicated that a romanisation directive was forthcoming. This unexpected demand created consternation in the Ministry and alarmed conservative language specialists committed to the status quo. Branch Chief Henderson quickly reassured Education Minister Maeda that GHQ had no intention of enforcing such an edict and the tension subsided, but Hall's *faux pas* would shorten the Occupation careers of both officers.[35]

Although most CI&E officials were conservative on the language issue, Hall surprisingly was permitted to work up a script proposal for the Stoddard Mission. The Chinese Central News Agency got wind of the endeavour, however and, in late January 1946, exposed it in a sensational scoop ('Plans to Replace Present Way of Writing Nippon Language by Alphabet'). Nonetheless, Hall was able to complete his study and present it to the US Mission in early March. The 44-page document concluded that because of the written language's 'excessive difficulty . . . the majority of Japanese people are actually unable to read anything beyond the simplest level and, accordingly, are politically uninformed'. The dual proposition that written Japanese 'constitutes a formidable obstacle to learning' and that a Latinised writing system is 'one of the most subtle and yet powerful allies of democracy' in the fight against nationalistic traditionalism was as dubious scientifically as it was ethnocentric.[36] Yet the US Mission was swayed by the force of Hall's arguments, and Stoddard's preliminary report called for the introduction of *rōmaji* in elementary schools and the publication of textbooks both in Japanese and Latin script. Philologist Andō Masatsugu generally agreed with Hall that the number of *kanji* should be reduced and replaced with *kana* script, but his colleagues on the Education Committee strongly opposed such radical meddling. Although amenable to the use of the Roman alphabet as a study tool, they objected to the elimination of Chinese characters. Committee Chair Nanbara ultimately prevailed upon Bowles to modify the Mission's finding. Consequently, while Stoddard's final report noted 'that in time Kanji should be wholly abandoned in the popular written language and that a phonetic system should be adopted', it actually recommended only 'that some form of Romaji be brought into common use by all means possible', leaving actual changes to the Japanese themselves.[37]

Sir George Sansom, who had briefed the US Education Mission at its inception, was taken aback by the Americans' language assumptions, which he declared to be unjustified. MacArthur, too, took a cautious view of the language issue. In his preface to the Stoddard Report, he noted that some of the US Education Mission's ideas on script revision were 'so far-reaching that they can only serve as a guide for long-range study and future planning.' General Chu Shih-ming, the Nationalist Chinese representative, raised the issue in the Allied Council for Japan on 30 April, but was reassured by CI&E Chief Dyke that language reform was a matter for the Japanese to decide. Pressure for more radical change emerged from another quarter, however. Dooman and the Japan Crowd having vacated the corridors of power, Hall's ideas now found a receptive audience in the State Department. In November 1946, the Department submitted a policy paper to SWNCC urging a more vigorous overhaul of the written language, but MacArthur objected forcefully through Diplomatic Section, successfully killing the proposal. When Washington submitted the Stoddard recommendations to the Far Eastern Commission in late March 1947, script reform was the only proposal not included.[38] GHQ would not interfere in language questions, which were to be an exclusively Japanese concern.

Language simplification nonetheless went forward. The Japanese Language Council, commissioned by the Education Ministry in 1934 to study ways of simplifying written Japanese, was resurrected after the surrender and worked energetically to streamline *kanji* by reducing the number of strokes per character and substantially lessening the amount to be mastered in elementary and middle school. A romanised script was introduced into Japanese language courses but as an adjunct to, not a substitute for, the traditional writing system (a long-standing demand of many Japanese educators). The resulting limited reform, then, was a compromise between the conservative foes of any kind of script modification and the liberal proponents of a far more thorough-going reform. Japanese and Americans educators found themselves ranged on both sides of the controversy, giving the issue a complexity that is often ignored.[39]

THE EDUCATION REFORMS

Textbook and curricula revision
Japan's capitulation occurred during the summer school break. In September 1945, the Education Ministry ordered the nation's children back to class to finish the second half of the school year (the Japanese school term begins in April and ends in March). On 3 October 1945, in line with the Ministry's New Education Policy, teachers were instructed to have students ink over or cut out sections in their textbooks deemed 'inappropriate', a euphemism for militaristic content. This policy, subsequently sanctioned by CI&E, continued until acceptable makeshift texts could

Photo 49. Children resume school in an outdoor classroom, 25 September 1945. Many schools were destroyed by Allied bombing. Students initially were confused by the abrupt switch to a democratic curriculum (Kyodo).

be provided. In some cases, frequent effacements produced non sequiturs, and extensive deletions rendered entire sections unintelligible. The psychological impact of these 'blackened-over primers' (*suminuri-kyōkasho*) on children was considerable. Education specialist Nakamura Kikuji recalls: 'The inked-over school books impressed indelibly on youthful minds the harsh finality of defeat. For many pupils, that moment of truth had a lasting influence on their lives.' Before the surrender, children had been admonished to take scrupulous care of their texts. 'Now we were suddenly told to smear the books with ink. . . . I felt as if I were defiling myself' wrote another Japanese. 'That day for the first time, I felt besieged by a jumble of contending values, a feeling that has persisted ever since.'[40]

On 10 November 1945, Civil Information and Education Section initiated a policy of recall and review. It instructed the Ministry to suspend the printing of objectionable texts while the Section had them translated into English and vetted for content. References to Royal authority now would be eliminated systematically. Predictably, stopping the presses produced an immediate shortage of school primers. On 31 December, SCAPIN-519 ('The Suspension of Courses in Morals (<u>Shushin</u>), Japanese History, and Geography') ordered the recall and pulping of old books still in use. It also required the Ministry to prepare and submit for approval provisional texts in pamphlet form and to prepare a comprehensive plan for school-book revision. The confusion created by so many sudden changes was compounded by an acute paper shortage, with the result that pupils were forced to use crude stopgap texts and in some instances to do without educational materials altogether. Thus, 'blackened-over primers' gave way to 'temporary school books' – flimsy folded pamphlets that disintegrated easily. With the start of the new school year in April 1946, however, revised texts became available, and by summer more than 400 had been cleared for publication. Geography courses were resumed in June 1946, and in October, schools began teaching Japanese history again using the freshly minted *Kuni no ayumi* (Our Nation's Progress) duly approved by CI&E censors and published by the Education Ministry.[41]

The new school programme introduced integrated core subjects, such as social studies (including civics), science and mathematics, in order to raise social awareness and cultivate a sense of individual responsibility as well as provide a basic education. Social studies, the primary core subject, replaced compartmentalised courses in geography, ethics and history. Ethics courses were abolished for the duration of the Occupation. To help teachers perform their new duties effectively, a curriculum guide, 'The Course of Study', was compiled for each grade. Instructors discouraged rote memorisation and emphasised 'problem solving' and free discussion. World history and current events courses dissolved the insularity that had characterised prewar instruction. Classroom hours devoted to foreign language study were increased, and English generally replaced German as the dominant second language. The number of required courses was reduced, elective subjects were added and the school week was shortened from six days to five. Under CI&E guidance, the American home-room system was introduced to teach proper behaviour and good citizenship, and student councils were established to encourage democratic self-government. Military drills and traditional martial arts (*budō*), including *jūdō* and *kendō*, were banned on 6 November 1945 and replaced by physical education. Vocational courses (industrial arts and homemaking for *both* boys and girls) were introduced at all levels to 'help create the same respect for those who work with tools as for those who work only with their minds'.[42] Intent on democratising all aspects of school life, CI&E introduced club activities ranging from sports to drama and English conversation.

Through classroom instruction, student self-government and extracurricular activities, the new programme of study strove to instil democratic values, foster a spirit of cooperation and teach respect for human dignity and the rights of minorities. Not all of these innovations were successful, however. The integration of vocational training proved difficult, and by the end of the Occupation, a trend toward specialised technical schools had reasserted itself. Respect for minority rights was interpreted as respect merely for minority opinions, and a proper awareness of Japan's cultural and ethnic minorities never developed. Finally, in 1958, the Ministry would revive ethics courses. Despite these developments, the Occupation's transformation of educational content was dramatic, thorough-going and enduring. Compared with the pre-1945 school programme, it was revolutionary.

CI&E undertook textbook reform by requiring the Education Ministry to submit a list of prospective authors and then screening the candidates' background and views. The Section exercised pre-publication censorship, reviewing the texts in manuscript form and, where necessary, insisting on revisions. In a dramatic break with past practice, however, writers were given broad discretion. CI&E laid down the basic guidelines, but within these limits, authors generally were free to determine editorial policy and content and to supply their own facts and figures. In November 1946, the Education Ministry published 'General Principles for Instruction in Japanese History', a teachers' guide that spelled out CI&E expectations for history courses. Ishiyama Shūhei, chief of the Second Editorial Branch of the Education Ministry's Textbook Bureau, and one of the authors of 'General Principles', later recalled: 'About a third of what I wrote was at the behest of GHQ, a third was a compromise and a third was of my own initiative.' Okiyama Hikaru, a Ministry bureaucrat who compiled a primer on Japanese language and literature, remarked, 'CI&E insisted on four criteria: clarity, a lively presentation, simplicity of expression and intelligibility. Beyond that, we were allowed to write as we pleased.'[43]

CI&E was slow in withdrawing certification authority from the Education Ministry, however. The Stoddard Report had specifically recommended against Ministry involvement in school-book selection. But when Japanese history courses resumed in late 1946, CI&E ordered the schools to use only books prepared by the Ministry and approved by GHQ. Occupation authorities looked askance at the Ministry's monopoly on textbook compilation but postponed corrective action, citing the press of more urgent tasks. It was not until July 1948 that the Board of Education Law transferred responsibility for school-book selection to individual schools. After the Occupation, the Ministry would reassert formal control over text certification, adopting GHQ's own screening process to censor content at variance with its neo-conservative philosophy (chapter 11).

The '6-3-3' system

Japan's prewar education system had required children of both sexes to attend school for six years. The Stoddard Mission recommended extending free coeducational and compulsory education from six years to nine: six years of elementary instruction plus three years of middle school, followed by an optional three years of high school for students desiring further study. It also urged that higher education be extended from three years to four. The so-called 6-3-3 (or 6-3-3-4) system was then in wide use in the United States, and this innovation is often cited as the Mission's most important reform. It is now clear, however, that the 6-3-3 proposal was of Japanese, not American, parentage.

Prewar education had been segregated by sex, with boys and girls attending separate institutions. It also was male-centred, élitist and multi-tracked, with five different orientations reflecting gender and class distinctions.[44] Liberal Japanese were keenly aware of the shortcomings of the nation's school system, and before the war, reform-orientated educators had advocated corrective action. In 1936, a well-known pedagogue, Abe Shigetaka of Tokyo Imperial University, had called for the adoption of the American 6-3-3 model. In 1937, the Education Reform Club (*Kyōiku Kaikaku Dōshi-kai*), an ad hoc association of some hundred like-minded academics, business people and other professionals, endorsed Abe's ideas and issued a similar set of recommendations. After the defeat, leaders of this group revived their reform agenda. Seven, including Toda Teizō, sociologist and Dean of Tokyo Imperial University's Faculty of Literature, were tapped for the Committee of Japanese Educators. Toda had been a student of Abe Shigetaka and was determined to carry on the work of his mentor. Together with Kaigo Tokiomi, he energetically lobbied the US Mission for an American-style reform.[45]

The Stoddard Mission arrived in Japan determined to leave the prewar 6-5-3 (elementary, middle, higher school) ladder in place but democratise it by making nine years of instruction (six years of elementary and three years of middle school) mandatory, coeducational and tuition-free. The remaining two years of middle school and all three years of high school were to be be neither prescriptive nor publicly funded. Mission members, however, were unable to resolve the complexities of Japan's multi-tiered education structure.[46] Both sides agreed on the need for nine years of schooling, but Stoddard was baffled by the five educational orientations and hesitated to dictate a unitary 6-3-3 ladder. This impasse was broken on 21 March 1946 when Japanese Chair Nanbara and Stoddard met secretly. Nanbara convinced the US Mission Chief to eliminate the multi-tracked system and adopt the American model. Stoddard agreed and incorporated the Japanese demand into his final report.[47] The Committee of Japanese Educators then presented the 6-3-3 reform as an American initiative, using the US Mission as a vehicle for its own project.

'The Government,' Nanbara later remarked with consummate understatement, 'was not pleased with our movement at all.'[48] Prime Minister Yoshida Shigeru and his new Education Minister, Takahashi Sei'ichirō (January to May 1947), stubbornly opposed the 6-3-3 reform. Nine years of mandatory, universal education, they argued, would place an insupportable strain on an already burdened national budget. The stalemate reportedly was broken when Takahashi paid a courtesy call on CI&E Chief Donald R. Nugent. Nugent greeted the Education Minister speaking rapidly in English and shook his hand. Taken aback by Nugent's verbal barrage and unable to understand it, Takahashi is said to have pumped Nugent's arm, nodded his head diplomatically and replied, 'Yes, yes', thereby inadvertently signalling approval of the 6-3-3 system. This account of Nugent's 'subterfuge' may be apocryphal, but the story, accepted as gospel in official circles, illustrates the widely held perception that the postwar education reforms were imposed unilaterally.[49]

The 6-3-3 system transformed Japanese education. Nine years of compulsory schooling was introduced in stages, seven years in 1947, eight in 1948 and nine in 1949. Multiple tracking was eliminated, and along with it discrimination based on gender, wealth and social standing. Elementary and middle schools were made coeducational, and higher learning became accessible via a single, graded school system. High schools resisted coeducation, however. By 1949, all junior high schools had integrated the sexes, but only 55 per cent of public senior high schools had done so. The former Imperial universities also opposed change, aggressively limiting female admissions to about 5 or 6 per cent of the student body.[50]

Higher education

The US Education Mission concentrated on primary and secondary education but had only general prescriptions for higher education. It recommended the introduction of liberal arts ('general education'), guarantees for academic freedom and the creation of more colleges and universities but proposed nothing specific. The details were left to the Japanese, and here again, the Committee of Japanese Educators seized the initiative. On 21 March, Nanbara asked Stoddard to 'model the whole scheme after the American plan, building up elementary schools, high schools, colleges and universities in a natural sequence with wide opportunities at all levels'.[51]

Nanbara formulated this and other demands in his final report, and after August 1946, the Japan Education Reform Council, the successor to the Committee of Japanese Educators, actively pressed for their implementation. In 1949, four-year universities became the norm, and in each prefecture, a single national university was established, absorbing the diverse curricula of former Imperial universities, women's colleges, technical institutes, normal schools and higher schools. A total of 250 institutions of higher learning were consolidated into 68 national universities. Prefectural and municipal governments also established public universities, which appeared alongside private four-year institutions. Of the new universities, two-thirds had been technical or normal colleges, and many struggled to upgrade their curricula, but eventually these institutions placed higher education within reach of everyone. Decentralisation enabled regional universities to assert their distinctive local features and accommodate students unable to afford the expense of studying in a large city. These schools were nicknamed *ekiben daigaku* after the box lunches sold at regional train stations, each featuring a local specialty.[52]

Another Japanese innovation was the junior college, which CI&E believed should be downgraded to senior high schools. Despite GHQ's misgivings, at the initiative of the Japan Education Reform Council, 148 junior colleges were established in 1950, some three-quarters of them exclusively for women. By the end of the Occupation, there were 205 junior colleges, including 7 national institutions, 31 prefectural and municipal schools and 167 private colleges. Thirty-four prewar women's colleges had been recognised as regular universities, and together with the new junior colleges they opened the doors of higher education to women. In 1950, only about 10 per cent of university students were female, but, within a few years, that figure would jump to 30 per cent.

Despite the American emphasis on decentralisation, the Education Ministry retained considerable authority over the universities, approving curricula modifications and exercising general oversight. Another vice that proved difficult to eradicate was the chair system, through which tenured professors exercised patriarchal control over their students, producing factionalism (the 'old boy' system) and élitism.

Eminent scholars, including many who sat on the Education Reform Council, were reluctant to eliminate their own base of power in the university. In 1935, nearly 90 per cent of government functionaries were graduates of Tokyo Imperial University. In 1948, that figure remained high, at 85 per cent, but by 1950, it had fallen to 45 per cent. Nonetheless, today, Tokyo University graduates continue to dominate the civil service and other élite professions.[53]

Mass participation
American and Japanese reformers encouraged parents, teachers and students to participate actively in the education process. Many of their efforts received enthusiastic popular endorsement. For instance, in late 1946, John M. Nelson, Chief of CI&E's Social Education Branch, proposed the introduction of Parent–Teacher Associations, which the Social Education Law legally mandated in 1949. By 1950, PTAs had been established in roughly 90 per cent of the country's school districts. To defend the position of women in higher education, Dr Lulu Holmes of Education Division's Higher Education Branch worked closely with prominent educator and feminist Fujita Taki of the New Japan Women's League (later, head of the Labour Ministry's Women's and Minors' Bureau). In October 1946, they established the Japanese Association of College Women. Renamed the Japanese Association of University Women in 1949, the organisation endeavoured to upgrade the academic standing of its members and improve other institutions of higher learning for women.[54]

To defend academic freedom, in December 1946, university teachers created the Japanese Association of University Professors, which by 1951 boasted more than 5,200 members in 92 public and private institutions. In October 1949, the Association would issue an unambiguous definition of academic freedom, which GHQ was then engaged in undermining with the Red Purge. The passive collaboration of many scholars with pre-1945 militant nationalism gave postwar academics a keen sense of personal and social responsibility for participating fully in politics outside of the classroom, and many expressed their views honestly and openly. The Japanese Association of University Professors was determined to defend that right, and to its credit, charges of 'ideological deviation' (left-wing ideas) never swayed the organisation from its duty.[55]

In the public school system, teachers, too, organised. On 1 December 1945, progressive historian Hani Gorō founded the All-Japan Teachers' Union (*Zenkyō*) to speed democratisation and secure better working conditions for teachers. On 2 December, old-style Christian Socialist Kagawa Toyohiko formed the Japan Educators' Union (*Nikkyō*), in part to defend the principle of Imperial sovereignty in education. Hani's radical initiative fired the imagination of the nation's teachers, and after joining the left-of-centre Congress of Industrial Unions (*Sanbetsu*) in February 1946, *Zenkyō* quickly eclipsed Kagawa's conservative organisation. Following the failed general strike of 1 February 1947, Hani's union and other left-of-centre teachers' groups merged to found the Japan Teachers' Union (*Nikkyōso*). Within a short time, virtually every primary and secondary school instructor had become a member. *Nikkyōso* enthusiastically supported the education reforms. As the largest government workers' union, however, it also led the opposition to GHQ's revision of the National Public Service Law in late 1948 and, by 1949, had been labelled a Communist front organisation. Many of its members fell victim to the Red Purge.

The US Education Mission and its Japanese counterpart both agreed on the need to protect the universities from encroachments by central authority. Consequently, the principle of university autonomy was instituted, with real decision-making powers vested in the faculty committee. Students, too, demanded and, were accorded, autonomous rights within the university. In fact, student militancy had preceded labour radicalism. Japan's first postwar strike was organised in September 1945 by students at Mito High School in Ibaraki Prefecture north of Tokyo. The protesters occupied a dormitory for one month, demanding that the Education Ministry dismiss the school's conservative principal. At the élite Peers' School, faculty and parents also petitioned the Education Ministry to remove the head master. In the early months of the Occupation, student agitation forced professors and officials to quit at more than 80 institutions, prompting the Ministry to call for the resignation of all educators who had supported militarism.[56]

In January 1947, Tokyo University allowed its students to form the first self-governing body (*jichikai*), and as that movement spread rapidly from campus to campus, student radicals began to organise nationally. On 18 September 1948, with GHQ's blessing, the All-Japan Federation of Student Self-Government Associations (*Zengakuren*) came into being to improve student life, defend academic freedom and university autonomy, reform education, fight fascism and promote democracy. Some 145 universities joined the national coordinating body. By May 1949, about 350 universities and roughly 60 per cent of the student population would belong to the organisation. GHQ quickly changed its view of *Zengakuren* when the federation began protesting not only at local measures such as tuition fee hikes but at national and even international issues, such as revision of the National Public Service Law and nuclear testing. Dominated by the Japan Communist Party, *Zengakuren* soon found itself in direct conflict with Occupation authorities (chapter 10).[57]

The implementing legislation

The Constitution, promulgated in early November 1946, had provided three educational guarantees. Article 20 prohibited the state from involvement in religious education. Article 23 ensured academic freedom and Article 26 established the right to universal, compulsory and free education. The Fundamental Law of Education (31 March, 1947) made these constitutional freedoms explicit, and its companion statute, the School Education Law of the same date, gave them concrete expression. Designed to replace the Imperial Rescript on Education, whose aim had been to produce 'good and faithful subjects of the Emperor', the Fundamental Law's 11 articles upheld democracy, the dignity of the person and world peace as supreme virtues. The statute was, as one scholar has phrased it, 'a new constitution for education'.[58]

The Education Ministry blanched at many of the law's provisions, notably coeducation, equality of educational opportunity and administrative decentralisation, but it was caught between a rock (CI&E's Education Division) and a hard place (the Japan Education Reform Council). Moreover, from June 1947 to October 1948, two Socialist-backed coalitions, the Katayama and Ashida Cabinets, gave the law their full support. Katayama and Ashida appointed as their Education Minister Morito Tatsuo, a Socialist who had been persecuted in the 1920s by Tokyo Imperial University for his research on Russian anarchist Peter Kropotkin. Morito strongly supported the reform agenda and enjoyed the confidence of the Japan Teachers' Union and the *Zengakuren*. In late June 1948, before the Diet, he would make a brave defence of student political activity, which he declared an inalienable constitutional right. The intrepid Education Minister also would resist pressure from GHQ to denounce left-wing radicalism in the schools, although eventually, even he was engulfed by the floodtide of anti-Communism.[59]

The Japan Education Reform Council (JERC), established in August 1946 to carry on the work of the US Education Mission, was now in the vanguard of change. Nanbara was vice chair for the first year of the Council's existence and chair thereafter. The 49-member body was given Cabinet rank, placing it beyond the machinations of the Education Ministry, and authorised to recommend basic policy to the government. Problems were discussed by a tripartite steering committee comprised of three members representing CI&E, JERC and the Education Ministry. Mark T. Orr, Chief of Education Division from May 1946, developed a particularly close relationship with Nanbara. 'It was our policy that we would not do anything without getting the full review by the JERC,' he later recalled. 'My feeling . . . was that our objectives . . . would not have much meaning unless there was strong Japanese support for every major reform. So I did not want any reforms that would not be supported, looking toward the future when there would no longer be an occupation.'[60]

The Fundamental Law of Education was a broad statement of principle. Enabling legislation was passed between 1947 and 1949 giving concrete form to the high ideals expressed in the charter. The School Education Law (31 March, 1947) supplied the details of the new 6-3-3 school structure and defined the objectives for each level of education. It also provided for special education, making prefectures responsible for assuring students with disabilities the same level and quality of education as other children.

Education of the handicapped had been a recognized right since 1872, but only a handful of national schools existed for the sight-, hearing- and speech-impaired, and many disabled pupils, particularly those with mental and emotional difficulties, were kept at home. Now the Education Reform Council insisted on the same period of compulsory schooling for all children. Implementation lagged considerably due to a shortage of teaching materials and qualified staff, but by May 1948, there were 74 schools for the blind and 64 for the deaf and mute, with a total enrollment of 12,400. The National Schools Establishment Law (31 May 1949), which created a four-year national university in each prefecture, also established a National School for the Education of the Blind in Tokyo and a National School for the Education of the Deaf in Chiba Prefecture, both offering teacher training and courses of higher learning.

The Social Education Law (10 June 1949), made learning accessible to the entire population by guaranteeing learning opportunities (including physical education, recreational activities and mail-correspondence courses) to out-of-school youths and adults. It also provided for government subsidies to municipalities in support of local educational and cultural activities, libraries, museums, and public halls, giving substance to the constitutional right of maintaining 'minimum standards of wholesome and cultured living' (Article 25).[61]

Three other laws boldly attacked the centralised administration of education. These were the Board of Education Law (15 July 1948), the Ministry of Education Establishment Law (1 June 1949) and the Private School Law (15 December 1949). The most radical of these was the Board of Education Law. At the firm insistence of the Education Reform Council and CI&E, the statute entrusted school administration to education boards elected by popular vote at prefectural and municipal levels. This provision effectively freed the schools from centralised authority and, in principle, limited the Education Ministry to an oversight role. Seven-member prefectural boards and five-member municipal boards were to determine curricula, textbook selection and the hiring of personnel. Elected to four-year terms, board members were subject to the Local Autonomy Law's recall provisions. The original bill had denied teachers the right to stand for election, but fierce opposition from the Japan Teachers' Union (*Nikkyōso*) forced the government to drop that measure.[62]

With board elections scheduled for 5 October 1948, however, Military Government raised a red flag. In August, an Eighth Army civil education officer had warned CI&E that the local electorate was ill-informed and indifferent to the upcoming balloting. Other MG units noted that *Nikkyōso* candidates and reactionary local bosses were likely to sweep the polls. Charles Kades and Justin Williams of Government Section, however, insisted that the elections go forward as planned: a postponement would imply a lack of faith in the ability of Japanese to choose their own representatives. The election of Communists, they said, was one of the risks inherent in a democracy. Unconvinced, General Charles W. Ryder, Commander of Eighth Army Military Government Section, wrote to MacArthur again expressing the Army's misgivings. The Supreme Commander replied via CI&E Chief Nugent that his headquarters was in no position to ignore or modify the Board of Education Law. The elections were held as scheduled for prefectures and major cities, but voter turnout was a disappointing 56 per cent, and conservative candidates won handily, capturing 72 per cent of the seats. Communists took a mere 2 per cent. Elections for remaining cities, towns and villages were to be held by 1 November 1950, but the Education Ministry manoeuvred to postpone them for two years. When the second round of balloting was finally held in October 1952, however, 10,000 new boards were empanelled, progressives made important gains (one third of all seats went to *Nikkyōso* candidates) and the system at last appeared ready to fulfil the role that the Education Reform Council and CI&E had envisaged for it.[63]

An incomplete reform

Despite its revolutionary character and overall success, the reform legislation was plagued by shortcomings and confronted with challenges both from within GHQ and from the central government. On 30 October 1948, for instance, CI&E and the Education Ministry published *Primer of Democracy*, a school reader containing a derogatory reference to the Soviet Communist Party and its paramount leader. In the screening process, the Education Ministry objected that the anti-Soviet content violated the Fundamental Law of Education, which required school curricula to remain ideologically neutral. When consulted, MacArthur remarked that the controversial passage also seemed to contravene GHQ's Press Code prohibiting 'false or destructive criticism of the Allied Powers'. In fact, in September of that year, SCAP's censors had unceremoniously removed the USSR from the list of Allies exempt from public criticism (below). At CI&E's insistence, the primer was published and came into wide use in high schools and adult education classes.[64]

Local education boards, the heart of the decentralisation programme, also encountered difficulties. Large numbers of teachers served on the boards that hired them and fixed their salaries, creating obvious conflicts of interest, and many board members, lacking a clear sense of public service, used their position to feather their own nests. At the same time, the Ministry of Education gradually reasserted its influence over the boards, which tended to 'look to Tokyo' for guidance. Education superintendents chosen by prefectural and municipal boards usurped local prerogatives, taking control of education policy and using the boards to ratify decisions made at higher levels. Finally, in 1956, the Ministry abolished elections and had local board members appointed by higher authority (chapter 11). The boards' fatal flaw, however, was their lack of financial independence, a problem that GHQ never was able to resolve, and ministerial control of local purse strings ultimately sounded the knell for the grass-roots control of education.[65]

RELIGIONS

In 1945, there were three large organised religions in Japan: Shintō (literally, the 'Way of the Gods'), an indigenous polytheistic form of nature worship based on rites of propitiation and purification; Mahayana, or Northern, Buddhism, officially introduced in the sixth century from Korea; and Christianity, brought by Jesuits in the sixteenth century and reintroduced by Catholic and Protestant missionaries in the late nineteenth century following the establishment of trade relations with the West. With the Meiji Restoration of 1868, Japan's ruling oligarchs attempted to institute a theocracy reconciling divine Imperial rule with modern government (*saisei-itchi*). The Imperial Rescript of 3 February 1870 proclaimed the Emperor to be the living embodiment of godhood and his Throne a holy office established by the ancestral Sun Goddess (Amaterasu Ōmikami) and handed down in unbroken succession to the present. The Meiji Constitution of 1890 described the sovereign as 'sacred and inviolable', thereby justifying the Emperor's actions – and by implication decisions of the government that represented him – as manifestations of divine will, subject neither to clarification nor dissent. This mythico-religious ideology was at the core of the 1890 Imperial Rescript on Education, which enjoined the people to 'guard and maintain the prosperity of Our Imperial Throne coeval with heaven and earth'.[66]

In 1882, the state formally placed all religions into one of three categories, Shintō, Buddhism and Christianity, but actively discouraged the growth of the latter two. Shintō was established as the national faith and integrated with the Imperial cult to serve as a unifying spiritual force for modernisation, much as Christianity had in Western society. Christianity, whose one god was absolute and stood above the Emperor, was viewed with particular hostility. Scorned as a foreign import, it suffered periodic persecution. The Meiji government asserted control over Shintō shrines and cults and divided the new state religion into Shrine (*Jinja*) Shintō and Sectarian (*Kyōha*) Shintō. Shrine Shintō was a hierarchical body of some 200,000 Imperial, national, prefectural, district and village shrines. Imperial shrines were funded by the Imperial household, national shrines by the government. Shintō priests were civil servants, and by the 1930s, roughly 10 per cent were highly trained professionals. Sectarian Shintō included Confucian groups, shamanistic mountain and purification cults, renascent messianic groups and highly organised sects with rigorous philosophical creeds, such as the influential Tenrikyō.[67]

At the pinnacle of the State Shintō system were the Great Shrines of Ise, home of the ancestral Sun Goddess and repository of the Imperial regalia (sword, mirror and jewel). The Yasukuni Shrine on Kudan Hill in Tokyo, under direct military control, enshrined the spirits of the nation's war dead, as did the national network of *Gokoku* (Defence of the Nation) Shrines. From 1937, an Army general was appointed chief priest at Yasukuni, and in 1945, Admiral Suzuki Kantarō, the former prime minister, assumed that post. As Japanese society shifted to a war footing in the 1930s, shrines dedicated to emperors and national military heroes, such as Meiji, Nogi and Tōgō, were used to fan militant nationalism. The village shrines and unranked sanctuaries at the bottom of this pyramid, however, were different in character. There, the spirit of Japan's age-old nature religion thrived, little affected by the social and political upheavals around it.

From 1900, State Shintō was regulated alternately by the Home and Education Ministries. In 1939, the Home Ministry created the Shrine Board (*Jingi'in*) to strengthen centralised control over this imposing but unwieldy edifice. At the same time, the Religious Bodies Law (1939) made all organised religious groups legal persons, required them to register and meet rigorous criteria and placed them under direct state supervision. The Religions Branch of the Education Ministry's

Photo 50. Imperial Army troops worship at Yasukuni Shrine in Tokyo a few months before the Kwantung Army's occupation of Manchuria. Dedicated to the souls of Japan's war dead, Yasukuni symbolised the ultra-nationalist ethos of the pre-defeat era. 24 April 1931 (Kyodo).

Indoctrination Bureau tightly regulated Buddhism and Christianity. In 1943, the three recognised religions were brought together under the Greater Japan Wartime Patriotic Association of Religions (*Dai Nippon Senji Shūkyō Hōkoku Kai*) and forced to cooperate in the myriad tasks of 'spiritual mobilisation'.[68]

Civil Information and Education Section's Religions Branch (later Division) under Dr William K. Bunce, then a Navy Lieutenant, was assigned the task of demilitarising State Shintō and ensuring basic religious freedoms. Bunce's instructions from Washington were minimal, however. Article 10 of the Potsdam Proclamation stated simply that freedom of religion would be guaranteed. The 'US Initial Post-Surrender Policy for Japan' of 22 September 1945 reiterated that 'Freedom of religious worship shall be proclaimed promptly on occupation' but added the proviso: 'At the same time it should be made plain to the Japanese that ultra-nationalistic and militaristic organisations will not be permitted to hide behind the cloak of religion.' The control document also prohibited discrimination based on creed or belief.

Freedom of belief
Allied thinking on religion was rudimentary and closely linked to discussions on education reform. Nonetheless, in mid-March 1944, the Inter-Divisional Area Committee on the Far East submitted a memorandum entitled 'Freedom of

Worship', drafted by Japan specialists Earle Dickover and Eugene Dooman. This paper did not reach MacArthur's headquarters until late 1945, but the Potsdam document, the 'US Initial Post-Surrender Policy' and the Joint Chiefs' 'Basic Directive' all drew on it, and its recommendations are worth considering briefly. The Memorandum noted that National Shintō had been promoted actively by the wartime state at the expense of Christianity and other religions. It distinguished between 'the harmless, primitive animism, which was the original Shinto' and 'a nationalistic emperor-worshipping cult which has been used by the militarists to develop the present fanatically patriotic, aggressive Japan'. The paper warned that National Shintō 'is a distinct source of danger to the peace of the Pacific and perhaps of the world'. The Memorandum recommended that while a few shrines used to foster extreme militarist sentiment (Yasukuni, Meiji, Nogi, Tōgō) might be closed down 'without any violation of the principles of religious worship', sanctuaries in general, including the Great Shrines of Ise, should remain open for individual worship but be denied state financial assistance. In short, the state was not to interfere in any way with individual religious practice, nor was it to favour one religion or religious organisation over another or to provide financial support in any form to such.[69]

On 4 October 1945, CI&E's Civil Liberties Directive suspended all laws restricting freedom of worship or belief, banned discrimination based on creed, abolished all organisations and government agencies involved in the suppression of religious freedom, and called for the release of all persons imprisoned because of their faith. Consequently, Christians, members of messianic sects such as Ōmotokyō and Tenri Honmichi and other religious leaders who had criticised the Emperor system were freed from prison. Shintō was not mentioned, however, and no action was taken against shrines, which the government insisted were patriotic organisations, not religious institutions. Interestingly, following the surrender, the Greater Japan Wartime Patriotic Association of Religions dismissed all government officials in its employ and reorganised its Buddhist, Christian and Shintō components as private cooperating federations in order to escape dissolution. The three groups subsequently formed the Religions League of Japan, an ecumenical body that would become a progressive force for change in the immediate postwar period.[70]

On 7 October, three days after the Civil Liberties Directive, John Carter Vincent, Chief of the State Department's Far Eastern Division, told an NBC commentator during a radio interview that Shintoism would be done away with as a state religion but not tampered with as an individual creed. 'Our policy goes beyond Shinto,' he then added. 'The dissemination of Japanese militaristic and ultra-nationalistic ideology in any form will be completely suppressed, and the Japanese government will be required to cease financial and other support of Shinto establishments.' The Vincent broadcast produced banner headlines in Tokyo the next day, catching CI&E unawares. Bunce subsequently was taken out of education work and asked to concentrate on the Shintō issue, and on 28 November, the Religions Branch was established as a separate unit inside CI&E (it would become Religions Division in June 1946).[71]

In line with the Vincent statement, Bunce was directed to disestablish Shintō as a national cult and prepare a statement formally separating state and religion. His first step was to draft a lengthy staff study on the Shintō directive. He was assisted in this task by Dr Kishimoto Hideo, a Harvard-educated religious scholar teaching at Tokyo Imperial University who had been recommended to CI&E by Education Minister Maeda Tamon. Kishimoto's cooperation was indispensable. An unpaid volunteer with no fixed hours, he made himself available to Bunce's staff on a regular basis. 'As time went on,' Bunce later reminisced, 'I became more and more dependent on Kishimoto for information.' He noted that, while the savant also worked closely with the Japanese government, 'after a time, this was not an important question at all because he was everybody's man, in a sense. He was seeking the best solution, and he would give me his views. . . . He was very independent and [the authorities] left him alone.' Kishimoto accompanied Bunce on field trips, served as interpreter at meetings with Japanese officials and used his prestige and credibility to argue the merits of reform with religious leaders and the public, becoming an unofficial spokesperson for Religions Division.[72]

Bunce also conferred regularly with Dr Anesaki Masaharu, head of the Religious Studies Department at Tokyo Imperial University and Kishimoto's father-in-law, and in the early months received several visits from renowned scholar and Zen master Suzuki Daisetsu, a bitter foe of the Shintō establishment. At the same time, Bunce corresponded with Dr Daniel C. Holtom, American missionary and expert on modern Shintō, who sent him a list of recommendations for the reform of Shrine Shintō (22 September 1945). These covered textbook revision, Shintō in the schools, and shrines and ceremonies and their administration. Bunce assigned Kishimoto and other Japanese advisers to the Special Projects and Research Branch, the Division's brain trust, and named William P. Woodard to head it.[73]

The Shintō Directive

Bunce and his staff completed their Shintō staff study on 3 December 1945. Based on it, they drafted the Shintō Directive (SCAPIN-448: 'Abolition of Governmental Support, Perpetuation, Control, and Dissemination of State Shintō'), which was issued on 15 December. Like many SCAP instructions, the document was worked up and finalised at the junior staff level. Many years later, Bunce remarked, 'My own directive, disestablishing State Shinto and prohibiting certain ultra-nationalistic teachings established by government, was written without any guidance from above and was not changed in any way by higher headquarters.'[74] It also reflected the views of Bunce's Japanese advisers and in this sense was a collaborative effort.

SCAPIN-448 banned official sponsorship or financial aid to shrines and any participation in Shintō rites or observances by government officials acting in their official capacity. It outlawed militaristic ideology in religious practice in general, annulled government orders pertaining to shrines, abolished the Home Ministry's Shrine Board, removed Shintō symbols from schools and public offices, and prohibited the dissemination of Shintō doctrine in educational institutions receiving public funds. The directive also banned use of the term 'Greater East Asia War' and other slogans connected with wartime ultra-nationalism. The document's second paragraph formulated rules for the separation of religion from the state 'to prevent the misuse of religion for political ends' and 'put all religions, faiths and creeds upon exactly the same legal basis, entitled to the same opportunities and protection'. The Emperor's renunciation of divinity on 1 January 1946, despite its Royal ambiguities, seemed to echo the Shintō Directive's bold tenor.[75]

The government promptly complied with the dissolution decree, transferring Shrine Board records to the Education Ministry's reconstituted Religious Affairs Bureau and suspending disbursements worth about ¥1 million to 200 Imperial and national shrines (nearly one quarter of these had gone to the Great Shrines of Ise alone). On 28 December, the Cabinet enacted the Religious Corporations Ordinance, enabling disestablished shrines and groups to became religious corporations. Some 80,000 shrines subsequently regrouped under the Association of Shintō Shrines (*Jinja Honchō*), a private body organised in late January 1946 by 200 shrine representatives from across Japan. Priests were stripped of their civil service rank and their privileges, and their semi-official training centre, the Institute for the Study of Imperial Writings (*Kōten Kōkyūsho*), was abolished. Unlike CI&E's Education Division, however, Religions Division never conducted a purge of religious leaders per se, Bunce believing it would do more harm than good.[76]

Education Ministry officials feared that CI&E would attempt to ban the Imperial family's private Shintō ceremonies and rituals and close down the Great Shrines of Ise. In late November, before the promulgation of SCAPIN-448, Sone Eki of the Central Liaison Office and I'inuma Issei, Vice President of the Shrine Board, visited the Religions Division chief with what a Bunce subordinate referred to as 'a remarkably progressive set of proposals' designed to pre-empt a formal SCAP directive. The recommendations had been worked out in cooperation with Anesaki, who had been acting as liaison between the Board and CI&E, and the Cabinet had ratified it on 20 November. The government proposals anticipated the provisions of the Shintō Directive to a surprising extent, but Bunce explained that the SCAPIN would be issued anyway as a formality. In the course of two conferences, the Japanese also broached the future of Yasukuni Shrine and impressed upon Bunce its importance to the country. Yasukuni, Meiji, Nogi and Tōgō Shrines, as well as the national *Gokoku* sanctuaries, were allowed to continue operating as places of individual worship, despite their militant past. 'Yasukuni,' Bunce later commented, 'was a national repository of the feeling of the whole nation who had lost members of their family. Therefore, Yasukuni had a legitimate place in Japanese life if the Japanese wanted to keep it.'[77]

This was a question of great personal importance to Bunce. GHQ's goal was to depoliticise Shintō belief and practice, removing chauvinistic and undemocratic elements, not to demean, discourage or restrict Shintō itself. A punitive policy would constitute discrimination against a specific faith, negating the principles of religious freedom and equality of belief. The injunction against state involvement in religion applied to all creeds, not just Shintō. Bunce later acknowledged that his prewar experience as an English teacher in Matsuyama, Ehime Prefecture had fostered in him an appreciation of both Buddhism and Shintoism but noted that his primary inspiration for the Shintō Directive was the US Constitution.[78]

SCAPIN-448 became the basis for the new Constitution's Article 14 (banning discrimination based on creed), Article 19 (freedom of thought and conscience), Article 20 (freedom of religion) and Article 89 (prohibiting the expenditure of public funds for 'the use, benefit or maintenance of any religious institution or association'). The directive's provisions also were written into the Fundamental Law of Education, the School Education Law, the Civil Code, the Local Autonomy Law and other statutes and ordinances covering religion.[79]

Christianity
While Bunce was guaranteeing to all religions equal opportunities and protection, the Supreme Commander was busy promoting Christianity, using his discretionary powers to make smooth its ways in the new Japan. To Bunce's dismay, MacArthur propagated the faith with astonishing candour. In October 1945, for instance, the General urged Protestant leaders to send 1,000 missionaries to convert the Japanese and gave them privileged access to the country. On 25 November 1946, he wrote to the Joint Chiefs that 'It is the policy of this theater to increase greatly the Christian influence.' On 24 February 1947, he told the US Congress in a radio message that 'Through the firm encouragement . . . of this yet frail spearhead of Christianity in the Far East lies hope that to hundreds of millions of backward peoples . . . may come a heretofore unknown spiritual strength.' MacArthur was elated by the ascension to power of Presbyterian and Socialist Katayama Tetsu in May of that year. In a public statement, he hailed as progress the fact that Japan was led by a Christian for the first time in its history and noted that 'Three great oriental countries now have men who embrace the Christian faith at the head of their governments, Chiang K'ai-shek in China, Manuel Roxas in the Philippines and Tetsu Katayama in Japan.' Katayama's premiership, he declared, offered hope that Christianity would prove 'an invincible spiritual barrier against the infiltration of ideologies which seek by suppression the way to power and advancement', an obvious reference to Communism. In October 1947, he wrote to a US missionary in Gifu Prefecture: 'I entertain the hope that Japan will become Christianised. Every possible effort to that end is being made and, had I my way, I would hope for a thousand missionaries for every one that is here now.'[80]

MacArthur's proselytising ardour stemmed partly from his own messianic proclivities, and partly from a sincerely felt moral obligation to rectify the damage done to mission schools and churches by the wartime régime. He believed fervently in the high ethical and humanitarian values of Christianity, and was convinced that, in their absence, the turmoil of defeat would drive Japan to the left. 'Japan is a spiritual vacuum', he told four Protestant leaders in the autumn of 1945. 'If you do not fill it with Christianity, it will be filled with Communism.' But his open support of church work in Japan also reflected a sensitivity to US public opinion as he prepared to enter the 1948 presidential elections. On MacArthur's orders, Religions Division facilitated the activities of evangelic groups, allowing them to use Occupation facilities and introducing their leaders to the Supreme Commander and even to the Emperor. MacArthur not only encouraged the churches to send missionaries but asked for, and received, 10 million Bibles and hymnals translated into Japanese. Although entry into Japan was strictly controlled, between August 1945 and December 1950, SCAP's G-1 and Religions Division invited 3,000 evangelists to Japan. Many also were allowed into south Korea until war broke out there in 1950. By June 1951, there were 4,000 in Japan, including large numbers who had taken refuge from the fighting in Korea. At the same time, prominent Japanese Christians – but not Buddhists – were allowed to visit the United States prior to the relaxation of entry and exit controls in 1949. Among them was Uemura Tamaki, a female activist who on her return presented the Empress with a Bible and lectured on it in the Imperial Palace. The first Japanese permitted to study abroad were Catholic seminarians. In late 1947, reacting to accusations of blasphemy from American church groups, MacArthur ordered CI&E Chief Nugent to reprimand the Education Ministry for publishing a textbook, *The History of the West*, suggesting that the New Testament was not entirely factual.[81]

Missionaries by and large were well-meaning, dedicated people. Among them were former prisoners of war, such as Jacob DeShazer, who had been captured after bombing Nagoya in April 1942 with the Doolittle Raiders. But many preached anti-Communism alongside the Gospel and denigrated Buddhism and Shintoism as pagan creeds based on superstition. Their growing presence immediately elicited charges from Japanese religious leaders that SCAP was favouring Christianity at the expense of traditional beliefs and in defiance of its own stated principles. On 20 January 1947, G-1 sent a check sheet to the Chief of Staff urging an official statement of non-assistance to the churches. It noted Buddhist and Shintō complaints that 'freedom of religion is only a theory with us because [Occupation authorities] are supporting the Christian movement'. Maintaining the appearance of non-support, G-1 asserted disingenuously, 'is strongly consistent with the policy of strengthening Christian influence in Japan'.

Bunce resolutely opposed such hypocrisy, prompting complaints from church dignitaries about CI&E's 'stiff-necked attitude of impartiality.' Religions Division clashed with Education Division over religious content in education, opposing what it viewed as an attempt to introduce Christian-derived teachings into the curriculum. In 1949, Bunce pressed Section Chief Nugent for a restatement of the policy of equal treatment and personally raised the issue with MacArthur. By that time, however, the Supreme Commander had concluded that 'pride of race . . . would prevent most Japanese from becoming Christian' and had stopped making public pronouncements in support of Christian missions.[82] And in fact, few Japanese responded to American efforts to propagate what was widely viewed as an alien religion. As of 31 December 1948, there were 343,000 Japanese Christians, a mere 0.6 per cent of the population, roughly the same figure as when MacArthur arrived in 1945. As one scholar has remarked cynically, 'Many Japanese accepted a free pocket Bible from the Americans, but they saw it as a cheap substitute for cigarette paper.'[83]

Where the Court was concerned, however, MacArthur and his staff discouraged proselytisation. In the wake of defeat, rumours abounded that the Emperor was considering conversion, sparking a fierce contest between foreign Catholic and Protestant leaders to win the monarch's favour. MacArthur's Counter-Intelligence Chief Elliott R. Thorpe reported escalating demands by the Papal Nuncio and Protestant bishops to visit Hirohito and fretted that 'whichever group got this potential convert, the other group would set up a protest that might well have resulted in MacArthur's relief as Commander-in-Chief in Japan'. In fact, MacArthur had flirted initially with the idea of winning an Imperial proselyte. On 10 July 1946, he confided to US Secretary of the Navy James Forrestal in Tokyo that he was thinking of asking the Emperor to join the Christian faith. The monarch, MacArthur said, was 'typical of any well-bred wealthy young club man in a Western society who was used by the military as their stooge'. The General evidently changed his mind, however. He later boasted to an American churchman that he had the power to make the Emperor and 70 million Japanese Christians overnight if he so chose, and he told American revivalist Billy Graham that Hirohito had indicated to him a willingness to adopt Christianity as Japan's new national creed. But the Supreme Commander rejected the offer, he told Graham, because it would be wrong to force any religion on a country. Such methods, he believed, would ruin the church's chances of ever developing properly in Japan. In any event, MacArthur appears to have decided that Imperial apostasy was poor policy.[84]

Nonetheless, the monarch met a long succession of US Christian leaders, including Cardinal Francis Spellman and Billy Graham, and reports of the Imperial family's impending conversion persisted. Nanbara Shigeru, himself a Christian, predicted in 1946 that Hirohito would embrace the faith, and in 1950, Kagawa Toyohiko, a Socialist reformer and Christian who had lectured to the Emperor on Christianity, told the media that the sovereign was studying the religion. The appointment, at Hirohito's request, of Philadelphia Quaker Elizabeth G. Vining as tutor to Crown Prince Akihito furthered such speculation, as did reports that the Empress Dowager believed Japan would be better off as a Christian nation.[85]

Problems, resolved and unresolved

The separation of religion and state posed a number of difficulties for Japan's traditional religions requiring the intervention of Religions Branch. The problem of state-owned shrine and temple precincts was especially complex. More than 30,000 Buddhist temples occupied 10,000 hectares of public land, and nearly 73,000 Shintō shrines were sited on 30,000 hectares. Without this property, many religious organisations could not operate, but an outright grant of land by the state would contravene Article 89 of the Constitution, which banned public assistance to religious institutions. Bunce got around this quandary by arguing that Article 20's guarantee of religious freedom was the more basic liberty. CI&E agreed, and on 12 April 1947, the Diet amended the 1939 Law for the Disposition of State-Owned Properties Used by Shrines and Temples. The revision allowed the government to transfer precinct titles to religious groups free of cost under certain conditions and enabled organisations to purchase other land at half its market value, saving many religious organisations from dissolution.[86] The land reform of October 1946 posed another problem, for it classified groups holding property received as religious offerings as absentee landlords. Religions Division convinced Natural Resources Section to allow churches, shrines and temples to retain such holdings if they were tilled or pastured by parish priests or other religious personnel.

The most pressing issue for Shintō groups was the loss of government revenues. Stripped of their subsidies, many sanctuaries came to rely on local neighbourhood associations (*tonari-gumi*) for maintenance costs and funds for shrine festivals. In the spring of 1946, Religions Division began receiving complaints from individuals that the *tonari-gumi* were exacting shrine dues and other contributions from families still organised in the wartime household networks. Failure to comply with such demands resulted in harassment and even threats of violence. As this was clearly a violation of the Shintō Directive, on 6 November 1946, Religions Division issued SCAPIN-1318 ('Sponsorship and Support of Shintō by Neighborhood Associations') prohibiting unauthorised levies. Under pressure from CI&E and Government Section, the Home Ministry finally disbanded the *tonari-gumi* on 31 May 1947, but the associations continued to operate informally, and the problem of forced contributions was never fully resolved.[87]

The Religious Corporations Ordinance of 28 December 1945 was an interim measure designed to facilitate the transition of shrines from state to private control. Through it, more than 200,000 sanctuaries became incorporated religious bodies. Among them were many messianic cults and new religions that proliferated in the confusion of the immediate postwar era. A number of these organisations applied for religious status solely in order to receive tax exemptions and other privileges. In 1947, Shinohara Yoshio, head of the Education Ministry's Religious Affairs Bureau, proposed to close some of the Ordinance's loopholes with a new law, but Bunce was not enthusiastic. He changed his mind when an inter-faith delegation of religious dignitaries visited him in the autumn of 1949 and requested his assistance in drafting a new law before the end of the Occupation. Bunce refused to undertake the task himself, however, suggesting that the religious leaders work with Shinohara to produce a draft. When the Ministry baulked at this suggestion, Bunce's Special Projects Officer William P. Woodard acted as go-between, inviting the Religions League of Japan to assist in formulating the proposal. League representatives in effect became consultants of Religions Division. The Religious Juridical Persons Law of 3 April 1951, enacted at the request of a private confederation and with the cooperation of leaders of all faiths, became the only religious statute passed by the Diet during the Occupation. Maintaining the separation of religion and state, the law met the varied needs of Japan's traditional creeds as well as its newer ones, treating all equally. It established firm criteria for incorporation but avoided regimentation, eliminating abuses under the 1945 Ordinance while enhancing the freedom and security of incorporated bodies. Coming late in the Occupation, this remarkable piece of legislation was an exercise in democratic self-regulation that exemplified the best of the postwar reforms.[88]

Religions Division left the Great Shrines of Ise intact, although divested of state support, and did not interfere with the ritual observances of the Imperial family itself, reasoning that this fell within the domain of individual freedom of worship. In November 1945, Hirohito journeyed to Ise to report the end of the war to the Sun Goddess and the spirits of his Imperial ancestors, and in June 1952, he made the trip again to announce the entry into effect of the San Francisco Peace Treaty. Religions Division interpreted these as private acts financed by the Imperial household, not official observances funded out of state coffers. The line between private and public acts quickly wore thin, however. Crown Prince Akihito's investiture ceremony in November 1952 was a solemn state function involving substantial government expenditures, but because the ceremony itself took place before the Imperial Shrine inside the Palace, the government claimed it was a private rite. Conservative post-Occupation governments would utilise this ambiguity to enhance the position of the Throne and its powerful symbolism, progressively blurring the crucial distinction between state and religion.[89]

A similar aura of uncertainty surrounded worship at Yasukuni Shrine, repository of the souls of Japan's war dead, and the legality of visits there by government officials would provoke controversy in the years that followed. In the autumn of 1951, with the Occupation nearing the end of its tenure, CI&E reversed its policy on the attendance of officials at funerals and other observances for deceased soldiers. In November 1946, the Section had issued verbal instructions to the Education and Home Ministries prohibiting local-government sponsorship of funerals and memorial services, including the presentation of condolence money or wreaths. It also had outlawed public ceremonies marking the return of funerary urns to bereaved families. In September 1951, Religions Division executed a perfect volte-face, informing the Education Ministry, again verbally, that it did not object to the 'appropriate commemoration' of the war dead by the government. Municipal authorities now were allowed to donate flowers, incense or wreaths on these occasions and give money to build tombs and ossuaries. Contributing to the erection of monuments or memorials later was authorised as well, provided the monuments were set apart from religious and educational institutions and did not bear religious symbols or nationalistic inscriptions. This dramatic policy shift alarmed Buddhist and Christian groups and drew a formal rebuke from the Religions League of Japan. Together with the Yasukuni issue, it would set the stage for a series of post-Occupation controversies over state involvement in religion (chapter 11).[90]

INFORMATION CONTROL AND THE MEDIA

Allied censorship and information controls, born of military necessity, originally were conceived as interim measures. Once instituted, however, they developed a life of their own, enduring until October 1949. Their extension beyond the initial military phase of occupation into peacetime was incongruent with the Potsdam guarantees of free speech and inquiry and, indeed, with the 1947 Constitution.

Wartime planning
In his State of the Union Speech of 6 January 1941, President Franklin Roosevelt listed free speech as one of the Four Freedoms constituting Allied war goals, but when war with Japan broke out eleven months later, that freedom became one of the first casualties. The US Office of Censorship, created on 19 December 1941 under the First War Powers Act, monitored and restricted information flows into and out of the United States as a wartime emergency measure. In mid-1943, its civilian director, Byron Price, a former Associated Press newsman, convinced military and civilian leaders to develop a post-defeat censorship policy for the Axis Powers.[91] Planning for Japan involved the Army and Navy, the State Department, the Office of War Information (OWI), and the Office of Strategic Services (OSS) and proceeded along two tracks. Early thinking was orientated to wake-of-battle military needs and assumed an invasion followed by a hostile occupation. Civilian planning was more broadly conceived: censorship and media guidance were viewed as extensions of US foreign policy directed at replacing fascist (and later, Communist) ideas with democratic values. The dual policy that emerged was strongly influenced by planning for postwar Germany.[92]

In July 1943, at the request of the US Office of Censorship, the Allied Combined Chiefs of Staff made the surveillance of civilian communications in occupied territories an official military duty. Censorship was to target the mails, telephone and telegraph, radio, press, films, and photographs and extend to both domestic and external communications. In May 1944, MacArthur received his first formal instructions on civil censorship from the War Department, and in November of that year, the Joint Chiefs issued a policy directive (JCS-873/3) on the subject to commanders in the Asian and Pacific theatres. The basic objectives of information control were to gather intelligence, insure military security, maintain internal order, prevent black-marketeering, enforce the terms of surrender, arrest suspected war criminals and disseminate information in support of military government. In the event of Japan's capitulation, all communications, domestic and external, were to be suspended temporarily, after which internal spot checks on the mails and tele-communications would be instituted. Unlike MacArthur's May instructions, JCS-873/3 also targeted the 'media of publicity' (newspapers, broadcasting, film), which were to be supervised closely and purged of ultra-nationalistic content.[93]

Based on JCS-873/3, on 31 December 1944, Brigadier General Thorpe, MacArthur's Counter-Intelligence chief, was directed to establish a Civil Censorship

Detachment. Lieutenant Colonel Donald D. Hoover, a former newspaper man and public relations expert who had helped organise the US Office of Censorship, was named to head the new unit. In April and July 1945, following the establishment of MacArthur's AFPAC headquarters in Manila, Hoover drafted the 'Basic Plan for Civilian Censorship in Japan.' His third revision (30 September) became the basis for the Occupation's censorship programme. Communications and media surveillance would be primarily a military endeavour assigned to Hoover's Civil Censorship Detachment.[94]

In the meantime, State Department planners working on Germany were stretching the concept of information management to include not only the extirpation of militaristic ideas but the inculcation in their place of democratic ones. Two State Department papers reflect this shift in emphasis. The first was a study drafted in July 1944 by Japan specialist Beppo Johansen and entitled 'Japan: Occupation: Media of Public Information and Expression' (CAC-237), which proposed moderate media controls and introduced the concept of prior clearance, or *pre*-censorship, of materials for domestic dissemination.[95] A year later, policy-makers had gone much farther and were openly advocating thought reform for postwar Germany, an idea that would shape the final draft of CAC-237. Leading this crusade was Archibald MacLeish, Secretary of State for Public and Cultural Relations. MacLeish was a fervent believer in ideological reorientation. The United States, he believed, had 'a duty now not only to occupy and police and feed and punish, but to convert and to persuade'. Even the Japan Crowd, whose lenient early proposals had stressed the liberation of the media from government control, now embraced this more radical point of view. In early 1945, Eugene H. Dooman, Chair of SWNCC's Subcommittee for the Far East, echoed MacLeish's concerns, asserting that 'It is our primary task in this war to change the basic thinking of the Japanese masses.'[96] In April 1945, Dooman's SFE requested a revision of CAC-237 specifying the concrete measures to be taken. This task was assigned to State Department officials working under MacLeish. Completed on 10 August 1945, 'Control of the Media of Public Information and Expression in Japan' spelled out a detailed programme of media surveillance designed, among other things, to redirect Japanese thinking along democratic lines via a positive policy of ideological guidance.

The new CAC-237 was followed in short order by 'Positive Policy for Reorientation of the Japanese' (SWNCC-162/D) of mid-July, which called for major changes in 'ideologies and attitudes of mind'. Extending well beyond formal schooling, this pro-active policy advocated utilising 'all possible media and channels' and was to be an integral part of military government activities. As one scholar has pointed out, it urged, in effect, the extension of wartime propaganda and psychological warfare techniques into the postwar era of peace in order to counter fascist and Communist ideology and secure America's long-term political interests in Japan. SWNCC-162/ D proposed enlisting the support of progressive Japanese, who with American shepherding would reforge the progressive elements in Japanese culture into a liberal democratic ethos, implying a long-range US commitment to the slow process of thought conversion. SWNCC-162 and CAC-237 were incorporated into early drafts of the Army's 'Basic Directive', which called for minimal surveillance and the use of the media of information to root out objectionable ideas and foster democratic principles.[97]

At the start of the Occupation, two organisations, one military, the other civilian, were responsible for information control. The Army's Civil Censorship Detachment performed the purgative function of eliminating undesirable ideas and influences from the media of publicity and expression. CI&E's Information Dissemination Branch (later, Information Division), the successor to Brigadier General Bonner F. Fellers's Psychological Warfare Branch (SWPA/AFPAC), was assigned the affirmative duty of realigning the nation's mental processes by providing books, magazine articles, radio scripts, films, plays, records and photographs extolling the virtues of the democratic (American) way of life.[98]

The Press and Radio Codes
Media control, a long-established practice in Japan, became pervasive with the beginning of the Pacific War. From December 1941, nothing could be published, broadcast or screened without prior approval. The Information Bureau, created in late 1940, employed 600 civilian and military censors to supervise print, broadcast and film media and engage in 'positive' propaganda in support of Japan's military objectives. The Bureau's propaganda lines were disseminated by the state-run news agency Dōmei (1936) and the Ministry of Communications's Japan Broadcasting Corporation (1926).[99]

Lieutenant Colonel Hoover's Civil Censorship Detachment (CCD) began operating from AFPAC headquarters in Yokohama on 1 September 1945, one day before the Instrument of Surrender was signed. On 3 September, the CCD created the Press, Pictorial and Broadcast Division to monitor the mass media. Pre-surrender planning had recommended utilising Dōmei and the Japan Broadcasting Corporation (*Nihon Hōsō Kyōkai*, dubbed 'NHK' to suit the American preference for acronyms) to disseminate Occupation directives, but MacArthur, on the advice of a senior American correspondent (reportedly anxious to destroy a rival), issued orders to shut down Dōmei. 'This would have been a very serious step indeed,' Counter-Intelligence Chief Thorpe later wrote, 'for we were using Domei as the only effective means of communicating the Commander-in-Chief's will to the nearly 60 million people in the Empire.' Thorpe and Hoover hastily arranged a meeting with MacArthur, and Hoover, 'with the earnest eloquence . . . of an old time revival preacher', persuaded the Supreme Commander to keep the news agency open.[100]

GHQ promptly replaced Japan's censorship and propaganda establishment with its own, retaining intact the full panoply of control mechanisms. On 11 September, CCD's Press, Pictorial and Broadcast Division moved into Dōmei and NHK offices. Meanwhile, GHQ/AFPAC transmitted its directives from Yokohama to Japan's media via the Information Bureau and the Home Ministry's Police Bureau (Censorship Section). MacArthur's Public Relations Office controlled the release of news to foreign correspondents (formal censorship of the foreign media ended on 6 October), and from 2 October, SCAP's Civil Communications Section assumed organisational control of NHK.[101] In a telling display of priorities, the Civil Information and Education Section itself took up residence in NHK's home offices in the Radio Tokyo Building, Hibiya.

On 10 September, the Supreme Commander issued the 'Freedom of Speech and Press Directive' (SCAPIN-16), drafted by the Civil Censorship Detachment. The 10-point memorandum pledged 'an absolute minimum of restrictions upon freedom of speech' but banned news that did not adhere to the truth, disturbed the public tranquillity, criticised the Allied powers or discussed Allied troop movements. Radio broadcasts were limited to news, music and entertainment, and Radio Tokyo was the only station allowed to broadcast news and commentary domestically. Violations of the order were punishable by suspension. Censorship of print and broadcast media began the same day. The CCD ordered Dōmei to cease overseas shortwave broadcasts. The English daily *Nippon Times* (shortly to become *The Japan Times*), a Foreign Ministry mouthpiece, was placed under pre-publication surveillance. Radio Tokyo, the nation's sole source of broadcast news, also was subjected to pre-censorship. Post-publication checks were imposed on books and pamphlets.[102]

Dōmei came in for particular scrutiny. Army censors were irate at its frequent reporting of GI crimes and misdemeanors. They hammered the state news agency for following the Foreign Ministry line that Japan's surrender had been conditional and for describing SCAP's communications to the government as 'negotiations'. On 13 September, CCD received 'Magic' intercepts of a message from Foreign Minister Shigemitsu Mamoru to Japanese legations in Berne, Stockholm and Lisbon informing them that Tokyo intended to 'make every effort to exploit the atomic bomb question in our propaganda' through Dōmei's overseas network. On 14 September, CCD charged the agency with disseminating untruthful news (misbehaviour by Occupation troops) and disturbing the public tranquillity (reports of Hiroshima and Nagasaki), suspended it for 24 hours and placed it under indefinite pre-publication censorship. Japan's premier daily, the *Asahi Shinbun*, also stood accused of criticising the atomic bombings and questioning reports of Japanese war crimes in the Philippines. It was suspended on 18 September. The next day, the *Nippon Times* met the same fate ostensibly for failing to submit a sensitive article to Thorpe's inspectors. Similarly, Ishibashi Tanzan's *Tōyō Keizai Shinpō* was shut down temporarily for running stories on the GI crime wave.[103]

To resolve the ambiguities in its media policy, on 19 September MacArthur's headquarters announced the 'Press Code for Japan' (SCAPIN-33), followed on 22 September by the 'Radio Code for Japan' (SCAPIN-43). The Codes were nearly identical in content, but the latter also covered programmes of information, education and entertainment. Additional 'freedom orders' were issued on 24 September, 27 September and 16 October liberating the mass media, including motion pictures, from government financial control and surveillance, wartime ordinances and other forms of central interference. The new Codes clarified the directive of 10 September but added prohibitions against articles liable to invite mistrust or resentment of Allied troops, news items based on editorial opinion and the colouring of stories with propaganda lines. CCD also ordered newspapers not to mention censorship or in any way indicate deletions. On 8 October, the Civil Censorship Detachment, now under Thorpe's Civil Intelligence Section (SCAP) placed Tokyo's five leading dailies on pre-censorship standing, and soon some 60 news agencies and papers were under pre-production scrutiny. From late October, all books (except school texts, which were the responsibility of CI&E) also were censored. Films, drama, phonograph records, lyrics, artwork and even paper lantern shows (*kamishibai*) were made subject to pre-performance or pre-release controls in the form of scenario and synopsis reviews, screenings, viewings and listening sessions.

On 4 October 1945, the Civil Liberties Directive abolished the Home Ministry's Police Bureau and its Censorship Section. In late October, Furuno Inosuke, the ultra-nationalist president of Dōmei, decided to liquidate the news agency, now bereft of government funding. On 1 November, SCAP ordered the reorganisation of the Information Bureau. Of no further use to the state, the Bureau was dissolved by the Shidehara government on 31 December. MacArthur's headquarters now was in sole command of the Japanese media.[104]

Civil censorship

Within a short time, the Army's censorship programme had moved well beyond the military's original counter-intelligence and security objectives, extending its prying eye into every nook and cranny of the public information industry. The overwhelming number of CCD personnel were Japanese and ethnic Koreans. In January 1947, they accounted for 8,132 out of 8,763 effectives, or about 93 per cent of the total. Some of these young men and women, particularly Koreans and Japanese of mixed parentage, had suffered under the military régime and now embraced Occupation goals with undisguised zeal. Others, including former newsmen, were of a more conservative hue. Koji Kawaguchi, one of several Nisei CCD personnel assigned to Fukuoka, Kyushu, later recalled that Japanese staff included many former newspaper editors, reporters, film directors and other media professionals. Although hired by SCAP, they were paid by the Japanese government. Many of these individuals performed their work perfunctorily with little understanding of Occupation objectives. A 1950 Military Intelligence survey of CCD activities complained that such people, 'unable to cast off the mental shackles of their reverence for the concept of a divine Emperor, considered any criticism of or levity with the Imperial institution to be a gross sacrilege ... and, furthermore, a violation of censorship policy'. These screeners injected a conservative bias into the review process that their American supervisors, Military Intelligence assessments notwithstanding, were inclined to tolerate (below).[105]

The Civil Censorship Detachment was run by the Army, but only about one third of its personnel were on active duty, the vast majority consisting of Department of the Army civilians, many of them women. Under CCD guidance, Japanese spied on other Japanese, but unlike the state's repressive wartime censors, MacArthur's legions were charged with fostering the conditions under which freedom of expression could flourish. In principle, information control was designed to maintain military security, determine the extent of compliance with Occupation policies, assist in the free and factual reporting of the news, and prevent a resurgence of ultra-nationalism. But in fact, CCD censorship frequently clashed with those ideals. Article 21 of the new Constitution stated unequivocally that 'No censorship shall be maintained, nor shall the secrecy of any means of communication be violated.' Yet, for four years, the Detachment's Telecommunications Division instituted wiretaps and listened in on 800,000 telephone conversations, and the Postal Division, which had taken over the operation of Japan's postal system on 13 September 1945, spot-checked 330 million pieces of mail, violating the civil rights and personal privacy of millions of citizens.

The Press, Pictorial and Broadcast (PPB) Division monitored a wide variety of media according to standards that seemed to change capriciously from one month to the next, compromising in many instances freedom of individual and collective expression.[106] The extent of surveillance was staggering. In mid-1947, at the height of its activities, PPB was scanning on a *monthly* basis (pre- and post-publication) 16 news agencies, 69 daily newspapers, 11,111 non-daily news publications, 3,243 magazines, 1,838 books, 8,600 radio programmes, 673 films, 2,900 drama scenarios and 514 phonograph records. *Kamishibai* (literally, 'paper shows'), an indigenous art form that tells a story via a series of illustrated paper panels often illuminated by lanterns, also were subjected to scrutiny because of their broad popular appeal. Between November 1945 and February 1947, PPB censors in District I (Tokyo and areas north) screened 8,821 such shows.[107]

Japanese examiners scoured this material diligently, referring questionable, objectionable and sensitive items to their American supervisors, who ordered a full or partial translation of the suspect text, words, dialogue or scene. After a review process entailing as many as 31 steps, the district censor could order a full or partial deletion or suppress the item in its entirety. He or she might also place it on hold, for a few days or indefinitely. To assist the monitors, PPB compiled secret censorship manuals with 'key logs', which were lists of proscribed subjects. The key logs changed frequently and without warning or explanation, reflecting shifting Occupation priorities.

Heading the list of taboo subjects was censorship itself. Other 'categories of deletion and suppression' included misconduct by Allied personnel, the atomic bombings, food shortages, black-market activities, fraternisation, mixed-blood children, population control, Japanese Americans, defence of war criminals, reparations, and peace treaty discussions. Also off limits were references to the Ogasawara, Ryukyu and Kuril Islands, critical US press commentary on MacArthur or the Occupation, and suggestions that SCAP had anything at all to do with elections, Cabinet changes, the operation of the government or the enactment of new laws, notably the Constitution. Even the foreign press was watched closely on these issues. In mid-March 1946, for example, Haru Matsukata (later, Reischauer) was blacklisted for informing her boss, Gordon Walker of the *Christian Science Monitor*, that the draft constitution MacArthur had just announced to the public as the work of the government was in fact an American initiative. The fiction of Japanese authorship, she later recalled, was 'a major falsehood that merited exposure'. Not only was Matsukata labelled a Communist for her trouble, but Walker was denied re-entry to Japan after a brief visit to China. Several journalists, American and British, would meet similar fates. Although many, like Walker, eventually were allowed to return, the threat of expulsion was an effective deterrent to printing the whole truth.[108]

Discussion of the mechanics of Occupation control and the operations of specific SCAP staff sections also was banned. Consequently, few Japanese understood how the Occupation super-government really worked. In December 1946, a district censor blue-pencilled the term 'Occupation costs' and told editors to replace it with 'costs of termination of war', which was subsequently changed to 'other costs', in order to disguise the source of 30 per cent of the 1947 budget. Indeed, to the extent possible, the Occupation itself was to be erased from the public consciousness and rendered if not invisible, then at least opaque. This was particularly evident in films, where English signs could not be shown, even inadvertently, and background shots of Military Police, Eighth Army troops, the Dai-Ichi Insurance Building, jeeps and bombed-out areas were regularly snipped by the censors' scissors. Even the dialogue line 'Ah! An airplane!' was excised from one scene, since Japanese air space was the exclusive domain of the US military. Among the most frequently suppressed information was news of specific world events, especially strikes in Allied countries, Allied policy disagreements, the Chinese revolution, US–Soviet relations and heightening Cold War tensions in Europe. In short, not only were the Japanese shielded from unwholesome (to the American eye) social and political events in their own country, but they were kept ignorant of international developments with a direct bearing on the nation's future.[109]

The key logs were a closely guarded military secret, and prohibited categories were not shown to Japanese editors, radio announcers or other media people, who were forced to second-guess PPB inspectors. US censorship officers regularly met media leaders to outline what constituted inappropriate discourse, and newspapers, movie companies and theatres developed their own coping mechanisms. During the war, editors and directors had established in-house 'censorship desks' to work with police and Information Bureau inspectors. The same specialists now worked with PPB officials, anticipating Occupation demands, interpreting media directives to co-workers and keeping their companies out of trouble. The film industry produced its own set of guidelines, which were circulated secretly among the studios. Self-censorship became a permanent feature of the editorial process in diverse media.

Censoring democracy
SCAP's treatment of specific topics, such as the atomic bombings and the Emperor, reveal the deeper logic of Japan's 'censored democracy'.[110] One of the Occupation's

first tasks was to suppress and control news of the nuclear holocaust. MacArthur's command was especially sensitive to the issue of radioactivity and other aftereffects. On 6 September 1945, Australian journalist Wilfred Burchett, who had managed to visit Hiroshima on his own, smuggled past US censors the first foreign eyewitness account of the devastation, noting that people not injured directly were dying of an acute but mysterious illness, which he ascribed to atomic radiation. Six days later, General Thomas F. Farrell, having just returned from a survey of the two cities, arranged a press conference to refute those charges. In February 1946, SCAP confiscated and sent to Washington chilling documentary footage of Hiroshima and Nagasaki shot by the Nippon Film Company (Nichiei) in the weeks immediately following the cities' destruction (chapter 9). For four years, Colonel Putnam's media custodians routinely struck down lay and scientific reports on the effects of the bomb. Although literary works dealing with the subject were not banned outright, the maze of pre-censorship requirements made publication difficult, and until 1949, only a handful of such works appeared in print. When Catholic physician Nagai Takashi submitted his eyewitness account, *The Bells Toll for Nagasaki* (*Nagasaki no kane*), in 1947, the CCD withheld the book from publication even though Economic and Scientific Section and Public Health and Welfare had cleared it. Finally, in 1948, General Willoughby agreed to publish the work but only on condition that a story on the Sack of Manila be appended, 'an unwitting tacit admission', a contemporary scholar has remarked, 'that the dropping of the atomic bomb on Japanese civilians was the moral equivalent of Japan's wartime atrocities'.[111]

From October 1946, PPB attitudes stiffened perceptibly. Examiners had cleared an editorial in the paper *Jiji Shinpō* warning against worshipping MacArthur as a god, but when the *Nippon Times* attempted to run an English version a few days later, an enraged Willoughby had the edition confiscated and ordered a new printing with an amended text. Thereafter, writes a former press censor, a chastised Press, Pictorial and Broadcast Division expanded its Tokyo staff, introduced more levels of decision-making and developed an obsessive concern with minor inaccuracies that further hampered its work.

Two months earlier, Willoughby had intervened forcibly in another controversial issue, criticism of the Emperor. In mid-August 1946, on the G-2 chief's orders, PPB suppressed a documentary by veteran film-maker Kamei Fumio entitled 'The Tragedy of Japan' (*Nihon no higeki*). Willoughby was acting at the behest of Prime Minister Yoshida, who had seen the film at a private screening and been shocked by its explicit treatment of Japanese war crimes and its implicit portrayal of the Emperor as a war criminal. The film's completion coincided with the 'placard' controversy and the Yoshida Cabinet's attempt to apply the charge of high treason to Imperial critics (chapter 6). Although CI&E's David Conde had actively promoted production of the film and PPB censors had approved it with certain modifications, Willoughby initiated a new round of vetting that overturned the earlier decision and led to the seizure of Kamei's prints. CCD Chief Putnam protested that the work did not exceed legitimate discussion of the Emperor and that suppression ran counter to SCAP's policy of supporting free expression, but to no avail. Kamei's producer at Nichiei, Iwasaki Akira, later recorded his bitter impressions of the 'occupied screen'. 'The American military clique', he wrote, 'is less democratic than the [wartime] Japanese were.'[112]

Willoughby's action sent an unmistakable message to the media (and to CCD). Even implied criticism of the Emperor and the Occupation's decision to preserve the Throne was off limits and could entail heavy penalties – banning of the documentary, for instance, nearly bankrupted its studio, Nichiei. As if those points needed further emphasis, in May 1947, with the new Constitution now in effect, CCD heavily censored another film by Kamei (with Yamamoto Satsuo) commissioned by Tōhō Studio to commemorate the entry into force of Article Nine. 'Between War and Peace' (*Sensō to heiwa*) was a strongly anti-militaristic film, but PPB discerned in its scenes of contemporary strikes, demonstrations and moral decadence a Communist propaganda line. Particularly objectionable was the assignment of responsibility for Japan's postwar plight to those who had manipulated the emperor system for their personal gain during the war. Willoughby's hard-knock lessons on the sanctity of the Imperial institution were not lost on PPB inspectors, who justified excising a shell-shocked soldier's demented and subversively satirical cry of 'Long Live the Emperor!' by noting that 'SCAP has recognised the Emperor system, and the scene is an attempt to belittle the system. . . .' Nonetheless, the movie survived to become one of the best films of 1947.[113]

The arts, too, were subject to the censor's whims. One of the most dramatic examples of myopic manipulation was the Press, Pictorial and Broadcast Division's attempt to outlaw Kabuki, Japan's traditional popular drama. PPB's Captain Earle Ernst and Lieutenant Hal Keith of CI&E both agreed that Kabuki, with its severed arms and heads, gruesome *harakiri* scenes and emphasis on *Bushidō*-inspired loyalty and vengeance, was feudalistic and nefarious to public morals. In mid-November 1945, after a PPB inspector had attended a performance of the Kabuki classic 'The Temple School' (*Terakoya*) featuring the famous actors Matsumoto Kōshirō (VII) and Nakamura Kichiemon (I), Japanese police strode onto the Tokyo Theatre stage after a scene in which a box containing the severed head of a child is opened and stopped the performance. PPB had already issued a banning order, and Military Police were there to help the Japanese officers enforce it. In deference to SCAP's censors, Shōchiku, the company that ran Kabuki, gratuitously offered to suspend all future plays indefinitely, confirming the dictum that old habits die hard.[114]

These events appalled Major Faubion Bowers – interpreter, military aide to MacArthur, aspiring musician and Kabuki aficionado from a prewar stay in Tokyo. Soon after his arrival at MacArthur's headquarters, Bowers befriended Kichiemon and other impecunious actors, supplying them with food scavenged from the US Embassy kitchen. He attempted personally to convince MacArthur to rescind the ban on Kabuki, but the Supreme Commander had no interest in the theatre (in later life, Bowers would characterise him as 'a cultural barbarian'). Finally, in November 1946, Bowers resigned his position and his commission and went to work with Ernst in CCD's Press, Pictorial and Broadcast Division, determined to save Kabuki from oblivion. His supreme achievement as censor was to authorise a performance of *Chūshingura* ('The Legend of the 47 Samurai') in November 1947 with an all-star cast, effectively lifting the prohibition on this vital art form. By that time, the official Occupation attitude had changed. A noted art critic summed up the new outlook ironically: 'Sure, it might be a little feudal, but at least it isn't Communist.' Other traditional arts, such as Bunraku and Noh attracted less public attention and therefore fared better under occupation. Modern drama (*shingeki*) and literature, by contrast, benefited enormously from the removal of repressive wartime restrictions and basically were left alone, although several playwrights and authors of leftist persuasion eventually were purged. Benign neglect characterised painting and sculpture, as well.[115]

From imposed censorship to self-censorship
SCAP phased out its censorship activities unceremoniously in stages. Only those with a demonstrated 'need to know' were informed of the changes. For the Japanese, censorship did not officially exist to begin with, and editors, reporters, columnists and radio heads were summoned by CCD officers and told only to continue exercising their own judgment based on past policy. The first major relaxation of controls occurred in August 1947 when broadcasting stations were transferred to post-censorship control. In mid-October, book publishers also were placed under post-publication vigilance, with the exception of 14 ultra-rightist and left-wing houses (the category 'Leftist Propaganda' had been added to the key log in mid-1947). In December, 97 per cent of all magazines were placed on the same footing (2 right-wing and 26 leftist publications remained under pre-censorship constraints, including such leading intellectual journals as *Chūō Kōron*, *Kōzō* and *Sekai*). Newspapers finally were switched to post-publication status in late July 1948. All censorship restrictions were abolished on 31 October 1949, in line with SCAP's policy of easing administrative controls and enlarging the Japanese government's freedom of action. The decision to end censorship had been taken in mid-1948 by Washington, however, not SCAP. The State Department, in particular, was concerned that the ponderous surveillance apparatus had 'the effect of continuing the authoritarian tradition in Japan', and the US National Security Council's Cold War manifesto of 8 October 1948, NSC-13/2 (chapter 10), reiterated that censorship was alienating a potential anti-Communist ally and doing more harm than good.[116]

Despite Japanese complaints, however, GHQ's programme of information management was benign compared to the government's wartime media policies, and while writers were not completely free to express their views, they were freer than they had been since 1931. Only a tiny percentage of materials published between late 1945 and late 1949 were actually suppressed, the great bulk being passed routinely. One newspaper staff writer compared working under Occupation vigilance to 'a severe brown out' – hardly satisfactory but much better than the 'complete black-out' imposed by pre-1945 Japanese surveillance. The grant of relative press free-dom, however conditional, produced a renaissance in print journalism. When the Sino-Japanese War engulfed China in 1937, there were 1,700 newspapers in Japan, but by 1942, through a process of state-imposed elimination and consolidation, that number had plummeted to 55. In September 1945, the Civil Censorship Detachment monitored 4 news agencies and 74 newspapers, but a year later, it was screening the output of 26 agencies and 7,685 papers. Before the defeat, there had been 600 magazines with a circulation of 5.9 million. By early 1947, there were more than 3,000. (In 1949, the number of periodicals would stabilise at 1,800 titles with a readership of approximately 22 million.) In October 1945, 21 books were submitted to CCD inspectors for vetting; in October 1946, that figure was 1,902. An explosion of creativity occurred in virtually all forms of media expression.[117]

Did censorship have a dampening effect on intellectual freedom? The answer, of course, is yes. Used to internal policing as a condition of survival under both wartime and postwar régimes, newspapers and magazines continued to exercise vigilance and self-control even after the lifting of formal constraints, for as the occupiers went to great lengths to explain, they could be reimposed at any time. Japanese editors got their first taste of genuine press freedom in 1952 when the Occupation ended, but by then, self-restraint had become a conditioned reflex. AP correspondent Russell Brines wrote at the time that the elimination of pre-censorship had resulted in 'a noticeable ultra-conservatism in all papers except the official Communist [press]'. Responsible editors, he noted, 'prefer to suppress a controversial story rather than risk . . . retali-ation for violating headquarters' injunctions against criticising the Occupation or publishing "inaccurate" news'.[118]

On the silver screen, too, self-censorship became the norm. In June 1949, with production controls gone, the film industry established the autonomous Film Ethics Regulation Control Committee (*Eirin*) ostensibly to maintain standards of decency. In fact, SCAP kept a close eye on *Eirin* for the duration of its tenure, and the Film Ethics Committee, which retained the CCD practice of assigning a censorship num-ber to each approved film, eschewed controversial themes such as labour strife. Equally problematic was the information barrier SCAP had erected around Japan. Outside news events were carefully filtered for domestic consumption, and Japanese could not communicate freely with the rest of the world about happenings inside their own country. Everything passed through the distorting lens of the military censor. Etō Jun has characterised occupied Japan as a 'closed linguistic space' where Japanese were separated from their own past and from important world develop-ments, producing a warped social and historical consciousness that robbed the nation of its identity. There is some truth in that assertion, but the question remains, com-pared to what? For all its obvious internal inconsistencies, flaws and abuses, American censorship was designed to eliminate the infinitely more repressive Old Order, allow-ing a new ethos to take root in its place. SCAP's brokered democracy was imperfect but nonetheless liberating compared to the police state of the 1930s. After all, it was the unstinting cooperation of Japan's reactionary wartime media with militarism that had made some kind of post-defeat censorship inevitable to begin with.[119]

After 1948, however, the ugly, repressive side of 'occupation control' emerged as the conqueror shifted ground from 'fascist cleansing to Communist chasing.' In September of that year, the CCD eased surveillance of anti-Soviet propaganda: thenceforth, the USSR would not be included in the key-log category 'strongly critical of the Allied Powers'. Even as it began to phase out media controls, Civil Censorship Detachment stepped up its surveillance of domestic telephone, telegraph and postal communications, focusing on 'violence, strikes, Communist activities or any other developments which were of a subversive or possible subversive nature'. These spot reports produced a constant flow of 'action leads', which were forwarded to concerned staff sections and agencies in SCAP. In early 1948, this massive invasion of personal privacy was yielding 4 million intercepts per month. Even after the lifting of surveillance in October 1949, GHQ continued to monitor and harass left-wing journals and papers, forcing many progressive publications to close down or adopt more conservative editorial policies. From the autumn of 1949, the Occupation wielded another potent weapon of thought control, the Red Purge, which in mid-1950 shut down the Communist Party organ *Akahata* (The Red Flag) and 1,387 left-wing publications and dismissed more than 1,000 editors, journalists, broadcasters and film-makers. (chapter 10).[120]

Nor was there anything benign about the punishments MacArthur's headquarters meted out to those it prosecuted for the crime of expressing unacceptable ideas. Not by coincidence, most of these show trials occurred in the last year of censorship. In the period from 1 June to 30 November 1948, GHQ found 148 'flagrant violations' of its censorship policies, most involving publications with left-wing or Communist sympathies. In January 1949, SCAP set up a Joint Board composed of G-2, CCD, CI&E and Legal Section to prosecute offenders in military courts. In August and September of that year, the Board had three editors (two of them Koreans) arraigned by the Eighth Army Provost Marshal. The accused received sentences ranging from two to five years at hard labour and, in the case of the Koreans, deportation.

Finally, Occupation authorities cracked down on *kamishibai* street plays. These stories, drawn or printed on illuminated paper panels, had a broad popular appeal and broached subjects, including prohibited themes, that the established media shied away from. This form of street art, resembling American guerrilla theatre of the 1960s, was ideally suited to radical grass-roots social criticism, and from 1949, with the shutting down of its censorship programme, GHQ pressured prefectural governments to enact ordinances outlawing *kamishibai* performances. The first banning order was passed in March 1949 by Kanagawa Prefecture, and Chiba, Osaka and others followed suit. The ordinances were a blatant violation of Occupation policy and the constitutional injunction against government interference with freedom of expression, but times had changed, and the local laws were allowed to stand. Film

Photo 51. Children gather to watch a portable *kamishibai* paper-lantern show, 1 September 1948. The illuminated children's stories often featured democratic themes. Many also were critical of Japan's conservative political régime and, with the onset of the 'reverse course', were suppressed on orders from GHQ (Kyodo).

critic Satō Tadao, looking back on the Occupation, characterised this later period of cultural and intellectual oppression as the stage of 'repressed democracy', as opposed to the early phase of 'encouraged democracy'.[121]

Thought reform, American-style

Censorship was only one form of information control. The Civil Information and Education Section also was involved heavily in media management, but of a different sort. As one historian has characterised it, whereas the Civil Censorship Detachment was 'telling the Japanese what they could not do', CI&E was telling them 'what they should and must do'. CI&E's mission statement charged the Section with creating 'a positive Japanese public knowledge of and belief in democracy in all walks of life – political, economic and cultural'. It was no coincidence that its first chief, Kermit Dyke, was a former NBC public relations specialist who had worked for the Office of War Information. Under him, a contemporary noted, the Section tackled 'the job of selling democracy as though it were an advertising campaign for a new soap'. The task of reorientation fell to CI&E's Information Division. Unlike CCD, which suppressed undemocratic ideas, the Division's primary function was ideological conversion, and it served as GHQ's agitation-propaganda arm.

In the first two months of occupation, Bradford Smith, former OWI officer, played a role in CI&E comparable to that of Colonel Hoover in the CCD, establishing the basic pattern of post-defeat information control. Smith had been chief of the OWI's Central Pacific Operations in Manila, joining the State Department when it absorbed the OWI in late August 1945. Picked up by Fellers's Information Dissemination Section (IDS) in AFPAC, Smith followed the IDS when it was incorporated into CI&E on 22 September as Information and Dissemination Branch (later, Information Division), serving as special adviser to Dyke. Smith brought with him a team of OWI propaganda experts that included his successor Don Brown, a former newspaperman and 'psywar' specialist and, like Smith, a State Department 'plant'. Other former OWI operatives were Captain Arthur Behrstock of Policy and Programmes Branch, former newsman Robert H. Berkov of Press and Publications Branch and David W. Conde of Motion Picture and Drama (later, Motion Picture and Theatrical) Branch. Radio Branch was staffed initially by Irving C. Correll, another OWI psywar expert and included such Voice of America veterans as Radio Programme Officer Frank S. Baba. These men were liberals, and by late 1946, most would be gone, some for arousing the suspicions of Willoughby's G-2.[122]

Information Division endeavours were keyed to the State Department's worldwide information and propaganda network. In early 1946, an inter-departmental agreement was reached whereby the Department would send its media directives to the War Department, which would forward them to MacArthur for transmission to CI&E. Coordinating this flow of information was Behrstock's Policy and Programmes Branch. To facilitate this mission, the War Department's Civil Affairs Division created a Reorientation Branch (later, Division), which in turn established a New York Field Office to supply CI&E with carefully selected books, magazines, newspaper editorials, model radio scripts, feature films, documentaries, plays and musical recordings.[123]

Information Division regulated these cultural imports, licensing only those it considered suitable for reorientation work. Japanese editors were advised to use these materials, and the Division swamped their desks with articles from over 100 middle-range US magazines, including *Life*, *Newsweek*, *Time* and *Reader's Digest*. Material from Allied countries and editorial commentary from UN and SCAP sources also were supplied to the Japanese media for priority release. The Division circulated from 350 to 400 such items every month. The regular appearance of so many foreign articles and news items in the mainstream media of a single country was an unprecedented event. At the grass-roots level, Information Division, in cooperation with Education Division, established CI&E Information Centres in cities and major universities across the country, stocking them with between 5,000 and 10,000 volumes and some 400 periodicals. The centres were staffed by friendly American librarians, who also collected films and phonograph records and organised lectures and concerts in an effort to diffuse American culture and values. An estimated 2 million Japanese frequented these libraries.[124]

At the same time, the Division strictly controlled the translation into Japanese of books and feature films. Prohibited works included John Steinbeck's *Grapes of Wrath*, Erskine Caldwell's *Tobacco Road*, Edgar Snow's *Red Star Over China*, and John Hershey's *Hiroshima*, which could not be read in Japanese translation until 1949. Films such as *Citizen Kane* and *Mr Smith Goes to Washington* also were suppressed on the grounds that they might lend themselves to Communist propaganda. This focus of activity sometimes brought CI&E into conflict with the Army's Civil Censorship Detachment, which claimed exclusive jurisdiction. CI&E 'suggestions' were in fact orders and were obeyed to the letter, infringing on CCD authority. CCD retaliated by blue-pencilling, snipping or suppressing materials that CI&E had taken a direct hand in shaping, such as Kamei Fumio's epic 'The Tragedy of Japan'. In late 1946, CCD vetoed a foreign policy speech by Secretary of Commerce Henry A. Wallace that CI&E had released to the media on instructions from the State Department. Ultimately, MacArthur's intervention was required to clear the talk.[125]

Reorientation at work

A major focus of reorientation work was the inculcation of war guilt. Beginning in December 1945, CI&E's Press and Publications Branch ordered newspapers to carry a serialised history of the war, prepared by CI&E researchers and their Japanese advisers, that emphasised the social, economic and political causes of Japanese aggression but also discussed atrocities, such as the Rape of Nanjing and the Sack of Manila. Magazines, documentary films, newsreels and books dealing with these subjects also were produced in large quantities on orders from Information Division. The war guilt programme stood in contrast to the positive work of selling American-style democracy and probably alienated as many Japanese as it convinced. Later in the Occupation, this aggressively propagandistic approach would find a fresh outlet in straightforward anti-Communist indoctrination.[126]

In addition to the activities outlined above, Press and Publications was intimately involved in monitoring the Japanese press. Branch Chief Berkov was a former journalist and took a firm stand in favour of press freedom, supporting workers and editors of the *Yomiuri* and other dailies in their struggle to purge management of ultra-nationalist elements and democratise production. Berkov was replaced in June 1946 by the conservative Major Daniel C. Imboden, who worked behind the scenes to break the *Yomiuri* strike and reinstate its discredited management. Imboden expanded the scope of censorship and tightened surveillance of the print media, exhorting editors and columnists to stress American views on Communism and American methods for combating it. He inundated news rooms with anti-Communist materials and articles extolling the superiority of the American way of life. Under his sway, management was able to reassert control over editorial content, and while press reform proceeded, it did so within the narrowly circumscribed limits defined by the owners.

In the field of visual media, David Conde's Motion Picture and Drama Branch rapidly dissolved the impediments to freedom of the screen. On 16 October, SCAPIN-146 ('Memorandum Concerning Elimination of Japanese Government Control of the Motion Picture Industry') removed wartime supervision and annulled the repressive 1939 Film Law, and on 16 November, Conde issued a directive banning 236 ultra-nationalistic, militaristic and feudalistic films made after 1931 and confiscated the prints. All but one each of the prints were burned, and the surviving copies were not returned to the Education Ministry until August 1952. Finally, in early December, the Film Corporation, the wartime industry control body, was dismantled.[126]

The hyperactive Conde wielded the censor's scissors with great energy and flair based on a CI&E list of prohibited subjects, but he was particularly zealous in the area of democratisation and reorientation, proposing film projects, outlining plots, suggesting changes, demanding innovations. And banging the table with his fists when his Japanese interlocutors objected or failed to grasp a point quickly enough. In October, Conde visited movie studios with a list of recommended themes that included the Sino-Japanese War (especially the struggle between militarists and anti-war activists) and women, who were to be portrayed in roles other than of child-bearing and housework. Controversial subjects, such as war orphans, however, were to be treated carefully, highlighting only 'good examples', and Japanese-American characters were off limits. Motion Picture and Theatre Branch also encouraged films on the Constitution and, somewhat incongruously, baseball.[127]

Under Conde's supervision, Japanese directors produced features condemning the *zaibatsu*, criticising the Emperor and promoting the rights of labour. Imai Tadashi's first postwar film, 'The People's Enemy' (*Minshū no teki*), was an exposé of the *zaibatsu* produced by Tōhō Studio on direct orders from Conde. Other works, some of them 'crudely propagandistic', dealt with wartime corruption but also included satirical pieces on the militarists. A major hit was Kurosawa Akira's 'No Regrets for My Youth' (*Waga seishun ni kui nashi*), a Tōhō film that dealt with the persecution of Takigawa Yukitoki, a Kyoto Imperial University law professor purged for his liberal beliefs in 1933. In the film, one of Takigawa's students was modelled on Ozaki Hotsumi, the brilliant intellectual and accomplice of German spy Richard Sorge who was executed in 1944. Mizoguchi Kenji also produced socially significant films, notably a moralising trilogy on women's liberation and 'Women of the Night' (*Yoru no onna-tachi*), a sensitive portrayal of a prostitute's life. Despite their some-times heavy symbolism, such films created new images of a self-aware, self-confident womanhood that resonated with the promise, if not the reality, of Japan's emerging democratic spirit.[128]

One of Conde's more controversial innovations was the 'kissing film' (*seppun eiga*). Kissing had been banned by the militarist régime as a decadent Western practice, and like public displays of affection in general, such intimate embraces offended the traditional Japanese sense of decorum. Conde, however, preached that kissing was liberating and democratic and literally ordered passionate Hollywood-style scenes included in feature films. Consequently, in late May 1946, two simul-taneous releases, Shōchiku Studio's 'Twenty-Year-Old Youth' (*Hatachi no seishun*) by Sasaki Yasushi and Daiei Studio's 'A Certain Night's Kiss' (*Aru yo no seppun*) by Chiba Yasuki, became the first movies to include necking on screen. Audiences appreciated such themes, which encouraged an atmosphere of sexual emancipation, but the kissing films also spawned a quasi-pornographic genre dubbed 'grotesque eroticism' (*ero-guro*), whose nude scenes and titillating dialogues kept the CI&E film-clippers busy.[129]

Information Division's Radio Branch played an even greater role in ideological redirection, for during the Occupation, radio was the pre-eminent means of mass information. The Branch worked closely with SCAP's Civil Communications Sec-tion in liberalising NHK, which was reorganised in October 1947 as a public corporation free of government control, along the lines of the British Broadcasting Corporation. In April 1946, the distinguished scholar and Socialist, Takano Iwasa-burō of the University of Tokyo, was named to head the organisation, which he purged of its conservative wartime staff. His general manager was Furukaki Tetsurō (NHK president from 1949), a former member of the League of Nations Secretariat and London correspondent for the *Asahi Shinbun*. Under Frank Baba, Radio Programme Officer, standards were set for announcers and efforts made to simplify broadcasting language, the norm adopted being a level of discourse comprehensible to a 14-year old. Branch Chief Dwight Herrick and Baba also encouraged com-mercial broadcasting, but SCAP custodianship preserved NHK's monopoly of the air waves for most of the Occupation, and rival private stations did not begin broadcasting until 1951. Baba drafted the Japanese Code of Broadcasting Ethics for commercial broadcasters, the equivalent of the *Eirin* Film Ethics Code.[130]

Radio Branch, too, pursued both negative and positive re-education policies. An early war-guilt programme was 'Now It Can Be Told' and its spin-off, 'Now It Can

Be Told Truth Box', which adapted the CI&E war history to the air waves in weekly instalments. Although the series shocked many Japanese, its blunt, 'in-your-face' style offended many more, and Baba recalls that NHK was inundated with complaints, its Japanese staff even receiving bomb and assassination threats. In October and November 1945, 'The Patriots' Hour', cast in the same mould, went on the air. Designed to allow the Japanese to relate their own wartime experiences, it began by featuring recently released political prisoners, included several Communists. G-2 quickly ended the experiment in December, and the programme's originators – Dyke, Bradford Smith and Conde – were branded as left liberals.

Predictably, affirmative propaganda met with a far more enthusiastic response. The American quiz show format proved especially popular with audiences, and in November 1947, Radio Branch's Ralph Hunter teamed up with veteran NHK announcer Fujikura Shūichi to produce 'Twenty Gates' (*Nijū no tobira*). The programme was Fujikura's idea and involved interviewing the 'man and woman in the street'. Fujikura later recalled, 'The war had ended, but Japanese retained their prewar mentality of deferring to superiors. No one thought of asking the ordinary person what he or she was thinking. Ralph Hunter was the first to hand people a mike and let them speak for themselves.' Programmes tailored to women and working people also were aired for the first time. 'The Women's Hour', produced by Egami Fuji and begun in October 1945, featured talks by feminists Katō Shizue, Ichikawa Fusae and Miyamoto Yuriko on women's issues, the Constitution, the new Civil Code and the importance of voting. Information programmes such as as 'Labour Hour', 'The Farmers' Hour', 'The Miners' Hour', 'The Teachers' Hour' and 'Children's Hour' opened broadcasting to the concerns of average Japanese. Fora, round-table discussions and current affairs quiz programmes, such as 'Fountain of Knowledge', also attracted large listening audiences. Nor was popular entertainment neglected, as comic monologues (*rakugo*), comedian duos (*manzai*) and ballads (*naniwa-bushi*) staged a dramatic comeback. American-style soap operas also made their debut, winning high ratings. SCAP's turn to the right after 1948 was reflected in a proliferation of anti-Communist themes, loyalty checks for NHK staff and, eventually, the Red Purge, but in the domain of radio broadcasting, CI&E policies generally succeeded in nurturing a deeper understanding of democratic thought and ideals.[131]

MEDIA AND DEMOCRATISATION

Historically, occupiers have imposed their language on the occupied in order to facilitate civil and military administration. This was the policy adopted by Imperial Japan in the areas it held during the Asia–Pacific War.[132] GHQ also might have insisted that English become the official language of occupation in Japan, as the US Army did in southern Korea from 1945 to 1948, but, apart from requiring that street names and public signs be rendered in English, it did not adopt a 'positive' language policy. In the absence of language constraints, the Japanese themselves set about learning English with unbridled enthusiasm. During the war, censors had banned the public use of English loan words, and while English had been taught in some schools in order to better know the enemy, its study outside of the classroom was an act of disloyalty. Immediately following the surrender, however, instruction in the adversary's tongue was revived in 'every town and village', according to newspaper accounts. On 23 September 1945, the *Tokyo Shinbun* reported that all the railway employees at Tokyo Station were attending morning drills in English conversation. An enterprising editor, Ogawa Kikumatsu, hastily compiled a list of words and phrases and put together a 33-page pamphlet entitled *A Handbook of Japanese-American Conversation* (*Nichi-Bei kaiwa techō*), which had sold 3.6 million copies by the end of 1945. Ogawa had little English himself, but his booklet remained Japan's all-time best seller until 1981 (ironically, its format was based in part on a prewar Japanese-Chinese language manual).[133] Allied missionaries followed in the footsteps of Allied troops, and Japanese flocked to their churches, not to contemplate the sermons but to develop their English skills. Middle-echelon bureaucrats in their 30s and 40s also struggled to acquire some mastery over the new tongue, which they polished in their daily contacts with GHQ officials. Although both sides relied heavily on interpreters, many of these functionaries became adept at English and at dealing with Americans. Several would be responsible for managing Japan–US relations through the post-Occupation decades.

'Come, come everybody'
On 1 February 1946, Hirakawa Tada'ichi launched what was destined to become one of the major cultural phenomena of the early postwar era. On that day, he inaugurated a new daily radio programme at NHK called 'Come, Come English', which began with the following invitation to listeners:

> Come, come everybody –
> How do you do, and how are you?
> Won't you have some candy?
> One and two and three, four, five.
> Let's all sing a happy song –
> singing tra la la.

The programme closed with the farewell:

> Goodbye, everybody,
> Goodnight until tomorrow.
> Monday, Tuesday, Wednesday, Thursday,
> Friday, Saturday, Sunday,
> Let's all come and meet again.
> Singing tra la la.

Photo 52. Hirakawa Tada'ichi broadcasts an English-language programme at NHK. 'Come, Come Everybody' enjoyed a phenomenal success during the early part of the Occupation, offering entertainment and practical lessons in democratic thought. 1 February 1946 (Mainichi).

These light-hearted words were set to a popular children's tune, 'The Badger Drummers of Shōjō Temple' (*Shōjōji no tanuki-bayashi*), whose familiar, upbeat melody inspired a sense of optimism. And this was Hirakawa's intention. 'I was hard pressed to find something that would lighten people's hearts and take their minds off the postwar gloom', he said in an interview. 'Unless Japanese could recover their sense of optimism and find something positive in their lives, a reason to believe in the future, there seemed little hope of trying to rebuild the nation.'[134] The 'Apple Song', the wildly popular theme tune from a film released in October 1945, had captured the nation's fancy with its naive lyrics, cheerful airiness and bright imagery, but Hirakawa felt the 'Apple' craze was sentimental and decadent and chose a well-known children's song instead of a pop melody. Written in 1925, the 'The Badger Drummers of Shōjō Temple' had been inspired by a folk tale and evoked the sunny promise of Taishō democracy and the insouciance of a prewar childhood.[135]

'Come, Come English' was aired for 15 minutes every day, Monday through Friday, between 6 and 6:15 pm. It took four days to complete one story sequence, and on the fifth day, Friday, Hirakawa invited a native English speaker to take part. Each segment introduced about 30 new words. Hirakawa urged people to relax, enjoy the experience and adjust naturally to the sounds and cadences of spoken English.[136] Hirakawa chose his themes carefully, sometimes staying up all night before a broadcast to find a humorous angle that all Japanese could identify with. In one skit, for instance, a young man visits a friend in the hospital and brings him a ripe tomato that he has grown himself. Through the dialogue, it emerges that they first met at the nursery where the young man bought the seedling. His friend was wearing a 'Come, Come English' badge and they struck up an acquaintance. Even amidst the hardships of daily life, Hirakawa was saying, one can find meaningful experiences. Such themes may appear frivolous to the contemporary sensibility, but the storyline, a visit to the hospital leavened by a budding friendship based on a mutual interest and conveyed through the medium of English, was novel, refreshing and a refutation of the martial values of wartime Japan that had stifled personal expression.

Finding enough to eat was a daily obsession for most Japanese, and this preoccupation reverberated through the programme's dialogues. Hirakawa began his broadcasting career in February 1946 just after the first emergency shipment of US wheat from Manila had reached Japan. In a show aired in April, a father and his daughter Mariko are discussing their day. Father asks where Mother is, and Mariko replies that she has gone to fetch the daily food ration. 'What is it? Dried herrings again?' Father asks. When Mariko says, 'No, it's white bread, I think', Father is astounded. Mariko explains; 'Yes. It's made of the flour that came from General Headquarters.' Father wonders where the flour came from, and Mariko tells him, 'From the Philippines, I think.' 'How do you know?' he queries. Mariko answers, 'I've read it in the paper.' Whereupon Father comments, 'Well, the paper does tell the truth nowadays, doesn't it?' This artless dialogue, broadcast just seven months after the defeat, was fraught with meaning for ordinary Japanese. Rigid censorship controls had been a fact of life during the war, and few believed much of what they read in the newspapers. A simple English conversation reminded people how dramatically life had changed. Hirakawa's genius lay in his ability to encourage the democratic impulse and convey a sense of internationalism through elementary English conversations based on real-life situations.

Democratisation from below

A liberal and a Christian, Hirakawa was able to present the best face of American democracy to the Japanese. His avuncular bearing, gentle nature and warm smile won him admirers of all ages. The programme enjoyed consistently high ratings, but among teenagers and children, it was NHK's top-rated broadcast. In 1947, 'Come, Come English' boasted an estimated audience of 5.7 million families, and a newspaper popularity poll ranked its host higher than all public figures except MacArthur and the Emperor. That year, the show's textbooks sold more than 500,000 copies, and Hirakawa was inundated by fan letters. In 1948 alone, he received more than 30,000 missives, some accompanied by gifts of fruit, medicine, clothing and wine, and many written in English. Half a million avid listeners would write him during the Occupation. *Time* and the *New York Times Magazine* ran feature stories on the 'Come, Come' phenomenon.[137]

Hirakawa's radio programme appealed to all ages, but children in particular were drawn to its humorous and instructive depictions of everyday life. Hirakawa referred to these young fans as 'Come, Come babies'. Within a short time, 'Come, Come' clubs had sprung up across the country composed of men and women from all stations of life and of all political persuasions. By 1947, more than 1,000 of these organisations were in existence, with a total membership of over 1 million. Branches were set up in offices, schools and neighbourhoods. They attracted office workers, housewives, young mothers and their children, and even pre-schoolers (dubbed 'acorn clubs'), but a large number were created by enthusiastic school children. At least one club, the Suginami branch in Tokyo, still exists today. A monthly magazine, *The Come, Come Club*, edited by Hirakawa and distributed by Metro Publishing House, carried news items from the various branches, including accounts of local activities and membership lists, and provided readers with a forum where they could exchange views in English on a wide range of topics. It also featured substantive articles covering subjects such as American and British comic books, drama, etiquette, films, literature and sports. Many prominent public figures of today got their start in the 'Come, Come' clubs, among them popular singer Peggy Hayama and Kunihiro Masao, former Diet member and international journalist. Ishihara Shintarō, novelist, conservative ideologue and Governor of Tokyo, also recalls with nostalgia Hirakawa's 'entertaining and unique' English lessons in an age when 'people struggled mightily to master what until recently had been considered a taboo – the language of our foe.'[138]

'Come, Come babies' gained more than a rudimentary knowledge of English. One former club member wrote that language study gave him a sense of personal empowerment. By imbibing the essence of the democratic spirit, he was contributing to Japan's recovery. Participation in club activities helped him overcome a sense of inferiority towards Westerners, made him more outgoing and brought lifelong friendships. In an age of privation, psychological exhaustion and moral confusion, these were positive values, indeed. 'Come, Come English' was a cultural movement that emerged spontaneously from the grass roots, transforming the social and political consciousness of young people, including this author, a junior high school student in rural Nagano Prefecture at the time.[139] For us, Hirakawa's broadcasts were our first genuine encounter with American democracy, and they enabled us to embrace the new creed in a way that was intimate, immediate and compelling. In short, we made these values our own and through self-directed cultural activities spread this ethos among a new generation. The transition from wartime controls to postwar freedom was one of ebullient revolutionary change, and it is difficult for younger Japanese today to understand how thoroughly liberated we felt. The Occupation reforms were introduced from the outside and from above, creating a broad framework for change, but as young people, our direct experience of transformation came from programmes like Hirakawa's, which tapped a deep idealistic vein that would have been difficult to reach through other means.

'Come, Come English' remained with NHK for five years, until 1951, after which Hirakawa switched to a commercial station, finally retiring the show in 1955. With the advent of the Cold War and GHQ's shift in priorities, Hirakawa's ratings began to decline. Economic stabilisation policies, the Red Purge and the Occupation's manipulation of the media tarnished the programme's image and menaced the bright future its early broadcasts had promised the country. Later, critics would see in English a tool of cultural imperialism, not an ally of democracy, and there may be more than a little truth to that assertion. Nevertheless, for Japanese now in their late 50s and 60s, Hirakawa remains indissolubly associated with the early reform phase of the Occupation, when English briefly was an instrument not of ideological domination but of personal discovery and social liberation.

CHAPTER 9

The Welfare Reforms and Minorities

One of GHQ's least-known but most successful ventures in social engineering was the revamping of Japan's public health and welfare system, an effort that produced immediate and dramatic results. Here, Japanese-American cooperation reached its zenith, resulting in brilliant advances that rivalled and in some cases even surpassed developments in the United States. Here, too, however, collaboration hit its nadir. The Occupation's use of Japanese scientists involved in wartime medical experiments on human beings, its unstinting support for the Atomic Bomb Casualty Commission and its tacit approval of eugenics legislation afford a glimpse at the dark underside of both societies. Minority rights was another area where bilateral cooperation produced bitter fruit, as MacArthur's staff, preoccupied with changing political priorities, turned a blind eye to social discrimination, deviating both from the Potsdam principles and from the US Army's 'Basic Directive'.

THE DDT REVOLUTION

GHQ's innovations in public health and welfare were among the most remarkable of the postwar reforms. Being fundamentally apolitical in nature, they encountered the least resistance from the Japanese bureaucracy and therefore achieved one of the highest rates of implementation, but they remain the least understood of SCAP's democratisation projects. Article 25 of the 1947 Constitution guaranteed all Japanese the right to minimum standards of wholesome living and required the state to 'use its endeavours for the promotion and extension of social welfare and security, and of public health'. GHQ's Public Health and Welfare Section (PH&W) under Crawford F. Sams was responsible for designing the legislation that would make these guarantees a reality.

PH&W concentrated its efforts in four major areas: preventive medicine, medical and health care, social welfare and social security. In this ambitious undertaking, the Section went well beyond what US pre-surrender planners had imagined. At the same time, it relied heavily on Japan's public health establishment. Sams' staff introduced important innovations, but more often they systematised and improved upon existing welfare institutions, sometimes retaining, sometimes eliminating past practices in a complex and dynamic process that involved close Japanese cooperation and ultimately preserved some of the best features – and in a few instances the worst – of both societies.

In September 1945, three problems of particular urgency confronted MacArthur's headquarters: providing disaster relief to millions of hungry and destitute war sufferers, preventing the spread of communicable diseases, which constituted a palpable threat to the security of Occupation forces, and demilitarising and democratising the health-care field. PH&W's massive DDT dusting programme, introduced in the autumn of 1945 to protect Allied personnel from infectious illnesses, came to epitomise this health and welfare revolution.

Emergency relief

Consonant with the punitive nature of the early reforms, Washington initially adopted a hands-off policy towards emergency assistance. The Joint Chiefs had specifically instructed MacArthur that 'the administration of relief . . . is not the function of the Supreme Commander and no gratuitous distribution of supplies as direct relief should be made' (JCS-1534, 25 October 1945).[1] This injunction reflected the pre-surrender US position that Japan alone was to blame for its plight and that the Allies had no obligation to alleviate suffering that was self-inflicted. Nonetheless, MacArthur promptly removed from military control all Imperial Army and Navy stores and equipment not essential for war and turned them over to the Home Ministry for civilian relief. An estimated 70 per cent of these stocks had been looted shamelessly immediately after the defeat by gangsters and corrupt officials (chapter 2), but the Ministry readied remaining supplies of food, clothing and medicines for distribution to the needy.[2]

The situation in Japan was desperate, indeed. Some 14.5 million people, or one out of five, were indigent with no means of steady employment, and 10 million of these were on the verge of starvation. Moreover, returning soldiers aggravated crowded conditions in urban areas already inundated with orphans and the war-displaced. Civilian repatriates from Japan's overseas empire were allowed to bring with them only what they could carry plus the equivalent of ¥1,000 in currency. Few had any means of sustaining themselves in Japan. Moreover, transportation was disrupted and families were scattered and unable to perform their habitual role of assisting close relatives in time of need. Traditional poor-relief institutions, run almost exclusively by non-governmental agencies, had virtually collapsed. In October 1945, US military officials warned of the possible total breakdown of Japan's supply and distribution system by the latter half of 1946, estimating that the Occupation mission itself would be endangered should 10 per cent of the population require emergency supplies in a given month. Doubtless it was this fear rather than purely humanitarian concerns that prompted MacArthur to disregard official policy and assign the organisation of relief activities top priority.[3]

The Welfare Ministry, socially and morally obliged to care for the war-distressed, quickly organised its own emergency relief activities, but these were piecemeal and ineffectual. On 8 December, SCAP's G-4 Section issued SCAPIN-404 ('Relief and Welfare Plans') instructing the government to develop a comprehensive scheme for providing food, clothing, housing, medical care, shelter and financial aid to the indigent from January through June 1946. The order also specified that such assistance be rendered without discrimination. On 31 December, Tokyo submitted a detailed proposal naming the Welfare Ministry as the central relief agency, established criteria of eligibility and designated traditional district welfare volunteers (*hōmen-i'in*) as primary aid distributors. The Ministry estimated that more than 800,000 households and some 3.4 million people were in urgent need of succour. GHQ approved the Ministry plan, which became the point of departure for Japan's postwar welfare system.

On 27 February 1946, PH&W issued a supplementary directive, SCAPIN-775 ('Public Assistance'), outlining desired legislative measures. The February instruction also introduced three new principles of public assistance: 1 operational responsibility of the state, which was prohibited from delegating authority to private or quasi-official agencies as in the past; 2 no discrimination or preferential treatment; and 3 no limitations on the amount of aid furnished. The non-discrimination clause was intended partly to eliminate special government support for war veterans and their families. The SCAPIN-775 principles had no roots in pre-surrender Japanese thinking. Nor, indeed, were they well-established even in the United States. The Public Health and Welfare Section based this directive largely on the 1945 platform of the progressive American Public Welfare Association, to which most of Sams' Welfare Division belonged. These officers were determined to avoid the shortcomings of US welfare policy and provide Japan with a system of public assistance second to none. Their idealism was shared by few policy-makers in Washington, however, and the notion that the state should guarantee all of its citizens a livelihood and decent standard of living was radical for the time.[4]

On the basis of SCAPINs 404 and 775, the Welfare Ministry drafted the Livelihood Protection Bill and presented it to the Diet in late July 1946. Under the supervision of Kasai Yoshisuke of the Welfare Ministry's Social Affairs Bureau,[5] the bill was prepared 'in an atmosphere of professional partnership and cooperation', as one Japanese expert has described it. Mutual misunderstandings about basic terminology abounded, however, complicating the legislative process and producing different interpretations of its significance. The English version ostensibly established the principle of state responsibility for public welfare, but the concept of public assistance as a state obligation and individual right was alien to the Japanese experience. Meiji officials had enacted the Relief Ordinance in 1874, replacing it with the Relief Law in 1929 following the onset of the Great Depression, but welfare activities were grounded in paternalistic concepts of mercy strongly associated with Imperial benevolence and implying state surveillance. The act of receiving charity was stigmatising, and the criteria for assistance were not need per se but social status, an assessment of the recipient's character and the reasons for seeking help. Consequently, Kasai's staff substituted the Japanese phrase 'livelihood protection' (*seikatsu hogo*) for the English 'livelihood security', enabling them to maintain the traditional gloss. The legislation was enacted on 9 September 1946 as the Daily Life Protection Law, with all the paternalistic overtones of the old system.[6]

Moreover, the new law was administered locally by volunteer district commissioners (*hōmen-i'in*), who actually determined, often arbitrarily, the size of livelihood doles. The district commissioner system had been established in the wake of the 1918 rice riots as a means of tightening social control at the local level, and 'social work' gradually replaced charity as the dominant form of relief. The law's implementing machinery continued this tradition. The commissioners were subsequently reorganised under separate legislation (29 July 1948) as social welfare commissioners (*minsei-i'in*, literally, 'people's life representatives') to assist local officials in administering the assistance programme. A total of 150,000 volunteers were made commissioners, and by 1949, they had given emergency aid and employment guidance to more than 3 million paupers and extended livelihood loans to 1.6 million repatriates. Nonetheless, the new commissioners retained the old aura of authority.[7]

Kasai also attempted to exclude from the purview of the law the able-bodied, those of loose morals and others who refused to work for a living. When PH&W objected, the Ministry's Social Affairs Bureau dropped the Japanese term for indolence (*taida*) from the draft legislation, but after the statute had passed, it issued a guideline that disqualified applicants for lazy or improper behaviour or for having relatives able to provide assistance. Finally, offended by the notion of unrestricted aid, Kasai managed to impose a ceiling on spending, with the national government bearing 80 per cent of relief costs and the prefectural and municipal governments each shouldering a 10 per cent share. Despite initial resistance, however, the programme was successful, and in 1950, at the suggestion of a US advisory mission, the Daily Life Protection Law was revised and strengthened. Community welfare commissioners were replaced by trained welfare experts subordinate to municipal authorities, disqualification criteria were eased and an explicit guarantee to an adequate livelihood (income security and welfare services) was added.[8]

Occupation health authorities could have established refugee camps for the displaced, unemployed millions as in Okinawa (chapter 3). To preclude that necessity, on 8 January 1946, PH&W issued SCAPIN-563 ('Control of Population Movements') ordering the government to outlaw travel from rural areas to cities of more than 100,000 unless individuals could show proof of a job and place to live. Exceptions were made for government officials, students and teachers, and those engaged in rehabilitation work. Rural inhabitants were not issued ration cards, essential for survival in the city, and could not purchase train tickets, making enforcement a relatively easy matter. GHQ renewed the prohibition on internal migration in June 1946, and the Cabinet extended it through 1947. On 22 December 1947, the Diet enacted a law formalising the travel ban through 31 December 1948. Japanese did not completely regain their freedom of movement until 1 January 1949, by which time the cities had been largely rebuilt and jobs were once more available.[9]

An even more serious problem was the looming spectre of mass starvation. The autumn harvest of 1945 had been the worst in decades, and the Japanese government and Sams prevailed on MacArthur to release an initial 100,000 tons of wheat from supplies that the US Army had stockpiled in the Philippines. The first emergency shipment reached Tokyo in late January 1946, and GHQ eventually distributed 400,000 tons. Japanese authorities, too, released 30,000 tons of canned meat, fish and biscuits (blankets and winter clothing were not handed out until late February 1946 due to distribution difficulties). The bulk of Army-donated food arrived in June and July but proved inadequate. By the summer of 1946, military stocks were nearing depletion and food shortages had become critical. MacArthur's headquarters desperately lobbied Washington for assistance, and in September, the Army's Government and Relief in Occupied Areas (GARIOA) programme began food deliveries, taking up the slack and narrowly averting famine. In December, under PH&W supervision, the Japanese government organised a school lunch programme designed to improve child nutrition. By 1949, some 7 million had benefited from the protein-rich meals of powdered skim milk and fish soup.[10] In the late summer of 1946, international relief agencies also began to assist in feeding and clothing the needy.[11]

Disease control and preventive medicine

Preventive medicine enjoyed a long tradition in Japan. The Meiji-era Infectious Diseases Law (1897) had created sanitation societies (*eisei-kumiai*) under police control to monitor outbreaks of contagious illness and, later, to run immunisation programmes. Japanese health authorities achieved considerable success in curbing typhoid fever and smallpox and fighting dysentery and diphtheria. Even at the height of the Asia–Pacific conflict, they managed to prevent cholera epidemics, eliminate scarlet fever and contain typhus. By August 1945, however, the nation's health-care infrastructure was a shambles, and sanitation control had virtually collapsed. Before the war, only six cities boasted sewage treatment plants, and most of these, together with municipal water supply facilities, had been heavily damaged or destroyed by wartime bombing. Three quarters of the population depended on shallow wells, springs or surface streams for their water, whose quality was under constant assault in rural areas from 'night soil', raw human waste used as fertiliser. In the cities, millions of repatriates from overseas exacerbated cramped, insalubrious conditions, providing an ideal breeding ground for life-threatening illnesses. Into this medical tinder box stepped returnees from Southeast Asia infected with cholera, smallpox and typhus. In the first three years of occupation, more than 650,000 people contracted a communicable disease and nearly 100,000 died.[12]

In 1945, dysentery, enteric disorders and other so-called filth diseases were surpassed in virulence only by tuberculosis. Japan had never attempted to eradicate systematically flies, mosquitoes, fleas, mites, lice or rodents, and these pests had multiplied beyond control. (The presence of rats around one's home traditionally was considered a sign of affluence.) Parasite infestation was widespread. Vaccine production had come to a standstill during the war, amplifying the threat of such 'wildfire' maladies as cholera, smallpox, typhoid and typhus. Mosquito-borne viruses caused intermittent outbreaks of malaria and Japanese B encephalitis. Meningitis, polio and scarlet fever also claimed many victims. Finally, chronic malnutrition left the population prey to diphtheria, pneumonia and tuberculosis. The last, the archetypal poor person's disease, was the number one killer in Japan, accounting for 12 to 15 per cent of all deaths since the mid-1930s.

The paramount duty of Public Health and Welfare Section was to safeguard the health and security of Allied forces, and epidemics posed an imminent threat to the Occupation mission. Not only did such calamities endanger the well-being of military personnel, but they were capable of inciting civil disorder among the Japanese public. DDT was the weapon of choice in the war against infectious diseases, and it was first deployed to protect Allied troops. One of the initial tasks of US military health teams was to disinfect thoroughly the areas into which Navy and Army units were scheduled to move. On 28 August 1945, the US Third Fleet ordered the Imperial Navy to place designated Allied disembarkment points off limits to local residents and informed it that 24 hours prior to the landings, US aircraft would spray those sites with insecticide. In early September, airplanes flying low dusted Tachikawa and other military installations with DDT. Aerial dispersal would continue into 1946, and between June and August of that year, C-46 transports dumped 200 tons of DDT on densely populated urban areas and Allied military bases across Japan. (Such was the American dread of contamination that, in early 1946, when MacArthur's military aide Major Faubion Bowers arranged a special Kabuki viewing for US military personnel in Tokyo, Occupation authorities disinfected the theatre with DDT three times before the performance.)[13]

Prior to Japan's surrender, Sams had stored large quantities of this powerful chemical in the Philippines, along with dusting equipment and typhus vaccine, but the first substantial consignments of DDT did not reach Japan until November. In early October, PH&W ordered the Japanese government to begin producing its own insecticide and, following the arrival of stocks from Manila, launched a programme of systematic dusting. By May 1946, Japan was producing enough DDT to meet most of the country's needs. In the meantime, public health officers in Military Government units had reorganised Japanese sanitary teams, and by 1948, there was one six-man unit for every 15,000 inhabitants. Formed around the prewar sanitary societies, the teams were responsible now to local health authorities, not the police. Under municipal supervision, quarantine stations were set up at 14 major ports of entry to delouse repatriating soldiers and civilians. Children were assembled in school yards and hosed down. Dusting stations were set up in large cities, where teams sprayed train stations, subways, streetcars, dormitories, theatres, public bath houses, roadside ditches and open sewers, and entered private homes to disinfect drains and lavatories. By 1949, about 50 million people, or roughly two-thirds of the population, had been doused with DDT.[14]

The American obsession with sanitised environments conveyed to the Japanese the message that they were dirty and disease-ridden. To a people traditionally priding themselves on physical cleanliness and propriety, this was one more insult compounding the injury of defeat. Children particularly resented the affront to their dignity as nozzles were thrust into collars and sleeves and DDT was pumped into their clothes and hair, turning them as white as the proverbial miller's apprentice.

Photo 53. A Japanese sanitation team dust with DDT while Military Government health officials observe from the sidelines. The DDT programme prevented a major outbreak of infectious illness, but the carcinogen's long-term effects on humans were never assessed. 5 March 1946 (Kyodo).

Teachers did their best to explain to children why spraying was necessary. In Tottori Prefecture, a village instructor composed a ditty, 'The DDT Song', which went: 'Tai, tai typhus, typhus all around! We hate it worse than the Devil himself! Everyone out now, let's go get dusted! DDT! DDT!' The pupils would sing the tune before going to the playground to be deloused. The lyrics drove home the point that typhus, which was carried by body lice, was even more unpleasant than the insidious white powder, which really was a friend in disguise.[15] Roving sanitation teams armed with pumps and dispensing billowy clouds of insecticide became a metaphor for the modernisation of pubic health practices in Japan. Sadly, as we know today, the chemical also is a powerful carcinogen, and although the resulting short-term benefits to public health were dramatic, its long-term effects on the human organism and the environment have not been assessed.

Where epidemics broke out, Military Government Teams intervened decisively. In December 1945, for example, typhus fever erupted in the Osaka region. The Osaka MG Team promptly banned travel into and out of Osaka, Sakai and Fuse (East Osaka) cities, began a delousing and inoculation programme and sent sanitary teams to dust public places, including court houses and detention centres, with DDT. More than 7,000 people were infected, of whom 615 died, but the epidemic was contained, and by May 1946, typhus had virtually disappeared.

Cholera was an equally potent threat. In April 1946, repatriation ships from China carrying cholera-stricken passengers docked in Kagoshima, Kyushu, creating a major scare in PH&W. Sams had the 'cholera ships' and those that came after diverted to special 'cholera ports', where more than 230,000 returnees eventually were quarantined. In all, over 700 cases of cholera, 250 of typhus and more than 100 of smallpox were isolated and treated. In response to the cholera menace, repatriation from Japan to Korea was temporarily suspended in June 1946. Due to PH&W's quick action, only 1,229 cases of the ailment surfaced in Japan in July and August, but in Korea, repatriates from China started an epidemic that spread along the rail line to Seoul, infecting 17,000 people within a few weeks and killing 11,000. Malaria, too, was endemic in the Hiroshima region and parts of Shikoku and Kyushu, and an epidemic of Japanese B encephalitis broke out in the Kanto region in the summer of 1948, affecting 7,000. Another 5,000 were stricken in 1950. DDT spraying dramatically reduced the incidence of both maladies.[16]

At the same time, PH&W initiated the domestic production of vaccines for cholera, smallpox, typhus, typhoid and tuberculosis. In 1946, PH&W and the Welfare Ministry organised large-scale inoculation programmes for a variety of diseases. On 1 July 1948, the Diet enacted the Preventive Vaccine Law, making mandatory immunisations against diphtheria, tuberculosis, typhoid, paratyphoid and smallpox for all Japanese between the ages of three and 60. Sams also oversaw the establishment of more than 1,700 modern venereal disease clinics across the country, procured newly developed drugs and organised educational campaigns to discourage the spread of sexually transmitted illnesses. Finally, Sams's staff, in tandem with Natural Resources Section, encouraged the domestic production and use of chemical fertilisers to replace night soil.[17] Together, these relatively inexpensive but effective measures enabled Japan to avoid a major epidemic during the Occupation and sharply reduced the incidence of infectious diseases.[18]

THE MEDICAL REFORMS

Demilitarisation and democratisation

Demilitarisation was a top PH&W priority. Particularly urgent was the liberation of Japan's hospital system from military control, both in order to free beds for civilian use and to end the system of priority treatment for veterans. In late September 1945, Sams reopened civilian hospitals and took steps to break the military's monopoly on medical services. In November and December, his staff issued a series of directives ordering the transfer of some 320 military hospitals, clinics, convalescence homes and related facilities to Welfare Ministry control. These were converted into national or prefectural institutions and opened to the general population. PH&W disbanded the Greater Japan Association for the War Disabled and dissolved the Japan Medical Corporation, which had exercised emergency wartime control over the nation's medical establishment. Sams's staff

Photo 54. General Crawford F. Sams directs a spraying operation to prevent the spread of Japanese encephalitis in Tokyo's Shiba-Shirogane district, today an affluent residential area. Sams's ambitious health and welfare reforms may have saved some 3 million lives (Kyodo).

purged high-ranking military personnel from the hospital system, but the medical corps had under its care some 78,000 wounded ex-combatants, and complete removal would have paralysed its services. Sams obtained a purge waiver from Government Section for doctors below the rank of lieutenant colonel. Lasting a year and a half, the exemption enabled hospitals to phase out former Army and

Navy doctors and replace them with civilians without sacrificing continuity of care.[19]

Another PH&W priority was the reorganisation of the Welfare Ministry. Here, however, Japanese bureaucrats took the first steps towards reform. The Konoe Cabinet had created the Ministry in January 1938 out of the Home Ministry's Labour and Social Bureaux. This was done partly in response to pressure from social bureaucrats involved in public health work and partly at the insistence of the Army, which had become alarmed at the deteriorating health of its rural recruits. The Ministry introduced a number of reform measures designed to stabilise living conditions and ensure a healthy military and work force. Its welfare specialists represented, in the context of the times, a progressive edge for social change but one that sought solutions within limits tolerable to the existing order. As defeat approached, these officials prepared to resurrect a social agenda put forward in the liberal 1920s but curtailed in the 1930s.

Sams's staff oversaw a mild purge of Welfare Ministry, but the programme affected mainly labour bureaucrats and resulted in the removal of only 23. Most social welfare officials remained on the job, and in late October 1945, at their initiative, Welfare Minister Ashida Hitoshi (October 1945 to April 1946) reorganised the Ministry, eliminating all military functions imposed by the wartime régime. As the Occupation got underway, the Ministry took over emergency relief activities from the Home Ministry, and bureaucratic restructuring was kept to a minimum. In mid-May 1946, GHQ directed the Ministry to reorganise again, and in November, it added three new bureaux: Public Health, Medical Affairs and Preventive Medicine. Sams was adamant that each prefecture establish both a health department and a welfare department to insure policy implementation at the regional level, and in December 1947, the Local Autonomy Law was amended to accommodate the new prefectural agencies.[20] In September 1947, the Ministry transferred its labour functions to the Labour Ministry and, following the dissolution of the Home Ministry in December, assumed responsibility for public sanitation and other former police functions. At the same time, it took over vital statistics, another police duty, from the Justice Ministry. Now fully removed from military and police control, the Ministry assumed its expanded role as guardian of the nation's health.[21]

A vital institution carried over from the prewar era was the network of health consultation centres the Home Ministry had established in 1937. In April 1947, GHQ directed the government to strengthen those centres, and on 5 September of that year, the Health-Care Centre Law was revised. The amendment established 800 health-care (HC) districts, each organised around an HC centre serving 100,000 people and supervised by the prefectural health and welfare departments. A district health officer was appointed to administer each establishment, which was organised into 17 service divisions ranging from medical affairs to environmental sanitation and health education. In January 1948, PH&W ordered the government to create a model HC centre in each prefecture. By the end of the Occupation there were 724 such centres across the country divided into three categories depending on the size of the population served, the largest having a staff of about 60, the smallest, 35. Members typically included doctors, dentists, public health nurses, veterinarians, sanitation experts, nutritionists, X-ray technicians and administrative support personnel.[22]

To provide staff for the HC centres, in early 1946 the Welfare Ministry established the Institute of Public Health, which organised a series of short-term and long-term training programmes. In late May 1947, the Ministry created the National Institute of Health to conduct basic research in public health medicine and produce vaccines (below). Other Ministry research organs were the Institute of Population Problems, the National Institute of Nutrition and the National Institute of Mental Health. At the same time, Navy Commander F. E. Linder of PH&W's Health and Welfare Statistics Division helped the Ministry develop a national reporting system for vital statistics.[23] Japan had maintained health statistics since 1877, when the Home Ministry's Sanitation Bureau began publication of an annual bulletin giving basic figures on births, deaths, illnesses and contagious and sexually transmitted diseases. The yearly report also included surveys of hospitals, pharmacies, drugs and medical practitioners. With Japanese assistance, PH&W was able to build on that foundation and install a modern system of statistical analysis and reporting. Under the new regime, the Health Statistics Division in each regional health-care centre collected data locally and forwarded them via the prefecture to the Welfare Ministry, which collated, analysed and published the national results annually.[24]

Medical and health care

PH&W revolutionised the practice of medicine, dentistry, pharmacy, nursing and veterinary medicine using the same original and highly effective formula. First, it recruited a council of progressive specialists, many of them trained in the United States, to set educational and professional standards, including national licensing requirements. The new council then reorganised the dominant professional association in each area to enforce standards and act as an oversight body. The revitalised professional association pressed for enabling legislation to codify these innovations in law. Finally, Sams's staff established a prefectural model training institution offering hands-on instruction in every field of medicine.[25]

PH&W's Medical Services Division under Colonel Harry G. Johnson began its reform of medical practice by inspecting medical schools at 18 universities and some 50 technical colleges. The Division closed down about half of the technical colleges (Class B schools) and placed the others on probation until they could attain the standards of the regular medical faculties (Class A schools). Johnson then introduced the American system of six-year medical studies followed by a one-year internship at an accredited hospital. To set modern standards, his staff established the Council on Medical Education and appointed a progressive specialist, Dr Kusama Yoshio, to head it. The Council cooperated in drafting a national licensing exam for which only graduates of Class A medical schools were eligible to sit. The Medical Practitioners Law of 30 July 1948 codified this and other educational requirements. The Medical Service Law of the same date created new norms for hospitals, clinics and midwifery homes. In September 1948, PH&W oversaw the creation of the School of Hospital Administration in Tokyo's First National Hospital and set up similar model institutions in each prefecture. Finally, the Council on Medical Education was absorbed into a restructured and liberalised Japan Medical Association, which strove to maintain high standards and advise the government on medical policy.

In similar fashion, Lieutenant Colonel Dale B. Ridgely's Dental Affairs Division modernised the practice of dentistry, assisted by the despatch of a special mission from the American Dental Association, and Major Grace E. Alt of the Nursing Affairs Division helped reform public health nursing, general nursing and midwifery.[26] Under Colonel Oness H. Dixon of the Veterinary Affairs Division, licensing norms and standardised training soon transformed the practice of veterinary medicine as well. Dixon created a new category of specialist, the 'health veterinarian', who was responsible for controlling animal diseases that affect humans directly or impair the food supply. He also introduced techniques and norms for inspecting meats and other perishables. The pharmaceutical industry, too, was reorganised, with licensed pharmacists now required by law to write out prescriptions. With the support of the respective professional associations, a series of statutes, passed simultaneously in mid-1948, institutionalised these changes. By convincing the Japanese to create different and clearly defined standards and licensing systems for medicine, dentistry and pharmacy, PH&W assured the autonomy of each profession, thereby improving the overall quality of medical and health care.[27]

Finally, PH&W instituted a stringent system of narcotics control. After World War I, Japan had encouraged the development of a local opium industry, and Osaka became the centre of domestic poppy cultivation. The Government Monopoly Corporation also imported hemp, opium and coca leaves from Formosa, Iran, Iwo Jima, Manchuria, Mongolia, the Ryukyus and Turkey, processing these intoxicants for domestic medical purposes and for export. By the mid-1930s, Japanese firms were producing about 10 per cent of the world's morphine and 37 per cent of its heroin. Just as the Western powers had profited from drug trafficking in their colonies, so, too, Imperial Japan sought to regulate and exploit this lucrative market in Korea, Manchuria and Taiwan and, later, in China, Inner Mongolia and Southeast Asia. Both the *zaibatsu* and the Imperial Army became deeply involved in this nefarious trade, making Japan one of the world's primary sources of illicit drugs. On 6 October 1945, PH&W directed the government to locate and itemise existing stores of narcotics and turn over past production records. In November, the Section ordered the destruction of heroin stocks, eliminating a sizable proportion of the international supply. Other impounded drugs eventually were released to the government for supervised medical use. PH&W's Narcotics Control Branch (later Division) and the Welfare Ministry drafted the Narcotics Control Bill based on US legislation. Enacted on 10 June 1948, the law severely restricted the production and sale of dangerous drugs and provided stiff penalties for violators.[28]

Photo 55. Plainclothes police round up roving bands of homeless children. War-displaced minors were a major source of petty crime. This boy, caught in a railway station at night, will be placed in an orphanage. Clutching a *geta* (wooden clog) in one hand, he protests angrily, but to no avail. 22 July 1947 (New York Times).

WELFARE LEGISLATION

In addition to the Daily Life Protection Law, two other pillars of social welfare reform were established under PH&W's tutelage: the Child Welfare Law, promulgated in December 1947, and the Law for the Welfare of the Physically Disabled, which was enacted two years later in December 1949. The mission statement of Sams' Welfare Division had called for such measures, but the real momentum for change came from the Japanese side. Kasai Yoshisuke of the Welfare Ministry's Social Affairs Bureau consulted frequently with Welfare Division Chief Colonel Nelson B. Neff and his staff and played a central role in drafting and shepherding both bills through the Diet. The Ministry's social bureaucrats had come into their own, and they left their distinctive imprint on each.

The Child Welfare Law
Protective measures for children were a pressing issue. War-displaced minors, many of them orphans, roamed the streets of Japan's cities in large numbers, subsisting in squalid conditions. A Welfare Ministry survey of June 1947, estimated their number at about 12,000, and in 1948, it found that from 20 to 30 per cent were under 10 years old. Street waifs subsisted by begging, collecting cigarette butts, shining shoes and selling newspapers, but many also picked pockets and engaged in petty theft to survive. On 10 September 1945, the Welfare Ministry outlined a programme of emergency relief for homeless children. The plan not only assigned the government a central role but sought to make such youngsters self-supporting – a forward-looking goal that anticipated GHQ's emergency relief directives of December and February (SCAPINs 404 and 775). The Ministry's Social Affairs Bureau implemented these emergency measures on a limited scale in Tokyo, Osaka and other large urban areas. At the same time, it began work on a more ambitious legislative programme designed to protect children in general.[29]

Out of the drafting process emerged the idea for a Children's Bureau. In a series of bilateral meetings held in the autumn of 1946, Kasai and his staff convinced Sams and Neff to endorse the establishment of a specialised agency for minors. Both sides subsequently agreed on the need to expand the principle of relief from one of protecting children to one of insuring their overall welfare.[30] The Children's Bureau was established on 19 March 1947 and a career bureaucrat named to head it, but Kasai tapped a non-bureaucrat veteran welfare activist, Yoshimi Shizue, to lead the Bureau's important Childcare Section, and she became the first woman to hold a position of high responsibility in government. As Childcare Section Chief, Yoshimi contributed to the enactment of a law that would meet the special needs of homeless minors while fostering the healthy development of all children.[31]

To generate public support, Sams enlisted the aid of Father Edward J. Flanagan, the founder of Boys' Town for homeless children in Omaha, Nebraska, who arrived in Tokyo in April 1947 as a PH&W consultant. Flanagan's appeal for more orphanages and protective legislation helped stimulate interest in the issue, and in

Photo 56. War orphans vie for a living as shoeshine boys on the streets of Tokyo, 5 May 1947. The Child Welfare Law of January 1948 provided relief for most, and by the end of the Occupation, homelessness had been eliminated as a major social problem (New York Times).

August of that year, the Ministry submitted its childcare bill to the Diet. Enacted in mid-December, the Child Welfare Law entered into force on 1 January 1948. It extended special protection to abandoned, abused and neglected children; abolished the practice of indentured labour; outlawed the employment of minors in dangerous occupations; provided for prenatal care; established health-care programmes for mothers and children; and guaranteed the privacy rights of minors adopted or born out of wedlock. It also laid the institutional foundation for a nationwide system of childcare centres, created standards for foster parentage and made the state responsible for creating and supervising orphanages and other juvenile institutions.

To oversee implementation of the law, the Ministry established Child Welfare Committees at the national and prefectural levels and Child Welfare Bureaux and consultation centres at prefectural and municipal levels. By early 1948, more than 100 childcare centres were in operation, and over 600 professional childcare workers (*jidō-i'in*), most of them women, had been assigned to every city, town and village in the country. In October 1949, PH&W enlisted the services of a United Nations social affairs specialist with experience in Britain and the United States to survey the work of the childcare agencies, which he pronounced highly effective. As a result of these measures, the number of war-displaced minors declined steadily. In 1946, only 33,000 children had found shelter in orphanages, but by 1949, that figure had grown to about 175,500, and by the end of the Occupation, homelessness among the young was no longer a pressing social issue.[32]

Japanese with disabilities

The third mainstay of welfare reform was the Law for the Welfare of the Physically Disabled. Like the child welfare statute, it represented a departure from the paternalistic Daily Life Protection Law of 1946, stressing not relief and income maintenance but rehabilitation. Here, the legislative process was characterised by a high degree of bilateral cooperation and internal consensus-building on both sides. In this instance, however, the Japanese side fought for progressive legislation that MacArthur's command, now committed to economic stabilisation, was reluctant to enact.

The Welfare Ministry led the effort to legislate protection for the disabled, but it was motivated initially by a perceived social responsibility to maimed war veterans. Japan had no state-sponsored rehabilitation programmes for the handicapped apart from military hospitals and convalescent homes. GHQ had not only dismantled the military hospital system but in February 1946 had eliminated military pensions and survivors' benefits, as well. Desperate to assist the war-disabled, Kasai's Social Affairs Bureau submitted a relief plan for the physically impaired to PH&W in August 1947, but Sams's staff rejected the proposal, which, it said, favoured veterans and violated the non-discrimination principle. By the autumn of 1947, however, Kasai's efforts had produced a change of heart in PH&W. In addition to Japanese with congenital handicaps were many who had been disabled as a result of Allied wartime bombing, and Sams's staff acknowledged the need for special legislation. When the Ministry proposed a new relief measure in February 1948, Sams and Neff agreed on condition that it be expanded to include the physically handicapped in general. The legislation would cover some 500,000 disabled, of whom 325,000 were former soldiers and sailors, many of them amputees.[33]

To develop a comprehensive proposal, the Ministry created an ad hoc advisory body, the National Rehabilitation Commission, and appointed private citizens and bureaucrats to sit on it. Pressure groups, such as the National League for the Rehabilitation of the Handicapped (*Zenkoku Shintai-shōgaisha Kōsei Dōmei*), helped shape the debate, lobbying for a law that made no distinction regarding sex, former occupation or type of disability. In October, a private organisation, the Nippon Lighthouse Foundation (below), invited Helen Keller to visit Japan. The militant Socialist, suffragette and champion of the disabled toured the country, raising public awareness of the problems faced by the blind, deaf and mute. By late 1948, these diverse currents had merged to form an irresistible movement for change. It remained to hammer out the details.[34]

In late 1948, Ferdinand Micklautz, Welfare Organisation and Rehabilitation Officer, convened a series of meetings with concerned Japanese to discuss the government plan. Held in the PH&W conference room at SCAP headquarters, the sessions were attended by Welfare Ministry officials, hospital directors, and heads of organisations for the blind, including Iwahashi Takeo, a lifelong friend of Keller who was himself unsighted. Iwahashi represented the Nippon Lighthouse Foundation, a self-help group he had founded in 1935 as a student after losing his sight.[35] The conferees established a Working Group inside the National Rehabilitation Commission to draft the bill, and in December 1948, the group met PH&W and other concerned GHQ staff sections several times in January and February 1949, refining a legislative draft it hoped to present to the Diet by March. Many of the proposals that emerged in these intense sessions were advanced for their day: Japanese and American welfare experts were contemplating reforms that would not be enacted in the United States until the Americans With Disabilities Act of 1990.[36]

The goal of this legislation was not to shelter the disabled but to reintegrate them into society as self-sufficient, productive members. Moreover, the Working Group draft called for cooperation among the Education, Labour and Welfare Ministries to assure basic services, a requirement that promised to overcome bureaucratic sectarianism. Such innovative concepts did not translate readily into Japanese practice, but the Welfare Ministry and the Working Group persevered. Among the changes they proposed was a programme of affirmative action that would require employers to hire a certain percentage of handicapped workers. The government would scrutinise labour contracts and provide funds for shopfloor vocational guidance, training and special equipment. A national braille library, a national centre for seeing-eye dogs and a priority housing policy also were envisaged. Unfortunately, these measures were never implemented, but their formulation attests to the farsightedness of their authors.[37]

By February 1949, PH&W and the Ministry had reached basic agreement on a bill, but the greatest opposition now came from inside MacArthur's headquarters.

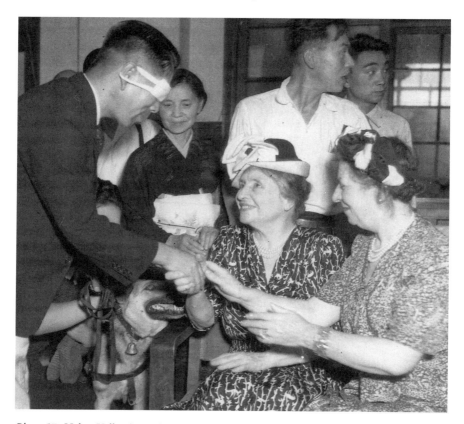

Photo 57. Helen Keller (centre) is introduced to a man with a seeing-eye dog, 3 September 1948. At the right is her Scottish companion and guide, Polly Thompson. Keller's visit to Tokyo gave a boost to government efforts to enact the Law for the Welfare of the Physically Disabled (December 1949). She came at the invitation of a Japanese organisation for the blind (Kyodo).

That month, the conservative financier Joseph M. Dodge arrived in Tokyo to inaugurate his Economic Stabilisation Programme, whose budgetary cuts and other deflationary measures soon plunged the economy into deep recession. When PH&W circulated a check sheet soliciting the concurrence of other staff groups, Economic and Scientific Section protested that the proposed legislation would inflate the budget that Dodge and ESS now were committed to balance. ESS and Civil Information & Education Section also raised the objection that Sams had voiced in 1947: the bill appeared to be a back-door way of providing relief to handicapped veterans. PH&W was advised to eliminate many of the proposal's most innovative aspects and make better use of existing programmes and facilities.

SCAP reticence retarded further progress for most of 1949. The Ministry held out for a more progressive statute, but finally accepted the ESS changes in order to pass the new law in time for the 1950 budget.[38] Enacted on 22 December 1949, the Law for the Welfare of the Physically Disabled failed to incorporate affirmitive action and other sought-after measures but nonetheless represented a dramatic advance over past practice. The handicapped were no longer to be regarded as a drain on the public coffers but as potentially productive citizens and taxpayers. National and regional rehabilitation centres were established, vocational training programmes and sheltered workshops set up and new employment opportunities created. National, regional and local governments were enjoined to organise braille libraries. Both the right to a subsistence and the right to work were codified in law. An Advisory Council on the Welfare of the Physically Disabled was established to monitor implementation and advise the Welfare Ministry on basic policy. Welfare and counselling offices for the handicapped, the latter staffed by professionals, were created in prefectural and municipal governments. People with disabilities received identity cards entitling them to special services, medical care, pensions and rehabilitation and welfare allotments. Families raising disabled children became eligible for special cash allowances.[39]

Social security
Japan already possessed the institutional rudiments of a modern social security system. The Meiji-era Mining Law (1905) and Factory Law (1911) had provided workers with limited protection, which was enlarged by the Health Insurance Law of 1922 (enforced in 1927). As the nation shifted to a war footing in the late 1930s, the Welfare Ministry introduced an ambitious reform package designed to bind workers to the shopfloor, improve health conditions and build a capital reserve to help finance the war effort.[40] These measures included the National Health Insurance Law (1938), the National Medical Care Law (1938), the Seamen's Insurance Law (1939), the Clerical Workers' Health Insurance Law (1939) and the Workers' Pension Insurance Law (1941), which was extended to women in 1944. By 1945, most working-age Japanese were covered by some form of insurance. The administration of social security programmes, however, generally was entrusted to non-governmental agencies, and in the absence of minimal standards, procedures were inconsistent, confusing and frequently ineffectual. From an American perspective, the weakness of the system lay in its philosophical assumptions of state and employer benevolence and mutual assistance, which ignored the contractual rights of the insured.[41]

PH&W's Social Security Division under George F. Pollack set out to streamline and liberalise social security programmes in four areas: accident insurance, unemployment insurance, medical care and pensions. The Welfare Ministry's Social Security Bureau was equally intent on reorganising social assistance to compensate for the loss of military pensions. In December 1945, the Shidehara government set up a high-profile advisory body, the Social Insurance Deliberation Council, to study the issue, and in March 1946, the Council created a Social Insurance Working Group to draft a set of preliminary proposals.[42]

In October 1947, the group submitted its proposals, many of them inspired by

Britain's 1942 Beveridge Report ('Social Insurance and Allied Services'). Drafted by Sir William Beveridge, the British study had called for the unification of health and unemployment insurance and pension schemes and, after 1945, became the basis of the Labour government's welfare-state proposals. Following the British example, the Working Group recommended integrating all existing programmes into a comprehensive and uniform national system covering virtually every type of social insurance and welfare disbursement. To finance this endeavour, it advocated spending the equivalent of 36 per cent of the 1947 GNP, a suggestion that was greeted with derision. The existing system, with its overlapping provisions, multiple jurisdictions and inequities, proved too complex to allow of a single, elegant solution, and the government decided to deal with the various programmes individually.[43]

By this time, Japanese and American officials already had completed a set of basic social security guarantees as part of the labour reforms. Enacted in 1947, the Workman's Compensation Insurance Law (April), the Employment Security Law (November) and the Unemployment Insurance Law (December) systematised and expanded pre-1945 worker insurance programmes. Coverage was not complete, however, and workers in enterprises of fewer than five employees were excluded from the scope of this legislation.

In August 1947, at Sams's invitation, Dr William H. Wandel of the US Department of Labour's Social Security Administration brought the US Social Security Mission to Tokyo to recommend further action. In December, following lengthy consultations with Welfare Ministry officials, the Mission submitted its conclusions to MacArthur, which were formally transmitted to the government in July 1948. The Wandel Report recommended 1 that Japan's various social security schemes be streamlined, 2 that the Daily Life Protection Law be strengthened, 3 that public health activities be improved, 4 that a single agency be established to administer social security and 5 that a Cabinet-level consultative body be created to advise the government on social security policy. The report also proposed compulsory health insurance for every worker and the full reimbursement of family medical costs.[44]

Based on the Wandel proposals, in May 1949 the government set up the Social Security Council inside the Prime Minister's Office to oversee Japan's emerging social security system.[45] The Dodge deflation of 1949 and 1950 slowed the Council's work, but in July 1950, it submitted the first of several reports whose recommendations eventually were implemented by the revised National Health Insurance Law of December 1958 and the National Pensions Law of April 1959. By the end of the Occupation, health insurance schemes covered more than 80 per cent of the population, but the 1958 law made medical coverage available to every citizen, and its companion statute of 1959 paved the way for a universal pension plan.

Wandel's proposals on mandatory national health insurance aroused the ire of the American Medical Association (AMA) and other US groups, who charged that compulsory medical coverage was an infringement on individual freedom of choice and an invitation to state socialism. Sams felt constrained to invite an AMA mission to Tokyo in August 1948 to review his public health and social security schemes, and he later appeared before the AMA in the United States to defend his Section's policies. The Association eventually gave PH&W a clean bill of heath, but Sams remained highly defensive on the issue, and as Cold War realities impinged, PH&W toned down its activist stance on social security.[46]

Sams's staff demonstrated consistent resolve, however, in its refusal to lift the Occupation ban on veterans' benefits. This remained a bone of contention with the Welfare Ministry, and as soon as the Occupation ended, Ministry officials presented draft legislation to restore many veterans' rights. On 30 April 1952, two days after Japan regained its independence, the Diet enacted the Law for War Invalids and Families of the War Dead, and in August 1953, it revised the Public Officials Pension Law, reinstating military pensions some six years ahead of the national system.

A MIXED LEGACY

In their ensemble, these reforms revolutionised Japan's health-care system. Sams estimated that without the modern practices PH&W introduced in concert with Japanese authorities, some 3 million people – more than the total number of war-related deaths – would have died needlessly between 1945 and 1952.[47] In retrospect, PH&W's health and welfare innovations were strikingly original, both in their conception and execution, but not all initiatives were successful; some were ill-conceived, and a few were misguided and even sinister.

The balance sheet

The PH&W reforms were not a carbon copy of statutes and practices then current in the United States. Sams and and his staff, influenced by the liberal American Public Welfare Association, sought solutions to Japan's health problems that did not yet exist in the United States. In 1947, the Wandel Mission specifically warned Japanese officials against imitating the American social security system, urging them to build on existing institutions, and the ensuing National Health Insurance Law of 1958 still has no parallel in US practice. The Law for the Welfare of the Physically Disabled, despite its defects, was well in advance of American legislation, although it failed to keep pace with subsequent progress in the West. In the medical field, Sams was critical of the American tendency towards over-specialisation, which had produced a relative dearth of general practitioners. Family doctors, he believed, ideally should meet 85 per cent of a community's medical needs, but in the United States fewer and fewer medical school graduates went into general practice. He did his best to counter the trend towards excessive specialisation in Japan, opposing the creation of advanced postgraduate programmes and the specialty board-certification system.[48]

Sams was a shrewd and innovative administrator. To break up the bureaucratic authoritarianism that permeated Japan's medical establishment, he actively discouraged the appointment of career administrators to top positions in the health-care field, naming instead physicians, dentists, pharmacists, veterinarians, nurses and others with hands-on experience. The resulting decentralisation of power opened up new opportunities for professionals and technicians, insuring an infusion of fresh ideas into each field.

Some PH&W endeavours were ill-conceived, such as the Section's attempt to regulate the field of traditional medicine,[49] and others fell on infertile soil. The US internship system, for instance, failed to take root. Sams had directed the government to institute the new system in May 1946, and in August of that year, one-year clinical training programmes were introduced. PH&W arranged internships for medical school graduates at 11 US military hospitals, but the programme proved unpopular with students and was discontinued after 1968, when radicals at the University of Tokyo's Medical Faculty attacked the system head-on.[50]

A few PH&W initiatives backfired. One of these was the Section's reliance on local sanitation societies (*eisei-kumiai*) to implement early health-care measures. In February 1947, some 57,600 such groups served nearly 10 million people. With the dissolution of the neighbourhood associations (*tonari-gumi*) in May of that year, the *eisei-kumiai* were placed under the jurisdiction of municipal health authorities, but by late 1947, many had been co-opted by the local conservative élite. Membership in the sanitation teams had remained compulsory, and municipal bosses were using them as vote-gathering machines, much as they had the *tonari-gumi*. On 16 August 1948, GHQ disbanded the societies, and PH&W had them gradually replaced with professional sanitation workers.[51]

Even major PH&W successes were not unqualified. In November 1948, more than 600 children receiving diphtheria shots became ill in Kyoto and Shimane Prefectures due to improper sterilisation techniques, and 68 eventually died. PH&W suspended the manufacture of Japanese vaccines in December, but tragedy struck again. In January 1949, 62 children out of more than 200 inoculated for whooping cough in Iwagasaki Township, Miyagi Prefecture developed active clinical tuberculosis, leading to three deaths. Sams charged that local Communists had sabotaged the vaccine batch with human TB bacilli in order to discredit the Occupation, but Japanese health authorities were never able to pinpoint the cause of the misfortune.[52]

Darker undercurrents

PH&W's positive legacy must be balanced against other more sinister endeavours, one of which involved the use of scientists associated with the Kwantung Army's notorious Unit 731, commanded by Lieutenant General Ishii Shirō (chapter 6). In late 1946 or early 1947, Sams directed the Welfare Ministry to establish the National Institute of Health (NIH) partly in order to oversee vaccine production. At Sams's insistence, the NIH was carved out of the prestigious Institute of Infectious Diseases (IID), which had been established in 1892 by Kitasato Shiba-saburō to study contagious illnesses and preventive medicine. Attached to Tokyo Imperial University during World War II, the IID was harnessed to the Imperial Army's biological war (BW) effort and many of its leading scientists experimented on prisoners for Unit 731. On 22 May 1947, with the reluctant agreement of

Tokyo University President Nanbara Shigeru, the National Institute of Health was formally established inside the IID's Toyama laboratories in Shinjuku Ward, Tokyo.[53]

A key role in the establishment of the NIH was played by its first Deputy Director Kojima Saburō, an Ishii collaborator, who recruited former Unit 731 personnel for the new Institute. Between 1947 and 1983, seven of eight NIH directors and six of eight vice directors either were members of the Ishii network or had assisted it in some way during the war.[54] Their grisly medical experiments had made these men leaders in the field of immunology, and it was to them that Sams and his staff turned to supervise the production of vital biologicals. Under PH&W's guidance, the Ishii group produced penicillin and vaccines for cholera, plague, tuberculosis and typhus. PH&W also helped two Ishii lieutenants, Kitano Masaji and Naitō Ryōichi, create the Japan Blood Bank, Inc. (reorganised in 1951 under American tutelage as the Green Cross Corporation) to manufacture plasma for US troops in Korea. Kitano, who had held command positions in Unit 731 and Unit Ei-1644 (Nanjing), ran the Corporation's Tokyo factory. Interviewed in Kyoto shortly before his death, the former bio-warrior openly acknowledged his and his colleagues' wartime role and boasted of their contribution to the development of preventive medicine in postwar Japan.[55]

Sams and others in PH&W not only knew of these men's sordid pasts but actively solicited their cooperation to further PH&W goals. 'The Institute', an NIH director told a researcher in 1987, 'was under the supervision of GHQ, and GHQ watched everything we did'. Indeed, PH&W and the Far East Command's Medical Section (which replaced PH&W in mid-1951) commissioned research from former Ishii scientists in the NIH on the tropical *tsutsugamushi* mite and typhus, areas where Japanese expertise was unrivalled. These projects were coordinated through the US Army's 406 Medical General Laboratory set up in 1946. Early in the Occupation, the Laboratory moved to the Mitsubishi Higashi Building in downtown Tokyo close to PH&W headquarters. The 406 Medical Laboratory developed diagnostic tests, plasma products and vaccines for US forces in Japan and Korea, and its staff included specialists in epidemiology, bacteriology and viral and ricketsial diseases, fields in which the Ishii group had conducted much of its wartime work. When haemorrhagic fever broke out in Korea in April 1951 and again in May and June of 1952, the 406 Medical Laboratory sought help from Ishii stalwart Kasahara Shirō, an expert from Manchurian days.[56] The National Institute of Health played a pivotal role in this research. In the past half century, the NIH has made important contributions to public health medicine in Japan, but its links with the wartime crimes of medical science cast a long shadow over this achievement. The key role PH&W played in these and other questionable medical initiatives compromised its integrity, clouding its considerable accomplishments with a legacy of doubt and suspicion.[57]

The Atomic Bomb Casualty Commission

PH&W's involvement in the work of the Atomic Bomb Casualty Commission (ABCC) was another controversial commitment. The ABCC had its origins in the diverse efforts by Japanese and American scientists to assess the destructive impact of the atomic bombings. On 8 August, two days after the first blast, Imperial General Headquarters despatched a 30-man team led by Military Intelligence Chief Arisue Seizō and Dr Nishina Yoshio of the Institute of Physical and Chemical Research (*Riken*) to Hiroshima. Their job was to determine the military nature of the dooms-day weapon. After 15 August, Japanese universities and research institutes also sent teams to study the medical effects of the bombings and, more importantly, to provide emergency relief. On 3 September, the day after the surrender ceremony, the Japanese government voluntarily submitted the results of its preliminary findings on Hiroshima and Nagasaki to MacArthur's headquarters in Yokohama. The following day, General Thomas F. Farrell of the Manhattan Project arrived in Japan to conduct his own studies on residual radiation and other potential hazards to occupying troops. Sams received the Farrell team and coordinated its activities.[58]

Farrell's group entered the devastated cities on 8 and 9 September accompanied by Japanese scientists and protected by prefectural security personnel. On 12 September, Farrell told a press conference in Tokyo that lingering radiation did not pose a creditable threat to human health, although Japanese physicians were documenting overwhelming evidence to the contrary. Later that month, a joint Japan–US commission was set up to examine the aftereffects of the bomb, and from late 1945 through early 1946, six US missions arrived to conduct separate studies, each assisted by Sams and his staff.[59]

GHQ was highly sensitive to the psychological impact of the bombings. In February 1946, Occupation authorities confiscated 20,000 feet of 35mm film on Hiroshima and Nagasaki shot by the Nippon Film Company (Nichiei). The Nichiei team had begun work in late August on orders from the Education Ministry, which was anxious to gather its own scientific data on the weapon, and it later joined the scientific survey organised by Nishina. In December, the Nagasaki Military Government Team arrested the Nichiei cameramen, confiscated their film and delivered it to the US Strategic Bombing Survey in Tokyo. The footage provided dramatic documentation of the immediate medical effects of the atomic blasts, and on 19 December, War Department Intelligence in Washington ordered SCAP to have Nichiei complete the film, edit one copy in English and hand it over. No other prints were to be made. GHQ attempted to acquire every foot of film Nichiei had taken, and the documentary was sent to Washington for analysis by military medical scientists (all of this at Japanese government expense). Entitled 'Effects of the Atomic Bomb on Hiroshima and Nagasaki', the film would not be recovered and shown in its entirely in Japan until the early 1980s.[60]

In July 1946, the United States resumed nuclear testing at the Bikini Atoll in the Marshalls, and in November of that year, President Truman ordered a major research effort to determine the long-term biological and medical effects of nuclear weapons on human beings. In January 1947, the National Research Council (National Academy of Sciences), under contract to the US Atomic Energy Commission, established the Atomic Bomb Casualty Commission (ABCC) to study cancers, shortened lifespans, developmental disorders, genetic mutations, sterility, visual impairments, abnormal pigmentation and other medical sequelae of the bomb. Sams was intimately involved in the activities of the ABCC from its inception. Under his direction, the Commission established research laboratories at Hiroshima (January 1948) and Nagasaki (July 1948). The city of Kure near Hiroshima, which had escaped destruction, was chosen as an experimental control and a research centre established there, as well. American ABCC researchers were attached to PH&W as consultants, and the Section provided administrative guidance and technical support. Several of its staff later went to work for the ABCC.[61]

At Sams's behest, the National Institute of Health formed a Japanese counterpart group to work with the Americans, and in August 1948, NIH created the Atomic Bomb Effects Research Institute, setting up its own branches at Hiroshima, Nagasaki and Kure. The Welfare Ministry contributed directly to the Commission's work, arranging funding, securing scientific and technical support personnel, and planning basic research. ABCC directors were Americans, but their deputies were Japanese, and Japanese staff outnumbered American participants by a ratio of eight to one. In seeking NIH cooperation, Sams's purpose was to discourage independent parallel research by Japanese scientists and assure access to Welfare Ministry resources, particularly its modern system of statistics collection and analysis.

From the start, however, this bilateral effort was one-sided. Research findings on radiation effects were classified as 'atomic secrets', and American scientists withheld sensitive data and other information not only from their Japanese colleagues but also, incredibly, from each other. The ABCC confiscated the autopsy records, organ specimens and other biological data gathered by Japanese researchers and shipped them to Washington for analysis. Japanese scientists could not publish or discuss publicly their own findings until very late in the Occupation. SCAP suppressed this material even after reports had been declassified and distributed in the United States, where some of the Japanese researchers had prewar reputations. As a result, the medical repercussions of the bomb remained a closely guarded secret, preventing a wider knowledge of its destructive force and impeding the development of medical procedures and treatments of benefit to *hibakusha*. This veil of secrecy would not be lifted until the end of the Occupation. Ironically, the secretive character of the ABCC and the high turnover among American specialists hampered its work, and results obtained during the Occupation era later were adjudged scientifically unreliable. In 1955, the Commission was restructured but continued to conduct research until 1975, when it was reorganised as a private group, the Radiation Effects Research Foundation.[62]

The ABCC failed to achieve its goals partly because of the distrust and ill-will its activities generated locally. The Commission's authoritarian methods aroused particular antipathy. ABCC personnel, travelling in military jeeps and exuding an aura

of authority, fetched parents and their children from their homes and delivered them
to local research stations. There, *hibakusha* were asked to undress and mount examining tables, where their burns, scars, malignancies and other injuries were probed,
measured, photographed and filmed. ABCC doctors exposed wounds for the camera,
drew blood samples, performed biopsies and took sperm counts. Examinations often
lasted all day, but subjects received no compensation. When *hibakusha* died, ABCC
workers, notified by local governments, sought permission from next of kin to perform autopsies. At Kure, the control city, Japanese unaffected by the bombings were
subjected to the same indignities in order to scientifically validate the findings at
Hiroshima. Thus, the Commission ran a vast controlled medical experiment, induct-
ing both victims of the bomb and non-victims into America's atomic research
programme.[63]

Researchers were especially concerned with the impact of the bomb on the human
reproductive system, and sterility, genetic damage and mutations became primary
areas of inquiry. Young children and women, especially pregnant ones, were a major
focus of attention. From 1948 to 1952, scientists surveyed and analysed statistic-
ally the pregnancies of more than 70,000 women. Midwives received a government
payment of between ¥20 and ¥50 for each pregnancy they reported and monitored,
and post-mortem exams of stillborn and aborted foetuses were carried out routinely.
Some 73,000 people were examined directly for genetic damage. More than 10,000
children were evaluated for adverse effects to their growth. Another 65,000 adults
were screened for radiation illness.[64]

Tokyo ordered municipal governments to assist the ABCC, and local officials
asked *hibakusha* to cooperate dutifully 'for the good of society'. In some instances,
the recalcitrant were threatened with military tribunals. Informed consent was not
on the agenda, and neither the authorities nor the subjects were told the purpose of
the experiments. This was not simply because 'atomic secrets' were involved but also
because such disclosure would threaten the professional goals and career ambitions of
the researchers. Dr William Silverman, who worked briefly for the ABCC, later
explained this philosophy: 'There's a conflict between informed consent and the
ability to conduct research, and the physician is not interested in the patient's
welfare, he's interested in his [own]. So he doesn't inform him.'[65]

The ABCC also was widely reviled for refusing to provide medical care. Its mission
was to conduct 'pure' research for military, not humanitarian, purposes, and scientists were under explicit orders not to render medical assistance to the people they
examined. This was a political decision taken in Washington, where officials feared
that aiding victims of the bomb would imply an admission of US guilt, undermining
America's moral leadership. In fact, however, American and Japanese doctors often
disobeyed orders and dispensed treatment, although this was done almost surreptitiously. The Commission refused to budge from basic policy. *Hibakusha* who came
to ABCC research stations seeking medical attention were turned away routinely.
The lack of assistance reinforced the *hibakusha*'s feelings of victimisation and lent
credence to claims that they were being used as human guinea pigs.[66]

No official system of relief, Japanese or American, existed for the survivors of Hiroshima and Nagasaki during the Occupation. Initially, bombing victims had received two-months' free treatment under the 1942 Wartime Casualties Care Law, but that aid expired in October 1945, forcing sufferers to seek medical attention at their own expense. In the early months of occupation, universities and private research institutions had combined studies of the bomb's impact with emergency treatment, but the creation of the ABCC curtailed many of these activities. Through the tireless efforts of Marcel Junod, the International Red Cross representative in Japan, the IRC and the American Red Cross supplied penicillin, sulfa drugs and plasma, with GHQ's cooperation, to hospitals in Hiroshima and Nagasaki, but a programme of subsidised medical care for *hibakusha* would not be established until 1957, and even then, Korean victims of the bomb, Japanese subjects at the time of the blasts, would be excluded on the grounds that they were now foreign nationals (chapter 10).[67]

Ultimately, the government found Hiroshima and Nagasaki useful in two senses. The bombings enabled it to portray the country as nuclear victim, deflecting popular attention away from Japan's wartime aggression in Asia and directing it inward towards the country's own suffering, unprecedented and ineffable. At the same time, the destruction of the two cities allowed government officials to cooperate with the Americans in acquiring vital knowledge about the physical and medical effects of atomic weaponry. As one historian has expressed it, the government 'exploited the *hibakusha* to gain the trust and good will of the world's only nuclear power'. Moreover, by failing to provide official medical relief to the victims and ignoring the plight of the bomb's Korean victims, 'the government and the Japanese people, too, compounded in their own way the tragedy of Hiroshima and Nagasaki'.[68]

The Eugenic Protection Law
Another questionable PH&W decision was its passive support for the 1948 Eugenic Protection Law, designed to prevent the birth of 'defective' and unwanted offspring. The postwar statute was a revision of the 1940 National Eugenic Law, which had been modelled on Nazi legislation designed to purify the racial stock by sterilising the mentally and physically disabled and culling potentially 'flawed' progeny through abortions. The 1948 law preserved many of the features of its 1940 predecessor. Abortions were encouraged if either parent was disabled, had genetic defects or suffered from personality disorders, or if the parents of either mother or father displayed such traits. Pregnancies also could be terminated legally if the mother had been raped, if either parent had leprosy (a feature that was absent in the 1940 law), or if the birth represented an unacceptable threat to the health of the mother.

The eugenics law was a hybrid creature, part product of the war era, part product of the unsettled social and economic conditions of the early postwar period. Demobilisation, repatriation and the return of war evacuees from the countryside produced a baby boom in the years between 1947 and 1949. Poverty, malnutrition and disease, however, made childbirth itself a risky undertaking, and the loss of male providers, soaring inflation and unemployment rendered childrearing an impossible task for many. This environment produced a flourishing trade in unwanted children, as bogus orphanages and welfare institutions scrambled to collect government childcare subsidies. In June 1948, it was revealed that the owners of two orphanages had been arrested for starving to death more than 100 babies in order to capitalise on this source of income. At the same time, rape and prostitution led thousands of women to seek back-room abortions at the hands of former military medics, veterinarians, eye doctors and outright quacks. Predictably, the crude, unsanitary procedures produced a steady stream of deaths and maimings.[69]

Among the conservative bureaucrats and lawmakers who backed this legislation were many who looked askance at the large number of mixed-blood children being born to prostitutes, GI rape victims and repatriates from China, Korea and Manchuria. Chauvinist elements forged an alliance of convenience with the group of Lower House social activists around Katō Shizue, Ōta Tenrei (inventor of the inter-uterine device) and Fukuda Masako, medical doctor and feminist, who together had unsuccessfully submitted a liberal family-planning bill to the Diet in late August 1947. The Katayama Cabinet, busy on other fronts, did not back the Katō–Ōta proposal, and it died in committee. When right-of-centre politicians sponsored a far more conservative proposal in June 1948, Katō, Ōta and other leaders of the planned parenthood movement seized the opportunity. Although privately critical of the bill's eugenic provisions, Katō's group was willing to tolerate them in return for even a minimalist birth-control programme, and it mobilised support from Akamatsu Tsuneko and other progressive lawmakers. The final draft of the bill, however, emphasised abortion, not contraception.

Enacted on 13 July 1948, the Eugenic Protection Law became effective on 11 September, and the number of legally terminated pregnancies soared in its wake, rising from 24,600 cases in 1949 to nearly 64,000 in 1951. The statute was amended twice, in June 1949 and May 1952, establishing Eugenic Protection Councils at the national and prefectural levels and Eugenic Protection Counselling Offices in municipalities and health-care centres. The 1949 revision approved the sale of contraceptive pharmaceuticals but also authorised abortions where birth would pose an undue economic hardship on the mother. The 1952 changes made the physician who would perform the abortion the sole judge of eligibility, assuring that this method remained the preferred mode of birth control in Japan for many years to come.[70]

On 15 July 1948, two days after the revision of the eugenic statute, the Diet enacted the Venereal Disease Control Law. Socialist Diet women had struggled to include that legislation in a single package together with family-planning and anti-prostitution measures, but conservative lawmakers addressed these issues separately to diminish their impact. Progressive on the surface, the Venereal Disease Control Law was fundamentally punitive. It instituted demeaning compulsory pre-marital and pre-nuptial VD examinations and required prospective couples to disclose past incidences of the disease and receive treatment under threat of fine and imprisonment. The Prostitution Prevention Law was not enacted until 1956, and conservative footdragging delayed its implementation until 1958.

Planned parenthood was a contentious moral issue in the United States, and PH&W avoided open involvement in the eugenics controversy. Sams personally believed that economic stability was impossible without some form of population control but was convinced that reindustralisation would solve the problem in the long run by lowering birth rates. Following the enactment of the Eugenic Protection Law, US Catholics accused Sams of promoting abortion, and in June 1948, reacting to harsh criticism from religious pressure groups, MacArthur's headquarters announced that population control was beyond the jurisdiction of the Occupation. GHQ also distanced itself publicly from family planning advocates, denying entry in 1949 to Margaret Sanger, who had been invited by Katō Shizue and the *Yomiuri Shinbun*.

Behind the scenes, however, PH&W worked to promote the aims of Katō and Ōta. Through the Rockefeller Foundation, which extolled population control as a prerequisite for economic growth (and investment opportunity), Sams brought a number of demographic consultants to Japan, attaching one of them full-time to his Welfare Division. At PH&W's invitation, John D. Rockefeller Jr visited Japan from late 1946 to early 1947 with two demographers in tow, and in September 1948, the Foundation despatched the Rockefeller Mission to Tokyo to study the population problem. From January to April 1949, with economic stabilisation now the number one Occupation priority, world authority and neo-Malthusian Warren S. Thompson and two colleagues teamed up with the Welfare Ministry's Institute of Population Problems and toured Japan. In meetings with local officials, business executives and opinion leaders across the country, this high-profile delegation delivered the message that family planning was the primary condition for economic rehabilitation.[71]

The Leprosy Prevention Law

PH&W sidestepped the sensitive issue of leprosy control, allowing Japan's archaic Leprosy Prevention Law to stand unchallenged. The Meiji government had passed the first Leprosy Prevention Law in 1907 patterned on similar legislation in Western countries. In the West, leprosy was viewed as the quintessential 'Oriental' malady,[72] and Japanese leaders considered its existence an affront to the nation's pride. Without controlling legislation, it was argued, Japan would never shed the image of an uncivilised, disease-blighted country. The law was amended in 1916, 1929 and 1931, becoming progressively repressive with each revision. The quarantine policy of 1907 was changed to compulsory lifelong incarceration, forced labour became the norm and disobedience, including attempts at escape, were punished by lengthy confinement in unheated isolation cells, where inmates sometimes froze to death in winter. Pregnancies were forcibly terminated, and from 1915, many institutions routinely conducted vasectomies on male inmates. Sterilisation also was a condition for marriage. The National Eugenic Law of 1940 had eliminated 'eugenic surgery' for lepers, but the 1948 statute ironically restored it.[73]

Nonetheless, under Occupation rule, conditions improved for patients in small but significant ways. In 1947, Communist Diet members drew attention to the practice of solitary confinement and the resulting deaths, sparking nationwide protests from leprosy sufferers. The practice was abolished the same year. The administration of leprosaria also was liberalised, and internees were able to elect representatives to the patients' committees that now helped run the institutions. This led in 1951 to the formation of the National Council of Leprosaria Inmates, which began to organise politically and trans-regionally. By this time, medical science had achieved major breakthroughs in the treatment of Hansen's disease. Sulfone and other drug therapies had appeared in the 1940s, making it possible to slow and, in many cases, arrest the progress of the illness. Cases of actual improvement also were recorded. Armed with this information, the National Council began work on a legislative draft reflecting the new realities. The statute as it then stood was in clear violation of Article 25 of the Constitution, which not only guaranteed a minimum standard of wholesome living but obliged the state to extend basic social protections to all citizens.

When the Welfare Ministry learned that a lawmaker intended to present a member's bill to Parliament, it hastily convened hearings in November 1951 and introduced pre-emptive legislation of its own. In line with postwar reforms, the government bill included an anti-discrimination clause, expanded family relief and assistance programmes and provided for the education of children, but it retained many of the degrading and oppressive features of the old law. The draft repeated the old assertion that leprosy is an incurable disease. It continued to oblige physicians to report carriers to the government and retained compulsory labour requirements, prohibitions on operating a business, permanent incarceration, decontamination procedures and punishments for violators. Despite protests from sufferers and their supporters, the revised Leprosy Prevention Law was enacted on 15 August 1953.[74]

PH&W appears to have watched these proceedings from afar. In 1949, the Welfare Ministry decided to retain its policy of complete sequestration, but Sams and his staff posed no objections. That the Section refrained from offering guidance is all the more surprising in light of social developments in the United States. In 1946, the Federal Security Agency (forerunner of the Department of Health, Education and Welfare) had set up a National Advisory Committee on Leprosy to review the policy of segregation and forcible confinement. By 1949, veterans' groups, labour unions and patients' associations were lobbying to pass a National Leprosy Bill. Distinguishing between cured, arrested and latent cases, activists demanded a medical discharge policy, the elimination of travel restrictions, rehabilitation and vocational training. The proposal was never enacted, but PH&W must have known of its existence. The late start of the debate on Hansen's disease in 1951 as the Occupation was winding down and the prominent involvement of the Communist Party may partially explain PH&W's reticence. A fuller answer must await further inquiry.[75]

MINORITIES

The Occupation reforms failed to achieve their full promise for indigenous Ainu, Okinawans, the *Buraku* minority (*Burakumin*) and ethnic Formosans and Koreans. Progressive intellectuals and the left in general assumed that liberalisation, by eradicating the vestiges of feudal ideology and privilege, would complete the 'bourgeois revolution' begun in 1868 and eliminate such pre-modern residues as cultural and ethnic discrimination.[76] MacArthur's command, however, failed to challenge racism in its various dimensions, tacitly condoning, and in some cases abetting, prejudicial attitudes and behaviour.

A promise of reform

Japan's insular exclusiveness towards ethnic minorities was partially a reaction to the humiliations it had suffered itself at the hands of Western imperialism since the late nineteenth century. The rage this inequitable treatment engendered was easily displaced onto Okinawans, Formosans and Koreans as Japan successively incorporated their homelands into its Empire. Attitudes towards colonial and semi-colonial subjects also were coloured by long-standing prejudice against *Burakumin*, a group formerly stigmatised as outcastes, and the indigenous Ainu inhabitants of the northern frontier, the first victims of Japan's modern expansion.

Under Imperial rule, Japan ostensibly was a multi-ethnic society, and all non-Yamato groups were, in principle, Japanese nationals and subjects of the Emperor. Policies of forcible assimilation, however, first imposed on the Ainu, were extended successively to Okinawans, Formosans and Koreans. Designed to minimise cultural and ethnic differences while preserving Yamato supremacy, these measures actually reinforced such distinctions by creating a dual standard of citizenship and treatment. From the late 1930s, social-control policies were intensified in order to transform non-Yamato nationals into loyal and obedient 'children of the Emperor', a process known as *kōminka*. Formosans and Koreans were compelled to adopt Japanese names (*sōshi-kaimei*), dress and manners; to speak only Japanese in public places; and to inscribe their families in Japanese-style household registries (*koseki*). Just as the Allies had incorporated colonial subjects and other marginalised groups into their armed forces, so the Imperial Army conscripted its minorities, organising them into segregated ethnic units and assigning them labour, guard and other menial duties.

Between 1944 and the summer of 1945, US Army and State Department planners commissioned a number of studies on the Japanese underclass. Relatively little was known about the Ainu. The *Buraku* problem drew more attention. In 1942 the Office of Strategic Services (OSS) had prepared two reports on the latter ('The Eta – A Persecuted Group in Japan'), and William Karpinsky, SCAP's first Labour Division chief, had discussed the issue in his graduation paper for Harvard's Civil Affairs Training School, comparing *Buraku* groups to African Americans. In 1944, Yale cultural anthropologist George P. Murdock surveyed the literature available on Okinawa and compiled a dossier on the Ryukyus. The OSS also prepared studies on 'aliens', which dealt almost exclusively with Formosans and Koreans, whom the OSS categorised as foreigners despite their nominal Japanese nationality. The OSS report became the basis of a US Army Civil Affairs Guide on aliens in Japan, published in the summer of 1945.[77] Pre-surrender studies were fragmentary, however, and MacArthur began the Occupation without a detailed, programmatic position on minorities.

Nonetheless, prewar planners were aware of cultural and ethnic discrimination. As indicated in chapter 8, SWNCC-162/D of July 1945 had linked Japan's Imperial cult with 'an extreme racial consciousness and an anti-foreign complex'. Basic US policy documents reflected the same concern. SWNCC's 'US Initial Post-Surrender Policy for Japan' of 22 September 1945 and GHQ's Civil Liberties Directive of 4 October expressly forbade laws that established discrimination on grounds of race or nationality. The constitutional control document SWNCC-228 ('The Reform of the Japanese Governmental System') of January 1946 was even more explicit. It stipulated that not only Japanese subjects but '*all persons within Japanese jurisdiction*' (emphasis added) be guaranteed the same fundamental civil and political rights. The Meiji Constitution, the SWNCC document said, fell short of other national charters because it applied only to Japanese subjects and left non-Japanese without adequate rights: '[T]he guarantee of fundamental civil rights both to Japanese subjects and to all persons within Japanese jurisdiction would create a healthy condition for the development of democratic ideas and would provide foreigners in Japan with a degree of protection which they have not heretofore enjoyed'.[78]

Surprisingly, before the end of the war, the Japanese government, too, had considered extending equal rights to colonial subjects, albeit for different reasons. Colonial law had distinguished between *naichijin*, nationals enjoying full citizenship by virtue of maintaining household registers in Japan proper, and *gaichijin*, second-class nationals registered in Japan's colonies and having relatively few rights. In 1922, the Governor General of Korea outlawed the transfer of colonial registers to Japan proper, thereby institutionalising this distinction. When the government began conscripting Koreans in 1942, however, it was compelled to emphasise ethnic equality in an effort to ensure the loyalty of colonial soldiers and workers. In November 1944, the Cabinet approved plans to eliminate shopfloor discrimination, remove restrictions on travel between Japan and Korea and permit Koreans in Japan to transfer their family registers from the colonial periphery to the Imperial metropolis. The relocation of colonial records to Japan effectively would have granted resident Koreans and Formosans voting and other civil rights, but the war ended before this programme could be implemented.[79]

Following the defeat, Japanese leaders moved quickly to close that door of opportunity, eliminate multi-ethnic vestiges and disempower erstwhile colonial subjects, convinced that their presence now was a threat to the survival of the Imperial Order. The revision of the Lower House Election Law on 17 December 1945 abrogated the right of resident Koreans and Formosans to vote or hold office.

It was feared that, armed with the ballot, former colonials would join Communists in pressing for the abolition of the emperor system. The new law's recondite jargon 'suspended for the time being' the voting rights of any resident whose household register was not kept in the Japanese main islands, thereby disfranchising the vast majority of Formosan and Korean residents.[80]

Not only did SCAP fail to challenge this law, but three months later Government Section allowed Japanese legal experts to veto constitutional proposals for the protection of minorities. Based on US pre-surrender planning documents, the GS Civil Rights Subcommittee incorporated in its February 1946 draft of the MacArthur Constitution explicit human rights guarantees for Koreans, Formosans and *Burakumin*. Article 13 read 'All natural persons are equal before the law. No discrimination shall be authorised or tolerated in political, economic or social relations on account of race, creed, social status, *caste or national origin*' (emphasis added). Article 16 stated simply 'Aliens shall be entitled to the equal protection of law.' As the Japanese side revised the working draft in March, it modified the language of the GS document, eliminating from Article 13 the term 'national origin' and altering 'all natural persons' (*shizenjin*) to 'all of the people'. For the English term 'people', however, it substituted the Japanese word 'nationals' (*kokumin*), thereby restricting the scope of this provision to Japanese citizens. Unlike *shizenjin* ('person' in natural law) or *jinmin* ('people', but with a leftist connotation), *kokumin* carries the paternalistic nuance of an ethnically homogeneous *Volk* indivisible from the nation-state. Article 16 with its equal rights provisions was simply deleted. Satō Tatsuo, Deputy Chief of the Cabinet Legislation Bureau and the government's leading constitutional specialist, later wrote that 'the idea of treating foreigners equally was bad enough in itself, but having to include Article 16 in the Japanese draft was particularly objectionable'. Satō almost certainly had in mind Korean and Formosan residents, whose legal status had become ambiguous since the liberation of their homelands from Japanese rule.[81]

During subsequent Diet debates, the Cabinet Legislation Bureau insisted that a clause, Article 10, be inserted at the beginning of Chapter 3 (Rights and Duties of the People), stating that 'the conditions necessary for being a Japanese national shall be determined by law'. Unlike US legal practice, which grants citizenship automatically to anyone born on US soil (*jus solis*), until 1985, Japanese law based nationality on the principle of patrilineal consanguinity (*jus sanguinis*). Thus, only someone born of a Japanese father was legally Japanese. The Cabinet Legislation Bureau added Article 10, Government Section's Charles Kades said later, 'to be very sure that it would be difficult for aliens to become Japanese citizens'.[82]

Burakumin, too, were denied specific protection. For the word 'caste' in GHQ's original Article 13, Japanese legists substituted the vague and almost meaningless expression 'family origin', thereby expunging from the Constitution an explicit guarantee of equality for Japan's 1 million former outcastes.[83] Nor did the Constitution recognise the indigenous status of the Ainu, who were lumped together in the undifferentiated category of 'Japanese national'. Okinawans, too, were Japanese nationals, but SCAP had detached the Ryukyus from the home islands and placed them under direct US military administration, denying their inhabitants any constitutional protection at all.

Government Section's constitutional drafting committee deferred to strong Japanese feelings on the question of minority rights, just as it did on the issue of guarantees for women (chapter 6). Afraid of provoking a backlash and endangering provisions deemed more important, it did not contest these changes. Many years later, Kades recalled that, while GS preferred the original wording, his orders from Whitney were to object only if a basic principle were involved. On the elimination of GHQ's Article 16, he noted laconically that '[t]here was no controversy between Mr Sato and me'. Kades asserted his belief that the final Japanese version, now Article 14, was adequate to protect the rights of minorities. It reads: 'All of the people [in Japanese, *'all nationals'*] are equal under the law and there shall be no discrimination in political, economic or social relations because of race, creed, sex, social status or family origin'. In a subsequent interview, however, Kades remarked candidly that in the United States at the time, 'aliens were not 100 per cent equal to American citizens. So I felt how can we insist that it is a basic principle to put [aliens in Japan] on the same level with Japanese people?' The Far Eastern Commission in Washington criticised the absence of explicit rights guarantees for non-Japanese in its review of the Constitution, which began in January 1949. On 5 May of that year, the Commission sent a query to SCAP entitled 'Position of Aliens Under the Constitution', noting that the charter was 'not clear' on this point, but the review itself was a pro forma exercise to begin with, and MacArthur's staff, by then engaged in a crack-down on leftist Koreans, had no intention of addressing the issue.[84]

The Ainu

The Ainu are an indigenous people who once occupied most of northeastern Japan. Following the Meiji Restoration of 1868, the central government aggressively colonised the Ainu homeland (*Ainu moshir*) in Hokkaido to consolidate its control of the archipelago and discourage Russian designs on the Far North. Ainu groups were forcibly relocated and their lands subsequently declared *terra nullius* and parcelled out to impoverished Japanese settlers who converged on Hokkaido in search of free homesteads. In 1899, Tokyo enacted the Hokkaido Former Aborigines' Protection Act to fully assimilate these displaced former hunters and gatherers into the Japanese way of life by offering them 'grants' of their own land and imposing on them an agrarian lifestyle. The Act allocated 5 hectares to each family, but that property was to revert to the state after 15 years if it were not improved upon. About 70 per cent of Hokkaido's Ainu received such land. The allotments could not be sold, but plots could be rented out, and within a decade, the bulk of Ainu land had been transferred to Japanese tenants.[85] The Act also placed Ainu children in segregated schools, where Japanese was taught and the Ainu language rigidly suppressed. These 'Schools for Former Aborigines' were finally abolished when the Act was revised in 1937, by which time relatively few Ainu were able to speak their native tongue fluently. Discrimination was compounded by poverty, and in the 1930s, to escape

Photo 58. An Ainu woman in traditional headdress casts her vote in the general elections of April 1946 at an elementary school in Shiraoi Village, southern Hokkaido. Occupation reforms raised the hopes of Ainu for greater equality but failed to actively defend minority rights or address the problem of ethnic discrimination (Kyodo).

endemic racism and seek new opportunities, a few successful Ainu farmers led Ainu settlement groups to Manchuria, where they farmed alongside Japanese colonists.

Following Japan's defeat in 1945, the Ainu immediately pressed for full social equality. In February 1946, for instance, 200 Ainu from across Hokkaido met to form the Hokkaido Ainu Association. In the spring of 1947, Major General Joseph M. Swing, Commander of the 11th Airborne Division, summoned four Ainu representatives to Sapporo and questioned them about independence. When the elders disavowed any such ambitions, Swing gave each ¥100,000 and dismissed them, presumably in an effort to purchase immunity from Soviet propaganda. Other groups, however, agitated for an 'Ainu Republic'. In July 1948, an Ainu representative addressed a petition for emancipation to the Chinese delegate to the Allied

Council for Japan. The document asked for land and 'a sphere of autonomy based on the right of self-determination of minorities' in order to preserve the Ainu identity and achieve genuine independence. The proposal was forwarded to the US State Department, which filed it without comment.

On the whole, the Ainu looked favourably on the Occupation. One group, for instance, sent MacArthur a deer skin and antlers 'as a token of our grateful appreciation for what he has done to secure land for our people and give to Japan a democratic society, based on law and order'. This gratitude appears misplaced in light of what the Occupation could have done for the Ainu people. Under Allied control, they enjoyed the same freedoms as other Japanese in the main islands, and some ran (unsuccessfully) for local office, but GHQ failed to take positive measures to defend their rights. Herbert Passin of Civil Education and Information Section, meeting young Ainu during a tour of Hokkaido, commented on the dilemma faced by 'despised minority groups . . . not strong enough to control their own destinies: assimilation or preservation of their identity'. Yet GHQ left the paternalistic Hokkaido Former Aborigines' Protection Act intact. Minor revisions implemented in 1946 and 1947 actually penalised the Ainu by abolishing certain welfare measures and tax exemptions.[86]

In one important area, Occupation policy actually discriminated against Japan's indigenous inhabitants. Under the Protection Act, the state had confiscated Ainu land and then returned a part of it to individual families on condition that it be developed for agriculture. The 1946 land reform classified Ainu farmers tilling only part of their grants as absentee landlords and redistributed those holdings to tenants, mainly Yamato Japanese (*wajin*). Despite organised protests to GHQ, many Ainu who farmed primarily for subsistence and engaged in seasonal labour for a living lost their land in this way. Successful Ainu cultivators were treated as large landlords, and they, too, saw large parts of their estates awarded to *wajin* tenants. SCAP reformers ignored minority interests, confirming Japanese ownership and control of the most productive Ainu farmland. In Hokkaido's southern Hidaka region, which boasts the highest concentration of Ainu residents in Japan, the 1946 land reform redistributed more than 30 per cent of the Meiji land grants to Japanese farmers.[87]

Okinawans

During the war, Professor George Murdock and a small group of anthropologists involved in Yale University's Cross Cultural Survey (1937–41) prepared a total of eight Civil Affairs Handbooks for the US Army. Among these was the 334-page *Civil Affairs Handbook, Ryukyu (Loochoo) Islands*, published in November 1944. As with other Handbooks, the authors relied on Japanese sources for more than 95 per cent of their data, thus reproducing many of the stereotypes held by Japanese writers, who regarded Ryukyuans as a backward, inferior breed of Japanese. Unlike Japanese anthropologists and linguists who stressed the similarities with Yamato Japanese, however, Murdock ignored considerable evidence to the contrary and characterised Okinawans as culturally, linguistically and racially distinct. From July through

October 1945, as a Navy Lieutenant Commander, he headed the Civil Affairs Department in the Ryukyus Military Government, where his ideas perpetuated the notion that the Ryukyus were a separate cultural and political entity.[88]

Okinawans fared poorly under occupation compared to Japanese in the home islands, both economically and in terms of civil and political freedoms. Agricultural production increased dramatically after the defeat, but US installations gradually crowded out prime farmland, and by 1947, more than one third of Okinawa's arable surface lay under roads and runways or behind barbed wire. During the garrison phase of occupation, which began in September 1945, US military authorities enforced restrictions on land use in the vicinity of military bases. One of these, the 'one-mile limit', prohibited the maintenance of any Okinawan building within a one-mile (1.6 km) radius of military billeting or dependent housing projects of more than 100 people. Army public health officials intended to create a sanitary cordon around base areas to combat mosquito-borne and epidemic diseases, but this measure imposed an enormous hardship on local farmers, who were forced from their homes into cramped, insalubrious resettlement centres far from their fields. In Okinawa's fertile farm belt in the central Nakagami District, more than half of the land under crops fell within this no-man's zone.[89]

To Ryukyuans, landownership was more than a livelihood. An integral part of the Okinawan identity, it was heavily freighted with ancestral and communal values. The alienation of this property tore at the very fabric of Okinawan society. With nothing but their labour to sell, many Ryukyuans found themselves employed on military bases and construction sites, building airfields, military highways and housing for American soldiers and their families. Until 1949, the cost of this work was borne by Tokyo, not Washington. Under-Secretary of the Army William H. Draper glibly explained in August 1948 that, although administratively detached from the mainland, 'the Ryukyu Islands, as a prefecture of Japan, remain a legal responsibility of the Japanese Government'. From 1946 through 1948, MacArthur's headquarters pursued a policy of studied neglect towards the archipelago, and with basic installations in place, military construction fell off precipitously and, with it, jobs. Economically, the region stagnated. This period in island life has been characterised by an American military historian as one of 'apathy and neglect', during which Okinawa became a scrap yard for discarded World War II equipment and, in his words, 'human cast-offs from the Far East Command'.[90]

Many GIs held the Okinawans in open contempt. Initially, such disdain reflected the savage fighting that had taken place in the archipelago in the closing months of the war. Rape became so commonplace in the wake of battle that the Army decreed the death penalty for offenders in an attempt to curb its incidence. Serious crime remained endemic throughout the American tenure. During one six-month period in 1949, *Life Magazine*, in an article entitled 'Okinawa Junk Heap', reported 16 robberies, 33 assaults, 18 rapes and 29 murders committed by GIs. The Army's rigid segregation policies, even more stringent than in the Japanese home islands, aggravated racial animosities between white and African-American troops, and these tensions were displaced onto Okinawans. When Philippine Scouts replaced black soldiers in early 1947, they, too, found the local population a convenient target on which to vent their frustrations (the Scouts remained until 1949).[91]

Denied basic constitutional protections, Ryukyuans enjoyed relatively few of the liberties taken for granted in Japan proper. Equal treatment, the Pentagon feared, would impede construction of the permanent military bases it sought on Okinawa. As one historian has commented, 'The democratic rights guaranteed to other Japanese applied to Okinawans only to the extent necessary to secure the cooperation of local workers on whom the bases depended.'[92] The programme of democratic reform SCAP implemented in the main islands and the very different policies of neglect and repression the US command pursued in Okinawa were two sides of the same coin. With the Ryukyus safely in US military hands, MacArthur could afford to espouse pacifism and govern Japan proper indirectly and in a spirit of leniency. Predictably, gross insensitivity to Ryukyuan rights and culture sparked frequent outbursts of popular resentment. When base workers attempted to strike, however, they found themselves facing Yankee bayonets. (Paradoxically, however, while this unequal relation of force limited the scope of union activism, it produced a labour movement more militant and tenacious than that in the home islands.)

Direct military governance meant military control of all aspects of Okinawan life. SCAP's purge programme was not operative in the Ryukyus, and US civil affairs officers relied on the old conservative élite in establishing the local political structures of civil administration. Thus, in many instances, the transition from Japanese to American military rule was seamless. For example, the Ryukyus Military Government appointed Naha's wartime mayor Tōma Jūgō to continue in that position after the war. A former member of the Imperial Rule Assistance Association, Tōma later became chief executive of the Okinawan government.

The US military divided the Ryukyus into 16 Military Government Districts (12 of them on Okinawa Island), and in August 1945, it authorised the creation of an Okinawan Advisory Council to assist the Deputy MG Commander. Under Navy tutelage (September 1945 to July 1946), the rudiments of local self-government were put in place.[93] A mission from SCAP's Government Section recommended electoral reform, and in January 1948, an election law was promulgated by military decree, allowing popular balloting for local mayors and assembly members. February's elections gave rise to Okinawa's first postwar political parties, which included Socialists and a leftist labour grouping, the Okinawa People's Party. Under military control, genuine self-government, with its implications for independence, was not permitted to emerge, however, and the machinery of local self-rule served primarily to speed the implementation of military decrees.[94]

In light of the Imperial Army's depredations, many Okinawans initially hailed the Americans as liberators, but the US Military Government's style of neo-colonial rule soon eroded what goodwill existed. To parry anti-American sentiment, US authorities attempted to foster separatist sentiment, utilising arguments similar to those advanced in 1944 by Murdock's Yale group. Okinawans were fiercely proud of their distinctive cultural heritage, but many also felt a cultural affinity for Japan despite the wartime horrors they had suffered. The overbearing American presence reinforced those feelings. As an American anthropologist of Okinawan descent has noted, the US attempt to force Okinawans to choose a semi-colonial, marginalised Ryukyuan identity over a Japanese identity was viewed 'as a thinly veiled "racist" contempt for Okinawans as an inferior people'. *Uchinanchu* (Okinawans) emphasised their distinctive language and culture with respect to *Yamatonchu* (Yamato Japanese), but that was not the affair of the United States. 'It was wrong', the anthropologist writes, 'for Americans to manipulate Japanese-Okinawan differences in ways prejudicial to Okinawans.' Whence the assertion, *vis-à-vis* the United States, of an intrinsically problematic loyalty to Japan. From 1948, Okinawans would attempt to rid the islands of de facto American colonial rule by demanding reversion to Japan (chapter 10).[95]

Okinawa as political pawn

American military authorities made no apologies for the subservient status of Okinawa. Brigadier General William E. Crist, appointed Deputy Commander for Military Government after the islands' capture in June 1945, explained US aims there as achieving military objectives at the least possible cost to the United States. 'We have no intention of playing Santa Claus for the residents of the occupied territory', he remarked, setting the tone for America's long and unpopular tenure in the archipelago. On 1 January 1947, the Ryukyus Command was placed under MacArthur's reorganised Far East Command and instructed to maintain exclusive American control of the archipelago until its future was decided. The Ryukyus Command's first objective was the 'liquidation of political, social and economic ties with the Japanese mainland'. The reasons for this separation became clear on 1 September when MacArthur protested a State Department proposal to return the Ryukyus to Japan with the signing of a peace treaty. In a cable to Secretary of State George C. Marshall, he wrote: 'Control over this group must be vested in the United States as absolutely essential to the defence of our Western Pacific Frontier. It is not indigenous to Japan ethnologically, does not contribute to Japan's economic welfare, nor do the Japanese people expect to be permitted to retain it. It is basically strategic and, in my opinion, failure to secure it for control by the United States might prove militarily disastrous.'[96] With the onset of the Cold War, American strategists came to view the Ryukyus as the lynchpin in a chain of island territories stretching from Micronesia and the former Japanese mandates in the Pacific to Japan proper. This strategic arc was perceived as America's first line of defence against Communism in the Far East, and Washington stubbornly denied the other Allies any voice in administering the 'keystone of the Pacific'.

In September 1947, as MacArthur was advocating the need for long-term control over the archipelago, Emperor Hirohito despatched Imperial aide Terasaki Hidenari to deliver a secret message from the monarch to William Sebald arguing for protracted American rule there. On 20 September, Sebald sent MacArthur a memorandum summarising the Imperial Note. Entitled 'Emperor of Japan's Opinion Concerning the Future of the Ryukyu Islands', it stated: 'the Emperor hopes that the United States will continue the military occupation of Okinawa and other islands of the Ryukyus. In the Emperor's opinion, such an occupation would benefit the United States and also provide protection for Japan.' The Note explained that after the Occupation, Russia would emerge as the primary menace to the security of Japan. US control of Okinawa would discourage Moscow from direct interference in Japanese affairs. Hirohito was remarkably precise about the modality of US control. 'The Emperor further feels that United States military occupation of Okinawa (and such other islands as may be required) should be based upon the fiction of a long-term lease – 25 to 50 years or more – with sovereignty retained in Japan.' According to Sebald's memorandum, Terasaki then made a personal proposal: 'Mr. Terasaki felt that the acquisition of "military base rights" (of Okinawa and other islands in the Ryukyus) should be by bilateral treaty between the United States and Japan rather than form part of the Allied peace treaty with Japan.'[97]

In short, the Emperor was proposing to support American bases in the Ryukyus in return for a demilitarised mainland. This irresponsible and reckless act of intervention belied the Emperor's supposedly depoliticised status under the 1947 Constitution and indicates the influence that the Court, shorn of its former authority but assured of 'symbolic' continuity, was capable of wielding behind the scenes. Washington had considered a strategic trusteeship for the Ryukyus under UN auspices, but now Hirohito was offering direct military control for up to half a century. Since mid-1945, the State Department had argued for the early return of the Ryukyus to Tokyo. By late 1947, however, George F. Kennan, director of the Department's Policy Planning Staff, was counselling a reassessment of America's long-term goals in Japan and Asia. On 15 October, three weeks after Sebald informed Washington of Hirohito's proposal, Kennan noted in a policy document for discussion that the Emperor's 'formula might well be explored as an alternative to strategic trusteeship'.[98] This suggestion appears to have been acted on, for, in 1951, secret bilateral negotiations effectively ceded control of the Ryukyus to the United States, with Japan retaining 'residual sovereignty', for an additional 20 years beyond the end of the Occupation (chapter 10).

Coming shortly after MacArthur's impassioned plea to Secretary of State Marshall to retain Okinawa as an American base, the Imperial Note may have reflected prior discussions between the Supreme Commander and the Japanese sovereign. Certainly, the Emperor had nothing to lose by making such a request. Hirohito had been absolved of war complicity in June 1946, but in the autumn of 1947, pressure to have him testify before the Tokyo War Crimes Tribunal was mounting. This concern may explain Sebald's comment in his cover letter to Marshall of 22 September that the Emperor's Okinawa proposal 'undoubtedly is largely based upon self-interest'. In any event, one week later, on 30 September, Special Prosecutor Joseph Keenan announced that the Tribunal would not summon the monarch as a witness.[99]

Photo 59. An Okinawa peasant tills her land under the shadow of an American aircraft. Ever expanding base installations robbed many islanders of their livelihood, creating deep animosity towards US military rule. Kadena Air Base, Okinawa. Undated (Asahi).

Burakumin
Defeat ostensibly liberated Japan's more than 1 million *Burakumin* from prewar oppression. *Buraku* persecution dated from pre-modern times, when feudal lords compelled certain non-agrarian occupational groups to live in segregated settlements (*buraku*) and perform such tasks as butchery, leather tanning and meat processing. Buddhist thought considered these activities ritually defiling, and such special-status groups were required to live apart from and avoid contact with commoners. This status hierarchy solidified in the seventeenth century, but the boundaries defining 'polluted' groups were continually redrawn throughout the Tokugawa period to assure a system of effective but decentralised control.[100] In 1871, following the Meiji Restoration, *Burakumin* were freed from feudal restraints and declared 'new commoners' but continued to live in ghettos and perform work society considered base, particularly meat and leather processing. *Buraku* militants challenged their caste-like untouchable status in 1922 with the creation of the *Suiheisha* (Levelling Society), but political activism, often leftist-orientated and anti-imperialist, was severely suppressed under the Peace Preservation Law. Japan's defeat in 1945 seemed to offer *Buraku* communities the possibility of a fuller emancipation.

Few Americans had more than a rudimentary awareness of the *Buraku* problem when the Occupation began. Government Section's Kades first learned of 'the Suiheisha issue' from Canadian diplomat E. H. Norman. In early 1946, however, *Buraku* organisations in southwestern Japan inundated General Headquarters with appeals to end oppressive treatment, many of them addressed directly to the Supreme Commander. Several SCAP groups, including Civil Information and Education, Civil Intelligence, Government, Legal, and Public Health and Welfare, received reports of *Buraku* persecution and demands for redress. Internal Government Section memoranda indicate that staff officers initially were committed in principle to eradicating informal social as well as institutional discrimination, but from 1948, GS increasingly took a hands-off attitude towards such issues. In part, American officials did not grasp the full dimensions of the *Buraku* problem. Karpinsky, in his March 1945 'Survey of Japanese Labor', for instance, failed to understand why *Burakumin* should be treated as black Americans were in the United States since they were physically and culturally indistinguishable from other Japanese. At the local level, Military Government and Civil Affairs Teams compiled the occasional report on *Buraku* discrimination but did not recommend remedial action.[101]

A rare SCAP official who advocated counter-measures was CI&E's Herbert Passin, who encountered the *Buraku* problem when he surveyed 13 farm villages between 1947 and 1948 to evaluate the land reform. Six of the hamlets were *Buraku* settlements. Passin subsequently wrote three reports on the issue and attempted to pressure the government into undertaking its own survey, but Section Chief Donald Nugent refused to support the proposal, which was quietly abandoned, and the government took no action on the problem during the Occupation. (A national census of *Buraku* communities would not be conducted until 1975.) Sams's Public Health and Welfare Section also showed little sensitivity to *Buraku* discrimination. In

March 1946, the Welfare Ministry instructed municipalities to discontinue special subsidies the government had authorised in 1936 as part of a 10-year programme to alleviate the appalling conditions in *Buraku* ghettos. PH&W apparently failed to challenge this decision, or consider palliative measures of its own.[102]

Kades and other high-ranking staff officers believed that the Constitution's Article 14 had eliminated *Buraku* persecution as a social problem. Nonetheless, Kades and other GS staff initially encouraged the activities of *Buraku* leader Matsumoto Ji'ichirō. Assuming leadership of the *Suiheisha* in the 1920s, Matsumoto had been elected to the Diet in 1938 representing the Social Masses Party, a moderate left-wing political formation. After the war, he helped reorganise the *Suiheisha* as the National Committee for *Buraku* Liberation (from 1955, the *Buraku* Liberation League). Between 1946 and 1948, GS intervened energetically on three occasions to prevent the government from purging Matsumoto as a putative rightist. In the second post-war general elections of April 1947, Matsumoto, running as a Socialist, won a seat in the Upper House and was promptly elected Vice President of that body, an unprecedented turn of events suggestive of the visionary temper of the times. As the Occupation shifted course, however, SCAP's patronage of the activist wavered, and by early 1949, the *Buraku* liberation movement and GHQ had come to blows in the political arena (chapter 10).[103]

Like the Ainu, *Burakumin* also were penalised by the land reform, which discriminated against small tenancies. About 30 per cent of all *Buraku* tenants worked less than 0.3 hectares, a figure that Occupation reformers considered disqualifying for successful ownership. As a result, these small-scale producers were excluded from the land reallotment programme, although many later renegotiated a transfer of land with local agricultural land commissions.[104] *Burakumin* were disproportionately represented among the 7 per cent of Japanese farmers who continued in tenancy arrangements after the reform.

Koreans and Formosans

By the war's end, there were an estimated 2.4 million Koreans and some 40,000 Formosans and other Chinese living in Japan – the vast majority 'slave labourers', as a 1946 Counter-Intelligence Corps survey described them. Of the 2.4 million Koreans, 1.16 million were male labourers, 1 million women and 240,000 small entrepreneurs, white-collar workers and students. The US Army's *Civil Affairs Guide: Aliens in Japan* (June 1945) had called for positive steps to protect Koreans from social and economic discrimination and Japanese reprisals after the war, noting that 'after the 1923 earthquake, widespread violence against Koreans occurred' (in fact, more than 6,000, or half of the Kanto region's Korean population, had been massacred by Japanese police and vigilante groups). Paradoxically, however, the Guide also urged their continued interim use as coolie labour for such strategic tasks as railway and road maintenance.[105]

In keeping with the Cairo Declaration of 1943, which had declared that 'in due course Korea shall become free and independent', the Army's 'Basic Directive' of

Photo 60. Korean girls between the ages of 8 and 14 await repatriation at Hakata, Kyushu. Members of a children's 'volunteer' labour corps mobilised by Japanese authorities for factory work, they are returning home to Cholla Namdo in southern Korea. Some 650,000 Koreans opted to remain in Japan. 19 October 1945 (Mainichi).

November 1945 declared Koreans and Formosans to be 'liberated peoples'. The document also stipulated, however, that, although they were not included in the term Japanese as used in the directive, they could be treated as enemy nationals should military security require it.[106] In practice, this implied that, while former colonials were free to repatriate and would receive rations and free rail transport to embarkation points, they would be treated as Japanese should they opt to remain. In fact, SCAP regarded former colonials as displaced persons or 'wards of the United States',[107] not as long-term residents with acquired rights of domicile. Subsequent Occupation policy perpetuated that ambiguous status, treating Koreans alternately as Japanese nationals and as aliens, as was convenient.

SCAP's official repatriation programme began in December 1945, but tens of thousands of Koreans already had converged on Japan's southern ports to await transportation, and by the end of 1945, more than 1.3 million had returned home. In February 1946, Public Health and Welfare Section instructed Japan's Welfare Ministry to register all Koreans, Chinese, Formosans and Ryukyuans to determine whether or not they intended to repatriate (SCAPIN-746: 'Repatriation of Koreans, Chinese, Ryukyuans, and Formosans'). The Ministry's tally, announced in March, recorded a total of 647,000 Koreans and some 30,000 Chinese and Formosans. Of the Koreans, only 133,000 expressed a desire to remain in Japan, but in fact, some

650,000, mainly long-term residents with prewar roots in the country, eventually opted to stay. Various factors prompted the decision to remain. In November 1945, GHQ had imposed a ¥1,000 limit on the amount of property returnees – Japanese and Koreans – could take home with them. The equivalent of 20 packs of cigarettes, this sum would barely support a family for one week in inflation-ridden Korea. Floods, epidemic diseases, rice riots, lack of housing and jobs, prejudice against repatriates, political instability and a homeland occupied by US and Soviet troops convinced many to stay in Japan, or, having departed, to return as soon as possible.[108]

In November 1945, ESS Labour Division Chief Karpinsky issued SCAPIN-360 ('Employment Policies') specifically banning employment discrimination against Koreans, Formosans and Chinese. By SCAP order, former colonials also were eligible to receive emergency relief supplies. Such protective measures were exceptional, however, and Japanese authorities made little effort to enforce them. When it became clear in early 1946 that large numbers of Koreans intended to remain in Japan, SCAP's attitude towards this minority changed perceptibly. In February and March, Legal Section made Koreans, ostensibly liberated people, subject to Japanese criminal jurisdiction, and G-2 issued a series of directives between April and June authorising police to tighten surveillance over their social and political activities. In June, a G-3 directive (SCAPIN-1015: 'Suppression of Illegal Entry') designed to prevent the spread of cholera outlawed the movement of people between Japan and Korea and ordered the government to detect entry violations and deport illegal entrants. Finally, in July, PH&W announced that Koreans would receive the same rations as Japanese, and ESS declared they would have to pay the same taxes.

The G-3 directive on illegal entry marked a turning point. Although intended as an emergency health decree, the SCAPIN assumed a life of its own. A sequel issued in December 1946 considerably strengthened the earlier instruction. By then cholera had been eliminated as a major health threat, but SCAP found the travel ban useful for other purposes: the suppression of smuggling and the entry of 'subversive elements'. This directive entailed enormous hardships for war-divided families anxious to be reunited, and the threat of deportation that now hung over the head of every Korean unable to prove residence in Japan gave police a powerful lever in dealing with this minority.

The government, having disenfranchised Korean and Formosan residents in late 1945 and written them out of its constitutional draft in early 1946, now sought to expel as many as possible. In June 1946, the Home Ministry via the Central Liaison Office asked SCAP for sweeping powers in deporting Korean 'troublemakers'. GHQ rejected the proposal on the grounds that 'it was discriminatory and was not designed to be universally applied to all foreign nationals'.[109] From that point onward, however, American and Japanese authorities began to consult closely on the so-called Korean problem. In October 1945, SCAP had set up a Korean Division inside Government Section to coordinate the repatriation programme with the US Military Government in southern Korea. In February 1947, the Division was relieved of its responsibilities, but its small core of Korean experts would continue to deal with Koreans in Japan throughout the Occupation. Among them was then-Captain Jack P. Napier, who developed a tight working relationship with veteran Korean handlers in the Home Ministry's Survey and Analysis Section, which had exercised jurisdiction over colonial subjects prior to the surrender.

In November 1946, MacArthur's headquarters made public an internal policy decision (taken secretly in May) that Koreans refusing repatriation would be considered as retaining their Japanese nationality 'for purposes of treatment' until such time as a duly established Korean government accorded them recognition as Korean citizens. The creation of a Korean state would resolve the question of legal status, but until then, Koreans would be treated as Japanese nationals and required to obey all Japanese laws. This move infuriated Koreans residents, who, having just been emancipated from Japanese rule, were now being returned arbitrarily to their pre-liberation status of Japanese nationals second-class.

The government pressed SCAP to take even stronger action, however, and in early 1947, having just declared Koreans to be Japanese nationals, Occupation officials now directed the government to register them as aliens 'for the time being'. The Alien Registration Ordinance (ARO) of 2 May 1947 was drafted 'for administrative and control purposes' by the GS Korean specialists and their counterparts in the Home Ministry. The Ministry proposed giving police broad powers to administer the registration. Government Section's Alfred C. Oppler and others objected to this provision, and that authority was transferred instead to the heads of municipal governments. The Ministry also sought for prefectural governors the right to deport violators of the ordinance, a unilateral power that Oppler criticised as unconstitutional. He insisted that an appeals procedure be instituted at the district-court level.[110] Despite such modifications, however, the resulting legislation aroused immediate controversy. Enacted as an Imperial ('Potsdam') decree in order to avoid parliamentary debate on the issue, the ARO entered into force one day before the new Constitution went into effect. It became the last Imperial Ordinance promulgated under the Meiji Constitution, an irony that was not lost on Koreans.

The 1947 Alien Registration Ordinance appeared on the surface to be a national version of an earlier Osaka statute requiring Koreans to register,[111] but its real inspiration was the US Alien Registration (Smith) Act of 1940, which had introduced alien registration, complete with fingerprinting, in the United States on the eve of World War II (chapter 10). The ARO pointedly did not include fingerprinting, but it mirrored other provisions of the US statute. Koreans and Formosans were obliged to register at age 14 and carry an alien passbook at all times. Failure to comply was a deportable offence, a stipulation that implicitly undermined the legal status of former colonials as Japanese nationals. Moreover, the passbook was virtually identical in format to that issued between 1936 and 1945 by the Racial Harmony Association (*Kyōwakai*) as part of the government's efforts to control and 'Japanise' these minorities. The Ordinance, as a SCAP summary put it, also 'gave the police a register of potential [*sic*] troublesome aliens'. Koreans deeply resented the statute, which they saw as an extension of the *Kyōwakai* system, and widespread opposition delayed its implementation by nearly half a year. The 'dog-tag registration' was so violently resisted, a G-2 report concluded, that 'Koreans succeeded in virtually defeating the purpose of the law'.[112]

A 'restless, uprooted minority'

Like Koreans, Japan's 30,000-strong Chinese community, primarily Formosans, had been declared liberated people, and although technically they should have been classified as Allied nationals, SCAP initially treated them as it did Koreans. Japanese pejoratively referred to both groups as 'third-country nationals' (*daisan-kokujin*), since they fell into neither the Allied nor enemy category. Two thirds of Koreans were unemployed, and Formosans fared no better. With no means of subsistence, many turned to black-market activities and the illegal distillation of liquor. In early 1946, an Osaka survey indicated that of 16,000 'open-air merchants', 70 per cent were Japanese and 30 per cent Koreans and Formosans, but 'third-country nationals' made handy scapegoats for these disruptive activities, and for rising urban crime rates as rival Korean, Formosan and Japanese gangs jockeyed for control of this lucrative but illegal trade. In June 1946, Formosan street vendors clashed with Japanese gangsters in the vast black market near Shibuya Station in Tokyo. As tensions escalated, in July, several hundred black-marketeers, some armed with pistols, iron bars and wooden clubs, clashed with police in front of the Shibuya Police Station, resulting in the death of seven Formosans and one police officer.[113]

More than 40 Formosans were arrested in connection with the incident and indicted by an Allied Military Commission, but the Chinese Liaison Mission in Tokyo intervened energetically on their behalf. As a result, the trial was prolonged and a Chinese diplomat appointed to sit on the Military Commission. Chinese pressure also forced GHQ to place on trial the police officers responsible for opening fire on the Formosans. According to the official SCAP statement, these gestures were made 'pursuant to General MacArthur's desire to give all possible assistance and consideration to Chinese interests in Japan'. Thirty-five Formosans eventually were convicted, sentenced to hard labour and deported, but the trial illustrates the relatively favourable position pro-Nationalist Chinese enjoyed after 1946. In February 1947, following intense pressure from the Chinese Mission, GHQ agreed to recognise as United Nations nationals all resident Formosans and Chinese registered by the Mission as Nationalist citizens. By that time, the Mission had issued certificates of nationality to about 20,000, or two-thirds of Japan's Chinese community. Chinese residents were required to register as foreigners under the Alien Registration Ordinance, but as recognised UN nationals, they acquired diplomatic representation, were removed from Japanese criminal jurisdiction and, in January 1948, were granted extra rations, rights not enjoyed by Koreans.[114]

SCAP's refusal to treat Koreans and pro-Communist Chinese as UN nationals heightened tensions between the authorities, Japanese and American, and these groups. The government's announcement in November 1946 that Koreans would have to pay a special capital levy, or 'war tax', brought massive protests. Although only a few high-income individuals were actually affected, Koreans bitterly resented the idea of having to pay for the crimes of their oppressor. On 20 December, some 30,000 Koreans rallied in front of the Imperial Palace to protest at the loss of voting rights, the war tax and the imposition of Japanese-national status. As they filed past Prime Minister Yoshida's residence, a scuffle broke out with police, leading to the arrest of 10 leaders. The 10 were charged with acts prejudicial to the Occupation under Imperial Ordinance 311 of 12 June. Tried by an Eighth Army military tribunal, they were deported to southern Korea on the orders of Eighth Army Commander Robert Eichelberger. The use of superordinate Occupation courts to deport ostensibly Japanese nationals subject in principle to Japanese law signalled a hardening of American attitudes towards the Korean minority. Unlike the Formosans charged in the Shibuya disturbance, the accused had no Korean mission to plead their cause.[115]

As early as the spring of 1946, MacArthur's headquarters had concluded that '[t]he presence of a restless, uprooted Korean minority in Japan, disdainful of law and authority, was . . . a serious obstacle to the success of the Occupation'.[116] Consequently, GHQ made no sustained effort to combat public prejudice against Koreans. When the Japanese media launched a hate campaign in the summer of 1946, the Civil Censorship Detachment watched silently from the sidelines. Among the prohibited subjects CCD censors were duty-bound to suppress were chauvinistic and anti-foreign propaganda, but the Japanese press was given free rein to slander Korean residents as hooligans and scofflaws prone to mob violence. On 17 August, Shi'ikuma Saburō, a Progressive Party Diet member, delivered a vitriolic diatribe in which he declared, 'We refuse to stand by in silence watching Formosans and Koreans . . . swaggering about as if they were nationals of victorious nations.' Their misbehaviour, he said, 'makes the blood in our veins, in our misery of defeat, boil'. The press gave these sensational comments front-page coverage. Former CI&E officer David Conde, intimately familiar with GHQ's key logs, was appalled by this tacit encouragement of racist sentiment. 'SCAP censors have read and approved the attacks on Koreans', he noted in a magazine article. 'SCAP itself has expressed anti-Korean sentiments . . . and many Americans do not conceal their preference for the Japanese.'[117]

The Korean League and ethnic education

One reason for SCAP's growing antipathy towards the Korean minority was the activities of the League of Korean Residents in Japan (*Choryŏn*), which had been created in mid-October 1945 to defend the rights of liberated nationals. The League's primary purpose was summed up by its most prominent member, Kim Ch'ŏn-hae, who had been freed from Fuchū Prison with other Communist leaders on 10 October. This was, he said 'to make Japan a decent place for Koreans to live'. The League set itself three major objectives: to help compatriots return to their homeland, to secure social equality and livelihood rights for those in Japan and to establish an independent government in Korea. By January 1946, the organisation had established 47 regional branches throughout Japan and soon commanded the allegiance of 400,000 Koreans, or two-thirds of the resident population.[118]

Without waiting for guidance from GHQ, *Chŏryŏn* undertook its own repatriation activities, negotiating rations, relief supplies and free rail transport with the Welfare Ministry and other government agencies. It confronted companies that had exploited Korean slave labour in mines and factories during the war, demanding back wages, and interceded with police on behalf of Koreans arrested for black-market activities. The League also established people's courts to mete out its own brand of justice to malefactors and war collaborators. *Chŏryŏn*'s top leadership was closely associated with the Japan Communist Party, but its rank and file included both leftist sympathisers and anti-Communists. In December 1945 and January 1946, two rightist groups split off from the Korean League to form their own organisations, and in early October 1946, the largest of these formed the Korean Residents' Union in Japan (*Mindan*) under the leadership of Pak Yŏl, a devout nationalist who had spent 23 years in prison for his anarchist ideas.[119]

The League, however, emerged as the most radical and consistent defender of Korean rights in Japan. It organised Korean participation in demonstrations against the Yoshida government and the May Day and Food May Day rallies of 1946 and took part in planning for the abortive general strike of 1 February 1947. One of the organisation's top priorities from early 1946, however, was the creation and maintenance of ethnic schools. The schools gave both form and substance to the aspirations of a liberated people. Their establishment was a spontaneous but deeply felt response to the intense psychological assault Japan had waged on the Korean national identity during the colonial period. Parents intent on returning to Korea were determined that their children, many of whom could speak only Japanese, learn their native tongue, shed the negative self-image that *kōminka* education had fostered and reclaim the rich cultural heritage that 35 years of Japanese rule had attempted to extinguish. By April 1948, the League was operating 541 elementary, 9 middle and 36 youth schools, with a teaching staff of some 1,360 and an enrolment of over 60,000 students. *Mindan* and other nationalist groups had organised 52 elementary schools, 2 middle schools and 2 training institutions, with more than 6,800 students in attendance.[120]

Koreans objected strongly to Japanese textbooks, such as the GHQ-approved *Kuni no ayumi* (Our Nation's Progress) of 1946, which depicted Japan's annexation of Korea as an exercise in mutual cooperation and failed to criticise the Imperial ideology that had legitimated colonial domination. *Chŏryŏn*'s Cultural Division wrote school books from a Korean perspective and submitted them to the censors in Civil Information and Education Section. CI&E approved the texts, which by and large emphasised democratic and nationalistic themes. By April 1948, the League had published 1 million copies of some 90 different textbooks on a wide range of subjects. The books were carefully edited and produced, and many were used by the *Mindan* schools, as well. *Chŏryŏn* also adhered to the School Education Law of March 1947, reorganising its schools on the 6-3-3 model and establishing educational standards in conformity with the new statute. The Korean community set up its own teacher-training programmes, and most ethnic schools strove to hire qualified instructors and meet minimum Education Ministry requirements, although they were hampered by a chronic lack of funds, basic equipment and experienced administrators and personnel.[121]

In Osaka and other areas where large numbers of Koreans lived, local Japanese school authorities sometimes helped set up ethnic classrooms, offering Korean students space in Japanese buildings, and education officials authorised the establishment of ethnic schools. Initially, the Occupation took scant notice of the Korean education system. By 1947, however, SCAP and Eighth Army had come to view *Choryŏn* with growing suspicion. Korean attempts to establish a sphere of cultural autonomy, with the self-governing ethnic school system at its core, seemed to challenge the principle of Occupation control. In June 1947, the Counter-Intelligence Corps warned of the League's 'tenuous self-granted extra-territoriality' and accused it, in effect, of establishing a parallel government complete with separate police powers. Occupation authorities were equally leery of *Choryŏn's* leftist sympathies. In the summer of 1947, US Army Intelligence alleged that the League had become heavily involved in illegal entry, smuggling and black-marketeering and was funnelling the proceeds from these illicit activities to the Communist Party. The Far East Command was particularly concerned that, as the date for UN-santioned general elections in Korea drew near, leftist agitation in the south would spill over into Japan and vice versa. *Choryŏn*, it alleged, was serving as a conduit for radical forces on both sides of the Korean straits. These fears contributed to SCAP's crackdown on ethnic education in 1948, leading to a series of sometimes violent confrontations over the issues of cultural autonomy and political allegiance (chapter 10). After 1948, one scholar has noted, 'Koreans in Japan found themselves trapped between the Cold War in Japan and the Cold War in Korea, and the policies developed to deal with them grew out of the distortions produced by the differences in these two sets of competing exigencies'.[122]

PART V

Policy Shift and Aftermath

CHAPTER 10

Changing Course

By late 1947, MacArthur's headquarters had largely achieved the policy objectives outlined in the US Army's 'Basic Directive'. A major exception was the economic deconcentration programme, which carried over into 1948. By this time, however, a broad policy reorientation was under way in Washington. Reflecting heightening East–West tensions, the ensuing change of pace would alter the character of the Occupation and prolong its duration.

WASHINGTON TAKES CHARGE

A bulwark against communism
A harbinger of the widening ideological divide that would soon become the Cold War was the speech delivered by Winston Churchill on 5 March 1946 at Fulton, Missouri. With President Truman by his side, the former British prime minister, speaking as a private citizen, declared that 'an iron curtain has descended across the continent' from the Baltic to the Adriatic and warned the Free World of the danger of Communist fifth columns operating everywhere. By early 1947, the concrete signs of a major policy shift in Washington could be discerned. In March, President Truman unveiled the Truman Doctrine, a plan to provide American military and economic aid to Greece and Turkey to help combat the growing influence there of the left. In May, Under-Secretary of State Dean Acheson called for the 'reconstruction of those two great workshops of Europe and Asia – Germany and Japan.' And in June, Secretary of State George C. Marshall announced the European Recovery Programme, a four-year multi-billion dollar aid package providing reconstruction assistance to cash-starved European economies. The object of the so-called Marshall Plan was to build up US export markets, prevent the Europeans from drifting into an accommodation with Soviet power and forestall the economic chaos that might lead to Communist-dominated governments on the continent. In July, the European Conference for Economic Reconstruction convened to oversee the flow of dollars to 16 war-devastated Western European countries. The Soviet Union and eight Socialist states in Eastern Europe boycotted these events. In October 1947, Moscow responded by establishing the Communist Information Bureau (Cominform) to coordinate strategy among national Communist movements worldwide, and in February 1948, it began the Berlin blockade.

The US National Security Act of July 1947 abolished the War and Navy Departments, merged the Army, Navy and Army Air Forces into a single Department of

Defense and streamlined the Joint Chiefs of Staff organisation. It also created the Central Intelligence Agency, which assumed many of the functions of the Office of War Information and the Office of Strategic Services, and the National Security Council (NSC), which took over some of the work of the State–War–Navy Coordinating Committee. SWNCC was reorganised as the State-Army-Navy-Air Force Coordinating Committee (SANACC). This restructuring completed the institutional armature for America's new policy of containing Communism and enhanced the authority of the Defense and State Departments. The author of the containment doctrine was Soviet specialist George F. Kennan, who in May 1947 gained ascendancy in the State Department as head of its newly created Policy Planning Staff. The erudite, patrician Kennan believed that the United States should eschew cooperation with the Soviet Union and attempt to contain Soviet influence wherever it manifested itself. His hawkish ideas found ready acceptance in the wake of the Republican Party's sweep of the November 1946 Congressional elections, which had given the Grand Old Party its first majority in Congress since 1930. The GOP victory coincided with the onset of the domestic Cold War, which Truman helped launch in March 1947 with his loyalty programme for Federal employees.[1]

The Truman Administration's foreign policy was heavily skewed towards Europe, which was viewed as the front line in the struggle against Soviet hegemonist ambitions. US objectives in Japan from 1947 through 1949, the period of 'soft' Cold War policy, were primarily to deny Moscow a foothold there and keep the country out of the Soviet orbit. Kennan and other State Department strategists intended to transform the 'Japanese workshop' into a pro-American centre of regional power from which the spread of Soviet influence in Asia could be checked. With China in the throes of revolution, an economically dynamic and politically stable Japan now was deemed vital to American national interests. Japan had displaced Nationalist China as the cornerstone of US strategic thinking in Asia, and its internal stabilisation and rehabilitation as Cold War ally were considered matters of vital concern.[2]

In January 1948, Secretary of the Army Kenneth Royall, speaking in San Francisco, praised the prewar military and industrial élite that had built up Japan's war machine and suggested that the task of economic recovery might require their services once again. *Zaibatsu* dissolution, he warned emphatically, must not be allowed to go too far: 'We cannot afford to sterilise the business ability of Japan.' Royall concluded: 'We hold to a . . . definite purpose of building in Japan a self-sufficient democracy, strong enough and stable enough to support itself and at the same time to serve as a deterrent against any other totalitarian war threats which might hereafter arise in the Far East.'[3] These declamatory remarks were picked up and amplified by the Japanese press and became known as the 'Bulwark Against Communism' speech.

The 'Kennan Restoration'
In early March 1948, Policy Planning Chief George Kennan visited MacArthur in Tokyo. His mission was to engineer a shift away from such 'destabilising reforms' as the purge, reparations, the dismantling of the Home Ministry, police decentralisation,

zaibatsu dissolution and liberal trade unionism. Kennan's ideas would set the tone for America's Japan policy for the duration of the Occupation. Through a series of deft manoeuvres, and in concert with the Pentagon and US business interests, he engineered what one scholar has called the Kennan Restoration, a change of pace and orientation that would later become known as the 'reverse course'.[4]

Kennan was convinced that MacArthur's liberal programmes were ruining the economy and exposing Japan to internal subversion by the left. 'SCAP had proceeded on a scale, and with a dogmatic, impersonal vindictiveness, for which there were few examples outside of the totalitarian countries themselves', he later wrote. Japanese life, he asserted, 'had been thrown into turmoil and confusion, producing a serious degree of instability.' Kennan's views, formulated in a Policy Planning Staff study, PPS-28, of 25 March, found solid support from the new Defense Secretary, James V. Forrestal, a former Wall Street executive with the investment firm Dillon, Read and Company, and his protégé, Under-Secretary of the Army William H. Draper Jr, a former vice president of the same company. Good bankers all, Forrestal and Draper were determined to restore Japan's capitalist class to undisputed authority, make the economy self-sufficient and reduce the cost to the US taxpayer of administering the Occupation.

Together, Kennan, Forrestal and Draper conspired to curb SCAP's powers. They found a ready ally in the American Council on Japan, the so-called Japan Lobby, which had been founded in late June 1948 at the Harvard Club in New York City. The ACJ's honorary chair was Joseph Grew, and the group counted among its associates a number of high-profile opinion-makers, Congressmen, bureaucrats and Japan hands. Among these were *Newsweek* Foreign Editor Harry Kern, *Newsweek's* bureau chief in Tokyo, Compton Pakenham, and New York lawyer James Kauffman, all spokesmen for big business. Other prominent members included Senator William F. Knowland, a Kern intimate and arch foe of MacArthur's anti-trust programme; Japan Crowd stalwarts Joseph Ballantine and Eugene Dooman; leading members of State's Far Eastern Division; and Army Secretary Royall and Under-Secretary Draper. The Japan Lobby also maintained ties with Eighth Army Commander Robert L. Eichelberger, who would lend the group his expertise following his retirement in the summer of 1948 and, via Kern and Pakenham, with the Imperial household. The ACJ quickly became a hive of anti-SCAP activity. While Kern and Pakenham hammered MacArthur's policies in the pages of *Newsweek* and Knowland scoured him on the Senate floor, the General's superiors in the Pentagon organised a succession of special missions designed to bring him to heel.[5]

In March 1948, Clifford S. Strike, a US engineer and industrial expert hired by Washington, completed a review of the Occupation's reparations programme (he had issued an initial report in February 1947). Strike's conclusions, prepared by his firm Overseas Consultants Inc., dramatically toned down the reparations demands of the 1946 Pauley Mission, calling for the removal only of military rather than 'war-supporting' industries and urging a 33 per cent cut in the Pauley targets. Strike rejected Pauley's contention that excess industrial capacity existed in Japan and

Photo 61. Diplomatic Section Chief William Sebald (right) greets George F. Kennan at Haneda airport, 1 March 1948. Kennan's visit to Japan signalled a shift in emphasis away from democratic reform towards economic stability, internal security and rearmament. This policy reorientation, epitomised by the Red Purge and the creation of a de facto Japanese army in 1950, became known as the 'reverse course' (US National Archives).

recommended that supporting industries such as pig iron, steel, machine tools, ball bearings and chemicals be exempted from war reparations altogether in order to jump start domestic production.[6] The Strike proposals would prepare the way for the elimination of reparations altogether in May 1949.

MacArthur personally took a dim view of reparations, and Strike's recommendations caused him no particular discomfort, but Under-Secretary of the Army Draper was another matter. In December 1947, Draper had coordinated the assault on

MacArthur's anti-trust programme through *Newsweek* and his Japan Lobby contacts (chapter 7). Now he quickly broadened the attack on the MacArthurian project. With State Department support, in March he asked Congress to bankroll an Economic Recovery in Occupied Areas (EROA) programme for one year beginning in April 1948. The goal of this assistance, touted as a Marshall Plan for Japan, was not only to develop export-orientated industries but generally to 'stimulate the economic revival of the Far East.'[7] In late March, Draper personally led a team of hand-picked business executives under Chemical Bank Chairman Percy H. Johnston to Tokyo. The high-powered fact-finding mission released its conclusions in April. Citing the need to create a self-supporting Japanese economy weaned of US subsidies, the so-called Johnston–Draper Report proposed a range of initiatives designed to boost production, end reparations, rollback anti-monopoly measures and place curbs on union activity. To offset the impending loss of the China market and promote trade ties with non-dollar areas in the region, the report urged improved access to raw materials and export markets in Southeast Asia. In May, Draper sent Ralph Young of the Federal Reserve Board to Tokyo with a group of government economists to study Japan's hyperinflation. In June, to MacArthur's chagrin, Young recommended drastic budget cuts and a fixed yen–dollar exchange rate.

Draper and Kennan had both informed MacArthur in Tokyo that *zaibatsu* dissolution could go no further. To mollify Washington, the Supreme Commander reluctantly agreed to a proposal by Draper that the Department of the Army create a Deconcentration Review Board (DRB) to study the impact of the anti-trust legislation on economic rehabilitation. Headed by Roy Campbell, a former shipping magnate from New York, and including five business leaders chosen by Draper for their conservative views, the DRB arrived in Tokyo in early May 1948. Within a relatively short time, the Board had succeeded in gelding SCAP's deconcentration programme. As a result, Japan's Holding Company Liquidation Commission, established in 1946 to dispose of *zaibatsu* shares, ultimately designated a mere 18 of the 325 largest non-finance subsidiaries slated for disbanding as 'excessively concentrated'. Of the 18, only 11 were actually divided into smaller firms; four had their stock holdings liquidated; three had some of their industrial assets dispersed; and, for a period thereafter, Mitsui and Mitsubishi were prohibited from using their corporate trademarks.[8] Moreover, in defiance of Edward C. Welsh of ESS's Anti-Trust and Cartels Division, ESS Financial Division's Walter LeCount manoeuvred to exempt banks from the deconcentration law, as well.[9] By the end of 1948, the State Department had rescinded its FEC-230 paper – never formally adopted by the Far Eastern Commission – and announced that the anti-trust programme had achieved its objectives. MacArthur's 'classic laissez-faire ideal of petit bourgeois capitalism', as one scholar has described it[10], had been soundly defeated by civilian and military leaders in Washington – but perhaps equally by the lack of any serious political or public support for decartelisation in Japan.[11]

Draper was not finished. In February 1948, Secretary of Defense Forrestal had ordered a feasibility study on rearming Japan, and in March, Draper broached the idea of establishing a small defence force to the Supreme Commander, who was visibly offended by the idea. The General remained firmly committed to Article Nine, and, while he supported the retention of Okinawa as integral to the US defence posture in Asia, he was unalterably opposed to raising a Japanese army. MacArthur also disagreed sharply with his superiors on the issue of Communism. In August 1948, in a personal note to Army Secretary Royall, he declared 'I do not regard the danger of Communism sweeping Japan as great. . . . I have little concern that it will develop into a threatening menace to Japanese society.'[12]

Nonetheless, the Supreme Commander now was on the defensive. In the face of Draper's renewed challenge to his authority, he beat a tactical retreat. In July 1948, the General instructed Prime Minister Ashida to revise the National Public Service Law and deny public-sector workers – one third of organised labour – the right to strike and bargain collectively (chapter 7). MacArthur also condoned a crackdown on Korean popular movements and left-wing labour activity, creating what British diplomat Ivan Pink described as an 'almost hysterical' climate of anti-Communist tension. According to Pink, in the summer of 1948, General Willoughby's Counter-Intelligence Corps deliberately propagated a Red Scare, which was quickly amplified by the mass media.[13]

The long, hot spring and summer of '48
The build-up to the Occupation's get-tough policy began in the spring. Its first victims were not Japanese workers but resident Koreans, and the arena in which this confrontation took place was education. SCAP's reform of the Japanese school system had emphasised 'respect for the rights of others, particularly minorities' (*Education for the New Japan*, May 1948), but Civil Information and Education Section did not interpret that high ideal as allowing autonomous Korean schools to proliferate unchecked. In January 1947, shortly after SCAP had announced that Koreans would be treated as Japanese nationals, the Education Ministry, at CI&E's bidding, notified prefectural governors that Korean children would be subject to the same educational obligations as Japanese. Wisely, it left the decision of whether to recognise ethnic schools to the discretion of local authorities. One year later, however, in January 1948, again acting on instructions from SCAP, the Ministry ordered Korean children to attend the same schools as Japanese from 1 April, the start of the new academic year.

As indicated earlier, Koreans had attempted to bring their school system into line with Education Ministry requirements, but the Ministry's order of January 1948 meant that children now would be absorbed into the Japanese system and that the ethnic curriculum, including Korean history and language courses, would become extracurricular subjects taught as an adjunct to regular class work. The League of Korean Residents in Japan (*Chōryōn*) and other groups adamantly opposed the new policy. During the colonial period, they argued, Japanese had built schools in Korea for their exclusive use with money extorted from Korean peasants while keeping colonial subjects illiterate and uninformed. In the Japanese metropolis, Koreans in Japanese schools were treated with cruelty and contempt and taught to despise their homeland. Ethnic schools, the League insisted, were necessary to correct that imbalance. *Choryŏn* promptly began negotiations with the Katayama Cabinet's left-of-centre Education Minister Morito Tatsuo, but while Morito was sympathetic, he was powerless in the face of unrelenting pressure from SCAP.[14]

Few Americans sympathised with the Korean point of view, and those who did were quickly silenced. GHQ was determined that Koreans, as ostensible Japanese nationals, comply with Japanese law. Behind that argument, however, was the suspicion, widespread among Eighth Army Military Government Teams and in G-2, that despite evidence to the contrary, the Korean schools were potential hotbeds of Communist propaganda. Even more subtle, and to Korean interests corrosive, was the nearly universal American assumption that Koreans would assimilate into Japanese society and that the primary agent of absorption should be the schools, as in the United States. A separate education system, it was feared, would foster a strong and distinctive national identity, intensifying ethnic antagonisms and complicating the tasks of occupation.[15]

When the Korean League refused to comply and intensified talks with the Education Ministry, SCAP perceived a challenge to Occupation authority and ordered the government to close the ethnic schools by force. On 31 March, Yamaguchi Prefecture in southern Honshu issued the first eviction decree and mobilised police, sparking demonstrations that spread rapidly across the country. Koreans of all political stripes resisted the order, and police bodily dragged students and teachers from their classrooms and nailed the doors shut. In many instances, however, demonstrators prevailed and the schools remained open.

On 23 April, about 15,000 protesters rallied in Osaka, where a large group broke into the Prefectural Office to present their demands to the governor directly. The next day in Kobe, angry parents and students occupied the Hyogo Prefectural Office, holding the governor captive and forcing him to retract his school closure order. The local US Military Government Team was caught unprepared, and MacArthur's Chief of Staff Paul Mueller ordered Eighth Army Commander Eichelberger to invoke top-secret alert plans ('Tollbooth'), proclaim a limited state of emergency and despatch US military police. Arriving in Kobe the next day, Eichelberger railed that the 'riots' had been instigated by 'the Reds', an allegation that even his own intelligence analysts refuted in their after-action reports. The perplexed General told the press that Japan's Korean community should be shipped back to Korea, preferably 'on a big ship like the Queen Elizabeth'. On 26 April, faced with renewed protests by 30,000 Koreans, Eichelberger issued a shoot-to-kill order, and police subsequently opened fire on demonstrators, killing a 16-year old boy. Hundreds were injured, many seriously. A 14-year old girl was badly beaten by police and later succumbed to head injuries. Osaka police also deployed fire hoses against protesters, a crowd-control method borrowed from the Americans.[16]

In the days following the so-called Kobe riot, Japanese police and American MPs rounded up thousands of people, mainly Koreans but also Japanese sympathisers,

Photo 62. Korean pupils, teachers and parents march on the Hyogo Prefectural Office, Kobe, 24 April 1948, to protest the forcible closure of ethnic schools on orders from GHQ (US National Archives).

Formosans and Okinawans who happened to be in the vicinity. More than 1,700 were arrested, of whom 39 eventually were tried in Eighth Army Provost Courts or by Japanese tribunals under Imperial Ordinance 311 ('activities inimical to the Occupation'). The leaders received sentences ranging from 10 to 15 years at hard labour and deportation. Patrick Shaw, head of the Australian Mission in Tokyo and British Commonwealth representative on the Allied Council for Japan, complained to SCAP that the punishment was wildly disproportionate to the offence, but Diplomatic Section Chief William Sebald retorted that Shaw's special pleading was 'politically motivated' and summarily dismissed the complaint.

SCAP and Eighth Army subsequently directed municipal governments in areas with large Korean populations to enact 'public safety ordinances' requiring prior police permission to hold parades, demonstrations and other outside gatherings. Beginning with the Osaka Public Safety Ordinance of July 1948, local public order statutes were promulgated across Japan. The ordinances gave police a new weapon in the struggle to suppress popular dissent, including union militancy, and imposed limits on the freedoms of expression and assembly that many charged were unconstitutional and a violation of SCAP's Civil Liberties Directive. To many Japanese, the statutes represented an extension of the Kobe limited emergency decree into public life.[17]

Against this backdrop, Occupation authorities began their summer crackdown

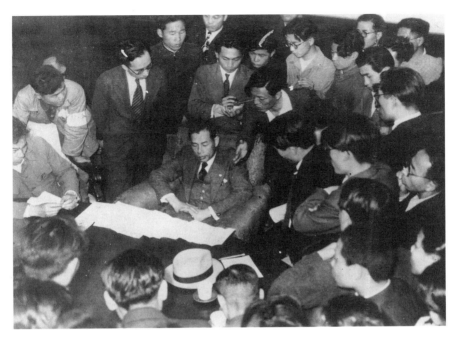

Photo 63. Koreans surround Governor Kishida Yukio of Hyogo Prefecture, 24 April 1948. Kishida was forced to repeal temporarily the school closure order, but the incident led to a GHQ-orchestrated attack on the Korean minority that would deprive it of basic civil and political rights (US National Archives).

on labour activism. In August 1948, Eighth Army mobilised troops to end a dispute at the Tōhō Motion Pictures Studios in Tokyo's Kinuta district. The Studio had been occupied since April by 1,500 actors, stagehands and other workers protesting against the company's unilateral scrapping of their union contract and its dismissal of 1,000 employees. Tōhō workers and their labour organisation, the Japan Movie and Theatre Workers' Guild, had taken over the shop and were running it themselves in a typical 'production struggle'. The company asked for a court order to remove the protesters, and on 13 August, the Tokyo District Court issued an eviction decree. Claiming that Americans living in the vicinity were endangered, Eighth Army pressed the Tokyo Military Government Team to intervene, whereupon Colonel Frank A. Hollingshead, Tokyo MGT Commander, instructed Tōhō management to request police action. When management complied, Hollingshead ordered the 1st Cavalry Division to despatch Military Police and a platoon of 50 dismounted cavalry backed by six armoured reconnaissance cars and five tanks to remove the striking workers. Another squadron was placed on stand-by alert at Camp Drake.[18] On 19 August, with three scout aircraft (one of them carrying the Division commander) circling overhead, US troops, armoured cars, tanks and 2,000 helmeted Japanese

Photo 64. Japanese police backed by US armoured personnel carriers and tanks arrive to suppress the Tōhō strike, 20 August 1948. The crushing of the strike action inaugurated a GHQ-sanctioned offensive by big business against the unions that would undermine labour democracy (Kyodo).

police armed with axes, saws, scaling ladders and battering rams moved into position. In the face of insurmountable odds, the strikers abandoned their action and left the studio peacefully, avoiding bloodshed. 'The only thing they didn't send was a battleship', quipped a Tōhō actress and union activist.[19]

The suppression of the Tōhō struggle was a prelude to the 'rationalisation' offensive and mass dismissals that management would unleash against organised labour in 1949. This hugely exaggerated display of armed might also was directed at *Sanbetsu Kaigi* (Congress of Industrial Unions), Japan's most powerful labour federation to which the Tōhō union belonged. Although only 10 per cent of the *Sanbetsu* membership was Communist, the organisation took consistently radical positions, advocating worker participation in production and policy-making.

The Eighth Army action accelerated two converging trends. In the autumn of 1947, ESS's Labour Division had begun fostering Democratisation Leagues (*Mindō*) inside *Sanbetsu* in an effort to marginalise its left-wing leadership. Now, in mid-1948, it welcomed the precedent-setting court ruling against worker takeovers. At the same time, corporate leaders had launched a coordinated drive to quell labour unrest and reassert the primacy of management over production. This initiative resulted in the creation in April 1948 of *Nikkeiren* (Japan Federation of Employers' Associations). *Nikkeiren* viewed the Tōhō dispute as a test case in the struggle to restore capital's 'right to manage' without worker participation and lobbied actively on behalf of the studio's embattled owners. Like SCAP, *Nikkeiren*'s real target was *Sanbetsu*. Under the banner of 'Fighting *Nikkeiren*', the giant employers' association would apply the lessons learned at Tōhō to larger, more significant labour actions in 1949, urging its members to break union contracts at will and fire uncooperative workers wholesale.[20]

Eighth Army organised the assault on the Tōhō union with Willoughby's G-2 watching from the wings, but Labour Division apparently had not been consulted. When the Division's Elizabeth Wilson later interviewed Tokyo MGT Commander Hollingshead about the anti-strike action, she was told bluntly that 'labour relations [are] largely a question of law enforcement' and that the MGT's 'primary purpose was to enforce the [13 August] court order by whatever methods were required'. Such muscular sentiments undoubtedly reflected the thinking of General Willoughby. Coming immediately after the interim revision of the National/Public Service Law (31 July), they also confirmed GHQ's dramatic departure from its early policy of non-intervention in labour disputes.[21]

Yoshida's conservative hegemony and NSC-13/2
In his August 1948 letter to Army Secretary Royall, MacArthur had downplayed Communist influence but basked in the reflected light of G-2's union-bashing actions, boasting that the summer offensive had broken 'this concentration of Communist power'. GHQ's hardline on labour contributed to a widening split in Socialist ranks, and on 7 October 1948, the Ashida Cabinet, beset by internal dissension and public furore over the National Public Service Law, collapsed under the Shōwa Denkō allegations. In September, high-ranking officials, including Ashida's vice minister of Agriculture, the director of the Economic Stabilisation Board and Deputy Prime Minister Nishio Suehiro, had been arrested on charges of receiving Shōwa Denkō gratuities and hush money for funnelling Reconstruction Finance loans to the giant fertiliser company. Ashida himself was arrested in December. Also apprehended were Fukuda Takeo, a senior Finance Ministry official (prime minister, 1976–8), and Democratic Liberal Party kingpin Ono Bamboku. Ashida, Fukuda, Nishio, Ono and almost all of the 64 businessmen, functionaries and politicians accused of bribery, fraud and perjury later were acquitted. To the chagrin of Government Section's Charles Kades, a champion of the Katayama and Ashida Cabinets, details of the scandal had been leaked to the media by Willoughby's G-2 in a bid to discredit the left and its supporters in GHQ.

With the moderate camp in disarray, Democratic Liberal Party (DLP) leader Yoshida Shigeru seized this opportunity to revive his premiership. Whitney and Kades opposed Yoshida's second bid for power with particular energy. Their disapproval stemmed in part from internal GHQ politics. Yoshida, through his clever and enterprising aide–confidant Shirasu Jirō, had won the ear and full support of

Willoughby. GS pushed its own candidate, Yamazaki Takeshi, the DLP's Secretary General, but both Yamazaki and MacArthur's apparent favourite, Miki Takeo of the People's Cooperative Party, deferred to the powerful Yoshida. To clinch the nomination, the DLP President arranged a personal audience with MacArthur and elicited an ambiguous nod from the General, which he publicly proclaimed a sign of official SCAP acceptance. On 15 October, Yoshida formed his second cabinet and the first solid single-party government of the postwar period, ushering in the so-called Yoshida Era. Shortly afterwards, Kades was reassigned to Washington at his personal request.[22] In November, the Tokyo War Crimes Tribunal delivered its verdict, and in December, seven convicted Class A war criminals were hanged, bringing to a close the first half of the Occupation. Yoshida would remain in power until 1954 as leader of a new conservative hegemony uniting right-of-centre political interests, big business and a civil service dominated by conservative bureaucrats – an alliance that Washington would find congenial and support fully.

As Yoshida prepared to take power, the policy shift announced by Kennan earlier in the year became irreversible with the formal adoption of his action programme for Japan. The National Security Council drew up a revised set of Kennan's PPS-28 recommendations as NSC-13/2, and President Truman signed the document on 7 October. Reflecting recent State and Defense Department thinking, NSC-13/2 listed 20 major policy objectives in Japan, including an end to the purge and reparations, a non-punitive peace treaty at some later time, reinforcement of the Japanese police establishment, concentration of more power in the hands of the government, and economic recovery driven by exports – a goal that was considered second in importance only to US security interests. The document called specifically for a 150,000-strong national police force and suggested that Japan might provide 'some degree of military assistance to the United States, at least to the extent of Japan's self-defense', themes that would be sounded again repeatedly between 1950 and 1951 as negotiations over a peace settlement got underway.[23]

NSC-13/2 marked a point of no return that even MacArthur was powerless to reverse. Indeed, the directive signalled the end of the General's ability to set and direct SCAP policy as he pleased. Substantive control over the Occupation had passed to Washington. The new policy statement also seemed to violate the Army's 'Basic Directive' in the areas of economic policy, political liberties and disarmament. From this point onwards, under Washington's vigilant eye, SCAP would intervene directly in the economy, suspend the civil liberties of suspected Communist sympathisers and, with the advent of war in Korea, raise a de facto Japanese army.

'REVERSE COURSE' OR SHIFT OF GEAR?

The 'stabilisation depression'
Determined to implement NSC-13/2 expeditiously, President Truman signed a nine-point stabilisation directive on 10 December 1948 for immediate execution by

SCAP. Originally drafted by Under-Secretary of the Army Draper, the order was issued to MacArthur as an 'interim directive', enabling Washington to bypass the Far Eastern Commission. This dubious procedure was roundly denounced by FEC members. Soviet representative Alexander Panyushkin attacked it as a unilateral modification of the régime of control in Japan and a violation of the FEC Charter. Australia, New Zealand and India also criticised the decree, noting that Washington's claim of urgency could not be justified. But the FEC was powerless to repudiate the order, and it stood. The stabilisation directive sought specifically to cut the costs of occupation, revive the economy and enable Japanese companies to compete again in world markets. Specifically, it called for 1 a balanced national budget, 2 a strengthened tax system, 3 tightening of credit, 4 wage stabilisation, 5 price controls, 6 a foreign exchange rate pegged at ¥360 to the dollar, 7 the promotion of exports, 8 increased industrial output and 9 more efficient food production and distribution. By ending costly subsidies to industry, Draper believed these pump-priming measures would force the economy to shake itself down, enabling Japan to make more efficient use of the EROA aid programme he proposed to implement.[24]

MacArthur was furious at this frontal attack on his authority, but, out-manoeuvred, he accepted the inevitable and informed Prime Minister Yoshida of the austerity plan. Yoshida advocated a Keynesian solution of deficit spending and opposed stabilisation in several areas, but by and large, he, too, acquiesced in the inevitable. In early 1949, the Premier appointed Ikeda Hayato as his Finance Minister and instructed him to carry out the reform. The Economic Stabilisation Programme (ESP) provided the springboard from which Ikeda would launch a brilliant political career, culminating in his premiership (1960–4) and the 'income-doubling plan' for which he is now known. Joseph M. Dodge, the orthodox Detroit banker selected to oversee this deflationary policy as 'economic tsar', also is remembered today, but his name evokes memories of hard times, dismissals, wage cuts and political turmoil. He proved to be, as a former Occupation official phrased it, 'the American whose impact on the Japanese during the occupation was second only to that of MacArthur'.[25]

On 1 February 1949, Dodge, who had just organised a major currency reform in Germany, arrived in Tokyo to implement the ESP. He had been recruited for this mission by fellow banker Draper. To free industry and the economy from dependence on government subsidies and US aid, Dodge proceeded to impose a Draconian budget that slashed public spending, curbed credit, severely restricted public consumption and reorientated industrial production away from domestic demand towards export-driven growth. Specifically, Dodge suspended industrial loans from the Reconstruction Finance Bank and replaced its bond-generated loans with a US Aid Counterpart Fund, which provided capital for long-term strategic investment and was financed by purchases of food and other US imports. In May 1949, the Ministry of International Trade and Industry (MITI) was created to ease Japan's re-entry into the world market. The Dodge system favoured the fittest, which not surprisingly turned out to be businesses with former *zaibatsu* connections. Unable to compete under deflationary conditions, many small- and medium-sized firms were forced under. Thus was created, in the words of former SCAP labour official Theodore Cohen 'the first postwar channel between the conservative Japanese big business elements and their bureaucratic and political allies in Japan and the top level of officials in the US government'.[26]

The Dodge Line, as it became known, rapidly 'disinflated' the economy, plunging the country into a severe 'stabilisation depression.' While the cutbacks mandated by Washington enabled the economic tsar to impose a balanced budget and eliminate trade and industrial subsidies within months, by June 1950, production had slumped to barely one third of the 1931 level, with investment at one half that of 1949. Ruthless cutbacks in the public and private sectors also created massive unemployment. The Dodge retrenchments coincided with the tail end of the unpopular civil service reform, and the government's 'personnel adjustment' policies resulted in the firing of tens of thousands for 'inadequate skills', 'uncooperative attitudes' and 'neglect of duty' – euphemisms for dissent. In the name of administrative streamlining, the government dismissed 250,000 civil servants and government workers and 410,000 municipal employees. Among these were some 95,000 members of the National Railways Workers' Union (*Kokurō*), one of *Sanbetsu*'s most militant labour groups. In the private sector, management discharged an additional 430,000 industrial workers. Dodge's perfectly balanced budget put more than 1 million people out of work. For those who remained employed, it meant wage freezes and, in some sectors, wage cuts running between 15 per cent and 20 per cent. Cohen recalled this aspect of the 'Dodge squeeze': 'The government wanted to fire workers in the railways, they wanted to fire people in other departments, but they couldn't do it because they would create a political storm. But with Dodge, of course, they could say it is Mr Dodge who is forcing us to do it. . . . [T]he labour unions could fight the Transport Minister, but they couldn't fight Joe Dodge.'[27]

The attack on left-wing unionism
As the government and 'Fighting *Nikkeiren*' applied the 'no-strike stabilisation programme' to eject radical workers from their jobs, the ESS Labour Division was summoning union leaders to General Headquarters and warning them not to oppose the project with strikes. Labour Division implied that the nine-point stabilisation directive, based on NSC-13/2, was official Occupation policy and that open defiance could be construed as inimical to Occupation objectives and prosecuted under Imperial Ordinance 311. In late December 1948, the new Division Chief Chester Hepler bluntly told workers' representatives that strikes were 'unpatriotic'. In March 1949, Robert Amis, head of the Division's Labour Relations Branch, delivered the same message to *Sanbetsu*, and in April, ESS Chief General William F. Marquat sent a similar letter to coal miners. In mid-March, the Austrian-born Valery Burati, a former organiser with the CIO-affiliated Textile Workers' Union, outlined a seven-point plan to help Tōshiba, one of Japan's big three manufacturers of electrical equipment, end a protracted strike by its left-leaning union. The plan proposed cancelling the company's labour agreement, refusing to bargain under

strike conditions and withdrawing government contracts.[28] In June, Burati pressured the National Railway Workers to cancel plans for a rail walkout.

Despite these blandishments, the labour movement bitterly resisted the 'disinflation' programme. Beginning in March and continuing through the summer, railway workers organised demonstrations, staged wildcat work stoppages and took over train operations. There was a dramatic surge in railway sabotage and other direct action. In June, employees occupied the Japan Steel Company in Hiroshima for 48 hours until police drove them out. Tōshiba had pursued an aggressive policy of 'rationalisation', producing severe labour turbulence. Slated for dismemberment under SCAP's anti-trust legislation, the company violated its union contract and began to fire 'surplus' workers in late 1948 in order to qualify for Reconstruction Finance Bank loans. At one of its Ni'igata plants, the union responded by taking over production and running the factory independently. When the Ni'igata District Court ruled in favour of management in June 1949, some 400 armed police arrived to evict the employees. A labour historian describes the resulting mêlée: 'Among the occupiers were many women workers who locked arms in scrimmage formation, which the police broke up by thrusting their night sticks under their skirts, kicking and beating them, and dragging them away by their hair. . . . In all 142 were arrested, fully half of them women.' By the end of the year, Tōshiba had scrapped two-thirds of all its plants and fired half of its national labour force.[29]

In June, as the government tightened the Dodge squeeze, the Diet revised the Labour Union Law (December 1945) and parts of the Labour Relations Adjustment Law (June 1946), broadly restructuring in the process Japan's labour-relations system. Labour Division had contemplated a revision of the 1945 law based on changes the US Advisory Committee on Labour had suggested in 1946. The amendment of the National Public Service Law in July 1948 and intensifying labour militancy prompted the Division to revive these recommendations. Its legislative draft of October 1948 sought to increase protection for workers while providing a means of ending extended disputes. The Division's proposal prohibited interference in union affairs by management, which was not allowed to offer financial aid to unions or discharge or otherwise discriminate against workers for union activities. The plan sought to reinforce labour democracy by making supervisors ineligible for union membership, insuring due process and requiring members to elect officials and determine strike actions by direct majority vote via secret ballots. It also provided for general meetings and the publication of financial reports at least once a year; banned discrimination on grounds of race, creed, sex, social status or family origin; and guaranteed freedom of political activity.

What began as a liberal attempt by GHQ labour officials to improve existing legislation, however, had become by early 1949 part of SCAP's stabilisation drive. The American proposal was promptly co-opted by social bureaucrats in the Labour Ministry and used to exclude left-wing radicals, bring labour into closer alignment with management and strengthen centralised control, all in the name of union democracy. Although many of the ESS draft's progressive measures were incorporated into the new law, others were altered or discarded and new stipulations were added as the Labour Ministry, with *Nikkeiren* looking over its shoulder, adapted the ESS programme to 'Japanese conditions'. Labour officials also exercised ministerial guidance, outlining their own criteria for labour unions to prefectural and municipal authorities. These administrative advisories preceded passage of the legislative revisions, facilitating their quick implementation.

Enacted on 1 June 1949, the revised law prohibited the payment of wages during strikes and generally strengthened the hand of employers in collective bargaining. It allowed the prime minister to designate companies providing vital services as 'public utilities enterprises' and impose a 30-day cooling-off period before strike action could be taken. The amendments bolstered the authority of the Labour Minister and prefectural governors to resolve labour disputes, gave the Ministry and central and prefectural labour relations commissions greater control over union certification and enabled the government to meddle directly in internal union business. Most importantly, the law refused to recognise unions 'which principally aim at carrying on political or social movements'. Ministry officials had excised language explicitly guaranteeing freedom of thought, substituting the word 'religion' (*shūkyō*) for the broader 'creed' (*shinjō*), with its nuance of political belief, in the GHQ draft and deleting the clause allowing political activity.[30]

For Labour Division, the Dodge Line made these changes 'tactically imperative', even if, as a former Division member expressed it, they 'looked increasingly like a grand design to restrain labour while industry rationalised'. Critics charged that the new statute was a Japanese version of the 1947 US Taft–Hartley Labour Act designed to rid the union movement of Communist influence. It is true that both SCAP and the government were determined to dismiss Communists, but the revision, with its clever *mélange* of liberal and restrictive provisions, was not a carbon copy of the unabashedly repressive US law (below). Its architects in the Labour Ministry were social bureaucrats committed to reintegrating labour into a Japanese system of top–down industrial relations amenable to state control but retaining a progressive veneer. This was a position, one historian has noted, that '[t]he Japanese government required neither American advice nor the new Cold War to arrive at'.[31]

Both left-wing and conservative unions opposed the labour-law revisions, even as anti-Communist groups attempted to use them to expel leftist rivals, and confrontations between capital and labour intensified in the second half of 1949. In June, Communist leaders announced a 'September Revolution' intended to rally workers and progressive forces against the newly installed Yoshida régime. That same month, 500 workers, including Communists and Koreans, seized a police station in Taira, Fukushima Prefecture and then occupied Taira City Hall for most of the day. Prefectural police called for Eighth Army intervention, but the demonstrators eventually dispersed, averting military action.

Amid mounting tensions, a series of mysterious and violent incidents, still unexplained, occurred in the summer. In July, the body of Japan National Railways President Shimoyama Sadanori was found on a railway line outside Tokyo. The same month, an unmanned train ploughed into a crowded railway station at Mitaka in western Tokyo, killing and injuring numerous bystanders. In August, a locomotive was sabotaged in Fukushima Prefecture, killing the driver and crew members (the Matsukawa Incident). No one was ever charged with Shimoyama's murder – in fact, many, including police and one of the doctors who performed the autopsy, concluded that he had committed suicide. Several railway unionists – mostly Communists – were arrested and tried for the Mitaka and Matsukawa incidents, but only one was actually convicted. These controversial incidents weakened the National Railway Workers Union, however, enabling SCAP-sponsored Democratisation Leagues to gain control of the Union's central committee and dampen effective opposition to retrenchment. The Dodge offensive and the accompanying crackdown on labour crippled *Sanbetsu* at the shopfloor level, and by 1950, the labour front was in disarray, its membership having plunged from 1.75 million to a mere 321,000.

The 'reverse course'
These diverse events marked the onset of what is widely referred to as the 'reverse course', a contested term that continues to generate controversy. Was there really such a thing? The short answer is yes but no. Yes, in the sense of economic intervention and, as discussed below, political repression and rearmament. No, in that such fundamental changes as legal and institutional reform, women's rights, land redistribution and health and welfare guarantees were not repealed and in many cases not even modified. Occupation policy after 1948 represented a change in emphasis, a course adjustment or shifting of gears, not a volte-face.

In a sense, the fundamental premises of the Occupation were conservative from the start. As one historian has commented: 'By retaining intact two of prewar Japan's privileged élites, the Imperial institution and the bureaucracy, the Truman administration insured that the formal democratisation of Japan would take place within the conservative framework of the old régime.'[32] Thus, so-called reform bureaucrats experienced no sense of reversal as GHQ adopted the anti-Communist, social-control programme they had espoused since the 1920s. Nonetheless, the policy switch was palpable and was felt immediately by those struggling from within to stretch and expand that framework: labour, the media, the Korean minority, the peace movement and progressive Japanese in general. 'Reverse course' (*gyaku-kōsu*) is a Japanese term that came into wide currency via a series of articles appearing in the *Yomiuri Shinbun* in November 1951. It is now used loosely to characterise the latter half of the Occupation, with its emphasis on economic recovery, anti-Communism and remilitarisation. The expression conveys the acute sense of betrayal felt by many Japanese who lived through those turbulent years and even today is heavily freighted with meaning and emotion.[33]

Although SCAP's later policies did not constitute a brusque rupture with the early phase of the Occupation, they responded precisely and inexorably to the imperatives of a new US strategy in Asia and the reorganisation of the world market. From 1949 to 1951, Washington pursued toward Japan a 'hard' Cold War policy designed not

Photo 65. Members of the National Railway Workers Union stage a sit-down hunger strike in downtown Tokyo, 19 December 1949, to protest at the government's failure to pay wages and bonuses as recommended by the Arbitration Board. The action was typical of the labour militancy, most of it principled and non-violent, that arose in response to the Dodge retrenchment programme and resulting layoffs and pay cuts (New York Times).

merely to keep the country out of the Soviet orbit but to make it an active partner in achieving US global objectives.[34] The basic outlines of this policy change, announced by Kennan's PPS-28 in early 1948, became clearly visible in 1949. In March of that year, the US Joint Chiefs of Staff recommended to Secretary of Defense Forrestal that measures be taken to utilise Japan's military potential should world events warrant it. In late April, Secretary of State Dean Acheson announced that Washington would give the Japanese government more authority by turning over many of the administrative functions performed by Occupation forces. In May, a revision of NSC-13/2 (entitled NSC-13/3) recommended that the United States not seek a definitive peace treaty with Japan in view of expanding Soviet influence (although in September, international pressure would force Washington to pay lip service to the idea of a settlement).

NSC-13/3 also announced another policy transmutation by unilaterally rescinding the advance transfers of Japanese reparations that Washington had initiated in April 1947. Primary war facilities now were to be reserved for economic recovery. Washington again used the expedient of an interim directive to override opposition in the Far Eastern Commission, a decision that was greeted by bitter denunciation from the Philippines and Nationalist China. General Carlos P. Romulo called it 'a flagrant repudiation by the United States of its commitments under the Potsdam Declaration', and Dr W. K. Lee noted archly that the US reversal would do 'gross injustice' to the victims of Japanese aggression.[35]

In June, another National Security Council paper, NSC-49, called for the use of Japan as a forward-deployed American base and again urged the creation of a Japanese military force able to assist the United States in the event of war with the Soviet Union. In July, SCAP began to phase out its 'eyes and ears' at the grass roots, the regional Military Government Teams, and by August was preparing for the return of Japanese sovereignty at some later date. In October 1949, with the establishment of the People's Republic of China, the US Congress appropriated funds for the construction of new military facilities on Okinawa. And, from late 1949, as high-ranking Pentagon officials declared that Japan now lay within America's defence perimeter, military planners were at work on an integrated trade scheme designed to link the 'Japanese workshop' with Southeast Asian markets. In early 1950, a new national security proposal, NSC-68, drafted by ex-Wall Street banker Paul H. Nitze, Kennan's replacement on the Policy Planning Staff, called for US economic support to Southeast Asia and massive military expenditures to contain and roll back Communism worldwide. By April 1950, Washington had committed itself to stabilising that region as a vital element in Japan's recovery and a means of denying its strategic resources to Communist insurgencies in Indo-China, laying the foundation for US intervention in Vietnam (1964–75).[36]

The brief liberal phase of the Occupation had peaked in 1947 and basically was over by 1948. By late 1949, MacArthur himself largely had acquiesced to Washington's Cold War project. Roger N. Baldwin of the American Civil Liberties Union summed up the misgivings of liberal-minded people on both sides of the Pacific when he complained to an Occupationaire in May 1950 that 'while many Occupation controls have been removed or transferred to Japanese authorities, the drive towards extension of democratic liberties has been slowed up'. Baldwin concluded that 'the essential difficulty under the artificial conditions of occupation lies in the drive for economic recovery, which strengthens conservatives and even reactionary forces at the expense of the progressive centre and the unions'.[37] A cogent expression, indeed, of what the 'reverse course' meant for Japan.

These developments pre-dated the outbreak of war in Korea and were played out against the backdrop of larger geo-political realities. In September and October 1949, Germany split into East and West régimes, whose mutual hostility was matched only by the two rival governments that had formed in Korea a year earlier. In mid-1949, the United States organised the North Atlantic Treaty Organisation and began arms aid to Western Europe, and in September, the Soviet Union broke the US monopoly on nuclear weapons by successfully exploding its first atomic bomb. In October, Communist forces liberated China, and the Nationalists assumed political control of Formosa (now Taiwan), completing their withdrawal there in December. In January 1950, President Truman authorised the production of hydrogen bombs, and in February, Moscow and Beijing signed a treaty of friendship, alliance and mutual assistance and recognised Ho Chi Minh's Vietminh as the official government of Vietnam.

PURGING 'REDS'

American anti-Communism
Washington's changing outlook on Japan reflected domestic as well as international developments, foremost among them a recrudescence of anti-Communist and xenophobic sentiment. The roots of this postwar phenomenon may be traced to the German-Soviet non-aggression pact of 1939. The following year, in an atmosphere of anti-Nazi, anti-Communist war hysteria, Congress passed the Alien Registration (Smith) Act, the first peacetime anti-sedition law in US history. The 1940 Smith Act required foreigners to be fingerprinted and carry an alien pass at all times, but it also banned membership in subversive organisations and the advocacy of subversive ideas. Applying to aliens and citizens alike, the law's anti-subversive clauses covered past as well as present actions and even beliefs. For aliens, violation of any of its provisions was a deportable offence. The Smith Act became one of the cornerstones of the postwar national security state.

Fear of the Soviet Union, a wartime ally, abated after Pearl Harbor but resurfaced with renewed vigour in 1945. Postwar anti-Communism was whipped up by a wave of strikes in 1946, the loss of prospects for cooperation with the Soviet Union and a renewed obsession with internal security. In January 1947, the House Committee on Un-American Activities (HUAC) announced an eight-point programme to ferret out and expose Communists in the Federal government. In March of that year, Truman, obsessed with 'Reds, phonies and parlour pinks', instituted a purge of suspected Communists and fellow-travellers in public service through FBI-administered loyalty tests and the Loyalty Review Board. The 1947 Labour-Management Relations (Taft–Hartley) Act required union members to pledge in writing that they were not Communists, instituting political purges in the labour movement, and imposed a wide array of restrictions on union activities in an effort to undermine collective bargaining. The Act, which organised labour condemned as a 'slave-labour law', imposed a 60-day cooling-off period at the end of a contract, during which time strikes were prohibited, and authorised the president to extend that period an additional 80 days if national security were threatened. In December 1947, the Attorney General's Office published its infamous List of Subversive Organisations.

In May 1948, Congress debated and nearly passed the Mundt–Nixon Bill requiring Communists and Communist front groups to register with Federal authorities. In July, twelve prominent American Communists were indicted under the 1940 Smith Act on charges of conspiring to overthrow the government. In August, HUAC hearings produced sensational accusations that Alger Hiss, a top State Department official, was a Soviet agent. As spy mania swept the nation, Congress launched a formal investigation into alleged Communist influence in the labour movement. Finally, with the collapse of Nationalist Chinese armies in 1949, Senator William Knowland of California and other Republican leaders linked the loss of China to 'Reds' in the government, heralding the advent of McCarthyism.

Anti-Communism seemed to pervade every facet of American life, becoming a national psychosis. In 1949, the National Education Association urged school boards across the country to fire suspected Communists from public schools, and New York State passed the Feinberg Law requiring state education officials to compile lists of subversive organisations, administer loyalty oaths and dismiss teachers for subversive acts or statements outside as well as inside the classroom. In 1950, the year Senator Joseph R. McCarthy, the Republican from Wisconsin, launched his anti-Communist crusade, Congress incorporated the Mundt–Nixon provisions into the Internal Security (McCarran) Act, whose powerful anti-subversion measures, like the Smith Act, applied to citizens and non-citizens alike. Included in its long list of offences was membership in or affiliation with treasonous or totalitarian organisations. The McCarran Act also empowered the state to denaturalise and deport without hearing any naturalised citizen or alien advocating totalitarian doctrines. Finally, the McCarran Act authorised the indefinite detention of suspected subversives in concentration camps during a state of emergency. It was, to quote a political scientist, 'one of the most massive onslaughts against freedom of speech and association ever launched in American history'.[38]

Japan's domestic Cold War
Waves from the anti-Communist tempest sweeping the United States reached Japanese shores, but initially they were buffered by the breakwater of Occupation policy. MacArthur considered Communism to be a manageable threat in Japan and, in

September 1949, declared that the 'small existent Communist minority' was 'no longer a major issue in Japanese life'. Many of his staff, however, were diehard anti-Communists to begin with, but even among those who were not, few, including the Supreme Commander himself, were entirely immune to the mood of America. In January 1950, MacArthur revised his earlier stance when the Communist Information Bureau denounced the Japan Communist Party (JCP) for its non-revolutionary parliamentary tactics and failure to oppose both the Occupation and American imperialism (Cominform Instruction no. 172). JCP Chair Nosaka Sanzō accepted that criticism and pledged to rebuild the Party as a 'link in the world revolutionary movement'. On 3 May 1950, the Supreme Commander responded to Communist-led demonstrations by publicly denouncing the Party as subversive and suggested that its days as a 'constitutionally recognised political movement' were over.[39] This veiled threat presaged the Red Purge that began in earnest in June of that year. The witch hunt, although instigated by SCAP, was conducted by the Japanese. The Dodge retrenchment, the labour law revisions and the government's tough new line on Communism had prepared the groundwork for a highly coordinated assault on basic civil liberties.

Soon after taking office, Yoshida launched his own domestic Cold War. New general elections in January 1949 had handed his recently formed Democratic Liberal Party a landslide victory, enabling the Prime Minister to put together a new government in February. The third Yoshida Cabinet would prove the longest-lived of any government since the Meiji era. In January's elections, the right-wing Socialists saw their Lower House representation plummet from 143 to 48, but the Communist Party registered unprecedented gains. Garnering nearly 2 million new votes, the JCP boosted its Lower House presence from four seats to 35. This leftward shift of progressive sentiment emboldened the radical labour movement and anti-government forces in general. With SCAP's help, Yoshida set out to curb the power of the left and make Japan safe for capitalism, politically as well as economically.

One of Yoshida's first actions in office was to purge Matsumoto Ji'ichirō, leader of the *Buraku* liberation movement and a member of the Upper House. A year earlier, in January 1948, as Upper House Vice President, Matsumoto had refused to bow to the Emperor during the formal opening of the Diet, and that tradition was discontinued as a result. Matsumoto's audacity infuriated Yoshida and the rightist camp. Conservatives were further incensed when, in late 1948, as the Tokyo Tribunal delivered its verdict on war crimes, Matsumoto declared that while the Emperor may not have been responsible for the war politically, he was accountable morally. On 1 January 1949, the new Premier wrote to MacArthur asking GHQ to purge this 'avowed opponent of the Emperor system' on the trumped-up charge that he had belonged to an ultra-nationalist organisation during the war.

Behind-the-scenes efforts to oust Matsumoto had begun on 11 December 1948, when Attorney General Ueda Shunkichi and Cabinet Secretary Satō Eisaku visited Government Section's Jack P. Napier. They told Napier that Matsumoto enjoyed Communist support and that purging him for alleged prewar rightist affiliations would discredit the Party on the eve of the general elections. Napier agreed but suggested that Yoshida seek Whitney's approval. Kades, a staunch Matsumoto defender, had just left Japan, and the resulting change in political climate inside GHQ proved decisive. Whitney advised Yoshida to wait until after January's election, which the Premier did, purging Matsumoto almost as soon as the polls closed. Massive protests – the largest since the Korean demonstrations of April 1948 – immediately erupted across the country, and more than 1 million dissenting signatures were collected, including those of two thirds of the lawmakers in the National Diet. Both the Soviet delegate to the Allied Council for Japan and the American Civil Liberties's Union denounced this unilateral action as unjust and undemocratic. Although Matsumoto was depurged in August 1951, the damage had been done: SCAP's high-handed behaviour had radicalised many *Burakumin*, confirming them both in their anti-Americanism and in their ties to the left.[40]

Yoshida quickly took steps to suppress open dissent and bolster the conservative status quo. He was assisted in this task by the influential anti-Communist ideologue Ueda Shunkichi, who had become Attorney General in October 1948. Ueda would direct the crusade against Communism through June 1950, when he was replaced by Ōhashi Takeo, a social bureaucrat from the wartime Home and Welfare Ministries (and future labour minister, 1962–4). In February 1949, Yoshida announced plans to create a Lower House Un-Japanese Activities Committee similar in design and purpose to its US equivalent, and a Diet Special Investigative Committee subsequently was empanelled for that purpose. Strong opposition from Socialist and Communist Diet members, however, prevented the Committee from fulfilling its intended role.[41]

In early April, the Prime Minister took more decisive action. Government Section's Napier and Yoshikawa Mitsusada, his counterpart in the Attorney General's Special Investigation Bureau (SIB), together drafted a special ordinance empowering the government to outlaw subversive organisations. On 4 April, Yoshida promulgated the Organisation Control Ordinance using the extra-parliamentary expedient of a Cabinet order. Based on Imperial Ordinance 101 of February 1946 authorising the disbanding of ultra-rightist organisations, Cabinet Order 64 enabled the state to dissolve any group that demonstrated subversive or anti-democratic tendencies. Specifically, it outlawed 'resistance or opposition to Occupation forces or to orders issued by the Japanese government in response to SCAP directives and attempts to change national policy by terroristic methods'.[42]

Shortly afterwards, Attorney General Ueda strengthened the Special Investigation Bureau, the agency responsible for applying the Organisation Control Ordinance. Consisting of former Home Ministry thought police, Korea experts and anti-Communist bureaucrats, the SIB had been transferred to the Prime Minister's Office following dissolution of the Home Ministry in December 1947 to function as a de facto FBI. It was incorporated into the Attorney General's Office in February 1948. The SIB was headed by Yoshikawa Mitsusada, the former Higher Thought Police officer credited with breaking the Sorge spy case in 1941. In June, following enactment of the Organisation Control Ordinance, Ueda doubled the SIB's staff, and the

group evolved quickly into a powerful internal intelligence directorate with privileged access to GS Executive Officer Jack Napier (Napier placed the SIB under direct
GS supervision and barred it from working with other GHQ intelligence groups).
That same month, under the revised Labour Union Law, employers began rewriting
union contracts and dismissing Communist-affiliated workers, and in July, at GHQ's
suggestion, Yoshida quietly began to remove 'Communists and fellow travellers' from
government service.[43] Finally, the Primer Minister urged MacArthur to depurge
some 32,000 rank-and-file ultra-nationalists and redeploy them in the struggle
against Communism. SCAP consented in principle but would not take action on the
request until October 1950, as the war in Korea entered a critical juncture.

The Red Purge
With an incipient national security apparatus in place, the Yoshida government and
MacArthur's command launched a multi-pronged assault on the enemies, real and
imaginary, of conservative rule. The purge machinery put in place to eliminate
militarists from public life in 1946 now was cranked up and redirected towards left-
of-centre liberals, labour activists and suspected Communists. The so-called Red
Purge began almost imperceptibly in April 1949 when the US commander of
the Yokosuka Naval Base attempted to force officials of *Sanbetsu*-affiliated unions to
sign Taft–Hartley style loyalty statements disavowing Communism. Union leaders
resisted, and GHQ's Labour Division openly sided with them, noting that the
loyalty oath and sanctions against those who refused to comply violated basic Japanese labour law. The issue was dropped, but it anticipated two subsequent steps
taken after mid-1949 to combat Communist influence in public life: the suppression
of left-wing ideas in education and the repression of Korean nationalism. Gaining
momentum, in 1950 the purge would spread from educators and Koreans to the
Communist Party and, ultimately, to public and private enterprises, the mass media
and even the arts. Coordinating this programme for SCAP were CI&E, ESS, GS,
and Willoughby's omnipresent G-2.[44]
    From late 1948, Military Government Teams had waged an intense but low-
profile campaign at the local level against the Japan Teachers' Union (*Nikkyōso*). In
November, Colonel Frank Hollingshead of the Tokyo MGT accused *Nikkyōso* of
having disgraced itself publicly 'by engaging in politically inspired issues having
nothing to do with the legitimate function of teachers' unions'. In February 1949,
Hollingshead's education officer Captain Paul T. Dupell told an academic audience
at Nippon University in Tokyo that Communism 'thrives like a disease festering in
filth' and urged the discharge of Communist teachers. 'We see no difference', he
asserted, between them and 'the former Nazi and Japanese militarists'. Joseph C.
Trainor, Deputy Chief of CI&E's Education Division, later restated the Occupation
position, indicating the extent to which anti-Communism had pervaded GHQ's
ranks. 'The Communist influence in and upon education in Japan was not a matter
of thin shades of pink, of fellow-travellers or of sympathetic intellectuals', he said; 'it
was rather a matter of the deep-dyed red Marxist and international Communist,

having ties with Moscow and prepared for action ranging from the haranguing debate to the tactics of the bully-boy.'[45] Few Japanese educators, Communist or non-Communist, could recognise themselves or their colleagues in the distorting mirror of such supercharged rhetoric, but by 1949, SCAP's education specialists were convinced that violent revolution from the left was imminent and that bold measures were required to counter the appeal of Communism in the schools and universities.

In July 1949, at the urging of CI&E Chief Donald R. Nugent, SCAP sent Dr Walter C. Eells, a professor of education from Stanford University, on a six-month speaking tour to denounce leftist influence in the schools, notably the Japan Teachers' Union. In his address at the inauguration of Ni'igata University on 19 July, he urged the new institution to remove leftist faculty members and attacked the *Zengakuren* as a Communist-controlled group. 'Must those who may believe in this dangerous doctrine be allowed in the name of academic freedom to teach such doctrines to the youth of the country?' he intoned self-righteously. Eells's lectures were met with boos and catcalls, by shouts of 'liar', 'enemy of democracy' and 'warmonger', but with true missionary grit he carried his anti-Communist vendetta to the far corners of the country.[46] On 7 September 1949, Education Minister Takase Sōtarō, acting on verbal orders from CI&E, secretly instructed prefectural education officials to begin discharging pro-Communist teachers. By March 1950, some 1,100 instructors had been removed from their jobs.

CI&E also targeted Korean schools. These had been allowed to remain open after the disturbances of April 1948 on condition that they register with the Education Ministry as private schools and introduce a basic Japanese curriculum in addition to ethnic courses. Following the creation of the Democratic People's Republic in September 1948, the schools had become a focus of pro-North Korean agitation and the stronghold of *Choryŏn*, the League of Korean Residents in Japan. The schools and the League had been particularly active in Yamaguchi Prefecture in southern Honshu. When Attorney General Ueda and SIB Chief Yoshikawa consulted Government Section's Napier about the situation in Yamaguchi in August 1949, Napier told them bluntly to dissolve the League. Consequently, on 8 September, Yoshikawa invoked the Organisation Control Ordinance and disbanded the group, depriving an overwhelming majority of Koreans of political leadership. *Choryŏn*'s leaders were purged, its property and other assets were confiscated and auctioned off and the proceeds deposited in the national treasury. On 19 October, under intense pressure from CI&E, the Education Ministry then extended the purge to Korean ethnic schools affiliated with the League, shutting them down as well.[47]

In late 1949, GHQ urged the government to 'decommunise' the civil service systematically but without establishing formal purge procedures. Since July, the government had targeted Communist sympathisers as part of its public-sector retrenchment programme, but now it expanded the scope of the exclusion programme. In June of 1950, before the start of the Korean War, MacArthur intervened personally. On 30 May, Communist-affiliated groups demonstrating in the 'People's Plaza' in front of the Imperial Palace had shouted anti-American slogans and roughed up several off-duty GIs. Simultaneously, the JCP organ *Akahata* launched a broadside attack on Occupation policy. The Communist Party appeared to be acting in conformity with Cominform Instruction no. 172. On 6 June, MacArthur sent Yoshida a letter ordering him to purge the JCP's Central Committee. 'I direct you', the message said, 'to make the necessary administrative measures to remove and exclude . . . the full membership of the Central Party of the Japan Communist Party from public service and render them subject to the prohibition, restrictions and liabilities of my directive of Jan. 4, 1946, and their implementing ordinances.' The list of 24 people included virtually every important Communist leader in Japan. Those purged were prohibited from holding public office or engaging in political activity. They could not belong to a political party, speak or write publicly on behalf of a political cause or even attempt privately to advance a political agenda. They were required to register their current address and any future changes of address with the government.[48] On 7 June, the General extended the purge directive to the editorial board of *Akahata*.

In late June, as SCAP proceeded with plans to expand its removal programme, events on the Korean peninsula took a dramatic turn. In the early morning hours of 25 June, some 90,000 North Korean soldiers supported by Soviet-made tanks swept across the 38th parallel, marking the beginning of the Korean War. On 27 June, the UN Security Council adopted a resolution condemning the breach of the peace, calling on North Korean forces to withdraw to the 38th parallel and requesting member states to assist South Korea. On 29 July, Truman ordered a naval blockade of Korea and the use of US ground troops, and on 7 July, the Security Council passed another resolution setting up a 'Unified Command' to organise a military response in Korea and turned full responsibility for that effort over to the United States. Truman immediately appointed MacArthur, his Far East Commander, to lead the Unified Command under the UN flag, and the Yoshida government pledged its full support for the US 'police action'.

The outbreak of war imparted fresh urgency to GHQ's crusade against Communism in Japan. On 26 June, *Akahata* itself was forced to suspend publication for one month due to allegedly one-sided reporting of events in Korea, and on 18 July, the paper was shut down indefinitely. On 24 July, Government Section's Napier, acting through SIB chief Yoshikawa, had told seven major newspapers and the Japan Broadcasting Corporation (NHK) to begin their own internal purges. Editors and broadcasters complied with the order on 28 July. Government Section also spearheaded the campaign to expel Communists from the shopfloor. GS Chief Whitney, Deputy Chief Frank Rizzo (Kades's replacement) and Jack Napier, with the full support of MacArthur and Willoughby, and in consultation with CI&E's Nugent and Charles N. Spinks of Diplomatic Section, ordered Japanese bureaucrats and corporate executives to proceed with 'decommunisation' on the highest authority. Napier's pro-active role as chief inquisitor earned him the sobriquet of 'Mr Purge'. GHQ was determined that as little blame as possible accrue to the Occupation, however, and purge orders invariably were communicated by word of mouth as informal guidance. The precise modality was left to the discretion of government agencies, boards of directors and Democratisation League cells, but Yoshikawa's Special Investigation Bureau and Willoughby's Counter-Intelligence Corps stood ready with lists of 'known subversives'.

On 10 August, 1950, SCAP extended 'decommunisation' to private industry, where the Korean War provided employers with a new excuse to discharge 'undesirable elements', for union organisers now represented an unacceptable security risk to companies holding US military special procurement contracts. Here, management and right-wing labour leaders, skilfully manipulating the revised Labour Union Law, conspired to rewrite union shop agreements and expel 'active troublemakers', a code word for leftists in general. The Labour Ministry played a double game, urging restraint on the one hand while promising not to interfere with the elimination of subversive unionists, on the other.

There were no legal grounds for the anti-Communist crusade. Its putative authority derived solely from SCAP's 1946 purge instruction, which had targeted rightists, not liberals and leftists. In late July, however, the Justice Ministry announced its support for MacArthur's policy. According to the private correspondence of ESS Labour Division's Valery Burati, with Vice Minister Teramoto Kōsaku serving as SCAP liaison, the Labour Ministry's reform bureaucrats agreed not to apply the so-called workers' bill of rights in Article 3 of the Labour Standards Law ('Stander's and Teramoto's baby') to discharged Communists. This decision, Burati wrote, had Labour Division's Golda Stander 'feeling thoroughly depressed and almost in tears'.[49]

Burati also confirmed that, in late July, GS Chief Whitney had taken unprecedented steps to protect MacArthur's headquarters from possible litigation. Whitney reportedly met secretly at that time with Tanaka Kōtarō, now Chief Justice of the Supreme Court (1950–60), and ordered him not to adjudicate lawsuits arising from the firings. The Legal Section officer present at the interview, which was 'entirely vocal', was instructed not to take notes of the conversation. Burati writes: 'Tanaka was told that the courts could not question management's designation of Communist. Anyone so designated by management was to be considered per se a Communist and the courts were not to touch his case'. Judge Tanaka apparently accepted this advice, for purge victims effectively were denied due process of law. 'The Legal Section also believes that Tanaka has instructed the lower courts, though not in writing', Burati noted. In early October, the Labour Ministry summed up the government position in an administrative guideline to prefectural and municipal authorities. The purge, it advised, was being undertaken on orders from SCAP. The dismissal of subversive elements was a defensive measure taken to protect the viability of private industry and should not be considered a violation of constitutional rights or basic labour law.[50]

As the removal campaign got underway, concern grew within ESS Labour Division that the 'discharging of Communists' might get out of hand. On 29 June 1950, shortly after MacArthur issued his purge instruction to Yoshida, Valery Burati sent ESS Chief Marquat a memorandum entitled 'Programme Against Communists in Japanese Labour'. The plan called for increased GHQ support of Democratisation Leagues and similar counter-measures but stopped short of recommending direct action. Burati, the only trade unionist in Labour Division, opposed the overt use of authoritarian methods to remove Communists and warned that managers should not be encouraged to fire left-leaning employees indiscriminately. 'We did not favour [their] retention', he said later, 'but if they were to be expelled, we wanted them expelled by democratic means.'[51] The State Department's labour specialist in Japan, Philip Sullivan, who had helped draft US pre-surrender plans for Japanese trade unions, also was critical of the purge. Why undermine the country's fragile labour democracy just as it had taken root, he wrote to Burati in November. Government Section, however, had no intention of relenting, and the purge was transformed into an extensive witch hunt that dismissed thousands of Communists, Socialists, left-leaning progressives and even liberals, robbing them of their careers, their livelihoods and often of their self-esteem. By the time the purge mania subsided in late 1950, about 11,000 public employees and another 11,000 workers in private industry had been thrown summarily out of work for their putative political beliefs. The human costs of this egregious abuse of civil rights are incalculable.

The government's ill-fated attempt to outlaw the Communist Party provides an ironic counterpoint to the 'success story' of the purge. In March 1950, Yoshida met MacArthur and asked him to ban the Party by invoking his executive powers as SCAP. Demurring on the grounds that he lacked the proper authority, the General remarked that he would not object, however, if the Diet were to take such action on its own by due process of law. The Prime Minister clearly hoped to use the Occupation to achieve this controversial objective (as it had in ending the second *Yomiuri* labour dispute in June 1946 and banning the general strike projected for 1 February 1947). MacArthur's statement of 3 May 1950 questioning the legality of the JCP seemed to augur well for Yoshida's scheme.

Convinced that Yoshida and his Attorney General (from June, Ōhashi Takeo) intended to enact banning legislation, GS Chief Whitney ordered Government Section's Osborne Hauge and Legal Section's Alfred Oppler and Kurt Steiner to draft a GHQ statement that could be presented to the Japanese as a basis for discussion. On 22 August 1950, the three submitted a lengthy study entitled 'Draft of the Essentials of a Bill Outlawing the Japan Communist Party and Other Organisations'. Attached to the bill, however, was a memorandum by Oppler and Steiner that explored the liabilities of enacting such legislation. An outright ban, they argued, could be construed as a form of thought control. It might infringe on basic constitutional liberties and could lend itself to other abuses unacceptable in a free society. In view of the Occupation's democratising mission, they suggested, such a measure would be self-defeating.[52]

In December 1950, Attorney Ōhashi instructed the SIB's Yoshikawa to study the possibility of invoking the Organisation Control Ordinance (Cabinet Order 64) to dissolve the Communist Party. When Yoshikawa broached the subject to Napier, however, the GS purge master reiterated MacArthur's insistence that only a

Diet-enacted law would be acceptable to SCAP. Consequently, on 10 January, Yoshida again sought MacArthur's advice, this time about the timing of such a bill. The Supreme Commander, however, apparently swayed by the Oppler–Steiner memo, replied that outlawing the JCP would be counter-productive. The government, he noted, had more to lose than to win, since the Party had lost much of its former influence and no longer posed a threat to Japan's security. The purge of Communists from the civil service, public enterprises, private industry and the media of information in 1950, he said, had precluded the necessity of an outright ban, which in any event probably would not pass the Diet and, additionally, would raise constitutional issues redounding to the discredit of the government.[53]

If banning Communism was constitutionally suspect, what then of the purge that in MacArthur's words had made such a measure redundant? The precipitous and arbitrary removal from public life of some 20,000 suspected leftists was a grave injustice. Ironically, however, it subsequently became the focus of complex manoeuvring by groups on both the left and the right who sought to exploit it for partisan ends. The Communists used the purge as ammunition in their campaign to turn public opinion against the Occupation and secure an early peace treaty. Some Socialists found it useful in asserting control over part of the labour movement. Reform bureaucrats saw in the dismissals a unique opportunity to suppress the left and consolidate their conservative agenda while using the ensuing social tensions to pry further concessions from SCAP. The purge debased the political process, diminishing not only those who helped implement it, but also those who attempted to profit by it or who condoned it through silence or inaction.

REARMING JAPAN

The Korean War and special procurements

Politically, the left had been contained. Economically, however, the outlook for Japan remained bleak. The Dodge austerity programme had balanced the budget but failed to generate the capital investment necessary to remedy slack industrial productivity, low export volume and chronic trade deficits. This failure was masked by the outbreak of fighting in Korea in June 1950, which reversed these trends almost overnight, as Japan was transformed into a vast supply depot and forward staging area for US combat forces. As a prominent Japanese economist has noted: 'the tragedy of war in a neighbouring country turned out to be a windfall boon for the Japanese economy'. Indeed, the conflict made believers of hard-headed pragmatists. Prime Minister Yoshida considered the war 'a gift of the gods', and Robert Murphy, America's first postwar ambassador to Japan, declared it 'a godsend'.[54] The engine driving recovery was the avalanche of rush orders for non-weapon goods and services, ranging from coal, scrap metal, textiles, chemical fertiliser, electrical products, and processed rubber to trucks, heavy transport, GI housing, ship and aircraft repair facilities, and communications equipment. Although the bulk of these 'special

Photo 66. Workers at Mitsui Heavy Industries' Sagamihara plant outside Tokyo repair war-damaged US tanks, *c.* 1950. Such work was typical of the Korean war procurements that refloated the economy, ending the Dodge recession (Kyodo).

procurements' were non-military, Japan also supplied barbed wire, incendiary bombs and napalm and by 1953 was manufacturing ammunition, small arms, machine guns and trench mortars disguised disingenuously as 'education orders'.[55]

The procurements boom, paid for in dollars and officially listed as 'invisible exports', enabled Japan to redress its balance of payments, reutilise much of the industrial plant capacity and equipment previously slated for removal as war reparations, boost employment and raise wages. War-matériel production alone generated jobs for an estimated 20,000 workers. During the conflict, imports of raw materials doubled and exports nearly trebled. In October 1950, industrial production exceeded the prewar level for the first time. Yoshida's 1946 priority production scheme favouring coal, steel, marine transport and electric power had foundered by time Joe Dodge arived in Tokyo in 1949. The Korean War boom refocused attention on heavy industry and strengthened the system of top-down industrial policy-making, which became a trademark feature of postwar economic growth.

On 20 February 1951, Economic and Scientific Section completed a report on Japan's latent industrial potential that called for an increase in the production of coal, steel and other heavy industrial goods of more than double the production levels of the 1932–6 period. In mid-May, ESS Chief Marquat, returning from a trip to Washington, announced the extension of new lines of credit and pledged US financial and technical support in developing strategic materials. US capital, he said, would not only provide technological assistance but stood ready to invest in selected Japanese companies. In order to keep the special procurements programme alive, on 12 February 1952, the Japanese government proposed reviving military production in certain areas and requested credit lines and the import of raw materials. Two days later, Marquat issued a directive allowing the revival of aircraft and armaments production, in response to which the Ministry of International Trade and Industry partially lifted its ban on such manufactures. These measures enabled the procurements scheme to survive into the post-treaty period.[56]

The National Police Reserve

Early fighting in Korea had gone badly for US forces. Leaving Kyushu for the peninsula with little advance preparation, the 24th Infantry Division lost 25 per cent of its strength in a single week's fighting in early July. By the end of that month, MacArthur had deployed virtually all of the Eighth Army's tactical forces – some 65,000 troops – across the straits to defend a shrinking perimeter on the southeastern tip of the peninsula around Taegu and the ports of Masan and Pusan. On 8 July, the day he was appointed to lead the UN Unified Command, MacArthur sent a letter to Yoshida 'authorising' the Prime Minister to augment Japan's 125,000-strong police force by a 'national police reserve of 75,000 men' and its Maritime Safety Board, established in 1948 as an embryonic Coast Guard, by 8,000. MacArthur asserted that a National Police Reserve (NPR) was needed to maintain 'public peace and security' but made no reference to the war. On 13 July, however, the Japanese government was told the new force would be placed under direct Cabinet control by Potsdam decree, not Diet legislation, and organised separately from the regular police. To avoid the constitutional issue, SCAP maintained the polite fiction that the force did not have military potential. The NPR came into being on 10 August, and by the end of the month, its first unit of 7,000 had been formed. Yoshida appointed former Home Ministry bureaucrat and Yoshida loyalist Masuhara Keikichi to head the Reserve. US planners, however, soon were urging Tokyo to expand the force to between 300,000 and 350,000 effectives, an augmentation that no internal security needs could possibly justify. It was clear to both American and Japanese officials – although Yoshida denied it to the end of his political career – that the National Police Reserve was an undercover army intended to serve as the core of a future fully equipped national military force.[57]

SCAP created a Civil Affairs Staging Area in a corner of the Dai-Ichi Mutual Life Insurance Building and appointed Major General Whitfield P. Shepard, then Chief of the Civil Affairs Section (CAS), and his executive officer, Colonel Frank Kowalski Jr, to create, direct and train the new army. Any illusions that the organisation was a mere police force were soon dispelled. After a visit to an NPR training camp, Diplomatic Section's Sebald recalled that 'The new Japanese Army . . . looked as though it had been made in the United States.' 'I thought at first I had stumbled into an American base', he wrote, 'for everything from guns to fatigues was GI. Only when I saw the Japanese soldiers eating with chopsticks did I fully realise that these were,

Photo 67. Japan's new National Police Reserve on review, 25 August 1950. The NPR, established at the outbreak of the Korean War on MacArthur's orders, signalled a decisive turning away from the early Occupation reforms, notably the Constitution's pacifist Article Nine (Kyodo).

indeed, soldiers of another Japanese generation, with a new mission.'[58] Drills were based on direct translations of US Army manuals, leading to some curious situations. The traditional Japanese command *kashira migi* (literally, 'heads right') became *man-ako migi* ('eyes right'), a stiff, archaic rendering of the English that caused some trainees to shift their eyes rightward on command but without moving their heads. Under CAS guidance, recruits were trained thoroughly in the use of such unpolice-like equipment as tanks (camouflaged in the manuals as 'special vehicles'), carbines, M-1 rifles, machine guns, bazookas and mortars. 'Americans managed these troops like a private army', Kowalski later commented. 'As battalions of infantry the NPR could have put on a whale of a fight.' The Police Reserve also opened the door to former military officers anxious to resume interrupted careers. Of the 400,000 people who applied in September 1951, over half had served in the Imperial Army. Moreover, about 800 candidates were invited to apply from among the unpurged former officers of the Japanese-led Manchukuo Army, their presumed anti-Communism recommending them for NPR work.[59]

The Old Guard attempted to reassert its influence via another route. Unknown to MacArthur or the Japanese government, in May 1946, General Willoughby had recruited Colonel Hattori Takushirō, the former Imperial General Staff officer, to build up a nationwide cadre of officers in hopes of reconstructing, at some later time, a Japanese army. A protégé of Ishiwara Kanji (ultra-rightist ideologue, Kwantung Army officer and architect of the 1931 Manchurian invasion), Hattori had served as military secretary to General Tōjō. After the war, the Colonel used his position on the Demobilisation Board to maintain active lists of some 70,00 former officers. In 1947, Willoughby confided to Government Section's Alfred Hussey that the Pentagon had ordered him to 'maintain the nucleus of the [Imperial] General Staff and . . . the records of the Japanese Army and Navy'. Charged by Willoughby with this task, Hattori quickly built an informal organisation, complete with prototype general staff, that came to include some 400 officers. When MacArthur ordered the creation of the Police Reserve, Willoughby attempted to instate Hattori as commander-in-chief and place his fellow officers in leadership positions. Kowalski, presented with a list of officer candidates for four divisions, consulted MacArthur's aide Colonel Lawrence E. Bunker, who brought the matter to the Supreme Commander's attention. A surprised MacArthur wisely overruled Willoughby and quashed the initiative, much to the relief of Yoshida, who reportedly was alarmed and deeply offended by the affair. Nonetheless, Willoughby apparently achieved some degree of success, for Civil Affairs Section later complained that 'the appointment of former police or political personnel to key . . . line and staff positions has been a constant block to progress'.[60]

The NPR moved into US military bases in Hokkaido and elsewhere abandoned in the wake of American troop deployments to Korea, and a special requisition programme was set up to equip it with military surplus and weapons from US stocks. Although the NPR operated only at the infantry company level, US and Japanese officials drafted coordinated plans to integrate this quasi-military force into larger Allied units in the event of an emergency. The Japan–US Military Security Assistance (MAS) agreement would formalise these arrangements in 1954, the year the integrated Self-Defence Forces were created. Japan, as one historian has remarked, now 'was set upon the path all military planners eventually march along, where the signposts point in a single direction and read: the best defence is a good offence – keep moving, keep moving'.[61]

Although the NPR never was directly involved in the fighting in Korea, Japan nonetheless cooperated wholeheartedly with the US war effort. The Maritime Safety Board, for example, deployed 20 minesweepers for demining operations in the waters around Korea under US Navy command. Japanese railroad, shipping, engineering, and communications specialists with first-hand knowledge of Korean conditions worked for UN forces, providing essential services. Many of these were former Japanese soldiers, now depurged. 'The Japanese were not asked or permitted to recruit soldiers to help us,' wrote Robert Murphy, 'but Japanese shipping and railroad experts worked in Korea with their own well-trained crews.' This was a top secret operation, he noted, adding that 'the Allied forces would have had difficulty remaining in Korea without this assistance from thousands of Japanese specialists who were familiar with that country'.[62] Another little-known area of cooperation was stevedoring. Japanese civilian seamen manned more than 120 power barges under Kitamura Masanori, President of East West Shipping Inc., for logistical support and other war-related activities. The barges were hired by the US Navy on the basis of secret contracts signed immediately after the Inchon landing of 15 September 1950. Japanese workers at home also performed vital support duties that otherwise would have required the presence of an estimated 260,000 American service troops.[63]

Ridgway and the integration of Cold War policy
The clearest indication that the Occupation had entered a new phase was SCAP's reinterpretation of Article Nine's absolute renunciation of arms and belligerency. Even before the Korean War began, however, MacArthur, a strict interpretationist, had modified his public views on Japan's defence arrangements. On 1 January 1950, he told the Japanese people in his New Year's address that 'by no sophistry of reasoning can [Article Nine] be interpreted as a complete negation of the inalienable right of self-defence against unprovoked attack'. Shortly afterward, Yoshida aired similar sentiments. Thenceforth, MacArthur's staff were at pains to lay responsibility for the strictly pacifist reading of Article Nine at the door of Shidehara Kijūrō, postwar Japan's second prime minister. According to Ambassador Murphy, in 1952, MacArthur himself vehemently rejected the notion that GHQ had anything to do with the no-war clause, saying that it was 'entirely a Japanese affair'. Toward the end of the Occupation, a high-ranking GHQ officer summed up the American view, telling a senior Japanese official that 'before the Korean War, the author was our old man. After the Korean War, the author was your old man.'[64]

From early 1950, Washington pressed Yoshida to accept long-term US bases in Japan, resume war production, rebuild a military force and join the United States in a collective regional defence arrangement. In early May 1950, Yoshida sent Finance Minister Ikeda Hayato, Ikeda's assistant Miyazawa Ki'ichi (prime minister, 1991–3) and Yoshida's personal aide Shirasu Jirō to Washington to sound out US views on ending the Occupation (MacArthur had forbidden Yoshida to negotiate directly on security questions). There, Ikeda told Joseph Dodge that the Japanese premier was ready to accept in principle the quid pro quo of post-treaty US bases for 'the earliest possible peace treaty'.

The idea of remilitarising, however, was anathema to Yoshida. On 22 June, three days before the Korean War began, Truman's special treaty envoy John Foster Dulles met Yoshida for the first time and repeated Washington's demand for a Japanese rearmament. Yoshida dismissed the notion airily and insisted on soliciting MacArthur's opinion. The Supreme Commander backed the Prime Minister, proposing 'industrial remilitarisation' as an alternative. Sometime between 21 and 23 June, however, MacArthur abandoned his hopes for permanent Japanese neutrality. In return for Defense Department support of an early peace accord, the General acquiesced in principle to a standing army and an unrestricted post-treaty US military deployment in Japan proper.[65] Even after the creation of the NPR, however, MacArthur refused to press for the high troops levels demanded by Washington.

The Korean War crystallised US policy towards Japan, but the shift to an integrated Cold War phase of occupation dates roughly from MacArthur's dismissal by President Truman in the spring of 1951. By late 1950, US forces had occupied most of the Democratic People's Republic in a bid, as MacArthur later expressed it, 'to clear out all North Korea, to unify it and to liberalise it'. Indeed, on 27 September, Washington had authorised the General to cross the 38th parallel and reunite the peninsula, short of provoking a Chinese or Soviet engagement.[66] In late November, however, as American troops approached the Yalu and Tumen Rivers on China's northeastern border with North Korea, some 250,000 Chinese People's Volunteers stormed southward, destroying the UN line and gradually pushing the Unified Command back to the 38th parallel, where in early 1951 both sides dug in for a long war of attrition. (A ceasefire would not be declared until 27 July 1953.)

MacArthur, however, had exceeded his mandate by bombing the Yalu River bridges and other sensitive targets. The Joint Chiefs protested that his rash actions had invited Chinese intervention in violation of their directive of September 1950. The General's subsequent calls to aggressively challenge China and widen the war in Korea brought him into direct conflict with Truman and the Pentagon, who were determined to end the war. Concluding that the Supreme Commander's bellicose actions had encroached on the authority of the President, the Joint Chiefs advised that he be relieved of his commands in Japan, Korea and the Far East. On 11 April, Truman complied with that recommendation, recalling MacArthur and naming General Matthew B. Ridgway, Eighth Army commander in Korea since December 1950, to replace him.[67]

Ridgway took over as SCAP in mid-April 1951, ending the quasi-autonomous status that MacArthur had arrogated for the Occupation by the sheer force of his personality. A team player lacking MacArthur's panache and overarching vision, the business-like Ridgway set about the task of rearming Japan and strengthening its internal security. With the departure of Whitney, who accompanied MacArthur into retirement, Frank Rizzo became GS chief and Jack Napier his deputy. One of the first priorities of the 'Ridgway–Rizzo régime' was to rehabilitate the nearly 200,000 ultra-nationalists GHQ had discharged from public life during the 'white purge'. In October 1950, MacArthur had agreed to release some 10,900 relatively harmless purgees in compliance with NSC-13/2's call for a relaxation of exclusion controls. In April 1951, soon after replacing MacArthur, Ridgway threw open the doors to all purged career military officers commissioned after 1937. By October 1951, a total of 359,530 ex-military men, politicians and ultra-nationalists had been returned to public life. Many former soldiers found employment with the National Police Reserve. Civil Affairs Section indicated that, by December 1951, it expected to integrate some 400 former field officers, all of them graduates of the pre-1945 Army and Navy military academies, into the force. Among those released from political limbo were Hatoyama Ichirō, Ishibashi Tanzan and Kishi Nobusuke, all of whom would serve as prime minister after the Occupation. In the first post-independence general elections of October 1952, more than 40 per cent of candidates elected to the

Photo 68 General Matthew B. Ridgway, fresh from the fighting in Korea, lands at Tokyo's Haneda Airport to relieve General MacArthur, recalled from his duties as Supreme Commander a few days earlier by President Truman. 15 April 1951 (Kyodo).

Lower House were former purgees. The Old Guard had staged a precipitous and dramatic comeback.[68]

Ridgway also worked to buttress the national security state in an effort to protect America's post-treaty interests in Japan. In May 1951, he set up the Committee on Counter-Measures Against Communism in the Far East, a top-secret SCAP-Eighth Army inter-staff group designed to coordinate SCAP policy in a wide range of areas deemed vital to America's post-Occupation interests in Japan. Among the issues it discussed were means of burnishing the Emperor's image, the surveillance and control of Communists, the deportation of Korean subversives, the Korean school problem, immigration and alien controls and psychological warfare strategies for Japan. The Counter-Measures Committee never fulfilled its Strangelovian ambitions, but its activities illuminate US thinking on Japan at this critical juncture.

With Ridgway's approval and encouragement, Attorney General Ōhashi strengthened the Special Investigation Bureau, and by August 1952, it had swelled from a staff of 260 (1949) to more than 1,700 and included many depurged police officers.[69] On 3 May 1951, Ridgway authorised the government to re-examine and propose modifications to laws and ordinances enacted during the Occupation. The Yoshida Cabinet promptly set up an Ordinance Review Committee, which recommended a further release of purged persons and changes to labour and anti-monopoly laws, land reform and the police and education reforms (chapter 11). The Committee continued its work well into the post-treaty era.

In at least once instance, the government actually strengthened a 'Potsdam Executive Order'. This was the 1949 Organisation Control Ordinance, which was repealed in July 1952 and replaced with the far harsher Subversive Activities Prevention Law. The new law was part of a package of 'peace preservation' statutes that Yoshida and Ōhashi had proposed to enact, including a prohibition on general strikes and the regulation of meetings and demonstrations, but these were never realised. Rizzo and Napier worked closely with Ōhashi in writing the Subversive Activities Prevention Bill, which was based in large part on the US Smith and McCarran Acts discussed earlier. Although many of its blatantly undemocratic features were eliminated in the drafting process, the law immediately bred constitutional controversy when it was passed on 21 July 1952. Directed primarily at Communists, labour agitators and Koreans, it represented the culmination of Yoshida's earlier campaign to outlaw the Communist Party. Responsibility for invoking the law passed from the Special Investigation Bureau, which was abolished, to the Public Security Investigation Agency, a more powerful organ attached to the Justice Ministry.[70]

In one area, SCAP's efforts to achieve greater Cold War integration failed spectacularly. This was the creation of *Sōhyō*, the General Council of Trade Unions of Japan, which ESS Labour Division's Valery Burati had worked hard to promote among left-orientated but non-Communist unionists. A foe of right-wing labour leaders, Burati threw his support to the left wing of the Democratisation Leagues and such Socialist radicals as Takano Minoru. His dream was to unify Japanese labour under a liberal, non-Communist leadership affiliated with the US- and British-backed International Confederation of Free Trade Unions (ICFTU), which had been created in late 1949 to oppose the Communist-dominated World Federation of Trade Unions (WFTU). But the democratisation movement had a mind of its own, and neither Burati nor Labour Division was able to control it. In July 1950, Hara Shigeru of the Japan Coal Mine Workers, Iwai Akira of the National Railways Workers, Ōta Kaoru of the Synthetic Chemical Workers, and other radical demo-cratic unionists inaugurated *Sōhyō*, with SCAP's approval. The new national centre incorporated nearly 4 million workers, or roughly half of organised labour. As Burati later recalled, however, 'The real foundation for *Sōhyō* was a strong feeling for independence . . . not GHQ initiative or permission.'[71]

The naive American assumption that all non-Communists were de facto allies proved a major miscalculation. MacArthur's staff expected *Sōhyō* to replace the left-wing *Sanbetsu*, whose leadership had been decimated by the Red Purge, but the new federation moved rapidly to the left. *Sōhyō*'s General Council promptly condemned the North Korean invasion of the south but called for peaceful reunification and non-involvement by Japan. As MacArthur's forces pushed beyond the 38th parallel in October 1950, occupying most of the Democratic People's Republic and precipitat-ing a Chinese counter-attack, any lingering sympathy for US war aims dissipated rapidly. The organisation also condemned the Red Purge for its indiscriminate dis-missals, although its opposition was largely rhetorical and it did little to contest the mass firings. In March 1951, *Sōhyō* adopted the Socialists' four-point peace policy (no peace treaty without China and the Soviet Union, a neutral foreign policy, no bases on Japanese soil and no rearmament) and rejected membership in the ICFTU. The labour front had begun as an earth-bound chicken, according to a popular analogy of the day, but had developed wings, metamorphosing into a duck that could fly.[72]

With *Sōhyō*'s leftward turning, Burati's days in Japan were numbered. In June 1951, he was 'put on the first ship home' for, among other things, publicly denouncing a decision by Ridgway and the Yoshida Cabinet to place the 'People's Plaza' at the Imperial Palace off limits during that year's May Day celebrations. Japanese workers, he later remarked, 'looked to the use of the Plaza as a [symbol] of the new freedom for labour. When this was suddenly denied them, they saw it as a return to the old repressive ways.' Even Ridgway harboured personal qualms about backing the government, fearing that SCAP endorsement of the decision 'would be interpreted as a slap to the working man'. The Emperor promptly assuaged those misgivings, however, telling Ridgway during their first meeting of his pleasure at the Supreme Commander's show of support.[73]

One year later, on 1 May 1952, three days after the restoration of Japanese sovereignty, 400,000 workers paraded through Tokyo to celebrate the nation's independence. Some 6,000 workers, barred again from the the 'People's Plaza', forcibly occupied this space so emblematic of Imperial authority and the Old Order, clashing with 5,000 riot police. Firing tear gas and small arms, police killed two demonstrators, injured some 2,300 and arrested more than 1,000, including large numbers of Communists and Koreans. *Sōhyō* was among the first to denounce the repression. The new labour centre took the government to court, charging it with abridging the constitutional right of freedom of assembly (the Supreme Court ruled in the state's favour in 1953). This turn of events epitomised the polarisation that reigned at the end of the Occupation, a product of the purge, war in Korea and Japanese rearmament.[74]

The Korean minority and the Cold War

Koreans were among the first victims of the Cold War, and their situation in Japan deteriorated as the reverse course proceeded. The minority's ambiguous legal status reflected a stark Cold War reality: the absence of a popularly elected government in its divided homeland. The Kobe and Osaka disturbances of April 1948 marked a watershed in the Korean community's relations with GHQ. The Occupation had 'bestowed' democracy on the defeated Japanese, but Koreans, ostensibly a liberated people, had been largely excluded from the process of reform. When they pressed for better treatment and a basic degree of cultural autonomy, they overstepped the bounds that SCAP had decreed acceptable for Japanese democracy.[75]

Following the Kobe–Osaka demonstrations, MacArthur asked Diplomatic Section to prepare a staff study on the status of Koreans in Japan. Sebald appointed his legal officer Richard B. Finn to draft the paper. Working closely with Jules Bassin of Legal Section, Finn finished his report in August 1948. 'The large Korean group in Japan, which is for the most part unassimilable ... and the source of dangerous friction with the Japanese', he concluded, 'constitutes a strong element of instability in the Far East and the cause of unfavourable propaganda directed against the United States as the principal occupying power in Japan.' With the establishment that month of a US-backed government in southern Korea, SCAP now was bound by State Department policy to define clearly the legal status of resident Koreans, but this Finn counselled against. 'If the treatment now accorded United Nations nationals or other foreigners in Japan were extended to Koreans', he said, 'the position of Koreans in Japan would become further entrenched in direct conflict with SCAP policy to encourage their return to Korea.' For the time being, 'Koreans in Japan should not be given any special rights or protection'. Even Finn, however, harboured doubts about the legality of Japan's Korean policy. The denial of voting rights in December 1945, he told the Foreign Ministry's Wajima Eiji in early February 1949, may have been desirable, but it 'set up a subordinate type of Japanese citizenship which seemed to me to violate the provisions of the new Constitution calling for complete equality of all Japanese nationals'. Wajima replied that the Japanese had always considered the Koreans 'an inferior race' and that this was the cause of Japanese 'uncertainty and hostility' towards the minority. Finn did not press the issue.[76]

Legal Section, however, took the position that Koreans should be offered the option of acquiring Japanese nationality. The device for accomplishing this, Jules

Bassin insisted, was the transfer of Korean household registers from Korea to Japan, a solution the Japanese government itself had contemplated in November 1944 (chapter 9). In May 1949, Bassin recommended that Koreans be offered three choices: repatriation (deemed unlikely), the acquisition of full Japanese citizenship, or the retention of permanent alien status. 'In this way', he argued, 'Koreans in Japan will eventually be divided into distinct legal groups and so divided will be subject to better control, both for purposes of repatriation and absorption.' Those who became Japanese citizens would be assimilated. The third option would 'accord the Occupation Forces and later the Japanese government, a lever in dealing with them'. Neither SCAP, Japan nor the Republic of Korea, however, intended to give Koreans a choice of citizenship. Following repeated démarches by the ROK Diplomatic Mission in Tokyo, SCAP briefly considered a request to register non-Communists as South Korean nationals and accord them foreign status, but in August 1949, acting on the advice of General Whitney, MacArthur vetoed the idea as beyond the Occupation's authority and inimical to Japan's long-term interests. The problem of legal status, he concluded, should be resolved by Seoul and Tokyo after the Occupation. Nothing was said about North Koreans, however, who presumably would become stateless persons.[77]

SCAP and the government, each for their own reasons, conspired to withhold from Koreans full civil and political rights. In June 1949, the Attorney General's Office suggested in a memorandum to Government Sction that 'it would be realistic and reasonable to treat [Koreans] sometimes as Japanese nationals and at other times as non-Japanese, as may fit the occasion, for the time being, and to extend the range of the latter treatment with all possible promptitude, so as ultimately to come to treat them as non-Japanese in every respect'. The memo urged that control over Koreans be tightened, on the one hand, while 'extending to them kind protection, on the other, so as to soften their feelings against Japan'. Concerning voting rights and alien registration, with its implicit threat of deportation, Koreans were to be considered non-Japanese. For purposes of taxation, education and property ownership, they would be treated as Japanese. One month earlier, Matsukata Makoto, scion of the Matsukata family, naturalised US citizen and GS staff officer, concluded after consulting concerned Japanese ministries that 'the Japanese, as a whole, still regard the Koreans as a tool of the Japanese people'. The government, he said, for the time being 'would rather have jurisdiction of the Koreans and recognise them as Japanese nationals in order that continued control may be exercised'.[78]

Following the creation of the Democratic People's Republic in September 1948, GHQ attempted to bolster the Pro-Seoul Korean Residents Union in Japan (*Mindan*) while orchestrating a crackdown on its leftist rival *Choryŏn*. Although the vast majority of Koreans in Japan had come originally from the southern part of the peninsula, their sympathies were overwhelmingly with the northern régime, which articulated the nationalist aspirations of workers and peasants. In the words of an American observer formerly with the US Army Military Government in Korea, 'The North Korean flag is the symbol of the only political orientation which has persistently fought to improve the position of Koreans in Japan. . . . Thus the fact that his leadership is Communist has not inclined the average Korean to disavow [the flag], but rather has counted in its favor.'[79] In SCAP's eyes, however, that flag represented a 'Soviet-established government,' and in October 1948, Willoughby ordered the Japanese police to suppress its use in public places. Almost immediately, in Sendai, Miyagi Prefecture, Eighth Army military police opened fire without warning on Koreans at an athletic meet where the northern flag was being paraded, wounding six participants, one of them critically. A series of flag-related incidents extending into 1949 resulted in violence and the arrests of dozens of Korean men and women for 'raising, condoning or failing to stop' displays of the banner. The prohibition extended even to lapel pins, badges and posters bearing a likeness of the emblem. Many violators of the banning order were convicted under Imperial Ordinance 311 and sentenced to hard labour and deportation – to South Korea.[80]

Largely indifferent to past colonial injustices, Occupation authorities failed utterly to comprehend the dynamics of Korean nationalism.[81] The government exploited this ignorance and American anti-Communism in a carefully contrived effort to expel virtually the entire Korean community. In July 1949, Yoshida's aide Shirasu Jirō visited Diplomatic Section and proposed 'a drastic attack upon Japan's Korean problem', calling for the deportation of 500,000 to 600,000 North and South Koreans. In late summer, Yoshida formally petitioned MacArthur to authorise this project, complaining that Koreans were mostly Communists, fellow-travellers, criminal elements, or parasites who contributed nothing to the economy. He proposed deporting all 650,000 to South Korea at government expense. In his response to the Premier, MacArthur agreed that Koreans should not be encouraged to remain in Japan but rejected the unilateral use of force to remove them.[82]

Meanwhile, as discussed earlier, the Attorney General dissolved the Korean League on 9 September on orders from Napier, and on 19 October, Japanese police closed down the League's ethnic schools, which CI&E Chief Donald R. Nugent accused of being run by 'agents of the Japan Communist Party' and spreading 'North Korean propaganda of a jingoistic nature'. To enforce these measures, Eighth Army stood ready to invoke its state of emergency powers and send tactical units into 'Korean ghettos'.

The repression of the Korean minority, like that of labour, was coordinated behind closed doors by a handful of top SCAP officials and their Japanese counterparts via informal agreements, verbal instructions and 'mutual understanding'. Napier later boasted that he applied the same methods to Koreans that he had developed for Communists. 'I had a job for General MacArthur that was something like [National Security Adviser] Oliver North had for President Reagan', he said. The Japanese, however, were anxious to shift the onus for these controversial measures onto the Occupation and pressed GHQ for written orders. GS and CI&E refused to put anything in writing, insisting that the government bear sole responsibility. Thus, the dissolution of *Choryŏn* and the shutting down of its schools were ostensibly Japanese actions that caught even some high-ranking GHQ staff officers unawares. Four days after the school closures, for instance, MacArthur himself reportedly had 'no know-ledge of the action being taken by the Japanese Government until it was announced'.[83]

In late 1949, the government revamped its alien control system. In September, it established an embryonic Immigration Control Bureau inside the Foreign Ministry designed to combat the illegal entry of Koreans. In December, on orders from SCAP, it revised the Alien Registration Ordinance. Enacted on 3 December, the new ARO required Koreans to re-register every three years and carry a standardised alien pass document, increased the criminal penalties for ARO violations, granted the Attorney General expanded powers of deportation and abolished the appeals procedure for deportees that Alfred Oppler had instated in 1947 (chapter 9).[84] Finally, in 1950, as the tougher ARO went into effect, the Justice Ministry enacted the Nationality Law. Despite its liberating protections for women and minors, the statute outlawed dual citizenship and stipulated that only persons born of a Japanese father could acquire Japanese nationality, upholding the prewar principle of patrilineal consanguinity (*jus sanguinis*) and effectively barring Koreans from obtaining full citizenship rights except through rigidly controlled and humiliating naturalisation procedures.

With their political organisation destroyed, their schools closed and tougher alien controls in place, a majority of Koreans saw their chances of achieving social and political equality with Japanese fade. Following the outbreak of the Korean War in June 1950, that hope vanished altogether, and many channelled their energies into the anti-war movement or joined the Communist underground, placing the Korean community once more on a collision course with the Occupation. In November and December 1950, Koreans in Kobe, Kyoto and Ōtsu (Shiga Prefecture) staged a series of rallies opposing tax levies and demanding ethnic education rights, jobs and assist-ance under the Daily Life Protection Law. Thousands of police were mobilised to suppress the demonstrations, leading to hundreds of arrests in what GHQ called the 'second Kobe riots'. In early 1951, with Government Section and the Special Investi-gation Bureau at work on a deportation scheme for Korean agitators, SCAP's G-1 Section invited a recently retired US Immigration and Naturalisation Service expert, Nicholas B. Collaer, to Japan to draft a comprehensive US-style immigration law complete with anti-subversive measures. Collaer coordinated his work with the Committee on Counter-Measures against Communism in the Far East, which cited stringent alien controls as 'one of the most important contributions the Committee can make in the battle against Communism in Japan.'[85]

In May 1951, Collaer presented the Japanese government with a draft of new immigration legislation based on the US Immigration and Naturalisation Bill, on which he had worked personally. Enacted in 1952 as the McCarran–Walter Act, the US law combined and reinforced two earlier alien control statutes discussed above, the 1940 Alien Registration (Smith) Act and the 1950 Internal Security (McCarran) Act, giving the state broad powers of surveillance and control, detention and deport-ation. Collaer retained Japan's Alien Registration Ordinance, to which he added fingerprinting, and brought immigration and deportation procedures together as a separate law. When the government attempted to insert an 'alien clause' in the

Immigration Control Bill declaring Koreans and Formosans to be foreigners subject to deportation, however, GHQ's Legal Section intervened, vetoing the proposal as 'totally unacceptable'. In a lengthy and highly nuanced brief, Jules Bassin proposed alternative measures for dealing with 'Korean subversives', including the enactment of an anti-sedition statute based on the US Smith and McCarran Acts and internment camps, but stressed that the arbitrary denationalisation of an ethnic minority would contravene the 1948 Universal Declaration of Human Rights. Not only would it constitute discrimination against a minority, he warned, but 'Red propaganda' might exploit such a measure 'to claim, among other things, that SCAP has established an American gestapo in Japan'.[86]

The Immigration Control Law went into effect on 1 November 1951, minus the infamous 'alien clause', and the new Alien Registration Law, replete with fingerprinting, came into force on 28 April 1952, the day Japan regained its independence. In October 1951, the Counter-Measures Committee concluded that, once enacted, the new laws would 'greatly reduce the potential of communist penetration [from abroad] and make possible the elimination [from Japan] of subversive aliens'. The task of training Japanese immigration officers, it said, 'is not a matter of trying to help the Japanese but one of trying to help ourselves by making a major contribution to the security of Japan'. Should the Occupation shirk this responsibility, the Committee warned, 'GHQ will have failed ... to provide Japan with the defensive weapon of alien and subversive control, without which our own security will be much more difficult to maintain'.[87]

THE PEACE SETTLEMENT

Negotiations, phase one

With Washington's primary goals for Japan attained, the last task facing US policy-makers was a peace settlement to end the Occupation, restore Japanese sovereignty and consolidate and safeguard US interests in post-treaty Japan. NSC-13/3 of May 1949 had counselled postponing a treaty in view of alleged Soviet expansionism, but Secretary of State Dean Acheson believed the time had come to grasp 'the nettle' of a negotiated peace, as the Occupation had become 'a rapidly diminishing asset'. MacArthur agreed with that assessment, having himself proposed in March 1947 an early treaty based on the principle of Japanese neutrality (the State Department prepared a treaty draft in August, but George Kennan vetoed it as out of step with Cold War realities). In April 1950, President Truman named John Foster Dulles to serve as foreign policy adviser to Acheson, assigning him special responsibility for opening treaty negotiations with Japan. A scion of the Eastern Establishment, Dulles had studied at Princeton and the George Washington Law School, becoming a high-powered corporate attorney for a Wall Street legal firm. In 1919, he attended the Versailles Peace Conference as a minor functionary and in 1945 served as senior adviser to the US delegation to the United Nations Conference in San Francisco.

Moreover, Dulles was a staunch Republican with impeccable party connections, an asset that would help him steer an eventual treaty through Congress.[88]

As noted earlier, in May 1950, Yoshida, under growing pressure from Washington, had agreed to concede the long-term maintenance of US bases in exchange for a prompt peace. Foreign military installations were the price Japan would pay for its sovereignty. This was a new demand, however, a consequence of Washington's 1948–9 policy realignment. During his tenure in the State Department, George Kennan had supported the retention of Okinawa as a military stronghold but opposed post-treaty bases in Japan proper. 'Given adequate police forces', he believed, 'the [main] islands could safely be left demilitarised and neutralised by international agreement.' Kennan's successor Paul Nitze, however, together with Acheson and Dulles, was committed not only to long-term base rights but a rapid and substantial rearmament.[89]

Dulles arrived in Tokyo on 21 June 1950 for a first round of shuttle diplomacy. When he met Yoshida on 22 June to sound him out on these issues, he was astounded by the Prime Minister's refusal even to consider the question of rearming as a condition for peace. Yoshida spoke 'with circumlocutory indirectness, with vagueness and with an astute use of parables' to get his views across. The Premier believed that Japan was not ready for remilitarisation. The country could not afford it, most people were against it and Japan's Asian neighbours would not tolerate it. Moreover, that a foreign power would attempt to impose such a condition was an affront to the nation's *amour-propre*.[90]

During Dulles's six-day sojourn, MacArthur, as noted above, came around to Yoshida's position of May, accepting in principle a treaty under which 'points in Japanese territory continue to be garrisoned by the Allied Powers . . . through the United States'. Nonetheless, both the Supreme Commander and the Premier were adamant in their opposition to a remilitarised Japan. *Newsweek*'s Foreign Editor Harry Kern had travelled to Tokyo on the same plane as Dulles, and now, on the evening of 22 June following Dulles's unhappy encounter with Yoshida, he invited the diplomat to a private party at the home of his Tokyo bureau chief, Compton Pakenham. The two men introduced Dulles to high-level officials in the Foreign and Finance Ministries, the National Rural Police and the Imperial household. On the day before Dulles left Tokyo, Matsudaira Yasumasa of the Imperial household asked Pakenham to deliver a verbal message to Dulles from the Emperor. The message, in effect, was a plea to release 'many intelligent Japanese', including former high-ranking military officers, from purge restraints (SCAP would comply a year later). In return, under the Imperial aegis, they would form an advisory council to promote US bases in Japan and work for other US objectives coinciding with their agenda. Kern's habile manoeuvring had opened an informal channel of communications between the Japan Lobby, Dulles and the Emperor that by-passed both MacArthur and Yoshida. The impact of Imperial intervention on later treaty deliberations is a matter of conjecture. Nonetheless, as with Okinawa, Hirohito appears once again to have engaged in high-stakes dual diplomacy behind the back of his government, showing utter disdain for his sworn constitutional duties.[91]

The eruption of hostilities in Korea on 25 June came as a rude shock to SCAP and the US defence establishment. Many Washington planners saw the war as directed ultimately against Japan and the US presence there, making the treaty a matter of special urgency. Determined to proceed promptly, Dulles and Acheson negotiated with the Pentagon, producing a basic agreement that President Truman approved on 8 September 1950. A 'brutally frank' document, NSC-60/1 gave the United States the right to keep armed forces in Japan 'for so long, and to such extent as it deems necessary'. Chinese intervention in force in Korea in November confirmed Washington in its resolve to restore peace with Japan and reach a quick agreement on the stationing of US forces there. On 10 January 1951, Truman appointed Dulles his personal treaty representative, noting in his letter of instruction to the envoy that the 'principal purpose in the proposed settlement is to secure the adherence of the Japanese nation to the free nations of the world and to assure that it will play its full part in resisting the further expansion of Communist imperialism'. The letter also affirmed the US desire that 'Japan should increasingly acquire the ability to defend itself'. Dulles arrived in Tokyo on 25 January for a second round of treaty talks, accompanied by two senior Defense Department officials. Yoshida and Dulles met a total of five times, deadlocking on the issue of rearmament.[92]

Negotiations, phase two
Washington was committed to a short, non-punitive peace instrument and a security arrangement that would serve US strategic interests in Asia. In September 1950, Dulles had incorporated a seven-point statement of principle into his treaty draft, and in November he presented these to the Far Eastern Commission. They stipu-lated that all nations at war with Japan were to be parties to the agreement. Japan would seek entry to the United Nations, recognise the independence of Korea, agree to an American-administered UN trusteeship for the Ryukyu and Ogasawara Islands, and accept the Allied disposition of Formosa, southern Sakhalin and the Kurils. Finally, Japan would provide the United States and 'perhaps other forces' with mili-tary facilities, abide by international fishery, narcotics and trade treaties, and agree to a mutual waiver of claims. This became the basic US negotiating position, and all seven points would be included in the final settlement. The security issue, together with the question of who would sign the treaty, however, immediately raised prob-lems between Washington and Tokyo, on the one hand, and between Washington and the Commonwealth countries, on the other, for Dulles had proceeded to Tokyo in January 1951 without properly briefing the Allies.[93]

Yoshida demanded a US defence commitment to an unarmed Japan sanctioned by the UN Charter. United Nations approval of such an 'international legal obligation' would, he believed, circumvent the Article Nine difficulty and leave the country free to develop its trade and industry under America's nuclear umbrella. Yoshida and Dulles first locked horns on 29 January, Yoshida's 'puff ball performance' producing an immediate stalemate. That evening, Yoshida, MacArthur and Dulles met to iron out their differences, with the Supreme Commander acting as mediator. To break the impasse, the General suggested, as he had nearly a year earlier, that industrial remilitarisation, not rearmament, was the answer. Japan should contribute industrial capacity, manpower and facilities, not troops. The next day, Yoshida took the initiative, submitting a five-point position paper that rejected rearmament until after the conclusion of peace and the achievement of economic independence, at which time the collective will of the Japanese people would be the deciding factor. He asked for an international collective security agreement centred on the United States and for American economic assistance and promised not to press the Okinawa–Ogasawara issue despite popular pressure for the return of these islands.[94]

Dulles back-pedalled from his demand for immediate rearmament. In return, on 2 February, Yoshida modified his stance on a standing army by pledging Japan's commitment to a modest military build-up. Specifically, he proposed the creation of land and sea security forces, 50,000-strong, to operate independently of the National Police Reserve, and the establishment of a National Security Ministry. Yoshida and his negotiators in the Foreign Ministry's Treaty Bureau, however, strenuously resisted Dulles's demand for land forces of between 300,000 and 350,000. Japan alone would determine the scope and pace of rearmament. Nonetheless, Yoshida's concession broke the log jam, and on this basis, both sides reached consensus on the broad outlines of a multilateral peace treaty to be accompanied by a separate bilateral security arrangement. On 9 February, Yoshida and Dulles initialled five documents setting out areas of basic agreement. From these would emerge three instruments: a multilateral peace treaty, a bilateral security accord and a bilateral administrative (status of forces) agreement.[95]

Dulles next set off for Manila, Canberra and Wellington to generate support for the treaty and explore a multi-national collective defence scheme in the Pacific. In Manila, President Elpidio Quirino, still smarting over Washington's unilateral rescission of advance reparations payments in May 1949, criticised the treaty proposal for not including a reparations provision. The Philippines eventually agreed to a bilateral defence treaty with the United States in return for a reparations clause in the peace treaty with Japan. Australia and New Zealand, which Dulles visited in mid-March, were alarmed by his plan for an 'island chain' pact to include Australia, Japan, the Philippines, New Zealand and the United States. The sticking point was nervousness over Japanese rearmament. Dulles attempted to overcome that objection by arguing the need to combat Communist aggression in the region and retain Japan as a Free-World ally. Japan and the Philippines, he argued, would serve as a screen between the Sino-Soviet bloc and the southwestern Pacific. Canberra and Wellington, however, feared renewed Japanese aggression more than they did the Communist menace and found the Dulles proposal unpalatable. London, too, frowned on a Pacific pact that excluded Hong Kong and Malaya and in which Britain would have no part. Dulles replied with a draft for a trilateral defence arrangement between Australia, New Zealand and the United States. The so-called ANZUS Pact was signed by the three governments in early September 1951, excluding Britain and confirming American ascendancy in the Pacific.[96]

In the meantime, the British were at work on their own treaty draft for Japan. In April, British and American specialists met in Washington to consider the two documents. The British version was broader and more precise but lacked the liberal, non-punitive character of the American version. On 3 May 1951, the joint working group came up with a combined draft that subsequently was shown to the Japanese, who asked for minor modifications. In August, Dulles insisted that Tokyo insert a reparations article requiring Japan to pay war damages in the form of goods and services, including technical assistance. The final treaty then was prepared for signing in September.

American and British views differed, however, on the question of which China should attend the San Francisco peace parlay. London, which had recognised the People's Republic in early 1950, insisted that Beijing sign for China. This also was the Japanese position, Yoshida being determined to restore trade and diplomatic relations with that country. Washington recognised only the Chiang Kai-shek (Jiang Jieshi) régime in Taipei and was resolutely opposed to the British plan. Since 1950, US policy planners had been haunted by the prospect of Japan's seeking independent trade ties with China and moving out of the American economic orbit. To forestall that event, Washington and SCAP were labouring mightily to draw Japan into an integrated regional trade scheme in Southeast Asia, with Dulles suggesting that Tokyo pay war reparations there in the form of commodities to pry open the region's markets. In mid-June, Dulles and British Foreign Secretary Herbert Morrison meeting in London were unable to reach agreement. They side-stepped the issue by deciding that neither of the Chinas should be invited to San Francisco. Tokyo would be allowed to choose with which government it wished to make peace so long as such a treaty were signed after but within three years of the main settlement's entry into force. The same principle held for other non-signatories. Dulles and Morrison also agreed that Japan would renounce its sovereignty over Formosa, southern Sakhalin and the Kurils but that the treaty would make no final disposition of these territories (below).[97]

The treaty and the security agreement

In the summer of 1951, Washington attempted to give the bilateral security pact an aura of mutuality, but no mutuality was involved. The base agreement was one-sided and riddled with inequalities. The US Joint Chiefs inserted what became known as the 'Far East clause', a purposely vague provision that allowed Washington to use American forces in Japan to insure 'international peace and security in the Far East'. In other words, the United States could use its installations in Japan to support military operations in other parts of Asia without consulting Tokyo beforehand. US troops would be stationed on Japanese soil for an indefinite period as an automatic right not contingent on Japanese assent. Thus, the treaty could not be terminated by Japan alone but required the consent of the United States. Moreover, Japan was prohibited from granting base or military privileges to a third country without Washington's permission. The Pentagon made no explicit commitment to defend Japan in the event of external aggression but acquired the right to put down, at Tokyo's request, 'large-scale internal riots and disturbances . . . caused through instigation or intervention by an outside power or powers' (this latter was scrapped when the accord was renewed in 1960).[98]

For five days in early September, 51 nations formerly at war with Japan met in the San Francisco Opera House to make peace with the defeated nation. The Soviet Union attended but boycotted the proceedings when its grievances were ignored. Dulles had promised to support Moscow's claims to southern Sakhalin and the Kurils if it joined the Peace Conference. The Soviets complained that in its final form, the treaty stated only that Japan relinquished its claims over the islands. They also raised objections to the stationing of foreign troops in post-treaty Japan and insisted that the Ryukyus and Ogasawaras be restored to their pre-defeat status. Finally, Deputy Foreign Minister Andrei Gromyko demanded a clause prohibiting Japan from joining an alliance directed against any Allied Power and called for the demilitarisation of the straits around Japan. The treaty was not open to debate, however, and the Conference President Dean Acheson ruled him out of order. Consequently, the Soviet Union and its allies, Poland and Czechoslovakia, refused to sign the document. Burma, India and Yugoslavia had been invited but refused to attend, neutralist India in large part because of disagreement over the fate of Okinawa and the base and rearmament issues. Beijing and Taipei had been excluded, as had the two Koreas.

In the end, 49 nations, including Japan, initialled the instrument of peace on 8 September. The multi-national pact restored Japanese independence. It was non-punitive and contained no war-guilt clause, although Japan agreed to pay reparations and give up nearly half of its former territory. Nor was the government required to retain the Occupation reforms. The country also pledged to work for peace within the framework of the UN Charter. In June 1952, India signed a separate peace, effective from August, and in 1956, Tokyo initialled an interim peace agreement with Moscow ending their state of war and paving the way for Japan's entry into the United Nations on 18 December (Tokyo time) of that year.

In the late afternoon of 8 September, four hours after signing the Peace Treaty, Yoshida for Japan and Acheson, Dulles and two US senators for the United States affixed their signatures to the Japan–US Security Treaty in a private ceremony at the San Francisco Presidio. A few days earlier, the United States had inked defence pacts with the Philippines and the ANZUS countries. The return of Japanese sovereignty was partial and conditional, a kind of 'subordinate independence' that made Japan, in effect, a permanent client state of the United States. In 1960, when the security treaty came up for renewal, Secretary of State Christian Herter was forced to admit that it contained 'provisions . . . pretty extreme from the point of view of an agreement between two sovereign nations'.[99]

Two major hurdles remained to be cleared, ratification and the Administrative Agreement governing US forces in Japan. The Japanese Diet approved the peace and

Photo 69. Prime Minister Yoshida Shigeru shakes hands with John Foster Dulles after signing the Security Treaty. To Yoshida's left rear is Finance Minister Ikeda Hayato. In the centre is Senator H. Styles Bridges of the Senate Armed Services Committee. To Dulles' left (far right) stands Dean Acheson. 8 September 1951 (US National Archives).

security treaties in late October 1951, but the US Congress was reluctant to ratify them in the absence of a pledge by Tokyo not to recognise the People's Republic of China. London, on the other hand, had instructed its diplomats in Tokyo to oppose any attempt by Yoshida to acknowledge the Nationalist government in Taiwan. To break this impasse, Dulles reneged on his earlier pledge to the British and, on 18 December, handed Yoshida a letter he had ghost-written and told the Prime Minister to send it to Washington. The so-called Yoshida Letter stated simply that Japan had 'no intention to conclude a bilateral treaty with the Communist régime of China'. This assurance was sufficient to insure ratification of the treaties in both houses of Congress in late March 1952.

The final obstacle was the bilateral Administrative Agreement provided for in Article 3 of the Security Treaty. In January 1952, President Truman appointed Assistant Secretary for Far Eastern Affairs Dean Rusk to negotiate this accord with the Japanese. In the ensuing talks, Rusk prevailed over Foreign Minister Okazaki Katsuo, producing a one-sided agreement whose exemptions and privileges granted US troops what amounted to limited extra-territoriality. Article 15 allowed the US military to arrest Japanese nationals outside of base areas, but more importantly, it gave American authorities exclusive jurisdiction over US service personnel and dependants for crimes committed anywhere in Japan. Article 22 of the Rusk draft established a 'combined command' under a US supreme commander 'in the event of hostilities or immediately threatened hostilities in the Japan area'. The combined command was dropped due to fierce Japanese opposition, and the jurisdiction provisions were modified to allow Japanese courts to assert authority in special cases (with US approval), but the final document was no less humiliating, reminding many of the unequal treaties Japan had been forced to sign with the Western powers in the late nineteenth century (it was brought into line with the NATO Status of Forces Agreement in September 1953, but many glaring inequalities remained). The accord subsequently was revised in 1960 as the Status of Forces Agreement.[100]

Washington and Tokyo signed the Administrative Agreement on 28 February 1952, and the San Francisco Peace Treaty and the Japan–US Security Treaty went into effect two months later on 28 April 1952, one day before Emperor Hirohito's 51st birthday. On the same date, Japan and the Republic of China (Taiwan) initialled a bilateral treaty restoring diplomatic and trade relations. Dulles's dream of bringing Japan into the Free-World fold had been realised, but at a very high cost to Japan, for two of its closest neighbours and potential trade partners, the People's Republic of China and the Soviet Union, now were political, economic and ideological foes.

An alternative future: the peace movement
Organised opposition to war and nuclear arms began in Japan soon after the defeat. *Hibakusha* joined local peace groups, and Hiroshima resident Kurihara Sadako, an anti-war poet from the pre-1945 era, launched a local literary review devoted to the atomic bombings.[101] Morito Tatsuo, later Education Minister, and other liberal and left-wing intellectuals founded the Hiroshima Peace Culture Association, and housewives and women labour leaders established the Hiroshima Democratic Women's Council. These grass-roots initiatives soon forged links with the international peace movement. In April 1949, intellectuals from East and West, meeting in Paris and Prague, held the First World Assembly to Protect the Peace, calling for an absolute ban on atomic weapons, and in May 1950, the Assembly issued the Stockholm Appeal denouncing the use of nuclear arms as a crime against humanity and launched an international signature campaign. SCAP prevented Japanese delegates from travelling abroad to attend the World Assembly, but in October of that year, ten local organisations created the Hiroshima Assembly to Protect the Peace, which was joined by hundreds of residents, including *hibakusha* and Koreans.

Following the start of the Korean War in June 1950, Occupation authorities attempted to suppress the peace movement as Communist-inspired, but unauthorised peace rallies by people of diverse political persuasions were held in Hiroshima and Nagasaki on 6 and 9 August of that year. On 30 November, following Chinese intervention in Korea, President Truman told a press conference that the United States was considering the option of atomic weapons. This stunning announcement galvanised the peace movement, intensifying anti-war activities across the nation. 'Illegal' remembrance events were staged again in early August 1951 in the two bombed cities, and in October, peace activists organised the Hiroshima Colloquium on Peace Problems, in which the mayor of Hiroshima participated.[102]

These diverse activities formed a core of anti-war dissent around which opposition to the San Francisco treaties would converge. This broad-based coalition of political parties, labour unions, academics, student groups, citizens' associations and religions organisations, united through bitter wartime experience, was committed to preserving Article Nine. It argued for a peace negotiated from a position of equality and mutual respect that all nations could sign. The coalition put forward four 'principles of peace': a comprehensive peace treaty signed by both Communist and non-Communist nations, opposition to rearmament, opposition to foreign military installations on Japanese soil and a foreign policy based on permanent, unarmed and 'inviolable' neutrality.

In the vanguard of the peace movement was the Colloquium on Peace Problems (*Heiwa Mondai Danwa-kai*), which was established in January 1950 by prominent thinkers, including philosopher Abe Yoshishige, political theorist Maruyama Masao and economist Tsuru Shigeto In its influential peace manifesto, the group defined the concept of inviolable neutrality as entailing support for the Universal Declaration of Human Rights, adherence to 'the spirit of peace in our Constitution' and the right to have 'broad, close and free trading relations with Asiatic countries, in particular with China, in order to achieve economic self-sufficiency' as quickly as possible. The manifesto declared that 'such things as the military agreement with a specific country or the leasing of bases for military purposes to a specific country . . . are, regardless [of the] pretext . . . against the Preamble and the Article Nine of our Constitution, and are likely to contribute towards the ruination of both Japan and the world'.[103] The Colloquium noted that the advent of modern warfare had made belligerency a self-destructive enterprise. It asserted that nuclear deterrence was a dangerous illusion, the Cold War a passing phenomenon and China too powerful to be subordinated to any political bloc. Finally, it concluded that Japan should not take sides in the East–West confrontation.

Opinion leaders such as Nanbaru Shigeru, President of Tokyo University; Marxist economist Ōuchi Hyōe; and Shimizu Ikutarō, a leading literary and social figure, argued strenuously on behalf of these principles. From today's post-Cold War vantage point, these positions have a truly prophetic ring to them. Yoshida, however, attacked his opponents as 'literary sycophants' and denounced unarmed neutralism as 'the babbling of a sleepwalker'. A 38th parallel, he declared later, ran through the heart of the Japanese people. Ironically, Hatoyama Ichirō and Ishibashi Tanzan, soon to lead governments of their own, advocated a militarily strong Japan, and they, too, accused Yoshida of subordinating Japan's independence to the whims of the American superpower.[104]

Photo 70. The Occupation ends with a whimper, then a bang. A street scene in Tokyo's Ueno district as Japan regains its independence, 28 April 1952. The sign between the US and Japanese flags announces the entry into force of the Peace Treaty, but passers-by, absorbed in their own affairs, greet the event with apparent indifference. A few days later, violent confrontations erupted between left-wing demonstrators and police (Kyodo).

Photo 71. Bloody May Day, 1 May 1952. Some 6,000 demonstrators protest against the exclusion of the People's Republic of China and the Soviet Union from the Peace Treaty and the signing of a bilateral Japan–US defence pact. Police broke up the rally in front of the Imperial Palace with tear gas, batons and sidearms. Two workers were shot to death. More than 2,300 were injured, and some 1,000 were arrested. The violence was symptomatic of the divisive legacy of the late Occupation era (Mainichi).

Against this background, in the autumn of 1951, opposition parties challenged the peace and security treaties in the Diet. The right wing of the Socialist Party favoured ratification without Soviet participation but opposed linking the peace accord to the security agreement. The Party's left-wing objected to the exclusion of the Soviet Union and to the security treaty itself. The Communist Party strongly opposed both instruments on the grounds that they did not include all of the powers concerned and allowed the indefinite garrisoning of foreign military forces in Japan. The conservatives, however, wielded sufficient votes to ratify both treaties formally in October, handing the Yoshida government a major victory.

The defeat of the peace faction, which probably represented the views of a majority of Japanese, was inevitable. Forced to operate with the framework imposed by the American occupier, activists were limited in what they could accomplish. Pacifist sentiment in Japan ran strong but was powerless to stop the war in Korea, alter the course of secret Japan–US security negotiations or prevent the deflection of Japanese trade away from China towards Southeast Asia. Nonetheless, the anti-war movement, with its emphasis on non-violence, non-alignment and the abolition of nuclear weapons, has served as an important barometer of the vitality of Japan's postwar democracy (chapter 11).

A divided peace (1): a post-colonial settlement deferred
The San Francisco Peace Treaty ushered in a divided peace. Externally, this truth was reflected in the exclusion of the major Communist countries of Asia from the settlement. Domestically, it was evidenced by the gap – Yoshida's '38th parallel' – that yawned between the treaty's conservative supporters and its liberal opponents. Another, deeper divide also ran through post-Occupation Japan. This was the absence of a post-colonial settlement for Japan's Korean minority and the continued occupation of Okinawa and the Northern Territories by American and Soviet troops.

In April 1951, following MacArthur's recall, Yoshida and Dulles met to discuss the question of whom to include in the peace process. President Syngman Rhee of the Republic of Korea was insistent that his country be represented at the treaty conference, and Dulles agreed, viewing Seoul's participation as a first step towards normalising relations between Japan and South Korea. To Dulles' surprise, Yoshida countered forcefully that Korea was not one of the Allied Powers and should not be included under any conditions. If South Korea became a signatory, the Prime Minister said, Koreans in Japan, most of whom were Communists, would acquire all the compensation and property rights accruing to Allied nationals. He noted that his government would like to deport most of these residents, but that MacArthur had opposed forcible mass repatriation to the south on the grounds that North Koreans 'would have their heads cut off'. Yoshida punctuated his remarks with the unsubstantiated assertion that it was a Korean who had assassinated Shimoyama Sadanori, President of the Japan National Railways, in the summer of 1949.[105] Swayed in part by Yoshida's invective, Dulles eventually agreed to drop the Republic of Korea from the list of treaty delegates.

Dulles, it should be noted, was no champion of oppressed former colonials. In his first memorandum concerning Japan, dated 6 June 1950, he had written that it might 'be difficult to preserve human rights, fundamental freedoms, and individualism in Japan'. To break down what he termed 'the racial barrier' that threatened to hinder Japan's full participation in the Western alliance, he suggested that 'it might be possible to capitalize on the Japanese feeling of racial and social superiority to the Chinese, Koreans, and Russians, and to convince them that as part of the free world, they would be in equal fellowship with a group which is superior to the members of the Communist world'.[106] In short, the United States might profitably enlist Japanese ethnic prejudices in the cause of anti-Communism.

Two other factors mitigated against Korean participation. President Rhee's advisors did not submit a formal statement of Korean goals to Washington until June 1951, by which time the shape of the peace conference largely had been determined. More importantly, in March, London had raised objections to the inclusion of the Republic of Korea as a signatory on the grounds that it was not a member of the Far Eastern Commission. The primary motive for London's reticence was British ire over American opposition to Chinese participation. The Nationalist government represented China on the Far Eastern Commission, not the People's Republic. If Beijing, a non-FEC member, could not attend the San Francisco Conference,

London reasoned, then neither should Seoul. Moreover, South Korean representation was certain to anger Moscow, increasing the likelihood of Soviet obstructionism. The combination of Japanese and British opposition proved determinant. In mid-June, Washington agreed to postpone the question of Korean participation, and Seoul was eliminated as a cosignatory from the American draft.[107]

With the Republic of Korea no longer a party to the peace, the San Francisco settlement avoided the contentious issue of Koreans in Japan. In early November 1951, Foreign Ministry official Nishimura Kumao told the Diet that the government purposely had not included a clause in the treaty offering ex-colonials a choice of citizenship. As independence drew near, Tokyo quietly engineered its own solution to this problem. On 28 April 1952, the day the San Francisco Peace Treaty entered into force, the Justice Ministry unilaterally stripped Koreans and Chinese of their Japanese nationality. The authorisation for this act of radical denationalisation was an internal ministerial directive, Circular No. 438 of 19 April, that stated simply, 'With the coming into effect of the Peace Treaty, Koreans and Formosans shall lose their Japanese nationality.' Many Japanese women married to former colonials also were denationalised, since by law they were listed in their husband's family register (*koseki*) in Korea or Formosa.[108]

As aliens, Koreans and Chinese became subject immediately to the Immigration Control Law (November 1951) and to the more powerful Alien Registration Law, which entered into force together with the Treaty on 28 April. Simultaneously, the government enacted Law no. 126, which 'permitted' Koreans living continuously in Japan from 2 September 1945 through 28 April 1952 to remain in the country 'for the time being' pending an ultimate resolution of their legal status. Finally, Koreans, together with Communists, were targeted by the Subversive Activities Prevention Law of 21 July 1952.

The tragedy of this disposition is that an American-style alien control system complete with anti-sedition provisions and based on the *jus soli* concept of nationality by birthplace was imposed on a society where *jus sanguinis* (patrilineal consanguinity) was the rule. This meant that not only first-generation Koreans but also their children and grandchildren would be subject ad infinitum to these potent and onerous controls, barring the difficult and demeaning option of naturalisation (chapter 11). To discuss legal status and related problems, on 15 February 1952, SCAP's Diplomatic Section brokered the first formal bilateral negotiations between Tokyo and Seoul, but the talks ended in acrimony, and an agreement on the status of South Korean residents would not be reached until the Japan–ROK Normalisation Treaty of 1965. Since Japan does not entertain diplomatic relations with the Democratic People's Republic of Korea, North Koreans, in effect, remained stateless persons. Their legal status would not be regularised until 1982, when Japan ratified the UN Convention Relating to the Status of Refugees (chapter 11).

Finally, central and local governments immediately inserted exclusionary 'nationality clauses' in a wide range of laws and ordinances in order to deny Koreans and Chinese basic social protection and other rights. As foreigners, Koreans and Chinese veterans were excluded from the purview of the Law for War Invalids and Families of the War Dead, enacted on 30 April 1952, and from the Public Officials Pension Law of 1 August 1953. They also were disqualified from assistance under the revised Daily Life Protection Law of 1950, with the Welfare Ministry's announcement that the term 'all people' in the statute really meant only Japanese citizens. Likewise, former colonials were denied such benefits as child welfare, old age assistance, aid to handicapped children and access to public housing. (At the discretion of local governments, those in distress might file for special consideration, the Ministry explained.) Nationality provisions barred non-Japanese from most public-sector and many private-sector occupations, as well.[109] In education, Korean children, formerly ordered to attend Japanese schools, now were told that, as aliens, they were no longer entitled to free public instruction.

In October 1952, Wajima Eiji, the Foreign Ministry official responsible for Japan–ROK negotiations, told US Ambassador Robert Murphy that he was 'having difficulties restraining other Ministries from measures aimed at Koreans'. The Welfare Ministry, Wajima said, was preparing to cut Koreans from the dole. The Education Ministry was taking steps to close down the remaining privately operated Korean schools. The Justice Ministry was considering sanctions against politically active Koreans under the Subversive Activities Prevention Law, and the new Immigration Control Agency was building stockades for Korean deportees.[110]

A divided peace (2): Okinawa and the Northern Territories

The Ryukyu Islands loomed large in Washington's treaty calculations. The Pentagon was determined to keep the archipelago as an American protectorate and expand its military position there, and Dulles was insistent with Yoshida about retaining the territory in order to bring the US military establishment into the peace process. Consequently, Article 3 of the Peace Treaty gave the United States 'the right to exercise all and any powers of administration, legislation and jurisdiction over the territory and all inhabitants' until such time as the US government proposed a UN trusteeship for the islands. In fact, Washington never intended to take such a step, assuring itself of complete control. At the same time, perhaps not by chance, the treaty seemed to mirror Emperor Hirohito's Okinawa gambit of September 1947 by granting Japan 'residual sovereignty' over the islands, an expedient that did nothing to alter the harsh reality of American rule.

The advent of the Cold War had brought major changes to Okinawa. In October 1948, NSC-13/2 recommended that the United States retain the archipelago on a long-term basis as a strategic asset, echoing MacArthur's plea to the Defense Secretary of a year earlier (chapter 9). At a press conference on 1 March 1949, MacArthur reiterated the importance of Okinawa to the United States. The 'Pacific', he told reporters, 'was looked upon as the avenue of possible enemy approach. Now the Pacific has become an Anglo-Saxon lake and our line of defense runs through the chain of islands fringing the coast of Asia. It starts from the Philippines and continues through the Ryukyu Archipelago, which includes its broad main bastion, Okinawa.' (In January 1950, Secretary of State Dean Acheson would elaborate on this definition but reverse the polarity: 'This defensive perimeter runs along the Aleutians to Japan and then goes to the Ryukyus. . . . The defensive perimeter runs from the Ryukyus to the Philippines,' he said.)[111]

Shortly afterwards, in early May 1949, NSC-13/3 called for the establishment of 'economic and political security' in the archipelago to make Okinawa politically safe for the projected long-term American custodianship there. The State Department feared that years of US neglect compounded by strong anti-American feeling would render the islands ungovernable. Military rule indeed had generated intense resentment among Ryukyuans. In September 1948, the Far East Command had set up a G-5 Military Government Section in an attempt to minimise friction between US troops and the civilian population, but American authorities continued to deny base workers the right to organise and strike and to appropriate vast tracts of private property for base facilities. In May 1949, the State Department sent anthropologist Douglas L. Oliver to survey local conditions and recommend necessary changes. Oliver delivered a scathing indictment of substandard social and economic conditions, prompting the Pentagon to begin pumping money into the economy – primarily in the form of military housing and other base-related projects cleverly financed out of Government and Relief in Occupied Areas (GARIOA) funds. In October, following the Communist victory in China, the Pentagon embarked on a $58 million programme of strengthening Okinawa's military reservations, lengthening runways to accommodate long-range bombers and expanding air-base installations in anticipation of a Communist attack on Formosa.[112]

The outbreak of war in Korea intensified the militarisation of the Ryukyus. US strategic interests dictated a need for aggressive land acquisition, and this brought the Army into direct conflict with Okinawan landholders. The Americans claimed that the Laws of Land Warfare precluded the need to compensate owners for land use. By 1950, the situation had become intolerable for Okinawans, producing a highly charged atmosphere of confrontation, and in October, the Joint Chiefs relented and ruled that rents must be paid for private land. In December, however, MacArthur ordered the Ryukyus Command to acquire title to all US-occupied land, whether by purchase or through condemnation, and land appropriation continued unabated.[113]

On 5 December 1950, acting on State Department recommendations, MacArthur issued a directive transforming the Military Government of the Ryukyus into the US Civil Administration of the Ryukyus (USCAR), which adopted a formula of quasi-direct rule. In reality, however, little had changed. Like its predecessor, USCAR was controlled from Washington and staffed entirely by Americans. The Military Governor of the Ryukyu Islands, for instance, became Governor of the Ryukyu Islands, but that position continued to be held by the Far East Commander in Tokyo (MacArthur). The Deputy Governor was the Commanding General of the Ryukyus Command, and the newly created Civil Administrator was a US Army general. Under USCAR was a Provisional Central Government of the Ryukyu Islands, created on 1 April 1951, which became the Government of the Ryukyu Islands (GRI) a year later, but the GRI's chief executive was appointed by the Americans.[114]

As the Korean War progressed, USCAR accelerated land acquisition. To convince farmers and other owners to part with their property, in 1952 the Civil Administrator introduced 20-year leases amounting to 6 per cent annually of the appraised land value, but a majority of Okinawans refused to sign the contracts. When landlords rejected negotiations altogether, USCAR mobilised troops and sometimes tanks to evict them from their holdings. Those who resisted were arrested. Farmers watched helplessly as their homes and villages were razed by bulldozers to make way for the new facilities. Some 57,000 landowners lost their property through expropriation or were forced to sign non-negotiable 'leases' imposed unilaterally by the military. Such policies inflamed anti-American sentiment, and most islanders came to prefer Japanese to American control. In 1951, as the return of sovereignty approached, Amami–Ōshima islanders staged hunger strikes, and on Okinawa, 199,000 people, or 72 per cent of the electorate, and 88 per cent of the voters on Miyako Island petitioned US and Japanese authorities to be reunited with the main islands. The appeals were sent to Japanese and American delegates attending the San Francisco Peace Conference, but the archipelago would not be returned until 1972.[115]

The disposition of the Ryukyus and the Ogasawaras was intimately linked to Japan's relinquishment of its claims to southern Sakhalin and the Kurils, areas under Soviet occupation. The Peace Treaty awarded Washington control of Japan's southernmost territories but very pointedly skirted the issue of the northern islands. To American policy planners, the northern territories were a useful bargaining chip. In 1947, the United States had turned a blind eye to the Soviet annexation in return for Kremlin support in the United Nations of a US-administered trust territory in Japan's former Micronesian colonies. When treaty discussions got underway in 1950, John Foster Dulles took a very different tack in order, as one historian has put it, 'to channel Japan's irredentism from the south into the north against the Soviet Union'.[116]

Yoshida's negotiating position was that the four southern Kurils, today's so-called Northern Territories, were an integral part of the Japanese homeland and should be fully recovered. Dulles ostensibly acknowledged this claim, but in October 1950, in negotiations with Soviet UN delegate Jacob Malik, he proposed to cede southern Sakhalin and the Kurils to Moscow in return for Soviet participation in the peace settlement. In the Yoshida–Dulles agreement of early February 1951, however, Dulles modified that position and, in the preliminary accord, called only for the return of southern Sakhalin. The Kurils were not to be handed over to Moscow until their geographical boundaries had been clarified, by international law if necessary. Moreover, the Kremlin would take possession of the territories only if it signed the treaty.

In June 1951, while in London, Dulles made further changes, which were incorporated into the San Francisco agreement. With British consent, he decided that Japan would simply renounce all right, title and claim to the Kurils and southern Sakhalin (Article 2). These territories would not be defined, nor would the treaty specify to which country they should be transferred. Moreover, a nation that did not sign the accord was not entitled to seek clarification of this issue from the International Court of Justice (Article 22). Thus, unless Moscow initialled the peace settlement, the matter could not even be adjudicated. Japan would lose the possibility of defining and reclaiming the four southern Kurils, and the Soviet Union would be denied formal treaty rights over the territories it had seized at the end of the war. The payoff for Washington would be perpetual mutual animosity between Tokyo and Moscow over the Northern Territories. On 5 September in San Francisco, Dulles put the finishing touches on this masterpiece of duplicity by stating that neither Japan nor the other allies were bound by the Yalta accord. He also noted that the United States did not consider the southernmost Habomai Group to be a part of the Kurils but that the question of boundaries should be resolved by the International Court. Predictably, the Soviet Union refused to sign the San Francisco Peace Treaty, in large part because of Article 2, making demarcation a moot point and deferring closure of the issue to a future but problematic bilateral accord.[117]

CHAPTER 11

The Legacy of Occupation

On 8 September 2001, Japanese and American leaders gathered in the Opera House in San Francisco to commemorate the signing of the Peace Treaty fifty years ago. Looking back on that event, Japanese can take pride in the peaceful, prosperous and democratic society they have constructed since then from the ashes of the Old Order. But pride in this accomplishment must be tempered by an awareness of the magnitude of the problems – some of them a direct threat to the viability of Japanese democracy itself – that still confront us. Many of these contemporary issues have their roots in the Occupation era, in the reorientation of US priorities after 1948 and in the subtle but stubborn and corrosive resistance with which Japan's conservative élite has opposed full implementation of the Allied reform programme.[1]

TERRITORIAL ISSUES

Following its surrender in August 1945, Japan lost all rights and titles to its former colonial possessions in Asia and the Pacific. The Greater Japanese Empire was reduced to the four main islands of Japan proper, and the Imperial government became, simply, the government of Japan. SCAP arbitrarily deprived Japan of the Ryukyu, Amami and Ogasawara archipelagos – traditional parts of the Japanese homeland – and placed them under exclusive US administration. The Amami Islands were returned to Japan on 25 December 1953, followed by the Ogasawaras on 26 June 1968 and, finally, some twenty seven years later by the Ryukyus on 15 May 1972, restoring Japan's basic territorial integrity.

In the north, however, Russia continues to occupy unlawfully other historical Japanese possessions – the Northern Territories – as a consequence of the secret Yalta protocol. With the restoration of Japanese sovereignty in April 1952, the fate of Etorofu, Kunashiri, Shikotan and the Habomai Group followed the twists and turns of Cold War realpolitik. Prime Minister Hatoyama Ichirō revived the question in 1955 and 1956 during normalisation talks with the Soviet Union. At that time, Moscow indicated it would acknowledge Japan's claims to the Habomais and Shikotan once bilateral ties were restored, but talks broke down when the Japanese side unilaterally demanded not only repossession of Kunashiri and Etorofu as well, but an international conference to discuss the disposition of southern Sakhalin and the northern Kurils. US prodding prompted Japan's surprising audacity. Fearing a thaw in Soviet–Japan relations, Secretary of State John Foster Dulles pressed Tokyo to assert its sovereignty claims over the other islands in hopes of alienating Moscow and thwarting a bilateral peace initiative. On 19 August 1956, Dulles, nervous that Tokyo might trade territory for a treaty, bluntly informed Foreign Minister Shige-mitsu Mamoru that, 'if Japan recognises Kunashiri and Etorofu as Soviet territory, the US will ask her to confirm Okinawa to be American territory'.[2]

On 19 October 1956, Japan and the Soviet Union signed a joint interim declar-ation ending hostilities and restoring diplomatic ties but deferred the territorial issue until the conclusion of a final peace settlement. Moscow pledged to return Shikotan and the Habomais at that time and even evacuated thousands of islanders from both territories in anticipation of their return to Japan, but a treaty never materialised.[3] In January 1960, Premier Nikita Khrushchev offered to give back the two islands in exchange for a Japanese promise to secure the withdrawal of US troops, but in June of that year, Washington and Tokyo revised their bilateral security accord, now the Japan–US Mutual Security Treaty, and Khrushchev's offer became a moot issue. The absence of a formal peace has hindered Japanese attempts to recover the southern Kurils. Russian control of the Habomai Group is particularly difficult to justify. Administered directly by Hokkaido before September 1945, these islets belong to Japan both historically and by virtue of international treaty.

In 1991, the Russian Foreign Ministry reversed its policy on the four contested islands, acknowledging Japan's traditional ownership. In 1993, the two countries signed a joint declaration pledging to resolve outstanding bilateral differences, including the Northern Territories issue, and in November 1997, Tokyo and Mos-cow affirmed the year 2000 as a target date for signing a peace treaty. In April 1998, Prime Minister Hashimoto Ryūtarō met Russian President Boris Yeltsin in Japan and proposed to draw the international boundary line north of the four southernmost islands – the historical demarcation point – but Moscow refused to link a treaty to the Northern Territories issue. Bilateral talks in Tokyo in September 2000 between Prime Minister Mori Yoshirō and Russian President Vladimir Putin ended in an impasse, and a quick resolution of the problem appears unlikely. In negotiating the future of these islands, Japan should insist on its traditional ownership rights, which Tsar Nicholas I formally recognised in 1853, and eschew any easy formula for joint management. At the same time, when an accord finally is reached, Japan must be prepared to safeguard the ethnic rights of Ainu, Nivhks (Gilyak), Oroks (Uilta) and other national groups living there.

A related issue is the fate of Koreans stranded on Sakhalin after Japan's defeat, survivors of the 40,000 to 60,000 workers the Imperial government sent to the island for forced labour in the early 1940s and then abandoned after the war. Postwar Japanese Cabinets have refused to acknowledge the problem of the Sakhalin Koreans. Diplomatic documents released by the Foreign Ministry in December 2000, for instance, show that, in 1957, the Ministry rejected a request by Seoul to help return this population, asserting there was no evidence they had suffered undue hardship. In the early 1990s, Russia allowed Koreans to visit their homeland, and after tedious negotiations with Seoul, Tokyo finally pledged financial assistance to help build apartments and a retirement home in South Korea to help resettle returnees. Such efforts are perfunctory and parsimonious in view of Japan's moral responsibility. Today, thousands of Koreans remain on Sakhalin. Japan must work with Korean and Russian authorities to facilitate repatriation and compensate these and other former slave labourers for their tribulations.

Another source of friction between Tokyo and Seoul is the unresolved territorial dispute over ownership of Takeshima (Tokto in Korean), two islets equidistant from Japan and the Republic of Korea. The Occupation failed to clarify the postwar status of Takeshima, a part of Shimane Prefecture since 1905. On 18 January 1952, President Syngman Rhee proclaimed the imposition of the so-called Rhee Line, which extended South Korea's territorial waters nearly 100 kilometres from its coastline (50 kilometres then was the international norm). When the Occupation ended in 1952, Seoul declared the islets a part of its continental shelf and sent troops to occupy them.

A similar controversy revolves around the Senkakus (Diaoyutai in Chinese), an island group near Taiwan blessed with rich fishing grounds and underground oil reserves, which Japan absorbed into Okinawa Prefecture in 1895. The United States took control of the islets in 1945 but returned them to Japan in 1972 with the reversion of Okinawa. Today, Taiwan and the People's Republic of China claim this territory as their own. Both Takeshima and the Senkakus have sparked inter-mittent diplomatic rows since 1952. The most recent flare-up occurred in 1996 following a Cabinet decision to extend Japan's exclusive economic zone to within 320 kilometres of its shoreline.

THE CONSTITUTION

Constitutional revision was the capstone of the Occupation's political reform programme, and of the GHQ-initiated changes, it has exerted the most profound influence on postwar Japanese society. Despite the 1947 Constitution's wide accept-ance, retention of the emperor system has provided ultra-nationalists with an insti-tutional base from which to propagate chauvinist ideals, but few Japanese today embrace that discredited ideology. Article Nine, which renounces the state's right of belligerency, however, continues to stir controversy.

The Emperor

The new Constitution overhauled the machinery of government, laying the founda-tion for a democratic polity. The division of executive, legislative and judicial powers, the election of Cabinet officials from among active members of the National Diet and the designation of the latter as the highest organ of state power today are taken for granted. These innovations rested on an even more fundamental reform, that of the emperor system, which divested an absolutist monarchy of its paramount temporal authority and replaced it with the principle of popular sovereignty.

SCAP's decision to retain the Imperial institution in the form of a 'symbolic' emperor, with exclusively representational and ceremonial duties, and to exempt Hirohito from war-crimes prosecution had lasting consequences for Japan's fledgling postwar democracy. In the light of recent research, there is no longer any doubt that Hirohito was involved intimately in planning and directing Japan's war effort.[4] MacArthur spared the monarch because he feared that, without him, the public would not cooperate as willingly with his reform agenda, necessitating perhaps direct military government and a difficult and protracted occupation. This also is undoubtedly the reason Occupation authorities rejected a third and eminently viable alternative, that of retaining the monarchy but obliging Hirohito to abdicate. Had SCAP pressed for abdication, the Japanese people might well have accepted, even welcomed, that decision.[5] GHQ's decision not to bring the Emperor to account for his wartime actions helped preserve and legitimate conservative rule – established with Occupation collusion in late 1948 – making it difficult for many Japanese to acknowledge their individual and national war responsibility. The Occupation's position that it was the militarists, not the Throne or the people, who brought about the Asia–Pacific conflict encouraged this collective evasion, and the country as a whole still has not addressed the war issue forthrightly. The task of atonement is further compounded by the ambiguities inherent in the so-called emperor-as-symbol system, for these have allowed conservatives to associate the postwar monarchy with the transcendent social and political values of the patriarchal state.

After 1952, ultra-conservative politicians attempted to reverse key Occupation reforms, openly advocating a military force independent of US control and an emperor who was not merely a symbol of national unity but also political head of state. They were led by the recently depurged Hatoyama Ichirō, who replaced Yoshida Shigeru as prime minister in December 1954, and Kishi Nobusuke, a wartime member of the Tōjō Cabinet and an unindicted war crimes suspect who became prime minister in 1957. In November 1954, Hatoyama formed the Japan Democratic Party with himself as president and Kishi as secretary general. One year later, in November 1955, Kishi engineered an alliance with Yoshida's Liberal Party to forge a new conservative coalition, the Liberal Democratic Party (*Jiyū Minshutō*, or *Jimintō*), which governed Japan virtually unchallenged until the early 1990s. Constitutional revision, rearmament and a politically revitalised emperor system remain at the top of the conservative agenda.[6]

After the Occupation, the Japanese government redoubled its efforts to anchor the Imperial institution in the popular consciousness. The marriage of Crown Prince Akihito to a commoner and Christian, Shōda Michiko, in 1959 received extensive press coverage, creating a 'Michiko Boom'. This royal fever was carefully stage-managed by the state and sustained by the media long after the event. During the 1960s, years of rapid economic growth, Hirohito became the symbol not only of national unity but also of economic prosperity and, following the Emperor's European tour of 1971 and his US tour of 1975, of Japan's efforts to 'internationalise'. In 1979, the traditional system of Imperial era names by which pre-1945 Japan reckoned its history (Meiji, Taishō, Shōwa, etc.) was reinstituted in law, lending new authority to the Throne and reinforcing the principle of dynastic succession. In the 1980s, this trend was strengthened by Prime Minister Nakasone Yasuhiro, a former Imperial Navy officer, avowed neo-nationalist and ex-director general of the Defence Agency, who proclaimed the Emperor to be a symbol of racial unity and the spiritual fountainhead of the nation.

The Shōwa Emperor's death in 1989 ended one of the longest Imperial reigns in Japanese history. Conservative forces seized on the event as an opportunity to infuse Imperial ideology with new life. The media obligingly created a pervasive mood of 'self-restraint', and the public submissively complied, cancelling weddings, sporting events, local festivals, *karaoke* parties and other leisure activities during the monarch's lengthy illness and subsequent funerary rites. But the real trend-setters were banks, large corporations and major department stores, not rightist ideologues, and their motives were a mixture of competitive commercialism (a refusal to be upstaged by rivals) and the fear of ultra-nationalist reprisals for failing to show the proper degree of respect.[7]

In the early postwar era, SCAP abolished the crime of *lèse majesté*, but critical comment on the Emperor's wartime activities, while not rare in academic circles, is still a risky venture in the public arena. Rightist vigilantes vigorously enforce this 'Chrysanthemum Taboo' through intimidation and violence in defiance of the constitutional guarantee of free speech. In December 1988, as the monarch lay dying, the mayor of Nagasaki, Motojima Hiroshi, responding to a question from a city assemblyman, stated his belief that Hirohito bore responsibility for the war. Later, he told journalists that had Hirohito 'resolved to end the war earlier, there would have been no Battle of Okinawa, no nuclear attacks on Hiroshima and Nagasaki'. He then criticised his own actions during the conflict, including orders he personally had given to troops to die for the Emperor. For his candour, Motojima was subjected immediately to death threats and harassment by rightist groups. In January 1990, a would-be assassin shot and seriously wounded the mayor. During this turbulent period, with the exception of the mayor of Yomitan in Okinawa, Socialist Party Chair Doi Takako and a few others, political figures were conspicuous by their silence on the issue of Imperial war guilt.[8]

Shōwa, the 'Era of Radiant Peace', gave way to Heisei, the 'Era of Achieving Peace', and the reign of Hirohito's eldest son, Akihito. Upon acceding to the throne, the new Emperor pledged to honour the Constitution and make the monarchy more accessible to the people. Some scholars have seen in this process of Imperial succession a skilfully orchestrated attempt by ultra-nationalists to enhance the political as well as symbolic authority of the emperor system.[9] That well may be, but while neo-nationalist machinations are a palpable concern, we may take Akihito at his word. Today popular sovereignty resides firmly in the people, not the Throne, and the reform of the Imperial institution under the Occupation aegis, despite its obvious limitations, remains one of the preconditions of democratic government in Japan.

Photo 72. Crown Prince Akihito woos commoner and Christian Shōda Michiko on the tennis courts of the mountain resort Karuizawa, 28 July 1958. Their marriage on 10 April 1959 helped to entrench the institution of the Throne by popularising it. The union also wed the monarchy to big business, for Michiko's father was a prominent businessman (Mainichi).

Article Nine

Article Nine survives despite repeated assaults from the right and even though conservative régimes have persisted in their attempt to undermine the spirit and the
letter of the no-war clause. Ironically, MacArthur himself struck the first blow when
he ordered the creation of the National Police Reserve in 1950. The government
reorganised the NPR in 1954 as the Self-Defence Forces (SDF) in direct contraven-
tion of the ban on arms. In 1955, the just-formed Liberal Democratic Party (LDP)
incorporated constitutional revision and the legalisation of the SDF into its political platform. In 1956, Parliament established the Commission on the Constitution
through which the LDP intended to enhance the status of the Emperor and rewrite
Article Nine. Surprisingly, the Commission's final report, issued in 1964, con-
founded conservative expectations by emphasising the Japanese contribution to the
Constitution and cautioning restraint in revising it. By then, the Liberal Democrats
no longer commanded the parliamentary votes (a two-thirds majority in both
houses) necessary to amend the charter. Conservatives since have attempted to skirt
Article Nine by reinterpreting it to suit their purposes (*kaishaku-kaiken*).

The government argues, for instance, that the SDF are for defensive purposes only
and therefore legitimate, but there is no disguising the fact that Japan's standing
234,000-strong land, sea and air forces violate the Constitution. The SDF budget
has grown steadily but has generally remained within 1 per cent of the gross domestic
product (as of 1999, it stood at 0.99 per cent of the GDP). The so-called 1 per cent
ceiling, imposed in 1976 and broken momentarily in 1987, is considered to represent the upper permissible limit of support for a purely defensive military force –
but this in itself serves as a rather clever justification for the de facto existence of a
military establishment.

The Liberal Democrats used the 1991 Gulf War as an excuse to weaken Article
Nine further and build a national consensus for rearmament. During that conflict,
Japan provided $13 billion to help finance the US-led multinational force that
bombed and invaded Iraq but was criticised loudly by Washington for refusing to
contribute military muscle as well. Using American pressure as a lever, the government proposed the despatch of SDF troops to the Middle East. When a groundswell
of domestic protest made that impossible, Tokyo deployed a squadron of four minesweepers to the Gulf, a token gesture but one that reinforced an old precedent
established during the Korean War (chapter 10). In June 1992, over fierce opposition, the government railroaded a bill through the Diet authorising the Self-Defence
Forces to take part in non-military UN peacekeeping actions. The International
Peace Cooperation Law opens the way for the eventual projection of Japanese military force abroad.

A measure of such import should have been submitted to the test of a national
referendum, or at the very least of new general elections.[10] So far, Japanese troops have
been sent on non-military missions to Cambodia (1992–3), Mozambique (1993–5),
Zaire and Kenya (1994), and the Golan Heights (1996), where they are currently
stationed. In 1998, the SDF were deployed to Honduras for disaster relief in the wake of

Hurricane Mitch, establishing another precedent, and in late January 2001, Japanese troops were flown to India to help that country recover from a devastating earthquake. Many here consider such participation in unarmed peace-keeping operations one way of fulfilling the nation's duties as a world citizen. Unfortunately, the government and Liberal Democratic Party hope to lever this involvement into a full-fledged combat role. In late 1998, Prime Minister Obuchi Keizō confirmed this intention when he indicated that his Cabinet was studying legislation that would allow the SDF to join in future UN military operations, as well. The 11 September 2001 terrorist attacks on New York and Washington have accelerated that process. Under US prodding, the government of Koizumi Jun'ichirō has enacted a legislative package that gives Japan's uniformed services a more active non-combat role abroad, and sent armed SDF units to operate in a foreign war zone for the first time ever. There seems to be no effective means of contesting these incremental faits accomplis.

The institutional groundwork for closer Japan–US cooperation was laid down in the late 1990s. In 1996, Tokyo and Washington initialled the Japan–US Acquisition and Cross-Servicing Agreement (upgraded in 1998), requiring each country to comply with bilateral requests for military services and materials. In September 1997, Japanese and American defence officials revised the Guidelines for Japan–US Defence Cooperation (1978). Less than two years later, in May 1999, the Diet enacted three laws to implement the updated Guidelines, and the government is determined to expand SDF emergency powers in the event of both domestic and regional crises.

This continual testing of the limits brings Article Nine ever closer to de facto abrogation. The 1997 Guidelines amount to a collective defence pact, which the Constitution clearly forbids. In the event of an attack on Japan proper or a hostile 'situation in the areas surrounding Japan', they give the US military access to civilian harbours, airports and key transportation and communications facilities. Local governments now are required by law not only to cooperate but to keep details of such collaboration secret, and Japan's Defence Agency is considering plans that will allow US forces in Japan to expropriate land and public facilities and flout domestic aviation and traffic laws in the event of a 'contingency'.

Under the Guidelines, bilateral military action will be coordinated by an integrated command structure charged with overseeing logistics support, intelligence sharing, minesweeping and combat operations. The integrated command scheme is strongly reminiscent of the 'combined command' provision that Washington attempted unsuccessfully to insert in the 1952 Administrative Agreement. Peacetime military cooperation also will be strengthened. Equally problematic is the US proposal to make theatre missile defence (TMD) a key element in the new Japan–US security arrangement. The TMD implies a joint command and control infrastructure and a reintegrated SDF. In late December 1998, the Obuchi Cabinet agreed to promote joint research on the project with the United States after declaring there to be no legal obstacles in doing so. These moves are yet another attempt by ruling circles to arrogate the right of belligerency denied them under law.

Another onerous legacy of the Occupation is the Status of Forces Agreement (SOFA), which originated in the Administrative Agreement of February 1952. Revised as SOFA when the Security Treaty was renewed in 1960, the accord enables the United States to garrison its troops in Japan in support of the SDF and its own strategic interests in the region. SOFA permitted the Pentagon, through its extensive repair, communications, arms and oil storage, and other Japan-based facilities, to make this country an indirect participant in the Vietnam War and, more recently, the Gulf War – conflicts that many Japanese felt were politically misguided and morally wrong. With US military intervention in Afghanistan in late 2001, Japan now has been dragged into another 'regional' conflict far from its shores.

Okinawans have borne the brunt of the US military deployment. Today, 75 per cent of all American bases in Japan are located in the Ryukyus, which occupy a minuscule 0.6 per cent of the country's total land area. Moreover, the US military controls 20 per cent of the archipelago's prime farmland and 40 per cent of its air space. The social problems caused by the presence of 27,000 foreign troops and their military installations are staggering. Rape, murder, theft, hit-and-run accidents and other offences by US service people are rife, but SOFA (notably Articles 17 and 25) gives Japanese courts jurisdiction only over crimes committed by off-duty personnel. In practice, Japanese authorities have tended to bow to US pressure and waive jurisdiction even over these cases, frustrating Okinawans in their efforts to see justice done. Furthermore, under SOFA, many of the prefecture's landowners are forced to lease their property to the bases.[11]

In September 1995, three US Marines kidnapped and raped a 12-year-old Okinawan girl, provoking consternation and rage across Japan. In Okinawa, 85,000 people demonstrated against SOFA and the American presence. The premeditated crime compelled Washington to agree to a partial revision of SOFA's legal jurisdiction provisions. It also provoked a massive backlash against the bases, leading Governor Ōta Masahide, in defiance of Tokyo and Japan's treaty obligations, to refuse to renew land leases and to call for a phased withdrawal of all US forces by the year 2015. The Pentagon responded by agreeing to return about 20 per cent of its holdings in the islands and to reduce troop levels over a 10-year period, but it refused to remove its forces altogether, insisting as it has for the past half century that this 'forward-deployed presence' is an integral part of the US defence perimeter in Asia.

In early July 2000, a US Marine broke into an Okinawan home and molested a 14-year-old girl in her sleep, sparking renewed outrage and calls for a US pullout. Occurring just before the Group of Eight summit in Okinawa, the incident highlighted once again the plight of Ryukyuans. One of the paradoxes of Japan's postwar democracy is that, while the Japanese people as a whole disapprove of rearmament and the stationing of US troops on their soil, they seem indifferent to the American bases in Okinawa and the problems they create for the island's 1.3 million inhabitants. Displaying a lamentable lack of principle, Japan's foreign policy supinely accommodates every US demand and refuses to address this problem.

The same absence of nerve characterises Tokyo's attitude towards US nuclear

Photo 73. Okinawans in Ginowan City, enraged at the rape of a school girl by three US servicemen, take to the streets to demand justice and a reduction in American forces, 21 October 1995. The crime was one of more than 5,000, many involving violence against women, that have been commited by US troops in Okinawa since the prefecture reverted to Japan in 1972 (Mainichi).

arms. In 1967, the government of Satō Eisaku committed the country to uphold three non-nuclear principles, pledging neither to possess nor manufacture nuclear arms or allow their introduction into the country. In the early 1960s, however, a US government analyst discovered that nuclear weapons were being stored on a barge off the coast of Kyushu. The bombs were held ready for emergency use by US aircraft at the Marine air base in Iwakuni. Their targets were North Korea, China and the Soviet Union. In 1966, US ambassador to Japan Edwin O. Reischauer got wind of the nuclear cache and threatened to resign unless the weapons were removed. In 1981, Reischauer disclosed the fact that successive Japanese Cabinets had tacitly condoned the introduction of nuclear warheads aboard US naval vessels during port calls and their transit through Japanese waters based on a secret bilateral understanding dating from the 1950s. Similarly, when Washington returned the Ogasawara Islands to Japan in 1968, Tokyo reportedly agreed verbally not to oppose the storage of nuclear arms there for emergency use should the United States demand privileged access.[12]

To defend the Constitution, Japan must scale down the Self-Defence Forces, create a service-orientated organisation for non-military peacekeeping purposes, demand the complete withdrawal of US troops and enforce the three non-nuclear principles. Every people enjoys the intrinsic right of self-defence, but in Japan, the people, through their support of the Constitution, have denied that right to the state for the past half century. Our most reliable defence is to develop the potential of Article Nine, make Japan a truly pacifist power and, through an enlightened peace diplomacy, demonstrate that the principles of disarmament and non-belligerency are not only desirable but workable. In cases such as Afghanistan, that means responding to US requests for assistance with humanitarian aid and eschewing military support, which can only compound the suffering.

This lofty – some would say unrealistic – goal eludes us at present, and in light of the current world crisis, some degree of constitutional revision seems likely in the near future. In 1999, conservative lawmakers established the Research Commission on the Constitution in both houses as a first step in that direction. Amending the national charter will not be simple, however. Acceptance requires the assent of two-thirds of all Diet members and the test of a national referendum. In May 2000, the Commission invited Beate Sirota Gordon and Richard A. Poole, two of the authors of the 1946 MacArthur draft constitution, to its Upper House session. Sirota recalled her role in writing the guarantees for women. When Government Section's Charles Kades read her proposals, she reminisced, he was stunned: 'Beate, your draft contains more than the American Constitution.' Sirota replied: 'Naturally. The American Constitution does not even include the word "woman".' Were the Japanese people pleased with the Japanese Constitution? Sirota asked. 'Of course, they were. The Japanese Government at that time was not so happy . . . but the Japanese people were.' In concluding she said, 'I think this Constitution should become the model of the world, and that is why it has not been revised for as long as 50 years.' This author is convinced that for most Japanese, non-belligerency remains a moral and psychological imperative.[13]

HUMAN RIGHTS

A scholar of the Occupation has remarked that Japan's postwar social structure is dualistic, consisting of areas where SCAP-induced reform was decisive and areas where it was stillborn, leaving prewar patterns intact. Both aspects, he notes, are inextricably bound together.[14] This observation seems especially apt where human rights are concerned.

Problems and prospects

The Constitution guarantees basic civil, political and other fundamental rights to Japanese citizens, and our judicial system is committed to upholding these liberties as the basis of a free society. Over the past two decades, the government has ratified a series of international human rights instruments, including the International Covenants on Human Rights (1979), the UN Convention Relating to the Status of Refugees (1982), the UN Convention on the Elimination of All Forms of Discrimination Against Women (1985), the UN Convention on the Rights of the Child (1994) and the International Convention on the Elimination of All Forms of Racial Discrimination (1996). These agreements take precedence over domestic law, requiring Japan to bring its legal system into line with international practice. There are many areas, however, where injustices cry out for redress.

For instance, Japan retains the death penalty in defiance of the current world trend against capital punishment. Inmates on death row cannot appeal an execution order once it has been issued, and names and date of execution are not made public even after the order has been carried out. In November 1998, the UN Human Rights Committee in Geneva criticised Japan for its overly harsh prison conditions and frequent recourse to brutal punitive measures, such as the use of leather handcuffs during prolonged solitary confinement, abuses that verge on cruel and inhuman treatment. Also problematic is the practice of obtaining confessions from suspects who are detained for long periods in police-station holding cells where they may be subjected to around-the-clock interrogations without benefit of legal counsel and under highly stressful conditions (see below).

Despite the landmark Law for the Welfare of the Physically Disabled of 1949, today physically and mentally handicapped Japanese do not enjoy many of the special legal protections their counterparts are afforded in the United States and other Western countries. The 1949 law was revised in 1970, but Japan has not made the substantial investments in social infrastructure that the disabled require in order to lead active, productive lives. Paternalism and institutional dependence, not independence, have been the result. In an attempt to remedy these shortcomings, in 1993, the government enacted the Fundamental Law for Disabled Persons. The new statute was designed to integrate the handicapped more effectively into society and enhance self-reliance ('normalisation'), but it failed to make equal treatment a right and has not lived up to its promise. The government also issues guidelines on the hiring of people with disabilities in both public and private sectors, but such directives are not legally binding and therefore not widely adhered to.

A problematic Occupation legacy is the 1948 Eugenic Protection Law. Although the statute decriminalised abortion, it also prescribed the termination of pregnancy for those whose physical or mental handicaps made them likely to produce 'defective progeny'. Until recently, hysterectomies were performed routinely on women diagnosed as having certain genetically caused disabilities. The law's sterilisation ('eugenic surgery') provision also targeted people with personality disorders and leprosy. Based on a Nazi eugenics ordinance, this regressive measure finally was abolished in 1996 and the legislation itself renamed the Motherhood Protection Law. The revision was prompted by a combination of factors, among them international criticism, plans to repeal the 1953 Leprosy Prevention Law and implementation of the Fundamental Law for Disabled Persons. Unfortunately, the Motherhood Protection Law did not repudiate the eugenic theory underlying the old statute, nor did it entrench the principle of women's reproductive health and rights. These demands require further legislative action.[15]

In April 1996, the government also abolished the Leprosy Prevention Law, ending an 88-year policy of forcibly segregating victims of Hansen's Disease. By the 1950s, most lepers had been cured as a result of new drug therapies, but the 1953 statute continued to deny them basic rights, and many were forced to undergo sterilisation or abortions under the Eugenic Protection Law. In 1998, thirteen former sufferers filed suit against the government at the Kumamoto District Court in Kyushu, demanding financial compensation and a formal apology for this breach of their human rights. Law suits proliferated, and in mid-May 2001, the Kumamoto Court held the state liable for violating the plantiffs' constitutional liberties and ordered it to pay them ¥1.8 billion in compensation. In late May, the government announced it would not appeal the verdict and acknowledged state culpability, an unprecedented move.

Women

The postwar reforms liberated women from traditional roles and granted them the same legal rights and entitlements as men, yet gender-based discrimination remains pervasive. Women's rights received renewed attention in 1985 when Japan ratified the UN Convention on the Elimination of All Forms of Discrimination Against Women. That year the government amended the Occupation-era Nationality Law (1950), which had conferred nationality only through the paternal line, so that today children of mixed marriages are able to acquire Japanese citizenship through either parent, although the principle of *jus sanguinis* remains in force.

Minor changes also have been made to the Civil Code, but more substantial reform is in order. In 1975, the International Year of Women, the law was changed to enable divorced women to keep their married name if they apply to do so within three months of a divorce. In 1980, a wife's legal share in family inheritance was increased, reflecting a re-evaluation of women's contribution to marriage. Many

Photo 74. With the 1999 revision of the Equal Employment Opportunity Law, office workers for Mitsui Life Insurance shed their obligatory company uniforms and come to work for the first time in casual attire. Most women remain tied to clerical positions, however, and are expected to quit when they get married. 1 April 1999 (Mainichi).

legal inequalities persist, however. The minimum age for marriage is 18 for men but 16 for women, and the latter cannot remarry for six months following a divorce, although men are free to do so. Illegitimate children are discriminated against in inheritance. Women are now pressing for the right to maintain separate surnames in marriage and to make a physical separation of five years grounds for divorce. In February 1996, the Legislative Council, a Justice Ministry advisory body, proposed measures to rectify these inequities, but as of this writing, LDP conservatives continue to block further Civil Code revisions.

In 1985, the Diet enacted the Equal Employment Opportunity Law, effective from 1986, to correct the blind spots in the postwar labour laws. The new legislation lacked an effective enforcement mechanism, however, and failed to eliminate sex-based disparities in the workplace. Women entered the job market en masse in the 1980s and 1990s and now account for half of the nation's labour force, but 36 per cent of female employees are relegated to unstable, poorly paid part-time work, and even full-time workers rarely participate in decision-making. A major problem is the so-called track-hiring system, where women are assigned clerical tasks but rarely managerial jobs. In 1997, only 9.5 per cent of working women held management-level positions, and even élite career-track women encounter serious obstacles. In 1995, Ishida Kuniko sued the Sumitomo Chemical Company (unsuccessfully) because male colleagues with the same educational and work background not only were being promoted faster but earned twice her salary.

To resolve these problems, in April 1999 the government revised the Equal Employment Opportunity Law, making labour arbitration obligatory if either party to a dispute requests it (until then, both sides had to agree, and management often refused to seek mediation). Other improvements include a ban on gender-specific job descriptions in public advertising and the prohibition of discriminatory treatment in employment, placement, promotion and job training. Employers also are obliged take positive steps to prevent sexual harassment. In 1991, the Child Care Leave Act was passed, allowing either parent to take a one year's absence to care for a newborn child, but there is no salary guarantee. Whereas in 1996, more than 44 per cent of working mothers giving birth availed themselves of this right, less than 0.2 per cent of working fathers did so. In other areas, women have registered slow but steady gains. In government, 16 per cent of national civil servants were women in 1999, up from 2 per cent in 1976, and the proportion of female assistant judges rose from 5 per cent to 22 per cent in the same period. As of April 2000, only 5 per cent of Lower House lawmakers were women, however, far fewer than in Sweden (42 per cent), Britain (18 per cent) or the United States (13 per cent).[16]

Minorities
Another paradox of democracy in Japan is that the Constitution's basic human rights provisions apply only selectively to non-Japanese, who remain subject to a system of subtle apartheid that Occupation policy tacitly condoned in the interests of preserving internal order.[17]

This is not to imply that Japanese society has not made significant progress in the past half century. International legal conventions ratified since 1979 have forced the government to make substantive changes in some areas. Following ratification of the 1982 Refugee Convention, for instance, North Koreans were permitted to acquire 'general permanent residence', a status more secure than de facto statelessness but less so than the formal treaty rights enjoyed by South Koreans. In January 1991, Tokyo and Seoul initialled a joint memorandum in which Japan pledged to take positive action to improve the social and political status of the Korean minority. Since 1992, all long-term inhabitants, whether South or North Korean nationals, have received 'special permanent resident status', although deportation is still possible for certain offences (such as a crime carrying a prison term of seven years or more). Residence, thus, remains a privilege, not an acquired right. Under the Refugee Convention, Koreans, Chinese and other foreign residents became eligible for state health, pension and disability benefits; government housing services; child-rearing allotments; and other entitlements formerly reserved for Japanese nationals.[18]

Many problems persist, however. Nationality clauses bar even third-generation Koreans and Chinese from most public-sector jobs, including the teaching profession. Nor are foreigners allowed to vote, hold elective office or make financial contributions to political parties, even though they pay the same state and local taxes as

Japanese. The Education Ministry does not honour the high school diplomas of Korean and Chinese ethnic high schools, obliging their graduates to take an equivalency exam to enter state-run universities. Paradoxically, however, it accepts the high school graduation certificates of foreign exchange students. Until recently, non-Japanese were forcibly fingerprinted every five years under the Alien Registration Law, a legacy of the Occupation period. Widespread non-violent civil disobedience by Koreans in the 1980s, however, forced the government to abolish this practice for permanent residents in 1993. Korean rights groups continued the campaign against fingerprinting until it was ended for all foreigners in 2000. The requirements, strictly enforced by police, to register changes of residence and to carry an alien pass card at all times remain in effect, although for permanent residents violations are no longer criminal offences.

North Korean residents, in particular, have been subjected to systematic police surveillance.[19] In 1990, mobile police units in full riot gear were sent into a pro-P'yŏngyang middle school in Tokyo during classes to apprehend a teacher suspected of not reporting a change of address to municipal authorities. In 1997, it was revealed that local government officials near Korea University in Tokyo routinely allowed police to check the alien registration records of North Korean residents. When P'yŏngyang fired a *Taepodong*-class missile over a part of Japanese territory in August 1998, North Korean students received death threats, and female students wearing traditional gowns (*ch'ima chŏgori*) were physically assaulted by enraged Japanese. These attacks mirrored those that followed in the wake of the so-called pachinko scandal of 1989, in which North Korean pachinko-parlour owners were accused of making illegal campaign donations to the Socialist Party (it was subsequently disclosed that the pachinko industry had made contributions across the political spectrum, including to the ruling Liberal Democratic Party).

Since the colonial era, Japan has pursued a policy of forcibly assimilating ethnic Koreans and Chinese. Today, the Justice Ministry pressures applicants for naturalisation to adopt a Japanese name, demonstrate a 'Japanese lifestyle' and, in effect, renounce their ethnic heritage as a condition for obtaining citizenship. The revised Nationality Law allows children of international marriages to choose their nationality at the age of 22, but the Ministry instructs local governments to register such children under the name of the Japanese parent at birth, thereby influencing that choice. This assimilationist policy is designed to gradually absorb the Korean minority, transforming potential Korean critics into obedient Japanese. The government recently has promised to simplify naturalisation procedures. To Koreans, however, obtaining citizenship still means accepting Japanese claims of racial superiority and embracing, publicly at least, the same ethnocentric values that have oppressed them as a people – a form of ethnicide that explains why many choose to retain their alien status rather than naturalise and become second-class Japanese.[20]

In November 1998, the UN Human Rights Committee took Japan to task once again for failure to acknowledge its roughly 550,000 long-term Korean residents as an ethnic minority and to redress these inequalities. The historic summit between

South Korean President Kim Dae Jung and North Korean leader Kim Jong Il in June 2000 and the reopening of normalisation talks that followed in August offer hope that the deep ideological division in Japan's Korean community can be healed and that further progress will be made in securing the political and civil rights of former colonial subjects. In September 2000, Japanese women married to Koreans living in the Democratic People's Republic were allowed to visit relatives in Japan for the first time in decades, and two bitter ideological rivals, the pro-Seoul Korean Residents Union in Japan (*Mindan*) and the pro-P'yŏngyang General Association of Korean Residents in Japan (*Chongryun*), announced an unprecedented plan to establish ties and discuss future cooperation.

Another group denied many Constitutional protections are Third-World migrant labourers, who entered Japan in large numbers after 1985 as the value of the yen rose dramatically against the dollar. Most of the currently estimated 300,000 foreign labourers residing illegally in Japan (1999) have overstayed tourist visas to work in the entertainment industry or at manual jobs eschewed by most Japanese as dirty, difficult and dangerous. Undocumented migrants are subject to violence, forced prostitution, unpaid wages, kickbacks and other abuses by unscrupulous labour brokers, employers and criminal syndicates. Most work under scandalous conditions in open violation of Japan's US-inspired labour laws. The incidence of industrial accidents is high for these workers, but in the past hospitals have refused to admit even those with serious injuries. Today, with the economy in recession, employers sometimes fire accident victims rather than accept financial responsibility for their treatment and recovery.[21] In January 1998, the police and Immigration Control Bureau established a special task force to locate and deport undocumented workers. This has forced the migrants underground, where they are more vulnerable than ever to exploitative labour practices. In September 1998, the Labour Standards Act was amended, lifting the ceiling on the number of hours an employee can be asked to work. Other changes to Occupation-inspired labour laws have undermined the principle of job security and legitimated the activities of labour brokers and placement agencies, on whom most foreign workers depend (see below).

An estimated 3 million *Buraku* people and some 24,000 indigenous Ainu also live marginalised existences. Occupation reforms failed to address the specific problems of either minority, and today these groups experience discrimination in education, marriage, employment, housing and general quality of life.

Ethnically indistinguishable from other Japanese, *Burakumin* remain segregated in some 6,000 ghettos, euphemistically called 'assimilation districts' (*dōwa-chiku*), which are concentrated in the Kansai region and southwestern Japan. While many pursue traditional occupations in the meat- and leather-processing industries, others attempt to 'pass' as Japanese. In 1969, the government enacted the Special Measures Law for Assimilation Projects to alleviate the social and economic misery of *Buraku* communities and assimilate their inhabitants into mainstream society. The law, renewable every 10 years, made funds available to repair roads, improve housing, upgrade community facilities and promote educational and cultural activities. It did

Photo 75. Kayano Shigeru, Upper House Diet member, sits in the Niputani Documentation Centre in Biratori Township, Hokkaido, recording Ainu epic poems (*yukar*). The first Ainu ever to hold a Diet seat, Kayano was one of the moving forces behind passage in 1996 of the New Ainu Cultural Promotion Law. 11 February 1998 (Kyodo).

not, however, grant new legal rights to individuals or impose new obligations on the state and was more a political statement than a substantive human rights initiative.[22] Prejudice remains difficult to eradicate. Although the practice is illegal, companies still circulate secret registers giving the names and locations of ghettos, enabling prospective employers to identify *Burakumin* job applicants. Marriage consultants maintain similar lists.

Most Ainu live in Hokkaido, many in small, segregated rural communities (*kotan*), although, like the *Buraku* people, in recent years increasing numbers have sought the anonymity of large cities. Prime Minister Nakasone Yasuhiro's assertion in 1986 that the Japanese were a homogeneous people with no ethnic minorities astounded and incensed the Ainu community. Adding injury to insult, in 1987, Biratori Township in southern Hokkaido began construction of a dam on land traditionally sacred to local Ainu. This gross insensitivity to native feelings added fuel to a campaign by Ainu for formal recognition as an indigenous people, the return of tribal lands and the restoration of former hunting, fishing and other rights. Through this movement, in 1994, prominent Ainu activist Kayano Shigeru won a seat in the Upper House, becoming the first indigenous legislator to sit in Parliament.[23] In 1996, after 14 years of intensive lobbying by Ainu groups, the Diet abolished the discriminatory and anachronistic Hokkaido Former Aborigines' Protection Act of 1899, replacing it with the New Ainu Cultural Promotion Law. The 1996 statute is the first to acknowledge the existence of an ethnic minority in Japan. Although it recognises the distinctive cultural heritage of the Ainu, however, it stops short of granting them official indigenous status, which under international law mandates special rights to land, natural resources and cultural protection. (The designation 'indigenous' was tacked onto the law as a non-binding resolution to avoid that particular obligation.)

LATER POLITICAL REFORMS

SCAP programmes such as bureaucratic restructuring and the broadening of political participation have had a determining influence on Japanese political life, but many reform projections were sabotaged, deflected or even reversed in the post-treaty era.

Local autonomy
With the return of Japanese sovereignty, SCAP's ambitious effort to promote decentralisation and municipal reform was quickly challenged by conservatives, who applied 'a combination of neglect and legislative revision' to undo them.[24] In 1952 and 1956, the Local Autonomy Law underwent two major revisions that subordinated local entities to prefectural authority. By 1956, the Hatoyama government had reduced the number of independent local governments by two-thirds through a radical programme of municipal amalgamation. The creation in 1960 of the Minis-

try of Home Affairs crowned the effort to reimpose centralised control. An equally telling blow to local self-governance was the systematic gutting of fiscal autonomy. Local entities together collect only about 30 per cent of the nation's total tax revenues but spend twice that amount in carrying out their obligations. Thus, the bulk of local funds consists of large-scale disbursements from the central government, most of which come with strings attached. This lopsided fiscal dependence on national coffers, which has been characterised as '30-per cent local autonomy', severely constricts the range of effective home rule.[25]

National authorities have used their control of the purse strings to make municipal governments responsible for a number of central functions, such as alien registration, Self-Defence Force recruitment and, in the case of Okinawa, the forcible extension of land leases for US bases. Some local entities have refused to fulfil these duties. In 1985, for instance, the mayor of Machida City (Tokyo), Ōshita Katsumasa, disobeyed a Home Affairs Ministry order to report Korean fingerprint refusers to higher authorities and impose other administrative sanctions.[26] Mayor Ōshita's position was that fingerprinting only foreigners violated the spirit of the Constitution. Other municipalities in the Kanto and Kansai areas followed suit, openly defying the central government, and one third of Japan's 3,300 local assemblies passed resolutions condemning fingerprinting and calling for a fundamental reform of the Alien Registration Law.

Faced with this revolt at the grass roots, central authorities attempted to revise the Local Autonomy Law so that the Home Affairs Ministry could bypass the legal procedures – including a formal court hearing – needed to bring the wayward municipalities to heel. This measure would have eliminated the process of judicial review, enabling the central government to intervene directly in local affairs with no possibility of appeal. Fortunately, the proposal was defeated. In 1996, when Okinawa Governor Ōta Masahide refused to authorise the extension of military land leases, Prime Minister Hashimoto Ryūtarō was forced to observe due process and go to court to resolve the issue. Although the Supreme Court ruled in the Prime Minister's favour, permitting him to finalise the lease contracts by proxy in Ōta's stead, the resulting publicity alerted Japanese to the gravity of the problem.[27]

Today, a few local governments, such as Kawasaki City (Kanagawa Prefecture) near Tokyo, ignore ministerial guidelines and employ Koreans and other foreigners in city jobs that do not involve policy-making. Some prefectural boards of education accept qualified Koreans as public school teachers, although not at the same salary and without the same prospects for advancement as their Japanese colleagues. Such decisions require courage, however, and many municipalities simply do as they are told for fear of losing vital subsidies.

At the community level, Japanese in general have not exercised aggressively enough their constitutional right of petition to remove public officials or enact, repeal and revise local ordinances.[28] Exceptions abound, however, such as citizen challenges to municipal support of Shintō ceremonies (below). In rare cases, communities have openly defied state policies. An example is the struggle of Miyake islanders to halt construction of facilities for night-landing practice (NLP) by US Navy aircraft. This anti-base movement began in 1983 when the government proposed to shift NLP exercises from Atsugi Naval Air Base just outside of Tokyo to Miyake Island. In 1987, the state despatched riot police to forcibly survey a site for the new facilities. The threat of expropriation brought police into direct confrontation with the islanders, who responded with non-violent tactics. In the face of overwhelming local opposition, the government was compelled to back down, and in 1989, it moved half of the NLP manoeuvres to remote Iwo Jima. This success shows what is possible when residents rely on their own resources to defend their rights through non-violent action.[29]

In a few instances, individuals have taken matters into their own hands. As the government was despatching riot troops to Miyake Island, Chibana Shōichi, a young supermarket owner from Yomitan Village, Okinawa, set fire to the Rising Sun flag. Chibana was protesting the government's decision to hold the 1987 National Athletic Meet in Okinawa. For this 'offence' (the Rising Sun did not become Japan's official flag until 1999), he was jailed, indicted and brought to trial, to the accompaniment of death threats and harassment from rightists, who set fire to his store and intimidated customers. Chibana made this non-violent gesture to remind Japanese in general of the suffering Okinawans had endured under the same flag during the war, and to oppose government efforts to make flag-raising and anthem-singing obligatory in public schools (below).[30]

In the 1990s, local networks of residents banded together to form suprapartisan coalitions at the national level to press for greater bureaucratic transparency and strengthen individual rights. These efforts produced the Products Liability Law of 1994 and the Non-Profit Organisation Law of 1998. Another victory for local groups was the National Information Disclosure Law of 1999, which gives citizens the right to demand access to official information.

Momentum for the freedom of information statute was generated in the early 1980s by grass-roots activists angry at the misuse of public funds by local officials to defray lavish entertainment expenses. Often these abuses involved prefectural officials attempting to woo their national counterparts (*kankan-settai*) or bogus business junkets paid for out of public expense accounts (*kara-shutchō*). Citizens' groups such as the Japan Federation of Housewives' Associations (*Shufuren*) and the Consumers' Union of Japan (*Nihon Shōhisha Renmei*) challenged these practices through lawsuits and demands for the release of government data on public spending. Their efforts forced towns, cities and prefectures to enact local public disclosure ordinances and spawned a freedom of information campaign that propelled the issue into the national arena. Political realignments of the early 1990s and the government's own administrative reform programme provided an opening through which activists could apply leverage, securing passage of a national statute in May 1999.

The law, which entered into force in April 2001, does not specifically guarantee the citizen's right to know, nor does it apply to government corporations, and its purview has been kept purposely vague to protect bureaucratic prerogatives. Nonetheless, the importance of citizen-enacted laws in a era of political apathy and low voter turnout should not be underestimated. When the new statute went into effect, hundreds filed requests for hitherto secret information. Concludes one scholar, 'inter-governmental relations in policy areas that have not been clearly delineated by national law can be independent, dynamic and unpredictable'. This 'bottom-to-top' political initiative is an example of a local issue whose resolution at the national level has benefited all citizens.[31]

Police and administrative reform
Although local voices occasionally have made themselves heard in national politics, the dominant trend since the Occupation has been one of recentralisation. Nowhere is this more evident than in law enforcement. In 1954, an amendment to the Police Law abolished the Local Municipal Police and the National Rural Police, which were incorporated into the Prefectural Police and placed under the direct authority of the newly created National Police Agency. This revision concentrated formerly independent city, town and village law agencies at the prefectural level and centralised the police chain of command. Its chief proponent was Nadao Hirokichi, an élite social bureaucrat who had served in the wartime Home and Welfare Ministries and who would soon become education minister (1957–9) in the Kishi Nobusuke Cabinet. So controversial was the reform that it led to rioting on the floor of the Diet, which ironically was quelled by police intervention.

Following recentralisation, the Occupation-era concern with democratic law enforcement and respect for basic human rights receded steadily, and many abusive prewar practices crept back into standard police procedure. For instance, under the 1908 Prison Law, which SCAP failed to abolish, police can detain a suspect for up to 23 days before asking for an indictment; that period can be prolonged considerably by adding charges of convenience. Moreover, the suspect is detained in a police-station holding cell instead of a pretrial confinement facility – the so-called substitute custody system (*daiyō kangoku*) – and interrogators routinely use high-pressure methods to obtain confessions. Access to legal counsel is limited (lawyers are barred from interrogation sessions), and visitors, mail and reading materials are prohibited. The surrogate detention system explains why about 86 per cent of criminal convictions are based on confessions, and why miscarriages of justice are regular occurrences. Recent years have seen a growing number of acquittals on the grounds of involuntary confessions, yet the government continues to sponsor bills that would give police even greater power over police-cell detainees.[32]

In August 1999, the Diet augmented police authority by pushing through a controversial wiretapping law that permits law officers to intercept communications via telephone, fax and the Internet. Although the statute ostensibly targets only suspected members of organised criminal groups, civil libertarians fear a broader violation of the constitutional provision insuring the secrecy of communications and privacy rights. The bill was bitterly contested by Socialists, Communists and the Democratic Party of Japan.

Bureaucratic restructuring is another SCAP initiative that fell wide of the mark. GHQ's reliance on the existing machinery of government to implement its programmes ultimately was self-defeating. Despite the dismantling of the Home Ministry and the remodelling of the civil service along American lines, the ministries gradually reclaimed many of their former prerogatives through the Cabinet Law (1947), the National Administrative Organisation Law (1948) and implementing legislation establishing the various ministries. Created in 1952, the Justice Ministry and Autonomy Agency, for example, assumed many of the functions of the defunct Home Ministry. Other ministries, too, recovered much of their former authority.[33]

Some scholars assert that the new civil service created a democratic framework for government, cooperating with rather than resisting Occupation reforms, but that is an overly optimistic view.[34] In a democracy, civil servants must maintain a cautious balance between political parties, on the one hand, and private pressure groups, on the other. Japan has never achieved that equilibrium. Radical change is needed to eliminate the tyranny of entrenched interests, endemic corruption and other vestiges of bureaucratic authoritarianism that characterise the Japanese way of government.

The task of taming the bureaucracy is enormous, but in January 2001, the Cabinet of Mori Yoshirō took the first decisive steps in that direction. Acting on the recommendations of an ad hoc advisory body established in 1997, the Mori administration streamlined government ministries and agencies, reducing their number from 23 to 13 and placing 68 elected lawmakers in top decision-making positions. This epoch-making change is intended to make the bureaucracy more responsive to the National Diet and the public will. The Education Ministry, for instance, has been combined with the Science and Technology Agency to form the Ministry of Education, Culture, Sports, Science and Technology. The former Health and Welfare Ministry and the Labour Ministry are now the Ministry of Health, Labour and Welfare. Other new super-agencies are the Ministry of Public Management, Home Affairs, Posts and Communications; the Ministry of Economy, Trade and Industry (formerly, the Ministry of International Trade and Industry); and the Ministry of Land, Infrastructure and Transport. This represents the most ambitious attempt at administrative reform since the Meiji era, but its effectiveness remains to be seen.

Political participation

The reform of the electoral law in December 1945 broadened the nation's electoral base to include women and produced Japan's first free general elections. At the same time, the reform denied suffrage to ethnic Koreans and Chinese. In early 1946, the inhabitants of Okinawa, the Amami islands, and the Ogasawaras, then under direct US control, also were disenfranchised. With the liberalisation of political life in the main islands, however, Japan became a participatory democracy, and political parties flourished, although the right retained its grip on power.

The conservative hegemony established in late 1948 was consolidated by the formation in 1955 of the Liberal Democratic Party, whose ascendancy lasted until the early 1990s. During most of this period, the Communist Party held only a few seats, and the sole effective opposition came from the Socialists, who were never able, however, to control more than about one third of the Diet. The result was the so-called one-and-a-half party system, in which the LDP held a two-thirds majority in the Lower House and the Socialists a one-third representation there.[35] This balance of power continued uninterrupted despite the debut of the Democratic Socialist Party (*Minshatō*, 1960) and the Clean Government Party (*Kōmeitō*, 1964) and the emergence of a quasi-multiparty system. The United States continued to favour the conservative régime and help it parry challenges from the left. During the late 1950s and early 1960s, for instance, the Central Intelligence Agency channelled between $2 million and $10 million a year into LDP coffers. This money was used to fund pro-American Diet candidates and acquire political intelligence. From the late 1960s, as the war in Vietnam escalated, the CIA pumped $1 million annually in secret funds into a media campaign supporting pro-American editors and politicians in order to mute criticism of the war.[36]

What amounted to one-party rule warped the structure of democratic governance in several ways. For instance, the LDP, the bureaucracy and big business became enmeshed in a self-serving system of patronage and influence-peddling that has enabled corporate Japan to evade regulatory constraints on economic activity. This collusion has made corruption pervasive, producing a series of scandals that began with the Shōwa Denkō bribery affair of 1948 and continued with a shipbuilding scam in the 1950s that tainted two future prime ministers, Ikeda Hayato and Satō Eisaku. The 'black mist' transactions of the 1960s brought further notoriety to the Satō government, and the Lockheed bribery case of the 1970s toppled Prime Minister Tanaka Kakuei. The Recruit shares-for-favours incident of the late 1980s peaked as the Shōwa Emperor lay dying, reports of the antics of greedy politicians providing an ironical counterpoint to daily updates on the ailing monarch's condition. In the late 1990s, Defence Agency officials became embroiled in a procurement-billing scheme that cut short the careers of more high-ranking bureaucrats. In early 2001, the Mori government was rocked by a major embezzlement incident in the Foreign Ministry and a massive bribery scandal involving a Cabinet minister and LDP Diet members. So-called structural corruption has led to the resignation or arrest and indictment over the years of a long list of corporate executives, prime ministers, Cabinet officials, lawmakers and top-echelon functionaries, undermining public faith in the nation's political institutions.

Another impediment to good government is 'money politics', shorthand for the fund-raising and vote-garnering machinery the LDP has implanted in each prefecture to purchase the continued support of farmers and local merchants. This system of patronage reflects the disproportionate influence of rural constituencies, which were mapped out in the 1950s before the explosive growth of Japan's urban population. Consequently, rural electoral districts have a lower ratio of voters per Diet seat than urban districts, creating inequality in the value of ballots. To rectify this situation, in 1982, a proportional formula was introduced allocating a fixed number of Lower House seats awarded according to a party's share of the national vote, and in March 1994, the electoral system was revised, introducing Lower House single-seat constituencies and enhancing the proportional-representation system.[37] The Political Funds Control Law also has been strengthened to eliminate some of the system's worst abuses.

Since the early 1990s, a plethora of new parties and shifting political alliances have weakened LDP hegemony, fragmented traditional political groupings and altered the face, albeit not the substance, of Japanese politics. In 1989, the LDP lost its majority in the Upper House for the first time. Reflecting public anger over the introduction of a 3 per cent consumption tax, that defeat was followed by the loss of its Lower House majority in 1993 and the defection of leading conservatives, who established their own faction, the Renewal Party (*Shinseitō*). In 1993, a coalition of eight opposition groups named maverick Hosokawa Morihiro prime minister, ending the conservatives' postwar monopoly on power. One year earlier, Hosokawa had formed the Japan New Party (*Nihon Shintō*) to combat LDP corruption.

In 1994, a revivified Socialist Party (rechristened the Social Democratic Party of Japan) did the unthinkable and forged an alliance with the LDP. The new grouping ousted Hosokawa, who was now dogged by scandal allegations of his own, and named Socialist leader Murayama Tomi'ichi to head the first coalition Cabinet under a Socialist prime minister since the Katayama government of 1947. To retain his influence, Murayama promptly abandoned key Socialist policies, including opposition to the Japan–US security alliance. In 1995, the LDP mainstream, led by Hashimoto Ryūtarō, wrested back control through a series of realignments with the Socialists and such LDP break-away groups as the New Harbinger Party (*Shintō Sakigake*) and the successor to the Renewal Party, the New Frontier Party (*Shin Shintō*). In January 1998, the New Frontier Party dissolved, giving birth to six new political formations, including Ozawa Ichirō's splinter group, the Liberal Party (*Jiyūtō*). LDP stalwart Obuchi Keizō led the government from July 1998 but in January 1999 was forced to form a coalition Cabinet with Ozawa's Liberal Party to retain a Lower House majority. In April 2000, the Liberal Party broke ranks with the government, but more than half of its members seceded from the Liberals to form the New Conservative Party, which remained in the ruling coalition. That month, Prime Minister Obuchi died suddenly of a stroke at age 62, and LDP arch-conservative Mori Yoshirō replaced him as premier. Finally, as this book goes to press (October 2001), Japan has yet a new prime minister, the conservative reformer Koizumi Jun'ichirō.

In the last thirteen years, Japan has had eleven prime ministers, all but one of them from the LDP stable, prompting criticisms of a 'revolving-door premiership'. Yet if the LDP is still omnipresent, it is no longer omnipotent. In 1996, the liberal Kan Naoto and two moderate-conservative leaders, Hata Tsutomu and Hatoyama Yukio, launched yet another group, the Democratic Party of Japan (*Minshutō*), a centrist alternative to the LDP that has replaced the Socialists as the largest opposition group, and today the political field is in flux. The old distinction between conservatives and progressives seems to have disappeared, with the Socialists and the new parties all staking a claim on power. These amorphous groupings lack not only a clear political vision, however, but internal consensus as well. Until recently, the only true parliamentary opposition in the traditional sense was the Japan Communist Party, which successfully attracted voters disillusioned with the present topsy-turvy party system. Yet in late 2000, the JCP revised its 1958 party constitution, dropping scientific socialism and recognising for the time being the existence of the Self-Defence Forces. The Communists, too, appear to be clearing the way for participation in a future coalition government. The continuity of neo-conservative politics amid this chaotic reshuffling of allegiances has confused the public. The result is increased distrust of the nation's leadership, voter apathy and general disaffection with the political process itself. In the area of political participation, the Occupation reforms must be adjudged a partial success.

THE ECONOMIC REFORMS

Economic democratisation hinged on three major initiatives: *zaibatsu* dissolution, the land reform and new labour laws. These policies enabled a stricken Japan to restore domestic production and rebuild a shattered economy. They also laid the groundwork for the frenetic industrial growth that began in the mid-1950s and continued undiminished until the oil crisis of 1973.

Recovery and zaibatsu *dissolution*
Zaibatsu dissolution stopped short of the far-reaching goals SCAP originally had set. The Dodge Economic Stabilisation Plan reined in rampant inflation after 1949 and accelerated *zaibatsu* reorganisation but dealt small- and medium-sized firms a devastating blow. The economy did not really recover until the Korean War, when US military procurements funnelled millions of dollars into the investment funds of big business. From the mid-1950s, Japan embarked on a programme of 'scrap and build', ushering in the so-called Japanese miracle – the period of rapid, protracted growth of the 1960s and early 1970s. This sustained economic boom was led by new industrial organisations, remnants of the former holding companies, now regrouped around large banks that had escaped dissolution. Economic deconcentration originally was intended to undermine the competitiveness of Japanese capitalism, but from 1948, with the onset of the 'reverse course', Washington actively pressed Japan to develop an export-orientated industrial policy. Tokyo was encouraged to protect domestic industries from external competition while exporting to the vast American and potentially vast Southeast Asian markets. President Dwight D. Eisenhower, for example, reportedly urged such leading US companies as Motorola to buy Japanese-made products and cultivate special relationships with Japanese suppliers even though these commodities were not yet up to US standards.[38] Ultimately, limited deconcentration and the absence of military spending dramatically enhanced Japan's competitive position in the world market, and the business élite has been remarkably successful in transferring the martial spirit of the pre-1945 era to the postwar corporate board room.[39]

In the 1980s, as the US trade deficit with Japan swelled to unprecedented propor-
tions, Washington had cause to regret its Occupation-era promotion of managed
trade, with its industrial targeting, predatory marketing strategies and protectionist
policies. Today, only about 20 per cent of Japanese firms compete fully in the world
market, but they are among the world's largest and most efficient. The remaining 80
per cent are geared to domestic production, although many are affiliates or subsidiaries of major exporters. Interlocking directorates, cross-shareholding, collusive and
exclusionary *keiretsu* groupings of manufacturers and suppliers, bid-rigging (*dangō*)
and other such 'non-tariff barriers' that block foreign access to the Japanese market
are a product of this developmentalist strategy.[40] Washington viewed the markets of
Southeast Asia as vital to Japan's complete economic recovery and its usefulness as a
Free-World ally. The rise of Communist-led forces in French Indo-China committed
to national liberation appeared to threaten that goal. If the Southeast Asian 'dom-
inoes' fell, it was feared, Japan might turn to China and the Communist bloc to
secure its long-term trade interests. In an important sense, the origins of the second
Indo-China War (1964–75) lie in flawed assumptions spawned between 1949 and
1950 tying Japan's future to the fate of these peripheral emporia.[41]

Labour reform
The Labour Union Law, the Labour Relations Adjustment Law and the Labour
Standards Law liberated the Japanese worker and brought the rights of working
people into line with internationally accepted norms. There were limits to reform,
however, beyond which the Occupation would not go. GHQ promptly outlawed
strike actions it deemed 'prejudicial to Occupation objectives' or, in the alarm-
ist rhetoric of the time, 'liable to endanger the security of Occupation forces'.
MacArthur banned the general strike planned for 1 February 1947 because he
believed it could disrupt the economy and threaten lives. SCAP also denied civil
servants the right to strike and bargain collectively. (This fundamental prerogative
was restored to some employees with the privatisation of the Japan National Railways, the Nippon Telegraph and Telephone Public Corporation and the Japan
Tobacco and Salt Public Corporation between 1985 and 1987.) Nor did SCAP
succeed fully in eliminating paternalistic employment practices or the hierarchical
shopfloor division of labour, both of which exert a negative influence on labour
relations today. Its attempt to bring in the American labour-management model and
US-style trade unionism also foundered as social bureaucrats in the Labour Ministry
reintroduced the group-orientated 'Japanese labour relations system' to counter
worker militancy. Enterprise unionism became the rule, with exclusive in-house
unions (including both workers and managers) narrowly focused on intra-company
problems.

During the 1970s and early 1980s, organised labour moved to the right. From the
mid-1980s, privatisation of the large public corporations accelerated this trend. In
1989, the left-of-centre *Sōhyō* (General Council of Trade Unions of Japan), representing about 37 per cent of all organised workers (3.6 million), dissolved and

merged with its bitter right-wing rival, *Dōmei* (Japanese Confederation of Labour). The result was *Rengō* (Japan Trade Union Confederation), a broad anti-Communist labour front advocating labour–management cooperation and boasting a membership of 8 million. Since then, the gap between union leadership and the rank and file has widened. Opposing *Rengō* is *Zenrōren* (National Confederation of Trade Unions), a small left-leaning federation of 1.4 million workers that separated from *Sōhyō* to form its own more politically orientated national centre.

In the early 1990s, the speculative bubble of the late 1980s burst, bringing on the worst recession of the postwar period. By 2001, the slow-down was being compared to the 1949–50 Dodge deflation, as the unemployment rate soared to an unprecedented 5 per cent. In this climate of sluggish growth, downsizing and bankruptcies, firms have moved to eliminate such traditional practices as lifetime employment, the seniority system and enterprise unionism. Ironically, the slack economy has brought Yoshida Shigeru's quip about GHQ ('Go Home Quickly') back into vogue as young employees with little work to do, known as 'GHQers', routinely leave the office early. Industrial restructuring has precipitated a decline in union membership, which dropped from 35 per cent of the work force in 1975 to about 22 per cent in 1998. The changing labour market also has encouraged the

Photo 76. On Japan's 65th May Day, foreign labourers, many of them undocumented, demonstrate alongside Japanese workers. Their banner reads: 'Through workers' solidarity, we can protect our rights, living standards, and peace'. Their presence indicates the changing composition of Japan's unskilled labour force and the stirrings of a multi-cultural society. A number of Japanese unions now include foreign workers in their membership regardless of residence status. With their assistance, Bangladeshis, Filipinos, Iranians and Latin Americans have formed their own unions. Hibiya, 1 May 1994 (Kyodo).

growth of new kinds of labour groups, such as cross-enterprise unions that organise part-time workers, foremen and foreign workers across company lines.[42]

In the late 1980s, as globalisation intensified, the government made deregulation and institutional reform national priorities and began revising key labour laws. In 1986, it rewrote the Temporary Staff Labour Law to enable employers to despatch superfluous workers to subsidiaries and affiliates (this was revised in July 1999, extending the authorised period of such transfers by up to one year). In 1987, the Employment Security Law was amended to allow the use of 'flexible' part-time contract labour hired at lower wages and with fewer benefits. In September 1998, the Labour Standards Law was amended, extending the working day from 8 to 10 hours, thereby eliminating the 40-hour work week. At the same time, the job-placement industry is being deregulated and the category of tasks subject to discretionary work schedules enlarged. SCAP's labour legislation was designed to protect workers from the vagaries of the market and the worst excesses of the capitalist system. Recent amendments are designed to streamline the economy, give big business maximum flexibility in dealing with the current crisis and subordinate workers' rights more completely to the needs of industry.

Land reform
Perhaps the Occupation's single most successful endeavour was the 1946 land reform. Although Japan had planned a modest restructuring of the land-tenure system during and immediately after the war, SCAP ultimately took that idea farther than even it had originally anticipated. The land-to-the tiller programme liberated 2 million hectares of agricultural land, redistributed it to former tenants at a fraction of its actual value, installed more than half of the nation's food producers on their own farms and virtually eliminated tenancy as an institution. The reform democratised rural life, raised living standards, improved labour efficiency and increased agricultural output. It failed, however, to remedy the problem of tiny dispersed land parcels. Today, full-time cultivators till on average a mere 2.8 hectares, and the vast majority manage a minuscule 1.6 hectares, impeding mechanisation and the development of scale economies. Forested property, on the other hand, was not confiscated and redistributed in the reform. As a result, this land escaped parcellisation and now plays a crucial role in preserving the rural ecology.[43]

The land reform was unequivocally beneficial in that it transformed poor tenant farmers into a class of self-reliant and economically viable family farmers, eliminated parasitic landlordism and boosted farm productivity. Once that judgement is behind us, however, ambiguities creep in. The reform weakened the farmers' movement and cost the Socialist Party, whose fortunes were closely linked with that movement, its rural electoral base. Land reform shifted rural political sympathies from the Socialists and Communists to the conservative alliance that took power in 1948. Former landlords watched with resentment as land values soared in the 1960s and 1970s and their ex-tenants enriched themselves by selling off the plots they had acquired in the reform.

Despite postwar improvements, farming remains synonymous with hard work and low income. The Basic Agriculture Law of 1961 encouraged large-scale rice mono-culture and mechanisation in order to facilitate the transfer of rural labour to urban manufacturing. To maintain living standards, many food producers were compelled to take part-time jobs outside of the farm sector. Today, for the majority, agriculture itself is a sideline activity, and full-time cultivators represent a mere 16 per cent of all farm households. Young farmers have difficulty attracting wives, and this has prompted some villages to recruit brides from China, South Korea, the Philippines, Sri Lanka and Thailand. Finally, few young men are willing to assume responsibility for the family farm, and if present trends continue, in many rural areas, the current generation of professional farmers may be the last.

As the land reform was completed, producers formed agricultural cooperatives (*Nōkyō*) to market their crops, acquire farm supplies cheaply, bank their income and pressure the government to maintain an elaborate system of price supports and other subsidies. Recent research shows that an intense debate took place within SCAP's Economic and Scientific Section and Natural Resources Section concerning the wisdom of encouraging the co-ops. Those who warned that the *Nōkyō* would monopolise the farm market were proved right by subsequent events. Since their inception, the co-ops have been a bastion of conservative rule, funnelling rural votes and funds into the LDP party machine.

In the 1980s, however, the Uruguay Round and subsequent trade liberalisation agreements forced the conservatives to slash subsidies and lower Japan's excessively high food prices to world-market levels (in 1998, the consumer's price of rice was still 2.4 times higher than in the United States). Today, shifting priorities are eroding rice-roots support for the LDP in its so-called Conservative Kingdom.[44]

THE CULTURAL REFORMS

The Occupation was determined to extirpate ultra-nationalist dogmas, and extensive reforms in education, religion and the mass media largely accomplished that goal. Many of the changes SCAP wrought, however, were gradually rolled back following the return of Japanese sovereignty.

Education
The education reforms dismantled the highly centralised and élitist prewar school system, making instruction co-educational, uniform and compulsory for nine years through junior high school. This decentralising project struck at the enormous authority of the Education Ministry by abolishing state-controlled textbooks, scrap-ping ethics and other courses that had promoted ultra-nationalist values and permit-ting individual schools to choose their own curricula and texts. Finally, Occupation authorities placed the responsibility for making school policy in the hands of locally elected boards of education.

Some Japanese scholars assert that the school reforms were dualistic. On the one hand, SCAP's basic education plan signalled a radical departure from past Japanese practice. On the other, it created a framework that tied educational policy to US global strategy. In the words of one academic, 'The introduction of an American-style education system furthered these strategic goals by providing a platform for the Occupation's own propaganda effort and the propagation of the democratic ideals fostered by Western (primarily American) capitalist society. The new system's ultimate objective was to transform Japan into a strong, anti-Communist state capable of countering the influence of China and the Soviet Union.'[45] It is true that the 1946 US Education Mission played a central role in setting the reform agenda, but this programme was not imposed unilaterally. Forward-looking Japanese educators and officials adapted the US proposals to Japanese realities, using the Occupation's immense authority to overcome conservative opposition and achieve meaningful change. In fact, in both form and content, this was in many respects a Japanese initiative.

The Yoshida government acquiesced in some of these momentous changes but successfully forestalled others. The conservatives objected strenuously to the idea of independent boards of education and succeeded in postponing their full introduction until October 1952, by which time Japan had regained its independence. In 1956, the ultra-conservative Hatoyama Cabinet abolished elective school boards altogether under the Local Educational Administration Law. Thereafter, local boards were appointed by municipal mayors and school superintendents by prefectural boards, which now controlled the hiring and firing of local teaching staff. The 1956 law proved so unpopular that the government had to introduce 500 police into the Upper House to restrain angry lawmakers in chaotic scenes reminiscent of the 1954 police reform.

The Education Ministry quickly recovered much of its former authority via enhanced powers of advice, guidance and consent. In 1958, it reasserted control over course content and textbook selection and reintroduced ethics into school curricula. Recentralisation was met with stiff resistance, most notably from the left-leaning Japan Teachers' Union (*Nikkyōso*). To curb the union's influence, the Yoshida government rammed through the Diet a controversial law – honoured in the breach – banning political activity by public school teachers during and after school hours, with the sole exception of voting.

Textbook screening, another SCAP innovation, became a tool for recasting educational content in a conservative mould. In the early phase of occupation, censors screened school texts to purge them of militarist ideology. Since 1958, the Education Ministry, through its Textbook Review Council, a conservative advisory body of teachers and scholars, has purged texts of materials deemed harmful to the nation's self-image. Until the late 1980s, the Ministry routinely suppressed passages discussing Japan's colonial conquests and wartime behaviour; these inconvenient facts were, in effect, written out of the history books. In 1965, historian Ienaga Saburō, a textbook writer who had contributed to the 1946 history primer *Kuni no ayumi* (Our Nation's Progress), took the Education Ministry to court for excising as inappropriate more than 300 passages or expressions from a text he had submitted. In 1989, the

Tokyo District Court, ruling on the third Ienaga suit, handed the historian a limited victory by declaring the censors wrong in one instance. Although the Court rejected his treatment of the colonisation of Korea, Unit 731's biological warfare experiments and the battle of Okinawa, upholding the government's right in principle to vet school texts and dictate course content, it allowed his account of the Nanjing massacre and other misdeeds. The verdict was a milestone that imposed clear limits on the extent of censorship. The same year, in the face of widespread criticism, the Education Ministry issued new standards for history education, requiring schools to focus more on the twentieth century and particularly the war era.[46]

Most textbooks of the 1990s have included brief references to colonial rule, the Nanjing massacre, 'comfort women' and other war issues, although discussion of the Emperor's role remains taboo. In 2000, the Ministry introduced further modifications that have shortened the textbook review period from one year to one month or less and require inspectors to state their reasons for deleting information or demanding revisions. But the crux of the problem, state censorship of educational content, is unresolved. Since the late 1990s, nationalistic scholars, opinion leaders and even popular cartoonists have disputed war atrocities and lobbied to reverse textbook revisions in order to create a neo-conservative consensus justifying Japan's wartime conduct. Reflecting that trend, the most recent textbooks, scheduled for release in 2002, devote less space to the war years. Only three of eight publishers have included material on wartime sexual slavery, and of the six that mention the Nanjing atrocities, only one gives a concrete figure for the number of victims (current texts cite figures ranging from 100,000 to 200,000).

One of the eight texts is an aggressively revisionist junior high history book submitted by a group of rightwing educators, the Japanese Society for History Textbook Reform. In early April 2001, the Education Ministry surprised the book's many critics by approving it for use in 2002. The text emphasises the importance of the emperor system, omits any reference to the 'comfort women' issue and downplays the scale and significance of atrocities such as the Nanjing rampage. The Ministry's decision brought ringing condemnation from Asian capitals, and a week later, Seoul protested by recalling its ambassador for consultations. Koreans were particularly offended by the textbook's attempt to sanitise Japan's colonial conquest of their country, and as of this writing, the controversy continues to rage, threatening to undo the recent efforts of ROK President Kim Dae Jung and others to reconcile the two countries and move the bilateral relationship forward.

The new texts also glorify the flag and national anthem. In the 1980s, Prime Minister Nakasone (1982–7) revised the school curriculum to emphasise 'Japanese identity' and respect for the then-unofficial Rising Sun banner (*Hinomaru*) and the de facto national hymn (*Kimigayo*, literally 'The Imperial Reign'), paramount symbols of the Old Order. In 1985, the Education Ministry instructed public schools to observe flag and anthem rituals at entrance and graduation ceremonies, and in 1989, a ministerial directive made these observances mandatory and prescribed punishments for wayward school officials. After a decade of acrimonious debate, in

August 1999, the Obuchi Cabinet pushed through two bills legally recognising the *Hinomaru* and the *Kimigayo* and immediately issued a circular requiring government organisations, including municipalities and public corporations, to raise the flag and sing the national hymn at government-sponsored events. New teaching guidelines, effective from 2002, will oblige teachers to emphasise these observances in an effort to forge a deeper sense of loyalty to the state. Students in some schools have boy-cotted graduation ceremonies to protest against these rites, however, and teachers affiliated with the Japan Teachers' Union also have expressed strong opposition. In August 2000, the Tokyo Board of Education reprimanded 17 public school teachers for wearing blue 'peace ribbons' and distributing leaflets that explained the close association of these militaristic symbols with the emperor system and wartime aggression.

The recentralisation of education has created other long-term problems, as well. Further tightening of ministerial control in the 1980s and 1990s has produced a thoroughly controlled school environment, where students' lives are closely moni-tored and regulated down to the finest detail of dress, hairstyle and behaviour, both in and outside of the classroom. An excessive emphasis on rote memorisation and unrelenting parental pressure to enter a top university, seen as the sole guarantee of a good job, stifle creativity. Test scores seem to have become the only accepted measure of individual worth. In recent years, this highly regimented system has led young people to acts of desperation and rebellion. Bullying at school and after class is a serious problem. Drug use now is common in middle schools, something unthink-able a few years ago, and long-term truancy is endemic. Many students appear aggressively self-centred and display little of the self-control on which Japanese trad-itionally have prided themselves. In 1997, violent incidents occurred at 30 per cent of the nation's middle schools and at 37 per cent of its high schools, directed mainly at other students but also at teachers and school property.

There have been positive developments, as well, such as the proliferation of preparatory academies, specialised trade schools, two-year junior colleges, 'freedom' schools and adult education programmes. Since 1985, the University of the Air has made advanced instruction available to anyone willing to apply themselves and learn. These institutions meet the diversified needs of a larger public, providing an alternative to the current rigid tracking system designed to turn out obedient citizens. In December 2000, the National Commission on Education Reform, an advisory panel to Prime Minister Mori, recommended overhauling the 1947 Fun-damental Law on Education in order to nurture creativity and eliminate excessive competition in college entrance exams. Reform, indeed, is long overdue, but here we must be careful to preserve the best of the Occupation-era law. This is its overarch-ing vision of a school system that insures the 'full development of the personality' and strives to produce a citizenry 'who shall love truth and justice, esteem individual value . . . and be imbued with an independent spirit, as builders of a peaceful state and society'.

Freedom of worship and belief
SCAP's Shintō Directive of December 1945 outlawed State Shintō, guaranteed freedom of worship and belief and mandated state neutrality in religious matters. These reforms were written into the Constitution's Article 20, which states unambiguously that: 'No religious organisation shall receive any privileges from the State' and that 'The State and its organs shall refrain from . . . religious activity'. Article 89 further stipulates that 'No money or other property shall be expended or appropriated for the use, benefit or maintenance of any religious institution'. The prewar tradition of conflating Shintō rites and nationalist ideology revived quickly, however, once the Occupation ended. Yasukuni Shrine in Tokyo, founded by the Emperor Meiji and dedicated to the spirits of those who have died in the Emperor's service, is a prime example. Formerly a state shrine, it was used by the militarists to glorify Japan's foreign conquests and promote patriotism. Disestablished during the Occupation, Yasukuni has enjoyed the moral support of successive conservative governments since 1952. In 1968, the shrine added the names of 2 million Japanese killed during World War II to its roster of 'heroic souls' (*eirei*), including some 50,000 Koreans and Chinese who were enshrined as Shintō deities (*saishin*) over the vehement protests of surviving family members. Since 1969, the LDP has submitted bills to the Diet almost annually seeking to restore state funding for Yasukuni, so far without success. In 1978, the names of 14 Class A war criminals were added to the rolls, and the following year, Prime Minister Ōhira Masayoshi (1978–80) paid an 'unofficial' visit to the sanctuary.

On 15 August 1985, Prime Minister Nakasone became the first postwar premier to worship publicly at the shrine in his official capacity. Nakasone was accompanied by his entire Cabinet, and the visit, which drew vitriolic comment from China, the two Koreas and other Asian countries, escalated into a major diplomatic incident. In 1986, Nakasone's newly appointed education minister, Fujio Masayuki, blamed the Occupation's education reforms for what he termed the 'Yasukuni allergy'. At the same time, he made statements minimising Japan's wartime brutality, implied that Chinese and Koreans had committed similar atrocities in the course of their own history and suggested that Koreans had welcomed and collaborated actively in their own colonisation. Nakasone's successors, however, prudently adopted a low profile and avoided the annual pilgrimage.

Buddhist and Christian groups promptly sued the government over the Nakasone visit, charging that in effect it treated the Shintō war shrine as a state institution and undermined the legal standing and rights of other religions. District courts dismissed the complaint, but in 1992, both the Fukuoka and the Osaka High Courts threw out the earlier verdicts and determined that the act of homage and the Prime Minister's monetary gift to Yasukuni were 'very likely' unconstitutional. The courts pointedly avoided a clear-cut judgement, however, leaving an area of ambiguity that conservative politicians have been able to exploit, strengthening the symbolism of state involvement with the shrine.

In 1993, Prime Minister Miyazawa Ki'ichi (1991–3) prayed secretly at the sanctuary to keep a promise to the Japan Association of War-Bereaved Families. In July 1996, Prime Minister Hashimoto Ryūtarō (1995–8) visited Yasukuni on his birthday. Although he went as a private citizen, he signed the guest register using his official title, a sign that the pendulum has begun to swing the other way. On 15 August 2000, Prime Minister Mori stayed away from the sanctuary to avoid controversy pending a state visit by Chinese Premier Zhu Rongi, but 10 members of his Cabinet venerated the war dead there. They were joined by Tokyo Governor Ishihara Shintarō, the first Tokyo head of government to worship in his official capacity. In 2001, Prime Minister Koizumi Jun'ichirō prayed publicly at the shrine on 13 August, two days before the official anniversary of Japan's capitulation, angering supporters and foes alike and drawing fresh rebukes from Asian neighbours.

With the exception of the ambiguous Nakasone ruling, the top court has not supported citizens contesting state-religion issues. In 1977, for example, the Supreme Court declared that the use of public funds to sponsor Shintō ritual is not unconstitutional per se. The controversy erupted when a city councillor in Tsu City, Mie Prefecture sued municipal authorities for financing a 1965 Shintō ground-purification ceremony. The Tsu District Court ruled that the event was a secular ritual commonly accompanying construction projects and therefore permissible under law. In 1971, the Nagoya High Court overturned that decision. The ceremony, despite its social function, also was a Shintō religious observance, the Court found, and therefore could not be funded publicly. When Tsu City appealed the verdict, however, the Supreme Court found in its favour, upholding the court of first instance.

Judges also have sided with the state in cases involving freedom of worship. In 1968, a Self-Defence Force officer, Nakaya Takafumi, was killed in a traffic accident while on duty. In 1972, the SDF informed his widow, Nakaya Yasuko, that against her wishes – she was a Christian – her deceased husband had been enshrined as a deity in the Yamaguchi prefectural Defence of the Nation Shrine (*Gokoku Jinja*) along with 26 other SDF dead. Nakaya Yasuko sued, but while two lower courts ruled that enshrinement was a religious activity and therefore illegal, the Supreme Court reversed these decisions in 1988, allowing the state, in effect, to apotheosise her deceased husband into a Shintō spirit.[47]

With the end of the Occupation, local governments began openly disbursing municipal funds for rites honouring the war dead. In 1977 residents of Mino'o City in Osaka Prefecture brought suit against the city for using public funds for that purpose, but in 1993, the Supreme Court ruled the practice to be within constitutional limits. During the Occupation, Mino'o authorities had concealed a war memorial (*chūkonhi*) erected in 1916 to the nation's war dead, a common practice at that time in prefectural cities and rural areas. In 1952, the city took the cenotaph out of wraps. When it decided to move the memorial to a new location and bought land for that purpose in 1975, anti-war residents invoked the Local Autonomy Law and challenged municipal authorities in court. They also sued the mayor and other city officials, including the chair of the local board of education, for attending a religious ceremony at the monument in their official capacity and for providing financial aid to a religious organisation – the Association of War-Bereaved Families, an affiliate of the nationalistic Japan Association of War-Bereaved Families. These actions, the anti-war group charged, violated Articles 20 and 89 of the Constitution.

In March 1982, Osaka District Court found that the allocation of public funds for such purposes violated the Constitution. The Court also ruled that the Association of Bereaved Families is a religious body and that public financial assistance to such organisations, too, is unconstitutional. In July 1987, however, the Osaka High Court overturned that decision on the grounds that the cenotaph was not an object of religious veneration but a simple monument and that the use of public funds to transfer it therefore was legitimate. The Court also declared that ceremonies honouring the war dead are not religious in nature but customary. The presence of the mayor and other city officials thus did not constitute state involvement in a religious rite. Finally, the Court held that the Association of Bereaved Families was not a religious body. The plaintiffs appealed their case to the Supreme Court, which upheld the High Court decision in February 1993.

The judiciary, then, generally has moved towards a looser interpretation of the constitutional guarantees affecting religious freedoms. In at least one area, however, superior courts have sided with citizens' groups against the state. In 1991, the Sendai High Court rejected decisions by the Morioka District Court sanctioning government visits to Yasukuni and allowing the payment of a shrine fee (*tamagushi-ryō*) by Iwate prefectural assembly members. The visits and the official disbursement, the High Court said, violated the principle of separation of religion and state. Similarly, in 1997, the Takamatsu High Court determined that *tamagushi* payments constituted a religious act favouring a specific cult.[48] The Supreme Court has yet to rule on this question, however.

The sarin poisoning incident in Tokyo posed a different challenge to postwar religious freedoms. On 20 March 1995, members of Aum Shinrikyō, a doomsday cult with thousands of young followers, released deadly sarin nerve gas on a Tokyo subway line, killing 12 commuters and injuring more than 5,500. Following the incident, the government promptly revised the 1951 Religious Corporation Law, placing religious groups under the jurisdiction of the Education Ministry instead of the prefectural governor and strengthening centralised control over religious activities in general. The government railroaded the reform bill through the Diet, enacting it in late 1996. In the United States, legislation of this magnitude would have required Congressional hearings lasting at least three years. The state next attempted to dissolve Aum Shinrikyō under the 1952 Subversive Activities Prevention Law. Such a measure would have created a dangerous precedent and was opposed successfully by a broad coalition of civil libertarians, progressive political parties and Christian, Buddhist and other religious groups.[49]

The mass media

SCAP's Press and Radio Codes of September 1945 abolished state control of the mass media, but the Occupation immediately imposed it own constraints on information.

Censorship was a necessary evil that helped nurture democratic ideals, but it had unintended consequences. Even after Japan recovered its independence, the media remained circumspect in their coverage of the Establishment, and the Chrysanthemum Taboo quickly reasserted itself. Consequently, the Fourth Estate has not played an effective watch-dog role in post-treaty Japan. The government, for its part, closely regulates the release of state information through the exclusive press clubs operated by each ministry and state agency and can deny access to reporters who stray too far from the official line. The mass media seem incapable of internal reform, but the public, too, is partly to blame for not holding editors to a higher standard of truth.

Few mainstream news organisations, for instance, question seriously Japan's political and diplomatic subservience to the United States. The media's uncritical acceptance of the 1997 Guidelines for Japan-US Defence Cooperation and the Theatre Missile Defence proposal is just one recent example. Another sacred cow is the United Nations. Editors and opinion leaders seem to believe that Japan's UN commitment is almighty. If the General Assembly sanctions armed intervention, as during the Gulf War, Tokyo must follow its lead, they imply, or suffer isolation and world condemnation. Behind the United Nations, however, stands the United States. Indeed, in many Japanese minds, the two are inseparable. Blind support for the United Nations clearly is dangerous, but as Japan's power élite manipulates that potent symbol and clamours for a seat on the Security Council, the mass media lend it their tacit support.[50]

Media abuses abound. Reporters tend to develop close relationships with the police, on whom they rely for leads on crime stories. Newspapers frequently sensationalise such reports, creating the impression that law officers are acting on the basis of established evidence, when in fact, suspects may be detained on a charge of convenience. Arrest becomes tantamount in the public mind to an admission of guilt, inviting miscarriages of justice. An example of irresponsible reporting is the Matsumoto incident. In July 1994, an innocent white-collar employee was virtually tried and convicted by the media of releasing poison gas into an apartment complex in Matsumoto City, Nagano Prefecture, killing seven people and injuring 270. In March 1995, the real culprit was discovered to be Aum Shinrikyō, which had used Matsumoto as a trial run for its assault on Tokyo commuters.

HEALTH, WELFARE AND THE PURSUIT OF HAPPINESS

GHQ's innovations in health and welfare were ahead of their time and are among the most remarkable of the postwar reforms. Article 25 of the 1946 Constitution states unequivocally that 'All people shall have the right to maintain the minimum standards of wholesome and cultured living. In all spheres of life, the State shall use its endeavours for the promotion and extension of social welfare and security, and of public health.' Similar guarantees were not incorporated into international law until later: the World Health Organisation Charter dates from 1951 and the International Covenants on Human Rights (Covenant A, Article 12) from 1966.

The eighteenth-century philosopher Jean-Jacques Rousseau once commented that the true measure of a nation's cultural development was to be found in its vital statistics, notably the ratio between birth and mortality rates. In that sense, the Occupation reforms helped Japan attain a very high level of cultural maturity. For instance, in 1947 the ratio of births to deaths per 1,000 people was 34.3 to 14.6; in 1960, it was 19.4 to 7.8; and in 1998, it was 9.6 to 7.5. Both rates have declined rapidly at approximately the same pace. (During the six-and-half years of Occupation control, the death rate alone dropped from 18.7 per 1,000 to 8.1.) The infant mortality rate has fallen even more dramatically, from 76.7 in 1947, to 39.8 in 1960 and to 3.6 in 1998. The lifespan of the average Japanese has grown proportionately and today is the longest in the world. In 1947, men lived an average of 50 years, but by 1998, that figure was 77.2 years. The figures for women, respectively, are 54 years and 84 years.[51]

Behind these data lie major advances in nutrition and the war against disease. In 1947, the average daily intake of animal protein was 6.7 grams in rural areas and 14.7 grams in the cities, but in 1950, that figure was 17 grams in both, and by 1997, it had more than doubled to 43.9 grams. With the shift from a traditional diet to a mixed regimen based on Western as well as Japanese foods, average height, weight and build have increased, and our young people now approach Western norms in body size and physical strength. Major infectious diseases also have been virtually eliminated. Cases of dysentery and diphtheria, for example, dropped from 50.2 and 36.3 victims, respectively, per 10,000 people in 1947 to 1.0 and 0.0 in 1997. Tuberculosis, another deadly disease for which there once was no cure, also has declined sharply, falling from 146.4 people per 10,000 in 1947 to 3.1 in 1997. These advances may all be traced to the ambitious public health programme instituted by the Occupation.[52]

While medical care, pubic health and social welfare have made impressive strides in the past half century, new problems such as pervasive industrial pollution also have arisen. In the 1950s and 1960s, the Chisso Corporation in Minamata, Kumamoto Prefecture pumped hundreds of thousands of tons of raw mercury effluent into Minamata Bay, poisoning the fish in the Ariake Sea, killing more than 900 local inhabitants and crippling or disabling many thousands of others. A Shōwa Denkō factory on the Agano River in Ni'igata Prefecture also caused a serious outbreak of 'Minamata disease'. In Yokkaichi, Mie Prefecture, a major petrochemical complex fouled the air, producing severe cases of asthma over a large area, and cadmium poisoning affecting the bones (*itai-itai* disease) led to widespread suffering in Toyama Prefecture. In 1980, there were 80,000 officially recognised victims of pollution-related diseases. By 1988, an additional 100,000 had been certified as suffering from atmospheric pollution alone, 94 per cent of them concentrated in the three industrial conurbations of Tokyo, Nagoya and Osaka.[53]

Since the 'hollowing out' of the economy in the 1980s, many smokestack industries have moved offshore, exporting their poisonous emissions to Southeast Asia. In

Japan today, pollution is increasingly invisible, but the air and land remain danger-ously contaminated by dioxin, polychlorinated biphenyls (PCBs), benzine and other industrial carcinogens. Even the country's contours have been altered, its once-beautiful coastlines having virtually disappeared. Although two thirds of our moun-tainous archipelago is forested, we find it cheaper to import timber from Southeast Asia, destroying local ecosystems there as well. Concrete and asphalt cover much of the country, and housing developments crowd out prime farmland. Consequently, we now import 60 per cent of our food.

In 1988, the government began construction of a dam on the Nagara River in Mie Prefecture, the longest natural river system remaining in Japan. The state has proceeded with the project despite protests from local residents and national and international conservation groups. Construction has adversely affected water quality, resulting in the loss of local fish species and damaging the regional habitat. In 1993, the government enacted the Basic Environmental Law in an effort to balance indus-trial activity and environmental protection, and in 1997, the Environmental Assess-ment Law was passed making ecological impact surveys mandatory. Yet even as the 1997 statute went into force, a new state reclamation project began draining some 3,550 hectares of the vast Isahaya tidal flats in Nagasaki Prefecture to create new farmland, destroying marine life unique to the bay ecology of Japan's largest remain-ing wetland. Scheduled for completion in 2006, the project has disrupted the local seaweed harvest and threatens other marine industries. Environmental laws not only lack effective enforcement mechanisms but also deny local residents a voice in the development projects that menace their communities. Despite Japan's material affluence, true prosperity – the peace of mind and generosity of spirit that come from co-existing harmoniously with nature – eludes us.[54]

The computer age brings with it new health threats of which we are only beginning to be aware. As birth and death rates have fallen and life expectancy has climbed, the care and rights of the elderly have become pressing issues. The coffers of the National Health Insurance programme are already badly strained, and many of us wonder who will pay the ballooning health-care costs of the future. We are hard pressed to deal with the growing incidence of cancer and other life-threatening diseases, and the concept of death with dignity and the hospice movement are still novel ideas here.

Japan, too, has its AIDS crisis. Open discussion of the problem is a social taboo, and those living with HIV are openly discriminated against, with many hospitals refusing to treat HIV-positive patients. The number of hidden carriers is expected to rise dramatically as the AIDS epidemic explodes in Asia. In the early 1980s, Health and Welfare Ministry officials knowingly allowed unheated blood products from the United States to enter Japan without testing them for HIV. As a result more than 2,000 haemophiliacs have contacted the immuno-deficiency virus through transfu-sions. In 1995, the Tokyo and Osaka District Courts ordered the government and five pharmaceutical companies, including the controversial Green Cross Corporation (chapter 10), to pay extensive damages to the victims and their families. In February 1996, Health and Welfare Minister Kan Naoto admitted the Ministry's responsibility for the tragedy and issued a formal apology, and the government subsequently brought criminal charges against a doctor, a Ministry official and three Green Cross executives.

These are a few of the problems of a postmodern society at century's end. Many of them reflect the highly managed, authority-orientated society we have built since 1952. Economism, embodied in the modern 'enterprise state,' has shifted popular loyalties from the emperor system to the corporation while weakening the social fabric of family and community life.[55] For many, the only alternative seems to be hedonism and the narrow pursuit of selfish, even antisocial, goals. Despite the very real gains Japan has made since the Occupation, issues such as the exclusion of cultural and ethnic minorities and the nation's war responsibility seem intractable. Nevertheless, if we continue working in the spirit of the postwar reforms, Japanese democracy is robust enough to meet such challenges. One of the keys to resolving these and future problems lies in our endogenous tradition of local-level activism.

GRASS-ROOTS DEMOCRACY

In May 1945, former ambassador to Japan Joseph C. Grew told President Truman that 'from the long range point of view, the best we can hope for in Japan is the development of a constitutional monarchy, experience having shown that democracy . . . would never work'. Nearly three years later, in February 1948, George F. Kennan, head of the State Department's Policy Planning Staff, wrote in a similar vein that 'We should cease to talk about vague and – for the Far East – unreal objectives such as human rights, the raising of the living standards, and democratization. The day is not far off when we are going to have to deal in straight power concepts. The less we are hampered by idealistic slogans, the better.'[56] Such cynical views were not shared by the forward-looking men and women in SCAP who oversaw the early reforms, or by the equally progressive Japanese who implemented and embraced them. Our postwar history is proof that the prospect of democracy was neither vague nor unreal.

The birth of citizens' movements
Critics of Occupation policy speak dismissively of 'trickle-down democracy', but what happened at the grass roots as the years passed was more of a drenching than a dribbling. The mid-1950s witnessed the florescence of a nationwide anti-war citizens' movement that MacArthur's headquarters had sought to suppress. Popular revulsion at US nuclear testing in the Pacific turned to outrage in March 1954 when a hydrogen bomb blast at the Bikini Atoll in the Marshalls irradiated islanders and the crew of a Japanese fishing vessel, Lucky Dragon (*Fukuryū Maru*) No. 5, which happened to be in the vicinity. In May, a non-partisan women's group in Tokyo's Suginami Ward launched a national signature campaign, and the so-called Suginami Appeal signalled the beginning of a mass movement to abolish nuclear weapons and war. By the end of 1954, more than 20 million signatures had been collected, and

many Japanese had turned their attention to the forgotten victims of Hiroshima and Nagasaki. In August 1955, the World Conference Against Atomic and Hydrogen Bombs was convened in Hiroshima, and in September of that year, the Japan Council Against Atomic and Hydrogen Bombs (*Gensuikyō*) was formed, linking groups across the political, religious and intellectual spectrum and including many *hibakusha*. The organisation was instrumental in securing passage in 1957 of the Atomic Bomb Victims' Medical Care Law, the first official relief programme for victims of the bombings. Backed by the Communist and Socialist Parties and *Sōhyō*, *Gensuikyō* also played a major role in the 1960 struggle against renewal of the Japan–US Security Treaty (*Anpō*). In 1964, Socialist-led groups, protesting Communist support nuclear testing by Communist states, left *Gensuikyō* to form a rival organisation, the Japan Congress Against Atomic and Hydrogen Bombs (*Gensuikin*).[57]

The year 1960 marked the rise of people's movements seeking democratic change through direct collective action. These began with the struggle of the Mi'ike miners in Kyushu, who struck for more than nine months to win decent working conditions and stop mine closures. The confrontation became a national cause célèbre pitting Japan's labour movement against big business and the state. As the Mi'ike strike progressed, roughly 5 million students, farmers, workers, housewives and highly diverse groups of citizens across the country joined forces to oppose renewal of the Security Treaty. The unprecedented outpouring of popular dissent prompted the Kishi Nobusuke Cabinet to resort to police force and ram the treaty through Parliament in May. The ensuing political upheavals of June, with bloody confrontations in front of the Diet, obliged US President Dwight D. Eisenhower to cancel a scheduled visit to Japan and precipitated the collapse of the Kishi government in July. The 1960 protests marked a shift away from mass movements dominated by workers and opposition parties towards smaller coalitions in which citizens occupied centre stage as they struggled to redefine Japanese democracy on their own terms.[58]

From the mid-1960s, national coalitions of local residents, students and citizens' groups, acting independently of existing political parties, rallied in support of the victims of mercury poisoning at Minamata, opposed the expansion of US military bases and contested the forcible expropriation of land for the construction of the Narita International Airport at Sanrizuka, Chiba Prefecture. In the 1970s, sustained economic growth produced a culture of complacency, and as the labour and student movements waned, the victory seemed to go to corporate Japan and the state. Since the 1980s, however, there has been a remarkable upswing in grass-roots activism, with local residents tackling a bewildering range of issues, from ethnic discrimination, the emperor system and rearmament to the environment, consumers' rights, information disclosure, gender equality and police abuses. Of these, the movement to atone for the past and make just restitution to the victims of Japan's wartime aggression is of special significance.

The movement for redress

The 1990s saw a veritable explosion of lawsuits filed by Koreans, Chinese and other non-Japanese intent on seeking justice. This civil rights litigation has placed the state itself on trial. Some 100 lawsuits demanding apologies and redress for war-related military conscription, compulsory labour and sexual slavery are currently being heard in the nation's courtrooms. Former Korean B- and C-class war criminals, ordered by Japanese superiors to carry out war crimes and jailed by US military judges, also have contested their postwar treatment.[59] Legal action has been initiated by former Allied prisoners of war from Australia, Britain, the Netherlands, New Zealand and the United States; Hong Kong residents compelled to convert wartime wages and savings into worthless military scrip; Taiwanese seeking payment of Japanese military postal savings; Filipinos, Malaysians, Pacific Islanders and Papua New Guineans seeking compensation for atrocities; and Chinese survivors of Unit 731's chemical and biological warfare experiments.

Japanese citizens' groups have been intimately involved in supporting these claims, offering legal advice, paying court fees, publicising the issues and bringing pressure to bear on the government. In 1993, more than 100 residents of Shinjuku Ward in Tokyo filed a restraining order to prevent the government from disposing of human bones unearthed at the site of the former Institute of Infectious Diseases. The remains were believed to include those of Asians killed in biological warfare tests in China and shipped back to Tokyo for post-mortem analysis. Citizens also have gone to court to win release of state-held documentary evidence on forced labour and sexual slavery, including the names of victims.

In July 1995, responding to pressure from Japanese civil rights groups, the coalition Cabinet of Socialist Murayama Tomi'ichi announced the establishment of the Asian Women's Fund to solicit private contributions with which to compensate surviving former 'military comfort women' (*jūgun ianfu*). The Murayama government also set up an unofficial state fund to provide medical and welfare services to the women. By limiting its campaign to corporate and private donations, however, the government purposely sidestepped the question of state responsibility for the sex-slave programme. Many human rights groups in Japan and abroad oppose the fund for that reason, and to date only 170 Asian women have accepted money from it. In August 2000, the UN Human Rights Committee in Geneva acknowledged in a resolution on the 'comfort women' problem that Japan has made partial efforts to atone for military prostitution but concluded that it has not adequately discharged its obligations under international law.[60]

The government contends that compensation issues were laid to rest by the 1952 San Francisco Peace Treaty and subsequent bilateral war reparations agreements. Diplomatic records declassified in 2000, however, suggest otherwise. According to the documents, the Netherlands threatened to boycott the San Francisco Peace Conference unless Japan vouchsafed the right of its nationals to seek personal redress. In a letter to the Dutch government, Prime Minister Yoshida temporised by endorsing the view that the Peace Treaty did not prevent individuals from filing private war claims. Today, momentum continues to build for a general settlement of outstanding claims as Japan enters the new century. In May 2000, the Diet enacted landmark legislation awarding a lump-sum ¥4 million ($37,000) payment to Koreans, Formosans and other Asians who served in the Japanese military during World War II. Widows of veterans will receive ¥2.6 million ($24,000) in compensation. The new law is expected to benefit between 2,000 and 3,000 people but applies only to permanent residents of Japan. Former Korean and Chinese soldiers – Imperial subjects at the time – are demanding the same level of compensation as their Japanese counterparts. (Between 1952 and 1994, a total of ¥39 trillion, or $361 billion, in assistance was paid out to former Japanese combatants and their families, of which three quarters went for military pensions.)[61]

Shortly afterwards, in July, in another precedent-setting decision, the Supreme Court ordered a Japanese company, Nachi-Fujikoshi, to reach an out-of-court settlement with three South Koreans seeking compensation for wartime forced labour at the company's munitions factory in Toyama Prefecture. The firm agreed to pay an unspecified sum but refused to offer an apology, which the plaintiffs had demanded as well. In late November, taking its cue from the Supreme Court's intercession in July, the Tokyo High Court announced that it had brokered an even more dramatic settlement. Following a lengthy civil suit, the Kajima Corporation agreed to apologise to survivors of the June 1945 massacre of Chinese labour conscripts at the Hanaoka Mine in Akita Prefecture (chapter 7). It also promised to pay an indemnity totaling ¥500 million (about $4.5 million) to *all* victims or their heirs, not merely the 11 plaintiffs who initiated the action.

A sincere act of contrition by the state for past misdeeds, however, has not been forthcoming. In 1993, amid the groundswell of agitation to acknowledge Japan's war responsibility, Hosokawa Morihiro, a reform-orientated conservative from Kyushu, became prime minister. The grandson of Prince Konoe Fumimaro, Hosokawa was seven when Konoe committed suicide in 1945 to avoid war crimes prosecution. One of Hosokawa's first official acts upon taking office was to call a press conference and announce candidly that Japan had been wrong to wage a war of aggression. Hosokawa's frank admission of culpability was followed in 1995 by a similar statement of regret from Prime Minister Murayama, leader of the first Socialist-LDP coalition. Since then, however, pro forma apologies have become a diplomatic ritual – politically correct but generally devoid of substance. The most recent expressions of remorse were offered by Prime Minister Koizumi in October 2001 during visits to Beijing and Seoul. These conciliatory gestures were widely viewed, however, as an effort to deflect criticism over the premier's pledge to mobilise the SDF in support of American military involvement in Afghanistan.

The National Diet has yet to pass a resolution atoning for the past, and the LDP is bitterly opposed to any such blanket confession of guilt. During President Jiang Zemin's visit to Tokyo in November 1998, the Chinese government asked for an unambiguous apology from Japan. The text proposed by Prime Minister Obuchi fell short of Chinese expectations, however, and Jiang refused to sign the joint communiqué. The Chinese President later told an audience at Waseda University in Tokyo that the Japanese atrocities he personally witnessed during the war compelled him to speak out against the possible resurgence of Japanese militarism. What has prevented most Japanese leaders from doing likewise?

Looking to the future

Many Japanese remain ambivalent about the war. One reason is the troubling legacy of the atomic bombings. In the United States, the official story of the A-bomb is that its use in the 'Good War' was justified, and most Americans still regard nuclear arms as 'the ultimate symbol of victory'.[62] In Japan, the official line is one of abject victimisation. This victim-consciousness prevents us from locating our experience of nuclear holocaust in the broader perspective of Japan's war of aggression in Asia. The Bomb was an unmitigated evil, but so were our wartime actions in Asia and the Pacific. This remains a difficult lesson for many. SCAP's censorship policies, which discouraged meaningful discussion of the bombings; its preservation of the monarchy; and its courting of the conservative élite as a Cold War ally deepened this fundamental ambiguity.

Rightist politicians have mined the fault line that runs through the national psyche, using the bombings and the dual humiliations of defeat and occupation to foster a backward-looking, narcissistic nationalism. In April 2000, Tokyo Governor Ishihara Shintarō told members of a Ground Self-Defence Force unit in the city that their responsibility in the event of an earthquake or other national emergency was to crack down on '*sankokujin*' (so-called third-country nationals) and other illegal immigrants, who could be expected to riot, and 'show the Japanese people and the inhabitants of Tokyo what the military is for in a state'. Ishihara's spontaneous use of *sankokujin*, the pejorative Occupation-era term for resident Koreans and Chinese, his confusion of these minorities with Third-World migrant workers and his suggestion that foreigners in general were potential enemies of the state stunned human rights groups and alarmed Koreans, Chinese and foreign labourers' organisations. Sadly, few Japanese seemed troubled by the fact that Ishihara's comments could be taken as an incitement to violence and evoked the spectre of the massacre of Koreans after the 1923 Great Kanto Earthquake – a criticism that was levelled by the UN Committee on Human Rights in March 2001. Most considered his remarks as typical of the brash ultra-nationalist politician, and many privately applauded him for his candor.

In almost perfect counterpoint, one month later, Prime Minister Mori Yoshirō told a political action group affiliated with the Association of Shintō Shrines that Japan is a 'divine nation centred on the Emperor'. Unlike Ishihara's pronouncement, Mori's comments created a national furore. The premier was forced to apologise for 'causing misunderstanding', but he refused to retract the sentiments behind his statement and shortly afterwards embellished another speech with the term *kokutai* ('national polity'), the pre-1945 euphemism for Imperial rule. Despite the ensuing controversy, the LDP and its allies commanded sufficient votes in the Diet to defeat a non-confidence motion, and Mori was returned to office in the general elections of June 2000.

Imperial conservatives, Ishihara and Mori are products of the Occupation period and Japan's myopic postwar political culture. Ishihara dreams of restoring Japan's military prowess, and Mori is an open admirer and one-time protégé of Colonel Tsuji Masanobu, the jingoistic ideologue and unindicted war crimes suspect.[63] Such politicians seem to command a substantial audience these days, but in this author's view, they represent Japan's past, not its future.

In April 2001, a younger politician, one who grew up in the 1950s, became prime minister. The sudden rise to power of Koizumi Jun'ichirō as we enter the 21st century seemed to herald a turning point of sorts. The maverick politician appointed the outspoken Tanaka Makiko as Japan's first female Foreign Minister. He also has declared war against LDP factionalism and pledged to further streamline the bureaucracy, making it more responsive to lawmakers, and to overhaul the nation's economic, financial and social institutions. These are laudable goals, for genuine political and structural reform are long overdue, and the only way out of the Heisei recession, the longest of the postwar period. However, just as his alterego, the ultranationalist Nakasone Yasuhiro, did in the 1980s, Koizumi has announced his intention to draw up a balance sheet and 'settle accounts' with the Occupation reforms. He openly advocates official visits to Yasukuni Shrine, constitutional revision and a strong collective defence arrangement with the United States. The Prime Minister's New Right political philosophy will make it difficult for Japan to assert moral or political leadership in Asia anytime soon.

Less than a week after Japanese dignitaries observed the Peace Treaty celebrations in San Francisco, an extremist group wreaked horrifying destruction on the United States. The terrorist strikes have placed that country on a war footing and prompted calls from Washington for Japan to 'show the flag' and join in retaliating against those it considers responsible. With this dark and tragic event – a defining moment that truly marks the end of the postwar era – a point of no return appears to have been reached that bodes ill for the demilitarised, liberal society we have struggled to create. The verdict on Japanese democracy is not yet in, however, for it is the people, not the politicians, who will have the final word. Many Japanese continue to regard the 1947 Constitution, with its guarantee of popular sovereignty, extensive civil liberties and war-renouncing Article Nine, as an achievement of universal significance. They are determined to work within that framework to make Japan a more just society and regain the trust of their Asian neighbours, despite the resistance of an entrenched conservatism and intense pressures from our American ally to participate militarily in an expanding war on terrorism.

Notes

Introduction

1. Takemae Eiji, *GHQ*, Iwanami Shinsho, 1983.
2. Kawai Kazuo, *Japan's American Interlude*, University of Chicago Press, 1960.
3. Use of the expression dates from 1933, when MacArthur, then Army Chief of Staff, and General Hugh A. Drum, Deputy Chief of Staff, referred to the headquarters of the new air component they were planning as GHQ. The acronym stuck and the term became official in 1935 with the creation of General Headquarters, US Army Air Forces (GHQ/USAF), a unified combat command directly under the Army General Staff. For a short time in 1941 or 1942, Army Chief of Staff George C. Marshall referred to the War Department's War Plans Division (WPD) as GHQ, but that appellation was dropped when the WPD was renamed Operations Division. See D. Clayton James, *The Years of MacArthur*, vol. 1: 1880–1941, Houghton Mifflin, 1970, pp. 458–60.
4. GHQ/AFPAC was reorganised as General Headquarters, Far East Command (GHQ/ FECOM) in January 1947.
5. The expression is Mark Gayn's. *Japan Diary*, Charles E. Tuttle, 1981 (William Sloane, 1948), p. 340.
6. Maeda Tamon, 'The Direction of Postwar Education in Japan', in *The Japan Quarterly*, no. 3, 1956, pp. 415–16; Kawai (1960), p. 189.
7. During the war, the Japanese term for the conflict was the Greater East Asia War, which militarists dated from the invasion of China in 1937. On 15 December 1945, GHQ's Shintō Directive outlawed the use of this phrase because of its association with State Shintō and ultra-nationalism. The Occupation directed that 'Pacific War' be used instead. Because this expression denotes the conflict with the United States and its Allies (1941–5) but minimises Japan's Asian conquests, many historians have adopted the blanket term Fifteen Years' War, which covers the period from the takeover of Manchuria in 1931 until Japan's defeat in 1945 (see Ienaga Saburō, *The Pacific War*, 1931–1945, Pantheon Books, 1978, pp. 247–8). I, too, prefer the latter when writing in Japanese, but Asia–Pacific War sufficiently conveys this sense in English.
8. The International Military Tribunal for the Far East, which tried Japanese war crimes, placed the number of dead at 200,000. The official Chinese figure is 300,000. Some Japanese historians propose a much lower number. Hata Ikuhiko, for instance, states that only 38,000 to 42,000 deaths can accurately be documented (*Nanjing jiken* [The Nanjing Incident], Chūō Kōronsha, 1986, chapter 7), but the lesser figures do not include the killing of prisoners of war or

civilians outside the city limits (see the brief discussion in Honda Katsuichi, *The Nanking Massacre: A Japanese Journalist Confronts Japan's National Shame*, M. E. Sharpe, 1999, p. 284). The severe breakdown in military discipline alarmed even Imperial General Headquarters. Although news of the Nanjing atrocities was kept from the public, several commanders involved were recalled to Tokyo, as were the recently formed reserve units that had run amok. An overview of the massacre and its interpretations is Joshua A. Fogel, ed., *The Nanjing Massacre: Its History and Historiography*, University of California Press, 2000. See also Timothy Brook, ed., *Documents on the Rape of Nanjing*, University of Michigan Press, 1999.

9. Emperor Hirohito ascribed the underlying causes of World War II to Japan's inability to achieve equality with the West. Specifically, he cited the refusal of the United States and other Western powers to insert a racial equality clause in the Versailles Peace Treaty, America's Oriental exclusion laws and the discriminatory treatment of Japanese immigrants on the West Coast. See Terasaki Hidenari and Mariko Terasaki Miller, eds, *Shōwa Tennō dokuhakuroku – Terasaki Hidenari, goyōgakari nikki* (The Shōwa Emperor's Soliloquy and the Diary of Terasaki Hidenari), Bungei Shunjūsha, 1991, p. 20.

10. Iriye Akira, *Power and Culture: The Japanese-American War, 1941–1945*, Harvard University Press, 1981, p. 13.

11. Alvin D. Cox, *Nomonhan: Japan Against Russia, 1939*, Stanford University Press, 1985, vol. 1, chapter 7 and vol. 2, pp. 915, 923, 929.

12. Ienaga (1978), p. 132.

13. Dean Acheson, *Present at the Creation: My Years in the State Department*, New American Library, 1970 (W. W. Norton, 1969), p. 64.

14. In English, see the discussion in Ben-Ami Shillony, *Politics and Culture in Wartime Japan*, Clarendon Press (Oxford), 1982, p. 198.

15. Hillis Lory, *Japan's Military Masters: The Army in Japanese Life*, Viking Press, 1943, p. 132.

16. See John W. Dower, *Japan in War and Peace: Selected Essays*, The New Press, 1993, pp. 104–5. Some reform-orientated bureaucrats found scope for their ambitions in the puppet state of Manchukuo, where they eschewed industrial capitalism and experimented with Socialist ideas. On the links between Japan's Manchurian empire and political forces and ideologies in the Japanese metropolis, see Louise Young, *Japan's Total Empire: Manchuria and the Culture of Wartime Imperialism*, University of California Press, 1998.

17. On the 2 July conference, see Herbert Feis, *The Road to Pearl Harbor: The Coming of the War Between the United States and Japan*, Princeton University Press, 1950, pp. 215–16. On the 6 September conference, see Takafusa Nakamura, *A History of Shōwa Japan, 1926–1989*, University of Tokyo Press, 1998, pp. 251–3.

18. On Japan–US negotiations prior to war, see Robert J. C. Butow, *Tojo and the Coming of the War*, Princeton University Press, 1961, chapter 11. A careful

discussion of planning for the Pearl Harbor strike is Peter Wetzler, *Hirohito and War: Imperial Tradition and Military Decision-Making in Prewar Japan*, University of Hawai'i Press, 1998, chapter 3.

19. John W. Dower, *War Without Mercy: Race and Power in the Pacific War*, Pantheon Books, 1986, p. 24.

20. Gotō Ken'ichi, 'Indonesia Under the "Greater East Asia Co-Prosperity Sphere"', in Donald Denoon, Mark Hudson, Gavan McCormack and Tessa Morris-Suzuki, eds, *Multicultural Japan: Paleolithic to Postmodern*, Cambridge University Press, 1996, pp.163–4; Ooi Keat Gin, *Rising Sun Over Borneo: The Japanese Occupation of Sarawak, 1941–1945*, Macmillan, 1999, pp. 39–40. In general, see Joyce C. Lebra, ed., *Japan's Greater East Asian Co-Prosperity Sphere in World War II: Selected Readings and Documents*, Oxford University Press (Kuala Lumpur), 1975, pp. 55–104 and Alfred W. McCoy, ed., *Southeast Asia Under Japanese Occupation*, Monograph Series no. 22, Yale University Southeast Asian Studies, 1980.

21. Dower (1986), p. 286; Akashi Yōji, 'Japanese Military Administration in Malaya: Its Formation and Evolution in Reference to Sultans, the Islamic Religion and the Moslem Malays, 1941–1945' in *Asian Studies*, no. 7, 1969, pp. 72–6.

22. See Paul H. Kratoska, *The Japanese Occupation of Malaya: A Social and Economic History*, University of Hawai'i Press, 1997, pp. 59, 83. Figures are from Akashi Yōji, 'Japan and "Asia for Asians"', in Harry Wray and Hilary Conroy, eds, *Japan Examined: Perspectives on Modern Japanese* History, University of Hawai'i Press, 1983, p. 325.

23. Ooi (1999), p. 44.

24. In French Indo-China, Ho Chi Minh organised the Vietminh to combat Japanese imperialism, led a general revolt in August 1945 and declared independence on 2 September. On 16 August, the Indonesian Army for Defenders of the Homeland burned the Rising Sun flag, arrested Japanese collaborators and carved out the country's first liberated zone, from which Indonesia's independence movement would spread. See Ienaga (1978), pp. 178–80. On the long-term benefits of Japanese occupation, see Akashi (1983), pp. 323–30. The quotation is from Richard Storry, *A History of Modern Japan*, Penguin Books, 1982, p. 220.

25. A grisly overview of Japanese atrocities is Yuki Tanaka, *Hidden Horrors: Japanese War Crimes in World War II*, Westview Press, 1998.

26. Utsumi Aiko, 'Japanese Army Internment Policies for Enemy Civilians During the Asia–Pacific War', in Denoon, *et al.*, eds (1996), pp. 174–209.

27. Japanese conduct towards prisoners of war and civilians was exemplary during the Russo-Japanese War, historians characterising it as generous and humane. During the battle for Port Arthur in 1904, for instance, General Nogi Maresuke gave strict orders to his troops to protect civilian life and property and punished infractions severely. See Storry (1982), pp. 139–40. A general treatment of

this subject is Olive Checkland, *Humanitarianism and the Emperor's Japan, 1877–1977*, St Martin's Press, 1994, Part 2, pp. 45–94.

28. On the figures for China, see Dower (1986), pp. 295–7. Robert P. Newman includes a recent review of war deaths in Asia in *Truman and the Hiroshima Cult*, Michigan State University Press, 1995, pp. 134–9, especially the table on p. 138. On the Indo-China famine, see Bui Minh Dung, 'Japan's Role in the Vietnamese Starvation of 1944–45', in *Modern Asian Studies*, vol. 29, no. 3, 1995, pp. 573–618.

29. Dower (1986), pp. 295–301. Arisawa Hiromi and Inaba Hidezō, eds, *Shiryō: sengo nijūnen-shi* (A Documentary History of the Two Postwar Decades), vol. 2 (Economics), Nihon Hyōronsha, 1966, pp. 2–5; Andō Yoshio, *Shōwa keizai-shi* (An Economic History of the Shōwa Era), Nihon Keizai Shinbunsha, 1976, pp. 241–4.

30. Occupation scholar Iokibe Makoto distinguishes between three types of reform. The first are those where Japanese officials seized the initiative in order to implement their own ideas or to pre-empt anticipated SCAP actions. These reforms include the Lower House Electoral Law and the Labour Union Law. A second category is legislation developed conjointly by GHQ and the concerned ministry, such as the Local Autonomy Law and land reform. A final group are measures imposed by Occupation fiat: constitutional revision, the Police Law, *zaibatsu* dissolution and anti-monopoly legislation. See 'Senryō seisaku no san ruikei' (Three Patterns in Occupation Policy), in *Revaiasan* (Leviathan), no. 6, Bokutakusha, 1990, pp. 97–120. My own research has highlighted the dynamic interplay between American and Japanese officials in drafting Japan's labour reform programme, where all three patterns are observed. See Takemae Eiji, *Sengo rōdō-kaikaku: GHQ rōdō seisaku-shi* (The Postwar Labour Reforms: A History of GHQ's Labour Reform Policy), Tōkyō Daigaku Shuppankai, 1982.

31. The historian is Takafusa Nakamura (1998), p. 285. See also Edwin O. Reischauer, 'The Allied Occupation: Catalyst, not Creator', in Wray and Conroy, eds (1983), pp. 335–42, Sheldon Garon, *The State and Labor in Modern Japan*, University of California Press, 1987, pp. 229–48, and John W. Dower, 'The Useful War', in Carol Gluck and Stephan R. Graubard, eds, *Showa: The Japan of Hirohito*, W. W. Norton, 1992, pp. 49–70. I develop this theme in greater detail in 'Early Postwar Reformist Parties', in Robert E. Ward and Sakamoto Yoshikazu, eds, *Democratizing Japan: The Allied Occupation*, University of Hawai'i Press, 1987, pp. 339–40.

32. One important task is a comprehensive comparison of the occupations of Korea, Okinawa and the Northern Territories, characterised by direct military governance, and the occupation of the Japanese main islands, where indirect rule was practised. These experiences should be contrasted in turn with Japan's wartime occupations of the Philippines, Malaya, the Dutch East Indies and other Southeast Asian countries. This is only a small part of the work ahead. For a fuller

discussion, see Takemae Eiji, *Senryō sengo-shi* (A History of the Occupation and Postwar Era), Iwanami Shoten, 1992, pp. 416–20.

33. My interest in the Allied Occupation of Japan began more than forty years ago as a graduate student in the United States. The catalyst was the discovery of two doctoral dissertations written by former Occupation officials: Ralph J. D. Braibanti's 'The Occupation of Japan – A Study in Organization and Administration', Syracuse University, 1949 and Martin T. Comacho's 'Administration of SCAP Labour Policy in Occupied Japan', Harvard University, 1954. These exhaustive, empirical studies on postwar Allied policy towards Japan were based on the authors' personal experiences in the Occupation and on internal GHQ/SCAP documents then unavailable to students. They proved a veritable treasure trove of information about a period that had profoundly influenced postwar Japan's political and socio-economic institutions, culture and values. Yet many of these facts were unknown to Japanese researchers. My curiosity piqued, I began to explore existing archival materials and interview former US and Japanese officials with first-hand knowledge of this period. Conducted over many years, this research took me to Australia, Britain, Mexico and the United States.

Two developments greatly facilitated my work. In the late 1960s, the US government began to declassify diplomatic and military documents relating to the Occupation, including top-secret materials. Nearly a decade later, in 1976, the Japanese government belatedly opened up a part of its own archives to the public. Access to this wealth of data removed the veil of secrecy that had shrouded many aspects of the Occupation. Using a vast array of memoranda, staff studies, committee minutes, internal circulars, inter-sectional check sheets and hand-written personal notes, it became possible to analyse in depth the organisational structure of GHQ; the ideas, actions and personalities of the officials who staffed this vast organisation; and the policy-making process itself. Moreover, scholars could now examine some of the most controversial events of this era, taking into account the full sweep of SCAP policy and the wider geopolitical context within which it was shaped.

SCAP's internal papers also highlighted errors of fact and interpretation that had plagued early Japanese research. Few specialists here fully grasped GHQ's organisational structure or knew very much about the backgrounds and responsibilities of the key players. Even such senior officials as section and division chiefs often were identified incorrectly. In the early 1970s, the Japanese economy entered a period of recessionary growth in the wake of the first oil crisis. A sense of impending doom encouraged scholars to take a fresh, critical look at the Occupation era and its significance for postwar Japanese society. This effort was facilitated by the declassification of more government files, both in Tokyo and Washington. The publication of the diaries, memoirs and other personal documents of central Occupation figures also opened new vistas.

My first concern in writing *Inside GHQ*, was to rectify common mistakes and misconceptions. This book marked a departure from my earlier empirical studies of SCAP's labour reforms by attempting to integrate new themes and motifs into a broader, more complex social and political mosaic. I also was determined to limn the careers and personalities of the outstanding men and women who administered GHQ's programmes. Since then, my research has focused on the impact of Occupation policies on the development of democracy in Japan and on popular attitudes towards society and the state. The English edition of *Inside GHQ* recapitulates this work while considerably expanding its scope.

34. Several important works have appeared as this monograph goes to press. Among them are Herbert P. Bix, *Hirohito and the Making of Modern Japan*, HarperCollins, 2000 and Iokibe Makoto, *Sensō, senryō, kōwa 1941–1955* (War, Occupation and the Peace Settlement, 1941–1955), Chūō Kōronsha, 2001. Two new books on Okinawa also came to the author's attention too late to benefit this monograph. They are Chalmers Johnson's *Blowback: The Cost and Consequences of American Empire*, Owl Books, 2001 and Robert D. Eldridge, *The Origins of the Bilateral Okinawa Problem: Okinawa in Postwar U.S.–Japan Relations, 1945–1952*, Garland Publishers (New York), 2001. For an English Review of Japanese-language materials through the 1980s, see Takemae Eiji, 'The Occupation', in National Committee of Japanese Historians, ed., *Historical Studies in Japan (VII), 1983–1987*, Yamakawa Shuppansha, 1990, pp. 267–88. A survey of the Japanese literature is Takemae Eiji, 'Senryō sōsetsu: senryō to GHQ' (An Overview of the Occupation: The Occupation and GHQ), in *GHQ: Nihon senryō-shi josetsu* (GHQ: An Introduction to the History of the Occupation of Japan), Nihon Tosho Sentā, 1996.

Chapter 1 The Pacific War and the Origins of GHQ

1. US Department of the Army (Historical Section, G-2, FECOM), ed., *Reports of General MacArthur*, vol. 1: Supplement (MacArthur in Japan – The Occupation: Military Phase), US Government Printing Office, 1966, p. 29. This four-volume series, compiled by MacArthur's staff in Japan but not published until 1966, is given below as *Reports of MacArthur*.
2. D. Clayton James, *The Years of MacArthur*, vol. 2: 1941–1945, Houghton Mifflin, 1975, p. 778.
3. On MacArthur's career, see in addition to D. Clayton James's three-volume study (1970–1985), William Manchester, *American Caesar: Douglas MacArthur, 1880–1963*, Little, Brown, 1978 and Michael Schaller, *Douglas MacArthur: The Far Eastern General*, Oxford University Press, 1989. On US colonial rule in the Philippines, see Teodoro A. Agoncillo and Milagros C. Guevro, *History of the Filipino People*, R. P. Garcia (Quezon), 1977.
4. Manchester (1978), p. 470.
5. Justin Williams Sr, *Japan's Political Revolution Under MacArthur: A Participant's Account*, University of Tokyo Press, 1979, p. 271.
6. MacArthur compared the success of his command to that of Caesar's in a

conversation with George F. Kennan. See Kennan's *Memoirs, 1925–1950,* Atlantic Monthly (Little, Brown), 1967, p. 384 and also D. Clayton James, *The Years of MacArthur,* vol. 3 Triumph and Disaster: 1945–1964, Houghton Mifflin, 1985, pp. 61–2. The historian is Richard Storry, *A History of Modern Japan,* Penguin Books, 1982, p. 240. Storry, a member of the Australian Diplomatic Mission in Tokyo during MacArthur's reign, characterised the General as 'the American version of the traditional British grandee . . . with a tendency towards complacent self-dramatisation' (ibid.). The lieutenant was Elliott R. Thorpe, *East Wind, Rain,* Gambit Inc. (Boston), 1969, p. 252. The oft-cited Truman quotations are from Robert H. Ferrell, ed., *Off the Record: The Private Papers of Harry S. Truman,* Harper & Row, 1980, p. 47.

7. Manchester (1978), pp. 512–16. Quotation is from p. 515. The MacArthur household was not always harmonious. Aide Bowers, for instance, found little Arthur insufferable, describing him in later life as a 'pampered rowdy brat'. Okamoto Shirō, *Kabuki o sukutta otoko: Makkāsā no fukukan Fōbian Bawāzu* (The Man Who Saved Kabuki: MacArthur's Military Aide Faubion Bowers), Shūeisha, 1998, p. 55.

8. Faubion Bowers, ''The Late General MacArthur, Warts and All', in *Esquire,* January 1967, p. 168.

9. MacArthur's 1947 quotation is from Government Section, SCAP, ed., *The Political Reorientation of Japan, September 1945 to September 1948* (below, given as *PRJ*), US Government Printing Office, 1949, vol. 2, p. 764. On MacArthur's unguarded comments to the US Scientific Advisory Group (9 December 1948), see Bowen C. Dees, *The Allied Occupation and Japan's Economic Miracle: Building the Foundations of Japanese Science and Technology, 1945–1952,* Curzon Press, 1997, p. 187. MacArthur's words were jotted down in memo form. The frequently cited statement before Congress is from the US Senate Committee on Armed Services and the Committee on Foreign Relations, *Hearing to Conduct an Inquiry into the Military Situation in the Far East,* 82nd Congress, 1st session, 1951. On MacArthur's stewardship in Japan, see Sodei Rinjirō, *Makkāsā no nisen nichi* (MacArthur's 2,000 Days) Chūō Kōronsha, 1975 and Sodei Rinjirō and Fukushima Jūrō, *Makkāsā kiroku: sengo Nihon no genten* (The MacArthur Records: Postwar Japan's Point of Departure), Nihon Hōsō Shuppan Kyōkai, 1982.

10. Douglas MacArthur, *Reminiscences,* McGraw-Hill, 1964, pp. 282–4, 310–11.

11. James (1985), p. 64.

12. Theodore Cohen, *Remaking Japan: The American Occupation as New Deal,* The Free Press, 1987, p. 64.

13. Ibid., p. 56.

14. A detailed American account of the events leading up to Pearl Harbor is Gordon W. Prange, *At Dawn We Slept: The Untold Story of Pearl Harbor,* Penguin Books, 1981, chapters 44–61. See also John Costello, *The Pacific War, 1941–1945,* New York, Quill, 1981, chapters 6 and 7.

15. The Chicano troops belonged to the 200th and 515th US Coast Artilleries. About 500,000 Mexican Americans served in World War II. Those in the 25th, 27th, 37th and 43rd National Guard Divisions would fight at Guadalcanal, New Guinea, Bougainville and elsewhere. Many also served with Eighth Army's 11th Airborne Division in the Philippine campaigns. See Raul Morin, *Among the Valiants: Mexican-Americans in WW II and Korea*, Borden Publishing (California), 1966, pp. 34–40, 203. Refer also to Ronald T. Takaki, *Double Victory: A Multicultural History of America in World War II*, Little, Brown, 2000, chapter 5.

16. On Tsuji's role, see Ward (1996), pp. 334–8. Death March statistics are from Stanley L. Falk, *Bataan: The March of Death*, Jove Publications (New York), 1983. In general, see Bōeichō Bōei-kenkyūsho Senshi-shitsu-hen (War History Office, Defence Agency), ed., *Senshi Sōsho (2): Hitō kōryaku sakusen* (War History Series, no. 2: Strategic Operations in the Philippine Islands), Asakumo Shinbunsha, 1966, chapters 4–6 and Louis Morton, *The Fall of the Philippines* (The US Army in World War II: The War in the Pacific), US Army Office of the Chief of Military History, US Government Printing Office, 1953, pp. 245–454.

17. On Japanese war planning and operations see *Reports of MacArthur*, vol. 2: Japanese Operations in the Southwest Pacific Area, Part 1.

18. Concerning the ADBA and development of the Joint Chiefs of Staff, see Louis Morton, *Strategy and Command: The First Two Years* (The US Army in World War II: The War in the Pacific), US Army Office of the Chief of Military History, US Government Printing Office, 1962, pp. 86–9, 125 164–9, 172–3, 607–10. See also Grace P. Hayes, *The History of the Joint Chiefs of Staff in World War II: The War Against Japan*, Naval Institute Press (Annapolis), 1982, pp. 44–50.

19. The North and Central Pacific Areas were directly under Nimitz's command. The South Pacific Area initially was assigned to Admiral Robert L. Ghormley and later to Nimitz protégé Admiral William F. ('Bull') Halsey. On US Navy planning, see Elmer B. Potter, *Nimitz*, Naval Institute Press (Annapolis), 1976, pp. 78–107.

20. GHQ/SWPA consisted of the Allied Land Forces (ALF), the Allied Air Forces (AAF) and the Allied Naval Forces (ANF). The ALF, led by General Sir Thomas Blamey, Commander in Chief of the Australian Army, was composed mainly of the Australian First and Second Armies and the Australian III Corps. ALF combat forces consisted of the Australian 6th and 7th Divisions, recalled from the Middle East, and the US 41st and 32nd Divisions, later regrouped as I Corps. The AAF, commanded by Lieutenant General George H. Brett, an American, was an amalgamation of air forces from the United States, Australia and the Dutch East Indies. Its principal strength was two American heavy bomber groups, two American medium bomber groups and three American fighter groups, backed by seventeen Australian squadrons and one Netherlands bomber squadron. The ANF, under Admiral Herbert F. Leary, also an American, included two Australian heavy cruisers, one Australian light cruiser, one

American heavy cruiser and several destroyers. *Reports of MacArthur*, vol. 1: The Campaigns of MacArthur in the Pacific, pp. 31–3.

21. Other late comers included Colonel Lester J. Whitelock, future SCAP Deputy Chief of Staff; Colonel Elliott R. Thorpe, later SCAP's Counter-Intelligence Chief; Brigadier General Spencer B. Akin, subsequently SCAP's Chief of Civil Communications; and Colonel Burdette M. Fitch, SCAP's Adjutant General. The Bataan Gang took its name from MacArthur's aircraft, of which there were two: *Bataan I*, a B-17, and *Bataan II*, a specially modified C-54 cargo transport. Most historians assume the name came from the Bataan Peninsula, but it may also have been inspired by the fragrant *bataan* tree, whose broad, bifurcated leaves resemble the wings of an aircraft.

22. Eichelberger began his Army career with a year on the US-Mexican border during the Pancho Villa rebellion. From 1918 to 1920, he was Chief of Staff to the US Expeditionary Force in Siberia, where he formed an active dislike of the Japanese military. Following duty in the Philippines, he attended the 1921 Washington Naval Conference as military aide to the Chinese delegation and later served as Superintendent of West Point. Robert L. Eichelberger and Milton MacKaye, *Our Jungle Road to Tokyo*, Viking Press, 1950, pp. xi–xiv.

23. The appointment of Krueger to head Sixth Army was a de facto demotion for Eichelberger, whom MacArthur had sidelined following the Buna offensive for not being a team player. On the Eichelberger–Krueger rivalry, refer to Paul Chwialkowski, *In Caesar's Shadow: The Life of General Robert Eichelberger*, Greenwood Press, 1993, pp. 74–82.

24. On Midway and Guadalcanal, see generally Bōeichō Bōei-kenkyūsho Senshi-shitsu-hen (War History Office, Defence Agency), ed., *Senshi Sōsho (6): Chūbu Taiheiyō rikugun sakusen (1) – Mariana gyokusai made* (Army Operations in the Central Pacific, Part 1 – To Defeat in the Marianas), Asakumo Shinbunsha, 1967, section 2, chapters 1–2; *Senshi Sōsho (7): Rikugun kōkū sakusen – tōbu Nyūginia-hōmen* (War History Series, no. 7: Army Air Operations – Around Eastern New Guinea), Asakumo Shinbunsha, 1967, section 1, chapters 1–3; and *Senshi sōsho (43) – Middouei-kaisen* (War History Series, no. 43: The Battle of Midway), Asakumo Shinbunsha, 1971. In English, see *Reports of MacArthur*, vol. 1, pp. 46–50, 59–66, 70–1, 91–9, 101, 105. The MacArthur quotation is from Eichelberger and MacKaye (1950), p. 21. On Nomonhan and Buna, see Storry (1982), p. 220.

25. Reno I was drawn up in February 1943, Reno II in August 1943, Reno III in October 1943, Reno IV in March 1944 and Reno V in June 1944. Musketeer I was drafted in July 1944 and Musketeer II in August of that year. *Reports of MacArthur*, vol. 1, pp. 168–70, 170–2.

26. Agoncillo and Guerrero (1977), pp. 452–7.

27. Important guerrilla bases were set up in Mindanao (under Colonel Wendel W. Fertig and Commander Charles Parsons), Samar (Colonel Pedro V. Merritt and Lieutenant Colonel Juan Causing), Negros (Colonel Gabriel Gador and

Captain Salvador Abcede), Cebu (Lieutenant Colonel James H. Cushing), Bohol (Major Ismael Ingeniero), northern Luzon (Major Russell W. Volckmann), central Luzon (Major Robert Lapham) and Leyte (Colonel Rupert K. Kangleon). *Reports of MacArthur*, vol. 1, pp. 295–326.

28. Agoncillo and Guerrero (1977), pp. 462–3, 471.
29. See Ienaga Saburō, *The Pacific War, 1931–1945*, Pantheon Books, 1978, p. 172.
30. Allison Ind, *Allied Intelligence Bureau: Our Secret Weapon Against Japan*, David McKay, 1958, pp. 11–12, 174. On Filipino Americans and the war, see Ronald T. Takaki, *A History of Asian Americans: Strangers from a Different Shore*, Little, Brown, 1998, pp. 359–60 and Takaki (2000), chapters 4 and 6.
31. See Allison B. Gilmore, *You Can't Fight Tanks with Bayonets: Psychological Warfare Against the Japanese Army in the Southwest Pacific*, University of Nebraska Press, 1998, pp. 18–20. Chapter 7 examines the effectiveness of Allied propaganda. Fellers's Psychological Warfare Branch should not to be confused with the Psychological Warfare Branch created by the US Office of War Information.
32. During World War II, 25,000 Native Americans entered the ranks, and many were used to transmit front-line messages in their native tongue, but they spoke Chippewa, Cherokee, Chocktaw, Comanche, Creek, Hopi and Menominee, not a specially encrypted language. The Navajo code was so effective that it remained a military secret until the 1960s. See Doris A. Paul, *The Navajo Code Talkers*, Dorrance Publishing (Pennsylvania), 1973, pp. 5–9, 36, 49, 73–5 and Takaki (2000), pp. 64–72.
33. Ind (1958), p. 185. Mashbir had learned Japanese during a four-year assignment in Tokyo with US Army Military Intelligence (1920–4). See his memoir, *I Was an American Spy*, Vantage Press, 1953.
34. Federal Bureau of Investigation searches uncovered no evidence of subversion, but even the absence of proof was used to justify anti-Japanese hysteria. Curiously, DeWitt's reading of the FBI finding was that: 'The very fact that no sabotage has taken place to date is a disturbing and confirming indication that such will be taken later.' (Commission on Wartime Relocation and Internment of Civilians, *Personal Justice Denied: Report of the Commission on Wartime Relocation and Internment of Civilians*, Civil Liberties Public Education Fund, 1997, p. 6.) On Nisei in the Pacific, see Joseph D. Harrington, *Yankee Samurai: The Secret Role of Nisei in America's Pacific Victory*, Pettigrew Enterprises (Detroit), 1979. A recent look at individual Nisei experiences during the war is Hawaii Nikkei History Editorial Board, ed., *Japanese Eyes, American Heart: Personal Reflections of Hawaii's World War II Nisei Soldiers*, Tendai Educational Foundation (Honolulu), 1998.
35. Looking back, a Nisei instructor characterised the Language School as 'a racist-motivated institution'. The Japanese-American instructors were not commissioned, yet the Caucasian students they taught became officers upon graduation, outranking their teachers overnight. (James Oda, *Heroic Struggles of*

Japanese Americans: Partisan Fighters from America's Concentration Camps, KNI, Inc., 1980, p. 116.) Experts trained in the MISL programme not of Japanese ancestry included academics and businessmen with experience in prewar Japan. Several played a role in the Occupation, and a few became outstanding scholars in the field of Japanese and Asian studies after the war. (See Allen H. Meyer, 'MIS: Non-Nikkei', in *Unsung Heroes: Military Intelligence Service, Past, Present, Future*, MIS-Northwest Association (Seattle), 1996 pp. 97–104 and Herbert Passin, *Encounter with Japan*, Kodansha International, 1982.)

36. See Suzuki Akira and Yamamoto Akira, *Hiroku-bōryaku senden-bira: Taiheiyō Sensō no kami no bakudan* (Secret Strategy and Propaganda Leaflets: Paper Bombs in the Pacific War), Kōdansha, 1977, pp. 152–75.

37. In April 1943, Harold Fudenna, for example, intercepted and translated a Japanese radio message at Port Moresby, New Guinea, giving the estimated time of arrival at Bougainville of Imperial Navy Admiral Yamamoto Isoroku. This information enabled US pilots to ambush and shoot down Yamamoto's aircraft on 18 April, dealing a serious blow to Japanese morale. On Willoughby's assessment of Japanese-Americans, see Bradford Smith, *Americans from Japan*, Lipincott, 1948, p. 325. See also Matsui Mitzi, 'The Military Intelligence Service Story', in *Unsung Heroes* (1996), pp. ix–xv and Suzuki and Yamamoto (1977), op. cit. In Europe, Nisei soldiers fought with the 100th Infantry Battalion and the 442nd Regimental Combat Team.

38. Eugene B. Sledge, *With the Old Breed at Pelieu and Okinawa*, Oxford University Press, 1990 (Presidio Press, 1981), pp. 34, 115, 120–1.The former war correspondent is Edgar L. Jones, cited in John W. Dower, *War Without Mercy*, Pantheon Books, 1986, p. 64.

39. The Allied summits are discussed in depth in Hayes (1982). Each of the meetings was given a code name. These were: Washington (1), 'Arcadia'; Casablanca, 'Symbol'; Washington (2), 'Trident'; Quebec (1), 'Quadrant'; Cairo, 'Sextant'; Teheran, 'Eureka'; Quebec (2), 'Octagon'; Malta and Yalta, 'Argonaut'; and Potsdam, 'Terminal'.

40. On the war in the Marshalls and Carolines, see Mark R. Peattie, *Nan'yō: The Rise and Fall of the Japanese in Micronesia, 1885–1945*, University of Hawai'i Press, 1988, pp. 265–77.

41. See generally, Bōeichō Bōei-kenkyūsho Senshi-shitsu-hen (ed.), no. 6, section 3, chapter 1 and Philip A. Crowl and Edmund G. Love, *The Campaign in the Marianas* (The US Army in World War II: The War in the Pacific), Office of the Chief of Military History, US Army, US Government Printing Office, 1960, pp. 163–266.

42. Peattie (1988), p. 286 and Bōeichō Bōei-kenkyūsho Senshi-shitsu-hen (ed.), no. 6, pp. 374–513.

43. See the account in Costello (1981), pp. 479–83. Quotation is from *Reports of MacArthur*, Vol. 1, p. 223.

44. Potter (1976), pp. 315–20.

45. See Edward J. Drea, *In the Service of the Emperor: Essays on the Imperial Japanese Army*, University of Nebraska Press, 1998, pp. 39–43.
46. US Strategic Bombing Survey (Pacific), *Summary Report*, Report no. 1, Washington DC, 1946, p. 16.
47. The LeMay quotation is from Curtis E. LeMay with MacKinlay Kantor, *Mission with LeMay: My Story*, Doubleday, 1965, p. 387. The Japanese rescuer was Captain Kubota Shigenori, head of the Army Medical School's No. 1 Rescue Detachment. His story is related by Edoin Hoito (Edwin Hoyt), *The Night Tokyo Burned: The Incendiary Campaign Against Japan, March–August 1945*, St Martin's Press, 1987, p. 100. The Fellers quotation is from Gar Alperovitz, *The Decision to Use the Atomic Bomb*, Vintage Books, 1995, p. 352.
48. Robert R. Smith, *Triumph in the Philippines* (The US Army in World War II: The War in the Pacific), US Army Office of the Chief of Military History, US Government Printing Office, 1991, pp. 9–17.
49. James (1975), p. 557.
50. See the discussion in Richard B. Frank, *Downfall: The End of the Imperial Japanese Empire*, Random House, 1999, pp. 178–80.
51. *Reports of MacArthur*, vol. 1, p. 196.
52. Dower (1986), p. 44–5. For its part, the US Army attacked the leftist Hukbala-hap guerrillas in early March, slaughtering a large number. The fiercely nationalistic Huks, a part of the Filipino Resistance, opposed both Japanese and American imperialism. See Ienaga (1978), p. 172.
53. On the role of Eighth Army in the Philippines, see *Reports of MacArthur*, vol. 1, pp. 451–60 and Chwialkowski (1993), pp. 120–37. On MacArthur's unauthorised invasions, see Smith (1991), pp. 584–5 and Manchester (1978), p. 429. Casualty figures are from Smith (1991). During the war, a total of 486,000 Imperial Army and Navy personnel perished in the Philippines. An additional 12,000 died after 15 August 1945. Kuwata Etsu and Maebara Tōru, eds, *Nihon no sensō: zukai to dēta* (*Japan's Wars: Graphs and Statistics*), Hara Shobō, 1986, p. 21.
54. A vivid description of this strategy is found in Sledge (1981) pp. 53, 172.
55. See Bōeichō Bōei-kenkyūsho Senshi-shitsu-hen (War History Office, Defence Agency), ed., *Senshi Sōsho (13): Chūbu Taiheiyō; rikugun sakusen (2) – Pereriu, Angauru, Iwojima* (War History Series, no. 13: Army Operations in the Central Pacific, Part 2 – Peleliu, Angaur, Iwo Jima), Asakumo Shinbunsha, 1968, pp. 259–416. See also Potter (1976), pp. 352–67 and Costello (1981), pp. 542–7.
56. *Reports of MacArthur*, vol. 2: Japanese Operations in the Southwest Pacific Area, Part 2, p. 575.
57. Geiger's III Amphibious Corps included troops who had fought at Cape Gloucester (New Britain), Guadalcanal, Bougainville, Guam and Peleliu. XXIV Corps had seen action at Guadalcanal and Leyte. The naval contingent consisted of the Central Pacific Task Force, which included the Fifth Fleet and the

British Pacific Fleet; Task Force Fifty; and the Joint Expeditionary Force under Rear Admiral Richmond K. Turner.

58. Ushijima's Thirty-Second Army was divided into four divisions, five mixed divisions and one artillery corps. See Bôeichō Bōei-kenkyūsho Senshi-shitsu-hen (War History Office, Defence Agency), ed., *Senshi Sōsho (11): Okinawa-hōmen rikugun sakusen* (War History Series, no. 11: Army Operations Around Okinawa), Asakumo Shinbunsha, 1968, chapter 7, and *Senshi Sōsho (17): Okinawa-hōmen kaigun sakusen* (War History Series, no. 17: Navy Operations Around Okinawa), Asakumo Shinbunsha, 1968, chapters 4 and 5.

59. See Ienaga (1978), p. 185. Kinjō, Professor Emeritus of Okinawa Christian Junior College, recounted this traumatic experience to Haruko Taya Cook and Theodore F. Cook, *Japan at War: An Oral History*, The New Press, 1992, pp. 365–6. See also his interview with Kajimoto Tetsushi in *The Japan Times*, 23 August 1996, p. 3.

60. Costello (1981), pp. 558–9.

61. Sledge (1981), pp. 260, 277–8.

62. Cook and Cook (1992), p. 360.

63. Hattori Takushirō, *Dai Toa Sensō-zenshi* (A History of the Greater East Asian War), Masu Shobō, vol 7, 1953, chap. 6 and Okinawa-ken, ed., *Okinawa: kunan no gendaishi* (Okinawa: A Troubled Modern History), Iwanami Shoten, 1996, pp. 20–5. See also the interview with Ōta Masahide in Cook and Cook (1992), pp. 458–61.

64. On Japanese casualties, refer to Ōta Masahide, *Sōshi Okinawa-sen* (A Comprehensive History of the Battle of Okinawa), Iwanami Shoten, 1982, pp. 213–20. American casualty figures are from Roy E. Appleman, James M. Burn, Russell A. Gugeler and John Stevens, *Okinawa: The Last Battle* (The US Army in World War II: The War in the Pacific), US Army Office of the Chief of Military History, US Government Printing Office, 1948, p. 473. On Colonel Chō Isamu, see Honda Katsuichi, *The Nanjing Massacre: A Japanese Journalist Confronts Japan's National Shame*, M. E. Sharpe, 1999, p. 169 and the introduction by Frank B. Gibney, p. xxi.

65. See Kase Toshikazu, *Eclipse of the Rising Sun*, Jonathan Cape, 1951, pp. 161–6 and, especially, George A. Lensen, *The Strange Neutrality: Soviet–Japanese Relations During the Second World War, 1941–1945*, Diplomatic Press (Tallahassee), 1972, pp. 134–5.

66. Allied cryptanalysts had cracked Japanese diplomatic and military codes in 1941. On US intercepts of Japanese diplomatic overtures, see Alperovitz (1995), pp. 18–22 and chapter 7.

67. On the Hirota-Malik talks, see Tsuyoshi Hasegawa, *The Northern Territories Dispute and Russo-Japanese Relations*, vol. 1: Between War and Peace, 1697–1985, University of California Press, 1998, pp. 53–4 and David Rees, *The Soviet Seizure of the Kuriles*, Praeger, 1985, pp. 70–1. For two different interpretations of the peace initiatives, see Herbert P. Bix, 'Japan's Delayed Surrender: A

Reinterpretation', in Michael J. Hogan, ed., *Hiroshima in History and Memory*, Cambridge University Press, 1996, pp. 98–106 and Takafusa Nakamura, *A History of Shōwa Japan, 1926–1989*, University of Tokyo Press, 1998, pp. 222–31.

68. Supply commands also were reorganised. In June 1945, US Army Forces in the West Pacific was set up in Manila under Lieutenant General Wilhelm D. Styer. The following month US Army Forces in the Mid-Pacific was established in Honolulu under Lieutenant General Robert C. Richardson. These replaced US Army Services of Supply and US Army Forces in the Far East.

69. Hayes (1982), p. 714.

70. See the discussion in Frank (1999), chapter 8. Quotations are from pp. 117, 140–1.

71. Under *Ketsu-6* (Decisive Battle Plan no. 6) for the defence of Kyushu, by early August 1945, Imperial General Headquarters had deployed 14 divisions, 6 independent mixed brigades, 3 independent armoured brigades, 1 anti-aircraft division and 25 infantry battalions attached directly to the commander of the Japanese Second Army. In the Kanto region, *Ketsu-3* (Decisive Battle Plan no. 3) called for 18 divisions, 2 armoured divisions, 7 independent mixed brigades, 3 independent tank brigades, 2 independent infantry regiments, 1 anti-aircraft division, 3 national guard brigades directly attached to the Army Commander and 18 combined amphibious units from the Yokosuka District Navy. See Bōeichō Bōei-kenkyūsho Senshi-shitsu-hen (War History Office, Defence Agency), ed., *Senshi Sōsho (51): Hondo kessen junbi (1) – Kantō no bōei* (War History Series, no. 51): Preparations for the Final Battle for the Homeland, Part 1 – The Defence of the Kanto Region), Asakumo Shinbunsha, 1971, chapter 6. For the invasion of Kyushu, the US Joint Chiefs planned to mobilise 14 divisions, including 3 US Marine divisions and 1 airborne division. The Allied attack on the Kanto Plain called for 25 divisions, including 2 armoured divisions, 3 Marine divisions and 1 airborne division. US air and sea forces deployed off Japan included 23 battleships, 26 aircraft carriers, 64 special aircraft carriers, 52 cruisers, 323 destroyers, 298 escort ships, 2,783 landing craft, 14,847 fleet aircraft, General George C. Kenney's Far Eastern Air Force and General Carl A. Spaatz's Strategic Air Forces. Against this, Japan could muster only 19 destroyers, 38 submarines, 3,300 special attack ships and 10,000 aircraft, 7,500 of which were no more than upgraded trainers. See Bōeichō Bōei-kenkyūsho Senshi-shitsu-hen (War History Office, Defence Agency), ed., *Senshi Sōsho (57): Hondo kessen junbi (2) – Kyūshū no bōei* (War History Series, no. 57): Preparations for the Final Battle for the Homeland, Part 2 – The Defence of Kyushu), Asakumo Shinbunsha, 1971, chapters 5–7 and *Reports of MacArthur*, vol. 1, pp. 405, 419, 430, 433–5.)

72. See *Reports of MacArthur*, vol. 2, Part 2, pp. 600–12, 648–65 and Frank (1999), especially chapters 12 and 13. By mid-August, Japan had an estimated 735,000 troops deployed on the island, outnumbering the US Sixth Army's 650,000

men, who would constitute the main invasion force. Walter Krueger, *From Down Under to Nippon: The Story of Sixth Army in World War II*, Combat Forces Press, Washington, 1953, p. 333.

73. Quotation is from the diary of Secretary of War Henry Stimson, 10 August 1945, cited by Frank (1999), p. 342.

74. *Reports of MacArthur*, vol. 1, pp. 436–9.

75. Krueger (1953), p. 335.

76. Manhattan Project scientists expected an explosive force of up to 1,700 tons of TNT. The Alamogordo blast produced a yield in the vicinity of 20,000 tons. The chief administrator was Major General Leslie R. Groves. His comment of 18 July 1945 is cited by Martin J. Sherwin, *A World Destroyed: Hiroshima and the Origins of the Arms Race*, Vintage Books, 1987 (Knopf, 1975), p. xiii.

77. The Churchill quotation is from Leon V. Sigal, *Fighting to a Finish: The Politics of War Termination in the United States and Japan*, Cornell University Press, 1988, p. 138. London and Washington had established scientific liaison offices in early 1941, and by October of that year, both sides were working together to produce a bomb. In 1942, Washington imposed restrictions on the exchange of information, but bilateral cooperation resumed in mid-1943. In August 1943 at Quebec, Washington promised to seek London's consent before using the weapon. At the Hyde Park Conference in September 1944, Churchill and Roosevelt agreed to continue bilateral nuclear collaboration after the war. By the end of that year, Britain was deeply involved in the Manhattan Project, providing technological support and helping the United States corner world supplies of uranium. See Sherwin (1987), pp. 68–88, 109–11.

78. US Department of State, *Foreign Relations of the United States* (below, given as *FRUS*): *The Conference of Berlin (The Potsdam Conference)*, vol. 2, US Government Printing Office, 1945, pp. 1474–6.

79. Charles L. Mee Jr, *Meeting at Potsdam*, M. Evans and Co. (New York), 1975, pp. 243–4. On Stalin and the bomb, see Hasegawa, vol. 1 (1998), p. 56.

80. The Americans had developed two different types of atomic weapon. The first was an untested uranium device with a gun-like trigger, the second an implosion-type plutonium bomb used in the Trinity blast. The US military was determined to test both on Japan in order to assess their relative destructiveness (Sigal, 1988, pp. 182–98). Hiroshima was a military centre, but its population of roughly 350,000, swollen by military personnel, commuters, temporary residents, Korean labourers and Allied prisoners of war, was overwhelmingly noncombatant. Nagasaki, a city of about 270,000, was of lesser military significance (see Committee for the Compilation of Materials on Damage Caused by the Atomic Bombs in Hiroshima and Nagasaki, *Hiroshima and Nagasaki: The Physical, Medical, and Social Effects of the Atomic Bombings*, Basic Books, 1981, pp. 344–69, 462–83). Concerning Korean casualties of the bomb, S. Pak, K. Kwak and W. Sin estimate that as many as 40,000 perished in the blast and its

aftermath (see *Hibakusha Kankokujin* [Koreans Exposed to the A-Bomb], Asahi Shinbunsha, 1975, p. 296). Recent research suggests figures of between 20,000 and 30,000 (Lisa Yoneyama, 'Memory Matters: Hiroshima's Korean Atom Bomb Memorial and the Politics of Ethnicity', in Laura Hein and Mark Selden, eds, *Living With the Bomb: American and Japanese Cultural Conflicts in the Nuclear Age*, M. E. Sharpe, 1997, p. 205). Roughly 1,000 Japanese American victims were said to be living in the United States alone (*Hiroshima and Nagasaki*, p. 482).

81. The Truman citation is from *Public Papers of the Presidents: Harry S. Truman, 1945*, US Government Printing Office, 1961, p. 149. Nishina is quoted in Monica Braw, *The Atomic Bomb Suppressed*, M. E. Sharpe, 1991, p. 12. Tokyo's protest omitted the fact that Japan, too, had joined the nuclear race. As early as 1940, Japanese scientists had discussed the possibility of developing atomic weapons, and in 1943, the government concluded that production was possible. By 1944, Japan had assembled four cyclotrons, but the nation's weapons programme never got beyond the laboratory stage due to its inability to acquire sufficient quantities of uranium and a dearth of human, physical and financial resources. The effort was, in the words of John W. Dower, 'puny and almost pathetic' (*Japan in War and Peace: Selected Essays*, The New Press, 1993, p. 57; see also Dees, 1997, chapter 2).

82. Arguments justifying the bombings on grounds of military necessity are advanced by Newman (1995) and Frank (1999).

83. The Manhattan Project and its logic are explained by Leslie R. Groves, *Now It Can Be Told: The Story of the Manhattan Project*, Harper, 1962 and Sherwin (1987), pp. 145, 194–5.

84. See Alperovitz (1995), pp. 325–6. James Hershberg analyses the reasoning of Conant, Vannevar Bush and other Interim Committee members in *James B. Conant: Harvard to Hiroshima and the Making of the Nuclear Age*, Knopf, 1993, pp. 219–29.

85. The Leahy citation is from his memoir, *I Was There: The Personal Story of the Chief of Staff to the Presidents Roosevelt and Truman, Based on his Notes and Diaries Made at the Time*, McGraw-Hill, 1950, p. 441. Alperovitz, ibid., pp. 225–6, 327, 352–6. On Bard's dissent, see Sherwin (1987), pp. 307–8.

86. MacArthur is quoted by Weldon E. Rhoades, *Flying MacArthur to Victory*, Texas A&M University Press, 1987, p. 428.

87. The Truman quotations are cited by Alperovitz (1995), pp. 6 and 563, respectively. Alperovitz introduces important new evidence concerning Truman's political motivations.

88. Hasegawa, vol. 1 (1998), p. 43.

89. John J. Stephan, *The Russian Far East: A History*, Stanford University Press, 1994, pp. 241–2 and Hasegawa, vol. 1 (1998), p. 52–3. Kase (1951), p. 224.

90. See David M. Glantz, *August Storm: The Soviet 1945 Strategic Offensive in Manchuria*, Paper no. 7, Combat Studies Institute, US Army Command and

Staff College, Fort Leavenworth, Kansas, 1983, pp. 5–7, 136–7, 141–2, 196–7.

91. *Reports of MacArthur*, vol. 2, Part 2, p. 728.

92. The First Cavalry, the 11th Airborne Division and the 77th Division were reassigned from Sixth Army to Eighth Army, which also included IX, X and XIV Corps. (The 11th Airborne originally was an Eighth Army command but had been attached temporarily to Sixth Army during the battle for Luzon.) The Eichelberger Papers, Duke University.

93. XXIV Corps was detached from Tenth Army in Okinawa, assigned to AFPAC and sent to operate independently as the US occupation force in southern Korea; the First Army Service Command was sent to Okinawa; and Lieutenant General Styer's US Army Forces in the Mid-Pacific assumed combat responsibility for the Southwest Pacific, relieving Eighth Army of all duties outside of Japan.

94. Williams (1979), p. 2. GHQ/SCAP, *History of the Nonmilitary Activities of the Occupation of Japan, 1945–1951*, vol. 2: Administration of the Occupation, Tokyo, 1951, pp. 21–2.

95. See James (1985), p. 63.

96. The Yalta pact ('Agreement Regarding Entry of the Soviet Union into the War Against Japan'), signed by Churchill, Roosevelt and Stalin, is reproduced in *FRUS: The Conferences at Malta and Yalta*, 1945, p. 984.

Chapter 2   Occupation: the First Weeks

1. On the Manila mission, see US Department of the Army (Historical Section, G-2, FECOM), ed., *Reports of General MacArthur*, vol. 1: Supplement (MacArthur in Japan – The Occupation: Military Phase), US Government Printing Office, 1966, pp. 19–23 (below, given as *Reports of MacArthur*).

2. Courtney Whitney, *MacArthur: His Rendezvous with History*, Knopf, 1956, p. 212.

3. Sidney F. Mashbir, *I Was an American Spy*, Vantage Press, 1953, pp. 304–10.

4. On Willoughby and Arisue, see Harry E. Wildes, *Typhoon in Tokyo: The Occupation and its Aftermath*, Macmillan, 1954, p. 52 and John Welfield, *An Empire in Eclipse: Japan in the Postwar American Alliance System – A Study in the Interaction of Domestic Politics and Foreign Policy*, Athlone Press, 1988, pp. 66–8.

5. Quotation is from Takemae Eiji, 'C. G. Tilton and the Occupation of Japan', in *The Journal of Tokyo Keizai University*, no. 146, 1986, p. 553.

6. Douglas MacArthur, *Reminiscences*, McGraw-Hill, 1964, pp. 282–3.

7. Thomas T. Sakamoto, 'The MIS Aboard the Battleship USS *Missouri*', in *Unsung Heroes: Military Intelligence Service, Past, Present, Future*, MIS-Northwest Association (Seattle), 1996, p. 32. The Yokohama Customs House is described by Crawford F. Sams, *'Medic': The Mission of an American Military Doctor in Occupied Japan and War-torn Korea*, edited by Zabelle Zakarian, M. E. Sharpe, 1998, p. 14.

8. On initial Japanese resistance to surrender, see Robert J. C. Butow, *Japan's Decision to Surrender*, Stanford University Press, 1954, pp. 222–4 and Kase Toshikazu, *Eclipse of the Rising Sun*, Jonathan Cape, 1951, pp. 258–64. Hirohito sent Prince Kan'in to Southeast Asia, Prince Asaka to China and Prince Takeda to Manchuria.

9. *Reports of MacArthur*, p. 118. The Eichelberger quotation is from Robert L. Eichelberger and Milton MacKaye, *Our Jungle Road to Tokyo*, Viking Press, 1950, p. 262. The MacArthur quotation is from his speech, 'Demobilization of Japanese Armed Forces', reproduced in Government Section, SCAP, *The Political Reorientation of Japan, September 1945 to September 1948* (below, given as *PRJ*), US Government Printing Office, 1949, vol. 1, p. 742.

10. Mark Gayn, *Japan Diary*, Charles E. Tuttle, 1981 (William Sloane, 1948), pp. 1–2.

11. Sams (1998), p. 12 and Bowen C. Dees, *The Allied Occupation and Japan's Economic Miracle: Building the Foundations of Japanese Science and Technology, 1945–1952*, Curzon Press, 1997, p. xiii.

12. Sakamoto (1996), p. 33.

13. See Kase's account (1951).

14. The Allied signatories were General Sir Thomas Blamey (Australia), Colonel L. Moore-Cosgrove (Canada), General Hsu Yung-chang (Republic of China), General Jacques LeClerc (France), Admiral Conrad Helfrich (Netherlands), Air Vice-Marshal Sir Leonard Isitt (New Zealand), Lieutenant General K. N. Derevyanko (Soviet Union), Admiral Sir Bruce Fraser (United Kingdom), and Admiral Chester W. Nimitz (United States).

15. 'Statement by General MacArthur to Surrender Delegates Aboard Battleship *Missouri*', in *PRJ*, vol. 2, p. 736.

16. Cited in Takafusa Nakamura, *A History of Showa Japan, 1926–1989*, University of Tokyo Press, 1998, p. 248.

17. John K. Emmerson, *The Japanese Thread: A Life in the US Foreign Service*, Holt, Rinehart & Winston, 1978 pp. 251, 274–5.

18. Beate Sirota Gordon, *The Only Woman in the Room: A Memoir*, Kodansha International, 1998, p. 11.

19. This was the reaction of Iwao Peter Sano, a Japanese American drafted into the Imperial Army while studying in Japan and sent to Manchuria. See his *1000 Days in Siberia: the Odyssey of a Japanese-American POW*, Bison Books (University of Nebraska Press), 1999, pp. 60–1.

20. Justin Williams Sr, *Japan's Political Revolution Under MacArthur: A Participant's Account*, University of Tokyo Press, 1979, p. 5.

21. Shigemitsu Mamoru, *Japan and Her Destiny: My Struggle for Peace*, edited by F. S. G. Piggott, E. P. Dutton, 1958, p. 375.

22. A lively account of this incident in English is Tsurumi Shunsuke, *A Cultural History of Postwar Japan, 1945–1980*, Kegan Paul International, 1987, pp. 5–6.

23. Shigemitsu (1958), p. 376.

24. Justin Williams basically accepts Shigemitsu's account of the meeting (1979, loc. cit). On the AFPAC directive, see *Reports of MacArthur*, p. 75.

25. Brigadier General George A. Lincoln of Operations Division reportedly glanced at a map in his office and within 10 seconds determined that the dividing line should fall along the 38th parallel. His subordinates Colonel Charles Bonesteel and Colonel Dean Rusk agreed and lobbied aggressively for acceptance of this boundary. See the account by Michael C. Sandusky, *America's Parallel*, Old Dominion Press, 1983, pp. 226–7.

26. Bruce Cumings, *The Origins of the Korean War: Liberation and the Emergence of Separate Regimes, 1945–1947*, Princeton University Press, 1981, pp. 123–8, 137–40. Citation is from p. 128.

27. Theodore Cohen, *Remaking Japan: The American Occupation as New Deal*, The Free Press, 1987, pp. 82, 133.

28. Eichelberger and MacKaye (1950), pp. 273–4.

29. *Mainichi Shinbun* (Kanagawa edition), 8 September 1945. Examples are from Yuki Tanaka, *Hidden Horrors: Japanese War Crimes in World War II*, Westview Press, 1998, p. 105.

30. Gayn (1981), p. 233. Hayato's comment is cited in Yukiko Koshiro, *Trans-Pacific Racisms and the U.S. Occupation of Japan*, University of Columbia Press, 1999, p. 69.

31. Yamada Mieko, *Senryōgun ianfu* (Comfort Women of the US Occupation Army), Kōjinsha, 1992, pp. 7, 42–3.

32. Some Allied forces also availed themselves of the sex slaves they 'liberated' from Japanese troops on Asian battlegrounds. See George Hicks, *The Comfort Women*, Yenbooks, 1995, pp. 72, 119–22, 127. The former Occupationaire is Cohen (1987), p. 127. The US Marine is Edwin L. Neville Jr, 'Japanese and GI Rapport', in William F. Nimmo, ed., *The Occupation of Japan: The Grassroots*, General Douglas MacArthur Foundation, 1992, p. 138. On New Zealand troops, see Laurie Brocklebank, *Jayforce: New Zealand and the Military Occupation of Japan, 1945–48*, Oxford University Press, 1997, p. 182.

33. The American observer is Michael S. Molasky. Molasky makes these points with particular cogency, describing prostitutes, black-marketeers and war orphans as icons of postwar life. See *The American Occupation of Japan and Okinawa: Literature and Memory*, Routledge, 1999, pp. 104–5, 107. The quotation is from p. 103. On the lives of these women, see the first-hand accounts in Mizuno Hiroshi, ed., *Shi ni nozonde uttaeru* (Our Dying Words Accuse!), Tōgosha, 1982 (originally published as *Nihon no teisō: gaikokuhei ni okasareta joseitachi no shuki* [Japan's Moral State: Women Raped by Foreign Soldiers and Their Stories], Sōjusha, 1953).

34. On the Tokyo, Yokohama and Kyoto VD sweeps, see Cohen (1987), p. 131 and Sams (1998), pp. 106–7. On the closure of the RAAs, Refer to Duus Masayo, *Makkāsā no futatsu no bōshi: tokushu ian-shisetsu RAA o meguru senryō-shi no sokumen* (The Two Hats of MacArthur: A History of RAA Comfort Stations

During the Occupation), Kōdansha Bunko, 1985, p. 280 and Inoue Etsuko, *Senryōgun ianjo: kokka ni yoru baishun shisetsu* (Comfort Stations for the Occupation Army: State-Operated Brothels), Shinhyōron, 1995, pp. 27–35.

35. On anti-prostitution legislation, consult Nishi Kyōko, *Senryōka no Nihon fujin seisaku* (Policies Affecting Japanese Women Under the Occupation), Domesu Shuppan, 1985, pp. 34–40. On women's welfare homes, see GHQ/SCAP, *History of the Nonmilitary Activities of the Occupation of Japan, 1945–1951*, vol. 18: Public Welfare, 1952, pp. 40–2.

36. Gayn (1981), pp. 245–53.

37. Whitney (1956), p. 216. One SCAP official: Takemae Eiji, 'J. Napier and the Purge in Japan', in *The Journal of Tokyo Keizai University*, no. 153, November 1987, p. 79. The Occupationaire is Justin Williams Sr (1979), p. 13. The *Yomiuri* account is from *Reports of MacArthur*, p. 24. Instances of loathsome behaviour by US forces in outlying regions were occasionally recorded. As late as September 1947, a SCAP official described 'a mild reign of terror' in Sapporo, Hokkaido, where troops of the 11th Airborne Division seemed 'determined to practice their martial arts on the helpless Japanese civilians' by beating, knifing or mauling them 'for a trivial or imagined reason, or for no reason at all'. Such outrages were exceptional, however. The incident is cited in Toshio Nishi, *Unconditional Democracy: Education and Politics in Occupied Japan, 1945–1952*, Hoover Institution Press (Stanford University), 1982, pp. 47–8.

38. Ball (1988), p. 98. The Australian press characterisation is from Peter Bates, *Japan and the British Commonwealth Occupation Force, 1946–52*, Brassey's (UK), 1993, p. 115.

39. Sodei Rinjirō, 'The Occupier and the Occupied', in William F. Nimmo, ed. (1992), pp. 5–6. On jeeps and children, see John W. Dower, *Embracing Defeat: Japan in the Wake of World War II*, W. W. Norton and the New Press, 1999, p. 110.

40. Statistics are from Walt Sheldon, *The Honorable Conquerors: The Occupation of Japan 1945–1952*, Macmillan, 1965, pp. 114–15, and GHQ/SCAP and FECOM, *Selected Data on the Occupation of Japan*, Tokyo, 1950, p. 107. Sheldon reports that the Occupation's extensive housing programme, which included the construction of new American-style accommodation, sparked a construction boom that by 1949 had consumed one third of Japan's iron and cement, one fifth of its steel and one tenth of its lumber and glass. The analogy with the British Raj is from Meirion and Susie Harries, *Sheathing the Sword: The Demilitarisation of Japan*, Heinemann, 1989, p. xxv. On Kennan: Letter from Kennan to W. Walton Butterworth, 9 March 1948, cited in Michael Schaller, *The Origins of the Cold War in Asia: The American Occupation of Japan*, Oxford University Press, 1985, p. 125. Faubion Bowers's comment is from 'Discussion', in Thomas W. Burkman, ed., *The Occupation of Japan: Arts and Culture*, General Douglas MacArthur Foundation, 1988, p. 204.

41. Gayn (1981), p. 17. High-buttoned shoes: Carmen Johnson, *Wave-Rings in the Water: My Years With the Women of Postwar Japan*, Charles River Press, 1996, p. 12.
42. Gayn (1981), p. 47.
43. This description is from William Costello, *Democracy vs. Feudalism in Postwar Japan*, Itagaki Shoten, 1948, p. 153. See also the discussion in Christopher Aldous, *The Police in Occupation Japan: Control, Corruption and Resistance to Reform*, Routledge, 1997, pp. 95–106, 214.
44. SCAP's report to the Famine Emergency Committee on 6 May 1946 is in *PRJ*, vol. 2, p. 749.
45. Figures on food rations are from Nakamura (1998), p. 281. On GHQ's release of food stores, see Yoshida Shigeru, *Japan's Decisive Century, 1867–1967*, Frederick A. Praeger, 1967, pp. 51–2 and Takemae Eiji, ed., *C. F. Samsu, DDT kakumei: senryō-ki no iryō fukushi seisaku o kaisō suru* (C. F. Sams, The DDT Revolution: Looking Back at the Reform of Medicine and Social Welfare During the Occupation), Iwanami Shoten, 1986, pp. 106, 113. The quotation is from Irokawa Daikichi, *The Age of Hirohito: In Search of Modern Japan*, The Free Press, 1995, p. 45.
46. Irokawa, ibid., and Sams (1998), p. 60.
47. Sams (1998), pp. 54, 59, 60–2. Also refer to Dower (1999), pp. 93–4. On GARIOA, see Jerome B. Cohen, *Japan's Economy in War and Reconstruction*, University of Minnesota Press, 1949.
48. The 'six-inch rule' is described by Donald Richie, 'The Occupied Arts', in Mark Sandler, ed., *The Confusion Era: Art and Culture of Japan During the Allied Occupation, 1945–1952*, Smithsonian Institution, 1997, p. 15. The MacArthur quotation is from Faubion Bowers, 'The Late General MacArthur, Warts and All', in *Esquire*, January 1967, p. 168. On MacArthur's attitude toward fraternisation, see W. MacMahon Ball, *Intermittent Diplomat: The Japan and Batavia Diaries of W. MacMahon Ball*, Alan Rix, ed., Melbourne University Press, 1988, p. 75.
49. *Reports of MacArthur*, pp. 51–2.
50. See Whitney (1956), p. 214.
51. The Eichelberger quotation is from official correspondence: 'Reports', 23 March 1946, cited in Roger Buckley, *Occupation Diplomacy: Britain, the United States and Japan 1945–1952*, Cambridge University Press, 1982, p. 235. The Occupationaire citation is from Sheldon (1965), p. 107. The historian is Yukiko Koshiro (1999), p. 159.
52. Richard L.-G. Deverall, *The Great Seduction: Red China's Drive to Bring Free Japan Behind the Iron Curtain*, International Literature Printing Co. (Tokyo), 1953, p. 97. Deverall, a former official in GHQ's Labour Division, gives no sources but cites this as the commonly accepted figure at the end of the Occupation.
53. See Bates (1993), pp. 112–14 and Cohen (1987), pp. 123, 132. The Gascoigne citation is from Bates, p. 84.

54. See Tsuyoshi Hasegawa, *The Northern Territories Dispute and Russo-Japanese Relations*, vol. 2: Neither Peace Nor War, 1985–1998, University of California Press, 1998, pp. 517–18.

55. John J. Stephan, *The Kuril Islands: Russo-Japanese Frontier in the Pacific*, Clarendon Press (Oxford), 1974, p. 151–2.

56. David Rees, *The Soviet Seizure of the Kuriles*, Praeger, 1985, pp. 58–9; Tsuyoshi Hasegawa, *The Northern Territories Dispute and Russo-Japanese Relations*, vol. 1: Between War and Peace, 1697–1985, University of California Press, 1998, pp. 44–5; Marc S. Gallicchio, 'The Kuriles Controversy: US Diplomacy in the Soviet–Japan Border Dispute, 1941–1956', in *Pacific Historical Review*, vol. 60, no. 1, 1991, pp. 74–6.

57. Rees (1985), pp. 76, 82 and Stephan (1974), p. 158.

58. On the May 1943 study, see Gallicchio (1991), p. 73. The Blakeslee Memorandum is reproduced in Stephan (1974), pp. 240–4.

59. Stephan (1974), p. 155. On Churchill's role, see Rees (1985), pp. 63–4.

60. This is the position taken by Stephan, Rees and other scholars based on the memoirs of Charles E. Bohlen, who accompanied Roosevelt to Yalta. See Bohlen, *Witness to History, 1929–1969*, W. W. Norton, 1973, pp. 196–7.

61. Gallicchio (1991), pp. 75 and Hasegawa, vol. 1 (1998), p. 44.

62. See Gallicchio (1991), pp. 75, 77 and note 18 on p. 77. On the Joint Chiefs at Potsdam, see Grace P. Hayes, *The History of the Joint Chiefs of Staff in World War II: The War Against Japan*, Naval Institute Press (Annapolis), 1982, pp. 720–1.

63. US Department of State, *Foreign Relations of the United States* (below, given as *FRUS*): *The Conference of Berlin (The Potsdam Conference)*, vol. 2, US Government Printing Office, 1945, pp. 1284–5.

64. The actual drafting of the Order was the work of the S&P's Colonel Charles Bonesteel, who was determined to retain at least some of the Kurils as a site for future US bases. Gallicchio (1991), pp. 83–4.

65. Hasegawa, vol. 1 (1998), pp. 61, 63–4. On Stalin's strategy, see David M. Glantz, 'The Soviet Invasion of Japan', in *Military History Quarterly*, vol. 7, no. 3, 1995, pp. 96–7, 136–7.

66. On Truman's motivation, refer to Wada Haruki, 'Nisso sensō' (The Japanese-Soviet War), in Hara Teruyuki and Togawa Tsugo, eds, *Kōza: Surabu no sekai* (The Slavic World), vol. 8: Surabu to Nihon (The Slavic Peoples and Japan), Kōbundō, 1995, p. 123. Concerning US air bases, see Rees (1985), pp. 76–7. On Stalin's order to Beria, see Hasegawa, vol. 1 (1998), p. 65.

67. Boris Slavinsky, *The Soviet Occupation of the Kuril Islands, August-September 1945: A Documentary Research*, Kennedy School of Government, Harvard University, 1993, p. 50.

68. Tsutsumi's force had lost more than half of its normal strength due to redeployments to the main islands. In August 1945, he had at his disposition 10 infantry battalions, an artillery division consisting of 18 rapid-fire 47mm can-

nons, an artillery unit with 53 mountain and field pieces, an engineering corps, an air defence corps and an armoured regiment.

69. See Stephan (1974), pp. 162–4 and, particularly, Slavinsky, (1993), pp. 56–65.

70. Suizu Mitsuru, *Hoppō ryōdo dakkan e no michi* (Recovering the Northern Territories), Nihon Kōgyō Shinbunsha 1979, p. 83.

71. Slavinsky (1993), pp. 76–84.

72. D. F. Ustinov, *Istoriia Vtoroi Mirovoi Voiny – 2* (History of the Second World War, 1939–45, vol. 2), Moscow, 1980.

73. Pravda, 3 September 1945, cited in Rees (1985), p. 82.

74. On the indigenous peoples of this region, see generally Ch. M. Taksami and V. D. Kosarev, *Ainu minzoku no rekishi to bunka: hoppō shōsū minzoku-gakusha no shiza yori* (The History and Culture of the Ainu People: Minorities of the Northern Islands from an Anthropological Viewpoint), Akashi Shoten, 1998. Bukawa Tsurunosuke, an émigré from Kunashiri who witnessed the Soviet occupation, claims that Soviet officers of Japanese descent from Sakhalin and Vladivostok were given high positions in the local military government to minimise friction with the populace. The garrison chief at Kunashiri, for example, was a Captain Utsunenko of the Soviet Pacific Fleet, reportedly of Japanese ancestry.

75. See Hokkaidō Keisatsubu Jōhōka, *Soren-gun senryō-ka ni okeru Chishima oyobi Habomai ritō gaikyō* (A General Survey of Conditions in the Kuril Islands and the Offshore Islets of Habomai Under Soviet Military Occupation), October 1945.

76. On the number of captured Japanese soldiers, see Slavinsky (1993), p. 83. Concerning local conditions, refer to Nemuro-shi Sōmubu Ryōdo Taisaku-gakari-hen (ed.), *Hoppō ryōdo: shūsen zengo no kiroku* (The Occupation of the Northern Territories: A Record of Events Before and After the End of the War), Nemuro-shi, vol. 1, 1970 and vol. 2, 1971.

77. Stephan (1974), p. 166–68.

78. See Nemuro-shi Sōmubu Ryōdo Taisaku-gakari-hen (ed.), *Nihon no ryōdo, Hoppō-ryōdo* (The Northern Territories: Japanese Homeland), Nemuro-shi, 1980.

79. Ibid.

Chapter 3   The Occupational Dynamic

1. Hugh Borton, *American Presurrender Planning for Postwar Japan*, Occasional Papers of The East Asian Institute, Columbia University, New York, 1967, p. 7. On French, Dutch and Portuguese ambitions, see Grace P. Hayes, *The History of the Joint Chiefs of Staff in World War II: The War Against Japan*, Naval Institute Press (Annapolis), 1982, p. 716.

2. US Department of State, *Foreign Relations of the United States* (below, given as *FRUS*), vol. 6, US Government Printing Office, 1945, pp. 630, 667–8, 670.

3. SWNCC-70/5, 'National Composition of Forces to Occupy Japan Proper in

the Post-Defeat Period', cited in Yukiko Koshiro, *Trans-Pacific Racisms and the U.S. Occupation of Japan*, University of Columbia Press, 1999, pp. 20–1, 231.

4. Joint War Plans Committee, 'Ultimate Occupation of Japan and Japanese Territory', 16 August 1945. Record Group 213, CCS 383.21, Japan, National Archives Records Administration, Washington DC.

5. Harry S. Truman, *Memoirs: Year of Decisions, 1945*, Doubleday, 1955, pp. 431–2.

6. Concerning the FEAC and its successor, the Far Eastern Commission, see George H. Blakeslee, *The Far Eastern Commission: A Study in International Cooperation 1945–1952*, US Department of State (US Government Printing Office), 1953.

7. Theodore Cohen, *Remaking Japan: The American Occupation as New Deal*, The Free Press, 1987, p. 56. In Japanese, the definitive study of the origins of the FEAC and FEC is Toyoshita Narahiko, *Nihon senryō kanri taisei no seiritsu: hikaku senryō-shi josetsu* (The Origins of the Control System for the Occupation of Japan: An Essay in Comparative Occupation History), Iwanami Shoten, 1992.

8. As of mid-July 1947, the subcommittee chairs and deputy chairs were as follows. Committee no. 1, Reparations: Major J. Plimsol (Australia), Dr R. H. van Gulik (Netherlands); Committee no. 2, Economic and Financial Affairs: F. C. Everson (Britain), Roswel H. Whitman (United States); Committee no. 3, Constitutional and Legal Reform: B. R. Sen (India), Ralph E. Collins (Canada); Committee no. 4, Strengthening of Democratic Tendencies: G. G. Dolbin (Soviet Union), Dr T. T. Mar (Republic of China); Committee no. 5, War Criminals: Liu Hsuan-tsui (Republic of China), F. C. Rodriguez (Philippines); Committee no. 6, Aliens in Japan: Francis Lacoste (France), F. C. Everson (Britain); and Committee no. 7, Disarmament of Japan: O. Reuchlin (Netherlands), Rear Admiral S. S. Ramishvili (Soviet Union). From 'Activities of the Far Eastern Commission', Report by the Secretary General, 26 February 1946 – 10 July 1947. After 1949, Burma was represented by U So Nyun and Pakistan by M. A. H. Ispahani. Other notable FEC members included Dr Herbert Evatt (1946) of Australia, Lord Halifax (1946) and Sir George Sansom (1946–7) of Britain, Lester Pearson (1946) of Canada, Dr V. K. Wellington Koo (1946–9) of Nationalist China, Brigadier General Carlos P. Romulo (1946–52) of the Philippines and Andrei Gromyko (1946) of the Soviet Union. See Blakeslee (1953), pp. 31, 239–40.

9. Ann Trotter, *New Zealand and Japan, 1945–1952: The Occupation and the Peace Treaty*, Athlone Press, 1990, pp. 38–43.

10. Asakai Kōichirō in Gaimushō-hen (ed.), *Shoki tai-Nichi senryō seisaku* (Early Occupation Policy Towards Japan), vol. 1, Mainichi Shinbunsha, 1978, pp. 211–52.

11. Quotations are from, respectively, Kawai Kazuo, *Japan's American Interlude*, University of Chicago Press, 1960, p. 18 and W. MacMahon Ball, *Japan: Enemy or Ally?*, Cassell (New York), 1949, pp. 23, 33.

12. W. MacMahon Ball, *Intermittent Diplomat: The Japan and Batavia Diaries of W. MacMahon Ball*, Alan Rix, ed., Melbourne University Press, 1988 p. 19. MacArthur himself used the term 'knock-down-dragout' when he instructed US officials to retaliate in kind against Soviet attacks. See Justin Williams Sr, *Japan's Political Revolution Under MacAthur: A Participant's Account*, University of Tokyo Press, 1979, pp. 80–81.
13. Ball (1988), p. 64 and note in same by Alan Rix, pp. 288–9; Cohen (1987), p. 308 and Mark Gayn, *Japan Diary*, Charles P. Tuttle, 1981 (William Sloane, 1948), pp. 217–18.
14. See Roger Buckley, *Occupation Diplomacy: Britain, the United States and Japan 1945–1952*, Cambridge University Press, 1982, p. 80–4 and Ball (1988), p. 47. On Whitney's attitude towards Ball and Chu, see Williams (1979), p. 81.
15. William J. Sebald with Russell Brines, *With MacArthur in Japan: A Personal History of the Occupation*, W. W. Norton, 1965, pp. 141–7.
16. Dean Acheson, *Present at the Creation: My Years in the State Department*, New American Library, 1970 (W. W. Norton, 1969) pp. 177–8.
17. Blakeslee (1953), p. 51.
18. See GHQ/SCAP, *History of the Nonmilitary Activities of the Occupation of Japan, 1945–1951* (below, given as *HNMA*), vol. 2: Administration of the Occupation, 1952, pp. 146–51. Government Section, SCAP, *The Political Reorientation of Japan, September 1945 to September 1948* (below, given as *PRJ*), US Government Printing Office, 1949, vol. 1, pp. 1–7.
19. Robert L. Eichelberger and Milton MacKaye, *Our Jungle Road to Tokyo*, Viking Press, 1950, p. 260.
20. On the role of Colonel Hattori, see Gayn (1981), pp. 445–6. See also the suggestive comments in Meirion and Susie Harries, *Sheathing the Sword: The Demilitarisation of Japan*, Heinemann, 1987, pp. 226–7.
21. US Department of the Army (Historical Section, G-2, FECOM), ed., *Reports of General MacArthur*, US Government Printing Office, 1966, vol. 1: Supplement (MacArthur in Japan – The Occupation: Military Phase), pp. 166–86 (below, given as *Reports of MacArthur*), pp. 136–43.
22. Cohen (1987), pp. 146–9; *Reports of MacArthur*, pp. 214–16 and Blakeslee (1953), pp. 123–30.
23. See Blakeslee, ibid., pp. 139–54.
24. GHQ/SCAP and FECOM, *Selected Data on the Occupation of Japan*, Tokyo, 1950, pp. 91–2. On Korean repatriates, see William J. Gane, *Repatriation, From 25 September 1945 to 31 December 1945*, Headquarters, US Army Military Government in Korea (Foreign Affairs Section, Seoul, 1946.
25. *Reports of MacArthur*, p. 191.
26. *HNMA*, vol. 2: Administration of the Occupation, p. 163. On Japanese Americans repatriated to Japan, see Sodei Rinjirō, *Were We the Enemy? American Survivors of Hiroshima*, Westview Press, 1998, pp. 52–3, 57.
27. Sodei, ibid., p. 50.

28. This was the intended result of a Kremlin policy decision taken in February 1945 following Stalin's Yalta pledge to enter the war against Japan. At that time, the Marshal ordered the Soviet State Prison Administration to prepare for the internment of German and Japanese war prisoners. On 23 August, one week after Japan's capitulation, GKO (State Committee of Defence) Order 9898 instructed Soviet commanders to deport Japanese POWs to the Soviet Union for hard labour. Tsuyoshi Hasegawa, *The Northern Territories Dispute and Russo-Japanese Relations*, vol. 1: Between War and Peace, 1697–1985, University of California Press, 1998, pp. 62–3. See also *Reports of MacArthur*, pp. 179–86.

29. Hane Mikiso cites the figure 500,000 based on recent archival research in the Soviet Union but does not provide a source. See *Eastern Phoenix: Japan Since 1945*, Westview Press, 1996, p. 14.

30. See William F. Nimmo, *Behind a Curtain of Silence: Japanese in Soviet Custody, 1945–1956*, Greenwood Press, 1988, pp. 115–20 and *Reports of MacArthur*, pp. 187–90.

31. Iwao Peter Sano, *1,000 Days in Siberia: the Odyssey of a Japanese-American POW*, Bison Books (University of Nebraska Press), 1999, p. 198.

32. *Reports of MacArthur*, pp. 166–86. See also Nimmo (1988), p. 125. A first-hand account by a Japanese POW who spent nearly two years with the British in Southeast Asia is Aida Yūji, *Prisoner of the British – A Japanese Soldier's Experiences in Burma*, Cresset Press, 1966.

33. On the history of the CLO, see Ara Takashi, *Nihon senryō-shi kenkyū josetsu* (An Introduction to Research on the History of the Occupation of Japan), Kashiwa Shobō, 1994, pp. 103–4.

34. *PRJ*, vol. 1, pp. 192–3. Yoshida Shigeru, *Japan's Decisive Century, 1867–1967*, Frederick A. Praeger, 1967, pp. 47, 57–8.

35. Yoshida, ibid., p. 315. The 'working model' quotation is from John W. Dower, *Embracing Defeat: Japan in the Wake of World War II*, W. W. Norton and the New Press, 1999, p. 212.

36. See Cohen (1987), pp. 100, 237 and Yoshida Shigeru, *The Yoshida Memoirs: The Story of Japan in Crisis*, Heinemann, 1961, p. 55. On Williams's intervention, see Maeda Hideaki, *Meiji, Taishō, Shōwa, Heisei: Episōdo de tsuzuru Kokkai no hyakunen* (One Hundred Years of Diet History Seen Through Episodes from Meiji to Heisei), Hara Shobō, 1990, pp. 74, 288–92.

37. Faubion Bowers, 'Discussion', in Thomas W. Burkman, ed., *The Occupation of Japan: Arts and Culture*, General Douglas MacArthur Foundation, 1988, p. 203.

38. For example, the headquarters of the 106th MG Group, formerly a part of Eighth Army's XI Corps in Kawasaki, became the Kanto Regional MG Headquarters. It was transferred to Maebashi, Gunma Prefecture and placed under the MGS of Eighth Army's IX Corps. Eighth Army also exercised direct jurisdiction over the Tokyo–Kanagawa region, and over the regional MG headquarters for the Chūgoku and Shikoku regions, which were administered by the British Commonwealth Occupation Force. A case study of an early regional team is

Takemae Eiji, 'Nihon senryō shoki gunsei no kenkyū: Nagano chūryū Dai 78 Gunsei Chūtai no katsudō shōkai' (Studies in Military Government During the Early Stage of the Occupation: An Introduction to the 78th Military Government Headquarters Stationed in Nagano), in *Gendai Hōgaku*, no. 1, 2000, pp. 163–212

39. In 1946, major MG teams consisted of 47 members (10 commissioned officers, 37 enlisted men), not counting Japanese employees, who generally outnumbered the Americans; intermediate teams had 40 members (8 officers, 32 enlisted personnel); and minor teams consisted of 31 members (6 officers, 25 enlisted personnel). Major MG teams were assigned to 12 prefectures (Hokkaido, Aomori, Miyagi, Yamagata, Gunma, Aichi, Shizuoka, Kyoto, Hyogo, Hiroshima, Fukuoka, Nagasaki) and one urban district (Kyoto). Medium teams were sent to 18 prefectures (Akita, Iwate, Toyama, Gifu, Fukushima, Ni'igata, Tochigi, Ibaragi, Chiba, Saitama, Nagano, Mie, Okayama, Yamaguchi, Ehime, Kumamoto, Oita, Kagoshima). Minor teams went to 13 prefectures (Nara, Shiga, Wakayama, Fukui, Ishikawa, Yamanashi, Miyazaki, Saga, Kagawa, Kochi, Tokushima, Tottori, Shimane). Two special MG detachments were set up to supervise the districts of Tokyo–Kanagawa (subdivided in 1948) and Osaka. The Tokyo–Kanagawa MG detachment consisted of 215 members (65 officers, 150 enlisted personnel); the Osaka MG team had 58 members (16 officers, 42 enlisted personnel). See Ralph J. D. Braibanti, 'Administration of Military Government in Japan at the Prefectural Level', in *American Political Science Review*, vol. XLIII, No. 2, April 1949.

40. The quotation is Eichelberger's, loc. cit.

41. *Yomiuri Shinbun*, Osaka Edition, 8 July 1988.

42. Miriam Farley, *Aspects of Japan's Labour Problems*, John Day, 1960, pp. 51–2.

43. Tanaka Hiroshi, *Zainichi gaikokujin: hō no kabe, kokoro no kabe* (Foreigners in Japan: Legal and Psychological Obstacles to Equality), Iwanami Shinsho, 1995, pp. 82–3.

44. From June 1951, CAS would be involved primarily in supervising Japan's National Police Reserve (see chapter 9).

45. In English, see Douglas H. Mendel, *The Japanese People and Foreign Policy: A Study of Public Opinion in Post-Treaty Japan*, University of California Press (Berkeley), 1961, pp. 146–7.

46. An introduction to Okinawan history in English is George Kerr, *Okinawa: The History of an Island People*, Charles E. Tuttle, 1958.

47. Arnold G. Fisch Jr, *Military Government in the Ryukyu Islands, 1945–1950*, US Army Center for Military History, US Government Printing Office, 1988, pp. 54–6.

48. Miyagi Etsujirō, *Okinawa senryō no 27-nenkan: Amerika-gunsei to bunka no henyō* (Twenty-Seven Years of Occupation in Okinawa: US Military Government and the Transformation of Okinawan Culture), Iwanami Shoten, 1992, pp. 11–17. Initially, the US Navy refused a request from MacArthur to

repatriate some 160,000 islanders who had been evacuated to Japan proper towards the end of the war, citing a lack of food and shelter in the archipelago. MacArthur persisted, however, and when the US Army assumed permanent control of the Ryukyus in July 1946, he initiated a relief programme that had returned about 140,000 Okinawans by the end of the year. The influx of repatriates, most of them carrying only the clothes they wore, imposed a further burden on the crippled economy. *Reports of MacArthur*, pp. 169–70 and Fisch (1988), p. 57.

49. See Watanabe Akio, *The Okinawa Problem: A Chapter in Japan–US Relations*, Melbourne University Press, 1970, pp. 18–19 and Oguma Eiji, '*Nihonjin*' *no kyōkai: Okinawa, Ainu, Taiwan, Chōsen – shokuminchi kara fukki undō made* (The Boundaries of the 'Japanese': Okinawa, the Ainu, Taiwan, Korea – From Colonies to the Reversion Movement), Shinyōsha, 1998, p. 462.

50. Fisch (1988), pp. 70–1, 106.

51. Ibid., pp. 72–6.

52. Ienaga Saburō, *The Pacific War, 1931–1945*, Pantheon Books, 1978, p. 238.

53. Tsuyoshi Hasegawa, *The Northern Territories Dispute and Russo-Japanese Relations*, vol. 2: Neither Peace Nor War, 1985–1998, University of California Press, 1998, pp. 77–8.

54. In January 1946, Under-Secretary of State Dean Acheson repeated Truman's admonition of August 1945 that the Soviet occupation was not a final territorial disposition but did not raise the issue publicly. The same year, however, Secretary of State James Byrnes and Soviet Foreign Minister V. M. Molotov tacitly agreed to recognise each others' territorial acquisitions in Japan. In exchange for a pledge of support from Byrnes for Moscow's Yalta claims at a future peace conference, Molotov refrained from attacking Washington's designation of Japan's Pacific mandates as US trust territories. In 1947, when the State Department proposed an early peace settlement with Japan, Washington could have broached the question but chose not to. James F. Byrnes, *Speaking Frankly*, Harper, 1947, p. 221.

55. Takemae Eiji, 'Sengo shoki no senkyo seido kaikaku' (Initial Postwar Reforms in Japan: GHQ and the 1945 Election Law Amendment), in *The Journal of Tokyo Keizai University*, no. 129, 1983, pp. 63–159.

56. Ōnuma Yasuaki, *Saharin kimin: sengo sekinin no tenkei* (The Displaced of Sakhalin: Fulfilling Japan's Post-Colonial Responsibility), Chūko Shinsho, 1992, pp. 24–5. On the Kuril repatriation, see Chishima Habomai Shotō Kyojūsha Renmei-hen (ed.), *Moto tōmin ga kataru warera hōppō yontō: Soren senryō-hen* (Former Islanders Remember Our Four Northern Islands: Under the Soviet Occupation), Chishima Habomai Shotō Kyojūsha Renmei (Sapporo), 1988, chapter 8.

57. Ōnuma (1992), pp. 10–11, 30–40.

58. See Dower (1999), p. 115 and George F. Kennan, *Memoirs, 1925–1950*, Atlantic Monthly (Little, Brown), 1967, p. 387.

59. Sixth Army, formed in Texas in February 1943 under Lieutenant General Walter Krueger, had fought in the southwestern Pacific and the Philippines. It consisted of the First Marine Division, the 32nd and 41st Infantry Divisions, two anti-aircraft brigades, a special engineer brigade, an airborne infantry regiment and a field artillery battalion. From September to December 1945, when the force was disbanded, Sixth Army was stationed in western Japan. Eighth Army, commanded by Lieutenant General Robert L. Eichelberger, was formed in the late summer of 1944. After successful campaigns in the southwestern Pacific and the Philippines, it was transferred to Okinawa and then to Yokohama.

US Naval forces in Japan included the Third and Fifth Fleets, which had operated independently of the US Pacific Fleet during the war. Established in August 1943 under Admiral William Halsey, the Third Fleet consisted of 6 battleships, 5 aircraft-carriers, 13 cruisers, the Seventh Division and about 500 aircraft belonging to the 13th Air Force. It was responsible for bombarding Japan's Pacific coastline during July and August of 1945. The Fifth Fleet, commanded by Admiral Raymond Spruance, took part in campaigns in the central Pacific and Okinawa. During the Occupation, it was assigned to Sasebo in Kyushu. The main Occupation air force was General George C. Kenney's US Fifth Air Force. Established in September 1942, it comprised the major part of SWPA's Allied Air Force. During the Occupation, the Fifth operated under the US Army's Pacific Air Command, which became the Far East Air Force in 1947.

60. This figure is cited by Cohen (1987), p. 123.

61. See generally Nishi Kyōko, *Senryōka no Nihon fujin seisaku* (Policies Affecting Japanese Women Under the Occupation), Domesu Shuppan, 1985.

62. Bettie J. Morden, *The Women's Army Corps, 1945–1978*, US Army Center for Military History, US Government Printing Office, 1990, pp. 47, 67, 107. On Nisei WACs, see Yaye F. Henman, 'The WAC Experience', in *Unsung Heroes: Military Intelligence Service, Past, Present, Future*, MIS-Northwest Association (Seattle), 1996, p. 7.

63. A seminal study of women in the Occupation is Susan J. Pharr, 'The Politics of Women's Rights', in Robert E. Ward and Sakamoto Yoshikazu, eds, *Democratizing Japan: The Allied Occupation*, University of Hawai'i Press, 1987, pp. 221–52. See also Susan J. Pharr, 'A Radical US Experiment: Women's Rights and the Occupation of Japan', in L. H. Redford, ed., *The Occupation of Japan: Impact of Legal Reform*, General Douglas MacArthur Foundation, 1977, pp. 125–34. Pharr (1987), pp. 239–41.

64. In many cases, Johnson relates in her memoir, simply indicating concern about an issue was sufficient to bring action. Often, problems were pointed out to the civil affairs officers by Japanese women. In one instance, a prefectural official of the local Women's and Minors' Bureau informed Johnson that recent labour legislation had failed to rectify the prewar practice in rural areas of indenturing daughters as collateral for a loan. Johnson promptly organised a visit to factories in the region to highlight the problem, which in at least one instance was

addressed immediately. 'Isn't it amazing what a casual visit can do?', one of her Japanese staff later remarked. Carmen Johnson, *Wave-Rings in the Water: My Years with the Women of Postwar Japan*, Charles River Press, 1996, pp. 97–8.

65. Ibid., p. 59. American female Occupationaires in Military Government included Rilma Buckman, Assistant Welfare Officer at Eighth Army MG Headquarters in Yokohama and Edna K. Callow, Public Welfare Officer for the Tokyo Military Government Team.

66. On the history of the 24th Infantry Regiment, see Ulysses Lee, *The Employment of Negro Troops* (The US Army in World War II), US Army Office of the Chief of Military History, US Government Printing Office, 1966, pp. 47, 366–7, 475, 479. Bill Stevens is quoted in Mary P. Motley, ed., *The Invisible Soldier: The Experience of Black Soldiers in World War II*, Wayne State University Press, 1975, p. 76.

67. Sherie Mershon and Steven Schlossman, *Foxholes and Color Lines: Desegregating the U.S. Armed Forces*, John Hopkins University Press, 1998, pp. 226–8 and Robert R. Smith, *MacArthur in Korea: The Naked Emperor*, Simon & Schuster, 1982, p. 228.

68. Gerald Astor, *The Right to Fight: A History of African Americans in the Military*, Presidio Press, 1998, pp. 346–9 and Smith (1982), ibid. See also the discussion in Koshiro (1999), pp. 55–6, 60–1.The Eichelberger quotation is from Paul Chwialkowski, *In Caesar's Shadow: The Life of General Robert Eichelberger*, Greenwood Press, 1993, p. 152.

69. On Japanese images of African Americans, see John R. Russell, *Nihonjin no kokujin-kan: mondai wa 'Chibikuro Sanbo' dake de wa nai* (Concerning Japanese Images of Black People: 'Little Black Sambo' is not the Only Problem), Shin Hyōron, 1991. These points also are made by Michael S. Molasky in his study of African Americans in the Japanese literary imagination during the Occupation (*The American Occupation of Japan and Okinawa: Literature and Memory*, Routledge, 1999, chapter 3). The quotation is from Molasky, p. 74.

70. Concerning black culture and Japanese jazz, see Joe B. Moore, 'Studying Jazz in Postwar Japan: Where to Begin?', in *Japanese Studies*, vol. 18, no. 3, 1998 and 'Reflections on Jazz in Postwar Japan: Blues People and Company Men', unpublished manuscript, 1998. During the war, black American leaders had been quick to note the racist thinking that underlay much anti-Japanese propaganda. They sought a 'double victory': the defeat of fascism abroad would bring an end to apartheid at home. Horace Cayton, a noted black sociologist, later remarked that, while the Japanese were imperialists, they had 'more right to the Orient than white imperialists', explaining that 'the Japanese at least tried to break the colour line'. Many black Americans, states a historian, were not pro-Japanese, but neither were they anti-Japanese and, at the war's end, 'many African Americans emerged ready and eager for reconciliation' with the former enemy. On Cayton's views, see Horace R. Cayton, *Long Old Road*, University of Washington Press, 1970, pp. 271–6. On black attitudes towards the Japanese,

refer to Reginald Kearney, *African American Views of the Japanese: Solidarity or Sedition?*, State University of New York Press, 1998. The quotation is from Kearny, p. 127. See also the landmark study by Ronald T. Takaki, *Double Victory: A Multicultural History of America in World War II*, Little, Brown, 2000, pp. 22–57.

71. During the war, the air, land and sea forces of Great Britain, Australia, New Zealand and India that would later form the BCOF fought the Japanese in India, Burma, Malaya, Borneo and elsewhere in South and Southeast Asia. Commonwealth troops in the Malaya Theatre Command under Lieutenant General Arthur Percival surrendered to General Yamashita Tomoyuki at Singapore in February 1942. Others fought with Commonwealth Forces in Southeast Asia under Admiral Lord Louis Mountbatten. These soldiers avenged Percival's humiliation by accepting the surrender of General Itagaki Seishirō, Commander of Japan's Seventh Route Army, in Singapore on 12 September 1945. Both surrenders are commemorated by wax effigies, the Dioramas, at the Singapore History Museum on Sentosa, a small island in Singapore Bay. The display dramatises the horror and ultimate banality of war.

72. On the question of Commonwealth participation, see Hayes (1982), pp. 714–15 and Buckley (1982), pp. 86–7, 102. A recent discussion of the BCOF is Takemae Eiji, 'Eirenpō Nihon senryōgun (BCOF) no seiritsu (1)' (The Formation of the British Commonwealth Force, Part 1), in *The Journal of Tokyo Keizai University*, no. 207, 1998, pp. 173–83. See also Chida Takeshi, *Eirenpō-gun no Nihon shinchū to tenkai* (The British Commonwealth Occupation Force in Japan: Its Deployment and History), Ochanomizu Shobō, 1997. On Australia's role, refer generally to James Wood, *Forgotten Force: The Australian Military Contribution to the Occupation of Japan*, Allen & Unwin, 1998.

73. Hamish Ion, 'Canada and the Occupation of Japan', in Ian H. Nish, ed., *The British Commonwealth and the Occupation of Japan*, International Centre for Economics and Related Disciplines, London School of Economics and Political Science, 1983, pp. 44–68. See also Takemae Eiji, 'Canadian Views on Occupation Policies and the Japanese Peace Treaty: Interview with Dr. Arthur K. Menzies', in *The Journal of Tokyo Keizai University*, no. 144, January 1986, pp. 331–2.

74. See Trotter (1990), pp. 7–23 and Laurie Brocklebank, *Jayforce: New Zealand and the Military Occupation of Japan, 1945–48*, Oxford University Press, 1997, pp. 1–15, 28.

75. See Peter Bates, *Japan and the British Commonwealth Occupation Force, 1946–52*, Brassey's (UK), 1993, p. 45–7 and Ian H. Nish, 'India and the Occupation of Japan', in Nish, ed. (1983), pp. 69–87.

76. Bates (1993), p. 68. The BCOF Army Component consisted of a mixed British-Indian division from the Fifth British Brigade, the 268th Indian Infantry Brigade and the Seventh Light Cavalry of the Indian Armoured Corps, and independent brigade groups from both Australia and New Zealand. The Air Component included Spitfire squadrons from the Royal Air Force and the Royal

Indian Air Force, Mustang squadrons from the Royal Australian Air Force and a Corsair squadron from the Royal New Zealand Air Force. The BCOF's naval contingent was made up of a squadron from the British Pacific Fleet, including warships from the Royal Navy, the Royal Australian Navy and the Royal Indian Navy. It has been suggested that the BCOF was deployed to the Chugoku region, which includes Hiroshima, because the United States wished to keep its troops out of the area devastated by the atomic bomb. See Sodei Rinjirō, *Were We the Enemy? American Survivors of Hiroshima*, Westview Press, 1998, p. 48.

77. Takemae Eiji, 'Ball's View on the Allied Occupation of Japan: Interview with W. MacMahon Ball', in *The Journal of Tokyo Keizai University*, no. 151 (June 1987), pp. 21–2.

78. Buckley (1982), p. 93.

79. A thriving BCOF economy sprang up based on sterling notes down to 3d, below which Australian copper coins were used. Food, basic commodities and other supplies were procured in Australia, and even American quartermasters turned to this source to provide perishable items for US soldiers, making the BCOF system a dollar-earner rather than a drain on the sterling bloc. See 'British Commonwealth Occupation Force', in *The Australian Encyclopedia*, Collins, 1984, pp. 130–4.

80. Bates (1993), pp. 134–5.

81. Ibid., pp. 118, 153–5. See also the assessment by Rajendra Singh, *Post-war Occupation Forces: Japan and South East Asia* (Official History of the Indian Armed Forces in the Second World War, 1939–45), Orient Longman (New Delhi), 1958, chapters 8 and 11.

82. Buckley (1982), pp. 102–3, Bates (1993), p. 223 and Brocklebank (1997), pp. 214–16.

83. Bates (1993), p. 227.

84. Takemae, 'Interview with Dr. Arthur R. Menzies' (1986), pp. 353–4 and Bates (1993), chapter 22.

85. For instance, Colonel Kermit R. Dyke briefly doubled as chief of AFPAC's Information and Education Section and SCAP's Civil Information and Education Section. Until May 1946, Brigadier General Elliott R. Thorpe headed AFPAC's Counter-Intelligence Section and SCAP's Civil Intelligence Section. Major General Stuart B. Akin was in charge of AFPAC's Signal Section and SCAP's Civil Communications Section, and Major General William F. Marquat simultaneously served as chief of AFPAC's Anti-Aircraft Section and SCAP's Economic and Scientific Section.

86. On Bower's linguistic abilities, see Sidney F. Mashbir, *I Was an American Spy*, Vantage Press, 1953, p. 317. On Diller, see William J. Coughlin, *Conquered Press: The MacArthur Era in Japanese Journalism*, Pacific Books (Palo Alto), 1952, pp. 114–18. The description of Baker is by Cohen (1989), p. 247. At MacArthur's personal request, Baker was made Deputy Chief of the ESS Foreign Investment Board, where his high-handed tactics earned him further

notoriety. He later served as adviser to Marquat. On Baker's checkered career, see Williams (1979), pp. 94–7.

87. See Sidney L. Huff with Joe Alex Morris, *My Fifteen Years with General MacArthur*, Paperback Library (New York), 1964.

88. On Fellers' and Bunker's political views, see Cohen (1987), p. 73 and Williams (1979), pp. 88–9.

89. *HNMA*, vol. 2: Administration of the Occupation, pp. 25–34.

90. See Laura E. Hein, *Fueling Growth: The Energy Revolution and Economic Policy in Postwar Japan*, Council on East Asian Studies, Harvard University, 1990, pp. 75–8.

91. For example, in early 1946, following the creation of the International Prosecution Section, Legal Section was raised from the special to the general staff level and placed directly under the SCAP Chief of Staff. Diplomatic Section also was added to the General Staff at this time. By 1946, there were five General Military Staff Sections in addition to the G-1 through G-4 segments and 12 civil staff sections, an organisational structure that would not change appreciably until 1951 when SCAP began to phase out the Occupation. A major exception occurred in January 1950, when Civil Affairs Section (CAS) was created to oversee the Civil Affairs Teams. There were minor changes, as well. In 1946, the Office of the Civil Property Custodian (CPC), Adjutant General's Section (AG), General Accounting Section (GAS) and the Civil Transportation Section (CTS) were created as special staff groups. The General Procurement Agency was transferred to staff section level, and the Civil Intelligence Section was temporarily disbanded (in Japan, this was widely believed to have happened in 1950). The Public Relations Office (sometimes referred to as the Public Relations Section) also was established in 1946 as SCAP's official spokes organ. In 1947, a new group, the Reparations Section (RS), was added, bringing the number of special staff sections to 13, where it stood through 1948. In 1949, with the completion of the war crimes trials, the International Prosecution Section was abolished, and Legal Section returned to special staff level. That year, the Office of the Comptroller was added to the General Staff on orders from the Department of the Army to help implement the Dodge Plan, and the General Accounting Section and the Reparations Section, their work done, were dissolved. In 1950, Legal Section was bumped to general staff level again, and the Statistical and Reports Section was rechristened the Civil and Historical Section. In 1951, as the Occupation wound down, staff groups were pared to a minimum. Economic and Scientific Section, which absorbed many of the personnel and functions of discontinued groups, alone retained something of its former size and importance. At the Military General Staff level, only the G-1 through G-4 Sections remained until the end.

92. *FRUS*, vol. 6, 1948, p. 673.

93. See Toshio Nishi, *Unconditional Democracy: Education and Politics in Occupied Japan, 1945–1952*, Hoover Institution Press (Stanford University), 1982, p. 207.

94. Courtney Whitney, *MacArthur: His Rendezvous with History*, Knopf, 1956, p. 300. Faubion Bowers, ''The Late General MacArthur, Warts and All', in *Esquire*, January 1967, p. 95.

95. A caustic but perceptive account of the Occupation's public relations machine, its handling of important visitors and efforts to mould American opinion is Robert B. Textor, *Failure in Japan: With Keystones for a Positive Policy*, Greenwood Press, 1972 (John Day, 1951), chapter 2.

96. See Ray A. Moore, 'Discussion', in Thomas W. Burkman, ed., *The Occupation of Japan: Arts and Culture*, General Douglas MacArthur Foundation, 1988, pp. 38–9. On the Supreme Court Mission, refer to Alfred C. Oppler, *Legal Reform in Occupied Japan: A Participant Looks Back*, Princeton University Press, 1976, pp. 255–75.

Chapter 4   Inside the Special Staff Sections

1. This was Colonel Crawford F. Sams of Public Health and Welfare. See Crawford F. Sams, *'Medic': The Mission of an American Military Doctor in Occupied Japan and War-torn Korea*, edited by Zabelle Zakarian, M. E. Sharpe, 1998, p. 36.

2. Takemae Eiji, 'The Kades Memoir on the Occupation of Japan', in *The Journal of Tokyo Keizai University*, no. 148, November 1986, p. 263.

3. Susan Deborah Chira, *Cautious Revolutionaries: Occupation Planners and Japan's Post-War Land Reform*, Tokyo: Agricultural Policy Research Center, 1982, chapter 3.

4. Unless otherwise indicated, data on GHQ's staff sections and personnel are from the following sources: GHQ/SCAP, *History of the Nonmilitary Activities of the Occupation of Japan, 1945–1951*, Tokyo, 1951; GHQ/SCAP and Far East Command, *Organization and Activities of GHQ*, Tokyo, 1950; GHQ/SCAP and Far East Command, *Selected Data on the Occupation of Japan*, 1950; and GHQ/SCAP, *Tokyo Telephone Directory (1945–1951)*, Tokyo. The multi-volume *History of the Nonmilitary Activities of the Occupation of Japan, 1945–1951* (below given as HNMA) is unreliable in tracing the evolution of staff sections and their administrative divisions, staff responsibilities and personnel assignments. The information presented here has been cross-referenced with the more accurate Tokyo telephone directories published annually during the Occupation.

5. George F. Kennan, *Memoirs, 1925–1950*, Atlantic Monthly (Little, Brown), 1967, p. 382. Elliott R. Thorpe, *East Wind, Rain*, Gambit Inc. (Boston), 1969, p. 195.

6. Max W. Bishop, 'Memorandum of Conversation: Reorganization of the Office of the United States Political Advisor' (4 April 1946), in US Department of State, *Foreign Relations of the United States* (below, given as *FRUS*), US Government Printing Office, vol. 8, 1946, pp. 188–90.

7. See William J. Sebald with Russell Brines, *With MacArthur in Japan: A Personal History of the Occupation*, W. W. Norton, 1965.

8. Charles N. Spinks, 'Indoctrination and Re-Education of Japan's Youth', in *Pacific Affairs*, March 1944 and *The Brocade Banner*, US Army Forces Pacific (Tokyo), 1946.

9. See Fearey's memoir, *The Occupation of Japan: Second Phase, 1948–50*, Macmillan, 1950.

10. Norman's works include *Japan's Emergence as a Modern State*, Institute of Pacific Relations, 1940; *Soldier and Peasant in Japan: The Origins of Conscription*, Institute of Pacific Relations, 1943; and *The Feudal Background of Japanese Politics*, Institute of Pacific Relations, 1945. Government Section's Deputy Chief Kades reportedly derived most of his knowledge of Japan from Norman's writings. So great was Norman's intellectual authority that, from 1947 to 1949, the diplomat–scholar was asked to tutor Prince Mikasa, Hirohito's younger brother, in Japanese history. See John Dower's essay, 'E. H. Norman, Japan and the Uses of History', in John W. Dower, ed., *Origins of the Modern Japanese State: Selected Writings of E. H. Norman*, Pantheon Books, 1975, pp. 3–101. Norman and Emmerson were associated with two other eminent Asia experts, Owen Lattimore and Andrew Roth, whose ideas also helped mould Allied attitudes toward Japan. Lattimore's *Solution in Asia* and Roth's *Dilemma in Japan*, both published by Little, Brown in 1945, were required reading for serious Occupationaires.

11. Richard B. Finn, *Winners in Peace: MacArthur, Yoshida and Postwar Japan*, University of California Press, 1992.

12. Justin Williams Sr, *Japan's Political Revolution Under MacArthur: A Participant's Account*, University of Tokyo Press, 1979, p. 7.

13. Ibid., pp. 56–67.

14. Quotations are from Hans H. Baerwald, 'Reminiscence of a Misspent Youth: Tokyo 1946–1949', in Ian H. Nish, ed., *Aspects of the Allied Occupation of Japan*, London School of Economics and Political Science, 1985, p. 31. On Whitney's anti-semitism, see Robert R. Smith, *MacArthur in Korea: The Naked Emperor*, Simon & Schuster, 1982, p. 228.

15. Whitney later compiled a lengthy panegyric to his boss, *MacArthur: His Rendezvous with History*, Knopf, 1956. His uncritical adulation of MacArthur and absolute intolerance of any criticism of the Supreme Commander prompted some historians to dismiss him and the Bataan clique as sycophants. See Richard Storry, *A History of Modern Japan*, Penguin, 1982, p. 240.

16. According to Williams, without Kades's leadership qualities, keen mind, idealism and imagination, Whitney might never have considered drafting a model constitution for Japan. (1979), p. 36.

17. Before the war, Tsukahara had worked as a Longshoreman and been active in the labour movement, eventually joining the Communist Party. In 1942, he was interned at the Tule Lake Relocation Center, a punishment camp in California for 'disloyal elements', where he helped to defuse a major disturbance before volunteering for military service. See Sodei Rinjirō, 'Nihon senryō to Nikkei-nisei' (Japanese-Americans and the Occupation of Japan), in Hata Ikuhiko and

Sodei Rinjirō, eds., *Nihon senryō hishi* (A Secret History of the Occupation of Japan), vol. 2, Asahi Shinbunsha, 1979, pp. 284–7.

18. Williams (1979), pp. 188–9. William's personal account of GS provides an intimate glimpse of the personalities and day-to-day workings of MacArthur's headquarters.

19. Ibid., pp. 54–5, 69–70 and Alfred C. Oppler, *Legal Reform in Occupied Japan: A Participant Looks Back*, Princeton University Press, 1976, pp. 29–30.

20. Hoover, after serving for over twenty years in business corporations and public commissions as a management and personnel expert, became a consultant in 1946 to the US Civil Service Commission and then President of the Civil Service Assembly of the United States and Canada. He came to Japan in 1947 at the invitation of Government Section to study ways of modernising the Japanese bureaucracy.

21. Maki had studied in Japan from 1937–39 and during the war worked for the Foreign Broadcast Intelligence Service and the OWI. He drew on his Occupation experience to write *Government and Politics in Japan: The Road to Democracy*, Frederick A. Praeger, 1962 and *Court and Constitution in Japan: Selected Supreme Court Decisions, 1948–1960*, University of Washington Press, 1964.

22. Quotations are from Oppler (1976), p. 31. The Baerwald study is *The Purge of Japanese Leaders Under the Occupation*, University of California Press, 1959.

23. Koseki Shōichi, *The Birth of Japan's Postwar Constitution*, Westview Press, 1997, p. 86 and Williams (1979), p. 58.

24. Harry E. Wildes, *Social Currents in Japan: With Special Reference to the Press*, University of Chicago Press, 1927. Wildes later wrote *Typhoon in Tokyo: The Occupation and its Aftermath*, Macmillan, 1954.

25. Beate Sirota Gordon, *The Only Woman in the Room: A Memoir*, Kodansha, 1997.

26. Eleanor M. Hadley, *Anti-Trust in Japan*, Princeton University Press, 1970.

27. Bisson's works included *Basic Treaty Issues in Manchuria Between Japan and China*, Foreign Policy Association, 1931; *Japan in China*, Macmillan, 1938; and *Japan's War Economy*, Institute of Pacific Relations, 1945. He subsequently wrote *Prospects for Democracy in Japan*, Macmillan, 1949. Bisson's representative postwar work, *Zaibatsu Dissolution in Japan* (University of California Press, 1954), complements Hadley's account of the anti-trust programme.

28. Oppler's 1976 memoir, cited above, provides important insights into the process of legal reform.

29. Meirion and Susie Harries, *Sheathing the Sword: The Demilitarisation of Japan*, Heinemann, 1987, p. 222. The quotation on Mussolini is from Charles A. Willoughby, *Maneuver in War*, Military Service Publishing Company (Harrisburg), 1939, p. 235.

30. Takemae (1986), pp. 300–1.

31. Charles A. Willoughby and John Chamberlain, *MacArthur, 1941–1951: Victory in the Pacific*, McGraw-Hill, 1954, p. 323; Takemae (1986), pp. 304, 313. The Hussey quotation is from the Harrieses (1987), p. 224.

32. On the early history of Counter-Intelligence, see Thorpe (1969), pp. 91–5.
33. Ibid., p. 248–9.
34. Robert B. Textor, *Failure in Japan: With Keystones for a Positive Policy*, Greenwood Press, 1972 (John Day, 1951), p. 190.
35. On the G-2 censorship order, see Williams (1979), p. 191. The only published account of the Canon Unit, by one of its operatives, should be consulted with caution. See Yon Cheong, *Kyanon kikan kara no shōgen* (Inside the Canon Unit), Banchō Shobō, 1973, pp. 70–3, 89–127.
36. Fifteen of these volumes have been published in a reprint edition by the US Army Office of the Chief of Military History: *War in Asia and the Pacific, 1937–1949*, Garland, 1980. One of Arisue's staff, Colonel Hattori Takushirō, alone produced an eight-volume history of the war between 1953 and 1956 based in part on military documents he had acquired surreptitiously and secreted from his employer. These were later abridged as *Dai Toa Sensō zenshi* (A History of the Greater East Asian War), Hara Shobō, 1965.
    Clarke Kawakami was the son of one of the founders of the Japan Socialist Party, Kawakami Kiyoshi. The elder Kawakami left politics and emigrated to the United States, where he studied journalism at the University of Minnesota and married an Irish-American. Clarke graduated from Harvard and worked as a journalist for the official Japanese news agency Dōmei. When war broke out, he joined the Office of War Information. Attached to GHQ at war's end, Kawakami became deputy to the ATIS chief before being recruited by G-2's Historical Section. After the Occupation, he worked for the United States Information Agency. Sodei (1979), op. cit., pp. 254. 278–9. On MacArthur's war-history project, see Jerome Forrest and Clarke H. Kawakami, 'General MacArthur and His Vanishing War History', in *Reporter*, 14 October 1952, pp. 20–5.
37. See Mark Gayn, *Japan Diary*, Charles P. Tuttle, 1981 (William Sloane, 1948), pp. 445–6 and Harry E. Wildes, *Typhoon in Tokyo: The Occupation and its Aftermath*, Macmillan, 1954, pp. 52–3, 307–9.
38. Aiso retired from the Army as a Lieutenant Colonel and in 1953 became America's first Nisei judge. In 1968, he was appointed to the California Court of Appeals. See the interview with Aiso in Takemae Eiji, *Nihon senryō: GHQ kōkan no shōgen* (The Occupation as Told by Senior GHQ Officials), Chūō Kōronsha, 1988, chapter 7. On Aiso's career, see also Tad Ichinokuchi, ed., *John Aiso and the M.I.S. – Japanese-American Soldiers in the Military Intelligence Service, World War II*, MIS Club of Southern California, 1988, pp. 4–35.
39. GHQ/SCAP, *A Brief History of G-II Section*, Tokyo, 1948.
40. The Willoughby quotation is from Willoughby and Chamberlain (1954). p. 322. CIC activities are detailed in US Army Intelligence Center, *History of the Counter-Intelligence Corps*, Fort Halabird, Maryland, 1960 (RG 319, CIC, National Archives Records Administration, Washington DC).
41. Williams (1979), pp. 193–5.

42. Harries (1987), pp. 109, 115.
43. See Richard M. Minear, Victor's *Justice: The Tokyo War Crimes Trial*, Tuttle, 1972, chapter 2.
44. Harries (1987), pp. 106, 115.
45. Ibid., pp. 147–9. On Justice Northcroft's views, see Ann Trotter, *New Zealand and Japan, 1945–1952: The Occupation and the Peace Treaty*, Athlone Press, 1990, pp. 82–3. Prominent defence lawyers included J. G. Brannon, counsel for Nagano Osami; Owen Cunningham, counsel for Ōshima Hiroshi; J. N. Freeman, counsel for Satō Kenryō; G. A. Furness, counsel for Shigemitsu Mamoru; D. F. Smith and G. Yamaoka, counsels for Hirota Kōki; W. Logan, counsel for Kido Kōichi; and G. F. Blewett, counsel for Tōjō Hideki. The defence was assisted by a Japanese legal team led by Kiyose Ichirō, famous for his prewar legal battles on behalf of extreme rightists. After the Occupation, he would serve as minister of education (November 1955 to December 1956).
46. See Minear (1972), chapter 4.
47. Pal graduated from Presidency University and taught mathematics at the University of Anandmohan before completing a law degree at the University of Calcutta. He subsequently was professor of law, vice president of the university and justice of the Calcutta Supreme Court.
48. Oppler (1976), pp. 69, 220–1. After the Occupation, Steiner went on to an academic career. His representative work is *Local Government in Japan*, Stanford University Press, 1965.
49. Before the war, Kramer had been chair of the Beldin Hemingway Company, a member of the Board of Directors of Gimbel Brothers and a director of Interstate Department Stores. When war broke out, he entered the US Army, serving as head of the Joint Supply Survey Board for the South Pacific and assistant to the US Deputy Chief of Staff in Australia.
50. Sebald (1965), p. 131.
51. Theodore Cohen, *Remaking Japan: The American Occupation as New Deal*, The Free Press, 1987, pp. 86–7.
52. Finance Division chiefs were C. F. Thomas, Walter K. Lecount (a banker who succeeded Thomas) and J. R. Allison (who succeeded Lecount in 1950 after handling legal affairs and public security for the 32nd MG Company). Head of the Finance Division's Fiscal Policy Branch was Eugene M. Reed, a specialist in local government and former adviser to the National Urban League and budget assessor for the Federal Government. A Navy Commander during the war years, Reed went through the Military Government School at Princeton, Japanese language school at the Stanford CATS and the Civil Affairs Staging Area in Monterey. The Money and Banking Branch Chief was Orville J. McDiarmid, who later assisted the Young Mission. Public Finance Branch was led by Henry Shavell, a Washington economist responsible for assessing property taxes and drawing up a schedule for indemnity payments. Shavell aided the Shoup Mission, which came to Japan in 1949 to revamp the tax system.

The Section's Internal Revenue Division Chief was Lon H. Moss, a personal friend of MacArthur from Manila days. Moss had worked in the Internal Revenue Division, US Army Military Government in Korea, before joining GHQ. In Tokyo, he was involved largely with tax reform. He also developed close contacts with Ikeda Hayato, the future Japanese finance minister (1949–52). The heads of the Budget Management Branch were Arthur M. McGlauflin and Edmond C. Hutchinson, who helped draft the Dodge Plan. Price Control and Rationing Division was headed by H. F. Alber, who entered GHQ as a civilian after service in the Philippines and with the Okayama Prefectural Military Government Team.

53. Cohen (1989), pp. 356–66.
54. On Cohen's reassignment, see Takemae Eiji, *Sengo rōdō-kaikaku: GHQ rōdō seisaku-shi* (The Postwar Labour Reforms: A History of GHQ's Labour Reform Policy), Tōkyō Daigaku Shuppankai, 1982, p. 184. The 'pathological fear' quotation is from Gayn (1981), p. 331. On Cohen's anti-Communism, see Takemae, 'The U.S. Occupation Policies for Japan: Interview with Mr. Theodore Cohen', in *Tokyo Metropolitan University Journal of Law and Politics*, Vol. 14, no. 1, 1973, p. 43.
55. Howard B. Schonberger, *Aftermath of War: Americans and the Remaking of Japan, 1945–1952*, Kent State University Press, 1989, pp. 119–20.
56. Takemae Eiji, 'Senryō shūketsuki no rōdō-seisaku: GHQ saigo no rōdō kachō Ēmisu ni kiku' (Labour Policy Towards the End of the Occupation: An Interview with Robert Amis, GHQ's Last Labour Division Chief), in *Tōkyō Keidai Gakkaishi*, nos. 116–17, 1980, pp. 196–9.
57. Key staff members included Paul Stanchfield, who helped Cohen draft the 1946 Labour Relations Adjustment Law; Dr Edgar C. McVoy and Sterling D. Collette, who assisted Hepler improve employment security; G. G. Becker, who collaborated on the 1947 Labour Standards Law; Leon Becker (in charge of the labour purge); H. G. Ihrig (public works); Alice W. Schurcliff (vocational training); and S. Balicka (labour statistics).
58. See the interviews with Stander and Smith in Takemae Eiji, *GHQ rōdōka no hito to seisaku* (Personnel and Policies of GHQ's Labour Division), Emutei Shuppan, 1991, pp. 205–8.
59. The Science Council was elected by some 44,000 certified academics and researchers in fields ranging from the humanities, law and economics to the theoretical and applied sciences. Its job was to promote the peaceful development of science and technology and advise the government on basic science policy. The Scientific and Technical Commission, staffed by an equal number of bureaucrats and non-government scientists, was created inside the Prime Minister's Office to act on Science Council recommendations and coordinate the implementation of science policy among the various ministries. Both bodies were established by law in the latter half of 1948 and became active in January 1949. See Bowen C. Dees, *The Allied Occupation and Japan's Economic Miracle:*

Building the Foundations of Japanese Science and Technology, 1945–1952, Curzon Press, 1997, chapter 8.

60. Dees, ibid., pp. 31–9, 49–60.

61. Ibid., pp. 60–2 and chapter 6.

62. Marlene J. Mayo, 'American Wartime Planning for Occupied Japan: The Role of the Experts', in Robert Wolfe, ed., *Americans as Proconsuls: United States Military Government in Germany and Japan, 1944–1952*, Southern Illinois University Press, 1984, p. 83.

63. The 1946 divisions were Administration, Education, Religions, Information (combining Press and Publications, Radio, Motion Picture and Theatrical, Libraries, Central Motion Picture Exchange, and Policy and Planning), Arts and Monuments, and Analysis and Research. In late 1947, Arts and Monuments was merged with Religions to form the Religions and Cultural Resources Division. In late 1948, Analysis and Research was rechristened Public Opinion and Sociological Research Division.

64. The Education and Information Divisions each were subdivided into six branches. In the Education Division, these were: School Education (elementary and secondary education, administration and finance), Higher Education (teacher training, universities, women's education and two-year colleges), Adult Education (youth organisations, vocational education, adult education and libraries), Specialist Education (language reform, curriculum and textbooks and the promotion of the natural and social sciences), Education Research, and Liaison and Investigation. The Information Division consisted of Press and Publications, Radio, Motion Pictures and Theatre, the Information Centre, Policy and Programmes, and the Central Motion Pictures Exchange.

65. William J. Coughlin, *Conquered Press: The MacArthur Era in Japanese Journalism*, Pacific Books (Palo Alto), 1952, p. 81.

66. Donald R. Nugent and Reginald Bell, eds, *The Pacific Area and its Problems: A Study Guide*, Institute for Pacific Relations, 1936.

67. See William M. Baltz, 'The Role of American Educators in the Decentralization and Reorganization of Education in Postwar Japan (1945–1952)', PhD dissertation, State University of New York (Buffalo), 1965, pp. 40–1 and Mayo (1982), p. 91. Hall recounted his experiences in *Education for a New Japan*, Yale University Press, 1949. Wunderlich completed a PhD in education at Stanford in 1952. His dissertation, 'The Japanese Textbook Problem and Solution', was based on his experience in CI&E.

68. Takemae Eiji, 'Kyōiku kaikaku no omoide: GHQ Kyōiku-kachō M. T. Oa hakase ni kiku' (Reminiscences of the Education Reforms: An Interview with Dr Mark T. Orr, GHQ's Education Division Chief), in *Tōkyō Keidai Gakkaishi*, no. 115, March 1980, p. 132. After the Occupation, Orr completed his doctorate, writing a dissertation on the CI&E reforms: 'Education Reform in Occupied Japan', Department of Political Science, University of North Carolina, 1954.

69. Marlene J. Mayo, 'Civil Censorship and Media Control in Early Occupied Japan: From Minimum to Stringent Surveillance', in Wolfe, ed. (1984), pp. 285, 301–4.

70. Kyoko Hirano, *Mr. Smith Goes to Tokyo: Japanese Cinema Under the American Occupation, 1945–1952*, Smithsonian Institution Press, 1992, pp. 41, 102–3, 148–9.

71. Marlene J. Mayo, 'The War of Words Continues: American Radio Guidance in Occupied Japan', in Thomas W. Burkman, ed., *The Occupation of Japan: Arts and Culture*, General Douglas MacArthur Foundation, 1988, pp. 55–6.

72. See Kurt Steiner, 'The Occupation and the Reform of the Japanese Civil Code', in Robert E. Ward and Sakamoto Yoshikazu, eds, *Democratizing Japan: The Allied Occupation*, University of Hawai'i Press, 1987, pp. 196, 200 and Susan J. Pharr, 'The Politics of Women's Rights' (1987), in Ward and Sakamoto, ibid., pp. 239–40, 251.

73. Gary H. Tsuchimochi, *Education Reform in Postwar Japan: The 1946 US Education Mission*, University of Tokyo Press, 1993, pp. 76–7.

74. Toshio Nishi, *Unconditional Democracy: Education and Politics in Occupied Japan, 1945–1952*, Hoover Institution Press (Stanford University), 1982, pp. 154–5.

75. Baltz (1965), pp. 57–9, 60–1, 63. Other female educators, some of them later replacements, included Edna Ambrose from Harvard University; Rebecca Barnhart, an education administrator; Luana Bowles from the US Office of Education who had lived in prewar Japan; Major Hazel B. Bundy, a guidance expert in charge of secondary school education; Edith Divelbiss, an education researcher; Jane Fairweather, a library specialist; Helen Hosp from the American Association of University Women; Major Stella Ware; and Dr Maude Williamson of Colorado State College. See Joseph C. Trainor, *Educational Reform in Occupied Japan: Trainor's Memoir*, Meisei University Press, 1983, pp. 423–45. The quotation is from Trainor, p. 424.

76. See Sherman E. Lee, 'My Work in Japan: Arts and Monuments, 1946–1948', in Mark Sandler, ed., *The Confusion Era: Art and Culture of Japan During the Allied Occupation, 1945–1952*, Smithsonian Institution, 1997, pp. 91–102.

77. Nishi Kyōko, *Senryōka no Nihon fujin seisaku* (Policies Affecting Japanese Women Under the Occupation), Domesu Shuppan, 1985, pp. 81–9.

78. After the Occupation, Passin pursued an academic career at Columbia University. His best known works are *Society and Education in Japan*, Columbia University Press, 1965 and *The Legacy of the Occupation – Japan*, Occasional Papers of the East Institute, Columbia University, 1968.

79. Colonel Edward H. Farr, Deputy Chief of Division until June 1946, graduated from the University of California and worked as a high school principal and city school-district superintendent. Major Roy W. Arrowood had been chairman of the mathematics department at a Texas high school before joining Education Division as Liaison Officer. Lieutenant Colonel Bernard A. Schmitz,

an Education Branch teaching specialist, had been a school instructor. Captain John W. Barnard, who held a PhD in education, assisted the Education Branch in drawing up teacher-training plans and preparing new textbooks. Captain Harry E. Griffith had taken a leave of absence from a teaching job at a California junior college to help CI&E reform Japan's teacher-training programmes at the normal school level.

Even lower-ranking officers were well-qualified for the work they did. Second Lieutenant Scott George (PhD in English, Vanderbilt University) was the Education Division's Vocational Training Officer and worked on simplifying the Japanese language. Second Lieutenant James B. Gibson, an Education Division liaison officer, was a one-time instructor of history and government at a California junior college. John W. Norviel, the Division's Recreation Officer, had a Master's degree in education from the University of Southern California.

80. William P. Woodard, *The Allied Occupation of Japan, 1945–1952, and Japanese Religions*, E. J. Brill, 1972.

81. Eells recounts his experiences in *Communism in Asia, Africa and the Far Pacific*, American Council on Education, 1954.

82. Jacob Van Staaveren, *An American in Japan, 1945–1948: A Civilian View of the Occupation*, University of Washington Press, 1994, pp. 156, 175.

83. Lawrence J. Hewes, *Japan: Land and Men*, Iowa State College Press, 1955.

84. *HNMA*, vol. 2: Administration of the Occupation, p. 80. Sams (1998), p. 33.

85. On Sams's contribution, see Takemae Eiji's comments in his translation of Sams's memoir, *C. F. Samsu, DDT kakumei: senryō-ki no iryō fukushi seisaku o kaisō suru* (C. F. Sams, The DDT Revolution: Looking Back at the Reform of Medicine and Social Welfare During the Occupation), Iwanami Shoten, 1986, pp. 419–29. See also the introduction and chronology by Zebelle Zakarian in Sams (1998), pp. ix–xxi.

86. Other women in the Section included Florence Brugger, Social Work Training Supervisor; Agnes O'Donnell, Assistant Nutrition Consultant; and Dorothy Toom, Medical-Surgical Nursing Consultant.

87. Sams, ibid., chapter 30.

88. Public Health and Welfare Division, Medical Section, *Public Health and Welfare in Japan: Final Summary, 1951–52*, GHQ/SCAP, Tokyo, 1952, pp. 1–2. On Sams's resignation and the post-Occupation assignment of technical advisers to the US Embassy, see Sams (1998), pp. 255, 260.

89. Economics Division monitored directives on industry, natural resources, labour and commerce. Legal and Government Division oversaw the courts, political parties, government bodies and local officials. Social Affairs Division supervised the implementation of GHQ information, education, and public health and welfare directives.

90. In the Public Information Section, military information was handled by the Information and Education Branch (domestic news) and the Public

Information Branch (foreign news), both of which also belonged to the Far East Command's Information Division.

91. The Hannah Memorandum recommended the establishment of a committee of civilian experts to oversee NHK's reorganisation, the formation of a working committee to assist the chair in carrying out his or her duties, as well as specific proposals for choosing the committee chair, establishing a broadcasting code of ethics and allocating radio frequencies. The Feissner Memorandum argued that broadcasting should be unregulated and unbiased, serve the public and meet certain technical standards for air waves and frequencies based on the Broadcasting Law, the Wireless Telegraphy Law and the statute creating the Radio Regulatory Committee. All of these measures were implemented with CCS assistance.

92. Division heads were Lieutenant Colonel J. E. Gonseth (Industry Division), Major W. C. Boese (Radio Division), Major B. E. Small (Domestic Radio Division), M. G. Cooke (International Radio Division) and Lieutenant Colonel W. L. Wardell (Telephone and Telegraph Division).

93. CTS carried out this duty with the close cooperation of Eighth Army Rail Transportation Offices (RTOs), which had been set up at major stations to handle special rail traffic. RTOs were responsible, in particular, for the running of troop trains, which were identified by signs reading 'US Army' or 'Allied Forces' affixed to the sides of the cars. The trains were under the jurisdiction of Major J. L. Rankin's Third Transportation Military Railway Unit located in the Nihon Yusen Building in Tokyo.

94. Serving as Executive Officer and, from 1949, as Railway Transportation Division Chief was Lieutenant Colonel D. R. Changnon, a University of Illinois engineering graduate who had studied accounting at Northwestern University and worked for the Illinois Central Railroad. During World War I, Changnon fought as a Second Lieutenant with US Army Air Forces in Europe. During World War II, he was assigned to GHQ/AFPAC in Manila as Transportation Planning Officer. Had the Allies invaded Japan, Changnon would have secured and operated the Japanese railway system.

95. Wildes (1954), pp. 309–16.

96. Leading members were drawn from Government Section (Major W. E. Monagan, Lieutenant Colonel Jack P. Napier), G-2 (R. P. Wheeler, Colonel E. C. Ewert), Civil Information and Education Section (Lieutenant Colonel Donald R. Nugent), Economic and Scientific Section (H. J. Irig), LS (S. A. Reese), Diplomatic Section (Dr Charles N. Spinks), Public Information Office (Colonel G. P. Welch), Public Health and Welfare (Colonel C. S. Mollohan), the Provost Marshal (Major C. F. Vail), the Psychological Warfare Unit (Major H. H. Deering) and a legal adviser (Major C. A. Nye). GHQ/SCAP, Government Section, 'Counter-Measures Against the Subversive Potential in Japan – 1946 to 1951 Inclusive' (RG 331, Box 8497, Washington National Records Center, Archives II, College Park, Maryland).

Chapter 5   The Genesis of Reform
 1. See Takemae Eiji, ed., *Beikoku Riku-Kaigun: gunsei-minji manyuaru* (The United States Army and Navy Manual of Military Government and Civil Affairs), Misuzu Shobō, 1998. Takemae's translation includes the original English and a commentary.
 2. Refer generally to Marlene J. Mayo, 'American Wartime Planning for Occupied Japan: The Role of the Experts', in Robert Wolfe, ed. *Americans as Proconsuls: United States Military Government in Germany and Japan, 1944–1952*, Southern Illinois University Press, 1984, pp. 3–51. On Hornbeck's reputation, see p. 11. The Pence quotation is from p. 23.
 3. Ibid., p. 18.
 4. Ibid., p. 32.
 5. *Suye Mura, A Japanese Village*, University of Chicago Press, 1939.
 6. On the organisation of early planning for Japan, see Hugh Borton, *American Presurrender Planning for Postwar Japan*, Occasional Papers of the East Asian Institute, Columbia University, 1967.
 7. Borton was known for *Japan Since 1931: Its Political and Social Development*, Institute of Pacific Relations, 1940, and 'Peasant Uprisings in Japan of the Tokugawa Period', in *Transactions, Asiatic Society of Japan*, 1938 (reprinted in book form by Paragon in 1968).
 8. Mayo (1984), pp. 20–1.
 9. Ibid.
10. Arnold G. Fisch Jr, *Military Government in the Ryukyu Islands, 1945–1950*, US Army Center for Military History, US Government Printing Office, 1988, pp. 14–15.
11. See Ralph J. D. Braibanti, 'The Occupation of Japan: A Study in Organisation and Administration', PhD dissertation, Syracuse University, 1949, chapter 2.
12. Takemae Eiji, 'Kyōiku kaikaku no omoide: GHQ Kyōiku-kachō M. T. Oa hakase ni kiku' (Reminiscences of the Education Reforms: An Interview with Dr Mark T. Orr, GHQ's Education Division Chief), in *Tōkyō Keidai Gakkaishi*, no. 115, March 1980, pp. 133–4.
13. Takemae Eiji, 'C. G. Tilton and the Occupation of Japan', in *The Journal of Tokyo Keizai University*, no. 146, 1986, pp. 550–2.
14. Justin Williams Sr, *Japan's Political Revolution Under MacArthur: A Participant's Account*, Tokyo, University of Tokyo Press, 1979, p. 2 and Braibanti (1949), p. 71.
15. A list of published Handbooks and Guides is found in Iokibe Makoto, ed., *The Occupation of Japan: US Planning Documents, 1942–1945*, Congressional Information Service and Maruzen Publishing Co., 1987, pp. 18–21.
16. See the discussion in Joe B. Moore, *Japanese Workers and the Struggle for Power, 1945–1947*, University of Wisconsin Press, 1983, pp. 63–5.
17. See Theodore Cohen, *Remaking Japan: the American Occupation as New Deal*, the Free Press, 1987, pp. 37–42.

18. Mayo (1984), pp. 34–5.
19. Cited in John H. Backer, 'From the Morgenthau Plan to the Marshall Plan', in Robert Wolfe, ed. (1984), p. 155.
20. See Borton (1967), pp. 19–20.
21. On the Morgenthau Plan and its impact on JCS-1380, refer to Cohen (1987), pp. 27–31.
22. Borton (1967), p. 21.
23. Cohen (1987), p. 42.
24. US Department of State, *Record of Hearings Before the Committee on Foreign Relations* (United States Senate, 78th Congress, Second Session, 12 and 13 December 1944), US Government Printing Office, Washington, 1944, pp. 18–19.
25. John K. Emmerson, *The Japanese Thread: A Life in the US Foreign Service*, Holt, Rinehart & Winston, 1978, p. 175.
26. US Department of State, *Foreign Relations of the United States* (below, given as *FRUS*), US Government Printing Office, vol. 6, 1945, pp. 545–7.
27. See Nakamura Masanori *The Japanese Monarchy: Ambassador Grew and the Making of the 'Symbol Emperor System', 1931–1991*, M. E. Sharpe, 1992, pp. 73–4.
28. The JCS memorandum is 'JCS 1388' (*FRUS: The Conference on Berlin – The Potsdam Conference*), 1945, vol. 1, pp. 903–10. Truman reviewed the memorandum at the conference of 18 June.
29. Concerning the opinion of the British General Staff, see Alperovitz (1995), p. 370. On the views of Truman's top military advisers, see Mayo (1984), p. 44. A recent discussion is Richard B. Frank, *Downfall: The End of the Imperial Japanese Empire*, Random House, 1999, pp. 217–21.
30. Grace P. Hayes, *The History of the Joint Chiefs of Staff in World War II: The War Against Japan*, Naval Institute Press (Annapolis), 1982, pp. 722–3. The principal author of the Proclamation was reported to be Colonel Charles Bonesteel of the Army's Strategy and Policy Group (Operations Division), which was headed by Brigadier General George A. Lincoln. See Marc S. Gallicchio, 'The Kuriles Controversy: US Diplomacy in the Soviet–Japan Border Dispute, 1941–1956', in *Pacific Historical Review*, vol. 60, no. 1, 1991, pp. 81–2, especially Note 34 on p. 82.
31. *FRUS: The Conference of Berlin (The Potsdam Conference)* vol. 1, 1945, pp. 889–94.
32. The MacLeish quotation is from *FRUS*, ibid. p. 895. Dean Acheson, *Present at the Creation: My Years in the State Department*, New American Library, 1970 (W. W. Norton, 1969), p. 162.
33. This process is analysed in detail by Yamagiwa Akira, 'Potsudamu sengen no sōan ni tsuite' (Concerning the Draft of the Potsdam Proclamation), in *Yokohama Shiritsu Daigaku Ronsō (Jinbun-Shakai-hen)*, no. 10, vol. 39, pp. 35–71.

34. See Cordell Hull, *The Memoirs of Cordell Hull*, Macmillan, vol. 2, 1948, pp. 1589–93.
35. 'JCS Memorandum to the President', 18 July 1945, *FRUS: The Conference of Berlin (The Potsdam Conference)*, vol. 2, 1945, p. 1269. On the importance of this document, refer to Frank (1999), pp. 219–20.
36. *FRUS*, ibid., pp. 1277, 1284–9. On this point, see Leon V. Sigal, *Fighting to a Finish: The Politics of War Termination in the United States and Japan*, Cornell University Press, 1988, p. 143.
37. See Roger Buckley, *Occupation Diplomacy: Britain, the United States and Japan 1945–1952*, Cambridge University Press, 1982, pp. 10–13, 59–60.
38. Williams (1979), pp. 98–9. Another possible interpretation is that the phrase was retained as a subtle way of evading just such a commitment, since in the view of US military planners and civilian hardliners there was no 'freely expressed will' in Japan. Thus, the paragraph may be seen as a clever means of preparing the ground for extensive 'top-down' democratic reforms. John W. Dower, personal communication to the author, 23 January 1999.
39. Quotation is from Robert Smith, *MacArthur in Korea: The Naked Emperor*, Simon & Schuster, 1982, p. 210. As the American scholar Andrew Roth noted in 1946, the terms 'moderate' and 'liberalist' are misleading as they apply to Japanese leaders of this period and should not be confused with conventional Anglo-American usage. Both moderates and militarists, he noted, shared the goal of establishing Japanese hegemony in the Far East. For moderates, the use of military force to achieve that goal was a question of expediency, involving a shrewd calculation of the costs and rewards. (Andrew Roth, *Dilemma in Japan*, Victor Gallancz, 1946, pp. 33–4.) A contemporary discussion of this question is Germaine A. Hoston, 'The State, Modernity, and the Fate of Liberalism in Prewar Japan', in *The Journal of Asian Studies*, no. 51, 1992, pp. 287–316. 'Moderates' generally viewed the Soviet Union as Japan's ultimate enemy and believed that war with Britain and the United States was a strategic error.
40. Notable for the role they would play in the closing days of the war were Hirota Kōki, who served as prime minister from March 1936 to February 1937; Prince Konoe Fumimaro (June to January 1937, July 1940 to July 1941, July to October 1941); Baron Hiranuma Ki'ichirō (January to August 1939); Admiral Yonai Mitsumasa (January to July 1940); General Tōjō Hideki (October 1941 to July 1944); and General Koiso Kuniaki (July 1944 to April 1945). These former heads of government advised the Emperor, recommended new prime ministers and served as a buffer between the Throne and the formal government.
41. On fears of a popular revolt at home, see Kido Nikki Kenkyūkai-hen (ed.), *Kido Kōichi Nikki (Diary of Marquis Kido Kōichi)*, Tōkyō Daigaku Shuppankai, 1966 p. 1171 and Kido Nikki Kenkyūkai, ed., *Kido Kōichi kankei bunsho* (Documents Concerning Kido Kōichi), Tōkyō Daigaku Shuppankai, 1966, p. 459. The

English translation of the Konoe Memorial is from Robert J. C. Butow, *Japan's Decision to Surrender*, Stanford University Press, 1954, p. 47.

42. See John W. Dower, *Empire and Aftermath: Yoshida Shigeru and the Japanese Experience, 1878–1954*, Council on East Asian Studies, Harvard University, 1979, pp. 235–45, 252–4.
43. See Frank (1999), pp. 90–1.
44. Ibid., pp. 95–6.
45. See Butow (1954), pp. 119–20.
46. Richard Storry, *A History of Modern Japan*, Penguin Books, 1982, p. 230.
47. Detailed accounts of the 9 August conferences in English are found in Butow (1954), pp. 160–1 and, especially, Frank (1999), chapter 18. Frank summarises and interprets recent materials in Japanese and English.
48. Herbert P. Bix, 'Japan's Delayed Surrender: A Reinterpretation', in Michael J. Hogan, ed., *Hiroshima in History and Memory*, Cambridge University Press, 1996, p. 111.
49. Hirohito's words have been carefully reconstructed from several sources by Butow (1954), p. 176. On this process, see Terasaki Hidenari and Mariko Terasaki Miller, eds, *Shōwa tennō dokuhakuroku – Terasaki Hidenari, goyōgakari nikki* (The Shōwa Emperor's Soliloguy and the Diary of Terasaki Hidenari), Bungei Shunjūsha, 1991, pp. 125–6. A concise account in English is Frank (1999), pp. 308–15. See also Bix (1996).
50. Kase Toshikazu, *Eclipse of the Rising Sun*, Jonathan Cape, 1951, p. 243.
51. Byrnes–Grassli, 11 August 1945. *FRUS*, vol. 6, 1945, pp. 631–2. Frank (1999), p. 302.
52. Gaimushō-hen (ed.), *Shūsen shiroku* (A Historical Record of the End of Hostilities), Shinbun Gekkansha, 1952, pp. 630–7. In English, see Shigemitsu Mamoru, *Japan and Her Destiny: My Struggle for Peace*, edited by F. S. G. Piggott, E. P. Dutton, 1958, p. 362.
53. Butow (1954), pp. 207–8.
54. *FRUS*, vol. 6, 1945, pp. 584–6.
55. Mayo (1984), pp. 44–5.
56. Emmerson (1978), p. 252.
57. Later documents included 'The Treatment of the Emperor of Japan' (SWNCC-55), 'Apprehension and Punishment of War Criminals' (SWNCC-57), 'Initial Allied Control Machinery for Japan Proper' (SWNCC-70), 'Treatment of Japanese Workers' Organisations' (SWNCC-92), 'Treatment of the Institution of the Emperor' (SWNCC-209), 'The Reform of the Japanese Governmental System and Constitutional Reform in Japan' (SWNCC-228), 'Policy for the Reform of the Japanese Educational System' (SWNCC-108), and 'Reduction of Japanese Industrial War Potential' (SWNCC-302), which urged economic decentralisation through *zaibatsu* dissolution.
58. Cohen (1987), pp. 13, 48.
59. Ibid., p. 13, and Takemae Eiji, 'The US Occupation Policies for Japan: Interview

with Mr. Theodore Cohen', in *Tokyo Metropolitan University Journal of Law and Politics*, vol. 14, no. 1, 1973, pp. 11–12.

60. Takafusa Nakamura, *A History of Shōwa Japan, 1926–1989*, University of Tokyo Press, 1998, p. 265.

61. Government Section, SCAP, *The Political Reorientation of Japan, September 1945 to September 1948* (below, given as *PRJ*), US Government Printing Office, 1949, vol. 2, p. 419.

62. The Emperor's speech is reproduced in US Department of the Army (Historical Section, G-2, FECOM), ed., *Reports of General MacArthur*, vol. 2: Japanese Operations in the Southwest Pacific Area, Part 2, US Government Printing Office, 1966, p. 728.

63. Cited in Toshio Nishi, *Unconditional Democracy: Education and Politics in Occupied Japan, 1945–1952*, Hoover Institution Press (Stanford University), 1982, pp. 146–7. The Emperor's 24 August statement is from Thomas A. Bisson, 'Winning the Peace in Japan', in *Amerasia*, September 1945, p. 246. On Ishibashi Tanzan, see Nakamura (1998), p. 258.

64. Even before Potsdam, Navy Captain Ellis M. Zacharias had exploited the ambiguity in Allied demands in his 'psywar' broadcasts to Japan. In these radio emissions, he 'slipped the leash of official policy' and asserted that unconditional surrender was a technical term and that the Atlantic Charter's pledge of self-determination implied the right to retain the emperor system. These broadcasts appear to have had virtually no effect on Japan's top leadership, however. Frank (1999), pp. 220–1, 231–2.

65. See Cohen (1987), pp. 8–9.

66. Acheson (1970), p. 162.

67. 'Authority of General MacArthur as Supreme Commander for the Allied Powers', 6 September 1945, in US Department of State, ed., *Occupation of Japan: Policy and Progress*, Greenwood Press, 1969, pp. 88–9.

68. These provisions are found, respectively, in Articles 6 to 12 of the Proclamation.

69. Gerhard von Glahn, *The Occupation of Enemy Territory: A Commentary on the Law and Practice of Belligerent Occupation*, Minneapolis: University of Minnesota Press, 1957, pp. 286–7.

70. Charles L. Kades, 'Representative Government in Japan', in *PRJ*, vol. I, p. xxv.

71. See Andō Nisuke, *Surrender, Occupation, and Private Property in International Law*, Clarendon Press (Oxford), 1991, chapter 5.

72. This is spelled out in Glahn (1957), op. cit. and Andō (1991), chapter 4.

73. GHQ/SCAP, *History of the Nonmilitary Activities of the Occupation of Japan, 1945–1951*, vol. 2: Administration of the Occupation, 1951, pp. 171–8.

74. See, for instance, Etō Jun, *Mō hitotsu no sengo-shi* (An Alternative History of the Postwar Era), Kōdansha, 1978; *Wasureta koto to wasurerareta koto* (What We Forgot and What We Were Made to Forget), Bungei Shunjūsha, 1979; and *Senryō shiroku* (A Documentary History of the Occupation), Kōdansha, vols. 1–4, 1981–2.

Chapter 6   The Political Reforms

1. Douglas MacArthur, *Reminiscences*, McGraw-Hill, 1964, p. 288. A transcript of the meeting was prepared by Imperial Household interpreter Okumura Katsuzō, and in the early 1970s, historian Kojima Noboru acquired and published a copy ('Tennō to Amerika to taiheiyō sensō' [The Emperor, America and the Pacific War], in *Bungei Shunjū*, November 1975, pp. 115–19). The quotation is from Faubion Bowers, "The Late General MacArthur, Warts and All', in *Esquire*, January 1967, p. 166.

2. See William P. Woodard, *The Allied Occupation of Japan, 1945–1952, and Japanese Religions*, Leiden: Brill, 1972, pp. 259–68, 317–21. A detailed account of the Emperor's statement on divinity is found in John W. Dower, *Embracing Defeat: Japan in the Wake of World War II*, W. W. Norton and the New Press, 1999, pp. 309–14. See also Nakamura Masanori, *The Japanese Monarchy: Ambassador Joseph Grew and the Making of the 'Symbol Emperor System', 1931–1991*, M. E. Sharpe, 1992, pp. 109–10.

3. This point is elaborated on by Dower (1999), pp. 12–14 and Note 25 on p. 601.

4. MacArthur's comment on the Imperial Rescript is from GHQ/SCAP, *Political Reorientation of Japan, September 1945 to September 1948* (below, given as *PRJ*), Tokyo, vol. 2, 1949, p. 471. See Dower's trenchant critique, op. cit., pp. 314–18.

5. *PRJ*, vol. 2, pp. 463–5. On Behrstock, see Kyoko Hirano, *Mr. Smith Goes to Tokyo: Japanese Cinema Under the American Occupation, 1945–1952*, Smithsonian Institution Press, 1992, p. 112.

6. See Takemae Eiji, 'Nihon Kyōsantō no kaihō sareta hi' (The Day the Communist Party was Liberated), in *Chūō Kōron*, July 1978 and Takemae, *Senryō sengo-shi* (A History of the Postwar Occupation), Iwanami Shoten 1992, pp. 93–170. On the role of the Korean community, see Pak Kyŏng-sik, *Kaihō-go: Zainichi Chōsenjin undō* (The Korean Movement in Japan Following Liberation), San'ichi Shobō, 1989, pp. 51–4.

7. John K. Emmerson, *The Japanese Thread: A Life in the US Foreign Service*, Holt, Rinehart & Winston, 1978, pp. 257–60, chapter 12.

8. See Takemae Eiji, 'Early Postwar Reformist Parties', in Robert E. Ward and Sakamoto Yoshikazu, eds, *Democratizing Japan: The Allied Occupation*, University of Hawai'i Press, 1987, pp. 339–65 and Takemae Eiji, 'J. K. Emāson-shi danwa sokkiroku' (Stenographic Record of a Talk with J. K. Emmerson), in *Tōkyō Keidai Gakkaishi*, no. 99, 1977, pp. 45–79.

9. In his youth, Katō Kanjū had advocated democratic reform domestically but supported military expansion abroad. After military service in Siberia during Japan's intervention there (1918–22), he moved quickly to left and took a job with the country's first labour organ, *Rōdō Sekai* (The World of Labour). He later became a union organiser and committed Socialist. Katō Shizue, former spouse of Baron Ishimoto Keikichi, was an early feminist who became an active proponent of birth control after a visit to the United States (1919–20) during

which Agnes Smedley introduced her to Margaret Sanger. During the war, she refused to cooperate with the government-controlled women's movement and was jailed briefly in 1937. After divorcing Baron Ishimoto, she married Katō Kanjū in 1944. In the United States, the Army's Civil Affairs Training Schools employed her autobiography as a textbook, and following the surrender, she was one of the first people GHQ approached for advice. Shizue spoke English well, and GHQ frequently used her as an interpreter. On her prewar activities, see Baroness Ishimoto Shidzué, *Facing Two Ways: The Story of My Life*, Stanford University Press, 1984 (Holt, Rinehart and Winston, 1938). Concerning her relations with SCAP, refer to Takemae (1987), p. 354 and Helen M. Hopper, 'Katō Shizue, Socialist Party MP, and Occupation Reforms Affecting Women, 1945–1948: A Case Study of the Formal vs. Informal Political Influence of Japanese Women', in Thomas W. Burkman, ed. *The Occupation of Japan: Education and Social Reform*, General Douglas MacArthur Foundation, 1982, pp. 375–400. See also Katō's interview with Ōsuga Mizuo, 'Minshuteki datta GHQ' (GHQ Was Democratic) in *Tokyo Shinbun*, 25 July 1993, p. 11. On Kishimoto, see Woodard (1972), pp. 26, 40.

10. Tanaka Sumiko, *Josei kaihō no shisō to kōdō* (Women's Liberation: Theory and Praxis), Jiji Tsūshinsha, 1975, pp. 6–8. Ichikawa's position in the postwar feminist movement was an ambiguous one. Following Japan's invasion of China in 1937, she had written, 'Now we are forced to choose one of three alternatives. The choices are: to go to prison by publicly opposing the war, to withdraw completely from the [women's] movement, or to cooperate with the state to a certain extent by acknowledging things as they are.' Ichikawa and such leading feminists as Akamatsu Tsuneko and Kawasaki Natsu opted to struggle for equal rights by cooperating with the government as fully as men. For this, she would be purged by GHQ. Fujieda Mioko, 'Japan's First Phase of Feminism', in Fumiko Fujimura-Fanselow and Atsuko Kameda, eds, *Japanese Women: New Feminist Perspectives on the Past, Present, and Future*, The Feminist Press (City University of New York), 1995, p. 336.

11. The placard incident is analysed by David J. Danelski, 'Purakādo jiken o meguru seiji to hō' (Political and Legal Ramifications of the Placard Incident), in *Hōritsu Jihō*, Parts 1 (pp. 40–47) and 2 (pp. 63–68), July and August 1988. The April directive from SWNCC and Nugent's suppression of the CI&E proposal were reported by Mark Gayn, *Japan Diary*, Charles P. Tuttle, 1981 (William Sloane, 1948), pp. 260–1. Emperor's broadcast: *Asahi Shinbun*, 25 May 1946. Concerning government resistance to abolition of the *lèse-majesté* statute, see Koseki Shōichi, *The Birth of Japan's Postwar Constitution*, Westview Press, 1997, pp. 231–2.

12. Emmerson (1978), p. 254.

13. Sumiya Yukio, Akazawa Shirō, Utsumi Aiko, Ogata Naokichi and Otabe Yūji, eds, *Tōkyō saiban handobukku* (A Handbook of the Tokyo Tribunal), Aoki Shoten, 1989, p. 8. On Japanese–American collaboration, see Dower (1999),

p. 325, chapter 15. On the history of Sugamo Prison: John L. Ginn, *Sugamo Prison, Tokyo: An Account of the Trial and Sentencing of Japanese War Criminals in 1948, by a US Participant*, McFarland & Co., 1992, pp. 1–13.

14. See Richard M. Minear, *Victor's Justice: The Tokyo War Crimes Trial*, Tuttle, 1972, p. 40.

15. Emmerson (1978), p. 267. The justice and associate prosecutor for each country were as follows. Australia: Sir William Webb (President), Sir Alan Mansfield; Britain: Lord Patrick, Sir Arthur Comyns-Carr; Canada: Edward Stuart McDougall, H. G. Nolon; France: Henri Bernard, Robert Oneto; India: Radhabinod Pal, Govinda Menon; Netherlands: Bert V. A. Röling, W. G. F. Boegerhoff Mulder; New Zealand: Sir Erima Harvey Northcroft, Ronald H. Quilliam; Philippines: Delfin Jaranilla, Pedro Lopez; Republic of China: Mei Ju-ao, Hsiang Che-chun; USSR: Ivan Zaryanov; United States: Major General Myron C. Cramer, Joseph B. Keenan (Chief Prosecutor).

16. US Department of State, *Foreign Relations of the United States* (below, cited as *FRUS*), vol. 6, 1948, p. 897. See also William J. Sebald with Russell Brines, *With MacArthur in Japan: A Personal History of the Occupation*, W. W. Norton, 1965, pp. 168–9. The original sentences were as follows. Hanging: General Doihara Kenji , Hirota Kōki, General Itagaki Seishiro, General Kimura Heitaro, General Matsui Iwane, General Mutō Akira and General Tōjō Hideki. Life imprisonment: General Araki Sadao, Colonel Hashimoto Kingoro, General Hata Shunroku, Baron Hiranuma Ki'ichirō, Hoshino Naoki , Kaya Okinori, Marquis Kido Kōichi, General Koiso Kuniaki, General Minami Jiro , Admiral Oka Takasumi, Baron Ōshima Hiroshi, General Satō Kenryō, Admiral Shimada Shigetarō, Shiratori Toshio, General Suzuki Tei'ichi and General Umezu Yoshijirō. Twenty years' imprisonment: Tōgō Shigenori. Seven years' imprisonment: Shigemitsu Mamoru. Matsuoka Yōsuke and Admiral Nagano Osami died during the Tribunal, and Ōkawa Shūmei was declared mentally unfit to stand trial. Minear (1971), pp. 200–3.

17. Typical of the war criminals who found their way into this underworld was Colonel Tsuji Masanobu, a former Imperial Army officer who had written a key propaganda booklet for the Imperial Army in 1942 entitled *Read This and the War is Won*. Deeply implicated in atrocities in Singapore and the Philippines (he reportedly ordered the Bataan Death March), Tsuji had evaded arrest by escaping to Southeast Asia and China, where he worked for the Chinese Nationalist Army. In mid-1946, he re-entered Japan and lived incognito (with the knowledge of General Willoughby, who was secretly recruiting an experienced military cadre for a future Japanese army). In early January 1950, US authorities dropped all charges against this fugitive, granting him a de facto pardon. Tsuji later became a best-selling author and Diet member, a dramatic career reversal experienced by many of the Old Guard after the Occupation. On Tsuji's wartime role, see Ward (1996), pp. 78, 80–2, 84, 334–8. See also Dower (1999), pp. 511–13.

18. Minear (1972), pp. 41–2, 50–3. For the trial proceedings, refer to R. John

Pritchard and Sonia M. Zaide, eds, *The Tokyo War Crimes Trial: The Complete Transcripts of the Proceedings of the International Military Tribunal for the Far East in Twenty-Two Volumes*, Garland, 1981.

19. Elliott R. Thorpe, *East Wind, Rain*, Gambit Inc. (Boston), 1969, p. 196. The Kennan quotation is from Dower (1999), p. 453.

20. See Minear (1972), chapter 4.

21. On missed days in court, see Meirion and Susie Harries, *Sheathing the Sword: The Demilitarisation of Japan*, Heinemann, 1987, p. 149. On the revolt of Commonwealth justices: Ann Trotter, *New Zealand and Japan, 1945–1952: The Occupation and the Peace Treaty*, Athlone Press, 1990, pp. 83–4.

22. These points are argued with particular clarity and insight by Dower (1999), chapter 15. On Pedro Lopez, see the Harrieses (1987), p. 121. The quotation is from the Harrieses, p. 108.

23. On the Tribunal's segregated facilities, see Yukiko Koshiro, *Trans-Pacific Racisms and the U.S. Occupation of Japan*, University of Columbia Press, 1999, p. 61.

24. For the judgment and dissenting opinions, see B. V. A. Röling and C. F. Ruter, eds, *The Tokyo Judgment: The International Military Tribunal for the Far East (I.M.T.F.E.), 29 April 1946–12 November 1948*, 2 vols, APA University Press (Amsterdam), 1977.

25. On this point, consult Ienaga Saburō, *The Pacific War, 1931–1945*, Pantheon Books, 1978, pp. 201, 249–50. The noted philosopher is Tsurumi Shunsuke, 'What the War Trials Left to the Japanese People', in C. Hosoya, N. Andō, Y. Ōnuma and R. Minear, eds, *The Tokyo War Crimes Trial: An International Symposium*, Kodansha International, 1986, pp. 134–45. A detailed discussion in English of Japanese views of the Tribunal is Tsurumi Shunsuke, *A Cultural History of Postwar Japan, 1945–1980*, Kegan Paul International, 1987, pp. 13–27.

26. Gavan McCormack, Hank Nelson, eds, *The Burma–Thailand Railway*, Allen & Unwin, 1993, p. 1 and chapter 7 (Yoshinori Murai, 'Asian Forced Labour'). Comparative statistics on Allied POW death rates are from *Kyokutō Kokusai Gunji Saiban sokkiroku* (Stenographic Record of the International Military Tribunal for the Far East), Yūshōdō, 1968, vol. 10, p. 766.

27. Takemae Eiji, 'Kaisetsu' (Commentary), in *Beikoku Riku-Kaigun: gunsei-minji manyuaru* (The United States Army and Navy Manual of Military Government and Civil Affairs), Misuzu Shobō, 1998, pp. 72–3. On the psychology of cruelty, see Yuki Tanaka, *Hidden Horrors: Japanese War Crimes in World War II*, Westview Press, 1999, pp. 70–8 and Utsumi Aiko, 'Japanese Army Internment Policies for Enemy Civilians During the Asia–Pacific War', in Denoon *et al.*, eds, *Multicultural Japan: Palaeolithic to Postmodern*, Cambridge University Press, 1996, pp. 199–211. A British perspective is the Harrieses (1987), chapter 19. The quotation is from the latter, p. 179.

28. See discussion and figures in Awaya Kentarō, *Tōkyō Saiban-ron* (An Analysis of the Tokyo Tribunal), Ōtsuki Shoten, 1989, p. 288. For a list of those actually executed, see Cha'en Yoshio, 'The Research on the Justice of Japan War Criminals

After the Second World War', PhD dissertation, Pacific Western University, 1996, p. 103. Refer also to Toyoda Sumio, *Sensō saiban yoroku* (Supplementary Documents on the War Trials), Taiseisha, 1986, chapter 14.

29. Tanaka (1996), p. 217. For the 3,000 figure, see Dower (1999), p. 449. On the Soviet trials of Unit 731 operatives, see Peter Williams and David Wallace, *Unit 731: Japan's Secret Biological Warfare in World War II*, The Free Press, 1989, p. 220. The statistics on Japanese POWs in the People's Republic of China are from Sumiya Yukio *et al*, eds (1989), pp. 128–31, 218–25.

30. The citation is from William Manchester, *American Caesar: Douglas MacArthur, 1880–1963*, Little, Brown, 1978, pp. 484–5. Utsumi (1996), pp. 202, 209, comments on the severity of sentences. The Nishimura case is examined in Ward (1996), especially chapters 14–16.

31. Awaya (1989), pp. 286–7. On Indonesian 'auxiliaries', see Utsumi (1996).

32. The first Japanese American to be tried for treason was Tomoya Kawakita, a Kibei who had left California in 1939 to study at Meiji University in Tokyo. Following the attack on Pearl Harbor, he was drafted and later assigned to the Ōeyama POW camp near Kyoto because of his English ability. In August 1946, Kawakita returned home with the first group of Nisei to be repatriated. In 1947, a former POW whom Kawakita had mistreated recognised him in Los Angeles, and he was arrested, tried and condemned to death. The sentence was later commuted, however, and Kawakita was deported to Japan in the early 1960s. Sodei Rinjirō, *Were We the Enemy? American Survivors of Hiroshima*, Westview Press, 1998, pp. 54–55. On Iva Toguri: Masayo U. Duus, *Tokyo Rose: Orphan of the Pacific*, Kodansha International, 1979.

33. See generally Yoshimi Yoshiaki, ed., *Jūgun-ianfu shiryōshū* (Basic Documents on the Military Comfort Women), Ōtsuki Shoten, 1992 and *Jūgun ianfu* (The Military Comfort Women), Iwanami Shoten, 1995. In English, see Tanaka (1996), chapter 3. The precursors of the military prostitutes were impoverished 'China-bound' Japanese women (*Karayuki-san*) sold into indentured servitude in China and Southeast Asia in the late nineteenth and early twentieth centuries (Yamazaki Tomoko, *Sandakan Brothel No. 8: An Episode in the History of Lower-Class Japanese Women*, M. E. Sharpe, 1999). Estimates of the number of women hired or conscripted as military prostitutes during World War II vary considerably, and an accurate assessment is probably not possible. Figures as low as 30,000 have been advanced, but these are not cumulative. Nor do they include replacements, which must have been considerable as women died, escaped or in some cases returned home, or account for the large numbers of women captured and kept as sex slaves for relatively short periods by roving Army units. In light of these difficulties, Yoshimi has revised his estimates to as few as 50,000 and as many as 200,000 (personal communication to the author, 7 June, 1999). See also Yoshimi (1995), pp. 78–81.

34. B. V. A. Röling, 'The Tokyo Trial in Retrospect', in Susumu Yamaguchi, ed., *Buddhism and Culture*, Nakano Press (Kyoto), 1960, p. 248.

35. Williams and Wallace (1989), pp. 207–10 and Sheldon H. Harris, *Factories of Death: Japanese Biological Warfare, 1932–45, and the American Cover-up*, Routledge, 1994, pp. 18–21, 33–9, 49–51, 63–72, 93–4, 167.

36. Williams and Wallace, ibid., p. 301. The debriefings of Ishii are detailed in Edward Regis, *The Biology of Doom: The History of America's Germ Warfare Project*, Henry Holt, 1999, pp. 85–113. See also pp. 126–30. The Fell quotation is from p. 129. On the Subcommittee for the Far East report, see Wallace (1989), p. 220. Military Intelligence's appraisal of Ishii is reported in Stephen Endicott and Edward Hagerman, *The United States and Biological Warfare: Secrets from the Early Cold War and Korea*, Indiana University Press, 1998, p. 40.

37. Quotations are from Minear (1972), pp. 116–17, 162.

38. The 170-page transcription was found among the personal papers of Terasaki Hidenari in the United States at the home of his daughter, Mariko Terasaki Miller. The discovery was made public in late 1990. See Terasaki Hidenari and Mariko Terasaki Miller, eds, *Shōwa Tennō dokuhakuroku – Terasaki Hidenari, goyōgakari nikki* (The Shōwa Emperor's Soliloquy and the Diary of Terasaki Hidenari), Bungei Shunjūsha, 1991. See also Fujiwara Akira, Awaya Kentarō, Yoshida Yutaka and Yamada Akira eds, *Tettei-kenshō: Shōwa Tennō 'dokuhakuroku'* (Conclusive Evidence: The Shōwa Emperor's 'Soliloquy'), Ōtsuki Shoten, 1991, pp. 35–75; Herbert P. Bix, 'Japan's Delayed Surrender: A Reinterpretation', in Michael J. Hogan, ed. *Hiroshima in History and Memory*, Cambridge University Press, 1996, p. 87; and Irokawa Daikichi, *The Age of Hirohito: In Search of Modern Japan*, The Free Press, 1995, pp. 94–8.

39. Two recent studies of Hirohito's military role in English are Edward J. Drea, *In the Service of the Emperor: Essays on the Imperial Japanese Army*, University of Nebraska Press, 1998, chapter 12 and Peter Wetzler, *Hirohito and War: Imperial Tradition and Military Decision-Making in Prewar Japan*, University of Hawai'i Press, 1998, Introduction, chapters 2 and 3. In Japanese, see Terasaki and Miller (1991). Herbert P. Bix's monumental work, *Hirohito and the Making of Modern Japan*, HarperCollins, 2000, Part III, summarises the recent scholarship with especial force and acumen.

40. See Masumi Junnosuke, *Shōwa Tennō to sono jidai* (The Emperor Shōwa and His Era), Yamakawa Shuppansha, 1998, pp. 141–218 and Fujiwara and Awaya, eds (1991). The quotation is from a military attaché to Imperial Vice Chamberlain Kinoshita Michio. See Kinoshita, *Sokkin nisshi* (A Vice Chamberlain's Diary), Bungei Shunjūsha, 1990, p. 34. The translation is John Dower's (1999), p. 291.

41. The US opinion survey is in George H. Gallup, *The Gallup Poll: Public Opinion 1935–1971*, New York: Random House, 1972, vol. 1, p. 512. On the JCS message, refer to Robert E. Ward, 'Presurrender Planning: Treatment of the Emperor and Constitutional Change', in Ward and Sakamoto, eds (1987), p. 65. MacArthur's response of 25 January is in *FRUS* (1946), vol. 8, pp. 395–7. On the FEAC mission, see Trotter (1990), p. 78.

42. Masumi (1998), pp. 233–8.
43. This is how Bonner Fellers, writing in 1947, described Hirohito. Cited in Herbert P. Bix, 'The Shōwa Emperor's "Soliloquy" and the Problem of War Responsibility', in *The Journal of Japanese Studies*, no. 18, 1992, pp. 86–7.
44. On Fellers's early ideas concerning the Emperor, see Allison B. Gilmore, *You Can't Fight Tanks with Bayonets: Psychological Warfare Against the Japanese Army in the Southwest Pacific*, University of Nebraska Press, 1998, pp. 51–2. The Fellers Memorandum is reproduced in Woodard (1972), pp. 360–1.
45. Awaya Kentarō, 'Emperor Shōwa's Accountability for War', in *The Japan Quarterly*, October–December, 1991, p. 390.
46. Dower dubs the blaming of the military for the war and the depiction of the Emperor as a pacifist the 'wedge' strategy. Dower (1999), chapter 9. A recent overview of this process is Masumi (1998), pp. 74–82. On the abdication debate, see Dower (1999), pp. 320–30 and Irokawa (1995), pp. 98–9.
47. *FRUS*, loc. cit.
48. Takemae (1987), pp. 355–8 and Joe B. Moore, *Japanese Workers and the Struggle for Power, 1945–1947*, University of Wisconsin Press, 1983, pp. 114–19, 123–4.
49. Takemae, ibid., pp. 330–55.
50. See Uchida Kenzō, 'Japan's Postwar Conservative Parties', in Ward and Sakamoto, eds. (1987), pp. 306–38.
51. Justin Williams Sr, *Japan's Political Revolution Under MacArthur*, University of Tokyo Press, 1979, pp. 10–11, pp. 75–7.
52. *PRJ*, vol. 1, p. 316.
53. Ibid., p. 345.
54. Tanaka (1975), p. 9.
55. Richard B. Finn, *Winners in Peace: MacArthur, Yoshida, and Postwar Japan*, University of California Press, 1992, p. 108. On the 1947 electoral reform, see Williams (1979), pp. 175–6.
56. Courtney Whitney, *MacArthur: His Rendezvous with History*, Knopf, 1956, p. 245.
57. See Hans H. Baerwald, *The Purge of Japanese Leaders under the Occupation*, University of California Press, 1959. The Kades quotation is from Takemae Eiji, 'The Kades Memoir on the Occupation of Japan', in *The Journal of Tokyo Keizai University*, no. 148, 1986, pp. 264–5.
58. Captain Arthur Behrstock and Lieutenant Tom Tsukahara of CI&E reportedly were behind Hatoyama's removal. Tsukahara had found a book Hatoyama had authored in 1938 following a visit to Germany and Italy in which he praised Hitler and Mussolini. Behrstock attempted to mobilise opinion against the politician inside GHQ but failed to elicit much interest. He then informed Mark Gayn of *The Chicago Tribune*, who questioned Hatoyama about the book at a Foreign Correspondents' Club press dinner. The issue was taken up by the media, and MacArthur decided to purge Hatoyama just as he was to become premier. See Gayn (1981), pp. 161–4, Kyoko Hirano, *Mr. Smith Goes to Tokyo:*

Japanese Cinema Under the American Occupation, 1945–1952, Smithsonian Institution Press, 1992, pp. 188, 305 (Note 28) and Masuda Hiroshi, *Seijika tsuihō* (The Purge of the Politicians), Chūō Kōron Shinsha, 2001, chapter 1.

59. On the economic purge, refer to Theodore Cohen, *Remaking Japan: The American Occupation as New Deal*, The Free Press, 1987, pp. 161–8.

60. Takemae (1986), pp. 266–7. On Yoshida and Ishibashi, see Sumimoto Toshio, *Senryō hiroku* (The Secret Story of the Occupation), vol. 2, Mainichi Shinbunsha, 1952, p. 101. The reasons for Ishibashi's purge are cited by Marlene J. Mayo, 'Civil Censorship and Media Control in Early Occupied Japan: From Minimum to Stringent Surveillance', in Robert Wolfe, ed., *Americans as Proconsuls: United States Military Government in Germany and Japan, 1944–1952*, Southern Illinois University Press, 1984, Note 50 on p. 509. Ichikawa's purge is discussed in depth in Masuda (2001), chap. 7. On Japanese participation in the purge, see Yoshida Shigeru, *The Yoshida Memoirs: The Story of Japan in Crisis*, William Heinemann, 1961, p. 63. Concerning the exclusion of women, refer to the comment by Helen M. Hopper in Burkman, ed. (1982), p. 438. Purge figures are from *PRJ*, vol. 2, p. 553.

61. Susan J. Pharr, 'The Politics of Women's Rights', in Ward and Sakamoto, eds (1987), p. 225.

62. See discussion in Koseki (1997), pp. 26–44 and the analysis by Dower (1999), pp. 355–60.

63. Koseki (1997), p. 41.

64. Ibid. p. 70. On the GS reaction, refer to Takayanagi Kenzō, Ōtomo Ichirō and Tanaka Hideo, eds, *Nihonkoku kenpō seitei no katei* (The Making of the Constitution of Japan), vol. 1, Yūhikaku, 1972, p. 36. See also PRJ, vol. 1, pp. 94–8.

65. Takayanagi *et al.* (1972), pp. 412–18. See also Williams (1979), p. 100–1, and Koseki (1997), p. 71.

66. On the FEAC's Tokyo interview with MacArthur, see Koseki (1997), pp. 73–6.

67. Ibid., pp. 77–80 and also Dower (1999), p. 369.

68. Beate Sirota Gordon, *The Only Woman in the Room: A Memoir*, Kodansha International, 1998, pp. 107–18. In fact, Sirota was not the only woman in the room, although her contribution was immense. The role of Ruth Ellerman, one of three other women present, awaits further study.

69. Ibid., pp. 121–4. On Japan's Constitution and the protection of women, see Susan Pharr, 'A Radical US Experiment: Women's Rights and the Occupation of Japan', in L. H. Redford, ed. *The Occupation of Japan: Impact of Legal Reform*, The Douglas MacArthur Foundation, 1977, pp. 125–7.

70. See interview with Karpinsky in Takemae Eiji, 'Senryō kaimaku-ki no rōdō seisaku' (Labour Policy at the Opening of the Occupation), in *Nihon Rōdō Kyōkai Zasshi*, no. 252, 1980.

71. See Takayanagi Kenzō *et al.* (1972), pp. 320–36 and Hideo Tanaka, *The Japanese Legal System: Introduction: Cases and Materials*, University of Tokyo Press, 1976, p. 676.

72. Whitney's atomic sunshine comment is from Whitney (1956), p. 251. According to Kades, Whitney was running a high fever that day and 'tended to say things he ordinarily wouldn't say'. Takemae (1986), pp. 282–3.
73. Takayanagi *et al.*, eds (1972), op. cit.
74. Koseki (1997), pp. 107–8.
75. Ibid., p. 109. *PRJ*, vol. 2, p. 657.
76. MacArthur (1964), pp. 287–8 and Gayn (1981), pp. 125–7.
77. Nakamura (1992), chapter 9.
78. Mears had written the prewar work, *The Year of the Wild Boar: An American Woman in Japan*, J. B. Lippincott, 1942 and later authored the influential *Mirror for Americans: Japan*, Houghton Mifflin, 1948. On the impact her essay had on Drew, see Nakamura, ibid., pp. 87–94, 103–6.
79. Nakamura, ibid., pp. 168–9. Yoshida (1961), p. 145.
80. Quotation is from Takayanagi *et al.* (1972), p. 393. On Imperial democracy, see Dower (1999), pp. 378, 384–5, 388.
81. The historian is Irokawa (1995), p. 101. The journalist is Allen Raymond in *The New York Herald Tribune*, 17 December 1947, cited in Thomas A. Bisson, *Prospects for Democracy in Japan*, Macmillan, 1949, p. 25. On Blyth's role, see Dower (1999), pp. 331–2.
82. See Theodore H. McNelly, 'General Douglas MacArthur and the Constitutional Disarmament of Japan', in *The Transactions of the Asiatic Society of Japan*, third series, vol. 17, 1982, p. 2. Quotation is from Takemae (1986), pp. 277, 279.
83. See Dower (1979), pp. 379–81. Yoshida (1961), p. 145.
84. On this controversy, see, respectively, MacArthur (1964), pp. 302–3; Williams (1979), pp. 107–8; Tanaka (1976), pp. 695–7; McNelly (1982), pp. 1–34; and Charles L. Kades, 'The American Role in Revising Japan's Imperial Constitution', in *Political Science Quarterly*, vol. 104, no. 2, 1989, pp. 215–47. See especially Theodore H. McNelly, *The Origins of Japan's Democratic Constitution*, University Press of America, 2000, chapter 5. According to McNelly and Kades, the GS Deputy Chief had been profoundly influenced by the Pact of Paris as a law student at Harvard. The Emperor's formal renunciation of divinity on 1 January 1946 and his pledge to build a new Japan based on pacifism also had left a deep impression. Kades reportedly proposed to Whitney that Hirohito issue an Imperial rescript renouncing Japan's war-making powers in order to mitigate worldwide hostility to the monarch and fulfil the demilitarisation provisions of the Potsdam Proclamation. According to this scenario, Whitney solicited Shidehara's opinion on 28 January 1946 and then conveyed the proposal to MacArthur, who subsequently incorporated the anti-war clauses into his three-point note to Government Section.
85. See Nakagawa Gō, 'Nichi-Fi ryōkoku kenpō ni miru ruien' (Similarities Observed in the Constitutions of Japan and the Philippines), in *Chūō Kōron*, May 1987, pp. 177–89 but, especially, p. 185; Kataoka Tetsuya, *The Price of a Constitution: the Origin of Japan's Postwar Politics*, Crane Russak (Taylor &

Francis), 1991, p. 37; and Koseki (1997), p. 85. Japan was not the only postwar state to foreswear war-making. Under the 1945 United Nations Charter, 50 nations renounced aggressive war in similar terms, and the present-day constitutions of France, Germany and Brazil also include explicit anti-war clauses, albeit none so ambitious as the Japanese charter.

86. *PRJ*, vol. 2, pp. 747–8.
87. A contemporary pacifist interpretation is C. Douglas Lummis, 'Japan's Radical Constitution', in *Nihonkoku kenpō o yomu* (Reading the Constitution of Japan), Kashiwa Shobō, 1993, pp. 155–94. See generally, Koseki Shōichi, *Kyūjō to anpō hoshō* (Article Nine and National Security), Shōgakkan, 2000.
88. Gayn (1981), p. 130.
89. See Satō's account in Satō Tatsuo, 'The Origin and Development of the Draft Constitution of Japan', in *Contemporary Japan*, vol. 24, nos 4–6 (pp. 175–87) and nos. 7–9 (pp. 371–87), 1956. Refer also to Irie Toshirō, *Kenpō seiritsu no keii to kenpōjō no sho-mondai* (The Writing of the Constitution and Constitutional Problems), Dai'ichi Hōki, 1976.
90. Kades (1989), p. 234; Inoue Kyoko, *MacArthur's Japanese Constitution*, University of Chicago Press, 1991, chapters 3 and 5; Koseki Shōichi, 'Japanizing the Constitution', in *The Japan Quarterly*, vol. 35, no. 3, 1988, pp. 234–40. A recent overview of the problem is Takemae Eiji and Okabe Fuminobu, *Kenpō seitei-shi: Kenpō wa oshi-tsukerareta ka* (A History of the Drafting of the Constitution: Was it Really Imposed on Japan?), Shōgakkan Bunko, 2000.
91. Williams (1979), p. 115.
92. Koseki (1997), pp. 173–9.
93. Ibid., pp. 181–3.
94. Kades (1989), p. 236; Koseki (1988), p. 239; Takemae (1986), pp. 279–80.
95. Koseki (1988), pp. 237–8; Koseki (1997), pp. 202–3; Theodore H. McNelly, ' "Induced Revolution": The Policy and Process of Constitutional Reform in Japan', in Ward and Sakamoto, eds (1987), pp. 94–5; and McNelly (2000), op. cit.
96. George H. Blakeslee, *The Far Eastern Commission: A Study in International Cooperation – 1945–1952*, US Department of State (US Government Printing Office), 1953, pp. 48–65. See also McNelly (1987), p. 87 and, especially, Koseki (1997), pp. 243–54.

Chapter 7   Institutional and Economic Reforms
 1. The quotations are from, respectively, GHQ/SCAP, *The Political Reorientation of Japan, September 1945 to September 1948* (below, given as *PRJ*), Tokyo, vol. 1, 1949, pp. 292 and 284. A comprehensive study of Occupation-era law enforcement in English is Christopher Aldous, *The Police in Occupation Japan: Control, Corruption and Resistance to Reform*, Routledge, 1997.
 2. ESS Labour Division (GHQ/SCAP), *Monthly Report*, November and December 1945. See Amakawa Akira, 'Senryō-seisaku to kanryō no taiō' (Occupation

Policy and the Response of the Bureaucracy), in Shisō no Kagaku Kenkyūkai-hen (ed.), *Kyōdō kenkyū: Nihon senryōgun: sono hikari to kage* (Two Faces of the Occupation Army of Japan: Joint Research), vol. 1, Tokuma Shoten, 1978, pp. 225–7. Aldous (1997), p. 47. Takemae Eiji, *Sengo rōdō-kaikaku: GHQ rōdō seisaku-shi* (The Postwar Labour Reforms: A History of GHQ's Labour Reform Policy), Tōkyō Daigaku Shuppankai, 1982, pp. 114–15.

3. On pre-surrender planning for police reforms, see Takemae Eiji, *Senryō sengo-shi* (A History of the Postwar Occupation), Iwanami Shoten, 1992, chapter 7. A detailed discussion of the reforms is found in Hironaka Toshio, *Sengo nihon no keisatsu* (The Police in Postwar Japan), Iwanami Shoten, 1968, chapter 1 and Chihō-jichi Kenkyū Shiryō Sentā-hen (ed.), *Sengo jichi-shi* (A History of Postwar Local Government Reform), Bunsei Shoin, 1977, chapter 5.

4. The Occupationaire is Harry E. Wildes, *Typhoon in Tokyo: The Occupation and its Aftermath*, Macmillan, 1954, p. 185. 'A certain pulling and hauling' is Kurt Steiner's expression: *Local Government in Japan*, Stanford University Press, 1965, p. 90. Pulliam's hyperbolic utterance is from Wildes (1954), p. 186. The other quotations are from *PRJ*, vol. 1, p. 296. Refer also to Aldous (1997), p. 212.

5. MacArthur letter to Katayama, 16 September 1947 (*PRJ*, pp. 298–9).

6. The organic statutes included the Law Concerning the Organisation of Urban and Rural Prefectures, the Law Concerning the Organisation of Cities, the Law Concerning the Organisation of Towns and Villages, the Law Concerning the Tokyo Metropolis and the Law Concerning the Hokkaido Assembly. See *PRJ*, vol. 1, pp. 266–7 and Steiner (1965), pp. 77–8.

7. The Kades quotation is from Takemae Eiji, 'Kades Memoir on the Occupation of Japan', in *The Journal of Tokyo Keizai University*, no. 148, 1986, p. 290. The characterisations of Rowell and Kades are from the GS document, 'Meeting of the Steering Committee on the Chapter on Local Government, Monday 11 February 1946', cited in Takayanagi Kenzō, Ōtomo Ichirō and Tanaka Hideo, eds, *Nihonkoku kenpō seitei no katei* (The Making of the Constitution of Japan), vol. 1, Yūhikaku, 1972, pp. 236.

8. See Steiner (1965), pp. 81–4.

9. Japanese theories of local self-rule are discussed in Teruhisa Horio, *Educational Thought and Ideology in Modern Japan*, University of Tokyo Press, 1988, pp. 139–42. On the Communist Party's position, see Steiner (1965), pp. 79–80.

10. Takemae Eiji, 'C. G. Tilton and the Occupation of Japan', in *The Journal of Tokyo Keizai University*, no. 146, 1986. See also *PRJ*, vol. 1, pp. 270–84 and Amakawa Akira, 'The Making of the Postwar Local Government System', in Robert E. Ward and Sakamoto Yoshikazu, eds, *Democratizing Japan: The Allied Occupation*, University of Hawai'i Press, 1987, pp. 253–83.

11. Justin Williams Sr, *Japan's Political Revolution Under MacArthur: A Participant's Account*, University of Tokyo Press, 1979, pp. 55–6.

12. Thomas A. Bisson, *Prospects for Democracy in Japan*, Macmillan, 1949, pp. 72–4.

13. Steiner (1965), pp. 72–5.
14. Ibid., pp. 136–7. *PRJ*, vol. 1, p. 29.
15. Taikakai-hen (ed.), *Naimushō-shi* (A History of the Home Ministry), vol. 3, Hara Shobō, 1980, pp. 997–1028.
16. Ibid., p. 578.
17. See T. J. Pempel, 'The Tar Baby Target: "Reform" of the Japanese Bureaucracy', in Ward, Sakamoto, eds (1987), pp. 166–7. See generally, John M. Maki, *Government and Politics in Japan: The Road to Democracy*, Frederick A. Praeger, 1962.
18. *PRJ*, vol. 2, p. 433.
19. Ibid.
20. Tsuru Shigeto, *Japanese Capitalism: Creative Defeat and Beyond*, Cambridge University Press, 1993, pp. 15–16. On the reform bureaucrats, see John W. Dower, *Empire and Aftermath: Yoshida Shigeru and the Japanese Experience, 1878–1954*, Council on East Asian Studies, Harvard University, 1979, pp. 362–3 and Takafusa Nakamura, *A History of Shōwa Japan, 1926–1989*, University of Tokyo Press, 1998, pp. 58, 193–5, 279. On the social bureaucrats, see Sheldon Garon, *The State and Labor in Modern Japan*, University of California Press, 1987, chapter 6.
21. Special Survey Committee (Ministry of Foreign Affairs), *Basic Problems for Post-war Reconstruction of Japanese Economy* (March 1946), Japan Economic Research Center, 1977. See the discussion in Laura E. Hein, *Fueling Growth: The Energy Revolution and Economic Policy in Postwar Japan*, Council on East Asian Studies, Harvard University, 1990, pp. 111–16.
22. Ishibashi was purged by SCAP from 1947 to 1951. After the Occupation, he was Minister of International Trade and Industry and served as prime minister briefly in 1956. See Masuda Hiroshi, *Kōshoku tsuihō* (The Purge of Public Officials), Tōkyō Daigaku Shuppankai, 1996, chapter 2. For a detailed discussion of priority production and the RFB, see Hein (1990), pp. 116–24.
23. James Hoover, cited in Takemae Eiji, 'SCAP Labour Policy for Japan: A Memoir by an ex-GHQ Labour Official', in *Toritsu Kōgyō Kōtō Senmon Gakkō kenkyū hōkoku* (Research Bulletin of the Tokyo Metropolitan Junior College of Industrial Arts), no. 8, March 1972, p. 61.
24. See Andrew Gordon, *The Evolution of Labor Relations in Japan: Heavy Industry 1853–1955*, Council on East Asian Studies, Harvard University, 1985, chapter 8.
25. ESS Labour Division (GHQ/SCAP), *Monthly Report*, November 1945. See also Takemae (1982), pp. 79–80. A general reference is Iwao Ayusawa, *A History of Labor in Modern Japan*, University of Hawai'i Press, 1966.
26. Theodore Cohen, *Remaking Japan: the American Occupation as New Deal*, The Free Press, 1987, pp. 215–16.
27. A detailed account of the Hanaoka revolt is Nozoe Kenji, *Hanaoka jiken o ou: Chūgokujin kyōsei renkō no sekinin o toinaosu* (The Truth About the Hanaoka Incident: Rethinking Responsibility for the Forcible Conscription of Chinese

Labourers), Ochanomizu Shobō, 1996, chapter 1 and *Kikigaki Hanaoka jiken* (Witness to the Hanaoka Incident), Ochanomizu Shobō, 1993, pp. 142–237.

28. See Joe B. Moore, *Japanese Workers and the Struggle for Power, 1945–1947,* University of Wisconsin Press, 1983, pp. 41–3.

29. Itō Ken'ichi, *Nankatsu kara Nanbu e* (From South Katsushika to South Tokyo), Iryō Tosho Shuppan, 1974; Miriam Farley, *Aspects of Japan's Labour Problems,* John Day, 1960, pp. 89–90.

30. In English, see Joe B. Moore, 'Production Control: Workers' Control in Early Postwar Japan', in Joe B. Moore, ed., *The Other Japan: Conflict, Compromise, and Resistance Since 1945,* M. E. Sharpe, 1997, pp. 15–19.

31. On the originality of production control, see Sumiya Mikio, 'Mitsubishi Bibai sōgi' (The Mitsubishi Bibai Labour Dispute), in Tōkyō Daigaku Shakai Kagaku Kenkyūjo-hen (ed.), *Sengo shoki rōdō sōgi chōsa* (Survey of Labour Disputes in the Early Postwar Period), Tōkyō Daigaku Shuppankai, 1971. See also Takemae Eiji, 'GHQ Labour Policy During the Period of Democratization, 1946–1948: The Second Interview with Mr Theodore Cohen', in *The Journal of Tokyo Keizai University,* no. 122, 1981, p. 117.

32. Hein (1990), pp. 6–8, chapter 4.

33. Moore (1997), p. 14.

34. Ibid., pp. 31–3.

35. The MacArthur quotations are cited, respectively, in Richard B. Finn, *Winners in Peace: MacArthur, Yoshida, and Postwar Japan,* University of California Press, 1992, p. 54 and *PRJ,* vol. 2, p. 750.

36. Cohen (1989), pp. 246–50.

37. See Takemae (1981), pp. 108–14 and Cohen, ibid., pp. 250–1.

38. GHQ/SCAP, *Monthly Summation of Non-Military Activities in Japan and Korea,* no. 13, October, pp. 37–8.

39. The FEC document is reproduced in Farley (1960), pp. 245–7. On MacArthur's comment (9 December 1948), see Bowen C. Dees, *The Allied Occupation and Japan's Economic Miracle: Building the Foundations of Japanese Science and Technology, 1945–1952,* Curzon Press, 1997, p. 187.

40. Takemae Eiji, 'The U.S. Occupation Policies for Japan: Interview with Mr. Theodore Cohen', in *Tokyo Metropolitan University Journal of Law and Politics,* vol. 14, no. 1, 1973, pp. 28–9.

41. Takemae, 'GHQ Labour Policy During the Period of Democratization, 1946–1948: The Second Interview with Mr. Theodore Cohen' (1981), p. 127.

42. *PRJ,* vol. 1, p. 323.

43. Howard B. Schonberger, *Aftermath of War: Americans and the Remaking of Japan, 1945–1952,* Kent State University Press, 1989, pp. 121–3. Richard L.-G. Deverall, *The Great Seduction: Red China's Drive to Bring Free Japan Behind the Iron Curtain,* International Literature Printing Co. (Tokyo), 1953, p. 227.

44. For a critique of the general strike leadership, see Takemae (1982), pp. 172–3. On *Zenrōren,* see Ayusawa (1966), pp. 285–6.

45. On the 'web of rules', consult Moore (1983), pp. 61–70. A discussion of GHQ's pre-systematised industrial relations is found in Anthony Woodiwiss, 'A Revolution in Labour Law? The Fate of the Trade Union Act in Post-War Japan', in Ian Neary, ed. *War, Revolution and Japan*, Japan Library (Kent), 1993, p. 117 and, generally, Woodiwiss, *Labour and Society in Japan: From Repression to Reluctant Tolerance*, Routledge, 1992. See also Garon (1987), pp. 232–7.

46. Takemae (1982), pp. 93–102.

47. Cohen (1987), pp. 231–3 and Takemae, ibid., pp. 103–13.

48. Tanaka Sumiko, *Josei kaihō no shisō to kōdō* (Women's Liberation: Theory and Praxis), Jiji Tsūshinsha, 1975, p. 16. See interviews with Stander and Smith in Takemae Eiji, *GHQ rōdōka no hito to seisaku* (Personnel and Policies in GHQ's Labour Division), Emutei Shuppan, 1991, pp. 205–8. Teramoto later emphasised that, without the backing of ESS and MacArthur's headquarters in general, passage of the law would have been difficult, if not impossible (interview with the author, 18 November 1981). On prewar social policy, see Garon (1987), chapters 4 and 5.

49. On the establishment of the Labour Ministry, see Takemae (1982), pp. 177–96 and Cohen (1987), pp. 236–7. Curiously, although Cohen supported the proposal, Stander distanced herself from discussions of the WMB. In frequent disagreement with CI&E's Ethel Weed over labour reform legislation, she appears to have taken a back seat on the issue.

50. A former organiser for the Japan Seamen's Union, Yonekubo had been a delegate and adviser to the ILO before the war and served in the wartime Diet (unendorsed by the Imperial Rule Assistance Association). Takemae (1982), loc. cit.

51. See Tanaka (1975), p. 13.

52. Susan J. Pharr, 'The Politics of Women's Rights', in Ward and Sakamoto, eds (1987), pp. 242–5.

53. Nishi Kyōko, *Senryōka no Nihon fujin seisaku* (Policies Affecting Japanese Women Under the Occupation), Domesu Shuppan, 1985, chapter 3.

54. See *PRJ*, vol. 1, pp. 214–21; Pharr (1987), op. cit.; Kurt Steiner, 'The Occupation and the Reform of the Japanese Civil Code', in Ward and Sakamoto, eds (1987), pp. 188–220; and Alfred C. Oppler, *Legal Reform in Occupied Japan: A Participant Looks Back*, Princeton University Press, 1976, pp. 74, 95, 111–29. Quotations are from Oppler, p. 77.

55. Wagatsuma Sakae, ed., *Sengo ni okeru minpō no keika* (The Revision of the Postwar Civil Code), Nihon Hyōronsha, 1956, p. 83.

56. *PRJ*, vol. 2, p. 582.

57. As noted earlier, the Labour Relations Adjustment Law restricted strikes by some public employees but only in cases where such action would clearly endanger the public welfare.

58. Quotations cited in Schonberger (1989), p. 127.

59. *PRJ*, vol. 1, p. 357. Dees (1997), p. 187.

60. Australia, unwilling to embarrass the United States, prevented the question from

coming to a vote. George H. Blakeslee, *The Far Eastern Commission: A Study in International Cooperation 1945–1952*, US Department of State (US Government Printing Office), 1953, pp. 170–5.

61. Takemae (1982), pp. 236–40; Cohen (1987), pp. 392–7.
62. Mitsubishi Economic Research Institute, ed. *Mitsui–Mitsubishi–Sumitomo: Present Status of the Former Zaibatsu Enterprises*, Mitsubishi Economic Research Institute, 1955, p. 6.
63. See Thomas A. Bisson, *Zaibatsu Dissolution in Japan*, University of California Press, 1954, pp. 69–71. The Big Four *zaibatsu* also were directly involved in the war. In 1938, Mitsui and Mitsubishi allegedly imported Iranian opium for the Imperial Army and distributed it to Chinese in occupied areas to increase addiction and facilitate pacification (on the narcotics trade, refer to chapter 8). Moreover, all of the combines profited immensely from the use of Chinese and Korean conscript labour, both in Manchuria and Japan. Cohen (1987), p. 157–8.
64. This was defined more precisely as a company or grouping of companies with combined assets of over ¥2 billion or capitalised at ¥500 million but having a controlling interest in several fields of business activity.
65. Eleanor M. Hadley, *Anti-Trust in Japan*, Princeton University Press, 1970, pp. 495–514.
66. Eleanor M. Hadley, 'Zaibatsu Dissolution', *Kodansha Encyclopedia of Japan*, Kodansha, 1983, pp. 365–6.
67. Cohen (1989), p. 358.
68. Ibid., pp. 360–3.
69. The Kern quotation is from *Newsweek*, 23 June 1947. On the FEC-230 controversy and the Japan Lobby, see Schonberger (1989), pp. 64, 75 and chapter 5 and John G. Roberts, 'The "Japan Crowd" and the Zaibatsu Restoration', in *The Japan Interpreter*, vol. 12, nos. 3–4, 1979, pp. 384–415.
70. Ōkurashō Zaisei-shi Shitsu-hen (ed.), *Shōwa zaisei-shi: shūsen kara Kōwa made* (The Financial History of the Shōwa Era: From the War's End to the Peace Treaty), vol. 2, Tōyō Keizai Shinpōsha, 1981, p. 495.
71. In 1943, Grew and Dooman rejected a proposal by Fearey to eliminate tenancy and improve rural conditions and objected to further study of the question. In July and August of 1945, Mark B. Williamson, later chief of Agriculture Division, Natural Resources Section, prepared two papers while at CASA in Monterey, California urging an even more radical reform of the land tenure system. The ideas of both men were strongly influenced by Dr Wolf I. Ladejinsky, a Russia-born agronomist with a deep knowledge of rural Japan then with the US Department of Agriculture. Williamson's Monterey proposals, too, met with disapproval. See Susan Deborah Chira, *Cautious Revolutionaries: Occupation Planners and Japan's Post-War Land Reform*, Tokyo: Agricultural Policy Research Center, 1982, chapter 3.
72. Yoshida Shigeru, *The Yoshida Memoirs: The Story of Japan in Crisis*, William Heinemann, 1961, p. 197.

73. On Ladejinsky's ideas, see Louis J. Walinsky, ed., *Agrarian Reform as Unfinished Business: The Selected Papers of Wolf I. Ladejinsky*, Oxford University Press, 1977. Refer also to Chira (1982), pp. 22–4, 140.

74. Chira, ibid., pp. 38–9.

75. See Mark Gayn, *Japan Diary*, Charles E. Tuttle, 1981 (William Sloane, 1948), pp. 18–19. *PRJ*, vol. 2, p. 575.

76. Chira (1982), pp. 92–3.

77. Kon Hidemi, *Yoshida Shigeru*, Kōdansha, 1967, pp. 147–53. Wada, a Socialist, headed the Economic Stabilisation Board in 1947 under the Katayama Cabinet and also was associated with the so-called Yoshida School. In March 1949, he joined the left wing of the Socialist Party and in 1954 was elected Secretary-General. On Wada's career, in English, see Alan B. Cole, George O. Totten and Cecil H. Uyehara, *Socialist Parties in Postwar Japan*, Yale University Press, 1966, pp. 282–6 and Masumi Junnosuke, *Contemporary Politics in Japan*, University of California Press, 1995, pp. 307–8.

78. Personal comment from Ward to Alan Rix, 20 April 1985, cited in W. Mac-Mahon Ball, *Intermittent Diplomat: The Japan and Batavia Diaries of W. MacMahon Ball*, Alan Rix, ed., Melbourne University Press, 1988, pp. 287–8.

79. Chira (1982), p. 96.

80. Ibid., p. 99–102. Letter from Eric Ward to Ball, cited in Takemae Eiji, 'Ball's View on the Allied Occupation of Japan: Interview with W. MacMahon Ball', in *The Journal of Tokyo Keizai University*, no. 151, June 1987, pp. 222–3.

81. See Ogura Takekazu, *Can Japanese Agriculture Survive? A Historical and Comparative Approach*, Agricultural Policy Research Centre, 1982, pp. 412–13.

82. The standard reference for the land reform is Nōchi Kaikaku Kiroku I'inkai, ed., *Nōchi kaikaku tenmatsu gaiyō* (A Synopsis of the Progress of the Land Reform), Nōsei Chōsakai, 1951. Statistics are from vol. 14. The representative work in English is Ronald P. Dore, *Land Reform in Japan*, Oxford University Press, 1959. Also valuable are the studies by direct participants Andrew J. Grad [Grajdanzev], *Land and Peasant in Japan: An Introductory Survey*, Institute of Pacific Relations, 1952 and Lawrence J. Hewes, *Japan: Land and Men*, Iowa State College Press, 1955.

83. *PRJ*, vol. 2, p. 760.

Chapter 8   The Cultural Reforms

1. US Army Service Forces, *Civil Affairs Handbook Japan*, Section 15: Education, 23 June 1944, p. 5.

2. Marlene J. Mayo, 'Psychological Disarmament: American Wartime Planning for the Education and Re-Education of Defeated Japan, 1943–1945', in Thomas W. Burkman, ed., *The Occupation of Japan: Education and Social Reform*, General Douglas MacArthur Foundation, 1982, p. 23.

3. The drafting committee included Japan Crowd stalwart Eugene H. Dooman; Frances A. Gulick, a China-born student of Blakeslee who had entered the State

Department from the Office of Strategic Services; Hillis Lory of the Japan Desk, who had taught for four years at Hokkaido Imperial University and authored *Japan's Military Masters: The Army in Japanese Life*, Viking Press, 1943; and Ralph Turner, a Yale economic historian who had worked on education reform for Germany. On the evolution of PCW-287, see Mayo (1982), pp. 35–46.

4. 'Japan: The Education System Under Military Government (PWC-287)', 15 July 1944, pp. 1–2, 7.

5. Ibid., pp. 10–11.

6. Bowles was an anthropologist and Asia specialist from Harvard. The son of missionaries, he had been raised in Japan, spoke Japanese fluently and shared with Hugh Borton a pacifist Quaker background that led him to eschew a front-line wartime role. On Bowles's role, see Mayo (1982), pp. 56–7, 62–6.

7. The Taishō readers were popularly known as 'dove and bean primers' because they opened on a picture of a dove, the symbol of peace, and beans, with which Japanese customarily fed the doves at shrines and other public places. The Shōwa textbooks were called '*sakura* primers' because the opening pages contained illustrations of cherry trees (*sakura*) in blossom, representing the Japanese martial spirit (the second and third pages depicted soldiers with rifles and the caption, 'Advance soldiers, advance').

8. 'Positive Policy for the Reorientation of the Japanese' (SWNCC-162). See the discussion in Mayo (1982), pp. 77–83. Quotations are from p. 78.

9. A short discussion of the post-surrender evolution of SWNCC-108 and SWNCC-162 is Takemae Eiji, *Senryō sengo-shi* (A History of the Occupation and Postwar Era), Iwanami Shoten, 1992, pp. 331–44 and Gary H. Tsuchimo-chi, *Education Reform in Postwar Japan: The 1946 US Education Mission*, University of Tokyo Press, 1993, p. 23. See also Mayo (1982), pp. 82–3.

10. Considered one of Japan's leading internationalists, Maeda had studied law at Tokyo Imperial University and served in the Home Ministry. He subsequently had represented Japan in the International Labour Organisation in Geneva (1923), worked as an editor for the *Asahi Shinbun* (1928–38) and headed the Japanese Cultural Library in New York (1938–41). During the war, he was Governor of Ni'igata Prefecture. A Christian, he became a Quaker after the war through the influence of an American missionary. Appointed Education Minister in the Higashikuni Cabinet on 18 August, Maeda would serve in that capacity until 13 January 1946, when, to the dismay of Bowles and other American friends, Government Section purged him for his wartime governorship.

11. Robert K. Hall, *Education for a New Japan*, Yale University Press, 1949, pp. 291–2.

12. On these points, refer to Toshio Nishi, *Unconditional Democracy: Education and Politics in Occupied Japan, 1945–1952*, Hoover Institution Press (Stanford University), 1982, pp. 147, 161–4. Maeda's views are expounded in Maeda Tamon, 'The Direction of Postwar Education in Japan', in *The Japan Quarterly*, vol. 3, no. 4, 1956, pp. 414–25.

13. On this process, see Joseph C. Trainor, _Educational Reform in Occupied Japan: Trainor's Memoir_, Meisei University Press, 1983, pp. 30–4 and Tsuchimochi (1993), pp. 89–94. The SCAPINs are reproduced in GHQ/SCAP, _History of the Nonmilitary Activities of the Occupation of Japan_ (given below as _HNMA_), no. 11: Education, 1952.
14. _HNMA_, no. 11: Education, ibid., pp. 59–68 and Ronald S. Anderson, _Education in Japan: A Century of Modern Development_, US Department of Health, Education and Welfare (US Government Printing Office), 1975, p. 63.
15. See Mark T. Orr, 'Education Reform Policy in Occupied Japan', PhD dissertation, Department of Political Science, University of North Carolina, 1954, pp. 207–8.
16. Herbert Passin, _The Legacy of the Occupation – Japan_, Occasional Papers of the East Asian Institute, Columbia University, 1968, p. 4; Trainor (1983), p. 68.
17. Tsuchimochi (1993), pp. 19–22.
18. On Orr's role, see Takemae Eiji, 'Kyōiku kaikaku no omoide: GHQ Kyōiku-kachō M. T. Oa hakase ni kiku' (Reminiscences of the Education Reforms: An Interview with Dr Mark T. Orr, GHQ's Education Division Chief), in _Tōkyō Keidai Gakkaishi_, no. 115, March 1980, p. 139. Tsuchimochi, op. cit., p. 28. Conant also is reported to have held pronounced anti-Japanese views. See Edward R. Beauchamp, 'Educational and Social Reform in Japan: The First United States Education Mission to Japan, 1946', in Burkman, ed. (1982), p. 180.
19. Ground-breaking research on the education reforms and the US Mission has been done by Kaigo Tokiomi, _Kyōiku kaikaku_ (The Education Reforms),Tōkyō Daigaku Shuppankai, 1975; Suzuki Ei'ichi, _Nihon senryō to kyōiku kaikaku_ (The Occupation of Japan and Education Reform), Keisō Shobō, 1983; Kubo Yoshizō, _Tai-Nichi senryō seisaku to sengo kyōiku kaikaku_ (Occupation Policy Towards Japan and the Reform of Postwar Education), Sanseidō, 1984; and Yomiuri Shinbun-hen (ed.), _Kyōiku no ayumi_ (Postwar Progress in Education), Yomiuri Shinbun, 1982. For more specialised works, refer to Satō Hideo, 'The Basic Source Materials on the Education Reform in Postwar Japan: Reports of the Surveys Conducted by the NIER Research Group', _Acta Asiatica_, no. 54, 1988, pp. 75–105.
20. Katherine Sansom, _Sir George Sansom: A Memoir_, Diplomatic Press (Tallahassee), 1972, p. 154.
21. These were Amano Teiyū, Kawai Michi and Nanbara Shigeru. See Anderson (1975), Note 4 on p. 87. Other Nitobe disciples were Education Minister Maeda Tamon and his successor Abe Yoshishige. Amano, too, would later serve in that position (May 1950 to August 1952).
22. Tsuchimochi (1993), pp. 71–7, and Trainor (1983), p. 62.
23. United States Education Mission to Japan, _Report of the United States Education Mission to Japan_, US Government Printing Office, 1946, pp. 1–62. The quotation is from p. 3. The report contained six sections: Aims and Contents, Language, Administration of Education, Teaching and the Education of Teachers,

Adult Education and Higher Education. See also the discussion in GHQ/SCAP, *Education in the New Japan*, Tokyo, May 1948.

24. Tsuchimochi (1993), p. 142.
25. The Stoddard quotation is from United States Education Mission to Japan (1946), p. 4. Japanese and American educators made a serious effort to harmonise their ideas before the final report was written, ironing out the details in a series of meetings held from 20 to 25 March during which the Japanese side presented its views informally as 'opinions'. Tsuchimochi (1993), p. 141–2. On Bowles's role, see Tsuchimochi (1993), pp. 95–107.
26. William K. Bunce, Chief of CI&E's Religions Division. Cited in William P. Woodard, *The Allied Occupation of Japan, 1945–1952, and Japanese Religions*, Leiden: Brill, 1972, p. 165.
27. Yoshida Shigeru, *The Yoshida Memoirs*, Heinemann, 1961, p. 131. The Abe citation is from Nishi (1982), p. 144.
28. Refer to Tsuchimochi (1993), pp. 83–4.
29. Tanaka's address is from the *Official Gazette Extra*, House of Representatives (English translation prepared by SCAP), 28 June 1946, p. 13. See also Nishi (1982), pp. 150–9.
30. Teruhisa Horio, *Educational Thought and Ideology in Modern Japan: State Authority and Intellectual Freedom*, University of Tokyo Press, 1988, pp. 135–7.
31. Trainor (1983), p. 297.
32. In English, this point is argued persuasively by J. Marshall Unger, *Literacy and Script Reform in Occupation Japan: Reading Between the Lines*, Oxford University Press, 1996.
33. Opinions generally fell into three categories. In 1873, Mori Arinori, Japan's first Education Minister (1885–9), proposed scrapping the Japanese language outright and replacing it with a simplified form of English. Mori's extremist and widely derided prescription found few advocates, but by the 1880s, a movement had appeared among academics, primarily scientists, to replace *kanji* and the two *kana* syllabaries with the Latin alphabet. As early as 1866, a second group of reformers had called for the abolition of *kanji* and the exclusive use of *kana*. A third tendency sought to reduce the number of *kanji* in use, standardise readings and streamline their basic components. All three arguments – romanisation, the exclusive use of *kana* and character simplification – continued to generate serious debate in official and academic circles until the early 1930s, when ultra-nationalist traditionalism drove discussion of script reform underground. Unger (1996), chapter 3.
34. At the University of Michigan, Hall had studied under linguist Charles C. Fries, a specialist on language simplification, who may have influenced his views on Japanese. Hall was particularly interested in the romanisation of Arabic transcription in Turkey under Kemal Atatürk, President of the Turkish Republic (1923–38). See Tsuchimochi (1993), pp. 109–10. The quotation is from Hall (1949), p. 352. See also Unger (1996), p. 71.

35. Hall's ideas on language reform are expounded in Hall (1949), pp. 293–410. On the controversy his ideas generated inside Education Division, see Trainor (1983), chapter 19. In 1950, Japanese language specialists conducted experiments indicating that the use of *rōmaji* has certain advantages over the traditional writing system in subjects such as mathematics. See Unger (1996), chapter 5. In December, Henderson was 'kicked upstairs' to the position of Special Advisor, and Lieutenant Colonel Donald R. Nugent stepped in to replace him as Chief of Education Branch (in May 1946, Nugent would become CI&E Chief of Section). Hall was relieved of operational duties and reassigned to the Section's Planning Division as Language Simplification Officer. Both men returned to the United States not long afterwards to resume academic careers.
36. Cited in Tsuchimochi (1993), pp. 111, 117–19.
37. United States Education Mission (1946), pp. 21–2. Tsuchimochi, ibid., pp. 75, 114–15.
38. United States Education Mission, ibid., p. iii. Nishi (1982), pp. 203–4.
39. Unger (1996). Hall, too, had urged that Chinese characters for everyday use be reduced to 1,500. Based largely on the JLC recommendations, in November 1946 the Education Ministry standardised the native *katakana* and *hiragana* syllabaries, modified a set of 1,850 characters (*tōyō kanji*) for ordinary use and adopted 881 characters for instruction in the lower grades (*kyōiku kanji*). Minor script modifications continued to be made during the Occupation and through the late 1950s.
40. Quoted by Kurita Wataru, 'Making Peace with Hirohito and a Militaristic Past', in *The Japan Quarterly*, April–June 1989, p. 189.
41. See Nishi (1982), pp. 176–84.
42. United States Education Mission (1946), p. 18.
43. Author's interview with Ishiyama and Okiyama, 2 January 1983. GHQ's liberal certification procedures resulted in the publication of some outstanding readers, such as *The New Constitution* and Yamamoto Yūzo's *Sun and Song* (*Taiyō to uta*). These textbooks elucidated the basic concepts of democracy in easy-to-understand language and challenged pupils to relate them to their everyday lives. They also expounded upon the evils of militarism and emphasised Japan's efforts to construct a civil society and rejoin the community of nations by embracing pacifist principles. Some primers were read not only by students but by adults in night-school classes and Parent–Teacher Associations.
44. At the end of six years of obligatory schooling, students continuing their studies were channelled into mass- and élite-orientated institutions. Mass-track students hit a dead end after two more years of study in higher elementary schools or two to seven years in youth schools (*seinen gakkō*), which taught lower-class youth industrial arts, agriculture and home economics. Élite-track students able to pass rigorous entrance exams went on to five years of middle school. Advanced technical training also was available in vocational schools. Only about

10 per cent of male elementary school graduates and 8 per cent of female graduates made the transition to middle school. Entry into higher schools, which provided three years of pre-university training and required students to live in dormitories, was even more selective. Less than 8 per cent of middle-school graduates managed to win acceptance to 32 state-run higher schools. Three years of university studies awaited the chosen few – less than 1 per cent of elementary school graduates. At the apex of the system were nine Imperial universities (including one each in Korea and Formosa) and below them a handful of prestigious private colleges. Women were barred from Tokyo and Kyoto Imperial Universities, but some 50 women's colleges existed, many of them founded by Christian missionaries. Women also had access to normal and technical schools, but only a small number pursued advanced studies. Education was intended to make women 'good wives' and 'wise mothers', and standards generally were lower than in boys' institutions. Academically, many women's colleges were colleges in name only, and the Education Ministry considered them on a par with boys' higher schools. In 1941, the Education Ministry attempted to extend compulsory education from six to eight years, but this measure could not be enforced because of the war. On 30 January 1946, just before the arrival of the Stoddard Mission, it announced that the prewar 6–5–3 (elementary, middle, higher school) ladder, with the first six years free and compulsory for all, would remain official policy. See *HNMA*, no. 11: Education, pp. 23–49 and Anderson (1975), chapter 2. Anderson was an Education Officer with a Military Government Team in southwestern Japan during the Occupation. His comments on Japanese education and the postwar reforms at the local level are particularly lucid.

45. On Japanese reformers, see Tsuchimochi (Gary) Hōichi, *Rokusansei kyōiku no tanjō: sengo kyōiku no genten* (The Origins of the 6–3 Education System: The Starting Point of Postwar Education), Yūshisha, 1992, pp. 96–100.
46. Tsuchimochi (1993), pp. 85, 107–9, 111.
47. Ibid., pp. 135–7.
48. Nanbara is quoted in Tsuchimochi, ibid., pp. 104, 107.
49. Author's interview with Kennoki Toshihiro. Kennoki was Education Minister from 1966 to 1967. See his *Ushi no ayumi: kyōiku ni waga michi o motomete* (At a Snail's Pace: For an Education System Suitable to Japan's Needs), Shōgakkan, 1973.
50. The Nanbara quotation is cited in Tsuchimochi (1993), p. 167.
51. *Ibid.* The Japanese side also insisted that specialised technical schools (*senmon gakkō*) be eliminated and integrated into higher-level institutions all enjoying the same academic standards. Normal schools and colleges, too, were to be phased out and teachers' training courses incorporated into university curricula. See Anderson (1975), pp. 75–8, 80.
52. To encourage the free exchange of ideas, from 1949 the Government and Relief in Occupied Areas (GARIOA) programme invited more than 1,000 Japanese

students and scholars to the United States to study in American universities. A smaller but constant stream of American educators also visited Japanese schools and institutions of higher learning.

53. American efforts to influence Japanese education continued long after the Stoddard Mission. Improvements for advanced science education were suggested by the six-man US Scientific Advisory Group (SAG), organised by the US National Academy of Sciences and led by chemist Roger Adams of the University of Illinois, which arrived in Tokyo in August 1947 at the invitation of Economic and Scientific Section. The SAG recommended dismantling the chair system, which it characterised as a feudalistic 'family-type' unit that stifled original thinking and narrowed the scope of scientific inquiry; increasing academic exchanges between institutions; and emphasising applied over pure science. In November 1948, a second SAG consisting of five members visited Tokyo to appraise the results of the first group. In September, a five-man US Cultural Science Mission, including historian Edwin O. Reischauer of Harvard and geographer Glen T. Trewartha of the University of Wisconsin, arrived to promote the social sciences. A second US Education Mission was despatched to Tokyo in August 1950, at the height of the Red Purge, but its primary function was to lend moral support to GHQ's anti-Communist crusade in the schools, and it made few substantive recommendations. On the SAGs, see Bowen C. Dees, *The Allied Occupation and Japan's Economic Miracle: Building the Foundations of Japanese Science and Technology, 1945–1952*, Curzon Press, 1997, chapter 9. A short description of the US Cultural Science Mission is found in Nishi (1982), pp. 230–2.

54. Nishi Kyōko, *Senryōka no Nihon fujin seisaku* (Policies Affecting Japanese Women Under the Occupation), Domesu Shuppan, 1985, p. 83.

55. Nishi (1982), p. 223.

56. San'ichi Shobō-hen (ed.), *Shiryō sengo gakusei undō (I), 1945–1949* (Basic Documents on the Student Movement, Part I: 1945), San'ichi Shobō, 1968, pp. 3–12.

57. See San'ichi Shobō-hen (ed.), ibid. In English, see also Shimbori Michiya, 'The Sociology of a Student Movement – A Japan Case Study', in *Daedalus*, vol. 97, Winter 1968, pp. 204–28 and Matsunami Michihiro, 'Origins of Zengakuren', in Stuart J. Dowsey, ed., *Zengakuren: Japan's Revolutionary Students*, Ishi Press (Berkeley), 1970, pp. 42–74.

58. Horio (1988), p. 129. Article 1 defined the aims of education as 'the full development of personality striving for the rearing of people . . . who shall love truth and justice, esteem individual value, respect labour and have a deep sense of responsibility, and be imbued with the independent spirit, as builders of the peaceful state and society'. Article 3 guaranteed equal opportunity and outlawed discrimination 'on account of race, creed, sex, social status, economic position or family origin'. Article 4 made education universal, compulsory and tuition-free; Article 5 provided for coeducation; Article 6 defined teachers as servants of

the community; Article 8 assured a political education necessary for 'intelligent citizenship'; Article 9 ordained religious tolerance and separation of church and state; and Article 10 made the school system and education in general 'directly responsible to the whole people'. *HNMA*, no. 11: Education, pp. 69–71.

59. Nishi (1982), pp. 213–14, 255–6.
60. Takemae (1980), pp. 140–1.
61. *HNMA*, no. 11: Education, pp. 168–9, 207–36, 292–306.
62. Kurt Steiner, *Local Government in Japan*, Stanford University Press, 1965, p. 95. The Ministry of Education Establishment Law gave the Ministry a purely advisory role and eliminated its authority to select textbooks and to certify and control administrative appointments and teacher promotions. The Private School Law assured a measure of autonomy to private schools by detaching them from direct state control. They were regulated by prefectural private-school councils composed of private-school teachers and administrators appointed by the governor.
63. See Nishi (1982), pp. 210–14 and Anderson (1975), pp. 68–9.
64. Ironically, Derevyanko's protestations in the Allied Council for Japan that officially sanctioned anti-Soviet literature violated basic Allied policy were dismissed as Soviet propaganda. Nishi, ibid., pp. 252–4.
65. Anderson (1975), pp. 69–70 and Steiner (1965), pp. 96–7. One consequence of the Dodge austerity programme of 1949 was a severe cut in the percentage of national funds allocated to local government. Diplomatic Section's Richard B. Finn, in a report to DS Chief William J. Sebald, noted in mid-1949 that more than 100 mayors and village heads had resigned and that 25 had been recalled by local assemblies for failure to procure adequate funding for education. In September 1949, the Shoup Mission recommended a system of block grants as a means of systematising national disbursements and reducing central control over local entities (chapter 10). In 1950, however, the government attempted to exempt educational funds from such grants. CI&E backed the government, preferring the system of local tax levies supplemented by special Ministry subsidies which it was in a position to control, but Government Section and other staff groups objected strenuously that such exceptions would jeopardise the entire scheme. Although MacArthur sided with Government Section, the Yoshida administration ignored GHQ and never implemented Shoup's recommendations. Finn's report of 25 July 1949 is cited in Nishi (1982), p. 215. On the block grant system, see Steiner (1965), loc. cit.
66. William K. Bunce, *Religions in Japan: Buddhism, Shinto, Christianity*, Charles E. Tuttle, 1955, pp. 27–34, 115–28. Bunce's book is based on a CI&E report he wrote in 1948 as a field guide for Military Government Teams. The pamphlet was prepared in cooperation with Kishimoto Hideo, a leading religious scholar.
67. On the divisions within Shintō, see generally Masaharu Anesaki, *The Religious Life of the Japanese People*, Kokusai Bunka Shinkōkai, 1961.
68. Bunce (1966), loc. cit.

69. US Department of State, *Foreign Relations of the United States* (below, given as *FRUS*), vol. 5, US Government Printing Office, 1944, pp. 1207–8.
70. Woodard (1972), pp. 51–2, 179.
71. Ibid, pp. 54–6 and Takemae Eiji, 'Religious Reform Under the Occupation of Japan: Interview with Dr. W. K. Bunce', in *The Journal of Tokyo Keizai University*, no. 150, March 1987, p. 195.
72. Takemae, ibid., pp. 199–200. Woodard (1972), pp. 26, 40, 341–2, 350, 354–5.
73. Holtom's book on Shintō was required reading for Occupationaires. Daniel C. Holtom, *The National Faith of Japan: A Study in Modern Shinto*, D. P. Dutton, 1938. Kishimoto was the author of *Japanese Religion in the Meiji Era*, Centenary Cultural Council Series, 1955.
74. Personal letter from Bunce to Dr Ebina Sugeo, 11 September 1994. Cited by courtesy of Dr Ebina.
75. *HNMA*, no. 20: Religion, pp. 6–10, 27–31.
76. Woodard (1972), pp. 57, 186–7, 193, 338–9.
77. Woodard, ibid., pp. 59–61. Takemae (1987), p. 202.
78. Bunce had taught at the Matsuyama High School from 1936 to 1939. It has been suggested that this experience sensitised him not only to Shintō practice but to the significance of Buddhism in Japanese religious life as well, convincing him of the folly of favouring one faith over another. Ebina Sugeo, 'Shūsen hiwa: Makkāsā to kyūsei Matsuyama kōkō no "Nenbutsu Ryōka"' (An Untold Story of the Early Postwar Era: MacArthur and the Former Matsuyama High School's 'Dormitory Sutra'), unpublished manuscript. Personal letter from Bunce to Dr Ebina Sugeo, ibid. Dr Ebina was a student at the high school.
79. Ironically, when SCAPIN-448 was publicised in mid-December, the careless mistranslation of a key clause appeared to outlaw Shintō in its entirety. The original English read: 'All teachers' manuals and textbooks now in use in any educational institution supported wholly or in part by public funds will be censored, and all Shinto doctrine will be deleted.' Education Ministry translators, however, truncated the sentence, rendering it simply as 'All Shinto doctrine will be deleted.' This, of course, was what the Shintō establishment had dreaded. The error was quickly corrected but misunderstanding lingered. Bunce also struggled with the word church and its Christian connotations. In the directive's first two drafts, he followed the US Constitution and used the phrase 'separation of church and state', but in the third draft, he changed 'church' to 'religion'. As he and his staff came to realise, Japanese and Western concepts of religion and worship differ significantly and cannot be used interchangeably.
80. Woodard (1972), pp. 243–5, 355–7.
81. Ibid., pp. 218–26, 231, 359; Douglas MacArthur, *Reminiscences*, McGraw-Hill, 1964, pp. 310–11; *HNMA*, no. 20: Religion, p. 48; Nishi (1982), pp. 44–5.
82. Woodard, ibid., pp. 351–3. Richard B. Finn, *Winners in Peace: MacArthur, Yoshida and Postwar Japan*, University of California Press, 1992, p. 168. Trainor (1983), pp. 284–7.

83. Christianity nonetheless won a number of prominent converts. A late and unlikely proselyte was Yoshida Shigeru. On his death bed, Yoshida summoned a Catholic priest, who arrived shortly after his death but baptized the deceased politician anyway. Yoshida's family included practising Catholics, and they chose the baptismal name Thomas More. Yoshida earlier had indicated a preference for Joseph, and the former premier was buried as Joseph Thomas More following funeral rites held at a Catholic cathedral in Tokyo. See John W. Dower, *Empire and Aftermath: Yoshida Shigeru and the Japanese Experience, 1878–1954*, Council on East Asian Studies, Harvard University, 1979, pp. 306, 547 (Note 3).

84. Elliott R. Thorpe, *East Wind, Rain*, Gambit Inc. (Boston), 1969, pp. 235–6. Woodard (1972), pp. 245, 272–5. Nishi (1982), pp. 43, 290. The MacArthur quotations are from the Forrestal Diary (Princeton University), as cited by Mikio Haruna, 'MacArthur Pondered Showa Conversion', in *The Japan Times*, 4 May 2000, p. 3.

85. The Supreme Commander did not oppose attempts to Westernise the Imperial family, however. In early 1949, he supported a request by the Empress to have Akihito educated in the United States. According to Diplomatic Section's William Sebald, MacArthur believed study in America would not only help Japan–US relations but wean the Prince from 'the enervating atmosphere of a royal court in which feudal customs may gradually reappear'. Walton Butterworth of the State Department's Far Eastern Division vetoed the proposal, suggesting that if the Prince must go abroad, he should choose Britain instead. (Akihito remained in Japan, but years later, his eldest son Hironomiya would study at Oxford.) Memorandum from William Sebald to W. Walton Butterworth, 18 February 1949 (894.0011/2–1849, National Archives Records Administration, Washington DC).

86. Woodard (1972), pp. 119–24.

87. Ibid., pp. 128–33, 227–9.

88. Ibid., pp. 91–102. See also Joseph M. Kitagawa, *Religions in Japanese History*, Columbia University Press, 1966, pp. 279–81.

89. Kitagawa, ibid., pp. 273–5.

90. Woodard (1972), pp. 149–56.

91. On the Office of Censorship, see Marlene J. Mayo, 'Civil Censorship and Media Control in Early Occupied Japan: From Minimum to Stringent Surveillance', in Robert Wolfe, ed., *Americans as Proconsuls: United States Military Government in Germany and Japan, 1944–1952*, Southern Illinois University Press, 1984, pp. 267, 499 (Note 4).

92. Information control is integral to the concept of military governance. The 1940 field guide, *The United States Army and Navy Manual of Military Government and Civil Affairs* (chapter 5), stipulated that '[t]o the extent that military interests are not prejudiced, freedom of speech and press should be maintained and instituted'. But the handbook forbade the transmission or receipt of 'any

message containing anything hostile, detrimental or disrespectful to the United States, its armed forces, their personnel, or the military government'. Takemae Eiji, ed., *Beikoku rikukaigun: gunsei-minji manyuaru* (The United States Army and Navy Manual of Military Government and Civil Affairs), Misuzu Shobō, 1998, p. 37.

93. See Mayo (1984), pp. 267–71. JSC-873/3 distinguished three phases of information management: invasion, occupation and indigenous government. The invasion and occupation phases would entail stringent media controls.

94. Monica Braw, *The Atomic Bomb Suppressed*, M. E. Sharpe, 1991, pp. 24–5. Mayo, ibid., pp. 278–9.

95. CAC-237 proposed strict information controls in the early emergency phase of occupation. Freedom of speech was to be guaranteed to the maximum extent possible, however, and censorship would be imposed only where there was a clear threat to the safety of the occupying forces or their mission. Moreover, such constraints were to be relaxed progressively during the post-emergency period and greater cooperation sought with liberal Japanese. Specific recommendations included the abolition of restrictive laws on freedom of expression, the monitoring of national newspapers (regional newspapers would not be watched), the use of Japan Broadcasting Corporation (NHK) facilities and the vetting of radio, theatre and film for militaristic content (film screenings would require prior military government approval).

96. Mayo (1984), pp. 277, 288–9, Note 18 on p. 510 and Marlene J. Mayo, 'The War of Words Continues: American Radio Guidance in Occupied Japan', in Thomas W. Burkman, ed., *The Occupation of Japan: Arts and Culture*, General Douglas MacArthur Foundation, 1988, p. 46.

97. At this time, the War Department's Civil Affairs Division set up an independent Reorientation Branch, and the State Department absorbed the Office of War Information, reorganising it as the Office of International Information and Cultural Affairs. Mayo (1982), pp. 77–83.

98. Fellers had been a ready convert to the notion of moral disarmament. On 27 August 1945, he transformed the Psychological Warfare Branch into the Information Dissemination Section. On 22 September, the IDS was incorporated into the Civil Information and Education Section, evolving into its Information Dissemination Branch. Mayo (1984), pp. 285–7.

99. Shortly after its inception, the Meiji state enacted the Press Ordinance of 1875, followed by the Press Law of 1909, imposing clear limits on freedom of speech. From the late 1930s, the government stepped up its surveillance of public media and from 1941, narrow restraints were placed on the media in conjunction with the 1938 National Mobilisation Law, which commandeered the human and physical resources necessary for war. The Censorship Section of the Home Ministry's Police Bureau tightly monitored public and private communications for anything disruptive of the public tranquillity, offensive to the sanctity of the Throne or critical of the institutions of private property and the family. Police

exercised pre-publication censorship of newspaper articles, radio scripts and film scenarios and post-publication controls over magazine pieces. See Lawrence W. Beer, *Freedom of Expression in Japan: A Study in Comparative Law, Politics, and Society,* Kodansha International, 1984, p. 67; Richard H. Mitchell, *Censorship in Imperial Japan,* Princeton University Press, 1983; and William J. Coughlin, *Conquered Press: The MacArthur Era in Japanese Journalism,* Pacific Books (Palo Alto), 1952, pp. 65–7.

100. Braw (1991), p. 35. Thorpe (1969), pp. 190–1.

101. See generally, Matsuda Hiroshi, *Hōsō sengo-shi* (A History of Postwar Broad-casting), Matagakisha, 1980 and NHK (Radio and TV Culture Institute), *50 Years of Japanese Broadcasting,* Nihon Hōsō Kyōkai, 1977.

102. Government Section, SCAP, ed., *The Political Reorientation of Japan, September 1945 to September 1948* (below, given as *PRJ*), US Government Printing Office, 1949, vol. 2, p. 460. Hailed by GHQ as the 'show window of the Occupation', *The Nippon Times* quickly became a mouthpiece for SCAP, with 30 per cent of its news emanating from MacArthur's Public Information Office. See Yamamoto Taketoshi, *Senryōki medeia bunseki* (A Study of the Media During the Occupation), Hōsei Daigaku Shuppankyoku, 1996, pp. 93–111.

103. Mayo (1984), p. 296. Coughlin (1952), pp. 20, 111–17.

104. Furuno claimed he was taking responsibility for Dōmei's wartime role as propaganda organ and espionage centre, but his real motive was to forestall more drastic action by SCAP. On 1 November, two new press agencies arose from the ashes, Kyōdō and Jiji, which survived by dividing the parent company's financial, material and human assets. Jiji tailored its activities to the business community, and Kyōdō quickly re-established much of Dōmei's former news monopoly. Furuno himself was arrested on Class-A war crimes charges but escaped conviction. See Yamamoto (1996), pp. 116–38, 292–7.

105. After establishing SCAP custodianship of the media, Hoover resigned in November 1945. In April 1946, Colonel William B. Putnam took charge of the Detachment, remaining in that position for most of the Occupation. In May 1946, Thorpe resigned and his Civil Intelligence Section was dissolved, and Putnam's CCD was transferred to G-2 Section's Civil Intelligence Divi-sion. Under Willoughby's watchful eye, the CCD divided its duties among the Postal Division, the Telecommunications Division and the Press, Pictorial and Broadcast Division. Putnam maintained established stations in four regions: Tokyo (District I, northern Japan), Osaka (District II, central Japan), Fukuoka (District III, southern Japan) and, in the early phase, Seoul (District IV, southern Korea). Data on CCD personnel are from Yamamoto (1996), p. 299. Kawaguchi was interviewed in Los Angeles by Takagi Kikurō, 'GHQ no ken'etsu: hōdō no "jiyū" to "tōei" to iu mujun' (GHQ Censorship: The Contradiction Between 'Freedom' and 'Control'), in Yomiuri Shinbun Henshūkyoku, *Sengo gojūnen: Nippon no kiseki* (Fifty Years After the War:

Japan's Path), vol. 1, 1995, p. 165. The Military Intelligence quotation is cited by Mayo (1984), p. 514.

106. On the objectives of censorship, see US Department of the Army (Historical Section, G-2, FECOM), ed., *Reports of General MacArthur*, vol. 1: Supplement (MacArthur in Japan – The Occupation: Military Phase), US Government Printing Office, 1966, pp. 232–3 (below, given as *Reports of MacArthur*). On 1 October and 27 November 1945, SCAP directives entitled 'Censorship of the Mails' and 'Regulations Governing Communications Over International, Foreign, and External Telegraph, Telephone and Wireless Facilities' authorised the CCD to screen mail as well as tap phones, and these became entrenched practices that continued until censorship was lifted in October 1949. Data are from Furukawa Atsushi, 'Nenpyō – Senryōka no shuppan, engeki, hōsō ken'etsu' (A Chronology of Censored Publications, Dramas and Broadcasts Under the Occupation), in *Tōkyō Keidai Gakkaishi* (The Journal of Tokyo Keizai University), no. 118, 1980, pp. 231–51.

107. Okuizumi Eizaburō and Furukawa Atsushi, 'Nihon senryōki no Kyokutō Beigun jōhō shūshū katsudō to soshiki' (Information-Gathering Activities and Organisation of the US Far East Command During the Occupation of Japan), in *Tōkyō Keidai Gakkaishi* (The Journal of Tokyo Keizai University), nos. 109–10, 1978, pp. 128–36; and Yamamoto (1996), pp. 263–4, 294–5, 329.

108. Haru Matsukata Reischauer, *Samurai and Silk: A Japanese and American Heritage*, Charles E. Tuttle, 1987 (Harvard University Press, 1986), pp. 312–13.

109. Braw (1991), pp. 55–8; Coughlin (1952), pp. 52–3, 79; Kyoko Hirano, *Mr. Smith Goes to Tokyo: Japanese Cinema Under the American Occupation, 1945–1952*, Smithsonian Institution Press, 1992, pp. 56–7.

110. The expression is John Dower's: *Embracing Defeat: Japan in the Wake of World War II*, W. W. Norton and the New Press, 1999, chapter 14.

111. Braw (1991), pp. 90–2, 94–9. The scholar is Mark Selden in the preface to Braw, p. x.

112. Robert M. Spaulding, 'CCD Censorship of Japan's Daily Press', in Burkman, ed. (1988), pp. 6–9. On 'Japan's Tragedy', see Hirano (1992), pp. 122–45. Iwasaki Akira, *Senryō sareta sukurīn* (The Occupied Screen), Shin Nihon Shuppansha, 1975, p. 83, translated by Hirano (1992), p. 102.

113. See the discussion in Hirano, ibid., pp. 54–5, 172–5 and, particularly, Dower (1999), pp. 429–31.

114. Earle Ernst also became an admirer of Kabuki and cooperated with Bowers in working to liberate it gradually from CCD control. He left SCAP for the University of Hawai'i shortly after Bowers joined PPB, becoming 'the pre-eminent Kabuki scholar in the West' (Donald Richie, 'The Occupied Arts', in Mark Sandler, ed., *The Confusion Era: Art and Culture of Japan During the Allied Occupation, 1945–1952*, Smithsonian Institution, 1997, p. 18). The art critic is Richie, ibid. On modern drama, see David G. Goodman, 'Shingeki Under the Occupation', in Burkman, ed. (1988), pp. 190–7.

115. Bowers left Japan in May 1948, his mission accomplished. Okamoto Shirō, *Kabuki o sukutta otoko: Makkāsā no fukukan Fōbian Bawāzu* (The Man Who Saved Kabuki: MacArthur's Military Aide Faubion Bowers), Shūeisha, 1998, pp. 157–8, 248, 268, 277, 367; Faubion Bowers, 'Discussion', in Burkman, ed. (1988), p. 204.
116. *Reports of MacArthur*, pp. 239–41. The State Department quotation is from Mayo (1984), p. 313.
117. Takakuwa Kōkichi, cited in Hirano (1992), p. 103. Yamamoto (1996), pp. 294–5.
118. Robert B. Textor, *Failure in Japan: With Keystones for a Positive Policy*, Greenwood Press, 1972 (The John Day Co., 1951), p. 110.
119. On *Eirin*, see Satō Tadao, *Nihon eiga-shi, 1941–1959* (The History of Japanese Cinema, 1941–1959), vol. 2, Iwanami Shoten, 1995, p. 230. Etō's arguments are developed in *Ochiba no hakiyose: haisen, senryō, ken'etsu to bungaku* (Raked Leaves: Defeat, Occupation, Censorship and Literature), Bungei Shunjūsha, 1981.
120. The quoted expression is Richie's, loc. cit. See also *Reports of MacArthur*, p. 241, Furukawa (1978), pp. 128–35 and, generally, Matsuura Sōzō, *Senryōka no genron dan'atsu* (Repression of Free Speech Under the Occupation), Gendai Jānarizumu Shuppankai, 1977, pp. 302, 309–11. Mayo (1984), p. 515 (Note 88).
121. Braw (1991), p. 75, chapter 7. Although the *kamishibai* ordinances gradually were repealed as television rendered that art form obsolete, Kanagawa Prefecture did not annul the ban until 1983. Yamamoto (1996), pp. 276–9. Satō Tadao, *Nihon no eiga: hadaka no Nihonjin* (The Japanese Cinema: The Japanese Revealed), Hyōronsha, 1978, p. 116, translated by Dower (1999), p. 439.
122. Harry E. Wildes, the quixotic Government Section scholar and rabid anti-Communist, later charged that '[o]fficial CIE publications, notably on press, radio, and movie development, favoured the Communist line, attacking conservatives as rightist, feudalistic, or reactionary while hailing radicals as progressives, liberals, and democrats'. *Typhoon in Tokyo: The Occupation and its Aftermath*, Macmillan, 1954, p. 274.
123. Mayo (1984), p. 308. Coughlin (1952), p. 45.
124. Mayo (1988), pp. 55–6.
125. On relations between CCD and CI&E, see Robert H. Berkov, 'The Press in Postwar Japan', in *Far Eastern Survey*, vol. 16, 1947, pp. 162–6. Coughlin (1952), p. 51. Shirasu Jirō suggested that David Conde's role in the film's development and his close association with Nichiei producer Iwasaki Akira precipitated his departure from CI&E in June 1946. See Hirano (1992), p. 134.
126. Mayo (1988), p. 58.
127. Conde was assisted by a British national of mixed ancestry, Hugh Walker (Japanese name: Ōkawa Shū) who had worked on the margins of the prewar Japanese cinema but knew the industry well and whose fluency in Japanese

made up for the Branch Chief's lack of language skills. A Formosan named Chen, a former physician, also worked under Conde, presumably as a translator and interpreter. Internal SCAP criticism of Conde's role in the production of *The Tragedy of Japan* hastened his resignation in June 1946. In November, George Gercke became Chief of Motion Picture and Drama Branch. A musician by training, he was one of the rare censors with actual experience in the film and entertainment industry, having managed productions in London and worked as assistant director for the musical *Show Boat*. Although Conde's tenure was brief, his influence on Japanese film was decisive and lasting. Hirano, ibid., pp. 39–44, 102–3, 134 and, by the same author, 'The Occupation and Japanese Cinema', in Burkman, ed. (1988), p. 149.

128. Hirano (1992), chapter 4.
129. Hirano, ibid. and Keiko McDonald, 'Whatever Happened to Passive Suffering? Women on Screen', in Sandler, ed. (1997), pp. 53–70.
130. Mayo (1988), p. 57; Baba (1988), p. 87.
131. Mayo, ibid., pp. 58–72. Baba, ibid., p. 86. Takagi (1995), p. 164.
132. In its prewar colonies, Japan had made Japanese the official public language as part of a policy of cultural and ethnic assimilation, actively discouraging national tongues. But in the Empire's wartime Pacific and Southeast Asian possessions, Japanese officials pursued a dual strategy. On the one hand, they imposed Japanese as the lingua franca of the Greater East Asia Co-Prosperity Sphere. Here, recognising the intrinsic difficulties of *kanji*, they drew from prewar ideas on language simplification, experimenting with romanisation and *kana*. On the other hand, Imperial authorities encouraged linguistic unity within each of the cultural spheres they controlled, establishing language blocs within which Tagalog, Indonesian, Vietnamese and Burmese were given ascendancy over other local languages. Takemae Eiji, *Senryō sengo-shi* (A History of the Occupation and Postwar Era), Iwanami Shoten, 1992, pp. 355–7.
133. *Reports of MacArthur*, pp. 51–2. Takemae (1992), pp. 358–9. On the success of Ogawa's book, see Dower (1999), pp. 188–9.
134. The author's interview with Hirakawa is reproduced in Takemae Eiji (1992), pp. 369–72. It was first published in 'Sengo demokurashī to Ei-kaiwa: "Kamu Kamu Eigo" no yakuwari (Postwar Democracy and English Conversation: The Role of 'Come, Come English'), in Shisō no Kagaku Kenkyūkai, ed., *Kyōdō kenkyū: Nihon senryō* (Joint Research: The Occupation of Japan), Tokuma Shobō, 1972, pp. 131–46.
135. Hirakawa Kiyoshi, *Kamu, kamu evuribadē: Hirakawa Tada'ichi to 'Kamu, Kamu Eigo' no jidai* (Come, Come Everybody: Hirakawa Tada'ichi and the Era of 'Come, Come English'), NHK Shuppan, 1995, pp. 16–19.
136. In the first three years, the programme presented 107 stories with a total vocabulary of more than 12,000 words, of which 600 were high-frequency core terms that were repeated systematically.

137. Hirakawa's own career exemplified the democratic values he attempted to instil in his listeners. As a young man of 16, he had gone to the United States to join his father, a migrant labourer. Settling in Seattle, Washington, he washed dishes, worked on the railroad and in a paper mill and sold automobiles. He began his education over again, entering elementary school and finally winning acceptance at Washington State University, where he majored in drama. After graduation, he moved to Los Angeles and worked as an actor in Hollywood, later marrying a compatriot. In 1937, when his wife's visa expired, Hirakawa accompanied her back to Japan. In Tokyo, he joined the Japan Broadcasting Corporation where his impeccable English soon made him the leading overseas broadcaster. When MacArthur's staff set up headquarters in Yokohama, Hirakawa was despatched to help the US Army set up its own broadcasting facilities and serve as liaison with NHK. Known to the Americans as Joe Hirakawa, he worked with CI&E's Radio Branch to renovate the broadcasting corporation. Hirakawa (1995), pp. 180–216; Mayo (1988), p. 78 (Note 36). Ibid., p. 76. Takemae (1992), pp. 359–60, 374–5, 378.

138. Ishihara Shintarō, introduction to Hirakawa (1995), pp. 1, 3.

139. As a junior high school student in those days, I was very busy. To make ends meet, I rolled cigarettes, made charcoal and gathered herbs in the mountains, which I sold together with rice on the black market. At the same time, I was reading Hegel and Marx. Hirakawa's programme so completely captured my fancy that I organised a 'Come, Come' club in Nagano. As president, I learned English. I also learned the rudiments of social science by negotiating a tax exemption with Japanese officials for a 'Come, Come' rally we were organising and to which we had invited members of the local Military Government Team. For me personally, the Occupation was a period of challenge and opportunity, not one of darkness and confusion, although later I would experience its sombre side, as well. 'Come, Come English' symbolised the sense of excitement, freedom and discovery that I and others my age felt in these early postwar years.

Chapter 9   The Welfare Reforms and Minorities

1. Cited in Tatara Toshio, 'The Allied Occupation and Japanese Public Welfare: An Overview of SCAP Activities During the Early Phase', in Thomas W. Burkman, ed., *The Occupation of Japan: Education and Social Reform*, General Douglas MacArthur Foundation, 1982, p. 314. SWNCC-107 ('Policy With Respect to Relief in Japan') of 1 October 1945 contained the same admonition.

2. Ibid., p. 324–5. After the European example, the Meiji state had instituted poor laws in 1874 and 1880, but care of the indigent was relegated primarily to Buddhist and Christian charitable organisations. See generally, Tatara Toshio, '1400 Years of Japanese Social Work From its Origins Through the Allied Occupation, 552–1952', PhD dissertation, Bryn Mawr College, 1975, chapters 2, 4 and 5.

3. Refer to the note by Zabelle Zakarian in Crawford F. Sams *'Medic': The Mission*

of an American Military Doctor in Occupied Japan and Wartorn Korea, Edited by Zabelle Zakarian, M. E. Sharpe, 1998, pp. 270–1.

4. See Ishida Takeshi, *Nihon no seiji to kotoba: 'jiyū' to 'fukushi'* (Politics and Language in Japan: 'Freedom and Welfare', vol. 1, Tōkyō Daigaku Shuppankai, Tokyo, 1989, pp. 287–90 and the discussion in Takahashi Mutsuko, *The Emergence of Welfare Society in Japan*, Ashgate, 1997, p. 56–8. Refer also to the analysis by former Health and Welfare Ministry official Murakami Kimiko, *Senryōki no fukushi seisaku* (Welfare Policy During the Occupation of Japan), Keisō Shobō, 1987, chapter 2 and to Kōseishō Gojūnen-shi Henshū I'inkai (below, given as Kōseishō), ed., *Kōseishō gojūnen-shi* (The Ministry of Health and Welfare: The First Fifty Years), Kōsei Mondai Kenkyūkai, 1988, pp. 584–5.

5. A graduate of Tokyo Imperial University's Law Faculty, Kasai began his career in the Home Ministry, transferring to Welfare at its creation in 1938. From 1945 until his retirement in 1951, he worked closely with PH&W. The quotation is from Tatara (1982), p. 321.

6. On the notion of Imperial mercy, see Ikeda Yoshimasa, *Nihon shakai fukushi-shi* (A History of Social Welfare in Japan), Hōritsu Bunkasha, 1986, pp. 163–8. Concerning the manipulation of phraseology, refer to Murakami (1987), pp. 42–8 and the discussion in Takahashi (1997), p. 60.

7. On the *hōmen-i'in*, see Tatara (1975), chapter 4 and Ishida (1989), p. 262–8. Statistics are from Public Health and Welfare Section, *Missions and Accomplishments of the Occupation in the Public, Health and Welfare Fields* (below, given as PH&W, *Missions and Accomplishments*), GHQ/SCAP, Tokyo, December 1949, p. 22.

8. See Kasai Yoshisuke, ' "Nomu, utsu, kau" to seikatsu hogo hōan' (Drunkards, Beggars and the Livelihood Protection Bill), in Kōseishō Nijūnen-shi Henshū I'inkai, ed., *Kōseishō nijūnen-shi* (The Ministry of Health and Welfare: The First Twenty Years), Kōsei Mondai Kenkyūkai, 1960, pp. 392–3, Tatara (1982), pp. 322–3 and the comments by Harold W. Fieldman, then chief of PH&W's Public Assistance Branch, in response to Tatara in Burkman, ed. (1982), p. 365. A concise summary in English is Takahashi (1997), pp. 60–2.

9. Sams (1998), pp. 158, 288 (Note 3) and Public Health and Welfare Section, *Public Health and Welfare in Japan*, GHQ/SCAP, Tokyo, 1949, pp. 212–22.

10. In May 1946, the average urban dweller consumed a mere 1,500 calories a day but, by November, that figure had jumped to 2,000 calories. See Takemae Eiji, ed., *C. F. Samsu, DDT kakumei: senryō-ki no iryō fukushi seisaku o kaisō suru* (C. F. Sams, The DDT Revolution: Looking Back at the Reform of Medicine and Social Welfare During the Occupation), Iwanami Shoten, 1986, pp. 106–7, 113. Takemae's translation of Sams's memoir includes sidebars with a running commentary on the text. The school lunch programme, for instance, originated with the visit of a United Nations Relief and Rehabilitation Agency mission to Japan in the summer of 1946 led by former US President Herbert Hoover. Hoover was appalled by the widespread malnutrition he encountered among

children and recommended remedial action to MacArthur. Japanese teachers, too, had petitioned the Education Ministry for school food relief. The Ministry approached CI&E, but when Section Chief Nugent showed little interest in the proposal, PH&W seized the initiative. On 14 October 1946, Sams ordered the government to establish a school meal programme, which was begun on 11 December in all state schools with assistance from Licensed Agencies for Relief in Asia (see Note 11 below). Students were asked to pay a modest ¥0.74 per lunch, but those with parents on the dole were exempted. Takemae, ibid., pp. 122–3.

11. On 30 August, PH&W directed the Welfare Ministry's Social Affairs Bureau to administer the distribution of food, clothing and medical supplies organised by an international aid consortium, the Licensed Agencies for Relief in Asia (LARA). Three LARA representatives, one each from the Catholic Church, the Quaker Friends Service Committee and the Protestant World Church Alliance, were attached to PH&W to assist in this work. By December 1949, LARA had supplied nearly 10.5 million tons of relief goods to 7 million people. In August 1947, PH&W began helping the Cooperative for American Remittances to Europe (CARE) distribute 'CARE packages' to destitute Japanese. In 1949, at Sams's invitation, the United Nations Children's Emergency Relief Fund (UNICEF) began providing surplus American skim milk to Japanese schools for the school lunch programme. The costs were borne by the Japanese government. On the food crisis and LARA, see Sams, ibid., pp. 59–64, 163–4 and PH&W, *Missions and Accomplishments*, p. 23.

12. Sōrifu (Prime Minister's Office), *Nihon tōkei nenkan* (Japan Statistical Yearbook), Tokyo, 1956, p. 477.

13. Takemae (1986), pp. 18–19 and Okamoto Shirō, *Kabuki o sukutta otoko: Makkāsā no fukukan Fōbian Bawāzu* (The Man Who Saved Kabuki: MacArthur's Military Aide Faubion Bowers), Shūeisha, 1998 p. 243.

14. Sams (1998), pp. 84–5, 93–4.

15. Takemae (1986), pp. 134–5.

16. Sams (1998), pp. 89–91, 207.

17. Sams, ibid., chapters 8–10. See also Harry E. Wildes, *Typhoon in Tokyo: The Occupation and its Aftermath*, Macmillan, 1954, chapter 19 and *HMNA*, no. 19: Public Health, pp. 49–51.

18. By 1949, dysentery had been reduced by 79 per cent. Cholera was effectively eliminated by December 1946, and smallpox, too, was brought quickly under control, falling from 17,000 cases in 1946 to 124 in 1949. In 1945, there were 58,000 instances of typhoid fever, but by 1949, that figure had plummeted by 90 per cent to fewer than 6,000. In 1945, a typhus epidemic broke out in Hokkaido among Korean miners, but the 32,000 cases reported in 1946 had dwindled to 212 by 1949. Diphtheria had afflicted 94,000 Japanese in 1944. Immunisation was begun in 1947, and by 1949, the incidence of this disease had dropped by 86 per cent. Japan had long suffered one of the world's highest death rates from

tuberculosis, but this scourge, too, was curbed following BCG vaccination programmes, and by 1949, the number of deaths had been slashed by 40 per cent.
PH&W, *Missions and Accomplishments*, pp. 2–13.

19. Sams's first obligation was to the Occupation forces, and on 12 September,
before instituting basic reforms, he helped the US Army requisition St Luke's
Hospital in Tokyo (the hospital would remain under American military control
until May 1956). In October, the Army took over Dōai Memorial Hospital in
Tokyo (returned in October 1955) and in early November it acquired the Osaka
Red Cross Hospital (returned in February 1955). On Sams's agreement with
Whitney, see Sams (1998), pp. 144–5. At the same time, PH&W demilitarised
the Japan Red Cross, the world's second largest national society. Responsible
primarily for the care of wounded soldiers, the Japan branch had been placed
under the Sanitation Commission of the Imperial Army and Navy. On 20 September 1945, Sams invited the American Red Cross to help restructure and
democratise its sister society. This task was undertaken by American Red Cross
personnel on loan to PH&W as consultants. The Japan Red Cross elected new
leaders for the first time in January 1947. Divested of its former military duties,
the organisation continued to operate hospitals and clinics and train nurses but
now included among its activities volunteer services, safety education (water
safety and first aid) and civilian disaster relief. Sams's Welfare Division also oversaw passage of the Disaster Relief Law of 18 October 1947. The statute established a
National Disaster Board with branches in each prefecture and made the central
government responsible for financing and coordinating relief activities. The
National Disaster Board proved its mettle during the devastating Ishikawa–Fukui
earthquake of June 1948. *HNMA*, no. 18: Public Welfare, pp. 94–5, 102–3.

20. Kōseishō, ed. (1960), pp. 94–6, and Yoshida Kyūichi, *Nihon shakai jigyō no
rekishi* (A History of Social Work in Japan), Keisō Shobō, 1994, chapter 13.
PH&W collided with Government Section over the issue of creating prefectural
health and welfare departments, GS being extremely reluctant to revise the
Local Autonomy Law it had just enacted in May 1947. After months of discussion, Sams eventually prevailed on GS Chief Whitney to amend the statute. The
Sams–Whitney impasse was related to the author by former Welfare Ministry
official Saita Noboru on 12 December 1985.

21. Tatara (1982), pp. 324–6 and Takemae (1986), pp. 214–15, 223.

22. Sams (1998), pp. 71–2 and Takemae (1986), pp. 218–20. In Tokyo, a model
health centre was set up in Suginami Ward consisting of the following divisions:
Administrative Affairs, Medical Affairs, Pharmaceutical Affairs, Environmental
Sanitation, Food and Animal Disease Control, Communicable Disease Control,
Venereal Disease Control, Prevention (Parasites), Maternal and Child Hygiene,
Dental Hygiene, Nutrition, Health Education, Public Health Statistics, Public
Nursing, Medical Social Science and Laboratories.

23. Katsumata Minoru, former Chief of the Welfare Ministry's Health Bureau,
played a crucial role in facilitating bilateral collaboration on the collection of

statistics. On Katsumata's role, see the memorial volume issued by his students, *Kindai kōshū-eisei no chichi: Katsumata Minoru* (Katsumata Minoru: The Father of Modern Public Health and Welfare), 1970.

24. Murakami (1987), pp. 151, 232 and Sams (1998), p. 79. When Dr Selwyn T. Collins, head statistician of the US Public Health Service, arrived in Tokyo at Sams's invitation to evaluate the reorganisation of vital statistics, he found a remarkably high level of reporting, which eventually achieved rates of completeness ranging from 95 to 99.8 per cent.

25. Sams (1998), p. 125 and Note 5 on p. 284, respectively.

26. The transformation of the nursing profession under Alt's supervision was stunning. Traditionally, nurses received little formal training and were looked down upon as menials. In June 1946, Alt set up the Tokyo Model Demonstration School of Nursing in the Central Red Cross Hospital and assigned American military nurses at St Luke's Hospital to key teaching positions. In 1949, as a result of improved nursing education and licensing standards, the Association of Japanese Midwives, Clinical Nurses and Public Health Nurses was admitted to the International Council of Nurses, enhancing the public image of these vital care-givers.

27. *HNMA*, no. 19: Public Health, pp. 128–43. The Pharmaceutical Affairs Law was enacted on 29 July, followed by the Dental Practitioners Law, the Dental Hygienists Law and the Public Health Nurse, Midwife and Nurses Law, which were passed together with the Medical Practitioners Law on 30 July.

28. See John M. Jennings, *The Opium Empire: Japanese Imperialism and Drug Trafficking in Asia, 1895–1945*, Praeger, 1997, pp. 99–107. After the war, Japan's civilian and former military drug lords managed to conceal large stores of narcotics and later made fortunes from their covert sale. Ironically, many buyers were GIs. Health and Welfare Ministry statistics show that in 1952, 11 per cent of all drug dealing in Japan took place in the vicinity of US military bases. A year later, that figure had jumped to 16 per cent. Wildes (1954), p. 198.

29. See Murakami (1987), pp. 102–8, 138–9 and Takemae (1986), pp. 56–7.

30. Although the Social Affairs Bureau championed the plan, the real impetus for the Children's Bureau came from a private citizens' coalition, the Forum on the Problems of Mothers and Children (*Boshi Mondai Kondankai*). After studying laws for minors in the United States and Europe, the Forum concluded that only an independent bureau could adequately safeguard the rights of children, and it energetically lobbied both PH&W and the Welfare Ministry. Murakami analyses the dovetailing of Japanese and American interests on this issue. Murakami (1987), pp. 127–9.

31. A former English teacher active in the Japan Christian Temperance Union, Yoshimi began her career as a social worker after graduating from the New York School of Social Work in 1929. During the depression years of the 1930s, she devoted herself to relief projects and volunteer work in Tokyo's impoverished popular quarters.

32. *HNMA*, no. 18: Public Welfare, pp. 53–63.
33. Kōseishō, ed. (1988), pp. 586–7 and *HNMA*, ibid., pp. 44–6.
34. See Kim Nan Goo, 'Sengo shōgaisha seisaku no seisei (The Origins of Japan's Postwar Policy for the Disabled), PhD dissertation, Tokyo Keizai University, 1995, pp. 67–8 and Murakami (1987), chapter 4.
35. Iwahashi Hideyuki, *Nippon Raitohausu yonjūnen-shi* (Nippon Lighthouse: The First 40 Years), Nippon Lighthouse, 1962. All of the consultants were highly accomplished in their respective fields. Hara Yasukazu (President, All-Japan Federation of Social Welfare Commissioners) had studied at Columbia and Yale Universities before the war. Kawamoto Unosuke (Principal, Tokyo School for the Blind) had undertaken research in Britain, Denmark, Germany and the United States. Ōno Kakuji was editor of the *Mainichi Shinbun*'s braille daily, the *Tenji Mainichi*. Representing GHQ were PH&W (Welfare Division's Neff), Civil Information and Education Section (Dr Louis Q. Moss, Vocational Education Officer, Education Division) and Economic and Scientific Section (Alice W. Shurcliff, Vocational Training Officer, Labour Division). Welfare Division's Micklautz took a personal interest in the Nippon Lighthouse Foundation and regularly conferred with professional associations and political action groups, including disabled veterans' organisations. Kim (1995), pp. 68–72.
36. In the late 1930s and early 1940s, the United States had enacted or revised three laws for the disabled: the Randolt–Sheppard Act (1936), the Wagner–O'Day Act (1938) and the revised Barden–LaFollette Act (1943, originally passed in 1920). A comprehensive Federal statute, however, did not appear until the Rehabilitation Act of 1973, which provided for vocational placement. The Act's Section 504 also outlawed discrimination against the disabled for the first time. The first legislation to codify the civil rights of the disabled was the 1990 Americans With Disabilities Act.
37. Kim (1995). pp. 68–72.
38. Kōseishō, ed. (1988), p. 587.
39. Despite the delay in enactment, some work-guarantee provisions of the disabilities bill were incorporated into revisions of the Employment Security Law (20 May 1949), the Emergency Unemployment Counter-Measures Law (20 May 1949) and the Unemployment Insurance Law (1 June 1949). The legislative process also produced a number of spin-off measures. In May 1949, the Ministry created a Rehabilitation Section inside the Social Affairs Bureau to administer its evolving programme for the handicapped and appointed Kuroki Toshikatsu to head it. Kuroki had just returned from a five-month tour of the United States, where he had studied American legislation for the disabled and rehabilitation work. The same month, the Ministry created the National Rehabilitation Centre for the Physically Disabled (31 May). In mid-1949, the scope of the disability bill was narrowed to include only individuals with physical impairments, but the Mental Health Law (1 May 1950) and the Tuberculosis Prevention Law (31 March 1951) were later passed as extensions

of the earlier draft of the disabilities statute. Kim (1995), pp. 84–6, 105 (Note 49).

40. Yoshida (1994), pp. 175–83.
41. *HNMA*, no. 20: Social Security, pp. 10–16.
42. The Social Insurance Working Group included Morito Tatsuo (Socialist parliamentarian and future education minister), Shimizu Gen (former chief of the Welfare Ministry's Social Security Bureau) and liberal economist Ōkōchi Kazuo. Murakami (1987), pp. 218–20.
43. See discussion in Takahashi (1997), p. 69.
44. Wandel held a PhD in economics from Columbia University. During the war, he was chief of the Labour Department's Unemployment Compensation Division, and from 1947, he headed the Programme Division in the Labour Department's Bureau of Employment Security. From May 1947, he also served as consultant to PH&W's Social Security Division. On the Wandel Report, refer to Shakai Hoshō Kenkyūjo-hen (ed.), *Nihon shakai-hoshō shiryō* (Data on Japan's Social Security System), vol. 1, Shiseidō, 1975, pp. 23–97.
45. The new Council included Health and Welfare officials Katsumata Minoru and Shimizu Gen, and Marxist economist Ōuchi Hyōe of Tokyo University.
46. Sams (1998), pp. 171–2.
47. Cited by Zabelle Zakarian in her introduction to Sams, ibid., p. xv.
48. *HNMA*, no. 20: Social Security, pp. 17–19. On specialisation, refer to Sams, ibid., pp. 127–8.
49. Sams and his staff displayed little understanding of Japanese midwifery and bone-setting (*hone-tsugi*) or Chinese acupressure (*shiatsu*), acupuncture (*hari*) and moxa-cautery (*kyū*), time-honoured alternative medical practices in Japan. PH&W originally had intended to curtail or eliminate these ancient professions altogether, but pressure from Japanese professional associations prevented it from doing so. Instead, the Section introduced a highly restrictive licensing system to discourage their practice. Acupressure, acupuncture and moxa-cautery normally were taught to the visually disabled as a means of livelihood, and about half of Japan's roughly 76,000 traditional practitioners were blind. Curiously, some Occupation officials took this as disqualifying factor. Sams, ibid., pp. 176–7 and Ōbayashi Michiko, *Josampu no sengo* (Midwifery in the Postwar Era), Keisō Shobō, 1989, pp. 116–17. Most Americans were simply ignorant of Chinese medicine. American POWs treated with acupuncture and moxa-cautery later charged that they had been tortured. Sams had to explain to US war crimes prosecutors that this was accepted medical practice in Asia (Sams, 1998, p. 130). Other shortcomings of the medical reforms are discussed briefly in Sugiyama Akiko, *Senryōki no iryō kaikaku* (Medical Reforms During the Occupation), Keisō Shobō, 1995, pp. 220–2.
50. Takemae (1986), pp. 244–5.
51. *HNMA*, no. 19: Public Health, pp. 63–4.
52. In January 1952, the victims sued the government, and the case eventually was

settled out of court. In October 1951, the Science Council of Japan's Medical Section urged the Welfare Ministry to discontinue compulsory BCG tuberculosis shots because of their potentially dangerous side effects. When Welfare Minister Hashimoto Ryūgo publicly considered a temporary suspension, Sams's replacement, Colonel Cecil S. Mollohan, intervened forcefully in defence of the programme's safety. As the controversy raged, mandatory vaccinations became an issue in the Diet, but in January 1952, Hashimoto declared the risks were minimal and announced that the programme would be continued, bringing the affair to a close. Kōseishō (1988), p. 592. See the discussion in Takemae (1986), pp. 200–1, 378–9.

53. Takemae, ibid., pp. 293–4.
54. Former bio-war scientists returned to their universities carrying their data with them, and several went on to brilliant careers in medical science. One became president of the reformed Japan Medical Association, another vice president of that body. Four became presidents of Kanazawa University, Nagoya Municipal Medical College and Kyoto Medical College, and others deans of medical faculties in prestigious universities. A few went to work in the private sector. See Takasugi Shingo, *731 butai: saikinsen no ishi o oe* (Unit 731: On the Trail of the Bio-war Doctors), Tokuma Shoten, 1982, chapter 1 and Shibata Shingo, ' "Akuma no hōshoku" no sensō hanzai' (War Crimes: The 'Devil's Gluttony'), in Shibata Shingo, ed., *Sensō to heiwa no ronri* (The Logic of War and Peace), Keisō Shobō, 1992, pp. 114–16.
55. See Tsuneishi Kei'ichi, *Igakusha-tachi no soshiki hanzai: Kantōgun Dai 731 Butai* (The Organised Crime of [Japan's] Medical Scientists: The Kwantung Army's Unit 731), Asahi Shinbunsha, 1994, pp. 199–219 and *731 Butai: seibutsu heiki hanzai no shinjitsu* (Unit 731: The Truth Behind the Crime of Biological Weapon's Development), Kōdansha, 1995, pp. 188–98. In the early 1990s, the Green Cross Corporation would be accused of knowingly importing and selling American blood products tainted with the human immunodeficiency virus.
56. The 1987 interview was conducted by Shibata (1995), p. 116. On the 406 Medical General Laboratory, see Stephen Endicott and Edward Hagerman, *The United States and Biological Warfare: Secrets from the Early Cold War and Korea*, Indiana University Press, 1998, pp. 141–8.
57. PH&W also used the wartime findings of the Ishii group to conduct its own medical trials on healthy subjects. In November 1946, Sams ordered the Welfare Ministry and the Institute of Infectious Diseases to organise a typhus experiment using inmates in Fuchū Prison outside of Tokyo. That year, typhus had stricken some 32,000 people, resulting in more than 3,300 deaths, and PH&W was desperate for new ways to combat the disease. The experiments, set up to track the spead of typhus by lice and the disease's transmutations, reportedly were conducted by the Institute over a one- to two-year period on 12 volunteers serving terms for non-capital offences. At Japanese insistence, informed consent

was obtained, but the medical trials reportedly replicated those conducted by Kitano Masaji on Chinese prisoners awaiting execution in wartime Manchuria, some of which had involved vivisections. The PH&W tests were benign compared to the murderous work of Ishii and Kitano, but they illustrate once again the readiness with which American authorities turned for help to those involved in Japan's bio-war programme. Sams and his staff became, in effect, co-conspirators after the fact in those wartime crimes. Takasugi (1982), chapter 3. See also the summary in Takemae (1986), pp. 152–4.

58. On 6 September, following independent confirmation of the human toll from Marcel Junod of the International Red Cross, Sams issued a Military Government directive in MacArthur's name ordering Tokyo to cooperate with the Farrell Mission. The directive also authorised the release of 12 tons of medical supplies for immediate distribution to the stricken areas by the IRC. Takemae (1986), pp. 32–3.

59. Surveys were conducted during this period by the Atomic Energy Commission, the Joint Commission on Atomic Effects, the US Public Health Service, the Strategic Bomb Survey, Army Medical Corps Intelligence and Navy Medical Corps Intelligence.

60. See Furukawa Atsushi, 'Senryō to chōhō: "Genbaku eiga" fuirumu to kiroku eiga no yukue' (The Occupation and Military Intelligence: The Fate of the 'Atomic Bomb' Footage and Documentary), in *Senshū Hōgaku Ronshū* (Occasional Papers, Law Faculty, Senshu University), nos 55 and 56, 1992, pp. 527–45.

61. On the origins of the ABCC, see M. Susan Lindee, *Suffering Made Real: American Science and the Survivors at Hiroshima*, University of Chicago Press, 1994, pp. 23–37. Concerning PH&W's role, see Zakarian's notes in Sams (1988), pp. 284–5.

62. Dr James Yamazaki, assigned to the ABCC in Nagasaki from 1949 to 1951 to study radiation illness, learned on leaving Japan that earlier US research on the bomb's aftereffects had been hidden from him. See *Children of the Atomic Bombs: An American Physician's Memoir of Nagasaki, Hiroshima, and the Marshall Islands*, Duke University Press, 1995. See also Monica Braw, *The Atomic Bomb Suppressed*, M. E. Sharpe, 1991, pp. 119–20, 130, 155–6; the Committee for the Compilation of Materials on Damage Caused by the Atomic Bombs in Hiroshima and Nagasaki, *Hiroshima and Nagasaki: The Physical, Medical, and Social Effects of the Atomic Bombings* (below, given as *Hiroshima and Nagasaki*), Basic Books, 1981, pp. 511–12; and Lindee, chapter 2.

63. Sasamoto Yukuo, *Beigun senryōka no genbaku chōsa: genbaku kagai-koku ni natta Nihon* (The US Military Atomic Bomb Survey during the Occupation: When Japan Became an Atomic Aggressor), Shinkansha, 1995, chapter 4. Sasamoto's study provides a critical in-depth study of the ABCC's work from a Japanese perspective.

64. Ibid.

648 Notes to Pages 430–434

65. Eileen Welsome, *The Plutonium Files*, The Dial Press, 1999, p. 212. See also p. 365.
66. Sasamoto (1995), pp. 195, 207. *Hiroshima and Nagasaki*, p. 535.
67. Takemae (1986), pp. 308–10. For American thinking on this question, which was openly debated inside the ABCC, see Lindee (1994), pp. 117–42.
68. Sasamoto (1995), pp. 7, 288.
69. Fujime Yuki, *Sei no rekishi-gaku* (The Historical Development of Gender in Modern Japan), Fuji Shuppan, 1997, p. 357.
70. Ibid., p. 358. Helen M. Hopper, 'Katō Shizue, Socialist Party MP, and Occupation Reforms Affecting Women, 1945–1948: A Case Study of the Formal vs. Informal Political Influence of Japanese Women', in Burkman, ed. (1982), pp. 388–91. See also Barbara Molony's afterword in Baroness Shidzué Ishimoto, *Facing Two Ways: The Story of My Life*, Stanford University Press, 1984 (Holt, Rinehart and Winston, 1938), pp. xxvi-xxvii.
71. Sams (1998), pp. 183–7 and Hopper (1982), p. 391–2. See also Deborah Oakley, 'The Development of Population Policy in Japan, 1945–1952, and American Participation', PhD dissertation, University of Michigan, 1977, pp. 151–3, 261–2. In this context, in 1947 Sams rejected a request by the Institute of Population Problems to survey children born to American fathers and Japanese mothers. The problem, he said, was too grievous a sore to probe and would raise uncomfortable questions about the 30,000 children Imperial troops were said to have left behind in Indonesia and the thousands more Japanese soldiers had fathered in China. Sams believed that such children would fare better if their American parentage were downplayed and they were assimilated quietly into Japanese society. GHQ imposed a blanket ban on public discussion of *konketsuji*, literally 'mixed-blood children' but with the nuance of 'half-caste'. The fate of these orphans was consigned to silence until censorship controls were lifted in 1949. In June 1948, a US journalist for *The Saturday Evening Post* was expelled from Japan for violating that taboo with an exposé on Japan's 'Occupation babies'. In August 1952, the Welfare Ministry's Children's Bureau finally conducted a survey, finding a total of 5,013 inter-racial children in Japan, of whom 84 per cent were part-Caucasian, 14 per cent part-African and 2 per cent of unknown ancestry. See Wildes (1954), p. 333 and Yukiko Koshiro, *Trans-Pacific Racisms and the U.S. Occupation of Japan*, East Asian Institute, Columbia University, 1999, pp. 162–4.
72. See Zachery Gussow, *Leprosy, Racism, and Public Health: Social Policy in Chronic Disease Control*, Westview Press, 1989, pp. 85–7.
73. On the origins of the pre-1945 system, see generally Fujino Yutaka, *Nihon fashizumu to iryō* (Japanese Fascism and the Medical Establisment), Iwanami Shoten, 1993. On postwar developments, consult Ōtani Fujirō, *Rai yobōhō haishi no rekishi* (A History of the Movement to Abolish the Leprosy Prevention Law), Keisō Shobō, 1996, pp. 42–77.
74. Hirasawa Yasui, *Jinsei ni zetsubō wa nai: Hansen-byō 100-nen no tatakai* (There is

Always Hope for One's Life: The 100-Year Struggle of Japan's Leprosy Sufferers), Kamogawa Shuppan, 1997, chapter 3. The lives of individual patients are recounted in Miyashita Tadako, *Kakuri no sato* (Segregated Villages), Ōtsuki Shoten, 1998.

75. A final twist to this puzzle was added in December 1951 by the arrival of two US Public Health Service officials on loan to Harvard's Leonard Wood Memorial Foundation, the only group in the United States then studying new chemotherapies for leprosy. From April 1952, the scientists conducted experiments on 342 patients involving the administration of untested drugs, biopsies and extensive photographing. Kōseishō (1988), p. 708. Gussow (1989), pp. 167–8. On the leprosy experiment, see Medical Section (Public Health and Welfare Division), *Public Health and Welfare in Japan: Final Summary, 1951–52*, GHQ/SCAP, Tokyo, 1952, pp. 77–9.

76. On the position of the Japan Communist Party, see Ian Neary, 'Burakumin in Contemporary Japan', in Michael Weiner, ed., *Japan's Minorities: The Illusion of Homogeneity*, Routledge, 1997, p. 60. An overview of research on minorities during the Occupation is Takemae Eiji, ' Senryō to mainoritei: kenkyū no dōkō to kadai' (Minorities under the Occupation: Research Trends and Topics), in *Buraku Kaihō Kenkyū*, no. 75, 1990, pp. 41–52.

77. Takemae (1990), p. 42–4. The OSS reports on 'Eta' are reproduced in Buraku Kaihō Kenkyūjo-hen (ed.), *Senryōki no Buraku mondai* (Documents on the *Buraku* Problem During the Occupation of Japan), Kaihō Shuppansha, 1991, pp. 260–87.

78. Takayanagi Kenzō, Ōtomo Ichirō and Tanaka Hideo, eds, *Nihonkoku kenpō seitei no katei* (The Making of the Constitution of Japan), vol. 1, Yūhikaku, 1972, pp. 430–2.

79. Koreans and Formosans registered in Japanese *koseki* in the main islands through adoption, marriage or other devices were eligible to vote in national and local elections. Some 200 Korean candidates stood in elections between 1929 and 1943, one winning a seat in the Lower House. On the colonial registration system, see Oguma Eiji, *'Nihonjin' no kyōkai: Okinawa, Ainu, Taiwan, Chōsen – shokuminchi kara fukki undō made* (The Boundaries of the 'Japanese': Okinawa, the Ainu, Formosa, Korea – From Colonies to the Reversion Movement), Shinyōsha, 1998, chapters 6 and 17. On pre-1945 electoral rights, see the brief summary in Kashiwazaki Chikako, 'The Politics of Legal Status: The Equation of Nationality with Ethnonational Identity', in Sonia Ryang, ed., *Koreans in Japan: Critical Voices from the Margin*, Routledge, 2000, p. 18.

80. Mizuno Naoki, 'Zainichi Chōsenjin-Taiwanjin sansei-ken "teishi" jōkō no seiitsu' (The Origin of the Clause Suspending the Electoral Rights of Koreans and Formosans in Japan), in *Sekai Jinken-mondai Kenkyū Sentā kenkyū kiyō* (Annals of the Centre for the Study of World Human Rights Issues), no. 1 (15 March), 1996, pp. 43–65 and no. 2, pp. 59–82.

81. Furukawa Atsushi, 'Gaikokujin no jinken (1): Sengo kenpō kaikaku to no kanren ni oite' (The Human Rights of Foreign Residents (1): In the Context of Postwar Constitutional Reform), in *The Journal of Tokyo Keizai University*, no. 146, 1986, pp. 63–80. See also Koseki Shōichi, 'Japanizing the Constitution', in *The Japan Quarterly*, vol. 35, no. 3, 1988, pp. 234–40.

82. Watanabe Toshio's interview with Kades, *Buraku mondai to Nihon senryō monjo kenkyū nyūsu* (News Bulletin on the *Buraku* Problem and Research on Occupation Documents), no. 14, 1989, pp. 7–8.

83. Watanabe Toshio, 'Senryō-ki no Buraku mondai' (The *Buraku* Problem During the Occupation) in *Buraku Kaihō-shi: Fukuoka* (The History of *Buraku* Liberation: Fukuoka), no. 58, June 1990, pp. 31–4.

84. Takemae Eiji, 'The Kades Memoir on the Occupation of Japan', in *The Journal of Tokyo Keizai University*, no. 148, November 1986, pp. 276–7 and Watanabe (1989), p. 7. On the FEC Note, see George H. Blakeslee, *The Far Eastern Commission: A Study in International Cooperation 1945–1952*, US Department of State (US Government Printing Office), 1953, p. 65.

85. See generally Takakura Sei'ichirō, 'The Ainu of Northern Japan: A Study in Conquest and Acculturation', in *The Transactions of the Philosophical Society of Philadelphia*, vol. 50, no. 4, 1960. See also Richard Siddle, *Race, Resistance and the Ainu of Japan*, Routledge, 2000, chapter 3.

86. Concerning the 1947 meeting in Sapporo, see Yoshihisa Masuko, 'Maboroshi no Ainu dokuritsu-ron o ou: chōrō ni shikin o okutta GHQ no shin'i' (In Search of the Mysterious Ainu Independence Proposal: GHQ's Real Intention in Sending Money to Ainu Elders), in *Asahi Jānaru*, 3 March 1989, pp. 87–90. For the petition, see 'Airgram from the American Consulate in Shanghai to the Department of State, A-683, 29 July 1948' (RG 54, 849.4016/7–2948, National Archives Records Administration, Washington DC). Gifts to MacArthur, are discussed in Sodei Rinjirō, *Haikei Makkāsā Gensui-sama: senryōka no Nihonjin no tegami* (Dear General MacArthur: Japanese Letters [to MacArthur] During the Occupation), Chūō Kōronsha, 1991, chapters 7 and 8. The Ainu example is cited and translated by John Dower in *Embracing Defeat: Japan in the Wake of World War II*, W. W. Norton and the New Press, 1999, p. 231. The Passin quotation is from Herbert Passin, *Encounter With Japan*, Kodansha International, 1982, p. 163.

87. Siddle (2000), pp. 148–51. Biratori-chō (ed.), *Hidaka chihō ni okeru Ainu-kei jūmin no seikatsu-jitai to sono mondai-ten* (Living Conditions and Problems of Ainu Residents in the Hidaka Region), 1965, p. 33.

88. Okinawa Kenritsu Toshokan Shiryō Henshūshitsu-hen (ed.), *Okinawa-ken shi: shiryō-hen* (History of Okinawa Prefecture: Documents), Okinawa-ken Kyōiku I'inkai, no. 2 (English), 1996, pp. 24–9 and discussion in Oguma (1998), pp. 462–6.

89. Arasaki Moriteru, *Dokyumento: Okinawa tōsō* (Documents on Okinawa's Struggle), Aki Shobō, 1969, chapters 1 and 2 and Arnold G. Fisch Jr, *Military*

Government in the Ryukyu Islands, 1945–1950, US Army Center for Military History, US Government Printing Office, 1988, pp. 169–70.

90. Fisch, ibid., pp. 77–9, 155–6.
91. Ibid., pp. 82–7. The *Life Magazine* article of 19 December 1949 is cited by Fisch, p. 82.
92. Sodei Rinjirō, *Rimembā Shōwa! Dōjidai-shi no oboegaki* (Remember Shōwa! A Memorandum on the History of Our Age), Marunouchi Shuppan, 1999, pp. 88–9.
93. In January 1946, popular elections were held for district governors and councillors based on universal suffrage. In April of that year, the Okinawan Advisory Council appointed a governor for the Okinawa Group, and a Central Okinawan Administration (later, the Okinawan Civilian Administration) was set up.
94. Fisch (1998), pp. 103–16.
95. Koji Taira, 'Troubled National Identity: The Ryukyuans/Okinawans', in Michael Weiner, ed., *Japan's Minorities: The Illusion of Homogeneity*, Routledge, 1997, pp. 160–1.
96. GHQ/SCAP and FECOM, *Selected Data on the Occupation of Japan*, Tokyo, 1950, p. 199 and *Reports of MacArthur*, p. 86. US Department of State, *Foreign Relations of the United States* (below, given as *FRUS*), US Government Printing Office, vol. 6, 1947, p. 512.
97. Shindō Ei'ichi, an Occupation scholar at Tsukuba University, discovered the Sebald Memorandum in the US National Archives in 1979. Opposition parties raised the issue in the Diet, producing shock and dismay in Okinawa and, in Tokyo, a storm of controversy. See Shindō Ei'ichi, 'Bunkatsu sareta ryōdo' (Japan's National Territory Divided) in *Sekai*, April 1979, pp. 31–51. A comprehensive treatment of this issue is Robert D. Eldridge, *The Origins of the Bilateral Okinawa Problem: Okinawa in Postwar U.S.–Japan Relations, 1945–1952*, Garland Publishing (New York), 2001, chapter 6.
98. Policy Planning Staff/10/1, cited by Ōta Masahide, 'War Memories Die Hard in Okinawa' in *The Japan Quarterly*, vol. 35, no. 1, 1988, p. 12.
99. See the discussion in Ōta, ibid., pp. 12–13 and Irokawa Daikichi, *The Age of Hirohito: In Search of Modern Japan*, The Free Press, 1995, pp. 99–101, 106.
100. Refer to Emiko Ohnuki-Tierney, 'A Conceptual Model for the Historical Relationship Between the Self and the Internal and External Others', in Dru C. Gladney, ed., *Making Majorities: Constituting the Nation in Japan, Korea, China, Malaysia, Fiji, Turkey, and the United States*, Stanford University Press, 1998, pp. 31–51 and Ian Neary (1997), p. 53.
101. See Buraku Kaihō Kenkyūjo-hen (ed.), 1991 and Akatsuka Yasuo, *Buraku Kaihō Kenkyū*, no. 60, 1988. On the GS memos, refer to Watanabe Toshio, 'Tokushū: Senryō-ki no Buraku mondai' (Special Feature: The *Buraku* Problem Under the Occupation), in *Buraku Kaihō Kenkyū*, no. 69, 1989, pp. 5–6, 7–10. See also his interview with Kurt Steiner in 'Senryō-ki no jinken hoshō to

Buraku mondai' (Human Rights Guarantees Under the Occupation and the *Buraku* Problem), in *Buraku Kaihō Kenkyū*, no. 73, 1990-a. In 1950, Carmen Johnson, an education officer in Shikoku, asked a Japanese scholar on her Civil Affairs staff to write a study of this problem, 'The Present Situation of *Eta* (or *Etta*) in Shikoku', but by her own admission, she did not fully understand it. See *Wave-Rings in the Water: My Years with the Women of Postwar Japan*, Charles River Press, 1996, pp. 158–60.

102. Watanabe Toshio, 'Senryō-ki no Buraku mondai', in *Buraku Kaihō-shi: Fukuoka*, no. 58, 1990-b, pp. 41, 47. Passin's reports are found in Buraku Kaihō Kenkyūjo-hen (ed.), 1991, pp. 388–409.

103. See Watanabe's interview with Kades in Watanabe (1989), p. 9 and, generally, Watanabe Toshio, *Gendai-shi no naka no Buraku mondai* (The *Buraku* Problem in Contemporary History), Kaihō Shuppansha, 1988. See also Watanabe (1990-b), pp. 41–2.

104. George De Vos and Wagatsuma Hiroshi, *Japan's Invisible Race: Caste in Culture and Personality*, University of California Press, 1966, pp. 73–4.

105. Population figures for Koreans are from William J. Gane, *Repatriation, From 25 September 1945 to 31 December 1945*, Headquarters, US Army Military Government in Korea (Foreign Affairs Section), Seoul, 1946, p. 14. Figures from Foreign Ministry archives in Tokyo released in December 2000 show a total of 2.18 million Koreans in Japan as of October 1945. See also Research and Analysis Branch, Office of Strategic Services, *Civil Affairs Guide: Aliens in Japan*, June 1945, pp. v–vi. Miyazaki Akira, 'Senryō shoki ni okeru Beikoku no Zainichi Chōsenjin seisaku: Nihon seifu no taiō to tomo ni' (The US Army's Korean Policy During the Occupation and the Japanese Government's Response), in *Shisō*, no. 734, August 1985, pp. 122–39.

106. Government Section, SCAP, ed., *The Political Reorientation of Japan, September 1945 to September 1948* (below, given as *PRJ*), US Government Printing Office, 1949, vol. 2, p. 432.

107. The quotation is from *HNMA*, no. 6: Treatment of Foreign Nationals, p. 103. On the view of Koreans as refugees, see Kim T'ae-gi, *Sengo Nihon seiji to Zainichi Chōsenjin mondai* (Postwar Japanese Politics and the Problem of Koreans in Japan), Keisō Shobō, 1997, pp. 54–73.

108. The origins of the prewar Korean community in Japan are discussed by Michael Weiner, *Race and Migration in Imperial Japan*, Routledge, 1994. On repatriation, see Gane (1946), Edward Wagner, *The Korean Minority in Japan, 1904–1950*, Institute of Pacific Relations, 1951, chapter 4 and Kim (1997), chapter 2.

109. *HNMA*, no. 6: Treatment of Foreign Nationals, p. 132.

110. Alfred C. Oppler, *Legal Reform in Occupied Japan: A Participant Looks Back*, Princeton University Press, 1976, p. 167.

111. The ARO had been preceded by a 'Korean registration' statute enacted locally by the Osaka Municipal government in November 1946 with the consent of

the Osaka Regional Military Government Team. The Osaka Korean Registration Ordinance required Koreans to give their fingerprints and carry an identification card, but fierce resistance made the fingerprinting requirement unenforceable, and the registration itself could only be partially completed. See Yang Yŏng-hu, 'Ōsaka-fu Chōsenjin tōroku jōrei seitei: 1946 no tenmatsu ni tsuite' (The Establishment of Municipal Osaka's Korean Registration Ordinance: Concerning the Events of 1946), in *Zainichi Chōsenjin-shi Kenkyū*, no. 16, 1986, pp. 104–26.

112. On the *Kyōwakai*, see Wagner (1951), pp. 37–8 and Weiner (1994), chapter 5. The definitive study of the ARO is Ōnuma Yasuaki, *Tan'itsu minzoku shakai o koete: Zainichi Kankoku-Chōsenjin to shūtsunyūkoku kanri-taisei* (Beyond the Myth of the Mono-ethnic Society: Koreans in Japan and the Immigration Control System), Tōshindō, 1992, chapter 3. The SCAP report referred to is *HNMA*, no. 6: Treatment of Foreign Nationals, p. 109. The G-2 assessment of the ARO is from Civil Intelligence Section, GHQ/FEC/SCAP, *Operations of the Civil Intelligence Section*, GHQ, FEC & SCAP, vol. IX, Intelligence Series (1), 1949, p. 119 (RG 319, Military History Section, Box 138, Washington National Records Centre, Archives II, College Park, Maryland).

113. The statistics on black-marketeering are supplied by former Osaka Metropolitan Police Chief Suzuki Eiji, *Sōkan rakudai-ki* (My Failures as Superintendent of Police), Masu Shobō, 1952, p. 16. A brief description of the Shibuya riot is found in Kōdansha, eds, *Shōwa: niman nichi no zenkiroku* (The Shōwa Era: A 20,000-Day Chronicle), vol. 7, Kōdansha, 1989, pp. 283–4. A detailed American account is included in POLAD documents, RG 84, boxes 7 and 17, Washington National Records Center, Archives II, College Park, Maryland.

114. POLAD, ibid. *HNMA*, no. 6: Treatment of Foreign Nationals, pp. 75–80.

115. Wagner (1951), pp. 65–6. In fact, the US Army Military Government in Korea's Office of Foreign Affairs attempted to intercede on behalf of Japan's Korean minority and frequently found itself in conflict with SCAP on this issue. In 1946, the Office established permanent liaison teams in Tokyo, Osaka and other cities in an effort to represent Korean interests in Japan. General John Hodge, US commander in southern Korea, personally protested SCAP's decision to treat Koreans as Japanese nationals, warning of 'violent repercussions' in Japan and Korea. MacArthur's staff generally ignored such pleas. See Cheong Sun-hwa, *The Politics of Anti-Japanese Sentiment in Korea*, Greenwood Press, 1991, chapter 5.

116. *HNMA*, no. 6: Treatment of Foreign Nationals, p. 26.

117. David Conde, 'The Korean Minority in Japan', in *The Far Eastern Survey*, 26 February 1947, pp. 43–5. Wagner (1951), p. 61.

118. Kim Ch'ŏn-hae is cited in Pak Kyŏng-shik, *Kaihōgo Zainichi Chōsenjin undō-shi* (The Postwar Movement of Koreans in Japan After Liberation), San'ichi Shobō, 1989, p. 56.

119. See Kobayashi Tomoko, '8–15 chokugo ni okeru Zainichi Chōsenjin to shin Chōsen kensetsu no kadai: Zainichi Chōsenjin Renmei no katsudō o chushin ni' (Koreans in Japan Immediately After 15 August 1945 and the Task of Building a New Korea: The Activities of the League of Korean Residents in Japan), in *Zainichi Chōsenjin-shi Kenkyū*, no. 21, 1991.

120. Ozawa Yūsaku, *Zainichi Chōsenjin kyōiku-ron: rekishi-hen* (Education and Koreans in Japan: Historical Background), Aki Shobō, 1973, pp. 186–99, 197–9, and Pak (1989), chapters 1 and 3.

121. In a review of Korean-language texts, an American historian found no 'appeals to anti-Americanism or calls for violent revolution'. The school books, he noted, examined both Soviet and American social and political institutions, and some included Biblical materials, as well. W. Donald Smith, 'Democracy Denied: The American Repression of Korean Education in Occupied Japan', unpublished essay (Graduate School of History, University of Washington), July 1993, pp. 14, 16–22. The statistics are from Uzawa (1973), p. 195.

122. On Occupation attitudes towards Koreans, see Robert Ricketts, 'Zainichi Chōsenjin no minzoku jishuken no hakai-katei: 1948–1949 o chūshin ni' (Koreans in Occupied Japan: The Destruction of Korean Cultural Autonomy, 1948–9), in *Seikyū gakujutsu ronshū*, no. 10, Kankoku Bunka Kenkyū Shinkō Zaidan, 1995, pp. 219, 228–30. The scholar is Mihashi Osamu, 'Joron: Senryō ni okeru tai-Zainichi Chōsenjin kanri-seisaku keisei-katei no kenkyū (1) (Introduction: An Analysis of the Establishment of Control Policies for Koreans in Occupied Japan), in *Seikyū gakujutsu ronshū*, no. 10, Kankoku Bunka Kenkyū Shinkō Zaidan, 1995, p. 202.

Chapter 10 Changing Course

1. On the national security state, see Robert J. Goldstein, *Political Repression in Modern America: From 1870 to the Present*, Schenkman Publishing Company, 1978, chapter 9. American globalism is discussed in Joyce and Gabriel Kolko, *The Limits of Power: The World and United States Foreign Policy, 1945–1954*, Harper & Row, 1972, chapter 4.

2. John Dower has characterised American strategy towards Japan between 1947 and 1949 as the era of soft Cold War policy: *Japan in War and Peace: Selected Essays*, The New Press, 1993, chapter 5. On Kennan and US strategy, refer to Bruce Cumings, *The Origins of the Korean War. Vol. II: The Roaring of the Cataract*, Princeton University Press, 1990, chapter 2.

3. Royall's speech is reproduced in Jon Livingston, Joe B. Moore and Felicia Oldfather, eds, *Postwar Japan: 1945 to the Present*, Pantheon Books, 1973, pp. 116–19.

4. Cumings (1990), p. 56.

5. George F. Kennan, *Memoirs, 1925–1950*, Atlantic Monthly (Little, Brown), 1967, pp. 388–9. Howard B. Schonberger, *Aftermath of War: Americans and the Remaking of Japan, 1945–1952*, Kent State University Press, 1989, 143–55.

6. Michael Schaller, *The American Occupation of Japan: The Origins of the Cold War in Asia*, Oxford University Press, 1985, p. 120.
7. Ibid., pp. 114, 127.
8. See Arisawa Hiromi, ed., *Shōwa keizai-shi* (A History of the Japanese Economy in the Shōwa Era), Nihon Keizai Shinbunsha, 1976, pp. 265–8.
9. Watanabe Takeshi, *Senryōka no Nihon zaisei-oboegaki* (A Memoir of Japanese Financial Policy Under the Occupation), Nihon Keizai Shinbunsha, 1966. See especially 'Watanabe Nikki' (The Watanabe Diary) of 31 May 1946, excerpted in Ōkurashō Zaisei-shi Shitsu-hen (Ministry of Finance, Financial History Office), ed. *Shōwa zaisei-shi: shūsen kara Kōwa made* (The Financial History of the Shōwa Era: From the War's End to the Peace Treaty), vol. 11, Tōkyō Keizai Shinpōsha, 1983, pp. 251–2.
10. John W. Dower, *Empire and Aftermath: Yoshida Shigeru and the Japanese Experience, 1878–1954*, Council on East Asian Studies, Harvard University, 1979, p. 298.
11. A final footnote would be written to SCAP's attempt to decentralise and democratise the economy with the Shoup Mission of May 1949. Dr Carl S. Shoup, a tax specialist from Columbia University, brought a team of financial experts to Japan to study the tax system and make recommendations. The mission's findings were presented in the Shoup Report, released in August 1949, which proposed a more equitable system of assessment, with greater government reliance on direct levies such as personal and corporate taxes for its revenues, and greater fiscal autonomy for municipalities. The need for the latter was acute, for by 1949, as a result of increasing expenditures and declining subsidies from Tokyo, the finances of local self-governing bodies were in a precarious state. To remedy this problem, Shoup suggested that independent local tax sources be increased and income-tax revenues shared with the central government (the so-called equalisation, or shared, tax). Shoup also recommended the creation of a strong Local Finance Commission to end the system of central government patronage and defend local prerogatives. In 1950, the Diet passed most of Shoup's recommendations, but the Yoshida government repealed or ignored the bulk of them. Yoshida effectively sabotaged the Local Finance Commission, which was absorbed into the Autonomy Agency in 1952 without ever fulfilling its intended function. Conservatives manipulated local fiscal reform to increase the reliance of municipal and prefectural authorities on central funding, and since the end of the Occupation, the central government has encroached steadily on local autonomy. See generally Tsuji Kiyoaki, *Nihon no chihō-jichi* (Local Autonomy in Japan), Iwanami Shoten, 1976. In English, see Shiomi Saburō, *Japan's Finance and Taxation*, Columbia University Press, 1957, pp. 82–92.
12. Letter to the Secretary of the Army, 14 August 1948 (RG319, Plans and Operations Division, Department of the Army, 1946–8, box 86, National Archives Records Administration, Washington DC).

13. Pink to Foreign Office, 26 August 1948 (FO 371/69823, Public Records Office, London). Cited in Schaller (1985), p. 134.

14. On the education controversy in general, see Kim Kyŏng-hae, ed., *Zainichi Chōsenjin minzoku-kyōiku yōgo tōsō shiryōshū* (Documents on the Struggle to Defend Korean Ethnic Education in Japan), vol. 1, Akashi Shoten, 1988 and Kim T'ae-gi, *Sengo Nihon seiji to Zainichi Chōsenjin mondai* (Postwar Japanese Politics and the Problem of Koreans in Japan), Keisō Shobō, 1997, chapter 4.

15. On the League's arguments, see *Educational Counter-Plan, Committee of Koreans Residing in Japan, Educational Real Situation of Korean Residents in Japan – In the Past and at Present*, 15 April 1948 (RG 331, Government Section Files, Japan National Diet Library Collection). Representative of American assumptions are those expressed in early 1948 by an education officer with the Yamanashi Military Government Team, who explained to local Koreans that: 'The teaching of the Japanese language was considered essential if they and their families elected to remain permanent residents of Japan.' America, he said, 'was a country of many races, but all children . . . learned English and American history'. Jacob Van Staaveren, *An American in Japan, 1945–1948: A Civilian View of the Occupation*, University of Washington Press, 1994, p. 183.

16. A detailed and compelling analysis of the limited emergency declared in Kobe under the 'Tollbooth' alert plan is Ara Takashi, *Nihon senryō-shi kenkyū josetsu* (An Introduction to Research on the History of the Occupation of Japan), Kashiwa Shobō, 1994, pp. 67–100. On police methods, see Ōsaka-fu Keisatsu-shi Henshū I'inkai-hen (ed.), *Ōsaka-fu keisatsu-shi* (A History of the Osaka Prefectural Police), vol. 3, Ōsaka-fu Keisatsu Honbu, 1973, pp. 234–49. A discussion in English is Inokuchi Hiromitsu, 'Korean Ethnic Schools in Occupied Japan, 1945–52', in Sonia Ryang, ed., *Koreans in Japan: Critical Voices from the Margin*, Routledge, 2000, pp. 140–53.

17. The Osaka Public Safety Ordinance was modelled on emergency public safety decrees promulgated by Fukui City and Fukui Prefecture in June 1948 at the prompting of the regional Military Government Team to prevent looting and other public disorders in the wake of the Ishikawa–Fukui earthquake. See Ozaki Isamu, *Kōan jōrei seitei hishi* (The Secret History of the Passage of the Public Safety Ordinances), Takushoku Shobō, 1978, chapters 3–4, 10–11.

18. These are the forces Eighth Army mobilised according to a G-2 Spot Intelligence report of 19 August. See Kyoko Hirano, *Mr. Smith Goes to Tokyo: Japanese Cinema Under the American Occupation, 1945–1952*, Smithsonian Institution Press, 1992, pp. 225–9 and Note 59 on p. 311. Observers at the scene reported a scout plane, four armoured reconnaissance cars and four Sherman tanks. Robert B. Textor, *Failure in Japan: With Keystones for a Positive Policy*, Greenwood Press (The John Day Co., 1951), 1972, p. 136.

19. Joe B. Moore, 'Purging Toho Cinema of the "Two Reds": A Case Study of the Reverse Course in the Japanese Labour Movement, 1947–1948', in *Canadian Journal of History*, vol. 26, December 1991, p. 456.

20. See Moore, ibid., pp. 469, 471–2 and his 'Nikkeiren and Restoration of the Right to Manage in Postwar Japan', in *Labour & Industry*, vol. 3, nos 2 & 3, 1990, pp. 281–301.

21. 'Memorandum of Conference: Tōho Movie Studio Dispute', 20 August 1948 (Chronological Files, May 48–December 48, RG 331, box no. 8477, Washington National Records Center, Archives II, College Park, Maryland). Cited in Chris Gerteis, 'Seeing Red: US Labor Policy and the Struggle for the Shopfloor at the Tōho Motion Picture Studios, 1948', MA dissertation, University of Iowa, 1995.

22. Just before Kades left Japan, he and Whitney would clash with Yoshida again over the latter's attempt to dissolve the House of Representatives without first obtaining a vote of no confidence. The Constitution, Kades said, gave the Diet alone the power to take such action. He was convinced that Yoshida's violation of Diet procedures, 'if not his arrogance', had eroded the principle of Diet supremacy. See Takemae Eiji, 'Possible Addendum to "Kades Memoir" ', in *The Journal of Tokyo Keizai University*, no. 150, March 1987, p. 222, Sodei Rinjirō, *Makkāsā no nisen-nichi* (MacArthur's 2000 Days), Chūō Kōronsha, 1989, pp. 257–63 and Justin Williams Sr, *Japan's Political Revolution Under MacArthur: A Participant's Account*, University of Tokyo Press, 1979, pp. 50–1.

23. National Security Council, *A Report to the President by the National Security Council*, 7 October 1948 (RG 319 POLAD Top Secret File, Washington National Records Center, Archives II, College Park, Maryland).

24. See George H. Blakeslee, *The Far Eastern Commission: A Study in International Cooperation – 1945–1952*, US Department of State (US Government Printing Office), 1953, pp. 163–6.

25. Richard B. Finn, *Winners in Peace: MacArthur, Yoshida and Postwar Japan*, University of California Press, 1992, p. 221.

26. Theodore Cohen, *Remaking Japan: The American Occupation as New Deal*, The Free Press, 1987, p. 441.

27. Takemae Eiji, 'GHQ Labour Policy During the Period of Democratization, 1946–1948: The Second Interview With Mr. Theodore Cohen', in *The Journal of the Tokyo Keizai University*, no. 122, 1981, p. 137.

28. See Cohen (1987), pp. 444–6. John Price, 'Valery Burati and the Formation of Sōhyō During the US Occupation of Japan', in *Pacific Affairs*, vol. 64, no. 2, 1991, pp. 209–10.

29. Joe B. Moore, 'The Toshiba Dispute of 1949: The "Rationalization" of Labor Relations', in *Labour, Capital and Society*, vol. 23, no. 1, 1990, p. 149.

30. See Takemae Eiji, *Sengo rōdō-kaikaku: GHQ rōdō seisaku-shi* (The Postwar Labour Reforms: A History of GHQ's Labour Reform Policy), Tōkyō Daigaku Shuppankai, 1982, pp. 251–98.

31. Takemae, ibid. and Cohen (1987), p. 449. The historian is Sheldon Garon, *The State and Labor in Modern Japan*, University of California Press, 1987, p. 237.

32. Herbert P. Bix, 'Japan: The Roots of Militarism', in Mark Selden, ed., *Remaking Asia: Essays on the American Uses of Power*, Pantheon Books, 1974, pp. 320–1.

33. The word originally applied to the depurging of ultra-nationalists in June 1951 but was enlarged to include the revival of militaristic themes in popular culture and the reassertion of traditional values and customs that occurred as independence drew near. The expression quickly acquired a broader dual meaning, referring to both the resetting of US policy goals for Japan after 1948 and the accompanying reactionary swing to the right of domestic politics that ushered in the second Yoshida Cabinet (October) and the era of domestic repression. In the late 1960s, younger American scholars borrowed the phrase to express their own misgivings about the evolution of US policy in Asia. See Takano Kazumoto, 'Nihon senryō kenkyū ni okeru "gyaku-kōsu"' (The Concept of 'Reverse Course' in Studies on the Occupation of Japan), in *Chūō Daigaku Daigakuin kenkyū nenpō* (Annals of the Graduate School, Chūō University), no. 15, March 1986, pp. 105–16.

34. Dower (1992), pp. 179–80.

35. Blakeslee (1953), pp. 167–8.

36. The US policy reversal on reparations also removed restrictions on the Japanese shipbuilding industry, which, over the vehement protests of Ausralia, Britain and New Zealand, was allowed to resume production. The industry became one of the engines driving Japan's economic recovery, and by 1960, its merchant tonnage had recovered to the 1941 level. See Miwa Ryōichi, 'Senryōki no Nihon zōsen kisei no jittai' (The State of Restrictions on Shipbuilding During the Occupation), in *Aoyama Keizai Ronshū*, nos 1–3, vol. 51, 1999, pp. 133–63. On US military pronouncements, see E. J. Lewe Van Aduard, *Japan: From Surrender to Peace*, Praeger, 1954, p. 109. Concerning US plans for Southeast Asia, refer to William S. Borden, *The Pacific Alliance: United States Foreign Economic Policy and Japanese Trade Recovery, 1947–1955*, University of Wisconsin Press, 1984, pp. 43–50 and chapter 3.

37. Letter of 12 May 1950 to Robert B. Textor, reproduced in *Failure in Japan: With Keystones for a Positive Policy*, Greenwood Press, 1972 (John Day, 1951), p. 124.

38. Goldstein (1978), p. 323.

39. The MacArthur quotations are from GHQ/SCAP and Far East Command, *Selected Data on the Occupation of Japan*, Tokyo, 1950, p. 11 and Robert A. Fearey, *The Occupation of Japan, Second Phase: 1948–1950*, Macmillan, 1950, p. 206. The text of the Cominform critique is reproduced in Tsuji Kiyoaki, ed., *Shiryō: sengo nijyūnen-shi* (A Documentary History of the Two Postwar Decades), vol. 1 (Politics), Nihon Hyōronsha, 1966, pp. 407–8.

40. Watanabe Toshio, 'Senryō-ki no Buraku mondai' (The *Buraku* Problem During the Occupation) in *Buraku Kaihō-shi: Fukuoka* (The History of *Buraku* Liberation: Fukuoka), no. 58, June 1990, pp. 43–5. An important recent study is that by Masuda Hiroshi, *Seijika tsuihō* (The Purge of the Politicians), Chūō Kōron Shinsha, 2001, pp. 240–77. See also George De Vos and Wagatsuma Hiroshi, *Japan's Invisible Race: Caste in Culture and Personality*, University of California Press, 1966, pp. 70–2.

41. Tsuji (1966), pp. 66–7.
42. Gendai Hōsei Shiryō Hensankai-hen (ed.), *Sengo senryō-ka hōritsu-shū* (Compendium of Laws Enacted Under the Postwar Occupation), Kokushokan Gyōkai, 1986, pp. 83–6.
43. On the SIB, see Yoshikawa Mitsusada's report, 'Hōmushō Tokubetsu Shinsa Kyoku', reproduced in Takemae (1982), pp. 421–38. See also Jack Napier, 'Counter-Measures Against the Subversive Potential in Japan, 1946 to 1951 Inclusive', no date (RG 331, box 8497, Washington National Records Center, Archives II, College Park, Maryland).
44. On the Yokosuka incident, see Takemae Eiji, *Senryō sengo-shi* (A History of the Occupation and Postwar Era), Iwanami Shoten, 1992, pp. 172–98. The following discussion is based on Takemae (1982), pp. 340–60 and Takemae (1992), pp. 201–32.
45. Hollingshead is quoted in Richard J. Smethurst, 'The Origins of the Japanese Teachers' Union', in Richard K. Beardsley, ed., *Studies in Japanese History and Politics*, University of Michigan Center for Japanese Studies, Occasional Papers, no. 10, 1967, p. 142. The Dupell quotation is from Toshio Nishi, *Unconditional Democracy: Education and Politics in Occupied Japan, 1945–1952*, Hoover Institution Press (Stanford University), 1982, p. 257. The Trainor citation is from Joseph C. Trainor, *Educational Reform in Occupied Japan: Trainor's Memoir*, Meisei University Press, 1983, p. 329.
46. Walter C. Eells, *Communism in Education in Asia, Africa and the Far Pacific*, American Council on Education, 1954, p. 12. Eells's speech is reproduced in Edward R. Beauchamp and James M. Vardaman Jr, eds, *Japanese Education Since 1945: A Documentary Study*, M. E. Sharpe, 1994, pp. 118–22.
47. Kim T'ae-gi, *Sengo Nihon seiji to Zainichi Chōsenjin mondai* (Postwar Japanese Politics and the Problem of Koreans in Japan), Keisō Shobō, 1997, pp. 561–3.
48. Cited in Courtney Whitney, *MacArthur: His Rendezvous With History*, Knopf, 1956, p. 310.
49. Letter from Valary Burati to Philip Sullivan dated '22 August 1950 and after', cited in Takemae Eiji (1982), p. 354. The letter is from the Burati Papers, Walter P. Reuther Library, Wayne State University.
50. Ibid. On the Labour Ministry circular of 9 October 1950, see Takemae (1982), pp. 418–20.
51. Takemae Eiji, 'Sōhyō and US Occupation Labour Policy: An Interview with Valery Burati' in *The Journal of the Tokyo College of Economics*, nos. 97–8, 1976, p. 265.
52. Takemae (1982), pp. 361–6.
53. Ibid., pp. 366–7.
54. Tsuru Shigeto, *Japan's Capitalism: Creative Defeat and Beyond*, Cambridge University Press, 1993, p. 58. The Yoshida quotation is from Dower (1979), p. 316. For the Murphy citation, see Robert Murphy, *Diplomat Among Warriors*, Doubleday, 1964, p. 347.

55. Herbert P. Bix, 'Regional Integration: Japan and South Korea in America's Asian Policy.', in Frank Baldwin, ed., *Without Parallel: The American-Korean Relationship Since 1945*, Pantheon Books, 1974, p. 197.

56. See Takafusa Nakamura, *A History of Shōwa Japan, 1926–1989*, University of Tokyo Press, 1998, pp. 306–7.

57. See generally Hata Ikuhiko, *Shiroku: Nihon saigunbi* (Historical Documents Pertaining to the Rearmament of Japan), Bungei Shunjūsha, 1976, chapter 6. In English, consult John W. Dower, 'The Eye of the Beholder', *The Bulletin of Concerned Asian Scholars*, vol. 2, no.1, October 1969, pp. 21–2 and Maeda Tetsuo, *The Hidden Army: The Untold Story of Japan's Military Forces*, Edition Q (Tokyo), 1995, chapters 1 and 2.

58. William J. Sebald with Russell Brines, *With MacArthur in Japan: A Personal History of the Occupation*, W. W. Norton, 1965, p. 198.

59. Frank Kowalski, *Nihon saigunbi: watakushi wa Nihon o saibusō shita* (The Remilitarisation of Japan: How I Rearmed Japan), Saimaru Shuppansha, 1969. Dower (1969), pp. 16–25. On the Manchukuo Army applicants, see John Welfield, *An Empire in Eclipse: Japan in the Postwar American Alliance System – A Study in the Interaction of Domestic Politics and Foreign Policy*, Athlone Press, 1988, p. 75.

60. Dower (1969), pp. 16–17. Alfred Rodman Hussey Papers, University of Michigan, cited in Harries (1989), p. 224. GHQ/SCAP (Civil Affairs Section), *A Report on the Japanese National Police Reserve*, October 1951, p. 9 (RG 319, Army Operations, 1950–1 (Top Secret, box 30).

61. Civil Affairs Section (1951), loc. cit. Dower (1979), p. 468.

62. Murphy (1964), pp. 347–8. A concise account in English is Welfield (1988), chapter 3.

63. See Takemae Eiji, Ozaki Tsuyoshi and Tanaka Kaori, 'Shōgen: sengo shoki kaiun hishi (A Witness to the Postwar History of Japanese Seamen: The Korean War and M. Kitamura), in *Shizen kagaku ronshū* (Occasional Papers in the Journal of Humanities and the Natural Sciences), Tōkyō Keizai Daigaku, March 1998, pp. 133–66. See also Transportation Section JLC 8000th Army Unit, 'JLC/TS Activities Report', September 1950, p. 11 (RG 407, box 4613, US National Archives and Records Administration, Washington DC).

64. Whitney (1956), p. 261. Charles L. Kades, 'The American Role in Revising Japan's Imperial Constitution', in *Political Science Quarterly*, vol. 104, no. 2, 1989, p. 224. The official cited by Kades was most likely Frank Rizzo, who replaced Whitney as chief of Government Section in 1951. See the interview with Rizzo in Osamu Nishi, *Ten Days inside General Headquarters (GHQ): How the Original Draft of the Japanese Constitution was Written in 1946*, Seibundo Publishing Company (Tokyo), 1989, p. 101. Murphy (1964), p. 341.

65. See discussion in Schaller (1985), pp. 276–8.

66. US Senate Committee on Armed Services and the Committee on Foreign Rela-

tions, *Hearing to Conduct an Inquiry into the Military Situation in the Far East,* 82nd Congress, 1st session, 1951, p. 19. See also Kolko (1972), pp. 593–607.
67. On the 'integrated' Cold War, see Dower (1993), pp. 189–93. On MacArthur's dismissal: Lawrence J. Korb, *The Joint Chiefs of Staff – The First Twenty-five Years,* Indiana University press, 1976, pp. 147–8.
68. GHQ/SCAP, *History of the Nonmilitary Activities of the Occupation of Japan, 1945–1951: 'The Purge',* Tokyo, 1951, pp. 122, 127. Civil Affairs Section (1951), loc. cit.
69. Miyauchi Yutaka, *Sengo chian rippō no kihonteki seikaku* (The Real Nature of the Postwar Public Security Laws), Yushindō, 1960, pp. 40–2, 55–7.
70. Miyauchi, ibid.; Dower (1979), pp. 366–8; and Takemae (1982), pp. 367–8.
71. Takemae (1976), p. 262.
72. Price (1991), 222–3.
73. Takemae (1976), p. 264. For a closer analysis of Burati's role, see Takemae Eiji, *Senryō sengo-shi* (A History of the Occupation and Postwar Era), Iwanami Shoten, 1992, chapter 4. Burati recognised the limits imposed by 'the overpowering weight of American capitalism working hand in hand through the Army with Japanese capitalism', but he himself had overstepped those bounds once too often. In 1949, he had testified against the US Navy on behalf of an alleged Communist union leader arrested in the Yokosuka incident. His close personal friendships with such left-leaning labour activists as Takano Minoru were another mark against him. Finally, his unstinting support for *Sōhyō* even after its drift to the left made his removal inevitable. Ridgway recounts his decision in Matthew B. Ridgway, *Soldier: The Memoirs of Matthew B. Ridgway,* Harpers, 1956, pp. 225, 227.
74. Lawrence W. Beer, *Freedom of Expression in Japan: A Study in Comparative Law, Politics, and Society,* Kodansha International, 1984, p. 178.
75. This process is detailed by Kobayashi Tomoko, 'GHQ no Zainichi Chōsenjin ninshiki ni kansuru ichi kōsatsu: G-2 Minkan Chōhō Kyoku teiki hōkokusho o chūshin ni' (Remarks on GHQ's Perception of Koreans in Japan: Periodic Reports of G-2's Civil Intelligence Section), in *Zainichi Chōsenjin-shi Kenkyūkai ronbunshū,* no. 32, 1994.
76. See Cheong Sung-hwa, *The Politics of Anti-Japanese Sentiment in Korea: Japanese–South Korean Relations Under American Occupation, 1945–1952,* Greenwood Press, 1991, chapter 5. Richard B. Finn, 'Memorandum of Conversation, Subject: Koreans in Japan', 3 February 1949, Enclosure no. 2 to dispatch no. 111, POLAD to State Department, 18 February 1949 (RG 54, 894.4016/5–1248, National Archives Records Administration, Washington DC). A fuller account of Finn's role, his views on Koreans and three interviews are given in Robert Ricketts, 'GHQ no tai-Zainichi-Chōsenjin seisaku o tsukutta otokotachi' (Cold Warriors and the Korean Minority in Occupied Japan: Part 1 – Richard B. Finn), in *Wakō Daigaku Ningen-kankei Gakubu kiyō* (Annals of the Faculty of Human Sciences, Wako University), no. 2, 1997, pp. 67–114.

77. Check Sheet (Subject: Status of Koreans in Japan), From: LS To: DS, 2 May 1949 (State Department Document no. 894.4016/8-1549, National Archives Records Administration, Washington DC). The outcome of the Finn–Bassin proposal is discussed at length in Kim (1997), pp. 610–59.

78. Government Section File: 'Status and Treatment of Koreans in Japan' and Matsukata Makoto, 'Memorandum for: Executive Officer, Government Section, Subject: Korean Situation in Japan', draft (RG 331, box 2190, Washington National Records Center, Archives II, College Park, Maryland).

79. Wagner (1951), p. 90.

80. Concerning the Sendai incident, see Yi Hyeong Nang, 'Miyagi-ken chi'iki ni okeru Zainichi-Chōsenjin no dōkō' (The Korean Community in Miyagi Prefecture), in *Seikyū gakujutsu ronshū*, no. 13, Kankoku Bunka Kenkyū Shinkō Zaidan, 1998, pp. 267–71. For other flag-related incidents, see Son Mun-gyu, 'Kokki o mamori-nuita hitobito: Chōsen Minshushugi Jinmin Kyōwa Koku kokki-keiyō jiken no shinsō' (People who Protected Their National Flag: The Truth About the DPRK Flag-Raising Incidents), in *Tōitsu Hyōron*, no. 60, 1978, pp. 66–73.

81. This was particularly evident in censorship policies towards Korean publications. Articles dealing with national identity, independence and reconstruction of the homeland were excised regularly from the beginning. By late 1947, however, the Korean left had become the main target of the censor's blue pencil, which deleted commentary critical of Japanese imperialism and the suppression of ethnic rights or favourable to the Soviet Union. A Civil Intelligence Section survey of December 1948 determined that fully 55 per cent of Korean daily papers and 41 per cent of other publications contained material hostile to the Occupation. This led to two showcase trials intended to bring the Korean media into line. In August 1949, a Military Court sentenced Kim Won-yun, a Korean editor in Osaka, to five years at hard labour followed by deportation to South Korea for a Press Code violation, and in September Eun Muam, a Korean editor in Tokyo, received a two-year sentence without deportation for a similar offence. See Kobayashi Tomoko, 'GHQ ni yoru Zainichi Chōsenjin kankō zasshi no ken'etsu' (The Censorship of Korean Publications by GHQ), in *Zainichi Chōsenjin-shi Kenkyūkai*, no. 22, 1992, pp. 84–98; Kim (1997), pp. 491–8; and Monica Braw, *The Atomic Bomb Suppressed*, M. E. Sharpe, 1991, pp. 87, 169. See also the examples cited by Yukiko Koshiro, *Trans-Pacific Racisms and the U.S. Occupation of Japan*, East Asian Institute, Columbia University, 1999, pp. 116–17.

82. The Shirasu memo is reproduced in Ricketts (1997), pp. 113–14. Yoshida is thought to have written his undated letter to MacArthur in late August 1949. The Prime Minister estimated that there were about 1 million Koreans in Japan 'of whom one half are illegal entrants'. Koreans, he claimed, were consuming huge amounts of US food imports, unfairly burdening future generations of Japanese who would have to shoulder that debt. Moreover, he asserted, a great

majority were 'not contributing at all to the economic reconstruction of Japan' and a large percentage were 'prone to commit political offences of the most vicious kind. More than 7,000 are always in jail.' The letter is published in Sodei Rinjirō, *Yoshida-Makkāsā ōfuku shokan-shū, 1945–1951* (Correspondence Between General MacArthur, Prime Minister Yoshida and Other High Japanese Officials, 1945–1951), Hōsei Daigaku Shuppankyoku, 2000, pp. 147–8.

83. Takemae Eiji, 'J. Napier and the Purge in Japan: Interview With Mr. Jack P. Napier', in *The Journal of Tokyo Keizai University*, no. 153, November 1987, pp. 73–99. The MacArthur citation is from POLAD, Tokyo, Dispatch 734, 21 October 1949 (RG 84, POLAD box 48, Washington National Records Center, Archives II, College Park, Maryland).

84. The revision stemmed from a series of conferences held by SCAP and Eighth Army between May and July 1949 to deal with the illegal entry of subversive elements from Korea. The resulting plan called for the reissuing of 'Korean registration certificates', tougher penalties and tighter police enforcement. At the July conference, Diplomatic Section's Richard Finn defended these measures as discriminatory but unavoidable and rejected a G-2 proposal to remove restrictions on travel between Japan and Korea as an alternative means of solving the problem. Takemae Eiji and Robert Ricketts, 'Robāto Riketto shimon-ōnatsu kyohi jiken kankei-shiryō' (Historical Documents Pertaining to Robert Ricketts's Trial for Fingerprint Refusal), in *The Journal of Tokyo Keizai University*, no. 161, June 1989, pp. 7–14. See also Kim (1997), pp. 666–71.

85. The Kobe–Kyoto–Ōtsu disturbances are discussed in Kim (1997), pp. 684–5. On the immigration law and subsequent measures against Koreans, see Takemae and Ricketts (1989), pp. 37–9.

86. Memorandum for Chief of Staff, Subject: Deportation of Subversive Aliens, 17 July 1951 (SCAP Records, Top Secret File, Sheets 00295–96, Japan National Diet Library). Although signed by Legal Section Chief Alva Carpenter, the brief was drafted by Bassin. See the discussion in Robert Ricketts, 'GHQ no Zainichi Chōsenjin seisaku' (GHQ's Korean Policy), in *Ajia Kenkyū*, Wakō Daigaku, 1994, pp. 15–16, 34.

87. Minutes of the Twenty-Third Meeting of the Committee on Countermeasures Against Communism in the Far East, 18 October 1951. GHQ/SCAP, Government Section, 'Counter-Measures Against the Subversive Potential in Japan – 1946 to 1951 Inclusive' (RG 331, box 8497, Washington National Records Center, Archives II, College Park, Maryland).

88. Dean Acheson, *Present at the Creation: My Years in the State Department*, New American Library, 1970 (Norton, 1969), p. 341. Finn (1992), pp. 156–7. On Dulles, see Schonberger (1989), p. 238.

89. Kennan (1967), p. 396.

90. William J. Sebald with Russell Brines, *With MacArthur in Japan: A Personal History of the Occupation*, Norton, 1965, p. 256–7. Yoshida's views on rearmament are discussed in Gerald L. Curtis, 'The Dulles–Yoshida Negotiations

on the San Francisco Peace Treaty', in *Columbia Essays in International Affairs*, vol. 2, Columbia University Press, 1967, pp. 37–61.

91. The MacArthur citation is from US Department of State, *Foreign Relations of the United States* (below, given as *FRUS*), US Government Printing Office, vol. 6, 1950, p. 1215. Pakenham was born in Kobe to a distinguished English family, and spoke fluent Japanese. A former member of Britain's élite Coldstream Guards, he had good contacts in the Imperial household and among ultra-conservative political leaders. He also was a bitter foe of MacArthur, having been denied re-entry into Japan in early 1948 for his caustic reporting on SCAP's economic reforms (the Japan Lobby intervened and Army Secretary Royall engineered his return). On the Emperor and Dulles, see Toyoshita Narahiko, *Anpō Jōyaku no seiritsu: Yoshida gaikō to Tennō gaikō* (The Drafting of the Security Treaty: Yoshida's Diplomacy and the Emperor's Diplomacy), Iwanami Shinsho, 1996, pp. 165–86. The message as reconstructed by Pakenham is reproduced in Schonberger (1989), pp. 154–6. The Dulles version is in *FRUS*, vol. 6, 1950, pp. 1236–7. In January 1951, the Emperor reportedly attempted to arrange a sequel to Pakenham's party of June 1950 through Matsudaira and Kern, but Dulles demurred. On 6 February, however, Pakenham introduced the US envoy to Hatoyama Ichirō and other Japanese conservatives committed to rearmament, who presented him with a statement of their goals. On 10 February, Dulles conferred informally with the Emperor in the Imperial Palace following preliminary bilateral agreement on the stationing of US forces in Japan. Upon hearing Dulles's account of the accord, Hirohito 'expressed his wholehearted agreement and appreciation to the United States' and said that he was 'fully in accord with the concepts mentioned'. Dulles met Hirohito again on 22 April and 18 December 1951. On 28 April 1952, the day the treaty went into effect, the special adviser sent Hirohito a message of his own, thanking the sovereign for affording him several opportunities to discuss bilateral issues. *FRUS*, vol. 6, Part 1, 1951, pp. 873–4 and Toyoshita (1996), pp. 180–1.

92. *FRUS*, vol. 6, Part 1, 1951, pp. 788–9.

93. See Frederick S. Dunn, *Peace-Making and the Settlement with Japan*, Princeton University Press, 1963, pp. 107–8 and, generally, Michael M. Yoshitsu, *Japan and the San Francisco Peace Settlement*, Columbia University Press, 1983, chapter 3.

94. *FRUS*, vol 6, Part 1, 1951, p. 832. Nishimura Kumao, *Sanfuranshisuko heiwa jōyaku* (The San Francisco Peace Treaty), in *Nihon gaikōshi* (Japanese Diplomatic History), vol. 27, Kajima Kenkyūjo Shuppankai, 1971, pp. 88–9. Kōsaka Masataka, 'Saisho Yoshida Shigeru ron' (Prime Minister Yoshida Shigeru: An Interpretation), Chūō Kōron, February 1965, p. 107.

95. The 2 February document is reproduced in Finn (1992), p. 279 and a slightly different version in Yoshitsu (1983), p. 60.

96. Ann Trotter, *New Zealand and Japan, 1945–1952: The Occupation and the Peace Treaty*, Athlone Press, 1990, pp. 157–62. See also Dunn (1963), p. 113.

97. *FRUS*, vol. 6, Part 1, 1951, pp. 1024–37, 1119–33. On economic reintegration, see Schaller (1985), chapter 16, especially pp. 294–8 and Borden (1984), pp. 143–65.
98. Yoshitsu (1983), chapter 4. See also discussion in Michael Schaller, *Altered States: The United States and Japan Since the Occupation*, Oxford University Press, 1997, chapter 2.
99. The Herter quotation is from US Senate, Committee on Foreign Relations, *Treaty of Mutual Cooperation and Security with Japan*, 86th Congress, 2nd Session (7 June 1960), pp. 30–1.
100. Yoshitsu (1983), pp. 83–100 and Schonberger (1989), pp. 265–78.
101. See Kurihara Sadako, *Black Eggs: Poems by Kurihara Sadako*, Center for Japanese Studies, University of Michigan, 1994.
102. Committee for the Compilation of Materials on Damage Caused by the Atomic Bombs in Hiroshima and Nagasaki, *Hiroshima and Nagasaki: The Physical, Medical, and Social Effects of the Atomic Bombings*, Basic Books, 1981, pp. 571–4.
103. 'A Statement by the Peace Study Group on the Problem of the Peace Settlement for Japan' in *Sekai* Editorial Staff, *Three Statements for World Peace*, Tokyo, 1950, pp. 18–22.
104. See discussion in Dower (1979), pp. 371–2.
105. 'Memorandum of Conversation by Mr. Robert A. Fearey of the Office of Northeast Asian Affairs', 23 April 1951, in *FRUS*, vol. 6, Part 1, 1951, 1006–8.
106. Dunn (1963), pp. 99–100.
107. Cheong (1991), pp. 92–3. In retrospect, by London's logic, it is ironical that Ceylon and Indonesia, neither of them FEC members, both were invited to the Peace Conference, an incongruity that seems to have escaped the treaty's Anglo-American planners.
108. On Nishimura's statement to the Diet, see Tanaka (1995), pp. 70–1. The Japanese Foreign Ministry had included the option of Japanese citizenship in its own treaty drafts between 1947 and 1950 on the assumption that the Americans would demand such a provision. In fact, however, the Ministry had envisaged citizenship for a select few, intending to forcibly repatriate the majority. Neither Japan nor the Republic of Korea was prepared to offer Koreans a choice in this matter, nor did the Korean movement in Japan ever formulate such a demand. All three parties regarded ethnicity and nationality as synonymous, conflating the very distinct concepts of ethnic identity, nationality and citizenship. On the nationality issue, see Matsumoto Kunihiko, 'Zainichi Chōsenjin no Nihon kokuseki hakudatsu' (The Denationalisation of Koreans in Japan), in *Hōgaku*, vol. 52, no. 4, 1988, pp. 645–79 and Kashiwazaki Chikako, 'The Politics of Legal Status: The Equation of Nationality with Ethnonational Identity', in Sonia Ryang, ed., *Koreans in Japan: Critical Voices from the Margin*, Routledge, 2000, pp. 20–30.
109. Changsoo Lee and George De Vos, *Koreans in Japan: Ethnic Conflict and Accommodation*, University of California Press, 1981, pp. 149–51. For instance,

today, non-Japanese generally are excluded from the civil service, the state school system, local boards of education, civil liberties commissions, welfare commissions and other public bodies. In recent years, qualified foreigners have been hired to teach in state schools but without the same rights and possibilities for promotion as Japanese. In the private sector, aliens cannot hold decision-making positions in mining, fishing, or telecommunications. Their employment is restricted in banking, the securities and insurance industries and aviation. Japanese nationality also is a condition for public accountants and ship pilots. See Gaimushō Jōyaku-kyoku-hen (ed.), *Waga kuni ni okeru gaikokujin no hōteki chi'i* (The Legal Status of Aliens in Japan), Nihon Kajo Shuppan, 1993, pp. 25–7.

110. The Wajima quotation is contained in a telegram from Ambassador Robert Murphy, US Embassy, Tokyo, to the Secretary of State, 2 October 1952 (State Department Central Files, Document no. 694.96B/10-252F, National Archives Records Administration, Washington DC). On the need for a post-treaty policy for former colonials, see Tanaka Hiroshi's seminal essay, 'Sengo Nihon to posuto-shokuminchi mondai' (Postwar Japan and the Post-Colonial Settlement Issue), in *Shisō*, no. 734, August 1985, pp. 38–52. A useful but dated treatment in English of Koreans in post-treaty Japan is Lee and De Vos (1981), chapter 7. See also Sonia Ryang's important monograph, *North Koreans in Japan: Language, Ideology, and Identity*, Westview Press, 1997, chapter 3.

111. The 'Anglo-Saxon lake' quotation is from *The New York Times*, 2 March 1949, cited in Acheson (1970), p. 465. Acheson's comment is on p. 466. On MacArthur's 'insular imperialism', see John W. Dower, 'Occupied Japan and the American Lake' in Edward Friedman and Mark Selden, eds, *America's Asia: Dissenting Essays on Asian-American Relations*, Vintage Books, 1971, p. 170.

112. See Arnold G. Fisch Jr, *Military Government in the Ryukyu Islands, 1945–1950*, US Army Center for Military History, US Government Printing Office, 1988, chapter 7; *FRUS*, vol. 7, Part 2, 1949, pp. 815–16; and Kenneth W. Condit, *The Joint Chiefs of Staff and National Policy, 1947–1949*, vol. 2 of *The History of the Joint Chiefs of Staff*, Michael Glazier, 1979, chapter 9.

113. Fisch (1988), p. 174.

114. The GRI's legislative branch, however, was composed of locally elected officials, allowing a limited degree of self-rule that complemented the system of municipal self-government established in 1948 (chapter 9). Watanabe Akio, *The Okinawa Problem: A Chapter in Japan–US Relations*, Melbourne University Press, 1970, p. 22.

115. Fisch, (1988), p. 169. In English, see the concise accounts by Watanabe (1970), pp. 13, 25 and Robert K. Sakai and Mitsugu Sakihara, 'Okinawa', in *The Kodansha Encyclopedia of Japan*, Kodansha, 1983, pp. 89–90. A recent discussion of the making of an American colony is Nicholas Evan Sarantakes, *Keystone: The American Occupation of Okinawa and US – Japanese Relations*, Texas A & M University Press, 2000 chapter 4. Of particular interest is Robert

D. Eldridge, *The Origins of the Bilateral Okinawa Problem: Okinawa in Postwar U.S.–Japan Relations, 1945–1952,* Garland Publishing (New York), 2001, chapter 7.

116. David Rees, *The Soviet Seizure of the Kuriles,* Praeger, 1985, p. 89. The Marshall Islands, in particular, would become a vast proving ground for American nuclear weapons. Between 1946 and 1958, the United States tested a total of 66 atomic and hydrogen bombs there. Today, the islands continue to serve as a test range for America's arsenal of intercontinental ballistic missiles. Jane Dibblin, *Day of Two Suns: US Nuclear Testing and the Pacific Islands,* New Amsterdam (New York), 1990, p. 20. The historian is Tsuyoshi Hasegawa, *The Northern Territories Dispute and Russo-Japanese Relations,* vol. 1: Between War and Peace, 1697–1985, University of California Press, 1998, p. 89.

117. Hasegawa, ibid., pp. 88–105.

Chapter 11   The Legacy of Occupation

1. The following is an abridged and updated version of Takemae Eiji's 'Senryō sōsetsu: senryō to GHQ' (An Overview of the Occupation: The Occupation and GHQ), in *GHQ: Nihon senryō-shi jōsetsu* (GHQ: An Introduction to the History of the Occupation of Japan), Nihon Tosho Sentā, 1996, pp. 74–95.

2. John J. Stephan, *The Kuril Islands: Russo-Japanese Fontier in the Pacific,* Clarendon Press (Oxford), 1974, p. 219.

3. Kyodo News Service, 'Moscow Wanted to Give Two Islands Back', in *The Japan Times,* 3 March 1993.

4. See, for example, Fujiwara Akira, Awaya Kentarō, Okada Akina and Yamada Akina eds., *Tettei-kenshō: Shōwa-tennō 'dokuhaku-roku'* (Conclusive Evidence: The Shōwa Emperor's 'Soliloguy'), Ōtsuki Shoten, 1991 pp. 36–77 and Yoshida Yutaka, *Shōwa-tennō no shūen-shi* (A Postwar History of the Shōwa Emperor), Iwanami Shinsho, 1992, Part I, chapters 1–2. A damning indictment of Hirohito's war complicity in English is the study by Herbert P. Bix, *Hirohito and the Making of Modern Japan,* HarperCollins, 2000, chapters 7–13.

5. Nakamura Masanori, *The Japanese Monarchy: Ambassador Grew and the Making of the 'Symbol Emperor System', 1931–1991,* M. E. Sharpe, 1992, pp. 175–84.

6. See discussion in Nakamura, ibid., pp. 121–2.

7. Watanabe Osamu, 'Gendai Nihon kokka no tokushu na kōzō' (The Peculiar Structure of the Modern Japanese State), in Tōkyō Daigaku Shakaikagaku Kenkyūjo-hen (ed.), *Gendai Nihon Shakai* (Contemporary Japanese Society), vol. 1, Tōkyō Daigaku Shuppankai, 1991, pp. 201–95.

8. See Norma Field's compelling personal account of Motojima, *In the Realm of a Dying Emperor: Japan at Century's End,* Vintage, 1993, chapter 3.

9. See, for instance, Koseki Shōichi, 'Kenpō o toi-naosu sengo gojūnen-me no "shiten"' (A Fresh Look at the Constitution Fifty Years Later), in Nihon Jānarisuto Kaigi-hen (ed.), *Masukomi no rekishi sekinin to mirai sekinin* (The

Mass Media's Responsibility for the Past and the Future), Kōbunken, 1995, pp. 93–125.

10. Takemae Eiji, *Senryō sengo-shi* (A History of the Occupation and Postwar Era), Iwanami Shoten, 1992, pp. 414–15.

11. For an overview of these problems, see Arasaki Moriteru, *Okinawa hansen-jinushi* (Okinawa and the Anti-War Landlords), Kōbunken, 1996, especially chapters 3, 6 and 7.

12. Edwin O. Reischauer, *My Life Between Japan and America*, Weatherhill, 1986, p. 299. A fuller account is Michael Schaller, *Altered States: the United States and Japan Since the Occupation*, Oxford University Press, 1997, pp. 196–7. On the Ogasawaras, see the news story in *The Japan Times*, 3 August 2000.

13. Minutes of the Research Commission on the Constitution, House of Councillors, 2 May 2000, pp. 21–2. A powerful endorsement of this view by an American observer is C. Douglas Lummis, *Kenpō to sensō* (The Constitution and War), Shōbunsha, 2000. See generally, Takemae Eiji, *Goken-kaiken-shi ron* (An Analysis of Arguments For and Against Constitutional Revision), Shōgakkan Bunko, 2001.

14. Nakamura Masanori, 'Sengo kaikaku to gendai' (The Postwar Reforms and Contemporary Japan), in *Senryō to sengo-kaikaku* (The Occupation and the Postwar Reforms), Yoshikawa Kobunkan, 1994, p. 16.

15. Udagawa Megumi, 'The Bitter Legacy of Eugenics', in *The Japan Views Quarterly*, The Asia Foundation Translation Series (Tokyo), vol. 2, no. 4, Winter 1993, pp. 37–8 and especially Matsubara Yōko, 'Nihon: sengo no Yūsei Hogo-hō (Japan: The Postwar Eugenics Protection Law – A Sterilisation Law in Disguise), in Yoneyama Shōhei, ed., *Yūseigaku to ningen shakai: seimei-kagaku no seiki wa doko e mukau ka* (Eugenics and Human Society: Where is the Century of Life Science Headed?) Kōdansha, 2000, pp. 229–33.

16. See Kinjo Kiyoko, 'Legal Challenges to the Status Quo', in Fumiko Fujimura-Fanselow and Atsuko Kameda, eds, *Japanese Women: New Feminist Perspectives on the Past, Present and Future*, The Feminist Press (City University of New York), 1995, pp. 353–63. See generally Prime Minister's Office, *The Present Status of Gender Equality and Measures*, 1999; Nakamura Akemi, 'New Equal Opportunity Law Called a Start', *The Japan Times*, 1 April 1999, p. 3; and Foreign Press Centre, Japan, ed., *Japan: A Pocket Guide*, 2000, pp. 173–4.

17. George Hicks, 'Japan, Land of Quiet Apartheid', *The International Herald Tribune*, 18 March 1992. A general discussion of ethnic and other minorities in Japan is Michael Weiner, ed., *Japan's Minorities: The Illusion of Homogeneity*, Routledge, 1997. See also John Lie, *Multiethnic Japan*, Harvard University Press, 2001, chapter 5.

18. Tanaka Hiroshi, *Zainichi Gaikokujin: hō no kabe, kokoro no kabe* (Foreigners in Japan: Legal and Psychological Obstacles to Equality), Iwanami Shinsho, 1995, chapter 6.

19. For a sensitive insider's account of North Koreans in Japan, see Sonia Ryang, *North Koreans in Japan: Language, Ideology, and Identity*, Westview Press, 1997

and on Koreans in general, Sonia Ryang, ed., *Koreans in Japan: Critical Voices from the Margin*, Routledge, 2000.

20. Kajimura Hideki, 'Confronting Japanese Racism: Toward a Korean Identity', in *Japan–Asia Quarterly Review (AMPO)*, vol. 20, nos 1–2, 1990, pp. 34–41. On naturalisation, see Kim Yŏng-dal, *Zainichi Chōsenjin no kika* (The Naturalisation of Koreans in Japan), Akashi Shoten, 1990.

21. Tanaka (1995), chapter 8. In English, see generally Komai Hiroshi, *Migrant Workers in Japan*, Kegan Paul International, 1995.

22. Frank K. Upham, *Law and Social Change in Postwar Japan*, Harvard University Press, 1987, chapter 3. On the *Buraku* people in general, see Roger I. Yoshino, *The Invisible Minority: Japan's Burakumin*, Buraku Kaihō Kenkyūsho, 1977.

23. The historical background to these changes is given in Kayano Shigeru, *Our Land Was a Forest: An Ainu Memoir*, Westview Press, 1994. On the Ainu ethnic revival, see Katarina Sjoberg, *The Return of the Ainu: Cultural Mobilization and the Practice of Ethnicity in Japan*, Harwood Academic, 1993. A discussion of recent developments is Richard Siddle, *Race, Resistance and the Ainu of Japan*, Routledge, 2000, chapter 7.

24. John W. Dower, *Empire and Aftermath: Yoshida Shigeru and the Japanese Experience, 1878–1954*, Council on East Asian Studies, Harvard University, 1979, p. 358.

25. Shibata Tokue and Miyamoto Ken'ichi pointed to this anomaly in the early 1960s. See their *Chihō zaisei* (Regional Fiscal Policy), Yūhikaku, 1963, p. 119. Journalists later coined the term. In English: Kurt Steiner, *Local Government in Japan*, Stanford University Press, 1965, p. 293.

26. Ōshita Katsumasa, *Machida-shi ga kawatta: chihō-jichi to fukushi* (Machida City Transformed: Local Autonomy and Social Welfare), Asahi Shinbunsha, 1992, chapter 4.

27. Takemae (1992), pp. 397–400.

28. Namie Ken, *Honmono no chihō-bunken/chihō-jichi* (Regional Decentralisation, Local Autonomy: The Real McCoy), BOC Shuppanbu, 1995. An overview of local action and national politics is Sheila A. Smith, ed., *Local Voices, National Issues: The Impact of Local Initiative in Japanese Policy-Making*, University of Michigan Press, 2000.

29. Hayakawa Noboru, *Ima Miyakejima: NLP kichi kensetsu keikaku ni hantai-suru shima-ikusa to kunō suru shima no genjitsu* (Miyakejima Now! An Island Opposes the Construction of an NLP Base: Miyake's Struggle and Travail), San'ichi Shobō, 1988.

30. Chibana Shōichi, *Yakisuterareta Hinomaru* (The Rising Sun Flag Burned to Ashes), Shakai Shisōsha, 1996. See also Norma Field's insightful account (1993), chapter 1.

31. See Patricia Maclachlan, 'Information Disclosure and the Center-Local Relationship in Japan', in Smith (2000), pp. 9–30. The quotation is from p. 29.

32. Gavan McCormack, 'Crime, Confession, and Control in Contemporary Japan',

in Gavan McCormack and Yoshio Sugimoto, eds, *Democracy in Contemporary Japan*, Hale & Ironmonger, 1986, pp. 186–214.

33. Akagi Suruki, *Kansei no keisei* (The Establishment of the Bureaucracy), Nihon Hyōronsha, 1991, pp. 39–402 and, generally, Okada Akira, *Gendai Nihon kanryō-sei no seiritsu* (The Establishment of the Modern Japanese Bureaucratic System), Hōsei Daigaku Shuppan-kyoku, 1994.

34. Amakawa Akira, 'Minshuka-katei to kanryō no taiō' (The Democratic Process and the Response of the Bureaucracy), in Nakamura Masanori, ed., *Sengo Nihon: senryō to sengo-kaikaku* (Postwar Japan: The Occupation and Postwar Reforms), vol. 2, Iwanami Shoten, 1995, pp. 233–66.

35. Robert A. Scalapino and Masumi Junnosuke, *Parties and Politics in Contemporary Japan*, University of California Press, 1962, pp. 47–9.

36. See the discussion in Schaller (1997), pp. 135–6, 195.

37. The number of Lower House seats was reduced from 511 to 500, of which 300 were single-seat constituencies where voters elect one candidate by name. The remaining 200 seats were allocated by party, voters selecting a party rather than a politician in 11 national blocs. The percentage of ballots each party receives determines the number of politicians it can put into office. Candidates are ranked for each bloc before the election. In February 2000, the number of seats was reduced further to 480 (300 single-seat members and 180 proportional representatives).

38. Stuart Auerbach, 'The US Created its "Japan Problem"', in *The Japan Times*, 26 July 1993 (reprinted from *The Washington Post*).

39. This point is made by C. Douglas Lummis, *Radical Democracy*, Cornell University Press, 1996, chapter 4.

40. On the Occupation reforms and the Japanese economy, see Bernard Bernier, *Le Japon contemporain: Une Economie nationale, Une Economie morale*, Les Presses de l'Université de Montréal, 1995, chapter 2. See also generally, Lonny E. Carlisle and Mark C. Tilton, eds, *Is Japan Really Changing its Ways? Regulatory Reform and the Japanese Economy*, Brookings Institution Press, 1998.

41. See Michael Schaller, *The Origins of the Cold War in Asia: The American Occupation of Japan*, Oxford University Press, 1985, chapter 8 and Schaller (1997), chapter 6. A similar argument is advanced cogently by William S. Borden, *The Pacific Alliance: United States Foreign Economic Policy and Japanese Trade Recovery, 1947–1955*, University of Wisconsin Press, 1984, chapter 3.

42. For more detail, see Takemae Eiji, *Shiryō Nihon no rōdō: seisaku, undō, hanrei* (Historical Documents on Japanese Labour: Policy, Labour Movements, Legal Precedents), Yūshisha, 1994.

43. Iwamoto Sumiaki and Teruoka Shuzō, 'Nōchi-kaikaku: jinushi-sei no shūen to jisakunō taisei' (The Land Reform: The Demise of the Landlord System and the System of Independent Farm Producers), in Sodei Rinjirō and Takemae Eiji, eds, *Sengo Nihon no genten: senryō-shi no genzai* (Postwar Japan: The Point of Origin–Occupation History Today), Yūshisha, vol. 2, 1992, pp. 61–126.

Figures are from Asahi Shinbun ed., *The Japan Almanac 2000*, Asahi Shinbunsha, 1999, p. 140.

44. Gōda Kimitsugu, 'Nōkyō-hō, dai'ichi kaisei-hō to GHQ no kyōdō-kumiai seisaku' (The First Farmers' Co-op Law and GHQ's Policy on Cooperatives), Parts 1 and 2, in *Ōita Daigaku keizai ronshū* (Ōita University Occasional Papers in Economics), no. 47, vols 1 and 3, 1995. Statistics are from *The Japan Almanac*, p. 142.

45. Kubo Yoshizō, *Shōwa kyōiku-shi* (A History of Education During the Shōwa Era), vol. 2, 1994, p. 42.

46. Nozaki Yoshiko and Inokuchi Hiromitsu, 'Japanese Education, Nationalism, and Ienaga Saburō's Textbook Lawsuits', in Laura Hein and Mark Selden, eds, *Censoring History: Citizenship and Memory in Japan, Germany, and the United States*, M. E. Sharpe, 2000, pp. 96–126. See also Ienaga Saburō, *Japan's Past, Japan's Future: One Historian's Odessey*, Rowman & Littlefield, 2001. Another useful account in English despite its lack of documentation is Peter J. Herzog, *Japan's Pseudo-Democracy*, Japan Library (Kent), 1993, pp. 208–17.

47. See Field (1993), chapter 2 and David M. O'Brien with Yasuo Ohkoshi, *To Dream of Dreams: Religious Freedom and Constitutional Politics in Postwar Japan*, University of Hawai'i Press, 1996, chapters 5 and 6.

48. Court cases in this section are discussed in Saikō Saibansho Sōkyoku-hen (ed.), *Gyōsei jiken saihanrei-shū* (Court Verdicts in Civil Suits), no. 38, vols 6 and 7, Zaidan Hōjin Hōsōkai, 1988, pp. 561–924. Saikō Saibansho Hanrei Chōsa I'inkai-hen (ed.), *Saikō Saibansho minji hanrei-shū* (Civil Verdicts of the Supreme Court), Saikō Saibansho Hanrei Chōsa I'inkai, no. 3, vol. 47, 1993, p. 1145 and Ashibe Nobuyoshi, *Kenpō* (The Constitution), Iwanami Shoten, 1999, pp. 150–3. See also O'Brien and Ohkoshi (1996), pp. 172–3.

49. Today, the Aum trials continue. In June and July 2000, four of five cultists convicted of the attack were sentenced to death, and two other members received the same penalty for their role in the 1989 murder of an anti-Aum lawyer and his family. Other Aum-linked killings are still being prosecuted, but the trial of the cult's guru, Asahara Shōkō, is expected to continue for some time. The organisation now operates under a different name, Aleph.

50. See Oda Makoto, 'Nihon wa "Kokuren" o yamete, "Kokuren" ni kyōryoku seyo' (Japan Should Quit, Then Cooperate With, the United Nations), *Gekkan Asahi*, January 1991, pp. 60–5 and Shindō Ei'ichi, 'Chi no suijaku ga motarasu sekai-zō no hizumi to hoshu e no kaiki' (Distortions in Our Worldview Caused by Intellectual Stagnation and Nostalgia for the Right) in Nihon Jānarisuto Kaigi, ed. (1995), pp. 127–71.

51. Statistics are from Ministry of Health and Welfare, *Statistical Abstracts on Health and Welfare in Japan*, 1999, pp. 35, 62.

52. Ibid., pp. 67, 73.

53. See, for example, Hoshino Yoshirō, 'Japan's Post-Second World War Environmental Problems', in Ui Jun, ed., *Industrial Pollution in Japan*, United Nations

University Press, 1992, pp. 64–76 and Ui Jun, 'Minamata Disease', in Ui Jun, ed., ibid., pp. 103–32. The data on victims of atmospheric pollution are from Miyamoto Ken'ichi, *Kōkyō seisaku no susume: gendai-teki kōkyōsei to wa nani ka* (For an Enlightened Public Interest Policy: A Query into the Modern Concept of Public Interest), Yūhikaku, 1998, pp. 218–19. The government admitted that the Minamata and Agano cases were caused by industrial pollution, but it subsequently devised excessively stringent medical criteria to identify sufferers in order to minimise the number eligible for compensation. From the start, local governments and the corporate polluters attempted to evade responsibility. Kumamoto Governor Teramoto Kōsaku, former Welfare Ministry official and author of the Labour Standards Law, played a central role in this cover-up in the early 1960s (see Mishima Akio, *Bitter Sea: The Human Cost of Minamata Disease*, Kosei Publishing Company, 1992, pp. 46, 102).

A partial solution was not reached until October 1995, when victims' organisations, opposition parties and the government agreed on a one-time-only compensation package for more than 8,000 people stricken with the disease. The settlement came 40 years after the outbreak of the malady and failed to answer the question of corporate and state responsibility. In April 2001, the Osaka High Court ruled that the state, Kumamoto Prefecture and Chisso Corp. were guilty of failing to prevent the Minamata tragedy and ordered them to pay damages to the plaintiffs. In May, however, the Justice Ministry announced it would appeal that verdict to the Supreme Court. On the structure of anti-pollution movements, see generally Jeffrey Broadbent, *Environmental Politics in Japan: Networks of Power and Protest*, Cambridge University Press, 1998.

54. A systematic critique of the modern Japanese scrap-and-build developmental state is Miyamoto (1998). In the early 1970s, social activists coined the term 'junkyard development' to characterise grandiose state schemes designed to promote economic integration at the expense of primary producers and local residents. See 'Junkyard Development', in *AMPO: A Report on the Japanese People's Movements*, no. 11, 1971, pp. 21–7.

55. This point is made by Nakamura Masanori, *The Japanese Monarchy: Ambassador Grew and the Making of the 'Symbol Emperor System', 1931–1991*, M. E. Sharpe, 1992, chapter 11.

56. Grew's remarks are in US Department of State, *Foreign Relations of the United States* (below, given as *FRUS*), US Government Printing Office, vol. 6, 1945, p. 545. See also Sebastian Swann, 'Democratisation and the Evasion of War Responsibility: The Allied Occupation of Japan', in *Reflections on the Allied Occupation of Japan*, STICERD Discussion Paper no. IS/99/370, London School of Economics and Political Science, October 1999, pp. 20–1. The Kennan quotation is from Policy Planning Staff Document no. 23 of 24 February 1948, reproduced in *FRUS*, vol. 1, Part 2, 1948, p. 524.

57. Committee for the Compilation of Materials on Damage Caused by the Atomic Bombs in Hiroshima and Nagasaki, *Hiroshima and Nagasaki: The*

Physical, Medical, and Social Effects of the Atomic Bombings, Basic Books, 1981, pp. 542–4, 554–5, 575–81.

58. See the ground breaking study on the *Anpō* struggle by Wesley Sasaki-Uemura, *Organizing the Spontaneous: Citizen Protest in Postwar Japan*, University of Hawai'i Press, 2001.

59. Koreans serving prison terms for B and C war crimes offences were not granted a remission of their sentences despite being arbitrarily deprived of Japanese nationality in April 1952. Article 11 of the San Francisco Peace Treaty obliged Japan to continue imposing on its nationals all penalties handed down by Allied military tribunals. Soon after the country recovered its sovereignty, 30 Korean and Taiwanese prisoners appealed their cases on the grounds that they were no longer Japanese. The Supreme Court (presided over by Tanaka Kōtarō), however, ruled that they had been Japanese nationals when they committed their crimes and therefore were not eligible for release. In a classic example of the double bind, in virtually all other instances, the government has justified its denial of basic civil and political liberties to former colonial subjects using the opposite argument: their 'loss' of Japanese nationality. See Utsumi Aiko, *Chōsenjin BC-kyū senpan no kiroku* (A Documentary Record of Class B and C Korean War Criminals), Keisō Shobō, 1982, pp. 213–46.

60. Recent news reports indicate that the Fund is running out of money. To date it has raised only about ¥448 million ($4 million), most of which is now gone. Japan's efforts pale beside those of Germany to compensate of Jews and East Europeans for Nazi depredations. Under a 1956 Federal relief law, that country has contributed a total of ¥6 trillion ($50 billion) to Jewish and non-German war victims.

61. On the Yoshida letter to the Dutch government, see John Price, 'Fifty Years Later, it's Time to Right the Wrongs of the San Francisco Peace Treaty,' in *The Japan Times*, 6 September 2001. On the compensation issue, see generally Odabe Yūji, Hayashi Hiroshi and Yamada Akira, *Kīwādo: Nihon no sensō hanzai* (Keywords: Japan's War Crimes), Yūsankaku, 1997, pp. 214–15.

62. Laura Hein and Mark Selden, eds, *Living with the Bomb: American and Japanese Cultural Conflicts in the Nuclear Age*, M. E. Sharpe, 1997, p. 3.

63. Concerning Tsuji, see note 17, chapter 6.

Translators' Note

Inside GHQ has evolved into a very different work from the slim monograph that Professor Takemae Eiji published in Japanese in 1983. With characteristic modesty, the author made few references in the original version to his own pioneering research in labour policy and other areas of Occupation history. In adapting the present work, the translators have drawn extensively from this impressive corpus of scholarship as well as from the in-depth interviews Professor Takemae has conducted with former SCAP and Japanese officials since 1983. The incorporation of recent scholarship on the Occupation, background information and copious endnotes has imparted additional depth, and volume, to the English edition.

The draft translation of the original Japanese text devolved largely upon Sebastian Swann in Washington DC, who also compiled the bibliography and index and coordinated the project with Athlone. The task of reorganising, updating and editing the text was undertaken by Robert Ricketts in Tokyo, under the close supervision of the author. Ricketts also integrated relevant materials from Professor Takemae's other writings, compiled endnotes and added the Introduction and chapters 9 and 11 based on the author's recent research. In the process, *Inside GHQ's* four original chapters ballooned to eleven, the English typescript from 270 pages to 1,200. Both translators have reviewed each other's work and contributed to the adaptation of the text as a whole; both are responsible for the final product.

We gratefully acknowledge the generous assistance of Andō Rei, Lonny Carlisle, Victor Carpenter, Alistair Graham, Inoue Teruko, Iwase Fusako, Deborah Kaplan, Koh Myong-shin, Matsuno Masako, Joe B. Moore, Naitō Kazuko, Ian H. Nish, Nishioka Takeo, Thaddeus Yoneji Ohta, Nina Raj, Lynne Riggs, Susan Schmidt, Lynne Wakabayashi, and Wendy Zeldin. Sasamoto Yukuo and Tanaka Kaori, Occupation scholars and Professor Takemae's assistants, provided services above and beyond the call of duty in tracking down difficult-to-locate sources, verifying facts and figures and encouraging the translators. We owe a special debt of gratitude to John W. Dower for his strong moral support and painstaking, insightful critique of the final draft. His sharp eye caught many inaccuracies, subtle and manifest, in the translation. We also are grateful to Brian Southam of Athlone Press and to Caroline Wintersgill and Jeremy Albutt of Continuum International Publishing Group for their kind assistance and remarkable patience in seeing this project to fruition. Finally, a heartfelt 'thank you' to the author, Professor Takemae Eiji, and his spouse, Atsuko, for their encouragement, guidance and refusal to lose faith in us during difficult times.

Robert Ricketts (Tokyo)
Sebastian Swann (Washington DC)

Bibliography

Acheson, Dean, *Present at the Creation: My Years in the State Department*, New American Library, 1970 (W. W. Norton, 1969).

Agoncillo, Teodoro A. and Milagros C. Guerrero, *History of the Filipino People*, R. P. Garcia (Quezon), 1977.

Aida Yūji, *Prisoner of the British – A Japanese Soldier's Experiences in Burma*, Cresset Press, 1966.

Akagi Suruki, *Kansei no keisei* (The Establishment of the Bureaucracy), Nihon Hyōronsha, 1991.

Akashi Yōji, 'Japanese Military Administration in Malaya: Its Formation and Evolution in Reference to Sultans, the Islamic Religion and the Moslem Malays, 1941–1945', in *Asian Studies*, no. 7, 1969.

Akatsuka Yasuo, *Buraku Kaihō Kenkyū* (*Buraku* Liberation Studies), no. 60, 1988.

Aldous, Christopher, *The Police in Occupation Japan: Control, Corruption and Resistance to Reform*, Routledge, 1997.

Alperovitz, Gar, *The Decision to Use the Atomic Bomb*, Vintage Books, 1995.

Amakawa Akira, 'The Making of the Postwar Local Government System', in Robert E. Ward and Sakamoto Yoshikazu, eds, *Democratizing Japan: The Allied Occupation*, University of Hawai'i Press, 1987.

——, 'Minshuka-katei to kanryō no taiō' (The Democratic Process and the Response of the Bureaucracy), in Nakamura Masanori, ed., *Sengo Nihon: senryō to sengo-kaikaku* (Postwar Japan: The Occupation and Postwar Reforms), vol. 2, Iwanami Shoten, 1995.

——, 'Senryō-seisaku to kanryō no taiō' (Occupation Policy and the Response of the Bureaucracy), in Shisō no Kagaku Kenkyūkai-hen (Shisō no Kagaku Research Group), ed., *Kyōdō kenkyū: Nihon senryō-gun: sono hikari to kage* (Two Faces of the Occupation Army of Japan: Joint Research), vol. 1, Tokuma Shoten, 1978.

Andō Nisuke, *Surrender, Occupation, and Private Property in International Law*, Clarendon Press (Oxford), 1991.

Andō Yoshio, *Shōwa keizai-shi* (An Economic History of the Shōwa Era), Nihon Keizai Shinbunsha, 1976.

Anesaki Masaharu, *The Religious Life of the Japanese People*, Kokusai Bunka Shinkō-kai, 1961.

Anonymous, 'Junkyard Development', in *AMPO: A Report on the Japanese People's Movements*, no. 11, 1971.

——, 'British Commonwealth Occupation Force', in *The Australian Encyclopedia*, Collins, 1984.

Appleman, Roy E., James M. Burn, Russell A. Gugeler and John Stevens, *Okinawa: The Last Battle* (The US Army in World War II: The War in the Pacific), Office of the Chief of Military History, US Army, US Government Printing Office, 1948.

Ara Takashi, *Nihon senryō-shi kenkyū josetsu* (An Introduction to Research on the History of the Occupation of Japan), Kashiwa Shobō, 1994.

Arai Naoyuki, *Shinbun sengo-shi* (A History of Postwar Newspapers), Keisō Shobō, 1979.

Arasaki Moriteru, *Dokyumento: Okinawa tōsō* (Documents on Okinawa's Struggle), Aki Shobō, 1969.

——, *Okinawa hansen-jinushi* (Okinawa and the Anti-War Landlords), Kōbunken, 1996.

Arisawa Hiromi, ed., *Shōwa keizai-shi* (A History of the Japanese Economy in the Shōwa Era), Nihon Keizai Shinbunsha, 1976.

Arisawa Hiromi and Inaba Hidezō, eds, *Shiryō: sengo nijūnen-shi* (A Documentary History of the Two Postwar Decades), vol. 2 (Economics), Nihon Hyōronsha, 1966.

Asahi Shinbun, ed., *The Japan Almanac 2000*, Asahi Shinbunsha, 1999.

Ashibe Nobuyoshi, *Kenpō* (The Constitution), Iwanami Shoten, 1999.

Astor, Gerald, *The Right to Fight: A History of African Americans in the Military*, Presido Press, 1998.

Auerbach, Stuart, 'The U.S. Created its "Japan Problem"', in *The Japan Times*, 26 July 1993.

Awaya Kentarō, 'Emperor Shōwa's Accountability for War', in *The Japan Quarterly*, October–December 1991.

——, *Tōkyō Saiban-ron* (An Analysis of the Tokyo Tribunal), Ōtsuki Shoten, 1989.

Ayusawa Iwao, *A History of Labor in Modern Japan*, University of Hawai'i Press, 1966.

Backer, John H., 'From the Morgenthau Plan to the Marshall Plan', in Robert Wolfe, ed., *Americans as Proconsuls: United States Military Government in Germany and Japan, 1944–1952*, Southern Illinois University Press, 1984.

Baerwald, Hans H., *The Purge of Japanese Leaders Under the Occupation*, University of California Press, 1959.

——, 'Reminiscence of a Misspent Youth: Tokyo 1946–1949', in Ian H. Nish, ed., *Aspects of the Allied Occupation of Japan*, London School of Economics and Political Science, 1985.

Ball, W. MacMahon, *Intermittent Diplomat: The Japan and Batavia Diaries of W. MacMahon Ball*, Alan Rix, ed., Melbourne University Press, 1988.

——, *Japan: Enemy or Ally?*, Cassell (New York), 1949.

Baltz, William M., 'The Role of American Educators in the Decentralization and Reorganization of Education in Postwar Japan (1945–1952)', PhD dissertation, State University of New York (Buffalo), 1965.

Bates, Peter, *Japan and the British Commonwealth Occupation Force, 1946–52,* Brassey's (UK), 1993.

Beauchamp, Edward R., 'Educational and Social Reform in Japan: The First United States Education Mission to Japan, 1946', in Thomas W. Burkman, ed. *The Occupation of Japan: Educational and Social Reform,* General Douglas MacArthur Foundation, 1982.

Beauchamp, Edward R. and James M. Vardaman Jr, eds, *Japanese Education Since 1945: A Documentary Study,* M. E. Sharpe, 1994.

Beer, Lawrence W., *Freedom of Expression in Japan: A Study in Comparative Law, Politics, and Society,* Kodansha International, 1984.

Berkov, Robert H., 'The Press in Postwar Japan', in *Far Eastern Survey,* vol. 16, 1947.

Bernier, Bernard, *Le Japon contemporain: Une Economie nationale, Une Economie morale,* Les Presses de l'Université de Montréal, 1995.

Biratori-chō, ed., *Hidaka chihō ni okeru Ainu-kei jūmin no seikatsu-jitai to sono mondai-ten* (Living Conditions and Problems of Ainu Residents in the Hidaka Region), 1965.

Bisson, Thomas A., *Basic Treaty Issues in Manchuria Between Japan and China,* Foreign Policy Association, 1931.

——, *Japan in China,* Macmillan, 1938.

——, *Japan's War Economy,* Institute of Pacific Relations, 1945.

——, *Prospects for Democracy in Japan,* Macmillan, 1949.

——, 'Winning the Peace in Japan', in *Amerasia,* September 1945.

——, *Zaibatsu Dissolution in Japan,* University of California Press, 1954.

Bix, Herbert P., *Hirohito and the Making of Modern Japan,* HarperCollins, 2000.

——, 'Japan's Delayed Surrender: A Reinterpretation', in Michael J. Hogan, ed., *Hiroshima in History and Memory,* Cambridge University Press, 1996.

——, 'Japan: The Roots of Militarism', in Mark Selden, ed., *Remaking Asia: Essays on the American Uses of Power,* Pantheon Books, 1974.

——, 'Regional Integration: Japan and South Korea in America's Asian Policy', in Frank Baldwin, ed., *Without Parallel: The American-Korean Relationship Since 1945,* Pantheon Books, 1974.

——, 'The Security Treaty System and the Japanese Military-Industrial Complex', in *The Bulletin of Concerned Asian Scholars,* vol. 2, no. 2, January 1970.

——, 'The Shōwa Emperor's "Soliloquy" and the Problem of War Responsibility', in *The Journal of Japanese Studies,* no. 18, 1992.

Blakeslee, George H., *The Far Eastern Commission: A Study in International Co-operation – 1945–1952,* US Department of State (US Government Printing Office), 1953.

Bōeichō Bōei-kenkyūsho Senshi-shitsu-hen (War History Office, Defence Agency), ed., *Senshi Sōsho (2): Hitō kōryaku sakusen* (War History Series, no. 2: Strategic Operations in the Philippine Islands), Asakumo Shinbunsha, 1966.

——, *Senshi Sōsho (6): Chūbu Taiheiyō rikugun sakusen (1) – Mariana gyokusai made* (Army Operations in the Central Pacific, Part 1 – To Defeat in the Marianas), Asakumo Shinbunsha, 1967.

——, *Senshi Sōsho (11): Okinawa-hōmen rikugun sakusen* (War History Series, no. 11: Army Operations Around Okinawa), Asakumo Shinbunsha, 1968.

——, *Senshi Sōsho (13): Chūbu Taiheiyō rikugun sakusen (2) – Pereriu, Angauru, Iwojima* (War History Series, no. 13: Army Operations in the Central Pacific, Part 2 – Peleliu, Angaur, Iwo Jima), Asakumo Shinbunsha, 1968.

——, *Senshi Sōsho (17): Okinawa-hōmen kaigun sakusen* (War History Series, no. 17: Navy Operations Around Okinawa), Asakumo Shinbunsha, 1968.

——, *Senshi Sōsho (51): Hondo kessen junbi (1) – Kantō no bōei* (War History Series, no. 51): Preparations for the Final Battle for the Homeland, Part 1 – The Defence of the Kanto Region), Asakumo Shinbunsha, 1971.

——, *Senshi Sōsho (57): Hondo kessen junbi (2) – Kyūshū no bōei* (War History Series, no. 57): Preparations for the Final Battle for the Homeland, Part 2 – The Defence of Kyushu), Asakumo Shinbunsha, 1971.

Bohlen, Charles E., *Witness to History, 1929–1969*, W. W. Norton, 1973.

Borden, William S., *The Pacific Alliance: United States Foreign Economic Policy and Japanese Trade Recovery, 1947–1955*, University of Wisconsin Press, 1984.

Borton, Hugh, *American Presurrender Planning for Postwar Japan*, Occasional Papers of The East Asian Institute, Columbia University, New York, 1967.

——, *Japan since 1931: Its Political and Social Development*, Institute of Pacific Relations, 1940.

——, 'Peasant Uprisings in Japan of the Tokugawa Period', in *Transactions, Asiatic Society of Japan*, 1938.

Bowers, Faubion, 'The Late General MacArthur, Warts and All', in *Esquire*, January 1967.

Braibanti, Ralph J. D., 'Administration of Military Government in Japan at the Prefectual Level', in *American Political Science Review*, vol. XLIII, no. 2, April 1949.

——, 'The Occupation of Japan – A Study in Organization and Administration', PhD dissertation, Syracuse University, 1949.

Braw, Monica, *The Atomic Bomb Suppressed*, M. E. Sharpe, 1991.

Broadbent, Jeffrey, *Environmental Politics in Japan: Networks of Power and Protest*, Cambridge University Press, 1998.

Brocklebank, Laurie, *Jayforce: New Zealand and the Military Occupation of Japan, 1945–48*, Oxford University Press, 1997.

Brook, Timothy, ed., *Documents on the Rape of Nanjing*, University of Michigan Press, 1999.

Buckley, Roger, *Occupation Diplomacy: Britain, the United States and Japan 1945–1952*, Cambridge University Press, 1982.

Bui Minh Dung, 'Japan's Role in the Vietnamese Starvation of 1944–45', in *Modern Asian Studies*, vol. 29, no. 3, 1995.

Bunce, William K., *Religions in Japan: Buddhism, Shinto, Christianity*, Charles E. Tuttle, 1955.

Buraku Kaihō Kenkyūjo-hen (*Buraku* Liberation Research Institute), ed., *Senryōki no Buraku mondai* (Documents on the *Buraku* Problem During the Occupation of Japan), Kaihō Shuppansha, 1991.

Burati, Valary, *The Burati Papers*, Walter P. Reuther Library, Wayne State University.

Butow, Robert J. C., *Japan's Decision to Surrender*, Stanford University Press, 1954.

——, *Tojo and the Coming of the War*, Princeton University Press, 1961.

Byrnes, James F., *Speaking Frankly*, Harper, 1947.

Carlisle, Lonny E. and Mark C. Tilton, eds, *Is Japan Really Changing its Ways? – Regulatory Reform and the Japanese Economy*, Brookings Institution Press, 1998.

Cayton, Horace R., *Long Old Road*, University of Washington Press, 1970.

Cha'en Yoshio, 'The Research on the Justice of Japan War Criminals After the Second World War', PhD dissertation, Pacific Western University, 1996.

Checkland, Olive, *Humanitarianism and the Emperor's Japan, 1877–1977*, St Martin's Press, 1994.

Cheong Sun-hwa, *The Politics of Anti-Japanese Sentiment in Korea*, Greenwood Press, 1991.

Chibana Shōichi, *Yakisuterareta Hinomaru* (The Rising Sun Flag Burned to Ashes), Shakai Shisōsha, 1996.

Chida Takeshi, *Eirenpō-gun no Nihon shinchū to tenkai* (The British Commonwealth Occupation Force in Japan: Its Deployment and History), Ochanomizu Shobō, 1997.

Chihō-jichi Kenkyū Shiryō Sentā-hen (Local Autonomy Documentation Centre), ed., *Sengo jichi-shi* (A History of Postwar Local Government Reform), Bunsei Shoin, 1977.

Chira, Susan Deborah, *Cautious Revolutionaries: Occupation Planners and Japan's Post-War Land Reform*, Tokyo: Agricultural Policy Research Center, 1982.

Chishima Habomai Shotō Kyojūsha Renmei-hen (Kuril-Habomai Islanders League), ed., *Moto tōmin ga kataru warera hōppō yontō: Soren senryō-hen* (Former Islanders Remember Our Four Northern Islands: Under the Soviet Occupation), Chishima Habomai Shotō Kyojūsha Renmei (Sapporo), 1988.

Chwialkowski, Paul, *In Caesar's Shadow: The Life of General Robert Eichelberger*, Greenwood Press, 1993.

Cohen, Jerome B., *Japan's Economy in War and Reconstruction*, University of Minnesota Press, 1949.

Cohen, Theodore, *Remaking Japan: The American Occupation as New Deal*, The Free Press, 1987.

Cole, Alan B., George O. Totten and Cecil H. Uyehara, *Socialist Parties in Postwar Japan*, Yale University Press, 1966.

Comacho, Martin T., 'Administration of SCAP Labour Policy in Occupied Japan', PhD dissertation, Harvard University, 1954.

Commission on Wartime Relocation and Internment of Civilians, *Personal Justice Denied: Report of the Commission on Wartime Relocation and Internment of Civilians*, Civil Liberties Public Education Fund, 1997.

Committee for the Compilation of Materials on Damage Caused by the Atomic Bombs in Hiroshima and Nagasaki, *Hiroshima and Nagasaki: The Physical, Medical, and Social Effects of the Atomic Bombings*, Basic Books, 1981.

Conde, David, 'The Korean Minority in Japan', in *The Far Eastern Survey*, 26 February 1947.

Condit, Kenneth W., *The Joint Chiefs of Staff and National Policy, 1947–1949*, vol. 2 of *The History of the Joint Chiefs of Staff*, Michael Glazier, 1979.

Cook, Haruko Taya and Theodore F., *Japan at War: An Oral History*, The New Press, 1992.

Costello, John, *The Pacific War, 1941–1945*, Quill (New York), 1981.

Costello, William, *Democracy vs. Feudalism in Postwar Japan*, Itagaki Shoten (Tokyo), 1948.

Coughlin, William J., *Conquered Press: The MacArthur Era in Japanese Journalism*, Pacific Books (Palo Alto), 1952.

Cox, Alvin D., *Nomonhan: Japan Against Russia, 1939*, Stanford University Press, 1985.

Crowl, Philip A. and Edmund G. Love, *The Campaign in the Marianas* (The US Army in World War II: The War in the Pacific), Office of the Chief of Military History, US Army, US Government Printing Office, 1960.

Cumings, Bruce, *The Origins of the Korean War: Liberation and the Emergence of Separate Regimes, 1945–1947*, Princeton University Press, 1981.

——, *The Origins of the Korean War*. vol. II: The Roaring of the Cataract, Princeton University Press, 1990.

Curtis, Gerald L., 'The Dulles–Yoshida Negotiations on the San Francisco Peace Treaty', in *Columbia Essays in International Affairs*, vol. 2, Columbia University Press, 1967.

Danelski, David J., 'Purakādo jiken o meguru seiji to hō' (Political and Legal Ramifications of the Placard Incident), in *Hōritsu Jihō*, Parts 1 & 2, July and August 1988.

Dees, Bowen C., *The Allied Occupation and Japan's Economic Miracle: Building the Foundations of Japanese Science and Technology, 1945–1952*, Curzon Press, 1997.

Deverall, Richard L.-G., *The Great Seduction: Red China's Drive to Bring Free Japan Behind the Iron Curtain*, International Literature Printing Co. (Tokyo), 1953.

De Vos, George and Wagatsuma Hiroshi, *Japan's Invisible Race: Caste in Culture and Personality*, University of California Press, 1966.

Dibblin, Jane, *Day of Two Suns: U.S. Nuclear Testing and the Pacific Islands*, New Amsterdam (New York), 1990.

Dore, Ronald P., *Land Reform in Japan*, Oxford University Press, 1959.

Dower, John W., 'E. H. Norman, Japan and the Uses of History', in John W. Dower, ed., *Origins of the Modern Japanese State: Selected Writings of E. H. Norman*, Pantheon Books, 1975.

——, *Embracing Defeat: Japan in the Wake of World War II*, W. W. Norton and the New Press, 1999.

——, *Empire and Aftermath: Yoshida Shigeru and the Japanese Experience, 1878–1954*, Council on East Asian Studies, Harvard University, 1979.

——, 'The Eye of the Beholder', *The Bulletin of Concerned Asian Scholars*, vol. 2, no. 1, October 1969.

——, *Japan in War and Peace: Selected Essays*, The New Press, 1993.

——, 'Occupied Japan and the American Lake', in Edward Friedman and Mark Selden, eds, *America's Asia: Dissenting Essays on Asian-American Relations*, Vintage Books, 1971.

——, 'Reform and Consolidation', in Harry Wray and Hilary Conroy, eds, *Japan Examined: Perspectives on Modern Japanese History*, University of Hawai'i Press, 1983.

——, 'The Useful War', in Carol Gluck and Stephan R. Graubard, eds, *Showa: The Japan of Hirohito*, W. W. Norton, 1992.

——, *War Without Mercy: Race and Power in the Pacific War*, Pantheon Books, 1986.

Drea, Edward J., *In the Service of the Emperor: Essays on the Imperial Japanese Army*, University of Nebraska Press, 1998.

Dunn, Frederick S., *Peace-Making and the Settlement with Japan*, Princeton University Press, 1963.

Duus, Masayo U., *Makkāsā no futatsu no bōshi: tokushu ian-shisetsu RAA o meguru senryō-shi no sokumen* (The Two Hats of MacArthur: A History of RAA Comfort Stations During the Occupation), Kōdansha Bunko, 1985.

——, *Tokyo Rose: Orphan of the Pacific*, Kodansha International, 1979.

Ebina Sugeo, 'Shūsen hiwa: Makkāsā to kyūsei Matsuyama kōkō no "Nenbutsu Ryōka"' (An Untold Story of the Early Postwar Era: MacArthur and the Former Matsuyama High School's 'Dormitory Sutra'), unpublished manuscript.

Eells, Walter C., *Communism in Education in Asia, Africa and the Far Pacific*, American Council on Education, 1954.

Eichelberger, Robert L., 'The Eichelberger Papers', Duke University.

Eichelberger, Robert L. and Milton MacKaye, *Our Jungle Road to Tokyo*, Viking Press, 1950.

Eldridge, Robert D., *The Origins of the Bilateral Okinawa Problem: Okinawa in Postwar U.S.–Japan Relations, 1945–1952*, Garland Publishing (New York), 2001.

Embree, John F., *Suye Mura, A Japanese Village*, University of Chicago Press, 1939.

Emmerson, John K., *The Japanese Thread: A Life in the US Foreign Service*, Holt, Rinehart & Winston, 1978.

Endicott, Stephen and Edward Hagerman, *The United States and Biological Warfare: Secrets from the Early Cold War and Korea*, Indiana University Press, 1998.

Etō Jun, *Mō hitotsu no sengo-shi* (An Alternative History of the Postwar Era), Kōdansha, 1978.

——, *Ochiba no hakiyose: haisen, senryō, ken'etsu to bungaku* (Raked Leaves: Defeat, Occupation, Censorship and Literature), Bungei Shunjūsha, 1981.

——, *Wasureta koto to wasurerareta koto* (What We Forgot and What We Were Made to Forget), Bungei Shunjūsha, 1979.

Etō Jun, ed., *Senryō shiroku* (A Documentary History of the Occupation), vols 1–4, Kōdansha, 1981–1982.

Falk, Stanley L., *Bataan: The March of Death*, Jove Publications (New York), 1983.

Farley, Miriam, *Aspects of Japan's Labour Problems*, John Day, 1960.

Fearey, Robert A., *The Occupation of Japan: Second Phase, 1948–50*, Macmillan, 1950.

Feis, Herbert, *The Road to Pearl Harbor: The Coming of the War Between the United States and Japan*, Princeton University Press, 1950.

Ferrell, Robert H., ed., *Off the Record: The Private Papers of Harry S. Truman*, Harper & Row, 1980.

Field, Norma, *In the Realm of a Dying Emperor: Japan at Century's End*, Vintage, 1993.

Finn, Richard B., *Winners in Peace: MacArthur, Yoshida and Postwar Japan*, University of California Press, 1992.

Fisch, Arnold G. Jr, *Military Government in the Ryukyu Islands, 1945–1950*, US Army Center for Military History, US Government Printing Office, 1988.

Fogel, Joshua A., ed., *The Nanjing Massacre: Its History and Historiography*, University of California Press, 2000.

Forrest, Jerome and Clarke H. Kawakami, 'General MacArthur and His Vanishing War History', *Reporter*, 14 October 1952.

Frank, Richard B., *Downfall: The End of the Imperial Japanese Empire*, Random House, 1999.

Fujieda Mioko, 'Japan's First Phase of Feminism', in Fumiko Fujimura-Fanselow and Atsuko Kameda, eds, *Japanese Women: New Feminist Perspectives on the Past, Present, and Future*, The Feminist Press (City University of New York), 1995.

Fujime Yuki, *Sei no rekishi-gaku* (The Historical Development of Gender in Modern Japan), Fuji Shuppan, 1997.

Fujino Yutaka, *Nihon fashizumu to iryō* (Japanese Fascism and the Medical Establishment), Iwanami Shoten, 1993.

Fujiwara Akira, Awaya Kentarō, Yoshida Yutaka and Yamada Akira, eds, *Tettei-kenshō: Shōwa-tennō 'dokuhakuroku'* (Conclusive Evidence: The Shōwa Emperor's 'Soliloquy'), Ōtsuki Shoten, 1991.

Furukawa Atsushi, 'Gaikokujin no jinken (1): Sengo kenpō kaikaku to no kanren ni oite' (The Human Rights of Foreign Residents in the Context of Postwar Constitutional Reform, 1), in *The Journal of Tokyo Keizai University*, no. 146, 1986.

——, 'Nenpyō – Senryōka no shuppan, engeki, hōsō ken'etsu' (A Chronology of Censored Publications, Dramas and Broadcasts Under the Occupation), in *Tōkyō Keidai Gakkaishi* (The Journal of Tokyo Keizai University), no. 118, 1980.

Furukawa Atsushi, 'Senryō to chōhō: "Genbaku eiga" fuirumu to kiroku eiga no yukue' (The Occupation and Military Intelligence: The Fate of the 'Atomic Bomb' Footage and Documentary), in *Senshū Hōgaku Ronshū* (Occasional Papers, Law Faculty, Senshu University), nos 55 and 56, 1992.

Gaimushō-hen (Ministry of Foreign Affairs), ed., *Nihon senryō kanri jūyō bunsho-shū* (Major Documents Pertaining to the Allied Occupation and Control of Japan), vols 1–4, Tōyō Keizai Shinbunsha, 1949.

——, *Shoki tai-Nichi senryō seisaku* (Early Occupation Policy Towards Japan), vols 1–2, Mainichi Shinbunsha, 1978.

——, *Shūsen shiroku* (A Historical Record of the End of Hostilities), Shinbun Gekkansha, 1952.

Gaimushō Jōyaku-kyoku-hen (Treaty Bureau, Ministry of Foreign Affairs), ed., *Waga kuni ni okeru gaikokujin no hōteki chi'i* (The Legal Status of Aliens in Japan), Nihon Kajo Shuppan, 1993.

Gallicchio, Marc S., 'The Kuriles Controversy: U.S. Diplomacy in the Soviet–Japan Border Dispute, 1941–1956', in *Pacific Historical Review*, vol. 60, no. 1, 1991.

Gallup, George H., *The Gallup Poll: Public Opinion 1935–1971*, vol. 1, New York: Random House, 1972.

Gane, William J., *Repatriation, From 25 September 1945 to 31 December 1945*, Headquarters, US Army Military Government in Korea (Foreign Affairs Section), Seoul, 1946.

Garon, Sheldon, *The State and Labor in Modern Japan*, University of California Press, 1987.

Gayn, Mark, *Japan Diary*, Charles E. Tuttle, 1981 (William Sloane, 1948).

Gendai Hōsei Shiryō Hensankai-hen (Editorial Committee for Modern Legal Documents), ed., *Sengo senryō-ka hōritsu-shū* (Compendium of Laws Enacted Under the Postwar Occupation), Kokushokan Gyōkai, 1986.

General Headquarters, Supreme Commander for the Allied Powers (GHQ/SCAP), *A Brief History of G-II Section*, 1948.

——, Civil Affairs Section, *A Report on the Japanese National Police Reserve*, October 1951.

——, Civil Historical Section, *History of the Nonmilitary Activities of the Occupation of Japan, 1945–1951*, 1951.

——, Civil Information and Education Section, *Education in the New Japan*, May 1948.

——, Economic and Scientific Section (Labour Division), *Monthly Reports.*

——, Economic and Scientific Section (Advisory Committee on Labor). *Final Report: Labor Policies and Programs in Japan,* 30 June 1946.

——, Government Section, *Political Reorientation of Japan, September 1945 to September 1948,* vols 1–2, US Government Printing Office, 1949.

——, Medical Section (Public Health and Welfare Division), *Public Health and Welfare in Japan: Final Summary, 1951–52,* 1952.

——, *Monthly Summation of Non-Military Activities in Japan and Korea,* 1945–1948.

——, Natural Resources Section, *Mission and Accomplishments of the Occupation in the Natural Resources Field,* September 1949.

——, Public Health and Welfare Section, *Missions and Accomplishments of the Occupation in the Public, Health and Welfare Fields,* December 1949.

——, Public Health and Welfare Section, *Public Health and Welfare in Japan,* 1949.

——, *Tokyo Telephone Directory,* 1945–1951.

General Headquarters, Supreme Commander for the Allied Powers (GHQ/SCAP), and Far East Command (FECOM), *Operations of the Civil Intelligence Section,* vol. IX, Intelligence Series (1), 1949.

——, *Organization and Activities of GHQ,* 1950.

——, *Selected Data on the Occupation of Japan,* 1950.

Gerteis, Chris, 'Seeing Red: US Labor Policy and the Struggle for the Shopfloor at the Tōho Motion Picture Studios, 1948', MA dissertation, University of Iowa, 1995.

Gilmore, Allison B., *You Can't Fight Tanks with Bayonets: Psychological Warfare Against the Japanese Army in the Southwest Pacific,* University of Nebraska Press, 1998.

Ginn, John L., *Sugamo Prison, Tokyo: An Account of the Trial and Sentencing of Japanese War Criminals in 1948, by a US Participant,* McFarland & Co., 1992.

Glahn, Gerhard von, *The Occupation of Enemy Territory: A Commentary on the Law and Practice of Belligerent Occupation,* University of Minnesota Press, 1957.

Glantz, David M., *August Storm: The Soviet 1945 Strategic Offensive in Manchuria,* Paper no. 7, Combat Studies Institute, US Army Command and Staff College, Fort Leavenworth, Kansas, 1983.

——, 'The Soviet Invasion of Japan', *Military History Quarterly,* vol. 7, no. 3, 1995.

Gōda Kimitsugu, 'Nōkyō-hō, dai'ichi kaisei-hō to GHQ no kyōdō-kumiai seisaku' (The First Farmers' Co-op Law and GHQ's Policy on Cooperatives), Parts 1 and 2, *Ōita Daigaku keizai ronshū* (Ōita University Occasional Papers in Economics), no. 47, Vols 1 and 3, 1995.

Goldstein, Robert J., *Political Repression in Modern America: From 1870 to the Present,* Schenkman Publishing Company, 1978.

Goodman, David G., 'Shingeki Under the Occupation', in Thomas W. Burkman, ed. *The Occupation of Japan: Education and Social Reform,* MacArthur Memorial, 1982.

Gordon, Andrew, *The Evolution of Labor Relations in Japan: Heavy Industry 1853–1955*, Council on East Asian Studies, Harvard University, 1985.

Gotō Ken'ichi, 'Indonesia Under the "Greater East Asia Co-Prosperity Sphere"', in Donald Denoon, Mark Hudson, Gavan McCormack and Tessa Morris-Suzuki, eds, *Multicultural Japan: Paleolithic to Postmodern*, Cambridge University Press, 1996.

Grad, Andrew J., *Land and Peasant in Japan: An Introductory Survey*, Institute of Pacific Relations, 1952.

Groves, Leslie R., *Now It Can Be Told: The Story of the Manhattan Project*, Harper, 1962.

Gussow, Zachery, *Leprosy, Racism, and Public Health: Social Policy in Chronic Disease Control*, Westview Press, 1989.

Hadley, Eleanor M., *Anti-Trust in Japan*, Princeton University Press, 1970.

——, 'Zaibatsu Dissolution', *Kodansha Encyclopedia of Japan*, Kodansha, 1983.

Haga Shirō, ed., *Nihon-kanri no kikō to seisaku* (The Control of Japan: Structure and Policy), Yūhikaku, 1951.

Hall, Robert K, *Education for a New Japan*, Yale University Press, 1949.

Hane Mikiso, *Eastern Phoenix: Japan Since 1945*, Westview Press, 1996.

Harries, Meirion and Susie, *Sheathing the Sword: The Demilitarisation of Japan*, Heinemann, 1987.

Harrington, Joseph D., *Yankee Samurai: The Secret Role of Nisei in America's Pacific Victory*, Pettigrew Enterprises (Detroit), 1979.

Harris, Sheldon H., *Factories of Death: Japanese Biological Warfare, 1932–45, and the American Cover-up*, Routledge, 1994.

Hasegawa Tsuyoshi, *The Northern Territories Dispute and Russo-Japanese Relations*, vols 1–2, University of California Press, 1998.

Hata Ikuhiko, *Nanjing jiken* (The Nanjing Incident), Chūō Kōronsha, 1986.

——, *Shiroku: Nihon saigunbi* (Historical Documents Pertaining to the Rearmament of Japan), Bungei Shunjūsha, 1976.

Hata Ikuhiko and Sodei Rinjirō, eds, *Nihon senryō hishi* (A Secret History of the Occupation of Japan), vol. 2, Asahi Shinbunsha, 1977.

Hattori Takushirō, *Dai Toa Sensō-zenshi* (A History of the Greater East Asian War), Masu Shobō, vol. 7, 1953.

Hawaii Nikkei History Editorial Board, ed., *Japanese Eyes, American Heart: Personal Reflections of Hawaii's World War II Nisei Soldiers*, Tendai Educational Foundation (Honolulu), 1998.

Hayakawa Noboru, *Ima Miyakejima: NLP kichi kensetsu keikaku ni hantai-suru shima – Ikusa to kunō suru shima no genjitsu* (Miyakejima Now! An Island Opposes the Construction of a NLP Base – Miyake's Struggle and Travail), San'ichi Shobō, 1988.

Hayes, Grace P., *The History of the Joint Chiefs of Staff in World War II: The War Against Japan*, Naval Institute Press (Annapolis), 1982.

Hein, Laura E., *Fueling Growth: The Energy Revolution and Economic Policy in Post-war Japan*, Council on East Asian Studies, Harvard University, 1990.

Hein, Laura and Mark Selden, eds, *Living With the Bomb: American and Japanese Cultural Conflicts in the Nuclear Age*, M. E. Sharpe, 1997.

——, *Censoring History: Citizenship and Memory in Japan, Germany, and the United States*, M. E. Sharpe, 2000.

Herman, Yaye F., 'The WAC Experience', in *Unsung Heroes: Military Intelligence Service, Past, Present, Future*, MIS-Northwest Association (Seattle), 1996.

Hershberg, James, *James B. Conant: Harvard to Hiroshima and the Making of the Nuclear Age*, Alfred A. Knopf, 1993.

Herzog, Peter J., *Japan's Pseudo-Democracy*, Japan Library (Kent), 1993.

Hewes, Lawrence J., *Japan: Land and Men*, Iowa State College, 1955.

Hicks, George, 'Japan, Land of Quiet Apartheid', *The International Herald Tribune*, 18 March 1992.

Hirakawa Kiyoshi, *Kamu kamu evuribadē: Hirakawa Tada'ichi to 'Kamu Kamu Eigo' no jidai* (Come, Come Everybody: Hirakawa Tada'ichi and the Era of 'Come, Come English'), NHK Shuppan, 1995.

Hirasawa Yasuji, *Jinsei ni zetsubō wa nai: Hansen-byō 100-nen no tatakai* (There is Always Hope for One's Life: The 100-Year Struggle of Japan's Leprosy Sufferers), Kamogawa Shuppan, 1997.

Hirano Kyoko, *Mr. Smith Goes to Tokyo: Japanese Cinema Under the American Occupation, 1945–1952*, Smithsonian Institution Press, 1992.

Hironaka Toshio, *Sengo Nihon no keisatsu* (The Police in Postwar Japan), Iwanami Shoten, 1968.

Hogan, Michael J., ed., *Hiroshima in History and Memory*, Cambridge University Press, 1996.

Hoito Edoin (Hoyt, Edwin), *The Night Tokyo Burned: The Incendiary Campaign Against Japan, March–August 1945*, St Martin's Press, 1987.

Hokkaidō Keisatsubu, Jōhōka (Hokkaido Police Agency, Intelligence Section), *Soren-gun senryō-ka ni okeru Chishima oyobi Habomai ritō gaikyō* (A General Survey of Conditions in the Kuril Islands and the Offshore Islets of Habomai Under Soviet Military Occupation), October 1945.

Holtom, Daniel C., *Modern Japan and Shinto Nationalism*, University of Chicago Press, 1947.

——, *The National Faith of Japan: A Study in Modern Shinto*, E. P. Dutton, 1938.

Honda Katsuichi, *The Nanking Massacre: A Japanese Journalist Confronts Japan's National Shame*, M. E. Sharpe, 1999.

Hopper, Helen M., 'Katō Shizue, Socialist Party MP, and Occupation Reforms Affecting Women, 1945–1948: A Case Study of the Formal vs. Informal Political Influence of Japanese Women', in Thomas W. Burkman, ed., *The Occupation of Japan: Education and Social Reform*, MacArthur Memorial, 1982.

Horio Teruhisa, *Educational Thought and Ideology in Modern Japan*, University of Tokyo Press, 1988.

Hoshino Yoshirō, 'Japan's Post-Second World War Environmental Problems', in Ui Jun, ed., *Industrial Pollution in Japan*, United Nations University Press, 1992.
Hōsōhō Seitei Katei Kenkyūkai (Study Group on Broadcasting Legislation), ed., *Shiryō: senryōka no hōsō rippō* (Documents on Broadcasting Legislation Under the Occupation), Tōkyō Daigaku Shuppankai, 1980.
Hoston, Germaine A., 'The State, Modernity, and the Fate of Liberalism in Prewar Japan', in *The Journal of Asian Studies*, no. 51, 1992.
Huff, Sidney L., with Joe Alex Morris, *My Fifteen Years with General MacArthur*, Paperback Library (New York), 1964.
Hull, Cordell, *The Memoirs of Cordell Hull*, Macmillan, vol. 2, 1948.

Ichinokuchi, Tad, ed., *John Aiso and the M.I.S. – Japanese-American Soldiers in the Military Intelligence Service, World War II*, MIS Club of Southern California, 1988.
Ienaga Saburō, *Japan's Past, Japan's Future: One Historian's Odyssey*, Rowman & Littlefield, 2001.
——, *The Pacific War, 1931–1945*, translated by Frank Baldwin, Pantheon Books, 1978.
Ikeda Yoshimasa, *Nihon shakai fukushi-shi* (A History of Social Welfare in Japan), Hōritsu Bunkasha, 1986.
Ind, Allison, *Allied Intelligence Bureau: Our Secret Weapon Against Japan*, David McKay, 1958.
Inokuchi Hiromitsu, 'Korean Ethnic Schools in Occupied Japan, 1945–52', in Sonia Ryang, ed., *Koreans in Japan: Critical Voices from the Margin*, Routledge, 2000.
Inoue Etsuko, *Senryōgun ianjo: kokka ni yoru baishun shisetsu* (Comfort Stations for the Occupation Army: State-Operated Brothels), Shinhyōron, 1995.
Inoue Kyoko, *MacArthur's Japanese Constitution*, University of Chicago Press, 1991.
Iokibe Makoto, 'Senryō seisaku no san ruikei' (Three Patterns in Occupation Policy), *Revaiasan* (Leviathan), no. 6, Bokutakusha, 1990.
——, *Sensō, senryō, kōwa, 1941–1955* (War, Occupation and the Peace Settlement, 1941–1955), Chūō Kōronsha, 2001.
Iokibe Makoto, ed., *The Occupation of Japan: U.S. Planning Documents, 1942–1945*, Congressional Information Service and Maruzen Publishing Co., 1987.
Ion, Hamish, 'Canada and the Occupation of Japan', in Ian H. Nish, ed., *The British Commonwealth and the Occupation of Japan*, International Centre for Economics and Related Disciplines, London School of Economics and Political Science, 1983.
Iriye Akira, *Power and Culture: The Japanese-American War, 1941–1945*, Harvard University Press, 1981.
Irie Toshirō, *Kenpō seiritsu no kei'i to kenpōjō no sho-mondai* (The Writing of the Constitution and Constitutional Problems), Dai'ichi Hōki, 1976.
Irokawa Daikichi, *The Age of Hirohito: In Search of Modern Japan*, The Free Press, 1995.

Ishida Takeshi, *Nihon no seiji to kotoba: 'jiyū' to 'fukushi'* (Politics and Language in Japan: 'Freedom and Welfare', vol. 1, Tōkyō Daigaku Shuppankai, Tokyo, 1989.

Ishimoto Shidzué, *Facing Two Ways: The Story of My Life*, Stanford University Press, 1984 (Holt, Rinehart and Winston, 1938).

Itō Ken'ichi, *Nankatsu kara Nanbu e* (From South Katsushika to South Tokyo), Iryō Tosho Shuppan, 1974.

Iwahashi Hideyuki, *Nippon Raitohausu yonjūnen-shi* (Nippon Lighthouse: The First 40 Years), Nippon Lighthouse, 1962.

Iwamoto Sumiaki and Teruoka Shuzō, 'Nōchi-kaikaku: jinushi-sei no shūen to jisakunō taisei' (The Land Reform: The Demise of the Landlord System and the System of Independent Farm Producers), in Sodei Rinjirō and Takemae Eiji, eds, *Sengo Nihon no genten: senryō-shi no genzai* (Postwar Japan: The Point of Origin – Occupation History Today), vol. 2, Yūshisha, 1992.

Iwanami Kōza, *Nihon rekishi* (Japanese History), Iwanami Shoten, vols 22–3, 1977.

Iwasaki Akira, *Senryō sareta sukurīn* (The Occupied Screen), Shin Nihon Shuppansha, 1975.

James, D. Clayton, *The Years of MacArthur*, vol. 1: 1880–1941, Houghton Mifflin, 1970.

——, *The Years of MacArthur*, vol. 2: 1941–1945, Houghton Mifflin, 1975.

——, *The Years of MacArthur*, vol. 3: Triumph and Disaster, 1945–1964, Houghton Mifflin, 1985.

Jennings, John M., *The Opium Empire: Japanese Imperialism and Drug Trafficking in Asia, 1895–1945*, Praeger, 1997.

Johnson, Carmen, *Wave-Rings in the Water: My Years With the Women of Postwar Japan*, Charles River Press, 1996.

Johnson, Chalmers, *Blowback: The Costs and Consequences of American Empire*, Owl Books, 2001.

Johnson, Chalmers, ed., *Okinawa: Cold War Island*, Japan Policy Research Institute, 1999.

Kades, Charles L., 'The American Role in Revising Japan's Imperial Constitution', in *Political Science Quarterly*, vol. 104, no. 2, 1989.

——, 'Representative Government in Japan', in *Political Reorientation of Japan, September 1945 to September 1948*, vol. 2, US Government Printing Office, 1949.

Kaigo Tokiomi, *Kyōiku kaikaku* (The Education Reforms), Tōkyō Diagaku Shuppankai, 1975.

Kajimura Hideki, 'Confronting Japanese Racism: Toward a Korean Identity', *Japan–Asia Quarterly Review* (AMPO), vol. 20, nos 1–2, 1990.

Kasai Yoshisuke, ' "Nomu, utsu, kau" to seikatsu hogo hōan' (Drunkards, Beggars and the Livelihood Protection Bill), in Kōseishō Nijūnen-shi Henshū I'inkai (Ministry of Health and Welfare Twenty-Year History Editorial Committee), ed.

Kōseishō nijūnen-shi (The Ministry of Health and Welfare: The First Twenty Years), Kōsei Mondai Kenkyūkai, 1960.

Kase Toshikazu, *Eclipse of the Rising Sun*, Jonathan Cape, 1951.

Kashiwazaki Chikako, 'The Politics of Legal Status: The Equation of Nationality with Ethnonational Identity', in Sonia Ryang, ed., *Koreans in Japan: Critical Voices from the Margin*, Routledge, 2000.

Kataoka Tetsuya, *The Price of a Constitution: The Origin of Japan's Postwar Politics*, Crane Russak (Taylor & Francis), 1991.

Kawai Kazuo, *Japan's American Interlude*, University of Chicago Press, 1960.

Kayano Shigeru, *Our Land was a Forest: An Ainu Memoir*, Westview Press, 1994.

Kearney, Reginald, *African American Views of the Japanese: Solidarity or Sedition?*, State University of New York Press, 1998.

Kennan, George F., *Memoirs, 1925–1950*, Atlantic Monthly (Little, Brown), 1967.

Kennoki Toshihirō, *Ushi no ayumi: kyōiku ni waga michi o motomete* (At a Snail's Pace: For an Education System Suitable to Japan's Needs), Shōgakkan, 1973.

Kerr, George, *Okinawa: The History of an Island People*, Charles E. Tuttle, 1958.

Kido Nikki Kenkyūkai-hen (Kido Diary Editorial Committee), ed., *Kido Kōichi Nikki* (*Diary of Marquis Kido Kōichi*), vols 1–2, Tōkyō Daigaku Shuppankai, 1966.

——, *Kido Kōichi kankei bunsho* (Documents Concerning Kido Kōichi), Tōkyō Daigaku Shuppankai, 1966.

Kim Kyŏng-hae, ed., *Zainichi Chōsenjin minzoku-kyōiku yōgo tōsō shiryōshū* (Documents on the Struggle to Defend Korean Ethnic Education in Japan), vol. 1, Akashi Shoten, 1988.

Kim Nan Goo, 'Sengo shōgaisha seisaku no seisei' (The Origins of Japan's Postwar Policy for the Disabled), PhD dissertation, Tokyo Keizai University, 1995.

Kim T'ae-gi, *Sengo Nihon seiji to Zainichi Chōsenjin mondai* (Postwar Japanese Politics and the Problem of Koreans in Japan), Keisō Shobō, 1997.

Kim Yŏng-dal, *Zainichi Chōsenjin no kika* (The Naturalisation of Koreans in Japan), Akashi Shoten, 1990.

Kimura Hiroshi, ed., *Hoppō ryōdo o kangaeru* (Considering the Northern Territories, Hokkaidō Shinbunsha, 1981.

Kinjo Kyoko, 'Legal Challenges to the Status Quo', in Fumiko Fujimura-Fanselow and Atsuko Kameda, eds, *Japanese Women: New Feminist Perspectives on the Past, Present, and Future*, The Feminist Press (City University of New York), 1995.

Kinoshita Michio, *Sokkin nisshi* (A Vice Chamberlain's Dairy), Bungei Shunjūsha, 1990.

Kishimoto Hideo, *Japanese Religion in the Meiji Era*, Centenary Cultural Council Series, 1955.

Kitagawa, Joseph M., *Religions in Japanese History*, Columbia University Press, 1966.

Kobayashi Tomoko, '8–15 chokugo ni okeru Zainichi Chōsenjin to shin Chōsen kensetsu no kadai: Zainichi Chōsenjin Renmei no katsudō o chūshin ni' (Koreans in Japan Immediately After August 15, 1945 and the Task of Building a New

Korea: The Activities of the League of Korean Residents in Japan), *Zainichi Chōsenjin-shi Kenkyūkai*, no. 21, 1991.

——, 'GHQ ni yoru Zainichi Chōsenjin kankō zasshi no ken'etsu' (The Censorship of Korean Publications by GHQ), *Zainichi Chōsenjin-shi Kenkyūkai*, no. 22, 1992.

——, 'GHQ no Zainichi Chōsenjin ninshiki ni kansuru ichi kōsatsu: G-2 Minkan Chōhō Kyoku teiki hōkokusho o chūshin ni' (Remarks on GHQ's Perception of Koreans in Japan: Periodic Reports of G-2's Civil Intelligence Section), *Zainichi Chōsenjin-shi Kenkyūkai ronbunshū*, no. 32, 1994.

Kōdansha, ed., *Shōwa: niman nichi no zenkiroku* (The Shōwa Era: A 20,000-Day Chronicle), vol. 7, Kōdansha, 1989.

Kojima Noboru, 'Tennō to Amerika to taiheiyō sensō' (The Emperor, America and the Pacific War), *Bungei Shunjū*, November 1975.

Kolko, Joyce and Gabriel, *The Limits of Power: The World and United States Foreign Policy, 1945–1954*, Harper & Row, 1972.

Komai Hiroshi, *Migrant Workers in Japan*, Kegan Paul International, 1995.

Kon Hidemi, *Yoshida Shigeru*, Kōdansha, 1967.

Korb, Lawrence J., *The Joint Chiefs of Staff – The First Twenty-five Years*, Indiana University press, 1976.

Kōsaka Masataka, 'Saisho Yoshida Shigeru ron' (Prime Minister Yoshida Shigeru: An Interpretation), *Chūō Kōron*, February 1965.

Kōseishō Nijūnen-shi Henshū I'inkai (Ministry of Health and Welfare Twenty-Year History Editorial Committee), ed., *Kōseishō nijūnen-shi* (The Ministry of Health and Welfare: The First Twenty Years), Kōsei Mondai Kenkyūkai, 1960.

——, *Kōseishō gojūnen-shi* (The Ministry of Health and Welfare: The First Fifty Years), Kōsei Mondai Kenkyūkai, 1988.

Koseki Shōichi, *The Birth of Japan's Postwar Constitution*, Westview Press, 1997.

——, 'Japanizing the Constitution', *The Japan Quarterly*, vol. 35, no. 3, 1988.

——, 'Kenpō o toi-naosu sengo gojūnen-me no "shiten"' (A Fresh Look at the Constitution Fifty Years Later), in Nihon Jānarisuto Kaigi-hen (Japan Conference of Journalists), ed., *Masukomi no rekishi sekinin to mirai sekinin* (The Mass Media's Responsibility for the Past and the Future), Kōbunken, 1995.

——, *Kyūjō to anpo hoshō* (Article Nine and National Security), Shōgakkan, 2000.

Koshiro Yukiko, *Trans-Pacific Racisms and the U.S. Occupation of Japan*, East Asian Institute, Columbia University, 1999.

Kowalski, Frank, *Nihon saigunbi: watakushi wa Nihon o saibusō shita* (The Remilitarisation of Japan: How I Rearmed Japan), Saimaru Shuppansha, 1969.

Kratoska, Paul H., *The Japanese Occupation of Malaya: A Social and Economic History*, University of Hawai'i Press, 1997.

Krueger, Walter, *From Down Under to Nippon: The Story of Sixth Army in World War II*, Combat Forces Press, Washington, 1953.

Kubo Yoshizō, *Shōwa kyōiku-shi* (A History of Education During the Shōwa Era), vol. 2, 1994.

——, *Tai-Nichi senryō seisaku to sengo kyōiku kaikaku* (Occupation Policy Towards Japan and the Reform of Postwar Education), Sanseidō, 1984.

Kurihara Sadako, *Black Eggs: Poems by Kurihara Sadako*, Center for Japanese Studies, University of Michigan, 1994.

Kurita Wataru, 'Making Peace with Hirohito and a Militaristic Past', in *The Japan Quarterly*, April–June 1989.

Kuwata Etsu and Maebara Tōru, eds, *Nihon no sensō: zukai to dēta* (Japan's Wars: Graphs and Statistics), Hara Shobō, 1986.

Lattimore, Owen, *Solution in Asia*, Little Brown, 1945.

Leahy, William, *I Was There: The Personal Story of the Chief of Staff to the Presidents Roosevelt and Truman, Based on his Notes and Diaries Made at the Time*, McGraw-Hill, 1950.

Lebra, Joyce C., ed., *Japan's Greater East Asia Co-Prosperity Sphere in World War II: Selected Readings and Documents*, Oxford University Press (Kuala Lumpur), 1975.

Lee Changsoo and George De Vos, *Koreans in Japan: Ethnic Conflict and Accommodation*, University of California Press, 1981.

Lee, Sherman E., 'My Work in Japan: Arts and Monuments, 1946–1948', in Mark Sandler, ed., *The Confusion Era: Art and Culture of Japan During the Allied Occupation, 1945–1952*, Smithsonian Institution, 1997.

Lee, Ulysses, *The Employment of Negro Troops* (The US Army in World War II), US Army Office of the Chief of Military History, US Government Printing Office, 1966.

LeMay, Curtis E., with MacKinlay Kantor, *Mission with LeMay: My Story*, Doubleday, 1965.

Lensen, George A., *The Strange Neutrality: Soviet Japanese Relations During the Second World War, 1941–1945*, Diplomatic Press (Tallahassee), 1972.

Lie, John, *Multiethnic Japan*, Harvard University Press, 2001.

Lindee, M. Susan, *Suffering Made Real: American Science and the Survivors at Hiroshima*, University of Chicago Press, 1994.

Livingston, Jon, Joe B. Moore and Felicia Oldfather, eds, *Postwar Japan: 1945 to the Present*, Pantheon Books, 1973.

Lory, Hillis *Japan's Military Masters: The Army in Japanese Life*, Viking Press, 1943.

Lummis, C. Douglas, ' Japan's Radical Constitution', in *Nihonkoku kenpō o yomu* (Reading the Constitution of Japan), Kashiwa Shobō, 1993.

——, *Kenpō to sensō* (The Constitution and War), Shōbunsha, 2000.

——, *Radical Democracy*, Cornell University Press, 1996.

MacArthur, Douglas, *Reminiscences*, McGraw-Hill, 1964.

——, *The Douglas MacArthur Papers*, MacArthur Memorial Bureau of Archives.

McCormack, Gavan, 'Crime, Confession, and Control in Contemporary Japan', in

Gavan McCormack and Yoshio Sugimoto, eds, *Democracy in Contemporary Japan*, Hale & Ironmonger, 1986.

McCormack, Gavan and Hank Nelson, eds, *The Burma-Thailand Railway*, Allen & Unwin, 1993.

McCoy, Alfred W., ed., *Southeast Asia Under Japanese Occupation*, Monograph Series no. 22, Yale University Southeast Asian Studies, 1980.

McDonald, Keiko I., 'Whatever Happened to Passive Suffering? Women on Screen', in Mark Sandler, ed., *The Confusion Era: Art and Culture of Japan During the Allied Occupation, 1945–1952*, Smithsonian Institution, 1997.

Maclachlan, Patricia, 'Information Disclosure and the Center-Local Relationship in Japan', in Sheila A. Smith, ed., *Local Voices, National Issues: The Impact of Local Initiative in Japanese Policy-Making*, University of Michigan Press, 2000.

McNelly, Theodore H., 'General Douglas MacArthur and the Constitutional Disarmament of Japan', *The Transactions of the Asiatic Society of Japan*, 3rd Series, vol. 17, 1982.

——, 'Induced Revolution: The Policy and Process of Constitutional Reform in Japan', in Robert E. Ward and Sakamoto Yoshikazu, eds, *Democratizing Japan: The Allied Occupation*, University of Hawai'i Press, 1987.

——, *The Origins of Japan's Democratic Constitution*, University Press of America, 2000.

Maeda Hideaki, *Meiji, Taishō, Shōwa, Heisei: Episōdo de tsuzuru Kokkai no hyakunen* (One-Hundred Years of Diet History Seen Through Episodes from Meiji to Heisei), Hara Shobō, 1990.

Maeda Tamon, 'The Direction of Postwar Education in Japan', in *The Japan Quarterly*, vol. 3, no. 4, 1956.

Maeda Tetsuo, *The Hidden Army: The Untold Story of Japan's Military Forces*, Edition Q (Tokyo), 1995.

Maki, John M., *Court and Constitution in Japan: Selected Supreme Court Decisions, 1948–1960*, University of Washington Press, 1964.

——, *Government and Politics in Japan: The Road to Democracy*, Frederick A. Praeger, 1962.

Manchester, William, *American Caesar: Douglas MacArthur, 1880–1963*, Little, Brown, 1978.

Martin, Edwin M., *The Allied Occupation of Japan*, Stanford University Press, 1948.

Mashbir, Sidney F., *I Was an American Spy*, Vantage Press, 1953.

Masuda Hiroshi, *Kōshoku tsuihō* (The Purge of Public Officals), Tōkyō Daigaku Shuppankai, 1996.

——, *Seijika tsuihō* (The Purge of the Politicians), Chūō Kōron Shinsha, 2001.

Masuko Yoshihisa, 'Maboroshi no Ainu dokuritsu-ron o ou: chōrō ni shikin o okutta GHQ no shin'i' (In Search of the Mysterious Ainu Independence Proposal: GHQ's Real Intention in Sending Money to Ainu Elders), *Asahi Jānaru*, 3 March 1989.

Masumi Junnosuke, *Contemporary Politics in Japan*, University of California Press, 1995.

——, *Shōwa Tennō to sono jidai* (The Emperor Shōwa and His Era), Yamakawa Shuppansha, 1998.

Matsubara Yōko, 'Nihon: sengo no Yūsei Hogo-hō to iu na no danshu-hō' (Japan: The Postwar Eugenic Protection Law – A Sterilisation Law in Disguise), in Yoneyama Shōhei, ed., *Yūseigaku to ningen shakai: seimei-kagaku no seiki wa doko e mukau ka* (Eugenics and Human Society: Where is the Century of Life Science Headed), Kōdansha, 2000.

Matsuda Hiroshi, *Hōsō sengo-shi* (A History of Postwar Broadcasting), Matagakisha, 1980.

Matsui Mitzi, 'The Military Intelligence Service Story', in *Unsung Heroes: Military Intelligence Service, Past, Present, Future*, MIS-Northwest Association (Seattle), 1996.

Matsumoto Kunihiko, 'Zainichi Chōsenjin no Nihon kokuseki hakudatsu' (The Denationalisation of Koreans in Japan), *Hōgaku*, vol. 52, no. 4, 1988.

Matsunami Michihiro, 'Origins of Zengakuren', in Stuart J. Dowsey, ed., *Zengakuren: Japan's Revolutionary Students*, Ishi Press (Berkeley), 1970.

Matsuura Sōzō. *Senryōka no genron dan'atsu* (Repression of Free Speech Under the Occupation), Gendai Jānarizumu Shuppankai, 1977.

Mayo, Marlene J., 'American Wartime Planning for Occupied Japan: The Role of the Experts', in Robert Wolfe, ed., *Americans as Proconsuls: United States Military Government in Germany and Japan, 1944–1952*, Southern Illinois University Press, 1984.

——, 'Civil Censorship and Media Control in Early Occupied Japan: From Minimum to Stringent Surveillance', in Wolfe, ed. (1984).

——, 'Psychological Disarmament: American Wartime Planning for the Education and Re-Education of Defeated Japan, 1943–1945', in Thomas W. Burkman, ed., *The Occupation of Japan: Education and Social Reform*, General Douglas MacArthur Memorial Foundation, 1982.

——, 'The War of Words Continues: American Radio Guidance in Occupied Japan', in Thomas W. Burkman, ed., *The Occupation of Japan: Arts and Culture*, General Douglas MacArthur Foundation, 1988.

Mears, Helen, *Mirror for Americans – Japan*, Houghton Mifflin, 1948.

——, *The Year of the Wild Boar: An American Woman in Japan*, J. B. Lippincott, 1942.

Mee, Charles L., Jr, *Meeting at Potsdam*, M. Evans & Co. (New York), 1975.

Mendel, Douglas, *The Japanese People and Foreign Policy: A Study of Public Opinion in Post-Treaty Japan*, University of California Press, 1961.

Mershon, Sherie and Steven Schlossman, *Foxholes and Color Lines: Desegregating the U.S. Armed Forces*, Johns Hopkins University Press, 1998.

Meyer, Allen H., 'MIS: Non-Nikkei', in *Unsung Heroes: Military Intelligence Service, Past, Present, Future*, MIS-Northwest Association (Seattle), 1996.

Mihashi Osamu, 'Joron: Senryō ni okeru tai-Zainichi Chōsenjin kanri-seisaku keisei-katei no kenkyū (1) (Introduction: An Analysis of the Establishment of Control Policies for Koreans in Occupied Japan), in *Seikyū gakujutsu ronshū*, no. 10, Kankoku Bunka Kenkyū Shinkō Zaidan, 1995.

Minear, Richard M., *Victor's Justice: The Tokyo War Crimes Trial*, Tuttle, 1972.

Ministry of Foreign Affairs (Special Survey Committee), ed., *Basic Problems for Post-War Reconstruction of Japanese Economy* (March 1946), Japan Economic Research Centre, 1977.

Ministry of Health and Welfare, *Statistical Abstracts on Health and Welfare in Japan*, 1999.

Mishima Akio, *Bitter Sea: The Human Cost of Minamata Disease*, Kosei Publishing Company (Tokyo), 1992.

Mitchell, Richard H., *Censorship in Imperial Japan*, Princeton University Press, 1983.

Mitsubishi Economic Research Institute, ed., *Mitsui-Mitsubishi-Sumitomo: Present Status of the Former Zaibatsu Enterprises*, Mitsubishi Economic Research Institute, 1955.

Miwa Ryōichi, 'Senryōki no Nihon zōsen kisei no jittai' (The State of Restrictions on Shipbuilding During the Occupation), in *Aoyama keizai ronshū*, nos 1–3, vol. 51, 1999.

Miyagi Etsujirō, *Okinawa senryō no 27-nenkan: Amerika-gunsei to bunka no henyō* (Twenty-Seven Years of Occupation in Okinawa: Military Government and the Transformation of Okinawan culture), Iwanami Shoten, 1992.

Miyamoto Ken'ichi, *Kōkyō seisaku no susume: gendai-teki kōkyōsei to wa nani ka* (For an Enlightened Public Interest Policy: A Query into the Modern Concept of Public Interest), Yūhikaku, 1998.

Miyashita Tadako, *Kakuri no sato* (Segregated Villages), Ōtsuki Shoten, 1998.

Miyauchi Yutaka, *Sengo chian rippō no kihonteki seikaku* (The Real Nature of the Postwar Public Security Laws), Yushindō, 1960.

Miyazaki Akira, 'Senryō shoki ni okeru Beikoku no Zainichi Chōsenjin seisaku: Nihon seifu no taiō to tomo ni' (The US Army's Korean Policy During the Occupation and the Japanese Government's Response), *Shisō*, no. 734, August 1985.

Miyazato Seigen, ed., *Amerika no taigai seisaku kettei katei* (The US Foreign Policy Decision-Making Process), San'ichi Shobō, 1975.

Mizuno Hiroshi, ed., *Shi ni nozonde uttaeru* (Our Dying Words Accuse!), Tōgosha, 1982 (originally published as *Nihon no teisō: gaikokuhei ni okasareta joseitachi no shuki* [Japan's Moral State: Women Raped by Foreign Soldiers and Their Stories], Sōjusha, 1953).

Mizuno Naoki, 'Zainichi Chōsenjin-Taiwanjin sansei-ken 'teishi' jōkō no seiritsu' (The Origin of the Clause Suspending the Electoral Rights of Koreans and Formosans in Japan), *Sekai Jinken-mondai Kenkyū Sentā kenkyū kiyō* (Annals of the Centre for the Study of World Human Rights Issues), no. 1 (March 15), 1996.

Molasky, Michael S., *The American Occupation of Japan and Okinawa: Literature and Memory*, Routledge, 1999.

Moore, Joe B., *Japanese Workers and the Struggle for Power, 1945–1947*, University of Wisconsin Press, 1983.

——, 'Nikkeiren and Restoration of the Right to Manage in Postwar Japan', *Labour & Industry*, vol. 3, nos 2 & 3, 1990.

——, 'Production Control: Workers' Control in Early Postwar Japan', in Joe. B. Moore, ed., *The Other Japan: Conflict, Compromise, and Resistance, Since 1945*, M. E. Sharpe, 1997.

——, 'Purging Toho Cinema of the "Two Reds": A Case Study of the Reverse Course in the Japanese Labour Movement, 1947–1948', *Canadian Journal of History*, vol. 26, December 1991.

——, 'Reflections on Jazz in Postwar Japan: Blues People and Company Men', unpublished manuscript, 1998.

——, 'Studying Jazz in Postwar Japan: Where to Begin?', *Japanese Studies*, vol. 18, no. 3, 1998.

——, 'The Toshiba Dispute of 1949: The "Rationalization" of Labor Relations', *Labour, Capital and Society*, vol. 23, no. 1, 1990.

Moore, Ray A., 'Discussion', in Thomas W. Burkman, ed., *The Occupation of Japan: Arts and Culture*, General Douglas MacArthur Foundation, 1988.

Morden, Bettie J., *The Women's Army Corps, 1945–1978*, US Army Center for Military History, US Government Printing Office, 1990.

Morin, Raul, *Among the Valiants: Mexican-Americans in WW II and Korea*, Borden Publishing Co. (California), 1966.

Morton, Lewis, *The Fall of the Philippines* (The US Army in World War II: The War in the Pacific), US Army Office of the Chief of Military History, US Government Printing Office, 1953.

——, *Strategy and Command: The First Two Years*, (The US Army in World War II: The War in the Pacific), US Army Office of the Chief of Military History, US Government Printing Office, 1962.

Motley, Mary P., ed., *The Invisible Soldier: The Experience of Black Soldiers in World War II*, Wayne State University Press, 1975.

Murakami Kimiko, *Senryōki no fukushi seisaku* (Welfare Policy During the Occupation of Japan), Keisō Shobō, 1987.

Nakagawa Gō, 'Nichi-Fi ryōkoku kenpō ni miru ruien' (Similarities Observed in the Constitutions of Japan and the Philippines), *Chūō Kōron*, May 1987.

Nakamura Akemi, 'New Equal Opportunity Law Called a Start', *The Japan Times*, 1 April 1999.

Nakamura Masanori, *The Japanese Monarchy: Ambassador Grew and the Making of the 'Symbol Emperor System', 1931–1991*, M. E. Sharpe, 1992.

——, *Keizai hatten to minshushugi* (Economic Development and Democracy), Iwanami Shoten, 1993.

——, 'Sengo kaikaku to gendai' (The Postwar Reforms and Contemporary Japan), in *Senryō to sengo-kaikaku* (The Occupation and the Postwar Reforms), Yoshikawa Kobunkan, 1994.

Nakamura Masanori, ed., *Sengo Nihon: senryō to sengo-kaikaku* (Postwar Japan: The Occupation and Postwar Reforms), vol. 2, Iwanami Shoten, 1995.

Nakamura Takafusa, *A History of Shōwa Japan, 1926–1989*, University of Tokyo Press, 1998.

Namie Ken, *Honmono no chihō-bunken/chihō-jichi* (Regional Decentralisation, Local Autonomy: The Real McCoy), BOC Shuppanbu, 1995.

Neary, Ian, 'Burakumin in Contemporary Japan', in Michael Weiner, ed., *Japan's Minorities: The Illusion of Homogeneity*, Routledge, 1997.

Nemuro-shi Sōmubu Ryōdo Taisaku-gakari-hen (Nemuro City Administrative Division, Territorial Section), *Hoppō ryōdo: shūsen zengo no kiroku* (The Occupation of the Northern Territories: A Record of Events Before and After the End of the War), Nemuro-shi, vol. 1, 1970 and vol. 2, 1971.

——, *Nihon no ryōdo, Hoppōryōdo* (The Northern Territories: Japanese Homeland), Nemuro-shi, 1980.

Neville, Edwin L., Jr, 'Japanese and GI Rapport', in William F. Nimmo, ed., *The Occupation of Japan: The Grassroots*, General Douglas MacArthur Foundation, 1992.

Newman, Robert P., *Truman and the Hiroshima Cult*, Michigan State University Press, 1995.

NHK (Radio and TV Culture Institute), *50 Years of Japanese Broadcasting*, Nihon Hōsō Kyōkai, 1977.

Nimmo, William F., *Behind a Curtain of Silence: Japanese in Soviet Custody, 1945–1956*, Greenwood Press, 1988.

Nish, Ian H., 'India and the Occupation of Japan', in Ian H. Nish, ed., *The British Commonwealth and the Occupation of Japan*, International Centre for Economics and Related Disciplines, London School of Economics and Political Science, 1983.

Nish, Ian H., ed., *Aspects of the Allied Occupation of Japan*, London School of Economics and Political Science, 1985.

Nishi Kyōko, *Senryōka no Nihon fujin seisaku* (Policies Affecting Japanese Women Under the Occupation), Domesu Shuppan, 1985.

Nishi Osamu, *Ten Days inside General Headquarters (GHQ): How the Original Draft of the Japanese Constitution was Written in 1946*, Seibundo Publishing Co. (Tokyo), 1989.

Nishi Toshio, *Unconditional Democracy: Education and Politics in Occupied Japan, 1945–1952*, Hoover Institution Press (Stanford University), 1982.

Nishimura Kumao, *Sanfuranshisuko heiwa jōyaku* (The San Francisco Peace Treaty), in *Nihon gaikōshi* (Japanese Diplomatic History), vol. 27, Kajima Kenkyūjo Shuppankai, 1971.

Nōchi Kaikaku Kiroku I'inkai (Land Reform Documentary Committee), ed., *Nōchi kaikaku tenmatsu gaiyō* (A Synopsis of the Progress of the Land Reform), Nōsei Chōsakai, 1951.

Nōchi Kaikaku Shiryō Hensan l'inkai (Land Reform Documents Editorial Committee), ed., *Nōchi kaikaku shiryō shūsei* (A Compendium of Documents on the Land Reform), vol. 14, Ochanomizu Shobō, 1982.

Norman, E. Herbert, *The Feudal Background of Japanese Politics*, Institute of Pacific Relations, 1945.

——, *Japan's Emergence as a Modern State*, Institute of Pacific Relations, 1940.

——, *Soldier and Peasant in Japan: The Origins of Conscription*, Institute of Pacific Relations, 1943.

Nozaki Yoshiko, and Inokuchi Hiromitsu, 'Japanese Education, Nationalism, and Ienaga Saburō's Textbook Lawsuits', in Laura Hein and Mark Selden, eds, *Censoring History: Citizenship and Memory in Japan, Germany, and the United States*, M. E. Sharpe, 2000.

Nozoe Kenji, *Hanaoka jiken no hitotachi* (Participants in the Hanaoka Incident), Shisō no Kagakusha, 1975.

——, *Hanaoka jiken o ou: Chūgokujin kyōsei renkō no sekinin o toi-naosu* (The Truth About the Hanaoka Incident: Rethinking Responsibility for the Forcible Conscription of Chinese Labourers), Ochanomizu Shobō, 1996.

——, *Kikigaki Hanaoka jiken* (Witness to the Hanaoka Incident), Ochanomizu Shobō, 1993.

Nugent, Donald R. and Reginald Bell, eds, *The Pacific Area and its Problems: A Study Guide*, Institute for Pacific Relations, 1936.

Oakley, Deborah, 'The Development of Population Policy in Japan, 1945–1952, and American Participation', PhD dissertation, University of Michigan, 1977.

Ōbayashi Michiko, *Josampu no sengo* (Midwifery in the Postwar Era), Keisō Shobō, 1989.

O'Brien, David M., with Yasuo Ohkoshi, *To Dream of Dreams: Religious Freedom and Constitutional Politics in Postwar Japan*, University of Hawai'i Press, 1996.

Oda, James, *Heroic Struggles of Japanese Americans: Partisan Fighters from America's Concentration Camps*, KNI, Inc., 1980.

Oda Makoto, 'Nihon wa 'Kokuren' o yamete, 'Kokuren' ni kyōryoku seyo' (Japan Should Quit, Then Cooperate With, the United Nations), *Gekkan Asahi*, January 1991.

Odabe Yūji, Hayashi Hiroshi and Yamada Akira, *Kīwādo: Nihon no sensō hanzai* (Keywords: Japan's War Crimes), Yūsankaku, 1997.

Oguma Eiji, *'Nihonjin' no kyōkai: Okinawa, Ainu, Taiwan, Chōsen – shokuminchi kara fukki undō made* (The Boundaries of the 'Japanese': Okinawa, the Ainu, Formosa, Korea – From Colonies to the Reversion Movement), Shinyōsha, 1998.

Ogura Takekazu, *Can Japanese Agriculture Survive? A Historical and Comparative Approach*, Agricultural Policy Research Center, 1982.

Ohnuki-Tierney, Emiko, 'A Conceptual Model for the Historical Relationship

Between the Self and the Internal and External Others', in Dru C. Gladney, ed., *Making Majorities: Constituting the Nation in Japan, Korea, China, Malaysia, Fiji, Turkey, and the United States*, Stanford University Press, 1998.

Okada Akira. *Gendai Nihon kanryō-sei no seiritsu* (The Establishment of the Modern Japanese Bureaucratic System), Hōsei Daigaku Shuppan-kyoku, 1994.

Okamoto Shirō, *Kabuki o sukutta otoko: Makkāsā no fukukan Fōbian Bawāzu* (The Man Who Saved Kabuki: MacArthur's Military Aide Faubion Bowers), Shūeisha, 1998.

Okinawa-ken (Okinawa Prefecture), ed., *Okinawa: kunan no gendaishi* (Okinawa: A Troubled Modern History), Iwanami Shoten, 1996.

Okinawa Kenritsu Toshokan Shiryō Henshūshitsu-hen (Okinawa Prefectural Library, Documentary Editorial Office), ed., *Okinawa-ken shi: shiryō-hen* (History of Okinawa Prefecture: Documents), no. 2 (English), Okinawa-ken Kyōiku I'inkai, 1996.

Okuizumi Eizaburō and Furukawa Atsushi, 'Nihon senryōki no Kyokutō Beigun jōhō shūshū katsudō to soshiki' (Information-Gathering Activities and the Organisation of the US Far East Command During the Occupation of Japan), *Tōkyō Keidai Gakkaishi* (The Journal of Tokyo Keizai University), nos 109–10, 1978.

Ōkurashō Zaisei-shi Shitsu-hen (Ministry of Finance, Financial History Office), ed., *Shōwa zaisei-shi: shūsen kara Kōwa made* (The Financial History of the Shōwa Era: From the War's End to the Peace Treaty), vol. II, Tōyō Keizai Shinpōsha, 1983.

Ōnuma Yasuaki, *Saharin kimin: sengo sekinin no tenkei* (The Displaced of Sakhalin: Fulfilling Japan's Post-Colonial Responsibility), Chūko Shinsho, 1992.

———, *Tan'itsu minzoku shakai o koete: Zainichi Kankoku-Chōsenjin to shūtsunykoku kanri-taisei* (Beyond the Myth of the Mono-ethnic Society: Koreans in Japan and the Immigration Control System), Tōshindō, 1992.

Ooi Keat Gin, *Rising Sun Over Borneo: The Japanese Occupation of Sarawak, 1941–1945*, Macmillan, 1999.

Oppler, Alfred C., *Legal Reform in Occupied Japan: A Participant Looks Back*, Princeton University Press, 1976.

Orr, Mark T., 'Education Reform in Occupied Japan', PhD dissertation, Department of Political Science, University of North Carolina, 1954.

Ōsaka-fu Keisatsu-shi Henshū I'inkai-hen (Osaka Prefectural Police Editorial Committee), ed., *Ōsaka-fu keisatsu-shi* (A History of the Osaka Prefectural Police), vol. 3, Ōsaka-fu Keisatsu Honbu, 1973.

Ōshita Katsumasa, *Machida-shi ga kawatta: chihō-jichi to fukushi* (Machida City Transformed: Local Autonomy and Social Welfare), Asahi Shinbunsha, 1992.

Ōta Masahide, *Sōshi Okinawa-sen* (A Comprehensive History of the Battle of Okinawa), Iwanami Shoten, 1982.

———, 'War Memories Die Hard in Okinawa' in *The Japan Quarterly*, vol. 35, no. 1, 1988.

Ōtani Fujirō, *Rai yobōhō haishi no rekishi* (A History of the Movement to Abolish the Leprosy Prevention Law), Keisō Shobō, 1996.

Ozaki Isamu, *Kōan jōrei seitei hishi* (The Secret History of the Passage of the Public Safety Ordinances), Takushoku Shobō, 1978.

Ozawa Yūsaku, *Zainichi Chōsenjin kyōiku-ron: rekishi-hen* (Education and Koreans in Japan: Historical Background), Aki Shobō, 1973.

Pak Kyŏng-sik, *Kaihō-go: Zainichi Chōsenjin undō* (The Korean Movement in Japan Following Liberation), San'ichi Shobō, 1989.

Pak, S., Kwak, K. and Sin, W., *Hibakusha Kankokujin* (Koreans Exposed to the A-Bomb), Asahi Shinbunsha, 1975.

Passin, Herbert, *Encounter With Japan*, Kodansha International, 1982.

——, *The Legacy of the Occupation – Japan*, Occasional Papers of the East Asian Institute, Columbia University, 1968.

——, *Society and Education in Japan*, Columbia University Press, 1965.

Paul, Doris A., *The Navajo Code Talkers*, Dorrance Publishing Co. (Pennsylvania), 1973.

Peattie, Mark R, *Nan'yō: The Rise and Fall of the Japanese in Micronesia, 1885–1945*, University of Hawai'i Press, 1988.

Pempel, T. J., 'The Tar Baby Target: "Reform" of the Japanese Bureaucracy', in Robert E. Ward and Sakamoto Yoshikazu, eds, *Democratizing Japan: The Allied Occupation*, University of Hawai'i Press, 1987.

Pharr, Susan J., 'A Radical US Experiment: Women's Rights and the Occupation of Japan', in L. H. Redford, ed., *The Occupation of Japan: Impact of Legal Reform*, General Douglas MacArthur Foundation, 1977.

——, 'The Politics of Women's Rights', in Robert E. Ward and Sakamoto Yoshikazu, eds, *Democratizing Japan: The Allied Occupation*, University of Hawai'i Press, 1987.

Potter, E. B., *Nimitz*, Naval Institute Press (Annapolis), 1976.

Prange, Gordon W., *At Dawn We Slept: The Untold Story of Pearl Harbor*, Penguin Books, 1981.

Price, John, 'Valery Burati and the Formation of Sōhyō During the U.S. Occupation of Japan', in *Pacific Affairs*, vol. 64, no. 2, 1991.

Prime Minister's Office, *The Present Status of Gender Equality and Measures*, Tokyo, 1999.

Pritchard, R. John and Sonia M. Zaide, eds, *The Tokyo War Crimes Trial: The Complete Transcripts of the Proceedings of the International Military Tribunal for the Far East in Twenty-Two Volumes*, Garland, 1981.

Rees, David, *The Soviet Seizure of the Kuriles*, Praeger, 1985.

Regis, Edward, *The Biology of Doom: The History of America's Germ Warfare Project*, Henry Holt, 1999.

Reischauer, Edwin O., 'The Allied Occupation: Catalyst, not Creator', in Harry

Wray and Hilary Conroy, eds, *Japan Examined: Perspectives on Modern Japanese History*, University of Hawai'i Press, 1983.

——, *My Life Between Japan and America*, Weatherhill, 1986.

Reischauer, Haru Matsukata, *Samurai and Silk: A Japanese and American Heritage*, Charles E. Tuttle, 1987 (Harvard University Press, 1986).

Rhoades, Weldon E., *Flying MacArthur to Victory*, Texas A&M University Press, 1987.

Richie, Donald, 'The Occupied Arts', in Mark Sandler, ed., *The Confusion Era: Art and Culture of Japan During the Allied Occupation, 1945–1952*, Smithsonian Institution, 1997.

Ricketts, Robert, 'GHQ no tai-Zainichi-Chōsenjin seisaku o tsukutta otoko-tachi' (Cold Warriors and the Korean Minority in Occupied Japan: Part 1 – Richard B. Finn), *Wakō Daigaku Ningen-kankei Gakubu kiyō* (Annals of the Faculty of Human Sciences, Wako University), no. 2, 1997.

——, 'GHQ no Zainichi Chōsenjin seisaku' (GHQ's Korean Policy), in *Ajia Kenkyū*, Wakō Daigaku, 1994.

——, 'Zainichi Chōsenjin no minzoku jishuken no hakai-katei: 1948–1949 o chūshin ni' (Koreans in Occupied Japan: The Destruction of Korean Cultural Autonomy, 1948–49), *Seikyū gakujutsu ronshū*, no. 10, Kankoku Bunka Kenkyū Shinkō Zaidan, 1995.

Ridgway, Matthew B., *Soldier: The Memoirs of Matthew B. Ridgway*, Harpers, 1956.

Roberts, John G., 'The "Japan Crowd" and the Zaibatsu Restoration', in *The Japan Interpreter*, vol. 12, nos 3–4, 1979.

Röling, B. V. A., 'The Tokyo Trial in Retrospect', in Susumu Yamaguchi, ed. *Buddhism and Culture*, Nakano Press (Kyoto), 1960.

Röling, B. V. A. and C. F. Ruter, eds, *The Tokyo Judgment: The International Military Tribunal for the Far East (I.M.T.F.E.), 29 April 1946–12 November 1948*, APA-University Press (Amsterdam), 2 vols, 1977.

Roth, Andrew, *Dilemma in Japan*, Little, Brown, 1945.

Russell, John R., *Nihonjin no kokujin-kan: mondai wa 'Chibikuro Sanbo' dake de wa nai* (Concerning Japanese Images of Black People: 'Little Black Sambo' is not the Only Problem), Shin Hyōron, 1991.

Ryang, Sonia., *North Koreans in Japan: Language, Ideology, and Identity*, Westview Press, 1997.

Ryang, Sonia, ed., *Koreans in Japan: Critical Voices from the Margin*, Routledge, 2000.

Saikō Saibansho Hanrei Chōsa I'inkai-hen (Supreme Court Verdicts Editorial Committee), ed., *Saikō Saibansho hanrei-shū* (Verdicts of the Supreme Court), Saikō Saiban-sho Hanrei Chōsa I'inkai, vol. 47, no. 3, 1993.

Saikō Saibansho Sōkyoku-hen (Supreme Court General Affairs Bureau), ed., *Gyōsei jiken saihanrei-shū* (Court Verdicts in Civil Suits), no. 38, vols 6 and 7, Zaidan Hōjin Hōsōkai, 1988.

Sakai, Robert K. and Mitsugu Sakihara, 'Okinawa', in *The Kodansha Encyclopedia of Japan*, Kodansha, 1983.

Sakamoto, Thomas T., 'The MIS Aboard the Battleship USS *Missouri*', in *Unsung Heroes: Military Intelligence Service, Past, Present, Future*, MIS-Northwest Association (Seattle), 1996.

Sams, Crawford F., *'Medic': The Mission of an American Military Doctor in Occupied Japan and Wartorn Korea*, edited by Zabelle Zakarian, M. E. Sharpe, 1998.

Sandusky, Michael C., *America's Parallel*, Old Dominion Press, 1983.

San'ichi Shobō-hen, ed., *Shiryō sengo gakusei undō (1), 1945–1949* (Basic Documents on the Student Movement, Part 1: 1945–1949), San'ichi Shobō, 1968.

Sano, Peter Iwao, *1,000 Days in Siberia: The Odyssey of a Japanese-American POW*, Bison Books (University of Nebraska Press), 1999.

Sansom, Katherine, *Sir George Sansom: A Memoir*, Diplomatic Press (Tallahassee), 1972.

Sarantakes, Nicholas Evan, *Keystone: The American Occupation of Okinawa and U.S.-Japanese Relations*, Texas A&M University Press, 2000.

Sasaki-Uemura, Wesley, *Organizing the Spontaneous: Citizen Protest in Postwar Japan*, University of Hawai'i Press, 2001.

Sasamoto Yukuo, *Beigun senryōka no genbaku chōsa: genbaku kagai-koku ni natta Nihon* (The US Military Atomic Bomb Survey During the Occupation: When Japan Became an Atomic Aggressor), Shinkansha, 1995.

Satō Hideo, 'The Basic Source Materials on the Education Reform in Postwar Japan: Reports of the Surveys Conducted by the NIER Research Group', in *Acta Asiatica*, no. 54, 1988.

Satō Tadao, *Nihon eiga-shi, 1941–1959* (The History of Japanese Cinema, 1941–1959), vol. 2, Iwanami Shoten, 1995.

——, *Nihon no eiga: hadaka no Nihonjin* (The Japanese Cinema: The Japanese Revealed), Hyōronsha, 1978.

Satō Tatsuo, 'The Origin and Development of the Draft Constitution of Japan', in *Contemporary Japan*, vol. 24, nos 4–6 and nos 7–9, 1956.

Scalapino, Robert A. and Masumi Junnosuke, *Parties and Politics in Contemporary Japan*, University of California Press, 1962.

Schaller, Michael, *Altered States: The United States and Japan Since the Occupation*, Oxford University Press, 1997.

——, *Douglas MacArthur: The Far Eastern General*, Oxford University Press, 1989.

——, *The Origins of the Cold War in Asia: The American Occupation of Japan*, Oxford University Press, 1985.

Schonberger, Howard B., *Aftermath of War: Americans and the Remaking of Japan, 1945–1952*, Kent State University Press, 1989.

Sebald, William J., with Russell Brines, *With MacArthur in Japan: A Personal History of the Occupation*, W. W. Norton, 1965.

Sekai Editorial Staff, *Three Statements for World Peace*, Tokyo, 1950.

Shakai Hoshō Kenkyūjo-hen (Social Security Research Institute), ed., *Nihon shakai-hoshō shiryō* (Data on Japan's Social Security System), vol. 1, Shiseidō, 1975.

Sheldon, Walt, *The Honorable Conquerors: The Occupation of Japan 1945–1952*, Macmillan, 1965.

Sherwin, Martin J., *A World Destroyed: Hiroshima and the Origins of the Arms Race*, Vintage Books, 1987 (Alfred A. Knopf, 1975).

Shibata Shingo, ' "Akuma no hōshoku" no sensō hanzai' (War Crimes: The 'Devil's Gluttony'), in Shibata Shingo, ed., *Sensō to heiwa no ronri* (The Logic of War and Peace), Keisō Shobō, 1992.

Shibata Tokue and Miyamoto Ken'ichi, *Chihō zaisei* (Regional Fiscal Policy), Yūhikaku, 1963.

Shigemitsu Mamoru, *Japan and Her Destiny: My Struggle for Peace*, edited by F. S. G. Piggott, E. P. Dutton, 1958.

Shillony, Ben-Ami, *Politics and Culture in Wartime Japan*, Clarendon Press (Oxford), 1982.

Shimbori Michiya, 'The Sociology of a Student Movement – A Japan Case Study', in *Daedalus*, vol. 97, Winter 1968.

Shindō Ei'ichi, 'Bunkatsu sareta ryōdo' (Japan's National Territory Divided), in *Sekai*, April 1979.

———, 'Chi no suijaku ga motarasu sekai-zō no hizumi to hoshu e no kaiki' (Distortions in Our Worldview Caused by Intellectual Stagnation and Nostalgia for the Right) in Nihon Jānarisuto Kaigi (Japan Conference of Journalists), ed., *Masukomi no rekishi sekinin to mirai sekinin* (The Mass Media's Responsibility for the Past and the Future), Kōbunken, 1995.

Shiomi Saburō, *Japan's Finance and Taxation*, Columbia University Press, 1957.

Shūkan Shinchō, ed., *Makkāsā no Nihon* (MacArthur's Japan), Shinchōsha, 1970.

Siddle Richard, *Race, Resistace and the Ainu of Japan*, Routledge, 2000.

Sigal, Leon V., *Fighting to a Finish: The Politics of War Termination in the United States and Japan*, Cornell University Press, 1988.

Singh, Rajendra, *Post-war Occupation Forces: Japan and South East Asia* (Official History of the Indian Armed Forces in the Second World War, 1939–45), Orient Longman (New Delhi), 1958.

Sirota Gordon, Beate, *The Only Woman in the Room: A Memoir*, Kodansha, 1997.

Sjoberg, Katarina, *The Return of the Ainu: Cultural Mobilization and the Practice of Ethnicity in Japan*, Harwood Academic, 1993.

Slavinsky, Boris, *The Soviet Occupation of the Kuril Islands, August–September 1945: A Documentary Research*, Kennedy School of Government, Harvard University, 1993.

Sledge, Eugene B., *With the Old Breed at Pelieu and Okinawa*, Oxford University Press, 1990 (Presidio Press, 1981).

Smethurst, Richard J., 'The Origins of the Japanese Teachers' Union', in Richard K. Beardsley, ed., *Studies in Japanese History and Politics*, University of Michigan Center for Japanese Studies, Occasional Papers, no. 10, 1967.

Smirnov, L. N. and E. V. Zaitsev, *Tōkyō Saiban* (The Tokyo Tribunal), Ōtsuki Shoten, 1980.

Smith, Bradford, *Americans From Japan*, Lippincott, 1948.

Smith, Robert, *MacArthur in Korea: The Naked Emperor*, Simon & Schuster, 1982.

Smith, Robert R., *Triumph in the Philippines* (The US Army in World War II: The War in the Pacific), Office of the Chief of Military History, US Army, US Government Printing Office, 1991.

Smith, Sheila A., ed., *Local Voices, National Issues: The Impact of Local Initiative in Japanese Policy-Making*, University of Michigan Press, 2000.

Smith, W. Donald, 'Democracy Denied: The American Repression of Korean Education in Occupied Japan', unpublished essay (Graduate School of History, University of Washington), July 1993.

Sodei Rinjirō, *Haikei Makkāsā Gensui-sama: senryōka no Nihonjin no tegami* (Dear General MacArthur: Japanese Letters [to MacArthur] During the Occupation), Chūō Kōronsha, 1991.

——, 'Nihon senryō to Nikkei-nisei', in Hata Ikuhiko and Sodei Rinjirō, eds, *Nihon senryō hishi* (A Secret History of the Occupation of Japan), vol. 2, Asahi Shinbunsha, 1977.

——, 'The Occupier and the Occupied', in William F. Nimmo, ed., *The Occupation of Japan: The Grassroots*, General Douglas MacArthur Foundation, 1992.

——, *Makkāsā no nisen-nichi* (MacArthur's 2,000 Days), Chūō Kōronsha, 1989.

——, *Rimembā Shōwa! Dōjidai-shi no oboegaki* (Remember Shōwa! A Memorandum on the History of our Age), Marunouchi Shuppan, 1999.

——, *Were We the Enemy? American Survivors of Hiroshima*, Westview Press, 1998.

——, *Yoshida-Makkāsā ōfuku shokan-shū, 1945–1951* (Correspondence Between General MacArthur, Prime Minister Yoshida and Other High Japanese Officials, 1945–1951), Hōsei Daigaku Shuppankyoku, 2000.

Sodei Rinjirō and Fukushima Jūrō, *Makkāsā kiroku: sengo Nihon no genten* (The MacArthur Records: Postwar Japan's Point of Departure), Nihon Hōsō Shuppan Kyōkai, 1982.

Sodei Rinjirō and Takemae Eiji, eds, *Sengo Nihon no genten: senryō-shi no genzai* (Postwar Japan: The Point of Origin – Occupation History Today), Yūshisha, vol. 2, 1992.

Son Mun-gyu, 'Kokki o mamori-nuita hitobito: Chōsen Minshushugi Jinmin Kyōwa Koku kokki-keiyō jiken no shinsō' (People who Protected Their National Flag: The Truth About the DPRK Flag-Raising Incidents), in *Tōitsu Hyōron*, no. 60, 1978.

Sōrifu (Prime Minister's Office), *Nihon tōkei nenkan* (Japan Statistical Yearbook), Tokyo, 1956.

Spaulding, Robert M., 'CCD Censorship of Japan's Daily Press', in Thomas W. Burkman, ed., *The Occupation of Japan: Arts and Culture*, General Douglas MacArthur Foundation, 1988.

Spinks, Charles N., *The Brocade Banner*, US Army Forces Pacific (Tokyo), 1946.

——, 'Indoctrination and Re-Education of Japan's Youth', in *Pacific Affairs*, March 1944.

Steiner, Kurt, *Local Government in Japan*, Stanford University Press, 1965.

——, 'The Occupation and the Reform of the Japanese Civil Code', in Robert E. Ward and Sakamoto Yoshikazu, eds, *Democratizing Japan: the Allied Occupation*, University of Hawai'i Press, 1987.

Stephan, John J., *The Kuril Islands: Russo-Japanese Frontiers in the Pacific*, Clarendon Press (Oxford), 1974.

——, *The Russian Far East: A History*, Stanford University Press, 1994.

Storry, Richard, *A History of Modern Japan*, Penguin, 1982.

Sugiyama Akiko, *Senryōki no iryō kaikaku* (Medical Reforms During the Occupation), Keisō Shobō, 1995.

Suizu Mitsuru, *Hoppō ryōdo dakkan e no michi* (Recovering the Northern Territories), Nihon Kōgyō Shinbunsha 1979.

Sumimoto Toshio, *Senryō hiroku* (The Secret Story of the Occupation), vol. 2, Mainichi Shinbunsha, 1952.

Sumiya Yukio, Akazawa Shirō, Utsumi Aiko, Ogata Naokichi and Otabe Yūji, eds, *Tōkyō Saiban handobukku* (A Handbook of the Tokyo Tribunal), Aoki Shoten, 1989.

Sumiya Mikio, 'Mitsubishi Bibai sōgi' (The Mitsubishi Bibai Labour Dispute), in Tōkyō Daigaku Shakai Kagaku Kenkyūjo-hen (Tokyo University Institute of Social Sciences), ed., *Sengo shoki rōdō sōgi chōsa* (Survey of Labour Disputes in the Early Postwar Period), Tōkyō Daigaku Shuppankai, 1971.

Suzuki Akira and Yamamoto Akira, *Hiroku-bōryaku senden-bira: Taiheiyō Sensō no kami no bakudan* (Secret Strategy and Propaganda Leaflets: Paper Bombs in the Pacific War), Kōdansha, 1977.

Suzuki Ei'ichi, *Nihon senryō to kyōiku kaikaku* (The Occupation of Japan and Education Reform), Keisō Shobō, 1983.

Suzuki Eiji, *Sōkan rakudai-ki* (My Failures as Superintendent of Police), Masu Shobō, 1952.

Swann, Sebastian, 'Democratisation and the Evasion of War Responsibility: The Allied Occupation of Japan and the Emperor', in *Reflections on the Allied Occupation of Japan*, STICERD Discussion Paper no. IS/99/370, London School of Economics and Political Science, October 1999.

Taikakai-hen, ed., *Naimushō-shi* (A History of the Home Ministry), vol. 3, Hara Shobō, 1980.

Taira Koji, 'Troubled National Identity: The Ryukyuans/Okinawans', in Michael Weiner, ed., *Japan's Minorities: The Illusion of Homogeneity*, Routledge, 1997.

Takagi Kikurō, 'GHQ no ken'etsu: hōdō no "jiyū" to "tōsei" to iu mujun' (GHQ Censorship: The Contradiction Between 'Freedom' and 'Control'), in Yomiuri Shinbun Henshūkyoku (Yomiuri Editorial Board), ed., *Sengo gojūnen: Nippon no kiseki* (Fifty Years After the War: Japan's Path), vol. 1, 1995.

Takaki, Ronald T., *Double Victory: A Multicultural History of America in World War II*, Little, Brown, 2000.

——, *A History of Asian Americans: Strangers from a Different Shore*, Little, Brown, 1998.

Takahashi Mutsuko, *The Emergence of Welfare Society in Japan*, Ashgate, 1997.

Takakura Sei'ichirō, 'The Ainu of Northern Japan: A Study in Conquest and Acculturation', in *The Transactions of the Philosophical Society of Philadelphia*, vol. 50, no. 4, 1960.

Takano Kazumoto, 'Nihon senryō kenkyū ni okeru "gyaku-kōsu"' (The Concept of 'Reverse Course' in Studies on the Occupation of Japan), *Chūō Daigaku Daigakuin kenkyū nenpō* (Annals of the Graduate School, Chūō University), no. 15, March 1986.

Takasugi Shingo, *731 Butai: saikinsen no isha o oe* (Unit 731: On the Trail of the Bio-war Doctors), Tokuma Shoten, 1982.

Takayanagi Kenzō, Ōtomo Ichirō and Tanaka Hideo, eds, *Nihonkoku kenpō seitei no katei* (The Making of the Constitution of Japan), vol. 1, Yūhikaku, 1972.

Takemae Eiji, *Amerika tai-Nichi rōdō seisaku no kenkyū* (A Study of US Labour Policy Towards Japan), Nihon Hyōronsha, 1970.

——, 'Ball's View on the Allied Occupation of Japan: Interview with W. MacMahon Ball', in *The Journal of Tokyo Keizai University*, no. 151, June 1987.

——, 'Canadian Views on Occupation Policies and the Japanese Peace Treaty: Interview with Dr. Arthur K. Menzies', in *The Journal of Tokyo Keizai University*, no. 144, January 1986.

——, 'Early Postwar Reformist Parties', in Robert E. Ward and Sakamoto Yoshikazu, eds, *Democratizing Japan: The Allied Occupation*, University of Hawai'i Press, 1987.

——, 'Eirenpō Nihon senryōgun (BCOF) no seiritsu (1)' (The Formation of the British Commonwealth Force, Part 1), in *The Journal of Tokyo Keizai University*, no. 207, 1998.

——, 'J. K. Emāson-shi danwa sokkiroku' (Stenographic Record of a Talk with J. K. Emmerson), in *Tōkyō Keidai Gakkaishi*, no. 99, 1977.

——, GHQ, Iwanami Shinsho, 1983.

——, 'GHQ Labour Policy During the Period of Democratization, 1946–1948: The Second Interview with Mr. Theodore Cohen', in *The Journal of Tokyo Keizai University*, no. 122, 1981.

——, *GHQ Rōdōka no hito to seisaku* (Personnel and Policies of GHQ's Labour Division), Emutei Shuppan, 1991.

——, *Goken-kaiken-shi ron* (An Analysis of Arguments For and Against Constitutional Revision), Shōgakkan Bunko, 2001.

——, 'The Kades Memoir on the Occupation of Japan', in *The Journal of Tokyo Keizai University*, no. 148, 1986.

——, 'Kaisetsu' (Commentary), in *Beikoku Riku-Kaigun: gunsei-minji manyuaru* (The United States Army and Navy Manual of Military Government and Civil Affairs), Misuzu Shobō, 1998.

——, 'Kyōiku kaikaku no omoide: GHQ Kyōiku-kachō M. T. Oa Hakase ni kiku' (Reminiscences of the Education Reforms: An Interview with Dr Mark T. Orr, GHQ's Education Division Chief), in *Tōkyō Keidai Gakkaishi*, no. 115, March 1980.

——, 'J. Napier and the Purge in Japan: Interview With Mr. Jack P. Napier', in *The Journal of Tokyo Keizai University*, no. 153, November 1987.

——, 'Nihon Kyōsantō no kaihō sareta hi' (The Day the Communist Party was Liberated), in *Chūō Kōron*, July 1978.

——, *Nihon senryō: GHQ kōkan no shōgen* (The Occupation as Told by Senior GHQ Officials), Chūō Kōronsha, 1988.

——, 'Nihon senryō shoki gunsei no kenkyū: Nagano chūryū Dai 78 Gunsei Chūtai no katsudō shōkai' (Studies in Military Government During the Early Stage of the Occupation: An Introduction to the 78th Military Government Headquarters Stationed in Nagano), in *Gendai Hōgaku*, no. 1, 2000.

——, 'The Occupation', in National Committee of Japanese Historians, ed., *Historical Studies in Japan (VII), 1983–1987*, Yamakawa Shuppansha, 1990.

——, 'Possible Addendum to "Kades Memoir"', in *The Journal of Tokyo Keizai University*, no. 150, March 1987.

——, 'Religious Reform Under the Occupation of Japan: Interview with Dr W. K. Bunce', in *The Journal of Tokyo Keizai University*, no. 150, March 1987.

——, 'SCAP Labour Policy for Japan: A Memoir by an ex-GHQ Labour Official', in *Toritsu Kōgyō Kōtō Senmon Gakkō kenkyū hōkoku* (Research Bulletin of the Tokyo Metropolitan Junior College of Industrial Arts), no. 8, March 1972.

——, 'Sengo demokurashī to Ei-kaiwa: "Kāmu Kāmu Eigo" no yakuwari' (Postwar Democracy and English Conversation: The Role of 'Come Come English'), in Shisō no Kagaku Kenkyūkai (Shisō no Kagaku Research Group), ed. *Kyōdō kenkyū: Nihon senryō* (Joint Research: The Occupation of Japan), Tokuma Shobō, 1972.

——, *Sengo rōdō-kaikaku: GHQ rōdō seisaku-shi* (The Postwar Labour Reforms: A History of GHQ's Labour Reform Policy), Tōkyō Daigaku Shuppankai, 1982.

——, 'Sengo shoki no senkyo seido kaikaku (Initial Postwar Reforms in Japan: GHQ and the 1945 Election Law Amendment), in *The Journal of Tokyo Keizai University*, no. 129, 1983.

——, *Senryō sengo-shi* (A History of the Occupation and Postwar Era), Iwanami Shoten, 1992.

——, 'Senryō shūketsuki no rōdō-seisaku: GHQ saigo no rōdō kachō Ēmisu ni kiku' (Labour Policy Towards the End of the Occupation: An Interview with Robert Amis, GHQ's Last Labour Division Chief), in *Tōkyō Keidai Gakkaishi*, nos 116–17, 1980.

——, 'Senryō sōsetsu: senryō to GHQ' (An Overview of the Occupation: The Occupation and GHQ), in *GHQ: Nihon senryō-shi jōsetsu* (GHQ: An Introduction to the History of the Occupation of Japan), Nihon Tosho Sentā, 1996.

——, 'Senryō to mainoritei: kenkyū no dōkō to kadai' (Minorities under the Occupation: Research Trends and Topics), in *Buraku Kaihō Kenkyū*, no. 75, 1990.

——, *Senryō to sengo kaikaku* (The Occupation and the Postwar Reforms), Iwanami Booklet no. 9, Iwanami Shoten, 1991.

——, *Shiryō Nihon no rōdō: seisaku, undō, hanrei* (Historical Documents on Japanese Labour: Policy, Labour Movements, Legal Precedents), Yūshisha, 1994.

——, *Shōgen: Nihon senryō-shi – Rōdōka no gunzō* (An Oral History of Japan Under Occupation: GHQ's Labour Division), Iwanami Shoten, 1983.

——, 'Sōhyō and US Occupation Labour Policy: An Interview with Valery Burati', in *The Journal of the Tokyo College of Economics*, nos 97–8, 1976.

——, 'Some Questions and Answers', in Harry Wray and Hilary Conroy, eds, *Japan Examined: Perspectives on Modern Japanese History*, University of Hawai'i Press, 1983.

——, 'C. G. Tilton and the Occupation of Japan', in *The Journal of Tokyo Keizai University*, no. 146, 1986.

——, 'The U.S. Occupation Policies for Japan: Interview with Mr. Theodore Cohen', in *Tokyo Metropolitan University Journal of Law and Politics*, vol. 14, no. 1, 1973.

Takemae Eiji, ed., *Beikoku Riku-Kaigun: gunsei-minji manyuaru* (The United States Army and Navy Manual of Military Government and Civil Affairs), Misuzu Shobō, 1998.

——, *C. F. Samusu, DDT kakumei: senryō-ki no iryō fukushi seisaku o kaisō suru* (C. F. Sams, The DDT Revolution: Looking Back at the Reform of Medicine and Social Welfare During the Occupation), Iwanami Shoten, 1986.

Takemae Eiji and Amakawa Akira, eds, *Nihon senryō hishi* (A Secret History of the Occupation of Japan), vol. 1, Asahi Shinbunsha, 1977.

Takemae Eiji and Okabe Fuminobu, *Kenpō seitei-shi: Kenpō wa oshi-tsukerareta ka* (A History of the Drafting of the Constitution: Was it Really Imposed on Japan?), Shōgakkan Bunko, 2000.

Takemae Eiji, Ozaki Tsuyoshi and Tanaka Kaori, 'Shōgen: sengo shoki kaiun hishi (A Witness to the Postwar History of Japanese Seamen: The Korean War and M. Kitamura), in *Shizen kagaku ronshū* (Occasional Papers in the Journal of Humanities and the Natural Sciences), Tōkyō Keizai Daigaku, March 1998.

Takemae Eiji and Robert Ricketts, 'Robāto Riketto shimon ōnatsu kyohi jiken kankei-shiryō' (Historical Documents Pertaining to Robert Ricketts' Trial for Fingerprint Refusal), in *The Journal of Tokyo Keizai University*, no. 161, June 1989.

Takemae Eiji and Sasamoto Yukuo, 'Chōsen Sensō to "Kokurengun" chi'i kyōtei – Nihon no ichi' (The Korean War and the Agreement on United Nations Forces Status: Japan's Position), *Tōkyō Keidai Gakkaishi (Keizaigaku)*, no. 17, Tōkyō Keizai Daigaku Keizai Gakkai, March 2000.

Taksami, Ch. M. and V. D. Kosarev, *Ainu minzoku no rekishi to bunka: hoppō shōsū minzoku-gakusha no shiza yori* (The History and Culture of the Ainu People: Minorities of the Northern Islands from an Anthropological Viewpoint), Akashi Shoten, 1998.

Tanaka Hideo, *The Japanese Legal System: Introduction: Cases and Materials*, University of Tokyo Press, 1976.

Tanaka Hiroshi, 'Sengo Nihon to posuto-shokuminchi mondai' (Postwar Japan and the Post-Colonial Settlement Issue), in *Shisō*, no. 734, August 1985.

——, *Zainichi Gaikokujin: hō no kabe, kokoro no kabe* (Foreigners in Japan: Legal and Psychological Obstacles to Equality), Iwanami Shinsho, 1995.

Tanaka Sumiko, *Josei kaihō no shisō to kōdō* (Women's Liberation: Theory and Praxis), Jiji Tsūshinsha, 1975.

Tanaka Yuki, *Hidden Horrors: Japanese War Crimes in World War II*, Westview Press, 1998.

Tatara Toshio, 'The Allied Occupation and Japanese Public Welfare: An Overview of SCAP Activities During the Early Phase', in Thomas W. Burkman, ed., *The Occupation of Japan: Education and Social Reform*, General Douglas MacArthur Memorial Foundation, 1982.

——, '1400 Years of Japanese Social Work From its Origins Through the Allied Occupation, 552–1952', PhD dissertation, Bryn Mawr College, 1975.

Terasaki Hidenari and Mariko Terasaki Miller, eds, *Shōwa Tennō dokuhakuroku – Terasaki Hidenari, goyōgakari nikki* (The Shōwa Emperor's Soliloquy and the Diary of Terasaki Hidenari), Bungei Shunjūsha, 1991.

Textor, Robert B., *Failure in Japan: With Keystones for a Positive Policy*, Greenwood Press, 1972 (The John Day Co., 1951).

Thorpe, Elliott R., *East Wind, Rain*, Gambit Inc. (Boston), 1969.

Tōkyō Daigaku Shakaikagaku Kenkyūjo (University of Tokyo Social Science Research Institute), ed., *Sengo kaikaku* (The Postwar Reforms), vols 1–8, Tōkyō Daigaku Shuppankai 1974.

Toyoda Sumio, *Sensō saiban yoroku* (Supplementary Documents on the War Trials), Taiseisha, 1986.

Toyoshita Narahiko, *Anpō Jōyaku no seiritsu: Yoshida gaikō to Tennō gaikō* (The Drafting of the Security Treaty: Yoshida's Diplomacy and the Emperor's Diplomacy), Iwanami Shinsho, 1996.

——, *Nihon senryō kanri taisei no seiritsu: hikaku senryō-shi josetsu* (The Origins of the Control System for the Occupation of Japan: An Essay in Comparative Occupation History), Iwanami Shoten, 1992.

Trainor, Joseph C., *Educational Reform in Occupied Japan: Trainor's Memoir*, Meisei University Press, 1983.

Trotter, Ann, *New Zealand and Japan, 1945–1952: The Occupation and the Peace Treaty*, Athlone Press, 1990.

Truman, Harry S., *Memoirs: Year of Decisions, 1945*, Doubleday, 1955.

——, *Public Papers of the Presidents: Harry S. Truman, 1945*, US Government Printing Office, 1961.

Tsuchimochi, Gary Hōichi, *Education Reform in Postwar Japan: The 1946 U.S. Education Mission*, University of Tokyo Press, 1993.

——, *Rokusansei kyōiku no tanjō: sengo kyōiku no genten* (The Origins of the 6–3 Education System: The Starting Point of Post-War Education), Yūshisha, 1992.

Tsuji Kiyoaki, *Nihon no chihō-jichi* (Local Autonomy in Japan), Iwanami Shoten, 1976.

Tsuji Kiyoaki, ed., *Shiryō: sengo nijyūnen-shi* (A Documentary History of the Two Postwar Decades), vol. 1 (Politics), Nihon Hyōronsha, 1966.

Tsuneishi Kei'ichi, *Igakusha-tachi no soshiki hanzai: Kantōgun Dai 731 Butai* (The Organised Crime of [Japan's] Medical Scientists: The Kwantung Army's Unit 731), Asahi Shinbunsha, 1994.

——, *731 Butai: seibutsu heiki hanzai no shinjitsu* (Unit 731: The Truth Behind the Crime of Biological Weapons Development), Kōdansha, 1995.

Tsuru Shigeto, *Japan's Capitalism: Creative Defeat and Beyond*, Cambridge University Press, 1993.

Tsurumi Shunsuke, *A Cultural History of Postwar Japan, 1945–1980*, Kegan Paul International, 1987.

——, 'What the War Trials Left to the Japanese People', in C. Hosoya, N. Andō, Y. Ōnuma and R. Minear, eds, *The Tokyo War Crimes Trial: An International Symposium*, Kodansha International, 1986.

Uchida Kenzō, 'Japan's Postwar Conservative Parties', in Robert E. Ward and Sakamoto Yoshikazu, eds, *Democratizing Japan: The Allied Occupation*, University of Hawai'i Press, 1987.

Udagawa Megumi, 'The Bitter Legacy of Eugenics', *The Japan Views Quarterly*, The Asia Foundation Translation Series (Tokyo), vol. 2, no. 4, Winter 1993.

Ui Jun, 'Minamata Disease', in Ui Jun, ed., *Industrial Pollution in Japan*, United Nations University Press, 1992.

Unger, J. Marshall, *Literacy and Script Reform in Occupation Japan: Reading Between the Lines*, Oxford University Press, 1996.

Upham, Frank K., *Law and Social Change in Postwar Japan*, Harvard University Press, 1987.

Urata Takeo and Ogawa Takeshi, *Toshokanhō seiritsu-shi shiryō* (Documents on the History of the Establishment of the Library Law), Nihon Toshokan Kyōkai, 1968.

US Army Intelligence Center, *History of the Counter-Intelligence Corps*, Fort Halabird, Maryland, 1960.

US Department of the Army (Historical Section, G-2, FECOM), ed., *Reports of General MacArthur*, vol. 1: Supplement (MacArthur in Japan – The Occupation: Military Phase), US Government Printing Office, 1966.

——, vol. 2: Japanese Operations in the Southwest Pacific Area, Parts 1 and 2, US Government Printing Office, 1966.

——, Office of the Chief of Military History, *War in Asia and the Pacific, 1937–1949*, Garland, 1980.

US Department of State, *Foreign Relations of the United States*, US Government Printing Office, 1945–52.

——, *Occupation of Japan: Policy and Progress*, US Government Printing Office, 1946 (Greenwood Press, 1969).

——, *Postwar Foreign Policy Preparation, 1939–1945*, US Government Printing Office, 1950.

——, *Record of Hearings Before the Committee on Foreign Relations* (United States Senate, 78th Congress, Second Session, 12 and 13 December 1944), US Government Printing Office, Washington, 1944.

——, *Report of the United States Education Mission to Japan*, US Government Printing Office, 1946.

——, *A Report to the President by the National Security Council*, 7 October 1948.

US Senate Committee on Armed Services and the Committee on Foreign Relations, *Hearing to Conduct an Inquiry into the Military Situation in the Far East*, 82nd Congress, 1st session, 1951.

US Senate Committee on Foreign Relations, *Treaty of Mutual Cooperation and Security with Japan*, 86th Congress, 2nd Session (7 June 1960).

US Strategic Bombing Survey (Pacific), *Summary Report*, Report no. 1, Washington D C, 1946.

Ustinov, D. F., *Istoriia Vtoroi Mirovoi Voiny* – 2 (History of the Second World War, 1939–45, vol. 2), Moscow, 1980.

Utsumi Aiko, *Chōsenjin BC-kyū senpan no kiroku* (A Documentary Record of Class B and C Korean War Criminals), Keisō Shobō, 1982.

——, 'Japanese Army Internment Policies for Enemy Civilians During the Asia-Pacific War', in Donald Denoon, Mark Hudson, Gavan McCormack and Tessa Morris-Suzuki, eds, *Multicultural Japan: Palaeolithic to Postmodern*, Cambridge University Press, 1996.

Van Aduard, E. J. Lewe, *Japan: From Surrender to Peace*, Praeger, 1954.

Van Staaveren, Jacob, *An American in Japan, 1945–1948: A Civilian View of the Occupation*, University of Washington Press, 1994.

Vasilevsky, A., *Delo Vsei Zhizni* (My Life Work), Moscow, 1978.

Wada Haruki, 'Nisso sensō' (The Japanese-Soviet War), in Hara Teruyuki and Togawa Tsugo, eds., *Kōza: Surabu no sekai* (The Slavic World), vol. 8: Surabu to Nihon (The Slavic Peoples and Japan), Kōbundō, 1995.

Wagatsuma Sakae, ed., *Sengo ni okeru minpō no keika* (The Revision of the Postwar Civil Code), Nihon Hyōronsha, 1956.

Wagner, Edward, *The Korean Minority in Japan, 1904–1950*, Institute of Pacific Relations, 1951.

Walinsky, Louis J., ed., *Agrarian Reform as Unfinished Business: The Selected Papers of Wolf I. Ladejinsky*, Oxford University Press, 1977.

Ward, Ian, *Snaring the Other Tiger*, Media Masters (Singapore), 1996.

Ward, Robert E., 'Presurrender Planning: Treatment of the Emperor and Constitutional Change', in Robert E. Ward and Sakamoto Yoshikazu, eds, *Democratizing Japan: The Allied Occupation*, University of Hawai'i Press, 1987.

Watanabe Akio, *The Okinawa Problem: A Chapter in Japan-US Relations*, Melbourne University Press, 1970.

Watanabe Osamu, 'Gendai Nihon kokka no tokushu na kōzō' (The Peculiar Structure of the Modern Japanese State), in Tōkyō Daigaku Shakaikagaku Kenkyūjo (Tokyo University Institute of Social Sciences), ed., *Gendai Nihon Shakai* (Contemporary Japanese Society), vol. 1, Tōkyō Daigaku Shuppankai, 1991.

Watanabe Takeshi, *Senryōka no Nihon zaisei-oboegaki* (A Memoir of Japanese Financial Policy Under the Occupation), Nihon Keizai Shinbunsha, 1966.

Watanabe Toshio, *Gendai-shi no naka no Buraku mondai* (The *Buraku* Problem in Contemporary History), Kaihō Shuppansha, 1988.

——, 'Interview with Charles Kades', *Buraku mondai to Nihon senryō monjo kenkyū nyūsu* (News Bulletin on the *Buraku* Problem and Research on Occupation Documents), no. 14, 1989.

——, 'Senryō-ki no Buraku mondai' (The *Buraku* Problem During the Occupation), *Buraku Kaihō-shi: Fukuoka* (The History of *Buraku* Liberation: Fukuoka), no. 58, June 1990.

——, 'Senryō-ki no jinken hoshō to Buraku mondai' (Human Rights Guarantees Under the Occupation and the *Buraku* Problem), *Buraku Kaihō Kenkyū*, no. 73, 1990.

——, 'Tokushū: Senryō-ki no Buraku mondai' (Special Feature: The *Buraku* Problem Under the Occupation), *Buraku Kaihō Kenkyū*, no. 69, 1989.

Weiner, Michael, *Race and Migration in Imperial Japan*, Routledge, 1994.

Weiner, Michael, ed., *Japan's Minorities: The Illusion of Homogeneity*, Routledge, 1997.

Welfield, John, *An Empire in Eclipse: Japan in the Postwar American Alliance System – A Study in the Interaction of Domestic Politics and Foreign Policy*, Athlone Press, 1988.

Welsome, Eileen, *The Plutonium Files*, The Dial Press, 1999.

Wetzler, Peter, *Hirohito and War: Imperial Tradition and Military Decision-Making in Prewar Japan*, University of Hawai'i Press, 1998.

Whitney, Courtney, *MacArthur: His Rendezvous with History*, Alfred A. Knopf, 1956.

Wildes, Harry E., *Typhoon in Tokyo: The Occupation and its Aftermath*, Macmillan, 1954.

Williams, Justin, Sr, *Japan's Political Revolution Under MacArthur: A Participant's Account*, University of Tokyo Press, 1979.

——, *The Justin Williams Papers*, University of Maryland.

Williams, Peter and David Wallace, *Unit 731: Japan's Secret Biological Warfare in World War II*, The Free Press, 1989.

Willoughby, Charles A., *Maneuver in War*, Military Service Publishing Company (Harrisburg), 1939.
——, *The Charles A. Willoughby Papers*, MacArthur Memorial Bureau of Archives.
Willoughby, Charles A. and Chamberlain, John, *MacArthur, 1941–1951: Victory in the Pacific*, McGraw-Hill, 1954.
Wood, James, *Forgotten Force: The Australian Military Contribution to the Occupation of Japan*, Allen & Unwin, 1998.
Woodard, William P., *The Allied Occupation of Japan, 1945–1952, and Japanese Religions*, E. J. Brill, 1972.
Woodiwiss, Anthony, *Labour and Society in Japan: From Repression to Reluctant Tolerance*, Routledge, 1992.
——, 'A Revolution in Labour Law? The Fate of the Trade Union Act in Post-War Japan', in Ian Neary, ed. *War, Revolution and Japan*, Japan Library (Kent), 1993.
Wunderlich, Herbert J., 'The Japanese Textbook Problem and Solution', PhD dissertation, Stanford University, 1952.

Yamada Mieko, *Senryōgun ianfu* (Comfort Women of the US Occupation Army), Kōjinsha, 1992.
Yamagiwa Akira, 'Potsudamu sengen no sōan ni tsuite' (Concerning the Draft of the Potsdam Proclamation), *Yokohama Shiritsu Daigaku ronsō (Jinbun-Shakai-hen)*, vol. 39, no. 10, 1986.
Yamamoto Taketoshi, *Senryōki medeia bunseki* (A Study of the Media During the Occupation), Hōsei Daigaku Shuppankyoku, 1996.
Yamazaki, James, *Children of the Atomic Bombs: An American Physician's Memoir of Nagasaki, Hiroshima, and the Marshall Islands*, Duke University Press, 1995.
Yamazaki Tomoko, *Sandakan Brothel No. 8: An Episode in the History of Lower-Class Japanese Women*, M. E. Sharpe, 1999.
Yang Yŏng-hu, 'Ōsaka-fu Chōsenjin tōroku jōrei seitei: 1946 no tenmatsu ni tsuite' (The Establishment of Municipal Osaka's Korean Registration Ordinance: Concerning the Events of 1946), *Zainichi Chōsenjin-shi Kenkyū*, no. 16, 1986.
Yi Hyeong-Nang, 'Miyagi-ken chi'iki ni okeru Zainichi Chōsenjin no dōkō' (The Korean Community in Miyagi Prefecture), *Seikyū gakujutsu ronshū*, no. 13, Kankoku Bunka Kenkyū Shinkō Zaidan, 1998.
Yomiuri Shinbun Sengo-shi Han (Yomiuri Shinbun Postwar History Project), ed., *Kyōiku no ayumi* (Postwar Progress in Education), Yomiuri Shinbun, 1982.
Yon Cheong, *Kyanon kikan kara no shōgen* (Inside the Canon Unit), Banchō Shobō, 1973.
Yoneyama, Lisa, 'Memory Matters: Hiroshima's Korean Atom Bomb Memorial and the Politics of Ethnicity', in Laura Hein and Mark Selden, eds, *Living With the Bomb: American and Japanese Cultural Conflicts in the Nuclear Age*, M. E. Sharpe, 1997.
Yoshida Kyūichi, *Nihon shakai jigyō no rekishi* (A History of Social Work in Japan), Keisō Shobō, 1994.

Yoshida Shigeru, *Japan's Decisive Century, 1867–1967*, Frederick A. Praeger, 1967.

——, *Kaisō jūnen* (Recollections of a Decade), vols 1–4, Shinchōsha, 1957.

——, *The Yoshida Memoirs: The Story of Japan in Crisis*, Heinemann, 1961.

Yoshida Yutaka, *Shōwa-tennō no shūsen-shi* (A Postwar History of the Shōwa Emperor), Iwanami Shinsho, 1992.

Yoshimi Yoshiaki, *Jūgun ianfu* (The Military Comfort Women), Iwanami Shoten, 1995 (published in English as *Comfort Women: Sexual Slavery in the Japanese Military During World War II*, Columbia University Press, 2000).

Yoshimi Yoshiaki, ed., *Jūgun-ianfu shiryōshū* (Basic Documents on the Military Comfort Women), Ōtsuki Shoten, 1992.

Yoshino, Roger I., *The Invisible Minority: Japan's Burakumin*, Buraku Kaihō Kenkyūsho, 1977.

Yoshitsu, Michael M., *Japan and the San Francisco Peace Settlement*, Columbia University Press, 1983.

Young, Louise, *Japan's Total Empire: Manchuria and the Culture of Wartime Imperialism*, University of California Press, 1998.

Index

Area (GHQ/SWPA), xxvii, 3, 11, 16, 23, 27, 37, 137, 163, 181; contacts with Philippine resistance, 17; dissolution of, 48; establishment of, 11; First Corps of, 14–15; island leap-frogging strategy of, 16, 24; rivalry with POA, 15
General Procurement Agent (GPA), GHQ, 196–7
General Staff, GHQ, 137, 139–41, 146, 153, 163; G-1, 137, 139–40, 378, 498; G-2, 11, 17–18, 53, 137, 139–40, 146, 148, 155–6, 161–8, 240, 267, 269, 298–9, 393, 395, 399, 451, 463, 467, 480; G-3, 110, 137, 449; G-4, 137–40, 195, 269, 406. *See also* Willoughby.
general strike, banning of, 140, 144, 168, 318–21, 323
General Superintenders Ordinance, 39
Geneva Convention on prisoners of war (1929), 251
Genrō, xxxiii, xxxiv, 271
George, Scott, 602
Gercke, George, 184
Germany, xxxi, xxxiii, 22, 36–7, 59, 93, 96, 132, 149, 172, 201–2, 206, 210, 212–13, 216–17, 227, 232, 245; German-Soviet Non-Aggression Pact, 476
GIs, 67–9, 72–5, 79–81, 385, 441, 482; crimes and misdemeanors of, 67, 385, 441; fraternisation with Japanese, 79–81; friendly attitude of, 72–3; mixed marriages, 80–1; and Okinawans, 441; segregated treatment of, 75, 80
Gibson, James, B., 602
Gilbert Islands, 10, 22; US capture of Makin, Tarawa, 22
Gilmartin, William, T., 190, 341
Ginza (Tokyo), 57
Gnechko, Aleksei, 86–7
Golunsky, S. A., 169
Gonseth, J. E., 603
Government and Relief in Occupied Areas (GARIOA). *See* emergency relief.
Government Section (GS), GHQ, 7, 49, 102, 105–6, 108, 115, 121, 123, 139, 141, 143, 146–8, 153–62, 168, 171, 189, 196, 206, 269, 276–9, 298, 301–5, 322, 327, 330, 337, 341, 437, 446–7, 480, 484, 496–8; Civil Rights Subcommittee, 277–9, 437; Civil Service Division, 154, 159, 331; commitment to democracy

tempered by promotion of administrative efficiency, 154; and Constitution, 105, 150, 274, 279–82, 287–8; Courts and Law Division of, 154, 171; Governmental Powers Division, 154, 157, 161; Judiciary Committee, 277; Korea Division, 123, 154, 159, 449–50; Korea-Ryukyus Division, 123; Legislative Division, 49, 157; Local Government Division, 49, 154, 159, 209, 301, 303, 343; Parliamentary and Political Division, 49, 154, 157–9, 165; Public Administration Division, 154, 159, 276; and purges, 267; Steering Committee of, 276, 282
Graham, Billy, 379
Grajdanzev, Andrew, J., 159, 342–3
grass roots, 301, 556–60
Gray, Gordon, 103
Greater East Asia Ministry, xxxvii, 47
Greater East Asia Co-Prosperity Sphere, xxxv, xxxvii, 16, 30, 123
Greater Japan Association for the War Disabled, 412
Greater Japan Wartime Patriotic Association of Religions (*Dai Nippon Senji Shūkyō Hōkoku Kai*), 373–4
Greater Japanese Empire, 219, 516
Green, J., Woodall, 187
Green Cross Corporation, 427, 555
Grew, Joseph, C., 151, 203–4, 210, 213–18, 225–6, 258, 283, 459, 555
Griffith, Harry, E., 602
Gromyko, Andrei, 504
Guadalcanal, 15, 129
Guam, 10, 25–6, 50
'Guidelines for Japan-US Defence Cooperation', 523, 552
'Guidelines for the Administration of the Southern Occupied Territories', xxxvi, 201
Guillain, Robert, 239
Gulf War, 522, 552
Gullion, Allen, W., 201

Habomai Islands, 516–17. *See also* Kuril Islands, Northern Territories
Hadley, Eleanor, M., 160, 162, 335
Hague Conventions (1907), 202, 232, 272, 277
Hakone talks (Japan-USSR), 36
Hall, Robert, K., 182–3, 350, 353–4, 360–1

sarin poisoning incident, 551
Sasagawa Ryōichi, 247
Sasaki Sōichi, 259
Sasaki Yasushi, 398
Sata Ineko, 265
Satō Eisaku, 318, 478, 524, 539
Satō Naotake, 35, 45, 222–3
Satō Tadao, 395
Satō Tatsuo, 287–9, 291, 302, 437–8
Satomi Kishio, 283
scandals, 539–40; 'black mist' scandal, 539;
    Recruit scandal, 539
SCAPINs (SCAP Index), 114–16, 124, 142,
    228, 255, 267, 340–1, 448–9
Schenk, Hubert, G., 189, 343
Schmitz, Bernard, A., 601
School Education Law. *See* education.
School for Government of Occupied Areas,
    208
schools, 303, 348, 356 (6–3–3), 361–8,
    438, 481; democratisation of, 348, 367;
    military training in, 348–50, 363;
    textbook reform, 183, 348, 356, 361–4
Schurcliff, Alice, W., 599
Science Advisory Group, US, 143
Science Council of Japan, 179
Scientific and Technical Advisory
    Commission, 179
Scientific and Technical Division. *See*
    Economic and Scientific Section.
Sebald, William, J., 100, 103, 150–1, 155,
    443–4, 460, 464, 487, 495
security treaty, Japan-US, 501–9, 540;
    bilateral administrative agreement of,
    504–6; extent to which treaty was forced
    upon Japan, 503–6; Far East clause of,
    503–4; renewal of, 504, 517, 556;
    socialists abandoning opposition to, 540;
    Status of Forces Agreement (SOFA), 502,
    504–6, 523–4; strengthening of, 523;
    terms of, 503–4. *See also* peace settlement.
Seidensticker, Edward, G., 153
Seiyūkai (Friends of Democratic
    Government Party), 262
Sekai (journal), 391
self-defence, right of, 490
Self-Defence Forces (SDF), 193, 291, 489,
    522–3, 526, 541, 558
Sendai, 207, 497
Sendai High Court, 551
Sendai telephone operators' strike, 313

Senkaku (Daioyutai) Islands, 518
Seoul, 5, 496, 518
Shanghai, 251
'shattering of the precious jewel' (*gyokusai*),
    23
Shavell, Henry, 598
Shaw, Patrick, 102, 464
Schenck, Hubert, G., 189, 343
Shepard, Whitfield, P., 193, 487
Sherman Anti-Trust Act (1890),
    334
Shidehara Kijūrō, 116, 203, 237–41,
    258, 262–3, 266–7, 271–2, 279–81, 286,
    309–11, 315, 331, 340–1, 351, 386, 423,
    490
Shiga Yoshio, 240, 261
Shigemitsu Mamoru, 35–6, 47, 58, 62–4,
    245–6, 257–8, 385, 517; and
    implementation of indirect Occupation
    rule, 62–3; role in unsuccessful
    appeasement of the Soviet Union, 35–6
Shi'ikuma Saburō, 452
Shikoku, 205, 412
Shikotan Island. *See* Kuril Islands, Northern
    Territories
Shimizu Ikutarō, 507
Shimoyama Sadanori, 472–3
Shinohara Yoshio, 380
Shintō, xl, 371–2, 377–80, 549–50, 559;
    disestablisment of, 375, 548; *Gokoku*
    shrines, 372, 376, 550; Ise Shrines, 372,
    374, 376, 381; Imperial regalia, 372; and
    militant nationalism, 372; National
    Shintō, 374, 549; original Shintō, 374;
    outlawing of in classrooms, 351; Sectarian
    Shintō (*Kyōha*), 372; Shintō Directive
    (1945), 181, 188, 211, 351, 375–7, 380,
    548; Shrine Board;, 372, 375–6; Shrine
    Shintō (*Jinja*), 372, 375; shrines: Meiji,
    Nogi, Tōgō, 374; 'Sponsorship and
    Support of Shinto by Neighborhood
    Associations' (1946), 380
Shipping Control Authority for the Japanese
    Merchant Marine (SCAJAP), 195
Shirasu Jirō, 113, 139, 279–80, 317, 467,
    490, 497
Shōchiku Film Studio, 390, 398
Shōda Michiko, 519, 521
Shoemaker, James, 208
Shōriki Matsutarō, 313
Shoup, Carl, S., 143; mission of, 144